Arrest, Search, and Investigation in North Carolina

Robert L. Farb   Fifth Edition 2016

The School of Government at the University of North Carolina at Chapel Hill works to improve the lives of North Carolinians by engaging in practical scholarship that helps public officials and citizens understand and improve state and local government. Established in 1931 as the Institute of Government, the School provides educational, advisory, and research services for state and local governments. The School of Government is also home to a nationally ranked Master of Public Administration program, the North Carolina Judicial College, and specialized centers focused on community and economic development, information technology, and environmental finance.

As the largest university-based local government training, advisory, and research organization in the United States, the School of Government offers up to 200 courses, webinars, and specialized conferences for more than 12,000 public officials each year. In addition, faculty members annually publish approximately 50 books, manuals, reports, articles, bulletins, and other print and online content related to state and local government. The School also produces the *Daily Bulletin Online* each day the General Assembly is in session, reporting on activities for members of the legislature and others who need to follow the course of legislation.

Operating support for the School of Government's programs and activities comes from many sources, including state appropriations, local government membership dues, private contributions, publication sales, course fees, and service contracts.

Visit sog.unc.edu or call 919.966.5381 for more information on the School's courses, publications, programs, and services.

For Bonnie, Debbie, Jessica,
Kevin, Chris, and Daphne

Summary Contents

Contents

Chapter 3

Law of Search and Seizure 193

Chapter 4

Search Warrants, Administrative Inspection Warrants, and Nontestimonial Identification Orders   403

Part I. Search Warrants   406

Chapter 5

Interrogation and Confessions, Lineups and Other Identification Procedures, and Undercover Officers and Informants   563

Chapter 6

Rules of Evidence in Criminal Cases   717

Preface

This book explains the legal rules that govern an officer's authority to enforce laws and to investigate criminal offenses. It also explains the basic rules of evidence in criminal cases. In addition, it provides—in the footnotes to the text and in the case summaries sections—appellate cases and statutory references to assist in researching particular issues. However, a new law enforcement officer need only read the text to understand the basic legal rules.

The text describes what I believe is the prevailing law in North Carolina state courts and, if the law is unclear, what appears likely to be the prevailing law. The text relies primarily on North Carolina and federal statutory law and on cases of the United States Supreme Court, North Carolina Supreme Court, and North Carolina Court of Appeals, although other appellate court cases are sometimes cited and discussed. The text is current with case law through June 2016 and statutory law through the 2016 legislative session.

I sometimes cite legal treatises. The reader should be aware, however, that treatises sometimes criticize United States Supreme Court and other appellate court rulings and thus disagree with prevailing law. Therefore, they do not necessarily state what is the law in North Carolina state courts. Still, they are valuable aids in understanding legal issues.

The footnotes may refer to appellate cases that are not mentioned in the case summaries, and vice versa. Thus, the reader may want to check both sources for reference material on particular issues.

This is the fifth edition of a book originally published in 1986. The second edition was published in 1992, the third edition in 2003, and the fourth edition in 2011. Relevant case summaries sections appear at the end of each chapter (there are no case summaries for Chapters 1 and 6).

I thank the following School of Government faculty members whose publications, blog posts, and other assistance facilitated my writing: Shea Denning, Jamie Markham, John Rubin, Jessica Smith, and Jeff Welty. I thank the many people in the School of Government publications division who contributed to the production of this book: Nancy Dooly, Jennifer Henderson, Katrina Hunt, Kevin Justice, and Daniel Soileau. I also thank Robby Poore in the School of Government marketing and communications division for the cover design.

I welcome comments about this book's scope, organization, or content. Comments may be sent to me at farb@sog.unc.edu.

Robert L. Farb
Chapel Hill
June 2016

An Introduction to Constitutional Law and North Carolina Criminal Law and Procedure

Chapter 1

An Introduction to Constitutional Law and North Carolina Criminal Law and Procedure

Before reading about an officer's authority to arrest, search, and investigate crimes, it is helpful to have a basic understanding of constitutional law and North Carolina criminal law and procedure. This chapter discusses the sources of criminal law, constitutional and statutory restrictions on an officer's enforcement authority, and criminal pretrial and trial procedure and appellate review.

Sources of Criminal Law

North Carolina criminal law comes from three main sources: (1) statutes enacted by the North Carolina General Assembly and, for prosecutions in federal courts in North Carolina, statutes enacted by the United States Congress; (2) the common law, which consists of decisions by appellate courts; and (3) ordinances enacted by county and city governments. However, these laws may be restricted by federal and state constitutional provisions.

Statutes

The North Carolina General Assembly, the state's legislative body, enacts the state's laws, which are called statutes.[1] Statutes passed in each session of the General Assembly are printed in *Session Laws of North Carolina*, a book published after each legislative session. They also are available on the legislature's website at www.ncleg.net/gascripts/EnactedLegislation/ELTOC.pl?sType=Law. Those statutes that affect all or most of the state are also published in *General Statutes of North Carolina*. The criminal statutes prohibit offenses against society. The most serious crimes (such as murder, rape, and robbery) are called *felonies*, and lesser crimes are called *misdemeanors* (minor assaults, shoplifting, and so on). Many violations of motor vehicle laws are *infractions*, which are noncriminal violations of the law that are not punishable by imprisonment.[2] Although infractions are not crimes, they normally are prosecuted in criminal court.

The United States Congress also enacts criminal statutes that apply throughout the country. Some crimes—for example, bank robbery[3]—violate both federal and state criminal laws and may be prosecuted and punished in both federal and state courts.[4]

Some of the material in this chapter comes from Thomas H. Thornburg, AN INTRODUCTION TO LAW FOR NORTH CAROLINIANS (UNC Institute of Government, 2d. ed. 2000).

1. Statutes sometimes provide that violations of rules issued by state and local government agencies, boards, commissions, etc., are criminal offenses. *See, e.g.*, N.C. GEN. STAT.

(hereafter, G.S.) § 130A-25(a) (violation of rules adopted by the Commission for Public Health or a local board of health is a misdemeanor).

2. Not all infractions are motor vehicle violations. *See, e.g.*, G.S. 113-291.8 (failing to display hunter orange a wildlife violation).

3. Section 2113 of Title 18 of the United States Code (hereafter, U.S.C.) (dates are omitted from U.S.C. cites); G.S. 14-87 & -87.1.

4. Bartkus v. Illinois, 359 U.S. 121 (1959); State v. Myers, 82 N.C. App. 299 (1986). Two states may also prosecute a defendant for the same criminal act. Heath v. Alabama, 474 U.S. 82

Common Law

Another source of criminal law is the common law. This body of law developed in the English courts over many centuries and was transported to this country by English colonists. It still survives with modifications by the respective states, including North Carolina.[5] Much of the common law has been written into our statutes. Thus, a statute that makes particular conduct a crime usually lists all of the elements that must exist before that crime may be charged; but if a statute does not state the elements fully, the courts look to the common law for further definition. For example, North Carolina's statutes on larceny set out the punishment for larceny depending on the kind of property taken, its value, or the manner in which it was taken. But they do not state the elements of that crime. One must look to the common law, as interpreted in court opinions, to know what the term *larceny* means.[6]

City and County Ordinances

City councils and boards of county commissioners also may adopt criminal laws, called *ordinances*, that apply in their cities or counties. These ordinances normally deal only with subjects not already covered by state law. Generally, a violation of an ordinance is a Class 3 misdemeanor and the maximum punishment is 20 days' imprisonment and a $500 fine.[7] The sentencing judge may impose an active term of imprisonment only if a defendant has a prior criminal record consisting of five or more convictions.[8]

Constitutional Restrictions on Enactment of Criminal Laws

For the most part, governments have a free hand in deciding what conduct they want to prohibit by enacting criminal laws. However, courts sometimes decide that a particular criminal law is invalid because it violates a person's constitutional rights. For example, a criminal law that outlaws sexually explicit publications might be invalid if it conflicts with the publisher's constitutional right to freedom of speech under the First Amendment to the United States Constitution. A law that makes it a crime to verbally interrupt a law enforcement officer may be unconstitutionally broad because it may criminalize a substantial amount of constitutionally protected speech.[9] (Constitutions are discussed in more detail in the next section.)

Constitutional and Statutory Restrictions on an Officer's Authority

An officer's authority to arrest, search, and investigate crimes generally comes from statutes[10] and the common law.[11] However, an officer's authority is limited by federal and state constitutional provisions that give people rights that may not be violated by governments or their officers. Some federal and state statutes also impose other restrictions.

(1985). However, there are statutory limitations on the State's authority to prosecute in such a situation. G.S. 90-97 provides that if a violation of G.S. Chapter 90, Article 5 (the North Carolina Controlled Substances Act), is a violation of a federal law or another state's law, a conviction or acquittal in that federal or state court for the same act bars prosecution in North Carolina. State v. Brunson, 165 N.C. App. 667 (2004). G.S. 15A-134 provides that if an offense occurs partly in North Carolina and partly in another state, a person charged with that offense may be tried in North Carolina if that person has not been placed in jeopardy for the identical offense in the other state.

5. G.S. 4-1.

6. For the elements of larceny, see Jessica Smith, NORTH CAROLINA CRIMES: A GUIDEBOOK ON THE ELEMENTS OF CRIME 323–24 (UNC School of Government, 7th ed. 2011).

7. G.S. 14-4. The maximum fine for an ordinance violation is $50 unless the ordinance expressly states that the maximum fine is a specified amount over $50, up to $500. A violation of an ordinance regulating the operation or parking of vehicles is an infraction with a maximum penalty of $50.

8. *See* G.S. 15A-1340.23.

9. *See* Houston v. Hill, 482 U.S. 451 (1987); Lewis v. New Orleans, 415 U.S. 130 (1974). The ruling in *Hill* does not make G.S. 14-223 (resisting, delaying, or obstructing a public officer) unconstitutional on its face, but the statute's application to a person's mere verbal argument with an officer ordinarily will be unconstitutional. *Cf.* Duran v. City of Douglas, 904 F.2d 1372 (9th Cir. 1990); Buffkins v. City of Omaha, 922 F.2d 465 (8th Cir. 1990). North Carolina cases recognize that G.S. 14-223 is not violated by communications that are intended merely to assert rights, clarify a misunderstanding, or obtain information in a peaceable and orderly manner. *See* State v. Leigh, 278 N.C. 243 (1971) (evidence sufficient to support conviction of G.S. 14-223); State v. Burton, 108 N.C. App. 219 (1992) (evidence sufficient); State v. Singletary, 73 N.C. App. 612 (1985) (evidence sufficient); State v. Allen, 14 N.C. App. 485 (1972) (evidence insufficient).

10. In North Carolina, most of these statutes are located in G.S. Chapter 15A.

11. Common law authority often comes from court cases that recognize that particular law enforcement actions do not violate constitutional restrictions. *See, e.g.,* Terry v. Ohio, 392 U.S. 1 (1968) (stop-and-frisk authority); G.S. 15A-231.

Constitutional Restrictions

A constitution is the basic charter for a government. It describes the government and the relationships of its different parts to each other. A constitution also limits the powers of the government, and it describes the basic rights of people that may not be infringed by the government and its officials, including its law enforcement officers.

United States Constitution

The United States Constitution describes the executive, legislative, and judicial branches of the federal government—the president, Congress, and the Supreme Court—how they are selected, and the powers of each. It also spells out certain fundamental rights: freedom of speech and religion, protection from unreasonable searches, due process of law, equal protection of the laws, and so forth. These federal constitutional rights are the supreme law in this country; many civil lawsuits and motions to suppress evidence in criminal cases are based on contentions that a government agency or officer violated one of these rights. (Suppression motions and exclusionary rules are discussed in Chapter 4.)

Of particular importance in this book are those restrictions on a law enforcement officer's authority contained in several amendments to the federal constitution. Although the first 10 amendments to the United States Constitution—known as the Bill of Rights—originally applied only to the federal government, court decisions after the Fourteenth Amendment was adopted have made some of these amendments applicable to state and local governments as well.[12] The amendments that apply particularly to an officer's authority are discussed below.

The First Amendment's freedom of speech provision protects a person's right to communicate ideas, opinions, and information. Although obscenity is not protected by the First Amendment, courts have developed special restrictive rules under the Fourth Amendment to govern law enforcement officers' arrest and search powers so that they will be less likely to "chill" a person's First Amendment right to produce or distribute nonobscene materials. (This subject is discussed in Chapters 2, 3, and 4.) The First Amendment also protects a person's freedom of religion, guarantees the right to demonstrate peaceably and to petition the government for redress of grievances, and assures freedom of the press.

The Fourth Amendment protects a person's right to privacy. It prohibits government officials, including law enforcement officers, from making *unreasonable* searches and seizures and prohibits the issuance of a search warrant unless it (1) is supported by information given under oath or affirmation that establishes probable cause and (2) particularly describes the place to be searched or persons or things to be seized. (The requirements of the Fourth Amendment are discussed extensively throughout Chapters 2, 3, and 4.)

The Fifth Amendment protects a person from being compelled to give testimonial evidence against himself or herself. This privilege against self-incrimination is the provision under which the United States Supreme Court has required officers to give *Miranda* warnings and to obtain a waiver of rights before they interrogate a person who is in their custody.[13] (This subject is discussed in Chapter 5.) The Fifth Amendment also contains a double jeopardy provision, which protects a person from being criminally tried or punished twice for the same offense.

The Sixth Amendment guarantees—under certain circumstances—the right to a lawyer during a trial and some pretrial proceedings. (The right to counsel at a lineup is discussed in Chapter 5.) The Sixth Amendment also guarantees the right to a speedy and public trial by an impartial jury, the right to be informed of the charges and to be confronted with the witnesses against oneself, and the right to have compulsory process (for example, subpoenas) issued for obtaining witnesses for one's defense.

The effect of the Fourteenth Amendment's Due Process Clause ("nor shall any State deprive any person of life, liberty, or property, without due process of law") is not easily described. Perhaps it is best summarized by saying that people have a right to have governmental agencies and officials deal fairly with them. In the context of law enforcement actions, it means that an officer may not obtain a confession from a defendant by unfair methods—physical abuse, psychological coercion, and the like. It also means that an officer may not conduct a lineup or other identification procedure by using unnecessarily

---

12. The United States Supreme Court has ruled that some or parts of some of the amendments that constitute the Bill of Rights apply to the states because they are "incorporated" into the Fourteenth Amendment through its Due Process Clause. That is, certain provisions of the Bill of Rights are also part of due process under the Fourteenth Amendment. *See, e.g.,* Wolf v. Colorado, 338 U.S. 25 (1949); Mapp v. Ohio, 367 U.S. 643 (1961).

13. Miranda v. Arizona, 384 U.S. 436 (1966).

suggestive procedures. (These subjects are discussed in Chapter 5.) The Fourteenth Amendment also prohibits a government from denying a person equal protection of the laws. In the context of criminal trials, this means, for example, that it is unconstitutional to exclude an identifiable racial group from a jury.

North Carolina Constitution

The North Carolina Constitution resembles the federal constitution. It sets out the organization of North Carolina government—how the governor, other state officers, the General Assembly, and the judicial branch (the General Court of Justice) are elected and what their powers are—and it lists rights of citizens that are similar to those listed in the United States Constitution. In the context of law enforcement officers' authority, North Carolina courts generally have not interpreted state constitutional provisions as imposing greater restrictions on officers' authority than the federal constitution does.[14] In at least one case, however, the North Carolina Supreme Court has parted company with the United States Supreme Court and has found that the North Carolina Constitution affords criminal defendants greater protections than does the United States Constitution. In that case,[15] the North Carolina Supreme Court strongly indicated that there is no "good faith" exception to the exclusion of evidence for a violation of the North Carolina Constitution like the "good faith" exception to the Fourth Amendment exclusionary rule under the United States Constitution (discussed in Chapter 4).[16]

Statutory Restrictions

Federal and North Carolina statutes are not merely sources of a law enforcement officer's authority to arrest, search, and investigate crimes. They also may impose restrictions on an officer's authority that are greater than those imposed by the United States and North Carolina constitutions. For example, federal statutes prohibit a North Carolina law enforcement officer from using certain wiretapping and eavesdropping equipment unless the state legislature permits its use under specified circumstances—which the North Carolina General Assembly has done.[17] Similarly, North Carolina statutes sometimes impose restrictions, such as the 48-hour time limitation on the execution of a search warrant, that are not constitutionally required.[18]

Criminal Pretrial and Trial Procedure
Misdemeanors and Infractions

Most misdemeanors and infractions are first tried in district court before a district court judge, who determines whether the defendant is guilty of a misdemeanor or responsible for the infraction. There is no jury trial in district court.

A defendant who is found guilty of a misdemeanor in district court may appeal to superior court for a new trial—called *trial de novo*. (An appeal is not permitted for an infraction.) The superior court trial is de novo; that is, it is a completely new proceeding in which the evidence must be presented again as though the district court trial had never occurred. A superior court misdemeanor trial must be conducted with a 12-person jury, although a defendant may waive the right to a jury trial.[19] A jury's verdict—whether guilty or not guilty—must be unanimous. If the jury cannot agree within a reasonable time, the judge will declare a mistrial—but the defendant may be tried again.

In a few limited situations, a misdemeanor may be tried in superior court without a district court trial being held first. The most common situation occurs when a defendant is being tried for a felony in superior court and the judge instructs the jury that it may instead find the defendant guilty of a misdemeanor that is a lesser-included offense of the felony.[20] For example, if a defendant is being tried for the felony offense of assault with a deadly

---

14. *See, e.g.*, State v. McClendon, 350 N.C. 630 (1999); State v. Kornegay, 313 N.C. 1 (1985); State v. Arrington, 311 N.C. 633 (1984); State v. Isleib, 319 N.C. 634 (1987).

15. State v. Carter, 322 N.C. 709 (1988).

16. Although the court appeared to have rejected a "good faith" exception in all cases, the court noted in *Carter* that the withdrawal of blood involved the most intrusive search and stated later in its opinion that "[w]e are not persuaded *on the facts before us* that we should engraft a good faith exception to the exclusionary rule under our state constitution." *Id.* at 724 (emphasis added). However, the court's opinion in State v. Garner, 331 N.C. 491 (1992), appeared to undermine the *Carter* ruling. See note 1 of Chapter 4.

---

17. 18 U.S.C. §§ 2510–21; G.S. 15A-286 through -298.

18. *See generally* 2 Wayne R. LaFave, Search and Seizure: A Treatise on the Fourth Amendment § 4.7(a) (5th ed. 2012); G.S. 15A-248.

19. G.S. 15A-1201.

20. G.S. 7A-271(a)(1).

weapon inflicting serious injury and the evidence is not definitive that the victim's injury was serious, the judge will instruct the jury to consider—if it does not convict the defendant of felonious assault—whether the defendant is guilty of the misdemeanor offense of assault with a deadly weapon. An infraction that is a lesser-included violation of a criminal offense also may be submitted to a jury without having been tried initially in district court.[21]

A misdemeanor also may be tried initially in superior court when a defendant is charged with a felony that occurred at the same time as the misdemeanor. For example, if a defendant is charged with the felony offense of involuntary manslaughter and the misdemeanor offense of impaired driving, and both charges arose out of the same automobile accident, the defendant may be tried for both charges in superior court without a district court trial of the impaired-driving charge.[22] A misdemeanor also may be tried initially in superior court if (1) a grand jury issues a *presentment* (an accusation that does not begin criminal proceedings but requires a district attorney to investigate the matter in question and allows the district attorney to submit an indictment for the grand jury's consideration) that charges a misdemeanor, (2) the district attorney then submits an indictment to the grand jury that charges that misdemeanor, and (3) the grand jury indicts the defendant for that offense.[23]

A defendant who is convicted of a misdemeanor or found responsible for an infraction in superior court has a right to appeal to the North Carolina Court of Appeals for review of the trial. (Appellate review is discussed later in this chapter.)

Felonies

Most felonies are processed initially through district court before they are tried in superior court or otherwise disposed of. Sometimes, however, a felony case begins with an *indictment*,[24] which is a written accusation by a grand jury, filed in superior court, charging a person with a criminal offense. The typical felony case begins when an officer arrests a person and takes that person before a magistrate, who—if the arrest was made without

a warrant—decides whether there is probable cause to charge the person and if so, sets conditions of pretrial release. The defendant either satisfies the conditions of pretrial release (by posting a secured bond, for example) or fails to do so and is jailed.

The next event usually is the *first appearance* in district court; if the defendant is in jail, the first appearance must be held within 96 hours or in the next session of district court, whichever occurs first.[25] A district court judge's most important duty during the first appearance is to determine whether the defendant has a lawyer. If the defendant wants an attorney and is *indigent* (that is, financially unable to hire an attorney), one will be appointed to represent the defendant. In counties with a public defender's office, a lawyer from that office normally represents the defendant. In other counties, a private lawyer who has agreed to accept court-appointed cases represents an indigent defendant. In a first-degree murder case in which the State is seeking the death penalty, the appointment of lead defense counsel and assistant defense counsel is made by the Office of Indigent Defense Services instead of by a judge.[26] The judge then normally schedules a *probable cause hearing* (explained in the next paragraph) to be held within one to three weeks.[27] A defendant may waive the right to a probable cause hearing.[28] If a prosecutor obtains an indictment before the scheduled probable cause hearing, no hearing is held.[29]

At the probable cause hearing, the state must present enough evidence to convince the district court judge that there is probable cause to believe that the defendant committed the charged felony or a lesser-included felony or misdemeanor. If probable cause is found for only a misdemeanor, the case may then be tried in district court.[30]

---

21. G.S. 7A-271(d)(1).

22. G.S. 7A-271(a)(3). *See* State v. Fearing, 304 N.C. 471 (1981); State v. Karbas, 28 N.C. App. 372 (1976).

23. G.S. 7A-271(a)(2). For a definition of a *presentment*, see G.S. 15A-641(c) and *State v. Birdsong*, 325 N.C. 418 (1989).

24. G.S. 15A-641(a).

25. G.S. 15A-601(c). A clerk of superior court may conduct a first appearance if a district court judge is not available in the county within 96 hours after the defendant is taken into custody. G.S. 15A-601(e).

26. G.S. 7A-452(a).

27. G.S. 15A-606(d) provides (with exceptions) that a probable cause hearing must be scheduled no sooner than five working days and no later than 15 working days following an initial appearance.

28. G.S. 15A-606.

29. State v. Lester, 294 N.C. 220 (1978).

30. A misdemeanor may be tried immediately with the consent of the prosecutor and the defendant. G.S. 15A-613(2). A prosecutor who still wanted to try the case as a felony could take a voluntary dismissal of the misdemeanor and seek an indictment from the grand jury—or obtain an indictment

If the judge finds that probable cause for a felony prosecution exists, then the prosecutor will submit a bill of indictment to the county's grand jury. Even if the judge does not find probable cause, the prosecutor still may seek an indictment because a finding of no probable cause is not a determination that the defendant is not guilty.

A district court judge has the authority to accept a defendant's guilty plea to a Class H or I felony if the prosecutor and the defendant consent to this procedure.[31] The guilty plea may be entered to a felony pending in district court or a felony pending in superior court that has been remanded to district court for this purpose.

The grand jury's role is to determine whether there is probable cause to indict the defendant. A defendant may not be tried for a felony unless he or she has been indicted—except that the defendant may waive an indictment for a *noncapital offense* (one that is not punishable by death) and be tried on an *information*, which is a written accusation by a prosecutor that charges a person with a criminal offense.[32]

An *arraignment* is a procedure to determine whether the defendant intends to plead guilty, no contest, or not guilty to the charge. (A plea of no contest is not an admission of guilt, but it authorizes the court to sentence the defendant; the plea may be entered only with the consent of the presiding judge and prosecutor.) An arraignment is required only if a defendant makes a written request for one.[33] If an arraignment is held, it is often the deadline when a defendant must file pretrial motions, including motions to suppress evidence.[34] These motions generally are heard before trial. If a judge grants a defendant's suppression motion before trial, a prosecutor may appeal that ruling to an appellate court to ask that court to reverse the judge's ruling.[35] The trial is delayed while the appellate court considers the prosecutor's appeal. If the judge denies a defendant's pretrial motion, the defendant generally may seek appellate review only after trial and conviction.[36]

A felony trial is always before a 12-person jury unless a defendant waives the right to a jury trial (a waiver is not permitted for a capital offense).[37] The jury's verdict—whether guilty or not guilty—must be unanimous. If the jury is unable to reach a unanimous decision—a situation that is sometimes called a *hung jury*—the judge will declare a mistrial, and the case may be tried again.

There is no trial if a defendant pleads guilty or no contest. Before accepting a guilty or no contest plea, a judge must determine whether the defendant understands the consequences—waiver of jury trial and other constitutional rights, potential punishment, and the like—of pleading guilty or no contest.

Appellate Review

A defendant in superior court who is found guilty of a crime or found responsible for an infraction has a right to *appellate review* of the trial. Appellate review is not another trial. The appellate court generally examines only alleged trial errors, such as whether the judge properly instructed the jury about the law applicable to the case or properly allowed or disallowed certain evidence to be heard, whether a confession was properly obtained or a search was properly conducted, or whether there was sufficient evidence to support the conviction. Almost all appeals go first to the North Carolina Court of Appeals (composed of 15 judges), where three-judge panels review cases. Convictions in which death is imposed for a conviction of first-degree murder are appealed directly to the North Carolina Supreme Court (composed of seven justices). If a court of appeals decision is not unanimous, the losing side automatically may have its case reviewed by the supreme court. Otherwise, the supreme court may choose whether it wants to hear a case.

Decisions of the North Carolina Court of Appeals are published in the *North Carolina Court of Appeals Reports* and are referred to by a series of numbers and letters called a *case citation*.[38] For example, a case citation

---

while the misdemeanor was pending in district court and then take a voluntary dismissal of the misdemeanor.

31. G.S. 7A-272(c); 15A-1029.1.

32. G.S. 15A-641(b).

33. G.S. 15A-941(d).

34. G.S. 15A-952(c). If an arraignment is to be held at the session of court for which the trial is calendared, the pretrial motions must be filed before 5:00 p.m. on the Wednesday before the session when the trial of the case begins.

35. G.S. 15A-979(c).

---

36. State v. Turner, 305 N.C. 356 (1982).

37. G.S. 15A-1201.

38. The *North Carolina Court of Appeals Reports* and the *North Carolina Reports* are published by the state. A commercial company (commonly known as West) also publishes

that reads 75 N.C. App. 504 (1985) refers to a decision that was issued in 1985 and published in volume 75, beginning on page 504. Decisions of the North Carolina Supreme Court appear in the *North Carolina Reports*. A supreme court case citation might read, for example, 314 N.C. 59 (1985). North Carolina appellate court opinions decided since 1996 are also available at the appellate division's website at https://appellate.nccourts.org/opinions/.

Appellate review of most criminal cases ends with the state supreme court. However, sometimes a defendant seeks appellate review of federal constitutional issues before the United States Supreme Court. A request to that Court to hear a case is called a *petition for a writ of certiorari*, and the Court's preliminary decision is whether to hear the case—that is, whether to grant or deny certiorari. Certiorari is granted for very few criminal cases. The Court's decisions are published in identical versions in three different publications, with the numbers indicating volume and page number respectively. For example, a citation may read United States v. Ross, 456 U.S. 598, 102 S. Ct. 2157, 72 L. Ed. 2d 572 (1982). The first set of numbers, 456 U.S. 598, refers to the Court's official reports, the *United States Reports*; 102 S. Ct. 2157 refers to the *Supreme Court Reporter*; and 72 L. Ed. 2d 572 refers to *United States Supreme Court Reports, Lawyers' Edition, Second Series*.

A defendant may then challenge the conviction by filing a motion for appropriate relief in state court,[39] and if unsuccessful, seek state appellate review and United States Supreme Court review of a denial of the motion. The grounds for challenging a conviction in a motion for appropriate relief are narrower than allowed on direct appeal of the conviction.

A defendant also may seek review of the conviction by filing a lawsuit (known as a *petition for a writ of habeas corpus*) in a federal district court in North Carolina. North Carolina has three federal districts—western, middle, and eastern—each with several judges. Review is limited to federal constitutional questions, except that a defendant generally may not obtain review of Fourth

Amendment search and seizure issues.[40] Federal district court decisions are published in the *Federal Supplement*. A case citation may read 164 F. Supp. 2d 734 (W.D.N.C. 2001), which refers to a decision in the western district (W.D.) of North Carolina (N.C.).

A decision of the federal district court may be appealed to the United States Court of Appeals, which is divided into 12 judicial circuits. North Carolina—along with South Carolina, Virginia, Maryland, and West Virginia—is included in the Fourth Circuit. Thus, an appeal from a North Carolina federal district court is to that court. Decisions of the federal circuit court of appeals are published in the *Federal Reporter*. For example, 233 F.2d 213 (4th Cir. 2000) refers to a Fourth Circuit decision. An appeal from one of these decisions is by a petition for a writ of certiorari to the United States Supreme Court.

Under certain circumstances, a defendant may again challenge the conviction in state court even after state appellate and federal post-conviction review have been unsuccessful, by filing a motion for appropriate relief in state court.[41]

North Carolina appellate cases in the *South Eastern Reporter*. A typical citation would appear as 553 S.E.2d 690, which refers to volume 553 of the *South Eastern Reporter*, Second Series, page 690.

39. *See* G.S. 15A-1415. *See generally* Jessica Smith, *Motions for Appropriate Relief, in* N.C. SUPERIOR COURT JUDGES' BENCHBOOK (UNC School of Government, Dec. 2013), http://benchbook.sog.unc.edu/criminal/motions-appropriate-relief.

---

40. In *Stone v. Powell*, 428 U.S. 465 (1976), the United States Supreme Court ruled that when a state court has provided a defendant with a full and fair opportunity to assert and to have considered a Fourth Amendment claim, the defendant may not be granted federal habeas corpus relief because evidence introduced at trial was allegedly obtained in violation of his or her Fourth Amendment rights. The Court reasoned that applying the exclusionary rule in a federal habeas corpus proceeding (as opposed to state trial and appellate proceedings, where the exclusionary rule still applies), which is held years after the criminal investigation was conducted, would have a minimal deterrent effect on an officer's conduct. Also, the societal costs—reversing a defendant's conviction because otherwise reliable evidence was obtained improperly—clearly outweigh this minimal deterrent effect.

41. *See supra* note 39.

Chapter 2

Law of Arrest and Investigative Stops

Chapter 2

Law of Arrest and Investigative Stops

The right of the people to be secure in their persons, houses, papers, and effects, against unreasonable searches and seizures, shall not be violated, and no Warrants shall issue, but upon probable cause, supported by Oath or affirmation and particularly describing the place to be searched and the persons or things to be seized.

—United States Constitution, Amendment IV

This chapter discusses law enforcement officers' territorial and subject-matter jurisdiction, their authority to arrest with and without warrants, and the legal standards for making investigative stops and arrests and completing custody of arrestees.

Introduction

The arrest of a person is a *seizure* under the Fourth Amendment; for it to be constitutional, it must be *reasonable*. Determining the reasonableness of an arrest involves balancing a person's right to be free and left alone by law enforcement officers with the officers' occasional need to interfere with personal freedom to investigate crime or to enforce laws. An arrest is unreasonable unless there is a factual basis for believing that the person to be arrested has committed a crime. The amount of factual information necessary to justify an arrest is called *probable cause*. Probable cause simply means a *fair probability*.[1]

Not all seizures of people are as serious as arrest. A brief stop of a person on a street for some investigative reason, such as questioning or identification, does not always constitute an arrest. Such stops, often called investigative stops or detentions, are legally justified by less factual information than is required for an arrest. Only *reasonable suspicion* of involvement in criminal activity is necessary to justify a brief detention of a suspect.

Law enforcement officers often interact with people without seizing them and therefore do not require any justification for their actions. For example, officers do not seize people by merely approaching them in a non-threatening manner on a street, in an airport, or on a bus; identifying themselves as law enforcement officers; and asking questions if the person is willing to answer them.[2]

Seizing people unlawfully can result in several undesirable consequences, including the following:

- The exclusion of resulting evidence from criminal proceedings[3]
- A civil lawsuit against the officer who made the illegal arrest or detention[4]

---

1. The United States Supreme Court in *Illinois v. Gates*, 462 U.S. 213 (1983), used the term "fair probability" in discussing the degree of certainty necessary to show that evidence of crime will be found in a particular place for purposes of determining whether there is probable cause to issue a search warrant. The Court also would likely use that term when discussing the degree of certainty to show probable cause to arrest. *See* State v. Crawford, 125 N.C. App. 279 (probable cause existed to arrest when there was fair probability defendant had committed criminal offense); Wilson v. Russo, 212

F.3d 781, 789 (3d Cir. 2000) ("probable cause exists if there is a 'fair probability' that the person committed the crime").

2. *See* United States v. Drayton, 536 U.S. 194 (2002); Florida v. Bostick, 501 U.S. 429 (1991); United States v. Waldon, 206 F.3d 597 (6th Cir. 2000).

3. *See* Mapp v. Ohio, 367 U.S. 643 (1961); N.C. Gen. Stat. (hereafter, G.S.) § 15A-974.

4. The most often used statute under which a person may sue a law enforcement officer is Section 1983 of Title 42 of the

- Criminal prosecution against the officer[5]
- Disciplinary action against the officer by the officer's employing agency

However, the fact that a seizure is found to be illegal does not cause automatic dismissal of criminal charges associated with that seizure; the person seized can still be prosecuted and convicted if there is sufficient admissible evidence of guilt.[6]

Jurisdiction

Officers may use their law enforcement authority over a person only within certain geographical areas and only with certain kinds of offenses. These limitations are called the officers' *jurisdiction*. Officers must have both *territorial* (geographical) and *subject-matter* (offense) jurisdiction to exercise their law enforcement powers lawfully.

Officers retain their law enforcement authority 24 hours a day, whether they are on duty or off duty (assuming, of course, they have both territorial and subject-matter jurisdiction).[7]

Limits on Law Enforcement Officers' Jurisdiction
Territorial Jurisdiction

(*See page 97 for case summaries on this topic.*)

Except in cases of hot pursuit, discussed on page 17, state and local law enforcement officers in North Carolina may not use their arrest powers outside the boundaries of the state. Within North Carolina, the officers' jurisdiction depends on their employing agency.

Several kinds of officers are discussed below.[8]

State law enforcement officers. State law enforcement officers may arrest anywhere within the state. State law enforcement officers include State Highway Patrol officers,[9] State Bureau of Investigation (SBI) agents,[10] alcohol law enforcement (ALE) agents of the State Department of Crime Control and Public Safety,[11] inspectors of the License and Theft Bureau of the Division of Motor Vehicles (DMV),[12] wildlife law enforcement officers,[13] marine fisheries enforcement officers,[14] and probation and parole officers.[15]

Local alcohol beverage control officers. Local alcohol beverage control (ABC) officers employed by county or city ABC boards may arrest anywhere in the county in which they are employed, except that city ABC officers' jurisdiction may be limited by a special legislative act that governs that city's ABC system.[16]

United States Code, which provides for a civil remedy against state and local government officials for deprivation of citizens' constitutional rights. *See, e.g.*, Messerschmidt v. Millender, 132 S. Ct. 1235 (2012); Malley v. Briggs, 475 U.S. 335 (1986); Graham v. Connor, 490 U.S. 386 (1989). Officers may also be sued under other federal and state statutes and for torts (civil wrongs) recognized by state law, such as false imprisonment, assault, and the like. *See* Myrick v. Cooley, 91 N.C. App. 209 (1988). Under certain circumstances, an officer's supervisors and the local government unit that employs the officer also may be held responsible for the officer's unconstitutional acts.

5. Two commonly used federal criminal statutes for prosecuting criminal violations of constitutional rights are Section 241 of Title 18 of the United States Code (hereafter, U.S.C.) (dates are omitted from U.S.C. cites) and 18 U.S.C. § 242. An officer may also be prosecuted under such state criminal laws as assault and battery.

6. *See* United States v. Crews, 445 U.S. 463 (1980); State v. Sutton, 244 N.C. 679 (1956).

7. *See* the court's statements in *State v. Gaines*, 332 N.C. 461 (1992) about the authority of off duty law enforcement officers. See also *State v. Lightner*, 108 N.C. App. 349 (1992), and cases from other states, such as *Duncan v. State*, 294 S.E.2d 365 (Ga. App. 1982); *Carr v. State*, 335 S.E.2d 622 (Ga. App. 1985); and *Sawyer v. Humphries*, 587 A.2d 467 (Md. App. 1991).

8. The list of officers is not all-inclusive. For a more complete list, see MICHAEL F. EASLEY & JEFFREY P. GRAY, TERRITORIAL AND SUBJECT MATTER JURISDICTION OF LAW ENFORCEMENT AGENCIES IN NORTH CAROLINA (North Carolina Department of Justice, May 1996).

9. G.S. 15A-402(a); 20-188.

10. G.S. 15A-402(a); 143B-917.

11. G.S. 15A-402(a); 18B-500(c).

12. G.S. 15A-402(a); 20-49.

13. G.S. 15A-402(a); 113-136(a). Although the latter statute describes these officers as wildlife protectors, they are also known as wildlife law enforcement officers.

14. G.S. 15A-402(a); 113-136(a). Although the latter statute describes these officers as marine fisheries protectors, they also are known as marine fisheries enforcement officers.

15. Because probation and parole officers (their common name, although they are also involved in post-release supervision) have the authority to arrest (G.S. 15-205, 15A-1368.6, and 15A-1376) and are state employees, they should be considered state law enforcement officers within the meaning of G.S. 15A-402(a), which provides for statewide territorial jurisdiction. In addition, they perform their duties within a uniform statewide court system, which further supports the view that they may exercise their arrest powers statewide.

16. G.S. 18B-501(c).

Sheriffs, deputy sheriffs, and county police officers. Sheriffs and their regularly employed deputies, county police, and officers of consolidated county–city law enforcement agencies may arrest anywhere in the state for felonies committed in their county and on any property and rights-of-way owned by the county outside its limits.[17] They may make other arrests only within their own county or on property or rights-of-way owned by the county outside its limits.[18] In addition, sheriffs and their deputies may arrest with a warrant on any river, bay, or creek adjoining their county.[19] Sheriffs have arrest jurisdiction in cities within their county as well as in the area outside the city, although as a matter of policy, they tend to exercise routine arrest authority only in those parts of the county not served by local police departments.

City law enforcement officers. City law enforcement officers may arrest in the city where they serve, in the property and rights-of-way that the city owns or leases outside its limits, and in the area within one mile of the city limits.[20] It would appear that officers may exercise arrest authority even when the extension of one mile from their city's limits would place them within an adjoining city, as the one-mile extension applies without limitation in the statutory language granting that authority.[21]

City law enforcement officers should check with their city attorney to determine whether they have any arrest jurisdiction beyond these limits; sometimes a special legislative act expands a particular city's limits beyond a mile.

City law enforcement officers are authorized to transport a person in custody to or from any place in North Carolina so that the person can attend a criminal court proceeding. Officers also are authorized to arrest that person for any offense he or she commits while being transported.[22]

Company police officers. North Carolina law authorizes corporations providing on-site security services, state institutions, and hospitals to apply to the attorney general to commission people to act as police officers for their company, hospital, institution, or the like.[23] These police officers must satisfy minimum basic law enforcement training requirements just like other law enforcement officers. Company police officers may arrest on property owned or possessed and controlled by (1) their employer and (2) a person who has contracted for their security services.[24] Railroad police officers are not subject to these limitations; they may arrest anywhere in the state.[25]

The territorial jurisdiction of company police officers of private universities and colleges (also known as campus police officers) also includes the portion of any public road or highway passing through or immediately adjoining property already subject to their jurisdiction; for example, property owned by or in possession and control of the university or college. The university or college board of trustees may enter into a joint agreement with a municipal governing board or county governing board (if a county governing board, with the consent of the sheriff) to extend campus police officers' law enforcement authority into part or all of the jurisdiction of the municipality

---

17. G.S. 15A-402(e).

18. G.S. 15A-402(b).

19. G.S. 162-14. Of course, a sheriff's territorial authority to arrest with or without a warrant extends to that part of a waterway that is included within the county. *See also* G.S. 15-129, which places the venue of an offense committed on any water or watercourse (or its sides or shores) that divides counties in either of the two counties nearest to the place where the offense was committed.

20. G.S. 15A-402(b) & (c); 160A-286. G.S. 160A-286 authorizes a city law enforcement officer to exercise all the powers of a law enforcement officer, not just arrest authority, within one mile of the city's corporate limits and on all property "owned by or leased" to the city, wherever located. G.S. 15A-402(b) speaks of arrest authority on property "owned" by the city outside the city's limits. Therefore, G.S. 160A-286 broadens an officer's arrest authority, beyond the provisions of G.S. 15A-402(b), to include property leased by the city that is outside the city's limits.

21. G.S. 15A-402(c); 160A-286. It would also appear that officers can exercise their authority within one mile of all property owned by or leased to the city, wherever located. Because the one-mile provision is designed in part to relieve officers from having to determine the precise location of a property line or else face potential legal liability for their actions, it is reasonable to interpret the legislature's intent that the provision applies to this property as well.

---

22. G.S. 15A-402(c).

23. G.S. 74E-1 through -13. College and university campus police officers who were company police officers for a campus police agency before the enactment of Chapter 74G (Campus Police Act) of the General Statutes may remain licensed as company police officers. G.S. 74E-6(b)(1). For a discussion of company police, see Michael F. Easley & Jeffrey P. Gray, Powers and Jurisdiction of Company Police in North Carolina (North Carolina Department of Justice, Jan. 1996).

24. G.S. 74E-6(c).

25. G.S. 74E-6(e).

or county and to determine the circumstances in which the extension of authority is granted.[26]

The University of North Carolina campus law enforcement officers. The board of trustees of any constituent institution of The University of North Carolina (UNC) is authorized to establish a campus law enforcement agency and to employ police officers.[27] (Under some circumstances, officers may be commissioned as company police officers;[28] see above.) These officers' territorial jurisdiction includes all property owned or leased to their institution and that portion of any public road or highway passing through the property or immediately adjoining it. The board of trustees may enter into a joint agreement with a municipal governing board or county governing board (if a county governing board, with the consent of the sheriff) to extend campus police officers' law enforcement authority into part or all of the jurisdiction of the municipality or county and to determine the circumstances in which the extension of authority is granted.[29] The board of trustees may also enter into a joint agreement with the governing board of any other UNC institution to extend the law enforcement authority of its campus police officers into any or all of the other institution's jurisdiction and to determine the circumstances in which this extension of authority may be granted.

Community college campus law enforcement officers. The board of trustees of a community college is authorized to establish a campus law enforcement agency and to employ police officers.[30] (Under some circumstances, officers may be commissioned as company police officers;[31] see above.) These officers' territorial jurisdiction includes all property owned or leased to their community college and that portion of any public road or highway passing through the property and immediately adjoining it. The board of trustees may enter into a joint agreement with a municipal governing board or county governing board (if a county governing board, with the consent of the sheriff) to extend campus police officers' law enforcement authority into part or all of the jurisdiction of the municipality or county and to determine the circumstances in which the extension of authority is granted.

Private nonprofit college campus police officers. Private nonprofit colleges are authorized to establish a campus law enforcement agency and to employ police officers.[32] These officers' territorial jurisdiction includes all property owned or possessed or controlled by the college and that portion of any public road or highway passing through the property or immediately adjoining it. The college governing board may enter into a joint agreement with a municipal governing board or county governing board (if a county governing board, with the consent of the sheriff) to extend campus police officers' law enforcement authority into part or all of the jurisdiction of the municipality or county and to determine the circumstances in which the extension of authority is granted. The board may also enter into joint agreements with the governing boards of other higher education institutions to extend the law enforcement authority of its campus police officers into any or all of the other institution's jurisdiction and to determine the circumstances in which this extension of authority may be granted.

---

26. G.S. 74E-6(d).

27. G.S. 116-40.5.

28. G.S. 74E-6(b)(1).

29. State v. Bernard, 236 N.C. App. 134 (2014) (NC A&T campus police had territorial jurisdiction to execute search warrant at defendant's off-campus private residence when A&T had entered into a mutual aid agreement with Greensboro Police Department; agreement gave campus police authority to act off campus concerning offenses committed on campus; offense of accessing computer occurred on campus because defendant sent electronic communication from residence to campus computer server).

30. G.S. 115D-21.1.

31. G.S. 74E-6(b)(1).

---

32. G.S. 74G-2. Police agencies at private institutions of higher education that were certified under G.S. Chapter 74E (Company Police Act) were automatically converted to campus police agencies when G.S. Chapter 74G was enacted (July 18, 2005), unless the institution's board of trustees elected not to have the agency converted. S.L. 2005-231, sec. 12. The North Carolina Supreme Court in *State v. Pendleton*, 339 N.C. 379 (1994), ruled that the state's delegation of its law enforcement power—through the law authorizing company police officers—to Campbell University, a religious institution, violated the First Amendment's Establishment Clause. *See also* State v. Jordan, 155 N.C. App. 146 (2002) (Pheiffer University is religious institution under *Pendleton* ruling); State v. Yencer, 365 N.C. 292 (2011) (court reversed court of appeals and ruled campus police laws, as applied to the defendant, who was arrested by Davidson College campus police officer for impaired driving, did not violate First Amendment's Establishment Clause; court noted that since its *Pendleton* ruling, discussed above, campus police agencies are now governed under different statutes, G.S. Chapter 74G, which have a secular legislative purpose; see the court's opinion for its extensive analysis of the First Amendment issues, including the status of Davidson College and Chapter 74G's provisions).

North Carolina General Assembly special police. Special police employed by the Legislative Services Office of the North Carolina General Assembly have the authority of city law enforcement officers within the City of Raleigh and a specified area of unincorporated Wake County. They also have authority throughout the state for a variety of activities, including accompanying a legislator who is conducting, or traveling to or from, his or her official duties.[33]

Expanded Territorial Jurisdiction for DWI-Related Offenses

Officers with subject-matter jurisdiction (discussed on page 18) who are investigating DWI-related offenses or vehicle crashes that occurred in their jurisdiction have expanded territorial jurisdiction.[34] For these offenses,[35] officers may investigate and seek evidence of the driver's impairment anywhere inside or outside the state and may make arrests anywhere in the state. Officers may take the arrested person to any place in the state (1) for one or more chemical analyses at the request of any law enforcement officer, medical professional, or other person to determine the extent or cause of the person's impairment; (2) to have the person identified; (3) to complete a crash report; and (4) for any other lawful purpose.[36]

Arrest After Continuous Flight (Hot Pursuit)

(*See page 98 for case summaries on this topic.*)

Law enforcement officers may arrest outside their territorial jurisdiction under certain circumstances.

Hot pursuit within the state. Local law enforcement officers, who normally are restricted to arresting within the

limits of the unit that employs them, may arrest outside that territory when the offender has committed a criminal offense within the territory and the arrest is made during hot pursuit while the offender is making an immediate and continuous flight from that territory.[37] Officers may pursue the offender throughout the state, but if they are to retain their authority to arrest, they must continue the pursuit and not stop to do something else. They need not keep the offender in sight at all times, however, so long as the offender remains in continuous flight. Officers also may await the arrival of assistance if they would be endangered by making the arrest without additional assistance.[38]

Company and campus police officers also may arrest outside their territorial jurisdiction if they are in hot pursuit of a person who committed an offense within their jurisdiction.[39]

Hot pursuit outside the state. Although normally North Carolina law enforcement officers may not arrest once they leave the state, they may arrest outside the state when they pursue a person who has committed an offense in North Carolina and is fleeing into an adjoining state whose laws permit an arrest to be made under these circumstances.[40] All four border states—Georgia,[41] South Carolina,[42] Tennessee,[43] and Virginia[44]—permit such arrests, but only for felonies (and certain impaired driving

---

33. G.S. 120-32.2.

34. G.S. 20-38.2.

35. Included among the offenses are G.S. 20-138.1 (impaired driving); G.S. 20-138.2 (impaired driving in commercial vehicle); G.S. 20-138.2A (operating commercial vehicle after consuming alcohol); G.S. 20-138.2B (operating school bus, school activity bus, or child care vehicle after consuming alcohol); G.S. 20-138.3 (driving by person under 21 years old after consuming alcohol or drugs); G.S. 20-138.5 (habitual impaired driving); G.S. 20-138.7 (transporting open container of alcoholic beverage); G.S. 20-141.4 (felony death by vehicle, felony serious injury by vehicle, and other offenses involving impaired driving); G.S. 20-12.1 (impaired supervision or instruction); G.S. 20-179.3(j) (violation of limited driving privilege by consuming alcohol); G.S. 14-17 (first-degree and second-degree murder) and 14-18 (involuntary manslaughter) when impaired driving is involved.

36. G.S. 20-38.3.

37. G.S. 15A-402(d).

38. State v. Melvin, 53 N.C. App. 421 (1981).

39. G.S. 15A-402(f); 74E-6(c)(3).

40. *See infra* notes 41 through 44.

41. GA. CODE ANN. § 35-1-15 (2010) (pursuit limited to offenses punishable in other states by death or imprisonment in excess of one year). This statute thereby limits the offenses to felonies under North Carolina sentencing laws, except that misdemeanor impaired driving (G.S. 20-138.1) and commercial impaired driving (G.S. 20-138.2) may also be included because they are punishable by up to two years' imprisonment under G.S. 20-179.

42. S.C. CODE ANN. § 17-13-47 (2010) (pursuit limited to offenses punishable in other states by death or imprisonment in excess of one year). This statute thereby limits the offenses to felonies under North Carolina sentencing laws, except that misdemeanor impaired driving (G.S. 20-138.1) and commercial impaired driving (G.S. 20-138.2) may also be included because they are punishable by up to three years' imprisonment under G.S. 20-179.

43. TENN. CODE ANN. § 40-7-203 (2011) (pursuit limited to felonies).

44. VA. CODE ANN. § 19.2-79 (2011) (pursuit limited to felonies).

misdemeanors mentioned in the accompanying note for pursuit into Georgia and South Carolina).[45]

When officers pursue a person into another state and arrest the person there, they may not simply bring the arrestee back to North Carolina. Instead, they must take the arrestee to a judicial official in that state and follow that state's procedures on completing custody.

Subject-Matter Jurisdiction

Some law enforcement officers may arrest only for certain kinds of offenses. Some of these limitations are discussed below. However, some statutes authorize all law enforcement officers, including those with limited arrest authority, to enforce specific laws. For example, all law enforcement officers generally have the authority to arrest for drug offenses contained in Article 5 of Chapter 90 of the North Carolina General Statutes (hereafter, G.S.).[46]

State Highway Patrol officers. With a warrant, officers of the Highway Patrol may arrest for any crime. In addition, they have general arrest jurisdiction for the following offenses: any offense committed in their presence, any crime committed on any street or highway, any other violation of laws that regulate travel and the use of vehicles or that protect the highways, highway robbery, bank robbery, murder or other crimes of violence, and littering.[47]

State Bureau of Investigation agents. State Bureau of Investigation (SBI) agents may arrest for any criminal offense.[48] Their authority to investigate on their own—without a request from local authorities, the governor, or the attorney general—is limited to arsons and other unlawful burnings, drug violations, thefts or misuse of state property, and assaults on state executive officers, legislators, or court officers.[49]

Alcohol law enforcement agents. Alcohol law enforcement (ALE) agents may arrest for any criminal offense, although their primary responsibility is to enforce ABC, lottery, and drug laws.[50]

Officers who specialize in enforcing motor vehicle laws. Officers of the Motor Carrier Enforcement Section of the State Highway Patrol and inspectors of the Division of Motor Vehicles License and Theft Bureau may arrest for all G.S. Chapter 20 (motor vehicle) violations and offenses committed in their presence when they are enforcing laws within their jurisdiction.[51]

Wildlife law enforcement officers. Wildlife law enforcement officers may arrest for any felony; offenses involving boating and water safety, hunting and trapping, and fishing (except for offenses under the jurisdiction of the Marine Fisheries Commission); any offense that either involves property owned or leased by the Wildlife Resources Commission or occurs on a wildlife refuge, game land, or boating and fishing access area managed by the Wildlife Resources Commission; any breach of the peace (an offense that disturbs public order and tends to incite others to break the peace); any assault committed against them or in their presence; carrying a concealed weapon; any offense, such as resisting an officer, that challenges their authority or interferes with their enforcement of the law; and any offense committed in their presence when they are enforcing laws within their jurisdiction.[52]

---

45. G.S. 15A-403 permits officers from other states to enter North Carolina to arrest a person fleeing from the other state only to the extent that the other state authorizes a North Carolina officer to enter that state. Because Georgia, South Carolina, Tennessee, and Virginia permit entry into their state only in hot pursuit to arrest for felonies (with the additional misdemeanors of impaired driving and commercial impaired driving for pursuit into Georgia and South Carolina, as discussed in notes 41 and 42, above), officers from these states may enter North Carolina only in hot pursuit to arrest for felonies (and the impaired driving misdemeanors previously mentioned for Georgia and South Carolina officers) committed in their respective states. *See generally* United States v. Goings, 573 F.3d 1141 (11th Cir. 2009) (irrelevant under Fourth Amendment if Georgia officers' arrest of defendant in Florida after pursuit violated state law; only issue under Fourth Amendment is whether probable cause existed to arrest defendant).

46. G.S. 90-113.5. Law enforcement officers are not permitted to enforce laws within Article 5 that are specifically delegated to others—for instance, the licensing of drug treatment facilities under G.S. 90-109.

47. G.S. 20-49, -188.

48. G.S. 14B-917 gives SBI agents the same authority to arrest as sheriffs, who may arrest for any crime.

49. G.S. 58-79-1, -2; 90-113.5; 143B-917, -919, -920. SBI agents may investigate any crime on request of law enforcement officers, district attorneys, or judges. When requested by the governor, they may investigate lynchings and mob violence, state Social Security frauds, and gambling and lottery violations. They may investigate election law frauds when requested by the State Board of Elections and directed by the governor. They may investigate any other crime when requested by the governor or the attorney general.

50. G.S. 18B-500(b).

51. G.S. 20-49, -49.1, -49.2, -183.10, -383.

52. G.S. 113-136; Parker v. Hyatt, 196 N.C. App. 489 (2009) (wildlife officer had subject-matter jurisdiction under G.S. 113-136(d) to stop vehicle driver and to arrest her for impaired

Marine fisheries enforcement officers. Marine fisheries enforcement officers may arrest for any felony; an offense arising out of any matter within the jurisdiction of the Marine Fisheries Commission; a stream-obstruction offense covered in G.S. Chapter 77; any offense involving property owned, leased, or managed by the Department of Environment and Natural Resources in connection with the conservation of marine and estuarine resources; any breach of the peace; any assault committed against them or in their presence; carrying a concealed weapon; and any offense, such as resisting an officer, that challenges their authority or interferes with their enforcement of the law.[53]

Sheriffs, deputy sheriffs, and county police officers. Sheriffs, deputy sheriffs, and county police officers may arrest for any criminal offense.[54]

Local alcohol beverage control officers. Local alcohol beverage control (ABC) officers may arrest for any criminal offense, although their primary responsibility is to enforce ABC and drug laws.[55]

City law enforcement officers. City law enforcement officers may arrest for any criminal offense.[56]

Company police officers. Company police officers may arrest for any criminal offense.[57]

Campus law enforcement officers. Whether sworn as company police officers, city law enforcement officers, or deputy sheriffs, campus law enforcement officers may arrest for any criminal offense. Officers of The University of North Carolina, community college, and private nonprofit college law enforcement agencies also may arrest for any criminal offense.[58]

Probation and parole officers. Parole officers may arrest a parolee only when the Post-Release Supervision and Parole Commission has issued an order of temporary or conditional revocation of parole for that person.[59] The same is true for officers supervising offenders on post-release supervision.[60] Probation officers may arrest a probationer for violating conditions of probation when a court has issued an order for arrest; in addition, probation officers may arrest "in the execution of [their] duties."[61] This language authorizes probation officers to arrest a probationer without an order for arrest;[62] it also suggests that they may arrest for such offenses as obstructing officers in the performance of their duties. However, because probation officers' authority to arrest for crimes that they may observe while performing their duties is unclear, they probably should not attempt to arrest for these offenses. Instead of getting an order for arrest, probation officers may make a written request to a law enforcement officer to make an arrest.[63]

Division of Adult Correction (formerly, Department of Correction)[64] policy provides that probation or parole officers must obtain a law enforcement officer's assistance in arresting a probationer or parolee whenever they reasonably believe that conducting the arrest alone might compromise their personal safety. Otherwise, officers may ask a law enforcement officer to make the arrest, or, if assistance is not needed or an emergency does not allow time to get a law enforcement officer's assistance, they may make the arrest.[65]

---

driving, which is an offense that satisfies the statutory language, "a threat to public peace and order which would tend to subvert the authority of the State if ignored"). The text does not describe all offenses that are within the jurisdiction of wildlife law enforcement officers. Under certain circumstances, an officer must issue a citation instead of making an arrest of a nonresident for some wildlife violations. G.S. 113-300.6.

53. G.S. 113-136(b), -136(d). The text does not describe all offenses that are within the jurisdiction of marine fisheries enforcement officers.

54. Sheriffs and their deputies derive their authority to arrest for any crime from common law. County police agencies derive their authority from local legislative acts. *See, e.g.,* 1929 N.C. Public-Local Laws, Ch. 93 (Gaston County police).

55. G.S. 18B-501(b).

56. G.S. 160A-285.

57. G.S. 74E-6(c).

58. G.S. 116-40.5(a); 115D-21.1; 74G-6(b).

59. G.S. 15A-1376(a).

60. G.S. 15A-1368.6.

61. G.S. 15-205; 15A-1345(a). The term "court" is not defined in G.S. 15A-1345 or elsewhere in Chapter 15A. At least in the context of G.S. 15A-1345(a), the legislature probably intended that the term includes all officials set out in G.S. 15A-305(a) (justice, judge, clerk, or magistrate), because G.S. 15A-305(a) (4) authorizes these officials to issue an order for arrest when a defendant has violated probation conditions.

62. State v. Waller, 37 N.C. App. 133 (1978).

63. G.S. 15A-1345(a). The written request is made with form DCC-12, Authority to Arrest.

64. The Department of Correction was renamed the Division of Adult Correction when several state departments were consolidated into a new Department of Public Safety by S.L. 2011-145.

65. Stevens H. Clarke, Law of Sentencing, Probation, & Parole in North Carolina 168 (UNC Institute of Government, 2d ed. 1997).

Special Jurisdictional Issues

Violations of federal laws. State and local law enforcement officers are authorized to arrest for violations of federal laws.[66] When officers make an arrest for a federal offense, they should follow the same rules of arrest that they would follow when arresting for a violation of state law. Although they may take the arrestee before a state magistrate,[67] they normally should take the arrestee before a federal judicial official such as a United States magistrate. Despite this formal authority to arrest for violations of federal laws, it is often advisable to leave arrests for federal offenses to federal officials, as they are more familiar with federal laws and arrest procedures.

Immigration enforcement by North Carolina law enforcement officers. North Carolina law provides that, when authorized by federal law, a state or local law enforcement agency may authorize its officers to perform functions of an officer under Section 1357(g) of Title 8 of the United States Code (immigration officer functions performed by state officers and employees) if the agency has a memorandum of agreement or memorandum of understanding for that purpose with a federal agency.[68] State and local law enforcement officers are authorized to hold any office or position with the applicable federal agency required to perform the functions.

Desertion and AWOL. State and local law enforcement officers may arrest a person who has deserted from the armed forces[69] and either deliver the person to armed forces personnel authorized to receive deserters or take the person before a state or federal magistrate so that the arrestee may be committed to a detention facility to await the arrival of military authorities.[70] Officers may arrest a person who is AWOL (away without leave) from the armed forces, although it is unclear whether their authority to arrest for being AWOL depends on a request to arrest by military authorities.[71]

Areas controlled by the federal government. Before discussing state and local law enforcement officers' authority to arrest on federally controlled land, it is helpful to understand a state's authority to prosecute crimes that are committed on federal land.

The jurisdiction of federal and state governments to prosecute crimes committed on federally controlled lands depends on the relationship of the federal government to the land.[72] Generally, there are three different

---

66. In the absence of a federal statute setting out the authority of a state officer to arrest for a federal offense, the law of the state where an arrest occurs determines the arrest's validity. United States v. DiRe, 332 U.S. 581 (1948); United States v. Swarovski, 557 F.2d 40 (2d Cir. 1977); United States v. Santana-Garcia, 264 F.3d 1188 (10th Cir. 2001) (court found that Utah state law, which authorizes law enforcement officer to arrest for "any public offense," authorized state law enforcement officer to arrest for federal immigration law violation; state law need not affirmatively authorize arrest for federal immigration law violation); United States v. Villa-Velazquez, 282 F.3d 553 (8th Cir. 2002) (similar ruling). Because there is no federal statute, and state law authorizes arrests for felonies and misdemeanors without limiting them to state crimes, North Carolina law enforcement officers may arrest for federal offenses. Other pertinent cases include United States v. Bowdach, 561 F.2d 1160 (5th Cir. 1977) (state law enforcement officer had authority to arrest defendant based on knowledge of outstanding federal arrest warrant) and United States v. Haskin, 228 F.3d 151 (2d Cir. 2000) (Vermont state police officer had authority to seize firearms for violation of federal firearms laws).

67. 18 U.S.C. § 3041.

68. G.S. 128-1.1. If an officer is not designated under federal law to perform the functions of an immigration officer, then the officer does not have the authority to detain or arrest a person subject to a civil immigration warrant absent Immigration and Customs Enforcement's express authorization or direction. Santos v. Frederick Cty. Bd. of Comm'rs, 725 F.3d 451 (4th Cir. 2013).

Although North Carolina has not enacted laws similar to Arizona's, the United States Supreme Court's ruling in Arizona

v. United States, 132 S. Ct. 2492 (2012), is of general interest. Four provisions of the Arizona law were at issue. One section made failure to comply with federal alien registration requirements a state misdemeanor. A second section made it a misdemeanor for an unauthorized alien to seek or engage in work in Arizona. A third section authorized officers to arrest without a warrant a person "the officer has probable cause to believe . . . has committed any public offense that makes the person removable from the United States" (quoting ARIZ. REV. STAT. ANN. § 13-3883(A)(5). A fourth section provided that officers who conduct a stop, detention, or arrest must in some circumstances make efforts to verify the person's immigration status with the federal government. The Court ruled that the first three provisions were preempted by federal law but that it was improper to enjoin the fourth provision "before the state courts had an opportunity to construe it and without some showing that enforcement of the provision in fact conflicts with federal immigration law and its objectives." 132 S. Ct. at 2510.

69. 10 U.S.C. § 808 (Art. 8, Uniform Code of Military Justice).

70. Military deserters may be confined in local detention facilities. G.S. 162-34; 45 N.C. Att'y Gen. Rep. 169 (1975). A military deserter has no right to bail. Huff v. Watson, 99 S.E. 307 (Ga. 1919).

71. Bledsoe v. Garcia, 742 F.2d 1237 (10th Cir. 1984); Myers v. United States, 415 F.2d 318 (10th Cir. 1969).

72. Basically there are three ways in which the federal government may acquire property within a state; the

method of acquisition determines the jurisdiction of the two governments.

First, the state may grant land owned by the state to the federal government. In this case, the remaining jurisdiction of the state is whatever is set out in the grant ceding the land. One must review the particular grant to determine the state's authority.

Second, the federal government may buy or condemn land within the state for a federal purpose. (This acquisition is made without the state's permission, which distinguishes it from the third method, discussed below.) In this second case, the federal government is treated no differently than any other property owner, and the state may enforce its laws on that land. However, the state may not interfere with the federal government's use of the land for the purpose for which it was purchased. Therefore, for example, the federal government may prosecute violations of congressional acts enacted to protect its property under the Property Clause (Art. IV, Sec. 3, Clause 2) of the United States Constitution. United States v. Gliatta, 580 F.2d 156 (5th Cir. 1978); Kleppe v. New Mexico, 426 U.S. 529 (1976).

The third method of acquisition is set out in Article I, Section 8, Clause 17, of the federal Constitution: "[Congress shall have the power] . . . to exercise [exclusive legislation] over all places purchased by the consent of the legislature of the state in which the same shall be, for the erection of forts, magazines, arsenals, dock-yards, and other needful buildings." This clause authorizes Congress to exercise exclusive jurisdiction over any land within a state that it purchases with the consent of the state legislature. Since 1940, however, statutory law (40 U.S.C. § 255, recodified as 40 U.S.C. § 3112) has required that the United States give its affirmative assent to the transfer of exclusive jurisdiction before such jurisdiction becomes effective.

North Carolina has had several legislative enactments concerning this issue. Before 1887, the General Assembly authorized the sale of specific tracts to the federal government by individual public laws. To determine the jurisdiction on property ceded before 1887, one must look at the specific grant. In 1887 (Pub. Laws of 1887, Ch. 136), the General Assembly consented to the federal government's acquisition of land in North Carolina for certain public buildings. Because the act was silent concerning jurisdiction, its effect was to grant exclusive federal jurisdiction through the constitutional clause discussed in the preceding paragraph.

In 1905, the legislature repeated the federal government's authorization to acquire land for various purposes, but it provided that the state would retain the authority to punish all violations of North Carolina law committed there—in effect giving the state concurrent jurisdiction with the federal government. This 1905 act remains codified as G.S. 104-1.

In 1907, the legislature changed the law. It again authorized federal acquisition of land, but the state reserved only the authority to serve criminal and civil process there. This 1907 act is now codified as G.S. 104-7. In 2005, major revisions were made to G.S. 104-7, the most pertinent to this discussion being that the state's consent to the United States' acquisition of land is conditioned on the state having concurrent power to enforce criminal law on the land. The 2005 change appears to apply prospectively to land obtained on or after May 27, 2005, the effective date of the legislation. *See* S.L. 2005-69.

Needless to say, the legislative acts through 1907 are somewhat contradictory. However, in 1945, the North Carolina Supreme Court clarified matters. In *State v. DeBerry*, 224 N.C. 834 (1945), the court ruled that a defendant could not be prosecuted under state law for an assault in the Winston-Salem federal courthouse because that building was under exclusive federal jurisdiction. To reach that decision, the court had to conclude that the acts of 1905 and 1907 were to be given prospective application only. The federal government acquired the Winston-Salem courthouse in 1899; thus, it was subject to the 1887 law that provided for exclusive federal jurisdiction.

In sum, if the property was acquired before 1887, the kind of jurisdiction is determined by the individual legislative act giving consent to the federal government to acquire the land. If the property was acquired between 1887 and 1905, there is exclusive federal jurisdiction. If it was acquired between 1905 and 1907, there is concurrent federal and state jurisdiction. If it was acquired between 1907 and 1940, there is exclusive federal jurisdiction. If it was acquired after 1940 and before May 27, 2005, the federal government obtains exclusive (or concurrent) jurisdiction only if it complies with the notification requirements of 40 U.S.C. § 255, recodified as 40 U.S.C. § 3112. *See generally* United States v. Johnson, 994 F.2d 980 (2d Cir. 1993) (sufficient compliance with 40 U.S.C. § 255, recodified as 40 U.S.C. § 3112). If the federal government does not comply with these statutory requirements, the state government generally prosecutes for crimes committed on such property. For land acquired on or after May 27, 2005, the state retains the authority to enforce its criminal laws on the land.

For cases on federal or state jurisdiction on certain property in North Carolina, see *State v. Burrell*, 256 N.C. 288 (1962) (U.S. Marine was properly prosecuted in state court for sexual assault when it occurred on property of U.S. Marine Corps Air Station at Cherry Point, acquired in 1958; federal government had not accepted jurisdiction under 40 U.S.C. § 255, recodified as 40 U.S.C. § 3112); *State v. Smith*, 328 N.C. 161 (1991) (defendant could not be prosecuted for murders committed on Camp Lejeune military reservation; in 1941, the United States purchased property where bodies were found, and federal government accepted exclusive jurisdiction in accordance with what is now G.S. 104-7 and 40 U.S.C. § 255, recodified as 40 U.S.C. § 3112); *State v. Graham*, 47 N.C. App. 303 (1980) (court affirmed state conviction for post office break-in when record did not reveal that federal government had accepted exclusive jurisdiction over post office under 40 U.S.C. § 255 [Author's note: 40 U.S.C. § 255, recodified as 40 U.S.C. § 3112, applies only to acquisitions after 1940], United States v. Johnson, 426 F.2d 1112 (7th Cir. 1970), and court did not discuss when post office was acquired); and *United States v. Raffield*, 82 F.3d 611 (United States and North Carolina governments have concurrent jurisdiction to prosecute crimes committed on national forest lands located within North Carolina [Author's note: National forests in North Carolina include Croatan, Uwharrie, Pisgah, and Nantahala]).

Pursuant to a July 27, 1984, agreement between the governor of North Carolina and the secretary of the Department of the Interior, the United States and North Carolina have concurrent jurisdiction in the following places: Blue Ridge Parkway, Cape Hatteras National Seashore, Cape Lookout National Seashore, Carl Sandburg Home National Historic Site, Fort Raleigh National Historic Site, Great Smoky Mountains National Park, Guilford Courthouse National Military Park, Moores Creek National Military Park, and Wright Brothers National Monument.

Specified federal officials have the authority under 40 U.S.C. § 1315 to authorize North Carolina law enforcement officers to enforce state criminal laws on federal property. Although the federal statute permits such an agreement with a state or local agency, such an agreement probably only can be made with the governor of North Carolina under G.S. 104-11.1.

There are special jurisdictional issues involving the Cherokee Indian Reservation in North Carolina. Although there are cases such as *United States v. Hornbuckle*, 422 F.2d 391 (4th Cir. 1970), and *State v. McAlhaney*, 220 N.C. 387 (1931), that have ruled or stated that federal and state governments have concurrent jurisdiction to prosecute criminal offenses committed on the Cherokee Indian Reservation, they are no longer valid in light of *United States v. John*, 437 U.S. 634 (1978), and *Eastern Band of Cherokee Indians v. Lynch*, 632 F.2d 373 (4th Cir. 1980). It appears that the State may prosecute a crime committed on the reservation only if it is committed by a non-Indian against a non-Indian. It also appears that state law enforcement officers may enter the reservation to arrest an Indian for a crime committed outside the reservation or to execute a search warrant related to a crime for which the state has jurisdiction. State v. Levier, 601 P.2d 1116 (Kan. 1979) (arrest); Nevada v. Hicks, 533 U.S. 353 (2001) (search warrant). Of course, law enforcement officers should consider seeking the cooperation and assistance of tribal law enforcement officers before executing such process.

The North Carolina Court of Appeals in *State v. Kostick*, 233 N.C. App. 62 (2014), ruled that a State Highway Patrol officer had jurisdiction to arrest the defendant, a non-Indian, for a DWI (driving while impaired) committed on the Cherokee reservation and that the State had the authority to try the defendant in North Carolina state courts. The court noted that pursuant to the Tribal Code of the Eastern Band of the Cherokee Indians and mutual compact agreements between the tribe and other law enforcement agencies, the North Carolina Highway Patrol has authority to patrol and enforce the motor vehicle laws of North Carolina within the Qualla boundary of the tribe, including the authority to arrest non-Indians who commit criminal offenses on the Cherokee reservation. Thus, the court concluded that North Carolina state courts have jurisdiction over the criminal offense of driving while impaired committed by a non-Indian, even when the offense

kinds of jurisdiction. First, when the federal government retains exclusive jurisdiction over its land, it has the sole power to prosecute crimes committed on that land. (Through the federal Assimilative Crimes Act,[73] the federal government prosecutes defendants under the criminal laws of the state on which the federal land is located.) Although the State may not prosecute crimes committed on such land, state or local law enforcement officers may enter the land to "execute criminal process" (for instance, making an arrest with an arrest warrant) for a defendant who committed a crime outside the federal land.[74] Second, federal and state governments may retain

---

and subsequent arrest occur within the Qualla boundary of the Cherokee reservation.

For an analysis of federal, state, and tribal jurisdiction over crimes committed on a reservation, see David T. Sentelle and Melanie T. Morris, *Criminal Jurisdiction on the North Carolina Cherokee Indian Reservation—A Tangle of Race and History*, 24 WAKE FOREST LAW REVIEW 335 (1989); *United States v. Welch*, 822 F.2d 460 (4th Cir. 1987); and *United States v. Johnson*, 637 F.2d 1224 (9th Cir. 1980). *See also* Jackson Cty. v. Swayney, 319 N.C. 52 (1987) (State did not have subject-matter jurisdiction to determine paternity when child, mother, and defendant were Cherokee Indians residing on reservation, but once paternity was established in tribal court, State had subject-matter jurisdiction in action brought by State under AFDC program to collect debt owed to the State for past public assistance and to obtain judgment for future child support). On the issue of a federal officer who was a criminal defendant in state court seeking removal of his state prosecution to federal court, see *State v. Ivory*, 906 F.2d 999 (4th Cir. 1990) (United States Marine could not remove to federal court a State prosecution arising from an accident that occurred while he was driving a military convoy on a state highway).

73. 18 U.S.C. § 13.

74. For property the federal government acquired from 1905 to 1907 and from 1907 to the present, G.S. 104-1 and G.S. 104-7 clearly reserve the state's right to serve criminal and civil process on land held under federal exclusive jurisdiction. For land acquired between 1887 and 1905, Pub. Laws of 1887, Ch. 136, did not reserve the right to serve criminal and civil process. Individual legislative acts before 1887 may have been silent also.

Despite the failure to reserve the right to serve criminal and civil process, the state retains such a right even without an express reservation. Since 1795, federal law, now codified as 33 U.S.C. § 728, has provided that "notwithstanding [that] any such cession of jurisdiction contains no such reservation, all process may be served and executed within the place ceded, in the same manner as if no cession had been made." Although this provision makes specific reference to another provision, 33 U.S.C. § 727, relating to federal acquisition of state land to build lighthouses, beacons, public piers, or landmarks, it

concurrent jurisdiction over federal land, which means that either government may prosecute crimes committed there. Third, the federal government may retain only a proprietary interest in federal land; the State generally prosecutes all crimes committed there, although the federal government may prosecute violations of federal law concerning the protection of its property.[75] In both concurrent and proprietary jurisdictions, state and local law enforcement officers clearly have the power to arrest for crimes committed on federal land and to arrest there a defendant who committed a crime elsewhere.

The federal government controls land in North Carolina in all three ways discussed above. Officers should consult with federal authorities in their area to determine the status of federal lands in their jurisdiction and to discuss mutually acceptable enforcement procedures.[76]

Offenses that occur in other states (extradition).[77] North Carolina law enforcement officers may arrest a person who flees to North Carolina after he or she has committed a misdemeanor or felony in another state if the officers obtain a fugitive warrant for the person's arrest from a North Carolina judicial official.[78] To obtain a fugitive warrant, officers must show either (1) probable cause

to believe that the person committed a crime in another state (the same standard for obtaining an arrest warrant for a crime committed in North Carolina) or (2) that the person has been charged in another state with committing a crime. A fugitive warrant also may be issued to arrest a person who has come from another state after escaping from imprisonment or violating conditions of probation or parole.[79]

If the fugitive warrant is issued because the person has been charged with a crime in another state, it must be supported by an affidavit to that effect, based on information from someone in the other state. A Division of Criminal Information (DCI) message or other reliable hearsay is sufficient to support a fugitive warrant.[80] A certified copy of the warrant or indictment from the other state should be attached to the fugitive warrant when it arrives, but its absence should not delay execution of the warrant. If a question exists about either the continuing validity of the charge in the other state or the other state's interest in having the person arrested, the officer should check with the appropriate authorities in that state before seeking a fugitive warrant. Verification of DCI messages in such instances is often advisable. Although the authority to arrest fugitives is not limited to felonies, most states normally will not extradite a misdemeanant.

Officers in North Carolina may arrest a fugitive from another state without a fugitive warrant if the person has been charged in the other state with a crime that is punishable there by more than one year's imprisonment.[81] Although the law does not require such an action, it is advisable to obtain a fugitive warrant in all cases unless taking the time to obtain the warrant would jeopardize the officer's ability to apprehend the fugitive.

A fugitive also may be arrested if the governor of North Carolina has issued a governor's warrant[82] for the fugitive's arrest. This warrant is usually issued after a person

---

reflects a congressional policy equally applicable to any federal land under federal exclusive jurisdiction, regardless of the purpose for which the land was acquired. Allowing a state to execute its criminal and civil process on federal land ordinarily would not interfere with any federal interest and would eliminate a federal enclave where a criminal defendant or civil party might hide. *See* Fort Leavenworth R.R. Co. v. Lowe, 114 U.S. 525 (1885); United States v. Unzeula, 281 U.S. 138 (1930); 7 Op. U.S. Att'y Gen. 628 (1856).

75. United States v. Gliatta, 580 F.2d 156 (5th Cir. 1978); Kleppe v. New Mexico, 426 U.S. 529 (1976).

76. If local federal authorities are unable to provide assistance, contact the United States General Services Administration.

77. For a more complete discussion of extradition, see Robert L. Farb, State of North Carolina Extradition Manual (UNC School of Government, 3d. ed. 2013).

78. Broadly defined, a person is a *fugitive from justice* when he or she commits a crime within a state and then leaves the state. It is unnecessary that the prosecution show that the person was charged before leaving the state or that the person fled to avoid prosecution. *In re* Sultan, 115 N.C. 57 (1894); Gee v. State of Kansas, 912 F.2d 414 (10th Cir. 1990); Dunn v. Hindman, 836 F. Supp. 750 (D.Kan. 1993). There is common law authority to arrest a person for a felony committed in another state even when a charge has not been brought against the person there. State v. Klein, 130 N.W.2d 816 (Wisc. 1964); Desjarlais v. State, 243 N.W.2d 453 (Wisc. 1976).

79. G.S. 15A-733.

80. 45 N.C. Att'y Gen. Rep. 236 (1976). An officer's telephone conversation with a knowledgeable person in the other state that provided information about the fugitive also could be used in the officer's affidavit to justify issuing a fugitive warrant.

81. G.S. 15A-734.

82. G.S. 15A-727. The majority view is that a person arrested pursuant to a governor's warrant has no right to bail, and judges have no common law or inherent authority to grant release on bail. See the cases cited in Farb, *supra* note 77, at 57. No right to bail exists when a fugitive waives the issuance of a governor's warrant and all other extradition proceedings and

is already in custody in North Carolina; it is based on a formal request for extradition from the governor of the requesting state to the governor of North Carolina.

The Administrative Office of the Courts (AOC) has published several forms used for processing fugitives that are of particular interest to law enforcement officers: AOC-CR-909M (magistrate's order for fugitive), AOC-CR-910M (arrest warrant for fugitive), AOC-CR-911M (fugitive affidavit) (to be used with either the magistrate's order or the arrest warrant), and AOC-CR-912M (waiver of extradition). These forms are also available to magistrates in their computer system and on the AOC's website at www.nccourts.org/Forms/FormSearch.asp.[83]

Foreign diplomats. Generally, the following foreign diplomatic personnel have complete criminal immunity from arrest and prosecution in the United States: (1) diplomatic agents (head of the diplomatic mission and members of the mission's diplomatic staff) and their families and (2) administrative and technical staff of the mission and their families.[84] Service staff have criminal immunity only for their official acts. Family members of the service staff and private servants of members of the mission have no immunity.

Federal officers and North Carolina's criminal laws. Certain federal law enforcement officers[85] are authorized to enforce North Carolina's criminal laws if (1) they are asked by the head of a state or local law enforcement agency, or designee, to provide temporary assistance, and the request is within the scope of that agency's jurisdiction; or (2) they are asked by state or local enforcement officers to provide temporary assistance when the state or local officers are acting within the scope of their jurisdiction.[86]

Expanded Jurisdiction through Cooperating Law Enforcement Agencies

Several statutes authorize the head of one law enforcement agency to provide temporary assistance to another agency upon its written request.[87] If this assistance includes officers' working temporarily with the other agency, the officers have the jurisdiction and authority of both the requesting agency and their own agency. Thus, a Raleigh police officer who was working for the Greensboro Police Department would have the jurisdiction and authority of both departments.[88]

---

consents to return to the demanding state. 50 N.C. Att'y Gen. Rep. 40 (1980).

When a fugitive is arrested by other than a governor's warrant, a magistrate or judge may set bail by bond, with sufficient sureties, before service of the governor's warrant unless the charged offense is punishable by death or life imprisonment under the laws of the state where it was committed. G.S. 15A-736.

83. Many other AOC forms are available at this website.

84. *See* Vienna Convention on Diplomatic Relations, Apr. 18, 1961, 23 U.S.T. 3227, T.I.A.S. No. 7502. This treaty became effective with respect to the United States on December 13, 1972. See the discussion of this treaty in 1978 U.S.C.C.A.N. at 1935–48. For a discussion of diplomatic immunity, see *Diplomatic and Consular Immunity: Guidance for Law Enforcement and Judicial Authorities* (United States Department of State, undated) www.state.gov/documents/organization/150546.pdf. *See also* Jonathan L. Rudd, *Diplomatic Immunity*, FBI LAW ENFORCEMENT BULL. 25 (Feb. 2008). This bulletin is available at https://leb.fbi.gov/in-each-issue/archive.

85. The federal law enforcement officers include special agents of the United States Secret Service; Federal Bureau of Investigation; Bureau of Alcohol, Tobacco, and Firearms; United States Naval Investigative Service; Drug Enforcement Administration; and the Internal Revenue Service. Also included are United States Postal Service inspectors; United

States Marshals Service marshals and deputies; and officers of the United States Customs Service, the United States Forest Service, the National Park Service, the Immigration and Naturalization Service, the United States Fish and Wildlife Service, the Tennessee Valley Authority, and the Veterans Administration.

86. G.S. 15A-406.

87. G.S. 90-95.2; 153A-212; 160A-288, -288.2. *See also* G.S. 18B-501(e). For a discussion of mutual aid agreements between law enforcement agencies, including sample resolutions and mutual assistance agreement forms, see Michael F. Easley and Jeffrey P. Gray, *Mutual Aid Agreements Between Law Enforcement Agencies in North Carolina* (North Carolina Department of Justice, Mar. 1996).

88. In *State v. Locklear*, 136 N.C. App. 716 (2000), a Robeson County deputy sheriff called for assistance in responding to a stabbing at a home three to four miles outside the Red Springs city limits. A Red Springs law enforcement officer responded to the call and was later assaulted by the defendant there. The defendant argued that the officer was outside his territorial jurisdiction (one mile beyond the city limits) when the assault occurred, and thus he could not be convicted of assault with a firearm on a law enforcement officer because he was not acting as an officer then. The court ruled that a mutual aid agreement between the Robeson County Sheriff's Department and the Red Springs Police Department permitted the officer to respond to the request for assistance, based on the agreement's permitting an oral request to be made for an "emergency." The court ruled that an emergency existed: the deputy sheriff was transporting a prisoner when he received the order to investigate the stabbing, and he was the only deputy in the vicinity of the residence.

A question that arises under these statutes is whether a standing written request may be made for specific types of temporary assistance or whether the requesting agency's head must make a written request for each individual situation. The attorney general has issued an opinion that a city or county governing body can adopt guidelines that enable the head of a law enforcement agency to make a standing written request for temporary assistance that will be valid for a specific period of time for specific types of assistance; the head of the requested agency can then furnish assistance within the guidelines without needing an individual written request each time.[89] Although long-term undercover work would require an individual written request, guidelines could provide for a standing written request for temporary assistance in making arrests, executing search warrants, and the like.

Officers without arrest authority may assist officers with arrest authority when assistance is requested. See the discussion on page 69 on assisting others in making an arrest.

Expanded Jurisdiction through Emergency Management Assistance Compact

The Emergency Management Assistance Compact provides for mutual assistance between states that are party to the compact in managing emergencies or disasters that are declared by the governor of the affected state or states.[90] The compact applies only to requests for assistance made by and to authorized representatives of each state. Law enforcement officers in one state who are sent to another state do not have the power to arrest in the other state unless specifically authorized by the other state.[91] All 50 states are members of the compact, as well as the District of Columbia, Puerto Rico, and the U.S. Virgin Islands.

Private Person's Authority to Detain

(*See page 98 for case summaries on this topic.*)

All people, whether or not they are law enforcement officers, are authorized to detain offenders under some circumstances. Law enforcement officers may use this authority when they do not have the authority to arrest.[92]

Private people may detain an offender whenever they have probable cause to believe that the offender has committed—in their presence—a felony, a breach of the peace (an offense that disturbs public order and tends to incite others to break the peace),[93] a crime involving physical injury to another, or a crime involving theft or destruction of property.[94] Private people may use only reasonable force in holding the offender and must immediately notify law enforcement officers and release the offender to them when the officers arrive.[95] Officers who attempt to use this authority to detain because they are not authorized to arrest someone must remember that they may detain the person only if the offense occurs in their presence, and they must release the offender as soon as possible to a law enforcement officer who has arrest authority. (A private person's authority to assist a law enforcement officer is discussed on page 69.)

A private person has the same authority as a law enforcement officer to arrest without a warrant a person who is charged in another state with a crime punishable by more than one year's imprisonment and who has fled from that state.[96] However, as a practical matter, a private person should simply detain the fugitive and call a law enforcement officer to take custody of the fugitive. A private person also has the authority to arrest a prisoner who has escaped from the state's prison system.[97]

89. 47 N.C. Att'y Gen. Rep. 181 (1978). The opinion specifically discussed G.S. 160A-288, but the other statutes cited in note 87, above, are similar.

90. G.S. Ch. 166A, Art. 4.

91. G.S. 166A-44(b).

92. Although there are no North Carolina cases supporting this statement, see the rulings in *Glazner v. State*, 318 S.E.2d 233 (Ga. 1984); *State v. Johnson*, 661 S.W.2d 854 (Tenn. 1983); and *State v. Horn*, 750 S.E.2d 248 (W.Va. 2013).

93. ROLLIN M. PERKINS & RONALD N. BOYCE, CRIMINAL LAW 477–78 (3d ed. 1982); State v. Mobley, 240 N.C. 476 (1954); State v. Tripp, 9 N.C. App. 518 (1970) (court ruled that breach of peace occurred when defendant deliberately forced another car off the roadway and then drove his car near the other driver's front door).

94. G.S. 15A-404.

95. State v. Wall, 304 N.C. 609 (1982); State v. Ataei-Kachuei, 68 N.C. App. 209 (1984).

96. G.S. 15A-734.

97. G.S. 148-40.

Legal Standards

Introduction

Before the legal standards for making investigative stops and arresting people are discussed, it is important to understand how a court analyzes the Fourth Amendment's prohibition against unreasonable seizures. A court must first decide whether the officer's conduct was such a significant interference with a person's freedom of movement that a seizure occurred under the Fourth Amendment.

The United States Supreme Court ruled in *Florida v. Royer* that a seizure occurs when, in view of all the circumstances surrounding the incident, a reasonable person, innocent of criminal activity, would have believed that he or she was not "free to leave."[98] However, the Court later ruled that an officer's interaction with a person that may otherwise constitute a seizure under the *Royer* free to leave definition is not a seizure unless additional circumstances exist. In *California v. Hodari D.*,[99] the Court ruled that an officer's "show of authority"—which occurs when an officer exercises authority without using physical force; for example, by chasing a suspect on foot or attempting to stop the driver of a vehicle by displaying a blue light—does not constitute a seizure unless the person submits to that show of authority. A person submits to a show of authority when a fleeing suspect stops pursuant to an officer's command or the driver stops a vehicle pursuant to a blue light.[100] Thus, a person who does not submit to an officer's show of authority under these circumstances has not been seized under the Fourth Amendment.[101]

If an officer grasps or applies physical force to the suspect, a seizure occurs even if the suspect does not submit to the officer's efforts to stop the suspect.[102] However, the Court in *Hodari D.* stated that if the suspect, once seized, breaks free or escapes from the officer's grasp, the seizure would terminate.

In *Florida v. Bostick*,[103] the Court adopted a definition of *seizure* to be applied when officers board a bus before its scheduled departure from the terminal to ask passengers whether they would be willing to consent to a search of their personal possessions. The Court determined that the free to leave definition was inappropriate in such a case because a passenger would not feel free to leave the bus when it was about to depart, even if law enforcement officers were not present there. The Court ruled that the appropriate definition of a seizure in these circumstances is whether a reasonable person, innocent of criminal activity, would feel free to decline the officers' requests (in this case, requests to inspect the bus ticket and ask for identification and a consent search) or otherwise terminate the encounter with the officers.[104]

Law enforcement officers often interact with people without seizing them and therefore do not require any justification for their actions. For example, officers do not seize people by merely approaching them in a nonthreatening manner on a street, in an airport, or on a bus, identifying themselves as law enforcement officers, and asking questions if the person is willing to answer them.[105] On the other hand, a seizure clearly occurs when

---

which did not occur under *Hodari D.* until defendant finally stopped his vehicle).

98. 460 U.S. 491 (1983). In *Florida v. Bostick*, 501 U.S. 429 (1991), the Court defined *reasonable person* as one who is innocent of criminal activity; that definition would apply as well to the *Royer* definition of a seizure.

99. 499 U.S. 621 (1991).

100. When an officer stops a vehicle, the passengers as well as the driver are seized under the Fourth Amendment. Brendlin v. California, 551 U.S. 249 (2007); State v. Jackson, 199 N.C. App. 236 (2009).

101. North Carolina appellate courts follow the *Hodari D.* ruling. *See, e.g.*, State v. Mewborn, 200 N.C. App. 731 (2009) (defendant did not submit to officers' authority before fleeing from them and thus was not seized until officers took physical control of him); State v. Atwater, __ N.C. App. __, 723 S.E.2d 582 (2012) (unpublished) (because the defendant did not stop his vehicle when officer activated his blue lights, defendant's misconduct thereafter was properly considered in determining whether reasonable suspicion supported an investigative stop,

102. However, an officer's mere tapping on a suspect's shoulder to get the suspect's attention is not necessarily a seizure. *See* 4 WAYNE R. LaFAVE, SEARCH AND SEIZURE: A TREATISE ON THE FOURTH AMENDMENT § 9.4(a), at 585 (5th ed. 2012).

103. 501 U.S. 429 (1991). *Bostick* did not decide whether the officers had seized the defendant. It remanded the case to the Florida Supreme Court so that court could initially determine that issue. *See* United States v. Drayton, 536 U.S. 194 (2002) (officers did not seize bus passengers during interaction on bus).

104. The Court stated that this definition of a seizure applies to encounters on city streets and in airport lobbies as well as on buses. It is unclear whether the Court intended to replace the free to leave definition for all officers' encounters with people. This book takes the conservative view and assumes that the free to leave definition still governs unless the encounters are the kinds discussed in *Hodari D.* and *Bostick*.

105. United States v. Drayton, 536 U.S. 194 (2002); Florida v. Bostick, 501 U.S. 429 (1991); Florida v. Royer, 460 U.S. 491

officers arrest people by physically taking them into custody and transporting them to a magistrate for an initial appearance. Even when officers have not made an arrest, a seizure also may occur when they restrain a person by physical force or display a weapon, or when their language or tone of voice indicates that their instructions must be followed.[106]

There are no simple rules or exact guidelines for determining when and whether a seizure has occurred. The most useful guide will come from carefully examining, case by case, the endless variation of law enforcement interactions with people that occur daily. This will help an officer understand some of the distinctions derived from appellate court cases and apply them in a principled manner in everyday duties.

The United States Supreme Court itself has difficulty deciding these issues—the Court's nine Justices rarely unanimously agree in search and seizure cases. Sometimes not even a majority (five Justices) can agree on a particular search and seizure principle. A quotation from a Court opinion is worth remembering:

> We do not suggest that there is a litmus-paper test for distinguishing a consensual encounter from a seizure or for determining when a seizure exceeds the bounds of an investigative stop [and thereby becomes an arrest that must be justified by probable cause]. Even in the discrete category of airport encounters, there will be endless variations in the facts and circumstances, so much variation that it is unlikely that the courts can reduce to a sentence or a paragraph a rule that will provide unarguable answers to the question whether there has been an unreasonable search or seizure in violation of the Fourth Amendment.[107]

Objective Standard

(See page 182 for case summaries on this topic.)

When a court analyzes a factual situation to determine whether a seizure occurred and, if so, whether the seizure was an arrest or an investigative stop, it uses an objective standard: how a "reasonable" person would view the circumstances. Thus, whether officers subjectively believed that they were or were not seizing a person—and if so, whether they were arresting or merely stopping the person—is not generally relevant. Instead, the court compares the objective facts surrounding the incident with the legal standards of what constitutes a seizure and considers, if the encounter was a seizure, whether it was an arrest or an investigative stop.[108] For example, officers may believe that their action in seizing a person was only an investigative stop, but a court may decide that the objective facts showed that their conduct was the equivalent of an arrest and, therefore, had to be justified by probable cause.[109] An objective standard also is used in determining whether people would have believed they were not free to leave. Although people who have been approached by officers may say that they believed they were not free to leave, a court may determine from the objective facts that a reasonable person in such a situation would not have felt that way and, therefore, no seizure occurred. (A *reasonable person* is defined as one who is innocent of criminal activity.)[110]

(1983). *See, e.g.,* State v. Perkerol, 77 N.C. App. 292 (1985) (officer's interaction with suspect in airport was not a seizure); State v. Thomas, 81 N.C. App. 200 (1986) (similar ruling).

106. Florida v. Royer, 460 U.S. 491 (1983).

107. *Id.* at 506–07. *See also* United States v. Sharpe, 470 U.S. 675 (1985) ("Much as a 'bright line' rule would be desirable, in evaluating whether an investigative detention is unreasonable, common sense and ordinary human experience must govern over rigid criteria.").

108. State v. Bone, 354 N.C. 1 (2001); State v. Peck, 305 N.C. 734 (1982); United States v. Analla, 975 F.2d 119 (4th Cir. 1992); United States v. Taylor, 956 F.2d 572 (6th Cir. 1992) (en banc) (officer's subjective intent to pursue defendant was irrelevant in considering whether defendant was seized unless officer conveyed that intent to defendant). The objective standard has at least one major exception. A court considers the particular officer's prior training and experience when it determines whether the officer had reasonable suspicion to make an investigative stop or probable cause to arrest. United States v. Cortez, 449 U.S. 411 (1981). Examples of United States Supreme Court cases using an objective standard involving other Fourth Amendment issues are *Devenpeck v. Alford*, 543 U.S. 146 (2004), and *Brigham City v. Stuart*, 547 U.S. 398 (2006).

109. Sibron v. New York, 392 U.S. 40 (1968); State v. Zuniga, 312 N.C. 251 (1982). On the other hand, an officer may believe that he or she had arrested a person at a particular time, but a court may decide that the objective facts showed that the officer's conduct was the equivalent of an investigative stop, requiring only reasonable suspicion.

110. Florida v. Bostick, 501 U.S. 429 (1991).

Officer's Objectively Reasonable Mistake of Fact or Law in Determining Reasonable Suspicion or Probable Cause

The United States Supreme Court and North Carolina appellate courts recognize that an officer's objectively reasonable mistake of fact when deciding to make an investigative stop or an arrest may still allow a court to determine that the investigative stop or arrest was reasonable under the Fourth Amendment. Examples include an officer's objectively reasonable mistake of fact about a vehicle driver's identity[111] or the identity of a person to be arrested.[112]

In 2014, the United States Supreme Court, affirming an earlier ruling of the North Carolina Supreme Court, ruled in *Heien v. North Carolina*[113] that an officer's objectively reasonable mistake of law in making an investigative stop or arrest is reasonable under the Fourth Amendment. The Court ruled, as had the North Carolina Supreme Court, that there was reasonable suspicion for an investigative stop of a vehicle. An officer had stopped a vehicle based on a nonfunctioning brake light. The evidence indicated that although the left brake light was operating, the right light was not. Interpreting various statutes, the North Carolina Court of Appeals had ruled[114] that a vehicle is not required to have more than one operating brake light. It concluded that because the law had not been violated, the stop was unreasonable under the Fourth Amendment. Before the North Carolina Supreme Court, the State did not appeal the court of appeals' interpretation of statutory law. Instead, the State appealed only the court's determination that the stop was unreasonable. Thus, the issue before that court and later before the United States Supreme Court was whether an officer's mistake of law may nonetheless establish reasonable suspicion to conduct a routine traffic stop. On this issue both courts ruled that an officer's objectively reasonable but mistaken belief that a traffic violation has occurred can provide reasonable suspicion for a stop (there were ambiguities in G.S. 20-129 as to whether a vehicle needed one or two operating rear lights). Applying this standard to the facts in this case, both courts found that the officer's mistake was

objectively reasonable and that the stop did not violate the Fourth Amendment.

Investigative Stop or Arrest

If a court determines that officers have seized a person, it then must decide whether their conduct constituted an investigative stop or an arrest. Officers may stop someone if they have reasonable suspicion that the person committed, is committing, or is about to commit a crime.[115] The stop must be brief, and the officers must pursue an investigation in a diligent and reasonable manner to confirm or dispel their suspicion quickly.[116] If officers detain a person beyond these limitations, a court may determine that the seizure was the functional equivalent of an arrest that must be justified by probable cause, even if the officers never formally arrested the person.

Sometimes the officers' interaction requires that a progression of legal questions be considered. The officers' initial conduct in approaching and talking to a person may not be a seizure under the Fourth Amendment, and therefore they do not need any justification for their actions. Later in the same encounter, the officers may interfere with the person's freedom in such a manner that they have seized the person, and therefore an investigative stop has occurred. The court then must determine whether the officers had reasonable suspicion or other authorization to stop the person. After stopping

---

111. State v. Williams, 209 N.C. App. 255 (2011). *See generally* Illinois v. Rodriguez, 497 U.S. 177 (1990); Brinegar v. United States, 338 U.S. 160 (1949).

112. Hill v. California, 401 U.S. 797 (1971). *See also* State v. Lynch, 94 N.C. App. 330 (1989).

113. 135 S. Ct. 530 (2014), *aff'g* State v. Heien, 366 N.C. 271 (2012).

114. 214 N.C. App. 515 (2011).

115. United States v. Cortez, 449 U.S. 411 (1981); United States v. Hensley, 469 U.S. 221 (1985).

116. United States v. Sharpe, 470 U.S. 675 (1985). The Supreme Court clearly stated in *Sharpe*, 470 U.S. at 686–87, that a reviewing court should not second-guess an officer when it considers whether the officer diligently pursued the investigation: "A creative judge engaged in post hoc evaluation of police conduct can almost always imagine some alternative means by which the objectives of the police might have been accomplished." In *Florida v. Royer*, 460 U.S. 491 (1983), the plurality opinion stated that the investigative techniques used during a stop may be no more intrusive than necessary to effectuate the stop. That statement was clarified in *United States v. Sokolow*, 490 U.S. 1 (1989), when the Court stated that for an investigative stop to be reasonable, officers are not required to use the least intrusive means available (for example, approaching a defendant without using force versus deciding to use force initially) to verify or dispel their suspicions. Such a rule would unduly hamper an officer's ability to make swift, on-the-spot decisions. The least intrusive means rule applies only to the length of the investigative stop, not to whether officers had a less intrusive means to verify their suspicions before stopping someone.

the person, the officers may interfere with the person's freedom to such a degree that the court will determine that an arrest occurred. It must then determine whether the officers had probable cause to arrest.[117]

Determination Made at the Time of the Arrest or Investigative Stop

It is important to remember that whatever incriminating evidence officers find after an arrest or investigative stop is not relevant when a court determines whether they had a legal justification when they stopped or arrested someone. For example, an arrest for possessing stolen goods cannot be justified on the basis of a post-arrest search that revealed the stolen goods.[118] Probable cause or reasonable suspicion must be determined from the facts known at the time of the arrest or investigative stop, not from the results of the later search.[119] (However, as discussed in Chapter 3 on page 250, officers who have probable cause to arrest may conduct a search incident to an arrest before the formal arrest if the arrest occurs at the same time the search is made. In addition, sometimes officers have both probable cause to arrest *and* probable cause to search; if so, a search may precede the arrest.)

The next two sections discuss the legal standards known as *reasonable suspicion* and *probable cause.* Understanding these standards is important because officers' lack of legal justification for their actions could result in the exclusion of evidence in a criminal proceeding, a civil lawsuit against the officers for money damages because they violated a person's constitutional rights, disciplinary action against the officers by the agency that employs them, or even criminal prosecution of the officers.

The Authority to Make an Investigative Stop: Reasonable Suspicion

(*See page 99 for case summaries on this topic.*)

The United States Supreme Court has recognized that law enforcement officers have the right to stop people on less than probable cause[120] (probable cause is discussed on page 39). It has ruled that officers may stop a person if they have reasonable suspicion that the person has committed, is committing, or is about to commit a crime.[121]

Definition

The United States Supreme Court has attempted to describe reasonable suspicion (a phrase used interchangeably with articulable suspicion, reasonable articulable suspicion, articulable reasonable suspicion, founded suspicion, and the like):

> Courts have used a variety of terms to capture the elusive concept of what cause is sufficient to authorize police to stop a person. . . . But the essence of all that has been written is that the totality of the circumstances—the whole picture—must be taken into account. Based upon that whole picture the detaining officers must have a particularized and objective basis for suspecting the particular person stopped of criminal activity. . . .
>
> The idea that an assessment of the whole picture must yield a particularized suspicion contains two elements, each of which must be present before a stop is permissible. First, the assessment must be based upon all of the circumstances. The analysis proceeds with various objective observations, information from police reports, if such

---

117. Florida v. Royer, 460 U.S. 491 (1983); State v. Perkerol, 77 N.C. App. 292 (1985). The uncommunicated intention of officers (for example, they would not have allowed the suspect to leave if the suspect had tried to do so) is irrelevant in determining whether an arrest had occurred. *See* 3 WAYNE R. LAFAVE, SEARCH AND SEIZURE: A TREATISE ON THE FOURTH AMENDMENT § 5.1(a), 11 (5th ed. 2012).

118. Henry v. United States, 361 U.S. 98 (1959); Beck v. Ohio, 379 U.S. 89 (1964).

119. Smith v. Ohio, 494 U.S. 541 (1990).

120. For a discussion of the difference between the standards of probable cause and reasonable suspicion, see *Alabama v. White*, 496 U.S. 325 (1990).

121. United States v. Cortez, 449 U.S. 411 (1981). An officer's right to stop a person for past criminal conduct constituting a felony was upheld in *United States v. Hensley*, 469 U.S. 221 (1985). The *Hensley* ruling is not limited to felonies. *See* State v. Blankenship, 757 S.W.2d 354 (Tenn. Crim. App. 1988), noted in 4 WAYNE R. LAFAVE, SEARCH AND SEIZURE: A TREATISE ON THE FOURTH AMENDMENT § 9.2(c), at 396 n.95 (5th ed. 2012). A useful publication on the multiple issues involved in traffic stops, including reasonable suspicion to stop a vehicle, is Jeffrey B. Welty, *Traffic Stops* (UNC School of Government, Aug. 2015), http://nccriminallaw.sog.unc.edu/wp-content/uploads/2015/09/2015-08-Traffic-Stops.pdf.

are available, and consideration of the modes or patterns of operation of certain kinds of lawbreakers. From these data, a trained officer draws inferences and makes deductions—inferences and deductions that might well elude an untrained person.

The process does not deal with hard certainties, but with probabilities. Long before the law of probabilities was articulated as such, practical people formulated certain common-sense conclusions about human behavior; jurors as factfinders are permitted to do the same—and so are law enforcement officers. Finally, the evidence thus collected must be seen and weighed not in terms of library analysis by scholars, but as understood by those versed in the field of law enforcement.

The second element . . . is . . . that the process just described must raise a suspicion that the particular individual being stopped is engaged in wrongdoing. Chief Justice Warren, speaking for the Court in Terry v. Ohio, . . . said that "[t]his demand for specificity in the information upon which police action is predicated is the central teaching of this Court's Fourth Amendment jurisprudence."[122]

Determination of Reasonable Suspicion

A court considers many factors when it determines whether an officer has reasonable suspicion to stop a person. Some of these factors are as follows:

- The officer's observation of conduct that, in light of the officer's training and experience, appears to be criminal
- Information the officer receives from other officers, citizens, or informants
- The time of day or night
- Whether the area is a high crime area
- The suspect's proximity to a location where a crime was recently committed or to a home, car, or business where criminal activity may be taking place
- Whether the suspect is a stranger to the area
- The suspect's reaction to the officer's presence, including flight after seeing the officer
- The officer's knowledge of the suspect's prior criminal record and activities, if they are relevant to the crime the suspect may be committing

- The suspect's flight from the scene of a crime
- Particularly in airport drug stops, the suspect's actions that may match factors set out in a profile of criminal behavior (for example, personal and behavioral traits associated with the commission of a particular crime)[123]

These and other factors all must be considered together in determining whether an officer has reasonable suspicion to make an investigative stop of a person.

Reasonable suspicion to stop a person who is in a vehicle is governed by the same legal principles discussed above. There are, however, some common misunderstandings about the legal grounds to make investigative stops of vehicle drivers for motor vehicle violations. First, it is mistakenly asserted that probable cause is necessary to stop a vehicle for a motor vehicle violation, when in fact only reasonable suspicion is required.[124] Second, it is also mistakenly asserted that reasonable suspicion exists to make an investigative stop of a vehicle for impaired driving only if there is evidence of another traffic violation—for example, driving left of center. Reasonable suspicion to stop a vehicle for impaired driving is determined by the totality of circumstances, which includes the officer's training and experience, indicating that a person is driving while impaired. The law does not require proof of another motor vehicle violation.[125]

Hearsay Evidence

When a court determines whether reasonable suspicion existed to justify an investigative stop, rules of evidence that are applicable at a trial do not apply. Thus, hearsay evidence that otherwise would be inadmissible at a trial is admissible at a suppression hearing.[126] For example, infor-

---

122. United States v. Cortez, 449 U.S. 411 (1981). *See also* United States v. Arvizu, 534 U.S. 266 (2002); Ornelas v. United States, 517 U.S. 690 (1996).

123. *See generally* 4 Wayne R. LaFave, Search and Seizure: A Treatise on the Fourth Amendment § 9.5 (5th ed. 2012).

124. State v. Styles, 362 N.C. 412 (2008) (court ruled that reasonable suspicion is standard for stops of vehicles for all traffic violations and disavowed statements in prior cases that probable cause is standard for stops of vehicles for readily observed traffic violations).

125. State v. Bonds, 139 N.C. App. 627 (2000).

126. The Fourth Amendment does not bar the use of hearsay evidence in determining reasonable suspicion or probable cause. Brinegar v. United States, 338 U.S. 160 (1949); Draper v. United States, 358 U.S. 307 (1959); Alabama v. White, 496 U.S. 325 (1990); Illinois v. Gates, 462 U.S. 213 (1983); 2 Wayne R. LaFave, Search and Seizure: A Treatise on the Fourth Amendment § 3.2(d), at 69 (5th ed. 2012). Under Rules 104(a)

mation given to an officer by another officer, a citizen, a confidential informant, or even an anonymous tipster may be considered. Because the law concerning the use of hearsay to assist in establishing reasonable suspicion is the same as the law concerning searches with and without a search warrant, this subject is discussed on page 425 of Chapter 4, which deals with search warrants, and is not repeated here.

Collective Knowledge of Officers

(*See page 181 for case summaries on this topic.*)

Sometimes an officer or law enforcement agency that possesses information about a suspect requests that another officer make an investigative stop. If the requesting officer's or agency's information establishes reasonable suspicion, the stop may be justified even though the stopping officer does not know the facts possessed by the requesting officer or agency. Also, if the collective knowledge of several officers or agencies working together on an investigation establishes reasonable suspicion, that generally may justify an investigative stop by one of the officers.[127] (The collective knowledge theory applies equally to probable cause to arrest.)

Appellate Court Cases on Reasonable Suspicion

(*See page 99 for case summaries on this topic.*)

The following facts in appellate court cases should provide some understanding of what constitutes reasonable suspicion. The reader should remember that the facts developed after the stops in these cases may not be used to supply reasonable suspicion to justify the stop.

Navarette v. California

After a 911 caller reported that a truck had run her off the road, a police officer located the truck the caller identified and executed a traffic stop. As officers approached the truck, they smelled marijuana. A search of the truck bed revealed 30 pounds of marijuana. The defendants moved to suppress the evidence, arguing that the traffic stop violated the Fourth Amendment because the officer lacked reasonable suspicion of criminal activity.

In *Navarette v. California*,[128] the United States Supreme Court, in what it termed a "close case," ruled that an officer had reasonable suspicion to make a vehicle stop based on a 911 call. Assuming that the 911 call was anonymous, the Court found that it bore adequate indicia of reliability, so that the officer could credit the caller's account that the truck ran her off the road. The Court explained: "By reporting that she had been run off the road by a specific vehicle—a silver Ford F-150 pickup, license plate 8D94925—the caller necessarily claimed eyewitness knowledge of the alleged dangerous driving. That basis of knowledge lends significant support to the tip's reliability." The Court noted that in this respect, the case contrasted with *Florida v. J.L.*[129] when the tip did not provide a basis to conclude that the tipster had actually seen the gun reportedly possessed by the defendant. It continued: "A driver's claim that another vehicle ran her off the road, however, necessarily implies that the informant knows the other car was driven dangerously." The Court noted evidence suggesting that the caller reported the incident soon after it occurred and stated: "That sort of contemporaneous report has long been treated as especially reliable." Again contrasting the case with *J.L.*, the Court noted that in *J.L.*, there was no indication that the tip was contemporaneous with the observation of criminal activity or made under the stress of excitement caused by a startling event. The Court determined that another indicator of veracity is the caller's use of the 911 system, which allows calls to be recorded and law enforcement to verify information about

---

and 1101(b)(1) of the North Carolina Rules of Evidence in G.S. 8C-1, the rules of evidence do not apply in a hearing that determines the admissibility of evidence, with the exception of rules concerning privileges. The following North Carolina cases recognizing the use of hearsay in establishing probable cause to arrest would apply equally to establishing reasonable suspicion to make an investigative stop: *State v. Roberts*, 276 N.C. 98 (1970); *Melton v. Hodges*, 114 N.C. App. 795 (1994); *Steinkrause v. Tatum*, 201 N.C. App. 289 (2009), *aff'd*, 364 N.C. 419 (2010).

127. *See* State v. Coffey, 65 N.C. App. 751 (1984); State v. Battle, 109 N.C. App. 367 (1993); State v. Bowman, 193 N.C. App. 104 (2008). *See also* 2 & 4 Wayne R. LaFave, Search and Seizure: A Treatise on the Fourth Amendment §§ 3.5, 9.5(j) (5th ed. 2012).

---

128. 134 S. Ct. 1683 (2014). The Court's ruling raised questions about the continuing validity of prior North Carolina cases that had found insufficient evidence or reasonable suspicion based on an anonymous 911 caller, including *State v. Blankenship*, 230 N.C. App. 113 (2013), and *State v. Peele*, 196 N.C. App. 668 (2009).

129. 529 U.S. 266 (2000).

the caller. Thus, "a reasonable officer could conclude that a false tipster would think twice before using such a system . . . [and a] caller's use of the 911 system is therefore one of the relevant circumstances that, taken together, justified the officer's reliance on the information reported in the 911 call." But, the Court cautioned, "None of this is to suggest that tips in 911 calls are *per se* reliable."

The Court noted that a reliable tip will justify an investigative stop only if it creates reasonable suspicion of criminal activity. It then determined that the caller's report of being run off the roadway created reasonable suspicion of an ongoing crime such as impaired driving. It stated:

> The 911 caller . . . reported more than a minor traffic infraction and more than a conclusory allegation of drunk or reckless driving. Instead, she alleged a specific and dangerous result of the driver's conduct: running another car off the highway. That conduct bears too great a resemblance to paradigmatic manifestations of drunk driving to be dismissed as an isolated example of recklessness. Running another vehicle off the road suggests lane positioning problems, decreased vigilance, impaired judgment, or some combination of those recognized drunk driving cues. . . . And the experience of many officers suggests that a driver who almost strikes a vehicle or another object—the exact scenario that ordinarily causes "running [another vehicle] off the roadway"—is likely intoxicated. . . . As a result, we cannot say that the officer acted unreasonably under these circumstances in stopping a driver whose alleged conduct was a significant indicator of drunk driving.

Florida v. J.L.

An anonymous phone call to a police department reported that a young black male standing at a particular bus stop and wearing a plaid shirt was carrying a gun. There was no audio recording of the call and nothing was known about the caller. Soon thereafter, officers went to the bus stop and saw three black males there. One (the defendant) of the three was wearing a plaid shirt. Officers did not see a firearm, and the defendant did not make any threatening or unusual movements. One offi-

cer stopped and frisked the defendant and seized a gun from his pocket.

The United States Supreme Court in *Florida v. J.L.*[130] ruled, distinguishing *Alabama v. White*, discussed below, and *Adams v. Williams*,[131] that this information was insufficient to support reasonable suspicion to make an investigative stop and frisk of the defendant. The court concluded that the tip in this case lacked the moderate indicia of reliability present in *White* and essential to the Court's ruling in that case. The tip was a bare report of an unknown, unaccountable informant who neither explained how he knew about the gun nor supplied any basis for believing that he had inside information about the defendant. Responding to the State's argument that the tip was reliable because its description of the suspect's visible attributes proved accurate, the Court stated that the reasonable suspicion at issue in this case required that a tip be reliable in its assertion of illegality, not just in its tendency to identify a determinate person. The Court

---

130. 529 U.S. 266 (2000). North Carolina cases concerning anonymous information since *Florida v. J.L.* include *State v. Johnson*, 204 N.C. App. 259 (2010) (anonymous information about person selling drugs at specific intersection was insufficient to stop vehicle for drug offense); *State v. Garcia*, 197 N.C. App. 522 (2009) (anonymous informant plus officer corroboration supported stop concerning marijuana at house); *State v. McArn*, 159 N.C. App. 209 (2003) (anonymous caller about illegal drugs in vehicle supplied insufficient information for vehicle stop); *State v. Allison*, 148 N.C. App. 702 (2002) (anonymous tip made in person to officer and officer's corroboration provided reasonable suspicion to make investigative stop and frisk for robbery suspect's weapon); *State v. Young*, 148 N.C. App. 462 (2002) (anonymous call and officer's corroboration provided reasonable suspicion to make investigative stop for armed robberies); *State v. Brown*, 142 N.C. App. 332 (2001) (anonymous phone call supplied insufficient information to support investigative stop under *Florida v. J.L.*); *State v. Hughes*, 353 N.C. 200 (2000) (similar ruling); *State v. Bone*, 354 N.C. 1 (2001) (anonymous call and officer's corroboration provided probable cause to arrest); and *State v. Peele*, 196 N.C. App. 668 (2009) (anonymous call about possible reckless or DWI driver headed for certain intersection and officer's following vehicle and seeing it weaving once within lane before stop was insufficient). Compare *Peele* with *Navarette v. California*, 134 S. Ct. 1683 (2014), discussed in the text above, and *United States v. Wheat*, 278 F.3d 722 (8th Cir. 2001) (anonymous phone call supported reasonable suspicion to stop vehicle for reckless driving, even though officer did not observe any traffic violation; court reviewed other cases decided since *Florida v. J.L.*).

131. 407 U.S. 143 (1972) (tip from known informant was sufficient to support stop and frisk for weapon).

also rejected the argument that there should be a "firearm exception" to standard reasonable suspicion analysis.

The Court specifically reserved the issue of whether a report of a person carrying a bomb must bear the same indicia of reliability as a report of a person carrying a firearm. The Court indicated that public safety officials in places where a reasonable expectation of privacy is diminished, such as airports or schools, may conduct protective searches with information that would be insufficient to justify searches elsewhere. The Court also stated that the requirement that an anonymous tip bear standard indicia of reliability to justify a stop in no way diminishes an officer's authority to conduct a protective search of a person who has already been legitimately stopped.[132] Its ruling in this case only concerns an officer's authority to make the initial stop. The Court restated its ruling that an anonymous tip lacking indicia of reliability of the kind contemplated in *White* and *Williams* does not justify a stop and frisk whenever and however it alleges the illegal possession of a firearm.

➤ **Illinois v. Wardlow**

Uniformed officers Nolan and Harvey of the Chicago Police Department were driving the last car of a four-car caravan of officers who were converging on an area known for heavy drug trafficking to investigate drug transactions. They anticipated encountering a large number of people in the area, including drug customers and people serving as lookouts. Officer Nolan saw the defendant standing next to a building and holding an opaque bag. The defendant looked in the direction of the officers and fled. Officers Nolan and Harvey turned their car, watched him as he ran through a gangway and an alley, and eventually cornered him on the street. Officer Nolan left his car and stopped the defendant.

The Court ruled in *Illinois v. Wardlow*[133] that these facts—the defendant's "unprovoked flight" on seeing the officers and his presence in an area of heavy drug trafficking—provided reasonable suspicion to stop the defendant to investigate criminal activity. The Court stated that "[h]eadlong flight—wherever it occurs—is the consummate act of evasion; it is not necessarily indicative of wrongdoing, but it is certainly suggestive of such."

➤ **Alabama v. White**

Police Officer B. H. Davis received an anonymous phone call stating that Vanessa White would be leaving a specified apartment at a particular time in a brown Plymouth station wagon with a broken right taillight lens, and she would be going to Dobey's Motel with an ounce of cocaine in a brown attaché case. The officer went with another officer to the apartment building and saw a car of that description parked in front of the building containing the specified apartment. The officers saw White leave the apartment building with nothing in her hands and get into the car. They followed it as White drove the most direct route to Dobey's Motel. The officers stopped the car when it was on the highway on which the motel was located.

The United States Supreme Court in *Alabama v. White*[134] ruled that these facts were sufficient verification of an anonymous phone call to provide reasonable suspicion to stop the defendant's vehicle to investigate her possession of illegal drugs. The officers' independent corroboration of significant aspects of the anonymous caller's information gave some degree of reliability to the other allegations by the caller. In addition, the Court noted that the caller was able to predict the defendant's future behavior (leaving her apartment, getting into the described car, and driving toward a particular motel), which demonstrated the caller's familiarity with the defendant's affairs. The Court also discussed the differences between reasonable suspicion and probable cause. It stated that although both standards are determined by examining the totality of circumstances, reasonable suspicion is a less demanding standard than probable cause because it may be established with information that is different in quantity or content and may be less reliable than that required to establish probable cause.

➤ **United States v. Sokolow**

When federal drug agent Richard Kempshall stopped the defendant at the Honolulu airport after he had flown from Honolulu to Miami and back to Honolulu, he and fellow officers knew that (1) the defendant, wearing a black jumpsuit and gold jewelry, had paid $2,100 for two airplane tickets (he had a woman companion) from a roll of

132. *See* Terry v. Ohio, 392 U.S. 1 (1968).
133. 528 U.S. 119 (2000).
134. 496 U.S. 325 (1990).

$20 bills; (2) he had traveled using a name that did not match the name under which his telephone number was listed; (3) his original destination was Miami, a source city for drugs; (4) he stayed in Miami for only 48 hours, even though the round-trip flight from Honolulu to Miami takes 20 hours; (5) he appeared nervous during the trip; and (6) he did not check any of his luggage.

The United States Supreme Court in *United States v. Sokolow*[135] ruled that these facts were sufficient to provide reasonable suspicion to stop the defendant in an airport to investigate his possession of illegal drugs. The Court stated that its analysis of whether reasonable suspicion existed was not adversely affected by the agents' belief when they stopped the defendant that his behavior was consistent with the drug courier profile (personal and behavioral traits associated with the commission of drug offenses). A reviewing court must require an officer to articulate factors leading to a conclusion that reasonable suspicion existed, but the fact that these factors—as understood by a trained officer—may be set forth in a profile does not detract from their evidentiary significance. That is, it is permissible that factors establishing reasonable suspicion may come from a profile.

The Court also noted that the reasonable suspicion standard requires an officer to articulate something more than an "unparticularized" suspicion or hunch. It requires some minimum level of objective justification considering the totality of circumstances, but the level of suspicion is considerably less than proof by a preponderance of evidence and less demanding than fair probability, the standard for probable cause. The Court concluded that although any one of the factors described above is not proof of illegal conduct and is quite consistent with innocent behavior, wholly lawful conduct may constitute reasonable suspicion.

Brown v. Texas
Officers Venegas and Sotelo were cruising in their patrol car during the afternoon. They saw the defendant and another man walking in opposite directions away from a third man in an alley. Although the two men were a few feet apart

when officers first saw them, the officers believed that they had been together or were about to meet until the patrol car appeared. The patrol car entered the alley. Officer Venegas got out and asked the defendant to identify himself and explain what he was doing there. The other man was not questioned or detained. Officer Venegas stopped the defendant because the situation "looked suspicious" and he had never seen him in his area, which had a high incidence of drug traffic. Officer Venegas had no additional facts to support his conclusion that the defendant looked suspicious.

The United States Supreme Court in *Brown v. Texas*[136] ruled that these facts were insufficient to provide reasonable suspicion, based on objective facts, that the defendant was involved in criminal activity. The mere fact that the defendant looked suspicious and was a stranger in a known drug area was not enough to establish reasonable suspicion to stop in this case.

United States v. Sharpe
Federal drug agent Luther Cooke was patrolling at 6:45 a.m. in an unmarked car on a coastal road near Sunset Beach, North Carolina—an area frequented by drug traffickers. He saw a pickup truck with an attached camper shell traveling on the highway with a Pontiac Bonneville. Cooke concluded that the truck was heavily loaded, because it was riding low in the rear and the camper did not bounce or sway appreciably when the truck drove over bumps or around curves. He noticed quilted material covering the camper's rear and side windows. Cooke knew from his experience as a drug agent that pickup trucks with camper shells often are used to transport large quantities of marijuana. He followed the two vehicles for approximately 20 miles as they went south into South Carolina. He decided to make an investigative stop and radioed the State Highway Patrol for assistance. Trooper Kenneth Thrasher, driving a marked car, responded to the call and caught up with the procession. Almost immediately, the Pontiac and the pickup turned off the highway onto a campground road. The two officers followed the two suspect vehicles as they drove at

135. 490 U.S. 1 (1989). *See also* United States v. Arvizu, 534 U.S. 266 (2002) (Border Patrol agent near Arizona–Mexico border had reasonable suspicion to stop vehicle to investigate drug and alien smuggling).

136. 443 U.S. 47 (1979).

55 to 60 miles per hour, exceeding the 35 miles per hour speed limit. The road looped back to the highway, where the two suspect vehicles turned and continued south. All four vehicles were in the middle lane of the three right-hand lanes of the highway. Thrasher pulled alongside the Pontiac (which was in the lead), turned on his flashing light, and motioned to the driver to stop. When the Pontiac moved into the right lane, the pickup truck cut between the Pontiac and Thrasher's car, nearly hitting the patrol car, and continued down the highway. Both suspect vehicles were eventually stopped.

The United States Supreme Court in *United States v. Sharpe*[137] stated that these facts supported a reasonable suspicion to stop the defendants' vehicles because they were trafficking in marijuana. The facts, taken together and as appraised by an experienced officer, provided clear justification to stop the vehicles and to pursue a limited investigation.

—◀ State v. Butler
Officer Ernesto Hedges and his partner saw the defendant, an unfamiliar person, standing with a group of people on a street corner known as a "drug hole," an area frequented by drug dealers and users. Hedges had been watching the area for several months. In the past six months, Hedges had made four to six arrests at the corner and knew that other arrests had been made there. As Hedges and his partner approached the group, the defendant and the officers made eye contact, and then the defendant immediately turned and walked away. The officers followed the defendant and asked him for identification. Before Hedges accepted the defendant's offer of his driver's license, he frisked the defendant.

The North Carolina Supreme Court in *State v. Butler*[138] ruled that these facts were sufficient, when considered in their totality, to provide reasonable suspicion to stop the defendant to investigate drug activity and to frisk him for weapons. The court particularly noted that offi-

cers saw the defendant not simply in a general high crime area, but on a specific corner known for drug activity and at the scene of recent, multiple drug-related arrests, and (distinguishing *Brown v. Texas*, discussed above) that the defendant immediately left the corner and walked away from the officers after making eye contact with them, thus providing evidence of flight.

—◀ State v. Fleming
A law enforcement officer first saw the defendant and his companion when they were standing in an open area between two apartment buildings in a housing project at approximately 12:10 a.m. The officer knew that many arrests for drug violations had been made in the housing project and that crack cocaine was sold there daily. The defendant and his companion stood there and watched the officer (and other officers who were with the officer) for a few minutes, walked between the two buildings, and then began walking down the public sidewalk in front of the apartment buildings. The officer decided to stop them because he had never seen them in the housing project. He stopped and frisked the defendant.

The North Carolina Court of Appeals in *State v. Fleming*[139] ruled that these facts were insufficient to provide a reasonable suspicion to stop and to frisk the defendant. Relying on *Brown v. Texas*, discussed above, the court stated that the evidence only showed that the defendant was standing in an open area of a housing project and then walked down a public sidewalk in a high drug area.

—◀ State v. Allison
An unidentified woman approached Officer Jamie Ledford at a convenience store and told him that about five minutes earlier she had been in a nearby restaurant where she had observed four African American males sitting in the bar area. She said that she had overheard them talking about robbing the restaurant, and she had seen the four men passing a black handgun among themselves. At the officer's request, the woman repeated her observations to Officer Richard Ivey. Ledford then obtained the woman's telephone number, which

---

137. 470 U.S. 675 (1985). Although the existence of reasonable suspicion was not an issue in the case, the Court clearly indicated that the drug agent had reasonable suspicion to stop the vehicles.

138. 331 N.C. 227 (1992).

---

139. 106 N.C. App. 165 (1992). *See also* State v. Hayes, 188 N.C. App. 313 (2008) (relying on *Fleming*, court ruled that officer did not have reasonable suspicion to stop defendant).

he wrote on the back of his hand. Ledford and other officers entered the restaurant and saw four African American males sitting in the bar area. Ledford identified the defendant as having been involved in prior gun-related incidents. He then approached the men and asked them to step into the restaurant's foyer. The defendant was "holding his pants up as though he had something dragging his pants down." Ledford began conducting a pat-down frisk of the defendant and asked him whether he was carrying any weapons. After the defendant responded "no," the officer continued frisking him and seized a 9 milliliter handgun from his waistband. Later, Ledford called the telephone number that he had written on the back of his hand, but there was no answer.

The North Carolina Court of Appeals ruled in *State v. Allison*[140] that these facts were sufficient to provide a reasonable suspicion to stop. Unlike the tip in *Florida v. J.L.*,[141] discussed above, the tip in this case was supplied in a face-to-face encounter rather than by an anonymous phone caller. Officer Ledford had an opportunity to observe the demeanor of the tipster to assess the tip's reliability. By engaging Ledford directly, the tipster significantly increased the likelihood that she would be held accountable if her tip proved to be false. Also, unlike the informant in *Florida v. J.L.*, the tipster offered a reasonable explanation as to how she was aware that criminal activity was possibly going to take place. In addition, the officer's knowledge that the defendant had been involved in gun-related incidents buttressed the tip.

State v. Rinck

Lieutenant Finger, along with several other law enforcement officers, arrived at a house around 1:45 a.m. where a homicide victim was found dead in his bed with two bullet wounds to his face. The homicide had occurred within the past half-hour. Finger left the house to return to the sheriff's office. As he drove from the house, he noticed

two men walking along a road. They were 200 feet from the victim's house. Finger turned on his blue light and stopped the two men.

The North Carolina Supreme Court in *State v. Rinck*[142] ruled that these facts were sufficient to provide a reasonable suspicion to stop. Two defendants were found walking along the road at an unusual time (early morning) near a house where a homicide had occurred recently. After they were stopped, an officer developed sufficient information to frisk one of them.

State v. Buie

At about 4:10 a.m., a woman awoke to find a man standing by her bed in her suite in the Downtowner Motor Inn. She screamed and the man ran from the suite. Several personal items were missing. The victim told Officer J. D. Harrell that the intruder was a black male wearing dark clothing, approximately 5 feet 11 inches tall, and weighing 190 pounds. She said he might have had a mustache but she was not sure.

Officer Marable heard this information when Officer Harrell transmitted it over police radio. Five to ten minutes later, around 4:30 a.m., Marable saw the defendant near the Downtowner Motor Inn. The defendant fit the burglar's description except that he was wearing a gold-colored leisure suit. Marable noticed that the defendant's T-shirt was wet, as if he had been running or perspiring heavily. He stopped the defendant and asked for some identification.

The North Carolina Supreme Court in *State v. Buie*[143] ruled that these facts provided a reasonable suspicion to stop the defendant, who fit the victim's general description of the burglar, was near the crime scene shortly after the crime, and looked as if he had been running. After

---

140. 148 N.C. App. 702 (2002). *See also* State v. Maready, 362 N.C. 614 (2008) (reasonable suspicion existed when unidentified minivan driver in face-to-face encounter with officers told them about erratic driving by Honda that she had just witnessed, and officers thereafter stopped Honda).

141. The court also distinguished *State v. Hughes*, 353 N.C. 200 (2000) (anonymous tip and officer corroboration did not support reasonable suspicion for investigative stop).

142. 303 N.C. 551 (1981). *See also* State v. Campbell, 188 N.C. App. 701 (2008) (reasonable suspicion supported stop of defendant about 3:40 a.m. in proximity of break-in); State v. Cooper, 186 N.C. App. 100 (2007) (reasonable suspicion did not support stop and frisk of defendant shortly after commission of armed robbery at nearby convenience store based solely on report that robber was black male, with no additional information provided, such as age, physical characteristics, or clothing, and defendant did not act suspiciously when officer approached him).

143. 297 N.C. 159 (1979).

the officer stopped the defendant, he developed sufficient information to frisk him.

State v. Douglas

About 12:34 a.m., Officer Galliher was in uniform and driving a marked patrol car. While he was stopped at an intersection, an Oldsmobile crossed it from his left. The patrol car's headlights shined directly on the car, and the officer saw that its trunk was open and a white object that appeared to be an appliance was in the trunk. The trunk was tied down, and a cloth was hanging out from it. Galliher also saw something white in the backseat. (He knew that there were several mobile home lots in that part of town, and several breaking and enterings and larcenies of appliances had occurred there recently.) Because the intersection was dark, Galliher pursued the Oldsmobile, seeking a well-lighted place in which to stop it. When the car approached a stoplight, a person got out of the car, came to the car's trunk, and also looked at Galliher's patrol car. After the car went through the intersection, Galliher put on his blue light and siren, stopped it, and walked to the vehicle.

The North Carolina Court of Appeals in *State v. Douglas*[144] found that these facts provided a reasonable suspicion to stop the defendant's car, which appeared to have an appliance in the trunk, late at night in an area where there had been recent break-ins. After the car was stopped, the officer developed sufficient information to arrest the defendant.

State v. Foreman

Officers set up a DWI checkpoint under G.S. 20-16.3A. Notice of the checkpoint was posted about one-tenth of a mile before the stop. At about 2:00 a.m., Officer Ipock saw a vehicle, immediately before the checkpoint's sign, make a "quick left turn" onto a street. The officer followed the vehicle, lost sight of it, but eventually saw it parked in a residential driveway. The officer directed his bright lights onto the vehicle

and also turned on his take-down lights, thereby enabling the officer to see that people were bent or crouched down inside the car. The vehicle's lights and ignition were off, and its doors were closed. Once backup arrived, the officer approached the vehicle and saw that the defendant was sitting in the driver's seat with the key in the ignition. There were several open containers of alcohol in the vehicle, and the vehicle emitted a strong odor of alcohol. In addition, the officer noticed that the defendant had a strong to moderate odor of alcohol about her person after she exited the vehicle and was unsteady on her feet.

The North Carolina Supreme Court in *State v. Foreman*[145] noted that the officer had never seized the vehicle at any point, and the defendant was not seized under the Fourth Amendment "until at least" the officer approached the vehicle. (The court did not decide precisely when the defendant was seized because it was not essential to the court's ruling; nonetheless, it is highly unlikely that the defendant was seized when the officer approached the vehicle.) Based on the incriminating circumstances that had occurred by then, the court ruled that the officer had reasonable suspicion to stop the driver of the vehicle. The court also ruled that "it is reasonable and permissible for an officer to monitor a checkpoint's entrance for vehicles whose drivers may be attempting to avoid the checkpoint," and "it necessarily follows that an officer, in conjunction with the totality of the circumstances or the checkpoint plan, may pursue and stop a vehicle which has turned away from a checkpoint within its perimeters for reasonable inquiry to determine why the vehicle turned away."

State v. Bonds

Officer Wyatt saw the defendant's vehicle stopped at an intersection. He noticed that the defendant's driver's side window was rolled down all the way, even though it was 28 degrees outside. The officer saw that the defendant had "a blank look on his face" and never turned his head to make eye contact with the officer. After the light changed, the officer followed the defendant's vehicle for about a

---

144. 51 N.C. App. 594 (1981), *aff'd*, 304 N.C. 713 (1982). *Compare with* State v. Murray, 192 N.C. App. 684 (2008) (reasonable suspicion did not support stop of vehicle about 3:41 a.m. near industrial park where there had been past break-ins when there were no break-in reports that night and there was nothing suspicious about vehicle to support stop).

145. 351 N.C. 627 (2000). *See also* State v. Bowden, 177 N.C. App. 718 (2006) (based on *State v. Foreman* and totality of circumstances in this case, reasonable suspicion supported stop of vehicle that turned before checkpoint).

half mile. The speed limit was 40 miles per hour, but the defendant's vehicle never exceeded 30 miles per hour. The officer stopped the vehicle to investigate the driver for DWI.

The North Carolina Court of Appeals ruled in *State v. Bonds*[146] that these facts supported reasonable suspicion to stop the vehicle. The court noted that this officer had been specifically trained to look for certain indicators of intoxication, including some of the indicators in this case, and that he had 10 years of experience and had made several arrests using these exact indicators. The court stated that an officer's training and experience must be considered in determining whether reasonable suspicion exists. The court noted that the National Highway Traffic Safety Administration, in its publication *The Visual Detection of DWI Motorists*, states that driving 10 miles per hour or more under the speed limit, in addition to staring ahead with fixed eyes, indicates a 50 percent chance of being legally intoxicated. (The court cited the publication's website address, but it is no longer valid. However, the publication can be found at www.nhtsa.dot.gov by typing "The Visual Detection of DWI Motorists" in the search function at the top of the page.) The court stated that this 50 percent statistic lends objective credibility to the officer's suspicions, demonstrating that his suspicions were in fact reasonable—something more than just a "hunch." The court rejected the defendant's argument that weaving, or some other form of aberrant driving, is required to satisfy the reasonable suspicion standard.

➤ State v. Watson

At approximately 2:30 a.m., Trooper Deans of the North Carolina Highway Patrol saw a 1971 Ford pickup truck driving on the dividing line of a two-lane highway near a nightclub. After the trooper turned to follow the vehicle, he noticed it weaving back and forth in its lane. After observing this behavior for approximately 15 seconds, the officer stopped the vehicle.

The North Carolina Court of Appeals in *State v. Watson*[147] ruled that these facts were sufficient to provide reasonable suspicion to stop the driver of the vehicle for impaired driving. The court noted the trooper's observation of the defendant's driving on the center line and

weaving back and forth within his lane for 15 seconds and that this activity took place at 2:30 a.m. on a road near a nightclub. The court stated that the totality of circumstances supported reasonable suspicion to stop the vehicle for impaired driving.

➤ State v. Jones

A trooper of the North Carolina Highway Patrol was patrolling Interstate 95 at about noon on September 30, 1987, when he saw the defendant's vehicle traveling in the opposite direction at a speed substantially slower than other vehicles normally travel on that highway. The trooper crossed the median to follow the car and measured its speed at 45 miles per hour, 20 miles per hour below the posted speed limit. He saw the car weave within its own lane from the white line on the shoulder to the center line. The trooper, who had 16 years of experience and had made several thousand arrests for impaired driving, stopped the vehicle. Based on his experience, he knew that low speed may indicate that a person is highly intoxicated, driving defensively, sleepy, or that there is difficulty with the car.

The North Carolina Court of Appeals in *State v. Jones*[148] found that these facts supported a reasonable suspicion to stop the defendant's car for impaired driving. In considering the totality of circumstances to determine whether reasonable suspicion existed, the court weighed the officer's articulated reasons based on his experience and training.[149] The court also noted that probable cause is *not* required to make an investigative stop of a vehicle; reasonable suspicion of criminal activity is sufficient.[150]

---

146. 139 N.C. App. 627 (2000).
147. 122 N.C. App. 596 (1996).

148. 96 N.C. App. 389 (1989).

149. *See also* State v. Aubin, 100 N.C. App. 628 (1990) (officer had reasonable suspicion to stop vehicle for impaired driving); State v. Barnard, 362 N.C. 244 (2008) (reasonable suspicion supported stop of vehicle based on vehicle's remaining stopped for 30 seconds after light had turned green and officer's testimony, based on his training and experience, that driver might be impaired); State v. Roberson, 163 N.C. App. 129 (2004) (officer did not have reasonable suspicion to stop defendant's vehicle for DWI based on vehicle remaining stationary for 8 to 10 seconds after red light turned green before proceeding through intersection).

150. The North Carolina Supreme Court later disavowed contrary statements in some prior cases and ruled in *State v. Styles*, 362 N.C. 412 (2008), that reasonable suspicion, not

---▋ State v. Fields

Around 4:00 p.m. an officer followed the defendant's vehicle for about one and a half miles. On three separate occasions, the officer saw the defendant's vehicle swerve to the white line on the right side of the traffic lane. The officer stopped the vehicle for impaired driving.

The North Carolina Court of Appeals in *State v. Fields*[151] ruled that the officer did not have reasonable suspicion to stop the vehicle for impaired driving. The vehicle's weaving within its lane, standing alone, was insufficient to support reasonable suspicion. The officer did not see the defendant violating any laws such as driving above or significantly below the speed limit. Furthermore, the defendant's vehicle was stopped about 4:00 p.m., which is not an unusual hour, and there was no evidence that the defendant was near any places to purchase alcohol.

---▋ State v. Hess

An officer on patrol at night ran a vehicle's registration plate and then the registered owner's driver's license, which was reported to be suspended. The officer could not determine the sex or race of the driver. The officer stopped the vehicle.

The North Carolina Court of Appeals in *State v. Hess*[152] ruled that the officer had reasonable suspicion to stop the vehicle. The court stated that it was reasonable for the officer under these circumstances to infer that the owner was driving the vehicle.

---

probable cause, is the standard to determine whether an officer has the authority to stop a vehicle for a traffic violation.

151. 195 N.C. App. 740 (2009). *See also* State v. Derbyshire, 228 N.C. App. 670 (2013) (one instance of weaving and other factors insufficient to support reasonable suspicion to stop for DWI). *Compare with* State v. Simmons, 205 N.C. App. 509 (2010) (distinguishing *State v. Fields*, court ruled officer had reasonable suspicion to stop vehicle for impaired driving when defendant was not only weaving within his lane but also weaving across and outside lanes of travel and once ran off the road); State v. Otto, 366 N.C. 134 (2012), *rev'g* 217 N.C. App. 79 (2011) (constant and continual weaving and other factors sufficient to support reasonable suspicion). For an analysis of cases involving a vehicle's weaving and reasonable suspicion to stop it, see Jeff Welty, *Weaving and Reasonable Suspicion*, NC CRIM. L. BLOG (June 19, 2012), http://nccriminallaw.sog.unc.edu/weaving-and-reasonable-suspicion-2/.

152. 185 N.C. App. 539 (2007).

The Authority to Arrest: Probable Cause

(*See page 172 for case summaries on this topic.*)

What constitutes probable cause—like what constitutes reasonable suspicion—cannot be reduced to a set formula of facts and circumstances. Each case is unique. The only way to learn the meaning of the phrase is to examine appellate court cases and to apply principles found in them to everyday situations.[153]

Courts sometimes refer to probable cause as reasonable grounds to believe or reasonable cause to believe. These terms are synonymous when used to refer to the probable cause standard that is required by the Fourth Amendment.[154]

Definition

The United States Supreme Court has defined *probable cause to arrest* as

> whether, at the moment the arrest was made, the facts and circumstances within [the officer's] knowledge and of which [the officer] had reasonably trustworthy information were sufficient to warrant a prudent [person] in believing that the [defendant] had committed or was committing an offense.[155]

Probable cause requires a showing—considering the totality of circumstances—that a crime was probably committed and the defendant probably committed it. Thus, the degree of certainty that corresponds to probable cause is *fair probability*; that is, the required amount of proof is *more* than the reasonable suspicion justification but less than for such other legal evidentiary standards as preponderance of evidence, more probable than

---

153. The United States Supreme Court in *Ornelas v. United States*, 517 U.S. 690 (1996), stated that probable cause and reasonable suspicion are fluid concepts that take their substantive content from the particular contexts in which the standards are being assessed.

154. Draper v. United States, 358 U.S. 307 (1959); Henry v. United States, 361 U.S. 98 (1959); State v. Crawford, 125 N.C. App. 279 (1997). The word "suspicion" also has been used, particularly in older United States Supreme Court cases. It should be avoided because it creates confusion with the standard for stopping someone, which is reasonable suspicion.

155. Beck v. Ohio, 379 U.S. 89 (1964).

not, more likely than not, prima facie evidence, clear or convincing evidence, or beyond a reasonable doubt.[156]

The factors a court considers when it determines whether an officer has probable cause to arrest are similar to those used to determine reasonable suspicion to stop:[157]

- The officer's observation of conduct that, in light of training and experience, appears to be criminal
- Information the officer receives from other officers, citizens, and informants
- The time of day or night
- Whether the area is a high crime area
- The suspect's proximity to a location where a crime recently was committed or to a home, car, or business where criminal activity may be taking place
- Whether the suspect is a stranger to the area
- The suspect's reaction to the officer's presence, including flight after seeing the officer[158]
- The officer's knowledge of the suspect's prior criminal record and activities, if they are relevant to the crime the suspect may be committing
- The suspect's flight from the scene of a crime
- Particularly in airport drug arrests, the suspect's actions that may match factors set out in a profile of criminal behavior

These and other factors all must be considered together in determining whether an officer has probable cause to arrest a person. An officer should remember that probable cause must exist for all the elements of an offense for the officer to have the authority to arrest.

Determination of Probable Cause with or without an Arrest Warrant

The determination of whether there is probable cause is the same whether an officer arrests with or without a warrant. However, a reviewing court may resolve a close case in favor of finding that probable cause existed if the arrest was made with a warrant.[159]

Hearsay Evidence

When a court determines whether probable cause existed to justify an arrest, rules of evidence that are applicable at a trial do not apply. Thus, hearsay evidence that otherwise would be inadmissible at a trial is admissible at a suppression hearing.[160] For example, information given to an officer by another officer, by a citizen, by a confidential informant, or even by an anonymous tipster may be considered.[161] Because the law concerning the use of hearsay to help establish probable cause to arrest is the same as the law concerning searches with and without a search warrant, this subject is discussed in on page 425 of Chapter 4, which deals with search warrants, and is not repeated here.

Collective Knowledge of Officers

(See page 181 for case summaries on this topic.)

Sometimes an officer or law enforcement agency that possesses information about a suspect requests that

---

156. State v. Crawford, 125 N.C. App. 279 (1997). Although the standard of certainty—fair probability—is the same whether the subject is probable cause to arrest or probable cause to search, one must remember that the inquiries underlying arrest (Was a crime committed, and did the defendant commit it?) and search (Is there evidence of a crime in the place or on the person to be searched?) focus on different facts. Therefore, probable cause to arrest does not automatically provide probable cause to search—and vice versa. *See* 2 WAYNE R. LAFAVE, SEARCH AND SEIZURE: A TREATISE ON THE FOURTH AMENDMENT § 3.1(b) (5th ed. 2012).

157. *See generally* 2 WAYNE R. LAFAVE, SEARCH AND SEIZURE: A TREATISE ON THE FOURTH AMENDMENT §§ 3.3 through 3.6 (5th ed. 2012).

158. *See, e.g.,* State v. Smith, 328 N.C. 99 (1991).

159. The principle is stated in *United States v. Ventresca,* 380 U.S. 102 (1964), concerning the determination of probable cause to support a search warrant, and certainly it also would apply to arrest warrants, because the United States Supreme Court has stated the constitutional preference for the use of warrants in making arrests and searches. *See also* Beck v. Ohio, 379 U.S. 89 (1964); 2 WAYNE R. LAFAVE, SEARCH AND SEIZURE: A TREATISE ON THE FOURTH AMENDMENT § 3.1(c) (5th ed. 2012).

160. The Fourth Amendment does not bar the use of hearsay evidence in determining reasonable suspicion or probable cause. Brinegar v. United States, 338 U.S. 160 (1949); Draper v. United States, 358 U.S. 307 (1959); Alabama v. White, 496 U.S. 325 (1990); Illinois v. Gates, 462 U.S. 213 (1983); 2 WAYNE R. LAFAVE, SEARCH AND SEIZURE: A TREATISE ON THE FOURTH AMENDMENT § 3.2(d), 68–71 (5th ed. 2012). Under Rules 104(a) and 1101(b)(1) of the North Carolina Rules of Evidence in G.S. 8C-1, the rules of evidence do not apply in a hearing that determines the admissibility of evidence, with the exception of rules concerning privileges.

161. State v. Roberts, 276 N.C. 98 (1970); Melton v. Hodges, 114 N.C. App. 795 (1994); Steinkrause v. Tatum, 201 N.C. App. 289 (2009), *aff'd,* 364 N.C. 419 (2010).

another officer make an arrest. If the requesting officer or agency's information establishes probable cause, the arrest may be justified even though the arresting officer does not know the facts possessed by the requesting officer or agency. Also, if the collective knowledge of several officers or agencies working together on an investigation establishes probable cause, that generally may justify an arrest by one of the officers.[162] (The collective knowledge theory applies equally to reasonable suspicion to stop.)

Appellate Court Cases on Probable Cause

(*See page 172 for case summaries on this topic.*)

The following facts in appellate court cases should provide some understanding of what constitutes probable cause. The reader should remember that the facts developed after the arrests in these cases may not be used to supply probable cause to arrest.

◄ Beck v. Ohio

Police officers arrested the defendant, took him to a nearby police station, searched him, and found illegal betting slips in his sock. The only evidence supporting probable cause was that an arresting officer knew what the defendant looked like and knew that he had a prior gambling record. The officer also had information and had heard reports about the defendant. But the officer gave no indication what information or reports he had received and did not give the source of the information and reports.

The United States Supreme Court in *Beck v. Ohio*[163] ruled that these facts were insufficient to provide probable cause to believe that the defendant illegally possessed gambling slips. The officer's knowledge of the defendant's physical appearance and his prior criminal record, while not inadmissible or irrelevant in determining probable cause, was not enough to establish probable cause. Otherwise, anyone with a prior record could be arrested at any time.

◄ Draper v. United States

An experienced federal narcotics agent used a paid informant to provide him with narcotics information. On September 3, 1956, the informant, who had worked for the agent for six months and had always given reliable and accurate information, told the agent that the defendant had moved to Denver and was selling narcotics. Four days later, the informant told the agent that the defendant had gone to Chicago by train the day before and would return by train on the morning of September 8 or 9, carrying 3 ounces of heroin. The informant described the defendant in detail, including the clothes that he would wear. He also said that the defendant would be carrying a tan zipper bag and that he habitually walked fast.

On the morning of September 8, the agent saw no one at the train station who fit the informant's description. But on September 9, he saw a person with the exact physical attributes and wearing the precise clothing described by the informant get off an incoming train from Chicago and start walking fast toward the exit. He was carrying a tan zipper bag in his right hand and his raincoat in his left hand. The agent arrested him. In a search incident to the arrest, heroin was found in his raincoat pocket and a syringe in the zipper bag.

The United States Supreme Court in *Draper v. United States*[164] ruled that these facts established probable cause to arrest. A reliable informant gave an officer detailed information about the defendant's involvement in illegal narcotics and told him when the defendant would return on a train from Chicago with narcotics in his possession. Although the informant had not told the officer how he had obtained his information, the officer's observation of the defendant at the train station corroborated the informant's information and thereby established probable cause to arrest the defendant.

---

162. *See* State v. Coffey, 65 N.C. App. 751 (1984); State v. Battle, 109 N.C. App. 367 (1993); State v. Bowman, 193 N.C. App. 104 (2008). *See also* 2 & 4 Wayne R. LaFave, Search and Seizure: A Treatise on the Fourth Amendment §§ 3.5, 9.5(j) (5th ed. 2012).

163. 379 U.S. 89 (1964).

164. 358 U.S. 307 (1959). It is not clear whether the Court held that probable cause existed before the police observed Draper at the train station or only after their observations corroborated what the informant had told them (see Justice White's concurring opinion in *Illinois v. Gates*, 462 U.S. 213 (1983)), but probable cause apparently existed only after the information was corroborated.

Maryland v. Pringle

After a vehicle was stopped by a law enforcement officer for speeding, a consent search revealed $763 of rolled-up cash in the glove compartment and five baggies of cocaine between the backseat armrest and the backseat. All three vehicle occupants—the driver; the defendant, a front seat passenger; and a backseat passenger—denied ownership of the cocaine and the money.

The United States Supreme Court in *Maryland v. Pringle*[165] ruled that the officer had probable cause to arrest the defendant as well as the other occupants. The Court stated that it was a reasonable inference from the facts that any or all three vehicle occupants knew and exercised dominion and control over the cocaine. A reasonable officer could conclude that there was probable cause to believe that the defendant committed the crime of possession of cocaine, either solely or jointly. The quantity of drugs and cash in the car indicated the likelihood of drug dealing, an enterprise to which a dealer would be unlikely to admit an innocent person with the potential to furnish evidence against him. Distinguishing *United States v. Di Re*,[166] the Court noted that no one in the car was singled out as the owner of the cocaine and cash in this case.

State v. Bone

An elderly woman was murdered in her apartment. An SBI agent found shoe print impressions left in blood at the apartment. A manager of a sporting goods store, along with a detective, examined a photograph of the impressions and determined that a Converse "Chuck Taylor" athletic shoe made the impressions. Within two months of the murder, an anonymous person called about this homicide and said that Tony Bone (the defendant), a black male, in his late 20s, climbed in an open window, punched an elderly female in the face so hard that her ears bled, and stole $5. The caller said that Bone worked for a moving company in Greensboro; lived in Trinity, North Carolina; was married; and was recently released from prison. The detective verified almost all of the anonymous caller's information before he approached the defendant. For example, he learned that the defendant was married and worked at a moving company in Greensboro. A criminal history check revealed that the defendant had been released from prison about one year before the murder. A cut screen at the murder scene indicated access through an apartment window. The victim was found with blood on her face, and the primary cause of death was a broken neck. The only incorrect information was that the defendant lived in Trinity, North Carolina, when he actually lived in Liberty—although both Trinity and Liberty are small communities in northern Randolph County. The detective approached the defendant at the moving company and asked him if he would come downtown to speak about an undisclosed matter; the defendant agreed. The detective noticed that the defendant was wearing Converse "Chuck Taylor" athletic shoes.

The North Carolina Supreme Court in *State v. Bone*[167] ruled that there was probable cause to arrest the defendant. The information given by the anonymous caller was substantially corroborated by the known facts. In addition, the detective saw the defendant wearing "Chuck Taylor" shoes.

State v. Tippett

A man committed a burglary in a Durham home about 1:00 a.m. while a husband and wife were sleeping there. The intruder attacked the wife and then fled. When Durham police officers arrived shortly thereafter, they noticed a man hiding behind a car parked on the street. When one of the officers got out of his police car, the man fled and escaped from him. The officer noticed that the man wore dark clothing and was barefoot. At about 3:00 a.m., two other police officers were driving along the second street over from the street on which the burglarized residence was located. They knew of the burglary and had been told that a barefoot white man, wearing coveralls, was the suspect. While looking for the suspect, they saw the defendant leaning against a brick wall behind a bush a few feet off the street and between two houses. He was wearing coveralls and was barefoot. He was arrested, and incriminating evidence was found when he was searched incident to the arrest.

---

165. 540 U.S. 366 (2003).
166. 332 U.S. 581 (1948).
167. 354 N.C. 1 (2001).

The North Carolina Supreme Court in *State v. Tippett*[168] ruled that there was probable cause to arrest the defendant, who was found in the neighborhood a few hours after a burglary occurred and whose description and clothing matched that of the suspected burglar.

State v. Harris

A home was broken into between 3:00 and 3:45 p.m., and two TVs, a radio, and various other goods were taken. Officer Kirkpatrick arrived about 4:00 p.m. to investigate the crime. He noticed that some strands of barbed wire on top of the backyard fence on the property had been mashed down, and he found two sets of fresh footprints leading into a newly plowed field between two overgrown areas. He followed the footprints into the woods. Beneath a tree and some bushes he found two TVs and a radio. When brought to the area, the victim of the break-in identified the items as his. The officer left the items there and set up surveillance about 6:00 p.m. Shortly after dark, between 7:15 and 7:30 p.m., the officer saw two men walk across the ball field into the wooded area about 100 yards from where he was sitting. They followed a path for a short distance and then cut across to the place where the TVs and radio had been left. After looking around, they retraced their steps, leaving the area the way they had come. When the officer intercepted them, they began to run. He was able to arrest one of them—the defendant. A search of the defendant incident to his arrest revealed items stolen during the break-in.

The North Carolina Supreme Court in *State v. Harris*[169] found probable cause to arrest the defendant because he was seen (within hours of the breaking and entering of the nearby house) going directly to the place in the woods where the stolen TVs and other goods had been concealed.

State v. Small

Officer Johnny Sharpless saw the defendant between 4:00 and 4:30 a.m. at the Sampson School in Kinston. He saw blood on the defendant's jacket, socks, trousers, and tennis shoes. The defendant said that he had been fighting with Leroy King. Sharpless told the defendant to get off the streets.

Sharpless was recalled to the school area about 6:55 a.m. and found a woman lying dead beside the basketball courts, which were located about 200 feet from the place where he had talked earlier with the defendant. The woman had been badly beaten and was bleeding from her head. Sharpless saw tennis shoe tracks around the area. Later, by looking through some high school annuals, Sharpless was able to tentatively identify the defendant as the man he had talked with earlier in the morning.

Sharpless and other officers went to the defendant's home that morning. The defendant's mother led them to the room in which he was sleeping. When he entered the room, Sharpless recognized the defendant as the person he had seen earlier in the morning. He also saw a pair of bloody socks and trousers spotted with blood and sand lying at the foot of the bed. The defendant was arrested.[170]

The North Carolina Supreme Court in *State v. Small*[171] found probable cause to arrest based on an officer's observations of the defendant near where a person was murdered and the officer's later observations of the defendant at his home after the murder.

State v. Bright

About 8:45 p.m. on April 7, 1979, a seven-year-old was abducted from a bowling alley in Gastonia while her parents were bowling. The abductor took her in his car and drove her to a dirt road, where he sexually assaulted her. Around 11:00 p.m., the child was found in a parking lot next to the bowling alley. She told Officer Rodney Parham that her assailant was a slender white male with red hair who wore green pants. The car in which she rode was a big blue two-door with a black, torn-up interior. She also said that there was a brown beer bottle in the car and that her assailant had been drinking. Parham talked to bowling alley employees and determined that another employee (the defendant) matched the child's

---

168. 270 N.C. 588 (1967).
169. 279 N.C. 307 (1971).

170. The court assumed, for the purpose of determining probable cause, that the defendant was arrested then.
171. 293 N.C. 646 (1977).

description. Parham learned the defendant's name, that he had been seen shortly before the child disappeared, and that he drove a Chevrolet automobile that matched her description. In the early morning hours of April 8, 1979, Parham went to the motel where the defendant resided and saw a 1967 Chevrolet in the parking lot that matched the child's description. PIN information showed that it was registered to the defendant. Parham looked inside the automobile and saw beer bottles. When the defendant walked outside his motel room, Parham noted that he matched the child's description. The defendant was arrested shortly thereafter.

The North Carolina Supreme Court in *State v. Bright*[172] found probable cause to arrest in this case because the sexual assault victim's description of her attacker and the car in which he abducted her matched the defendant's appearance and the appearance of his car. Also, the defendant worked at the bowling alley from which the child had been abducted.

State v. Williams
A member of the narcotics division was stationed in a motel to watch drug transactions in an area of substantial drug traffic. At about 3:30 p.m., he saw a confidential source make a drug purchase (but not involving the defendant in this case). This was a weekday afternoon when there was normal pedestrian traffic and stores were open for business. At about 4:00 p.m., the officer saw the defendant and an unidentified male meet. He did not know either man. He saw the defendant and the other man join hands but saw nothing in either man's hand. The defendant then put his left hand into his left coat pocket, withdrew it, crossed the street, and entered the manager's office of the motel where the officer was located.

When the defendant emerged, the officer met him in the lobby. He identified himself as a police officer and asked the defendant for identification. The defendant stated that he had none on him.

The North Carolina Court of Appeals in *State v. Williams*[173] found that in this case there was not probable

cause to arrest the defendant for possession of drugs. Although the defendant was in an area of high drug activity, the officer only saw two persons join hands and one of them put his hand in his pocket.

Note, however, that this evidence would likely support a finding of reasonable suspicion to make an investigative stop.

Pretextual Arrest, Investigative Stop, or Search
(See page 170 for case summaries on this topic.)

Before the United States Supreme Court issued its ruling in *United States v. Whren*,[174] a frequently litigated issue was whether an arrest or investigative stop, even when appropriately supported by probable cause or reasonable suspicion, was unreasonable under the Fourth Amendment if the officer made the arrest or investigatory stop as a pretext to accomplish some other purpose unrelated to the arrest or stop. The Court ruled in *Whren* that stopping a vehicle for a traffic violation, when there is probable cause to believe the traffic violation was committed, does not violate the Fourth Amendment regardless of the officer's motivation for doing so.[175] Thus, for example,

---

172. 301 N.C. 243 (1980).
173. 32 N.C. App. 204 (1977).

174. 517 U.S. 806 (1996).
175. In *State v. McClendon*, 350 N.C. 630 (1999) (officer had probable cause for stopping defendant's vehicle for speeding and following too closely and therefore was justified in stopping it, regardless of the officer's motivation for doing so), the North Carolina Supreme Court adopted the *Whren* ruling under the North Carolina Constitution. *See also* State v. Hamilton, 125 N.C. App. 396 (1997) (officer's motivation irrelevant under *Whren* when stop for seat belt violation). The court's ruling in *Whren* did not change Fourth Amendment law that an officer may make an investigative stop of a vehicle based on reasonable suspicion. State v. Styles, 362 N.C. 412 (2008) (court discussed *Whren* and ruled that reasonable suspicion is standard for stops of vehicles for all traffic violations and disavowed statements in prior cases that probable cause is standard for stops of vehicles for readily observed traffic violations). The Court in *Whren* stated that stopping a vehicle for an improper racial purpose must be considered under the Equal Protection Clause of the Fourteenth Amendment, not the Fourth Amendment. For the application of the Equal Protection Clause in a case involving law enforcement officers who allegedly enforced a bicycle headlamp statute in a racially discriminatory manner, see *United States v. Bell*, 86 F.3d 820 (8th Cir. 1996) (person asserting unequal enforcement of facially neutral statute must show both that the enforcement had a discriminatory effect and that it was motivated by a discriminatory purpose). *See also* United States v. Alcaraz-Arellano, 441 F.3d 1252 (10th Cir. 2006) (defendant failed to present evidence showing discriminatory intent). Although an officer's improper racial purpose in stopping a Hispanic defendant for a seat belt

a Fourth Amendment violation does not occur when a drug investigator who rarely enforces minor traffic violations decides to stop a car speeding at forty-five miles per hour in a thirty-five miles per hour speed zone because the officer knows the driver is a drug trafficker and wants to determine if drugs or drug paraphernalia are in the car. Although the Court in *Whren* did not decide whether an officer's motive is also irrelevant when the officer has reasonable suspicion, but not probable cause, to stop a vehicle for a traffic violation (or to make an investigative stop of a person or vehicle for any criminal violation), it likely would rule that way.[176]

The United States Supreme Court has also applied the *Whren* principle when an officer has probable cause to arrest—that is, the officer's motivation for making the arrest is irrelevant under the Fourth Amendment.[177]

On the other hand, when officers are authorized to conduct a search or seizure for which neither probable cause nor reasonable suspicion is required, their motive for doing so may be relevant. For example, the United States Supreme Court in *City of Indianapolis v. Edmond* ruled that a vehicle checkpoint whose primary purpose was to interdict illegal drugs violated the Fourth Amendment.[178] The Court noted that in prior cases it had directly

or indirectly approved of seizures of vehicles without reasonable suspicion at checkpoints to intercept illegal aliens, to remove impaired drivers from highways, and to check driver's licenses and vehicle registrations.[179] These seizures remain lawful after *Edmond*. However, the Court declined to approve a checkpoint whose primary purpose was to detect evidence of ordinary criminal wrongdoing, such as illegal drugs.[180]

Mandatory Duty to Arrest for Domestic Violence Offense

An officer generally has the discretion whether to make an arrest or charge an offense even if probable cause exists.[181] There is at least one restriction on this discretion. G.S. 50B-4.1(b) provides that an officer "shall" make an arrest, with or without a warrant, if the officer has probable cause to believe that the person knowingly violated a valid domestic violence protective order that excludes the person from the residence or household occupied by the domestic violence victim or directs the person from doing any of the acts specified in G.S. 50B-3(a)(9). Those acts include (1) threatening, abusing, or following the victim; (2) harassing the victim by telephone, visiting the home or workplace, or other means; (3) cruelly treating or abusing an animal owned, possessed, kept, or held as a pet by the victim or minor child residing in the household; or (4) otherwise interfering with the victim. A North Carolina Court of Appeals case interpreted "shall" to not impose a mandatory duty to arrest, at least in the absence of a stronger indication of legislative intent to impose a mandatory duty.[182] In response to this case, the legislature enacted a law that specifically mentioned

---

violation was an issue in *State v. Villeda*, 165 N.C. App. 431 (2004), the court ruled in favor of the defendant on a different ground and did not address the racial purpose issue.

G.S. 143B-903 requires certain state and local law enforcement officers to record detailed information about a vehicle driver when they conduct a traffic stop, including the driver's race, ethnicity, gender, and approximate age.

176. Ashcroft v. al-Kidd, 563 U.S. 731 (2011) (Court made clear that motive is irrelevant in application of reasonable suspicion standard, although that was not the issue decided in the case); *United States v. Knights*, 534 U.S. 112 (2001) (Court strongly indicated that the *Whren* ruling applies to Fourth Amendment actions supported by reasonable suspicion). In *United States v. Dumas*, 94 F.3d 286 (7th Cir. 1996), the Seventh Circuit Court of Appeals noted that any argument that an investigative stop based on reasonable suspicion was invalid as a mere pretext to search for drugs was foreclosed by *Whren v. United States*.

177. Arkansas v. Sullivan, 532 U.S. 769 (2001).

178. 531 U.S. 32 (2000). However, the Court stated that the inquiry about the primary purpose is limited to "the programmatic level and is not an invitation to probe the minds of individual officers at the scene." The Court noted that the ruling in *Whren v. United States*, 517 U.S. 806 (1996), does not apply to inventory and administrative searches that may be conducted without reasonable suspicion or probable cause. *See also* Ashcroft v. al-Kidd, 563 U.S. 731 (2011) (discussing *Edmond*).

In *United States v. Davis*, 270 F.3d 977 (D.C. Cir. 2001), the court of appeals made clear that it is constitutional to establish a roadblock for checking licenses even though a secondary purpose is to detect illegal drugs.

179. United States v. Martinez-Fuerte, 428 U.S. 543 (1976); Michigan Dep't of State Police v. Sitz, 496 U.S. 444 (1990); Delaware v. Prouse, 440 U.S. 648 (1979) (dicta).

180. The Court noted that a checkpoint set up for an emergency—such as to thwart an imminent terrorist attack or to catch a dangerous fleeing criminal—would likely not violate the Fourth Amendment.

181. For example, the court in *Ellis v. White*, 156 N.C. App. 16 (2003), noted that the officer exercised his discretion and did not charge the plaintiff with all the offenses for which probable cause existed.

182. Cockerham-Ellerbee v. Town of Jonesville, 176 N.C. App. 372 (2006).

the case and stated that G.S. 50B-4.1(b) creates a mandatory duty to arrest if the conditions set out in the statute are met.[183] Thus, it is highly likely that in a future case the North Carolina Court of Appeals would recognize that G.S. 50B-4.1(b) imposes a mandatory duty to arrest.

Special Aspects of Stopping Authority
Investigative Stop Based on Reasonable Suspicion

Assuming an investigative stop was based on reasonable suspicion, sometimes an officer's conduct after the stop is challenged as violating the Fourth Amendment. Two significant issues are (1) the length of time (duration) of the stop and (2) the scope of the stop, both of which are discussed below.

Length of Time Allowed for an Investigative Stop
(*See page 137 for case summaries on this topic.*)

The United States Supreme Court specifically has declined to impose a maximum limit on the length of time allowed for an investigative stop.[184] Instead, the Court has said that the permissible length of time will depend on the facts and circumstances of each case, which include the following:

- Whether an officer diligently pursues a means of investigation that is likely to confirm or dispel his or her suspicions quickly—but courts generally should not second-guess whether an officer should have used alternative investigative means that were available
- The suspect's reaction to the officer's stop
- The officer's need to adjust his or her response to what is happening[185]

For example, if—one minute after stopping a suspect—an officer realizes that the suspect is completely innocent of criminal activity, any further detention is improper. On the other hand, if an officer's suspicions remain or are increased after the stop—by the suspect's actions or words or by other information the officer learns—the stop may continue briefly to allow the officer time to determine whether there is probable cause to arrest. If probable cause is not established, the suspect must be released. Although appellate courts have approved stops of suspects that lasted as long as an hour or more,[186] an officer normally should not detain a suspect the officer has stopped longer than 20 minutes[187] unless (1) circumstances indicate that the investigation is about to establish probable cause to arrest (2) an investigative procedure (showup identification or the like) will soon be conducted that likely will confirm or dispel the suspicion of criminal activity; or (3) the suspect's evasive actions or untruthfulness have contributed to the length of the stop. Generally, an officer will be permitted more time to conduct an investigative stop involving a serious crime or dangerous

---

183. S.L. 2009-389.

184. United States v. Sharpe, 470 U.S. 675 (1985); United States v. Place, 462 U.S. 696 (1983).

185. United States v. Sharpe, 470 U.S. 675 (1985). In *Florida v. Royer*, 460 U.S. 491 (1983), the Court stated that during a stop officers must use the investigative methods that are the least intrusive means reasonably available to confirm or dispel their suspicions. The Court in *United States v. Sokolow*, 490 U.S. 1 (1989), explained that its statement in *Royer* applied only in determining the appropriateness of the length of the stop. The Court stated that for an investigative stop to be reasonable, officers are not required to use the least intrusive means available (for example, approaching a defendant without using force versus deciding to use force initially) to verify or dispel

their suspicions. Such a rule would unduly hamper an officer's ability to make swift, on-the-spot decisions.

186. See *United States v. Richards*, 500 F.2d 1025 (9th Cir. 1974), discussed in 4 WAYNE R. LaFAVE, SEARCH AND SEIZURE: A TREATISE ON THE FOURTH AMENDMENT § 9.2(f) (5th ed. 2012), and cases discussed in note 253 in the treatise. *See also* State v. Hernandez, 208 N.C. App. 591 (2010) (detention of defendant for approximately one hour and 10 minutes after traffic stop was proper because none of vehicle's occupants had a driver's license or other identification and officer could not write citation to driver until identification was determined); State v. Darack, 66 N.C. App. 608 (1984) (detention of defendant for 47 minutes was proper); United States v. McCarthy, 77 F.3d 522 (1st Cir. 1996) (detention for 75 minutes was proper); State v. Munoz, 141 N.C. App. 675 (2001) (detention for 45 minutes was proper); State v. Ray, 137 N.C. App. 326 (2000) (detention for 20 to 25 minutes was proper); United States v. Davies, 768 F.2d 893 (7th Cir. 1985) (detention for 45 minutes was proper); United States v. Hardy, 855 F.2d 753 (11th Cir. 1988) (50-minute detention of two occupants in car to await narcotics dog was proper); United States v. Vega, 72 F.3d 507 (7th Cir. 1995) (detention for 62 minutes was proper); United States v. Bloomfield, 40 F.3d 910 (8th Cir. 1994) (one-hour detention was proper).

187. The United States Supreme Court noted but rejected the American Law Institute's recommendation of a 20-minute maximum in *United States v. Place*, 462 U.S. 696 n.10 (1983). *See also* United States v. Sharpe, 470 U.S. 675 (1985). However, that recommendation is a good guideline (unless circumstances noted in the text exist) so that an officer would not likely violate a person's constitutional rights.

offender than one involving a minor crime or nondangerous offender.[188]

Officer's interaction with suspect after investigative stop is completed. If an officer detains a suspect beyond the time permitted under the Fourth Amendment, a court will likely exclude the introduction of evidence at trial that was obtained as a result of the Fourth Amendment violation.[189] However, sometimes an officer's interaction with a suspect may properly be continued beyond the permitted time if at least one of three justifications exists:[190]

1. An officer develops probable cause to arrest the suspect for a criminal offense and takes the suspect to a judicial official for an initial appearance
2. During the investigative stop an officer develops reasonable suspicion of other criminal activity to permit additional investigation and detention of the suspect (for example, reasonable suspicion of illegal drugs in a vehicle after a traffic stop)[191]
3. The suspect voluntarily remains with the officer

If the suspect voluntarily remains with the officer, a justification (such as reasonable suspicion) for the officer's continuing interaction is no longer required because the suspect is no longer seized under the Fourth Amendment.[192] A court may find that a suspect remained voluntarily based on the totality of circumstances or because an officer explicitly obtained the suspect's consent to remain. An officer is not required to tell the suspect that he or she is free to leave, although it would be a favorable factor in determining whether the suspect voluntarily remained.[193] (Of course, even if a suspect voluntarily remained with an officer, the interaction may later escalate into a seizure of the suspect that would require reasonable suspicion or probable cause.)

The voluntariness issue often arises after the completion of a traffic stop (for example, a citation or warning ticket has been given to the driver, no other reason exists to detain the driver, and the officer wants to request a consent search). If, after the completion of a traffic stop, the officer asks for consent to search the driver's vehicle while still possessing the driver's license and registration, a court will likely rule that the driver was being illegally detained, unless reasonable suspicion supported the continued detention.[194] On the other hand, it would generally be legally permissible to return the driver's license and registration and then request consent to search.[195]

---

188. *See* 4 Wayne R. LaFave, Search and Seizure: A Treatise on the Fourth Amendment § 9.2(f), at 446 (5th ed. 2012).

189. For example, if the continued detention of a defendant after the completion of a traffic stop violated the Fourth Amendment, evidence seized pursuant to a search conducted with the defendant's consent during the unlawful detention would be inadmissible. State v. Myles, 188 N.C. App. 42, *aff'd per curiam*, 362 N.C. 344 (2008); State v. Jackson, 199 N.C. App. 236 (2009).

190. The text does not discuss every possible justification.

191. State v. Hernandez, 208 N.C. App. 591 (2010) (reasonable suspicion supported detention after traffic stop of defendant, driver, and other passengers, based on multiple factors set out in opinion); State v. Euceda-Valle, 182 N.C. App. 268 (2007) (after writing warning ticket and delivering to defendant, officer had reasonable suspicion to detain defendant further so drug dog could conduct sniff of vehicle); State v. Wilson, 155 N.C. App. 89 (2002) (reasonable suspicion supported detention of defendant after officer issued warning ticket); State v. McClendon, 350 N.C. 630 (1999) (similar ruling); State v. Hernandez, 170 N.C. App. 299 (2005); Rousello v. Starling, 128 N.C. App. 439 (1998) (reasonable suspicion to detain driver after speeding stop to investigate discrepancy between rental agreement and vehicle's license tag; length of stop was 99 minutes). Cases not finding reasonable suspicion to continue detention include *State v. Falana*, 129 N.C. App. 813 (1998), and *State v. Fisher*, 141 N.C. App. 448 (2000).

192. In deciding whether the suspect is still being seized under the Fourth Amendment beyond the permissible bounds of an investigative stop, courts generally apply the *Florida v. Royer*, 460 U.S. 491 (1983), definition of a *seizure*: whether a reasonable person under the circumstances would believe that he or she was not free to leave. See the analysis in *State v. Jackson*, 199 N.C. App. 236 (2009).

193. In *Ohio v. Robinette*, 519 U.S. 33 (1996), the Court rejected a lower court ruling that an officer must advise a lawfully seized defendant that he or she is free to go before consent to search will be recognized as voluntary. It is clear that *Robinette* also would not require such an advisement to prove that a defendant remained voluntarily after a traffic stop had ended. The test in deciding voluntariness versus seizure is based on a totality of circumstances.

194. State v. Jackson, 199 N.C. App. 236 (2009) (defendant was illegally seized after traffic stop had ended when officer asked for consent to search while she still possessed defendant's license and registration; reasonable person would not believe he or she was free to leave without his or her driver's license and registration).

195. Taking a few seconds to request consent to search after the traffic stop is completed is not an illegal seizure of the suspect. United States v. Carrazco, 91 F.3d 65 (8th Cir. 1996) (three-second delay after handing warning ticket to defendant to request defendant's consent for drug dog to sniff truck's exterior was not illegal seizure). And the United States

(See the discussion of *Rodriguez v. United States*, below.) Although it is not necessarily legally required before an officer requests consent, an officer may want to specifically ask if the driver is willing to answer some questions or to remain for a few minutes.[196]

United States Supreme Court Case on Delay After Completed Traffic Stop. In *Rodriguez v. United States*,[197] the United States Supreme Court significantly limited the scope of a traffic stop. The officer in *Rodriguez* completed a traffic stop for driving on the shoulder of a highway after checking the vehicle registration and driver's licenses of the driver and passenger, conducting a warrant check, returning all documents, and issuing the driver a warning ticket. The officer then asked the driver for consent to walk his drug dog around the vehicle, but the driver refused to give his consent. Nonetheless, the officer told the driver to turn off the ignition, leave the vehicle, and wait for a second officer. When the second officer arrived, the first officer walked his drug dog around the car, and the dog alerted to the presence of drugs. A search of the vehicle revealed methamphetamine. Seven to eight minutes had elapsed from the time the officer issued the written warning until the dog's alert.

The Court recognized that during a traffic stop, in addition to determining whether to issue a traffic ticket, an officer's mission includes ordinary inquiries incident to the stop, such as

- checking a driver's license,
- inspecting a vehicle's registration and insurance, and
- determining whether there are outstanding warrants.[198]

The Court said that these checks serve the same objective as enforcement of traffic laws, ensuring that vehicles on the road are operated safely and responsibly. However, it noted that an officer must act reasonably in completing these authorized checks—that is, an officer cannot deliberately or unreasonably delay the checks to allow time, for example, for a drug dog to arrive at the scene.[199]

The Court ruled that an officer may not extend a completed traffic stop for any period of time, no matter how brief, to conduct a dog sniff[200]—absent reasonable suspicion of criminal activity[201] (or consent).[202] The Court rejected the government's argument that an officer may

---

Supreme Court in *Arizona v. Johnson*, 555 U.S. 323 (2009), made clear that questioning unrelated to a stop is permissible as long as it does not "measurably" extend the duration of the stop.

196. These requests are not necessarily legally required, because a court examines all the circumstances surrounding the encounter in deciding whether the driver remained voluntarily or was seized under the Fourth Amendment. In *State v. Morocco*, 99 N.C. App. 421 (1990), the officer, after issuing a warning ticket and returning the defendant's driver's license and registration, simply asked for consent to search.

197. 135 S. Ct. 1609 (2015).

198. The Court in *Rodriguez v. United States*, 135 S. Ct. 1609 (2015), somewhat unconvincingly justified a warrant check based on the fact that it can determine whether an apparent traffic violator is wanted for prior traffic offenses. However, earlier in its opinion the Court offered a better justification

when it recognized that the traffic mission may "attend to related safety concerns" in addition to addressing the traffic violation that warranted the stop. 135 S. Ct. at 1614. Warrant checks are certainly related to safety concerns, because an officer clearly needs to be alert to a potentially dangerous person who may be wanted for murder or other serious offenses.

199. The Court stated that authority for a seizure ends when tasks tied to the traffic violation "are—or reasonably should have been—completed." *Rodriguez*, 135 S. Ct. at 1614.

200. The *Rodriguez* ruling may also apply to questions unrelated to the traffic stop or to asking for consent during the stop, to the extent that these questions extend the duration of the stop (absent reasonable suspicion to extend the stop). For example, when an officer is examining a driver's license or registration, writing a citation, or awaiting a warrant check, if questioning about travel plans or requesting a consent search occurs while these lawful traffic stop functions are being performed, the stop is not being unlawfully prolonged. On the other hand, if an officer asks about travel plans or requests a consent search while not performing lawful traffic stop functions and the delay in doing so prolongs the traffic stop (and reasonable suspicion does not support extending the stop), the delay may be problematic under *Rodriguez*.

201. Post-*Rodriguez* cases decided by North Carolina appellate courts include *State v. Johnson*, ___ N.C. App. ___, 783 S.E.2d 753 (2016) (reasonable suspicion supported detention after traffic stop had been completed); *State v. Castillo*, ___ N.C. App. ___, 787 S.E.2d 48 (2016) (similar ruling); *State v. Warren*, 368 N.C. 736 (2016), *aff'g per curiam*, ___ N.C. App. ___, 775 S.E.2d 362 (2016) (similar ruling); *State v. Bedient*, ___ N.C. App. ___, 786 S.E.2d 319 (2016) (reasonable suspicion did not exist to support detention after traffic stop had been completed).

202. The Court did not mention in its opinion that consent, as well as reasonable suspicion, would authorize an officer to extend the stop. However, it is clear that a person may give voluntary consent to waive his or her Fourth Amendment rights, including during this type of encounter—and the Court clearly would so rule if presented with this issue. For pre-*Rodriguez* cases decided by North Carolina courts that upheld an officer's search after a person consented to answer questions or remain after a traffic stop had been completed, see *State v. Heien*, 226

incrementally prolong a traffic stop, which some lower courts, including North Carolina's, had justified as a de minimis intrusion.[203] The Court reasoned that a dog alert is not a permissible part of a traffic stop because it detects evidence of ordinary criminal wrongdoing, which is not part of an officer's traffic mission. The Court clearly indicated, however, that if a dog sniff or other non-traffic-related activity does not add any time to the stop (in this case, it added seven to eight minutes), then the dog sniff or other activity is valid under the Fourth Amendment, as it previously had ruled in *Illinois v. Caballes*.[204]

The court's ruling does not appear to bar an officer, after the traffic stop has been completed and all of the person's documents (driver's license, registration, and so forth) have been returned, from briefly asking for consent to search the vehicle (see similar discussion above). After the stop is completed, the person is free to leave (an officer could reinforce this by telling the person that he or she may leave), and mere questioning is not a seizure under the Fourth Amendment.[205]

Scope of Investigative Stop: Investigative Techniques
(*See page 137 for case summaries on this topic.*)

Ordering driver and passengers out of vehicle. (See page 151 for case summaries on this topic.) The United States Supreme Court has ruled that an officer who has lawfully stopped a vehicle may order the driver and passengers out of the vehicle without showing any reason to

do so under the Fourth Amendment.[206] Alternatively, an officer could order the driver and passengers to remain in the vehicle.[207]

Using force. Officers may use reasonable force, including touching or grabbing, to stop a person. However, if officers use more force than is reasonably necessary, a court may later determine that the seizure was an arrest that must be justified by probable cause. In such a case, if there was no probable cause, evidence obtained as a direct result of the arrest will be inadmissible in court proceedings.

Courts have permitted the following kinds of force in stopping a person, when the force was reasonable on the basis of the circumstances of each case: blocking the suspect's car with police cars, drawing a gun on the suspect for the officer's protection, and making the suspect lie on the ground.[208]

N.C. App. 280, *aff'd*, 367 N.C. 163 (2013); and *State v. Kincaid*, 147 N.C. App. 94 (2001).

Although there are no prescribed words that an officer must use to obtain consent in this situation, a cautious officer should consider—after returning any documents and issuing any citation or warning ticket—telling the person that he or she is now free to leave and then asking the person whether he or she is willing to remain to answer the officer's questions.

203. To the extent that the following cases upheld a dog sniff after a traffic stop had been completed because there was a de minimis delay (and reasonable suspicion or consent did not exist to support the post-traffic-stop dog sniff), their rulings are effectively overruled by *Rodriguez*: *State v. Sellars*, 222 N.C. App. 245 (2012); *State v. Brimmer*, 187 N.C. App. 451 (2007).

204. 543 U.S. 405 (2005) (traffic stop was not unconstitutionally extended because dog sniff was conducted by one officer while another officer was still executing the traffic stop).

205. Muehler v. Mena, 544 U.S. 93 (2005); Arizona v. Johnson, 555 U.S. 323 (2009).

206. Pennsylvania v. Mimms, 434 U.S. 106 (1977) (driver); Maryland v. Wilson, 519 U.S. 408 (1997) (passenger); State v. McGirt, 122 N.C. App. 237 (1996) (driver); State v. Pulliam, 139 N.C. App. 437 (2000) (passenger).

207. Rogala v. District of Columbia, 161 F.3d 44 (D.C. Cir. 1998) (officer ordered passenger back into vehicle); United States v. Moorefield, 111 F.3d 10 (3d. Cir. 1997) (officer ordered passenger to remain in car with hands in air).

208. United States v. Hensley, 469 U.S. 221 (1985) (drawn gun proper when officer stopped suspects reported to be armed and dangerous); United States v. Harley, 682 F.2d 398 (2d Cir. 1982) (use of weapons does not necessarily transform stop into arrest); United States v. Taylor, 716 F.2d 701 (9th Cir. 1983) (same); United States v. Sinclair, 983 F.2d 598 (4th Cir. 1993) (same); United States v. Jacobs, 715 F.2d 1343 (9th Cir. 1983) (fact that officer ordered defendants out of car at gunpoint did not, without further reason, make the stop an arrest when gun was justified by safety reasons); United States v. Nargi, 732 F.2d 1102 (2d Cir. 1984) (use of guns proper); United States v. Danielson, 728 F.2d 1143 (8th Cir. 1984) (use of drawn guns proper when suspected bank robbers were stopped); United States v. Serna-Barreto, 842 F.2d 965 (7th Cir. 1988) (officer did not exceed scope of investigative stop when he pointed gun at two drug trafficking suspects and ordered them out of their car; officer was alone at night, drug traffickers are usually armed, and other factors supported use of gun). *But see* United States v. Robertson, 833 F.2d 777 (9th Cir. 1987) (detention of defendant by 7 to 10 officers, one of whom aimed his gun at her nose, told her to freeze, and detained her from 5 to 15 minutes, exceeded scope of investigative stop (and thus was an arrest requiring probable cause when display of force) was unnecessary to ensure compliance with request to stop and there was no evidence that she was armed or dangerous). *See generally* 4 Wayne R. LaFave, Search and Seizure: A Treatise on the Fourth Amendment § 9.2(d) (5th ed. 2012).

Questioning. Officers may question a suspect they have stopped, although the suspect need not answer questions.[209] *Miranda* warnings are usually unnecessary because the suspect is not yet in custody for *Miranda* purposes.[210] (For a discussion of the custody requirement for *Miranda* warnings, see page 573 of Chapter 5.)

As discussed previously, the United States Supreme Court has made clear that an officer's questions about matters unrelated to the justification for an investigative stop (for example, questions posed to a vehicle occupant during a traffic stop as to whether there are drugs or guns in the vehicle) do not convert the encounter into an unlawful seizure as long as the questions do not measurably extend the duration of the stop.[211]

Moving or handcuffing a suspect for safety or security reasons. If, after stopping a suspect, officers move the suspect without his or her consent, a court may later determine that the investigative stop became an arrest for which probable cause was required. Generally, officers may move a suspect a short distance to another place if necessary for safety or security reasons or other legitimate purposes.[212] However, officers normally may not transport a suspect a significant distance (for example, to a law enforcement facility) without exceeding the scope of an investigative stop.[213]

Handcuffing a suspect during an investigative stop may be permissible if the defendant represents a flight or security risk.[214]

Using identification procedures. If officers believe that a crime was just committed in the area where the suspect was stopped and the suspect may be connected with that offense, witnesses may be brought to view the suspect or the officer may move the suspect a short distance to the scene of the crime for this purpose—if the time taken for the identification is relatively brief.[215] (Of course, officers may want to obtain the suspect's consent before they move the suspect so that their actions are justified on that ground as well.) But if officers took the suspect without his or her consent to a law enforcement facility for this purpose, a court probably would consider the action to have exceeded the scope of an investigatory stop.[216]

---

209. A lawfully stopped suspect also may be returned to the crime scene for brief questioning. United States v. Medina, 992 F.2d 573 (6th Cir. 1993).

210. Berkemer v. McCarty, 468 U.S. 420 (1984); State v. Benjamin, 124 N.C. App. 734 (1996) (defendant being frisked was not entitled to *Miranda* warnings because he was not in custody). For an excellent analysis of the distinction between a seizure for an investigatory stop and custody for *Miranda* purposes, see *United States v. Streifel*, 781 F.2d 953 (1st Cir. 1986), *later ruling*, 815 F.2d 153 (1st Cir. 1987); and *United States v. Bengivenga*, 845 F.2d 593 (5th Cir. 1988).

211. Arizona v. Johnson, 555 U.S. 323 (2009).

212. In *Florida v. Royer*, 460 U.S. 491 (1983), the plurality opinion stated that the record in this case did not show that the officers had legitimate safety or security reasons for moving the suspect without his consent from the airline boarding area to a small airport room, where they attempted to obtain his consent to search his luggage. In light of the later case of *United States v. Sharpe*, 470 U.S. 675 (1985), it is not clear that the officers' movement of the suspect was necessarily improper. Rather, the *Sharpe* Court indicated that the officers' detention of the suspect in a small room for questioning was an important reason why the stop in *Royer* became an arrest. *See also* 4 Wayne R. LaFave, Search and Seizure: A Treatise on the Fourth Amendment § 9.2(g) (5th ed. 2012); United States v. Vanichromanee, 742 F.2d 340 (7th Cir. 1984) (stopping of defendant and two other drug suspects in parking garage for 5 to 10 minutes and moving them to nearby apartment (where other drug suspects were located) for 5 to 10 additional minutes did not raise intrusiveness of stop to

arrest); United States v. Nurse, 916 F.2d 20 (D.C. Cir. 1990); United States v. Glover, 957 F.2d 1004 (2d Cir. 1992); United States v. Jones, 973 F.2d 928 (D.C. Cir. 1992).

A lawfully stopped suspect also may be returned to the crime scene for brief questioning. United States v. Medina, 992 F.2d 573 (6th Cir. 1993).

213. Dunaway v. New York, 442 U.S. 200 (1979). *See* 4 Wayne R. LaFave, Search and Seizure: A Treatise on the Fourth Amendment § 9.2(g), at 465 (4th ed. 2004).

214. State v. Campbell, 188 N.C. App. 701 (2008) (handcuffing during investigative stop was permissible when officer knew that defendant had previously fled from law enforcement, even though he had been cooperative during this stop); State v. Carrouthers, 213 N.C. App. 384 (2011) (upholding use of handcuffs); State v. Thorpe, 232 N.C. App. 468 (2014) (similar ruling). *See also* State v. Sanchez, 147 N.C. App. 619 (2001) (use of handcuffs did not exceed scope of investigative stop); United States v. Bautista, 684 F.2d 1286 (9th Cir. 1982) (handcuffing allowed); United States v. Jordan, 232 F.3d 447 (5th Cir. 2000) (handcuffing allowed to frisk defendant).

215. *See* 4 Wayne R. LaFave, Search and Seizure: A Treatise on the Fourth Amendment § 9.2(g) (5th ed. 2012), and cases cited in note 288 of that publication. *Florida v. Royer*, 460 U.S. 491 (1983), does not affect the validity of these cases because the officers, unlike in *Royer*, had a legitimate law enforcement justification to move the suspects. An additional case is *United States v. McCargo*, 464 F.3d 192 (2d Cir. 2006) (no Fourth Amendment violation when officers during *Terry* stop transported defendant a short distance for identification by burglary victim).

216. Dunaway v. New York, 442 U.S. 200 (1979). *See* 4 Wayne R. LaFave, Search and Seizure: A Treatise on the Fourth Amendment § 9.2(g), at 355 (5th ed. 2012).

Using drug dog. The use of a drug dog to sniff a vehicle during a traffic or other investigative stop is permissible while the driver is being lawfully detained for the issuance of a citation or warning ticket or for another lawful purpose.[217] However, if the use of a drug dog or awaiting the arrival of a drug dog occurs for any length of time after a traffic or other investigative stop has been reasonably completed, then consent or reasonable suspicion of criminal activity would be needed to support a suspect's continued detention.[218]

Checking Division of Criminal Information or other information source. After stopping a suspect, officers may check for outstanding warrants and other criminally related information through the DCI or other information source if the check does not unduly prolong the stop.[219]

Checking driver's license and other information during a vehicle traffic stop. After stopping a vehicle for a traffic violation, an officer may check the driver's license, vehicle registration (including the rental agreement if it is a rented vehicle), insurance, and identity. The officer may also check the DCI or other information source, as discussed above.[220]

Frisk after an investigative stop. Officers may frisk a person for weapons when they have reasonable suspicion that the person has a weapon and presents a danger to the officer or others. Although officers' authority to frisk may be exercised whether or not a stop has occurred, it usually arises after they have stopped someone.[221] (The authority to frisk is discussed on page 257 of Chapter 3.)

Stop without Reasonable Suspicion

Law enforcement officers may stop a person under certain circumstances when they do not have reasonable suspicion to believe that the person is committing a crime if there is a proper justification for interfering briefly with the person's freedom.

Service of Legal Process

Officers are authorized to stop a person to serve various kinds of legal process: criminal summonses,[222] citations,[223] nontestimonial identification orders,[224] subpoenas,[225] and any other kind of legal process that does not permit officers to take a person into custody.

Execution of a Search Warrant

During the execution of a warrant to search private premises, officers may detain those present for such time as is reasonably necessary to execute the warrant.[226] (This subject is discussed further on page 442 of Chapter 4.)

---

217. Illinois v. Caballes, 543 U.S. 405 (2005) (proper use of drug dog during traffic stop); State v. Branch, 177 N.C. App. 104 (2006) (proper use of drug dog at checkpoint when reasonable suspicion supported additional detention beyond initial stop at checkpoint).

218. Rodriguez v. United States, 135 S. Ct. 1609 (2015) (detaining for dog sniff a traffic stop defendant for seven to eight minutes after stop completed violated Fourth Amendment absent reasonable suspicion or consent).

219. Although involving a vehicle stop, the ruling in *Rodriguez v. United States*, 135 S. Ct. 1609 (2015) (discussed above in the text) generally supports the statement in the text. *See also* United States v. Hensley, 469 U.S. 221 (1985) (brief detention permitted to determine whether another jurisdiction had issued arrest warrant); United States v. Rutherford, 824 F.2d 831 (10th Cir. 1987) (delay of 25 minutes for computer registration check of car did not transform a legal investigatory stop into arrest when computer problem caused delay).

220. Rodriguez v. United States, 135 S. Ct. 1609 (2015) (discussed above in the text); Burton v. City of Durham, 118 N.C. App. 676 (1995); Rousselo v. Starling, 128 N.C. App. 439 (1998); State v. Hunter, 107 N.C. App. 402 (1992); State v. Jones, 96 N.C. App. 389 (1989).

221. The United States Supreme Court in *Terry v. Ohio*, 392 U.S. 1 (1968), recognized the constitutionality of stopping and frisking suspects. Interestingly, the majority opinion discussed only the frisk in that case and did not analyze the stop. But Justice Harlan's concurring opinion did discuss the right to make a forcible stop.

222. G.S. 15A-303. Although the statute does not specifically authorize an officer to stop a person to serve a criminal summons, that power naturally flows from the officer's duty to serve the summons.

223. G.S. 15A-302. Although the statute does not specifically authorize an officer to stop a person to serve a citation, that power naturally flows from the officer's duty to serve the citation. In most cases, of course, the officer would have stopped a person before issuing and serving the citation.

224. G.S. 15A-277. Although the statute does not specifically authorize an officer to stop a person to serve a nontestimonial identification order, that power naturally flows from the officer's duty to serve the order. Nontestimonial identification orders are discussed in Chapter 4.

225. G.S. 15A-801, -802; 1A-1, Rule 45(e), Rules of Civil Procedure. An officer who personally serves a subpoena clearly may stop a person to serve it.

226. G.S. 15A-256; Michigan v. Summers, 452 U.S. 692 (1981). *See also* Muehler v. Mena, 544 U.S. 93 (2005).

Public Emergencies

When officers reasonably believe that it is urgently necessary to save life, prevent serious bodily harm, or avert or control public catastrophe, they may enter buildings, vehicles, and other premises; limit or restrict where people may go; and take control over others' property.[227] This statutory authority may not be used for a law enforcement purpose. Instead, it allows an officer to control property and persons during emergencies such as floods, fires, and hurricanes or to enter a home where, for example, a neighbor has reported that an elderly person has not come out for a long time.

When the governor[228] or a local government official[229] declares a state of emergency during a disaster, riot, catastrophe, or similar public emergency, law enforcement officers are authorized to restrict the movement of people in public places.[230]

Stop of Vehicle under Community Caretaking Doctrine

The North Carolina Court of Appeals in *State v. Smathers*[231] upheld an officer's stop of a vehicle without probable cause or reasonable suspicion under the community caretaking doctrine, which had been recognized in a different context (a search of a trunk) by the United States Supreme Court in *Cady v. Dombrowski*,[232] discussed in Chapter 3 on page 260. The officer in *Smathers* saw the defendant driving her vehicle and striking a large animal that had run onto the road, causing the vehicle to bounce and produce sparks as it scraped the road. The officer pulled behind her and activated his blue lights to stop her vehicle to ensure that she and the vehicle were okay. As it

turned out, she was impaired and was later arrested for DWI. The court set forth the State's burden to satisfy the community caretaking doctrine: (1) a search or seizure under the Fourth Amendment occurred;[233] (2) an objectively reasonable basis (that is, an officer's subjective intent is not relevant) supports the community caretaking function; and (3) the public need or interest to make the stop outweighs the intrusion on a person's privacy. Included among the relevant factors in balancing the public need or interest with a person's privacy are (1) the degree of the public interest and the exigency of the situation; (2) the circumstances surrounding the seizure, including time, location, and the degree of overt authority and force displayed by an officer; and (3) the availability, feasibility, and effectiveness of alternatives to the type of intrusion actually accomplished.

Motor Vehicle Checkpoints, Including Driver's License and DWI Checkpoints

(*See page 162 for case summaries on this topic.*)

The constitutional and statutory issues concerning motor vehicle checkpoints are comprehensively discussed in a School of Government publication that is available online and cited in the accompanying footnote.[234]

Constitutional background. The United States Supreme Court ruled in *Delaware v. Prouse* that the Fourth Amendment prohibits officers, acting on their own initiative, from randomly stopping vehicles for the sole purpose of checking whether the driver has a proper driver's license and vehicle registration.[235] Therefore, officers ordinarily may not stop a vehicle unless they have at least reasonable suspicion that a driver or occupant has committed or is committing a criminal offense or infraction, as discussed on page 29. However, the Court indicated that a systematic roadblock type of stop to check licenses and registrations is permissible if all cars are stopped or if some patterned method of stopping is devised.[236]

---

227. G.S. 15A-285. *See* State v. Braswell, 312 N.C. 553 (1985) (officers' entry into home was justified under G.S. 15A-285 because they believed that person might be inside who was injured and needed assistance).

Another statute, G.S. 15A-401(b)(4), authorizes an officer to detain a person arrested for violating an order limiting freedom of movement or access under G.S. 130A-475 (public health threat that may have been caused by terrorist incident using nuclear, biological, or chemical agents) or G.S. 130A-145 (quarantine and isolation authority) to the area designated by the state health director or local health director. The person may be detained in the area until an initial appearance under G.S. 15A-511 and G.S. 15A-534.5.

228. G.S. 14-288.15(c).

229. G.S. 14-288.12(b), -288.13(b), -288.14(a).

230. The proclamation issued by the governor or local government official must authorize the restriction.

231. 232 N.C. App. 120 (2014).

232. 413 U.S. 433 (1973).

233. Of course, if neither a search nor seizure occurred, there is no Fourth Amendment issue to resolve.

234. Jeffrey B. Welty, *Motor Vehicle Checkpoints*, ADMIN. OF JUST. BULL. 2010/04 (Sept. 2010), http://sogpubs.unc.edu/electronicversions/pdfs/aojb1004.pdf.

235. 440 U.S. 648 (1979). To the extent that G.S. 20-183(a) could be interpreted to allow an officer to stop a vehicle when the stop is not permitted by the Fourth Amendment, it is unconstitutional.

236. *Prouse*, 440 U.S. at 663. *See also* Justice Blackmun's concurring opinion, 440 U.S. at 663. The Court recognized the *Prouse* dicta in *City of Indianapolis v. Edmond*, 531 U.S.

The Court also indicated that it generally did not question the constitutionality of roadside truck weigh stations and inspection checkpoints.[237] Although North Carolina courts have not decided this issue, courts in other jurisdictions have upheld the constitutionality of these activities.[238]

The United States Supreme Court in *Michigan Department of State Police v. Sitz* ruled constitutional an impaired-driving highway checkpoint conducted under guidelines that require officers to stop every vehicle and examine the driver briefly for signs of intoxication; reasonable suspicion is not needed to make this brief stop.[239] Detention of particular drivers for more extensive field sobriety testing may require satisfaction of a reasonable suspicion standard.

The United States Supreme Court in *City of Indianapolis v. Edmond* ruled unconstitutional a highway checkpoint whose primary purpose was to detect illegal drugs.[240] The Court did not decide in this case whether a checkpoint would be constitutional if the primary purpose was to detect impaired drivers or check drivers' licenses and the secondary purpose was to detect illegal drugs.[241]

The North Carolina Supreme Court has ruled that an officer may monitor a checkpoint's entrance for vehicles whose drivers may be attempting to avoid the checkpoint and may pursue and stop a vehicle that has turned away from a checkpoint within its perimeters to determine why the vehicle did so.[242] For example, an officer may pursue and stop a vehicle that avoids an impaired-driving checkpoint by making a legal left turn before the checkpoint if the driver could have observed the checkpoint ahead.

Other North Carolina appellate cases on checkpoints are discussed in the School of Government publication mentioned at the beginning of this section.

North Carolina statute authorizing motor vehicle checkpoints. North Carolina statutory law authorizes the use of checkpoints[243] to determine compliance with Chapter 20 (motor vehicle law) of the General Statutes.[244] If a law enforcement agency is conducting a checkpoint, it must:

1. Designate in advance the pattern both for stopping vehicles and for requesting drivers who are stopped to produce a driver's license, registration, or insurance information.

2. Ensure that the pattern is not based on a particular vehicle type (for example, motorcycles only). However, the pattern may designate any type of commercial motor vehicle.

3. Operate under a written policy[245] that provides guidelines for the pattern, although the pattern

---

32 (2000). *See generally* 5 Wayne R. LaFave, Search and Seizure: A Treatise on the Fourth Amendment § 10.8(a) (5th ed. 2012).

237. *Prouse*, 440 U.S. at 663 n.26.

238. *See generally* 5 Wayne R. LaFave, Search and Seizure: A Treatise on the Fourth Amendment § 10.8(c) (5th ed. 2012). *See also* United States v. Fort, 248 F.3d 475 (5th Cir. 2001) (warrantless and suspicionless stopping of commercial vehicles for regulatory inspection is constitutional); United States v. Castelo, 415 F.3d 407 (5th Cir. 2005); United States v. Delgado, 545 F.3d 1195 (9th Cir. 2008).

239. 496 U.S. 444 (1990). North Carolina courts have upheld the constitutionality of driver's license and impaired driving checkpoints. State v. Mitchell, 358 N.C. 63 (2004); State v. Colbert, 146 N.C. App. 506 (2001); State v. Tarlton, 146 N.C. App. 417 (2001); State v. Barnes, 123 N.C. App. 144 (1996). However, how a particular checkpoint was conducted will be subject to constitutional scrutiny. See, for example, *State v. Veazey*, 191 N.C. App. 181 (2008), and the same case later on appeal after remand to the trial court for additional findings and conclusions of law, *State v. Veazey*, 201 N.C. App. 398 (2009).

240. 531 U.S. 32 (2000). The Court declined to approve a checkpoint whose primary purpose was to detect evidence of ordinary criminal wrongdoing, such as illegal drugs. The Court noted that a checkpoint set up for an emergency (such as to thwart an imminent terrorist attack or to catch a dangerous fleeing criminal) would likely not violate the Fourth Amendment.

241. *Edmond*, 531 U.S. at 32 n.2. *See* United States v. Davis, 270 F.3d 977 (D.C. Cir. 2001) (court stated that checkpoint with a primary purpose of checking licenses and registrations and a secondary purpose of drug enforcement would be constitutional; court remanded case to district court for additional findings).

242. State v. Foreman, 351 N.C. 627 (2000). *See also* State v. Bowden, 177 N.C. App. 718 (2006).

243. Although the statute uses the term "checking stations," the text uses "checkpoint," the more commonly used term.

244. G.S. 20-16.3A.

245. In *State v. White*, 232 N.C. App. 296 (2014), officers of a local law enforcement agency conducted a driver's license checkpoint, but their agency did not have a written checkpoint policy as required by G.S. 20-16.3A(a)(2a), nor was it operating the checkpoint under another agency's policy. The court ruled that this statutory violation was substantial and required the suppression of evidence obtained at the checkpoint. The court rejected the State's argument that the suppression of evidence was not permitted because Chapter 20 of the General Statutes

itself need not be in writing.[246] The policy may be the agency's own policy, or if the agency does not have a written policy, it may be the policy of another law enforcement agency, and it may include contingency provisions for altering either pattern if actual traffic conditions differ from those anticipated.[247] However, an individual officer may not be given discretion concerning which vehicle is to be stopped or, if the vehicle is stopped, which driver is to be requested to produce a driver's license, registration, or insurance information.

4. Advise the public that an authorized checkpoint is being operated by having, at a minimum, one law enforcement vehicle with its blue light in operation during the conduct of the checking station.

The statute also provides:

1. An officer who has reasonable suspicion that a vehicle occupant has violated Chapter 20 or any other law may detain that person[248] to investigate further. A driver stopped at the checkpoint may be requested to submit to an alcohol screening test if during the course of the stop the officer determines that the driver had previously consumed alcohol or has an open container of alcoholic beverage in the vehicle. The officer must consider the results of the test or a refusal to take the test in determining if there is reasonable suspicion to investigate further.

2. The placement of checkpoints should be random or statistically indicated, and agencies must avoid placing them repeatedly in the same location or proximity. However, the statute provides that this provision is not a ground for a motion to suppress or a defense to any offense arising out of the operation of a checkpoint.

3. Law enforcement agencies may conduct any type of checkpoint or roadblock if it is established and operated in accordance with the United States and North Carolina constitutions.

Information-Seeking Checkpoints

(See page 168 for case summaries on this topic.)

The United States Supreme Court in *Illinois v. Lidster* approved the use of information-seeking checkpoints under certain circumstances.[249] For example, the Court in *Lidster* approved a checkpoint designed to obtain from motorists more information about an unsolved hit-and-run that had occurred around the same place and time of night about one week earlier. The checkpoint involved stopping each vehicle for 10 to 15 seconds, asking the occupants whether they had seen anything happen the prior weekend, and handing each driver a flyer describing the case and asking for assistance in identifying the vehicle and driver.

Wildlife and Marine Fisheries Officers

(See page 169 for case summaries on this topic.)

In North Carolina, wildlife law enforcement officers and marine fisheries enforcement officers have additional authority to stop people for wildlife and marine fisheries violations that are not available to other law enforcement officers when they investigate general criminal law violations.[250] Of course, wildlife and marine fisheries officers

---

does not contain express statutory language requiring suppression of evidence for a statutory violation.

246. Even if it is not legally required to do so, a law enforcement agency may want to provide written guidelines concerning the pattern.

247. The statute also provides that if officers of a law enforcement agency are operating under another agency's policy, it must be stated in writing.

248. Although G.S. 20-16.3A(b) refers to reasonable suspicion relating to an "occupant" but then refers to detaining the "driver," it is appropriate only to detain the person for whom reasonable suspicion exists, unless all occupants are being detained for officer safety reasons.

249. 540 U.S. 419 (2004).

250. The stopping authority of wildlife law enforcement officers and marine fisheries enforcement officers may be subject to constitutional question in light of *Delaware v. Prouse*, 440 U.S. 648 (1979). However, Justice Blackmun's concurring opinion (joined by Justice Powell) in *Prouse* stated that he did not believe that the *Prouse* ruling threw any "constitutional shadow" on game wardens who make largely random examinations in performing their duties. The Court would likely uphold a reasonable use of such stopping authority. *See* People v. Perez, 59 Cal. Rptr. 2d 596 (Cal. App. 1996); Drane v. State, 493 So. 2d 294 (Miss. 1986); State v. Keehner, 425 N.W.2d 41 (Iowa 1988); People v. Layton, 552 N.E.2d 1280 (Ill. App. 1990); United States v. Fraire, 575 F.3d 929 (9th Cir. 2009) (upholding checkpoint at entrance and exit of national park to check for illegal hunting). *See generally* State v. Nobles, 107 N.C. App. 627 (1992), *aff'd*, 333 N.C. 787 (1993) (G.S. 113-136(k), authorizing warrantless administrative inspections of licensed fish dealership, is constitutional on its face); State v. Pike, 139 N.C. App. 96 (2000) (wildlife officer made constitutional suspicionless stop of motor vessel under G.S. 75A-17(a) to conduct safety inspection).

also may stop a person when they have reasonable suspicion that a person has committed a violation of the law.

These officers usually may stop anyone they reasonably believe is engaging in an activity regulated by their respective agencies—for example, hunting, fishing, trapping, or transporting of taxable seafood—to see whether that person is complying with the law. If the person to be stopped is in a motor vehicle and the officers are in their vehicle, the officers must give notice by appropriate siren, light, or horn before they make the stop.[251]

Wildlife officers must satisfy a higher standard than described in the preceding paragraph to stop a vehicle on a primary highway (a highway designated by N.C., U.S., or Interstate numbers).[252] They must have "clear evidence" that the vehicle has been recently engaged in a regulated activity.[253]

A person who is stopped must allow the wildlife or marine fisheries officers to inspect licenses and equipment.[254]

A person commits a criminal misdemeanor if the person refuses to stop when ordered to do so[255] or refuses to show licenses or other items required to be carried by law or regulation.[256]

A person commits a criminal misdemeanor if the person refuses to allow an officer to inspect weapons or equipment that the officer reasonably believes to be possessed incident to a regulated activity and the officer has reasonable suspicion that a violation has been committed, except that an officer may inspect a shotgun to confirm whether it is plugged or unplugged without reasonable suspicion.[257]

A person commits a criminal misdemeanor if the person refuses to allow an officer to inspect fish or wildlife to ensure compliance with bag and size limits.[258]

Except as provided in G.S. 113-137 (search incident to arrest and seizing and confiscating property), officers may not inspect, in the absence of a person in apparent control of the item to be inspected, (1) weapons; (2) equipment (except equipment left unattended in its normal operation) including, but not limited to, traps, trot lines, crab pots, and fox pens; (3) fish; and (4) wildlife.[259]

Custody without Probable Cause

Sometimes an officer investigating a crime may want to take a person into custody even when probable cause does not exist to arrest the person for a crime. However, without probable cause, an officer may not require a person to come without the person's consent to a law enforcement facility for questioning; no "arrest on suspicion" or other similar kind of detention is allowed beyond that permitted by an investigative stop.[260] Thus, if an officer wants to take a murder suspect from his or her home to the law enforcement facility for questioning, the officer must obtain the suspect's consent to do so. It is sometimes best to explain to the suspect that he or she need not come with the officer and that he or she is not under arrest and is free to leave the officer's presence at any time the suspect wishes. An officer may want to obtain consent both orally and in writing to help the suspect fully understand the right not to come with the officer without the suspect's consent and to assist a later reviewing court in determining that the suspect voluntarily accompanied the officer to the law enforcement facility.[261]

---

251. G.S. 113-136(f).

252. *See* G.S. 136-44.2. The limitation in this section (that the highway must be outside a municipality) would not apply to the power to stop contained in G.S. 113-136(g).

253. G.S. 113-136(g).

254. G.S. 113-136(k). A person who does not allow the inspection commits a misdemeanor. *See generally* State v. Nobles, 107 N.C. App. 627 (1992), *aff'd*, 333 N.C. 787 (1993) (G.S. 113-136(k), authorizing warrantless administrative inspections of licensed fish dealership, is constitutional on its face).

255. G.S. 113-136(j).

256. G.S. 113-136(k).

257. *Id.*, as amended by S.L. 2015-263, effective for offenses committed on or after December 1, 2015. *See generally* State v. Colosimo, 669 N.W.2d 1 (Minn. 2003) (defendant's conviction for refusing to allow inspection of open areas of his boat for fish that defendant admitted transporting did not violate his Fourth Amendment rights).

258. G.S. 113-136(k), as amended by S.L. 2015-263, effective for offenses committed on or after December 1, 2015.

259. *Id.*

260. Dunaway v. New York, 442 U.S. 200 (1979) (taking person to police station without probable cause and without consent violates Fourth Amendment); State v. Simpson, 303 N.C. 439 (1981) (defendant voluntarily came to police station); State v. Davis, 305 N.C. 400 (1982) (same); State v. Reynolds, 298 N.C. 380 (1979) (same); State v. Jeffries, 55 N.C. App. 269 (1982) (same); State v. Freeman, 307 N.C. 357 (1983) (officer arrested defendant without probable cause when he went to suspect's house and told him that he was there to "pick him up" and then took him without his consent to sheriff's department for questioning; resulting confession was inadmissible).

261. *See, e.g.*, State v. Bromfield, 332 N.C. 24 (1992) (defendant voluntarily agreed to accompany officers back to police

When an officer has probable cause to believe that a crime has been committed but cannot arrest a suspect because the officer has only reasonable suspicion that that person committed the crime, a prosecutor may obtain a *nontestimonial identification order* from a judge. This document will require the suspect to submit to fingerprinting, lineups, handwriting samples, and similar identification procedures if the procedures will aid materially in establishing whether that person committed the offense.[262] Nontestimonial identification orders are discussed on page 459 of Chapter 4.

The Arrest Warrant and Other Criminal Process

Criminal Process

A person may be taken into custody (or in some cases directed to appear before a court) either with or without the authority of *criminal process*.[263] Criminal process includes arrest warrants, orders for arrest, criminal summonses, and citations. In essence, criminal process is a document indicating that a person has committed a criminal offense; it either directs that person to appear before a court or directs an officer to arrest and bring the person before a judicial official.

Except for citations, only a judicial official may issue criminal process, which is valid throughout the state.[264] Judicial officials include appellate justices and judges, superior and district court judges, clerks of superior court (including assistant and deputy clerks), and magistrates.[265] Because magistrates normally perform the judicial official's functions that are described in this book, the term "magistrate" generally will be used even though another judicial official legally may perform the function.

An officer who executes criminal process by serving it on the person named in the document must enter the date of execution on it and return it to the clerk of superior court's office—or to a magistrate, if the magistrate

agrees to forward it to the clerk's office. The return of service must be entered in the electronic repository.[266]

Arrest Warrant

(*See page 183 for case summaries on this topic.*)

An arrest warrant charges a person with a criminal offense—felony or misdemeanor—and orders an officer who has the authority and jurisdiction to execute the warrant to arrest the person and bring the person without unnecessary delay for an initial appearance before a judicial official to answer to the charge.

Criminal process other than an arrest warrant is issued in at least two common circumstances involving arrests. First, when a grand jury indicts a person, an order for arrest is issued instead of an arrest warrant because the indictment is the charging document; the only necessary criminal process is the authority to arrest. The second circumstance occurs when an officer arrests a person without a warrant and brings the person before a magistrate for the initial appearance. If the magistrate finds probable cause to charge the person with a criminal offense, the magistrate will issue a magistrate's order (discussed on page 86). An arrest warrant is unnecessary because the officer already has arrested the person; the only necessary criminal process is a charging document.

Paperwork. The Administrative Office of the Courts prepares and prints forms for the court system. It also maintains an electronic repository (commonly known as NCAWARE),[267] which allows criminal process to be created electronically and printed as needed and also allows criminal process originally created in paper form to be entered into the electronic repository.[268] The standard arrest warrant form is AOC-CR-100, which provides a blank space on which to charge any criminal offense. The

---

station). Of course, oral consent is sufficient; written consent is not required.

262. G.S. Ch. 15A, Art. 14 (G.S. 15A-271 through -282). For juvenile nontestimonial identification orders, see G.S. 7B-2103 through -2109.

263. G.S. 15A, Art. 17 (G.S. 15A-301 through -305).

264. G.S. 15A-303(f), -304(f), -305(d).

265. G.S. 15A-101(5).

266. G.S. 15A-301.1(k).

267. The acronym refers to the North Carolina Warrant Repository. Although the term "warrant" is used, the repository includes all criminal process other than a citation. However, a citation's contents would appear in the repository when an officer arrests a person and takes him or her to a magistrate for an initial appearance, and the magistrate issues a magistrate's order after finding probable cause for the misdemeanor alleged in the citation.

268. G.S. 15A-301.1. Other relevant statutes involving the electronic repository are G.S. 15A-101.1 (definitions) and G.S. 15A-301 (criminal process).

AOC also has other arrest warrant forms for charging specific offenses.[269]

For arrest warrants initially created and existing only in paper form, North Carolina law requires that the issuing judicial official prepare an original and two copies of the arrest warrant[270] (an officer may assist in completing the paperwork). The magistrate forwards one copy to the clerk of court's office as a record that the arrest warrant was issued. The magistrate gives two copies to the officer for service.

For arrest warrants originally created in electronic form or originally created in paper form but later entered into the electronic repository, paper copies of the arrest warrant may be printed by any judicial official, law enforcement officer, or other authorized person.[271]

When the officer arrests the defendant, the officer gives a copy of the arrest warrant to the defendant and then fills out the return-of-service on the original copy and returns it to the clerk's office or to a magistrate, if the magistrate has agreed to forward it to the clerk's office.

For arrest warrants initially created and existing only in paper form, if the warrant is not executed (that is, if the defendant has not been arrested) within 180 days of issuance, it must be returned to the clerk. The purpose of this provision is to reduce the amount of outstanding criminal process that may exist within law enforcement agencies. But failure to return the warrant does not invalidate it, and thus a lawful arrest may be made with it.[272] If a warrant is returned, a new one may be issued or the old warrant may be reissued.[273] The requirement that the warrant be returned within 180 days does not impose a time limit on when the arrest may be made; the 180-day limit only concerns the handling of paperwork.

For arrest warrants originally created in electronic form or originally created in paper form but later entered into the electronic repository, the warrant must be served not later than 24 hours after it has been printed. If the process is not served within 24 hours, that fact promptly must be recorded in the electronic repository and all copies in paper form must be destroyed. (It is unclear whether the printed warrant is no longer valid for service after 24 hours, but an officer should assume so until an appellate court rules on the issue.)[274] If the warrant was never executed, it may again be printed in paper form at a later time. When service of the warrant is no longer being actively pursued, that fact must promptly be recorded in the repository.[275]

Issuance and content. Before a magistrate may issue an arrest warrant—or criminal summons (discussed on page 59)—the person (sometimes referred to as the complainant) who is seeking the warrant or criminal summons must present testimony under oath or affirmation. This testimony may be presented in person or—in the case of an arrest warrant—by means of an audio and

---

269. The forms are available in paper and in the electronic repository. Most AOC forms are also available at www.nccourts.org/Forms/FormSearch.asp. The School of Government issues a publication that provides charging language for many criminal offenses: JEFFREY B. WELTY, ARREST WARRANT AND INDICTMENT FORMS (UNC School of Government, 6th ed. 2010). There are online updates to this publication available at www.sog.unc.edu/publications/updates-and-supplements.

270. The original copy of the arrest warrant is the document that normally will be used as the criminal pleading at trial.

271. G.S. 15A-301.1(e).

272. G.S. 15A-301(d)(3). However, officers who deliberately fail to return the warrant after 180 days may be committing a misdemeanor under G.S. 14-242.

273. G.S. 15A-301(d)(4), -301(e)(1).

274. It is unclear whether the language in G.S. 15A-301.1(m), enacted in 2002, that "[f]ailure to enter any information as required by subsection (i) or (k)" limits the later statutory language that the failure does not "invalidate the process, nor does it invalidate service or execution made after the period specified in subsection (k)," which includes the 24 hours language. If it is a limitation, then the latter language applies only to a failure to enter information and does not apply as well to a mere failure to serve or execute the process within 24 hours. Thus, the particular paper warrant is no longer valid if not served within 24 hours, and, as a result, an officer must have another warrant printed. On the other hand, a different interpretation of G.S. 15A-301.1(m) may be derived from examining the statute governing paper criminal process that has existed since its enactment in 1974. The legislature that enacted G.S. 15A-301(d)(2) required criminal process to be returned in a certain number of days, depending on the type of process. However, to protect officers from civil liability and other consequences, it also provided in G.S. 15A-301(d)(3) that a failure to return process in the required number of days did not invalidate the process nor its service or execution. One can argue that the legislature in 2002 intended to carry forward the same principle in G.S. 15A-301.1(m), however awkwardly the statutory subsection reads. Compare these provisions with the search warrant provision in G.S. 15A-248, in which the legislature explicitly stated that a search warrant not executed within 48 hours is "void." One can argue that the legislature is aware when it needs to clearly state when a process is void, as it has done with search warrants. But it did not explicitly do so in any subsection of G.S. 15A-301.1.

275. G.S. 15A-301.1(k).

video transmission in which both the person and the magistrate can see and hear each other.[276] The person's testimony must contain facts from which the magistrate can find probable cause to believe that a crime has been committed and probable cause to believe that the defendant committed it. When a person presents these facts to the magistrate, the facts either must appear in an affidavit—a written, signed statement made under oath or affirmation—or must be stated orally under oath or affirmation to the official.[277] Almost always, the facts are presented orally under oath or affirmation rather than by written affidavit, and therefore the complainant's signature is not required when an arrest warrant or criminal summons is issued. Only the issuing magistrate's signature is required.

An arrest with an arrest warrant is valid only if the facts that support probable cause for the arrest were presented to the issuing official when the warrant was issued. Thus, an officer should not expect a magistrate to issue an arrest warrant automatically just because the officer asks for it. The Fourth Amendment requires the magistrate to make an independent judgment, on the basis of information given under oath or affirmation, that there is probable cause to arrest.

Generally, most requirements about the content of an arrest warrant will be met if the warrant form is followed. Two items in the warrant that merit special attention, however, are the statement of the offense being charged and the identity of the person to be arrested.

To understand why the offense being charged must be stated with specificity, it is necessary to remember that a warrant serves two basic purposes: (1) it authorizes an officer to arrest a person; and (2) it informs a defendant of the offense with which he or she is charged and, for a misdemeanor, provides the formal charge for trial. For the first purpose, it is necessary only to set out the offense being charged clearly enough so that the person being arrested knows why he or she is being arrested (for example, "trespassing"). For the second purpose, if the warrant is also to serve as a trial document (known as the criminal pleading), then the charge must assert facts that support every element of a criminal offense clearly enough to inform the defendant what conduct he or she allegedly committed.[278] Normally, an officer should assume that the warrant is to serve both purposes and therefore should set out the charge completely. But if the warrant does not state the charge completely enough, a prosecutor can later correct the problem in court by amending the warrant[279] or filing a statement of charges, which may charge either the misdemeanor originally charged or an additional or different misdemeanor.[280] However, a prosecutor normally must file the statement of charges before arraignment in district court.[281]

---

276. G.S. 15A-304(d)(3). The use of this procedure and the equipment must be approved by the Administrative Office of the Courts.

277. G.S. 15A-304(d), -303(c). A written affidavit is not constitutionally required for the issuance of an arrest warrant. Oral sworn testimony is sufficient. There even is some authority that oral sworn testimony is constitutionally sufficient when a search warrant is issued (of course, however, North Carolina statutory law requires that a written affidavit be supplied with a search warrant). *See Tygart v. State*, 451 S.W.2d 225 (Ark. 1970); *United States ex rel. Gaugler v. Brierley*, 477 F.2d 516 (3d Cir. 1973); *United States v. Goyett*, 699 F.2d 838 (6th Cir. 1983); *Sherrick v. Eyman*, 389 F.2d 648 (9th Cir. 1968); 2 Wayne R. LaFave, Search and Seizure: A Treatise on the Fourth Amendment § 4.3(b), (c), & (e) (5th ed. 2012). The Court's ruling in *Malley v. Briggs*, 475 U.S. 335 (1986) (officer may be civilly liable for obtaining arrest warrant and making arrest when reasonably well-trained officer would have known that information failed to establish probable cause), does not either explicitly or implicitly require that an affidavit be submitted with an arrest warrant.

278. G.S. 15A-924(a)(5).

279. A warrant, statement of charges, criminal summons, citation, or magistrate's order may be amended at any time before or after final judgment when the amendment does not change the nature of the offense charged. G.S. 15A-922(f).

280. G.S. 15A-922(d). Although a fatally defective arrest warrant may not be amended, a statement of charges may substitute for a fatally defective arrest warrant. State v. Madry, 140 N.C. App. 600 (2000).

A statement of charges may not charge a felony. A district court judge ordinarily would allow a prosecutor to amend a felony warrant to make it possible for district court proceedings to be conducted, because (1) the defendant's guilt is not being determined and the defendant normally is not prejudiced by an amendment and (2) a properly prepared indictment must be returned before the case may be prosecuted in superior court.

281. G.S. 15A-922(d). A prosecutor may be required to file a statement of charges if the defendant objects to being tried when a citation is the criminal pleading. G.S. 15A-922(c). If—at or after arraignment in district court or on trial de novo in superior court—the defendant objects to the sufficiency of the charge contained in a criminal summons, warrant, or magistrate's order, and the judge rules that the criminal pleading is insufficient, the prosecutor may file a statement of charges. But the statement of charges may not change the nature of the offense. G.S. 15A-922(e); State v. Caudill, 68 N.C. App. 268

The person to be arrested must be identified sufficiently in the warrant so that it is unlikely that the wrong person will be arrested. If the person's name is unknown, a description may be used if it is an adequate identification. Both the first and last name, if known, of the person to be arrested should be given. The identification will likely be sufficient when the first and last names are reversed if the mistake is obvious. A nickname or alias also may be used, if the person to be arrested is known by that name and may be identified properly. Finally, a misspelling of a name does not affect the validity of a criminal pleading if the misspelling, when pronounced, sounds like the correct name.[282]

Validity of warrant. (See page 183 for case summaries on this topic.) If a warrant is valid on its face—that is, if all the formal requirements relating to the form and appearance of a warrant are satisfied—officers are protected from civil liability in serving it even if it is later proved that the warrant is invalid because, for example, a witness was not sworn properly before giving testimony before the magistrate.[283] However, officers are expected to know at least some of the legal requirements, so they should not expect to escape liability if the warrant is clearly invalid on its face.

A warrant is valid on its face if it satisfies certain requirements.[284] The warrant must

1. be in writing and signed[285] by an authorized issuing official (the arresting officer needs to check whether the warrant has been signed properly);
2. be issued in the name of the state (note that the AOC warrant form prints the state's name);
3. be directed to a specific officer or class of officers authorized to execute it (this information is printed on the AOC warrant form);
4. either name or accurately describe the person to be arrested (see above); and
5. charge a recognizable criminal offense, even though the charging language may be defective for use as a criminal pleading at trial (for example, "did unlawfully and willfully trespass" charges a recognizable criminal offense, even though it is a defective criminal pleading).[286]

Even if a warrant is valid on its face under state law, officers may be civilly liable under federal law for violating a person's constitutional rights if they obtain an arrest warrant and make an arrest with it when a reasonably well-trained officer in their position would have known that their information failed to establish probable cause to arrest.[287]

Criminal Summons

A criminal summons may legally charge a felony, a misdemeanor, or an infraction, but note the practical issues charging a felony or infraction in the accompanying footnote.[288] (An infraction is a noncriminal violation that

---

(1984) (statement of charges was improper at superior court trial de novo when it charged nonsupport of illegitimate child after district court trial for nonsupport of legitimate child).

282. *See, e.g.*, State v. Taylor, 61 N.C. App. 589 (1983) (description by nickname proper).

283. G.S. 15A-301(f).

284. The requirements of a warrant valid on its face so that an officer properly may execute it are set out in *State v. McGowan*, 243 N.C. 431 (1956) (warrant void because no evidence that judicial officer signed it). Although *McGowan* also lists as a requirement that testimony be taken under oath, an officer examining an arrest warrant ordinarily would have no way of knowing whether the testimony was so taken. In any event, all AOC-printed arrest warrant forms state that the warrant was issued with information furnished under oath. Other cases include *State v. McDonald*, 14 N.C. 469 (1831) (officer bound to know search warrant void on its face because justice of peace had no authority to issue it); *Alexander v. Lindsey*, 230 N.C. 663 (1949) (arrest was valid under arrest warrant that was defective in charging criminal offense—"did unlawfully and willfully trespass"—but warrant was not void on its face because it charged a recognizable criminal offense); *Robinson v. City of Winston-Salem*, 34 N.C. App. 401 (1977) (arresting officer is liable for false imprisonment only when he does not use reasonable diligence in determining whether the person

arrested was actually the same person described in the arrest warrant); *State v. Truzy*, 44 N.C. App. 53 (1979) (no right to resist arrest pursuant to arrest warrant even if warrant may not in fact state a crime; however, it appears that the warrant in this case sufficiently charged the common law offense of public nuisance).

285. Criminal process in the electronic repository may contain an electronic signature. See G.S. 15A-101.1(5), -301.1. *See also* State v. Watts, 289 N.C. 445 (1976) (mechanical reproduction of public officer's signature was sufficient to authenticate public document if officer intended to adopt it as his or her signature).

286. Alexander v. Lindsey, 230 N.C. 663 (1949).

287. Malley v. Briggs, 475 U.S. 335 (1986).

288. G.S. 15A-303. However, the AOC criminal summons form (AOC-CR-113) does not permit charging a felony because of the immediate need to fingerprint a person who is charged with a felony, which is permitted under G.S. 15A-502(a) only when a person is arrested. In addition, NCAWARE does not permit charging a stand-alone infraction in a criminal summons; it would need to be produced manually.

is not punishable by imprisonment. A person may not be arrested for an infraction. Infractions are discussed in more detail on page 88.)

Unlike an arrest warrant, a criminal summons does not authorize an officer to take the defendant into custody. Instead, it orders the defendant to appear in court on a specified date. If the defendant willfully fails to appear, an order for arrest may be issued when the charge is a felony or misdemeanor, and the defendant may also be held in contempt of court after a court hearing is held.[289] If the defendant willfully fails to appear when the charge is an infraction, another criminal summons may be issued—but not an arrest warrant—and the defendant may also be held in contempt of court after a court hearing is held.[290]

A criminal summons should be used instead of an arrest warrant when it appears that the defendant will come to court as required without the need to arrest the defendant and set conditions of pretrial release.

An officer or law enforcement agency employee[291] serves the criminal summons on a defendant by giving a copy to him or her.

A criminal summons initially created and existing only in paper form must be returned if it is not executed within 90 days or by the time specified on it for the defendant's court appearance, whichever is earlier.[292] However, as with an arrest warrant, failure to return a criminal summons does not invalidate it. If a criminal summons is returned, a new one may be issued or the old criminal summons may be reissued.

A criminal summons originally created in electronic form or originally created in paper form but later entered into the electronic repository must be served not later than 24 hours after it has been printed. If the process is not served within 24 hours, that fact promptly must be recorded in the electronic repository and all copies in paper form must be destroyed. (It is unclear whether the printed summons is no longer valid for service after 24 hours, but an officer should assume so until an appellate court rules on the issue.)[293] If the summons was never executed, it may again be printed in paper form at a later time. When service of the summons is no longer being actively pursued, that fact must promptly be recorded in the repository.[294]

Citation

A citation is a directive, issued by an officer or other person authorized by law to do so, that a person appear in court and answer a misdemeanor charge or an infraction.[295] An officer who issues a paper citation must give the defendant a copy, but the defendant is not required to sign a receipt that is printed on the original citation to indicate that he or she has received a copy.[296] If the defendant refuses to sign, the officer effectively certifies delivery by signing the original citation that must be filed in the clerk of superior court's office. North Carolina law specifically prohibits an officer from arresting, without further reason, a defendant who refuses to sign the receipt on the original citation.[297] (Remember, of course, that a person may not be arrested for an infraction under any circumstance.)

If an officer issues a citation by using a computer and entering the pertinent data (commonly known as an eCITATION®), the officer prints and gives the defendant a copy, but an original citation is not printed for the defendant to sign.[298]

If, after a citation charging a misdemeanor has been served, it appears likely that the defendant will not appear in court, an arrest warrant or criminal summons may be issued just as if a citation had never been issued.[299] If

---

289. G.S. 15A-303(e); 5A-15.

290. Criminal contempt proceedings are separate from the trial of the infraction charged in a criminal summons. A judicial official who institutes plenary criminal contempt proceedings through a show cause order may also issue an order for arrest for the defendant if the official finds, from a sworn statement or affidavit, probable cause that the person will not appear in response to the order to appear. G.S. 5A-16(b). This provision would apply to proceedings instituted for failing to appear in court pursuant to a criminal summons, even if the offense charged in the criminal summons is an infraction.

291. When a defendant is called into a law enforcement agency to receive a criminal summons, any employee designated by the agency's chief executive officer may serve a criminal summons at the agency's office. G.S. 15A-301(b).

292. G.S. 15A-301(d)(2).

---

293. *See supra* note 274.

294. G.S. 15A-301.1(k).

295. G.S. 15A-302(a).

296. G.S. 15A-302(d). This subsection also provides that if the citation charges a parking violation, a copy of the citation must be delivered to the operator of the vehicle who is present at the time of service or must be delivered to the registered owner of the vehicle if the operator is not present by affixing a copy of the citation to the vehicle in a conspicuous place.

297. G.S. 15A-302(d).

298. As indicated in the prior paragraph in the text, a defendant's signature is not a prerequisite for a legally valid citation.

299. G.S. 15A-302(f).

a person charged with a misdemeanor fails to appear in court, an order for arrest may be issued.[300] If a person charged with an infraction fails to appear in court, only a criminal summons may be issued.[301]

If a defendant who is charged with a motor vehicle criminal offense or infraction (whether the offense or infraction is charged in an arrest warrant, criminal summons, or citation) fails to appear for trial or fails to pay a fine, a penalty, or court costs imposed for the charge, the defendant's license will be revoked by the Division of Motor Vehicles.[302] The revocation of the license does not prohibit a later prosecution of the defendant; it is an administrative action separate from the trial of the motor vehicle violation. The license will remain revoked until the defendant disposes of the charge; pays the fine, penalty, or court costs; or meets other statutory criteria that may rescind the revocation.

The citation is legally sufficient to serve as the trial charging document without a magistrate's signature on it or without the issuance of a warrant or other process.[303] A prosecutor may dismiss a citation at any time before trial, or the prosecutor may file a statement of charges in place of the citation to correct any errors in the charge or to charge additional or different offenses.[304]

Issuing a citation is appropriate when there is probable cause to believe that a person has committed a misdemeanor but it would be unnecessary to make an arrest.

In at least two situations,[305] North Carolina law prohibits an officer from making a warrantless misdemeanor arrest (remember that an officer may not arrest for an infraction). First, when an officer stops a person who is licensed in a state[306] that is party to reciprocal provisions concerning the arrest of nonresidents and the person has committed a motor vehicle misdemeanor (for example, driving without a valid driver's license) that would not result in revocation of the offender's driver's license, the officer may not arrest but instead must issue a citation.[307] Second—except for certain specified offenses—an officer may not make a warrantless arrest when a misdemeanor is committed out of the officer's presence unless the officer has probable cause to believe that the offender will not be apprehended or will harm himself or herself or others or damage property unless immediately arrested.[308] (See the discussion of warrantless misdemeanor arrests on page 63.)

For example, a merchant, Linda Arnold, reports to a law enforcement agency that she has just detained John Gray, a lifelong resident of the community, for misdemeanor larceny of a $200 camera.[309] When the officer arrives at the store, Arnold tells the officer the facts concerning the larceny and says that she has recovered the camera from Gray. Although the officer has probable cause—based on Arnold's account—to believe that Gray committed misdemeanor larceny, the officer is not authorized to make a warrantless arrest. The officer does not have this authority because the facts in this case do not support probable cause to believe that Gray will not be apprehended or that he will injure himself or others or damage property unless he is immediately arrested. However, although the officer may not make a warrantless arrest, the officer may issue a citation to Gray for misdemeanor larceny. If the officer does not choose to issue a citation, the officer or Arnold may testify about the theft before a magistrate so that a criminal summons or arrest warrant may be issued. But the officer has no authority to require Gray to come with the officer to the magistrate's office against his will because such a prolonged detention clearly would be considered an illegal arrest.

---

300. *Id.*; G.S. 15A-305(b)(3).

301. G.S. 15A-1116(b).

302. G.S. 20-24.1, -24.2. These provisions do not apply to an offense in which a cash bond, posted as a condition of pretrial release for that offense, was forfeited. In such a case, the forfeiture of the cash bond is a conviction; G.S. 20-4.01(4a)a.3.

303. G.S. 15A-922(a), (c).

304. G.S. 15A-302(e), -922(d).

305. Another situation not discussed in the text is that under certain circumstances, an officer must issue a citation instead of making an arrest of a nonresident for some wildlife violations. G.S. 113-300.6.

306. As of the time of the preparation of this book, the District of Columbia and all states except Alaska, California, Michigan, Montana, Oregon, and Wisconsin had reciprocal agreements with North Carolina.

307. G.S. 20-4.19. G.S. 20-4.18(5) was amended by S.L. 1999-452 to delete the requirement that a person's agreement to comply with the terms of a citation must be signed.

308. G.S. 15A-401(b)(2).

309. If the offense was concealment of merchandise under G.S. 14-72.1, then an officer has the authority under G.S. 15A-401(b)(2)c. to make a warrantless arrest of the defendant without any of the justifications set out in G.S. 15A-401(b)(2)b.

Order for Arrest

An order for arrest is an order issued by a judicial official that directs an officer to take a person into custody.[310] It differs from an arrest warrant in that it does not charge the person with a crime. Although an order for arrest may be issued for various reasons,[311] it is most often issued when a defendant fails to appear in court when required. It also may be issued when a grand jury indictment begins a criminal case: copies of the bill of indictment and order for arrest must be given to the defendant when the officer makes the arrest.[312]

An order for arrest created and existing only in paper form must be returned if it is not executed within 180 days. It may be reissued in the same manner as an arrest warrant.[313]

An order for arrest originally created in electronic form or originally created in paper form but later entered into the electronic repository must be served not later than 24 hours after it has been printed. If the process is not served within 24 hours, that fact promptly must be recorded in the electronic repository and all copies in paper form must be destroyed. (It is unclear whether the printed order for arrest is no longer valid for service after 24 hours, but an officer should assume so until an appellate court rules on the issue.)[314] If the order was never executed, it may again be printed in paper form at a later time. When service of the order is no longer being actively pursued, that fact must promptly be recorded in the repository.[315]

Restriction on Obscenity Offenses

North Carolina law prohibits the issuance of criminal process for the obscenity offenses in G.S. 14-190.1 (disseminating obscenity), G.S. 14-190.4 (coercing acceptance of obscene publication), and G.S. 14-190.5 (preparing obscene materials) unless a district attorney or an assistant district attorney requests that it be done.[316] This restriction also applies to search warrants for evidence related to these offenses. Although North Carolina law permits an officer to make a warrantless arrest without a prosecutor's request for these offenses (because a magistrate's order is not criminal process), the constitutionality of warrantless arrests for obscenity offenses is unclear.[317] Therefore, an officer normally should not make a warrantless arrest without consulting with a prosecutor or the legal advisor for the officer's agency.

Arrest without a Warrant or Order for Arrest

Although the preferred way to make an arrest is with an arrest warrant in the officer's possession, the law recognizes several instances when an officer may arrest without a warrant.

Warrant or Order for Arrest Has Been Issued

If law enforcement officers know that an arrest warrant has been issued for a person, whether for a felony or a misdemeanor, they may make the arrest even though they do not have the warrant in their possession[318] (but note the restrictions on entering premises to arrest, discussed on page 71). Mere knowledge that the arrest warrant exists is sufficient to justify the arrest; no additional probable cause is needed. When making such an arrest, officers must inform the arrestee that the warrant has been issued and must later serve the warrant (or have it served) on the arrestee. Although the statute that provides this arrest authority does not explicitly permit arrest with knowledge of an outstanding order for arrest, it is likely that a court would rule that such authority exists, as a warrant and an order for arrest provide functionally equivalent arrest authority.

---

310. G.S. 15A-305(a).

311. G.S. 15A-305(b) specifies the purposes for which an order for arrest may be issued.

312. G.S. 15A-305(b)(1), -305(c)(2). An order for arrest is not to be issued after an indictment is returned if the defendant already had been released from custody on the same charge in district court and the case had been bound over for action by the grand jury.

313. G.S. 15A-301(d)(2).

314. See *supra* note 274.

315. G.S. 15A-301.1(k).

---

316. G.S. 14-190.20.

317. *See* Maryland v. Macon, 472 U.S. 463 (1985) (court states that it does not decide in this case whether warrantless arrest for misdemeanor obscenity offense violates Fourth Amendment); Penthouse Int'l, Ltd. v. McAuliffe, 610 F.2d 1353 (5th Cir. 1980); Wood v. State, 240 S.E.2d 743 (Ga. App. 1977).

318. G.S. 15A-401(a)(2).

Felony

An officer may arrest without a warrant when the officer has probable cause to believe that a felony has been committed and that the person to be arrested has committed it. And it is not necessary that the felony actually have been committed (or any part of it have taken place) in the officer's presence.[319] Thus, an officer who receives reliable information establishing probable cause that a person committed an armed robbery several months ago could arrest that person without a warrant, even though the officer did not witness the robbery. But the officer may have to obtain an arrest or search warrant, or both, if the officer needs to enter the defendant's or a third party's home to make the arrest (see the discussion of entering premises to arrest on page 71).

Misdemeanor

(See page 184 for case summaries on this topic.)

General Rules

Generally, an officer may make a warrantless arrest for a misdemeanor in the following circumstances:

I. When the officer has probable cause to believe that the person has committed a misdemeanor in the officer's presence, or

II. When the officer has probable cause to believe that the person has committed a misdemeanor out of the officer's presence and also has probable cause to believe that one of the following conditions exists:

    A. The offender committed one of the following offenses:

      1. Concealment of merchandise (G.S. 14-72.1); or

      2. Impaired driving (G.S. 20-138.1); or

      3. Commercial impaired driving (G.S. 20-138.2); or

      4. Domestic criminal trespass (G.S. 14-134.3); or

      5. Simple assault or affray (G.S. 14-33(a)), assault inflicting serious injury (G.S. 14-33(c)(1)), assault with a deadly weapon (G.S. 14-33(c)(1)), assault on a female (G.S. 14-33(c)(2)), or assault by pointing a gun (G.S. 14-34), when the offense was committed by a person with whom the alleged victim has a *personal relationship* as defined in G.S. 50B-1;

      A *personal relationship* includes:

      a. Current or former spouses;

      b. People of the opposite sex who live together or have lived together;

      c. People who are related as parents and children, including others acting in loco parentis to a minor child, or as grandparents and grandchildren;[320]

      d. People who have a child in common;

      e. People who are current or former household members;

      f. People of the opposite sex who are in a dating relationship or have been in a dating relationship;[321]

      6. Violation of domestic violence protective order (G.S. 50B-4.1(a));[322] or

    B. The person will not be apprehended unless immediately arrested; or

    C. The person may cause physical injury to himself or herself or others unless immediately arrested; or

    D. The person may damage property unless immediately arrested.[323]

---

319. G.S. 15A-401(b)(2)a. In *State v. Narcisse*, 90 N.C. App. 414 (1988), the court analyzed whether officers had probable cause to believe a felony had been committed *in their presence* to make a warrantless arrest. The court correctly concluded that the offense was committed in their presence because they heard the offense being committed—voices describing a drug sale through a transmitter hidden on an informant. However, this analysis was unnecessary because G.S. 15A-401(b)(2)a. specifically authorizes an officer to make a warrantless arrest for a felony even if it has not been committed in the officer's presence.

320. G.S. 50B-1(b)(3) provides that an aggrieved party may not obtain an order of protection against a child or grandchild under the age of 16.

321. G.S. 50B-1(b)(6) provides that a *dating relationship* is one in which the parties are romantically involved over time and on a continuous basis during the course of the relationship. A casual acquaintance or ordinary fraternization between people in a business or social context is not a dating relationship.

322. As discussed in the text of this chapter on page 45, an officer has a statutory duty to arrest for this offense under certain circumstances.

323. G.S. 15A-401(b)(2)b. through f. A warrantless misdemeanor arrest for an offense not committed in the officer's

"In [the officer's] presence." A person commits an offense in an officer's presence when the officer witnesses the crime through one or more of the senses of sight, hearing, smell, touch, or taste. For example, when an officer smells marijuana smoke in a vehicle the officer has stopped, the offense of possessing marijuana is being committed in the officer's presence. If an officer hears a slapping sound, turns, and sees a person who is yelling "why did you hit me," an assault has been committed in the officer's presence.[324] If a reliable informant gives an officer information that establishes probable cause that a person possesses a misdemeanor amount of marijuana and the officer sees shortly thereafter a person who matches the description provided by the informant, the offense is being committed in the officer's presence even though the officer has not yet seen the marijuana.[325]

A typical example of an offense not generally committed in an officer's presence is a misdemeanor larceny seen by a merchant, who then reports it to a law enforcement officer.[326] Note, however, if the offense is concealment of merchandise (shoplifting) under G.S. 14-72.1, the officer may make a warrantless misdemeanor arrest even if the offense is not committed in the officer's presence.

When a misdemeanor is not committed in the officer's presence and it is not one of the offenses listed in II.A. above, the officer must satisfy one of the conditions listed in II.B., II.C., or II.D. above if the officer wants to make a warrantless arrest.

"Will not be apprehended unless immediately arrested." The phrase "will not be apprehended unless immediately arrested" means that if the officer went to a magistrate and obtained an arrest warrant to arrest a person instead of immediately arresting the person without a warrant, the person probably would not be found in order to be arrested later with the warrant. Clearly an officer could make a warrantless arrest when the person's name is unknown or when the person is leaving the scene of the crime in a car.[327] In most cases, a warrantless arrest also could be made, even when the person's identity is known, if the person lives in another state—but that may not apply to a college student or other out-of-state person who lives in the area for a temporary but extended period.

When a person is known and lives in or near the community where the crime occurred, it is unlikely that the person could not be apprehended unless immediately arrested. Thus, warrantless arrests would not be permitted *for this reason* in some cases involving misdemeanor larceny and other common misdemeanors committed by local residents, if the offenses were not committed in the officer's presence. Of course, a warrantless arrest may be allowed for some other reason, as discussed below.

"May cause physical injury to himself [or herself] or others." In a factually appropriate case, an officer could make a warrantless arrest for a misdemeanor assault that was not committed in the officer's presence if the person may cause physical injury to himself or herself or others unless immediately arrested.

"May damage property." This condition may be satisfied in misdemeanor larceny cases if the offender has

---

presence that violated this statute probably is not a federal constitutional violation if the arrest was supported by probable cause. Woods v. City of Chicago, 234 F.3d 979 (7th Cir. 2000); Pyles v. Raisor, 60 F.3d 1211 (6th Cir. 1995); Barry v. Fowler, 902 F.2d 770 (9th Cir. 1990); Fields v. City of South Houston, 922 F.2d 1183 (5th Cir. 1991); Street v. Surdyka, 492 F.2d 368 (4th Cir. 1974). However, the United States Supreme Court has not definitively decided this issue. *See* Atwater v. City of Lago Vista, 532 U.S. 318 (2001); Virginia v. Moore, 553 U.S. 164 (2008). The Fourth Amendment's exclusionary rule would not bar evidence seized as a result of a statutory violation if there was not a Fourth Amendment violation. Virginia v. Moore, 553 U.S. 164 (2008) (Virginia law enforcement officers who had probable cause to arrest defendant for a misdemeanor did not violate Fourth Amendment when they arrested him and conducted a search incident to arrest, although state law did not authorize an arrest). However, the exclusionary rule under G.S. 15A-974(a)(2) may apply.

324. Cases in which a sense of hearing justified a finding that an offense was committed in an officer's presence are *State v. McAfee*, 107 N.C. 812 (1890) (assault); *State v. Crockett*, 82 N.C. 599 (1880) (assault); and *State v. Narcisse*, 90 N.C. App. 414 (1988) (monitoring conversations of drug transaction).

325. State v. Wooten, 34 N.C. App. 85 (1977). Although this case was decided under a former statute concerning a felony committed in an officer's presence, it clearly applies to the "in [an officer's] presence" language in present law. *See also* State v. Roberts, 276 N.C. 98 (1970).

326. Under certain circumstances, a larceny could be committed in the officer's presence when reported by a merchant. If the officer had probable cause to believe that the alleged thief still possessed the stolen item while the person was in

the officer's presence, then under the ruling in *State v. Wooten*, which is discussed in the text and cited in note 325, above, the offense is being committed in the officer's presence because larceny is a continuing offense.

327. State v. Tilley, 44 N.C. App. 313 (1979) (defendant committed a crime in Dare County; Tyrrell County officers could make warrantless misdemeanor arrest of defendant traveling in car away from Dare County).

not returned, or refuses to return, the property allegedly taken.

Arrest of a Resident of a Reciprocal State

As discussed on page 61, when an officer stops a person who is licensed in a state[328] that is party to the reciprocal provisions concerning arrest of nonresidents and the person has committed a motor vehicle offense—for example, driving without a valid driver's license—that would not result in revocation of the person's license, the officer may issue a citation. However, the officer may not make a warrantless arrest, even if the offense was committed in the officer's presence, unless the person will not agree that he or she will comply with the terms of the citation.[329] (Remember that an officer has no authority to arrest for an infraction.)

Delay in Making a Warrantless Misdemeanor Arrest

An officer who wants to make a misdemeanor arrest without a warrant must make the arrest within a reasonable time or lose the authority to proceed without a warrant.[330] For example, if an officer sees a person smoking marijuana at an outdoor concert and does nothing then, the officer may not the next day make a warrantless arrest for that offense of misdemeanor possession of marijuana. Instead, the officer must obtain an arrest warrant or criminal summons or may issue a citation. On the other hand, an officer who delays making an immediate arrest for a law enforcement purpose associated with the arrest (for example, an unruly crowd is impeding the arrest, or the officer must pursue the offender to make the arrest) would still retain the authority to make a warrantless arrest as long as the officer does not become involved in unrelated matters before making the arrest. Also, a temporary hesitation in making a warrantless arrest—for example, arresting a person who had walked about 75 yards away from an officer after committing an assault—would not prohibit the warrantless arrest.[331]

Violation of Pretrial Release Order

An officer may arrest without a warrant a person who the officer has probable cause to believe has violated a pretrial release order entered under G.S. 15A-534 (general pretrial release conditions) or G.S. 15A-534.1(a)(2) (conditions imposed in pretrial release order concerning crimes of domestic violence). The officer may exercise this arrest authority whether or not the violation occurred in his or her presence.[332]

Escape from Arrest

Although the law is not entirely clear on this point, an officer generally may rearrest without a warrant any person who escapes from the officer's custody after the officer has made an arrest.[333] Apparently, however, an officer may not rearrest without a warrant unless the officer has actually taken the person into custody and not just attempted to arrest. The authority to rearrest does not require that the officer be in fresh pursuit of an escapee, or that the escapee present the danger of evading arrest entirely, or that the escapee present a danger of injuring others. An officer could, for example, rearrest without a warrant a misdemeanant who had escaped from the officer's custody two days earlier even though the escapee was no longer likely to evade arrest and was completely harmless. However, an officer should consider obtaining an arrest warrant once the officer stops looking for the person who has escaped from the officer's custody, as a warrant may be needed to make an arrest if the defendant is at his or her home or a third party's home (see the discussion on page 71).

Escapees from prison or jail present a different situation. Because escape is a continuing criminal offense, when an officer sees a prison escapee, the offense is being committed in the officer's presence.[334] Therefore,

---

328. See the list of states cited in note 306, above.

329. G.S. 20-4.18(5) was amended by S.L. 1999-452 to delete the requirement that a person's agreement to comply with the terms of a citation must be signed. Another situation not discussed in the text is that under certain circumstances, an officer must issue a citation instead of making an arrest of a nonresident for some wildlife violations. G.S. 113-300.6.

330. State v. Warren, 709 P.2d 194 (N.M. App. 1985). There are no North Carolina cases directly on point.

331. State v. McClure, 166 N.C. 321 (1914). *See also* Annotation, *Peace Officer's Delay in Making Arrest Without a Warrant for Misdemeanor or Breach of Peace*, 58 A.L.R. 2d 1056 (1958); ROY G. HALL, JR., THE LAW OF ARREST § 20 (UNC Institute of Government, 2d ed. 1961).

332. G.S. 15A-401(b)(1), -401(b)(2)f.

333. *Cf.* State v. Finch, 177 N.C. 599 (1919); ROY G. HALL, JR., THE LAW OF ARREST § 32 (UNC Institute of Government, 2d ed. 1961).

334. State v. White, 21 N.C. App. 173 (1974).

even with a misdemeanor escape, an officer may make a warrantless arrest without the additional justifications needed when the crime is not being committed in the officer's presence.

Probation, Parole, or Post-Release Supervision Violation

Convicted offenders may be given some degree of freedom on probation, parole, or post-release supervision. However, they often are required to accept various restrictions on the way they live.

Law enforcement officers may arrest a probationer without a warrant for violating the conditions of probation on the written request of a probation officer, accompanied by a written statement signed by the probation officer that the probationer has violated specified probation conditions.[335] Officers also may arrest a probationer with an order for arrest issued by a judicial official. Officers who arrest a probationer must bring him or her before a magistrate so that conditions of pretrial release may be determined.[336]

Officers may arrest a post-release supervisee or parolee for violating supervision conditions only when the Post-Release Supervision and Parole Commission has issued a temporary or conditional revocation order.[337] It is unclear whether the arresting officers must have the order in their possession when they make the arrest; however, it appears that they need not possess it if they know that it has been issued, they inform the arrested post-release supervisee or parolee that the order has been issued, and they serve it on the person as soon as possible after the arrest.[338] A

parolee or post-release supervisee arrested pursuant to a revocation order has no right to pretrial release pending the revocation proceedings.[339]

Taking Custody of Juveniles for Delinquent Acts and Other Matters

The concepts surrounding taking custody of a juvenile are similar to those of adult arrests, but some words and phrases differ.

Officers may take temporary custody of a juvenile under the age of 16[340] without a court order when they have probable cause to believe that the juvenile is delinquent and the same reasons exist to justify temporary custody as would justify a warrantless arrest of an adult.[341] After officers take a juvenile into custody without a court order, (1) they must notify the juvenile's parent, guardian, or custodian that the juvenile is in custody and that the person has a right to be present with the juvenile until it is determined whether a secure or nonsecure custody order is needed; (2) they must release the juvenile to a parent, guardian, or custodian if they determine that custody is no longer necessary; or (3) if they do not release the juvenile, they must request a court counselor to prepare a petition alleging that the juvenile is delinquent.[342] The juvenile may not be held for more than 12 hours (or more than 24 hours if any of the 12 hour period falls on a weekend or legal holiday) unless the court counselor has filed a petition and a judge has issued a secure or nonsecure custody order.[343]

---

335. G.S. 15A-1345(a). The Fourth Circuit Court of Appeals in *Jones v. Chandrasuwan*, 820 F.3d 685 (4th Cir. 2016), ruled that the Fourth Amendment requires that probation officers have reasonable suspicion to arrest a probationer for allegedly violating probation conditions. Although North Carolina appellate courts are not bound by this ruling, they often give weight to Fourth Circuit rulings and may therefore adopt this ruling. In any event, the policy of the Section of Community Corrections of the Division of Adult Correction requires probation officers to use the probable cause standard involving arrests of probationers.

336. G.S. 15A-1345(b).

337. G.S. 15A-1368.6(a), -1376(a). G.S. 143B-721(d) sets out the commission's authority to issue warrants, which would include an order to arrest a parolee or post-release supervisee.

338. The Post-Release Supervision and Parole Commission order is functionally equivalent to an arrest warrant, and thus the provisions of G.S. 15A-401(a)(2) would likely apply. *See also* G.S. 148-63.

339. G.S. 15A-1376 and 15A-1368 do not provide a right to release pending the hearing on an alleged parole or post-release supervision violation, respectively. *See also* Stevens H. Clarke, Law of Sentencing, Probation, and Parole in North Carolina 180 (UNC Institute of Government, 2d ed. 1997).

340. A *juvenile* is a person under the age of 18 who is not married, emancipated, or in the military. A *delinquent juvenile* is a juvenile who has committed a criminal offense or infraction under state law or local ordinance or indirect criminal contempt and who was under the age of 16, but at least 6, at the time of the offense. G.S. 7B-1501(7) & -1501(17).

341. G.S. 7B-1900.

342. G.S. 7B-1901. Under certain circumstances, the petition may be prepared by a clerk or magistrate. A court counselor must approve the filing of the petition, and the petition must be filed with the clerk or, if the clerk's office is closed, a magistrate. G.S. 7B-1803, -1804.

343. G.S. 7B-1901(b). A chief district court judge may delegate the power to issue secure and nonsecure custody orders

Officers also are authorized to take temporary custody of a juvenile without a court order if they have reasonable grounds to believe that the juvenile (1) is undisciplined;[344] (2) is abused, neglected, or dependent and would be injured or could not be taken into custody if officers first had to obtain a court order;[345] or (3) is an absconder from a residential facility operated by the Division of Juvenile Justice or an approved detention facility.[346] Officers who take an undisciplined juvenile into custody must follow the same procedures that apply when a delinquent juvenile is in custody; that is, notify the parent, guardian, or custodian and either seek a petition and obtain a custody order within 12 (or 24) hours or release the juvenile.[347] Officers who take custody of a juvenile they have cause to suspect is abused, neglected, or dependent must (1) notify the juvenile's parent, guardian, or custodian; (2) release the juvenile to the parent, guardian, or custodian if the officers determine that continued custody is not necessary; and (3) immediately contact the county department of social services.[348]

When officers take custody of an absconder, a secure custody order must be obtained and the juvenile must be transported to an approved detention facility. Then officers must contact the administrator of the residential facility or detention facility from which the juvenile absconded, and that administrator is responsible for returning the juvenile to the facility.[349]

The Arrest Procedure
Use of Force
(See page 185 for case summaries on this topic.)

Generally
The following discussion of the use of force sets out general principles and forgoes specific advice, for at least two reasons. First, cases deciding whether an officer properly used force often are dependent on the unique facts of each case.[350] Second, officers should know and follow their own agency's policy on the use of force. Sometimes that policy may impose greater restrictions than required by constitutional, statutory, or common law.

Every arrest that officers make involves either a threatened or an active use of force. Essentially, officers themselves decide how much force is necessary under the circumstances to bring the arrestee within their custody and control. However, they are entitled to use only as much force as is reasonably necessary to secure the arrestee, overcome resistance, prevent escape, recapture the arrestee, or protect themselves from bodily injury.[351] They may never use more force than is necessary to accomplish this purpose.[352] Authority to use force that is likely to kill the arrestee is limited to special situations. Except in those special situations discussed below, deadly

---

for alleged delinquent or undisciplined juveniles to the chief court counselor or the counseling staff. G.S. 7B-1902.

344. G.S. 7B-1900(2). *Undisciplined juvenile* is defined in G.S. 7B-1501(27).

345. G.S. 7B-500. *Abused juvenile, neglected juvenile,* and *dependent juvenile* are defined respectively in G.S. 7B-101(1), -101(15), and -101(9).

346. G.S. 7B-1900(3).

347. G.S. 7B-1901. Undisciplined petitions are generally filed by a juvenile court counselor, but a clerk may do so as well. G.S. 7B-1803.

348. G.S. 7B-501. Abuse, neglect, and dependency petitions generally are prepared and filed by the director of the county social services department or the department's attorney. G.S. 7B-403(a). *See also* G.S. 7B-404 (authorizing magistrate to issue petition under specified circumstances).

349. G.S. 7B-1901(c).

350. For example, the United States Supreme Court noted in *Brosseau v. Haugen,* 543 U.S. 194, 201 (2004), that whether an officer's use of force violated the Fourth Amendment "depends very much on the facts of each case." For cases on deadly force, see 3 Wayne R. LaFave, Search and Seizure: A Treatise on the Fourth Amendment § 5.1(d) (5th ed. 2012).

351. State v. Miller, 197 N.C. 445 (1929); State v. Belk, 76 N.C. 11 (1877). *See* G.S. 15A-401(d)(1). *See also* Graham v. Connor, 490 U.S. 386 (1989) (all claims that law enforcement officers have used excessive force in course of an arrest, investigatory stop, or other seizure of a free person must be analyzed under Fourth Amendment standard of objective reasonableness—in other words, without regard to an officer's intent or motivation—not under substantive due process); Scott v. Harris, 550 U.S. 372 (2007) (officer's use of force to terminate high-speed chase threatening lives of innocent bystanders was reasonable under Fourth Amendment even though it placed fleeing motorist at risk of serious injury or death); *Plumhoff v. Rickard,* 134 S. Ct. 2012 (2014) (officers did not use excessive force in violation of Fourth Amendment when using deadly force to end high speed car chase, which ended when officers shot and killed fleeing driver).

352. State v. Miller, 197 N.C. 445 (1929).

force may not be used, even if the arrestee will escape if such force is not used.

In determining the amount of force required, an officer may consider all the circumstances surrounding the arrest, such as the type of offense, the arrestee's reputation and words or actions, and whether the arrestee is armed. The amount of force used must not be excessive, considering the circumstances.

If officers are making an unlawful arrest, their use of force against the arrestee is also unlawful and may constitute an assault.[353]

Resistance or Flight from Arrest

If officers are attempting to make an unlawful arrest, the prospective arrestee may lawfully resist and use whatever force may be necessary to become free, but the arrestee may not use deadly force when the arrestee reasonably knows that a law enforcement officer is attempting to make an arrest.[354] An arrestee's resistance is unlawful if the original arrest was lawful or if the arrestee uses excessive force in resisting the arrest, whether lawful or unlawful.

If the arrestee resists a lawful arrest, the arresting officers are allowed to use the amount of force they reasonably believe is necessary to take the person into custody, but no more. Physical force may be used to overcome the resistance, place the person under arrest, or defend the officer or a third person from physical force that the arrestee may use.[355]

Deadly force (including firing in the direction of the arrestee)[356] may be used only when it is in fact necessary or appears to be reasonably necessary (1) to protect against deadly force that the arrestee is using to resist arrest or (2) to take into custody, or keep in custody, a person who either is using a deadly weapon in an attempt to escape or presents an imminent threat of death or serious physical injury to others unless apprehended immediately.[357] The United States Supreme Court has indicated

that a warning, if feasible, must be given before officers use deadly force.[358]

Officers need not back off from making an arrest if the arrestee is threatening to use deadly force, regardless of the offense for which the officers are seeking to make the arrest. If the person resisting the arrest is using deadly force, officers may use deadly force to overcome that resistance. The use of deadly force is not related directly to the kind of crime the arrestee is believed to have committed. Instead, the law focuses on the kind of force being used by the arrestee and the officers.

Whether officers may use deadly force when it is not reasonably necessary in self-defense depends on whether

---

recklessly through city streets and his collisions with civilian and officers' vehicles could have caused officers to reasonably believe they faced imminent risk of deadly physical force); Forrett v. Richardson, 112 F.3d 416 (9th Cir. 1997), *rev'd on other grounds*, Chroma Lighting v. GTE Prods. Corp., 127 F.3d 1136 (9th Cir. 1997) (evidence supported officers' use of deadly force to capture suspect who had committed violent crime); Smith v. City of Hemet, 394 F.3d 689 (9th Cir. 2005) (definition of *deadly force* is that which creates a substantial risk of causing death or serious bodily harm).

358. In *Tennessee v. Garner*, 471 U.S. 1 (1985), the Court made the following statements, which were dicta (in other words, unnecessary to its ruling that deadly force was improperly used against an unarmed, nondangerous, fleeing suspect): "Where the officer has probable cause to believe that the suspect poses a threat of serious physical harm, either to the officer or others, it is not constitutionally unreasonable to prevent escape by using deadly force. Thus, if the suspect threatens the officer with a weapon or there is probable cause to believe that he has committed a crime involving the infliction or threatened infliction of serious physical harm, deadly force may be used if necessary to prevent escape, and if, where feasible, some warning has been given." Note that the constitutionally permissible use of deadly force, reflected in these statements, may permit a broader use of deadly force than North Carolina statutory law allows. For a case when an officer's warning helped justify his using deadly force, see *Ford v. Childers*, 855 F.2d 1271 (7th Cir. 1988) (en banc). Other cases on an officer's warning before using deadly force include *Krueger v. Fuhr*, 991 F.2d 435 (8th Cir. 1993) (absence of warning immediately preceding shooting did not make use of deadly force constitutionally unreasonable); *Colson v. Barnhart*, 130 F.3d 96 (5th Cir. 1997) (officer's failure to give warning was not objectively unreasonable); *Vathekan v. Prince George's County*, 154 F.3d 173 (4th Cir. 1998) (failure to give verbal warning before deploying police dog to seize someone was objectively unreasonable under Fourth Amendment); and *Vaughan v. Cox*, 343 F.3d 1323 (11th Cir. 2003) (reasonable jury could find that it was feasible for officer to warn truck's occupants before shooting into truck to stop it).

---

353. State v. Simmons, 192 N.C. 692 (1926).

354. G.S. 15A-401(f); State v. Mobley, 240 N.C. 476 (1954); State v. Allen, 166 N.C. 265 (1914).

355. G.S. 15A-401(d)(1).

356. *See* State v. Simmons, 192 N.C. 692 (1926); State v. Wall, 304 N.C. 609 (1982).

357. G.S. 15A-401(d)(2). *See generally* Turner v. City of Greenville, 197 N.C. App. 562 (2009) (officers' use of deadly force to stop vehicle driver was objectively reasonable when driver had disregarded officers' commands and driven

the arrestee will be immediately dangerous to the life of another if he or she escapes. It is difficult to describe exactly what circumstances will indicate that an arrestee presents an imminent threat of death or serious injury. But officers can be sure that under North Carolina law, the mere fact that the offense committed was a felony does not by itself entitle them to use deadly force against an escaping offender. A person may have just committed a burglary, but if the person is clearly unarmed and not dangerous and simply runs away from the crime scene, officers are not justified in using deadly force to prevent the escape.[359]

Whenever officers use force to make an arrest, to prevent a person from fleeing arrest, or to defend themselves or others,[360] the after-the-fact judgment of whether they properly used reasonable force (whether deadly or nondeadly) focuses on whether a reasonable person in the officers' position would have believed it was actually necessary *or* apparently necessary to use the force that was actually used. The phrase "actually necessary" means that the situation *in fact* required the officers' use of force—for example, the defendant pointed a shotgun at the officers and threatened to kill them, and the officers then used deadly force to defend themselves. If the shotgun was loaded and working properly, the officers *in fact* faced deadly force when they defended themselves. The phrase "apparently necessary" means that although the force used was not *in fact* necessary, the circumstances as they appeared to the officers were sufficient to create a belief in a reasonable person standing in their shoes that the force used was necessary.[361] For example, suppose that officers approached a suspect and said, "You're

under arrest for robbery," and the suspect reached into a pocket, pulled out what appeared to be a weapon, pointed the weapon at the officers, and told the officers, "I'm going to kill you." If the officers used deadly force, they would be justified even if the weapon was unloaded or was only a toy. In this case their lives were not *in fact* threatened, but the officers properly used deadly force because it was apparently necessary to do so.[362]

Escape of Convicted Felon from Custody

North Carolina law allows officers to use deadly force when they believe that it is actually or apparently necessary to prevent the escape of a person from custody that was imposed as a result of a felony conviction.[363] When a convicted felon is attempting to escape from a prison unit, for example, deadly force may be used if it is actually or apparently necessary to prevent the escape. Deadly force also may be used when an officer is transporting a convicted felon who attempts to escape and deadly force is actually or apparently necessary to prevent the escape. However, officers should consider—before they use deadly force on an escaping convicted felon—how dangerous the felon is to the officers and others, the nature of the offense for which the felon was convicted, and the likelihood that the felon will be apprehended if deadly force is not used to prevent the escape.[364]

Assistance from Private People

North Carolina law authorizes a private person to assist law enforcement officers in making an arrest or preventing an escape from arrest when officers request assistance.[365] However, a private person is not legally obligated to assist and is entitled to ignore their request. A person who assists requesting officers has the same legal rights

---

359. The Fourth Amendment to the United States Constitution also prohibits the use of deadly force in such a case. Tennessee v. Garner, 471 U.S. 1 (1985).

360. Hinton v. City of Raleigh, 46 N.C. App. 305 (1980) (police officers ordered two armed robbers to halt, but both refused to do so; one robber pointed a gun at officer, who killed robber; next robber crouched and raised his arm toward the same officer, and officer then killed him; court ruled that officer was justified in killing both robbers in self-defense).

361. The phrase in G.S. 15A-401(d)(2) (regarding deadly force) that is equivalent to "apparently necessary" is "appears to be reasonably necessary." The equivalent phrase in G.S. 15A-401(d)(1) is "reasonably believes it necessary." *See also* State v. Ellis, 241 N.C. 702 (1955) (officer may use no more force than reasonably appears to be necessary); State v. Norris, 303 N.C. 526 (1981) (sets out general principles of self-defense to homicide).

362. For another example of an officer's proper use of deadly force when an officer reasonably believed a suspect had a weapon (when, in fact, he did not have a weapon) and presented a deadly threat to the officer, see *Anderson v. Russell*, 247 F.3d 125 (4th Cir. 2001).

363. G.S. 15A-401(d)(2)c. *See also* G.S. 148-46.

364. It is unlikely that the rationale of *Tennessee v. Garner*, 471 U.S. 1 (1985)—which ruled unconstitutional the use of deadly force on an unarmed, nondangerous, fleeing suspect—applies to the use of deadly force that is actually or apparently necessary to prevent the escape of a convicted felon. However, an officer should consider the factors mentioned in the text, because a later reviewing court may decide otherwise.

365. G.S. 15A-405.

as the officers do. That is, the person has the same authority to make an arrest or to prevent an escape from an arrest and is entitled to the same benefits as the officers, such as death benefits and worker's compensation. In fact, the person is protected more than the officers, because the person is not subject to any civil or criminal penalty if the arrest was unlawful, unless the person knew that it was unlawful. Thus, the person would not suffer any penalty even if it later turned out that the officers themselves were making an unlawful arrest.

An officer who does not have either territorial or subject-matter jurisdiction to arrest may assist an officer with jurisdiction to arrest when the second officer requests assistance; the officer without jurisdiction is in the same legal position as a private person. An officer without jurisdiction should remember that this law permits only assistance to arrest or to prevent an escape from arrest; it does not permit assistance in executing search warrants and the like. For a discussion of expanding jurisdiction through cooperating law enforcement agencies, see page 24.

Notice of Authority
Before Stopping a Vehicle

North Carolina law requires that city or county officers in a motor vehicle use a warning device when they overtake another vehicle outside municipal limits for the purposes of stopping the vehicle or arresting the driver for a motor vehicle violation.[366] Although that device could be any number of things, as a practical matter this requirement generally is satisfied by using a blue (or other color) light or a siren.

When an Arrest Is Made

(*See page 186 for case summaries on this topic.*)

When officers make an arrest with or without a warrant, they must tell the arrestee that they are law enforcement officers, that the person is under arrest, and why the person is being arrested.[367] There are two exceptions to these requirements. First, if the officers' appearance clearly indicates that they are law enforcement officers, they need not say so. But if their uniform is one that some people may not recognize as an officer's uniform, then giving notice that they are law enforcement officers is still a good idea. Second, officers may delay stating the reason

for an arrest if giving it immediately would not be reasonable under the circumstances. For example, if officers must pursue or subdue the arrestee, they may wait until the person has been brought completely under control and the situation has calmed down before stating the reason for arrest. On the other hand, if the person asks the reason for the arrest and the officers respond only, "You know why," they have violated their duty to inform the person of the reason for the arrest.[368]

One other kind of notice is sometimes required. When officers arrest with an arrest warrant or an order for arrest that is not in their possession, they must inform the arrestee that such a warrant or order is outstanding and must later serve it (or have it served) on the arrestee, as discussed on page 62.

North Carolina law requires that the arrest warrant be served on and a copy be given to the arrestee.[369] Although officers need not read the warrant to the arrestee, it is a good practice to read at least the charging language when serving the warrant. If a person is arrested without a warrant and a magistrate later finds probable cause and issues a magistrate's order, the same practice should be followed when serving the arrestee with a copy of the magistrate's order.[370]

Before Entering a Dwelling

(*See page 186 for case summaries on this topic.*)

Sometimes officers must enter a private dwelling or other private premises to arrest someone who is inside. Generally, officers must give notice before they enter. They must state both their authority (that they are law enforcement officers) and their purpose in being there (that they have come to arrest the person for a certain crime).[371] This notice is required regardless of the offense for which the person is to be arrested.

Officers need not give notice before entering when they have reasonable grounds to believe that giving the notice would present a clear danger to human life.[372] Two exam-

---

366. G.S. 20-183(a).
367. G.S. 15A-401(c)(2).

368. State v. Ladd, 308 N.C. 272 (1983).
369. G.S. 15A-301(c)(1).
370. Although G.S. 15A-511(c) does not specifically require that a copy of the magistrate's order be given to the arrestee, it clearly should be done.
371. G.S. 15A-401(e)(1)c.
372. *Id.* This statute appears to set a higher standard than the Fourth Amendment (assuming a court would determine that "reasonable grounds to believe" sets a higher standard than reasonable suspicion), which likely only requires

ples of situations in which notice would *not* be required are (1) when the person to be arrested is holding a hostage and is threatening to kill the hostage if an attempt is made to take the person into custody and (2) when a suspect is known to be armed and dangerous and giving notice would allow the suspect to attack the arresting officers. Notice is not excused if the only purpose in not giving it is to prevent the arrestee from fleeing or from destroying evidence, but these factors may affect how long officers must wait for a response after they give notice.[373]

The North Carolina Court of Appeals has recognized another circumstance in which notice is not required. The court ruled that officers were not required to give notice to a fleeing suspect of their authority and purpose when they followed her into her house while in immediate pursuit to arrest her and she knew during the entire pursuit that they were State Highway Patrol officers and knew why they had entered her house.[374]

Entering Premises to Arrest

(See page 186 for case summaries on this topic.)

Although officers may make arrests in public places without a warrant,[375] the United States Supreme Court

has stated that the "physical entry of the home is the chief evil against which the wording of the Fourth Amendment is directed" and that "searches and seizures inside a home without a warrant are presumptively unreasonable."[376] Therefore, officers generally may not enter a home or other place of residence (for example, a motel room) without a warrant to make a routine arrest. Two exceptions are when (1) officers receive consent to enter, or (2) exigent (emergency) circumstances justify entering without a warrant.

Entering premises without a warrant because there are exigent circumstances to assist someone who may be seriously injured or to prevent the infliction of serious injury is discussed in Chapter 3 on page 260.

Entering Defendant's Home or Other Place of Residence without Consent or Exigent Circumstances

When consent has not been given and there are no exigent circumstances, officers who want to enter the defendant's home or another place where the defendant is residing[377] must

   1. a. have in their possession an original arrest warrant or order for arrest for the defendant, which

---

reasonable suspicion that giving notice would present a clear danger to human life. *Cf.* Richards v. Wisconsin, 520 U.S. 385 (1997) (officers are not required to knock and announce their presence before entering home to execute search warrant if they have *reasonable suspicion* that doing so would be dangerous or futile, or that it would inhibit the effective investigation of crime by, for example, allowing the destruction of evidence). The *Richards* reasonable suspicion standard likely would be applied to the knock-and-announce requirement when entering premises to make an arrest. Thus, in some cases a violation of the statute would not require the application of the Fourth Amendment's exclusionary rule if the officer had reasonable suspicion—but not reasonable grounds to believe—to excuse giving notice. In any event, the exclusionary rule would not apply to the execution of an arrest warrant. Hudson v. Michigan, 547 U.S. 586 (2006) (exclusionary rule does not apply to seized evidence when officer violated knock-and-announce requirement in executing search warrant); United States v. Pelletier, 469 F.3d 194 (1st Cir. 2006) (applying *Hudson* to execution of arrest warrant); United States v. Jones, 523 F.3d 31 (1st Cir. 2008) (similar ruling). In such cases, only the statutory exclusionary rule in G.S. 15A-974 would be implicated.

373. *See* State v. Edwards 70 N.C. App. 317 (1984), *rev'd on other grounds*, 315 N.C. 304 (1985).

374. Lee v. Greene, 114 N.C. App. 580 (1993).

375. United States v. Watson, 423 U.S. 411 (1976) (warrantless felony arrest may be made in public place even if officer had time to obtain arrest warrant). The *Watson* ruling probably

also applies to warrantless misdemeanor arrests in public places, including misdemeanors not committed in an officer's presence. See Justice White's dissenting opinion in *Welsh v. Wisconsin*, 466 U.S. 740 (1984), and *Atwater v. City of Lago Vista*, 532 U.S. 318 (2001) (recognizing but not deciding issue of warrantless arrests for misdemeanors not committed in an officer's presence).

376. Payton v. New York, 445 U.S. 573 (1980). Officers do not necessarily enter premises when the person to be arrested appears at the door and is arrested there. *See* United States v. Santana, 427 U.S. 38 (1976). Also, officers may sometimes attempt to use deception to get inside the premises or to get the person to step outside the premises so that the arrest is made without entering. *See* 3 Wayne R. LaFave, Search and Seizure: A Treatise on the Fourth Amendment § 6.1(c), (e) (5th ed. 2012).

377. A person who is staying at another's residence as an overnight guest has a Fourth Amendment privacy interest that requires officers to have an arrest warrant to enter the residence. Minnesota v. Olson, 495 U.S. 91 (1990). However, the officers also must have a search warrant to enter that residence because the permanent resident also has a Fourth Amendment privacy interest. Steagald v. United States, 451 U.S. 204 (1981); Perez v. Simmons, 884 F.2d 1136 (9th Cir. 1989), *opinion amended*, 900 F.2d 213 (9th Cir. 1990), *and* 998 F.2d 773 (9th Cir. 1993).

includes a document (i) first created and existing only in paper form, (ii) printed through facsimile transmission, or (iii) existing in electronic form in the Administrative Office of the Courts electronic repository (NCAWARE), including the electronic form of the document and any copy printed from the electronic form;[378] or

b. have a photocopy[379] of the arrest warrant or order for arrest if the original warrant or order is possessed by a member of a law enforcement agency in the county where the officers are employed and the officers verify with the agency that the warrant or order is valid;[380] and

2. reasonably believe that the place to be entered is the defendant's residence;[381] and

3. reasonably believe that the person to be arrested is present inside;[382] and

4. give notice before entering of their authority and purpose unless they have reasonable cause to believe that giving notice would endanger the life or safety of any person.[383]

---

378. G.S. 15A-401(e)(1)a, -301(e)(1), -301.1, -101.1(9) (definition of *original*). Officers have ready access to an original in the electronic repository, because G.S. 15A-301.1(e) provides that any criminal process in the repository may at any time and place in the state be printed in paper form by any judicial official, law enforcement officer, or other authorized person.

Note that the statute does not permit officers to enter without consent a defendant's private premises to arrest when they know of an outstanding arrest warrant or order for arrest but do not possess it. Leon H. Corbett, Jr., *Criminal Process and Arrest under the North Carolina Pretrial Criminal Procedure Act of 1974*, 10 Wake Forest Law Review 377, at 401 (1974). This restriction is not necessarily constitutionally required. *See* Commonwealth v. Sawyer, 452 N.E.2d 1094 (Mass. 1983) (ruling in *Payton v. New York*, 445 U.S. 573 (1980), did not apply to Maine officers' entry into defendant's hotel room to arrest defendant, even though they did not have New York arrest warrant in their possession).

In *State v. Hewson*, 88 N.C. App. 128 (1987), the court ruled that officers could not enter the defendant's home to arrest him based on their knowledge of an outstanding order for arrest for civil contempt when they did not possess the order for arrest, they did not have consent to enter, and exigent circumstances did not exist. The court's ruling is clearly correct, but the implication in its opinion that the officers' entry into the home would have been permissible if they had probable cause to believe a *crime* had been committed is inconsistent with the statute. Such an interpretation would negate the statutory requirement that an officer must possess the arrest warrant or order for arrest unless there is consent to enter or exigent circumstances exist.

Under certain circumstances, a forcible warrantless entry into a civil committee's residence to enforce an involuntary civil commitment order in an officer's possession does not violate the Fourth Amendment. McCabe v. Life-Line Ambulance Serv., Inc., 77 F.3d 540 (1st Cir. 1996) (officers' warrantless forcible entry into a person's house to serve a licensed psychiatrist's signed application for a 10-day involuntary commitment of that person—based on the finding of a likelihood of serious harm—was reasonable under the Fourth Amendment).

379. The word "copy" in G.S. 15A-401(e)(1)a. means a photocopy. If an officer has a printed criminal process (which includes an arrest warrant or order for arrest) from the electronic repository, a faxed copy, or a certified copy of an arrest warrant or order for arrest under G.S. 15A-301(e)(1), then the process is valid as set out in 1.a. in the text.

380. G.S. 15A-401(e)(1)a. also permits a third way that is not mentioned in the text: the officer is authorized to arrest a person without an arrest warrant or order for arrest having been issued. Although that way is a proper justification when the officer has exigent circumstances to enter the residence to arrest or consent to enter, it is not a permitted justification under the ruling in *Payton v. New York*, 445 U.S. 573 (1980). Remember that this statute was enacted before the *Payton* ruling and has not been amended to conform with it.

381. For an excellent analysis of factors 2 and 3 set out in the text, see *United States v. Bervaldi*, 226 F.3d 1256 (11th Cir. 2000). Note that factor 2 set out in the text is not in G.S. 15A-401(e)(1)a., but it is required by the Fourth Amendment. United States v. Magluta, 44 F.3d 1530 (11th Cir. 1995). For pertinent cases on these issues, see *United States v. Lauter*, 57 F.3d 212 (2d Cir. 1995) (officers were not required to obtain new arrest warrant with new address when they learned that defendant had moved to new apartment; officers only needed to have reasonable belief that defendant was residing and present in new apartment); *United States v. Risse*, 83 F.3d 212 (8th Cir. 1996) (even though defendant maintained permanent residence elsewhere, officer had reasonable belief that defendant possessed common authority with her boyfriend over another residence to permit officer to enter that residence with arrest warrant).

Federal appellate courts are almost evenly split on whether establishing a reasonable belief requires probable cause or less evidence than probable cause. See the discussion in United *States v. Vasquez-Algarin*, 821 F.3d 467 (3rd Cir. 2016).

382. *See* United States v. Litteral, 910 F.2d 547 (9th Cir. 1990) (officers had reasonable belief that defendant was in mobile home—informant told officers that if defendant's car was there, he would be there; officers saw defendant's car before they entered property); United States v. Gay, 240 F.3d 1222 (10th Cir. 2001) (informant's information supplied reasonable belief). See note 381, above, as to whether reasonable belief is the same as probable cause.

383. G.S. 15A-401(e)(1)c.

Most commonly, an order for arrest will be issued in connection with a criminal offense because a case has begun with an indictment or a defendant has failed to appear in court. It would also appear that an officer may enter premises to arrest—if the conditions set out above are satisfied—when an order for arrest has been issued in conjunction with proceedings for civil or criminal contempt under Chapter 5A of the General Statutes, for example, arising from actions for nonsupport of children.[384]

Entering a Third Party's Home without Consent or Exigent Circumstances

When consent has not been given and there are no exigent circumstances, officers who want to enter the home of a third party to arrest a person who does not live there must have a search warrant to do so.[385] The reason an arrest warrant for the defendant is not sufficient to enter a third party's home is that it does not adequately protect the third party's Fourth Amendment privacy interests.[386] Thus, before entering the home of a third party, officers must

1. a. have in their possession an original arrest warrant or order for arrest for the defendant, which includes a document

(i) first created and existing only in paper form, (ii) printed through facsimile transmission, or (iii) existing in electronic form in the Administrative Office of the Courts electronic repository (NCAWARE), including the electronic form of the document and any copy printed from the electronic form;[387] or

b. have a photocopy[388] of the arrest warrant or order for arrest if the original warrant or order is possessed by a member of a law enforcement agency in the county where the officers are employed and the officers verify with the agency that the warrant or order is valid; or

c. be authorized to arrest the defendant when an arrest warrant or order for arrest has not been issued;[389] and

2. have a search warrant to search the third party's premises for the defendant; and

3. have reasonable grounds to believe that the defendant is inside.[390]

Then, before entering, officers must give notice of their authority and purpose by stating their identity and that

---

384. G.S. 5A-16(b) authorizes, under certain circumstances, the issuance of an order for arrest in conjunction with plenary proceedings for criminal contempt. A judge also has the authority to issue an order for arrest for a person who failed to appear in response to a show cause order for either criminal or civil contempt proceedings.

385. Steagald v. United States, 451 U.S. 204 (1981). To the extent that G.S. 15A-401(e) would permit entry into a third party's home without a search warrant, contrary to *Steagald*, it is unconstitutional.

If officers violate the third party's constitutional rights in entering that person's premises, they may be civilly liable to the third party. *See, e.g.,* Perez v. Simmons, 884 F.2d 1136 (9th Cir. 1989), *opinion amended,* 900 F.2d 213 (1990), *and* 998 F.2d 773 (9th Cir. 1993). However, if officers seize evidence to be used against the defendant during their violation of the third party's rights, the defendant has no standing to suppress such evidence unless the defendant's constitutional rights also were violated. *Cf.* Minnesota v. Olson, 495 U.S. 91 (1990).

386. It can be argued that a search warrant also should be required to enter a defendant's home because an arrest warrant does not adequately protect the defendant's privacy interest in his or her home. But the Supreme Court rejected that argument in *Payton v. New York*, 445 U.S. 573 (1980), and ruled that only an arrest warrant is required.

387. *See supra* note 378.

388. *See supra* note 379. It is highly unlikely that the statutory requirements set out in 1.a. and 1.b. in the text are required by the Fourth Amendment. *See* United States v. Winchenbach, 197 F.3d 548 (1st Cir. 1999); Russell v. Harms, 397 F.3d 458 (7th Cir. 2005). If so, a violation of these requirements would not invoke the Fourth Amendment's exclusionary rule to bar evidence seized as a result of the violation, but a court would consider the application of G.S. 15A-974.

389. G.S. 15A-401(e)(1)a. The ruling in *United States v. Winchenbach*, 197 F.3d 548 (1st Cir. 1999) (officers obtained search warrant to search residence for drugs; they did not obtain arrest warrant for defendant who lived there, although they did have probable cause to arrest him; upon entering residence to execute search warrant, they arrested defendant without an arrest warrant; court ruled, distinguishing *Payton v. New York*, 445 U.S. 573 (1980), that warrantless arrest did not violate Fourth Amendment) supports the constitutionality of this statutory provision in a case when officers enter the premises with a search warrant and then arrest the defendant without an arrest warrant or order for arrest having been issued.

390. Although the search warrant must be supported by reasonable grounds to believe that the defendant is in the premises, officers may obtain the search warrant and find out later—but before they execute the search warrant—that the defendant is no longer there. If this occurs, the officers must not enter the home. *See also* G.S. 15A-401(e)(1)b.

they are there to arrest the defendant.[391] This notice is not required if they have probable cause to believe that giving notice would endanger the life or safety of any person.[392]

Consent to Enter Premises

When officers want to enter the defendant's or a third party's home to arrest the defendant, they may not need an arrest or search warrant if they receive consent to enter from someone who has authority to give it. If officers want to enter the defendant's home, they normally may receive consent from the defendant's spouse, mother, father, adult sibling, or live-in friend or any other person who has equal privacy interests in the defendant's home. (Consent to search is discussed on page 224 of Chapter 3.) Once officers receive consent, they may search in any place within the home where a person may be found, subject to whatever restrictions the person who consents may impose. Even when consent is given, officers will need an arrest warrant to arrest the defendant for certain misdemeanors that were not committed in their presence (see the discussion on page 63).

When officers want to enter the home of a third party to arrest a person who does not live there, they must receive consent to enter from a person who has a privacy interest in that home—generally an adult who lives there.

Exigent Circumstances That Justify Entering Premises
(*See page 188 for case summaries on this topic.*)

When exigent circumstances exist to make an arrest, officers may enter a defendant's or third party's home or other place of residence even though they do not have an arrest warrant, search warrant, or consent. Although the term "exigent circumstances" is not easily described, it generally means that officers need to act immediately. The following discussion of appellate court cases may provide some understanding of exigent circumstances.

Entering premises without a warrant because there are exigent circumstances to assist someone who may be seriously injured or to prevent the infliction of serious injury is discussed in Chapter 3 on page 260.

— **Payton v. New York**
After two days of intensive investigation, New York City detectives established probable cause to believe that the defendant had murdered the

manager of a gas station two days earlier. At about 7:30 a.m. on the next day, six officers went to the defendant's apartment without a warrant, forced their way in, and arrested him.

The United States Supreme Court in *Payton v. New York*[393] ruled that exigent circumstances did not exist to enter the defendant's apartment to arrest him without a warrant.

— **Riddick v. New York**
In June 1973 the victims identified the defendant as the robber in two armed robberies that occurred in 1971. In January 1974 detectives discovered the defendant's address. On March 14, 1974, four officers entered the defendant's house without a warrant and arrested him.

The United States Supreme Court in *Riddick v. New York*[394] ruled that exigent circumstances did not exist to enter the defendant's home to arrest him without a warrant.

— **Welsh v. Wisconsin**
In Wisconsin, on the night of April 24, 1978, a witness saw a car that was being driven erratically swerve off the road and come to a stop in a field, without damaging property or injuring any person. The witness suggested to the driver-defendant that he wait for assistance in removing his car, but the driver walked away from the scene. When the police arrived a few minutes later, the witness told them that the driver was either heavily intoxicated or sick. The police checked the car's registration, learned that it was registered to the defendant, and noted that his residence was within a short walking distance from the scene. Without a warrant, the police entered the defendant's home and arrested him. The only exigent circumstance that could justify an immediate warrantless entry into the home to arrest was that the defendant's blood alcohol level might dissipate while the police obtained a warrant.

The United States Supreme Court ruled in *Welsh v. Wisconsin*[395] that the seriousness of an offense is an important factor in determining whether exigent circum-

---

391. G.S. 15A-249.
392. G.S. 15A-251(2).

393. 445 U.S. 573 (1980).
394. *Id.* (companion case to *Payton v. New York*).
395. 466 U.S. 740 (1984).

stances exist to permit a warrantless entry into a home to arrest. Because the offense in this case was extremely minor (in Wisconsin, the first offense of driving under the influence of an intoxicant was a noncriminal violation punishable by a maximum $200 fine), the imminent destruction of evidence by the dissipation of the defendant's blood alcohol level was not a sufficient reason to justify the warrantless entry.[396] The Court also noted that this case involved neither hot pursuit of the defendant from the scene of the crime nor a threat to public safety, as the defendant had abandoned his car at the scene and already was at home when the police arrived.[397]

----

396. Note that the maximum punishment for misdemeanor impaired driving in North Carolina is two years' imprisonment, and thus it is not an extremely minor offense like the Wisconsin offense in *Welsh*.

397. The Court made clear in *Stanton v. Sims*, 134 S. Ct. 3, 6 (2013), that "despite our emphasis in *Welsh* on the fact that the crime at issue was minor—indeed, a mere nonjailable civil offense—nothing in the opinion establishes that the seriousness of the crime is equally important *in cases of hot pursuit*." For cases on exigent circumstances in entering premises to arrest for traffic violations, see *People v. Thompson*, 135 P.3d 3 (Cal. 2006) (*Welsh* limited to nonjailable offenses); *Howard v. Dickerson*, 34 F.3d 978 (10th Cir. 1994) (no exigent circumstances to make warrantless entry into house to arrest person for minor traffic misdemeanors—no hot pursuit in this case); *Norris v. State*, 993 S.W.2d 918 (Ark. 1999) (similar ruling); *City of Middletown v. Flinchum*, 765 N.E.2d 330 (Ohio 2002) (court ruled that exigent circumstances supported officers' entry into house in hot pursuit to arrest defendant for reckless driving; defendant had fled into house to avoid officers); *State v. Paul*, 548 N.W.2d 260 (Minn. 1996) (similar ruling involving entry into house in hot pursuit to arrest defendant for impaired driving); *Beachwood v. Sims*, 647 N.E.2d 821 (Ohio Ct. App. 1994) (distinguishing *Welsh v. Wisconsin*, court ruled exigent circumstances supported warrantless entry into home to arrest defendant for driving under influence of alcohol, an offense punishable by imprisonment); and *Goines v. James*, 433 S.E.2d 572 (W.Va. 1993) (court noted that officer may make warrantless entry into defendant's home in hot pursuit of defendant to arrest for serious misdemeanor of driving under the influence). *See generally* Illinois v. McArthur, 531 U.S. 326 (2001) (upholding an officer's seizure of the defendant while another officer sought a search warrant to search the defendant's home, the Court rejected the defendant's argument, relying on *Welsh v. Wisconsin*, that the minor misdemeanor involved in this case required a ruling for the defendant; the Court distinguished the nonjailable misdemeanor involved in *Welsh* from the jailable misdemeanors involved in the case before it). *See also* 3 Wayne R. LaFave, Search and Seizure: A Treatise on the Fourth Amendment § 6.1(f), at 419 (5th ed. 2012).

- ◀ Warden v. Hayden

  Police were informed that an armed robbery had just taken place at a cab company and the suspect had run from the scene into a house nearby. Police arrived within five minutes after the suspect entered the house; they entered the house without a warrant and searched for the suspect and any weapons that he had used in the robbery or that might be used against them.

The United States Supreme Court in *Warden v. Hayden*[398] ruled that exigent circumstances supported the warrantless entry to arrest a robbery suspect and search the house for weapons. It stated:

> The Fourth Amendment does not require police officers to delay in the course of an investigation if to do so would gravely endanger their lives or the lives of others. Speed here was essential, and only a thorough search of the house for persons and weapons could have insured that [the suspect] was the only man present and that the police had control of all weapons which could be used against them or to effect an escape.[399]

- ◀ United States v. Santana

  An undercover drug officer arranged a heroin buy from Patricia McCafferty. McCafferty told him (not knowing that he was an officer) that she would get the heroin from the defendant at the defendant's house. The officer took her there, and she purchased the heroin in the house, came out, and gave it to him. The officer drove away from the area with McCafferty and then arrested her. He and other officers returned to the defendant's house to arrest the defendant, who was standing in the doorway of her house with a brown paper bag in her hand. The police pulled up within 15 feet of the defendant and shouted, "Police!" The defendant retreated into her house; the police entered without a warrant and arrested her.

The United States Supreme Court in *United States v. Santana*[400] first decided that the defendant was in a public place when she stood in the doorway of her house

----

398. 387 U.S. 294.
399. *Id.* at 298–99.
400. 427 U.S. 38 (1976).

and that the officers, therefore, could make a warrantless arrest. The Court then ruled that the officers' warrantless hot pursuit into the home was justified to prevent the destruction of evidence—namely, marked money used in the drug transaction and other drugs that might be in the house. Once the defendant saw the police, she no doubt would have destroyed the evidence if the police had taken the time to obtain an arrest warrant.

— Minnesota v. Olson
Police officers entered without consent the upper unit of a duplex to arrest the defendant inside. The defendant had been staying there as an overnight guest. The officers knew that the residents of that unit were not endangered by the defendant's presence. In addition, police squads surrounded the duplex, and thus the defendant could not escape. Although grave crimes (murder and robbery) had been committed the day before, the defendant was not the murderer but was thought to be the driver of the getaway car. The officers already had recovered the murder weapon. Also, the officers had not been in hot pursuit of the defendant.

The United States Supreme Court in *Minnesota v. Olson*[401] affirmed the Minnesota Supreme Court's finding that the facts in this case were insufficient to justify the officers' warrantless entry of the duplex to arrest the defendant. The Court also ruled that an overnight guest has a reasonable expectation of privacy in a residence to contest the legality of officers' warrantless entry of that residence to arrest the guest.

— State v. Guevara
Officers West and Medlin went to the defendant's home with information that there were outstanding felony arrest warrants for him. They saw the defendant, accompanied by a young boy, standing outside his mobile home. Although the defendant denied being the subject of the arrest warrants, the officers believed otherwise. After confirmation from a dispatcher that the defendant was still wanted, officer Medlin stated to the dispatcher that they would arrest him. The defendant, having

heard officer Medlin's words, retreated into his home and slammed the door. Officer West pushed the door open and entered the home, where he was shot and killed by the defendant. Officer Medlin was shot and seriously injured by the defendant while the officer was outside the mobile home.

The North Carolina Supreme Court in *State v. Guevara*[402] ruled that exigent circumstances supported officer West's entry into the defendant's home to arrest him. The court stated that the defendant's actions—suddenly withdrawing into his home and slamming the door—created the appearance that he was fleeing or trying to escape and, coupled with the young child's presence, established exigent circumstances to enter the defendant's home to arrest him.

— State v. Worsley
Officers arrived at a murder scene and discovered the victim's body, the subject of a brutal stabbing, lying in a common area of an apartment complex. An eyewitness to the murder identified the defendant as the killer. Another witness informed the officers that he had seen the defendant running toward the defendant's apartment shortly after the murder. The officers went to the defendant's nearby apartment and discovered fresh blood on the doorknob of the back door. The officers knocked loudly on the defendant's door and identified themselves as officers but received no response. They then entered the apartment.

The North Carolina Supreme Court in *State v. Worsley*[403] ruled that the officers had exigent circumstances to enter the defendant's home, without consent or an arrest warrant, to arrest the defendant.

— State v. Woods
Officers were dispatched to investigate an alarm sounding at the defendant's residence. After arriving at the residence, an officer heard the alarm and saw that the rear door of the residence was open. He heard no response from inside the residence after announcing his presence and identity. He conducted a cursory search of the residence for potential victims or suspects. He found no

---

401. 495 U.S. 91 (1990). Although the Court affirmed the state court's judgment that the facts did not establish exigent circumstances to enter to arrest, it did not affirm the entirety of the state court's legal standard for determining exigent circumstances.

402. 349 N.C. 243 (1998).
403. 336 N.C. 268 (1994).

one but saw evidence of a break-in. He and other officers reentered the residence to conduct a more thorough search, looking again for victims and suspects.

The North Carolina Court of Appeals in *State v. Woods*[404] ruled that the officers' warrantless entries into the residence to investigate a possible break-in were justified by exigent circumstances and thus were reasonable under the Fourth Amendment. It was clear that a break-in had occurred, and the officers had reason to believe that the intruders or victims could still be in the residence.

State v. Allison
Responding to a telephone call that a murder had occurred, Deputy Sheriff Smith arrived and talked to the homicide victim's son. The son told Smith that the defendant, the victim's husband, had shot his mother. When Smith asked the son where she had been shot, the son pointed to the defendant's trailer about 150 to 200 feet away. Deputy Sheriff Autrey then arrived. Smith told Autrey to check the defendant's trailer to see whether he was there. (Neither of the officers was aware then that the son had already checked the trailer.) Autrey went to the trailer. After knocking on the door and getting no response, he opened the unlocked door and went in. He saw a .22 caliber rifle on a couch to the right of the door. Autrey seized the rifle, announced his presence and authority, and searched the trailer for the defendant. No one was there. Autrey had no arrest or search warrant when he entered the trailer.

The North Carolina Supreme Court in *State v. Allison*[405] ruled that exigent circumstances supported Deputy Sheriff Autrey's warrantless entry. Autrey had probable cause to believe that the defendant had committed murder, was armed and in the trailer, and would likely escape if not immediately arrested.

State v. Nowell
A drug courier working with law enforcement officers and wearing a body wire delivered approximately 50 pounds of marijuana to a residence where the purchaser and his accomplice were waiting for the delivery of the marijuana. When an officer heard through a radio transmitter that the purchaser and his accomplice were about to roll a marijuana cigarette from the marijuana and smoke it, law enforcement officers entered the residence without a search warrant.

The North Carolina Court of Appeals ruled in *State v. Nowell*[406] that exigent circumstances did not exist to enter the house without a warrant. The court stated that the destruction of the amount of marijuana required to roll one marijuana cigarette from the approximately 50 pounds of marijuana inside the residence was not an exigent circumstance to permit the officers to enter the residence without a search warrant. (Although this ruling involved an entry without a search warrant, it would be equally applicable to an entry without an arrest warrant.)

State v. Yananokwiak
A law enforcement officer and an anonymous informant attempted to buy cocaine from Mark Klouda. Klouda was arrested after he agreed to sell the officer some cocaine for $3,800. Shortly thereafter, Klouda agreed to help the officer arrest his drug supplier, the defendant. Although Klouda did not know the defendant's street address, he offered to guide police to the house. Klouda, who was equipped with a concealed microphone,

---

404. 136 N.C. App. 386 (2000). The court also ruled that the officers' search of a chest of drawers, chair, and cabinet exceeded the scope of the permissible search for suspects and victims. It was unreasonable to believe that a small child could have been found in the cabinet, based on the facts in this case.

405. 298 N.C. 135 (1979). Although this case was decided before *Payton v. New York* and *Welsh v. Wisconsin*, its ruling is consistent with those decisions.

406. 144 N.C. App. 636 (2001), *aff'd*, 355 N.C. 273 (2002). The court's ruling appeared to be based on the insignificant amount of marijuana that might be destroyed from smoking one joint compared to the amount of marijuana from the 50 pounds that still would remain. Compare the *Nowell* ruling with the later case of *State v. Stover*, 200 N.C. App. 506 (2009). In *Stover*, the court ruled that officers had probable cause and exigent circumstances to enter the home without a warrant. Officers stopped a vehicle and noticed a passenger with marijuana, who then told them the location of the house at which she had purchased the marijuana. Officers went to the house to conduct a knock and talk. When they arrived there, they perceived a strong odor of marijuana emanating from the house. An officer heard a noise from the back of the house and saw the defendant, whose upper torso was partially out of a window. The court noted that the officers could reasonably believe that the defendant was attempting to flee the scene, and they were also concerned about a possible destruction of evidence.

entered the house alone. The officers heard Klouda tell the defendant that he had made the sale and that the money was outside in his car. Klouda came out of the house, retrieved the $3,800, and went back inside. The officers then heard Klouda say, "They want another ounce; here's your money." Next they heard the sounds of someone counting money and shaking something. Then Klouda asked, "[I]s that enough for a whole ounce? Is it good as the other stuff? . . . What's that?" A voice identified as the defendant's responded, "The cut." The officers then rushed into the house and arrested the defendant.

The North Carolina Court of Appeals in *State v. Yananokwiak*[407] ruled that exigent circumstances did not exist to enter the house without a warrant. The officers knew that Klouda and the defendant had conducted drug deals before, and the overheard conversations did not indicate that the defendant suspected Klouda of being an informant or was uneasy over the time lapse between Klouda's "sale" to Simons and his return to the defendant's home. Nor did the evidence reveal that the defendant was about to escape or destroy the drugs. Although drug dealers frequently own guns and are violent, there was no evidence that this defendant was armed or dangerous.

⎯▌ State v. Wallace
Charlotte police officers arrested Charles Alexander, who had been staying at the New Imperial Motel in Charlotte and had been involved in several armed robberies in the Charlotte area. At 9:45 a.m. Alexander gave information to the police that gave them probable cause to arrest the defendant for two armed robberies. Alexander also told the police that the defendant was sharing a room with him at the New Imperial Motel. At 10:00 a.m. the motel clerk informed the police that the defendant had recently left the motel with another person. The police were preparing a warrant to arrest the defendant when the clerk called around 10:15 a.m. and told them that the defendant had returned and was taking articles from his motel room as if he intended to leave. The officers immediately went to the motel room and, without a warrant, arrested the defendant there.

The North Carolina Court of Appeals in *State v. Wallace*[408] ruled that exigent circumstances permitted the warrantless arrest of the defendant in his motel room. The defendant was preparing to check out of the motel and leave the area, and he was suspected of having committed violent offenses.

Summary

These and other cases indicate that the factors[409] a court will consider in determining exigent circumstances include the following:

- Hot pursuit of a suspect
- Danger to the public or law enforcement officers outside or inside the dwelling if an immediate warrantless entry is not made
- The need to prevent the imminent destruction of evidence
- The need to prevent a suspect's escape
- Whether the suspect is armed
- The gravity of the offense for which the suspect is being arrested; exigent circumstances will rarely be found to justify entry into a home to arrest for extremely minor offenses, particularly offenses not punishable by imprisonment

Entering Premises to Accompany the Arrestee
(See page 191 for case summaries on this topic.)

When officers arrest someone, they may accompany the arrestee wherever he or she goes. Thus, the United States Supreme Court has ruled that if the arrestee wants to go home to get a change of clothes or identification, for example, officers automatically may enter the residence with the arrestee.[410] Officers need not justify their entering with the arrestee—for example, by showing that the arrestee might obtain a weapon there or attempt to escape.

---

407. 65 N.C. App. 513 (1983).

408. 71 N.C. App. 681 (1984).

409. *See generally* 3 WAYNE R. LaFAVE, SEARCH AND SEIZURE: A TREATISE ON THE FOURTH AMENDMENT § 6.1(f) (5th ed. 2012); United States v. MacDonald, 916 F.2d 766 (2d Cir. 1990) (en banc); United States v. Coles, 437 F.3d 361 (3d Cir. 2006).

410. Washington v. Chrisman, 455 U.S. 1 (1982). *See also* State v. Worsley, 176 N.C. App. 642 (2006) (defendant was not fully clothed when officers arrived at her residence; officer had right to accompany her into residence while she got dressed (citing *Chrisman*)).

Entering Premises with News Media

(*See page 192 for case summaries on this topic.*)

The United States Supreme Court has ruled that officers violate the Fourth Amendment when they bring news media or other third parties into a home during the execution of a warrant when the third parties' presence is not aiding the warrant's execution.[411] This ruling clearly also would apply when officers are entering premises to arrest without an arrest warrant.

Use of Force When Entering Premises to Arrest

When officers are authorized to enter premises to make an arrest, they also are authorized to use whatever force is necessary to enter. After giving any required notice, they may forcibly enter the premises as soon as they believe that their admittance is being denied or unreasonably delayed.[412] They also may forcibly enter premises when they are not required to give any notice—that is, when doing so would present a clear danger to life.[413]

Completion of Custody of the Arrestee
Searching and Investigating Incident to Arrest or Stop

Depending on the type of arrest or stop that has been made and its purpose, various kinds of searches and further investigations of a person may be authorized. Among the most important are a full search of the arrestee and the area and containers within the arrestee's immediate control and the frisk of an apparently dangerous person who has been stopped. These and other searches are discussed on pages 249 and 257 of Chapter 3.

Securing the Arrestee and Dealing with Companions of the Arrestee

Arresting officers generally may take reasonable steps to secure a person they have arrested, even though that person may have submitted peaceably when he or she was arrested. What steps are reasonable is a matter of the arresting officers' judgment, but their judgment should be based on the degree of likelihood that the person will try to escape. It might include consideration of such factors as the arrestee's reputation and past criminal history, the crime for which he or she was arrested, and the arrestee's attitude when taken into custody. But no rule prohibits handcuffing an arrestee, even if he or she submitted peaceably to arrest.

The arresting officer may transfer custody to another officer who will complete the appropriate processing of the arrestee. The officer taking custody of the arrestee may do so automatically without needing independent justification for taking custody. For example, if the arresting officer properly makes a warrantless misdemeanor arrest for a misdemeanor larceny offense that was not committed in the officer's presence, the officer taking custody does not have to justify taking custody of the arrestee under the statutory requirements for making such a warrantless arrest (discussed on page 63).

The legal duties of officers to take care of the safety of companions of an arrestee are unclear.[414] However, there are some situations when officers should consider taking on this responsibility. For example, officers arrest the driver of a vehicle for impaired driving late at night in a high crime area and impound the vehicle because the passenger is unable to drive it. The officers should consider transporting the passenger to a safe place or providing a means for the passenger to call for assistance; abandoning the passenger may subject the officers to civil liability if the passenger is harmed.[415]

---

411. Wilson v. Layne, 526 U.S. 603 (1999).

412. G.S. 15A-401(e)(2); State v. Sutton, 34 N.C. App. 371 (1977) (officers properly broke down door to serve orders for arrest when they knocked, demanded entry, received no response from occupants, and heard sounds that would justify conclusion that admittance was being unreasonably delayed so that occupants could escape). For cases on the knock-and-announce requirement under the Fourth Amendment, see *Wilson v. Arkansas*, 514 U.S. 927 (1995), and *Richards v. Wisconsin*, 520 U.S. 385 (1997). *See generally* Hudson v. Michigan, 547 U.S. 586 (2006) (Fourth Amendment exclusionary rule inapplicable to violation of knock-and-announce requirement when serving search warrant).

413. G.S. 15A-401(e)(2).

414. *See, e.g.,* Courson v. McMillan, 939 F.2d 1479 (11th Cir. 1991); Gregory v. City of Rogers, 974 F.2d 1006 (8th Cir. 1992) (en banc); Hillard v. City and Cty. of Denver, 930 F.2d 1516 (10th Cir. 1991).

415. Wood v. Ostrander, 879 F.2d 583 (9th Cir. 1989).

Detention of Defendant Arrested for Violation of Order Limiting Freedom of Movement Involving Terrorist Attack or Isolation Order for Health Reasons

Law enforcement officers are authorized to detain a person arrested for violating an order limiting freedom of movement or access in an area designated by the state health director or local health director when the order involves a terrorist attack using nuclear, biological, or chemical agents or when confining a person for health reasons pursuant to an isolation order or quarantine. The person may be detained in the area until the initial appearance before a magistrate.[416]

Care of Minor Children Present When Adult Supervising Them Is Arrested

When a law enforcement officer arrests an adult who is supervising minor children present at the time of the arrest, the minor children must be placed with a responsible adult approved by a parent or guardian of the children. If it is not possible to place the minor children in that manner within a reasonable time, the officer must contact the county department of social services.[417]

Protecting the Unconscious Arrestee

North Carolina law gives a special responsibility to officers who arrest a person who is unconscious or semiconscious or for any other reason is unable to communicate with them.[418] Officers must examine the arrestee to see whether the arrestee is wearing a medical symbol indicating that he or she suffers from diabetes, epilepsy, a heart condition, or any other disabling condition. If the arrestee wears such a tag, the officers must make a reasonable effort to have medical care provided. Jailers have the same duty with inmates.[419] In most cases, officers must have an unconscious or semiconscious arrestee medically examined to assure that the condition is not dangerous and that the arrestee needs no further medical care.

Obtaining an Interpreter for a Deaf Person

North Carolina law requires an officer who arrests a deaf person to secure a qualified interpreter before the person is notified of his or her rights, interrogated, and the like.[420]

Informing the Arrestee of the Charge

North Carolina law requires arresting officers to inform the arrestee of the offense for which he or she has been arrested.[421] Usually this requirement will be met when the person is notified of the arrest. Giving the arrestee a copy of the arrest warrant or magistrate's order also satisfies this requirement. Officers who make an arrest pursuant to an outstanding warrant or order for arrest not in their possession must give the arrestee a copy of the warrant or order for arrest as soon as reasonably possible, even if they must take it to the jail. Delivery need not be made by the arresting officers themselves, but they should make certain that someone has done so.

Informing a Foreign National of the Right to Have Consular Official Notified

A *foreign national* is a person who is not a United States citizen. The Vienna Convention on Consular Relations requires that government authorities who have arrested[422] a foreign national inform that person of the right to have authorities notify his or her consular officials of the arrest.[423] Such a responsibility would generally belong to

---

416. G.S. 15A-401(b)(4). *See also* G.S. 130A-145, -475. For pretrial release provisions concerning these matters, see G.S. 15A-534.5.

417. G.S. 15A-401(g).

418. G.S. 15A-503.

419. G.S. 153A-225.1.

420. G.S. 8B-2(d). The statute also provides that any answer, statement, or admission taken from a deaf person without a qualified interpreter present and functioning is inadmissible in court for any purpose.

421. G.S. 15A-501(1).

422. Although the convention applies to detentions as well as arrests, the manual cited in the next footnote states that the Department of State does not consider a "detention" to include a brief traffic stop or similar event in which a foreign national is questioned and then allowed to resume his or her activities.

423. Article 36, Vienna Convention on Consular Relations, April 24, 1963, 21 U.S.T. 77, T.I.A.S. No. 6820. There are some countries in which the notification of the consular officials is mandatory, regardless of the foreign national's request (for example, nationals of the United Kingdom, Costa Rica, Jamaica, and Nigeria); see page 4 of the manual described in the next sentence. The United States Department of State has published a comprehensive manual entitled *Consular Notification and Access* (4th ed. 2014), available at https://travel.state.gov/content/dam/travel/CNAtrainingresources/CNAManual_Feb2014.pdf. This manual lists Department of State telephone numbers for assistance to officers and others; describes the treaty obligations, countries that are parties to the treaty, steps

the arresting law enforcement officer or his or her agency.[424] The United States and most other countries, including our neighboring countries of Canada and Mexico, are parties to this treaty.[425] Issues that are involved if the treaty is not followed are discussed in the accompanying note.[426]

Taking Fingerprints and Photographs
Adults

With one exception, discussed in the paragraph below about Class 2 and 3 motor vehicle misdemeanors, an adult[427] arrested for any crime—felony or misdemeanor—

---

to follow when a foreign national is arrested, and suggested statements to arrested foreign nationals (including statements in several foreign languages); and provides consular locations in the United States and other useful information. *See also* Jonathan L. Rudd, *Consular Notification and Access: The International Golden Rule*, FBI LAW ENFORCEMENT BULL. 22 (Jan. 2007), www.fbi.gov/publications/leb/leb.htm.

The North Carolina Court of Appeals in *State v. Aquino*, 149 N.C. App. 172 (2002), ruled that the defendant was not detained or arrested to require an officer to comply with the treaty, which is not triggered unless there is an arrest or similar kind of detention. The defendant was free to leave at any time when he talked with the officer.

424. See page 15 of the manual discussed in note 423, above.

425. For a list of countries, see the manual discussed in note 423, above.

426. In *Sanchez-Llamas v. Oregon*, 548 U.S. 331 (2006), the United States Supreme Court ruled that (1) suppression of a defendant's statements to law enforcement is not a remedy for a violation of the Vienna Convention on Consular Relations, and (2) a state may subject claims of treaty violations to the same procedural default rules that apply generally to other federal law claims. The Court assumed without deciding that the international treaty, which requires law enforcement to inform an arrested foreign national of the right to consular notification, creates judicially enforceable rights. *See also* State v. Herrera, 195 N.C. App. 181 (2009) (relying on *Sanchez-Llamas*, court ruled that violation does not result in suppression of confession).

The United States Supreme Court has not decided whether a foreign national may civilly sue law enforcement officers and agencies when the national was not notified of the right to consular notification. However, a majority of federal courts of appeals that have considered the issue have ruled that the foreign national has no right to sue. *Compare* Gandara v. Bennett, 528 F.3d 823 (11th Cir. 2008) (no right to sue); Mora v. New York, 524 F.3d 183 (2d Cir. 2008) (same ruling); Cornejo v. County of San Diego, 504 F.3d 853 (9th Cir. 2007) (same ruling), *with* Jodi v. Voges, 480 F.3d 822 (7th Cir. 2007) (right to sue under § 1983).

427. Although the term "adult" is not used in the statutes, for ease of reading it is used in the text—concerning the

may be fingerprinted and photographed for law enforcement records. When the crime is a felony, the arresting law enforcement agency is *required* to see that the arrestee is fingerprinted and the fingerprints forwarded to the State Bureau of Investigation.[428]

An arresting law enforcement agency is *required* to fingerprint a person charged with the following misdemeanors and forward the fingerprints to the SBI: G.S. 14-134.3 (domestic criminal trespass); G.S. 15A-1382.1 (offenses involving domestic violence); G.S. 50B-4.1 (violation of domestic violence protection order); G.S. 20-138.1 (impaired driving); G.S. 20-138.2 (commercial impaired driving); G.S. 20-138.2A (operating commercial vehicle after consuming alcohol); G.S. 20-138.2B (operating various specialized vehicles after consuming alcohol); and G.S. 90-95(a)(3) (possessing controlled substance).[429]

An arresting law enforcement agency is *required* to cause a person charged with a misdemeanor assault, stalking, or communicating a threat and held under G.S. 15A-534.1 (pretrial release restrictions for certain domestic violence offenses) to be fingerprinted so the fingerprints can be forwarded to the SBI.[430]

An officer is also *required* to fingerprint and photograph a person who cannot be identified by a valid form of identification and has been arrested for (1) an

---

authority to fingerprint or photograph an adult who has been arrested—to refer to (1) a person who commits a criminal offense on or after his or her 16th birthday; (2) a juvenile who commits a criminal offense and is emancipated, married, or in the armed services; or (3) a juvenile who commits a criminal offense and has been previously convicted of an offense in superior court; *see* G.S. 7B-1604.

428. G.S. 15A-502(a1). G.S. 15A-1382(a) provides that when a defendant is fingerprinted pursuant to G.S. 15A-502 before the disposition of the case, a report of the disposition must be made to the State Bureau of Investigation (SBI). G.S. 15A-1382(b) provides that when a defendant is convicted of any felony, a report must be made to the SBI; if the defendant was not fingerprinted under G.S. 15A-502 before the felony conviction, fingerprints must be taken and forwarded to the SBI along with the report of the conviction.

429. G.S. 15A-502(a2), as enacted by S.L. 2015-195 and S.L. 2015-267, effective October 1, 2015.

For a discussion of this statute, see Jeff Welty, *Must Officers Now Arrest, Rather Than Cite, for Misdemeanor Marijuana Possession?*, NC CRIM. L. BLOG (Oct. 7, 2015), http://nccriminallaw.sog.unc.edu/must-officers-now-arrest-rather-than-cite-for-misdemeanor-marijuana-possession/.

430. G.S. 15A-502(a4), as enacted by S.L. 2015-195 and S.L. 2015-267, effective October 1, 2015.

offense involving impaired driving[431] or (2) driving while license revoked if the revocation is an impaired driving revocation under G.S. 20-28.2.[432] If a defendant refuses to provide fingerprints when arrested for a felony or for the impaired driving and driving while license revoked offenses described in the prior sentence, then the magistrate must make submission to fingerprinting a condition of pretrial release.[433]

An arrestee who is charged with a motor vehicle offense may not be fingerprinted or photographed if the offense is a Class 2 or Class 3 misdemeanor.[434] This prohibition applies only when fingerprints or photographs are taken solely for law enforcement records. Photographs or fingerprints may be taken for evidentiary use, such as photo or video to show a defendant's intoxication.[435]

An arresting law enforcement agency must cause a person charged with a crime to provide to the magistrate as much as possible of the following information: (1) name, including first, last, middle, maiden, and nickname or alias; (2) address; (3) driver's license number and issuing state; (4) date of birth; (5) sex; (6) race; (7) social security number; and (8) relationship to the alleged victim and whether it is a "personal relationship" as defined by G.S. 50B-1(b).[436]

Despite the prohibition against fingerprinting and photographing for Class 2 and 3 misdemeanor motor vehicle offenses, a photograph may be taken of a person who operates a motor vehicle on a street or highway if (1) the person is cited by an officer for a motor vehicle moving violation,[437] (2) the person does not produce a valid driver's license pursuant to an officer's request, and (3) the officer has a reasonable suspicion about the person's true identity.[438]

Although there is some uncertainty about what age constitutes an adult for the purpose of fingerprinting and photographing, clearly the more persuasive view is that an adult is a person 16 years old or older (thus, the juvenile provisions, discussed below, apply only to a person under 16 years old).[439] Officers may wish to consult

---

431. The term "offense involving impaired driving" is defined in G.S. 20-4.01(24a). Among the offenses included in the definition are impaired driving, commercial impaired driving, habitual impaired driving, murder and manslaughter involving impaired driving, and felony and misdemeanor offenses in G.S. 20-141.4, such as misdemeanor and felony death by vehicle and felony serious injury by vehicle.

432. G.S. 15A-502(a6).

433. G.S. 15A-534(a).

434. G.S. 15A-502(b).

435. G.S. 15A-502(d).

436. G.S. 15A-502(a3), as enacted by S.L. 2015-195, effective October 1, 2015.

437. The term "motor vehicle moving violation" does not include the offenses listed in the third paragraph of G.S. 20-16(c) for which no points are assessed (for example, improper plates and registration), nor does it include equipment violations in Part 9, Article 3, of Chapter 20 of the General Statutes. G.S. 15A-502(b).

438. G.S. 15A-502(b). The photograph is subject to the limitations set out in G.S. 15A-502(b1).

439. G.S. 15A-502(a) clearly should be interpreted to apply to arrestees who are sixteen years old or older. A 1996 legislative amendment (1996 N.C. 2nd Extra Sess. Laws, Ch. 18) to G.S. 15A-502(c), which specifies the circumstances when an adult may be photographed and fingerprinted, lends support to the statement that an adult is a person sixteen years old or older. The legislative amendment specifically stated that G.S. 15A-502 does not authorize the taking of photographs or fingerprints of a juvenile *alleged to be delinquent* (the emphasized words were added by the legislative amendment). Only a juvenile under sixteen years old may be alleged to be delinquent. However, as discussed below, North Carolina appellate decisions may indicate otherwise.

The North Carolina Supreme Court ruled in *State v. Fincher*, 309 N.C. 1 (1983), that the custodial interrogation warnings listed in G.S. 7A-595 (now, G.S. 7B-2101) must be given to a person *under 18* (who is unemancipated, unmarried, and not in the armed forces) because the court interpreted the word "juvenile" in the statute to mean the same as *juvenile* as defined in G.S. 7A-517(20) (now, G.S. 7B-1501(17)). The court noted that the preface to G.S. 7A-517 (now, G.S. 7B-1501) states: "Unless the context *clearly* requires otherwise, the following words have the listed meanings . . . [emphasis in original]." The court then concluded that the term "juvenile" in G.S. 7A-595 must be given the definitional meaning in G.S. 7A-517(20), as its context does not require or suggest a different interpretation.

The concurring opinion in *Fincher* persuasively argued that the General Assembly did not intend to expand warnings for 16- and 17-year-olds beyond that required for other adults. It pointed out that G.S. 7A-595 and Article 48 (now, Article 15 of G.S. Chapter 7B), in which the statute appears, apply only to juvenile delinquency proceedings—a *delinquent juvenile* is a person under 16 who is unemancipated, unmarried, and not in the armed forces.

The term "juvenile" almost certainly was used instead of the term "delinquent juvenile" simply for drafting simplicity; it is somewhat wordy and awkward to use "alleged juvenile delinquent" throughout statutes. It *clearly* appears that neither the Juvenile Code Revision Committee, which drafted the Juvenile Code bill, nor the North Carolina General Assembly intended that any provisions in Article 48 would apply to criminal procedure applicable to adults—which includes, of course, 16- and 17-year-olds. It is instructive to read the commentary to the draft of this article in *The Final Report of the Juvenile Code Revision Committee* (N.C. Department of Crime Control and Public Safety, 1979) (hereafter, *Report*), at 181–92. (None of the opinions in *Fincher* refer to the *Report*.) First, the commentary reveals no basis for concluding that the committee was broadening the rights of adults beyond those contained in *Miranda*. Second, the nontestimonial identification procedures (which appear in the same article), as drafted and as indicated in the commentary, *clearly* apply only to juveniles *under 16*. For example, the commentary to proposed G.S. 7A-551 (as enacted, G.S. 7A-597, and now, G.S. 7B-2104) stated: "A request for an order may be made prior to the *adjudicatory hearing or prior to trial of the case when it is transferred to Superior Court for trial as in the case of adults* [emphasis added]." Clearly, 16- and 17-year-olds do not have adjudicatory hearings or have their cases transferred to superior court—they are treated just as other adults are. (The legislature later amended G.S. 7A-597 to delete the reference to superior court transfer, leaving just the reference to an adjudicatory hearing.) Although a statute's caption is not dispositive when interpreting a statute, the caption of G.S. 7A-596 (now, G.S. 7B-2103) is "Authority to issue nontestimonial identification order where juvenile alleged to be delinquent." Note also the complete lack of references in G.S. 7A-601 (now, G.S. 7B-2108) (destruction of records resulting from nontestimonial identification procedures) to any provision that conceivably could refer to 16- or 17-year-olds; nor is there any indication in the commentary to the *Report* that this age group was deliberately exempted from the records-destruction provisions.

The better conclusion is that both the legislative history and the statutes considered in their context clearly require that the term "juvenile" not be given the definitional meaning in G.S. 7A-517(20).

Since *Fincher*, the North Carolina Court of Appeals in *State v. Norris*, 77 N.C. App. 525 (1985), has stated in dicta that the nontestimonial identification procedures in the Juvenile Code apply to a 16-year-old. For the reasons discussed above, the *Fincher* ruling is questionable. However, even conceding the correctness of *Fincher* concerning interrogation procedures (the North Carolina Supreme Court specifically declined to reconsider *Fincher* in *State v. Smith*, 317 N.C. 100 (1986)), the *Norris* dicta clearly are contrary to the legislative history and statutes discussed above. If the *Norris* dicta become binding law, all nontestimonial identification procedures—which include fingerprinting and photographing—would apply to 16- and 17-year-olds. The General Assembly clearly did not intend such a result when it passed the Juvenile Code, particularly when G.S. Chapter 15A already was effective and included a provision for fingerprinting and photographing 16- and 17-year-olds (and all other adults) under G.S.15A-502. Note also that the legislature, when it enacted G.S. 7B-2103 in 1998, explicitly exempted from the provisions requiring a

their agency's legal advisor or their district attorney to determine how they should handle photographing and fingerprinting 16- and 17-year-olds.

Juveniles

A juvenile who is taken into custody may not be fingerprinted or photographed unless a judge issues a nontestimonial identification order.[440] However, there are three exceptions to the necessity of obtaining a nontestimonial identification order. First, a law enforcement officer or agency must fingerprint and photograph a juvenile who was 10 years old or older when the juvenile allegedly committed a *nondivertible offense*, defined as first-degree and second-degree murder, rape, sexual offense, arson, first-degree burglary, crime against nature, a felony drug violation, or any felony involving the willful infliction of serious bodily injury or that was committed with a deadly weapon.[441] The duty to fingerprint occurs when a complaint has been prepared for filing as a petition and the juvenile is in the physical custody of law enforcement or the Division of Juvenile Justice. Second, a juvenile may be fingerprinted and photographed if the juvenile has been charged as an adult[442] or the juvenile's case has been transferred to superior court for trial as an adult.[443] Third, a law enforcement officer or agency must fingerprint and photograph a juvenile who has been adjudicated delinquent if the juvenile was 10 years old or older when the juvenile committed a felony (there is no duty to fingerprint and photograph if the juvenile has previously been fingerprinted and photographed because he or she was charged with a felony that was a nondivertible offense).[444]

See the discussion above under "Adults" concerning the age when a person is considered a juvenile or adult.

---

nontestimonial identification order a "juvenile [who] has been charged as an adult." A person who commits an offense while he or she is 16 or 17 years old is always charged as an adult.

440. G.S. 7B-2103; 15A-502(c).

441. G.S. 7B-2102(a). The definition of a *nondivertible offense* is in G.S. 7B-1701.

442. Under G.S. 7B-1604, a juvenile who is emancipated must be prosecuted as an adult and a juvenile who has been convicted of an offense in superior court must be prosecuted as an adult for offenses committed thereafter. Also, G.S. 7B-2103 excepts from its provisions requiring a nontestimonial identification order a "juvenile [who] has been charged as an adult."

443. G.S. 7B-2103.

444. G.S. 7B-2102(b).

A law enforcement officer or other person who willfully fingerprints or photographs a juvenile without a nontestimonial identification order, when such an order is required, is guilty of a Class 1 misdemeanor.[445]

Obtaining a nontestimonial identification order for a juvenile is discussed on page 459 of Chapter 4.

Taking DNA Samples for Certain Offenses

An officer must obtain, or cause to be obtained, a DNA sample from a person arrested for certain offenses,[446] which include first- and second-degree murder, voluntary and involuntary manslaughter, rape and other sex offenses,[447] specified felony assaults,[448] kidnapping and related offenses,[449] first- and second-degree burglary and related offenses,[450] first- and second-degree arson and related offenses,[451] armed and common law robbery, discharging barreled weapon or firearm into occupied property, certain child abuse felonies,[452] any offense that would require the person to register as a sex offender,[453] cyberstalking, and stalking. Attempt, solicitation, conspiracy, or aiding and abetting these offenses are also included.[454]

If an officer makes an arrest without a warrant, the DNA sample may not be taken unless and until a magistrate or other judicial official finds probable cause at the initial appearance. Also, a DNA sample should not be taken if the officer knows that a sample has previously been obtained, the DNA record is stored in the state DNA database, and the record and sample have not been expunged.[455]

The DNA sample must be taken by a cheek swab unless a court orders that a blood sample be obtained. The cheek swab may be taken without a court order or search warrant. The person taking the DNA sample must complete a form[456] for the case file[457] and provide the arrestee with a written notice of the procedures for seeking an expunction of the DNA sample.[458] The arresting officer must forward, or cause to be forwarded, the DNA sample to the appropriate laboratory for DNA analysis and testing.

---

445. G.S. 7B-2109.

446. The United States Supreme Court in *Maryland v. King*, 133 S. Ct. 1958 (2013), ruled that when officers arrest a defendant based on probable cause for a "serious offense," taking and analyzing a cheek swab of the arrestee's DNA is, like fingerprinting and photographing, a legitimate police booking procedure that is reasonable under the Fourth Amendment. The Court did not define *serious offense.*"

United States Supreme Court cases that have used the term "serious offense" in constitutionally based rulings include those that have ruled that a defendant has a Sixth Amendment right to a jury trial for a "serious offense," defined as an offense punishable by more than six months' imprisonment. Lewis v. United States, 518 U.S. 322 (1996); Blanton v. City of N. Las Vegas, 489 U.S. 538 (1989); Codispoti v. Pennsylvania, 418 U.S. 506 (1974). The Court's opinion in *Maryland v. King* did not cite these cases, so it remains uncertain what the Court meant by the term.

For analysis of *Maryland v. King*, see Jeff Welty, *Supreme Court Upholds Taking DNA Upon Arrest*, NC CRIM. L. BLOG (June 4, 2013), http://nccriminallaw.sog.unc.edu/?p=4294.

447. Any offense in Article 7B of Chapter 14 of the General Statutes is included. Thus, misdemeanor sexual battery is included as well.

448. Assault with a deadly weapon with intent to kill or inflicting serious injury (G.S. 14-32); assault inflicting serious bodily injury (G.S. 14-32.4(a)); assault with a firearm or deadly weapon on a governmental officer and others (G.S. 14-34.2); assault with a firearm on a law enforcement officer and others (G.S. 14-34.5); assault on a firefighter and others (G.S. 14-34.6); assault by strangulation (G.S. 14-32.4); habitual misdemeanor assault (G.S. 14-33.2); and assault inflicting serious injury on a law enforcement officer and others (G.S. 14-34.7).

449. Any offense in Article 10 (kidnapping and abduction) and Article 10A (human trafficking) of Chapter 14 of the General Statutes is included.

450. Breaking out of dwelling house burglary (G.S. 14-53); breaking or entering a place of religious worship (G.S. 14-54.1); and burglary with explosives (G.S. 14-57) are included.

451. Any offense in Article 15 (arson) of Chapter 14 of the General Statutes is included.

452. Child abuse inflicting serious injury (G.S. 14-318.4(a)) and child abuse inflicting serious bodily injury (G.S. 14-318.4(a3)).

453. *See* Article 27A of Chapter 14 of the General Statutes.

454. G.S. 15A-266.3A(g).

455. G.S. 15A-266.3A(a).

456. The SBI is required to promulgate the form, which must record the date and time the sample was taken, the name of the person taking the sample, the name and address of the person from whom the sample was taken, and the offense(s) for which the person was arrested. G.S. 15A-266.3A(b1).

457. The meaning of "case file" in G.S. 15A-266.3A(b1) is unclear. By stating that the form must be maintained in the case file and must be available to the prosecuting attorney, it implies that the case file is maintained by whoever completed the form, which is the person who obtained the DNA sample. As a practical matter, the original or a copy of the form should be sent to the district attorney's office so that it may be given to the prosecutor in charge of the case.

458. The grounds and procedure for an expunction are set out in G.S. 15A-266.3A(f) through 15A-266.3A(g3). Expunction requires destroying any retained biological samples and removing a person's DNA record from the state DNA database and DNA databank.

If an arrestee refuses to provide a DNA sample, then the magistrate must require as a condition of pretrial release that the defendant provide a DNA sample.[459]

These DNA procedures do not apply to a juvenile taken into custody and processed in juvenile court. However, if jurisdiction over a juvenile is transferred to superior court for trial as an adult, a DNA sample must be taken from the juvenile if any of the offenses for which the juvenile is transferred are the same as those for which adults must provide a sample.

Taking the Arrestee to a Judicial Official

(See page 191 for case summaries on this topic.)

Officers who make an arrest with or without a warrant must take the arrestee for an initial appearance before a magistrate "without unnecessary delay,"[460] but the law does not impose a specific time limit. Officers, if they choose, first may take the arrestee somewhere else that the arrestee wants to go, such as to a residence to obtain clothing, or they may take the arrestee somewhere for a reasonable period of time for identification, interrogation, medical assistance, blood alcohol testing, and the like.[461]

For DWI and related cases,[462] there is specific statutory authority providing that an officer is not required to take the arrestee before a judicial official for an initial appearance until the completion of all investigatory procedures, crash reports, and chemical analyses.[463]

Sometimes officers arrest a person with probable cause but receive further information after the arrest—but before taking the person to a magistrate—that clearly shows that probable cause no longer exists to charge the person with a crime; for example, they learn that the arrestee is not the person who is wanted for the crime. North Carolina statutory law literally requires officers to take the person to a magistrate for an initial appearance despite clear evidence that probable cause no longer exists.[464] However, federal constitutional law appears to require that officers must release an arrestee when probable cause clearly no longer exists. In such a situation, because federal constitutional law would override North Carolina statutory law, officers should release the arrestee in a safe place instead of taking the arrestee to a magistrate.[465]

---

459. G.S. 15A-534(a).

460. G.S. 15A-501(2), -511(a)(1).

461. G.S. 15A-501(3), -501(4). The reasons for delay provided in these two subdivisions are not exhaustive. State v. Wallace, 351 N.C. 481 (2000) (court ruled that the officers did not violate G.S. 15A-501(2) by taking the defendant to a magistrate 19 hours after his arrest; because of the number of crimes to which the defendant confessed and the amount of time needed to record the details of the crimes, along with the officers' accommodation of the defendant's request to sleep, the delay was not unnecessary); State v. Reynolds, 298 N.C. 380 (1979) (no unnecessary delay occurred in the two to three hours during which officers questioned defendant and took hair and blood samples); State v. Martin, 315 N.C. 667 (1986) (no unnecessary delay during two hours when confession was obtained); State v. Sings, 35 N.C. App. 1 (1978) (seven-hour delay after arrest was not unnecessary delay when officers took codefendant to recover stolen property, recaptured him when he escaped from their custody, and then took confession from defendant).

462. Under G.S. 20-38.1, the law enforcement processing duties set out in G.S. 20-38.3 apply to all implied consent offenses as defined in G.S. 20-16.2. In G.S. 20-16.2(a1), an *implied consent offense* is defined as an offense involving impaired driving (defined in G.S. 20-4.01(24a)) and an alcohol-related offense made subject to G.S. 20-16.2. Offenses involving impaired driving include impaired driving, commercial

impaired driving, habitual impaired driving, murder and manslaughter involving impaired driving, and felony and misdemeanor offenses in G.S. 20-141.4, such as misdemeanor and felony death by vehicle and felony serious injury by vehicle.

463. G.S. 20-38.3. For example, an officer may take the arrestee to any place in the state for one or more chemical analyses; for an evaluation by an officer, medical professional, or other person to determine the extent or cause of the arrestee's impairment; to have the arrestee identified; to complete a crash report; or for any other lawful purpose.

464. G.S. 15A-511(a)(1).

465. Thompson v. Olson, 798 F.2d 552 (1st Cir. 1986) (dicta); BeVier v. Hucal, 806 F.2d 123 (7th Cir. 1986) (dicta); McConney v. City of Houston, 863 F.2d 1180 (5th Cir. 1989) (if officer determines beyond a reasonable doubt that person arrested for public intoxication was not intoxicated, officer must release that person); 2 Wayne R. LaFave, Search and Seizure: A Treatise on the Fourth Amendment § 3.2(d), at 62 (5th ed. 2012). *See also* Duckett v. City of Cedar Park, 950 F.2d 272 (5th Cir. 1992) (constitutional violation may be proved if officers arrest person with arrest warrant and fail to release person after receiving information that establishes beyond a reasonable doubt that arrest warrant had been withdrawn). Officers who fail to release a person in these circumstances may be civilly liable not only for federal constitutional violations but also for state torts, such as false imprisonment. *But see* Peet v. City of Detroit, 502 F.3d 557 (6th Cir. 2007) (police do not have Fourth Amendment duty to release arrestee the moment new exculpatory evidence is revealed).

Conducting an Initial Appearance

A magistrate (or other judicial official) conducts an initial appearance for a person arrested with or without a warrant. When a person has been arrested without a warrant, the magistrate first must determine whether to issue a magistrate's order. Whether the person has been arrested with or without a warrant, the magistrate must inform the arrestee of the charges, the right to communicate with counsel and friends, and the circumstances under which the arrestee may secure pretrial release.[466]

An initial appearance for an offense other than first-degree murder may be conducted by an audio and video transmission between the magistrate or other judicial official and the defendant in which both people can see and hear each other.[467] If the defendant has counsel, the defendant must be allowed to communicate fully and confidentially with counsel during the proceeding.

Issuing a Magistrate's Order When the Arrest Is without a Warrant

An officer must take a person arrested without a warrant to a magistrate so that the magistrate may determine whether to issue a magistrate's order. A magistrate's order is a document that charges a person with a criminal offense; it is issued only if the magistrate determines that probable cause exists to believe that a criminal offense was committed and that the defendant committed that offense.[468] The arrestee must be released from custody if the magistrate finds no probable cause to charge a crime. An officer may, but is not required to, return the arrestee and anyone who accompanied the arrestee to the scene of the arrest.[469]

The uniform traffic citation in paper or electronic form may be converted into a magistrate's order when an officer decides to arrest a person instead of charging the person by using a citation. The citation normally will be used this way when an officer arrests a person for driving while impaired. The magistrate will take the officer's sworn testimony, decide whether probable cause exists,

and charge the offense by creating a magistrate's order in NCAWARE (discussed on page 56).

A magistrate's order is inappropriate and unnecessary when an officer arrests a person with an arrest warrant because a judicial official already has determined that probable cause exists to charge the arrestee with a criminal offense.

Delaying the Initial Appearance of a Drunk or Disruptive Arrestee

If an arrestee is grossly intoxicated or otherwise unable to understand the proceedings, a magistrate may delay the initial appearance and order the arrestee detained for a short time until he or she can understand the proceedings.[470] The same delay also may occur if the defendant becomes disruptive after the magistrate begins the proceedings.

Considering Pretrial Release Conditions

At the initial appearance, a magistrate must determine which conditions of pretrial release (written promise to appear, unsecured or secured appearance bond, custody release, house arrest with electronic monitoring) the arrestee must satisfy to be released from custody. A magistrate must set pretrial release conditions for all arrested persons, whether arrested with or without a warrant. The primary exception occurs when a person is charged with first-degree murder; only a judge may set pretrial release conditions for that crime.[471]

North Carolina law permits detention of a person charged with impaired driving under certain circumstances before the person is allowed the opportunity to satisfy the conditions of pretrial release.[472] If a magistrate finds by clear and convincing evidence that the impairment of the arrestee's physical or mental faculties presents a danger of physical injury to himself or herself or others or damage to property if the arrestee is released, the mag-

---

466. G.S. 15A-511(b). Under certain circumstances, a magistrate may be designated to appoint an attorney for a defendant except in potentially capital offenses. G.S. 7A-146(11), -292(15).

467. G.S. 15A-511(a1). The use of this procedure and the equipment must be approved by the Administrative Office of the Courts.

468. G.S. 15A-511(c).

469. G.S. 15A-504.

470. G.S. 15A-511(a)(3).

471. G.S. 15A-533(b), -533(c). G.S. 15A-533(a) provides that a person involuntarily committed to a mental health facility has no right to pretrial release when he or she is charged with a crime allegedly committed while residing in, after his or her escape from, or during an unauthorized absence from the facility.

472. G.S. 15A-534.2. For an analysis of this statute and its pertinent case law, see SHEA RIGGSBEE DENNING, THE LAW OF IMPAIRED DRIVING AND RELATED IMPLIED CONSENT OFFENSES IN NORTH CAROLINA 99–115 (UNC School of Government, 2014).

istrate must order the arrestee to be held in custody until one of the following conditions occurs: (1) the arrestee's physical and mental faculties are no longer impaired to the extent that the arrestee presents a danger of physical injury to himself or herself or others or damage to property if the arrestee is released; or (2) a sober, responsible adult is willing and able to assume responsibility for the arrestee until his or her physical and mental faculties are no longer impaired. An arrestee may not be detained for longer than 24 hours under this provision.

North Carolina law provides that only a judge may set conditions of pretrial release for defendants arrested for domestic violence offenses. However, if a judge has not set conditions of pretrial release within 48 hours of arrest, then a magistrate must set conditions. Domestic violence offenses include the following:

- Assaulting, stalking, or communicating a threat to a spouse or former spouse or a person with whom the arrestee lives or has lived as if married
- Domestic criminal trespass
- Violation of a domestic violence protective order entered under Chapter 50B of the General Statutes
- Any felony in General Statutes Chapter 14, Article 7B (rape and other sex offenses); Article 8 (assaults); Article 10 (kidnapping and abduction); and Article 15 (arson and other burnings) when the felony is committed on a spouse or former spouse or person with whom the arrestee lives or has lived as if married[473]

There are other special provisions involving certain offenses or arrests of probationers, which are cited in the accompanying footnote.[474]

---

473. G.S. 15A-534.1. A violation of a domestic violence protective order is a criminal offense under G.S. 50B-4.1, and thus that offense is included within the provision discussed in the text. There also is authority under G.S. 15A-534.1(1) to detain for a reasonable time period a defendant who poses a danger of injury or intimidation if immediately released.

474. The special provisions include (1) G.S. 15A-533(d) for certain drug trafficking offenses; (2) G.S. 15A-534(d1) for a defendant who failed to appear on one or more prior occasions for one or more charges to which the pretrial release conditions apply; (3) G.S. 15A-534(d2) for a defendant charged with a felony and currently on probation for a prior offense; (4) G.S. 15A-534.4 for sex offenses and crimes of violence against child victims; (5) G.S. 15A-534.6 for manufacture of methamphetamine; and (6) G.S. 15A-1345(b1) for a probationer arrested for a violation of a probation condition who

See pages 81 and 84 for a discussion of when a defendant must be required as a condition of pretrial release to submit to fingerprinting or to give a DNA sample.

Permitting the Arrestee to Communicate with Counsel and Friends

The arresting officer must tell the arrestee of the right to communicate with counsel and friends and must also give the arrestee a reasonable chance to do so.[475] This requirement does not mean that an officer must tolerate attempts to delay or that the state must pay for long distance telephone calls. But the arrestee must be given a reasonable opportunity, with a reasonable amount of assistance, to call lawyers and friends. There is no legal basis for a "one telephone call only" rule, and applying such a rule would be inconsistent with North Carolina law.

Informing a Minor's Parent and School Principal of a Criminal Charge
Notifying a Minor's Parent of a Criminal Charge

North Carolina law requires an officer who has charged a minor (a person under 18 years old) with a criminal offense to notify the minor's parent or guardian of the charge as soon as practicable, in person or by telephone.[476] If the minor has been taken into custody, the officer or immediate supervisor must notify the parent or guardian in writing—within 24 hours of the minor's arrest—that the minor is in custody. If the parent or guardian cannot be found, then the officer or immediate supervisor must notify the minor's next-of-kin of the minor's arrest as soon as practicable. This notification requirement does not apply if any of the following conditions exist:

- The minor has been emancipated by court order or because the minor is married
- The minor has not been taken into custody and has been charged with a motor vehicle moving violation for which fewer than four driver's license points are

---

has a pending charge for a felony or has been convicted of an offense that requires registration as a sex offender or would have required registration but for the effective date of the sex offender registration law.

475. G.S. 15A-501(5). A magistrate at the initial appearance also must inform the defendant of the right to communicate with counsel and friends. G.S. 15A-511(b)(2).

476. G.S. 15A-505(a), (b).

assessed (except that the parent or guardian must be notified of an offense involving impaired driving)

- The minor has been charged with a motor vehicle offense that is not a moving violation

The notification duty described in the preceding paragraph does not apply to a person charged in juvenile court.[477] An officer's duty to notify a juvenile's parent, guardian, or custodian after taking a juvenile into custody without a court order is discussed on page 66.

Notifying the School Principal of a Felony Charge

A law enforcement officer who charges a student with a felony (excluding a felony under Chapter 20 of the General Statutes) must notify the principal of the student's North Carolina public or private school of the charge.[478] The notification may be made in person or by telephone, and it must be made as soon as practicable but at least within five days of the charge. However, if the student is arrested—which would occur with almost all felonies—the officer or the officer's supervisor must notify the principal in writing within five days of the student's arrest. If the principal receives notification under the statute, the district attorney's office must notify the principal of the final disposition of the case at the trial court level, and the notification must be in writing and must be made within five days of the disposition.

The requirement that an officer must notify a principal would apply only to students who are 16 years old or older when they commit an offense, because the law does not apply to students who are charged in juvenile court.[479] A juvenile court counselor, not a law enforcement officer,

has the responsibility to notify a principal when a petition is filed against a juvenile that alleges delinquency for an offense that would be a felony if committed by an adult.[480]

Completing Custody of a Person Arrested in Another State

A North Carolina officer who pursues a person who has committed a felony and arrests the person in an adjoining state (Georgia, South Carolina, Tennessee, or Virginia) under the circumstances discussed on page 17 may not return the person to North Carolina. Instead, the officer must take the person to a judicial official in the state where the arrest was made. That official then determines whether the arrest was lawful and, if it was, commits the person to jail or another confinement facility (unless the person is entitled to have bond set and posts bond) in that state to await a request for extradition by the governor of North Carolina. In some cases, the person might agree to waive extradition—that is, agree to return to North Carolina without waiting for the governor to request extradition. If the waiver occurs before a judicial official in the other state, the officer may return the person directly to North Carolina.

Procedure for Charging and Processing People for Infractions

Many minor motor vehicle violations are infractions.[481] There are non-motor-vehicle infractions (for example, a hunter failing to display hunter orange material).[482] An infraction is a noncriminal violation of law that is not punishable by imprisonment; unless otherwise provided by law, the maximum penalty for an infraction is a penalty of $100.[483] An officer may detain a person for a reasonable period to issue and serve a citation that charges an infraction, but the officer has no authority to arrest the person. A person charged with an infraction also may not be required to post an appearance bond if the person is (1) a North Carolina resident or (2) licensed in a state

---

477. None of the provisions in G.S. 15A-505 apply to a person charged in juvenile court, because the section is located in Chapter 15A and the section uses the terms "arrest" and "criminal offense," which clearly indicate that the statute is referring to offenders in the adult court system. Also, G.S. 7B-1901 and G.S. 7B-1904 address notification requirements when a juvenile is taken into custody.

478. G.S. 15A-505(c).

479. None of the provisions in G.S. 15A-505 apply to a person charged in juvenile court, because the section is located in Chapter 15A and it uses the terms "arrest" and "criminal offense," which clearly indicate that the statute is referring to offenders in the adult court system. Also, G.S. 7B-3101 addresses notification requirements when a juvenile is taken into custody. Although such a scenario is highly unlikely, the requirement to notify the school principal in G.S. 15A-505(c) could also apply to a student under 16 years old who was married, otherwise emancipated, or subject to prosecution as

an adult under G.S. 7B-1604, because such a person would be prosecuted in adult court.

480. G.S. 7B-3101.

481. The infraction procedure is codified in Article 66 of Chapter 15A of the General Statutes (G.S. 15A-1111 through -1118).

482. G.S. 113-291.8.

483. G.S. 14-3.1.

that is a member of the nonresident violator reciprocal agreement (see page 61) and the charged infraction is subject to the provisions of that agreement.[484] Any other person charged with an infraction may be required to post a bond, and the officer may require the person to come with the officer to a magistrate to determine what bond is appropriate, if any. However, if the magistrate finds that the person is unable to post a secured bond, the magistrate must allow the person to be released upon posting an unsecured bond.[485]

---

484. G.S. 15A-1113(c).
485. *Id.*

Chapter 2 Appendix: Case Summaries

Chapter 2 Appendix: Case Summaries

Arrests, Investigative Stops, and Related Issues

Jurisdiction
Territorial Jurisdiction
(*This topic is discussed on page 14.*)

Generally

State v. Eubanks, 283 N.C. 556 (1973). Illegal, although constitutional, arrest for impaired driving did not require suppression of evidence found after the arrest. [Author's note: G.S. 15A-974(a)(2) did not exist when this case was decided.] *See generally* Virginia v. Moore, 553 U.S. 164 (Virginia law enforcement officers who had probable cause to arrest defendant for a misdemeanor did not violate Fourth Amendment when they arrested him and conducted a search incident to arrest, although state law did not authorize an arrest).

State v. Bernard, 236 N.C. App. 134 (2014). The court ruled that North Carolina A&T University (A&T) campus police had territorial jurisdiction to execute a search warrant at the defendant's off-campus private residence when A&T had entered into a mutual aid agreement with local police. The agreement gave campus police authority to act off-campus concerning offenses committed on campus. The statutes governing unauthorized access to a computer—the crime in question—provide that any offense "committed by the use of electronic communication may be deemed to have been committed where the electronic communication was originally sent or where it was originally received." (See G.S. 14-453.2.) The defendant "sent" an "electronic communication" when she accessed the email account of an A&T employee and sent a false email. The court concluded that the offenses were "committed on Campus" because she sent the email through the A&T campus computer servers.

State v. Scruggs, 209 N.C. App. 725 (2011). The court ruled that even if a stop and arrest of the defendant by campus police officers while off campus violated G.S. 15A-402(f), the violation was not substantial under G.S. 15A-974 to require the exclusion of evidence resulting from the stop and arrest, which were constitutionally authorized.

State v. Locklear, 136 N.C. App. 716 (2000). A Robeson County deputy sheriff called for assistance in responding to a stabbing at a home three to four miles outside the Red Springs city limits. A Red Springs law enforcement officer responded to the call and was later assaulted by the defendant there. The defendant argued that because the Red Springs officer was outside his territorial jurisdiction (a city officer's jurisdiction is generally limited to one mile beyond a city's limits) when the assault occurred, the officer was not acting as an officer and thus the defendant could not be convicted of assault with a firearm on a law enforcement officer. The court ruled that a mutual aid agreement between the Robeson County Sheriff's Department and the Red Springs Police Department permitted the officer to respond to the request for assistance, based on the agreement's permitting an oral request to be made for an "emergency." The court ruled that an emergency existed: the deputy sheriff was transporting a prisoner when he received the order to investigate the stabbing, and he was the only deputy in the vicinity of the residence.

State v. Pearson, 131 N.C. App. 315 (1998). An officer arrested the defendant for DWI. When an Intoxilyzer malfunctioned, he took the defendant outside the officer's territorial jurisdiction to administer the Intoxilyzer test. The court ruled, relying on *State v. Satterfield*, 300 N.C. 621 (1980), that the defendant's failure to file an affidavit with his motion to suppress the chemical test result, based on an allegation of a substantial statutory violation, was a ground to deny the motion. The court also ruled, relying on *State v. Afflerback*, 46 N.C. App. 344 (1980), that even if the officer's actions were a statutory violation (which the court said it did not believe to be true), it was not a substantial violation to require suppression of the chemical test result under G.S. 15A-974. [Author's note: G.S. 20-38.3(2), enacted in 2006, authorizes an officer to take a defendant anywhere in the state for a chemical analysis.]

State v. Gwyn, 103 N.C. App. 369 (1991). An officer arrested the defendant for impaired driving just inside the boundary of the state of Virginia after he had seen the defendant driving in North Carolina. However, the officer did not know that he was in Virginia when he arrested the defendant. The court ruled that although the arrest was illegal, it was constitutionally valid because it was supported by probable cause. Evidence seized as a result of the arrest—the officer's detection of alcohol on the defendant's breath and the Breathalyzer test reading—was admissible under the balancing test of G.S. 15A-974(2). [Author's note: This statute was recodified as G.S. 15A-974(a)(2) in S.L. 2011-6, which added a good faith exception to the application of G.S. 15A-974.] The defendant's driving, which was a menace to public safety, outweighed the defendant's illegal arrest under the balancing test of G.S. 15A-974(a), and the officer's violation was neither extensive nor willful because he did not know the defendant was in Virginia.

State v. Afflerback, 46 N.C. App. 344 (1980). No federal or state constitutional right was violated when Raleigh police officers undertook undercover drug transactions with a defendant in Zebulon (and therefore presumably outside the officers' jurisdiction). [Author's note: North Carolina's statutory exclusionary rule in G.S. 15A-974 was not discussed.]

State v. Harris, 43 N.C. App. 346 (1979). Even assuming that a Stokes County deputy sheriff's stop of a defendant in Forsyth County was included within the term "arrest" in G.S. 15A-402(b) and therefore was unlawful, it was constitutional; any possible violation of G.S. 15A-402(b) was not "substantial" under G.S. 15A-974 so as to require that evidence be excluded under North Carolina's statutory exclusionary rule.

State v. Mangum, 30 N.C. App. 311 (1976). Although a city officer's arrest of a defendant three miles outside the city violated G.S. 15A-402(b), the arrest was constitutionally valid because it was supported by probable cause. [Author's note: North Carolina's statutory exclusionary rule in G.S. 15A-974 was not discussed.]

Arrest after Continuous Flight (Hot Pursuit)

(*This topic is discussed on page 17.*)

State v. Melvin, 53 N.C. App. 421 (1981). A Burlington police officer's arrest of the defendants 1.67 miles outside the city boundary was justified because the defendants were in "immediate and continuous flight" (G.S. 15A-402(d)) from Burlington after they had committed an armed robbery.

Private Person's Authority to Detain

(*This topic is discussed on page 25.*)

State v. Wall, 304 N.C. 609 (1982). A convenience store cashier (the defendant) shot at a car leaving the store's parking lot with a person inside the car who had committed misdemeanor larceny in the store in the cashier's presence. The court ruled that the shooting was not justified under a private person's authority to detain, because the cashier stated that he fired the weapon to force the victim to bring the beer back—not to prevent the victim from leaving. The court alternatively ruled that even if the cashier's acts constituted an attempt to detain, deadly force was unreasonable because even a law enforcement officer would not have had authority to shoot at the fleeing misdemeanant under these circumstances.

State v. Ataei-Kachuei, 68 N.C. App. 209 (1984). The court ruled that the jury should consider whether the defendant used reasonable force as a private person when he shot at a car to detain its driver, who had committed larceny from the defendant and a felonious assault with his car. [Author's note: The court's ruling is questionable because it appeared that the defendant's use of deadly force was unreasonable as a matter of law because (1) he shot at the car as it was moving away from him, (2) there was no justification (such as self-defense) in using deadly force, and (3) it was unclear whether even a law enforcement officer in this case would have been entitled under G.S. 15A-401(d)(2) to use deadly force to arrest the driver, a fleeing felon. And even if an officer properly could have used deadly force to prevent an escape from an arrest under the same circumstances that should not make "reasonable" a private person's use of deadly force to detain.]

The Authority to Make an Investigative Stop: Reasonable Suspicion

(This topic is discussed on page 29.)

Determination of Reasonable Suspicion
Generally
UNITED STATES SUPREME COURT

Navarette v. California, 134 S. Ct. 1683 (2014). The Court, in what it termed a "close case," ruled that an officer had reasonable suspicion to make a vehicle stop based on a 911 call. After a 911 caller reported that a truck had run her off the road, a police officer located the truck the caller identified and executed a traffic stop. As officers approached the truck, they smelled marijuana. A search of the truck bed revealed 30 pounds of marijuana. The defendants moved to suppress the evidence, arguing that the traffic stop violated the Fourth Amendment because the officer lacked reasonable suspicion of criminal activity. Assuming based on the court record that the 911 call was anonymous, the Court found that it bore adequate indicia of reliability, so the officer could credit the caller's account that the truck ran her off the road. The Court explained: "By reporting that she had been run off the road by a specific vehicle—a silver Ford F-150 pickup, license plate 8D94925—the caller necessarily claimed eyewitness knowledge of the alleged dangerous driving. That basis of knowledge lends significant support to the tip's reliability." The Court noted that in this respect, the case contrasted with *Florida v. J. L.*, 529 U.S. 266 (2000), where the tip did not provide a basis to conclude that the tipster had actually seen the gun reportedly possessed by the defendant. It continued: "A driver's claim that another vehicle ran her off the road, however, necessarily implies that the informant knows the other car was driven dangerously." The Court noted evidence suggesting that the caller reported the incident soon after it occurred and stated: "That sort of contemporaneous report has long been treated as especially reliable." Again contrasting the case with *J.L.*, the Court noted that in *J.L.*, there was no indication that the tip was contemporaneous with the observation of criminal activity or made under the stress of excitement caused by a startling event. The Court determined that another indicator of veracity is the caller's use of the 911 system, which allows calls to be recorded and law enforcement to verify information about the caller. Thus, "a reasonable officer could conclude that a false tipster would think twice before using such a system . . . [and a] caller's use of the 911 system is therefore one of the relevant circumstances that, taken together, justified the officer's reliance on the information reported in the 911 call." But the Court cautioned: "None of this is to suggest that tips in 911 calls are *per se* reliable."

The Court noted that a reliable tip will justify an investigative stop only if it creates reasonable suspicion of criminal activity. It then determined that the caller's report of being run off the roadway created reasonable suspicion of an ongoing crime such as impaired driving. It stated:

> The 911 caller . . . reported more than a minor traffic infraction and more than a conclusory allegation of drunk or reckless driving. Instead, she alleged a specific and dangerous result of the driver's conduct: running another car off the highway. That conduct bears too great a resemblance to paradigmatic manifestations of drunk driving to be dismissed as an isolated example of recklessness. Running another vehicle off the road suggests lane positioning problems, decreased vigilance, impaired judgment, or some combination of those recognized drunk driving cues. . . . And the experience of many officers suggests that a driver who almost strikes a vehicle or another object—the exact scenario that ordinarily causes "running [another vehicle] off the roadway"—is likely intoxicated. . . . As a result, we cannot say that the officer acted unreasonably under these circumstances in stopping a driver whose alleged conduct was a significant indicator of drunk driving.

[Author's note: The Court's ruling raises questions about the continuing validity of prior North Carolina cases that had found insufficient evidence or reasonable suspicion based on an anonymous 911 caller, including *State v. Blankenship*, 230 N.C. App. 113 (2013), and *State v. Peele*, 196 N.C. App. 668 (2009).]

United States v. Arvizu, 534 U.S. 266 (2002). A Border Patrol agent stopped a vehicle in Arizona near the Arizona-Mexico border to investigate illegal activity, including drug and alien smuggling. The Court reviewed the detailed facts in this case and ruled that the agent had reasonable suspicion to stop the vehicle. (See the Court's discussion of the facts in its opinion.) The Court expressly disavowed the method of analysis of the Ninth Circuit

Court of Appeals, which had ruled that 7 of the 10 factors used by the trial court in considering the legality of the stop carried little or no weight in a reasonable suspicion analysis. The Court stated that the Ninth Circuit's approach departed sharply from the totality of circumstances analysis mandated by such cases as *United States v. Sokolow*, 490 U.S. 1 (1989). The Ninth Circuit appeared to believe that each of the agent's observations that was by itself readily susceptible to an innocent explanation was entitled to no weight. The Court stated that although each of the factors alone is susceptible to innocent explanation, and some factors are more probative than others, taken together they established reasonable suspicion to stop the vehicle.

Florida v. J.L., 529 U.S. 266 (2000). An anonymous phone call to a police department reported that a young black male standing at a particular bus stop and wearing a plaid shirt was carrying a gun. There was no audio recording of the call and nothing was known about the caller. Soon thereafter, officers went to the bus stop and saw three black males there. One of the three (the defendant) was wearing a plaid shirt. Officers did not see a firearm, and the defendant did not make any threatening or unusual movements. One officer stopped and frisked the defendant and seized a gun from his pocket. The Court ruled, distinguishing *Alabama v. White*, 496 U.S. 325 (1990) (reasonable suspicion to make investigative stop was supported by anonymous call predicting suspect's future conduct and officers' corroboration of caller's information), and *Adams v. Williams*, 407 U.S. 143 (1972) (tip from known informant was sufficient to support stop and frisk for weapon), that this information was insufficient to support reasonable suspicion to make an investigative stop and frisk of the defendant. The Court concluded that the tip in this case lacked the moderate indicia of reliability present in *Alabama v. White* and essential to the Court's ruling in that case. The tip was a bare report by an unknown, unaccountable informant who neither explained how he knew about the gun nor supplied any basis for believing that he had inside information about the defendant. Responding to the State's argument that the tip was reliable because its description of the suspect's visible attributes proved accurate, the Court stated that the reasonable suspicion at issue in this case required that a tip be reliable in its assertion of illegality, not just in its tendency to identify a determinate person. The Court also rejected the argument that there

should be a "firearm exception" to standard reasonable suspicion analysis.

The Court specifically reserved the issue of whether a report of a person carrying a bomb must bear the same indicia of reliability as a report of a person carrying a firearm. The Court stated that it did not hold that public safety officials in places where the reasonable expectation of privacy is diminished, such as airports or schools, are prohibited from conducting protective searches with information that would be insufficient to justify searches elsewhere. The Court also stated that the requirement that an anonymous tip bear standard indicia of reliability to justify a stop in no way diminishes an officer's authority, in accord with *Terry v. Ohio*, 392 U.S. 1 (1968), to conduct a protective search of a person who has already been legitimately stopped. Its ruling in this case concerns only an officer's authority to make the initial stop. The Court restated its ruling that an anonymous tip lacking indicia of reliability of the kind contemplated in *Adams v. Williams* and *Alabama v. White* does not justify a stop and frisk whenever and however it alleges the illegal possession of a firearm.

Illinois v. Wardlow, 528 U.S. 119 (2000). Uniformed officers A and B were driving the last car of a four-car caravan of officers who were converging on an area known for heavy drug trafficking to investigate drug transactions. They anticipated encountering a large number of people in the area, including drug customers and people serving as lookouts. Officer A saw the defendant standing next to a building and holding an opaque bag. The defendant looked in the direction of the officers and fled. Officers A and B turned their car, watched the defendant as he ran through a gangway and an alley, and eventually cornered him on the street. Officer A left his car and stopped the defendant. The Court ruled that these facts—the defendant's unprovoked flight on seeing the officers and his presence in an area of heavy drug trafficking—provided reasonable suspicion to stop the defendant to investigate criminal activity. *See also* United States v. Gordon, 231 F.3d 750 (11th Cir. 2000) (defendant's making eye contact with officer, thereafter moving quickly toward an adjacent car, entering that car, and then driving away in the opposite direction from the officers, coupled with the officers' knowledge of frequent unlawful activity in neighborhood where defendant had been standing, supported reasonable suspicion to stop defendant; court's ruling relied on *Wardlow* and stated that *headlong* flight is not always required—running or walking very quickly was sufficient in this case to establish unprovoked flight from the officers); United States v. Jordan, 232 F.3d 447 (5th Cir. 2000) (defendant's running at full sprint from grocery store in high crime area, while looking back over his shoulder, provided reasonable suspicion under *Wardlow* to make investigative stop for robbery of store).

Ornelas v. United States, 517 U.S. 690 (1996). The Court ruled that an appellate court must exercise de novo review of a trial court's determination of whether reasonable suspicion or probable cause existed. However, the court noted, an appellate court should review findings of historical fact (that is, the facts underlying the issue of the existence of reasonable suspicion or probable cause) only for clear error and should give due weight to inferences drawn from those facts by trial courts and law enforcement officers.

Alabama v. White, 496 U.S. 325 (1990). An officer received an anonymous phone call stating that Vanessa White would be leaving a specified apartment at a particular time in a brown Plymouth station wagon with a broken right taillight lens, and that she would be going to Dobey's Motel with an ounce of cocaine in a brown attaché case. This officer and another officer went to the specified building and saw a car of that description parked in front. The officers saw White leave the apartment building with nothing in her hands and get into the car. They followed it as White drove the most direct route to Dobey's Motel. The officers stopped the car when it was on the highway on which the motel was located.

The Court ruled that there was sufficient verification of the anonymous call to support reasonable suspicion to stop the vehicle. The Court noted that reasonable suspicion is a less demanding standard than probable cause, because reasonable suspicion may be established not only with information different in quantity or content than that for probable cause, but also with information less reliable than that for probable cause. In this case, the officers' independent corroboration of significant aspects of the anonymous caller's information gave some degree of reliability to the caller's allegations. In addition, the caller was able to predict White's future behavior (leaving her apartment, getting into the described car, and driving toward Dobey's Motel), which demonstrated the caller's familiarity with White's affairs. The Court concluded that the anonymous call, as corroborated, exhibited sufficient indicia of reliability to justify the investiga-

tory stop of White's car. *See also* State v. Maready, 362 N.C. 614 (2008) (witness was not completely anonymous informant because she provided information to officers through face-to-face encounter with them).

United States v. Sharpe, 470 U.S. 675 (1985). The Court stated that the following facts supported a conclusion that a drug agent had reasonable suspicion that the defendants were involved in marijuana trafficking: (1) he saw two vehicles traveling together for 20 miles in an area near the coast known to be frequented by drug traffickers; (2) the agent knew that pickup trucks with camper shells (one of the vehicles he was watching was such a truck) are often used to transport large quantities of marijuana; (3) the pickup truck appeared to be heavily loaded and the camper's windows were covered with a quilted material instead of curtains; and (4) both vehicles took evasive actions and started speeding when another officer began following them in his marked car.

United States v. Hensley, 469 U.S. 221 (1985). The informant supplied great detail about a robbery to a law enforcement agency, and her admission of tangential participation in the robbery established that she was sufficiently reliable and credible to supply reasonable suspicion that the defendant had driven the getaway car during a robbery. Therefore, the agency's "wanted flyer" for the defendant provided valid grounds to stop the defendant for further investigation.

United States v. Cortez, 449 U.S. 411 (1981). Border Patrol officers had reasonable suspicion to stop a vehicle to check for illegal aliens. The Court stated that reasonable suspicion is determined from the totality of circumstances based on evidence as it is perceived by law enforcement officers, and the suspicion must focus on criminal wrongdoing of the particular person being stopped. For other cases concerning border searches, see *United States v. Villamonte-Marquez*, 462 U.S. 579 (1983) (custom officer's boarding of vessel without reasonable suspicion was proper); *United States v. Martinez-Fuerte*, 428 U.S. 543 (1976) (stopping vehicles at permanent checkpoints without reasonable suspicion was proper); *United States v. Ortiz*, 422 U.S. 891 (1975) (conducting warrantless vehicle searches of cars without probable cause or consent at traffic checkpoints removed from the border and its functional equivalents was improper); *Almeida-Sanchez v. United States*, 413 U.S. 266 (1973) (roving patrol's conducting warrantless vehicle searches without probable cause or consent 20 miles from Mexican border was improper).

Brown v. Texas, 443 U.S. 47 (1979). Officers lacked reasonable suspicion of criminal activity to stop the defendant when they saw him and another person in an alley in an area where there was a high incidence of drug traffic; they had no reason to suspect any specific misconduct.

Delaware v. Prouse, 440 U.S. 648 (1979). The Court ruled that an officer had no authority to stop a car on a public highway to check the operator's driver's license or the car's registration when the officer had neither probable cause nor reasonable suspicion that the occupant was violating the law. The Court did not decide the legality of conducting supervised roadblocks or spot checks without reasonable suspicion. For later cases addressing highway checkpoints, see *Michigan Department of State Police v. Sitz*, 496 U.S. 444 (1990) (Court upheld impaired-driving highway checkpoint), *City of Indianapolis v. Edmond*, 531 U.S. 32 (2000) (recognizing statements in *Delaware v. Prouse* approving of driver's license checkpoints). See also the case summaries under "Conducting Impaired-Driving and Driver's License Checkpoints" on page 162.

United States v. Brignoni-Ponce, 422 U.S. 873 (1975). Except at the border or its functional equivalents, the Border Patrol must have reasonable suspicion to stop vehicles that may contain illegal aliens. The Court defined reasonable suspicion as follows: "[Officers] are aware of specific articulable facts, together with rational inferences from those facts, that reasonably warrant suspicion."

Adams v. Williams, 407 U.S. 143 (1972). An officer had authority to stop forcibly a person sitting in a car in a high crime area late at night when a person known to the officer told him that the occupant of the car was carrying narcotics and had a gun at his waist.

Peters v. New York, 392 U.S. 40 (1968). The Court ruled that an officer had probable cause to arrest the defendant for attempted burglary based on his own observations and the defendant's furtive actions, including fleeing from an apartment hallway. Justice Harlan's more persuasive concurring opinion stated that there was no probable cause to arrest, but the officer had reasonable suspicion to stop the defendant forcibly and frisk him.

Terry v. Ohio, 392 U.S. 1 (1968). The Court in *Terry* recognized the authority of law enforcement officers to stop and frisk suspects with less than probable cause; the Court's opinion did not articulate the standard, although it became known in later cases as "reasonable suspicion."

The opinion narrowly focused on the officer's proper frisk of the defendant for weapons based on evidence that he and an accomplice were about to rob a store. However, Justice Harlan's concurring opinion discussed the officer's right to make a forcible stop with articulable suspicion, which requires less evidence to establish than probable cause.

NORTH CAROLINA SUPREME COURT

State v. Jackson, 230 N.C. 113 (2015). Reversing the court of appeals, *State v. Jackson*, 234 N.C. App. 80 (2014), the court ruled that an officer had reasonable suspicion for an investigative stop, which occurred at approximately 9:00 p.m. in the vicinity of Kim's Mart. The officer knew that the immediate area had been the location of hundreds of drug investigations. Additionally, the officer personally had made drug arrests in the area and was aware that hand-to-hand drug transactions occurred there. The officer saw the defendant and another man standing outside of Kim's Mart. Upon spotting the officer in his patrol car, the two stopped talking and dispersed in opposite directions. In the officer's experience, this is typical behavior for individuals engaged in a drug transaction. The officer tried to follow the men, but lost them. When he returned to Kim's Mart, they were standing 20 feet from their original location. When the officer pulled in, the men again separated and started walking in opposite directions. The defendant was stopped and, as a result, contraband was found. The court ruled that these facts were sufficient to support reasonable suspicion to justify the investigatory stop. The court noted that its conclusion was based on more than the defendant's presence in a high crime and high drug area.

State v. Maready, 362 N.C. 614 (2008). A witness was not a completely anonymous informant because she provided information to officers through a face-to-face encounter with them. (A detailed summary of this case is provided under "Non-DWI Traffic Stops," below.)

State v. Campbell, 359 N.C. 644 (2005). An Aiken, South Carolina, law enforcement officer arrived at a Kmart parking lot in Aiken in response to an employee's report of a suspicious person (the defendant) whose car had been parked for three to four hours in the parking lot with the person inside the entire time. The employee pointed toward the car as it left the parking lot. The officer followed the car until it stopped at a convenience store. The defendant got out of the vehicle and started walking toward the store. The officer pulled behind the defendant's vehicle and stopped without activating a siren or blue lights. She asked the defendant if she could speak with him. He walked toward her and a conversation ensued. The defendant told her that he had been sleeping in the Kmart parking lot. He said that he had stopped in Aiken to take a nap, and he was driving home to North Carolina after finishing a job in Columbia, South Carolina. (Aiken is 45 miles west of Columbia.) Responding to the officer's request for his driver's license and car registration, the defendant said that he did not have any identification, but he told the officer his name and date of birth. He said that the car belonged to a friend, but he could not recall the friend's name. As a result of this conversation, the officer asked the defendant to "hold up and she would be back up with him." He was later arrested for driving without a license.

(1) The court ruled, relying on *Florida v. Bostick*, 501 U.S. 429 (1991), and other cases, that the defendant was not seized under the Fourth Amendment when the officer approached him and conversed with him about his presence in the Kmart parking lot and about his driver's license and car registration. (2) The court ruled, assuming arguendo that the defendant had been seized under the Fourth Amendment when the officer asked him to "hold up and she would be back up with him," that reasonable suspicion of criminal activity supported the seizure based on the following: the defendant's activity in the Kmart parking lot; his statement about going to North Carolina but stopping in Aiken, which is not on the route to North Carolina; and the defendant's not having a driver's license and not knowing the name of his friend to whom the car belonged.

State v. Hughes, 353 N.C. 200 (2000). On the morning of March 13, 1998, Officer A was sitting in Officer B's office when Officer B received a phone call. At the call's conclusion, Officer B told Officer A that he had been talking with a confidential, reliable informant who said that a dark-skinned Jamaican (nicknamed "Markie"), weighing more than 300 pounds, about six feet tall, between 20 and 30 years old, with a short haircut, clean cut, and wearing baggy pants, would be arriving in Jacksonville with marijuana and powdered cocaine in his possession on a bus coming from New York City, possibly the 5:30 p.m. bus. The informant also indicated that Markie "sometimes" came to Jacksonville on weekends before it got dark, that he "sometimes" took a taxi from the bus station, that he "sometimes" carried an overnight bag, and that he would

be headed to North Topsail Beach (quotations are from the court's opinion).

Later in the day, Officer A relayed this information by telephone to Officer C and told him to go to the bus station. At the suppression hearing, Officer C could not recall whether he had been given a description of the defendant's clothing, nor could he recall whether he ever had been given the suspect's nickname. Officer C also testified at the suppression hearing that he did not know what time the defendant would arrive in Jacksonville or on which bus, only that he was coming in that afternoon.

When Officer C and his partner, Officer D, reached the bus station, one bus from New York had already arrived, but a bus coming from Rocky Mount was scheduled to arrive around 5:30 p.m. Officer C testified at the suppression hearing that he knew that Rocky Mount was a transfer point between New York and Jacksonville. When the bus arrived, it pulled in with its door facing away from the officers, blocking their view of the arriving passengers so that they could not see whether the defendant stepped off the bus. Officer C testified, however, that the defendant was not in the parking lot before the bus arrived and that he had stepped from behind the bus after it arrived. The defendant matched the exact description Officer C had been given and was carrying an overnight bag.

The defendant immediately stepped into a taxi that went on Highway 17 South, toward an area called the Triangle, where Highway 17 splits in two directions—toward Wilmington and Topsail Beach or toward Richlands. A vehicle must pass through the Triangle before it can be determined in which direction the vehicle is going. However, the officers stopped the defendant's taxi before it reached the Triangle. The officers discovered marijuana and cocaine in the defendant's possession after they stopped the taxi.

The court ruled, distinguishing *Alabama v. White*, 496 U.S. 325 (1990), and relying on *Florida v. J.L.*, 529 U.S. 266 (1999), that this information was insufficient to establish reasonable suspicion to stop the defendant in the taxi to investigate illegal drugs. The court upheld the trial judge's findings of fact and ruling, which had granted the defendant's suppression motion. The court stated that the telephone call from a confidential, reliable informant to Officer B that was given to Officer A must be treated as anonymous information, because there was no evidence to support Officer B's statement that the informant was reliable. The court noted that Officer B did not testify at the suppression hearing and Officer A was not given any information by Officer B about the informant's reliability. The court also rejected the State's argument that the informant made a statement against penal interest under G.S. 14-225. The court determined that the anonymous information by itself was insufficient to support reasonable suspicion. The information did not contain the range of details required by *White* to sufficiently predict the defendant's future action but was instead peppered with uncertainties and generalities. The court also determined that the officers' corroboration of the information was insufficient to support reasonable suspicion. The court, relying on *J.L.*, found that reasonable suspicion did not arise merely from the fact that the person met the description given to the officers. The court noted that the officers stopped the taxi before it could be determined in which direction it was going.

State v. Fletcher, 348 N.C. 292 (1998). The defendant sought to suppress statements that he made as a result of an investigative stop and arrest for breaking and entering a motor vehicle in front of a beauty salon. Officer A received information from Witness A that about the time a car was broken into, a tall black male with dark pants and a white T-shirt had been acting suspiciously nearby (walking back and forth in front of the salon). Officer A also received information from Witness B that a black male with a white T-shirt had picked up a cement block and walked toward the beauty salon and then, moments later, had run down an alley. Officer B received a transmission from Officer A to be on the lookout for such a person, giving him the description from Witnesses A and B and the location where the suspect had been seen. Moments later, Officer B saw a person fitting this description within two blocks of the location; he stopped him and put him in a patrol car. Fifteen minutes had elapsed since the reporting of the crime.

The court ruled that reasonable suspicion supported the investigative stop of the defendant for breaking and entering a motor vehicle, based on the proximity in time and location and the accuracy of the physical description of the race, gender, and clothing of the suspect. The court cited *State v. Lovin*, 339 N.C. 695 (1995), *State v. Rinck*, 303 N.C. 551 (1981), and *State v. Buie*, 297 N.C. 159 (1979). The court noted that the record showed that the defendant sat in the patrol car for a short period of time, "several minutes," while the officers waited for Witness A to arrive to attempt to identify him. Witness A identified the defendant as the person she had seen in front of the beauty shop. The court ruled that her identification, in conjunction with Witness B's description, gave the officers probable cause to arrest the defendant for breaking and entering the motor vehicle. The court cited *State v. Wrenn*, 316 N.C. 141 (1986), *State v. Joyner*, 301 N.C. 18 (1980), *State v. Bright*, 301 N.C. 243 (1980), and *State v. Tippett*, 270 N.C. 588 (1967). The court also ruled that the length of time during the investigative stop had been reasonable under the Fourth Amendment.

State v. Odum, 343 N.C. 116 (1996). The court, per curiam and without an opinion, reversed the decision of the court of appeals, 119 N.C. App. 676 (1995), that affirmed the defendant's conviction. The court stated that the decision was reversed for the reasons stated in the dissenting opinion in the court of appeals.

Officers were working drug interdiction at the Raleigh train station. They had received information from a ticket agent that the defendant had purchased a train ticket with cash using small bills, had departed Raleigh for New York City on April 27, and was to return on the afternoon of April 29. The officers also learned that the defendant had previously been arrested for attempted robbery in New Jersey, although the charge had been dismissed. When the train arrived in Raleigh on April 29, the defendant left the train carrying a red nylon gym bag and appeared to be headed toward a car in the parking lot in which a female was sitting. The officers approached the defendant, showed him their badges, and asked him to answer a few questions. The defendant agreed to talk to them, and they moved over to the sidewalk. When asked to produce his train ticket, the defendant showed them his ticket stub bearing the name D. Odum (his name was David Odum). When asked for identification, the defendant became visibly nervous when he could not find his identification. When he looked into his gym bag for identification, one of the officers saw that the defendant was apparently trying to conceal the contents of the bag. The defendant finally told the officers that he could not find any identification. Although the defendant objected, the officers then seized his gym bag (to await a drug detection dog to sniff it). They told him he was free to leave and that if he left an address, they would have the bag delivered to him. During this conversation, the defendant informed the officers that the woman sitting in the car was his ride. One officer testified at the suppression hearing that the woman neither spoke nor made eye contact with the defendant during the entire questioning.

The dissenting opinion concluded that reasonable suspicion did not exist to support the seizure of the gym bag. The evidence as a whole could easily be associated with many travelers. Many travelers daily embark on trips similar to the defendant's, and the fact that the defendant paid for his ticket in cash was not remarkable, considering the price was $107. The opinion noted that one officer testified that there was no evidence that the defendant had any prior involvement with drugs, and the prior robbery charge that was later dismissed was not a sufficient reflection of a person's propensity to be involved in drug trafficking.

The opinion also noted that one of the officers testified that the defendant did not give him any false information during the interaction at the train station. The officers never inquired about the nature of the defendant's trip, nor was there evidence of any questions that might have bolstered their suspicions. Although the defendant became visibly nervous when he could not find his identification, the opinion noted that it is not uncommon for a person to appear nervous when approached by a law enforcement officer. Also, the actions of the woman in the car and the defendant's reluctance to let the officers see what was in his bag did not provide reasonable suspicion.

State v. Lovin, 339 N.C. 695 (1995). The murder victim's body was discovered in the afternoon, and the victim's Porsche was reported missing. At 4:00 p.m. a person saw a Porsche that matched the description of the victim's car being driven by a male with a lot of hair, a gold watch, and large-frame glasses. She followed it until it turned toward the airport and then reported this information to a law enforcement agency. Officers went to the airport and found that the hood of the Porsche was still warm. A ticket agent reported that the defendant was acting suspiciously at the ticket counter. She described him as having long brown hair and wearing a gold watch. The court ruled that this and other information in the officers' possession provided reasonable suspicion to make an investigative stop of the defendant to investigate the murder.

State v. Watkins, 337 N.C. 437 (1994). An officer received a transmission on an official radio frequency stating that there was a "10-50" (suspicious vehicle) behind a well-drilling company. The officer arrived there and got out of his car. He saw a car with its lights off moving out of the company parking lot. It was 3:00 a.m., the area was generally rural, and the location was a business that the officer knew was normally closed at that hour. The officer got in his car and stopped the car on the highway. The court ruled, based on these facts and the comparable cases of *State v. Fox*, 58 N.C. App. 692 (1982),

aff'd per curiam, 307 N.C. 460 (1983); and *State v. Tillett*, 50 N.C. App. 520 (1981); that the officer had a reasonable suspicion to stop the car. The court noted, citing *Alabama v. White*, 496 U.S. 325 (1990), that an anonymous tip may provide reasonable suspicion when corroborated by independent law enforcement work. [Author's note: See the later case of *State v. Watkins*, 120 N.C. App. 804 (1995), discussed below.]

State v. Butler, 331 N.C. 227 (1992). The court upheld an officer's stop and frisk of a drug suspect, citing these factors: (1) the officer saw the defendant in the midst of a group of people congregated on a corner known as a "drug hole"; (2) the officer had watched the corner daily for several months; (3) the officer knew the corner was a center of drug activity because he had made four to six drug-related arrests there in the past six months; (4) the officer was aware of other arrests there as well; (5) the defendant was a stranger to the officer; (6) when the defendant made eye contact with uniformed officers, he immediately left the corner and walked away, behavior that is evidence of flight; and (7) the officer's experience was that people involved in drug traffic are often armed. The court stated that, in considering the legality of the frisk, the officer was entitled to formulate "common-sense conclusions" about "the modes or patterns of operation of certain kinds of lawbreakers" (citing *United States v. Cortez*, 449 U.S. 411 (1981)) in concluding that the defendant, reasonably suspected of drug trafficking, might be armed.

State v. Jones, 304 N.C. 323 (1981). Reasonable suspicion existed to stop the defendant, who was walking late at night with a brown paper bag in his hand from a closed convenience store toward an unoccupied car that was on the highway with its lights off and its motor running.

State v. Rinck, 303 N.C. 551 (1981). Reasonable suspicion existed to stop two men walking along a road late at night within 200 feet of a home where a homicide had occurred about 30 minutes earlier.

State v. Buie, 297 N.C. 159 (1979). Reasonable suspicion existed to stop the defendant, who generally fit the victim's description of the burglar, was near the crime scene shortly after the crime, and looked as if he had been running.

State v. Thompson, 296 N.C. 703 (1979). Officers had reasonable suspicion to stop and detain the occupants of a van parked near Fort Fisher in the public parking area at 12:30 a.m., because officers were aware that break-ins by persons using a van had been reported recently in the area. The court's finding of reasonable suspicion would have had more support if the facts had shown how recently the break-ins had occurred. The dissenting opinion noted that evidence did not link this particular van—or even one fitting its description—to the break-ins. The court noted that whether a seizure had occurred was problematic and assumed, for the purpose of deciding the case, that it had. [Author's note: If the majority had analyzed whether a seizure had occurred, it probably would have concluded that the officer did not seize the occupants. Therefore, the officer's initial actions need not be supported by reasonable suspicion or other justification.]

State v. McZorn, 288 N.C. 417 (1975). A reliable informant's information was sufficient to support a stop of a green Chevrolet Vega to investigate whether the driver was involved in a murder and armed robbery. The informant had told the officer less than an hour before the vehicle stop that the defendant had been at a "beer joint," was driving a 1974 green Chevrolet Vega, and had a .38 caliber revolver in his inside pocket that had been used to kill a person during a robbery that the defendant and another man had committed.

NORTH CAROLINA COURT OF APPEALS

State v. Sawyers, ___ N.C. App. ___, 768 S.E.2d 753 (2016). (1) The court ruled that an investigative stop of the defendant's vehicle was justified by reasonable suspicion. While on patrol in the early morning, an officer saw the defendant walking down a street. Directly behind him was another male, who appeared to be dragging a drugged or intoxicated female. The defendant and the other male placed the female in the defendant's vehicle, entered it, and drove away. The officer was unsure whether the female was being kidnapped or was in danger. Given these circumstances, the officer had reasonable suspicion that the defendant was involved in criminal activity. (2) The court alternatively upheld the stop based on the community caretaking doctrine; see *State v. Smathers*, 232 N.C. App. 120 (2014). The officer was attempting to ensure the female's safety, and the public need to seize the defendant by an investigative stop of the vehicle outweighed his privacy interest in being free from the intrusion.

State v. Crandell, ___ N.C. App. ___, 786 S.E.2d 789 (2016). The court ruled that reasonable suspicion supported the stop of the defendant's vehicle. The vehicle was stopped after the defendant left premises known as "Blazing Saddles." Based on his experience making almost two dozen arrests in connection with drug activity at Blazing

Saddles and on other officers' experiences there, an officer was aware of a steady pattern by people involved in drug transactions who would visit Blazing Saddles when the gate to the premises was down and stayed down for approximately two minutes. The defendant followed this exact pattern: he visited Blazing Saddles when the gate was down and stayed approximately two minutes. The court distinguished these facts from those when a defendant was simply observed in a high drug area, noting that Blazing Saddles was a "notorious" location for selling drugs and dealing in stolen property. It was an abandoned, partially burned building with no electricity, and there was no apparent legal reason for anyone to go there at all, unlike neighborhoods in high drug or crime areas where people live and naturally would be present.

State v. Travis, ___ N.C. App. ___, 781 S.E.2d 674 (2016). The court ruled that an officer had reasonable suspicion to stop a vehicle to investigate for a drug offense. The officer was in an unmarked patrol vehicle in the parking lot of a local post office and saw the defendant pull into the lot. The officer knew the defendant because he had previously worked for the officer as an informant and had executed controlled buys. When the defendant pulled up to the passenger side of another vehicle, the passenger of the other vehicle rolled down his window. The officer saw the defendant and the passenger extend their arms to one another and touch hands. The vehicles then left the premises. The entire episode lasted less than a minute, with no one from either vehicle entering the post office. The area in question was not known to be a crime area. Based on his training and experience, the officer believed that he had witnessed a hand-to-hand drug transaction, and he stopped the defendant's vehicle. Based on items found during the search of the vehicle, the defendant was charged with drug crimes. The trial court denied the defendant's motion to suppress. Although it found the case to be a "close" one, the court found that reasonable suspicion supported the stop. Noting that it had previously ruled that reasonable suspicion supported a stop when officers witnessed acts that they believed to be drug transactions, the court acknowledged that the present facts differed from those earlier cases; specifically, that the transaction in question occurred in daylight in an area that was not known for drug activity. Also, because there was no indication that the defendant was aware of the officer's presence, there was no evidence that he displayed signs of nervousness or took evasive action to avoid the officer. However, the court concluded that reasonable suspicion existed. It noted that the actions of the defendant and the occupant of the other car "may or may not have appeared suspicious to a layperson," but they were sufficient to permit a reasonable inference by a trained officer that a drug transaction had occurred. The court thought it significant that the officer recognized the defendant and had past experience with him as an informant in connection with controlled drug transactions. Finally, the court noted that a determination that reasonable suspicion exists need not rule out the possibility of innocent conduct.

State v. Sutton, 232 N.C. App. 667 (2014). The court ruled that an officer had reasonable suspicion to stop and frisk the defendant when the defendant was in a high crime area and made movements that the officer found suspicious. The defendant was in a public housing area patrolled by a Special Response Unit of the United States Marshals Service and the Drug Enforcement Administration concentrating on violent crimes and gun crimes. The officer in question had 10 years of experience and was assigned to the Special Response Unit. Many people were banned from the public housing area—in fact, the banned list was nine pages long. On a prior occasion, the officer heard shots fired near the area. In the present case, the officer saw the defendant walking normally while swinging his arms. When the defendant turned and "used his right hand to grab his waistband to clinch an item" after looking directly at the officer, the officer believed that the defendant was trying to hide something on his body. The officer then stopped the defendant to identify him, frisked him, and found a gun in the defendant's waistband.

State v. Blankenship, 230 N.C. App. 113 (2013). The court ruled that officers did not have reasonable suspicion to stop the defendant based on an anonymous tip from a taxicab driver. The taxicab driver anonymously contacted 911 by cell phone and reported that a red Mustang convertible with a black soft top, license plate XXT-9756, was driving erratically, running over traffic cones, and continuing west on a specified road. Although the 911 operator did not ask for the caller's name, the operator used the caller's cell phone number to later identify the taxicab driver as John Hutchby. The 911 call resulted in a "be on the lookout" being issued; minutes later officers spotted a red Mustang matching the caller's description, with "X" in the license plate, heading in the direction indicated by the caller. Although the officers did not observe the defendant violating any traffic laws or see evidence of improper driving that would suggest impair-

ment, the officers stopped the defendant. The defendant was charged with DWI.

The court stated:

> [T]he officers did not have the opportunity to judge Hutchby's credibility firsthand or confirm whether the tip was reliable, because Hutchby had not been previously used and the officers did not meet him face-to-face. Since the officers did not have an opportunity to assess his credibility, Hutchby was an anonymous informant. Therefore, to justify a warrantless search and seizure, either the tip must have possessed sufficient indicia of reliability or the officers must have corroborated the tip.

The court found that neither requirement was satisfied.

[Author's note: The later ruling in *Navarette v. California*, 134 S. Ct. 1683 (2014) (anonymous caller's report provided reasonable suspicion for vehicle stop), summarized above, raises questions about the continuing validity of the *Blankenship* ruling.]

State v. Knudsen, 229 N.C. App. 271 (2013). The court ruled that the trial court did not err by concluding that the seizure of the defendant by officers blocking the sidewalk on which he was walking was unsupported by reasonable suspicion. The officers observed the defendant walking down the sidewalk with a clear plastic cup in his hands filled with a clear liquid. The defendant entered his vehicle, remained in it for a period of time, and then exited his vehicle and began walking down the sidewalk, where he was stopped. The officers stopped and questioned the defendant because he was walking on the sidewalk with the cup and the officers wanted to know what was in the cup.

State v. Harwood, 221 N.C. App. 451 (2012). The court ruled that reasonable suspicion did not support the seizure of the defendant made as a result of an anonymous tip. When evaluating an anonymous tip in this context, the court must determine whether the tip taken as a whole possessed sufficient indicia of reliability. If not, the court must assess whether the anonymous tip could be made sufficiently reliable by independent corroboration. The tip at issue reported that the defendant would be selling marijuana at a certain location on a certain day and would be driving a white vehicle. The court ruled that given the limited details contained in the tip and the officers' failure to corroborate its allegations of illegal activity, the tip lacked sufficient indicia of reliability.

State v. Watkins, 220 N.C. App. 384 (2012). The court ruled that officers had reasonable suspicion to stop the defendant's vehicle. Officers had received an anonymous tip that a vehicle containing "a large amount of pills and drugs" would be traveling from Georgia through Macon County and possibly Graham County; the vehicle was described as a small- or mid-sized passenger car, maroon or purple in color, with Georgia license plates. Officers set up surveillance along the most likely route. When a small purple car passed the officers, they pulled out behind it. The car then made an abrupt lane change without signaling and slowed down by approximately 5–10 m.p.h. The officers ran the vehicle's license plate and discovered that the vehicle was registered to a person known to have outstanding arrest warrants. Although the officers were fairly certain that the driver was not the wanted person, they were unable to identify the passenger. They also saw the driver repeatedly looking in his rearview mirror and glancing over his shoulder. They then pulled the vehicle over. The court concluded that the defendant's lane change, the anonymous tip, and the defendant's other activities were sufficient to give an experienced law enforcement officer reasonable suspicion that some illegal activity was taking place. Those other activities included the defendant's slow speed in the passing lane, frequent glances in his rearview mirrors, repeated glances over his shoulder, and driving a car registered to another person. Moreover, noted the court, not only was the defendant not the owner of the vehicle, but the owner was known to have outstanding arrest warrants. It was reasonable to conclude that the unidentified passenger may have been the vehicle's owner.

State v. Hemphill, 219 N.C. App. 50 (2012). The court ruled that an officer had reasonable suspicion that criminal activity was occurring to make an investigative stop of the defendant. At 10:10 p.m. the officer learned of a report of suspicious activity involving two men at used car lot Auto America. When the officer arrived at the scene, he saw the defendant, who generally matched the description of one of the individuals reported, peering from behind a parked van. When the defendant spotted the officer, he ran, ignoring the officer's instructions to stop. After a 1/8-mile chase, the officer found the defendant trying to hide behind a dumpster.

State v. Brown, 217 N.C. App. 566 (2011). The court of appeals ruled that the trial court erred by denying the defendant's motion to suppress evidence of his alleged impairment when the evidence was the fruit of an illegal stop. An officer who was surveying an area in the hope of locating robbery suspects saw the defendant pull off to the side of a highway in a wooded area. The officer heard yelling and car doors slamming. Shortly thereafter, the defendant accelerated rapidly past the officer, but not to a speed warranting a stop for a traffic violation. Thinking that the defendant may have been picking up the robbery suspects, the officer followed the defendant for almost a mile. Although he observed no traffic violations, the officer pulled over the defendant's vehicle. The officer did not have any information regarding the direction in which the suspects fled, nor did he have a description of the getaway vehicle. The officer's reason for pulling over the defendant's vehicle was insufficient evidence of reasonable suspicion to support an investigative stop.

State v. White, 214 N.C. App. 471 (2011). The court of appeals ruled that the trial court erred by denying the defendant's motion to suppress evidence obtained from an unlawful stop. Officers responded to a complaint of loud music in a location they regarded as a high crime area. The officers did not see the defendant engaged in any suspicious activity, nor did they observe any device capable of producing loud music. Rather, the defendant was merely standing outside at night, with two or three other men. These facts did not provide reasonable suspicion to justify an investigatory stop of the defendant. Thus, the officer's encounter with the defendant was entirely consensual; the defendant was free to ignore the interaction by running away, which he did. Once the officer caught up with the defendant and handcuffed him for resisting arrest, a seizure occurred. However, because the defendant's flight from the consensual encounter did not constitute resisting, the arrest was improper.

State v. Ellison, 213 N.C. App. 300 (2011), *aff'd on other grounds*, 366 N.C. 439 (2013). The court ruled that an officer had reasonable suspicion to stop the defendant's vehicle. An informant told the officer that after having his prescriptions for hydrocodone and Xanax filled, a man named Shaw would immediately take the medications to defendant Treadway's residence, where he would sell the medications to Treadway. Treadway then sold some or all of the medications to defendant Ellison. The officer later learned that Shaw had prescriptions for Lorcet and Xanax, observed Shaw fill the prescriptions, and followed Shaw from the pharmacy to Treadway's residence. The officer watched Shaw enter and leave Treadway's residence. Minutes later the officer observed Ellison arrive. In stopping Ellison's vehicle, the officer also considered activities derived from surveillance at his place of work, which were consistent with drug-related activities. Although the officer had not had contact with the informant before this incident, one of his co-workers had worked with the informant and found the informant to be reliable—specifically, the informant had previously provided information that resulted in arrests.

State v. Brown, 213 N.C. App. 617 (2011). The court ruled that officers had reasonable suspicion to stop the defendant. When officers on a gang patrol noticed activity at a particular house, they parked their car to observe. The area was known for criminal activity. The defendant exited from the rear of the house and approached the officers' car. One of the officers had previously made drug arrests in front of this house. As the defendant approached, one officer feared for his safety and got out of the car to have a better defensive position. When the defendant realized that the individuals were police officers, his "demeanor changed" and he appeared very nervous: he started to sweat, began stuttering, and would not speak loudly. Additionally, it was late and there was little light for the officers to see the defendant's actions.

In re A.J. M-B, 212 N.C. App. 586 (2011). The court of appeals ruled that the trial court erred by denying the juvenile's motion to dismiss a charge of resisting a public officer when reasonable suspicion did not support a stop of the juvenile for criminal activity. An anonymous caller reported to law enforcement that "two juveniles in Charlie district . . . [were] walking, supposedly with a shotgun or a rifle" in "an open field behind a residence." A dispatcher relayed the information to an officer, who went to an open field behind the residence. The officer saw two juveniles "pop their heads out of the wood line" and look at him. Neither was carrying a firearm. When the officer called out for them to stop, they ran around the residence and down the road.

State v. Chlopek, 209 N.C. App. 358 (2011). The court ruled that an officer lacked reasonable suspicion to stop the defendant's vehicle. Around midnight, officers were conducting a traffic stop at Olde Waverly Place, a partially developed subdivision. While doing so, an officer noticed the defendant's construction vehicle enter the subdivision and proceed to an undeveloped section. Although officers had been put on notice of copper thefts from subdivisions under construction in the county, no such thefts had been reported in Olde Waverly Place. When the defendant exited the subdivision 20 to 30 minutes later, his vehicle was stopped. The officer did not articulate any specific facts about the vehicle or how it was driven that would justify the stop; the fact that there had been numerous copper thefts in the county did not support the stop.

State v. Huey, 204 N.C. App. 513 (2010). An officer was looking for two robbery suspects. The State stipulated at the suppression hearing that the officer knew the suspects were black males about 18 years old and that one suspect was wearing a light-colored hoodie and the other was wearing a darker hoodie. An officer stopped the defendant, who was wearing a light-colored hoodie. The defendant presented a North Carolina identification card, which revealed that he was 51 years old. The officer then ran a warrant check and arrested him on an outstanding arrest warrant. (Although the officer testified at the suppression hearing that he learned that the suspects were about 18 years old only after he discovered the defendant's outstanding arrest warrant, the court ruled that the trial court was bound by the State's stipulation.) Even if the officer could not have known the defendant's age when he initially saw the defendant with his hoodie on, he should have been able to recognize that the defendant was much older than 18 years of age when face-to-face with him. In any event, the court stated that as soon as the defendant provided his identification card with his birth date, the officer knew that the defendant did not match the descriptions of the suspects, and at that point the investigative stop should have ended because reasonable suspicion did not exist.

State v. Johnson, 204 N.C. App. 259 (2010). An anonymous caller at 12:14 p.m. reported that a black male wearing a white T-shirt and blue shorts was selling illegal drugs and guns at the corner of Pitts and Birch streets in the Happy Hill Garden community. The caller said that the sales were occurring out of a blue Mitsubishi with a license plate of WT 3456. The caller refused to provide a name, and officers could not contact the caller. The officers did not know how the caller obtained his or her information. The caller telephoned again at 12:32 p.m. and stated that the suspect had just left the area but would return shortly. Officers were stationed at the only two entrance points to the community. They saw a blue Mitsubishi with a license plate of WT 3453 being driven by a black male wearing a white T-shirt. An officer entered the license plate information into his computer, which revealed that the vehicle was registered to a Kelvin Johnson, black male, date of birth August 5, 1964. It also showed that Johnson's driver's license was suspended. Officers stopped the vehicle, arrested the defendant for driving while license revoked, placed him in the back of a patrol car, and searched the defendant's vehicle incident to his arrest.

(1) The court ruled, relying on *State v. Hughes*, 353 N.C. 200 (2000), and *State v. Peele*, 196 N.C. App. 668 (2009), that the anonymous information was insufficient evidence to support reasonable suspicion to stop the defendant's vehicle. The court stated that when an anonymous tip forms the basis for a traffic stop, the tip itself must exhibit sufficient indicia of reliability, or it must be buttressed by sufficient law enforcement corroboration. The court examined the facts and concluded that neither ground was satisfied. (2) The court ruled that even though the anonymous tip did not support the vehicle stop, the officers had reasonable suspicion to stop the vehicle based on their knowledge that the registered owner's driver's license was suspended. [Author's note: Although not cited by the court, see *State v. Hess*, 185 N.C. App. 530 (2007) (when officer ran vehicle's registration plate and then registered owner's driver's license, which was reported to be suspended, officer had reasonable suspicion to stop vehicle when there was no evidence that owner was not driving vehicle).]

State v. Crowell, 204 N.C. App. 362 (2010). A confidential informant phoned an officer and said that a black male with cocaine would arrive in a few minutes in a black Lexus SUV at a car wash on Highway 301 in Benson. The informant said that he had seen the cocaine. The officer had known the informant for 13 years and knew his mother and other family members. A month before this phone call, the informant had provided the officer with reliable information about illegal drug activity that resulted in an arrest. Fifteen minutes after the phone call, a black Lexus SUV pulled into the car wash and parked. The informant was also at the car wash, and he called the officer to confirm that the black Lexus SUV was the correct one and the defendant was the driver. Officers stopped the vehicle after it left the car wash. The court ruled that the officers had reasonable suspicion to stop the vehicle based on the confidential informant's information. The court noted that the informant's basis of knowledge was not an essential factor under the totality of circumstances test for determining reasonable suspicion (or probable cause). The informant's information correctly predicted the defendant's future actions, including his mode of transportation, destination, and time of arrival. This information, corroborated by the officers, sufficiently demonstrated that the informant had inside knowledge about the defendant, giving the officers a basis for believing that the rest of his information concerning the defendant's transportation of cocaine was also accurate.

State v. Mello, 200 N.C. App. 437 (2009), *aff'd*, 364 N.C. 421 (2010). The court ruled, relying on *State v. Butler*, 331 N.C. 227 (1992), that the following facts established reasonable suspicion to stop a vehicle to investigate an apparent drug transaction between the vehicle occupants and two pedestrians. An officer in a vehicle was patrolling a well-known drug location where he had previously made drug-related arrests. He saw two pedestrians approach a vehicle and put their hands into it. The officer did not know the vehicle driver but recognized the two pedestrians, although he did not know their names or whether he had previously arrested them. As the officer drove closer, the two pedestrians fled and the vehicle drove away in the opposite direction from the officer's vehicle. The court stated that the officer could reasonably have construed the facts to indicate that a hand-to-hand drug transaction had occurred.

State v. Garcia, 197 N.C. App. 522 (2009). A detective received information in May 2007 and on July 7, 2007, from an anonymous confidential informant that marijuana was being kept in a storage shed at a house at 338 Barnes Road and that the defendant was the seller of the marijuana. After searching the defendant's name on a law enforcement database, the detective found his picture and information that he lived at that address and had a lengthy history of police contact, including suspicion of drug and firearms offenses. Surveillance on July 26, 2007, at the house revealed two men who left and returned several times to the residence in a black BMW. The detective thought one of the men was the defendant. She also saw both men emerge from the area near the shed and enter the BMW. One of them had a black bag with large handles. Other officers who received this information from the detective followed the BMW to a place that was a known drug area. Two people (not the two who were in the BMW) fled when an officer told them he was an officer. Both men who arrived in the BMW, one of whom was the defendant, were placed in handcuffs. The court ruled, distinguishing *State v. Hughes*, 353 N.C. 200 (2000), that the officers had reasonable suspicion of the defendant's selling marijuana to make an investigative stop, based on the information from the anonymous confidential informant and the officers' corroboration of that information.

State v. Allen, 197 N.C. App. 208 (2009). An officer responded to an assault call from a motel at about 3:30 a.m. The victim told the officer that the suspect was a tall white male who left in a small dark car driven by a white female with blonde hair. The officer looked in the vicinity for about 10 minutes and then saw a small, light-colored vehicle operated by a white female with blonde hair driving away from the motel. The officer saw the vehicle enter the center turn lane and make an abrupt left turn into a parking lot and drive hastily over rough pavement. The driver was outside the vehicle when the officer approached. The officer saw a person in the passenger seat but could not determine whether the passenger was male or female. The officer directed the driver to come to his vehicle so that he could ask her questions about the assault. She was eventually arrested for DWI. The court ruled, relying on *State v. Allison*, 148 N.C. App. 702 (2002), and distinguishing *State v. Hughes*, 353 N.C. 200 (2000), that the officer had reasonable suspicion to conduct an investigatory stop based on the information supplied by the assault victim and the officer's observations. The court stated that although the record did not reveal the victim's name or give details about the victim's encounter with the officer, a face-to-face encounter with a crime victim affords a higher degree of reliability than an anonymous telephone call. In addition to the victim's information, the officer saw the driver's hurried actions, which indicated that the driver was trying to avoid him. In addition, the car was near the area in which the assault had occurred. The fact that the car was light colored and not dark colored as described by the victim did not detract from a finding of reasonable suspicion under all the circumstances.

State v. Williams, 195 N.C. App. 554 (2009). An officer heard a radio report of an armed robbery that had just occurred at a Hispanic store. Due to language barriers between the victims and law enforcement officers, there were two conflicting descriptions of the robber. The first described him as a white male wearing a hood and gloves and carrying a silver firearm. The second described him as an African American male about six feet tall with a medium build, wearing a green hooded jacket and gloves and carrying a silver gun. Just minutes later, the officer saw the defendant—an African American male approximately six feet tall with a medium build—a block or two from the robbery location, walking in the same direction that the robber was reportedly traveling, although he was walking down the middle of the street blocking traffic. The defendant was wearing a "blue-green" jacket made of a material that changed colors. He had his hands in his pockets, his hood was up, and he was wearing wraparound glasses. The officer approached the defendant and asked him to take his hands out of his pockets. The defendant stopped walking, kept his hands in his pockets, and did not say anything. After again being ordered to show his hands, the defendant took them out but also started to empty his pockets. As he was doing so, the officer saw the top of a plastic baggie in one of the pockets. When the officer frisked the defendant, he patted the defendant's front pocket and felt something hard to the touch, round, and possibly a quarter of an inch thick. Based on its feel, the officer believed the object to be a crack cookie and removed it. The court ruled, distinguishing *State v. Cooper*, 186 N.C. App. 100 (2007), that the officer had reasonable suspicion to make an investigative stop of the defendant for armed robbery and to frisk him for weapons.

State v. Hudgins, 195 N.C. App. 430 (2009). An officer received a call from dispatch at approximately 2:55 a.m. informing him that a man (hereafter, the caller) was driving his car and being followed by another vehicle. The caller did not identify himself but stated that he was being followed by a man armed with a gun in the vicinity of a specified intersection in Greensboro. The caller described the vehicle by make, model, and color and provided updates on its location. The officer advised the dispatcher to direct the caller to Market Street so that he could intercept the vehicles. The officer arrived there and saw the two vehicles at a red light. The officer activated his lights and siren, which caused both vehicles to stop, and approached the vehicle that was following the caller. The caller did not identify himself but exited his vehicle and identified the driver of the other vehicle as the man who had been following him. The officer removed the defendant from his car. The court ruled, relying on *State v. Maready*, 362 N.C. 614 (2008), that the officer had reasonable suspicion of criminal activity to stop the defendant's vehicle because (1) the caller telephoned police and remained on the telephone for about eight minutes; (2) the caller provided specific information about the vehicle following him and the location; (3) the caller carefully followed the instructions of the dispatcher, which allowed the officer to intercept the vehicles; (4) the defendant followed the caller over a peculiar and circuitous route that doubled back on itself, going in and out of residential areas between 2:00 a.m. and 3:00 a.m.; (5) the caller remained on the scene long enough to identify the defendant to the officer; and (6) by calling on a cell phone and remaining at the scene, the caller placed his anonymity at risk.

State v. Murray, 192 N.C. App. 684 (2008). An officer was performing a property check in an industrial park at 3:41 a.m. He saw a vehicle coming out of the area and decided to pull behind it and run its license plate to determine if it was a local vehicle. The officer conceded at the suppression hearing that the vehicle was not violating any traffic laws; was not trespassing, speeding, or making any erratic movements; and was on a public street. The license plate check showed that the vehicle was not stolen and was in fact a rental vehicle from a nearby city. Nevertheless, the officer stopped the vehicle. The court ruled that reasonable suspicion did not support the stop. Although the officer's patrol of the area was part of increased policing due to past break-ins, he saw no indication that night of damage to vehicles or businesses in the park and stopped the vehicle because he wanted to make sure there wasn't anything illegal taking place.

State v. Campbell, 188 N.C. App. 701 (2008). At approximately 3:40 a.m., Officer A responded to a report of a breaking and entering in progress at a residence. While driving to the residence (he arrived within three minutes of the report), the officer saw the defendant riding a bicycle on a road that was near the reported break-in (about a quarter-mile). The officer did not see anyone else in the vicinity. The officer continued to the dwelling without making any contact with the bicyclist. He saw that a window had been opened with a small, flathead screwdriver or a pry tool and he notified other officers of that information. Officer B, aware of Officer A's report about the bicyclist and the break-in, including the type of instrument that may have been used, eventually stopped the defendant, who had a backpack and was playing with something inside it. Officer C arrived and recognized the defendant as having an extensive history of breaking and entering as well as being a substance abuser. Officer B handcuffed the defendant and frisked him. A small flashlight and a Swiss Army–type knife were found in the defendant's pockets. The defendant was then arrested. The court ruled that Officer B had reasonable suspicion to stop the defendant, noting the defendant's proximity to the break-in, the time of day, and the absence of other people in the area.

State v. Hayes, 188 N.C. App. 313 (2008). An officer saw the defendant and his companion driving on a Sunday afternoon in an area where several prior drug-related

arrests had been made. They got out of the car and walked back and forth along a nearby sidewalk. The officer looked in the car and saw a gun under the seat where the companion had been sitting. The officer did not know anything about the defendant and his companion and did not believe that either man lived in the neighborhood. The court ruled, relying on *State v. Fleming*, 106 N.C. App. 165 (1992), that an officer did not have reasonable suspicion to make an investigative stop of the defendant.

State v. Cooper, 186 N.C. App. 100 (2007). During the late afternoon, a law enforcement officer heard a radio report that an armed robbery had been committed at a convenience store. The robber was described as a black male. The officer also heard over the radio that another officer had seen a black male walking on Lake Ridge Drive shortly after the robbery. The officer turned onto Deanna Drive to begin a sweep of the area. The robber had reportedly left the rear of the store, heading in the general direction of the area the officer was searching. The officer knew that there was a path running from the store through woods to Lake Ridge Drive. The officer approached the intersection of Deanna Drive and Lake Ridge Drive approximately five minutes after the robbery. The officer saw a black male near the point where the path exited onto Lake Ridge Drive. From the time the officer turned off Capital Boulevard until this point, the officer had seen no one else. He drove closer to the black male and motioned him to approach his car. In response, the defendant walked over to the car. The officer conducted a stop and frisk of the black male. The court ruled that the officer did not have reasonable suspicion to stop and frisk the defendant for the armed robbery. (See the court's discussion of the case law on this issue.)

State v. Blackstock, 165 N.C. App. 50 (2004). The court ruled, citing *State v. Fox*, 58 N.C. App. 692 (1982), *aff'd per curiam*, 307 N.C. 460 (1983), *State v. Tillett*, 50 N.C. App. 520 (1981), and other cases, that officers had reasonable suspicion to make an investigative stop of a vehicle. The court noted that two people wearing dark clothing (one of whom was the defendant) were observed loitering at a closed shopping center shortly before midnight in an area targeted by law enforcement officers as a high crime area. No other vehicles were in the shopping center parking lot. When a vehicle, which the two people may have recognized as a law enforcement vehicle, appeared, the men abruptly and hurriedly returned to their vehicle, which was parked out of general public view, and departed. Once in the vehicle, the passenger turned and looked behind as if trying to determine the identity of the officers following them. The court concluded that these cumulative factors, together with the other detailed findings by the trial judge, adequately supported the officers' reasonable belief that the two people were involved in criminal activity.

State v. Edwards, 164 N.C. App. 130 (2004). Suspecting that the defendant had committed sexual assaults on females on December 23, 2000, and December 26, 2000, based on information gathered from the victims, officers placed him under surveillance. On January 9, 2001, evidence from surveillance at about 2:50 a.m. indicated that the defendant's car had left his residence and was traveling toward a nearby town. About 4:00 a.m. officers heard an alert tone from that town's police that a female had been sexually assaulted by a person with a handgun whose general description met the defendant's. Officers saw no other vehicles on the road that night other than patrol cars (it was snowing). The defendant's vehicle then passed an officer's vehicle; it was coming from the other town and heading toward the defendant's residence. The officers stopped the defendant's vehicle. The defendant immediately put both of his hands underneath his seat and jumped out of the vehicle. Officers had to draw their weapons on the defendant because he failed to comply with their orders. After handcuffing the defendant, one of the officers searched under the front seat of the defendant's vehicle for a weapon and found a handgun.

(1) The court ruled that the officers had reasonable suspicion to stop the defendant to investigate the recent sexual assault. The court noted that the officers also had authority to stop the vehicle because it had an expired Illinois registration plate. (2) The court ruled that the officer had the authority to make a protective search of the defendant's vehicle for a weapon under *Michigan v. Long*, 463 U.S. 1032 (1983).

State v. McArn, 159 N.C. App. 209 (2003). An anonymous caller reported to a police department that a white Nissan vehicle at a specified location was involved in the sale of illegal drugs. Based on this information, and with no additional corroboration of the anonymous caller's information, an officer stopped the vehicle. The court ruled, relying on *State v. Hughes*, 353 N.C. 200 (2000), and other cases, that the officer did not have reasonable suspicion to make an investigative stop of the vehicle.

State v. Martinez, 158 N.C. App. 105 (2003). The court ruled that reasonable suspicion supported an officer's investigative stop of a vehicle for possible criminal activity. At 2:00 a.m., Officer A was on routine patrol in a marked vehicle when he saw and drove past a male pedestrian. The officer immediately turned around and pulled over on the side of the road behind the pedestrian. Upon seeing the officer, the pedestrian ran toward the woods in the direction of a mobile home park. About four minutes later, while the officer was driving through the mobile home park in an unsuccessful attempt to locate the pedestrian, Officer B contacted Officer A by radio and informed him that there was a motor vehicle parked on the right shoulder of the road near the mobile home park. Officer A then drove out of the mobile home park and saw a white vehicle leaving the right shoulder of the road near the mobile home park. This vehicle was located about 50 yards from the area where the officer had seen the pedestrian flee from him earlier. The officer then stopped the vehicle. The court stated that it was reasonable for the officer to infer that the person who had fled from him was in some way related to the stopped vehicle located a mere 50 yards from the fleeing pedestrian. The fact that the stop occurred around 2:00 a.m., when there was generally no foot traffic and there were no vehicles on the road except this vehicle and the patrol vehicles, contributed to the officer's suspicion.

State v. Summey, 150 N.C. App. 662 (2002). Officers were conducting surveillance in a known drug area. An officer was watching a residence that had been the subject of a nuisance abatement proceeding for drug-related activities. A group of men were standing in the residence's front yard. The officer saw a pickup truck stop at the residence. One man in the yard approached the truck and appeared to converse with the driver. A few moments later, the man returned to the yard and the truck drove away. Believing that he had witnessed a drug transaction, the officer radioed to other officers, who stopped the vehicle. The defendant was seated in the passenger seat with her left hand hidden underneath fabric. An officer recognized her from prior investigative stops. Concerned about small weapons in her hand, the officer asked her to show her hands. She lifted her hands but kept her left hand closed in a fist. The officer noticed a rock-like substance, which he believed to be crack cocaine, wedged in a gap between the defendant's fingers. She refused to open her left hand. The officer applied pressure to the back of her hand and forced it open. He recognized one piece of crack cocaine as it fell from her hand and another piece that remained stuck to her palm.

(1) The court ruled that reasonable suspicion existed to make an investigative stop of the vehicle for illegal drugs. (2) The court ruled that reasonable suspicion existed to search the defendant's closed hand for weapons. The court noted that at the suppression hearing the officers testified that they had been trained that a small knife or razor blade could be concealed in a clenched fist. Also, the search of the defendant's hand was justified by the officer's having seen crack cocaine wedged in her fingers. (3) The court ruled that reasonable force was used to open the defendant's closed hand to search for weapons and to prevent the destruction of evidence.

State v. Allison, 148 N.C. App. 702 (2002). An unidentified woman approached Officer A at a convenience store and told him that about five minutes earlier she had been in a nearby restaurant where she had observed four African American males sitting in the bar area. She said that she had overheard them talking about robbing the restaurant and that she had seen the four men passing a black handgun among themselves. At the officer's request, the woman repeated her observations to Officer B. Officer A then obtained the woman's telephone number, which he wrote on the back of his hand. Officer A and other officers entered the restaurant and saw four African American males sitting in the bar area. Officer A identified the defendant as having been involved in prior gun-related incidents. He then approached the men and asked them to step into the restaurant's foyer. The defendant was "holding his pants up as though he had something dragging his pants down." The officer began conducting a pat-down frisk of the defendant and asked him whether he was carrying any weapons. After the defendant responded "no," the officer continued to frisk him and seized a 9 millimeter handgun from his waistband. The defendant was arrested for carrying a concealed weapon. Later, Officer A called the telephone number that he had written on the back of his hand, but there was no answer. The court ruled, distinguishing *Florida v. J.L.*, 529 U.S. 266 (2000), and *State v. Hughes*, 353 N.C. 200 (2000), that reasonable suspicion supported Officer A's investigatory stop of the defendant. Unlike in *J.L.* and *Hughes*, the tip was supplied by a face-to-face encounter rather than by an anonymous phone call. Officer A had an opportunity to observe the demeanor of the tipster to assess the tip's reliability. By engaging Officer A directly, the tipster significantly increased the likelihood that she would be held accountable if her tip proved to be false. Also, unlike the informants in *J.L.* and *Hughes*, the tipster

offered a reasonable explanation of how she was aware that criminal activity was possibly going to take place. In addition, the officer's knowledge that the defendant had been involved in gun-related incidents buttressed the tip. The court also ruled that the officer's frisk was proper. The court rejected the defendant's argument that once Officer A had begun to frisk him and found nothing, the defendant should have been permitted to leave once he informed the officer that he was not carrying a handgun.

State v. Young, 148 N.C. App. 462 (2002). A Western Union office was robbed twice in a two-week period. Each robbery was committed by a person who was described similarly. A week after the second robbery, a female caller to 911, who would not identify herself because she feared for herself and her child, said that she knew who had committed both robberies. She said he was currently in the vicinity of a Wendy's restaurant near the Western Union and was driving a white 1998 Buick Century. Her description matched the prior descriptions. She also described the person's clothing and said that he was very dangerous and armed with a pistol. An officer then went to Wendy's and saw a vehicle and its driver that matched the anonymous caller's identifications. The officer followed the defendant when he drove away from Wendy's. He drove the wrong way down a one-way street. Eventually he pulled into a parking lot and was stopped after getting out of his car. The court ruled that the officer had probable cause to believe that the defendant violated G.S. 20-165.1 (willfully driving wrong way on one-way street) that justified the officer's stop of the defendant. The court also ruled, relying on *State v. Bone*, 354 N.C. 1 (2001), that the anonymous information and corroboration by the officer established reasonable suspicion to stop the defendant for the armed robberies.

State v. Brown, 142 N.C. App. 332 (2001). A detective received a call from his agency's 911 center stating that a "concerned citizen" had telephoned to complain that two black males were rolling marijuana cigarettes and selling crack cocaine on the porch of a vacant house under construction at a specified street corner. The citizen said that one of the black males was wearing a gray T-shirt and jeans and the other was wearing a black T-shirt and jeans. Two officers went to the house but did not see any black males on the porch. However, they saw three black males and a black female sitting on the porch of a house next door. Two of the males wore clothing fitting the description given by the caller. The defendant, the third male, was wearing a black pullover shirt and camouflage pants. The three men denied having any drugs. One officer frisked the defendant, and while being frisked, the defendant attempted to pull away from the officer. He was then arrested for resisting an officer, and cocaine was found incident to the arrest. The court, relying on *Florida v. J.L.*, 529 U.S. 266 (2000), ruled that the information from the anonymous phone call was insufficient to support the officer's stop and frisk of the defendant. Because the cocaine was discovered as a fruit of the officer's illegal stop and frisk, the evidence must be suppressed. [Author's note: Based on *Florida v. J.L.*, the information also was insufficient to support the stop and frisk of the two black males who matched the anonymous caller's description.] *See also In re* A.J.M.-B., 212 N.C. App. 586 (2011) (anonymous call that juveniles were walking with firearm in open field was insufficient to support investigative stop, based on *Florida v. J.L.*); United States v. Jones, 242 F.3d 215 (4th Cir. 2001) (anonymous call that "several black males" were drinking beer and causing a disturbance at an intersection was insufficient to stop vehicle in area).

State v. Covington, 138 N.C. App. 688 (2000). At approximately 3:00 a.m. on December 23, 1996, two Asheboro police officers received a call reporting that two males had broken into an apartment building in Asheboro and were leaving the apartment building heading toward Morgan Avenue. The officers drove to an intersection about 300 yards from the reported break-in and separated. Officer A went to the apartment building, and Officer B remained at the intersection. Officer A ordered Officer B to stop any pedestrians or vehicles entering the area. Two vehicles entered the area, and Officer B stopped them both by waving his flashlight. Officer B asked the driver of the first vehicle for his license, spoke with the driver and passengers briefly, and allowed them to proceed. The defendant's vehicle approached the intersection next, and Officer B again waved his flashlight. The defendant stopped and rolled down his window. Officer B explained that he was investigating a possible break-in in the area and was stopping all pedestrians and vehicles as part of the investigation. Without being asked to do so by Officer B, the defendant got out of his vehicle, staggering and talking about what he would do if someone had broken into his house. He was eventually arrested for DWI. The court ruled, citing *State v. Tillett*, 50 N.C. App. 520 (1981), and other cases, that Officer B had reasonable suspicion to stop the defendant's vehicle, based on the facts in this case. The court stated that it was reasonable for Officer B to stop and detain the defendant briefly to ascertain his identity and his possible involvement in criminal activity or to warn him as a resident.

State v. Parker, 137 N.C. App. 590 (2000). The court reviewed the facts of a long investigation of drug trafficking at a particular apartment and ruled that the officers had a reasonable suspicion of drug activity to make an investigative stop of a vehicle leaving that apartment, based on the following facts: (1) the accumulation of information received by the officers throughout their investigation led them to believe a "stash house" for drugs was located at the apartment; (2) within minutes of setting up surveillance of that location, the officers saw two men and the defendant leave the apartment complex at 1:00 a.m. and walk hurriedly to a parked vehicle in the parking lot; and (3) the detectives noticed the men placing what appeared to be a rifle wrapped in a blanket and a black tote bag, possibly containing controlled substances, in the trunk of the automobile.

State v. Willis, 125 N.C. App. 537 (1997). Officers were conducting surveillance of a residence while a search warrant was being sought to search it for drugs. The defendant, whom the officers did not recognize, left the residence on foot. Concerned that he might be involved in drug activity occurring in the residence, they followed him. When the defendant realized that he was being followed, he took evasive action by cutting through a parking lot. A detective then asked a uniformed officer to stop the defendant and ask him for identification. That officer approached the defendant on foot, told him he was conducting an investigative stop, and asked him for identification and for consent to a pat down for drugs and weapons. The defendant consented to the pat down. The officer began to pat down the exterior and then the interior of the defendant's leather jacket. Just as the officer began to check the jacket's interior pocket, the defendant lunged into the jacket with his hand. The officer, believing that the defendant might be reaching for a weapon and fearing for his safety, immediately locked his hands around the defendant's jacket, effectively locking the defendant's hand inside the pocket. Another officer arrived and assisted the officer. When the two officers managed to get the defendant's hand out of his pocket, they put the defendant's hands behind him and reached into the defendant's interior jacket pocket and emptied it, revealing several baggies of crack cocaine.

Relying on *State v. Butler*, 331 N.C. 227 (1992), the court ruled that the officer's investigative stop was supported by reasonable suspicion. The court noted that the defendant left a suspected drug house just before the search warrant was to be executed, took evasive action when he knew that he was being followed, and exhibited nervous behavior.

State v. Watkins, 120 N.C. App. 804 (1995). An officer stopped a vehicle for impaired driving. A prior appeal of this case determined that anonymous information and the officer's observations provided reasonable suspicion for the stop. See *State v. Watkins*, 337 N.C. 437 (1994), discussed above. In later proceedings, the defendant filed a supplemental suppression motion based on newly discovered evidence that the anonymous information had been supplied to the stopping officer by another officer and that the other officer had fabricated the information (there was no evidence that the stopping officer knew that the information was fabricated). The court ruled that reasonable suspicion that is based on information fabricated by a law enforcement officer and supplied to another law enforcement officer may not serve as a basis for the stop by the officer who received the fabricated information, even though that officer did not know that the information was fabricated.

State v. Clyburn, 120 N.C. App. 377 (1995). Officers were conducting surveillance at night at a place that had a reputation for drug activity and where officers had previously made drug arrests. Officers saw three males in front of a vacant duplex. As individuals approached one of the males, he would disappear behind the duplex with them. The other two males remained in front of the duplex as if acting as lookouts. Each time the defendant reappeared, the other two males conferred with him. Based on the officers' training and experience with similar activity, they believed that drug transactions were being conducted. After one such activity, one of the males and a female got into a car and drove away. The car was stopped and the male (the defendant) and female were frisked. An officer searched the passenger area of the car and found a .357 Magnum in the glove compartment. The male was arrested for carrying a concealed weapon. Following the arrest, the car was searched and crack cocaine was found in an ashtray.

The court ruled that (1) the officers had reasonable suspicion to stop the car to investigate drug activity; and (2) the search of the car for weapons was proper under *Michigan v. Long*, 463 U.S. 1032 (1983), because after the defendant had been frisked, he became belligerent, and the officers could reasonably believe that the defendant was potentially dangerous and might be armed because of

his involvement in drug trafficking. The court also cited *State v. Butler*, 331 N.C. 227 (1992).

State v. Jordan, 120 N.C. App. 364 (1995). An officer received a call that two black males, one wearing dark clothing and the other wearing a green jacket, had just left a Pick-N-Pay shoe store after committing an armed robbery. The officer, who was less than a mile away from the shopping center when he received the call, went there. As he drove toward the shoe store, the officer saw a small blue car come from behind Revco Drugs in the shopping center. The area from which the car came was not used for public parking. The blue car contained three black males. The officer saw no other black people in the area. The officer followed the car and noticed that the backseat passenger kept looking back at the police vehicle. When he saw an arm reach out of the passenger window and drop two small card-like objects, he stopped the car. The court ruled that the officer had reasonable suspicion to stop the car to investigate the armed robbery.

State v. Watson, 119 N.C. App. 395 (1995). Three officers approached a convenience store at night. Officer A had made 50 or more arrests for possession of cocaine in this area. Officer A knew that the defendant had previously been arrested for drug charges. The defendant, on seeing the officers, put items in his mouth and started to go back into the store. When Officer A grabbed the defendant's jacket, the defendant attempted to drink a soft drink. The officer took the drink away, ordered the defendant to spit the objects out of his mouth, and applied pressure to the defendant's throat so that he would spit out the items. The defendant spit out three baggies containing crack cocaine. Based on this and other evidence (for example, officers testified at the suppression hearing that drug dealers will attempt to conceal or to swallow drugs when they see officers), the court ruled that the officers had reasonable suspicion to stop the defendant; the court cited *State v. Butler*, 331 N.C. 227 (1992). The court also ruled that exigent circumstances supported the reasonableness of the officer's actions in applying pressure to the defendant's throat so that he would not swallow the drugs he had placed in his mouth (the court considered the officers' training and experience and their familiarity with the area, the defendant, and drug dealers' practice of hiding drugs in their mouths to elude detection).

State v. Taylor, 117 N.C. App. 644 (1995). Officer A knew that the defendant had been previously arrested for drugs and had a reputation in the community as a drug dealer. Officer A and other officers saw the defendant with others in an area known for drug trafficking. As officers approached the area in their marked car, the defendant left. The officers saw him at a nearby intersection. The defendant stopped as the police car approached him. As Officer A got out of the car, the defendant walked toward him and dropped something on the ground. The officer approached the defendant and brought him over to the police car. He determined that the dropped item was marijuana and arrested the defendant. He then noticed that the defendant was talking "funny" and ordered him to spit out whatever was in his mouth. The defendant spit out individually wrapped pieces of crack cocaine.

The court ruled that (1) the defendant was not seized until after he dropped the item to the ground, because he had not yielded to a show of authority before then; see *California v. Hodari D.*, 499 U.S. 621 (1991); (2) after the defendant dropped the item, Officer A had reasonable suspicion to detain the defendant, considering everything the officer knew; (3) Officer A had probable cause to arrest the defendant when he determined that the dropped item was marijuana; and (4) even if the defendant did not voluntarily spit out the cocaine, it was admissible as a search incident to arrest.

State v. Wilson, 112 N.C. App. 777 (1993). A police department received an anonymous phone call that several people were selling drugs in the breezeway of Building 1304 in the Hunter Oaks Apartments. The caller did not provide any names or descriptions of the alleged drug dealers. Two officers familiar with the area knew that if a police car entered the parking lot at one end of the breezeway, the suspects would run out the other end. They devised a plan whereby a police car would enter the parking lot and officers would position themselves so that they could stop anyone who ran out of the back of the breezeway. An officer stopped the defendant as he ran out of the back of the breezeway and conducted a frisk. During the frisk the officer felt a lump in the left breast pocket of the defendant's jacket and immediately believed that it was crack cocaine. The officer then asked the defendant if his coat had an inside pocket. The defendant did not respond verbally but instead opened his jacket so that the inside pocket was visible. The officer saw and removed a small plastic bag that contained crack cocaine.

(1) Distinguishing *State v. Fleming*, 106 N.C. App. 165 (1992), the court ruled that the officer had authority to stop and frisk the defendant based on the anonymous phone call, the flight of the defendant and others when the police car pulled into the parking lot, and the officer's

experience that weapons were frequently involved in drug transactions. (2) Distinguishing *Minnesota v. Dickerson*, 508 U.S. 366 (1993), the court noted that the officer in this case—unlike the officer in *Dickerson*—did not need to manipulate the item in the defendant's pocket to determine that it was cocaine; he immediately believed it was crack cocaine. The court ruled that the requirement in *Dickerson* that it must be "immediately apparent" to the officer that the item is illegal means that the officer must have probable cause to believe that the item is illegal. The court also ruled that the officer's tactile senses, based on his experience and the facts in this case, gave him probable cause to believe that the item was crack cocaine. Thus, the officer did not exceed the scope of a frisk under the *Dickerson* ruling.

State v. Pittman, 111 N.C. App. 808 (1993). Two officers were on patrol at a train station at 1:30 a.m. They saw the female defendant and a man speak and then part company when they saw the officers. Officer Gunn approached the defendant and Officer Ferrell approached the man. The defendant showed Gunn a train ticket and stated that she was traveling alone and did not know the man with whom she had been seen. Gunn noticed that the defendant was constantly looking over at the man, who was 20 feet away. The defendant consented to a search of her bag; nothing was found. Meanwhile, Ferrell spoke with the man, who said he was traveling alone and did not know the defendant. The man consented to a search of his bag; nothing was found. Later, a vehicle pulled up to the train station, and the man put his bag in the trunk. The man then motioned to the defendant to approach the car. He placed her bag in the trunk, and the two of them got in the car and left. The officers compared information that they had learned from their encounters with the man and the defendant and had the car stopped by a uniformed officer. The defendant refused to consent to a search and was taken to the police station and searched.

(1) The court, relying on *Florida v. Bostick*, 501 U.S. 429 (1991), ruled that Officer Gunn did not seize the defendant at the train station. He merely approached her and asked a few questions, and she voluntarily gave him her train ticket and consented to a search of her bag. (2) The court ruled that the officers had reasonable suspicion to stop the vehicle in which the defendant was a passenger, based on the facts discussed above. (3) The court ruled that the officers did not have probable cause to search the defendant for illegal drugs after the vehicle stop, based on the facts discussed above.

State v. Holmes, 109 N.C. App. 615 (1993). The court ruled that reasonable suspicion existed to stop a vehicle based on the following facts. A trained drug officer saw the defendant driving slowly into a neighborhood known for violence and illegal drugs. The defendant then engaged two different groups of people in conversation from a car and went inside a house personally known to the officer because he had made drug arrests there. The defendant returned to the car after a few minutes and lit a cigarette, which he shared with two passengers until it was gone and the car was filled with smoke. Based on his training, the officer believed that the cigarette was a marijuana cigarette. The defendant then placed a plastic bag in the trunk of the car and returned to the house alone for about 30 seconds. When the defendant returned to the car, he carefully concealed an object underneath the driver's seat.

State v. Fleming, 106 N.C. App. 165 (1992). Officers at 12:10 a.m. were in a housing project area where illegal drug activity was common. An officer saw the defendant and a companion, strangers to the area, standing in an open area between two apartment buildings. The two men watched the officer for a few minutes and began walking on a sidewalk away from him. The officer drove around to where the men were walking, got out of his car, and commanded them to come to him. They hesitated a minute and then approached him. The defendant acted "real nervous." As the officer was questioning the defendant about why he was in this area (to which the defendant responded that a friend had dropped him off and he was walking through), the officer frisked him and found crack cocaine. The court ruled, relying on *Brown v. Texas*, 443 U.S. 47 (1979), that the officer's stop and frisk of the defendant was not supported by reasonable suspicion of criminal activity. *See also* United States v. Davis, 94 F.3d 1465 (10th Cir. 1996) (defendant's actions in exiting car, making and breaking eye contact with officers, and then walking away from officers did not support reasonable suspicion to stop defendant).

State v. Swift, 105 N.C. App. 550 (1992). Officers had reasonable suspicion to stop the defendant for illegal consumption of beer after he emerged from his vehicle and placed a beer can on the ground of a convenience store parking lot; the store had only an off-premises license. His later flight from the officers gave them probable cause to arrest.

State v. Cornelius, 104 N.C. App. 583 (1991). An officer received a call from a police radio dispatcher that a black male in a black BMW with a temporary license tag was selling controlled substances from his car on Meridan Street. The street was in a neighborhood with a reputation as a high crime area for selling drugs (the court ruled that this reputation evidence is admissible in determining reasonable suspicion to stop). An officer arrived at that street within a minute and saw a black male driving a black BMW with a temporary license tag. The officer stopped the car, based on the radio dispatch and the officer's seeing a possibly illegal license tag. The court ruled that the officer, based on these facts, had reasonable suspicion to stop the car to investigate illegal drug activity. [Author's note: This ruling is now questionable in light of the later case of *Florida v. J.L.*, 529 U.S. 266 (1999).]

State v. Reid, 104 N.C. App. 334 (1991), *rev'd on other grounds*, 334 N.C. 551 (1993). The court upheld an investigatory stop of a vehicle based on officers' reasonable suspicion of the defendant's involvement in criminal activity. Officers responded at 2:25 a.m. to an alarm at a drugstore in a shopping center. While driving there, they noticed the defendant's vehicle parked 100 yards away, and there were no other cars or people in the shopping center's parking lot. After discovering that the meter box behind the store was missing, they noticed that the defendant's vehicle was no longer there. They shortly thereafter saw the vehicle on a highway without its headlights on and accelerating at a high rate of speed. They pursued and stopped the vehicle, which initially did not stop pursuant to the patrol car's siren and blue light. The court noted that officers need not have had reasonable suspicion of a specific break-in to stop a vehicle but simply reasonable suspicion of some illegal conduct.

State v. Drewyore, 95 N.C. App. 283 (1989). Reasonable suspicion supported the officers' stop of the defendant's vehicle. The defendant paid utilities for a beach cottage, and parked outside the cottage was a boat that officers believed to be a type used in drug smuggling. Three days before the stop, the defendant had driven a circuitous route with a vehicle for over 130 miles, including many U-turns and stops. The officers believed that the driving pattern was a counter-surveillance technique used by drug traffickers. On the day the defendant was stopped, she was driving an Oldsmobile, and later on that day the same car and another vehicle were traveling in tandem and using counter-surveillance techniques.

State v. Harrell, 67 N.C. App. 57 (1984). An officer had reasonable suspicion to stop the defendant, who was sitting in his car in a Cannon Mills parking lot late at night between employee shifts, when a security guard saw him apparently engage in a drug transaction and the parking lot was located in a high crime area.

State v. Davis, 66 N.C. App. 98 (1984). The court applied the totality of circumstances analysis set out in *Illinois v. Gates*, 462 U.S. 213 (1983), to determine that two informants' tips were reliable and supported a reasonable suspicion to stop the defendant's vehicle to investigate a robbery. The tips gave the defendant's name as the robber; his admission to the informants that he had been robbing people; his description; and the color, make, and location of his car—which the officers independently verified. The tips also gave accurate details of the robbery that had not been reported by newspapers.

State v. Fox, 58 N.C. App. 692 (1982), *aff'd*, 307 N.C. 460 (1983). An officer had reasonable suspicion to stop the driver of a car late at night in a business district where break-ins had occurred earlier that night. The defendant was driving slowly in a dead-end street where all businesses were closed. He was dressed shabbily but was driving a new car, and he appeared to avoid the officer's gaze when he passed him.

State v. McNeill, 54 N.C. App. 454 (1981). Two officers saw the defendant and another man walking quickly late at night. The defendant was carrying an armful of clothing, and the other man was carrying a television set. When the officers shined their car's headlights on the defendant, he dropped the clothing and ran. A third officer, who heard the defendant's description on the radio, saw him (he matched the description) walking on the wrong side of the road, sweating profusely and breathing hard. The court ruled that the officer had reasonable suspicion to stop and detain the defendant. After being stopped, the defendant ran from the officer. The court ruled that the officer then had probable cause to arrest him under G.S. 14-223, because he was obstructing the officer in performing his duties.

State v. Douglas, 51 N.C. App. 594 (1981), *aff'd*, 304 N.C. 713 (1982). Reasonable suspicion existed to stop the defendant's car, which appeared to have an appliance in the trunk and was in an area late at night where there had been several thefts of washers and dryers from a nearby mobile home business.

State v. Tillett, 50 N.C. App. 520 (1981). An officer had reasonable suspicion to stop a car at night based on the following facts: (1) the car entered a dirt road in seasonally unoccupied Nags Head Woods; (2) there were reports of firelighting deer (a wildlife violation) in that area; and (3) the officer later saw the car coming out of the area. The court ruled that an experienced officer would have had reasonable suspicion of criminal activity—burglarizing homes or firelighting deer.

In re Horne, 50 N.C. App. 97 (1980). Officers heard a radio dispatch at 1:00 a.m. that two males had been seen pushing or pulling a wagon with a box or television set on it. When an officer arrived, one of the males fled. The box on the wagon contained various merchandise. The officer had reasonable suspicion of larceny to detain the juvenile who was beside the wagon.

State v. Trapper, 48 N.C. App. 481 (1980). An officer had reasonable suspicion to stop a truck to investigate marijuana smuggling when (1) the officer had kept certain premises under surveillance and had been fired on while doing it (the shooting had occurred some days or weeks before the stop); (2) he had seen a boat aground near the premises without a good explanation, although this occurred sometime before the night of the stop; and (3) about midnight he saw a truck leave the premises. The court stated that it took judicial notice that the county in which these events occurred is on the North Carolina coast in an area that is regularly used by marijuana smugglers.

State v. Greenwood, 47 N.C. App. 731 (1980), *rev'd on other grounds*, 301 N.C. 705 (1981). An officer had reasonable suspicion to stop the defendant (by ordering the defendant to roll down his car window) when the officer arrived at a church in response to a report that a suspicious person was on the premises and churchgoers directed him to the defendant, who was alone in a car parked in the corner of the church parking lot. [Author's note: The court's finding of reasonable suspicion would have had more support if specific facts had been given to confirm the churchgoers' conclusion that the defendant was "suspicious."]

In re Beddingfield, 42 N.C. App. 712 (1979). An officer saw a 12-year-old in a car with an adult at night in a convenience store parking lot. When the adult went into the store to shop, the officer approached the car, identified herself as an officer, shined her flashlight on her badge, and said, "Please roll the window down." [Author's note: It is questionable whether this evidence supported the court's conclusion that the seizure (the court apparently assumed a seizure had occurred) was "reasonable" under the Fourth Amendment, because the facts do not support a reasonable suspicion that a crime had been or was about to be committed or otherwise justify the officer's conduct.]

FEDERAL APPELLATE COURTS

United States v. Christmas, 222 F.3d 141 (4th Cir. 2000). Officers A and B were investigating a homicide in a neighborhood. A resident approached Officer A and told him that "you need to come and deal with the drugs and the guns that these guys have on the porch two doors down from me." She said that the object of her complaint was two houses away from her home and located at 401 Canal Street. When the two officers arrived at that residence, they saw one woman and three men on the porch. Officer A advised them that he was investigating a report about narcotics and gun activity on the premises. He then stated that he was going to conduct a pat-down search for the safety of all concerned. His frisk of one of them (the defendant, whom the officer knew and found it odd that he would be present on Canal Street, given the tensions between gangs there and gangs from the defendant's part of town) resulted in the seizure of a handgun.

Distinguishing *Florida v. J.L.,* 529 U.S. 266 (2000), the court ruled that this informant supported the officer's stop and frisk. Unlike the facts in *J.L.,* Officer A's conversation with the tipster gave him the opportunity to assess her credibility and demeanor. Two factors supported her credibility. One was the close proximity of the informant's residence to the illegal activities—she would know if drugs were being sold from the porch there. The other was the informant's proximity to 401 Canal Street when she spoke to Officer A—by informing the officer about her neighbors' illegal activity, the informant exposed herself to the risk of reprisal. In addition, she could be held accountable for false statements to the officer—although she did not give her name, the officers knew that she lived at 309 Canal Street. The court also ruled that the frisk was justified, based on this information and the officer's reasonable belief that the defendant's presence on the porch created a potential for violence. *See also* United States v. Sims, 296 F.3d 284 (4th Cir. 2002) (anonymous call describing person who had just fired pistol and officer's observation of defendant, who matched description and acted evasively when he saw the officer, supported reasonable suspicion to stop defendant).

United States v. Wilson, 205 F.3d 720 (4th Cir. 2000). An officer did not have reasonable suspicion to stop the defendant's car simply because the car had a temporary paper license tag and the officer could not read the handwritten expiration date on the tag as he drove behind the car after dark. The officer had no suspicion that the defendant was driving without a license, operating an unregistered car, or otherwise violating the law, and nothing appeared illegal about the temporary tag.

United States v. Lender, 985 F.2d 151 (4th Cir. 1993). At approximately 12:50 a.m., officers were patrolling an area where they knew heavy drug trafficking occurred. They saw a group of four or five men, including the defendant, huddled on a street corner. The defendant had his hand stuck out with his palm up, and the other men were looking down toward his palm. Suspecting a drug transaction, officers approached the group. The group began to disperse, and the defendant walked away from the officers with his back to them. One officer called for the defendant to stop, but the defendant refused, telling the officer, "You don't want me; you don't want me." As the defendant continued to walk away, he brought his hands to the front of his waist as though reaching for or fumbling with something there. The officer again called for the defendant to stop. The defendant stopped briefly, and a loaded semiautomatic pistol fell from his waist to the ground. The court ruled that the officers had reasonable suspicion to stop the defendant for drugs.

DWI Stops

NORTH CAROLINA SUPREME COURT

State v. Verkerk, 367 N.C. 483 (2014), *rev'g* 229 N.C. App. 416 (2013). In a DWI case where the defendant was initially stopped by a firefighter, the court determined that the trial court properly denied the defendant's motion to suppress that had challenged the firefighter's authority to make the initial stop. After observing the defendant's erratic driving and transmitting this information to the local police department, the firefighter stopped the defendant's vehicle. After some conversation, the defendant drove away. When police officers arrived on the scene, the firefighter indicated where the vehicle had gone. The officers located the defendant, investigated her condition, and charged her with DWI. On appeal, the defendant argued that because the firefighter had no authority to stop her, evidence from the first stop was improperly obtained. However, the court determined that it need not consider the extent of the firefighter's authority to conduct a traffic stop or even whether the defendant's encounter with him constituted a "legal stop." The court reasoned that the firefighter's observations of the defendant's driving, which were transmitted to the police before making the stop, established that the police officers had reasonable suspicion to stop the defendant.

The court noted that this evidence was independent of any evidence derived from the firefighter's stop.

State v. Kochuk, 366 N.C. 549 (2013). The court, per curiam and without an opinion, reversed the decision of the North Carolina Court of Appeals, 223 N.C. App. 301 (2012), for the reasons stated in the dissenting opinion. An officer was on duty and traveling eastbound on Interstate 40, where there were three travel lanes. The officer was one to two car lengths behind the defendant's vehicle in the middle lane. The defendant momentarily crossed the right dotted line once while in the middle lane. He then made a legal lane change to the right lane and later drove on the fog line twice. The officer stopped the vehicle, and the defendant was later charged with DWI. The dissenting opinion stated that this case is controlled by *State v. Otto*, 366 N.C. 134 (2012), summarized immediately below. The defendant was weaving within his own lane, and the vehicle stop occurred at 1:10 a.m. These two facts coupled together, under *Otto*'s totality of circumstances analysis, constituted reasonable suspicion for the DWI stop.

State v. Otto, 366 N.C. 134 (2012), *rev'g* 217 N.C. App. 79 (2011). The court ruled that there was reasonable suspicion for a vehicle stop in this case. Around 11 p.m., an officer observed a vehicle drive past. The officer turned behind the vehicle and immediately noticed that it was weaving within its own lane. The vehicle never left its lane, but it was "constantly weaving from the center line to the fog line." The vehicle appeared to be traveling at the posted speed limit. After watching the vehicle weave in its own lane for about three-quarters of a mile, the officer stopped the vehicle. The defendant was issued a citation for impaired driving. The court of appeals determined that the traffic stop was unreasonable because it was supported solely by the defendant's weaving within her own lane. The supreme court disagreed, concluding that under the totality of the circumstances, there was reasonable suspicion for the traffic stop. The court noted that unlike other cases in which weaving within a lane was held insufficient to support reasonable suspicion, the weaving here was "constant and continual" over three-quarters of a mile. Additionally, the defendant was stopped around 11 p.m. on a Friday night.

State v. Barnard, 362 N.C. 244 (2008). An officer stopped his marked patrol vehicle behind the defendant's vehicle, which was stopped at a red light. When the light turned green, the vehicle remained stopped for approximately 30 seconds before making a legal left turn; the vehicle had remained at the light without any reasonable explanation for doing so. The officer initiated a stop of the vehicle. The court ruled that reasonable suspicion supported the stop of the vehicle based on these facts and the officer's testimony, based on his training and experience, that the driver might be impaired. The officer said that impairment slows reaction time, and that a red light turning green and the driver hesitating for 30 seconds would definitely be an indication of impairment. The court noted that it was irrelevant that part of the officer's motivation to stop the vehicle may have been for a perceived, though apparently nonexistent, statutory violation of impeding traffic. The court stated that the constitutionality of a traffic stop depends on objective facts, not an officer's subjective motivation; the court cited *Whren v. United States*, 517 U.S. 806 (1996), and *State v. McClendon*, 350 N.C. 630 (1999).

State v. Foreman, 351 N.C. 627 (2000). Officers set up a DWI checkpoint under G.S. 20-16.3A and posted notice of the checkpoint about one-tenth of a mile before the stop. At about 2:00 a.m., an officer saw a vehicle, immediately before the checkpoint's sign, make a "quick left turn" onto a street. The officer followed the vehicle, lost sight of it, but eventually saw it parked in a residential driveway. The officer directed his bright lights onto the vehicle and also turned on his take-down lights, thereby enabling the officer to see that people were bent or crouched down inside the car. The vehicle's lights and ignition were off, and its doors were closed. Once backup arrived, the officer approached the vehicle and saw that the defendant was sitting in the driver's seat with the key in the ignition. There were several open containers of alcohol in the vehicle, and the vehicle emitted a strong odor of alcohol. In addition, the officer noticed that the defendant had a strong to moderate odor of alcohol about her person after she exited the vehicle and she was unsteady on her feet.

(1) The court noted that the officer did not seize the vehicle or the defendant "until at least" the officer approached the vehicle. Based on the incriminating circumstances that existed by then, the court ruled that the officer had reasonable suspicion to stop the driver. (2) Disavowing contrary statements in the court of appeals' opinion in this case, the court stated: "[W]e hold that it is reasonable and permissible for an officer to monitor a checkpoint's entrance for vehicles whose drivers may be attempting to avoid the checkpoint, and it necessarily follows that an officer, in conjunction with the totality of the circumstances or the checkpoint plan, may pursue and

stop a vehicle which has turned away from a checkpoint within its perimeters for reasonable inquiry to determine why the vehicle turned away."

State v. White, 311 N.C. 238 (1984). An officer noticed a person in a parked car who appeared to be highly intoxicated. The officer watched the person as he drove away. The person failed to respond to the officer's blue light. The officer had reasonable suspicion to stop the person's car.

NORTH CAROLINA COURT OF APPEALS

State v. Wainwright, ___ N.C. App. ___, 770 S.E.2d 99 (2015). The court ruled that an officer had reasonable suspicion to stop the defendant's vehicle for DWI. The officer observed the defendant's vehicle swerve right, cross the line marking the outside of his lane of travel, and almost strike the curb. The court found that this evidence, along with "the pedestrian traffic along the sidewalks and in the roadway, the unusual hour defendant was driving, and his proximity to bars and nightclubs, support[ed] the trial court's conclusion that [the] Officer . . . had reasonable suspicion to believe defendant was driving while impaired."

State v. Weaver, 231 N.C. App. 473 (2013). The court ruled that the trial court, in granting the defendant's motion to suppress in a DWI case, erred by concluding that a licensed security guard was a state actor when he stopped the defendant's vehicle. In the alternative, the court ruled that even if the security guard was a state actor, reasonable suspicion supported the stop. The guard saw the defendant at 2:10 a.m. in rainy weather conditions, traveling approximately 25 m.p.h. in a 15 m.p.h. zone and crossing over the center street lines several times. The time, poor weather conditions, speed, and failure to maintain lane control provided the guard with reasonable suspicion to stop the defendant.

State v. Derbyshire, 228 N.C. App. 670 (2013). The court ruled in this DWI case that the officer lacked reasonable suspicion to stop the defendant's vehicle. At 10:05 p.m. on a Wednesday night, an officer noticed that the defendant's high beams were on. The officer also observed the defendant weave once within his lane of travel. When pressed about whether the defendant weaved out of his lane, the officer indicated that "just . . . the right side of his tires" crossed over into the right-hand lane of traffic going in the same direction. The State presented no evidence that the stop occurred in an area of high alcohol consumption or that the officer considered such a fact as a part of her decision to stop the defendant. The court char-

acterized the case as follows: "[W]e find that the totality of the circumstances . . . present one instance of weaving, in which the right side of Defendant's tires crossed into the right-hand lane, as well as two conceivable 'plus' factors—the fact that Defendant was driving at 10:05 on a Wednesday evening and the fact that [the officer] believed Defendant's bright lights were on before she initiated the stop." The court first noted that the weaving in this case was not constant and continuous. It then concluded that driving at 10:05 p.m. on a Wednesday evening and the officer's belief that the defendant's bright lights were on "are not sufficiently uncommon to constitute valid 'plus' factors" to justify the stop under a "weaving plus" analysis.

State v. Fields, 219 N.C. App. 385 (2012). The court ruled that an officer had reasonable suspicion to stop the defendant's vehicle when the defendant's weaving in his own lane was sufficiently frequent and erratic to prompt evasive maneuvers from other drivers. Distinguishing cases holding that weaving within a lane, standing alone, is insufficient to support a stop, the court noted that here "the trial court did not find only that defendant was weaving in his lane, but rather that defendant's driving was 'like a ball bouncing in a small room'" and that "[t]he driving was so erratic that the officer observed other drivers—in heavy traffic—taking evasive maneuvers to avoid defendant's car." The court determined that none of the other cases involved the level of erratic driving and potential danger to other drivers that was involved in this case.

State v. Simmons, 205 N.C. App. 509 (2010). The court ruled, distinguishing *State v. Fields*, 195 N.C. App. 740 (2009), that an officer had reasonable suspicion to stop a vehicle for impaired driving. The defendant was not only weaving within his lane but also was weaving across and outside the lanes of travel and at one point ran off the road.

State v. Peele, 196 N.C. App. 668 (2009). At approximately 7:50 p.m. on April 7, 2007, an officer responded to a dispatch concerning "a possible careless and reckless, D.W.I., headed toward the Holiday Inn intersection." The vehicle was described as a burgundy Chevrolet pickup truck. The officer immediately arrived at the intersection and saw a burgundy Chevrolet pickup truck. After following the truck for about a tenth of a mile and seeing the truck weave within its lane once, the officer stopped the truck. The court ruled that the officer did not have reasonable suspicion to stop the truck. The court noted that there was no information identifying the caller, what the caller had seen, or where the caller was located. The officer's observation of the truck's weaving within a lane once did not corroborate the caller's assertion of careless or reckless driving. [Author's note: The later ruling in *Navarette v. California*, 134 S. Ct. 1683 (2014) (anonymous caller's report provided reasonable suspicion for vehicle stop), summarized above, raises questions about the continuing validity of the *Peele* ruling.]

State v. Fields, 195 N.C. App. 740 (2009). Around 4:00 p.m., an officer followed the defendant's vehicle for about one and a half miles. On three separate occasions, the officer saw the defendant's vehicle swerve to the white line on the right side of the traffic lane. The officer stopped the vehicle for impaired driving. The court ruled that the officer did not have reasonable suspicion to stop the vehicle. The vehicle's weaving within its lane, standing alone, was insufficient to support reasonable suspicion. The court noted that the facts in this case were clearly distinguishable from the circumstances in *State v. Jacobs*, 162 N.C. App. 251 (2004) (reasonable suspicion of impaired driving existed when defendant's vehicle was weaving within lane at 1:43 a.m. in area near bars), and *State v. Watson*, 122 N.C. App. 596 (1996) (reasonable suspicion of impaired driving existed when defendant's vehicle was weaving within lane and driving on dividing line of highway at 2:30 a.m. near nightclub). In this case, the officer did not see the defendant violating any laws such as driving above or significantly below the speed limit. Furthermore, the defendant's vehicle was stopped about 4:00 p.m., which is not an unusual hour, and there was no evidence that the defendant was near any places to purchase alcohol.

State v. Fuller, 193 N.C. App. 670 (2009). The court ruled that exigent circumstances supported officers' warrantless entry into a mobile home to arrest the defendant pursuant to an outstanding arrest warrant when officers reasonably believed that the defendant was attempting to escape and also presented a danger to the officers and others in the home.

State v. Jones, 186 N.C. App. 405 (2007). The court ruled that an officer had reasonable suspicion for a DWI stop of a defendant operating a two-wheeled motorized vehicle, based on the following facts (quoted language is officer's testimony as recounted by the court): The officer saw the defendant operating a motorized vehicle in a "wobbly" manner, and the defendant had to "put her foot down" on the road to negotiate a right-hand turn and "almost dropped the moped." The officer equated her operation of the vehicle as she was turning to that of "a child learning to ride a bicycle" for the first time. After the

defendant made the turn, the officer saw the defendant for "two to three" minutes and followed her for "two to three blocks." During this time, he watched the defendant wobble on the moped and described her operation of it as "jerky."

State v. Roberson, 163 N.C. App. 129 (2004). At approximately 4:30 a.m., an officer was traveling southbound on High Point Road in Greensboro when he stopped for a red light at an intersection. The defendant's vehicle was also stopped at the red light on the opposite side of the intersection—northbound on High Point Road. There were no other vehicles in the area. When the light turned green, the officer proceeded through the intersection. As he passed the defendant's vehicle, he saw the defendant and could see that she was looking straight ahead. He later was unable to recall whether he saw her hands. After the officer had traveled one city block, the defendant's vehicle still had not moved. The officer made a U-turn and began to approach the defendant's vehicle from the rear. The officer estimated that the defendant's vehicle had delayed 8 to 10 seconds before proceeding through the intersection. Shortly thereafter the officer stopped the vehicle. The officer testified that many bars and restaurants were located in the immediate area and he believed that they were required to stop serving alcohol at 2:00 a.m. The court ruled, relying on cases from other jurisdictions, that the officer did not have reasonable suspicion to stop the defendant's vehicle for DWI. The court noted that a driver waiting at a traffic light can have her attention diverted for any number of reasons. Moreover, because there was not another vehicle behind the defendant to redirect her attention to the green light by honking a horn, a time lapse of 8 to 10 seconds did not appear so unusual as to establish reasonable suspicion for a vehicle stop. The court rejected in the consideration of reasonable suspicion in this case the State's advocacy of general statistics concerning time, location, and special events (the furniture market's presence in town) from which a law enforcement officer could draw inferences based on training and experience. The court also stated that it would not address the State's argument based on a reference to a National Highway Traffic Safety Administration (NHTSA) publication on statistics concerning slow responses to traffic signals, because neither the publication nor testimony about it were introduced at the suppression hearing. [Author's note: Concerning NHTSA publications and establishing reasonable suspicion, see *State v. Bonds*, 139 N.C. App. 627 (2000).]

State v. Jacobs, 162 N.C. App. 251 (2004). The defendant was convicted of several drug offenses. An officer stopped the defendant's vehicle, detained him for about three to five minutes, received consent to search the vehicle, and discovered evidence in the car and on the defendant's person.

(1) About 1:43 a.m. on November 8, 2001, a Burlington police officer saw a car continuously weaving back and forth in its lane over a distance of three-quarters of a mile. There were several bars in the area. The court ruled, relying on *State v. Watson*, 122 N.C. App. 596 (1996), that the officer had reasonable suspicion to stop the vehicle for DWI. [Author's note: Although the officer also had information that a suspect in a Johnson City, Tennessee, murder was in Burlington; the car's Tennessee license plate was registered to a Johnson City resident; and a substantial amount of drug trafficking occurred between Burlington and Johnson City; these facts had not also been used as the basis for the trial judge's ruling that the officer had reasonable suspicion to stop the vehicle.] (2) The court ruled that the length of the defendant's detention (about three to five minutes) during the investigatory stop was reasonable under the Fourth Amendment. During this time the officer asked the defendant questions about his impairment, the murder suspect, and drug trafficking. The defendant's responses did not fully resolve the officer's suspicions, and the defendant was acting very nervous—the court noted *State v. McClendon*, 350 N.C. 630 (1999), concerning the issue of nervousness as a factor in determining reasonable suspicion.

State v. Thompson, 154 N.C. App. 194 (2002). Two officers estimated the speed of the defendant's vehicle to be about 15 to 20 m.p.h. over the speed limit. They saw the vehicle weave within its lane and touch the left line separating the two eastbound lanes at least twice with both left tires. The court ruled, citing *State v. Watson*, 122 N.C. App. 596 (1996), that the officers had reasonable suspicion to make an investigative stop of the defendant's vehicle for DWI.

State v. Bonds, 139 N.C. App. 627 (2000). On December 27, 1997, an officer saw the defendant's vehicle stopped at an intersection. He noticed that the defendant's driver's side window was completely rolled down, even though it was 28 degrees outside. The officer saw that the defendant had "a blank look on his face" and never turned his head to make eye contact with the officer. After the light changed, the officer followed the defendant's vehicle for about a half mile. The speed limit was 40 m.p.h., but the defendant's vehicle never exceeded 30 m.p.h. The officer stopped the vehicle to investigate the driver for DWI.

The court ruled that these facts supported reasonable suspicion to stop the vehicle. The court noted that this officer had been specifically trained to look for certain indicators of intoxication, including some of the indicators in this case, and that he had 10 years of experience and had made several arrests using these exact indicators. Citing *State v. Thompson*, 296 N.C. 703 (1979), the court stated that an officer's training and experience must be considered in determining whether reasonable suspicion exists. The court noted that the National Highway Traffic Safety Administration, in its publication *The Visual Detection of DWI Motorists*, stated that driving 10 miles per hour or more under the speed limit and staring ahead with fixed eyes indicated a 50 percent chance that the driver was legally intoxicated. (The court cited the publication's website address, but it is no longer valid. However, the publication can be found at www.nhtsa.dot.gov by typing "The Visual Detection of DWI Motorists" in the search function at the top of the page.) The court stated that this 50 percent statistic lends objective credibility to the officer's suspicions, demonstrating that his suspicions were in fact reasonable—something more than just a "hunch." The court rejected the defendant's argument that weaving, or some other form of aberrant driving, is required to satisfy the reasonable suspicion standard.

State v. Rogers, 124 N.C. App. 364 (1996). An officer was directing traffic with hand signals when the defendant's vehicle approached the intersection where the officer was located. Instead of turning left as the officer directed, the defendant stopped his vehicle in the intersection. The officer approached the vehicle and noticed a strong odor of alcohol on the defendant's breath. The officer directed the defendant to drive to the shoulder of the road, and the defendant complied with that directive. The officer then administered an Alco-Sensor test, which revealed a reading of 0.13, and the officer arrested the defendant for impaired driving. The court upheld the trial judge's ruling that the officer had reasonable suspicion, based on the strong odor of alcohol on the defendant's breath, to stop the defendant's vehicle.

State v. Watson, 122 N.C. App. 596 (1996). At about 2:30 a.m., an officer saw a vehicle driving on the dividing line on a two-lane highway near a nightclub. After turning to follow the vehicle, the officer watched the vehicle weave back and forth in its lane for about 15 seconds. The officer then stopped the vehicle. The court ruled that this was sufficient evidence, based on the totality of the circumstances, to support an investigative stop of the vehicle for impaired driving.

State v. Battle, 109 N.C. App. 367 (1993). Officer Harmon responded to a disturbance call at a washerette and saw the defendant seated behind the steering wheel of a red Pontiac. The officer noticed the odor of alcohol on the defendant's breath, and the defendant performed physical tests poorly. The officer told the defendant not to drive the vehicle, because he believed the defendant was impaired by alcohol. The officer left the washerette, radioed Officer Beekin to be on the lookout for the Pontiac, and gave Beekin the vehicle's license plate number. Officer Beekin later saw the Pontiac leave the washerette, followed it for four blocks (and did not see anything unusual about its operation), and then stopped it.

The court ruled that Officer Harmon, before he communicated his request to be on the lookout for the Pontiac, had reasonable suspicion that the defendant, impaired by alcohol, would leave the parking lot operating the vehicle. Although Officer Beekin did not personally have the information to establish reasonable suspicion and had not been told that information by Officer Harmon, Officer Beekin validly stopped the Pontiac based on Harmon's request, which was based on reasonable suspicion.

State v. Aubin, 100 N.C. App. 628 (1990). An officer had reasonable suspicion of an impaired driving offense to stop a car that was going 45 m.p.h. and weaving within a lane on Interstate 95.

State v. Jones, 96 N.C. App. 389 (1989). Although the officer did not see the vehicle committing a traffic violation, his observations of the vehicle's traveling 20 miles per hour under the speed limit (45 m.p.h. in a 65 m.p.h. zone) on an interstate highway and weaving within a lane were sufficient, based on the officer's training and 16 years' experience, to support a reasonable suspicion to make an investigatory stop for DWI. The court noted that the officer's failure to charge the defendant with a DWI offense was irrelevant in determining whether the officer initially had reasonable suspicion to stop the vehicle.

State v. Adkerson, 90 N.C. App. 333 (1988). An officer was traveling east on a highway at 2:00 a.m. and saw the defendant's car as it was traveling west. The officer noticed that the headlights of the defendant's car were darting back and forth as though the car was weaving. The officer turned around and followed the car for about a quarter of a mile. It weaved back and forth in its lane five or six times and ran off the right side of the road once.

The court ruled that the officer had reasonable suspicion to make an investigatory stop for impaired driving.

FEDERAL APPELLATE COURTS

United States v. Wheat, 278 F.3d 722 (8th Cir. 2001). A motorist using a cell phone called 911 to report that a tan-and-cream-colored Nissan Stanza with a license plate beginning with the letters W-O-C was being driven erratically in the northward lane of Highway 169 near Fort Dodge, Iowa. The caller said that the car was passing on the wrong side of the road, cutting off other cars, and otherwise being driven as if by a "complete maniac." The 911 operator did not ask the caller to identify himself. The caller's information was relayed to patrolling officers. Shortly thereafter, an officer saw a tan Nissan Maxima with a license plate beginning with the letters W-O-C stopped in the northbound lane of Highway 169 at its intersection with Highway 20. The Nissan made a right turn, and the officer stopped it immediately, without having observed any incidents of erratic driving or other traffic violation. The defendant was driving the Nissan.

The court ruled, distinguishing *Florida v. J.L.*, 529 U.S. 266 (2000), that the officer had reasonable suspicion to stop the vehicle. The court noted that an anonymous caller extensively described a vehicle that, based on the caller's contemporaneous eyewitness observations, the caller believed was being operated dangerously. The caller cited specific examples of moving violations. When the officer caught up with the vehicle minutes later while it was stopped at an intersection, he corroborated all its innocent details, thus confirming that it was the vehicle identified by the caller. Within seconds after the vehicle resumed motion, the officer immediately stopped it before it could proceed and potentially endanger other vehicles.

Non-DWI Traffic Stops
UNITED STATES SUPREME COURT

Heien v. North Carolina, 135 S. Ct. 530 (2014) (citations omitted). Affirming *State v. Heien*, 366 N.C. 271 (2012), the Court ruled that because an officer's mistake of law was reasonable, it could support a vehicle stop. In *Heien*, an officer stopped a vehicle because one of its two brake lights was out, but a court later determined that a single working brake light was all the law required. The case presented the question of whether such a mistake of law can give rise to the reasonable suspicion necessary to uphold the seizure under the Fourth Amendment.

The Court answered the question in the affirmative. It explained:

> [W]e have repeatedly affirmed, "the ultimate touchstone of the Fourth Amendment is 'reasonableness.'" . . . To be reasonable is not to be perfect, and so the Fourth Amendment allows for some mistakes on the part of government officials, giving them "fair leeway for enforcing the law in the community's protection." . . . We have recognized that searches and seizures based on mistakes of fact can be reasonable. The warrantless search of a home, for instance, is reasonable if undertaken with the consent of a resident, and remains lawful when officers obtain the consent of someone who reasonably appears to be but is not in fact a resident. . . . By the same token, if officers with probable cause to arrest a suspect mistakenly arrest an individual matching the suspect's description, neither the seizure nor an accompanying search of the arrestee would be unlawful. . . . The limit is that "the mistakes must be those of reasonable men."
>
> But reasonable men make mistakes of law, too, and such mistakes are no less compatible with the concept of reasonable suspicion. Reasonable suspicion arises from the combination of an officer's understanding of the facts and his understanding of the relevant law. The officer may be reasonably mistaken on either ground. Whether the facts turn out to be not what was thought, or the law turns out to be not what was thought, the result is the same: the facts are outside the scope of the law. There is no reason, under the text of the Fourth Amendment or our precedents, why this same result should be acceptable when reached by way of a reasonable mistake of fact, but not when reached by way of a similarly reasonable mistake of law.

The Court then found that the officer's mistake of law was objectively reasonable, given the state statutes at issue:

> Although the North Carolina statute at issue refers to "*a* stop lamp," suggesting the need for only a single working brake light, it also provides that "[t]he stop lamp may be incorporated into a unit with one or more *other* rear lamps." N.C. Gen. Stat. Ann. § 20-129(g) (emphasis added). The use of "other" suggests to the everyday reader of English that a "stop lamp" is a type of "rear lamp." And another subsection of the same provision requires that vehicles "have all originally equipped rear lamps or the equivalent in good working order," § 20–129(d), arguably indicating that if a vehicle has multiple "stop lamp[s]," all must be functional.

NORTH CAROLINA SUPREME COURT

State v. Griffin, 366 N.C. 473 (2013). The court ruled that the defendant's act of stopping his vehicle in the middle of the roadway and turning away from a license checkpoint supported reasonable suspicion for a vehicle stop. The trial court denied the defendant's motion to suppress, finding the stop constitutional. In an unpublished opinion, the court of appeals reversed on grounds that the checkpoint was unconstitutional. That court did not, however, comment on whether reasonable suspicion for the stop existed. The state supreme court allowed the State's petition for discretionary review to determine whether there was reasonable suspicion to initiate a stop of the defendant's vehicle and reversed. It reasoned:

> Defendant approached a checkpoint marked with blue flashing lights. Once the patrol car lights became visible, defendant stopped in the middle of the road, even though he was not at an intersection, and appeared to attempt a three-point turn by beginning to turn left and continuing onto the shoulder. From the checkpoint [the officer] observed defendant's actions and suspected defendant was attempting to evade the checkpoint. . . . It is clear that this Court and the Fourth Circuit have held that even a legal turn, when viewed in the totality of the circumstances, may give rise to reasonable suspicion. Given the place and manner of defendant's turn in conjunction with his proximity to the checkpoint, we hold there was reasonable suspicion that defendant was violating the law; thus, the stop was constitutional. Therefore, because the [officer] had sufficient grounds to stop defendant's vehicle based on reasonable suspicion, it is unnecessary for this Court to address the constitutionality of the driver's license checkpoint.

State v. Burke, 365 N.C. 415 (2012). In a per curiam ruling without a written opinion, the state supreme court affirmed the decision in *State v. Burke*, 212 N.C. App. 654 (2011), in which the court of appeals ruled that the trial judge erred by denying the defendant's motion to suppress because reasonable suspicion did not support a stop of the defendant's vehicle. The officer stopped the vehicle because the numbers on its 30-day tag looked "low," and the low number led him to "wonder[] about the possibility of the tag being fictitious." The court of appeals noted that it had previously ruled that 30-day tags that were unreadable, concealed, obstructed, or illegible justified stops of the vehicles involved. In this case, however, although the officer testified that the 30-day tag was dirty and worn, he was able to read the tag without difficulty. The tag was not faded. The information was clearly visible and was accurate and proper.

State v. Maready, 362 N.C. 614 (2008). Two officers were on patrol and saw an apparently intoxicated man walking along a road. The man was staggering near the roadway, so the officers began driving toward him. As they did so, the officers saw in the opposite lane a minivan being driven at a slow speed with its hazard lights activated. Behind the minivan was a Honda Civic. The intoxicated man ran across the roadway and got into the Honda. After passing the minivan, which had stopped, the Honda continued down the road. The officers turned around, and as they pulled alongside the minivan, its driver signaled them to get their attention. The minivan driver appeared distraught and told the officers that they needed to check on the Honda's driver because he had been driving erratically, running stop signs and stop lights. The officers conducted an investigatory stop of the Honda, which the defendant was found to be driving.

The court ruled that the officers had reasonable suspicion of criminal activity to make the stop. (1) The driver of the minivan was in a position to view the alleged traffic violations; a firsthand eyewitness report is an indicator of reliability. Her cautious driving and apparent distress were consistent with a driver having witnessed another motorist driving erratically. (2) The court gave significant weight to the minivan driver's approaching the officers in person and providing information at a time and place near the scene of the alleged traffic violations. She had little time to fabricate her allegations. She was not a completely anonymous informant, because she provided the tip through a face-to-face encounter with the officers. It is inconsequential that the officers did not pause to record

her license plate number or other identifying information. Not knowing whether the officers would do so, the minivan driver willingly placed her anonymity at risk. Reviewing all the evidence, including the officers' observations, the court concluded that there was reasonable suspicion to make an investigative stop of the defendant's vehicle.

State v. Styles, 362 N.C. 412 (2008). The defendant, who was operating a vehicle moving in the same direction as and in front of an officer's vehicle, changed lanes without signaling. An officer stopped the defendant for that violation.

(1) The court ruled, relying on the rulings of several federal courts of appeal, that reasonable suspicion is the standard for stops of vehicles for all traffic violations. The court disavowed statements in prior court opinions and in cases of the North Carolina Court of Appeals that probable cause is the standard for the stop of a vehicle for a readily observed traffic violation. These cases include *State v. Ivey*, 360 N.C. 562 (2006); *State v. McClendon*, 350 N.C. 630 (1999); *State v. Young*, 148 N.C. App. 462 (2002); and *State v. Wilson*, 155 N.C. App. 89 (2003). (2) The court ruled that the officer had reasonable suspicion to stop the vehicle for changing lanes without signaling under G.S. 20-154(a). The defendant's failure to signal violated the statute, because changing lanes immediately in front of another vehicle may affect the operation of the trailing vehicle (in this case, the officer's vehicle).

State v. Ivey, 360 N.C. 562 (2006). A law enforcement officer stopped a vehicle driven by the defendant after observing that the defendant completely stopped at a stop sign at an intersection and then made a right turn without using a turn signal. The court ruled, relying on the standard of probable cause set out in *Whren v. United States*, 517 U.S. 806 (1996), that the officer did not have probable cause to stop the vehicle for a perceived traffic violation, specifically G.S. 20-154(a). The evidence did not indicate that any vehicle or pedestrian was, or might have been, affected by the turn—including the officer's vehicle, which was some distance behind the defendant's vehicle. [Author's note: Since the *Ivey* ruling, the North Carolina Supreme Court in *State v. Styles*, 362 N.C. 412 (2008), ruled that reasonable suspicion, not probable cause, is the standard for all traffic stops.]

State v. Steen, 352 N.C. 227 (2000). Officers responded to a call that a man was on a bicycle that was weaving on a specific street. Officers discovered the defendant on a bicycle on that street—weaving back and forth through heavy traffic—and stopped him. The court ruled that the officers had reasonable suspicion to stop the defendant; the defendant's dangerous operation of the bicycle constituted a motor vehicle offense (presumably, reckless driving under G.S. 20-140, which applies to a bicycle).

State v. McClendon, 350 N.C. 630 (1999). Officer A saw the defendant driving a station wagon on I-85 at a speed of about 72 m.p.h. in a 65 m.p.h. zone and following closely behind a minivan that was going the same speed. The officer believed that the two vehicles were traveling together. With the assistance of Officer B, both vehicles were stopped. Officer A questioned the driver of the minivan and then issued a warning ticket for speeding. Officer B questioned the defendant. The defendant appeared nervous, did not make eye contact, and was breathing heavily. He produced a driver's license and title to the vehicle but no registration. The defendant told the officer that the station wagon belonged to his girlfriend; however, he could not give the officer her name, even though the addresses on the defendant's driver's license and the vehicle's title were the same. As the defendant continued to answer questions, his nervousness increased. He fidgeted, answered evasively, and appeared very uncomfortable. The officer again asked the defendant for his girlfriend's name and for the name on the vehicle's registration. The defendant appeared to say "Anna." Although that name did not appear on the title, a radio check did not reveal any problems with the registration or the defendant's driver's license. The name on the title was Jema Ramirez. After communication with Officer A, Officer B issued a warning ticket to the defendant for speeding and following too closely. When asked to consent to a search of his vehicle, the defendant—sighing deeply, chuckling nervously, and looking down—muttered "no." Officer A arrived. The defendant was sweating and breathing rapidly and again refused to consent to a search of his vehicle. Approximately 15 to 20 minutes elapsed after the issuance of the warning ticket before a drug dog arrived and alerted to the vehicle, resulting in a search and the discovery of drugs.

The court adopted, in considering search and seizure issues under the North Carolina Constitution, the ruling in *Whren v. United States*, 517 U.S. 806 (1996), that stopping a vehicle for a traffic violation, when there is probable cause to believe that the traffic violation was committed, is constitutional regardless of the officer's motivation for doing so (for example, stopping a vehicle for a traffic violation when the officer's motivation for

the stop is to investigate illegal drugs). The court ruled that the officer in this case had probable cause to stop the defendant's vehicle for speeding and following too closely and therefore was justified in stopping it, regardless of the officer's motivation for doing so.

The court also ruled that the continued detention of the defendant from the time of the issuance of the warning ticket to the arrival of the drug dog was supported by reasonable suspicion of criminal activity. The court cited several factors that supported reasonable suspicion under the totality of the circumstances. First, when the officer questioned the defendant about who owned the car, the defendant said his girlfriend owned it but initially would not give a name. Then he gave the name Anna, but that name was not listed on the title. Second, although the defendant appeared unsure of who owned the car, the address of the owner listed on the title and the address on the defendant's driver's license were the same, which indicated that they both lived in the same residence. Third, the defendant was extremely nervous, sweating, breathing rapidly, sighing heavily, and chuckling nervously in response to questions. He also refused to make eye contact when answering questions. The court cited *State v. Butler*, 331 N.C. 227 (1992), and noted that nervousness was a factor in determining reasonable suspicion in that case.

The court distinguished its ruling from the ruling in *State v. Pearson*, 348 N.C. 272 (1998) (no reasonable suspicion to frisk defendant). The court stated that it would "revisit *Pearson* now in order to clarify its meaning . . . ." The court noted that it said in *Pearson* that "[t]he nervousness of the defendant is not significant. Many people become nervous when stopped by a state trooper." The court stated:

> Although the quoted language from *Pearson* is couched in rather absolute terms, we did not mean to imply there that nervousness can never be significant in determining whether an officer could form a reasonable suspicion that criminal activity is afoot. Nervousness, like all other facts, must be taken in light of the totality of circumstances. It is true that many people do become nervous when stopped by an officer of the law. Nevertheless, nervousness is an appropriate factor to consider when determining whether a basis for reasonable suspicion exists.

In *Pearson*, the nervousness of the defendant was not remarkable. Even when taken together with the inconsistencies in the statements of the defendant and his girlfriend, it did not support a reasonable suspicion. In the case before us, however, defendant exhibited more than ordinary nervousness; defendant was fidgety and breathing rapidly, sweat had formed on his forehead, he would sigh deeply, and he would not make eye contact with the officer. This, taken in the context of the totality of circumstances found to exist by the trial court, gave rise to a reasonable suspicion that criminal activity was afoot.

The court ruled that the duration of the detention—15 to 20 minutes from the warning ticket to the arrival of the drug dog—was reasonable. The officers acted quickly and diligently to obtain the drug dog, and they promptly put the drug dog to work on its arrival.

NORTH CAROLINA COURT OF APPEALS

State v. Johnson, ___ N.C. App. ___, 784 S.E.2d 633 (2016). The court ruled that the trial court in a DWI trial erred by denying the defendant's motion to suppress based on the officer lacking reasonable suspicion to make a traffic stop for motor vehicle violations. While on routine patrol, the officer saw the defendant's truck stopped at a traffic light waiting for the light to change. The defendant revved his engine, and when the light changed to green, abruptly accelerated into a left-hand turn. Although his vehicle fishtailed, the defendant regained control before it struck the curb or left the lane of travel. The officer was unable to estimate the speed of the defendant's truck. Snow was falling at the time and slush was on the road. These facts do not support the conclusion that the officer had reasonable suspicion that the defendant committed a violation of unsafe movement or traveling too fast for the conditions.

State v. Coleman, 228 N.C. App. 76 (2013). The court ruled that an officer lacked reasonable suspicion to stop the defendant's vehicle. A "be on the lookout" call was issued after a citizen caller reported that there was a cup of beer in a gold Toyota sedan with license number VST-8773 parked at the Kangaroo gas station at the corner of Wake Forest Road and Ronald Drive. Although the complainant wished to remain anonymous, the communications center obtained the caller's name as Kim Creech. An officer responded and observed a vehicle fitting the caller's description. The officer followed the driver as he pulled out of the lot and onto Wake Forest Road and then pulled him over. The officer did not observe any traffic violations. After a test indicated impairment, the defendant was charged with DWI. Noting that the officer's sole reason for the stop was Creech's tip, the court found that the tip was not reliable in its assertion of illegality because possessing an open container of alcohol in a parking lot is not illegal; the law applies only to highways, not public vehicular areas. It concluded: "Accordingly, Ms. Creech's tip contained no actual allegation of criminal activity." The court further found that the officer's mistaken belief that the tip included an actual allegation of illegal activity was not objectively reasonable. Finally, the court concluded that even if the officer's mistaken belief was reasonable, it still would find the tip insufficiently reliable. Considering anonymous tip cases, the court ruled that although Creech's tip provided the license plate number and location of the car, "she did not identify or describe defendant, did not provide any way for [the] Officer . . . to assess her credibility, failed to explain her basis of knowledge, and did not include any information concerning defendant's future actions."

State v. Hernandez, 229 N.C. App. 601 (2013). The court ruled, relying on *State v. Hess*, 185 N.C. App. 530 (2007), that an investigative stop of the defendant's vehicle was lawful. Officers stopped the defendant's vehicle because it was registered in her name, her license was suspended, and they were unable to determine the driver's identity.

State v. Royster, 224 N.C. App. 374 (2012). (1) The court ruled that an officer had reasonable suspicion to stop the defendant's vehicle for speeding. The court rejected the defendant's argument that because the officer only observed the vehicle for three to five seconds, the officer did not have a reasonable opportunity to judge the vehicle's speed. The court noted that after his initial observation of the vehicle, the officer made a U-turn and began pursuing it. He testified that during his pursuit, the defendant "maintained his speed." Although the officer did not testify to a specific distance that he observed the defendant travel, "some distance was implied" by his testimony concerning his pursuit of the defendant. Also, although it is not necessary for an officer to have had specialized training to be able to visually estimate a vehicle's speed, the officer in this case had specialized training in visual speed estimation. (2) The court rejected the defendant's argument that the officer lacked reasonable suspicion to stop his vehicle for speeding because there was insufficient evidence identifying the defendant as the driver. Specifically, the defendant noted that the officer lost sight of the vehicle for a short period of time. The officer only lost sight of the defendant for approximately 30 seconds, and when he saw the vehicle again, he recognized both the car and the driver. [Author's note: On this point the opinion discussed the court's earlier opinion in *State v. Lindsey*, 219 N.C. App. 249 (2012), which was later reversed by the North Carolina Supreme Court (see 366 N.C. 325 (2012)) four days before *Royster* was decided but not in time to be included in *Royster*. However, because the court distinguished *Lindsey*, its discussion of the reversed decision does not appear to undermine the ultimate ruling.]

State v. Canty, 224 N.C. App. 514 (2012). The court ruled that reasonable suspicion did not support a traffic stop. The State had argued that reasonable suspicion existed based on the driver's alleged crossing of the fog line on Interstate 40, the driver's and passenger's alleged nervousness and failure to make eye contact with officers as they drove by and alongside the patrol car, and the vehicle's slowed speed. The court found that the evidence failed to show that the vehicle crossed the fog line and, in the absence of a traffic violation, the officers' beliefs about the conduct of the driver and passenger were nothing more than an "unparticularized suspicion or hunch." It noted that nervousness, slowing down, and not making eye contact are not unusual reactions when passing law enforcement officers. The court also found it "hard to believe" that the officers could tell that the driver and passenger were nervous as they passed the officers on the highway and as the officers momentarily rode alongside the vehicle. The court also found the reduction in speed—from 65 m.p.h. to 59 m.p.h.—insignificant.

State v. Osterhoudt, 222 N.C. App. 620 (2012). The court ruled that an officer had reasonable suspicion to stop the defendant's vehicle based on observed traffic violations despite the officer's mistaken belief that the defendant also had violated G.S. 20-146(a) (drive on right side of highway). The officer's testimony that he initiated the stop after observing the defendant drive over the double yellow line was sufficient to establish a violation of G.S. 20-146(d)(1) (drive within single lane); (d)(3) (failure to obey direction of official traffic-control device regarding designated lanes); (d)(4) (failure to obey direction of official traffic-control device regarding changing lanes); and 20-153(a) (proper right turns at intersections). There-

fore, regardless of his subjective belief that the defendant violated G.S. 20-146(a), the officer's testimony established objective criteria justifying the stop. The stop was reasonable, and the superior court erred in holding otherwise. The court noted that because the officer's reason for the stop was not based solely on his mistaken belief that the defendant violated G.S. 20-146(a) but, rather, was also because the defendant crossed the double yellow line, the case was distinguishable from others that had ruled that an officer's mistaken belief that a defendant had committed a traffic violation is not an objectively reasonable basis for a stop. [Author's note: Concerning an officer's reasonable mistake of law, see *Heien v. North Carolina*, 135 S. Ct. 530 (2014), discussed above.]

State v. Williams, 209 N.C. App. 255 (2011). The court ruled that officers had reasonable suspicion to stop a vehicle in which the defendant was a passenger, based on the officers' good faith belief that the driver had a revoked license and information about the defendant's drug sales provided by three informants. Two of the informants were confidential informants who had provided good information in the past. The third was a patron of the hotel where the drug sales allegedly occurred and met with an officer face-to-face. Additionally, officers corroborated the informants' information. As such, the informants' information provided sufficient indicia of reliability. The officer's mistake about who was driving the vehicle was reasonable under the circumstances.

State v. Ford, 208 N.C. App. 699 (2010). The court ruled that the trial court properly denied the defendant's motion to suppress when officers had reasonable suspicion to believe that the defendant committed a traffic violation supporting the traffic stop. The stop was premised on the defendant's alleged violation of G.S. 20-129(d), which requires that a motor vehicle's rear plate be lit so that under normal atmospheric conditions it can be read from a distance of 50 feet. The trial court found that normal conditions existed when officers pulled behind the vehicle; officers were unable to read the license plate with the patrol car's lights on; when the patrol car's lights were turned off, the plate was not visible within the statutory requirement; and officers cited the defendant for the violation. The defendant's evidence that the vehicle, a rental car, was "fine" when rented did not controvert the officer's testimony that the tag was not sufficiently illuminated on the night of the stop.

State v. Hudson, 206 N.C. App. 482 (2010). The court ruled that an officer had reasonable suspicion to stop the defendant's vehicle for a violation of G.S. 20-146(a) (requiring vehicles to be driven on the right half of a highway) after the officer observed the vehicle twice cross the center line of the northbound lanes of I-95 and weave back over the fog line.

State v. McRae, 203 N.C. App. 319 (2010). The court ruled that Officer A had reasonable suspicion to stop a vehicle for two independent reasons. First, Officer A had the authority to stop the vehicle because the officer had reasonable suspicion that the defendant had committed a violation of G.S. 20-154(a) by failing to use his turn signal when he pulled off the highway into a gas station parking lot. There was medium traffic and the defendant's vehicle was a short distance in front of the officer. The court relied on *State v. Styles*, 362 N.C. 412 (2008), and distinguished *State v. Ivey*, 360 N.C. 562 (2006). Second, the officer also had the authority to stop the vehicle based on a confidential informant's tip to another officer (Officer B) that had been broadcast to Officer A and other officers before the stop telling them to be on the lookout for a black male driving a green Grand Am within the Pembroke city limits. The informant had worked with Officer B on several occasions and had provided reliable information in the past that led to the arrest of drug offenders. The informant identified the driver by name—a name that Officer B recognized as someone associated with the drug trade. The informant also described the specific car (a green Grand Am) and advised the officer that the defendant would be driving the car within the city limits of Pembroke with 60 grams of cocaine in his possession.

State v. Smith, 192 N.C. App. 690 (2008). An officer stopped a Ford pickup truck for failing to display a proper registration tag. The court noted the recent ruling in *State v. Styles*, 362 N.C. 412 (2008) (reasonable suspicion is standard for all vehicle stops), and ruled that the officer had reasonable suspicion to stop the defendant's vehicle for a violation of G.S. 20-79.1(e). The officer's testimony showed that it was dark when the officer saw the vehicle's license tag, the tag was just a piece of paper with "February 07" written on it, and the tag was not like a piece of cardboard that North Carolina auto dealers provide with a car purchase. [Author's note: The tag was issued by the state of Georgia. The court cited a federal case that had ruled that a traffic stop based on an officer's incorrect but reasonable assessment of facts does not violate the Fourth Amendment.]

State v. Johnson, 186 N.C. App. 673 (2007). An officer ran the tags on a Ford vehicle and discovered that they were registered to a Chevrolet. The court ruled that the officer had reasonable suspicion to stop the vehicle for improper tags.

State v. McLamb, 186 N.C. App. 124 (2007). An officer stopped a vehicle going 30 m.p.h. The officer believed that the speed limit was 20 m.p.h., but the legal limit was actually 55 m.p.h. The court ruled, relying on *State v. Ivey*, 360 N.C. 562 (2006), and cases from other jurisdictions, that the officer did not have probable cause to stop the vehicle for speeding. An officer's mistake of law may not support probable cause to stop a vehicle. [Author's note: This ruling may need to be reconsidered in light of the standard for a reasonable mistake of law set out in *Heien v. North Carolina*, 135 S. Ct. 530 (2014), discussed above.]

State v. Hess, 185 N.C. App. 530 (2007). An officer on patrol at night ran a vehicle's registration plate and then the registered owner's driver's license, which was reported to be suspended. The officer could not determine the sex or race of the driver. The officer stopped the vehicle. The court ruled, relying on cases from other jurisdictions, that the officer had reasonable suspicion to stop the vehicle. The court stated that it was reasonable for the officer to infer under these circumstances that the owner was driving the vehicle. See also State v. Herdnandez, 227 N.C. App. 601 (2013), discussed above.

State v. Parker, 183 N.C. App. 1 (2007). A narcotics detective was conducting surveillance of the defendant in response to a citizen's complaint that the defendant was trafficking in methamphetamine. He stopped a vehicle that the defendant was driving because it was going approximately 60 m.p.h. in a 45 m.p.h. zone and then passed another vehicle at approximately 80 m.p.h. in a 55 m.p.h. zone. The court ruled that the narcotics detective had probable cause to stop the defendant's vehicle for the speeding violations. The court noted prior case law (*Whren v. United States*, 517 U.S. 806 (1996); *State v. McClendon*, 350 N.C. 630 (1999)) that an officer's subjective motivation is irrelevant when a stop is supported by probable cause. Also, the fact that an officer conducting a traffic stop did not later issue a traffic citation is irrelevant to the validity of the stop under *State v. Baublitz*, 172 N.C. App. 801 (2005). [Author's note: Since the *Parker* ruling, the North Carolina Supreme Court in *State v. Styles*, 362 N.C. 412 (2008), ruled that reasonable suspicion, not probable cause, is the standard for all traffic stops.]

State v. Baublitz, 172 N.C. App. 801 (2005). An officer was conducting drug surveillance at a residence. The defendant and another person got into a vehicle and drove away. The officer followed the vehicle and saw it twice cross the center line of the highway. The officer stopped the vehicle, conducted a consent search, discovered cocaine in the vehicle, and arrested the defendant for possession of cocaine. He did not charge the defendant with the traffic violation. The court ruled that the officer had probable cause to stop the vehicle for the readily observed traffic violation under G.S. 20-146(a) (vehicle must be driven on right side of highway). The court noted that under *State v. McClendon*, 350 N.C. 630 (1999), the ulterior motive of the officer is irrelevant when there are objective circumstances justifying the officer's action. The court also ruled that the officer's failure to charge the defendant with the traffic violation was irrelevant to the validity of the stop. [Author's note: Since the *Baublitz* ruling, the North Carolina Supreme Court in *State v. Styles*, 362 N.C. 412 (2008), ruled that reasonable suspicion, not probable cause, is the standard for all traffic stops.]

State v. Hernandez, 170 N.C. App. 299 (2005). An officer stopped a vehicle driven by the defendant for a seat belt violation. While in the patrol car with the defendant, the officer ran a license and registration check, questioned the defendant about his travel plans, and issued him a citation. The defendant then gave consent to search the vehicle, and cocaine was found in the vehicle. The consent to search was given within six minutes of the defendant's detention in the vehicle. The court ruled that (1) the officer had probable cause to stop the vehicle for the seat belt violation (the officer saw the defendant remove the seat belt while still driving), a readily observed traffic violation; and (2) the officer had reasonable suspicion to detain the defendant after issuing the citation, based on the defendant's extreme nervousness, conflicting statements about his travel plans, and air fresheners in the defendant's vehicle emitting a strong odor. [Author's note: Since the *Hernandez* ruling, the North Carolina Supreme Court in *State v. Styles*, 362 N.C. 412 (2008), ruled that reasonable suspicion, not probable cause, is the standard for all traffic stops.]

State v. Barnhill, 166 N.C. App. 228 (2004). The court ruled that the officer had probable cause to stop the defendant's vehicle for speeding. The court rejected, as contrary to the rules of evidence, the trial judge's ruling that an officer must articulate objective criteria to corroborate his or her opinion of the vehicle's speed. The court stated that an officer's opinion may be based on personal observation. Also, the court stated that an officer need not have specialized training to be able to visually esti-

mate a vehicle's speed. The court then examined the facts in this case and upheld the officer's stop of the vehicle for speeding: the officer had an unobstructed view of the vehicle as it traveled on a street, and his personal observation of its speed, coupled with the sound of the engine racing and the bouncing of the car as it passed through an intersection, established probable cause to believe that the defendant was exceeding a speed that was reasonable and prudent under the existing conditions in violation of G.S. 20-141(a). [Author's note: Since the *Barnhill* ruling, the North Carolina Supreme Court in *State v. Styles*, 362 N.C. 412 (2008), ruled that reasonable suspicion, not probable cause, is the standard for all traffic stops.]

State v. Villeda, 165 N.C. App. 431 (2004). The court ruled that the officer did not have probable cause to stop the defendant's vehicle for a seat belt violation. Evidence showed that the officer could not see inside vehicles driving in front of him at night on the stretch of road on which the defendant was stopped; thus the evidence supported the trial judge's finding that the allegation that the defendant was not wearing a seat belt was incredible. [Author's note: Since the *Villeda* ruling, the North Carolina Supreme Court in *State v. Styles*, 362 N.C. 412 (2008), ruled that reasonable suspicion, not probable cause, is the standard for all traffic stops.]

State v. Wilson, 155 N.C. App. 89 (2002). A trooper saw a vehicle being driven less than one car length behind another vehicle while traveling at 69 m.p.h. The trooper stopped the car and issued a warning ticket for G.S. 20-152 (following too closely). Later, the defendant consented to a search of the vehicle, and cocaine was found in the vehicle's battery. The court ruled that the trooper had probable cause to stop the vehicle for this violation. [Author's note: Since the *Wilson* ruling, the North Carolina Supreme Court in *State v. Styles*, 362 N.C. 412 (2008), ruled that reasonable suspicion, not probable cause, is the standard for all traffic stops.]

State v. Kincaid, 147 N.C. App. 94 (2001). An officer saw the defendant driving a vehicle and attempting to conceal his face from the officer. The officer stopped the vehicle because he knew that the defendant's license had been revoked for two to three years. During the time the officer had known the defendant, he had seen him travel either as a passenger in a car or as the driver of a moped but never as the driver of a car. The court ruled that the officer had reasonable suspicion to stop the vehicle based on his information about the defendant and his driver's license despite the fact that, after the stop, the officer's information turned out to be incorrect.

State v. Schiffer, 132 N.C. App. 22 (1999). An officer saw a vehicle with windows and windshield that he believed were tinted darker than permitted by North Carolina law. Specifically, the officer saw that the windshield tinting extended approximately 10 inches from the top of the windshield, about 4 to 5 inches in excess of what is permitted under G.S. 20-127(b). Once he pulled behind the vehicle, the officer saw that it had Florida tags. He then pulled alongside the vehicle to see if the window displayed a sticker indicating that the tinting complied with Florida law. Seeing no such sticker, he stopped the vehicle. After the driver rolled down his window, the scent of unburned marijuana emanated from the vehicle. The officer asked for the defendant's consent to search the vehicle. The defendant said he did not know if he could consent to its search because he did not own the vehicle. The officer explained that the defendant could consent because he was in control of the vehicle. He further explained that he could search the vehicle even without the defendant's consent because he smelled marijuana, and that he could obtain a search warrant. The defendant then consented to a search of the vehicle.

The court reviewed North Carolina law at the time of this vehicle stop and concluded that the officer was acting under a good faith but mistaken belief that G.S. 20-127 required vehicles with tinted windows or windshields to display a label in each tinted window or windshield indicating that its tinting complied with North Carolina law. Such labels had been but were no longer required. In addition, a recently enacted statutory change had exempted North Carolina's window tinting restrictions for out-of-state vehicles that were in compliance with their state's tinting laws. However, the windshield tinting restrictions in G.S. 20-127 applied to out-of-state vehicles, and the officer therefore had reasonable suspicion to stop the vehicle based on his observation that the windshield tinting was excessive, and that was one of the reasons the officer stopped the vehicle.

State v. Hudson, 103 N.C. App. 708 (1991). An officer had reasonable suspicion to stop a vehicle when he saw that its 30-day temporary license tag was illegible because both the expiration date and the numbers were faded.

State v. Gray, 55 N.C. App. 568 (1982). An officer who received a report from another officer that the defendant was driving a vehicle with expired temporary license tags had reasonable suspicion to stop the vehicle.

Airport Investigative Stops

United States v. Sokolow, 490 U.S. 1 (1989). The Court ruled that reasonable suspicion supported the officers' stop of the defendant at the Honolulu airport after he had flown from Honolulu to Miami and back to Honolulu. When they stopped him, they knew that (1) the defendant had paid $2,100 for two airplane tickets (he had a woman companion) from a roll of $20 bills; (2) he had traveled using a name that did not match the name under which his telephone number was listed; (3) his original destination was Miami, a source city for drugs; (4) he stayed in Miami for only 48 hours, even though the round-trip flight from Honolulu to Miami takes 20 hours; (5) he appeared nervous during the trip; and (6) he did not check any of his luggage.

The Court stated that its analysis of whether reasonable suspicion existed was not adversely affected by the agents' belief, when they stopped the defendant, that his behavior was consistent with the drug courier profile. A reviewing court must require an officer to articulate factors leading to a conclusion that reasonable suspicion existed, but the fact that these factors may be set forth in a profile does not detract from their evidentiary significance as understood by a trained officer.

The Court stated that, for an investigative stop to be reasonable, officers are not required to use the least intrusive means available to verify or to dispel their suspicions—for example, approaching a defendant without using force rather than deciding to use force initially. Such a rule would unduly hamper an officer's ability to make swift, on-the-spot decisions. The least intrusive means rule applies only to the length of the investigative stop, not to whether officers had a less intrusive means to verify their suspicions before stopping someone.

Florida v. Rodriguez, 469 U.S. 1 (1984). This case involved an airport encounter between officers and people in an airport who possessed drugs. The Court ruled that even assuming that officers had seized the defendant and two other drug suspects, they had reasonable suspicion to do so because (1) experienced drug officers saw the three suspects at the Miami airport; (2) when the three suspects saw the officers, they spoke furtively to each other; (3) one suspect said to another, "Get out of here"; (4) the defendant tried to evade the officers; and (5) the suspects made contradictory statements about their identities.

Florida v. Royer, 460 U.S. 491 (1983). This case involved an airport encounter between officers and a deplaning passenger who possessed drugs. Eight justices (in four opinions) concluded that reasonable suspicion supported the stop of the passenger. His appearance, mannerisms, luggage, and actions fit certain characteristics of the drug courier profile, and the officers discovered that he was traveling under an assumed name. But five justices (in two opinions) concluded that sometime after the initial stop, the officers' actions exceeded the permissible bounds of a stop when they took the passenger (without his consent and without a security or safety justification) to a small airport room, removed his suitcase from the baggage area, and attempted to obtain his consent to search his suitcase while they retained his airline ticket and driver's license. The defendant was as a practical matter under arrest, so that probable cause was necessary to justify any further detention. [Author's note: In the later case of *United States v. Sharpe*, 470 U.S. 675 (1985), the Court indicated that an important factor in *Royer* when determining that the detention exceeded the scope of an investigative stop and had become an arrest was the confinement of the defendant without his consent in a small room for questioning after his luggage had been seized.]

Reid v. Georgia, 448 U.S. 438 (1980). This case involved an airport encounter between officers and a deplaning passenger who possessed drugs. The Court ruled that the following evidence was insufficient to support reasonable suspicion to stop the defendant outside the airport terminal to investigate drug activity: (1) the defendant and his companion arrived from a city that was a source of drugs, (2) they had no luggage other than their shoulder bags, and (3) they appeared to be trying to conceal the fact that they were traveling together as they walked through the airport terminal. [Author's note: Because the Court did not have before it the issue of whether a seizure had occurred when the drug agent approached the passenger outside the terminal, the Court's opinion assumed that a seizure had occurred. It was unclear whether a Court majority would have decided that the officer's actions constituted a seizure.]

United States v. Mendenhall, 446 U.S. 544 (1980). This case involved an airport encounter with a deplaning passenger who possessed drugs. Two justices concluded that the officers' actions in approaching and questioning a passenger were not a seizure requiring justification; a person is seized under the Fourth Amendment only if, in

view of all the circumstances surrounding the incident, a reasonable person would have believed that he or she was not free to leave. [Author's note: A majority of the Court adopted this definition of a seizure in later cases, but note that this definition was modified in *California v. Hodari D.*, 499 U.S. 621 (1991), and *Florida v. Bostick*, 501 U.S. 429 (1991).] Three justices assumed that the officers' actions were a seizure and concluded that reasonable suspicion supported stopping the passenger for questioning, based on the trained drug officers' observations of the passenger and the fact that drug couriers frequented this airport.

State v. Pope, 120 N.C. App. 462 (1995). An officer approached the defendant in an airport and identified himself. After the defendant agreed to talk with the officer, the defendant produced his airline ticket and identification on the officer's request. The officer returned the ticket and identification to the defendant and asked him to accompany the officer to a more private area. The defendant agreed and accompanied the officer to a private room. There the defendant consented to a search of his bag and person. The court ruled, relying on *Florida v. Royer*, 460 U.S. 491 (1983); *State v. Casey*, 59 N.C. App. 99 (1982); and *State v. Grimmett*, 54 N.C. App. 494 (1981); that the entire encounter between the officer and the defendant was consensual and therefore the defendant's Fourth Amendment rights were not violated.

State v. McDaniels, 103 N.C. App. 175 (1991), *aff'd*, 331 N.C. 112 (1992). Officers had reasonable suspicion to stop a vehicle as it was driving away from the Raleigh-Durham (RDU) airport when they had reliable information that (1) two men who were the driver and passenger of the stopped vehicle, using fictitious names, had chartered a plane to fly late at night to the New York City area, a source of about 90 percent of the illegal drugs brought into central North Carolina; (2) the men had made an identical trip the weekend before from RDU; (3) they paid $1,270 in cash for their flight; (4) they were dressed in "shiny," "silky," "flashy," business suits; (5) they gave the charter service two telephone numbers that could not be verified; (6) the car's license plate number was listed in a woman's name but was assigned to a different car, and the car's vehicle identification number was registered to an owner whose name was neither of the names given to the charter service; (7) one of the men had carried a briefcase on the flight to the New York City area late Saturday night, which suggested a business transaction but seemed to the officers an unusual time to conduct business when combined with other suspicious factors in the case; and (8) after their arrival to the RDU airport, the two men in the car, which had heavily tinted glass, circled the parking area, which the officers believed meant that the occupants were watching out for law enforcement. The court noted that the facts known to the officers at the time of the stop must be viewed through the eyes of a reasonable officer on the scene, guided by the officer's experience and training. For another airport stop case, see *State v. Hendrickson*, 124 N.C. App. 150 (1996) (reasonable suspicion existed to stop defendant and seize bag at airport).

State v. Allen, 90 N.C. App. 15 (1988). Even assuming that the officer's statement to the defendant in an airport, "Halt, police," was a seizure [Author's note: Such a statement would not by itself constitute a seizure under the later case of *California v. Hodari D.*, 499 U.S. 621 (1991).], the officer had reasonable suspicion to stop the defendant, based on the officer's information from an informant about the defendant's prior drug activity, the officer's prior experience with drug-related arrests, and the defendant's actions after deplaning, which included pushing people out of his way and running down an escalator. Later, the officer approached the defendant in the airport parking lot, identified himself, and asked the defendant for an airline ticket or other identification. These actions also were not a seizure.

State v. Russell, 84 N.C. App. 383 (1987). Reasonable suspicion existed to stop and detain an airplane and its occupants to investigate possession of illegal drugs. The airplane had landed late at night at a rural airport, and there were other suspicious circumstances, discussed in the court's opinion.

State v. Thomas, 81 N.C. App. 200 (1986). A deplaning passenger was not seized when officers asked for and returned his plane ticket and driver's license and he accompanied them without comment when they requested that he come to an office down the concourse. The court ruled that the defendant voluntarily consented to come to the office.

State v. Porter, 65 N.C. App. 13 (1983). The court ruled that the officers' initial encounter with the defendant at an airport was not a seizure; the defendant went to an office voluntarily and consented to a search of her pocketbook. It alternatively ruled that the officers had reasonable suspicion to stop based on an informant's information and the officers' corroboration of that information.

State v. Sugg, 61 N.C. App. 106 (1983). Reasonable suspicion supported an airport stop of the defendant, who met many characteristics of the drug courier profile and whose actions were suspicious to an officer with extensive experience in drug investigations.

State v. Casey, 59 N.C. App. 99 (1982). No seizure occurred during an officer's encounter with a deplaning passenger at an airport or when the passenger accompanied the officer to a basement office. *See also* State v. Grimmett, 54 N.C. App. 494 (1981); State v. Perkerol, 77 N.C. App. 292 (1985); State v. Poindexter, 104 N.C. App. 260 (1991).

School Search and Seizure Cases

Safford Unified School District v. Redding, 557 U.S. 364 (2009). After learning that a middle school student might have prescription strength and over-the-counter pain relief pills, school officials searched her backpack but did not find any pills. A school nurse then had her remove her outer clothing, pull out her bra and shake it, and then pull out the elastic on her underpants. The student's breasts and pelvic area were exposed to some degree by her compliance with these directives. No pills were found. The Court ruled that school officials had reasonable suspicion to search the student's backpack and outer clothing; however, because the facts did not indicate that the drugs presented a danger to students or were concealed in her bra or underpants, school officials did not have sufficient justification under the Fourth Amendment to make the student pull out her bra and underpants. The Court also ruled that school officials were protected from civil liability by qualified immunity because clearly established law when the search was conducted did not show that the search violated the Fourth Amendment.

New Jersey v. T.L.O., 469 U.S. 325 (1985). The Fourth Amendment requires that searches conducted by public school officials on students must be reasonable, but it does not require that the searches be supported by a search warrant or be based on probable cause. A teacher's report that a student had been observed smoking in a bathroom in violation of school rules provided reasonable suspicion to justify a school official's decision to open the student's purse to look for cigarettes. The official's observation of cigarette rolling papers in the purse provided reasonable suspicion that the student was carrying marijuana and justified a further search of the purse for contraband.

In re T.A.S., 366 N.C. 269 (2012). The state supreme court vacated and remanded the decision below, 213 N.C. App. 273 (2011) (holding that a search of a juvenile student's bra conducted by school officials and observed by a male law enforcement officer was constitutionally unreasonable), ordering further findings of fact. The court ordered the trial court to

> make additional findings of fact, including but not necessarily limited to: the names, occupations, genders, and involvement of all the individuals physically present at the "bra lift" search of T.A.S.; whether T.A.S. was advised before the search of the Academy's "no penalty" policy; and whether the "bra lift" search of T.A.S. qualified as a "more intrusive" search under the Academy's Safe School Plan.

The court further provided that "[i]f, after entry of an amended judgment or order by the trial court, either party enters notice of appeal, counsel are instructed to ensure that a copy of the Safe School Plan, discussed at the suppression hearing and apparently introduced into evidence, is included in the record on appeal."

In re D.L.D., 203 N.C. App. 434 (2010). An officer was assigned to a high school as a resource officer and had made many arrests for controlled substances at one of the school's bathrooms. The officer and an assistant principal (hereafter, principal) noticed on monitoring cameras that two male juveniles were entering the bathroom and one was standing outside. The principal told the officer that the situation "looked kind of fishy" and suggested they check it. As they approached the bathroom, they saw one male student outside the men's bathroom and another male student outside the women's bathroom, and both students stared at the officer and principal. They then saw the juvenile and two other male students leave the bathroom. When the juvenile saw the officer and the principal, he ran back into the bathroom, and they followed him. When the officer said that he saw the juvenile put something in his pants, the principal replied, "We need to check it." The officer frisked the juvenile and found a container used to hold BB gun pellets. Inside the container were three individually wrapped bags of marijuana worth $20 each. The officer handcuffed the juvenile and took him to a school office. The principal told the officer that they needed to check the juvenile to make sure that he did not have anything else. The officer searched the juvenile and discovered $59 in his pocket. The juvenile immediately stated that "the money was not from selling drugs" but was his mother's rent money. The court ruled that the Fourth Amendment reasonableness standard for school

searches applied to the searches by the officer, citing *New Jersey v. T.L.O.*, 469 U.S. 325 (1985); *In re D.D.*, 146 N.C. App. 309 (2001); and other cases, and that the searches at the bathroom and school office were constitutional.

In re J.L.B.M., 176 N.C. App. 613 (2006). The court ruled, relying on *State v. Fleming*, 106 N.C. App. 165 (1992), that the following evidence was insufficient to support reasonable suspicion to make an investigative stop of the juvenile. The stopping officer relied solely on a dispatch that there was a suspicious person at a gas station, the juvenile matched the "Hispanic male" description of the suspicious person, the juvenile was wearing baggy clothes, and the juvenile chose to walk away from the patrol car. The officer was not aware of any graffiti or property damage before the officer stopped the juvenile, and the officer noticed a bulge in the juvenile's pocket only after the stop.

In re S.W., 171 N.C. App. 335 (2005). The juvenile, a high school student, walked by a deputy sheriff who was assigned as a full-time school resource officer at the high school. The deputy noticed a strong odor of marijuana emanating from the juvenile. The deputy located two school administrators and in their presence asked the juvenile if he could search him. The juvenile agreed to the search, and the search revealed 10 small plastic bags of marijuana. The court noted that the deputy was exclusively a school resource officer, assisted school officials with school discipline, was present in the school hallways during school hours, and was advancing the school's educational goals when he stopped the juvenile. The deputy was not conducting an investigation at the behest of an outside law enforcement officer who was investigating a non-school-related crime. The court ruled, relying on *In re J.F.M.*, 168 N.C. App. 143 (2005), that the deputy lawfully searched the juvenile under *New Jersey v. T.L.O.*, 469 U.S. 325 (1985) (applying reasonable grounds to suspect as the standard for searches by school officials), and thus did not violate the United States or North Carolina constitutions. The court noted that the deputy did not need the juvenile's consent to conduct the search under the *T.L.O.* standard

In re J.F.M., 168 N.C. App. 143 (2005). A deputy sheriff, who was also a school resource officer, investigated an affray involving T.B. and another student. The affray occurred about 2:00 p.m., and although he did not see the affray, the officer observed a group of students gathered outside on the school campus. He saw T.B. leaving the grounds and gave her three commands to stop, which she ignored. Continuing his investigation, the officer spoke with a school administrator who told him that T.B. had been in the affray and was leaving the school campus. At approximately 3:00 p.m., the officer approached T.B. at a bus stop on the school campus and told her that she needed to come back to the school to talk to the school administrator about the affray. She refused to go with the officer, who responded by grabbing her arm and telling her that she needed to come with him. J.F.M. then pushed the officer and told T.B. to run. T.B. later returned and struck the officer with an umbrella. The court ruled, relying on *Wofford v. Evans*, 390 F.3d 318 (4th Cir. 2004) (extending reasonableness standard of *New Jersey v. T.L.O.*, 469 U.S. 325 (1985), to detentions of students), and *In re D.D.*, 146 N.C. App. 309 (2001) (extending *T.L.O.* to searches by resource officers working in conjunction with school officials), that the reasonableness standard of *T.L.O.* applied to a resource officer's detention of a student when acting in conjunction with a school official. The court examined the facts in this case and found that the resource officer was acting in conjunction with the school administration and that his detention of the student was reasonable under *T.L.O.*

In re D.D., 146 N.C. App. 309 (2001). A teacher told the principal about overhearing some students saying that a group of girls was coming to the school's campus to fight at the end of the school day—the students named one student who would be involved in the fight. The principal gathered three law enforcement officers, one of whom was the school resource officer. The other two were off-duty officers, one of whom was assigned to the school as a security officer. In the school's parking lot, the principal confronted a student of his school and three girls who were from another school in the city. There were additional encounters with these students, which included the finding of a box cutter in the purse of one of the students. The principal and the officers then took them to the principal's office. The principal ordered the girls to empty their pockets. The defendant, a juvenile, had a knife in her pocket. After reviewing case law in other jurisdictions, the court ruled that the Fourth Amendment's reasonableness standard in *New Jersey v. T.L.O.*, 469 U.S. 325 (1985), applied in this case when the officers acted in conjunction with the school principal to maintain a safe and educational environment and to report truants from other schools. The court also ruled that the search of the juvenile was reasonable under the *T.L.O.* standard.

In re Murray, 136 N.C. App. 648 (2000). A student told assistant principal Smith that Jason Murray had something in his book bag that he should not have at school. Smith found Murray alone in a room. Murray denied having a book bag, but Smith saw a book bag less than an arm's reach away from Murray and asked if it was his. When Murray responded affirmatively, Smith walked Murray to her office with Murray carrying his book bag. Smith then asked Murray if there was anything in the book bag that should not be there. He said no. Smith then advised him that she needed to search the bag. Murray responded that he did not want her to search it and asked that his father be called. Smith called in the school's dean of students and a resource officer, a deputy sheriff. They explained to Murray that they needed to search the book bag for safety reasons. When Smith attempted to take possession of the bag from Murray, he held on to it. The deputy grabbed Murray, struggled with him, and handcuffed him so that no one would get hurt. Smith then opened the bag and found a pellet gun. The court ruled, relying on cases from other jurisdictions, that this search was conducted by a school official, with only the assistance of the deputy, and thus the reasonable suspicion standard of *New Jersey v. T.L.O.*, 469 U.S. 325 (1985), applied. The court also ruled that the student's tip and Murray's lie about ownership of the bag were sufficient to establish reasonable suspicion. Finally, the court ruled that the search was conducted in a reasonable manner. Smith's search, which was confined to the book bag, was reasonable in scope. The use of handcuffs ensured that Smith could safely search the bag without interference and allowed the deputy to prevent harm to those present. *See also* DesRoches *ex rel.* DesRoches v. Caprio, 156 F.3d 571 (4th Cir. 1998) (reasonable suspicion existed to search student's backpack in investigation of missing shoes).

Special Aspects of Stopping Authority
Length of Time Allowed for an Investigative Stop
(*This topic is discussed on page 46.*)

Rodriguez v. United States, 135 S. Ct. 1609 (2015) (citations omitted). The Court ruled that a dog sniff that prolongs the time reasonably required for a traffic stop violates the Fourth Amendment. After an officer completed a traffic stop, including issuing the driver a warning ticket and returning all documents, the officer asked for permission to walk his police dog around the vehicle. The driver said no. Nevertheless, the officer instructed the driver to turn off his car, exit the vehicle, and wait for a second officer. When the second officer arrived, the first officer retrieved his dog and led it around the car, during which time the dog alerted to the presence of drugs. A search of the vehicle revealed a large bag of methamphetamine. About seven or eight minutes elapsed from the time the officer issued the written warning until the dog's alert.

The Court reasoned that an officer may conduct certain unrelated checks during an otherwise lawful traffic stop, but "he may not do so in a way that prolongs the stop, absent the reasonable suspicion ordinarily demanded to justify detaining an individual." The Court noted that during a traffic stop, beyond determining whether to issue a traffic ticket, an officer's mission includes "ordinary inquiries incident to [the traffic] stop," such as checking the driver's license, determining whether the driver has outstanding warrants, and inspecting the automobile's registration and proof of insurance. It explained: "These checks serve the same objective as enforcement of the traffic code: ensuring that vehicles on the road are operated safely and responsibly." A dog sniff, by contrast, "is a measure aimed at detect[ing] evidence of ordinary criminal wrongdoing." The Court continued: "Lacking the same close connection to roadway safety as the ordinary inquiries, a dog sniff is not fairly characterized as part of the officer's traffic mission."

The Court rejected the government's argument that an officer may "incremental[ly]" prolong a stop to conduct a dog sniff as long as the officer is reasonably diligent in pursuing the traffic-related purpose of the stop and provided that the overall duration of the stop remains reasonable in relation to the duration of other traffic stops involving similar circumstances. The Court dismissed the notion that "by completing all traffic-related tasks expeditiously, an officer can earn bonus time to pursue an unrelated criminal investigation." It continued:

> If an officer can complete traffic-based inquiries expeditiously, then that is the amount of "time reasonably required to complete [the stop's] mission." As we said in [*Illinois v.*] *Caballes* [, 543 U.S. 405 (2005)] and reiterate today, a traffic stop "prolonged beyond" that point is "unlawful." ... The critical question, then, is not whether the dog sniff occurs before or after the officer issues a ticket ... but whether conducting the sniff "prolongs"—*i.e.*, adds time to—"the stop."

In this case, the trial court ruled that the defendant's detention for the dog sniff was not independently supported by individualized suspicion. Because the federal appellate court did not review that determination, the Court remanded for a determination by that court as to whether reasonable suspicion of criminal activity justified detaining the defendant beyond completion of the traffic infraction investigation.

[Author's note: This case effectively overruled *State v. Brimmer*, 187 N.C. App. 451 (2007) (court ruled that the brief additional time (one and one half minutes for the dog sniff) did not prolong the detention beyond that reasonably necessary for the traffic stop).]

Illinois v. Caballes, 543 U.S. 405 (2005). The defendant was lawfully stopped for speeding. While the stopping officer was writing a warning ticket, another officer arrived and walked a drug detection dog around the defendant's vehicle. The dog alerted to the trunk and a search discovered marijuana. The entire incident lasted less than 10 minutes. The Court stated that the issue in this case was a narrow one: whether the Fourth Amendment requires reasonable, articulable suspicion to justify using a drug detection dog to sniff a vehicle during a legitimate traffic stop. The Court noted that a seizure justified solely by the interest in issuing a warning ticket can become unlawful if it is prolonged beyond the time reasonably required to complete that mission. The Court stated that the state court had reviewed the stopping officer's conversations with the defendant and the precise timing of his radio transmissions to the dispatcher to determine whether the officer had improperly extended the duration of the stop to enable the dog sniff to occur. The Court accepted the state court's conclusion that the duration of the stop in this case was entirely justified by the traffic offense and the ordinary inquiries incident to such a stop. The Court noted that the state appellate court had ruled, however, that the use of the drug detection dog converted the encounter from a lawful traffic stop into a drug investigation, and because the shift in purpose was not supported by reasonable suspicion that the defendant possessed illegal drugs, it violated the Fourth Amendment. The Court rejected this analysis and ruling. It stated that conducting a dog sniff would not change the character of a traffic stop that is lawful at its inception and otherwise conducted in a reasonable manner, unless the dog sniff itself violated the defendant's Fourth Amendment right to privacy. The Court ruled that the dog sniff did not do so, relying on *United States v. Jacobsen*, 466

U.S. 109 (1984); *United States v. Place*, 462 U.S. 696 (1983); and *City of Indianapolis v. Edmond*, 531 U.S. 32 (2000); and distinguishing *Kyllo v. United States*, 533 U.S. 27 (2001). The Court stated that a dog sniff conducted during a lawful traffic stop that reveals no information other than the location of a substance that a person had no right to possess does not violate the Fourth Amendment.

United States v. Sharpe, 470 U.S. 675 (1985). The Court stated in this case that there is no rigid time limitation for an investigative stop. While time is an important factor in determining whether a stop is reasonable under the Fourth Amendment, reviewing courts must consider the law enforcement purposes to be served by the stop as well as the time reasonably needed to effectuate those purposes. A court must examine whether officers diligently pursued a means of investigation that was likely to confirm or dispel their suspicions quickly during the time they detained the suspect. But a reviewing court also must consider whether the officers were involved in a swiftly developing situation, and it normally should not second-guess what they did. The fact that less intrusive alternative investigative means may have been available does not, by itself, make the stop unreasonable. A stop is unreasonable only when officers act unreasonably in not recognizing or pursuing alternatives.

The Court ruled that the 20-minute detention of the defendant in this case was reasonable under the Fourth Amendment. A drug agent attempted to stop two vehicles that he reasonably suspected were involved in drug trafficking. He stopped one vehicle, but the second vehicle took evasive action after being signaled to stop; another officer stopped the second vehicle (the defendant's) some distance down the road. About 15 minutes after investigating the first vehicle, the drug agent arrived at the defendant's vehicle and investigated. The defendant was detained a total of about 20 minutes from the time he was stopped until the time that probable cause developed from the odor of marijuana emanating from his vehicle. The Court ruled that the 20-minute detention was reasonable, because the case did not involve any delay that was unnecessary to accomplish the officers' legitimate investigative stop. The delay was attributable almost entirely to the defendant's evasive actions.

State v. Warren, 368 N.C. 736 (2016), *aff'g per curiam* ___ N.C. App. ___, 775 S.E.2d 362 (2015). The state supreme court affirmed per curiam the decision of the North Carolina Court of Appeals that had ruled that an officer had reasonable suspicion to extend a traffic stop to allow a dog sniff of a vehicle. The defendant did not contest the validity of the traffic stop. Instead, the defendant contended that the trial court erred in ruling that the officer had reasonable suspicion to extend the scope and length of time of a routine traffic stop to allow a dog sniff outside the defendant's vehicle. Before discussing whether reasonable suspicion existed, the court recognized that *Rodriquez* overturned prior rulings of lower appellate courts, including North Carolina's (see *State v. Brimmer*, 187 N.C. 451 (2007), and *State v. Sellars*, 222 N.C. App. 245 (2012)), to the extent that they permitted a de minimus time period to prolong a traffic stop for activities unrelated to a traffic stop, such as a dog sniff.

The court noted that it was unclear whether the officer's call for backup or waiting for backup to arrive prolonged the stop beyond what was necessary to complete the traffic stop. However, the court did not need to decide that issue, because it found that reasonable suspicion justified an extension of the traffic stop to execute a dog sniff based on the trial court's findings that (1) the defendant was observed and stopped in an area that the officer knew to be a high crime and drug area; (2) while writing a warning citation, the officer saw that the defendant appeared to have something in his mouth that he was not chewing and that affected his speech; (3) the officer had specific training in drug detection and during his six years of experience, he had made many drug stops and had seen suspects attempt to hide drugs in their mouths and swallow them to destroy evidence; and (4) during the officer's conversation with the defendant, he denied being involved in drug activity "any longer." The court stated that this case was similar to the facts in *In re I.R.T.*, 184 N.C. App. 579 (2007), which also upheld a finding of reasonable suspicion.

State v. Heien, 367 N.C. 163, *aff'g per curiam* 226 N.C. App. 280 (2013). [Author's note: The United States Supreme Court in *Heien v. North Carolina*, 135 S. Ct. 530 (2014), decided a different issue in this prosecution (reasonable mistake of law when making an investigative stop) than the ruling discussed in the text.] The state supreme court affirmed per curiam the decision of the North Carolina Court of Appeals that had ruled that a valid traffic stop was not unduly prolonged and that, as a result, the defendant's consent to search his vehicle was valid. The stop was initiated at 7:55 a.m. and the defendant, a passenger who owned the vehicle, gave consent to search at 8:08 a.m. During this time, the two officers present discussed a malfunctioning vehicle brake light with the driver, discovered that the driver and the defendant claimed to be going to different destinations, and observed the defendant behaving unusually (he was lying down on the backseat under a blanket and remained in that position even when approached by one of the officers requesting his driver's license). After each person's name was checked for warrants, their licenses were returned. One officer then requested consent to search the vehicle. The officer's tone and manner were conversational and nonconfrontational. No one was restrained, no guns were drawn, and neither person was searched before the request to search the vehicle was made. The supreme court ruled that the trial judge properly concluded that the defendant was aware that the purpose of the initial stop had been concluded and that further conversation between the officer and the defendant was consensual. The court also ruled that the defendant's consent to search the vehicle was valid even though the officer did not inform the defendant that he was searching for narcotics. [Author's note: Because the defendant's consent was given immediately after the traffic stop had been completed, it appears that the ruling in this case is not in conflict with *Rodriguez v. United States*, 135 S. Ct. 1609 (2015), discussed above.]

State v. McClendon, 350 N.C. 630 (1999). The court ruled that the duration of the detention—15 to 20 minutes from the warning ticket to the arrival of the drug dog—was reasonable. The officers acted quickly and diligently to obtain the drug dog, and they promptly put the drug dog to work on its arrival.

State v. Bedient, ___ N.C. App. ___, 786 S.E.2d 319 (2016). (1) Analyzing this case in light of *Rodriguez v. United States*, 135 S. Ct. 1609 (2015), summarized above, the court ruled that because reasonable suspicion did not exist to prolong the defendant's detention once the purpose of a traffic stop had concluded, the trial court erred by denying the defendant's motion to suppress evidence obtained as a result of a consent search of her vehicle during the unlawful detention. The court found that the evidence showed only two circumstances that could possibly provide reasonable suspicion for extending the duration of the stop: the defendant was engaging in nervous behavior, and she had associated with a known drug dealer. It found the circumstances insufficient to provide reasonable suspicion.

The officer had a legitimate basis for the initial traffic stop: addressing the defendant's failure to dim her high beam lights. Once the officer provided the defendant with a warning about using the high beams, the original mission of the stop was concluded. Although some of the officer's later follow-up questions about the address on her license were supported by reasonable suspicion (whether she was in violation of state law requiring a change of address on a driver's license), this "new mission for the stop" concluded when the officer decided not to issue her a ticket in connection with her license. At this point, additional reasonable suspicion was required to prolong the detention.

The court agreed with the defendant that her nervousness and association with a drug dealer did not support a finding of reasonable suspicion to prolong the stop. Among other things, the court noted that nervousness, although a relevant factor, is insufficient by itself to establish reasonable suspicion. It also concluded that "a person's mere association with or proximity to a suspected criminal does not support a conclusion of particularized reasonable suspicion that the person is involved in criminal activity without more competent evidence." These two circumstances, the court ruled, "simply give rise to a hunch rather than reasonable, particularized suspicion." (2) Concerning another issue, the court ruled that the defendant's consent to search the vehicle was not obtained during a consensual encounter, because the officer had not returned the defendant's driver's license when she consented.

State v. Castillo, ___ N.C. App. ___, 787 S.E.2d 48 (2016). Analyzing this case in light of *Rodriguez v. United States*, 135 S. Ct. 1609 (2015), summarized above, the court ruled that reasonable suspicion supported the officer's extension of the investigative stop's duration, based on the following: the officer smelled marijuana on the defendant's person, the officer learned from the defendant that he had an impaired driving conviction based on marijuana usage, the defendant provided a "bizarre" story regarding the nature of his travel, the defendant was extremely nervous, and the officer detected "masking odors." (2) Concerning another issue, the court ruled that the defendant's consent to search his car, given during the lawful extension of the stop, was clear and unequivocal.

State v. Velazquez-Perez, 233 N.C. App. 585 (2014). In a drug trafficking case, the court ruled that the trial court did not err by denying the defendant's motion to suppress drugs seized from a truck during a vehicle stop. The defendant argued that once the officer handed the driver a warning citation, the purpose of the stop was over and, accordingly, anything that occurred thereafter unconstitutionally prolonged the stop. The court noted that officers routinely check relevant documentation while conducting traffic stops. Here, although the officer had finished writing the warning citation, he had not completed his checks concerning the licenses, registration, insurance, travel logs, and invoices of the commercial vehicle. Thus, "The purpose of the stop was not completed until [the officer] finished a proper document check and returned the documents to [the driver and the passenger, who owned the truck]." The court noted that because the defendant did not argue the issue, it would not address which documents may be properly investigated during a routine commercial vehicle stop.

State v. Lopez, 219 N.C. App. 139 (2012). The court ruled that reasonable suspicion supported the length of the stop in this case. Also, the officer's initial questions concerning the defendant's license, route of travel, and occupation were within the scope of the traffic stop. Any further detention was appropriate based on the following facts. The defendant did not have a valid driver's license. Although the defendant said he had just gotten off work at a construction job, he was well kept with clean hands and clothing. The defendant "became visibly nervous by breathing rapidly[;] . . . his heart appeared to be beating rapidly[;] he exchanged glances with his passenger and both individuals looked at an open plastic bag in the back seat of the vehicle." An officer saw dryer sheets protruding from an open bag containing a box of clear plastic wrap, which, due to his training and experience, the officer knew were used to package and conceal drugs. The defendant told the officer that the car he was driving belonged to a friend but that he was not sure of the friend's name.

State v. Jacobs, 162 N.C. App. 251 (2004). An officer stopped the defendant's vehicle, detained him for about three to five minutes, received consent to search the vehicle, and discovered evidence in the car and on the defendant's person.

(1) About 1:43 a.m. on November 8, 2001, a Burlington police officer saw a car continuously weaving back and forth in its lane over a distance of three-quarters of a mile. There were several bars in the area. The court ruled, relying on *State v. Watson*, 122 N.C. App. 596 (1996), that the officer had reasonable suspicion to stop the vehicle for DWI. [Author's note: Although the officer also had information that a suspect in a Johnson City, Tennessee, murder was in Burlington; the car's Tennessee license plate was registered to a Johnson City resident; and a substantial amount of drug trafficking occurred between Burl-

ington and Johnson City; these facts had not also been used as the basis for the trial judge's ruling that the officer had reasonable suspicion to stop the vehicle.] (2) The court ruled that the length of the defendant's detention (about three to five minutes) during the investigatory stop was reasonable under the Fourth Amendment. During this time the officer asked the defendant questions about his impairment, the murder suspect, and drug trafficking. The defendant's responses did not fully resolve the officer's suspicions, and the defendant was acting very nervous. The court noted *State v. McClendon*, 350 N.C. 630 (1999), concerning the issue of nervousness as a factor in determining reasonable suspicion.

State v. Crenshaw, 144 N.C. App. 574 (2001). The defendant's vehicle was stopped for an inoperable taillight and illegal parking in an area known for drug activity. One of the officers involved with the stop of the vehicle knew that the defendant had previously been convicted of possession of a firearm by a felon. They checked his license and registration, which were valid. The officers then ordered the defendant out of his vehicle and frisked him. The court ruled, relying on *State v. Butler*, 331 N.C. 227 (1992), that the duration of the vehicle stop beyond the initial stop was reasonable, based on the officers' familiarity with the defendant, the defendant's presence in an area known for drug activity, and the defendant's having been illegally parked. The officers testified at the suppression hearing that the defendant verbally consented by answering "okay" when one of the officers stated that he wanted to search the defendant's vehicle. The defendant did not offer any evidence to refute the voluntariness of his consent. The court ruled that evidence supported the trial judge's ruling that the consent to search was voluntary.

State v. Munoz, 141 N.C. App. 675 (2001). The defendant was driving a tractor trailer truck with a car carrier on I-85 and was transporting a Ford Aerostar and a Nissan Sentra. A trooper stopped him for traffic violations, and later another trooper arrived. The defendant handed one of the troopers his license, registration, a notebook containing his log book, and a clipboard holding shipping documents and bills of lading. The troopers found inconsistencies in the defendant's log book and in the shipping documentation. The clipboard contained documents entitled "bill of lading" for the Aerostar and for other vehicles that were no longer on the carrier. There was no bill of lading for the Sentra. The defendant produced a fax that listed the Sentra's destination as Junior City, New Jersey, a contract number, and Miguel Angel as the contact person;

there was no other documentation concerning the Sentra. The defendant told the troopers that he did not know Angel. The troopers also noted that the defendant smelled strongly of grease or fuel. The defendant told the troopers that he was receiving $200 per vehicle to transport (from Texas) the Aerostar to Delaware and the Sentra to New Jersey. One trooper sent the defendant back to his truck while he checked the tags of the cars on the carrier and the other cars listed on the clipboard. After the checks were completed and the trooper received notice that the license and registration were valid, the trooper issued the defendant a warning citation for two motor vehicle violations and returned all the documentation to the defendant. About 45 minutes elapsed from the time the defendant was stopped until he was issued the citation. The defendant then consented to a search of the vehicles, one of which contained cocaine.

Relying on *State v. McClendon*, 350 N.C. 630 (1999), the court ruled that the 45-minute detention of the defendant was supported by reasonable suspicion of criminal activity because (1) the log book was not properly filled out and contained discrepancies, (2) the defendant did not have a bill of lading or an inspection for the Sentra but did have proper documentation for the Aerostar and other cars he had previously transported, (3) the defendant smelled like grease, and (4) the economics of traveling from Texas to Delaware and New Jersey for $200 per car appeared suspicious. *See also* State v. Castellon, 151 N.C. App. 675 (2002) (delay of 25 minutes to check motorist's driver's license was reasonable).

State v. Ray, 137 N.C. App. 326 (2000). Officers stopped a vehicle because one of its headlights was not working. Before the officers could give the driver a warning ticket, other officers arrived who had reasonable suspicion that the occupants had been involved in an armed robbery. The officers then received consent to search the vehicle. They ordered all three occupants out of the vehicle and required them to sit on the curb, cross their feet, and put their hands on their knees. The court ruled that the officers' seizure was no longer than necessary, the occupants were not handcuffed, and the officers did not draw their weapons even though they were armed. The elapsed time from the traffic stop until the occupants were arrested and transported to police headquarters was at most 20 to 25 minutes. Based on these facts, the seizure was not converted into an arrest requiring probable cause.

Rousselo v. Starling, 128 N.C. App. 439 (1998). The plaintiff sued an officer for a violation of his Fourth Amendment rights. An officer stopped a vehicle for speeding at 2:10 p.m. The officer noted a discrepancy between the vehicle's license tag number (TG0355) listed in the vehicle's rental agreement and the vehicle's actual license tag number (ZLN697). The officer placed the plaintiff in his vehicle. During the next 20 minutes, the trooper questioned the plaintiff about his background, where he was going, and so forth. The officer believed that the plaintiff was evasive and nervous. The officer called for backup at 2:34 p.m. While waiting for backup, the officer requested several record checks from the officer's agency dispatcher. The officer continued to question the plaintiff and also asked consent to search the car, which was denied. He received verification of the plaintiff's driver's license and, at 2:42 p.m., a drug intelligence center advised the officer that it had no information about the plaintiff. The backup officers arrived at 2:50 p.m. At 3:02 p.m., the officers asked for a canine unit. At 3:04 p.m., the dispatcher called the car rental company to determine if the plaintiff had rented the vehicle. At 3:15 p.m., the car rental company informed the dispatcher that the plaintiff had rented the vehicle. The drug dog arrived about that time and alerted to the presence of drugs, but a search of the vehicle until 3:47 p.m. did not discover any drugs. At that time, the officer was informed of the information from the rental company. Shortly thereafter, the plaintiff was allowed to leave.

The plaintiff argued on appeal that the officer did not have reasonable suspicion to detain him before the dog sniff. The court concluded that, based on the facts in this case, the discrepancy between the rental agreement and the vehicle's license tag furnished reasonable suspicion to detain the vehicle. In addition, the court stated that there was not a sufficient indication of the officer's lack of diligence to support the argument that the detention was too long.

State v. McDaniels, 103 N.C. App. 175 (1991), *aff'd*, 331 N.C. 112 (1992). The length of time, a maximum of 30 minutes, during the investigative stop for drug trafficking of a vehicle leaving an airport was reasonable.

State v. Morocco, 99 N.C. App. 421 (1990). An officer properly stopped the defendant's vehicle for a seat belt violation. The court ruled that the defendant was properly detained for three minutes while the officer wrote a ticket for the violation and also requested the defendant's consent to search his car for illegal weapons, alcohol, and contraband.

State v. Darack, 66 N.C. App. 608 (1984). The detention of the defendant for 47 minutes and his airplane for three hours was properly based on reasonable suspicion that the airplane had been stolen and controlled substances were on board.

Scope of an Investigative Stop

(*This topic is discussed on page 49.*)

UNITED STATES SUPREME COURT

Arizona v. Johnson, 555 U.S. 323 (2009). Three officers, members of a gang task force, were on patrol near a neighborhood associated with the Crips gang. They stopped a vehicle after a license plate check revealed that the vehicle's registration had been suspended for an insurance-related violation, which under Arizona state law was a civil infraction warranting a citation. There were three occupants in the vehicle: the driver, a front-seat passenger, and the defendant (a backseat passenger). When making the stop, the officers had no reason to suspect anyone of criminal activity. Each officer dealt with one of the occupants. The officer involved with the defendant had noticed on the officers' approach to the vehicle that the defendant had looked back and kept his eyes on the officers. She observed that the defendant was wearing clothing that was consistent with Crips membership. She also noticed a scanner in the defendant's back pocket, which she believed that most people would not carry in that manner unless they were involved in criminal activity or trying to evade law enforcement. The defendant answered the officer's questions (he provided his name and date of birth but had no identification; he said that he had served time in prison for burglary) and also volunteered that he was from an Arizona town that the officer knew was home to a Crips gang. The defendant complied with the officer's request to get out of the car. Based on her observations and the defendant's answers to her questions, the officer suspected that he might have a weapon and frisked him and discovered a gun.

(1) The Court reviewed its case law on stop and frisk beginning with *Terry v. Ohio*, 392 U.S. 1 (1968), particularly noting *Pennsylvania v. Mimms*, 434 U.S. 106 (1977) (officer may automatically order driver out of lawfully stopped vehicle); *Maryland v. Wilson*, 519 U.S. 408 (1997) (applying *Mimms* to passengers); and *Brendlin v. California*, 551 U.S. 249 (2007) (when vehicle is stopped, passengers as well as driver are seized). The Court stated that the combined thrust of these three cases is that an officer who conducts a routine traffic stop may frisk the driver and any passenger the officer reasonably suspects to be armed and dangerous. The officer need not additionally have cause to believe that any vehicle occupant is involved in criminal activity. (2) An Arizona state appellate court had ruled that while the defendant initially was lawfully seized, before the frisk occurred the detention had evolved into a consensual conversation about his gang affiliation because the officer's questioning was unrelated to the traffic stop. The Arizona court concluded that the officer did not have the right to frisk the defendant—even if she had reasonable suspicion that he was armed and dangerous—absent reasonable suspicion that the defendant had engaged in, or was about to engage in, criminal activity. The United States Supreme Court rejected that view and concluded that the seizure of the defendant during this traffic stop was continuous and reasonable from the time the vehicle was stopped to the time the frisk occurred. A traffic stop of a vehicle communicates to a reasonable passenger that he or she is not free to terminate the encounter with law enforcement and move about at will. Nothing occurred in this case that would have conveyed to the defendant that the traffic stop had ended before the frisk or that he was otherwise free to depart without the officer's permission. The officer was not constitutionally required to give the defendant an opportunity to depart the scene after he exited the vehicle without first ensuring that, in so doing, she was not permitting a dangerous person to get behind her. Citing *Muehler v. Mena*, 544 U.S. 93 (2005) (questioning of the plaintiff about her immigration status did not violate the Fourth Amendment because the plaintiff's detention during the execution of the search warrant was not prolonged by the questioning), the Court stated that an officer's questions about matters unrelated to the justification for a traffic stop do not convert the encounter into an unlawful seizure, as long as the questions do not measurably extend the duration of the stop. [Author's note: The Court's statement means, for example, that an officer's questioning of a vehicle occupant during a traffic stop as to whether there are drugs or guns in the vehicle is not an unreasonable seizure as long as the questioning does not measurably extend the duration of the stop. *See also* United States v. Olivera-Mendez, 484 F.3d 505 (8th Cir. 2007); United States v. Stewart, 473 F.3d 1265 (10th Cir. 2007); United States v. Everett, 601 F.3d 484 (6th Cir.

2010). To the extent that *State v. Parker*, 183 N.C. App. 1 (2007), implied that reasonable suspicion was required when an officer asked for a consent search of a lawfully detained defendant when the request was unrelated to the traffic violation for which the defendant was detained, it now appears inconsistent with *Johnson* as well as *Muehler v. Mena*, 544 U.S. 93 (2005) (mere questioning by law enforcement officers is not a seizure under the Fourth Amendment).]

Muehler v. Mena, 544 U.S. 93 (2005). Officers obtained a search warrant for a house and premises to search for deadly weapons and evidence of gang membership related to an investigation of a gang-related drive-by shooting. A SWAT team and other officers (a total of 18 officers altogether) executed the warrant. Aware that the gang was composed primarily of illegal immigrants, an INS officer accompanied the officers. One or two officers guarded four occupants detained at the scene, who were handcuffed for about two to three hours while the warrant was executed. In addition, the INS officer questioned the occupants about their immigration status while the warrant was executed. One of the occupants (the plaintiff in this case) sued the officers for allegedly violating her Fourth Amendment rights during the execution of the search warrant. The Court ruled that the detention of the plaintiff in handcuffs was reasonable under the Fourth Amendment. The two- to three-hour detention in handcuffs in this case did not outweigh the officers' continuing safety interests. The Court also ruled that the questioning of the plaintiff about her immigration status did not violate the Fourth Amendment because the plaintiff's detention during the execution of the search warrant was not prolonged by the questioning. Mere questioning by law enforcement does not constitute a seizure. [Author's note: Although this case did not involve the scope of an investigative stop, the ruling that mere questioning does not necessarily violate the Fourth Amendment has had an impact on case law involving investigative stops. See *Arizona v. Johnson*, 555 U.S. 323 (2009), discussed above.]

Illinois v. Caballes, 543 U.S. 405 (2005). The defendant was lawfully stopped for speeding. While the stopping officer was writing a warning ticket, another officer arrived and walked a drug detection dog around the defendant's vehicle. The dog alerted to the trunk and a search discovered marijuana. The entire incident lasted less than 10 minutes. The Court stated that the issue in this case was a narrow one: whether the Fourth Amendment requires reasonable, articulable suspicion to jus-

tify using a drug detection dog to sniff a vehicle during a legitimate traffic stop. The Court noted that a seizure justified solely by the interest in issuing a warning ticket can become unlawful if it is prolonged beyond the time reasonably required to complete that mission. The Court stated that the state court had reviewed the stopping officer's conversations with the defendant and the precise timing of his radio transmissions to the dispatcher to determine whether the officer had improperly extended the duration of the stop to enable the dog sniff to occur. The Court accepted the state court's conclusion that the duration of the stop in this case was entirely justified by the traffic offense and the ordinary inquiries incident to such a stop. The Court noted that the state appellate court had ruled, however, that the use of the drug detection dog converted the encounter from a lawful traffic stop into a drug investigation, and because the shift in purpose was not supported by reasonable suspicion that the defendant possessed illegal drugs, it violated the Fourth Amendment. The Court rejected this analysis and ruling. It stated that conducting a dog sniff would not change the character of a traffic stop that is lawful at its inception and otherwise conducted in a reasonable manner, unless the dog sniff itself violated the defendant's Fourth Amendment right to privacy. The Court ruled that the dog sniff did not do so, relying on *United States v. Jacobsen*, 466 U.S. 109 (1984); *United States v. Place*, 462 U.S. 696 (1983); and *City of Indianapolis v. Edmond*, 531 U.S. 32 (2000); and distinguishing *Kyllo v. United States*, 533 U.S. 27 (2001). The Court stated that a dog sniff conducted during a lawful traffic stop that reveals no information other than the location of a substance that a person had no right to possess does not violate the Fourth Amendment.

Hiibel v. Sixth Judicial District Court of Nevada, 542 U.S. 177 (2004). A caller to a sheriff's department reported seeing a man assault a woman in a truck on a certain road. When the officer arrived there, he found the truck parked on the side of the road, the defendant standing by the truck, and a young woman sitting inside. The defendant was stopped by the law enforcement officer based on reasonable suspicion that the defendant had committed the assault. The officer asked the defendant for identification, explaining that he wanted to determine who the man was and what he was doing there. The defendant refused to provide identification. The defendant was convicted of willfully obstructing and delaying the officer in attempting to discharge a legal duty—based on a Nevada statute that requires a person subject to an investigative stop to disclose his name.

(1) The Court ruled that the officer's request for the defendant's name was reasonably related in scope to the circumstances that justified the stop and did not violate the Fourth Amendment. (2) The Court ruled that the defendant's conviction did not violate the defendant's Fifth Amendment privilege against compelled self-incrimination because in this case the defendant's refusal to disclose his name was not based on any articulated real and appreciable fear that his name would be used to incriminate him or that it would furnish a link in the chain of evidence needed to prosecute him. The Court noted that a case may arise when there is a substantial allegation that furnishing identity at the time of an investigative stop would have given an officer a link in the chain of evidence needed to convict the defendant of a separate offense. In that case, a court can then consider whether the Fifth Amendment privilege applies and, if the privilege has been violated, what remedy must follow. But those questions need not be resolved in the case before the Court.

[Author's note: The ruling in this case that the Nevada law is constitutional does not resolve the issue of whether it is a violation of North Carolina law when a person refuses to give his or her name during an investigative stop. That is a matter for North Carolina state courts to decide. Unlike Nevada law, there is no North Carolina statute that requires a person who is the subject of an investigative stop based on reasonable suspicion to disclose his or her name. (There is a limited provision in G.S. 20-29 that it is a Class 2 misdemeanor for a person operating a motor vehicle, when requested by a uniformed officer, to refuse to write his or her name for identification or give his or her name.) Without such a statute, it does not appear that a person's mere refusal to disclose his or her name is sufficient evidence by itself to arrest or convict the person of violating G.S. 4-223 (resisting, delaying, or obstructing a public officer in discharging or attempting to discharge a duty of office) absent a showing how the mere refusal to disclose resisted, delayed, or obstructed the officer in that particular investigative stop. Although a mere refusal may be insufficient to arrest a person for violating G.S. 14-223, the refusal under certain circumstances may allow an officer additional time to detain the person to determine whether a crime was committed.]

Ohio v. Robinette, 519 U.S. 33 (1996). An officer stopped the defendant for speeding. The defendant gave his driver's license to the officer, who ran a computer check that revealed that the defendant had no prior violations. The officer asked the defendant to step out of his car, issued a verbal warning to the defendant, and returned his license. The officer then asked the defendant if he had any illegal contraband in his car. The defendant said no. When the officer then asked the defendant if he could search his car, the defendant consented. The Court rejected a lower court ruling that an officer must advise a lawfully seized defendant that the defendant is free to go before a consent to search will be recognized as voluntary. The Court noted that a consent to search must be voluntary, and voluntariness is a question of fact that must be determined from all the circumstances. An officer's warning before obtaining consent to search is not required by the Fourth Amendment for the search to be valid.

NORTH CAROLINA SUPREME COURT

State v. Williams, 366 N.C. 110 (2012), *aff'g* 215 N.C. App. 1 (2011) (reasonable articulable suspicion justified extending traffic stop). The officer stopped the vehicle in which the defendant was a passenger for having illegally tinted windows and issued a citation. The officer then asked for and was denied consent to search the vehicle. Thereafter, he called for a canine trained in drug detection. When the dog arrived, it alerted on the car and drugs were found. Several factors supported the trial court's determination that reasonable suspicion supported extending the stop. First, the driver told the officer that she and the defendant passenger were coming from Houston, Texas, which was illogical given their direction of travel. Second, the defendant's inconsistent statement that they were coming from Kentucky and were traveling to Myrtle Beach "raise[d] a suspicion as to the truthfulness of the statements." Third, the driver's inability to tell the officer where they were going, along with her illogical answer about driving from Houston, permitted an inference that she "was being deliberately evasive, that she had been hired as a driver and intentionally kept uninformed, or that she had been coached as to her response if stopped." Fourth, the fact that the defendant initially suggested that she and the driver were cousins but then admitted that they just called each other cousins based on their long-term relationship "could raise a suspicion that the alleged familial relationship was a prearranged fabrication." Finally, the vehicle, which had illegally tinted windows, was owned by a third person. The state supreme court concluded:

> Viewed individually and in isolation, any of these facts might not support a reasonable suspicion of criminal activity. But viewed as a whole by a trained law enforcement officer who is familiar with drug trafficking and illegal activity on interstate highways, the responses were sufficient to provoke a reasonable articulable suspicion that criminal activity was afoot and to justify extending the detention until a canine unit arrived.

State v. McClendon, 350 N.C. 630 (1999). The court ruled that the continued detention of the defendant from the issuance of a warning ticket to the arrival of the drug dog was supported by reasonable suspicion of criminal activity. The court cited several factors that supported reasonable suspicion under the totality of the circumstances. First, the officer questioned the defendant about who owned the car. The defendant said that his girlfriend owned the car but initially would not give a name. Then he gave the name "Anna," but that name was not listed on the title. Second, although the defendant appeared unsure of who owned the car, the address of the owner listed on the title and the address on the defendant's driver's license were the same, which indicated that they both lived in the same residence. Third, the defendant was extremely nervous, sweating, breathing rapidly, sighing heavily, and chuckling nervously in response to questions. He also refused to make eye contact when answering questions.

The court cited *State v. Butler*, 331 N.C. 227 (1992), and noted that nervousness was a factor in determining reasonable suspicion in that case. The court distinguished its ruling in this case with the ruling in *State v. Pearson*, 348 N.C. 272 (1998) (no reasonable suspicion to frisk defendant). The court stated that it would "revisit *Pearson* now in order to clarify its meaning. . . ." The court noted that it said in *Pearson* that "[t]he nervousness of the defendant is not significant. Many people become nervous when stopped by a state trooper." The court stated:

> Although the quoted language from *Pearson* is couched in rather absolute terms, we did not mean to imply there that nervousness can never be significant in determining whether an officer could form a reasonable suspicion that criminal activity is afoot. Nervousness, like all other facts, must be taken in light of the totality of circum-

stances. It is true that many people do become nervous when stopped by an officer of the law. Nevertheless, nervousness is an appropriate factor to consider when determining whether a basis for reasonable suspicion exists.

> In *Pearson*, the nervousness of the defendant was not remarkable. Even when taken together with the inconsistencies in the statements of the defendant and his girlfriend, it did not support a reasonable suspicion. In the case before us, however, defendant exhibited more than ordinary nervousness; defendant was fidgety and breathing rapidly, sweat had formed on his forehead, he would sigh deeply, and he would not make eye contact with the officer. This, taken in the context of the totality of circumstances found to exist by the trial court, gave rise to a reasonable suspicion that criminal activity was afoot.

NORTH CAROLINA COURT OF APPEALS

State v. Johnson, ___ N.C. App. ___, 784 S.E.2d 633 (2016). In this drug trafficking case, the court ruled that an officer had reasonable suspicion to extend a traffic stop. After Officer Ward initiated a traffic stop and asked the driver for his license and registration, the driver produced his license but was unable to produce a registration. The driver's license listed his address as Raleigh, but he could not give a clear answer as to whether he resided in Brunswick County or Raleigh. Throughout the conversation, the driver changed his story about where he resided. The driver was speaking into one cell phone and had two other cell phones on the center console of his vehicle. The officer saw a vehicle power control (VPC) module on the floor of the vehicle, an unusual item that might be associated with criminal activity. When Ward attempted to question the defendant, a passenger, the defendant mumbled answers and appeared very nervous. Ward then determined that the driver's license was inactive, issued the driver a citation, and told him that he was free to go. However, Ward asked the driver if he would mind exiting the vehicle to answer a few questions. Ward also asked the driver if he could pat him down, and the driver agreed. Meanwhile, Deputy Arnold, who was assisting, observed a rectangular shaped bulge underneath the defendant's shorts, in his crotch area. When he asked the defendant to identify the item, the defendant responded that it was his male anatomy. Arnold asked the defendant to step out of the vehicle so that he could do a pat down; before this could be completed, a ziplock bag containing heroin fell from the defendant's shorts. The extension of the traffic stop was justified: the driver could not answer basic questions, such as where he was coming from and where he lived; the driver changed his story; the driver could not explain why he did not have his registration; the presence of the VPC was unusual; and the defendant was extremely nervous and gave vague answers to the officer's questions.

State v. Fisher, 219 N.C. App. 498 (2012). The court of appeals ruled that the trial court erred by concluding that an officer lacked reasonable suspicion to detain the defendant beyond the scope of a routine traffic stop. The officer lawfully stopped the vehicle being driven by the defendant for a seat belt violation but then extended the detention in order to wait for the arrival of a canine unit. The State argued that numerous factors established reasonable suspicion that the defendant was transporting contraband: there was an overwhelming odor of air freshener in the car; the defendant claimed to have made a five-hour round-trip to go shopping but had not purchased anything; the defendant was nervous; the defendant had pending drug charges and was known as a distributor of marijuana and cocaine; the defendant was driving in a pack of cars; the car was registered to someone else; the defendant never asked why he had been stopped; the defendant was "eating on the go"; and a handprint indicated that something recently had been placed in the trunk. Although the officer did not know about the pending charges until after the canine unit was called, the court found this to be a relevant factor. It reasoned: "The extended detention of defendant is ongoing from the time of the traffic citation until the canine unit arrives and additional factors that present themselves during that time are relevant to why the detention continued until the canine unit arrived." Even discounting several of these factors that might be indicative of innocent behavior, the court found that other factors—nervousness, the smell of air freshener, inconsistency concerning travel plans, driving a car not registered to the defendant, and the pending charges—supported a finding that reasonable suspicion existed.

State v. Hernandez, 208 N.C. App. 591 (2010). The court ruled that the trial court properly denied a motion to suppress asserting that a vehicle stop was improperly prolonged. An officer stopped the truck after observing it following too closely and making erratic lane changes.

The occupants were detained until a Spanish language consent to search form could be brought to the location. The defendant challenged as unconstitutional this detention that lasted approximately one hour and 10 minutes. The court distinguished cases cited by the defendant, explaining that in both, vehicle occupants were detained after the original purpose of the initial investigative detention had been addressed, and the officer attempted to justify an additional period of detention based solely on the driver's nervousness or uncertainty about travel details, which does not provide reasonable suspicion that criminal activity is afoot. Here, however, because none of the occupants had a driver's license or other identification, the officer could not issue a citation and resolve the initial stop. Because the challenged delay occurred when the officer was attempting to address issues arising from the initial stop, the court determined that it need not address whether the officer had a reasonable suspicion of criminal activity sufficient to justify a prolonged detention. Nevertheless, the court went on to conclude that even if the officer was required to have such a suspicion to justify the detention, the facts supported the existence of such a suspicion. Specifically, (1) the driver did not have a license or registration, (2) a man was in the truck bed covered by a blanket, (3) the defendant handed the driver a license belonging to the defendant's brother, (4) the occupants gave inconsistent stories about their travel that were confusing given the truck's location and direction of travel, (5) no occupant produced identification or a driver's license, (6) the men had no luggage despite the fact that they were traveling from North Carolina to New York, and (7) the driver had tattoos associated with criminal gang activity.

State v. Jackson, 199 N.C. App. 236 (2009). An officer stopped a vehicle and, with other officers, checked the driver's license and registration of the driver and determined that they were valid and there were no outstanding warrants for the driver and two passengers, one of whom was the defendant. After the traffic stop had ended but before the driver's license and registration had been returned, an officer asked questions about illegal drugs and weapons in the vehicle and then asked for consent to search the vehicle, which was granted. Cocaine was found in the vehicle, the three occupants were arrested, and cocaine was found in the defendant's sock at the jail. The court ruled, relying on *Brendlin v. California*, 551 U.S. 249 (2007), that the defendant was seized during the stop of the vehicle and could challenge the duration of the seizure as violating the Fourth Amendment. The court also ruled that once the traffic stop had ended and the driver's license and registration had not been returned, the officer's questioning about illegal drugs and weapons in the vehicle was an extension of the seizure beyond the scope of the original traffic stop, and reasonable suspicion did not exist to justify the extension of the seizure. The court rejected the argument that the encounter had become consensual after the traffic stop had ended, because a reasonable person under the circumstances would not believe he was free to leave without his driver's license and registration. The vehicle search was tainted by the illegality of the extended detention. Because the defendant was arrested based on the discovery of cocaine and a weapon in the vehicle, the cocaine found in the defendant's sock at the jail was the direct result of the officer's illegal search of the vehicle. Thus, the exclusionary rule prohibited the admission of the evidence found in the vehicle and the defendant's sock.

State v. Hodges, 195 N.C. App. 390 (2009). Vice detectives were conducting drug surveillance at a residence and also had information from confidential informants about specific drug sellers and drug sales there. They believed that a vehicle leaving the residence contained a buyer of drugs, and they followed the vehicle to Interstate 40. The detectives saw the vehicle apparently speeding and asked an officer on routine patrol on the interstate to make his own observations about the vehicle's speed or another traffic violation and make a vehicle stop if a violation occurred. The officer followed the vehicle, saw it speeding, and turned on his lights to stop the vehicle. One of the detectives in the detectives' vehicle saw the passenger look back at the officer's vehicle, and the passenger appeared to conceal something underneath the passenger's seat. The detective radioed the officer that he believed the passenger was hiding either drugs or a weapon under the seat and warned him to be careful. After stopping the vehicle, the officer spoke with the driver (the defendant) and the passenger. The defendant stated that the passenger was his neighbor and identified his first name, which was inconsistent with the passenger's driver's license. The officer issued a verbal warning to the defendant for speeding. The officer further detained both the defendant and passenger and eventually the passenger consented to a search of the vehicle. The court ruled that based on these and other facts set out in its opinion, the officer had reasonable suspicion of criminal activity (specifically, drugs or other contraband

in the vehicle) to detain the occupants after the traffic stop had concluded. The court also ruled that the five-minute detention after the traffic stop had concluded was reasonable under the Fourth Amendment.

State v. Myles, 188 N.C. App. 42, *aff'd*, 362 N.C. 344 (2008). The court ruled that reasonable suspicion did not support an officer's continued detention of vehicle occupants (defendant was a passenger) after the completion of a traffic stop. An officer stopped a vehicle for weaving on Interstate 40 and running slightly off the highway. The officer did not detect an odor of alcohol on the driver, learned that the car was being operated under a rental agreement executed by the defendant-passenger that was one day overdue, told the driver to be more careful, and asked him to come to the officer's car so the officer could write a warning ticket. The officer noted that the driver was sweating profusely despite the fact that it was a cool day. The officer talked with the driver about his travel plans. The officer then went back to the driver's car and spoke to the defendant-passenger about the rental agreement and whether it had been extended. The defendant said he had done so. The officer noticed the defendant's heart beating through his shirt. The officer eventually obtained consent to search the car from the driver and defendant. The court ruled that both the driver and the defendant-passenger were seized under the Fourth Amendment after the completion of the traffic stop and the issuance of the warning ticket and that the totality of circumstances did not support reasonable suspicion for the continued detention of the driver and defendant—the nervous behavior of the driver was insufficient. The court distinguished the ruling in *State v. McClendon*, 350 N.C. 630 (1999). The nervousness of the defendant could not be considered in establishing reasonable suspicion because the officer observed that behavior after the traffic stop had been completed.

State v. Euceda-Valle, 182 N.C. App. 268 (2007). An officer stopped the defendant's vehicle for speeding and issued him a warning ticket. There was a passenger in the vehicle. After writing and delivering the warning ticket to the defendant, the officer ordered the defendant to remain so that a drug dog could conduct a sniff of the exterior of the vehicle. The court ruled, relying on *State v. McClendon*, 350 N.C. 630 (1999), and *State v. Hernandez*, 170 N.C. App. 299 (2005), that the officer had reasonable suspicion to detain the defendant. The defendant was extremely nervous and refused to make eye contact with the officer. The smell of air freshener was coming from the vehicle, and the vehicle was not registered to the occupants. Also, the defendant and the passenger disagreed about their itinerary.

State v. Hernandez, 170 N.C. App. 299 (2005). The defendant was convicted of trafficking in cocaine. An officer stopped a vehicle driven by the defendant for a seat belt violation. While in the patrol car with the defendant, the officer ran a license and registration check, questioned the defendant about his travel plans, and issued him a citation. The defendant then gave consent to search the vehicle, and cocaine was found in the vehicle. The consent to search was given within six minutes of the defendant's detention in the vehicle. The court ruled that (1) the officer had probable cause to stop the vehicle for the seat belt violation (the officer saw the defendant remove the seat belt while still driving), a readily observed traffic violation; and (2) the officer had reasonable suspicion to detain the defendant after issuing the citation, based on the defendant's extreme nervousness, conflicting statements about his travel plans, and air fresheners in the defendant's vehicle emitting a strong odor. [Author's note: Since the *Hernandez* ruling, the North Carolina Supreme Court in *State v. Styles*, 362 N.C. 412 (2008), ruled that reasonable suspicion, not probable cause, is the standard for all traffic stops.]

State v. Bell, 156 N.C. App. 350 (2003). Trooper A stopped a vehicle, driven by the defendant's brother, for speeding; the defendant was a passenger in the front seat. The backseat was filled with many personal belongings, including stereo equipment. After the stop, Trooper B arrived and assisted Trooper A. When the driver offered a New York learner's permit and a rental agreement for the vehicle, Trooper A asked him to come back to the patrol car so that he could check the permit and tag, and he questioned him there. Trooper B questioned the defendant while he was in the vehicle. The driver and the defendant told different stories to the troopers about their itinerary. Trooper B also noticed that the defendant's eyes wandered while he talked, resisting eye contact with the trooper. Upon considering that the backseat was filled with personal belongings, indicating that the trunk was full, and that the men told inconsistent stories, Trooper A became suspicious about illegal drugs, based on his experience and training in drug interdiction. After issuing a citation to the driver for speeding in a work zone and returning his learner's permit, Trooper A asked Trooper B to request the defendant's consent to search the vehicle because his name appeared on the rental agreement.

The court ruled that even if, as the defendant asserted, the traffic stop had concluded when the trooper asked for consent to search the vehicle, reasonable suspicion of criminal activity supported the detention. The court relied on *State v. McClendon*, 350 N.C. 630 (1999).

State v. Wilson, 155 N.C. App. 89 (2002). A trooper stopped a car and issued a warning ticket for a violation of G.S. 20-152 (following too closely). Later, the defendant consented to a search of the vehicle and cocaine was found in the vehicle's battery.

The court ruled that reasonable suspicion supported the detention of the defendant after the trooper issued the warning ticket. The court stated that the evidence established that (1) the vehicle had a strong odor of air freshener; (2) an atlas was in the backseat and screws were missing from the dashboard; (3) the vehicle was registered in Florida, but the defendant was from Ohio; (4) there were discrepancies in the descriptions by the defendant and accomplice of a vehicle left in Florida; and (5) the defendant was very nervous—tapping his hands and feet while in the trooper's car. In addition, the trooper had special knowledge of illegal drugs and knew that the defendant's actions were consistent with those of a drug trafficker.

State v. Kincaid, 147 N.C. App. 94 (2001). An officer saw the defendant driving a vehicle, attempting to conceal his face from the officer. The officer stopped the vehicle because he knew that the defendant's license had been revoked for two to three years. During the time the officer had known the defendant, he had seen him travel either as a passenger in a car or as the driver of a moped but never as the driver of a car. The defendant gave his license to the officer. The officer allowed the defendant to enter a convenience store while he ran a license check. The license was valid, and the officer returned it and the registration to the defendant when he returned. The officer then asked the defendant if he could answer some questions concerning another matter and the defendant consented. After being asked if he had anything in the car that the officer needed to be concerned about, the defendant admitted that he had marijuana under the front seat.

The court ruled that the officer had reasonable suspicion to stop the vehicle based on the officer's information about the defendant and his driver's license, despite the fact that the officer's information turned out to be incorrect after the stop. The court noted that the ground for the detention of the defendant ended when the officer learned that the defendant's license was valid. However, the defendant consented to questions after the officer had returned the driver's license and registration to the defendant. The court ruled that a reasonable person would have felt free to leave when the documents were returned. The court noted that the officer was neither prohibited from simply asking if the defendant would consent to additional questioning nor from questioning the defendant after receiving his consent. Based on the totality of circumstances, the court ruled that the defendant was not seized under the Fourth Amendment after the officer had returned the documents to him.

State v. Falana, 129 N.C. App. 813 (1998). A trooper stopped the defendant's vehicle because it weaved within its own lane twice and touched the lane divider line once. The defendant presented his driver's license and vehicle registration. The trooper asked the defendant whether he was fatigued or had been drinking. The defendant responded that he had been driving all night and was tired. The trooper did not detect that the defendant was under the influence of any impairing substance. The trooper saw that the defendant was breathing rapidly and would periodically pause in his speech and swallow. The trooper believed that the defendant was nervous. The trooper also checked the passenger's identification, which was proper. The trooper then radioed for backup assistance. He received no hits on warrants checks of the defendant and the passenger. The trooper then issued a warning ticket to the defendant and returned his license and registration. The defendant, in response to the trooper's inquiry, denied having anything illegal in his vehicle. The trooper became suspicious because the defendant continued to breathe rapidly and appeared to be nervous and also because the passenger had given the trooper a different statement than the defendant about when they had been in New Jersey. The trooper then asked the defendant if he could search the vehicle. The defendant refused. The trooper asked again for permission to search the vehicle. After the defendant asked the trooper whether he had a search warrant and received a negative response from the trooper, the defendant again refused to consent to a search of his vehicle. The trooper then told the defendant that he was going to have a drug dog walk around his vehicle. The dog alerted, and the defendant's vehicle was searched.

The court, assuming without deciding that the stop of the vehicle was proper, ruled that the continued detention of the defendant after the issuance of the warning ticket was not supported by reasonable suspicion and therefore violated the Fourth Amendment. Relying on the reasoning of *State v. Pearson*, 348 N.C. 272 (1998), the court ruled that the defendant's nervousness and the differing statements of the defendant and passenger about when they had been in New Jersey did not constitute reasonable suspicion to detain the defendant after the issuance of the warning ticket. *See also* State v. Fisher, 141 N.C. App. 448 (2000) (reasonable suspicion did not justify detention beyond initial traffic stop and thus dog sniff occurring during illegal detention was unconstitutional).

Burton v. City of Durham, 118 N.C. App. 676 (1995). The court ruled that an officer may conduct a registration check when the officer has properly stopped a defendant for committing an infraction (in this case, exceeding a safe speed).

State v. Aubin, 100 N.C. App. 628 (1990). The court ruled that an officer had reasonable suspicion of an impaired-driving offense to stop a car that was going 45 m.p.h. and weaving within a lane on an interstate highway. The officer asked the defendant to come to his patrol car so he could determine whether the defendant had the odor of alcohol about him. The officer asked the defendant about his plans for returning the rental car he was driving, whether he still lived in Quebec, and what he did for a living. The officer then attempted to obtain the defendant's consent to search his car. The court ruled that this conversation did not exceed permissible behavior of an officer conducting a stop of a vehicle for impaired driving.

State v. Hunter, 107 N.C. App. 402 (1992). A trooper stopped the defendant for illegal parking and questioned the defendant about the other two occupants of the car. The defendant initially misidentified them. Also, the rental agreement was in the name of a person who was not in the car. The court found that the trooper's questions about the other occupants in the car were legitimately aimed at confirming the defendant's identity, particularly as the rental contract was in the name of another person. The trooper then issued a warning ticket to the defendant and asked him if he would sign a consent to search form allowing a search of the car and all luggage. The court ruled that the trooper's initial investigation was reasonably related to the purpose of issuing a warning ticket for illegal parking and that asking for permission to search the defendant's vehicle did not exceed the permissible scope of the trooper's investigation.

State v. Jones, 96 N.C. App. 389 (1989). An officer properly stopped a vehicle based on reasonable suspicion that the driver was committing an impaired-driving offense. The scope of the investigatory stop was reasonably related to the impaired-driving offense because the defendant gave the officer two different names. The officer continued to investigate the defendant's identity and the vehicle's lease agreement, because an officer has the authority to determine a defendant's identity. The fact that the officer later obtained the defendant's consent to search the car did not make the scope of the stop impermissible.

Ordering People Out of a Vehicle after a Lawful Stop
(*This topic is discussed on page 49.*)

Arizona v. Johnson, 555 U.S. 323 (2009). Three officers, members of a gang task force, were on patrol near a neighborhood associated with the Crips gang. They stopped a vehicle after a license plate check revealed that the vehicle's registration had been suspended for an insurance-related violation, which under Arizona state law was a civil infraction warranting a citation. There were three occupants in the vehicle: the driver, a front-seat passenger, and the defendant (a backseat passenger). When making the stop, the officers had no reason to suspect anyone of criminal activity. Each officer dealt with one of the occupants. The officer involved with the defendant noticed upon the officers' approach to the vehicle that the defendant had looked back and kept his eyes on the officers. She observed that the defendant was wearing clothing that was consistent with Crips membership. She also noticed a scanner in the defendant's back pocket, which she believed most people would not carry in that manner unless they were involved with criminal activity or trying to evade law enforcement. The defendant answered the officer's questions (he provided his name and date of birth but had no identification; he said that he had served time in prison for burglary) and also volunteered that he was from an Arizona town that the officer knew was home to a Crips gang. The defendant complied with the officer's request to get out of the car. Based on her observations and the defendant's answers to her questions, the officer suspected he might have a weapon and frisked him and discovered a gun.

(1) The Court reviewed its case law on stop and frisk, beginning with *Terry v. Ohio*, 392 U.S. 1 (1968), particularly noting *Pennsylvania v. Mimms*, 434 U.S. 106 (1977) (officer may automatically order driver out of lawfully stopped vehicle); *Maryland v. Wilson*, 519 U.S. 408 (1997) (applying *Mimms* to passengers); and *Brendlin v.*

California, 551 U.S. 249 (2007) (when vehicle is stopped, passengers as well as driver are seized). The Court stated that the combined thrust of these three cases is that an officer who conducts a routine traffic stop may frisk the driver and any passenger whom the officer reasonably suspects to be armed and dangerous. The officer need not additionally have cause to believe that any vehicle occupant is involved in criminal activity. (2) An Arizona state appellate court had ruled that while the defendant initially was lawfully seized, before the frisk occurred the detention had evolved into a consensual conversation about his gang affiliation, because the officer's questioning was unrelated to the traffic stop. The Arizona court concluded that the officer did not have the right to frisk the defendant—even if she had reasonable suspicion that he was armed and dangerous—absent reasonable suspicion that the defendant had engaged, or was about to engage, in criminal activity. The United States Supreme Court rejected that view and concluded that the seizure of the defendant during this traffic stop was continuous and reasonable from the time the vehicle was stopped to the time the frisk occurred. A traffic stop of a vehicle communicates to a reasonable passenger that he or she is not free to terminate the encounter with law enforcement and move about at will. Nothing occurred in this case that would have conveyed to the defendant that the traffic stop had ended before the frisk or that he was otherwise free to depart without the officer's permission. The officer was not constitutionally required to give the defendant an opportunity to depart the scene after he exited the vehicle without first ensuring that, in so doing, she was not permitting a dangerous person to get behind her. Citing *Muehler v. Mena*, 544 U.S. 93 (2005) (questioning of the plaintiff about her immigration status did not violate the Fourth Amendment because the plaintiff's detention during the execution of the search warrant was not prolonged by the questioning), the Court stated that an officer's questions about matters unrelated to the justification for a traffic stop do not convert the encounter into an unlawful seizure, as long as the questions do not measurably extend the duration of the stop.

Maryland v. Wilson, 519 U.S. 408 (1997). The Court ruled that an officer who has lawfully stopped a vehicle may order the passengers out of the vehicle without showing any reason to do so under the Fourth Amendment.

Pennsylvania v. Mimms, 434 U.S. 106 (1977). The Court ruled that when an officer properly stopped a car to issue a traffic summons because it was being operated with an expired license plate, he had the right, for his safety, to order the driver out of the car, even though he had no grounds to suspect that the driver was a threat to him.

State v. Brewington, 170 N.C. App. 264 (2005). The defendant was convicted of the felony of assault on a governmental officer with a deadly weapon, reckless driving, and being a habitual felon. An officer stopped a vehicle for a seat belt violation by the driver; the defendant was a passenger. While talking to the driver, the officer made several observations of the defendant's suspicious conduct (see the facts set out in the court's opinion) and instructed him to remain in the vehicle. The driver was ordered out of the vehicle, and the officer conducted a consensual frisk and found cocaine on his person. While the officer was arresting the driver, the defendant moved behind the steering wheel and started to drive away. The officer attempted to stop the car by reaching for the key and was dragged by the moving vehicle. The defendant fled the scene and later was arrested in Ohio. The court ruled that the officer had reasonable suspicion to require the defendant to remain at the scene, based on the facts set out in the court's opinion (the court ruled, alternatively, that the car could be detained based on the discovery of cocaine on the driver, which provided probable cause to search the vehicle).

State v. Pulliam, 139 N.C. App. 437 (2000). Officers were conducting a driver's license checkpoint. The driver gave consent to a search of his vehicle. When the officer asked who his passenger was, the driver asserted that he did not know the defendant's name. The officer ordered the defendant-passenger, whom the officer knew to be a convicted drug trafficker, to get out of the vehicle. The defendant became belligerent, saying that the officer had no right to make him get out. The defendant smelled of alcohol, was loud and argumentative, and used profanity. When the defendant finally got out of the vehicle, he was unsteady on his feet and appeared to be intoxicated. The officer saw a large bulge, one inch wide and six or seven inches long, in the defendant's front pants pocket. He patted that place and discovered a utility razor knife.

(1) The court ruled, relying on *Maryland v. Wilson*, 519 U.S. 408 (1997), and other cases, that the driver's consent to search his vehicle allowed the officer to order the passenger out of the vehicle without the necessity of reasonable suspicion of criminal activity. (2) Based on the facts set out above, the court ruled that the officer had

reasonable suspicion that the defendant was armed and dangerous to justify the frisk.

United States v. Williams, 419 F.3d 1029 (9th Cir. 2005). The court ruled that an officer may order a passenger in a lawfully stopped car who has voluntarily gotten out of the car to get back into the car.

Rogala v. District of Columbia, 161 F.3d 44 (D.C. Cir. 1998). The court ruled that an officer has the authority to order a passenger to stay in a vehicle during a traffic stop, particularly when, as in this case, the officer is alone and feels threatened.

United States v. Moorefield, 111 F.3d 10 (3d Cir. 1997). Following *Maryland v. Wilson*, discussed above, the court ruled that an officer may require a vehicle's driver and passengers to remain in the vehicle with their hands up in the air during a traffic stop.

United States v. Stanfield, 109 F.3d 976 (4th Cir. 1997). Officers conducting a traffic stop of a vehicle with windows so heavily tinted that the officers are unable to view the interior may open the door of the vehicle and visually inspect its interior.

Taking a Person to a Law Enforcement Facility
(*This topic is discussed on page 50.*)

Kaupp v. Texas, 538 U.S. 626 (2003). The defendant, 17 years old, was a murder suspect. Three officers entered his bedroom at 3:00 a.m. and awakened him with a flashlight, and one officer said, "We need to go and talk." The defendant said, "Okay." He was handcuffed and taken—shoeless and dressed only in boxer shorts and T-shirt—to the crime scene and then to a law enforcement facility. He was given *Miranda* warnings, waived his rights, and then admitted to his involvement in the murder. The Court ruled, citing *Hayes v. Florida*, 470 U.S. 811 (1985), and other cases, that the officers' conduct in removing the defendant from his home and taking him to the law enforcement facility under these circumstances was a seizure requiring probable cause (which the State conceded did not exist). The Court rejected the State's argument that the defendant had validly consented to being taken to the law enforcement facility; his answer of "okay" was a mere submission to a claim of lawful authority. The Court also ruled, based on the factors set out in *Brown v. Illinois*, 422 U.S. 590 (1975), that unless the state on remand can point to testimony undisclosed in the record, the confession must be suppressed as a direct fruit of the arrest made without probable cause.

Hayes v. Florida, 470 U.S. 811 (1985). Officers took the defendant without his consent from his home to the police station and took his fingerprints without probable cause to arrest or judicial authorization to take his fingerprints. The Court ruled that the officers' action was an illegal seizure under the Fourth Amendment, but it noted that the Fourth Amendment may permit a judicial official to authorize a seizure of a person with less evidence than probable cause and to bring the person to a police station for fingerprinting. The Court also noted that the Fourth Amendment may permit officers to briefly detain a person for fingerprinting at the place where they stopped the person, when they reasonably suspect that the person committed a crime and reasonably believe that fingerprinting will establish or negate the person's connection with the crime.

Dunaway v. New York, 442 U.S. 200 (1979). When officers took the defendant involuntarily from a neighbor's home to the police station and interrogated him, their action required probable cause to arrest; reasonable suspicion that the defendant committed a crime could not justify this kind of detention. *See also* Taylor v. Alabama, 457 U.S. 687 (1982); Brown v. Illinois, 422 U.S. 590 (1975); State v. Freeman, 307 N.C. 357 (1983).

Davis v. Mississippi, 394 U.S. 721 (1969). Officers took the defendant without his consent to police headquarters and took his fingerprints. They had neither probable cause to arrest him nor judicial authorization to take his fingerprints. The Court ruled that the transportation and detention for fingerprinting was an illegal seizure under the Fourth Amendment, and the fingerprint evidence should not have been admitted at trial. The Court noted that it need not determine whether the Fourth Amendment would permit, under narrowly circumscribed procedures, fingerprinting of a person when probable cause to arrest does not exist.

State v. Simpson, 303 N.C. 439 (1981). The defendant was not arrested or otherwise seized under the Fourth Amendment when he voluntarily accompanied officers to a law enforcement building at their request and then was taken to an unlocked interrogation room and interviewed throughout the day; he was never arrested, handcuffed, or restrained or otherwise treated as if he were in custody until an arrest warrant was served in the evening. An officer's statement at a court hearing that the defendant was in his custody during the day was not dispositive when the evidence showed that the restraint on the defendant's freedom was not sufficient to constitute a seizure under the Fourth Amendment. *See also* State v. Bromfield, 332 N.C. 24 (1992); State v. Phipps, 331 N.C. 427 (1992); State v. Johnson, 317 N.C. 343 (1986); State v. Jackson, 308 N.C. 549 (1983), *later appeal*, 317 N.C. 1 (1986); State v. Davis, 305 N.C. 400 (1982); State v. Morgan, 299 N.C. 191 (1980); State v. Reynolds, 298 N.C. 380 (1979); State v. Cass, 55 N.C. App. 291 (1982); State v. Smith, 61 N.C. App. 52 (1983).

Using Weapons or Handcuffs

(*This topic is discussed on page 50.*)

United States v. Hensley, 469 U.S. 221 (1985). The Court stated that an officer's use of a drawn weapon to protect himself during a stop was proper because the suspects were reported to be armed and dangerous.

State v. Carrouthers, 213 N.C. App. 384 (2011). The court ruled that an officer's act of handcuffing the defendant during a *Terry* stop was reasonable and did not transform the stop into an arrest. The officer observed what he believed to be a hand-to-hand drug transaction between the defendant and another individual; the defendant was sitting in the backseat of a car, with two other people up front. While frisking the defendant, the officer felt an item consistent with narcotics, corroborating his suspicion of drug activity. The officer then handcuffed the defendant and recovered crack cocaine from his pocket. The circumstances presented a possible threat of physical violence, given the connection between drugs and violence and the fact that the officer was outnumbered by the people in the car. *See also* State v. Thorpe, 232 N.C. App. 468 (2014) (handcuffing defendant was permissible during investigative stop when single officer was also dealing with another suspect).

State v. Sanchez, 147 N.C. App. 619 (2001). The defendant was convicted of cocaine trafficking offenses. Based on information from an informant that supplied reasonable suspicion and also revealed that the defendant might be heavily armed, officers conducted an investigatory stop of a vehicle in which they drew their guns and handcuffed the defendant and other passengers. The handcuffing occurred for no more than five minutes. The court ruled, citing *United States v. Hensley*, 469 U.S. 491 (1985), that the use of weapons and handcuffs was permissible during the stop.

Burton v. City of Durham, 118 N.C. App. 676 (1995). The court ruled that the officers' use of handcuffs to subdue the arrestee after he resisted arrest was reasonable.

United States v. Crittendon, 883 F.2d 326 (4th Cir. 1989). An officer's use of handcuffs on the defendant, who was stopped for a burglary, was proper, because the officer reasonably anticipated that he might be needed to assist in capturing the defendant's accomplice, who had fled from the officers. The court stated that brief, even if complete, deprivations of a suspect's freedom do not convert a stop and frisk into an arrest, as long as the methods of restraint are reasonable under the circumstances. *See also* United States v. Jordan, 232 F.3d 447 (5th Cir. 2000) (handcuffing defendant after investigative stop because he was physically evasive was reasonable and did not convert stop into arrest requiring probable cause); United States v. Corrales, 183 F.3d 1116 (9th Cir. 1999) (officers' detaining defendant with handcuffs for 15 to 30 minutes was reasonable and did not convert stop into arrest requiring probable cause when weapons had been found, more weapons were potentially there, fleeing people were at large, and uncooperative people were inside a residence).

United States v. Taylor, 857 F.2d 210 (4th Cir. 1988). Using six law enforcement vehicles to block a drug dealer's car and drawing weapons on the car to order the occupants out were permissible actions during an investigative stop, based on the officers' knowledge of the defendant's propensity for violence. *See also* United States v. Lane, 909 F.2d 895 (6th Cir. 1990) (display of weapon proper during drug trafficking stop).

United States v. Robertson, 833 F.2d 777 (9th Cir. 1987). The detention of the defendant by 7 to 10 officers—one of whom aimed his gun at her nose, told her to freeze, and detained her between 5 to 15 minutes—exceeded the scope of an investigative stop (and thus was an arrest requiring probable cause) when the display of force was unnecessary to ensure compliance with the request to stop and there was no evidence that she was armed or dangerous.

United States v. Harley, 682 F.2d 398 (2d Cir. 1982). An officer's use of a weapon during a stop for safety reasons does not necessarily transform the stop into an arrest. *But see* State v. Wrenn, 316 N.C. 141 (1986) (state conceded that officer's use of a weapon transformed stop into an arrest when officer stopped the defendant's car, opened the door, ordered the defendant out of the car at gunpoint, and advised the defendant to keep his hands where the officer could see them).

When an Officer's Interaction with a Person Is a Seizure under the Fourth Amendment

(*This topic is discussed on page 26.*)

UNITED STATES SUPREME COURT

Brendlin v. California, 551 U.S. 249 (2007). Officers stopped a car in which the defendant was a passenger. The defendant remained in the vehicle and was eventually arrested. The Court ruled, reviewing its prior cases defining the seizure of a person under the Fourth Amendment, that the passenger was seized and therefore could contest the validity of the stop of the vehicle. The Court stated that any reasonable passenger in the defendant's position would have understood the officers to be exercising control to the extent that no one in the car was free to depart without their permission.

United States v. Drayton, 536 U.S. 194 (2002). Three law enforcement officers—dressed in plain clothes, carrying concealed weapons, and displaying visible badges—boarded a bus while it was stopped at a bus terminal. One officer knelt at the driver's seat (the bus driver was not in the bus) without blocking the aisle or obstructing the bus exit, while two officers went to the rear of the bus. One officer stayed there while the other worked his way toward the front, speaking to passengers as he went. To avoid blocking the aisle, the officer stood next to or just behind each passenger with whom he spoke. He explained that the officers were conducting a bus interdiction to deter drugs and illegal weapons from being transported on the bus. He did not inform passengers of their right to refuse to cooperate. Defendants Drayton and Brown were seated together. Brown consented to a search of a bag in the overhead luggage rack, which revealed no contraband. The officer noted that both defendants were wearing heavy jackets and baggy pants despite the warm weather. Due to his experience, the officer knew that drug traffickers often use baggy clothing to conceal weapons or narcotics. The officer received consent from Brown to search his person after asking, "Do you mind if I check your person?" He found hard objects similar to drug packages that he had detected on other occasions and arrested Brown. The officer then received consent from Drayton after asking, "Mind if I check you?" He discovered the same hard objects and arrested Drayton.

The Court ruled that (1) the officers did not seize the defendants during this bus-boarding procedure—a reasonable person would have felt free to terminate the encounter with the officer; (2) the Fourth Amendment does not require officers to advise bus passengers of their right not to cooperate and to refuse to consent to searches; and (3) the defendants voluntarily consented to the search of their luggage and their bodies.

County of Sacramento v. Lewis, 523 U.S. 833 (1998). The Court, relying on *California v. Hodari D.*, 499 U.S. 621 (1991), and *Brower v. County of Inyo*, 489 U.S. 593 (1989), ruled that a law enforcement officer did not seize a person under the Fourth Amendment when, during a high-speed chase, the person fell off a motorcycle being pursued by the officer and the officer's vehicle accidentally struck the person. There was no governmental termination of the person's movement *"through means intentionally applied."* The Court also ruled, relying on *Hodari D.*, that the Fourth Amendment does not encompass failed attempts to make a seizure.

Florida v. Bostick, 501 U.S. 429 (1991). Two officers boarded a bus bound from Miami to Atlanta during a stopover in Fort Lauderdale. They asked a passenger (for whom they did not have reasonable suspicion of criminal activity) for permission to inspect his ticket and identification. He consented to the inspection. The ticket, from Miami to Atlanta, matched the passenger's identification and was returned to him. The officers explained that they were narcotics agents looking for illegal drugs, and they requested the passenger's consent to search his luggage. He consented.

The Court noted two facts: (1) the officers specifically advised the passenger that he had a right to refuse to consent (although this fact may be relevant to the seizure issue in this case, such a warning is not required when obtaining consent to search, Schneckloth v. Bustamonte, 412 U.S. 218 (1973)); and (2) although one officer carried a zipper pouch containing a pistol, the pistol was never removed from the pouch, pointed at the passenger, or otherwise used in a threatening manner. The Court rejected a per se rule adopted by the Florida Supreme Court that bus passengers are seized when officers board a bus because the passengers do not feel free to leave the bus to avoid the officers' questioning. The Court also rejected the definition of a seizure from a prior case, *Michigan v. Chesternut*, discussed below, which provided that a seizure occurs when a reasonable person would reasonably believe that he or she is not "free to leave." Because the defendant in this case was a passenger on a bus that was scheduled to depart, he would not have felt free to leave the bus even if the officers had not been present. His movements essentially were confined as the natural result of his decision to take the bus—which is not related to the issue of whether the officers' conduct was coercive.

The Court ruled that the appropriate inquiry is whether a reasonable person would feel free to decline the officers' requests or otherwise terminate the encounter. It also stated that this inquiry applies equally to all encounters that occur on streets, on trains, at airports, and so forth. The Court also rejected the defendant's argument that he must have been seized, because a reasonable person would not freely consent to a search of luggage that the person knows contains drugs: the Court ruled that the proper "reasonable person" test presupposes an innocent person.

The Court remanded the case to the Florida Supreme Court to determine if a seizure occurred. For bus-boarding cases decided before *Bostick* in which findings that seizures did not occur during bus boardings are consistent with *Bostick*'s analysis, see *State v. Christie*, 96 N.C. App. 178 (1989), and *State v. Johnson*, 98 N.C. App. 290 (1990).

California v. Hodari D., 499 U.S. 621 (1991). A group of youths, including the defendant, fled at the approach of an unmarked police car with two officers inside. One of the officers, who was dressed in street clothes but was wearing a jacket with the word "Police" embossed on both front and back, left the car and chased them. Eventually, the officer and the defendant were face-to-face running toward each other. The defendant tossed away what appeared to be a small rock (which later was determined to be rock cocaine), and then the officer tackled him. The State of California conceded that the officer did not have reasonable suspicion to make an investigative stop until after the defendant tossed the rock cocaine (the Court, in footnote 1, appeared to disagree with the state's concession).

The Court ruled that the officer did not seize the defendant under the Fourth Amendment until he tackled him. The Court ruled that a seizure of a person occurs only when (1) an officer has applied actual physical force to the person (for example, touching or tackling), or (2) absent physical force, the defendant submits to an officer's "show of authority." While the Court's definition of *seizure* in prior cases had been that a person is seized if, in view of all the circumstances surrounding the incident, a reasonable person would have believed that he or she was not free to leave, in *Hodari D.* it clarified that definition by stating that facts satisfying the definition do not establish that a seizure occurs when a person simply interacts with an officer's show of authority. For example, the Court noted that a seizure does not occur when an officer shouts, "Stop, in the name of the law," and the person continues to flee. To constitute a seizure, there must be, in addition, a submission to the officer's show of authority—for example, the person stops as a result of the officer's command. The Court concluded in this case that the defendant had not been seized when he tossed the rock cocaine, because the officer did not apply physical force until he tackled the defendant, and the defendant did not submit to a show of authority until he was tackled (the Court assumed, without deciding, that an officer chasing a suspect is a show of authority).

Brower v. County of Inyo, 489 U.S. 593 (1989). The decedent (his heirs were suing the county and officers for damages) was killed when he drove a stolen car (in which he was speeding to elude the police) into a police roadblock. The roadblock consisted of an 18-wheel tractor trailer truck, which was set up behind a curve and completely blocked the road, and a police car with its headlights directed toward the decedent's car to blind him. The Court ruled that a government's termination of a person's movement through intentionally applied means is a seizure under the Fourth Amendment. Because the civil complaint alleged that the decedent was stopped by an instrumentality, the roadblock, that was set in motion or placed to stop him, it stated a sufficient claim that he was seized. However, the Court stated that a law enforcement pursuit in which a suspect unexpectedly loses control of his car and crashes is not a seizure; an intentional acquisition of physical control is required to constitute a seizure.

Michigan v. Chesternut, 486 U.S. 567 (1988). Officers in a patrol car saw a car pull over to the curb and a man get out of the car and approach the defendant, who was standing alone on the corner. When the defendant saw the patrol car near that corner, he turned and began to run. The patrol car followed the defendant around the corner so that the officers could see where the defendant was going. The patrol car caught up with the defendant and drove alongside him for a short distance. The defendant then threw a number of packets of drugs to the ground. Rejecting a bright-line test for determining whether an officer's pursuit is a seizure under the Fourth Amendment, the Court ruled—based on these facts—that the officers did not seize the defendant while pursuing him. The police conduct here—a brief acceleration to catch up

with the defendant followed by a short drive alongside him—was not so intimidating that a reasonable person in the defendant's position could reasonably have believed that he was not free to disregard the police presence and go about his business (note the later modification of the definition of *seizure* in *California v. Hodari D.* and *Florida v. Bostick*, discussed above). The officers' subjective uncommunicated intentions in pursuing the defendant were irrelevant in assessing whether a seizure occurred.

Immigration & Naturalization Service v. Delgado, 466 U.S. 210 (1984). Immigration and Naturalization Service agents did not seize an entire factory workforce when they stationed themselves near the factory's exits and questioned workers inside.

NORTH CAROLINA SUPREME COURT

State v. Icard, 363 N.C 303 (2009). At approximately 12:30 a.m., an officer noticed a vehicle parked in the parking lot of a food store in a high crime area known for prostitution and drug-related activity. The officer saw a person behind the steering wheel. The officer parked directly behind the vehicle in which the defendant was a passenger, with his blue lights flashing. The officer, who was in uniform and armed, told the driver in the defendant's presence that the two were being checked out because the area was known for drugs and prostitution. The officer requested from the driver his driver's license and registration and asked for and received the driver's explanation of why he and the defendant were there. After the officer requested law enforcement assistance, another officer arrived in a marked police car and used his take-down lights to illuminate the defendant's side of the vehicle. Both officers then approached the defendant. When the defendant twice failed to respond to one of the officer's attempts to initiate a conversation, the officer opened the defendant's door and made contact with her. The officer requested that the defendant produce her identification and then asked the defendant to come, bringing her purse, to the rear of the vehicle, where he and the other officer continued to ask questions. When one officer left the defendant to deal with the driver, he did not return her purse but instead handed it to the other officer. The court ruled that the encounter with the defendant constituted a seizure under the Fourth Amendment. The court stated, citing *Florida v. Bostick*, 501 U.S. 429 (1991), that a reasonable person in the defendant's position would have believed she was not free to leave or otherwise terminate the encounter.

State v. Campbell, 359 N.C. 644 (2005). An Aiken, South Carolina, law enforcement officer arrived at a Kmart parking lot in Aiken in response to an employee's report of a suspicious person (the defendant) whose car had been parked for three to four hours in the parking lot with the person inside the entire time. The employee pointed toward the car as it left the parking lot. The officer followed the car until it stopped at a convenience store. The defendant got out of the vehicle and started walking toward the store. The officer pulled behind the defendant's vehicle and stopped without activating a siren or blue lights. She asked the defendant if she could speak with him. He walked toward her and a conversation ensued. The defendant told her that he had been sleeping in the Kmart parking lot. He said that he had stopped in Aiken to take a nap, and he was driving home to North Carolina after finishing a job in Columbia, South Carolina. (Aiken is 45 miles west of Columbia.) Responding to the officer's request for his driver's license and car registration, the defendant said he did not have any identification, but he told her his name and date of birth. He said the car belonged to a friend, but he could not recall the friend's name. As a result of this conversation, the officer asked the defendant to "hold up and she would be back up with him." He was later arrested for driving without a license.

(1) The court ruled, relying on *Florida v. Bostick*, 501 U.S. 429 (1991), and other cases, that the defendant was not seized under the Fourth Amendment when the officer approached him and conversed with him about his presence in the Kmart parking lot and about his driver's license and car registration. (2) The court ruled, assuming arguendo that the defendant had been seized under the Fourth Amendment when the officer asked him to "hold up and she would be back up with him," that reasonable suspicion of criminal activity supported the seizure based on the following: the defendant's activity in the Kmart parking lot; the defendant's statement about going to North Carolina but stopping in Aiken, which is not on the route to North Carolina; and the defendant's not having a driver's license and not knowing the name of his friend to whom the car belonged.

State v. Brooks, 337 N.C. 132 (1994). An SBI agent accompanied other law enforcement officers in executing a search warrant for a nightclub to search for illegal drugs. On arriving at the nightclub, the agent saw the defendant sitting in the driver's seat of a vehicle parked in the parking lot. The agent walked over to the driver's side of the vehicle and shined his flashlight into the car's interior. He saw on the passenger side of the bucket seats an empty unsnapped holster within the defendant's reach. The agent asked the defendant, "Where is your gun?" The defendant replied, "I'm sitting on it." The agent was unable to see the gun although he shined his light all about the vehicle. He requested the defendant to get out of the vehicle; the defendant reached under his right thigh and handed the gun to the agent. The agent did not place the defendant under arrest for carrying a concealed weapon, but he eventually obtained permission to search the vehicle and found cocaine in a nylon pouch there. The court ruled, relying on *Florida v. Bostick*, 501 U.S. 429 (1991), that the agent's initial encounter with the defendant was not a seizure under the Fourth Amendment and therefore did not require justification, such as reasonable suspicion. There was no evidence tending to show that the agent made a physical application of force or that the defendant submitted to any show of force. Further, there was no indication that a reasonable person in the defendant's position would have believed he or she was not free to leave or otherwise terminate the encounter.

State v. Farmer, 333 N.C. 172 (1993). Based on facts in this case, the court ruled that the officers' encounter and conversation with the defendant on the roadside was not a seizure under the Fourth Amendment or the North Carolina Constitution. The defendant had no objective reason to believe that he was not free to end his encounter with the officers and to proceed on his way.

NORTH CAROLINA COURT OF APPEALS

State v. Price, 233 N.C. App. 386 (2014). The court ruled that the trial court erred by granting the defendant's motion to suppress. A wildlife officer on patrol in a pine forest approached the defendant, who was dressed in full camouflage and carrying a hunting rifle, and asked to see his hunting license. After the defendant showed his license, the officer asked how he got to the location. He replied that his wife transported him there. The officer then asked him whether he was a convicted felon, and the defendant admitted that he was. The officer seized the weapon, and the defendant was later charged with being a felon in possession of a firearm. The court ruled that the defendant was neither seized under the Fourth Amendment nor in custody under *Miranda* when the officer asked about his criminal history, and therefore the trial court erred by granting the motion to suppress.

State v. Knudsen, 229 N.C. App. 271 (2013). The court ruled that the trial court did not err by determining that the defendant was seized by two officers while walking on a sidewalk. Although the officers did not use physical force to restrain the defendant, both were in uniform and had weapons. One officer blocked the sidewalk with his vehicle and another used his bicycle to block the defendant's pedestrian travel on the sidewalk.

State v. Harwood, 221 N.C. App. 451 (2012). The court ruled that the defendant was seized under the Fourth Amendment when officers parked directly behind his stopped vehicle, drew their firearms, and ordered him and his passenger to exit the vehicle. After the defendant got out of his vehicle, an officer put him on the ground and handcuffed him.

State v. Eaton, 210 N.C. App. 142 (2011). The court ruled, citing *California v. Hodari D.*, 499 U.S. 621 (1991), that the defendant was not seized when he dropped a plastic baggie containing controlled substances. An officer was patrolling at night in an area where illegal drugs were often sold, used, and maintained. When the officer saw five people standing in the middle of an intersection, he turned on his blue lights, and they dispersed in different directions. When the officer asked them to come back, all but the defendant complied. When the officer repeated his request to the defendant, the defendant stopped, turned, and discarded the baggie before complying with the officer's show of authority by submitting to the officer's request.

State v. Williams, 201 N.C. App. 566 (2009). An officer saw the defendant driving a vehicle displaying a 30-day tag he suspected was expired because it was dirty and torn. Before a computer inquiry about the tag came back, the defendant pulled into a driveway. The officer did not activate his blue lights or siren, nor did he give any other indication for the defendant to stop. The officer stopped his vehicle on the other side of the street and approached the defendant's vehicle. The officer asked the defendant about the status of the 30-day tag, and the defendant said that it was expired. The officer then asked the defendant for his license, and the defendant handed him an expired registration and admitted that he did not have a driver's license. The officer asked the defendant to step out of his vehicle to speak with him. After a brief conversation, the defendant consented to a search of his person, which resulted in a seizure of cocaine. The court ruled, relying on *State v. Isenhour*, 194 N.C. App. 539 (2008), that

the officer did not seize the defendant under the Fourth Amendment during the encounter.

State v. Mewborn, 200 N.C. App. 731 (2009). Officers patrolling a high crime area in a marked car saw the defendant and another person walking in the middle of the street. They pulled alongside them and asked if they would wait a minute because they needed to speak with them for a few minutes. As the officers were getting out of their car, the defendant turned and started to run away. A chase ensued, and the officers eventually took physical control of the defendant. During the chase, the defendant appeared to throw a gun from his pocket. Based on this evidence, he was convicted of possession of a firearm by a felon. After he was stopped, he threw a bag of cocaine under the police car. Based on this evidence, he was convicted of possession of cocaine. The defendant moved to suppress all the evidence, arguing that the officers unconstitutionally stopped the defendant without reasonable suspicion. The court noted that the dispositive issue is a determination whether the defendant was seized under the Fourth Amendment before or after he ran from the officers. The court ruled, relying on *California v. Hodari D.*, 499 U.S. 621 (1991), that the defendant did not submit to the officers' authority before fleeing from them and was not seized until the officers took physical control of him. Thus, the flight from the officers could properly be considered in determining whether the officers had reasonable suspicion to stop the defendant, and the court ruled that the officers did have reasonable suspicion.

State v. Jackson, 199 N.C. App. 236 (2009). An officer stopped a vehicle and, with other officers, checked the driver's license and registration of the driver and determined that they were valid and there were no outstanding warrants for the driver and two passengers, one of whom was the defendant. After the traffic stop had ended but before the driver's license and registration had been returned, an officer asked questions about illegal drugs and weapons in the vehicle and then asked for consent to search the vehicle, which was granted. Cocaine was found in the vehicle, the three occupants were arrested, and cocaine was found in the defendant's sock at the jail. The court ruled, relying on *Brendlin v. California*, 551 U.S. 249 (2007), that the defendant was seized during the stop of the vehicle and could challenge the duration of the seizure as violating the Fourth Amendment. The court also ruled that once the traffic stop had ended and the driver's license and registration had not been returned, the officer's questioning about illegal drugs and weapons in the vehicle was an extension of the seizure beyond the scope of the original traffic stop, and reasonable suspicion did not exist to justify the extension of the seizure. The court rejected the argument that the encounter had become consensual after the traffic stop had ended, because a reasonable person under the circumstances would not believe he was free to leave without his driver's license and registration. The vehicle search was tainted by the illegality of the extended detention. Because the defendant was arrested based on the discovery of cocaine and a weapon in the vehicle, the cocaine found in the defendant's sock at the jail was the direct result of the officer's illegal search of the vehicle. Thus the exclusionary rule prohibited the admission of the evidence found in the vehicle and the defendant's sock.

State v. Isenhour, 194 N.C. App. 539 (2008). The defendant and a passenger were sitting in a car in the back corner of a fast food restaurant parking lot. Officers were patrolling the area near the parking lot and saw that neither the defendant nor the passenger had left the car for 10 minutes. They then pulled up to the defendant's car in their marked patrol car. They parked approximately eight feet from the defendant's car and approached on foot while in full uniform and armed. The court ruled that the officers' actions were not a seizure under the Fourth Amendment. The court agreed with the trial court's conclusion that the defendant's vehicle was not blocked by the officers' vehicle, and the defendant was free to drive away at any time.

State v. Leach, 166 N.C. App. 711 (2004). An informant advised law enforcement officers that he was going to make a drug purchase from the defendant at a specific location. When the defendant arrived there in his vehicle, the officers surrounded it. The defendant immediately backed away and led the officers on a high speed chase for nearly 30 miles. The court ruled, relying on *California v. Hodari D.*, 499 U.S. 621 (1991) (person is not seized under Fourth Amendment until he or she submits to an officer's show of authority or physical force is applied by an officer), that the defendant was not seized under the Fourth Amendment until the officers physically restrained him after the chase. Thus, the defendant's abandonment of cocaine during the chase was not the fruit of a seizure.

State v. Cuevas, 121 N.C. App. 553 (1996). Officers who were conducting drug surveillance followed the defendant and an acquaintance as they took a cab from a bus station. The cab stopped at a restaurant. The officers drove up in their car. An officer approached the cab,

opened its rear passenger door, identified himself as a police officer, and asked the defendant and the acquaintance for consent to search them and their luggage. Drugs were discovered and the defendant was arrested. The defendant argued that he had been illegally seized without reasonable suspicion before he consented to the search. The court ruled, relying on *State v. West*, 119 N.C. App. 562 (1995), that the defendant had not been seized before the consent search. The court noted that law enforcement conduct does not constitute a seizure unless "a reasonable person would not feel free to decline the officer's request or otherwise terminate the encounter." *See* Florida v. Bostick, 501 U.S. 429 (1991). In other words, the court said, a seizure does not occur until there is a physical application of force or submission to a show of authority. *See* California v. Hodari D., 499 U.S. 621 (1991). The court stated that the officer did not order the cab to stop, turn on the law enforcement car's siren, or order the defendant to stay in place. Rather, the officer opened the cab's rear door and asked the defendant and his acquaintance for consent to search them and their luggage. Nothing during this encounter suggested that the defendant was not free to leave.

State v. West, 119 N.C. App. 562 (1995). Two officers, dressed in civilian clothes, were at an airport with a drug interdiction unit. They noticed two suspicious males, one of whom was the defendant, at the terminal and followed them to the parking lot. They approached the defendant and his acquaintance as they stood on each side of a parked car. Officer Black presented his credentials, identified himself as a police officer, and requested to speak to the defendant. The defendant provided to the officer, at the officer's request, his airline ticket and identification. The defendant was extremely nervous and his hands were shaking. Black told the defendant that he was investigating drugs and asked the defendant for his consent to search his luggage. The defendant agreed and handed it to Black. As the defendant gave his luggage to Black, Black noticed the defendant's hands trembling and jerking back briefly. This jerking motion startled Black. Concerned for his safety, Black asked the defendant for permission to frisk him before checking his luggage. Without responding to Black, the defendant ran, throwing down a bag containing crack cocaine.

The court ruled that the defendant was not seized under the Fourth Amendment. Applying the ruling of *California v. Hodari D.*, 499 U.S. 621 (1991), that a seizure does not occur until there is a physical application of force or the submission to a show of authority, the court ruled that neither had occurred at the time the defendant ran from the officers. The court noted that while there was testimony that Black may have reached for the defendant, there was no evidence indicating that Black physically applied force or that the defendant submitted to any show of force. At the time Black asked for permission to frisk the defendant, the encounter was consensual and did not require reasonable suspicion. The court also rejected the defendant's argument that the ruling in *Hodari D.* should not be accepted in interpreting provisions of the North Carolina Constitution.

State v. James, 118 N.C. App. 221 (1995). An officer saw the defendant nervously pacing until he reboarded a bus. The defendant moved toward the rear of the bus and picked up a duffel-type bag from a seat and put it in the overhead luggage bin. Officers went through the typical bus boarding procedures designed to find illegal drugs. The defendant agreed to allow an officer to look in his bag. The officer removed a portable radio from the bag and noticed that screws on the radio had been unscrewed several times. The officer asked the defendant if he would get off the bus so they could talk privately. The defendant did not respond verbally but left the bus with the officer. They went to a private area of the bus terminal, where the officer again obtained a consent to search. The officer discovered cocaine in the radio.

(1) Relying on *State v. McDowell*, 329 N.C. 363 (1991), and other cases, the court reviewed the facts of the bus boarding and ruled that the defendant's consent to search was voluntarily given, although he had an IQ of 70. (2) Relying on *State v. Christie*, 96 N.C. App. 178 (1989), and *State v. Bromfield*, 332 N.C. 24 (1992), the court ruled that the defendant was not seized when he was on the bus or when he left the bus with the officers.

State v. Taylor, 117 N.C. App. 644 (1995). Officer A knew that the defendant had been previously arrested for drugs and had a reputation in the community as a drug dealer. Officer A and other officers saw the defendant with others in an area known for drug trafficking. As the officers approached the area in their marked car, the defendant left. The officers then saw him at a nearby intersection. The defendant stopped as the police car approached him. As Officer A got out of the car, the defendant walked toward him and dropped something on the ground. The officer approached the defendant and brought him over to the police car. He determined that the dropped item was marijuana and arrested the

defendant. He then noticed that the defendant was talking "funny" and ordered him to spit out whatever was in his mouth. The defendant spit out individually wrapped pieces of crack cocaine.

The court ruled that (1) the defendant was not seized until after he dropped the item to the ground, because he had not yielded to a show of authority before then; *see* California v. Hodari D., 499 U.S. 621 (1991); (2) after the defendant dropped the item, Officer A had reasonable suspicion to detain the defendant, considering everything the officer knew; (3) Officer A had probable cause to arrest the defendant when he determined the item was marijuana; and (4) even if the defendant did not voluntarily spit out the cocaine, it was admissible as a search incident to arrest.

State v. Johnston, 115 N.C. App. 711 (1994). An officer was conducting a license check at an intersection. He saw the defendant's car approach the checkpoint, turn off into an apartment complex parking lot about 200 yards before the intersection, and remain seated there about five minutes. The officer drove over to the defendant's car. As the officer got out of his car, the defendant got out of his car. The officer noticed that the defendant was unsteady on his feet. The officer approached the defendant and asked him why he turned off the road before the license check. The defendant responded that he lived at the complex. The officer noticed a strong odor of alcohol about the defendant's breath. When the officer asked the defendant for his driver's license, the defendant was unable to produce one. The officer then asked him to step back to his vehicle; he eventually arrested him for impaired driving.

Citing *Florida v. Bostick*, 501 U.S. 429 (1991), the court ruled that the officer did not seize the defendant when he approached him and asked him for his driver's license, noting that a seizure does not occur simply when an officer approaches a person and asks a few questions. Once the defendant admitted that he did not have a license, the officer had probable cause to arrest him. While the officer could have arrested him, he chose to ask the defendant to step back to his vehicle so he could investigate further. He then arrested the defendant after he failed field sobriety tests. The court concluded that the officer's actions were consistent with the Fourth Amendment.

State v. Pittman, 111 N.C. App. 808 (1993). Two officers were on patrol at a train station at 1:30 a.m. They saw the female defendant and a man speak and then part company when they saw the officers. Officer Gunn approached the defendant, and Officer Ferrell approached the man. The defendant showed Gunn a train ticket and stated that she was traveling alone and did not know the man with whom she had been seen. Gunn noticed that the defendant was constantly looking over at the man, who was 20 feet away. The defendant consented to a search of her bag; nothing was found. Meanwhile, Ferrell spoke with the man, who said he was traveling alone and did not know the defendant. The man consented to a search of his bag; nothing was found. Later, a vehicle pulled up to the train station, and the man put his bag in the trunk. The man then motioned to the defendant to approach the car. He placed her bag in the trunk, and the two got in the car and left. The officers compared information they had learned from their encounters with the man and the defendant and had the car stopped by a uniformed officer. After the defendant refused to consent to a search, she was taken to the police station and searched. Relying on *Florida v. Bostick*, 501 U.S. 429 (1991), the court ruled that Officer Gunn did not seize the defendant at the train station. He merely approached her and asked a few questions, and she voluntarily gave him her train ticket and consented to a search of her bag.

FEDERAL APPELLATE COURTS

United States v. Sullivan, 138 F.3d 126 (4th Cir. 1998). Following a traffic stop, and after its purpose—checking license and registration and returning them to the defendant—had been served, an officer, prompted by a lingering suspicion that something was amiss, asked the defendant whether he had anything illegal in the car. When the defendant would not directly answer the question, the officer repeated it several times. During the course of the dialogue, which lasted less than a minute, the officer advised the defendant that it would be better "to tell me now" and that he "would be cool" with the defendant. The questions culminated with the defendant's admission that he had a gun under the front seat. The court ruled that the defendant was not seized during the officer's dialogue with the defendant; that is, the encounter was consensual and the defendant was not in custody under *Miranda*. The court stated that the mere fact that the officer did not affirmatively advise the defendant that he could refuse to answer the officer's questions or that he was free to leave did not transform the encounter into a seizure or custodial interrogation.

The Officer's Personal Knowledge of Facts Constituting "Reasonable Suspicion"

(*This topic is discussed on page 31; also, see similar topic in the case summaries under "Collective Knowledge of All Officers" on page 181.*)

United States v. Hensley, 469 U.S. 221 (1985). An officer properly stopped a defendant for a felony based on a "wanted for investigation" flyer issued from another law enforcement agency. Even though the officer making the stop did not know the facts constituting reasonable suspicion, his action was proper because the agency issuing the flyer had facts to support reasonable suspicion to stop. [Author's note: This ruling also would allow a stop for a misdemeanor under similar circumstances.]

State v. Battle, 109 N.C. App. 367 (1993). Officer Harmon responded to a disturbance call at a washerette and saw the defendant seated behind the steering wheel of a red Pontiac. The officer noticed the odor of alcohol on the defendant's breath, and the defendant performed physical tests poorly. The officer told the defendant not to drive the vehicle, because he believed the defendant was impaired by alcohol. The officer left the washerette, radioed Officer Beekin to be on the lookout for the Pontiac, and gave Beekin the vehicle's license plate number. Officer Beekin later saw the Pontiac leave the washerette, followed it for four blocks (and did not see anything unusual about its operation), then stopped it.

The court ruled that Officer Harmon, before he communicated his request to be on the lookout for the Pontiac, had reasonable suspicion that the defendant, impaired by alcohol, would leave the parking lot operating the vehicle. Although Officer Beekin did not personally have the information to establish reasonable suspicion and had not been told that information by Officer Harmon, Officer Beekin validly stopped the Pontiac based on Harmon's request, which was based on reasonable suspicion.

The Authority to Make an Investigative Stop or Take Other Action without Reasonable Suspicion
Detaining People Present When a Search Warrant Is Executed or Is Being Sought

(*This topic is discussed on page 442.*)

Bailey v. United States, 133 S. Ct. 1031 (2013). The Court held that the ruling in *Michigan v. Summers*, 452

U.S. 692 (1981) (officers executing a search warrant may detain occupants on the premises while the search is conducted), does not justify the detention of occupants beyond the immediate vicinity of the premises covered by a search warrant. In this case, the defendant left the premises before the search began, and officers waited to detain him until he had driven about one mile away. The Court reasoned that none of the rationales supporting the *Summers* decision—officer safety, facilitating the completion of the search, and preventing flight—apply with the same or similar force to the detention of recent occupants beyond the immediate vicinity of the premises. It further concluded that "[a]ny of the individual interests is also insufficient, on its own, to justify an expansion of the rule in *Summers* to permit the detention of a former occupant, wherever he may be found away from the scene of the search." It stated: "The categorical authority to detain incident to the execution of a search warrant must be limited to the immediate vicinity of the premises to be searched." The Court continued, noting that *Summers* also relied on the limited intrusion on personal liberty involved with detaining occupants incident to the execution of a search warrant. It concluded that when officers arrest an individual away from his or her home, there is an additional level of intrusiveness. The Court declined to precisely define the term "immediate vicinity," leaving it to the lower courts to make this determination based on "the lawful limits of the premises, whether the occupant was within the line of sight of his dwelling, the ease of reentry from the occupant's location, and other relevant factors."

Illinois v. McArthur, 531 U.S. 326 (2001). Officers accompanied the defendant's wife to a trailer, where she lived with the defendant, so that she could peacefully remove her belongings. After collecting her belongings and leaving the trailer, she told the officers that she had seen the defendant slide some marijuana under the couch. An officer knocked on the door, told the defendant what his wife had said, and asked consent to search the trailer. The defendant refused. The officer then told another officer to get a search warrant and told the defendant that he could not reenter the trailer without an officer accompanying him. A search warrant was obtained within two hours.

The Court ruled that the officers' action in preventing the defendant from reentering the trailer was reasonable under the Fourth Amendment. First, the officers had probable cause to believe that the trailer contained illegal drugs. Second, they had good reason to fear that the defendant, unless restrained, would destroy the drugs before they could return with a search warrant. Third, the officers imposed a significantly less restrictive restraint than arresting the defendant or searching the trailer without a warrant. Fourth, they imposed the restraint for a limited period of time—two hours.

Michigan v. Summers, 452 U.S. 692 (1981). As officers arrived at a house to execute a search warrant for drugs, they saw the defendant go out the front door of the house and walk across the porch and down the steps. They asked him to let them in, and they detained him while they searched the house. The officers then arrested the defendant when they found drugs in the house and determined that he owned the house.

The Court ruled that a search warrant for contraband implicitly authorizes executing officers to detain occupants of premises while a search is conducted. *See also* State v. Guy, 54 N.C. App. 208 (1981); G.S. 15A-256 (which authorizes the detention of all persons present, not just occupants, during a search of premises not generally open to the public or of a vehicle other than a common carrier).

Ordering People Out of a Vehicle after a Lawful Stop

(*See same topic on page 49.*)

Conducting Impaired-Driving and Driver's License Checkpoints

(*This topic is discussed on page 52.*)

UNITED STATES SUPREME COURT

City of Indianapolis v. Edmond, 531 U.S. 32 (2000). Officers set up a vehicle checkpoint with the primary purpose of interdicting illegal drugs. An officer would approach a vehicle that was stopped at the checkpoint, advise the driver that he or she was being stopped briefly at a drug checkpoint, and ask the driver to produce a license and registration. The officer would also look for signs of impairment and conduct an open view examination of the vehicle from the outside. A drug dog would walk around the outside of the vehicle.

The Court ruled that this checkpoint violated the Fourth Amendment because its primary purpose was to interdict illegal drugs. The Court noted that it had directly or indirectly in prior cases approved of suspicionless seizures of vehicles at checkpoints to intercept illegal aliens, United States v. Martinez-Fuerte, 428 U.S. 543 (1976); to remove impaired drivers from highways, Michigan Dep't of State Police v. Sitz, 496 U.S. 444 (1990); and to check driver's licenses and vehicle registrations, Delaware v. Prouse, 440 U.S. 648 (1979) (dicta). The rationale in *Martinez-Fuerte* was based on the need to police the United States border, and the rationales in both *Sitz* and *Prouse* were based on highway safety. The Court declined to approve a checkpoint whose primary purpose was to detect evidence of ordinary criminal wrongdoing, such as possession of illegal drugs. The Court noted that a checkpoint set up to deal with an emergency—such as thwarting an imminent terrorist attack or catching a dangerous fleeing criminal—would not likely violate the Fourth Amendment.

The Court rejected the argument that its ruling in *Whren v. United States*, 517 U.S. 806 (1996) (officer's motivation in stopping vehicle is irrelevant when probable cause exists for traffic violation), bars inquiry into the primary purpose of a checkpoint. The Court noted that the *Whren* ruling does not apply to suspicionless inventory and administrative searches, and the Court stated that it also does not apply to an inquiry into the primary purpose of a checkpoint. However, the Court stated that the inquiry about primary purpose is limited to "the programmatic level and is not an invitation to probe the minds of individual officers at the scene." [Author's note: Federal appellate cases have applied the *Whren* ruling to seizures based on reasonable suspicion—see, for example, *United States v. Dumas*, 94 F.3d 286 (7th Cir. 1996)—and the Court did not address that issue in this case. And the United States Supreme Court in *United States v. Knights*, 534 U.S. 112 (2001), strongly indicated that the *Whren* ruling applies to Fourth Amendment actions supported by reasonable suspicion.]

The Court stated in footnote 2 of its opinion that it need not decide in this case whether a state may establish a checkpoint program with the primary purpose of checking licenses or impaired driving and a secondary purpose of interdicting illegal drugs. *See* United States v. Davis, 270 F.3d 977 (D.C. Cir. 2001) (court states that checkpoint with primary purpose of checking licenses and registrations and secondary purpose of drug enforcement would be constitutional; court remands to district court for additional findings).

Michigan Department of State Police v. Sitz, 496 U.S. 444 (1990). An impaired-driving highway checkpoint conducted under guidelines that require officers to stop every vehicle and briefly examine the driver for signs of intoxication is constitutional. Officers do not need reasonable suspicion to make the initial, brief stop of a vehicle at the checkpoint. The court noted that additional detention of drivers for more extensive field sobriety testing may require reasonable suspicion.

NORTH CAROLINA SUPREME COURT

State v. Griffin, 366 N.C. 473 (2013). The court ruled that the defendant's act of stopping his vehicle in the middle of the roadway and turning away from a license checkpoint supported reasonable suspicion for a vehicle stop. The trial court denied the defendant's motion to suppress, finding the stop constitutional. In an unpublished opinion, the court of appeals reversed on grounds that the checkpoint was unconstitutional. That court did not, however, comment on whether reasonable suspicion for the stop existed. The state supreme court allowed the State's petition for discretionary review to determine whether there was reasonable suspicion to initiate a stop of the defendant's vehicle and reversed. It reasoned:

> Defendant approached a checkpoint marked with blue flashing lights. Once the patrol car lights became visible, defendant stopped in the middle of the road, even though he was not at an intersection, and appeared to attempt a three-point turn by beginning to turn left and continuing onto the shoulder. From the checkpoint [the officer] observed defendant's actions and suspected defendant was attempting to evade the checkpoint. . . . It is clear that this Court and the Fourth Circuit have held that even a legal turn, when viewed in the totality of the circumstances, may give rise to reasonable suspicion. Given the place and manner of defendant's turn in conjunction with his proximity to the checkpoint, we hold there was reasonable suspicion that defendant was violating the law; thus, the stop was constitutional. Therefore, because the [officer] had sufficient grounds to stop defendant's vehicle based on reasonable suspicion, it is unnecessary for this Court to address the constitutionality of the driver's license checkpoint.

State v. Mitchell, 358 N.C. 63 (2004). A Belmont Police Department officer decided to conduct a driver's license checkpoint on U.S. 29/74 to check westbound traffic for valid licenses and registrations. The officer spoke with his shift sergeant before conducting the checkpoint to ensure that there were enough personnel to conduct it. The officer had standing permission from a department captain to conduct these checkpoints as long as the captain's oral guidelines were followed: at least three officers were present at the checkpoint; officers conducted the checkpoint in a safe area and wore traffic vests, held flashlights to direct vehicles to stop, and stopped every vehicle. These guidelines were not set out in writing. At 4:15 a.m., the defendant's vehicle approached the checkpoint where there were patrol cars with activated blue lights. An officer shined his flashlight on his left hand, directing the defendant to stop. The defendant did not stop; in fact, he speeded up and forced the officer to quickly move out of the path of the defendant's vehicle to avoid being struck. The officer got into his vehicle and pursued the defendant's vehicle, and the defendant eventually stopped 1.5 miles beyond the checkpoint. As a result of this and other evidence, the defendant was charged with DWI.

(1) The court ruled that written guidelines are not required under either the United States or North Carolina constitutions to conduct driver's license checkpoints. Adequate oral guidelines were followed in conducting the checkpoint in this case. (2) The court ruled that the officer received supervisory approval to conduct the checkpoint. The court noted the officer's having spoken with the staff sergeant about adequate personnel to conduct the checkpoint and the officer's standing permission from the captain to conduct driver's license checkpoints as long as he followed the captain's guidelines. These were sufficient restraints to keep the officer from abusing his discretion. (3) The court ruled that the driver's license checkpoint did not violate the Fourth Amendment, based on its rulings in (1) and (2) and the stopping of all oncoming traffic at the checkpoint. (4) The court ruled that the officer's stop of the defendant's vehicle was justified by reasonable suspicion of criminal activity irrespective of the constitutionality of the checkpoint: assault on a law enforcement officer, attempting to elude a law enforcement officer, and reckless driving.

State v. Foreman, 351 N.C. 627 (2000). Officers set up a DWI checkpoint under G.S. 20-16.3A. Notice of the checkpoint was posted about one-tenth of a mile before the stop. At about 2:00 a.m., an officer saw a vehicle, immediately before the checkpoint's sign, make a "quick left turn" onto a street. The officer followed the vehicle, lost sight of it, but eventually saw it parked in a residential driveway. The officer directed his bright lights onto the

vehicle and also turned on his take-down lights, thereby enabling him to see that people were bent or crouched down inside the car. The vehicle's lights and ignition were off, and its doors were closed. Once backup arrived, the officer approached the vehicle and saw that the defendant was sitting in the driver's seat with the key in the ignition. There were several open containers of alcohol in the vehicle, and the vehicle emitted a strong odor of alcohol. In addition, the officer noticed that the defendant had a strong to moderate odor of alcohol about her person after she exited the vehicle and she was unsteady on her feet. (1) The court noted that the officer had never seized the vehicle at any point, and the defendant was not seized under the Fourth Amendment "until at least" the officer approached the vehicle. Based on the incriminating circumstances that existed by then, the court ruled that the officer had reasonable suspicion to stop the driver of the vehicle. (2) Disavowing contrary statements in the court of appeals' opinion in this case, the court stated: "[We] hold that it is reasonable and permissible for an officer to monitor a checkpoint's entrance for vehicles whose drivers may be attempting to avoid the checkpoint, and it necessarily follows that an officer, in conjunction with the totality of the circumstances or the checkpoint plan, may pursue and stop a vehicle which has turned away from a checkpoint within its perimeters for reasonable inquiry to determine why the vehicle turned away."

NORTH CAROLINA COURT OF APPEALS

State v. McDonald, ___ N.C. App. ___, 768 S.E.2d 913 (2015). Although the court determined that the trial court properly found that the checkpoint had a legitimate purpose of checking for driver's license and vehicle registration violations, it concluded that the trial court failed to adequately determine the checkpoint's reasonableness. The court ruled that the trial court's "bare conclusion" on reasonableness was insufficient and vacated and remanded for appropriate findings as to reasonableness.

State v. White, 232 N.C. App. 296 (2014). The court ruled that the trial court did not err by granting the defendant's motion to suppress evidence obtained as a result of a vehicle checkpoint. Specifically, the trial court did not err by concluding that a lack of a written policy in full force and effect at the time of the defendant's stop at the checkpoint constituted a substantial violation of G.S. 20-16.3A (requiring a written policy providing guidelines for checkpoints). The court also rejected the State's argument that a substantial violation of G.S. 20-16.3A could not support suppression; the State had argued that evidence can be suppressed only if there is a constitutional violation or a substantial violation of G.S. Chapter 15A.

State v. Nolan, 211 N.C. App. 109 (2011). The court ruled that the trial court did not err by concluding that the vehicle checkpoint did not violate the Fourth Amendment. The trial court properly concluded (1) that the primary programmatic purpose of the checkpoint was "the detection of drivers operating a motor vehicle while impaired and that the 'procedure was not merely to further general crime control'" and (2) that this primary programmatic purpose was constitutionally permissible. Applying the three-pronged test of *Brown v. Texas*, 443 U.S. 47 (1979), the trial court properly determined that the checkpoint was reasonable.

State v. Jarrett, 203 N.C. App. 675 (2010). The defendant, accompanied by a passenger, approached a stationary driver's license checkpoint at approximately 11:16 p.m. An officer noticed an aluminum can located between the driver's and passenger's seats. The can was open and a light liquid residue was on the top of the can. The passenger leaned toward the defendant, apparently trying to conceal the can from view. The defendant provided the officer with his license, which revealed that the defendant was 18 years old, and the vehicle's registration. Before returning these items, the officer asked, "What is in the can?" Neither the defendant nor the passenger responded. When questioned again, the passenger raised the can, revealing that it was a Busch Ice beer. The officer directed the defendant to a nearby parking lot, where he was eventually arrested for DWI.

(1) The court ruled that the driver's license checkpoint was valid under the Fourth Amendment. It was conducted under a written department policy. Six officers with flashlights—two in each lane of traffic—stopped every car coming through the checkpoint to determine if drivers possessed a valid driver's license and vehicle registration. A supervisory officer was at the checkpoint. All officers wore uniforms and traffic vests. Their vehicles had activated blue lights. The court discussed the trial court's findings concerning the checkpoint's primary programmatic purpose and the reasonableness of the checkpoint. (2) The court ruled that the officer had reasonable suspicion to detain the defendant for further investigation based on the officer's observation of the beer can and the occupants' behavior involving the beer can.

State v. Veazey, 201 N.C. App. 398 (2009). The court upheld the trial court's ruling that the license checkpoint was constitutional. The trial court found that (1) the primary programmatic purpose of the checkpoint was valid (enforcement of state's motor vehicle laws), and (2) the checkpoint was reasonable: the state has a strong interest in enforcing motor vehicle laws, the checkpoint was tailored to meet this purpose, and the checkpoint constituted a minimal intrusion on drivers' liberty. [Author's note: This case was previously before the court in *State v. Veazey*, 191 N.C. App. 181 (2008), discussed below, and the court had remanded the case to the trial court for additional findings of fact and conclusions of law concerning the constitutionality of a checkpoint.]

State v. Gabriel, 192 N.C. App. 517 (2008). Members of the State Highway Patrol (SHP) established a driver's license checkpoint. Several armed robberies had occurred near the checkpoint location in the preceding week, and suspects in the most recent robbery were seen driving a stolen sports utility vehicle in the vicinity of the checkpoint's location. The court reviewed two cases involving checkpoints: *State v. Rose*, 170 N.C. App. 284 (2005), and *State v. Veazey*, 191 N.C. App. 181 (2008), and noted that when there is no evidence to contradict the state's proffered purpose for a checkpoint, the trial judge may rely on the officer's assertion of a legitimate primary purpose. However, when there is evidence that could support a finding of either a lawful or unlawful purpose, the trial judge cannot rely solely on an officer's bare assertion of the checkpoint's purpose. An SHP officer was the only witness to testify at the suppression hearing. He said that the reason for the checkpoint was that several armed robberies had been committed in the area, and the purpose of the checkpoint was to issue citations for "anything that came through." The officer also testified about using the checkpoint to check for driver's licenses. The court concluded that because the officer's testimony varied concerning the primary programmatic purpose of the checkpoint, the trial judge could not simply accept the state's invocation of a proper purpose but instead was required to make independent findings of fact and conclusions of law concerning the primary purpose. Because the trial judge had not done so, the court remanded the case to the trial court to make those findings and conclusions. The court, citing *Rose*, stated that if the trial judge finds that the checkpoint had a proper primary programmatic purpose, the judge must also enter findings of fact and conclusions of law concerning its reasonableness.

State v. Veazey, 191 N.C. App. 181 (2008). Two law enforcement officers established a checkpoint on a highway. The defendant was stopped and charged with DWI. The defendant made a motion to suppress, arguing that the checkpoint violated the Fourth Amendment. The trial judge ruled that the checkpoint was constitutional. The defendant pled no contest to DWI and preserved his right to appeal the trial judge's ruling on his suppression motion.

(1) The court remanded to the trial court for additional findings and conclusions of law on the constitutionality of the checkpoint. First, the court concluded, given the conflicting evidence, that the trial judge failed to make sufficient findings and conclusions of law concerning the officers' primary purpose in conducting the checkpoint. Second, relying on *Brown v. Texas*, 443 U.S. 47 (1979), and *State v. Rose*, 170 N.C. App. 284 (2005), the court concluded that the trial judge failed to properly apply the three-prong inquiry set out in *Brown* to determine whether the checkpoint itself was reasonable under the Fourth Amendment. (2) The court ruled, assuming without deciding that the checkpoint was constitutional, that an officer had reasonable suspicion of criminal activity at the checkpoint to detain the driver for additional investigation. When the defendant presented his driver's license during the initial checkpoint detention, the officer detected a strong odor of alcohol in the vehicle and also saw that the defendant's eyes were red and glassy. [Author's note: See the later case of *State v. Veazey*, 201 N.C. App. 398 (2009), discussed above.]

State v. Burroughs, 185 N.C. App. 496 (2007). The trial judge ruled that a checkpoint (at which the defendant was arrested for DWI) violated the Fourth Amendment based on the ruling in *State v. Rose*, 170 N.C. App. 284 (2005). The State appealed. The court noted that the trial judge's ruling was based on the absence of evidence to support the primary programmatic purpose of the checkpoint. The court stated that the ruling misconstrued the principles of *Rose* and *City of Indianapolis v. Edmond*, 531 U.S. 32 (2000), on which *Rose* heavily relied. The court stated that the *Rose* ruling provided that when contradictory evidence exists about a checkpoint's primary purpose, the trial judge must examine the available evidence to determine the actual purpose, because bare assertions of a constitutional purpose cannot be allowed to mask unconstitutional purposes. Neither *Rose* nor *Edmond* mandated that trial judges extensively inquire about the purpose of every checkpoint. The court in *Rose* required

additional findings of the checkpoint's purpose because substantial evidence indicated that the checkpoint's purpose was to impermissibly check for illegal drugs. The court concluded that from the available evidence in the case before it, the actual purpose of the checkpoint clearly was the same as its stated purpose: to check for impaired drivers. Because such a purpose has been expressly ruled constitutional and the trial judge misconstrued the *Rose* ruling, the court reversed the trial judge's ruling. However, the court ruled that there still remained on remand for the trial court to determine whether the individual circumstances surrounding the stop of the defendant at this checkpoint were constitutional; the court cited and quoted from *State v. Mitchell*, 358 N.C. 63 (2004).

State v. Bowden, 177 N.C. App. 718 (2006). Law enforcement officers established a driver's license checkpoint late at night at the bottom of a hill. It was not visible to motorists until they crested the hill about 250 feet away. One officer was assigned to identify drivers who might try to avoid the checkpoint. He saw a pickup truck driven by the defendant crest the hill and descend rapidly toward the checkpoint. The truck braked hard, causing the front headlights to dip low. The truck then made an abrupt turn into the parking lot of the nearest apartment complex. As the officer approached in his patrol car without blue lights on, he saw the truck pull out of a parking space into which it had apparently backed and travel toward the parking lot's exit but then drive headfirst into a new parking space as the patrol car drew near. The officer pulled his patrol car behind the truck and activated his blue lights. The court ruled, assuming without deciding that the officer had seized the defendant under the Fourth Amendment when pulling his patrol car behind the truck and activating blue lights, that the officer's seizure was supported by reasonable suspicion, based on the ruling in *State v. Foreman*, 351 N.C. 627 (2000). The totality of circumstances justified the officer's pursuing and stopping the defendant's vehicle to inquire why he turned before the checkpoint.

State v. Rose, 170 N.C. App. 284 (2005). The defendant was convicted of various offenses resulting from evidence seized from a vehicle at a license checkpoint. Four of the five law enforcement officers running the checkpoint were narcotics officers (see the court's opinion for details on how the checkpoint was planned and conducted). The trial judge denied the defendant's motion to suppress evidence based on the asserted unconstitutionality of the checkpoint. The court ruled that the case must be remanded to the trial court to determine the primary purpose of the checkpoint under *City of Indianapolis v. Edmond*, 531 U.S. 32 (2000), and the reasonableness of the checkpoint under *Illinois v. Lidster*, 540 U.S. 419 (2004), examining factors such as a plan, time frame, supervision, and directions on how to conduct a checkpoint. [Author's note: The court's remand to the trial court based on *Edmond* was clearly supported by the facts involving this checkpoint, especially the manner in which the checkpoint was conducted by the narcotics officers. However, the court's additional remand to the trial court for a multifactor analysis based on *Lidster* was questionable. The United States Supreme Court in *Lidster* had to decide whether an information-seeking checkpoint was reasonable under the Fourth Amendment. It is highly unlikely that the Court intended to engraft its *Lidster* analysis into the detailed multifactor test required by *Rose* of the reasonableness of all driver's license checkpoints.]

State v. Colbert, 146 N.C. App. 506 (2001). Law enforcement agencies collaborated in establishing a DWI checkpoint under G.S. 20-16.3A. [Author's note: the statute was substantially revised in 2006.] An officer stopped the defendant's vehicle at the checkpoint. Pursuant to the checkpoint plan, the officer (1) requested the defendant to produce his driver's license, (2) observed the defendant's eyes for signs of impairment, (3) conversed with the defendant to determine if he had the odor of alcohol on his breath and if his speech pattern indicated impairment, and (4) observed the defendant's clothing. The checkpoint plan provided that an Alco-Sensor test would be used only when an officer had reasonable suspicion that the driver had committed an implied consent offense. After these observations, the officer instructed another officer to conduct an Alco-Sensor test on the defendant. Based on the test results, the officer arrested the defendant for DWI. The court ruled that the checkpoint did not violate G.S. 20-16.3A(2) in failing to designate in advance a pattern for requesting drivers to submit to alcohol screening tests. The court stated that the fact that an officer must make a judgment as to whether there is reasonable suspicion does not vitiate the plan's validity nor offend the requirement that individual officers not exercise unbridled discretion under G.S. 20-16.3A(2). The court noted that the term "alcohol screening test" in G.S. 20-16.3A(2) is not limited to the administration of the Alco-Sensor test but also includes the four procedures in the plan, discussed above, that were administered to every driver who passed through the checkpoint. The court found that the checkpoint plan was constitutionally reasonable under *Michigan Department of State Police v. Sitz*, 496 U.S. 444 (1990).

State v. Tarlton, 146 N.C. App. 417 (2001). Two State Highway Patrol (SHP) officers were on preventive patrol and decided to establish a driver's license checkpoint. One officer called his supervisor and received permission to establish the checkpoint. The officers were aware that SHP policy required the checkpoint to be conducted by at least two officers, by a nonrandom method, and with a blue light on. During the checkpoint, they checked every vehicle in both directions except when they were writing citations. Blue lights were operating on both vehicles. The court ruled that the checkpoint was constitutionally valid. The court stated that (1) supervisory approval of a driver's license checkpoint is not constitutionally required and (2) a written guideline setting out a driver's license checkpoint is also not constitutionally required.

State v. Barnes, 123 N.C. App. 144 (1996). A Highway Patrol sergeant, who was acting shift supervisor, decided to organize a roadblock to check licenses and vehicle registrations. He considered the likelihood of detecting people who were violating motor vehicle laws, the traffic conditions, the traffic volume that would pass through the roadblock, and the convenience of the public. Patrol officers intended to stop all vehicles that approached the roadblock from either direction to detect driver's license and registration violations as well as other motor vehicle violations, including impaired driving. A roadblock was established on a road at about 12:45 a.m., taking into account that there is a higher incidence of impaired driving on weekend early morning hours. The sergeant's unmarked patrol car was parked in the paved median dividing the lanes of the road, and another unmarked patrol car was parked on the road's shoulder. At least one of the patrol cars had its blue lights on. The defendant's car was stopped and the defendant was asked to show his license and registration; his conduct led to his arrest and conviction for impaired driving. The court noted the provisions of G.S. 20-16.3A [Author's note: The statute was substantially revised in 2006.] and State Highway Patrol Directive No. 63. The directive requires that "[a]ll roadblocks shall be marked by signs, activated emergency lights, marked Patrol vehicles parked in conspicuous locations, or other ways to assure motorists are aware that an authorized roadblock is being conducted. A blue light on at least one Patrol vehicle shall be operated at all times."

Reviewing the facts set out above, the court ruled that the roadblock substantially complied with G.S. 20-16.3A and Directive 63 (the court noted its ruling in *State v. Sanders*, 112 N.C. App. 477 (1993)) and the stopping of the defendant's car did not violate the Fourth Amendment.

State v. Sanders, 112 N.C. App. 477 (1993). Two State Highway Patrol officers set up a driver's license check at a ramp off a highway. They did not post signs warning the public that a license check was being conducted. The officers checked every car that approached the checkpoint unless they were busy writing citations. The defendant entered the ramp, and as he approached the checkpoint, he stopped his car 150 feet from one of the troopers. The defendant then drove up to the checkpoint, stopped the car, and rolled down his window. In response to the trooper's request for driver's license and registration, the defendant said that he did not have the registration or any identification and that he was not the owner of the car. The passenger in the car also failed to produce any identification. The trooper asked the defendant to get out of the car. As he stepped out of the car, the trooper saw a bulge about the size of two fists in the right pocket of the defendant's jacket. The trooper then told the defendant to face the car and place his hands on the car so he could pat him down for weapons. As the defendant was doing so, the trooper saw plastic protruding from the right pocket. While frisking the defendant, the trooper touched the bulge and noted that it felt like "hard flour dough." The trooper removed the plastic bag from the defendant's pocket. It contained three smaller bags with cocaine inside.

Distinguishing *Delaware v. Prouse*, 440 U.S. 648 (1979), the court ruled that the stop of the defendant's vehicle for the license check was constitutional. The court noted that the troopers followed guidelines of their agency in selecting the location and time for the license check and detained every car that passed through, except for those that came through while they were issuing citations.

Conducting Information-Seeking Checkpoints

Illinois v. Lidster, 540 U.S. 419 (2004). Just after midnight, on Saturday, August 23, 1997, an unknown motorist struck and killed a bicyclist in an Illinois community. About one week later, at about the same time of night and at about the same place, law enforcement officers established a highway checkpoint designed to obtain from motorists more information about the unsolved hit-and-run. The checkpoint involved stopping each vehicle for 10 to 15 seconds, asking the occupants whether they had seen anything happen the prior weekend, and handing each driver a flyer describing the case and asking for assistance in identifying the vehicle and driver. When the defendant stopped his vehicle at the checkpoint, an officer smelled alcohol on his breath that eventually led to his conviction for driving under the influence of alcohol. The defendant argued that the checkpoint violated the Fourth Amendment. Distinguishing *City of Indianapolis v. Edmond*, 531 U.S. 32 (2000) (checkpoint whose primary purpose was to detect illegal drugs violated Fourth Amendment), the Court ruled that the brief, information-seeking vehicle checkpoint did not violate the Fourth Amendment. The Court noted that, unlike in *Edmond*, the primary purpose of the checkpoint in this case was not to determine whether a vehicle's occupants were committing a crime but to ask them, as members of the public, for their help in providing information about a crime in all likelihood committed by others. The checkpoint was neither presumptively constitutional or unconstitutional. Instead, its reasonableness is to be judged by the individual circumstances in this case, using the Fourth Amendment standard of examining the gravity of the public concerns served by the seizure, the degree to which the seizure advances the public interest, and the severity of the interference with individual liberty. The Court then examined these circumstances and ruled that the checkpoint did not violate the Fourth Amendment. The relevant public concern was grave—a fatal hit-and-run. The checkpoint's objective was to find the perpetrator of this specific crime, not the perpetrators of unknown crimes. The checkpoint significantly advanced this grave public concern. The court approvingly noted the checkpoint's similar time and place with the commission of the crime and that the officers used the checkpoint to obtain information from drivers, some of whom might well have been in the vicinity of the crime when it occurred. Most importantly, the checkpoint interfered only minimally with Fourth Amendment privacy rights; it involved only a few minutes waiting in line at the checkpoint, contact with officers for a few seconds, and the officers' simple request for information and distribution of a flyer. All vehicles were stopped systematically, and there was no allegation that the officers acted in a discriminatory or otherwise unlawful manner.

Stopping Vehicle under Community Caretaking Doctrine

State v. Sawyers, ___ N.C. App. ___, 786 S.E.2d 753 (2016). (1) The court ruled that an investigative stop of the defendant's vehicle was justified by reasonable suspicion. While on patrol in the early morning, an officer saw the defendant walking down a street. Directly behind him was another male, who appeared to be dragging a drugged or intoxicated female. The defendant and the other male placed the female in the defendant's vehicle, entered it, and drove away. The officer was unsure whether the female was being kidnapped or was in danger. Given these circumstances, the officer had reasonable suspicion that the defendant was involved in criminal activity. (2) The court alternatively upheld the stop based on the community caretaking doctrine; see *State v. Smathers*, 232 N.C. App. 120 (2014), summarized below. The officer was attempting to ensure the female's safety, and the public need to seize the defendant by an investigative stop of the vehicle outweighed his privacy interest in being free from the intrusion.

State v. Smathers, 232 N.C. App. 120 (2014). In a case where the State conceded that the officer had neither probable cause nor reasonable suspicion to seize the defendant, the court decided an issue of first impression and ruled that the officer's seizure of the defendant by stopping her vehicle was justified by the community caretaking doctrine. The officer stopped the defendant to see if she and her vehicle were okay after he saw her hit an animal on a roadway. Her driving did not give rise to any suspicion of impairment. During the stop the officer determined that the defendant was impaired and arrested her for DWI. The court noted that in adopting the community caretaking exception, "we must apply a test that strikes a proper balance between the public's interest in having officers help citizens when needed and the individual's interest in being free from unreasonable governmental intrusion." It went on to adopt the following test for application of the doctrine:

> [T]he State has the burden of proving that: (1) a search or seizure within the meaning of the Fourth Amendment has occurred; (2) if so, that under the totality of the circumstances an objectively reasonable basis for a community caretaking function is shown; and (3) if so, that the public need or interest outweighs the intrusion upon the privacy of the individual.

The court applied the test and found that the stop at issue fell within the community caretaking doctrine.

Stopping Vehicle for Safety Reason

State v. Wade, 198 N.C. App. 257 (2009). A police department issued a "be on the lookout" alert for the owner of a green Saturn bearing a specific license plate number and registered to a named 26-year-old white male whose photo had been distributed to the department's officers. He had been reported missing by his parents, who did not know where he was and believed that he was in danger. An officer saw a green Saturn with that license plate number. He saw a black male driving it, a white female in the front passenger seat, and a white male in a rear passenger seat. Another officer pulled behind the car and stopped it. Later events resulted in the driver, the defendant, being charged with a drug offense. The court ruled that the stop of the vehicle did not violate the Fourth Amendment. The court stated that having received the missing person report, it was perfectly appropriate for the officers to temporarily prevent the Saturn from being driven off, detain the occupants, and make sure that the missing person was not in any danger of harm. The mere fact that the officers did not observe that the missing person had sustained personal harm or that he was under direct physical restraint when he exited the vehicle did not make further investigative activities inappropriate, given the parents' concern that he might have been at risk of harm or consorting with people involved with illegal drugs.

Wildlife Law Enforcement Stopping Authority

State v. Pike, 139 N.C. App. 96 (2000). Wildlife law enforcement officers were patrolling a lake at night and were stopping every vessel for a safety inspection. They saw a pontoon boat, operated by the defendant, and signaled the operator to stop, which he did immediately. The officers activated their take-down lights, announced their presence, and informed the defendant that they were going to conduct a safety check of the vessel. They did so without boarding the vessel. After the safety inspection, the defendant was arrested for operating a motor vessel while impaired in violation of G.S. 75A-10(b1)(2).

Relying on *Schenekl v. State*, 996 S.W.2d 305 (Tex. Ct. App. 1999), the court ruled that the officers did not violate the Fourth Amendment by stopping the vessel, even though they did not have reasonable suspicion to conduct the stop. The court found that the government's interest in maintaining safety on its lakes and rivers substantially outweighed this defendant's reasonable expectation of privacy in his vessel. [Author's note: The court did not decide whether the officers could have boarded the motor vessel without reasonable suspicion or probable cause; *see* Klutz v. Beam, 374 F. Supp. 1129 (W.D.N.C. 1973) (warrantless boarding for inspection in landlocked lake of private boat used as a home and without consent or without basis for believing there was a law violation was unconstitutional).]

Pretextual Stop or Arrest

(This topic is discussed on page 44.)

Arkansas v. Sullivan, 532 U.S. 769 (2001). The Court made clear that its ruling in *Whren v. United States*, 517 U.S. 806 (1996), discussed below, applies to custodial arrests as well as traffic stops.

City of Indianapolis v. Edmond, 531 U.S. 32 (2000). Officers set up a vehicle checkpoint with the primary purpose of interdicting illegal drugs. An officer would approach a vehicle that was stopped at the checkpoint, advise the driver that he or she was being stopped briefly at a drug checkpoint, and ask the driver to produce a license and registration. The officer also would look for signs of impairment and conduct an open view examination of the vehicle from the outside. A drug dog would walk around the outside of the vehicle.

The Court ruled that this checkpoint violated the Fourth Amendment because its primary purpose was to interdict illegal drugs. The Court noted that it had directly or indirectly in prior cases approved of suspicionless seizures of vehicles at checkpoints to intercept illegal aliens, *United States v. Martinez-Fuerte*, 428 U.S. 543 (1976); to remove impaired drivers from highways, *Michigan Dep't of State Police v. Sitz*, 496 U.S. 444 (1990); and to check driver's licenses and vehicle registrations, *Delaware v. Prouse*, 440 U.S. 648 (1979) (dicta). The rationale in *Martinez-Fuerte* was based on the need to police the United States border, and the rationales in both *Sitz* and *Prouse* were based on highway safety. The Court declined to approve a checkpoint whose primary purpose was to detect evidence of ordinary criminal wrongdoing, such as possession of illegal drugs. The Court noted that a checkpoint set up to deal with an emergency—such as thwarting an imminent terrorist attack or catching a

dangerous fleeing criminal—would not likely violate the Fourth Amendment.

The Court rejected the argument that its ruling in *Whren v. United States*, 517 U.S. 806 (1996) (officer's motivation in stopping vehicle is irrelevant when probable cause exists for traffic violation), bars inquiry into the primary purpose of a checkpoint. The Court noted that the *Whren* ruling does not apply to suspicionless inventory and administrative searches, and the Court stated that it also does not apply to an inquiry into the primary purpose of a checkpoint. However, the Court stated that the inquiry about primary purpose is limited to "the programmatic level and is not an invitation to probe the minds of individual officers at the scene." [Author's note: Federal appellate cases have applied the *Whren* ruling to seizures based on reasonable suspicion—see, for example, *United States v. Dumas*, 94 F.3d 286 (7th Cir. 1996)—and the Court did not address that issue in this case. And the United States Supreme Court in *United States v. Knights*, 534 U.S. 112 (2001), strongly indicated that the *Whren* ruling applies to Fourth Amendment actions supported by reasonable suspicion.]

The Court stated in footnote 2 of its opinion that it need not decide in this case whether a state may establish a checkpoint program with the primary purpose of checking licenses or impaired driving and a secondary purpose of interdicting illegal drugs. *See* United States v. Davis, 270 F.3d 977 (D.C. Cir. 2001) (court states that checkpoint with primary purpose of checking licenses and registrations and secondary purpose of drug enforcement would be constitutional; court remands to district court for additional findings).

Whren v. United States, 517 U.S. 806 (1996). Drug officers stopped a vehicle for traffic violations. The Court ruled that stopping a vehicle for a traffic violation, when there is probable cause to believe the traffic violation was committed, does not violate the Fourth Amendment regardless of the officer's motivation for stopping the vehicle. The Court also stated that stopping a vehicle for an improper racial purpose must be considered under the Equal Protection Clause of the Fourteenth Amendment, not the Fourth Amendment. [Author's note: (1) This ruling effectively overruled *State v. Morocco*, 99 N.C. App. 421 (1990), which had ruled that the test for determining whether a stop is pretextual is what a reasonable officer *would* do rather than what an officer legally *could* do. The North Carolina Court of Appeals in *State v. Hamilton*, 125 N.C. App. 396 (1997), recognized that *Whren* effectively overruled *Morocco*. (2) The Court did not discuss whether its ruling also would apply when an officer has only reasonable suspicion to stop a vehicle for a traffic violation, although it likely would so rule; *see, e.g.*, Ashcroft v. al-Kidd, 563 U.S. 731 (2011) (Court made clear that motive is irrelevant in application of reasonable suspicion standard, although that was not the issue decided in the case); United States v. Dumas, 94 F.3d 286 (7th Cir. 1996) (*Whren* applies to a stop based on reasonable suspicion). (3) The Court's ruling did not change Fourth Amendment law that an officer may make an investigative stop of a vehicle based on reasonable suspicion. *See* State v. Styles, 362 N.C. 412 (2008).]

State v. McClendon, 350 N.C. 630 (1999). Officer A saw the defendant driving a station wagon on I-85 at a speed of about 72 m.p.h. in a 65 m.p.h. zone, and the defendant was following closely behind a minivan that was going the same speed. The officer believed that the two vehicles were traveling together. With the assistance of Officer B, both vehicles were stopped. Officer A questioned the driver of the minivan and then issued a warning ticket for speeding. Officer B questioned the defendant. The defendant appeared nervous, did not make eye contact, and was breathing heavily. He produced a driver's license and title to the vehicle but no registration. The defendant told the officer that the station wagon belonged to his girlfriend; however, he could not give the officer her name even though the addresses on the defendant's driver's license and the vehicle's title were the same. As the defendant continued to answer questions, his nervousness increased. He fidgeted, answered evasively, and appeared very uncomfortable. The officer again asked the defendant for his girlfriend's name and for the name on the vehicle's registration. The defendant appeared to say "Anna." Although that name did not appear on the title, a radio check did not reveal any problems with the registration or the defendant's driver's license. The name on the title was Jema Ramirez. After communication with Officer A, Officer B issued a warning ticket to the defendant for speeding and following too closely. When asked to consent to a search of his vehicle, the defendant—sighing deeply, chuckling nervously, and looking down—muttered "no." Officer A arrived. The defendant was sweating and breathing rapidly, and again refused to consent to a search of his vehicle. Approximately 15 to 20 minutes elapsed after the issuance of the warning ticket before a drug dog arrived and alerted to the vehicle, resulting in a search and the discovery of drugs.

The court adopted under the North Carolina Constitution the ruling in *Whren v. United States*, 517 U.S. 806 (1996), that stopping a vehicle for a traffic violation, when there is probable cause to believe that the traffic violation was committed, is constitutional regardless of the officer's motivation for doing so. The court ruled that the officer in this case had probable cause for stopping the defendant's vehicle for speeding and following too closely and therefore was justified in stopping it, regardless of the officer's motivation for doing so (that is, even if the officer's motive was to stop the vehicle for a drug investigation, it was properly stopped for the traffic violation).

State v. Smith, 346 N.C. 794 (1997). Officers received information that illegal drugs were located in a suitcase in a bedroom in the defendant's house. The source of the information, the defendant's girlfriend, who shared a bedroom with the defendant, told the officers that she would consent to a search. Officers decided to seek consent to search the house because they believed that they lacked probable cause to obtain a search warrant. [Author's note: The procedure of approaching a house to ask consent to search is commonly known as "knock and talk."] Officers arrived at the house with a drug dog. One of the residents—a person who lived there, but who was not the girlfriend or the defendant—let them into the house. The girlfriend allowed the officers' entry into and search of the bedroom she shared with the defendant. The drug dog alerted, and the officers seized illegal drugs there. The court, relying on *Schneckloth v. Bustamonte*, 412 U.S. 218 (1973), ruled that officers who approach a residence with the intent to obtain consent to conduct a warrantless search do not violate the Fourth Amendment by simply using such a procedure. [Author's note: This ruling would apply whether or not the officers had probable cause to obtain a search warrant; see the court's excerpt from *Schneckloth* included in its opinion.] The court also noted that the officers' subjective state of mind in using such a procedure is irrelevant, citing *Whren v. United States*, 517 U.S. 806 (1996).

State v. Parker, 183 N.C. App. 1 (2007). A narcotics detective was conducting surveillance of the defendant in response to a citizen's complaint that the defendant was trafficking in methamphetamine. He stopped a vehicle that the defendant was driving because it was going approximately 60 m.p.h. in a 45 m.p.h. zone and then passed another vehicle at approximately 80 m.p.h. in a 55 m.p.h. zone. The court ruled that the narcotics detective had probable cause to stop the defendant's vehicle for the speeding violations. The court noted prior case law (*Whren v. United States*, 517 U.S. 806 (1996); *State v. McClendon*, 350 N.C. 630 (1999)) that an officer's subjective motivation is irrelevant when a stop is supported by probable cause. Also, the fact that an officer conducting a traffic stop did not later issue a traffic citation is irrelevant to the validity of the stop under *State v. Baublitz*, 172 N.C. App. 801 (2005). [Author's note: Since the *Parker* ruling, the North Carolina Supreme Court in *State v. Styles*, 362 N.C. 412 (2008), ruled that reasonable suspicion, not probable cause, is the standard for all traffic stops.]

State v. Baublitz, 172 N.C. App. 801 (2005). An officer was conducting drug surveillance at a residence. The defendant and another person got into a vehicle and drove away. The officer followed the vehicle and saw it twice cross the center line of the highway. The officer stopped the vehicle, conducted a consent search, discovered cocaine in the vehicle, and arrested the defendant for possession of cocaine. The officer did not charge the defendant with the traffic violation. The court ruled that the officer had probable cause to stop the vehicle for the readily observed traffic violation under G.S. 20-146(a) (vehicle must be driven on right side of highway). The court noted that under *State v. McClendon*, 350 N.C. 630 (1999), the ulterior motive of the officer is irrelevant when there are objective circumstances justifying the officer's action. The court also ruled that the officer's failure to charge the defendant with the traffic violation was irrelevant to the validity of the stop. [Author's note: Since the *Baublitz* ruling, the North Carolina Supreme Court in *State v. Styles*, 362 N.C. 412 (2008), ruled that reasonable suspicion, not probable cause, is the standard for all traffic stops.]

State v. Hamilton, 125 N.C. App. 396 (1997). An officer involved in drug surveillance stopped a vehicle because the driver and front seat passenger were not wearing seat belts as required by law. The court ruled, based on *Whren v. United States*, 517 U.S. 806 (1996), that because the officer had probable cause to believe that the seat belt law had been violated, the stop was consistent with the Fourth Amendment even though a reasonable officer might not have made the stop. The court recognized that the *Whren* ruling had effectively overruled *State v. Morocco*, 99 N.C. App. 421 (1990), ruling that the test for determining whether a stop is pretextual is what a reasonable officer *would* do, rather than what an officer legally *could* do.

United States v. Scheetz, 293 F.3d 175 (4th Cir. 2002). Officers set up a checkpoint with two signs about 100 feet apart, both of which read "K-9 Check Point Ahead." Officers stationed at the checkpoint checked driver's licenses and looked for impaired drivers. There was no K-9 officer at the checkpoint. Narcotics officers in unmarked vehicles watched for motorists who threw items out of their vehicles or who made U-turns or took other evasive actions when they saw the signs. A vehicle executed an illegal U-turn after passing the first checkpoint sign but before reaching the checkpoint itself. The narcotics officers stopped the vehicle. The court ruled, distinguishing *City of Indianapolis v. Edmond*, 531 U.S. 32 (2000), and relying on *Whren v. United States*, 517 U.S. 806 (1996), that the commission of the illegal U-turn supported the stop of the vehicle.

United States v. Clayton, 210 F.3d 841 (8th Cir. 2000). An officer received an anonymous call that the defendant possessed methamphetamine and a sawed-off shotgun in his home. The officer then learned that there was an outstanding arrest warrant for the defendant for failure to appear on a speeding citation. The officer, along with several federal drug agents, executed the arrest warrant by arresting the defendant in his home and, with the defendant's consent to search, seized the methamphetamine and a sawed-off shotgun. The court ruled, relying on *Whren v. United States*, that the execution of the arrest was valid. The officer's motive in executing the arrest warrant was irrelevant.

The Authority to Arrest: Probable Cause
Determination of Probable Cause
(This topic is discussed on page 39.)

UNITED STATES SUPREME COURT

Maryland v. Pringle, 540 U.S. 366 (2003). After a vehicle was stopped for speeding by a law enforcement officer, a consent search revealed $763 of rolled-up cash in the glove compartment and five baggies of cocaine between the backseat armrest and backseat. All three vehicle occupants—the driver; the defendant, who was a front-seat passenger; and a backseat passenger—denied ownership of the cocaine and the money. The Court ruled that the officer had probable cause to arrest the defendant as well as the other occupants. The Court stated that it was a reasonable inference from the facts that any or all three vehicle occupants knew and exercised dominion and control over the cocaine. A reasonable officer could conclude that there was probable cause to believe that the defendant committed the crime of possession of cocaine, either solely or jointly. The quantity of drugs and cash in the car indicated the likelihood of drug dealing, an enterprise to which a dealer would be unlikely to admit an innocent person with the potential to furnish evidence against him. Distinguishing *United States v. Di Re*, 332 U.S. 581 (1948), the court noted that no one in the car was singled out as the owner of the cocaine and cash in this case.

Ornelas v. United States, 517 U.S. 690 (1996). The Court ruled that an appellate court must exercise de novo review of a trial court's determination of whether reasonable suspicion or probable cause existed. However, the Court noted, an appellate court should review findings of historical fact (that is, the facts underlying the issue of the existence of reasonable suspicion or probable cause) only for clear error and should give due weight to inferences drawn from those facts by trial courts and law enforcement officers.

Illinois v. Gates, 462 U.S. 213 (1983). The Supreme Court rejected the two-prong test of *Aguilar v. Texas*, 378 U.S. 108 (1964), and *Spinelli v. United States*, 393 U.S. 410 (1969), that had been used to analyze an informant's information to support probable cause to issue a search warrant. The Court substituted a totality of circumstances test, in which an issuing magistrate considers the informant's information along with other facts in determining probable cause. This test also is used in determining probable cause to arrest, including warrantless arrests. *See, e.g.,* United States v. Miller, 925 F.2d 695 (4th Cir. 1991) (court found probable cause to make warrantless arrest; officer was not required to corroborate information from first-time informant when informant's tip was substantially corroborated by officer's observations and officer had previously arrested defendant for drug charges).

Hill v. California, 401 U.S. 797 (1971). When officers mistake a person for someone else they seek to validly arrest, the arrest is constitutionally reasonable under the Fourth Amendment if the arresting officers have probable cause to arrest the person sought and reasonably believe that the person arrested is the person sought. *See also* State v. Lynch, 94 N.C. App. 330 (1989).

Peters v. New York, 392 U.S. 40 (1968). An officer had probable cause to arrest the defendant for attempted burglary, based on his own observations and defendant's furtive actions, including fleeing down an apartment hallway. Justice Harlan's more persuasive concurring opinion stated that the officer did not have probable cause to arrest, although the officer did have reasonable suspicion to stop the defendant forcibly and frisk him.

Sibron v. New York, 392 U.S. 40 (1968). An officer did not have probable cause to arrest when he observed the defendant talking with known narcotics addicts. He did not overhear the conversations and did not see anything pass between the defendant and any of the addicts.

Beck v. Ohio, 379 U.S. 89 (1964). An officer did not have probable cause to arrest when (1) his information showed only that the defendant had a prior gambling record, and (2) his hearsay information was not related specifically to criminal activity.

Henry v. United States, 361 U.S. 98 (1959). An officer did not have probable cause to arrest when his information vaguely referred to involvement of the defendant's accomplice in a crime and there was no other incriminating evidence. Probable cause to arrest may not be established with incriminating evidence that is seized after an arrest is made.

Draper v. United States, 358 U.S. 307 (1959). Probable cause to arrest existed when a reliable informant gave an officer detailed information and the officer's observations of the defendant when he arrived at the local train station corroborated that information. *See also* State v. Ketchie, 286 N.C. 387 (1975).

NORTH CAROLINA SUPREME COURT

State v. Biber, 365 N.C. 162 (2011). The court ruled that officers had probable cause to arrest the defendant for possession of a controlled substance found in a motel room. Officers responded to a motel based on a call from the motel manager that illegal activities, including drug use, were taking place in a room there. The officers' conversation with the manager when they arrived confirmed the possibility of these activities. When the motel room door was opened, officers saw a woman sitting on a bed with a crack pipe and drug paraphernalia next to her. (The male defendant and another woman also were in the room.) Upon seeing the officers, the woman fled into the bathroom and flushed the toilet. A search of the bathroom revealed a bag containing what appeared to be cocaine or methamphetamine. The male defendant ignored instructions to remain still and instead moved about the room. When asked, the defendant asserted that the room and a bag containing clothing were his. The court noted that the officers were confronted by the male defendant, who appeared to have brought two women and his own personal belongings into the room where drug use appeared to be taking place.

State v. Bone, 354 N.C. 1 (2001). An elderly woman was murdered in her apartment. An SBI agent applied dye to the apartment floor and it raised shoe print impressions left in blood. A manager of a sporting goods store, along with a detective, examined a photograph of the impressions and determined that a Converse "Chuck Taylor" athletic shoe made the impressions. Within two months of the murder, an anonymous person called about this homicide and said that Tony Bone (the defendant), a black male in his late 20s, climbed in an open window, punched an elderly female in the face so hard that her ears bled, and stole five dollars. The caller said that Bone worked for a moving company in Greensboro, lived in Trinity, North Carolina, was married, and was recently released from prison.

The court noted that a detective verified almost all of the anonymous caller's information before he approached the defendant. For example, he learned that the defendant was married and worked at a moving company in Greensboro. A criminal history check revealed that the defendant had been released from prison about one year before the murder. A cut screen at the murder scene indicated access through an apartment window. The victim was found with blood on her face, and the primary cause of death was a broken neck. The only incorrect information was that the defendant lived in Trinity, North Carolina, although both Liberty and Trinity are small communities in northern Randolph County. The detective approached the defendant at the moving company and asked him if he would come downtown to speak about an undisclosed matter; the defendant agreed to do so. The detective noticed that the defendant was wearing "Chuck Taylor" athletic shoes.

The court ruled, relying on *Illinois v. Gates*, 462 U.S. 213 (1983), that the officer had probable cause to arrest the defendant. The information given by the anonymous caller was substantially corroborated by the known facts. In addition, the detective saw the defendant wearing "Chuck Taylor" shoes.

Best v. Duke University, 337 N.C. 742 (1994). The plaintiff sued defendant Duke University for malicious prosecution and other torts based on his arrest and prosecution for trespass and larceny. An officer saw the plaintiff's vehicle enter Duke Faculty Club driveway at 5:00 a.m., turn its lights off, and continue down the driveway. Ten or fifteen minutes later, the officer saw the plaintiff's vehicle exit the driveway and go toward the rear of the Washington-Duke Hotel. The officer knew that the hotel was having problems with thefts. He decided to stop the vehicle by blocking it. However, the plaintiff drove his vehicle around the officer and sped away. The plaintiff did not stop even when the officer pulled beside him, rolled down his window, and flashed his badge. Eventually, the plaintiff stopped, and the officer saw wrought iron furniture inside the vehicle. The plaintiff said to another officer there (Russell) that he was taking the furniture to a friend's house. A check of the Faculty Club then indicated that there was no missing furniture. The plaintiff was allowed to leave. The next day Russell learned that furniture similar in description to the plaintiff's furniture had in fact been stolen from the Faculty Club the previous night. Arrest warrants for larceny and trespass were obtained, and the plaintiff was arrested. At the criminal trial, the State, at the close of the State's evidence, took a voluntary dismissal of the trespass charge without an explanation, and the judge found the defendant not guilty of the larceny charge.

The court examined the evidence and ruled that probable cause existed as a matter of law for the plaintiff's arrest for trespass and larceny and his later prosecution for larceny; thus defendant Duke University's motion for a directed verdict on the malicious prosecution claim should have been granted at trial. The court rejected the plaintiff's argument that the State's voluntary dismissal of a criminal charge without an explanation is a prima facie showing of absence of probable cause in a malicious prosecution claim. The court distinguished its ruling in *Pitts v. Village Inn Pizza, Inc.*, 296 N.C. 81 (1978) (disputed issue of whether probable cause existed in malicious prosecution claim when evidence showed prosecutor had voluntarily dismissed criminal charge before trial), because in *Pitts* the only evidence presented was the issuance of an arrest warrant charging a criminal offense and the prosecutor's dismissal of that charge. In this case, uncontroverted evidence established probable cause as a matter of law; thus the prosecutor's voluntary dismissal was not sufficient evidence of a lack of probable cause to establish a question of fact for the jury. The court stated that it disapproved *Pitts* to the extent that it may be read to suggest otherwise. The court also noted that, unlike the prosecutor in *Pitts*, the prosecutor in this case had prosecuted the plaintiff on a second charge, larceny.

State v. Medlin, 333 N.C. 280 (1993). Atlantic Beach officers arrested the defendant in a breezeway outside a motel room in Atlantic Beach for a murder and robbery committed in Wake County, based on mistaken belief that an arrest warrant had been issued in Wake County for these offenses. The court determined, however, that Atlantic Beach officers had sufficient information (see the court's opinion) to establish probable cause to arrest, based on the facts in this case. Therefore, the warrantless arrest was proper.

State v. Smith, 328 N.C. 99 (1991). The suspect in an armed robbery and murder committed around 5:30 a.m. in a rural area was described as a black male wearing blue jeans and a blue shirt. At 8:15 a.m., a uniformed officer in his patrol vehicle saw a person meeting that description walking on the side of a road two miles from the murder scene. The person stopped when he noticed the officer, and then he ran from the officer toward a farmhouse. At 9:30 a.m., officers saw a black male wearing blue jeans and a blue shirt running near the same farmhouse. They chased and apprehended him. When asked his name, the suspect responded, "I haven't shot anybody." The court ruled that probable cause existed to arrest the suspect, considering all the circumstances, including the suspect's flight from the officer.

State v. Primes, 314 N.C. 202 (1985). The court ruled that the detention of a prisoner within the prison confines for a recently committed murder was reasonable under the Fourth Amendment, based on the facts in this case. The detention did not have to be supported with facts constituting probable cause.

State v. Thompson, 313 N.C. 157 (1985). A missing child was last seen with the defendant. There was probable cause to arrest the defendant for kidnapping when officers saw him without the child 14 hours later and they knew about the defendant's prior history of sexual assaults.

State v. Freeman, 307 N.C. 357 (1983). An officer arrested the defendant without probable cause when he went to a suspect's house and told him that he was there to "pick him up" and then took him without his consent to the sheriff's department for questioning; the resulting confession was inadmissible. *Compare with* State v. Simpson, 303 N.C. 439 (1981) (defendant voluntarily went to police station).

State v. Zuniga, 312 N.C. 251 (1982). A seven-year-old was raped and murdered in a sparsely populated rural area near Taylorsville. The victim's grandfather, who previously had employed the defendant as a farm worker, had seen the defendant earlier that day traveling in a taxicab to the grandfather's home. (The victim's body was found near the grandfather's home.) Later that day, the defendant took a taxicab from Taylorsville to Statesville, where he boarded a bus destined for Arkansas.

The court ruled that the following facts established probable cause to arrest the defendant for murder when Tennessee officers took him into custody in a Tennessee bus station: the defendant's unexplained presence at the grandfather's home in a sparsely populated area, the discovery of the victim's body near the home that day, and the defendant's flight from the area by a bus. Although a defendant's location near the crime scene and other evidence in this case might support a reasonable suspicion to make an investigative stop of the defendant, the court's finding of probable cause was questionable.

State v. Bright, 301 N.C. 243 (1980). Probable cause existed to arrest when the defendant matched a child sexual assault victim's description of her assailant and his car matched the child's description of the car in which she was abducted. Also, the defendant worked at the bowling alley where the child was abducted.

State v. Reynolds, 298 N.C. 380 (1979). The defendant called the sheriff's department to report that he had found an elderly neighbor unconscious or dead in her house. Officers had probable cause to arrest him for murder after their investigation revealed that (1) he was not wearing shoes, and bare footprints were found in and around the house; (2) he was shirtless, and a blood-stained T-shirt was found in the house; (3) he was scratched about his face and torso, and there was evidence of a vigorous struggle; and (4) the only unsecured entrance to the house was the window that the defendant said he had used to break into the house to check on the woman.

State v. Mathis, 295 N.C. 623 (1978). A robbery suspect escaped into a wooded area. An officer saw the defendant, who roughly matched the description of one of the robbery suspects, come onto a street off a hill that led into the wooded area. The defendant looked as though he had been in the woods; he was covered with grass and lice. The court ruled that probable cause existed to arrest him.

State v. Small, 293 N.C. 646 (1980). There was probable cause to arrest the defendant when (1) an officer observed him before dawn at a school and his clothing was bloody; (2) a homicide victim was found shortly thereafter in the same area; and (3) the officer went to the defendant's home hours later and saw the bloody clothing again.

State v. Harris, 279 N.C. 307 (1971). There was probable cause to arrest the defendant when, within hours of a breaking and entering and larceny, he went directly to the place in the woods where the stolen items had been concealed.

State v. Roberts, 276 N.C. 98 (1970). A reliable informant's information that was corroborated by officers' observations gave them probable cause to arrest the defendant for possessing LSD, even though they had not seen drugs in his possession before the arrest. *See also* State v. Harrington, 283 N.C. 527 (1973); State v. Alexander, 26 N.C. App. 21 (1975); State v. Wooten, 34 N.C. App. 85 (1977); State v. Willis, 61 N.C. App. 23 (1983), *modified and aff'd*, 309 N.C. 451 (1983); State v. Hart, 64 N.C. App. 699 (1983).

State v. Tippett, 270 N.C. 588 (1967). There was probable cause to arrest the defendant for burglary when he was seen in the neighborhood a few hours after a burglary occurred and his description and clothing matched that of the suspected burglar.

NORTH CAROLINA COURT OF APPEALS

State v. Overocker, 236 N.C. App. 423 (2014). The court ruled that the trial court properly granted the defendant's motion to suppress when probable cause did not support the defendant's arrest for impaired driving and unsafe movement. The defendant was arrested after he left a bar, got in his SUV, and backed into a motorcycle that was illegally parked behind him. The officer relied on the following facts to support probable cause: the accident, the fact that the defendant had been at a bar and admitted to having three drinks (in fact he had four), the defendant's performance tests, and the odor of alcohol on the defendant. However, the officer testified that the alcohol odor was "light." Additionally, none of the officers on the scene observed the defendant staggering or stumbling, and his speech was not slurred. Also, the only error the defendant committed in the field sobriety tests was to ask the officer halfway through each test what to do next. When instructed to finish the tests, the defendant did so. The court concluded:

> [W]hile defendant had had four drinks in a bar over a four-hour time frame, the traffic accident . . .

was due to illegal parking by another person and was not the result of unsafe movement by defendant. Further, defendant's performance on the field sobriety tests and his behavior at the accident scene did not suggest impairment. A light odor of alcohol, drinks at a bar, and an accident that was not defendant's fault were not sufficient circumstances, without more, to provide probable cause to believe defendant was driving while impaired.

The court also rejected the State's argument that the fact that the officer knew the defendant's numerical reading from a portable breath test supported the arrest, noting that under G.S. 20-16.3(d), the alcohol concentration result from an alcohol screening test may not be used by an officer in determining if there are reasonable grounds to believe that the driver committed an implied consent offense, such as driving while impaired.

State v. Townsend, 236 N.C. App. 456 (2014). The court ruled that probable cause supported the defendant's arrest for DWI. When the officer stopped the defendant at a checkpoint, the defendant had bloodshot eyes and a moderate odor of alcohol. The defendant admitted to "drinking a couple of beers earlier" and that he "stopped drinking about an hour" before being stopped. Two Alco-Sensor tests yielded positive results, and the defendant exhibited clues indicating impairment on three field sobriety tests. The court rejected the defendant's argument that because he did not exhibit signs of intoxication such as slurred speech, glassy eyes, or physical instability, there was insufficient probable cause, stating that "as this Court has held, the odor of alcohol on a defendant's breath, coupled with a positive alco-sensor result, is sufficient for probable cause to arrest a defendant for driving while impaired."

State v. Williams, 225 N.C. App. 636 (2013). The court ruled that probable cause supported the defendant's arrest for DWI. Officers responded to a one-car accident at 4:00 a.m. The defendant was lying on the ground behind the car and appeared very intoxicated. His shirt was pulled over his head, and his head was in the sleeve hole of the shirt. He appeared unconscious. When an officer tried to arouse the defendant, he woke up and started chanting. He had a strong odor of alcohol. He stood up and fell back. The key was in the ignition, and the car was not running. No other person was present.

State v. Banner, 207 N.C. App. 729 (2010). The court ruled that if the underlying charges that form the basis for an order for arrest (OFA) for a failure to appear in court remain unresolved at the time the OFA is executed, the OFA is not invalid and an arrest made pursuant to it is not unconstitutional merely because a clerk or judicial official failed to recall the OFA after learning that it was issued erroneously. On February 22, 2007, the defendant was cited to appear in Wilkes County Court for various motor vehicle offenses (Wilkes County charges). On June 7, 2007, he was convicted in Caldwell County of unrelated charges and sent to prison. When a court date was set on the Wilkes County charges, the defendant failed to appear because he was still in prison on the unrelated charges, and no writ was issued to secure his presence. The court issued an OFA for the failure to appear. When the defendant was scheduled to be released from prison on the unrelated charges, Department of Correction employees asked the Wilkes County clerk's office to recall the OFA, explaining that the defendant had been incarcerated when it was issued. However, the OFA was not recalled, and on October 1, 2007, the defendant was arrested pursuant to that order, having previously been released from prison. When he was searched incident to arrest, officers found marijuana and cocaine on his person. The court rejected the defendant's argument that the OFA was invalid because the Wilkes County clerk failed to recall it as requested, concluding that because the underlying charges had not been resolved at the time of arrest, no automatic recall occurred. The court further noted that even if good cause to recall existed, recall was not mandatory and therefore a failure to recall did not nullify the OFA. Thus, the officers were entitled to rely on it, and no independent probable cause was required to arrest the defendant. The court declined to resolve the issue of whether there is a good faith exception to Article I, Section 20, of the North Carolina Constitution.

Steinkrause v. Tatum, 201 N.C. App. 289 (2009), *aff'd*, 364 N.C. 419 (2010). Officers arrived at a scene of an accident and found the driver's vehicle upside down in a ditch next to an exit ramp, where it had come to rest after having rolled several times. One officer smelled an odor of alcohol about the driver's person. The court ruled that the nature of the accident and the odor of alcohol provided probable cause to arrest the driver for DWI. The court also ruled that hearsay information (one officer told the arresting officer that the driver had the odor of alcohol about her person) was admissible to establish that the arresting officer had probable cause to arrest the driver for DWI.

State v. Brown, 199 N.C. App. 253 (2009). The court ruled that an officer had probable cause to arrest the defendant for murder based on information given by an anonymous caller who later revealed his identity to the officer before the arrest. The informant stated the name of the defendant, how he committed the murder, why he committed the murder, and exactly where he lived. The officer corroborated that information with facts gathered throughout the investigation.

State v. Hocutt, 177 N.C. App. 341 (2006). The defendant was convicted of first-degree murder. When officers left the murder scene around 11:30 p.m., they saw the defendant walking barefoot along a road. He had scratches all over his body, was very dirty, and was staggering. The officers recognized the defendant and saw that he was very intoxicated. They placed him in handcuffs and took him to jail for "detox purposes," "to sober up." The court ruled, distinguishing *Davis v. Town of Southern Pines*, 116 N.C. App. 663 (1994), that the officers lawfully seized the defendant under the public intoxication statute, G.S. 122C-303. The court concluded that the defendant met the statutory criteria because he was "apparently in need of and apparently unable to provide for himself" clothing and possibly shelter. The court rejected the defendant's argument that the officers only had the authority to take the defendant to his home, not to jail.

State v. Stanley, 175 N.C. App. 171 (2005). A law enforcement officer received a call from a confidential informant concerning a person selling drugs outside a local convenience store. The officer had worked with the informant for 14 years, and the informant's information had proven to be reliable, leading to at least one hundred arrests and convictions. The person was described by the informant as a black male wearing a blue ski hat, a dark jacket, and blue jeans and standing beside a Citgo gas station on Sugar Creek Road. The informant said that the person possessed crack cocaine and was selling it. Approximately 30 to 45 minutes later, the officer and another officer met with the informant a short distance from the Citgo. The informant told them that the person was still there and selling crack cocaine. The two officers went to the Citgo and saw a person (along with two or three others in the parking lot who did not match the informant's description), later identified as the defendant, matching the description given by the informant. The court ruled that this information provided the officers with probable cause to arrest the defendant.

State v. Chadwick, 149 N.C. App. 200 (2002). A reliable informant gave an officer information that the defendant would be delivering a large amount of cocaine to a specific location in about 50 minutes. The informant described the driver and the make of the vehicle in which the defendant would be a passenger, the direction of the vehicle's travel to the location, and where the vehicle would park. The informant said that the defendant would act as if he were there to use the telephone and then conduct a drug transaction. The officer had previously set up a drug deal with the defendant. The officer conducted surveillance at the place and corroborated all of the informant's information. The court ruled that the officer had probable cause to arrest and search the defendant, citing several cases, including *State v. Wooten*, 34 N.C. App. 85 (1977), and *State v. Mills*, 104 N.C. App. 724 (1991).

State v. Milien, 144 N.C. App. 335 (2001). On December 16, 1998, a drug officer conducting surveillance near a mobile home park saw the defendant bury a bag containing two or three ounces of an off-white, rocky substance in a wooded area. On December 18, 1998, two officers set up surveillance near the place where the bag was buried. Other officers went to the mobile home park and spoke with several men, including the defendant. The men consented to being frisked, but no drugs were found. An officer told the men that he was going to get a drug dog to search the wooded area. The officers then left in their cars. The officers conducting the surveillance watched the defendant go to the exact place where he had buried the bag two days earlier, dig up the bag, and place it in his jacket pocket. The defendant then got in his vehicle. The officers followed the defendant in their vehicle. The defendant threw the bag out of his vehicle into the woods. The defendant did not stop his vehicle when the officers put on their blue lights, but he stopped after they turned on their siren. The officers handcuffed the defendant, but they did not formally arrest him. One officer found the plastic bag after approximately 15 minutes. The defendant was then placed under arrest.

The trial judge ruled that reasonable suspicion supported the detention of the defendant before his formal arrest and denied the defendant's motion to suppress. The court stated that it was unnecessary to determine whether the detention of the defendant before his formal arrest exceeded the scope of an investigative stop and required probable cause, because probable cause existed to justify the seizure of the defendant when he was hand-cuffed. The court cited *State v. Harrington*, 283 N.C. 527 (1973), on the probable cause issue.

State v. Crawford, 125 N.C. App. 279 (1997). Responding to a call from a department dispatcher about a suspicious vehicle on the side of a road in a rural area, a deputy sheriff saw a car parked there with its engine off. The driver's door was open and the defendant was sitting in the driver's seat with one leg hanging out of the car. The defendant was in a semiconscious state. His knee and shirt were wet with drool, and his pants were undone. The deputy asked the defendant if he was okay. He was initially unresponsive and appeared to have trouble speaking. As the deputy looked for a medical alert bracelet, he detected a strong odor of alcohol on the defendant's breath. He then felt the hood of the car and, although the outdoor temperature was 26 degrees, the hood was warm. When the defendant finally spoke, he had a slight slur in his speech. The deputy asked him if he had been drinking, and the defendant replied, "Yes." When asked how much he had had to drink, the defendant replied, "Some." The deputy then asked the defendant several times to step out of the car. The defendant failed to respond to the deputy's first request to get out of the car and answered "no" to the second request. After the third request, the defendant replied, "I'm not going anywhere with you." The defendant then started to put a key into the ignition. The deputy removed the defendant from the car and arrested him for impaired driving. The court noted that the degree of certainty necessary for probable cause is a fair probability and ruled that this evidence supplied probable cause to arrest the defendant for impaired driving.

The court also ruled, relying on *In re Pinyatello*, 36 N.C. App. 542 (1978), that this evidence supported, under G.S. 15A-401(b)(2), the officer's warrantless arrest for the misdemeanor of impaired driving committed outside the officer's presence, because the defendant presented a danger to himself and others if not immediately arrested. [Author's note: Although not applicable to the date on which the offense in this case occurred, G.S. 15A-401(b)(2)(c) now authorizes an officer to make a warrantless impaired-driving arrest without any additional justification (such as danger to the defendant or others), even if the offense was committed outside the officer's presence.]

State v. Rogers, 124 N.C. App. 364 (1996). An officer was directing traffic with hand signals when the defendant's vehicle approached the intersection where the officer was located. Instead of turning left as the officer directed, the defendant stopped his vehicle in the intersection. The officer approached the vehicle and noticed a strong odor of alcohol on the defendant's breath. The officer directed the defendant to drive to the shoulder of the road, and the defendant complied with that directive. The officer then administered an Alco-Sensor test, which revealed a reading of 0.13, and the officer arrested the defendant for impaired driving.

(1) The court upheld the trial judge's ruling that the officer had reasonable suspicion, based on the strong odor of alcohol on the defendant's breath, to stop the defendant's vehicle. (2) The trial judge also ruled that the strong odor of alcohol was sufficient to establish probable cause to arrest the defendant for impaired driving. The judge declined to base a finding of probable cause on the Alco-Sensor test reading because the officer failed to give a second test in what the judge stated was a violation of G.S. 20-16.3(b). The court upheld the trial judge's ruling that there was probable cause to arrest the defendant for DWI. The court noted the evidence of the strong odor of alcohol on the defendant's breath but stated that the evidence of the Alco-Sensor reading could also be considered in establishing probable cause, even though the failure to give a second test violated G.S. 20-16.3(b). The court stated: "There is no prohibition against the results of this test being used by the officer to form probable cause, although this evidence may not have been admissible at trial."

State v. Taylor, 117 N.C. App. 644 (1995). Officer A knew that the defendant had been previously arrested for drugs and had a reputation in the community as a drug dealer. Officer A and other officers saw the defendant with others in an area known for drug trafficking. As the officers approached the area in their marked car, the defendant left. The officers then saw him at a nearby intersection. The defendant stopped as the police car approached him. As Officer A got out of the car, the defendant walked toward him and dropped something on the ground. The officer approached the defendant and brought him over to the police car. He determined that the dropped item was marijuana and arrested the defendant. He then noticed that the defendant was talking "funny" and ordered him to spit out whatever was in his mouth. The defendant spit out individually wrapped pieces of crack cocaine.

The court ruled that (1) the defendant was not seized until after he dropped the item to the ground, because he

had not yielded to a show of authority before then—*see* California v. Hodari D., 499 U.S. 621 (1991); (2) after the defendant dropped the item, Officer A had reasonable suspicion to detain the defendant, considering everything the officer knew; (3) Officer A had probable cause to arrest the defendant when he determined that the item was marijuana; and (4) even if the defendant did not voluntarily spit out the cocaine, it was admissible as a search incident to arrest.

Moore v. Hodges, 116 N.C. App. 727 (1994). A trooper arrived at the scene of a one-car accident and saw Moore's vehicle in the ditch on the side of the road. Moore was lying down in the back of a rescue squad vehicle while being treated for injuries. She told the trooper at the hospital that she was driving the vehicle and it went off the road. She admitted having had some liquor earlier in the day. The trooper noticed Moore's mumbled speech and detected a faint odor of alcohol about her. He administered an alcohol screening test, authorized for probable cause determinations under G.S. 20-16.3(d), using an Alco-Sensor, which is approved under N.C. Administrative Code title 15A, rule 19B.0503(a). The test registered a result higher than 0.10. The court ruled that, based on these facts, the trooper had probable cause to believe that Moore had committed impaired driving.

Davis v. Town of Southern Pines, 116 N.C. App. 663 (1994). The civil plaintiff sued law enforcement officers and the town for violating her Fourth Amendment rights by taking her to jail for allegedly being intoxicated in public. The evidence, taken in the light most favorable to the plaintiff on the defendant's motion for summary judgment, showed that the plaintiff was publicly intoxicated at 1:30 a.m. and that she tripped and fell while walking to a phone booth to call a cab. The plaintiff told the law enforcement officers that she was not bothering anybody and that she was going to call a cab to take her home. The plaintiff's sister offered to call a cab for the plaintiff and take care of her. The officers then took the plaintiff to jail against her will, which the court ruled constituted an arrest under the Fourth Amendment. The court also ruled that, based on these proffered facts, the officers did not have probable cause to believe that the plaintiff was in need of assistance under G.S. 122C-303. G.S. 122C-303 authorizes officers to take a publicly intoxicated person to jail (1) if the person is apparently in need of and apparently unable to provide for himself or herself food, clothing, or shelter but is not apparently in need of immediate medical care and (2) if no other facility is readily available to receive the person.

State v. Trapp, 110 N.C. App. 584 (1993). On January 3, 1991, a confidential informant advised Detective Hines that Steven James would be driving from Jacksonville to Maysville that night to make a cocaine purchase. The informant said James would return to Jacksonville and go to 106 Circle Drive and then to the Triangle Motel. Another confidential informant advised Detective Selogy that drugs were being sold at 106 Circle Drive and that James and his girlfriend, defendant Trapp, lived at that address. The informant also said that defendant Trapp hid the drugs in her vagina while they were being transported. [Author's note: It did not appear from the court's opinion that either informant told the detectives the basis of his or her knowledge about James's and defendant Trapp's activities.] That night the detectives saw people matching the description provided by one of the informants leave a car and enter 106 Circle Drive and later leave that address in the same car and arrive at the Triangle Motel. When they left the motel, Detective Selogy followed the car and activated his blue lights. He saw the female passenger, later identified as defendant Trapp, move closer to the driver, later identified as James, and then saw the male driver put his hand over the female's lap as he was looking in the rearview mirror. After the car was stopped, defendant Trapp was taken to the police station. The court ruled that, based on the informants' information and the officers' corroboration of that information, the detectives had probable cause to arrest the defendant when they stopped the car. The court relied on several cases, including *Draper v. United States*, 358 U.S. 307 (1959), and *Illinois v. Gates*, 462 U.S. 213 (1983).

State v. Mills, 104 N.C. App. 724 (1991). At about 11:00 p.m., two officers (Cruz and Brigman) in an unmarked car approached an intersection in an undercover attempt to purchase drugs. Another officer (Foster) followed the car at a distance. (Foster and Cruz had seen prior drug sales at the intersection. According to their observations, drug dealers approached cars at that intersection when the driver of a car pulled to the side of the road and turned off the headlights.) Cruz and Brigman approached the intersection, turned off the car's headlights, and saw the defendant and another man standing at the corner. (Foster previously had seen the defendant at the corner with other people soliciting cars parked at the intersection, and he had seen the defendant approaching cars. Foster also recognized the defendant's companion as a lookout for drug dealers.) When the defendant approached within one and one-half feet of the parked car occupied by Cruz and Brigman, his companion shouted a warning that they were the police. The defendant then turned and walked quickly away from the car. Foster blocked the defendant with his car and noticed that the defendant was "almost shaking" and acting very nervous. Foster searched the defendant's pockets and found a crack pipe and a $10 bill with crack cocaine inside.

The court upheld the search on two independent grounds. (1) The officer had probable cause to arrest the defendant, and the search was incident to arrest—a search may precede a formal arrest if probable cause to arrest exists before the search and the evidence seized is not considered in establishing probable cause. The court noted the following factors in considering probable cause: the time of day, the defendant's suspicious behavior, the defendant's flight from the officers, and the officers' knowledge of the defendant's past criminal conduct. (2) Probable cause existed to search the defendant for cocaine, and exigent circumstances permitted the officers to search him without a search warrant.

Richardson v. Hiatt, 95 N.C. App. 196 (1989). An officer had probable cause to arrest the defendant as follows: the defendant had been involved in a one-car accident, going off the road into a ditch; driving conditions were excellent; the officer noticed a strong odor of alcohol about the defendant; and the defendant admitted that he had fallen asleep at the wheel. For other cases finding probable cause to arrest a defendant for impaired driving, see *State v. Tappe*, 139 N.C. App. 262 (2000); *State v. Rogers*, 124 N.C. App. 364 (1996); *State v. Adkerson*, 90 N.C. App. 333 (1988).

State v. Turner, 94 N.C. App. 584 (1989). Officers boarded a commercial bus that was stopped at the Raleigh bus terminal while passengers were entering and leaving it. Officers interviewed the defendant and another man named Ricketts and learned that both had traveled from Fort Lauderdale, Florida, and were bound for Winchester, Virginia. Both had Jamaican accents. While speaking to Ricketts, one officer saw several bulges in his jacket. When the officer asked permission to search the jacket, Ricketts fled the bus and was arrested. Officers searched the jacket and found several ball-shaped objects containing crack cocaine. An officer went to the defendant's seat and asked him to stand. (The court ruled that the officer's action was not a seizure because the trial court had found that the defendant was free to leave then.) When the defendant stood, the officer noticed a bulge in the defendant's pants identical to the balls that had been removed from Rickett's jacket. The defendant refused to respond to the officer's questions about the bulge and whether he was traveling with Ricketts. The court ruled that, based on these facts, the officer had probable cause to arrest the defendant for possessing illegal drugs.

State v. Lynch, 94 N.C. App. 330 (1989). An officer mistakenly but reasonably believed that the defendant was another individual for whom arrest warrants had been issued; the court stated that this information was at least sufficient to provide a basis to stop the defendant and require him to identify himself. When the officer stopped the defendant's vehicle and asked him to identify himself, the defendant fled. The court ruled that the officer then had probable cause to arrest him for a violation of G.S. 14-223 (resisting, delaying, or obstructing an officer discharging an official duty). *See also* State v. McNeill, 54 N.C. App. 454 (1981) (similar ruling; officer stopped defendant with reasonable suspicion and defendant fled); State v. Swift, 105 N.C. App. 550 (1992) (similar ruling; defendant fled from officers who had reasonable suspicion to stop him); State v. Washington, 193 N.C. App. 670 (2008) (similar ruling; defendant fled from officers who had reasonable suspicion to stop him and defendant fled from them).

State v. Williams, 32 N.C. App. 204 (1977). There was no probable cause to arrest for possession of drugs when the evidence consisted of only an officer's observations in a drug area of two people joining hands and one of them putting his hand in his pocket.

State v. Cooper, 17 N.C. App. 184 (1972). Officers had probable cause to arrest the defendant, who was walking on a deserted street late at night near a shop that just had been broken into. The arrest occurred shortly after a security officer had seen two men loading clothes into a van parked at the shop's rear door and a few minutes after one of the suspects had eluded the security officer in the same area.

FEDERAL APPELLATE COURTS

S.P. v. City of Takoma, Md., 134 F.3d 260 (4th Cir. 1998). The court ruled that officers had probable cause to believe, based on the facts set out in the court's opinion, that there was a clear and imminent danger that the plaintiff (in this civil lawsuit against the city), as a result of a mental disorder, would harm herself if left alone. Thus, they had probable cause to detain her for the lim-

ited purpose of transporting her for an emergency mental evaluation. She was later involuntarily committed under Maryland law. *Compare with* Bailey v. Kennedy, 349 F.3d 731 (4th Cir. 2003) (no probable cause to seize person for emergency medical evaluation).

Collective Knowledge of All Officers

(*This topic is discussed on page 31.*)

United States v. Hensley, 469 U.S. 221 (1985). An officer who is making an arrest or an investigative stop for a felony need not know the facts constituting probable cause or reasonable suspicion if the other officer or the agency that issued a directive or flyer to arrest or to stop had the facts that constitute probable cause or reasonable suspicion. *See also* Whiteley v. Warden, 401 U.S. 560 (1971); State v. Zuniga, 312 N.C. 251 (1984); State v. Nixon, 160 N.C. App. 31 (2003); State v. Whitehead, 42 N.C. App. 506 (1979); State v. Tilley, 44 N.C. App. 313 (1979). [Author's note: The *Hensley* ruling would apply to a stop for a misdemeanor as well as for a felony.]

State v. Watkins, 120 N.C. App. 804 (1995). An officer stopped a vehicle for impaired driving. A prior appeal of this case determined that anonymous information and the officer's observations provided reasonable suspicion for the stop; *see* State v. Watkins, 337 N.C. 437 (1994). In later proceedings, the defendant filed a supplemental suppression motion based on newly discovered evidence that the anonymous information had been supplied to the stopping officer by another officer who had fabricated the information (there was no evidence that the stopping officer knew that the information was fabricated). The court ruled that reasonable suspicion that is based on information fabricated by a law enforcement officer and supplied to another law enforcement officer may not serve as a basis for a stop, even though the stopping officer did not know that the information was fabricated.

State v. Battle, 109 N.C. App. 367 (1993). Officer Harmon responded to a disturbance call at a washerette and saw the defendant seated behind the steering wheel of a red Pontiac. The officer noticed the odor of alcohol on the defendant's breath, and the defendant also performed physical tests poorly. The officer told the defendant not to drive the vehicle, because he believed the defendant was impaired by alcohol. The officer left the washerette, radioed Officer Beekin to be on the lookout for the Pontiac, and gave Beekin the vehicle's license plate number. Officer Beekin later saw the Pontiac leave the washerette, followed it for four blocks, did not see anything unusual about its operation, and then stopped it.

The court ruled that Officer Harmon, before he communicated his request to be on the lookout for the Pontiac, had reasonable suspicion that the defendant, impaired by alcohol, would leave the parking lot operating the vehicle. Although Officer Beekin did not personally have the information to establish reasonable suspicion and had not been told that information by Officer Harmon, Officer Beekin validly stopped the Pontiac based on Harmon's request, which was based on reasonable suspicion.

State v. Coffey, 65 N.C. App. 751 (1984). The information that justifies an arrest need not be personally known by the arresting officer when the collective knowledge of the officers of three different law enforcement agencies who were participating together in a drug investigation was sufficient to establish probable cause to arrest.

Objective Standard in Determining Reasonable Suspicion, Probable Cause, or the Fact of Arrest

(This topic is discussed on page 27.)

Devenpeck v. Alford, 543 U.S. 146 (2004). Based on information that the plaintiff had impersonated a law enforcement officer while using his own vehicle to stop a motorist, an officer stopped the plaintiff's vehicle to investigate. The officer's suspicions about the plaintiff's impersonating an officer increased based on information learned after the stop. Another officer joined the stopping officer and discovered that the plaintiff had been taping his conversations with the two officers. They arrested the defendant for what they believed was an unlawful taping violation. However, a state appellate court ruling at the time of this arrest had clearly established that the plaintiff's taping was not unlawful. There were two other offenses for which the officers could possibly have made an arrest: (1) impersonating an officer and (2) obstructing a law enforcement officer. The plaintiff sued the officers for making an arrest without probable cause under the Fourth Amendment. A federal appellate court ruled that the officers did not have probable cause to arrest. It rejected the officers' claim that there was probable cause to arrest the plaintiff for impersonating an officer and obstructing a law enforcement officer, because those offenses were not "closely related" to the offense (illegal taping) identified by the officers when they arrested the plaintiff. The Court reversed the federal appellate court's ruling. The Court ruled, relying on *Whren v. United States*, 517 U.S. 806 (1996), and *Arkansas v. Sullivan*, 532 U.S. 769 (2001), that the Fourth Amendment requires only that an officer arrest a person based on probable cause that a crime was or is being committed. The Court rejected a requirement that an offense establishing probable cause must be closely related to, and based on the same conduct as, the offense that the arresting officer identified when the arrest occurred. The Court stated that an officer's subjective reason for making an arrest need not be the criminal offense for which the known facts provide probable cause. The Court remanded the case for a determination as to whether there was probable cause for the two offenses for which the officers could have made an arrest. [Author's note: The Court's ruling effectively overrules the "sufficiently related" analysis in *Glenn-Robinson v. Acker*, 140 N.C. App. 606 (2000), discussed below.]

State v. Freeman, 307 N.C. 357 (1983). The subjective beliefs of the officer or suspect are not dispositive in determining whether a suspect was seized under the Fourth Amendment. The defendant was seized—arrested without probable cause—when an officer went to his home and told him he was there to "pick him up" and took him to the police station without his consent, where a confession was obtained. *See also* United States v. Holloway, 962 F.2d 451 (5th Cir. 1991) (officers' subjective intent to arrest was irrelevant in deciding when arrest occurred).

State v. Sanders, 295 N.C. 361 (1978). Although the officer informed the defendant that he was not under arrest, the court determined that his initial detention of the defendant was in fact an arrest unsupported by probable cause. *See also* State v. Bone, 354 N.C. 1 (2001) (officer's belief that he did not have probable cause to arrest is irrelevant; objective standard supported a finding of probable cause); State v. Zuniga, 312 N.C. 251 (1982) (although an officer testified that he detained the defendant but did not formally arrest him, the court ruled that he had in fact arrested him); Maryland v. Macon, 472 U.S. 463 (1985) (objective test is used to determine Fourth Amendment violation); Scott v. United States, 436 U.S. 128 (1978) (objective test is used to determine application of exclusionary rule under Fourth Amendment); Florida v. Royer, 460 U.S. 491 (1983) (fact that officers did not believe they had probable cause to arrest did not prevent government from showing that custody was based on probable cause); State v. Riggs, 328 N.C. 213 (1991) (officer's belief about what constitutes legal requirements to determine reliability of informant was irrelevant).

State v. Osterhoudt, 222 N.C. App. 620 (2012). The court ruled that an officer had reasonable suspicion to stop the defendant's vehicle based on observed traffic violations despite the officer's mistaken belief that the defendant also had violated G.S. 20-146(a) (drive on right side of highway). The officer's testimony that he initiated the stop after observing the defendant drive over the double yellow line was sufficient to establish a violation of G.S. 20-146(d)(1) (drive within single lane); (d)(3) (failure to obey direction of official traffic-control device regarding designated lanes); (d)(4) (failure to obey direction of official traffic-control device regarding changing lanes); and 20-153(a) (proper right turns at intersections). Therefore, regardless of his subjective belief that the defendant violated G.S. 20-146(a), the officer's testimony established objective criteria justifying the stop. The stop was reasonable, and the superior court erred in holding otherwise. The court noted that because the officer's reason for the stop was not based solely on his mistaken belief that the defendant violated G.S. 20-146(a) but, rather, was also because the defendant crossed the double yellow line, the case was distinguishable from others that had ruled that an officer's mistaken belief that a defendant had committed a traffic violation is not an objectively reasonable basis for a stop. [Author's note: Concerning an officer's reasonable mistake of law, see Heien v. North Carolina, 135 S. Ct. 530 (2014), discussed above.]

Glenn-Robinson v. Acker, 140 N.C. App. 606 (2000). In this case, the plaintiff sued a law enforcement officer and the officer's governmental unit for various torts related to the officer's alleged unconstitutional seizure and arrest of the plaintiff. The trial judge granted summary judgment for the civil defendants, and the plaintiff appealed. The plaintiff was a school bus driver whose bus was stopped in the traveled portion of a street, awaiting students to be dismissed from school. The officer was off duty in private employment driving a tractor trailer truck. The officer first ordered the plaintiff to move the school bus and later told the plaintiff that she was under arrest for violating a section of the city code (obstructing flow of vehicular traffic by stopping or parking a vehicle in the traveled portion of a street), an infraction under G.S. 14-4(b).

On appeal, the officer acknowledged that he had no authority to arrest the plaintiff for an infraction, but he contended that he had probable cause to arrest the plaintiff for a violation of G.S. 20-114.1(a) (violating order of law enforcement officer related to traffic control), a mis-

demeanor. The court ruled that an officer may seek to justify his arrest of the plaintiff under G.S. 20-114.1(a)—this statutory violation was based on the plaintiff's alleged refusal to move her bus from the travel lane and thus was sufficiently related to the infraction, which was parking the bus in the travel lane. The court relied on *Trejo v. Perez*, 693 F.2d 482 (5th Cir. 1982) (when officer arrested a person for offense A for which there was no probable cause, officer could still justify arrest for related offense B for which there was probable cause), and *Graham v. Connor*, 490 U.S. 386 (1989) (question is whether officer's actions are objectively reasonable). [Author's note: See the summary of *Devenpeck v. Alford*, 543 U.S. 146 (2004), above, and its impact on the reasoning (but not the result) in *Glenn-Robinson*.]

State v. Coffey, 65 N.C. App. 751 (1984). Although the officers told the defendant that they were detaining him, they in fact had arrested him. However, the officers had probable cause to arrest, even though they subjectively believed that they did not have probable cause.

The Arrest Warrant and Other Criminal Process
Arrest Warrants
Validity of Warrant
(*This topic is discussed on page 59.*)

Malley v. Briggs, 475 U.S. 335 (1986). An officer may be civilly liable under federal law for violating a person's constitutional rights if the officer obtains an arrest warrant and makes an arrest with it when a reasonably well-trained officer in that position would have known that the information failed to establish probable cause to arrest. *But see* Hunter v. Bryant, 502 U.S. 224 (1991) (qualified immunity for officers who had reasonable belief in probable cause to arrest).

State v. McGowan, 243 N.C. 431 (1956). An arrest warrant was void, because there was no evidence that it was signed by a judicial officer.

Alexander v. Lindsey, 230 N.C. 663 (1949). An arrest was valid when it was made with an arrest warrant that defectively charged a criminal offense ("did unlawfully and willfully trespass"). The warrant was not void on its face, because it charged a recognizable criminal offense.

State v. Taylor, 61 N.C. App. 589 (1983). The arrest warrant's description of the defendant by the defendant's nickname, Blood, was proper.

Service of Warrant

Robinson v. City of Winston-Salem, 34 N.C. App. 401 (1977). An arresting officer is liable for false imprisonment only when the officer is not reasonably diligent in determining whether the person arrested was actually the same person described in the arrest warrant. See also cases under "The Right to Resist an Illegal Arrest" on page 186.

Arrest without a Warrant for a Felony

United States v. Watson, 423 U.S. 411 (1976). A warrantless felony arrest may be made in a public place even if the officer had time to obtain an arrest warrant.

Arrest without a Warrant for a Misdemeanor

(*This topic is discussed on page 63.*)

In the Officer's Presence

Atwater v. City of Lago Vista, 532 U.S. 318 (2001). An officer made a warrantless arrest for a seat belt violation that was punishable only by a fine under Texas law. The Court ruled that the Fourth Amendment does not bar an officer from making a warrantless arrest for a misdemeanor that is punishable only by fine. [Author's note: This ruling has no practical effect in North Carolina. North Carolina law does not authorize an officer to arrest a person for an infraction, which is punishable by a penalty only.]

State v. McAfee, 107 N.C. 812 (1890). A crime is committed in the officer's presence if the officer heard it being committed. *See also* State v. Crockett, 82 N.C. 599 (1880).

State v. Wooten, 34 N.C. App. 85 (1977). If a reliable informant gives an officer information that establishes probable cause that a person possesses heroin, and the officer shortly thereafter sees a person who matches the informant's description, the offense is being committed in the officer's presence—even though the officer has not yet seen the drugs. (Although this case involved a felony, its discussion about an offense committed in an officer's presence applies to misdemeanor arrests as well.) *See also* State v. Roberts, 276 N.C. 98 (1970).

Outside the Officer's Presence: The Defendant "Will Not Be Apprehended Unless Immediately Arrested"

State v. Tilley, 44 N.C. App. 313 (1979). The defendant committed a crime in Dare County. Tyrrell County officers could make a warrantless misdemeanor arrest of the defendant as he traveled in a car away from Dare County.

In re Pinyatello, 36 N.C. App. 542 (1978), and *In re Gardner*, 39 N.C. App. 567 (1979). In both of these driving-under-the-influence cases, the court did not state why the defendants could not be arrested without a warrant based on the arresting officer's reason that they would not be apprehended unless immediately arrested. Apparently, however, the officers knew the defendants' identities and could easily have arrested them later with a warrant. In any event, the court in both cases ultimately upheld the out-of-presence misdemeanor warrantless arrests for other reasons—see the discussion of these cases below. [Author's note: After these cases were decided, G.S. 15A-401(b)(2) was amended to authorize an officer to make an out-of-presence arrest for both impaired driving and commercial impaired driving based solely on whether an officer had probable cause to make the arrest.]

"May Cause Physical Injury to Himself [or Herself] or Others"

[Author's note: After the cases below were decided, G.S. 15A-401(b)(2) was amended to permit an officer to make an out-of-presence arrest for both impaired driving and commercial impaired driving based solely on whether an officer had probable cause to make the arrest.]

State v. White, 84 N.C. App. 111 (1987). A security guard told an officer that the defendant had twice come to a studio making threats—the second time driving a car to the studio parking lot. The officer approached the defendant, who was not then in a car, saw that he was intoxicated, and arrested him for driving while impaired. The court ruled that the officer had authority to arrest under G.S. 15A-401(b)(2) because the defendant's car was nearby and the officer knew that the defendant had come and gone once already. Thus, he had probable cause to believe that the defendant would drive again in an impaired condition if he was not immediately arrested without a warrant.

State v. Spencer, 46 N.C. App. 507 (1980). The warrantless arrest of the defendant at a food store, after the defendant had driven under the influence and been involved in an accident, was upheld because he might have caused injury to himself or others unless immediately arrested.

State v. Matthews, 40 N.C. App. 41 (1979). The warrantless arrest of the defendant at a police station for driving under the influence was upheld because he might have caused injury to himself or others unless immediately arrested.

In re Gardner, 39 N.C. App. 567 (1979). The warrantless arrest of the defendant for driving under the influence—at the front steps of his house within 200 to 300 yards of an accident scene—was upheld because he might have caused injury to himself or others unless immediately arrested.

In re Pinyatello, 36 N.C. App. 542 (1978). The warrantless arrest of the defendant at the accident scene for driving under the influence was upheld because he might have caused injury to himself or others unless immediately arrested. *See also* State v. Crawford, 125 N.C. App. 279 (1997) (similar ruling).

"May Damage Property"

In re Gardner, 39 N.C. App. 567 (1979). The warrantless arrest of the defendant for driving under the influence—at the front steps of his house within 200 to 300 yards of the accident scene—was upheld because he might have damaged property unless immediately arrested. [Author's note: After this case was decided, G.S. 15A-401(b)(2) was amended to permit an officer to make an out-of-presence arrest for both impaired driving and commercial impaired driving based solely on whether an officer had probable cause to make the arrest.]

The Arrest Procedure
Use of Force, Including Deadly Force

(*This topic is discussed on page 67.*)

Plumhoff v. Rickard, 134 S. Ct. 2012 (2014). The Court ruled that officers did not use excessive force in violation of the Fourth Amendment when using deadly force to end a high-speed car chase. The chase ended when officers shot and killed the fleeing driver. The driver's daughter filed a civil rights action under Title 42, Section 1983, of the United States Code (hereafter, Section 1983), alleging that the officers used excessive force in terminating the chase in violation of the Fourth Amendment. Given the circumstances of the chase—among other things, speeds in excess of 100 m.p.h. when other cars were on the road—the Court found it "beyond serious dispute that [the driver's] flight posed a grave public safety risk, and . . . the police acted reasonably in using deadly force to end that risk." The Court rejected the respondent's contention that, even if the use of deadly force was permissible, the officers acted unreasonably in firing a total of 15 shots,

stating: "It stands to reason that, if police officers are justified in firing at a suspect in order to end a severe threat to public safety, the officers need not stop shooting until the threat has ended."

Scott v. Harris, 550 U.S. 372 (2007). The plaintiff sued an officer and others for allegedly violating his Fourth Amendment rights in a high-speed chase that resulted in injury to the plaintiff. The Court ruled, based on the facts in this case, that the officer did not violate the Fourth Amendment by ramming the plaintiff's vehicle from behind in an attempt to stop the plaintiff's vehicle from continuing its public-endangering flight.

Brosseau v. Haugen, 543 U.S. 194 (2004). The Court ruled that a law enforcement officer was entitled to qualified immunity in the defense of a civil lawsuit alleging the officer's improper use of deadly force under the Fourth Amendment. The Court stated that the issue in this case involved the officer's shooting a disturbed felon set on avoiding capture through vehicular flight, when people in the immediate area were at risk from that flight. (See the detailed facts set out in the Court's opinion.) The Court concluded that the case law at the time of the shooting did not "clearly establish" that the officer's conduct violated the Fourth Amendment.

Graham v. Connor, 490 U.S. 386 (1989). All claims that law enforcement officers have used excessive force in the course of an arrest, investigative stop, or other seizure of a free person must be analyzed under the Fourth Amendment standard of objective reasonableness (that is, without regard to an officer's intent or motivation), not under substantive due process.

Tennessee v. Garner, 471 U.S. 1 (1985). A Tennessee statute was unconstitutional because it authorized an officer to use deadly force against an apparently unarmed, nondangerous felony suspect who was fleeing from the scene of a recently committed nondangerous burglary.

State v. Ellis, 241 N.C. 702 (1955). An officer has no duty to retreat when the officer acts in self-defense while performing official duties. *See also* State v. Dunning, 177 N.C. 559 (1919).

State v. Miller, 197 N.C. 445 (1929). An officer who is making a lawful arrest may use whatever force is reasonably necessary to overcome resistance.

State v. Simmons, 192 N.C. 692 (1926). Deputy sheriffs were properly convicted of manslaughter for shooting and killing the occupant of a car when they had no authority to arrest the occupant or to search the car.

Hinton v. City of Raleigh, 46 N.C. App. 305 (1980). Two armed robbers, ordered by Raleigh police officers to halt, refused to do so. One robber pointed a gun at an officer, who then killed him. The other robber crouched and raised his arm toward the same officer, who then killed him. The court ruled that the officer was justified, by reason of self-defense, to kill both robbers.

The Right to Resist an Illegal Arrest

State v. Mobley, 240 N.C. 476 (1954). A person has the right to resist an illegal arrest but may not use excessive force. *See also* State v. Allen, 166 N.C. 265 (1914); State v. Polk, 76 N.C. 11 (1877); State v. Sparrow, 276 N.C. 499 (1970); State v. Hewson, 88 N.C. App. 128 (1987).

State v. Truzy, 44 N.C. App. 53 (1979). A person may not resist an arrest pursuant to an arrest warrant even if the warrant does not in fact charge a crime. [Author's note: However, it appears that the warrant in this case correctly charged the common law offense of public nuisance.] *See also* State v. Wright, 1 N.C. App. 479, *aff'd on other grounds*, 274 N.C. 380 (1968). For cases that appear to be in conflict with *Truzy* and *Wright*, see *State v. McGowan*, 243 N.C. 431 (1953); *State v. Honneycutt*, 237 N.C. 595 (1953); *State v. Queen*, 66 N.C. 615 (1872); *State v. Curtis*, 2 N.C. 471 (1797); and *State v. Carroll*, 21 N.C. App. 530 (1974).

Notice of Authority

When an Arrest Is Made

(This topic is discussed on page 70.)

State v. Kinch, 314 N.C. 99 (1985). Officers properly advised the defendant that he was being arrested for rape. It is not necessary to give *Miranda* warnings to make a lawful arrest.

State v. Ladd, 308 N.C. 272 (1983). An officer violated G.S. 15A-401(c)(2)c. (giving notice of arrest) by responding, "You know why," when the defendant asked why he was arrested.

Before Entering a Dwelling

(This topic is discussed on page 70.)

Wilson v. Arkansas, 514 U.S. 927 (1995). Officers made an unannounced entry into a home to execute a search warrant. The Arkansas Supreme Court ruled that the Fourth Amendment does not require officers to knock and announce before entering a home. The Court, rejecting the state court's ruling, ruled that an officer's unannounced entry into a home must be reasonable under the Fourth Amendment. Whether an officer announced his or her presence and authority before entering a home is among the factors to be considered in determining whether the entry was reasonable, along with the threat of physical harm to the officer, pursuit of a recently escaped arrestee, and the likely destruction of evidence if advance notice were given. The Court specifically stated that it will leave to lower courts the task of determining whether an unannounced entry was reasonable and remanded this case to the Arkansas Supreme Court for that purpose.

[Author's note: G.S. 15A-249 sets standards in entering private premises to execute a search warrant, and G.S. 15A-401(e) sets standards in entering private premises to arrest.]

Lee v. Greene, 114 N.C. App. 580 (1994). An officer arrested the suspect's husband in the driveway of their home. Because the suspect blocked the front door of the officer's car, in which the husband was sitting, the officers (another officer had arrived by then) decided to arrest her for obstructing and delaying the arrest of her husband. When the suspect began moving toward her house, they ran after her. As she entered her house and was closing the door, the officers grabbed the door and entered the house. The court ruled that under these circumstances, the officers were not required to give notice of their authority and purpose under G.S. 15A-401(e). The suspect knew the officers' identities and their reason for being at her house. Moreover, the officers were about to arrest the suspect as she entered her house and attempted to close the door. Compliance with G.S. 15A-401(e) was not required.

State v. Sutton, 34 N.C. App. 371 (1977). Officers properly broke down a door to serve an arrest order after they knocked, demanded entry, received no response from occupants, and heard sounds that would justify the conclusion that their admittance was being unreasonably delayed so that occupants could escape.

Entrance onto Premises to Arrest

(This topic is discussed on page 71; entering premises to search for evidence or weapons is discussed on pages 260 and 261; entering premises for a public safety reason is discussed on page 260.)

Generally

Steagald v. United States, 451 U.S. 204 (1981). An officer may not enter a third party's home—a place where the defendant does not reside—to arrest a defendant unless the officer has a search warrant or consent to enter or unless exigent circumstances justify entry without a search warrant.

Payton v. New York, 445 U.S. 573 (1980). An officer may not enter a defendant's residence to arrest the defendant unless the officer has an arrest warrant or consent to enter or unless exigent circumstances justify an entry without an arrest warrant. *See also* Kirk v. Louisiana, 536 U.S. 635 (2002).

United States v. Santana, 427 U.S. 38 (1976). The defendant, who was standing in the doorway of her home when officers sought to arrest her by shouting "Police" and displaying their identification, was in a public place under the Fourth Amendment. Therefore, the officers had the authority to arrest her without a warrant, and she could not defeat their authority to make the warrantless arrest by retreating into her home. The officers' entry into her home was justified because they were in hot pursuit of the defendant. *See also* United States v. Ramos, 933 F.2d 968 (11th Cir. 1991) (when defendant and confidential informant consummated drug deal outside house and defendant began moving rapidly toward house, officers could enter house to pursue and arrest her); United States v. Sewell, 942 F.2d 1209 (7th Cir. 1991) (undercover officer purchased drugs while standing in apartment hallway and while defendant was inside apartment, although the defendant may have crossed the threshold of the doorway to the apartment when completing the sale; defendant closed door on officer when he realized he had sold to an officer; exigent circumstances permitted warrantless entry to arrest); City of Middletown v. Flinchum, 765 N.E.2d 330 (Ohio 2002) (officers saw defendant driving recklessly and followed him to his house, where he got out of his car; ignoring officers' commands to stop, defendant ran into the house; court ruled that officers in hot pursuit could warrantlessly enter house to arrest defendant for misdemeanor motor vehicle violation).

State v. Workman, 344 N.C. 482 (1996). Officers had probable cause to believe that the defendant was inside his home when they entered late at night to execute an arrest warrant for two murders, based on the following facts. The defendant's accomplice in the murders pointed out the trailer as the defendant's home. Officers maintained surveillance on the trailer while another officer obtained an arrest warrant. They did not see anyone leave the trailer. As the officers approached the trailer, they saw lights on and heard noises inside.

State v. Basden, 8 N.C. App. 401 (1970). Within minutes of a robbery, officers arrived at a residence where the vehicle used in the robbery was parked in the driveway. All curtains on the residence windows were drawn. This was sufficient evidence that the robbers were inside the residence.

Watts v. County of Sacramento, 256 F.3d 886 (9th Cir. 2001). If a suspect named in an arrest warrant is a guest of a third party, then—absent exigent circumstances—officers must obtain a search warrant to enter the third party's dwelling. If the suspect is a co-resident of the third party, an arrest warrant is sufficient to enter the third party's dwelling and any evidence found in the dwelling is admissible against the third party.

United States v. Oaxaca, 233 F.3d 1154 (9th Cir. 2000). Officers violated the Fourth Amendment when they entered the defendant's attached garage and arrested him without an arrest warrant, even though the defendant had left the garage door open, when exigent circumstances did not support the entry into the garage.

United States v. Bervaldi, 226 F.3d 1256 (11th Cir. 2000). Officers had a reasonable belief (probable cause is not required) that (1) the dwelling they entered to arrest a person, for whom they had an arrest warrant, was that person's residence; and (2) the person was inside the dwelling when they entered it.

United States v. Winchenbach, 197 F.3d 548 (1st Cir. 1999). Officers obtained a search warrant to search a residence for drugs. They did not obtain an arrest warrant for the defendant who lived there, although they did have probable cause to arrest him. Upon entering the residence to execute the search warrant, the officers arrested the defendant without an arrest warrant. The court ruled, distinguishing *Payton v. New York*, discussed above, that the warrantless arrest did not violate the Fourth Amendment.

United States v. Risse, 83 F.3d 212 (8th Cir. 1996). Officers had a reasonable belief that the female person (Rhoads) for whom they had an arrest warrant resided with a male person (Risse) at his home, and therefore an arrest warrant was sufficient to enter Risse's home to arrest Rhoads. Rhoads had previously told the officers that she was "staying with" Risse and the officers could contact her there. In addition, a confidential reliable informant had told an officer that Rhoads was living with Risse. While officers twice successfully contacted Rhoads at Risse's residence, they were unable to contact her at her permanent residence elsewhere. The court rejected the defendant's argument that a person can have only one residence for Fourth Amendment purposes.

United States v. May, 68 F.3d 515 (D.C. Cir. 1995). Officers had a reasonable belief that the person (Thomas) named in an arrest warrant for murder was in the dwelling that they entered to execute the arrest warrant. Police records disclosed that Thomas lived there. Two witnesses placed Thomas at that dwelling after the murder. The murder occurred on a Saturday afternoon, the arrest warrant was issued on Monday, and officers entered the dwelling on Tuesday morning.

United States v. Gooch, 6 F.3d 673 (9th Cir. 1993). The defendant had a reasonable expectation of privacy in his tent located on a public campground, and the officers' warrantless entry into the tent to arrest him—without exigent circumstances or consent—violated the Fourth Amendment. *See also* United States v. Sandoval, 200 F.3d 659 (9th Cir. 2000) (similar ruling involving search of tent on government land). *But see* United States v. Ruckman, 806 F.2d 1471 (10th Cir. 1986) (warrantless search of cave on government land did not violate Fourth Amendment because defendant did not have reasonable expectation of privacy there).

Perez v. Simmons, 884 F.2d 1136 (9th Cir. 1989), *opinion amended*, 900 F.2d 213 (1990), 998 F.2d 773 (9th Cir. 1993). An officer may not enter a third party's home to arrest a defendant who is merely temporarily staying in the home unless the officer has a search warrant or consent to enter or unless exigent circumstances justify entry without a search warrant.

Exigent Circumstances

(*This topic is discussed on page 74.*)

UNITED STATES SUPREME COURT

Minnesota v. Olson, 495 U.S. 91 (1990). The Court affirmed the ruling of the Minnesota Supreme Court that exigent circumstances did not exist to justify the officers' warrantless, nonconsensual entry of the upper unit of a duplex where the defendant had been staying as an overnight guest. The officers knew that residents who were in the unit with the defendant were not endangered by his presence. In addition, police squads surrounded the duplex, and thus the defendant could not escape. Although grave crimes—murder and robbery—had been committed the prior day, the defendant was not the murderer but was thought to be the driver of the getaway car, and the officers had already recovered the murder

weapon. Also, the officers were not in hot pursuit of the defendant.

Welsh v. Wisconsin, 466 U.S. 740 (1984). There were no exigent circumstances sufficient to justify an officer's entry of a defendant's home to arrest him without a warrant when (1) the officer was not in hot pursuit; (2) the offense involved was relatively minor (Wisconsin punished impaired driving as a noncriminal civil violation); and (3) the defendant did not pose a threat to public safety. The imminent dissipation of the defendant's blood-alcohol content did not justify a warrantless entry to arrest for this minor offense, considering all the circumstances in this case. *See also* Howard v. Dickerson, 34 F.3d 978 (10th Cir. 1994) (no exigent circumstances to make warrantless entry into house to arrest person for minor traffic misdemeanors—no hot pursuit in this case); Norris v. State, 993 S.W.2d 918 (Ark. 1999) (similar ruling); People v. Thompson, 135 P.3d 3 (2006) (*Welsh* limited to nonjailable offenses); Beachwood v. Sims, 647 N.E.2d 821 (Ohio Ct. App. 1994) (distinguishing *Welsh v. Wisconsin*, court ruled exigent circumstances supported warrantless entry into home to arrest defendant for driving under influence of alcohol, an offense punishable by imprisonment); Goines v. James, 433 S.E.2d 572 (W.Va. 1993) (court noted that officer may make warrantless entry into defendant's home in hot pursuit of defendant to arrest for serious misdemeanor of driving under the influence); State v. Paul, 548 N.W.2d 260 (Minn. 1996) (similar ruling). *See generally* Illinois v. McArthur, 531 U.S. 326 (2001) (upholding an officer's seizure of the defendant while another officer sought a search warrant to search the defendant's home, the Court rejected the defendant's argument, relying on *Welsh v. Wisconsin*, that the minor misdemeanor involved in this case required a ruling for the defendant; the Court distinguished the nonjailable misdemeanor involved in *Welsh* from the jailable misdemeanors involved in the case before it).

Payton v. New York and ***Riddick v. New York***, 445 U.S. 573 (1980). Exigent circumstances did not exist in these cases to permit entry into the defendants' residences to arrest without an arrest warrant. The arrests were routine. There was no factual justification to justify the entries without a warrant.

United States v. Santana, 427 U.S. 38 (1976). Officers properly entered the defendant's house without a warrant to arrest her when (1) they shouted "Police" as she was standing in her doorway, (2) she retreated into her house, and (3) the officers entered to arrest her and to prevent the destruction of evidence (drugs and marked money used in a recently completed drug transaction).

Warden v. Hayden, 387 U.S. 294 (1967). The defendant committed an armed robbery and shortly thereafter ran into a house. Exigent circumstances allowed the officers to make a warrantless entry into a house when they arrived within minutes after the defendant entered the house.

NORTH CAROLINA SUPREME COURT

State v. Guevara, 349 N.C. 243 (1998). Officers A and B went to the defendant's home with information that there were outstanding felony arrest warrants for him. They saw the defendant, accompanied by a young boy, standing outside his mobile home's back door. Although he denied being the person who was the subject of the arrest warrants, the officers believed otherwise. After confirmation from a dispatcher that the defendant was still wanted, Officer B stated to Officer A that they would arrest him. The defendant, hearing Officer B's words, retreated into his home and slammed the door. Officer A pushed the door open and entered the home, where he was shot and killed by the defendant. Officer B was shot and seriously injured by the defendant while Officer B was outside the mobile home.

(1) The court, relying on *State v. Miller*, 282 N.C. 633 (1973), ruled that even if Officer A violated the Fourth Amendment in entering the defendant's home to arrest him, the exclusionary rule did not bar the testimony of Officer B about the killing of Officer A. (2) The court ruled that exigent circumstances supported Officer A's entry into the defendant's home to arrest him. The court stated that the defendant's actions—suddenly withdrawing into his home and slamming the door—created the appearance that he was fleeing or trying to escape and, coupled with the young child's presence, established exigent circumstances to enter the defendant's home to arrest him.

State v. Worsley, 336 N.C. 268 (1994). Officers arrived at a murder scene and discovered the victim's body, the subject of a brutal stabbing, lying in a common area of an apartment complex. An eyewitness to the murder identified the defendant as the killer. Another witness informed the officers that he had seen the defendant running toward the defendant's apartment shortly after the murder. The officers went to the defendant's nearby apartment and discovered fresh blood on the doorknob of the back door. The officers knocked loudly on the defendant's door and identified themselves as officers but received no response. They then entered the apartment. The court ruled that the officers had exigent circumstances to enter the defendant's home—without consent or an arrest warrant—to arrest the defendant.

State v. Allison, 298 N.C. 135 (1979). An officer had a right to enter the defendant's trailer to arrest him when the officer had probable cause to believe that the defendant had just committed a murder, was armed and in the trailer, and would probably escape if not immediately arrested.

NORTH CAROLINA COURT OF APPEALS

State v. Stover, 200 N.C. App. 506 (2009). The court ruled that officers had probable cause and exigent circumstances to enter a home based on the following facts. Officers stopped a vehicle and noticed a passenger with marijuana, who then told them the house at which she had purchased the marijuana. Officers went to the house to conduct a knock and talk. When they arrived, they perceived a strong odor of marijuana emanating from the house. An officer heard a noise from the back of the house and saw the defendant with his upper torso partially out of a window. The court noted that the officer could reasonably believe that the defendant was attempting to flee the scene and that the officers were also concerned about possible destruction of evidence.

State v. Fuller, 193 N.C. App. 670 (2009). The court ruled that exigent circumstances supported officers' warrantless entry into a mobile home to arrest the defendant pursuant to an outstanding arrest warrant when officers reasonably believed that the defendant was attempting to escape and also presented a danger to the officers and others in the home.

State v. Harris, 145 N.C. App. 570 (2001). An officer who had probable cause to believe that drugs were being sold in a hotel room telephoned the room and told the defendant that maintenance would be coming to the room to fix a smoke detector. The officer then knocked on the door. A voice from inside the room asked who was there. The officer responded, "Maintenance." One of the occupants opened the door. The officer, holding his credentials in his hand, identified himself as a police officer. The officer then observed activity that gave him exigent circumstances to enter the room to arrest and search. The court ruled that the officer's use of a ruse (trickery) to get one of the hotel room's occupants to open the door did not violate the Fourth Amendment. The court noted that the officer did not enter the room based on the ruse—the entry was based on exigent circumstances that existed after the door was opened.

State v. Nowell, 144 N.C. App. 636 (2001), *aff'd*, 355 N.C. 273 (2002). The court ruled that officers did not have exigent circumstances to enter a residence to seize marijuana, based on the following facts. A drug courier working with law enforcement officers and wearing a body wire delivered approximately 50 pounds of marijuana to a residence where the purchaser and his accomplice were waiting for the delivery of the marijuana. When an officer heard through a radio transmitter that the purchaser and his accomplice were about to roll a marijuana cigarette from the marijuana and smoke it, law enforcement officers entered the residence without a search warrant.

State v. Woods, 136 N.C. App. 386 (2000). Officers were dispatched to investigate an alarm sounding at the defendant's residence. After arriving at the residence, an officer heard the alarm and saw that the rear door of the residence was open. He heard no response from inside the residence after announcing his presence and identity. The officer conducted a cursory search of the residence for potential victims or suspects. He found no one but saw evidence of a break-in. He and other officers reentered to conduct a more thorough search, looking again for victims and suspects. In the master bedroom, they opened a drawer in a standing chest that was about 15 to 20 inches deep, 25 to 30 inches long, and 18 inches wide and discovered a bag of green vegetable material. In the kitchen and living room area, they saw a cabinet that was about 34 inches tall and 48 inches wide. While attempting to open the cabinet doors, an officer moved a chair and heard a noise underneath it. His flashlight revealed a tear on the bottom of the chair and a bag inside that appeared to contain money. He opened the cabinet door but found nothing. Officers later obtained a search warrant and discovered various drugs, money, and drug paraphernalia.

(1) Relying on *United States v. Dart*, 747 F.2d 263 (4th Cir. 1984), and other cases, the court ruled that the officer's warrantless entry into the residence to investigate a possible break-in was justified by exigent circumstances and thus was reasonable under the Fourth Amendment. It was clear that a break-in had occurred and the officers had reason to believe that the intruders or victims could still be in the residence. (2) The court ruled, relying on *Mincey v. Arizona*, 437 U.S. 385 (1978), that the officers' search of the chest of drawers, chair, and cabinet

exceeded the scope of the permissible search for suspects and victims. It was unreasonable to believe that a person could have been found in the cabinet, based on the facts in this case.

State v. Wallace, 71 N.C. App. 681 (1984). Officers, who had probable cause to arrest the defendant for two armed robberies, entered the defendant's motel room without a warrant to arrest him. The court ruled that exigent circumstances justified the officers' warrantless entry because a motel clerk had called the officers and told them that the defendant had recently returned to his motel room and was taking articles out of the room as if he were leaving (the officers were preparing arrest warrants when the clerk called).

State v. Yananokwiak, 65 N.C. App. 513 (1983). There were no exigent circumstances to justify a warrantless entry into a house to arrest the defendant for a drug offense, because there was no evidence that he was about to escape or destroy drugs or that he presented a danger to a police informant inside the house or to the police outside.

FEDERAL APPELLATE COURTS

McCabe v. Life-Line Ambulance Service, Inc., 77 F.3d 540 (1st Cir. 1996). The officers' warrantless forcible entry into a person's house to serve a licensed psychiatrist's signed application for a 10-day involuntary commitment of that person, based on the finding of a likelihood of serious harm, was reasonable under the Fourth Amendment.

United States v. McCraw, 920 F.2d 224 (4th Cir. 1990). Officers went to a hotel room without an arrest warrant and knocked on the door without announcing themselves. The defendant opened the door about halfway while standing inside his room. When he saw the officers, he attempted to close the door. The officers forced their way inside and arrested him. The court, distinguishing *United States v. Santana*, 427 U.S. 38 (1976), ruled that because the defendant was not in the threshold of the doorway, he was not in a public area, and a warrantless arrest was unconstitutional. The court also ruled that exigent circumstances did not support the warrantless arrest because (1) the defendant did not know of his accomplice having been arrested; (2) he did not know that his room was under surveillance; and (3) he had no reason to destroy evidence, and any risk of his destroying evidence was precipitated by the officers themselves when they knocked on the door.

Entrance onto Premises to Accompany the Arrestee

(This topic is discussed on page 78.)

Washington v. Chrisman, 455 U.S. 1 (1982). An officer arrested a college student, who then asked to return to his dormitory room to get his identification. The officer accompanied him into his room. The Court ruled that an officer has an automatic right to accompany an arrestee wherever the arrestee goes. This right is not dependent on evidence that the arrestee might have a weapon available there or might attempt to escape.

State v. Weakley, 176 N.C. App. 642 (2006). The defendant appeared at the front door of a residence and was told that officers had an arrest warrant for her. The defendant was not fully clothed. One of the officers accompanied her into the residence while she got dressed. Relying on *Washington v. Chrisman*, 455 U.S. 1 (1982), the court ruled that the officer's presence in the residence was lawful because the officer was entitled to monitor the defendant's movements while she got dressed.

Completion of Custody: Taking the Arrestee to a Magistrate without Unnecessary Delay

(This topic is discussed on page 85.)

County of Riverside v. McLaughlin, 500 U.S. 44 (1991). The detention for more than 48 hours of a defendant arrested without a warrant and without a determination of probable cause by a judicial official or a judicial body (for example, a grand jury) presumptively violated the Fourth Amendment.

State v. Wallace, 351 N.C. 481 (2000). The defendant was arrested on an arrest warrant for a larceny, but he also was a suspect in three murders. Before giving *Miranda* warnings, officers spoke with the defendant for about three hours, mostly about sports, his employment and military experience, and his biographical information. The defendant also voluntarily raised the issue of his drug use. The officers did not interrogate him about the murders for which he was a suspect and did not ask any questions designed to elicit incriminating responses. After having properly been given *Miranda* warnings, the defendant confessed to nine murders. He was given opportunities to use the restroom and was fed. At some point during the interrogation, the defendant requested to see his girlfriend and daughter. An officer told the defendant that the police would attempt to contact them but that they had no control over whether either of them would come to see him. The defendant was taken to magistrate 19 hours after his arrest—he had slept 4 hours just before being taken to the magistrate. The court ruled that the officers did not violate G.S. 15A-501(2) because of the number of crimes to which the defendant confessed and the amount to time needed to record the details of them. Given the officers' accommodation of the defendant's request to sleep, the 19-hour delay was not unnecessarily long under the statute.

State v. Chapman, 343 N.C. 495 (1996). At about 9:30 a.m., the defendant was arrested at a bank for attempting to cash a forged check. He waived his *Miranda* rights and admitted that he had attempted to cash a check that he had forged after taking it in a robbery. Officers took the defendant to a school to search for a purse that had been taken in the robbery. They then returned the defendant to the police station, where he confessed to forgery and uttering charges. A detective procured arrest warrants for these charges at 12:30 p.m. and served them on the defendant. The defendant then was questioned by another detective who was investigating the robbery in which the checks were taken, and the defendant confessed to the robbery at 1:27 p.m. Officers prepared an arrest warrant to charge the robbery, but it was not immediately presented to the magistrate. The defendant then was interviewed by another detective about an unrelated robbery and murder. The detective put nine photos of the murder victim on the walls of the interrogation room and one photo of the victim on the floor directly in front of the chair in which the defendant sat during the interrogation. Thus, the defendant saw a photo of the victim in every direction he turned. During the interview, the detective falsely implied to the defendant that handwriting analysis of a note found next to the victim's body showed it was written by the defendant and that the defendant's fingerprints were on the note. The defendant confessed to the murder at about 7:05 p.m. and was taken to the magistrate about 8:00 p.m.

(1) The court ruled that there was no unreasonable delay in a magistrate's determination of whether there was probable cause to issue an arrest warrant. Distinguishing *County of Riverside v. McLaughlin*, 500 U.S. 44 (1991), and *Gerstein v. Pugh*, 420 U.S. 103 (1975), the court noted that the defendant was arrested at 9:30 a.m. without a warrant and that a magistrate issued an arrest warrant based on probable cause at 12:30 p.m. This procedure satisfied the rulings in these cases that a magistrate promptly determine probable cause. The court noted that the defendant was then in lawful custody and could be interrogated about other crimes. (2) The court ruled that

the defendant's statutory right under G.S. 15A-501(2) to be taken to a magistrate without unnecessary delay was not violated. The court noted that much of the time between the defendant's arrest at 9:30 a.m. and his being taken before a magistrate at 8:00 p.m. was spent interrogating the defendant about several crimes. The court stated that the officers had the right to conduct these interrogations and that they did not cause an unnecessary delay by doing so. (3) The officers failed to advise the defendant of his right to communicate with friends, in violation of G.S. 15A-501(5). The court ruled that, based on *State v. Curmon*, 295 N.C. 453 (1978), the defendant was not prejudiced by this violation, based on the facts in this case.

State v. Littlejohn, 340 N.C. 750 (1995). The defendant was arrested for murder and other offenses; interrogated for 10 hours, during which time he confessed; and then taken to the magistrate. The total period of time from arrest to appearance before the magistrate was 13 hours. The court ruled, based on these and other facts (for example, the officers advised the defendant of his constitutional rights before they began interrogation), that the delay did not violate G.S. 15A-501(2).

State v. Daniels, 337 N.C. 243 (1994). An officer's one-hour delay between arresting the defendant and informing him of his rights under G.S. 15A-501(5) was not unnecessary, because during that time period the officer was involved in interactions with the defendant, including taking him to a house at the defendant's request.

State v. Reynolds, 298 N.C. 380 (1979). The two to three hours during which officers questioned the defendant and took hair and blood samples did not constitute "unnecessary delay" under G.S. 15A-501. *See also* State v. Martin, 315 N.C. 667 (1986).

State v. Sings, 35 N.C. App. 1 (1978). A seven-hour delay after the defendant's arrest was not "unnecessary delay" when the officers used that time to take the codefendant to recover stolen property, recaptured him when he escaped from their custody, and then obtained a confession from him.

State v. Wheeler, 34 N.C. App. 243 (1977). A one-hour delay between the defendant's arrest and his appearance before a magistrate was not "unnecessary delay."

State v. Sanders, 33 N.C. App. 284 (1977). Delay in taking the defendant to a magistrate was unnecessary when officers took him to another city for a showup after calling a local magistrate to come to the police station. The court interpreted "reasonably necessary" in G.S. 15A-501(4) (taking a person elsewhere before taking the person to a magistrate is permissible if it is reasonably necessary for identification) as limited to exigent circumstances—that is, when an eyewitness is critically injured. This ruling may not be sound because the court failed to note that the legislature did not adopt the more restrictive provision in the Model Penal Code, on which G.S. 15A-501(4) was based.

Bringing News Media during Execution of Warrant

(This topic is discussed on page 79.)

Wilson v. Layne, 526 U.S. 603 (1999). Law enforcement officers invited news media representatives to accompany them during the execution of an arrest warrant in a home. The Court ruled that officers violate the Fourth Amendment when they bring news media or other third parties into a home during the execution of a warrant when the third parties' presence is not aiding the warrant's execution. The news media clearly were not aiding the execution of the arrest warrant in this case. The court noted that third parties may properly aid the execution of a search warrant; for example, by identifying stolen property.

Law of Search and Seizure

Chapter 3

Law of Search and Seizure

The right of the people to be secure in their persons, houses, papers, and effects, against unreasonable searches and seizures, shall not be violated, and no Warrants shall issue, but upon probable cause, supported by Oath or affirmation and particularly describing the place to be searched, and the persons or things to be seized.

—United States Constitution, Amendment IV

This chapter discusses the legal standards for searching and seizing property and people—including search and seizure of abandoned property, searches with consent, vehicle and container searches, wiretapping and eavesdropping, and searches to protect officers and property—and whether a search warrant is needed to conduct a search and seizure.

Introduction

The law of search and seizure, like the law of arrest, protects a person's right to privacy—the right to be let alone—by restricting the power of law enforcement officers and other government officials[1] to search and seize a person and a person's property. The Fourth Amendment, however, does not apply to a search or seizure by a private person, no matter how unjustified, unless the private person acts as an agent of government officials or

acts with their participation or knowledge.[2] For example, a private mail courier who, without the instigation of law enforcement officers, opens a damaged package, discovers a white powdery substance, and then informs law officers of the discovery, has not conducted a search or seizure under the Fourth Amendment. And law enforcement officers do not conduct a search or seizure if they do not probe the contents of the package any further than the courier did.[3]

As discussed in Chapter 2, an arrest of a person is a *seizure* under the Fourth Amendment and, in order to be constitutional, must be *reasonable*. For a discussion of when a person is seized,[4] see page 26 in Chapter 2.

A search of a person or property or a seizure of property, to be constitutional, also must be reasonable under

---

1. For example, searches and seizures by OSHA inspectors, building inspectors, fire fighters, and teachers are governed by the Fourth Amendment, even though the standard governing the reasonableness of a search or seizure may differ from the standard that applies to law enforcement officers. Whether the exclusionary rule should apply to searches and seizures by these officials is a separate issue from whether the Fourth Amendment governs their conduct. See the discussion in *New Jersey v. T.L.O.*, 469 U.S. 325 (1985), and 1 Wayne R. LaFave, Search and Seizure: A Treatise on the Fourth Amendment § 1.8(e) (5th ed. 2012).

2. United States v. Jacobsen, 466 U.S. 109 (1984); Walter v. United States, 447 U.S. 649 (1980); State v. Sanders, 327 N.C. 319 (1990) (private person's entry by ruse into house was not attributable to law enforcement based on court's totality of circumstances test); State v. Peele, 16 N.C. App. 227 (1972) (crime victim searched defendant's attic without knowledge or instigation of law enforcement officers). *See generally* 1 Wayne R. LaFave, Search and Seizure: A Treatise on the Fourth Amendment § 1.8 (5th ed. 2012).

3. *Jacobsen*, 466 U.S. 109 n.1 (1984).

4. Pertinent United States Supreme Court cases on the seizure of a person include *Brendlin v. California*, 551 U.S. 249 (2007); *United States v. Drayton*, 536 U.S. 194 (2002); *Florida v. Bostick*, 501 U.S. 429 (1991); *California v. Hodari D.*, 499 U.S. 621 (1991); *United States v. Mendenhall*, 446 U.S. 544 (1980); *Immigration & Naturalization Service v. Delgado*, 466 U.S. 210 (1984); and *Florida v. Royer*, 460 U.S. 491 (1983).

the Fourth Amendment.[5] Determining the reasonableness of a search or seizure involves balancing the individual's right to be free and left alone by law enforcement officers with the officers' occasional need to interfere with personal freedom and property to investigate crime or to enforce laws.

Not all interactions of officers with people and their property are searches or seizures. Officers conduct a search only when they infringe on a person's expectation of privacy that society recognizes as reasonable. They make a seizure of property only when they interfere in a meaningful way with a person's possessory interests in his or her property.[6]

To be reasonable under the Fourth Amendment, some searches and seizures may be conducted only with *probable cause* (that is, reasonable grounds for believing that the object sought will be found in the place that is to be searched) and a search warrant; some may be conducted with probable cause but without a warrant; and some may be conducted with a lesser amount of factual information than probable cause—that is, with *reasonable suspicion*. This chapter will discuss the legal requirements for a variety of law enforcement actions that are considered searches or seizures.

The source of the law of search and seizure is not only the Fourth Amendment and court decisions that interpret its meaning but also statutes that set out additional guidelines. It is important to understand these statutory provisions, because they sometimes place greater restrictions on an officer's authority to search and seize than the restrictions imposed by the United States and North Carolina constitutions.[7]

An unlawful search or seizure may result in several undesirable consequences, including (1) the exclusion of evidence from criminal proceedings,[8] (2) a civil lawsuit for money damages against the officers who made an illegal search or seizure,[9] (3) a criminal prosecution against the officers,[10] and (4) a disciplinary action against the officers by their employing agency.

Observations and Actions That May Not Implicate Fourth Amendment Rights

The law of search and seizure protects a person's right to privacy. However, some observations and actions by officers involve such an insignificant interference with a person's privacy that the officers' conduct does not constitute a search or seizure under the Fourth Amendment and, therefore, needs no justification—the rules governing searches and seizures do not apply.

The United States Supreme Court has articulated two separate theories to evaluate whether a search has occurred under the Fourth Amendment: (1) the "legitimate expectation of privacy" theory and (2) the trespassory or physical intrusion theory. Either theory may support a finding that a search occurred.

A legitimate expectation of privacy has two components: (1) a person must have an actual (subjective) expectation of privacy—that is, a person must demonstrate that he or she wants to preserve something as private, *and*

---

5. The United States Supreme Court has stated that determining what is a reasonable search and seizure involves a balancing of the government's reason for intruding on a person's reasonable expectation of privacy and a person's interest in maintaining his or her privacy. The Court has rejected the argument that the Fourth Amendment requires that probable cause support all searches and seizures, including some "full-scale" searches. See the discussion of these issues and the Court's prior cases in *New Jersey v. T.L.O.*, 469 U.S. 325 (1985).

6. These definitions of search and seizure are set out in *United States v. Jacobsen*, 466 U.S. 109 (1984).

7. *See, e.g.*, N.C. GEN. STAT. (hereafter, G.S.) § 15A-248 (requiring that a search warrant be executed within 48 hours after it is issued; a precise 48-hour time limit is not constitutionally required). For a discussion of rights under the North Carolina Constitution, see note 1 in Chapter 4.

8. Mapp v. Ohio, 367 U.S. 643 (1961); G.S. 15A-974.

9. The most often used statute under which a person may sue a law enforcement officer is Section 1983 of Title 42 of the United States Code (hereafter, U.S.C.) (dates are omitted from U.S.C. cites), which provides for a civil remedy against state and local government officials for deprivations of citizens' constitutional rights. *See, e.g.*, Malley v. Briggs, 475 U.S. 335 (1986); Graham v. Connor, 490 U.S. 386 (1989); Anderson v. Creighton, 483 U.S. 635 (1987) (court ruled that the test set out in Harlow v. Fitzgerald, 457 U.S. 800 (1982), applies to officer who conducted warrantless search of third party's home: objective test is used to determine whether officer could have believed that search was lawful in light of clearly established law and searching officer's information). Officers also may be sued under other federal and state statutes and for torts (civil wrongs) recognized by state law, such as false imprisonment, assault, etc. *See* Myrick v. Cooley, 91 N.C. App. 209 (1988). Under certain circumstances, an officer's supervisors and the local government unit that employs the officer also may be held responsible for the officer's unconstitutional acts.

10. Two commonly used federal criminal statutes for prosecuting criminal violations of constitutional rights are 18 U.S.C. § 241 and 18 U.S.C. § 242. An officer also may be prosecuted under such state criminal laws as assault and battery.

(2) the person's subjective expectation of privacy must be one that society recognizes as reasonable—that is, the person's expectation, viewed objectively, must be justifiable under the circumstances.[11] Unless both components are satisfied, a person may not successfully assert that his or her right of privacy under the Fourth Amendment has been violated.[12] For example, a person subjectively may expect privacy when growing marijuana in an open field protected by a fence with a locked gate and "No Trespassing" signs.[13] But the United States Supreme Court has ruled that open fields generally are not areas involving intimate activities that the Fourth Amendment was intended to protect from government intrusion and, therefore, a person's asserted expectation of privacy there is not one that society recognizes as reasonable.[14]

The trespassory or physical intrusion theory, which is derived from common law trespass, was recognized in two recent United States Supreme Court cases, *United States v. Jones*[15] and *Florida v. Jardines*.[16] As indicated above, this theory is a ground for finding that a Fourth Amendment search occurred that is sufficient by itself and independent from the reasonable expectation of privacy theory. Thus, the two theories must be considered in cases when the facts may support one or both theories.

The Court in *Jones* ruled that the government's installation of a GPS tracking device on a vehicle and its use of that device to monitor the vehicle's movements on public streets constituted a "search" within the meaning of the Fourth Amendment. Officers who suspected that the defendant was involved in drug trafficking installed a GPS device without a valid search warrant on the undercarriage of a vehicle while it was parked in a public parking lot in Maryland. Over the next 28 days, the government

used the device to track the vehicle's movements and once had to replace the device's battery when the vehicle was parked in a public lot. By means of signals from multiple satellites, the device established the vehicle's location within 50 to 100 feet and communicated that location by cellular phone to a government computer. It relayed more than 2,000 pages of data over a four-week period.

The defendant was charged with several drug offenses. He unsuccessfully sought to suppress the evidence obtained through the GPS device. Before the United States Supreme Court, the government argued that a warrant was not required for the GPS device. Concluding that the evidence should have been suppressed, the Court characterized the government's conduct as having "physically occupied private property for the purpose of obtaining information." Thus, the Court had "no doubt that such a physical intrusion would have been considered a 'search' within the meaning of the Fourth Amendment when it was adopted."[17] The Court declined to address whether the defendant had a reasonable expectation of privacy in the undercarriage of his car and in the car's locations on the public roads, concluding that such an analysis was not required when the intrusion—as here—"encroached on a protected area."[18]

The Court in *Jardines* ruled that officers' use of a drug-sniffing dog on a homeowner's porch to investigate the contents of the home was a "search" within the meaning of the Fourth Amendment. The Court's reasoning was based on the theory that the officers engaged in a physical intrusion of a constitutionally protected area. Applying that principle, the Court ruled:

> The officers were gathering information in an area belonging to [the defendant] and immediately surrounding his house—in the curtilage of the house, which we have held enjoys protection as part of the home itself. And they gathered that information by physically entering and occupying the area to engage in conduct not explicitly or implicitly permitted by the homeowner.[19]

---

11. The concept of "reasonable expectation of privacy," developed in Justice Harlan's concurring opinion in *Katz v. United States*, 389 U.S. 347 (1967), was later adopted by the Supreme Court. *See, e.g.*, Oliver v. United States, 466 U.S. 170 (1984); United States v. Jacobsen, 466 U.S. 109 (1984); Smith v. Maryland, 442 U.S. 735 (1978).

12. Oliver v. United States, 466 U.S. 170 (1984).

13. Entering the curtilage of a person's property where there is a "no trespassing" sign and a closed gate may constitute a search. See the discussion of the case law from other jurisdictions in *State v. Smith*, ___ N.C. App. ___, 783 S.E.2d 504 (2016), although *Smith* did not find that a search occurred based on the facts in that case.

14. *Id.*

15. 132 S. Ct. 945 (2012).

16. 133 S. Ct. 1409 (2013).

---

17. *Jones*, 132 S. Ct. at 949.

18. *Id.* at 952.

19. *Jardines*, 133 S. Ct. at 1414. In *State v. Smith*, ___ N.C. App. ___, 783 S.E.2d 504 (2016), the court rejected the defendant's argument that a "no trespassing" sign on his gate expressly removed an implied license to approach his home. While the trial court found that a "no trespassing" sign was

The Court did not decide the case on a reasonable expectation of privacy analysis.

Abandoned Property and Garbage

(*See page 282 for case summaries on this topic.*)

The Fourth Amendment does not apply to searching or seizing abandoned property. The reason is fairly clear. A person cannot assert a violation of a legitimate expectation of privacy if he or she has intentionally relinquished an interest in the property. But officers sometimes may have difficulty determining when property has been abandoned.

Garbage is discussed separately because it is analyzed somewhat differently than abandoned property.

Abandoned Property

The following discussion suggests some factors that officers should consider so they may recognize correctly whether real or personal property has been abandoned.

Real property. It often is difficult to determine whether and when a person has abandoned real property, such as land, buildings, and the like. Therefore, abandonment is not often a sound basis for searching real property. An example of abandoned real property that could be searched without a Fourth Amendment justification, however, is a building that has been unoccupied for a long time and has been gutted by vandals.

If real property is rented, officers may be able to determine more readily when the renter abandoned a reasonable expectation of privacy there. For example, if the rented property is a hotel room, abandonment normally occurs when the guest checks out and removes his or her belongings.[20] The owner of a building ordinarily may not consent to a search of a rented room, but the owner may properly do so when the renter abandons the room. On the other hand, an apartment dweller who has simply not paid rent on time or a hotel guest who has stayed a few hours after checkout time has not ordinarily relinquished a reasonable expectation of privacy—unless the landlord or hotel manager has legally had the person removed from the property or other facts indicate that an expectation of privacy is no longer reasonable.[21]

---

posted on the day of the shooting, there was no evidence that the sign was present on the day the officers first visited the property. Also, there was no evidence that the defendant took consistent steps to physically prevent visitors from entering the property; the open gate suggested otherwise. Finally, the defendant's conduct upon the detectives' arrival belied any notion that their approach was unwelcome. Specifically, when they arrived, he came out and greeted them. For these reasons, the defendant's actions did not reflect a clear demonstration of an intent to revoke the implied license to approach. The court ruled that the officers' actions did not exceed the scope of a lawful knock and talk. Finally, the court rejected the defendant's argument that his Fourth Amendment rights were violated because the encounter occurred within the home's curtilage. The court noted that no search of the curtilage occurs when an officer is in a place where the public is allowed to be for purposes of a general inquiry. Here, officers entered the property through an open driveway and did not deviate from the area where their presence was lawful. See *State v. Pasour*, 223 N.C. App. 175 (2013) ("no trespassing" sign was evidence of homeowner's intent that side and back of home were not open to public).

---

20. Abel v. United States, 362 U.S. 217 (1960); United States v. Kitchens, 114 F.3d 29 (4th Cir. 1997) (although motel guest may have reasonable expectation of privacy even after rental period has terminated if there is pattern or practice that would make expectation reasonable, a reasonable expectation of privacy did not exist when motel had strict practice concerning checkout and thus officer's entry into motel room one-and-one-half hours after checkout time did not violate Fourth Amendment); United States v. Rambo, 789 F.2d 1289 (8th Cir. 1987) (defendant was asked to leave hotel by officers, acting at request and on behalf of hotel's manager, because of defendant's disorderly behavior; court ruled that defendant was properly ejected from hotel under Minnesota law, rental period had terminated, and hotel room had reverted to management; thus, defendant no longer had Fourth Amendment right of privacy and could not successfully contest the officers' warrantless entry into the hotel room to arrest and their later search under bed mattress); United States v. Rahme, 813 F.2d 31 (2d Cir. 1987) (defendant was arrested and a hotel room key was found in his possession; several days later, officer contacted hotel and learned that hotel personnel had taken possession of luggage in that room; luggage was lawfully in hotel's possession pursuant to its lien for unpaid rent under New York law; court ruled that hotel's lawful, exclusive, and adverse possession of luggage deprived defendant of any legitimate expectation of privacy); United States v. Hoey, 983 F.2d 890 (8th Cir. 1993) (defendant did not have reasonable expectation of privacy in apartment for which he had not paid rent for six weeks, he had had moving sale, and neighbor saw defendant leaving apartment for what appeared to be last time); United States v. Dorais, 241 F.3d 1124 (9th Cir. 2001) (when checkout time was noon and defendant said he would stay until 12:30 p.m., defendant did not have reasonable expectation of privacy after 12:30 p.m.).

21. United States v. Owens, 782 F.2d 146 (10th Cir. 1986) (defendant maintained reasonable expectation of privacy in motel room when he stayed a short time after checkout); United States v. Melucci, 888 F.2d 200 (1st Cir. 1989)

Personal property. Officers can often determine that personal property has been abandoned because it simply is thrown away. For example, a person who throws away personal property while being approached or pursued by a law enforcement officer has abandoned it under the Fourth Amendment, unless the person abandoned it as a direct result of an officer's illegal search or seizure.[22]

A person also abandons personal property when the person affirmatively denies an ownership or possessory interest in the property. For example, if a person affirmatively denies ownership of a suitcase at an airport or on a bus, the person has abandoned it, even if the suitcase in fact belongs to that person.[23] Officers then may inspect its contents without further justification, assuming that no other person has a privacy interest in the suitcase.[24] On the other hand, if a person does not clearly disclaim ownership,[25] or if the person continues to physically possess the suitcase while denying ownership,[26] officers may not consider the suitcase abandoned. Officers may, however, take other investigative actions that would allow them to examine a suitcase's contents: a search with consent or a brief investigative detention based on reasonable suspicion, if the investigative detention develops probable cause to search the suitcase with a search warrant.

A customer who has rented a car does not necessarily lose a reasonable expectation of privacy in the car after the rental agreement has expired, at least when the rental car company has not attempted to repossess the car and the parties to the agreement understand that the customer retains possession and control of the car and, in effect, continues to rent it.[27]

One point concerning abandoned cars deserves particular attention. North Carolina law declares that cars that remain illegally on private or public property for more than 10 days are "abandoned" and may be tagged and later removed if the owner does not intervene.[28] This law does not necessarily mean that the car has been abandoned under the Fourth Amendment and, therefore, may be searched. However, it may be proper to look for the car's identification or to inventory its contents if it is impounded—as discussed later in this chapter on page 261. Before officers may search the car based on the abandonment theory, they must be satisfied that the owner has relinquished an interest in it.[29]

Garbage

The United States Supreme Court has ruled that people do not have a reasonable expectation of privacy in garbage that they have placed for collection on the curb in front of their house.[30] The Court reasoned that it is

---

(defendant did not have reasonable expectation of privacy in his rented modular storage unit when he failed to pay rent, lessor took possession of unit, lease had terminated, and defendant had rented unit under false name); United States v. Mulder, 808 F.2d 1346 (9th Cir. 1987) (defendant—who overstayed his intended departure from his hotel room—did not abandon locked bag in room when he left room and returned 48 hours later; private security officer's search and discovery of pills within bag was private search and did not violate Fourth Amendment; however, a law enforcement officer's authorization of lab test to determine content of pills exceeded "field test" permitted under United States v. Jacobsen, 466 U.S. 109 (1984), and was unconstitutional because it was conducted without search warrant).

22. State v. Joe, 222 N.C. App. 206 (2012) (noting that the defendant was illegally arrested without probable cause, the court concluded that property abandoned as a result of illegal police activity cannot be held to have been voluntarily abandoned). *See generally* California v. Hodari D., 499 U.S. 621 (1991); Hester v. United States, 265 U.S. 57 (1924); State v. Cooke, 54 N.C. App. 33, *modified and aff'd*, 306 N.C. 132 (1982); State v. Cromartie, 55 N.C. App. 221 (1981); State v. Williams, 71 N.C. App. 136 (1984).

23. State v. Johnson, 98 N.C. App. 290 (1990); United States v. Flowers, 912 F.2d 707 (4th Cir. 1990).

24. *See, e.g.,* United States v. Tolbert, 692 F.2d 1041 (6th Cir. 1982). Of course, a defendant would not have a Fourth Amendment privacy interest to contest the search of a suitcase that he or she had abandoned even if another person had a privacy interest in it.

25. United States v. Sanders, 719 F.2d 882 (6th Cir. 1983).

26. State v. Casey, 59 N.C. App. 99 (1982).

27. United States v. Henderson, 241 F.3d 638 (9th Cir. 2000). Concerning a related rental car issue, the Fourth Circuit Court of Appeals in *United States v. Wellons*, 32 F.3d 117 (4th Cir. 1994), ruled that a person who is not listed in a rental agreement as an authorized driver does not have a reasonable expectation of privacy to challenge a search of the rental car. However, other courts may allow a nonauthorized driver to challenge a search under certain circumstances. *See* United States v. Thomas, 447 F.3d 1191 (9th Cir. 2006); United States v. Smith, 263 F.3d 571 (6th Cir. 2001). See rental car cases summarized in 6 Wayne R. LaFave, Search and Seizure: A Treatise on the Fourth Amendment § 11.3(e) n.325 (5th ed. 2012).

28. G.S. 20-137.6 through -137.14.

29. State v. McLamb, 70 N.C. App. 712 (1984) (defendants appeared to have abandoned vehicles in undeveloped area).

30. California v. Greenwood, 486 U.S. 35 (1988). The North Carolina Supreme Court ruled consistently with *Greenwood* in *State v. Hauser*, 342 N.C. 382 (1995). Cases decided before *Greenwood* but whose results are consistent with its ruling

common knowledge that garbage left on or at the side of a public street is readily accessible to scavengers and other members of the public. Moreover, people are aware when placing their trash for pickup by a third party, such as sanitation workers, that these people may sort through the garbage or permit others, including law enforcement officers, to do so. Garbage placed for collection in an area accessible to the public is not subject to an expectation of privacy that society recognizes as reasonable.

Law enforcement officers or sanitation workers acting at their direction may take and examine garbage without violating the Fourth Amendment in such places as dumpsters near office buildings and apartments and at or near the curbside of a home—even if the area near the curbside where the garbage has been placed for collection is within the curtilage.[31] (The curtilage, discussed in the next section of this chapter, is the area surrounding the home that is so tied to the home that it also receives Fourth Amendment protection.) However, an officer may not intrude significantly within the curtilage to take and examine garbage that is located at or near the home.[32] Of course, sanitation workers may remove the garbage there as part of their regular duties and give it to law enforcement officers to examine, and their examination would not violate the Fourth Amendment.[33]

Areas Outside the Home: Curtilage and Open Fields

(*See page 287 for case summaries on this topic.*)

The Curtilage

People have a reasonable expectation of privacy not only in their home but also in the curtilage of the home. The *curtilage* is the area immediately surrounding the home that is so intimately tied to the home itself that it deserves the Fourth Amendment's protection. For example, the area includes buildings such as unattached garages, storage sheds, and similar structures, if they are relatively close to the dwelling and serve the homeowner's daily needs.[34] Officers who enter the curtilage are conducting a search under the Fourth Amendment,[35] except when they use a common entranceway to a home.[36] But the physical intrusion or trespassory theory of the Fourth Amendment may bar the officer's entry under certain

---

include *United States v. Terry*, 702 F.2d 299 (2d Cir. 1983); *United States v. Kramer*, 711 F.2d 789 (7th Cir. 1983); and *United States v. Dela Espriella*, 781 F.2d 1432 (9th Cir. 1986).

31. United States v. Dunkel, 900 F.2d 105 (7th Cir. 1990), *vacated on other grounds*, 498 U.S. 1043 (1991) (defendant did not have reasonable expectation of privacy in dumpster located in parking lot of commercial building that was used by building's tenants); United States v. Hedrick, 922 F.2d 396 (7th Cir. 1991) (defendant did not have reasonable expectation of privacy in garbage cans permanently located in driveway 18 to 20 feet from the sidewalk, 20 feet from an unattached garage, and 50 feet from house, even though the cans were in the curtilage); United States v. Long, 176 F.3d 1304 (10th Cir. 1999) (even if garbage bags were within curtilage, defendant did not have reasonable expectation of privacy there to successfully challenge law enforcement officers who took bags; defendant's placement of bags exposed them not just to garbage collector but also to anyone traveling down the alleyway); United States v. Wilkinson, 926 F.2d 22 (1st Cir. 1991) (proper to search trash left for collection on lawn near curb), *overruled on other grounds by* Bailey v. United States, 516 U.S. 137 (1995); United States v. Comeaux, 955 F.2d 586 (8th Cir. 1992) (search of garbage can in alley near garage was proper, even if can was within curtilage). The physical intrusion theory recognized in *Florida v. Jardines*, 133 S. Ct. 1409 (2013), may be implicated in these kinds of searches.

32. State v. Rhodes, 151 N.C. App. 208 (2002) (officers' warrantless search of trash can located by side entry door of house violated Fourth Amendment). The physical intrusion theory recognized in *Florida v. Jardines*, 133 S. Ct. 1409 (2013), may be implicated in these kinds of searches.

33. State v. Hauser, 342 N.C. 382 (1995) (officer directed trash collector to bring trash to him after normal collection); United States v. Crowell, 586 F.2d 1020 (4th Cir. 1978) (similar ruling).

34. For a discussion of the curtilage concept involving multi-unit dwellings, see Jeff Welty, *Multi-Unit Dwellings and Curtilage*, NC CRIM. L. BLOG (Oct. 11, 2012), http://nccriminallaw.sog.unc.edu/multi-unit-dwellings-and-curtilage/, and Jeff Welty, *Do Multi-Unit Dwellings Have Curtilage?* NC CRIM. L. BLOG (May 18, 2011), http://nccriminallaw.sog.unc.edu/do-multi-unit-dwellings-have-curtilage/. See also *State v. Williford*, ___ N.C. App. ___, 767 S.E.2d 139 (2015) (parking lot in front of multi-unit apartment building was not located on the curtilage).

35. Although entry onto the curtilage is a search under the Fourth Amendment, the United States Supreme Court in *Oliver v. United States*, 466 U.S. 170 n.11 (1984), did not decide whether the degree of Fourth Amendment protection for the curtilage is as extensive as that afforded the home. Thus, the Court may decide in a later case that a search warrant, which generally is required to enter a home, is not required to enter the curtilage—probable cause without a warrant may be sufficient. *See also* Rogers v. Pendleton, 249 F.3d 279 (4th Cir. 2001) (probable cause is required to search curtilage of home; reasonable suspicion is insufficient); Penna v. Porter, 316 Fed. Appx. 303 (4th Cir. 2009) (unpublished).

36. *See generally* State v. Smith, ___ N.C. App. ___, 783 S.E.2d 504 (2016).

circumstances (see the discussion below under "Common Entranceway to Residence.")

Sometimes it is difficult to define precisely what area immediately surrounding a home is within the curtilage. In *United States v. Dunn*,[37] the United States Supreme Court adopted a four-part test to determine whether property is within a home's curtilage:

1. The proximity of the area to the home
2. Whether the area is within an enclosure surrounding the home
3. The nature and use to which the area is put
4. The resident's efforts to protect the area from observations by passersby

The Court in *Dunn* stated that these factors are useful analytical tools to determine whether an area is so intimately tied to the home itself that it should be placed under the home's Fourth Amendment protections. The Court applied these factors and ruled that a barn 60 yards from a home was not within its curtilage. The Court noted that the barn was 50 yards beyond the fence surrounding the house. The barn stood out as a distinct part of the defendant's ranch, quite separate from the house. Officers had objective information—a strong smell from the barn of phenylacetic acid, which is used in making illegal drugs—that the barn was not being used for intimate activities of the home. The defendant did little to protect the barn area from observations by those standing in open fields. Other interior fences on the defendant's property were designed and constructed to corral livestock, not to prevent people from observing the enclosed area. The Court ruled that the officers did not violate the

defendant's Fourth Amendment rights by crossing over five fences—not including the fence surrounding the house—before they got to the barn.

The Court next ruled—assuming without deciding that the barn, although not within the curtilage, was entitled to Fourth Amendment protection and could not be entered without a search warrant—that the officers did not violate the defendant's Fourth Amendment right of privacy when they stood next to the barn's locked front gates, shined a flashlight through opaque netting above the gates without entering the barn, and looked into the barn.[38] The officers then left, obtained a search warrant, and searched the barn with the warrant.

Open Fields and Woods

When officers are on private property *outside* the curtilage—for example, when they are walking through fields or woods—they are not conducting a search under the Fourth Amendment.[39] The United States Supreme Court has ruled that a person does not have a reasonable expectation of privacy in the area outside the curtilage.[40] The Fourth Amendment does not protect that area even if officers are committing a criminal trespass or even if the area is surrounded by a fence and "No Trespassing" signs.[41] Any evidence that (1) officers see in plain view and

---

37. 480 U.S. 294 (1987). *See* State v. Washington, 86 N.C. App. 235 (1987) (applying the curtilage test of *United States v. Dunn*, court ruled that tobacco barn, packhouse, and hog shelter that were 50 to 75 feet from house were not within curtilage). *See also* State v. Burch, 70 N.C. App. 444 (1984) (brush pile, concealing marijuana plants, was within curtilage when located 84 feet behind house, as a short distance beyond brush pile were small crib, privy, cider press, and cider barrels; beyond crib was recreation building containing piano, pool table, and refrigerator; and beyond recreation building was private garage with junked cars; sown and mowed grass was around house, between house and marijuana patch, alongside crib, and between farm road and recreation building). The expansive definition of *curtilage* in *Burch*, decided before *United States v. Dunn*, may have been implicitly modified by *Dunn* and *State v. Fields*, 315 N.C. 191 (1985) (tool shed located at least 45 feet from dwelling was not within curtilage for second-degree burglary offense).

38. *But see* State v. Tarantino, 322 N.C. 386 (1988), in which the North Carolina Supreme Court, distinguishing *United States v. Dunn*, ruled that a defendant had a reasonable expectation of privacy in a boarded-up store building, and an officer's peering through a quarter-inch crack in the store building's rear wall after entering the enclosed porch there violated the defendant's Fourth Amendment rights. Compare the *Tarantino* ruling with *United States v. Pace*, 955 F.2d 270 (5th Cir. 1992) (no search occurred when officers pressed their faces against small opening in barn to see inside) and *United States v. Taylor*, 90 F.3d 903 (4th Cir. 1996) (officers' observation through open blinds while standing at front door did not violate Fourth Amendment).

39. For the purposes of the Fourth Amendment, an open field may be any unoccupied or undeveloped area outside of the curtilage and need be neither "open" nor a "field" as those terms are used in common speech. United States v. Dunn, 480 U.S. 294 (1987).

40. Oliver v. United States, 466 U.S. 170 (1984). The Court also ruled that fields and woods outside the curtilage are not "effects" as that word appears in the Fourth Amendment; therefore, these areas are not within the scope of the amendment.

41. Officers who are conducting a legitimate law enforcement function on the property are not violating North Carolina's criminal trespass laws. *See* State v. Prevette, 43 N.C. App.

have probable cause to believe is evidence of a crime, such as marijuana plants, and (2) is outside the curtilage may be seized without a search warrant under the plain view justification.[42] However, evidence the officers see in plain view from outside the curtilage that is located within the curtilage generally may not be seized without a search warrant, unless there are exigent circumstances, because officers who enter the curtilage are conducting a search for which Fourth Amendment justification—probable cause and a search warrant—is required.[43]

---

450 (1979) (entry onto private property for inquiry or interview is proper; officers are not trespassers); State v. Church, 110 N.C. App. 569 (1993) (similar ruling); State v. Ellis, 241 N.C. 702 (1955). *Cf.* Parker v. McCoy, 188 S.E.2d 222 (Va. 1972); Alvarez v. Montgomery Cty., 147 F.3d 354 (4th Cir. 1998) (Maryland trespass law is not violated when officer is on private property performing law enforcement function). However, whether the officers are violating the physical intrusion or trespassory theory of the Fourth Amendment, discussed earlier in the text, is unclear. *But see* United States v. Mathias, 721 F.3d 952 (8th Cir. 2013) (when officer's trespass occurred outside curtilage to view activity within curtilage, trespassory theory of Fourth Amendment was not violated).

42. United States v. Jacobsen, 466 U.S. 109 (1984); G.M. Leasing Corp. v. United States, 429 U.S. 338 (1977); Payton v. New York, 445 U.S. 573 (1980) (noting distinction between permitting warrantless seizure of property in open area and requiring warrant to enter private property to seize property). *See also* State v. Perry, 69 N.C. App. 477 (1984) ((apparent) warrantless seizure of marijuana in area outside curtilage upheld); State v. Piland, 58 N.C. App. 95 (1982) (court upheld warrantless seizure of marijuana growing near defendant's house when officers saw it in plain view from neighbor's property; court questionably—*see* United States v. Whaley, 781 F.2d 417 (5th Cir. 1986)—stated that it is irrelevant whether defendant had reasonable expectation of privacy where marijuana was growing; although court probably could have upheld the warrantless search based on exigent circumstances if marijuana was growing on curtilage); United States v. Eng, 753 F.2d 683 (8th Cir. 1985) (implicitly recognizing that warrantless seizure of marijuana outside curtilage was proper); State v. Grindstaff, 77 N.C. App. 467 (1985) (although the shed may have been within the curtilage, the officers were lawfully there when they saw what appeared to be marijuana).

In *State v. Nance*, 149 N.C. App. 734 (2002), the defendant leased barns and paddocks for her horses. Animal control officers received a telephone call on December 18, 1998, that the horses were being treated cruelly. That same day they viewed the horses from a road. The horses were located in open, accessible areas on the defendant's leased property. They were emaciated and appeared to be starving. On December 21, 1998, the officers entered the property and seized the horses without a search warrant. The court noted that although the officers did not violate the Fourth Amendment when they initially viewed the horses on December 18, 1998, they deprived the defendant of her Fourth Amendment possessory interest in the horses when they removed them three days later. The court then ruled that exigent circumstances did not support the officers' seizure of the horses on the defendant's property without a search warrant. The court stated that the officers had ample time during the three days to secure a search warrant.

The court's ruling is questionable. First, the court's view that the second entry onto the defendant's property without a search warrant or consent violated the Fourth Amendment because it was "private property" is in direct conflict with *Oliver v. United States*, 466 U.S. 170 (1984) (person has no reasonable expectation of privacy in land beyond curtilage of his or her home, and, therefore, officer's presence there is not a search under the Fourth Amendment). Because the defendant had no reasonable expectation of privacy in the land on which the horses were located, officers could walk on that land without a search warrant or consent as often as they wanted without violating the defendant's Fourth Amendment rights. Second, the plain view doctrine does not require that the officers' seizure of the horses be supported by exigent circumstances. The plain view doctrine is the basis for upholding a warrantless seizure of evidence when (1) an officer is lawfully in a position to make a plain view observation (or touch, smell, etc.); (2) the officer has a lawful right of access to the object; and (3) the officer has probable cause to believe that the object to be seized is evidence of a crime. Horton v. California, 496 U.S. 128 (1990); United States v. Soussi, 29 F.3d 565 (10th Cir. 1994). There is no additional requirement of exigency to seize evidence of a crime in plain view if an officer's presence on property is lawful; the officer has lawful access to the object to be seized (in this case, the horses in an open, accessible area); and there is probable cause to seize it. *See* G & G Jewelry, Inc. v. City of Oakland, 989 F.2d 1093 (9th Cir. 1993) (upholding warrantless seizure of stolen property at pawn shop under plain view doctrine, which does not require showing of exigent circumstances); United States v. Perry, 95 Fed. Appx. 598 (5th Cir. 2004) (unpublished) (upholding warrantless seizure of marijuana in open field under plain view doctrine); United States v. Paige, 136 F.3d 1012 (5th Cir. 1998). The officers were lawfully on the land on December 21, 1998, when they approached the horses because the land was not a place where the defendant had a reasonable expectation of privacy. Thus, there was a valid intrusion onto the land where the officers made a plain view observation of the horses. They also had probable cause to believe that the property they seized (the horses) was evidence of the crime of cruelty to animals and that they could seize the horses under the plain view doctrine without a warrant or a showing of exigent circumstances.

43. United States v. Whaley, 781 F.2d 417 (5th Cir. 1986) (warrantless entry onto curtilage to seize marijuana plants seen in plain view from road violated Fourth Amendment when exigent circumstances did not authorize entry). As mentioned *supra* note 35, it is possible that the United States Supreme Court may not require a search warrant to enter the curtilage, but an officer should obtain a search

Although officers' *presence* on private land outside the curtilage is not a search under the Fourth Amendment, they conduct a search that requires appropriate justification under the Fourth Amendment (usually, a search warrant) if they enter a closed structure outside the curtilage.[44] On the other hand, officers are not conducting a search if they merely look through an opening in a closed structure or if they enter an open structure and look around, because a person does not have a reasonable expectation of privacy in an open structure outside the curtilage where a passerby is able to look inside.[45]

Common Entranceway to Residence

When officers go to a house by using the common entranceway (for example, a driveway or sidewalk to a door) for a legitimate purpose, such as to respond to a complaint, question a suspect in a criminal investigation, or conduct a "knock and talk"[46] (a procedure in which officers approach a residence with the intent to obtain consent to conduct a warrantless search of the residence), they are not conducting a search under the Fourth Amendment—even though they have entered the curtilage.[47] A person ordinarily expects a variety of people to enter private property for any number of purposes; therefore, the person does not have a reasonable expectation of privacy in the areas of private property commonly used by those who come there. On the other hand, if officers do something that is not ordinarily explicitly or implicitly permitted by the homeowner, such as bringing a drug dog to the front porch of a home to gather information on what is inside, such as illegal drugs, that conduct is ordinarily a search under the physical intrusion or trespassory theory of the Fourth Amendment.[48]

Knocking on the front and side doors without success and then going to the backyard and knocking on the back door, which is not used by visitors—particularly when officers have no reason to believe that knocking on the back door would produce a response—will likely constitute a search under the Fourth Amendment.[49]

Plain View Sensory Perceptions (Observation, Smell, Sound, Touch, and Taste)

(See page 297 for case summaries on this topic.)

The United States Supreme Court has stated that "[w]hat a person knowingly exposes to the public, even in

---

warrant—absent exigent circumstances—until an appellate court has approved an entry without a search warrant.

44. The Court noted in *Oliver v. United States*, 466 U.S. 214 n.10 (1984), that the Fourth Amendment protects activities in open fields that might implicate a person's privacy, such as a seizure of effects on a person's body. The Court also may recognize that a person has a reasonable expectation of privacy in effects, such as an enclosed building, that are located outside the curtilage. The United States Supreme Court deliberately did not decide this issue in *United States v. Dunn*, 480 U.S. 294 (1987). *See, e.g., State v. Tarantino*, 322 N.C. 386 (1988); *United States v. Santa Maria*, 15 F.3d 879 (9th Cir. 1994) (search of trailer outside curtilage violated Fourth Amendment). *But see State v. Kaplan*, 23 N.C. App. 410 (1974) (warrantless search of tent-like structure outside curtilage was permissible).

45. *State v. Boone*, 293 N.C. 702 (1977).

46. The North Carolina Supreme Court in *State v. Smith*, 346 N.C. 794 (1997), ruled that the knock-and-talk procedure in that case did not violate the defendant's Fourth Amendment rights. *See also* Hardesty v. Hamburg Twp., 461 F.3d 646 (6th Cir. 2006) (officers conducting knock and talk did not violate plaintiff's Fourth Amendment rights when, after knocking on the front door and not receiving an answer, they went to the back door and knocked because there was evidence someone was inside; see court's discussion of cases from other federal appellate courts); United States v. Taylor, 458 F.3d 1201 (11th Cir. 2006) (officer's minor departure from the front door during knock and talk did not violate defendant's Fourth Amendment rights). The use of the knock-and-talk procedure at night may be problematic after *Florida v. Jardines*, 133 S. Ct. 1409 (2013). *See* Jeff Welty, *Does the Trespass Theory of the Fourth Amendment Limit the Scope of Knock and Talks?* NC Crim. L. Blog (Dec. 3, 2013), http://nccriminallaw.sog.unc.edu/ does-the-trespass-theory-of-the-fourth-amendment-limit-the- scope-of-knock-and-talks/.

47. *See State v. Prevette*, 43 N.C. App. 450 (1979) (entry onto private property for inquiry or interview is proper); State v. Robinson, 148 N.C. App. 422 (2002) (similar ruling); State v. Church, 110 N.C. App. 569 (1993) (similar ruling); State v. Wallace, 111 N.C. App. 581 (1993) (similar ruling); State v. Tripp, 52 N.C. App. 244 (1981); State v. Carter, 66 N.C. App. 330 (1984) (officers' driving up driveway to house did not violate Fourth Amendment); United States v. Evans, 27 F.3d 1219 (7th Cir. 1994) (walking up driveway).

48. 133 S. Ct. 1409 (2013).

49. State v. Pasour, 223 N.C. App. 175 (2012) (officers violated Fourth Amendment by going to backyard and knocking on back door based on facts in this case). *See also* Jeff Welty, *Going to the Back Door*, NC Crim. L. Blog (Oct. 22, 2012), www.sog.unc.edu/blogs/nc-criminal-law/going-back-door; Alvarez v. Montgomery Cty., 147 F.3d 354 (4th Cir. 1998) (officer went to backyard to find occupant of residence when responding to report of underage drinking party); United States v. Daoust, 916 F.2d 757 (1st Cir. 1990) (officers lawfully went to back door when front door was inaccessible); United States v. Garcia, 997 F.2d 1273 (9th Cir. 1993) (officer walked to back door thinking it was front door); United States v. Raines, 243 F.3d 419 (8th Cir. 2001) (officer attempting to serve civil process walked to backyard after knocking on front door, believing that occupants might be there).

his own home or office, is not a subject of Fourth Amendment protection."[50] Everyday living results in a certain loss of privacy, and in certain circumstances law enforcement officers can obtain facts about someone by using opportunities to see, smell, touch, and hear that are available to all people. When officers are in a public place or another area,[51] such as an open field, that is not protected by the Fourth Amendment, or if the officers have legally intruded on someone's privacy, what they see,[52] smell,[53] touch,[54] and hear[55] generally is not a search under the Fourth Amendment. Knowledge gained by the sense of sight is commonly known as a plain view observation— and knowledge gained by the senses of smell, touch, or hearing is known by other appropriate descriptions.[56] The

sense of taste may be recognized as well.[57] (The sense of touch is discussed extensively on page 257 concerning a frisk of a person.)

Although a plain view observation or use of other senses is generally not a search, officers may need further justification to take possession of or look for the evidence they have seen in plain view, because their investigative actions after a plain view observation may constitute a search or seizure, or both, under the Fourth Amendment.[58] And if an investigative action is a search or seizure, it may require probable cause to support it.[59]

---

50. Katz v. United States, 389 U.S. 347 (1967).

51. Although the Court in *Katz* stated that "the Fourth Amendment protects people—and not simply 'areas'—against unreasonable searches and seizures" (389 U.S. 347, 353 (1967)), in later cases it has clearly considered areas when it has determined whether a person has a reasonable expectation of privacy. *See, e.g.,* Oliver v. United States, 466 U.S. 170 (1984).

52. *See, e.g.,* Texas v. Brown, 460 U.S. 730 (1983).

53. *See, e.g.,* United States v. Johns, 469 U.S. 478 (1985) (odor of marijuana supplied probable cause to search vehicle); State v. Greenwood, 47 N.C. App. 731 (1980) (odor of marijuana provided probable cause to search vehicle), *rev'd on other grounds,* 301 N.C. 705 (1981); State v. Trapper, 48 N.C. App. 481 (1980).

54. *See, e.g.,* Minnesota v. Dickerson, 508 U.S. 366 (1993); State v. Briggs, 140 N.C. App. 484 (2000); State v. Robinson, 189 N.C. App. 454 (2008). *Dickerson* and *Briggs* involved the sense of touch during an otherwise lawful frisk; *Robinson* involved feeling a cylindrical object that made a rattling sound when moved. Touching or feeling an object or person may be so intrusive that it constitutes a search. *See* Bond v. United States, 529 U.S. 334 (2000) (officer's squeeze of bag in exploratory manner in overhead bin on bus was search under Fourth Amendment for which officer did not have appropriate justification).

55. *See, e.g.,* United States v. Jackson, 588 F.2d 1046 (5th Cir. 1979) (officers did not conduct a search when they listened to a conversation taking place in an adjoining motel room by lying on a motel room floor and pressing their ears to crack at the bottom of connecting door; officers did not use any device to assist their aural surveillance); United States v. Fisch, 474 F.2d 1071 (9th Cir. 1973) (same).

56. The discussion of plain view in the text generally focuses on the issue of whether an officer's use of the senses—sight, smell, hearing, taste, and touch—constitutes a search under the Fourth Amendment; it then separately analyzes the justification for any resulting seizure or search. The plain view doctrine, on the other hand, is the basis for upholding a warrantless seizure of property when (1) an officer is lawfully in a position to make a plain view observation (or touch, smell,

etc.); (2) the officer has a lawful right of access to the object; and (3) the officer has probable cause to believe that the object to be seized is evidence of a crime. Horton v. California, 496 U.S. 128 (1990); United States v. Soussi, 29 F.3d 565 (10th Cir. 1994); State v. Beveridge, 112 N.C. App. 688 (1993). Probable cause is synonymous with the "immediately apparent" language in the now partially overruled case of *Coolidge v. New Hampshire,* 403 U.S. 443 (1971). *See* State v. White, 322 N.C. 770 (1988); State v. Wilson, 112 N.C. App. 777 (1993); Horton v. California, 496 U.S. 128 (1990). *See generally* 1 Wayne R. LaFave, Search and Seizure: A Treatise on the Fourth Amendment § 2.2(a) (5th ed. 2012); United States v. Jackson, 131 F.3d 1105 (4th Cir. 1997). The Court in *Horton* also ruled that the plain view doctrine does not require that an officer "inadvertently" discover the object to be seized. However, G.S. 15A-253 requires that evidence in plain view must be seized inadvertently during the execution of a search warrant. Unfortunately, North Carolina appellate courts continue to assert erroneously (*see, e.g.,* State v. Bone, 354 N.C. 1 (2001); State v. Castellon, 151 N.C. App. 675 (2002)) that the plain view doctrine requires that the evidence must be discovered inadvertently during a warrantless seizure even though G.S. 15A-253 is inapplicable, which was recognized in footnote 1 in *State v. Alexander,* 233 N.C. App. 50 (2014). For a definition of *inadvertence,* see the discussion of *State v. White* in note 70, below. For an analysis of the questionable ruling in *State v. Nance,* 149 N.C. App. 734 (2002), involving the seizure of horses on private property, see note 42, below.

57. An officer who lawfully possesses a mason jar of liquid— believing that it may be non-tax-paid liquor—probably does not conduct a search or seizure if the officer tastes the liquid to determine if it is liquor or not. *Cf.* United States v. Jacobsen, 466 U.S. 109 (1984) (test of white powder to determine whether it was cocaine was not a search or seizure).

58. *United States v. Jacobsen,* 466 U.S. 109 (1984), provides an excellent analysis of how to consider each law enforcement action separately; how to determine whether each action was a search or seizure; and, if an action was a search or seizure, what justification must be shown to support it.

59. In *Arizona v. Hicks,* 480 U.S. 321 (1987), the Court ruled that under the plain view doctrine an item may not be searched or seized with less than probable cause. Officers in *Hicks* properly entered an apartment where a shooting had

Sometimes a search warrant also may be needed. For example, an officer's initial observation of a computer file containing child pornography while executing a search warrant to search computer files for documentary evidence concerning the sale of controlled substances may be justified as a plain view observation. However, opening additional files that the officer knows will not contain items subject to search with the search warrant will require another search warrant.[60] Thus, one must carefully analyze each investigative action officers take after seeing (or using another sense to perceive) something in plain view to determine whether the action was proper under the Fourth Amendment.

A variety of everyday circumstances involve a plain view observation and a later investigative action that may involve a search or seizure, or both. It is useful to discuss a few common situations to help officers understand actions that they may properly take under the Fourth Amendment.

Observation into a Home from a Public Place

Officers may observe an object or activities in a home from an area, such as a sidewalk, where the public generally has access. An observation into the home from such an area, even with the use of binoculars—assuming that the binoculars are used merely to clarify an object that can be seen with unaided vision[61]—is not a search under the Fourth Amendment. The resident of a home does not have a reasonable expectation of privacy in what has been exposed to public view. If, for example, officers are standing on a sidewalk and see a plant through the window of a house, they have made a plain view observation that does not violate anyone's Fourth Amendment rights. If their training and experience provide them with a reasonable belief that it is a marijuana plant, they then have probable cause to seize it. But the authority to seize the plant does not automatically allow them to enter the home without a search warrant, because a warrantless entry into a home is unreasonable under the Fourth Amendment without consent to enter or exigent circumstances (a need for immediate action) that would permit officers to enter.[62] Thus, unless the officers obtain consent to enter the home to seize the marijuana plant or unless exigent circumstances exist—for example, officers reasonably believe that the plant may be imminently destroyed or removed[63]—a search warrant is needed to enter the home and to seize the plant.

---

occurred to search for the shooter and any victims or weapons. They seized three weapons and a stocking-cap mask. They noticed two expensive stereo components in the squalid apartment. An officer read serial numbers from some of the items without moving them; the Court ruled that this act was neither a search nor a seizure and therefore did not violate the defendant's Fourth Amendment rights. However, the officer also moved a turntable so that he could read its serial number. This act constituted a search that required probable cause (probable cause also was necessary to support the later seizure of the turntable from the apartment). Because the State had conceded that only reasonable suspicion existed to move the turntable, the Court ruled that the officer's actions violated the defendant's Fourth Amendment rights. However, the Court's ruling did not affect the validity of *United States v. Place*, 462 U.S. 696 (1983), which permits a brief seizure of luggage at an airport when there is reasonable suspicion that it may contain evidence of a crime—in this case, illegal drugs.

60. United States v. Carey, 172 F.3d 1268 (10th Cir. 1999) (officers obtained search warrant to search files on defendant's computers for "names, telephone numbers, ledger receipts, addresses, and other documentary evidence pertaining to sale and distribution of controlled substances"; upon opening a file labeled "JPG," officer discovered child pornography; officer then opened many more files with that label and discovered more child pornography; court ruled that seizure of additional child pornography files was not authorized by the search warrant; after opening the first child pornography file, officer was aware what label meant; when he opened additional files with that label, he knew that he was not going to find items related to drug activity as specified in search warrant). *See also* United States v. Walser, 275 F.3d 981 (10th Cir. 2001) (officer executing search warrant for drug documents found file with child pornography and then properly obtained search warrant to search computer for more child pornography). *But see* United States v. Williams, 592 F.3d 511 (4th Cir. 2010) (criticizing *Carey* ruling as improperly focusing on officer's subjective motivation for continuing to search computer files instead of whether warrant's terms objectively permitted continuing search).

61. *See* 1 Wayne R. LaFave, Search and Seizure: A Treatise on the Fourth Amendment § 2.2(c) (5th ed. 2012). *See generally* State v. Tarantino, 322 N.C. 386 (1988) (search occurred when officer peered through quarter-inch crack in boarded-up store building's rear wall after entering enclosed porch there).

62. Vale v. Louisiana, 399 U.S. 30 (1970). *See* United States v. Whaley, 781 F.2d 417 (5th Cir. 1986).

63. *See, e.g.*, United States v. Cuaron, 700 F.2d 582 (10th Cir. 1983); United States v. Webster, 750 F.2d 307 (5th Cir. 1984).

Observation into a Car

Officers who lawfully stop a vehicle and look inside with a flashlight do not conduct a search under the Fourth Amendment.[64] If the officers see an object in a vehicle that they reasonably believe is evidence of a crime, they have probable cause to seize it. They may enter the vehicle and seize the object without a search warrant[65] because (1) the vehicle and the object are mobile or capable of mobility and (2) the United States Supreme Court and the North Carolina Supreme Court have recognized that a person has a lesser expectation of privacy in a vehicle than in a home.[66] (Searches of vehicles will be discussed in more detail later in this chapter on page 236.)

As previously discussed, plain view also includes the sense of smell. Thus, the smell of the odor of marijuana emanating from a vehicle allows an officer to make a warrantless search of the vehicle for marijuana.[67]

A plain view observation (or use of other senses, such as smell) may also establish probable cause to arrest one or more occupants because it is illegal to possess the object (for example, illegal drugs) at any time or because the object was recently stolen and links an occupant to a

crime such as breaking or entering, larceny, or robbery. If officers arrest one of the occupants, they also may under certain circumstances[68] conduct a warrantless search of the entire interior of the car, including any containers within the interior, based on the search incident to arrest justification (discussed later in this chapter on page 252).

Observation in a Private Place after Legitimate Access

Officers who are lawfully in a home may seize evidence of a crime that they see in plain view. For example, officers who are lawfully in a home to investigate a domestic disturbance complaint may lawfully seize a white powdery substance that they see on a kitchen table if they have probable cause to believe that the substance is cocaine or another illegal drug.

Officers who are executing a search warrant may search every area in the house where they reasonably may find the objects the warrant permits them to seize. While doing so, officers also may seize any other object that they inadvertently see in plain view and have probable cause to believe is evidence of a crime—even if it is not evidence named to be seized under the search warrant.[69] Officers "inadvertently" seize an object not named in the warrant if, before the warrant was issued, they did not have probable cause to seize it and did not specifically intend to search for and seize it.[70] Officers' authority to seize objects

---

64. *See* Texas v. Brown, 460 U.S. 730 (1983); State v. Brooks, 337 N.C. 132 (1994); State v. Whitley, 33 N.C. App. 753 (1977).

65. *See, e.g.,* Colorado v. Bannister, 449 U.S. 1 (1980); United States v. Head, 783 F.2d 1422 (9th Cir. 1986).

66. United States v. Chadwick, 433 U.S. 1 (1977); California v. Carney, 471 U.S. 386 (1985); State v. Isleib, 319 N.C. 634 (1987) (upholding warrantless vehicle search under both United States and North Carolina constitutions).

67. *See* State v. Smith, 192 N.C. App. 690 (2008) (odor of marijuana provided probable cause to search vehicle); State v. Corpening, 200 N.C. App. 311 (2009) (similar ruling); State v. Cornelius, 104 N.C. App. 583 (1991) (similar ruling); State v. Trapper, 48 N.C. App. 481 (1980) (similar ruling); State v. Greenwood, 47 N.C. App. 731 (1980) (similar ruling; court rejected analyses in cases from other jurisdictions that distinguished, in determining probable cause, whether odor of marijuana emanated from unburned, burning, or burned marijuana), *rev'd on other grounds*, 301 N.C. 705 (1981); State v. Toledo, 204 N.C. App. 170 (2010) (discovery of odor of marijuana from spare tire in luggage area of Chevrolet Suburban provided probable cause to make warrantless search for marijuana in rest of vehicle, including second spare tire in vehicle's undercarriage). Although the odor of marijuana allows a warrantless search of a vehicle, it does not necessarily allow the warrantless search of an occupant. *See* State v. Malunda, 230 N.C. App. 355 (2013) (odor of marijuana emanating from driver's side of vehicle and marijuana being discovered on driver's side did not allow warrantless search of vehicle passenger when considering all the circumstances in this case).

68. A search incident to arrest of a vehicle occupant is subject to the limitations imposed by *Arizona v. Grant*, 556 U.S. 332 (2009), discussed later in this chapter.

69. In *Horton v. California*, 496 U.S. 128 (1990), the Court overruled *Coolidge v. New Hampshire*, 403 U.S. 443 (1971), and ruled that the plain view doctrine does not require that an officer "inadvertently" discover the object to be seized. However, G.S. 15A-253 requires that a discovery of evidence during the execution of a search warrant must be inadvertent. Because inadvertence is just a statutory requirement, only the statutory exclusionary rule in G.S. 15A-974 would apply in determining whether the evidence is admissible.

70. State v. White, 322 N.C. 770 (1988). Officers in *White* executed a search warrant for stolen property and seized stolen items that were not named in the warrant. The court ruled that *inadvertence* (which no longer is required under the Fourth Amendment but is required under G.S. 15A-253) under the plain view doctrine means that officers do not have probable cause to believe that evidence will be discovered until they actually observe it during an otherwise justified search. Judicial review involves a two-step inquiry: Before the search, did officers have probable cause to secure a search warrant for the later-seized items that were not named in the search warrant? If the answer is yes, the seizure is illegal. If the answer is no, then the review proceeds to the second inquiry: Did the

in plain view after a valid intrusion into an area is legally known as the *plain view doctrine*.[71]

Use of Special Devices or Animals

Generally, using special devices or animals to assist in seeing, smelling, or hearing is permissible if the use of the unaided eye, nose, or ear from the same place would have been legal. (This section will discuss the general use of special devices or animals, although not all of them necessarily fit under the plain view justification. Wiretapping, eavesdropping, and related issues are discussed later in this chapter on page 210.)

Binoculars, telescopes, and flashlights. An observation made with the aid of binoculars from the street into a place, such as a home, where there is a reasonable expectation of privacy, is permissible, just as an observation with an unaided eye would have been, if the binoculars are used merely to clarify an object that can be seen with unaided vision.[72] Similarly, using a flashlight is permissible.[73] However, using a sophisticated, high-powered telescope to look into a home may invade a person's reasonable expectation of privacy under certain circumstances and thus may be considered a search under the Fourth Amendment that requires appropriate justification (usually, a search warrant).[74]

On the other hand, using highly sophisticated devices does not violate anyone's Fourth Amendment rights if the place being observed is not one where anyone could have a reasonable expectation of privacy. For example, officers do not violate the Fourth Amendment when they use high-powered binoculars or a telescope to view activities occurring in an open field or on a street or sidewalk.

Thermal imagers. (See page 313 for case summaries on this topic.) The United States Supreme Court has ruled that the use of a thermal imager aimed at a private home to detect the relative amounts of heat within the home constitutes a search under the Fourth Amendment.[75] (A thermal imager is sometimes useful to determine if a person is growing marijuana in his or her home because indoor marijuana cultivation typically requires the use of high-intensity lamps.) Thus, absent exigent circumstances or consent, an officer must obtain a search warrant to use a thermal imager when it is directed at a place, such as a home, in which a person has a reasonable expectation of privacy.

Aircraft. Generally, aircraft surveillance is permissible to help officers make observations and does not constitute a search under the Fourth Amendment. For example, officers do not conduct a search when they fly (1) over open fields or (2) in lawful navigable airspace over the curtilage of a home and see with their unaided eyes marijuana plants in a fenced-in yard.[76] (Open fields and curtilage are discussed on page 200.) However, their actions may constitute a search requiring appropriate justification (usually, a search warrant) if they also use sophisticated cameras or similar devices to see intimate activities within the curtilage that they could not otherwise see.[77]

GPS tracking devices. (See page 308 for case summaries on this topic.) Because Global Positioning System (GPS) devices have largely supplanted beepers[78] in tracking

---

officers have probable cause to believe that the seized items were evidence of a crime when they seized them without a warrant? The court ruled that the officers' use of break-in incident reports when they were executing a search warrant did not violate the inadvertence standard because they did not have probable cause to seize the items named in these reports to list them in a search warrant. Therefore, the officers properly seized these items. The court ruled, however, that the officers did not have probable cause to seize some items not named in the reports until *after* they seized them; therefore the officers illegally seized them.

71. For a discussion of the plain view doctrine, see note 56, above.

72. *See* United States v. Lee, 274 U.S. 559 (1927) (dicta); Fullbright v. United States, 392 F.2d 432 (10th Cir. 1968); 1 Wayne R. LaFave, Search and Seizure: A Treatise on the Fourth Amendment § 2.2(c) (5th ed. 2012).

73. United States v. Dunn, 480 U.S. 294 (1987) (shining flashlight into barn did not violate defendant's Fourth Amendment rights); Texas v. Brown, 460 U.S. 730 (1983); State v. Brooks, 337 N.C. 132 (1994); State v. Whitley, 33 N.C. App. 753 (1977). *See* 1 Wayne R. LaFave, Search and Seizure: A Treatise on the Fourth Amendment § 2.2(b) (5th ed. 2012).

74. See the discussion in 1 Wayne R. LaFave, Search and Seizure: A Treatise on the Fourth Amendment § 2.2(c),

at 628 (5th ed. 2012). *See generally* California v. Ciraolo, 476 U.S. 207 (1986).

75. Kyllo v. United States, 533 U.S. 27 (2001). The Court noted that thermal imagers are not generally used by the public. It did not indicate whether its ruling would change if they became widely used by the public.

76. *See* California v. Ciraolo, 476 U.S. 207 (1986); Dow Chem. Co. v. United States, 476 U.S. 227 (1986); Florida v. Riley, 488 U.S. 445 (1989).

77. *See* 1 Wayne R. LaFave, Search and Seizure: A Treatise on the Fourth Amendment § 2.2(c), at 636 (5th ed. 2012).

78. For cases on beepers, see *United States v. Knotts*, 460 U.S. 276 (1983) (monitoring beeper signal from container in

vehicles, containers, and other objects, the following discussion will focus on GPS devices (although the legal principles applicable to GPS devices generally apply to beepers as well).[79] For an extensive discussion of GPS tracking, see Chapter 4 of *Digital Evidence*, a School of Government publication by Jeffrey B. Welty.

In *United States v. Jones*,[80] the United States Supreme Court ruled that the government's installation of a GPS tracking device on a vehicle and its use of that device to monitor the vehicle's movements on public streets constituted a "search" within the meaning of the Fourth Amendment. Officers who suspected that the defendant was involved in drug trafficking installed a GPS device without a valid search warrant on the undercarriage of a vehicle while it was parked in a public parking lot in Maryland. Over the next 28 days, the government used the device to track the vehicle's movements and once had to replace the device's battery when the vehicle was parked in a different public lot. By means of signals from multiple satellites, the device established the vehicle's location within 50 to 100 feet and communicated that location by cellular phone to a government computer. It

relayed more than 2,000 pages of data over the four-week period.

The defendant was charged with several drug offenses. He unsuccessfully sought to suppress the evidence obtained through the GPS device. Before the United States Supreme Court, the government argued that a warrant was not required for the GPS device. Concluding that the evidence should have been suppressed, the Court characterized the government's conduct as having "physically occupied private property for the purpose of obtaining information."[81] Thus, the Court had "no doubt that such a physical intrusion would have been considered a 'search' within the meaning of the Fourth Amendment when it was adopted."[82]

The Court's opinion declined to address whether the defendant had a reasonable expectation of privacy in the undercarriage of his car and in the car's locations on the public roads, concluding that such an analysis was not required when the intrusion—as here—"encroached on a protected area." But there were five votes in two concurring opinions that would treat long-term GPS surveillance even without a trespass as a violation of the Fourth Amendment's reasonable expectation of privacy theory.[83] It is unclear whether the Court will treat as a Fourth Amendment violation a short GPS search without a search warrant if it can be done without a trespass (for example, concealing a tracking device inside an object and then convincing a suspect to accept the object that is placed in a vehicle).

While the resolution of many aspects of the *Jones* ruling awaits future appellate cases, officers should consider the following conservative course of action to avoid constitutional violations, unless their agency's legal advisor provides different advice.

Officers should assume that judicial authorization is required before installing and using a GPS tracking device, whether stick-on or hard-wired, unless there are exigent circumstances that would obviate the need for

---

vehicle while it traveled on public highways to cabin was not search or seizure under Fourth Amendment); and *United States v. Karo*, 468 U.S. 705 (1984) (warrantless installation of beeper in can of ether with owner's consent and later transfer of can to defendant was not search under Fourth Amendment; however, monitoring beeper inside private residence was search requiring probable cause and a search warrant or other judicial authorization, absent exigent circumstances). The *Karo* Court, responding to the government's contention that it would be impossible to describe in advance the "place" to be searched, stated that the following information will suffice to permit the device's installation and surveillance: description of the object into which the device is to be placed; the reasons why the officers want to install the device (that is, probable cause to believe that using the device may discover criminal activity); and the length of time for which the device's surveillance is requested. In a case decided before *Karo*, the North Carolina Court of Appeals in *State v. Hendricks*, 43 N.C. App. 245 (1979), set out stricter requirements for obtaining a search warrant. The court clearly would need to modify those Fourth Amendment requirements in light of *Karo*.

79. A tracking device, which would include a GPS device, is specifically exempted from the definition of *electronic communication* in 18 U.S.C. § 2510(12)(C) and G.S. 15A-286(8)(c) and is clearly not a *wire communication* or *oral communication* as defined by federal and state laws. There is a federal law, 18 U.S.C. § 3117, that sets out the territorial scope of a federal court's search warrant or order authorizing the use of a tracking device.

80. 132 S. Ct. 945 (2012).

81. *Id.* at 949.

82. *Id.*

83. *Id.* at 952. See the discussion in Jeff Welty, *The Supreme Court on GPS Tracking:* United States v. Jones, NC Crim. L. Blog (Jan. 24, 2012), http://nccriminallaw.sog.unc.edu/the-supreme-court-on-gps-tracking-u-s-v-jones/. Concerning a separate GPS issue, see Jeff Welty, *Authentication and GPS Tracking*, NC Crim. L. Blog (June 2, 2014), http://nccriminallaw.sog.unc.edu/authentication-and-gps-tracking/.

such authorization.[84] And prior judicial authorization is necessary regardless of the length of the monitoring.

Judicial authorization can be secured either by a search warrant or a court order. As explained in a School of Government blog post cited in the accompanying footnote,[85] a court order issued by a superior court judge appears to be the better approach. The application for a court order should contain a factual statement, under oath, establishing probable cause to support the use of the tracking device. Although likely not legally required, it may be helpful to explain the need to use a tracking device instead of taking other actions, such as visual surveillance.

The court order should include a finding of probable cause and a statement authorizing the installation and monitoring of the tracking device, including the authorization to enter private property to install it, if necessary. The order probably should also:

- Set a time limit on monitoring—for example, 30 days, unless extended in a later order. The relevant Federal Rule of Criminal Procedure[86] provides for a 45-day renewable period of monitoring.
- Address whether and how the subject is to be notified of the use of the device. For example, the order could provide for service of the order when the monitoring is completed. The federal rule provides for service within 10 days of the completion of monitoring, unless the judge finds a reason to order otherwise.
- Require the officer to notify the issuing judge once installation and monitoring are complete. This would be similar to the return requirement for a search warrant.

It is not clear whether the authorization to use the tracking device would include the tracking of a suspect beyond North Carolina's borders, but it would appear to be permissible.

Dogs. (See page 309 for case summaries on this topic.) Allowing a trained narcotics-detection dog to sniff luggage in a public place, to walk around a vehicle in a public place, or to walk in a common area of a storage facility does not constitute a search under the Fourth Amend-

ment.[87] However, some courts have ruled that a dog's sniff of a person is a search.[88]

Officers should remember that they may not bring the dog into an area protected by the Fourth Amendment unless they have appropriate justification to enter that area.[89] For example, although officers are generally permitted to enter the curtilage of a home to access the front door to conduct a knock and talk, they are not permitted to take a drug detection dog to the front door or porch.[90] Also, when a dog alerts to an object—such as a suitcase or briefcase—probable cause may be established, but a search warrant or consent may still be needed to search the object[91] (see the discussion on page 242).

Officers may take a drug dog with them while executing a search warrant for illegal drugs or a dog trained for detecting explosives or accelerants with them when executing a search warrant for arson of a dwelling without needing any additional justification beyond the issuance of the search warrant.[92]

Courts will examine all the circumstances surrounding a person's consent to search a vehicle to determine if the consent included permission to allow a drug dog to

---

84. The future state of GPS law is unclear, especially considering the death of Justice Scalia, who wrote the Court's opinion.

85. Jeff Welty, *Advice to Officers after* Jones, NC Crim. L. Blog (Jan. 30, 2012), http://nccriminallaw.sog.unc.edu/advice-to-officers-after-jones/.

86. Fed. R. Crim. P. 41(e)(2)(C).

87. Illinois v. Caballes, 543 U.S. 405 (2005); United States v. Place, 462 U.S. 696 (1983); City of Indianapolis v. Edmond, 531 U.S. 32 (2000); State v. Washburn, 201 N.C. App. 93 (2009); State v. Fisher, 141 N.C. App. 448 (2000); United States v. Jeffus, 22 F.3d 554 (4th Cir. 1994); Jennings v. Joshua Indep. Sch. Dist., 877 F.2d 313 (5th Cir. 1989). Of course, if a vehicle was unlawfully stopped or a person unlawfully detained, the results of a positive alert by a dog may be suppressed as a fruit of the unlawful stop or detention. State v. Fisher, 141 N.C. App. 448 (2000). For discussion of dog alert legal issues, see 1 & 2 Wayne R. LaFave, Search and Seizure: A Treatise on the Fourth Amendment §§ 2.2(g), 3.3(d) at n.268 (5th ed. 2012).

88. *Compare* B.C. v. Plumas Unified Sch. Dist., 192 F.3d 1260 (9th Cir. 1999) (dog sniff of students is a search) *and* Horton v. Goose Creek Indep. Sch. Dist., 690 F.2d 470 (5th Cir. 1982) (similar ruling) *with* Doe v. Renfrow, 631 F.2d 91 (7th Cir. 1980) (court adopted as its own a district court opinion that dog sniff of student is not a search).

89. *See* 1 Wayne R. LaFave, Search and Seizure: A Treatise on the Fourth Amendment § 2.2(g), at 699-700 (5th ed. 2012); United States v. Winningham, 140 F.3d 1328 (10th Cir. 1998).

90. Florida v. Jardines, 133 S. Ct. 1409 (2013). See the discussion of this case earlier in this chapter.

91. *See* State v. McDaniels, 103 N.C. App. 175 (1991) (officers used search warrant to search briefcase after dog's positive alert), *aff'd*, 331 N.C. 112 (1992).

92. *See* 2 Wayne R. LaFave, Search and Seizure: A Treatise on the Fourth Amendment § 4.10(d), at 979 (5th ed. 2012).

enter the vehicle. These circumstances include: (1) If the drug dog was present when consent was given, whether the person made any objection to the use of the dog. (2) Whether the person objected when the dog entered the vehicle to begin the search.[93] Of course, officers may wish to obtain explicit consent to permit the drug dog to enter the vehicle even though such consent may not be legally required.

The use of a drug dog to sniff a vehicle during a traffic or other investigative stop is permissible while the driver is being lawfully detained for the issuance of a citation or warning ticket or for another lawful purpose[94] but not after the stop has been completed unless there is reasonable suspicion of criminal activity or consent is obtained.[95]

What are the constitutional requirements in assessing a dog's reliability? The United States Supreme Court in *Florida v. Harris*[96] ruled that the dog sniff in the case provided probable cause to search a vehicle. The Court rejected the ruling of the Florida Supreme Court that would have required the prosecution to present, in every case, an exhaustive set of records, including a log of the dog's performance in the field, to establish the dog's reliability. The Court found this "demand inconsistent with the 'flexible, common-sense standard' of probable cause."[97] It instructed:

> In short, a probable-cause hearing focusing on a dog's alert should proceed much like any other. The court should allow the parties to make their

best case, consistent with the usual rules of criminal procedure. And the court should then evaluate the proffered evidence to decide what all the circumstances demonstrate. If the State has produced proof from controlled settings that a dog performs reliably in detecting drugs, and the defendant has not contested that showing, then the court should find probable cause. If, in contrast, the defendant has challenged the State's case (by disputing the reliability of the dog overall or of a particular alert), then the court should weigh the competing evidence. In all events, the court should not prescribe, as the Florida Supreme Court did, an inflexible set of evidentiary requirements. The question—similar to every inquiry into probable cause—is whether all the facts surrounding a dog's alert, viewed through the lens of common sense, would make a reasonably prudent person think that a search would reveal contraband or evidence of a crime. A sniff is up to snuff when it meets that test.[98]

Applying that test to the drug dog's sniff in the case at hand, the Court found that it had been satisfied and ruled that there was probable cause to search the defendant's vehicle.[99]

Wiretapping, Eavesdropping, Access to Stored Electronic Communications, and Related Issues

(See page 365 for case summaries on this topic.)

Overview

In 2015, the School of Government published *Digital Evidence*, a book authored by faculty member Jeffrey B. Welty. This valuable resource covers the following topics:

- Search warrants for digital devices
- Warrantless searches of digital devices

---

93. Castro v. State, 755 So. 2d 657 (Fla. Dist. Ct. App. 1999) (use of drug dog to sniff vehicle's interior did not exceed scope of consent to search vehicle; defendant did not indicate to officers that his consent to search did not encompass the use of a drug dog and did not object when the dog began to search); United States v. Gonzalez-Basulto, 898 F.2d 1011 (5th Cir. 1990) (defendant did not object to use of dog to search interior of trailer of tractor trailer truck).

94. Illinois v. Caballes, 543 U.S. 405 (2005) (proper use of drug dog during traffic stop); State v. Branch, 177 N.C. App. 104 (2006) (proper use of drug dog at checkpoint when reasonable suspicion supported additional detention beyond initial stop at checkpoint).

95. *See* Rodriguez v. United States, 135 S. Ct. 1609 (2015), discussed in Chapter 2. *See also* State v. Euceda-Valle, 182 N.C. App. 268 (2007) (officer had reasonable suspicion to detain defendant after issuing warning ticket for speeding so drug dog could sniff vehicle's exterior).

96. 133 S. Ct. 1050 (2013).

97. *Id.* at 1053 (citations omitted).

---

98. *Id.* at 1058.

99. For an analysis of *Harris*, see Jeff Welty, *Supreme Court: Alert by a Trained or Certified Drug Dog Normally Provides Probable Cause*, NC CRIM. L. BLOG (Feb. 20, 2013), http://nccriminallaw.sog.unc.edu/?p=4111.

- Law enforcement access to and interception of electronic communications, including phone calls, emails, and text messages
- GPS tracking
- Admissibility of electronic evidence, including authentication, best evidence rule, and hearsay

Officers should be aware that the legal issues discussed in this section are complex and have been subject to different interpretations by courts.[100] Officers who are unsure of the legality of their proposed investigative activity may wish to consult their agency's legal advisor or other legal resource.[101]

Federal law[102] prohibits law enforcement officers of state and local governments from using devices to intercept—without consent of one of the parties to the communication—wire, oral, or electronic communications,[103] unless state law permits a device's use. These communications include telephone and cell phone calls, non-telephone conversations when the parties have a reasonable expectation of privacy, and real-time transmission of email and text messages. The North Carolina General Assembly has enacted legislation to permit officers to intercept communications with a state court order, but under limited circumstances.[104] Only the attorney general of North Carolina or his or her designee may apply for an order authorizing a state or local law enforcement agency to engage in a permitted interception; however, district attorneys and state and local law enforcement agencies may request that the attorney general apply for an order.[105] The attorney general must apply for an order from a judicial review panel composed of three judges appointed by the chief justice of the North Carolina Supreme Court. This panel is the only judicial body that may issue an order authorizing electronic surveillance—individual judges may not do so. (Hereafter, this order will be referred to as an extraordinary court order.) The legislation contains detailed provisions about the issuance and implementation of interception orders and the disclosure and use of intercepted communications.

Federal and state laws provide for criminal penalties and civil damages for unlawful interceptions of wire, oral, or electronic communications.[106] Exclusionary rules differ depending on the type of unlawful interception.[107]

---

100. The Fifth Circuit in *Steve Jackson Games, Inc. v. United States Secret Service*, 36 F.3d 457, 462 (5th Cir.1994), stated that the federal wiretapping law "is famous (if not infamous) for its lack of clarity." The Ninth Circuit in *United States v. Smith*, 155 F.3d 1051, 1055 (9th Cir. 1998), noted that the intersection of the federal wiretapping law and the federal stored communications law "is a complex, often convoluted, area of the law."

101. For a comprehensive discussion of pertinent issues, see the following publications and their annual supplements or pocket parts, if available: CLIFFORD S. FISHMAN & ANNE T. MCKENNA, WIRETAPPING AND EAVESDROPPING IN THE INTERNET AGE (3d ed. 2007) (annual loose-leaf updates through 2015–16); 2 WAYNE R. LAFAVE ET AL., CRIMINAL PROCEDURE §§ 4.1 through 4.9 (3d ed. 2007); SEARCHING AND SEIZING COMPUTERS AND OBTAINING ELECTRONIC EVIDENCE IN CRIMINAL INVESTIGATIONS (United States Department of Justice, 2009) (hereafter, Searching and Seizing Computers), www.justice.gov/criminal-ccips/ccips-documents-and-reports.

102. *See* 18 U.S.C. §§ 2510 through 2522.

103. For the definitions of *intercept, wire communication, oral communication,* and *electronic communication*, see 18 U.S.C. §§ 2510(1), (2), (4), and (12) and G.S. 15A-286(8), (13), (17), and (21). *Intercept* means the aural or other acquisition of the contents of any wire, electronic, or oral communication through the use of any electronic, mechanical, or other device. *Electronic, mechanical, or other device* is defined in 18 U.S.C. § 2510(5) and G.S. 15A-286(7).

104. *See* G.S. 15A-286 through -298.

105. *See* G.S. 15A-292.

106. *See, e.g.,* 18 U.S.C. §§ 2511, 2520, 2701, & 2707; G.S. 15A-287, -288, & -296. A plaintiff who sues for civil damages for intercepting an oral communication must prove that officers committed the act "willfully." Wright v. Town of Zebulon, 202 N.C. App. 540 (2010) (police department's interception of one of its own officer's oral communications in his vehicle to check if officer was tipping-off drug dealers about confidential police department information did not violate North Carolina's Electronic Surveillance Act because interception was not committed willfully).

107. G.S. 15A-294(g) provides that an "aggrieved party" (see G.S. 15A-286(1) and *Alderman v. United States*, 394 U.S. 165 (1969)) may move to suppress the contents of any intercepted wire, oral, or electronic communications, or evidence derived from the interception, on the grounds that (1) the communication was unlawfully intercepted, (2) the order of authorization for the interception was insufficient on its face, or (3) the interception was not made in conformity with the order of authorization. The federal statutory exclusionary rule applies only to the unlawful interception of wire or oral communications; unlike G.S. 15A-294(g), it does not apply to an interception of electronic communications. 18 U.S.C. §§ 2515, 2518(10). However, if an interception of an electronic communication violated the Fourth Amendment, the application of the Fourth Amendment's exclusionary rule would apply.

Federal appellate courts disagree as to whether evidence must be excluded under 18 U.S.C. §§ 2515 and 2518(10) if the government obtains evidence from a private party who unlawfully obtained evidence but without the government's involvement. (A majority of courts deciding the issue support

Wiretapping and Eavesdropping Law Exclusions

An officer or private person may use a device to intercept a wire, oral, or electronic communication if the officer or private person is a party to the communication or if one of the parties to the communication has given prior consent to the interception.[108]

---

exclusion.) *Compare* United States v. Vest, 813 F.2d 477 (1st Cir. 1987) (statutory exclusionary rule applies not only when the government obtains evidence as a result of violating federal wiretapping or eavesdropping laws but also when the government with "clean hands" (that is, the government was not involved in or did not procure the violation) receives evidence obtained by a private person who violated those laws); United States v. Crabtree, 565 F.3d 887 (4th Cir. 2009) (rejecting clean hands exception); *In re* Grand Jury, 111 F.3d 1066 (3d Cir. 1997) (rejecting clean hands exception); *and* Chandler v. U.S. Army, 125 F.3d 1296 (9th Cir. 1997) (similar ruling), *with* United States v. Murdock, 63 F.3d 1391 (6th Cir. 1995) (disagreeing with *United States v. Vest*, cited above, court ruled that statutory exclusionary rule does not apply to evidence that the government with "clean hands" receives from private person who obtained the evidence in violation of federal wiretapping and eavesdropping laws). *See also* United States v. Baftiri, 263 F.3d 856 (8th Cir. 2001) (evidence obtained through illegal wiretapping is admissible for impeachment purposes); Culbertson v. Culbertson, 143 F.3d 825 (4th Cir. 1998) (similar ruling).

North Carolina appellate courts have barred the use of illegally obtained evidence to obtain a search warrant, State v. Shaw, 103 N.C. App. 268 (1991), and in a divorce proceeding, Rickenbacker v. Rickenbacker, 290 N.C. 373 (1976) (court, however, specifically declined to decide whether illegally obtained evidence may be used for impeachment purposes). *But see* State v. McGriff, 151 N.C. App. 631 (2002) (inadvertent interception of defendant's telephone conversation with victim by person who was using her cordless telephone was not willful and therefore was not unlawful under G.S. 15A-287(a)(1) and 18 U.S.C. § 2511(1)(a); evidence of conversation was admissible); Kroh v. Kroh, 152 N.C. App. 347 (2002) (court adopted vicarious consent doctrine to permit interception of oral communications by one spouse of communications between other spouse and children under certain circumstances).

Only federal law regulates access to stored wire and electronic communications (18 U.S.C. §§ 2701 through 2711), discussed in the text on page 218. There is no statutory exclusionary rule for violations; *see* 18 U.S.C. § 2708; State v. Stitt, 201 N.C. App. 233 (2009); United States v. Meriwether, 917 F.2d 955 (6th Cir. 1990). Thus, evidence would be excluded at trial only if an officer violated the Fourth Amendment or other constitutional provisions.

108. 18 U.S.C. §§ 2511(2)(c), (d); G.S. 15A-287(a). Under 18 U.S.C. § 2511(2)(d), a private person may intercept a communication under the same circumstances as an officer but not if the communication is intercepted for the purpose of committing any criminal or tortuous act in violation of the United States Constitution or federal or state law.

Interceptions of communications through ham and CB radio broadcasts and other transmissions—such as police and fire—that are readily accessible to the public are specifically excluded from federal and state wiretapping and eavesdropping laws.[109]

Intercepting Phone Conversations
Intercepting Phone Conversations—Generally

Officers may not use a device to intercept—by listening to or recording—a phone conversation without an extraordinary court order unless one of the parties to the conversation has given prior consent to the interception. This prohibition applies to conversations on landline and cell phones, including the radio portion of a cordless phone communication that is transmitted between the cordless phone handset and its base unit.[110] Even though conversations on some of these phones may be readily intercepted by scanners and radios that many people own and use, it is a violation of both federal and state law to do so without an extraordinary court order.

Federal and state law and the Fourth Amendment are not violated if a party to a phone conversation consents to its interception with a recording or listening device.[111] For example, officers lawfully may record or listen to a phone conversation between their informant and a murder suspect when the informant has given prior consent to their recording or listening to the conversation. Officers also may record a phone conversation between themselves and another party to the conversation.[112] Note that offi-

---

109. 18 U.S.C. § 2511(2)(g); G.S. 15A-287(b)(2).

110. Federal legislation enacted in 1994 deleted the exclusion of cordless telephone communications from the definitions of *wire communication* and *electronic communication* in 18 U.S.C. §§ 2510(1) and (12). Pub. L. No. 103-414, § 202(a), 108 Stat. 4290 (Oct. 25, 1994).

111. 18 U.S.C. § 2511(2)(c); G.S. 15A-287(a); State v. Branch, 288 N.C. 514 (1975); United States v. Moncivals, 401 F.3d 751 (6th Cir. 2005); United States v. Miller, 720 F.2d 227 (1st Cir. 1983); Griggs-Ryan v. Smith, 904 F.2d 112 (1st Cir. 1990) (implied consent to record incoming phone calls).

112. Officers also do not violate federal law or the Fourth Amendment (1) if they answer a telephone while lawfully in a person's home, even if they misrepresent their identity (*see, e.g.,* United States v. Passarella, 788 F.2d 377 (6th Cir. 1986); United States v. Sangineto-Miranda, 859 F.2d 1501 (6th Cir. 1988)); (2) when they overhear clearly audible transmissions on an answering machine activated by telephone calls received while the officers are lawfully in the room where it is located (they also may replay and transcribe the tapes after lawfully seizing the answering machine; *see* United States v. Upton, 763 F. Supp.

cers may not communicate surreptitiously with defendants when doing so would violate the defendants' Sixth Amendment right to counsel; this subject is discussed in Chapter 5.

Intercepting Phone Conversations of Prisoners or Inmates

Intercepting or recording phone calls of prisoners and inmates has been generally upheld under either (1) an implied consent theory, when prisoners or inmates have been notified that their calls are subject to monitoring or recording, or (2) exceptions set out in federal and state wiretapping laws.[113] Intercepting or recording conversa-

tions within prisons and jails will not be discussed here; consult the cases and legal resource listed in the accompanying footnote.[114]

Searching Cell Phone Incident to Arrest

The United States Supreme Court in *Riley v. California*[115] ruled that the search incident to arrest exception to the search warrant requirement did not apply to a search of

---

232 (S.D. Ohio 1991)); or (3) when they overhear and record a person's telephone conversation when that person clearly realizes that officers, standing near the person, can hear every spoken word; *see* People v. Siripongs, 754 P.2d 1306 (Cal. 1988).

113. United States v. Hammond, 286 F.3d 189 (4th Cir. 2002) (taping of prisoner's telephone calls was lawful for two reasons: (1) law enforcement exception under 18 U.S.C. § 2510(5)(a)(ii), and (2) prisoner consented to taping based on signed consent form acknowledging that all calls may be monitored and recorded and that use of telephone constitutes consent to monitoring); State v. Hocutt, 177 N.C. App. 341 (2006) (while in jail, defendant made incriminating statements over the phone to his girlfriend and to his brother, which were recorded pursuant to jail policy; inmates receive an informational handbook concerning this policy; notices are posted in the cell blocks telling inmates that their telephone calls are monitored; and before being connected, both the caller and the person being called hear a recorded warning that "all calls are subject to monitoring and recording," except for "attorney calls"; court ruled that the defendant's recorded jail telephone conversations were properly obtained under the Fourth, Sixth, and Fourteenth Amendments); State v. Price, 170 N.C. App. 57 (2005) (while in jail awaiting trial, defendant placed telephone calls to his mother; the jail's phone system played, for all outgoing calls, a recording heard by both parties to the call that stated in pertinent part: "This call is subject to monitoring and recording"; these calls were recorded, as were all inmate calls at the jail, and introduced into evidence at the defendant's trial; court ruled that the defendant impliedly consented under both federal and state law to the monitoring and recording of the telephone calls); State v. Troy, 198 N.C. App. 396 (2009) (inmate impliedly consented to recording of telephone calls because he had been given notice that calls were subject to monitoring and recording when he had made prior calls); United States v. Eggleston, 165 F.3d 624 (8th Cir. 1999) (prisoner signed statement noting that all telephone calls were subject to monitoring and recording; prisoner consented to monitoring and recording); United States v. Workman, 80 F.3d 688 (2d Cir. 1996) (prisoner's consent to monitoring and recording of telephone calls implied when prisoner notified that calls may be monitored); United States v. Van Poyck, 77

F.3d 285 (9th Cir. 1996) (prisoner has no reasonable expectation of privacy under Fourth Amendment for telephone calls; recording of calls permitted under exceptions to federal wiretapping law); United States v. Noriega, 917 F.2d 1543 (11th Cir. 1990) (court remanded case to district court to determine if inmate had agreed to recording of all his telephone conversations, including those with his attorneys); United States v. Willoughby, 860 F.2d 15 (2d Cir. 1988) (inmate, a pretrial detainee, impliedly and expressly consented to interception and recording of telephone conversations when sign above telephone informed him that all conversations were monitored; no reasonable expectation of privacy under Fourth Amendment for inmate's telephone calls); United States v. Sababu, 891 F.2d 1308 (7th Cir. 1989) (telephone caller outside prison had no reasonable expectation of privacy in telephone conversation with prisoner). *But see* Campiti v. Walonis, 611 F.2d 387 (1st Cir. 1979) (monitoring of telephone call by inmate did not fit within any exemption of federal wiretapping law; monitoring was not done according to usual procedure in prison unit). *See also* Clifford S. Fishman & Anne T. McKenna, Wiretapping and Eavesdropping §§ 6:42 through 6:52 (3d ed. 2007) (annual loose-leaf updates through 2015–16).

Prison and jail policies generally exclude monitoring and recording telephone calls between prisoners or inmates and their lawyers to protect the attorney–client privilege and the Sixth Amendment right to counsel.

114. United States v. Harrelson, 754 F.2d 1153 (5th Cir. 1985) (recording of conversation between prisoner and visitor did not violate federal wiretapping law); United States v. Willoughby, 860 F.2d 15 (2d Cir. 1988) (recording of conversation between two inmates did not violate federal wiretapping law); State v. Rollins, 363 N.C. 232 (2009) (prisoner did not have reasonable expectation of privacy in conversation with wife in prison's visiting area); Clifford S. Fishman & Anne T. McKenna, Wiretapping and Eavesdropping in the Internet Age §§ 6:53 through 6:55 (3d ed. 2007) (annual loose-leaf updates through 2015–16); 4 Wayne R. LaFave, Search and Seizure: A Treatise on the Fourth Amendment § 10.9(d) (5th ed. 2012).

115. 134 S. Ct. 2473 (2014). Two separate cases were subsumed under this name, and both involved officers who examined electronic data on cell phones without a search warrant as a search incident to arrest.

The discussion of *Riley* in the text is substantially derived from Jeff Welty, *Supreme Court: Can't Search Cell Phones Incident to Arrest*, NC Crim. L. Blog

a cell phone.[116] The Court stated that searches incident to arrest generally are justified (1) to ensure that the arrestee does not have a weapon and (2) to prevent the arrestee from destroying evidence. Cell phone searches do not implicate those concerns. "[O]fficers remain free to examine the physical aspects of a phone to ensure that it will not be used as a weapon,"[117] but the data on the phone does not pose a risk of physical harm. And there is little risk that the data on a phone will be destroyed by the arrestee.

The government had argued that even seized phones could be locked or remotely wiped if not inspected immediately, but the Court found little reason to believe that these practices were prevalent or could be remedied by a search incident to arrest. Further, the risk of such practices can be managed by using Faraday bags (which block the radio waves that cell phones use to communicate) and other tools. Thus, the Court found little justification for allowing phones to be searched incident to arrest.

The Court also found a strong privacy interest militating against such warrantless searches. It noted that phones often contain vast quantities of data, making a search intrusive far beyond the mere fact of arrest itself and far beyond the level of intrusion associated with more traditional searches of pockets, wallets, and purses incident to arrest. Many phones can access data stored on remote servers, making a search extend beyond the immediate area of the arrestee. Emphasizing the need to establish a clear and workable rule, the Court therefore categorically exempted cell phones from the search incident to arrest doctrine.

How does the *Riley* ruling affect law enforcement practices beyond the need for a search warrant to search a cell phone incident to arrest?

First, the ruling clearly would apply to other data devices that a person possesses when arrested, such as tablets and laptops.

Second, if an officer has probable cause to believe that a cell phone or other data device contains evidence of a crime, the officer may warrantlessly seize the phone[118]

but must apply for a search warrant to search it, either by physically appearing before a judicial official or by applying remotely through an audio and video transmission under G.S. 15A-245(a)(3).[119]

If there is evidence supporting a Fourth Amendment exception to the search warrant requirement, such as exigent circumstances or consent to search, then an officer may warrantlessly seize the cell phone and search it. However, the Court made clear that exigent circumstances are not satisfied based merely on the possibility of remote wiping of data, locking of a phone, or data encryption—absent evidence, for example, of an imminent remote wiping attempt. The Court stated that if officers seize a phone in an unlocked state, they may be able to disable a phone's automatic-lock feature to prevent the phone from locking and encrypting data. Exigent circumstances may exist if there is an immediate need to search a cell phone to stop a serious crime in progress, such as kidnapping, violent acts, possible detonation of a bomb, or an imminent threat to officers.

Consent to search is another exception to the search warrant requirement. Because of the large and diverse amount of data that may be contained in a phone, an officer should make clear to the suspect the scope of the proposed search when obtaining consent. For example, an officer seeking a broad search could ask for consent to conduct "a complete search of the phone," while a more narrow request might ask for consent to search the "list of recent calls" or another limited kind of data.

The Court's opinion suggests that data stored in "the cloud" is protected by the Fourth Amendment. One of its justifications as to why cell phone searches are more intrusive than searches of physical objects is a phone's possible connection to a remote server (the cloud) that contains the phone's data. If this feature makes phone searches more intrusive, it may follow that the remote data is generally subject to a Fourth Amendment expectation of privacy.[120]

(June 26, 2014), http://nccriminallaw.sog.unc.edu/supreme-court-cant-search-cell-phones-incident-to-arrest/.

116. The North Carolina Supreme Court had previously permitted such a search. State v. Wilkerson, 363 N.C. 382 (2009).

117. 134 S. Ct. at 2485.

118. The Court clearly indicated that an arrestee's phone may be seized without a search warrant while an officer seeks a search warrant.

119. Officers need to check whether their respective counties have the capacity and approval to consider a search warrant application as set out in the statute cited in the text.

120. That may forecast a reconsideration in whole or in part of the third-party doctrine in cases such as *United States v. Miller*, 425 U.S. 435 (1976) (depositor has no reasonable expectation of privacy in copies of checks and other bank records that are in bank's possession), at least as it applies to privacy-sensitive information.

Whether the *Riley* ruling applies to cases that were final when *Riley* was decided[121] and the application of the Fourth Amendment's exclusionary rule to officers' searches conducted before the *Riley* ruling are discussed in the blog posts cited in the accompanying footnote.[122]

In a post-*Riley* case, the North Carolina Court of Appeals in *State v. Clyburn*[123] ruled that *Riley* applied to the digital contents of a car's Garmin GPS device in the pants pocket of a defendant who had been arrested. The court reasoned that although a GPS device does not store as much information as a cell phone, a person's expectation of privacy in the digital contents of a GPS device outweighs the government's interests in officer safety and the destruction of evidence.

Intercepting Oral Communications

An *oral communication* is essentially defined under federal and state law as an oral communication uttered by a person who has a reasonable expectation of privacy (note that this is the same standard as under the Fourth Amendment)[124] that the communication is not subject to interception. Thus, for example, federal and state law prohibit using a device,[125] such as a recorder or transmitter, to

make a nonconsensual interception of oral communications in a home or other place, such as an office,[126] where a person may have a reasonable expectation of privacy. Federal and state law also appear to prohibit the use of a parabolic microphone to listen from a distance to a quiet conversation between two people on a park bench.[127] On the other hand, a nonconsensual recording of a speech made in a public park or at an open city council meeting would not violate federal or state law.

Courts in other jurisdictions have uniformly ruled that officers may make a nonconsensual recording of conversations between two arrestees in the officers' law enforcement vehicle, because the arrestees do not have a

---

121. The date of the *Riley* ruling was June 25, 2014.

122. Jessica Smith, *Riley and Retroactivity*, NC CRIM. L. BLOG (July 29, 2014), http://nccriminallaw.sog.unc.edu/?p=4872; Jeff Welty, *Riley and Good Faith*, NC CRIM. L. BLOG (July 30, 2014), http://nccriminallaw.sog.unc.edu/?p=4873.

123. ___ N.C. App. ___, 770 S.E.2d 689 (2015).

124. The statutory phrase in 18 U.S.C. § 2510(2) and identical G.S. 15A-286(17) ("oral communication uttered by a person exhibiting an expectation that such communication is not subject to interception under circumstances justifying such expectation") is equivalent to the reasonable expectation of privacy standard under the Fourth Amendment. *See* United States v. Turner, 209 F.3d 1198 (10th Cir. 2000). There is no reasonable expectation of privacy component in the definitions of *electronic* and *wire communications*.

125. *Electronic, mechanical, or other device* means any device or apparatus that can be used to intercept a wire, oral, or electronic communication, with some exceptions. 18 U.S.C. § 2510(5) and G.S. 15A-286(7). Federal and state law is not violated if a device is not used. *See* United States v. McLeod, 493 F.2d 1186 (7th Cir. 1974) (officer's unaided listening to defendant's conversation in public telephone booth, while officer stood four feet away from booth, did not violate federal law or Fourth Amendment). Officers who listen on an extension telephone without the consent of the parties to the conversation may violate federal law, although an exemption exists when law enforcement officers do so in the ordinary course of their duties. *See* 18 U.S.C. § 2510(5)(a)(ii); United States v. Paul, 614

F.2d 115 (6th Cir. 1980); State v. Page, 386 N.W.2d 330 (Minn. App. 1986).

126. United States v. McIntyre, 582 F.2d 1221 (9th Cir. 1978) (officers violated federal law by placing microphone and transmitter in office of assistant chief of police). Cases on secretly taping a defendant and another person in a law enforcement interview room include *Belmer v. Commonwealth*, 553 S.E.2d 123 (Va. App. 2001) (secret recording of defendant's conversation with her mother and boyfriend in police interview room did not violate the defendant's reasonable expectation of privacy); *State v. Munn*, 56 S.W.3d 486 (Tenn. 2001) (secret recording of defendant's conversations with his parents in a police interview room violated the Fourth Amendment and federal wiretapping law; no evidence was offered that practice of recording conversations was justified by security reasons); *State v. Howard*, 728 A.2d 1178 (Del. Super. 1998) (secret recording of defendant's conversations with his spouse in police interview room violated reasonable expectation of privacy because of marital relationship; no evidence was offered that recording was justified by security reasons); *State v. Wilkins*, 868 P.2d 1231 (Idaho 1994) (secret taping of conversation between defendant and his parents while alone in police department booking room did not violate defendant's reasonable expectation of privacy or federal wiretapping law despite officer's promise to turn off tape recorder before leaving room); and *State v. Hauss*, 688 P.2d 1051 (Ariz. App. 1984) (secret taping of defendant's conversation with girlfriend in police interview room did not violate defendant's reasonable expectation of privacy or federal wiretapping law).

127. Even in public, people may have a reasonable expectation of privacy that their quiet conversations will not be intercepted by a device. *See generally* People v. Lesslie, 939 P.2d 443 (Colo. Ct. App. 1996) (unlawful to place listening device on windowsill of open window of men's restroom of bar and listen to conversations from nearby motel, despite fact that person outside in alley next to windowsill could be in position to overhear conversation; people in restroom would realize that window was open, know that someone was walking by alley, and lower their voices or terminate conversation); 1 WAYNE R. LAFAVE, SEARCH AND SEIZURE: A TREATISE ON THE FOURTH AMENDMENT § 2.2(f) (5th ed. 2012).

reasonable expectation of privacy that their conversations are not subject to interception.[128] North Carolina courts would likely agree with these rulings.

Federal and state law and the Fourth Amendment are not violated if a party to an oral communication consents to its interception with the use of a recording or transmitting device. For example, officers lawfully may record or listen to a conversation between their informant and a suspected drug dealer when the informant has agreed to be fitted with a device that records or transmits the conversation, even if the conversation occurs in the privacy of the suspected drug dealer's home.[129] Note that officers may not communicate surreptitiously with defendants when doing so would violate the defendants' Sixth Amendment right to counsel. This subject is discussed in Chapter 5.

Using Throw Phone during Emergency

Officers may wish to use a so-called throw phone[130] during an emergency. For example: A suspect is in a house with several hostages and is threatening to kill them. Officers want to open an avenue of communication with the suspect by means of a phone that permits the suspect and officers to talk with each other. The phone may also be configured as a listening device, secretly capturing conversations through a microphone in the phone that operates even when the phone is turned off. It can be argued that the microphone is a device that intercepts an oral communication and thus is prohibited by federal and state law without an extraordinary court order.[131] Both

federal and state law provide a means to obtain emergency approval from specified federal or state officials to use a device to intercept wire, oral, and electronic communications, as long as an official applies within 48 hours thereafter to an appropriate court for authorization.[132] One ground for emergency approval is an immediate danger of death or serious injury to a person. Under procedures established by the North Carolina Department of Justice, the head of a law enforcement agency must make an emergency request to the attorney general or his or her designee. This request is usually initiated when the agency head contacts a State Bureau of Investigation district office, which will communicate with the attorney general's designee.[133]

---

128. United States v. Dunbar, 553 F.3d 48 (1st Cir. 2009); State v. Turner, 641 S.E.2d 436 (S.C. 2007); State v. Wilson, 169 S.W.3d 870 (Mo. Ct. App. 2005); United States v. Turner, 209 F.3d 1198 (10th Cir. 2000); United States v. Clark, 22 F.3d 799 (8th Cir. 1994); United States v. McKinnon, 985 F.2d 525 (11th Cir. 1993); State v. Ramirez, 535 N.W.2d 847 (S.D. 1995); State v. Smith, 641 So. 2d 849 (Fla. 1994); People v. Crowson, 660 P.2d 389 (Cal. 1983); People v. Seaton, 194 Cal. Rptr. 33 (Cal. App. 1983); Brown v. State, 349 So. 2d 1196 (Fla. Dist. Ct. App. 1977); State v. Lucero, 628 P.2d 696 (N.M. Ct. App. 1981); K.F. v. State, 797 P.2d 1006 (Okla. Crim. App. 1990).

129. United States v. White, 401 U.S. 745 (1970); State v. Levan, 326 N.C. 155 (1990) (no violation of state constitution); On Lee v. United States, 343 U.S. 747 (1952); Lopez v. United States, 373 U.S. 427 (1963); United States v. Caceres, 440 U.S. 741 (1979).

130. It is commonly known as a throw phone because it is sometimes thrown through an open window to a suspect.

131. On the other hand, because the term "oral communication" is consistent with a reasonable expectation of privacy

under the Fourth Amendment, United States v. Turner, 209 F.3d 1198 (10th Cir. 2000), one can argue that even if a hostage taker subjectively believed that his conversations with hostages or other accomplices in a house would remain private from interception, that belief is not one that society would recognize as reasonable. *See generally* Illinois v. Rakas, 439 U.S. 128, 143 n.12 (1978); Minnesota v. Carter, 525 U.S. 83 (1998). If a court adopted this argument, using a throw phone as a listening device would not be subject to federal and state wiretapping and eavesdropping laws. However, because there is no case law on this issue and considering that violations of federal and state laws are subject to criminal and civil penalties, officers may want to seek an extraordinary court order through the North Carolina Department of Justice, as explained in the text.

132. 18 U.S.C. § 2518(7); G.S. 15A-291(b). There are few cases on these statutory provisions; none have involved throw phones. Nabozny v. Marshall, 781 F.2d 83 (6th Cir. 1986) (upholding emergency phone wiretaps when three suspects kidnapped bank manager and sought to extort bank moneys); United States v. Couch, 666 F. Supp. 1414 (N.D. Cal. 1987) (finding no emergency to support phone wiretaps when suspects were planning bank robbery but it was not imminent); United States v. Duffey, 2009 WL 2356156 (N.D. Tex. 2009) (unpublished) (upholding emergency cell phone wiretap when suspects were about to commit violent robberies).

133. A designated attorney in the North Carolina Department of Justice is on call at all times to receive requests for emergency authorizations. The agency head must complete a form (SBI-100) setting out the reasons for and the type of interception, as well as other information. If the attorney approves the request and the interception is initiated, the department within 48 hours will seek authorization of the interception before a three-judge panel of North Carolina judges, as previously described in the text on page 211.

Silent Video Surveillance

North Carolina law enforcement officers may conduct video surveillance without violating federal or state wiretapping or eavesdropping laws as long as the surveillance does not also intercept oral communications.[134] However, a search warrant will be needed when officers conduct silent video surveillance directed at or in a place where a person has a reasonable expectation of privacy, unless one of the participants present during the surveillance has given consent. For example, officers will need a search warrant to place a silent video camera on a utility pole to record all activities in a person's backyard when the backyard is surrounded by a 10-foot-high fence.[135] On the other hand, a silent video camera directed at people on a public street or sidewalk to observe possible drug transactions does not interfere with anyone's reasonable expectation of privacy and may be used without a search warrant or other legal authorization.[136]

Courts have imposed stringent requirements for such a search warrant or court order; therefore, officers should consider consultation with an attorney before applying for one.[137]

---

134. United States v. Falls, 34 F.3d 674 (8th Cir. 1994) (search warrant for silent video surveillance of apartment); United States v. Koyomejian, 970 F.2d 536 (9th Cir. 1992) (en banc) (court order for silent video surveillance of business office); United States v. Mesa-Rincon, 911 F.2d 1433 (10th Cir. 1990) (court order for silent video surveillance of warehouse); United States v. Biasucci, 786 F.2d 504 (2d Cir. 1986) (search warrant for silent video surveillance of business office); United States v. Torres, 751 F.2d 875 (7th Cir. 1984) (search warrant for silent video surveillance of safe houses used by terrorists).

135. United States v. Cuevas-Sanchez, 821 F.2d 248 (5th Cir. 1987).

136. State v. Augafa, 992 P.2d 723 (Haw. Ct. App. 1999). Other cases involving video surveillance include *United States v. Vankesteren*, 553 F.3d 286 (4th Cir. 2009) (motion-activated video surveillance in open fields of defendant's property did not violate his reasonable expectation of privacy); *Brannum v. Overton County School Board*, 516 F.3d 489 (6th Cir. 2008) (video surveillance and taping of middle school students changing clothes in locker rooms violated their Fourth Amendment rights); *United States v. Gonzales*, 328 F.3d 543 (9th Cir. 2003) (hospital employee did not have reasonable expectation of privacy in hospital mail room to challenge video surveillance); *Cowles v. State*, 23 P.3d 1168 (Alaska 2001) (video surveillance of defendant in university box office did not violate reasonable expectation of privacy); *United States v. Nerber*, 222 F.3d 597 (9th Cir. 2000) (video surveillance of defendant in hotel room violated reasonable expectation of privacy); *United States v. Jackson*, 213 F.3d 1269 (10th Cir. 2000), *judgment vacated and case remanded for consideration of unrelated issue*, 531 U.S. 1033 (2000) (video surveillance of activities occurring outside residence that were visible to people who passed by did not violate reasonable expectation of privacy); *State v. McLellan*, 744 A.2d 611 (N.H. 1999) (video surveillance

of school custodian in classroom did not violate reasonable expectation of privacy); *State v. Augafa*, 992 P.2d 723 (Haw. Ct. App. 1999) (video surveillance of defendant in street did not violate reasonable expectation of privacy); *United States v. McIver*, 186 F.3d 1119 (9th Cir. 1999) (video surveillance of defendant's presence near marijuana plants in national forest did not violate reasonable expectation of privacy); *State v. Holden*, 964 P.2d 318 (Utah Ct. App. 1998) (video surveillance of defendant's front yard open to public view did not violate reasonable expectation of privacy); *Vega-Rodriguez v. Puerto Rico Telephone Co.*, 110 F.3d 174 (1st Cir. 1997) (video surveillance of open and undifferentiated work area did not violate reasonable expectation of privacy); *Sacramento County Deputy Sheriffs' Association v. County of Sacramento*, 59 Cal. Rptr. 2d 834 (Cal. Ct. App. 1996) (video surveillance of deputy sheriffs in county jail's release office did not violate reasonable expectation of privacy); *Thompson v. Johnson County Community College*, 930 F. Supp. 501 (D. Kan. 1996), *aff'd*, 531 U.S. 1033 (10th Cir. 1997) (video surveillance of open security personnel locker area did not violate reasonable expectation of privacy); *State v. Thomas*, 642 N.E.2d 240 (Ind. Ct. App. 1995) (video surveillance of camp store in which defendant worked violated reasonable expectation of privacy); *State v. Bonnell*, 856 P.2d 1265 (Haw. 1993) (video surveillance of employee break room violated reasonable expectation of privacy); *United States v. Taketa*, 923 F.2d 665 (9th Cir. 1991) (video surveillance of law enforcement officer's private office violated reasonable expectation of privacy); and *Thornton v. University Civil Service Merit Board*, 507 N.E.2d 1262 (Ill. App. Ct. 1987) (video surveillance of police department office shared by officers did not violate reasonable expectation of privacy).

137. *See* United States v. Falls, 34 F.3d 674 (8th Cir. 1994); United States v. Koyomejian, 970 F.2d 536 (9th Cir. 1992); United States v. Mesa-Rincon, 911 F.2d 1433 (10th Cir. 1990); United States v. Cuevas-Sanchez, 821 F.2d 248 (5th Cir. 1987); United States v. Biasucci, 786 F.2d 504 (2d Cir. 1986); United States v. Torres, 751 F.2d 875 (7th Cir. 1984). For example, the court in *United States v. Falls*, cited above, ruled that a search warrant (or court order) authorizing silent video surveillance, based on probable cause, is sufficient to satisfy the Fourth Amendment if (1) the issuing official finds that normal investigative procedures have been tried and have failed or reasonably appear unlikely to succeed; (2) the warrant contains a particular description of the type of activity sought to be videotaped and a statement of the particular offense to which it relates; (3) the warrant does not allow a period of surveillance longer than is necessary, or in any event no longer than 30 days; and (4) the warrant requires that the surveillance be conducted in such a way as to minimize videotaping of activity not otherwise subject to surveillance. *See also* 1 Wayne R. LaFave, Search and Seizure: A Treatise on the Fourth Amendment § 2.2(f), at 678–79 (5th ed. 2012).

An analysis of video surveillance cases before and after the GPS case of *United States v. Jones*[138] (installation of a GPS tracking device on a suspect's vehicle was a Fourth Amendment search because it involved a physical intrusion into the vehicle to obtain information), discussed earlier in this chapter, is provided in a blog post cited in the accompanying footnote.[139]

Access to Stored Electronic Communications (Email and Text Messages) and Related Information

This topic is comprehensively discussed in the School of Government publication cited in the accompanying footnote.[140] The discussion here is a general overview of issues that are complex, evolving with rapid technological changes, and sometimes subject to conflicting court rulings. The United States Supreme Court and the North Carolina appellate courts have not issued many rulings on these issues.

Officers may not intercept and access the contents[141] of an electronic communication (for example, an email or text message) during its real-time transmission without an extraordinary court order, as described above for the interception of phone conversations.[142] However, an officer ordinarily does not need an extraordinary court

order once the communication has been transmitted. Under federal law—which solely regulates the legal issues discussed in this section—if a communication has been stored by an electronic communications service (for example, an Internet service provider providing services to the public)[143] for 180 days or less, a search warrant is necessary to access its contents.[144] If a communication has been stored for more than 180 days, then an officer may access the contents of the communication by obtaining a search warrant or, with notice to the recipient of the communication, by obtaining a subpoena or a court order[145] that is based on a standard less than probable cause.[146] The law allows delayed notice to the recipient under certain circumstances.[147] Federal law likely makes a North Carolina search warrant (and perhaps a court order based on probable cause as well) legally sufficient

---

138. 132 S. Ct. 945 (2012).

139. Jeff Welty, *Video Surveillance Cameras*, NC CRIM. L. BLOG (Dec. 12, 2013), http://nccriminallaw.sog.unc.edu/?p=4570.

140. JEFFREY B. WELTY, DIGITAL EVIDENCE (UNC School of Government, 2015) (*hereafter*, DIGITAL EVIDENCE). Because the legal issues discussed in this publication are still evolving, the reader may want to check for future blog posts at http://nccriminallaw.sog.unc.edu/ by typing a pertinent term in the search box.

141. What precisely constitutes the contents of an email (or text message) has not been settled. The actual message and subject line are contents, while noncontent information would likely include the Internet Protocol (IP) addresses, the email addresses, and the volume of files transferred. See the discussion in 2 WAYNE R. LAFAVE ET AL., CRIMINAL PROCEDURE §§ 4.4(c), (d) (3d ed. 2007); *United States v. Forrester*, 512 F.3d 500 (9th Cir. 2008); and *In re Application of United States for an Order Authorizing Use of a Pen Register*, 396 F. Supp. 2d 45 (D. Mass. 2005).

142. The discussion in this section concerns obtaining information from a public service provider, such as AOL or Google. The laws are somewhat different for nonpublic service providers. *See* Jeffrey B. Welty, *Prosecution and Law Enforcement Access to Information about Electronic Communications* 15, ADMIN. OF JUST. BULL. 2009/05 (Oct. 2009), www.sog.unc.edu/sites/www.sog.unc.edu/files/reports/aojb0905.pdf.

143. *Id.*

144. 18 U.S.C. § 2703(a). For what constitutes "storage," see DIGITAL EVIDENCE, *supra* note 140, at 96.

The execution of a search warrant by faxing it to a service provider, which then retrieves the email messages without the officer's presence and sends them to the officer, does not violate the Fourth Amendment. United States v. Bach, 310 F.3d 1063 (8th Cir. 2002).

145. 18 U.S.C. § 2703(b). Under North Carolina law, the only kind of subpoena that may be issued before a criminal charge has been brought is an administrative subpoena. The State Bureau of Investigation (SBI) is the only North Carolina law enforcement agency that is authorized to issue an administrative subpoena. *See* G.S. 15A-298, which specially authorizes subpoenas to a communications common carrier or electronic communications service to compel records if the records (1) disclose information concerning local or long distance toll records or subscriber information and (2) are material to an active SBI criminal investigation.

If criminal charges have been brought, then a regular trial subpoena may be issued.

Before criminal charges are brought, non-SBI law enforcement officers will need to obtain a search warrant (which, of course, requires probable cause that a crime has been committed) or a court order from a superior court judge. It is uncertain whether a district court judge may issue a court order. *See* DIGITAL EVIDENCE, *supra* note 140, at 97. Because of the uncertainty, officers should seek a search warrant or court order from a superior court judge unless a legal advisor directs otherwise.

146. Federal law (18 U.S.C. § 2703(d)) provides that a federal or state court order, unlike a search warrant, only requires reasonable grounds to believe that the contents of the email or text message are relevant and material to an ongoing investigation.

147. See 18 U.S.C. § 2705.

to access the contents of a communication even though a service provider is located in another state.[148]

The constitutionality of using a court order based on less than probable cause or a subpoena to access the contents of an email or text message, discussed in the prior paragraph, is an evolving legal issue. One federal court of appeals has ruled that the Fourth Amendment requires a search warrant and that, to the extent that federal law allows access with a court order based on less than probable cause or a subpoena, federal law violates the Fourth Amendment.[149] Although this case is not binding on federal or state courts in North Carolina, the reader will need to be aware of future cases on this issue to determine whether this ruling will be adopted by other courts and affect law enforcement practice in North Carolina.[150] As a practical matter, using a search warrant or court order based on probable cause to obtain the contents of an email or text message is the safest course.

Other statutory provisions allow a law enforcement officer to obtain transactional and subscriber information[151] and permit service providers to voluntarily disclose certain information to officers.[152]

Access to Stored Messages in Voice Mailbox

Federal legislation enacted in 2001 effectively provided that an officer may obtain access to stored messages in a voice mailbox under the same conditions as access to stored electronic communications, discussed above.[153] Before this legislation was enacted, some courts had ruled that an extraordinary court order was necessary and others had ruled that the provisions concerning access to stored electronic communications governed.[154] Absent consent, an officer should obtain a search warrant to access stored messages.

Pen Registers and Trap and Trace Devices

A comprehensive discussion of this topic is available in the School of Government publication cited in the accompanying footnote.[155] The discussion here provides a general overview.

A *pen register* as defined in federal law is a device that records or decodes the numbers dialed or routing, addressing, or signaling information transmitted by an instrument or facility from which a wire or electronic communication is transmitted; instruments such as a landline or cellular telephone or computer are included.[156] The North Carolina law definition is not as comprehensive, but state judges still have the authority to issue orders under the federal definition, as explained in the publication cited in the accompanying footnote.[157] A

---

148. *See* Digital Evidence, *supra* note 140, at 97–98.

149. United States v. Warshak, 631 F.3d 266 (6th Cir. 2010). For an analysis of *Warshak* and related cases, see Digital Evidence, *supra* note 140, at 92–94.

150. Even if service providers are not located in states in which the *Warshak* ruling is binding (Kentucky, Michigan, Ohio, and Tennessee), they may insist on a search warrant in any event.

151. Under 18 U.S.C. § 2703(c)(1), a search warrant or court order (based on reasonable grounds as described in note 146, above), must be used to obtain transaction records, which would include the electronic address of a person who sent an email message to the subscriber. Under 18 U.S.C. § 2703(c)(2), an administrative subpoena, trial subpoena, search warrant, or court order is sufficient to obtain the name, address, local and long distance telephone records, telephone number or other subscriber number or identity, length of service of a subscriber of such service, and types of services the subscriber utilized. For a discussion of these issues, see Digital Evidence, *supra* note 140, at 100–103.

Notice to the subscriber is not required when obtaining transactional or subscriber information, no matter what legal process is used under this statute.

152. For example, a service provider may divulge the contents of a communication (1) to a law enforcement agency if the provider inadvertently obtained the communication and it appeared to pertain to the commission of a crime or (2) to a government entity (which would include a law enforcement agency) if the provider has a good faith belief that an emergency involving danger of death or serious physical injury to a

---

person requires disclosure without delay of communications concerning the emergency. 18 U.S.C. §§ 2702(b)(7) & (8).

153. Uniting and Strengthening America by Providing Appropriate Tools Required to Intercept and Obstruct Terrorism (USA PATRIOT ACT) Act of 2001, Pub. L. No. 107-56, § 209, 115 Stat. 272. Section 209 amended 18 U.S.C. §§ 2510(1), (14), and 2703(a) and (b). This legislation removed "electronic storage" from the definition of *wire communication* to specifically exclude voice mailbox messages from the definition. The legislative change is noted in *United States v. Councilman*, 418 F.3d 67 (1st Cir. 2005), and *Noel v. Hall*, 568 F.3d 743 (9th Cir. 2009). The legislation was to expire on December 31, 2005, but it was made permanent by Pub. L. No. 109-177, § 102(a), 120 Stat. 195.

154. See the discussion in Clifford S. Fishman & Anne T. McKenna, Wiretapping and Eavesdropping in the Internet Age § 2.21 (3d ed. 2007) (annual loose-leaf updates through 2015–16).

155. Digital Evidence, *supra* note 140, at 117–20.

156. Thus, a pen register may also be used to track all the addresses to which a particular computer user sends emails. *See* Digital Evidence, *supra* note 140, at 118.

157. Digital Evidence, *supra* note 140, at 118–22.

pen register is needed to obtain, for example, a list of all the addresses to which email is sent from a particular account.[158]

A *trap and trace device* as defined in federal law reveals the phone numbers of calls made to a phone or routing, addressing, or signaling information transmitted to a landline or cellular phone or a computer. The North Carolina law definition is not as comprehensive, but state judges still have the authority to issue orders under the federal definition, as explained in the publication cited in the accompanying footnote.[159]

Neither a pen register nor a trap and trace device intercepts the contents of oral, wire, or electronic communications, and, therefore, they are not regulated by federal or state wiretapping and eavesdropping laws.[160] Also, their use is not governed by the Fourth Amendment because the United States Supreme Court has ruled that people do not have a reasonable expectation of privacy in the phone numbers they dial on their phones.[161] However, state law requires officers to obtain a court order from a superior court judge before using a pen register or a trap and trace device.[162] A court order must be supported by reasonable suspicion that a person has committed a felony or a Class A1 or 1 misdemeanor and that the results from using the pen register or trap and trace device will materially aid in determining whether the person committed the offense.[163] A person who willfully and knowingly violates the law—by using a pen register or trap and trace device without a court order—is guilty of a Class 1 misdemeanor.[164]

A court order is not required when the phone customer consents to the phone company's installation of a pen register or trap and trace device.[165]

Access to Real-Time (Prospective) or Historical Cell-Site Location Information

A comprehensive discussion of this topic is available in the School of Government publication cited in the accompanying footnote.[166] The discussion here provides a general overview.

Officers may want to obtain real-time (prospective) or historical information about a particular cell phone's contacts with cell towers to determine a cell phone's approximate location. By doing so, they can track a suspect in real time or learn from a cell provider's records if a suspect was near a location where a crime was committed.

The case law is evolving concerning what sort of legal process is needed before an officer may access this information, and the United States Supreme Court has not issued rulings on these issues. A search warrant or court order based on probable cause may be necessary to obtain real-time cell-site location information (unless the United States Supreme Court or North Carolina appellate courts issue a ruling otherwise), and the publication cited in the accompanying footnote sets out the advantages of using a court order instead of a search warrant.[167]

The North Carolina Court of Appeals in *State v. Perry*[168] ruled that a court order based on the federal law standard, which is similar to reasonable suspicion, is sufficient to obtain historical cell-site location information.[169] The

---

158. Although state law only requires orders for devices placed on telephone lines, North Carolina law enforcement officers also must comply with federal law's more encompassing coverage. Note that North Carolina judges are authorized under federal law to issue orders for placing devices on non-telephone lines as well as telephone lines because state law does not bar judges from doing so. DIGITAL EVIDENCE, *supra* note 140, at 119.

159. DIGITAL EVIDENCE, *supra* note 140, at 120.

160. United States v. New York Tel. Co., 434 U.S. 159 (1977).

161. Smith v. Maryland, 442 U.S. 735 (1979). The ruling case likewise would likely apply to routing, addressing, and signaling information involved with emails, text messages, and the like. *See* DIGITAL EVIDENCE, *supra* note 140, at 120.

162. G.S. 15A-260 through -264. Although federal officers may more easily obtain orders under federal law requirements, North Carolina law enforcement officers must follow the more demanding state law requirements.

163. State law is more stringent than federal law in requiring reasonable suspicion of a felony or a Class A1 or 1 misdemeanor. Federal law (18 U.S.C. § 3123) only requires that the information likely to be obtained by the use of the device is relevant to an ongoing criminal investigation.

164. Because a violation of this law is not a constitutional violation (*see* Smith v. Maryland, 442 U.S. 735 (1979)), evidence obtained as a result of a violation would only be subject to the statutory exclusionary rule in G.S. 15A-974.

165. G.S. 15A-261(b)(3).

166. DIGITAL EVIDENCE, *supra* note 140, at 91–123.

167. DIGITAL EVIDENCE, *supra* note 140, at 110–15.

168. ___ N.C. App. ___, 776 S.E.2d 528 (2015). Courts in other jurisdictions are split on whether a search warrant or court order based on probable cause is constitutionally required. It is not unlikely that the United States Supreme Court will eventually decide the issue.

169. The standard under 18 U.S.C. § 2703(d) is specific and articulable facts showing there are reasonable grounds to believe that the records or information sought are relevant and material to an ongoing criminal investigation. The court order should be sought from a superior court judge. Of course, a search warrant or court order based on probable cause would

court concluded that obtaining such information is not a search under the Fourth Amendment, and thus officers need only satisfy the federal statutory standard.[170] However, an officer still may wish to use a search warrant or a court order based on probable cause when seeking historical information as a precaution against a future contrary ruling by a higher court.

Phone Records

A comprehensive discussion of this topic is available in the School of Government publication cited in the accompanying footnote.[171] The discussion here is a general overview.

Federal law[172] prohibits a telephone company, cell phone provider, or other entity from providing to federal, state, and local law enforcement officers phone records and other information—for example, billing records and unlisted customer information—unless the company or provider has the consent of the customer or the officer obtains one of the following:

- An administrative subpoena authorized by federal or state law; North Carolina law authorizes State

Bureau of Investigation agents to issue an administrative subpoena.[173]
- A federal or state grand jury subpoena.
- A search warrant.
- A court order requiring the company or provider to disclose the records; a North Carolina law enforcement officer should obtain such a court order from a superior court judge.[174]
- A trial subpoena. Note that a trial subpoena may not be issued until a criminal charge has been brought.

Civil liability and exclusionary rules involved with a violation of this federal law are discussed in the accompanying footnote.[175]

---

also be sufficient because it satisfies a higher standard than the federal statute.

170. See the detailed summary of this case on page 308 in the appendix to this chapter. *See also* State v. Hurtado, ___ N.C. App. ___, 781 S.E.2d 351 (2015) (unpublished) (under *Perry*, acquisition of defendant's historical cell phone local records from AT&T was not search under Fourth Amendment). If there is a violation of the statute in obtaining historical cell-site location information that is not also a constitutional violation, there is no statutory exclusionary rule to bar the introduction of the information. United States v. Guerrero, 768 F.3d 351 (5th Cir. 2014).

171. *See* Jeffrey B. Welty, *Prosecution and Law Enforcement Access to Information about Electronic Communications* 2–4, ADMIN. OF JUST. BULL. 2009/05 (Oct. 2009), www.sog.unc.edu/sites/www.sog.unc.edu/files/reports/aojb0905.pdf.

172. 18 U.S.C. §§ 2703(c) & (d). The law applies to law enforcement access to records of other entities, such as cell phone providers, in addition to landline telephone companies. The law applies to all providers of an *electronic communication service*, defined in 18 U.S.C. § 2510(15), or a *remote computing service*, defined in 18 U.S.C. § 2711(2). See the discussion of access to stored electronic communications on page 218.

The federal statute requiring cost reimbursement to companies and providers for providing records, 18 U.S.C. § 2706, applies to state and local governments in addition to the federal government. Ameritech Corp. v. McCann, 403 F.3d 908 (7th Cir. 2005), *on remand*, 2005 WL 1398606 (E.D. Wis. 2005) (unpublished).

173. G.S. 15A-298 (authorizes SBI to issue an administrative subpoena to a communications common carrier or electronic communications service to compel records if the records (1) disclose information concerning local or long distance toll records or subscriber information and (2) are material to an active SBI criminal investigation). A subpoena may be issued without a showing of probable cause. *In re* Subpoena Duces Tecum, 228 F.3d 341 (4th Cir. 2000).

174. A court order should be obtained from a superior court judge because it is unclear whether a district court judge may issue the order. *See* Jeff Welty, *Can a District Court Judge Sign an Order for Phone Records?* NC CRIM. L. BLOG (Sept. 14, 2010), http://nccriminallaw.sog.unc.edu/can-a-district-court-judge-sign-an-order-for-phone-records/. A superior court judge would have the authority to issue such an order under *In re Superior Court Order*, 315 N.C. 378 (1986). The provisions of 18 U.S.C. § 2703(d) require that the government show that there is reason to believe the contents of the records being sought are relevant to a legitimate law enforcement inquiry. The phone company or cell provider may move to quash or modify the order if the information or records requested are unusually voluminous or compliance with the order otherwise would unduly burden the company.

175. The Fourth Circuit Court of Appeals in *Tucker v. Waddell*, 83 F.3d 688 (4th Cir. 1996), ruled that civil liability applies only to the telephone company for illegally providing the information, not to the law enforcement officer or his or her agency that obtained the information, at least in the absence of evidence that the officer or agency aided and abetted or conspired with the telephone company to violate the law. The *Tucker* ruling may now be questionable in light of federal legislation enacted after the ruling was issued. *See* Freedman v. America Online, Inc., 303 F. Supp. 2d 121 (D. Conn. 2004) (police officers who obtained plaintiff's subscriber information from Internet service provider using invalid search warrant were civilly liable for violation of Electronic Communications Privacy Act).

A violation of federal law does not require the exclusion of evidence at a criminal trial. The provisions of 18 U.S.C. § 2708 state that the remedies and sanctions set out in the law are the only judicial remedies and sanctions for nonconstitutional

Bank Records

(See page 314 for case summaries on this topic.)

North Carolina statutory law sets out procedures that government agencies and employees, including prosecutors and law enforcement officers, and financial institutions, including banks, savings and loans institutions, and loan companies, must follow to obtain or to provide access to a customer's financial records—that is, checks, deposit slips, and the like.[176] However, the law permits a financial institution, without complying with the law's procedures, to (1) notify a prosecutor or law enforcement officer that it has information that may be relevant to a possible violation of a law or regulation or (2) disclose the name, address, account number, and type of account of any customer. The financial institution also could probably reveal whether a customer has a security deposit box with the financial institution, because that fact is apparently not a financial record as defined by the law.

The law provides that government officials may not have access to a financial institution's records unless the record is described with reasonable specificity and access is sought with one of the following:

1. Customer authorization
2. A search warrant
3. A grand jury subpoena or court order connected with a grand jury proceeding
4. A court order[177] or subpoena
5. Other ways specified in the law

If access is sought by the process described in item 4 above, the law requires advance notice to the customer, although that notice may be delayed for a good reason—for example, if a customer might destroy evidence if given notice.

Whenever the process described in items 1 through 4 is used to obtain a financial record, the financial institution must be reimbursed for assembling and delivering the records, unless reimbursement is waived, in whole or in part, by the financial institution.[178] A person who violates the law in obtaining financial records may be civilly liable to the customer in an amount equal to the sum of (1) $1,000, (2) any actual damages sustained by the customer as a result of disclosing the record, and (3) punitive damages for willful or intentional violations.[179] However, a person is not civilly liable if the person acted in good faith in obtaining and relying on process to secure the records.

---

violations of the law. Because a customer does not have a Fourth Amendment right of privacy in the records held by a telephone company (United States v. Punk, 153 F.3d 1011 (9th Cir. 1998), and, by analogy to bank records, *United States v. Miller*, 425 U.S. 435 (1976)), this provision effectively makes the records admissible even if the officer violates the law in obtaining them.

176. G.S. 53B-1 through -10 (entitled "Financial Privacy Act"). Legislation enacted in 2013 (S.L. 2013-337) authorizes a law enforcement agency investigating a credible report of financial exploitation of a disabled adult or older adult to apply to a district court judge for a subpoena to obtain the adult's financial records from a financial institution. G.S. 53B-4(13); 108A-116, -117. A *disabled adult* is a person 18 years old or older or legally emancipated who is present in North Carolina and is physically or mentally incapacitated. G.S. 108A-113(2). An *older adult* is a person who is 65 years old or older. G.S. 108A-113(8).

177. *See, e.g., In re* Superior Court Order, 315 N.C. 378 (1986) (superior court judge has inherent authority to order

bank to disclose customer's bank records if reasonable suspicion exists that crime was committed and records probably will relate to investigation of that crime).

178. G.S. 53B-9(b) provides that the fee shall be at the rate established pursuant to 12 U.S.C. § 3415 and Section 219 of Title 12 of the Code of Federal Regulations (hereafter, C.F.R.) (dates are omitted for C.F.R. cites). The rates are set in 12 C.F.R. § 219.3, App. A, which provides as follows: (1) reproduction at 25 cents for each page photocopied and each paper copy of microfiche, per frame; 50 cents for duplicate microfiche, per microfiche; actual cost for storage media; and (2) search and processing at $22 per hour for a clerical/technical worker and $30 per hour for a computer support specialist or a manager/supervisory worker. This regulation should be checked occasionally to make sure the rates have not changed.

179. G.S. 53B-10. The law does not contain an exclusionary rule to bar unlawfully obtained evidence from being introduced in a criminal or civil proceeding. *See* United States v. Kington, 801 F.2d 733 (5th Cir. 1986) (Congress did not intend that evidence obtained in violation of federal Right to Financial Privacy Act be suppressed when it did not authorize that remedy; therefore suppression was inappropriate); United States v. Thomas, 878 F.2d 383 (6th Cir. 1989) (unpublished). The rationale of these rulings would probably apply to a violation of North Carolina's Financial Privacy Act.

Records in Federally Assisted Alcohol or Substance Abuse Program

Federal law restricts access by law enforcement officers and prosecutors to records of the identity, diagnosis, and treatment of a patient maintained in any federally assisted alcohol or substance abuse program.[180] Generally, a judge (which includes a state judge) must conduct a hearing, consider specified factors, and then decide whether to issue a court order requiring the disclosure of the patient's records.[181] Thus, a subpoena to obtain these records is not sufficient; a hearing must be held.[182]

Civil liability and exclusionary rules involved with a violation of this federal law are discussed in the accompanying footnote.[183]

Documents in Possession of News Media, Writers, and Publishers

Federal law restricts an officer's authority to search for and seize work product or documentary materials in the possession of a person reasonably believed to have a purpose to disseminate to the public a newspaper, book, broadcast, or other similar form of public communication.[184] In effect, it requires an officer to use a subpoena instead of a search warrant or warrantless search or seizure to obtain work product or documentary materials, unless one of the law's exceptions, which are discussed below, exists. This law is commonly known as the Privacy Protection Act or PPA.

Concerning both work product and documentary materials,[185] the law's general requirement that a

---

180. 42 U.S.C. § 290dd-2; 42 C.F.R. § 2.12(b) (describing what constitutes federal assistance). Federal law (42 U.S.C. § 290dd-2(e)) specifically authorizes the reporting of suspected child abuse and neglect to appropriate state or local authorities.

181. 42 U.S.C. § 290dd-2. A federal rule, 42 C.F.R. § 2.65(d), sets out the factors a judge must find to authorize disclosure after conducting a hearing: (1) the crime is extremely serious, such as one causing or directly threatening the loss of life or serious bodily injury; (2) there is a reasonable likelihood that the records will disclose information of substantial value in the investigation or prosecution; (3) other ways of obtaining the information are not available or would not be effective; (4) the public interest and need for disclosure outweigh the potential injury to the patient, the physician–patient relationship, and the program's ability to provide services to other patients; and (5) issues concerning counsel for the person possessing the records (see subsection (d)(5)).

Disclosure of records with a patient's consent is governed by 42 C.F.R. §§ 2.31 through 2.35.

182. 42 C.F.R. § 265(b). Cases on issues involving access to these records include *Doe v. County of Fairfax*, 225 F.3d 440 (4th Cir. 2000) (officer obtained records in violation of federal law); *United States v. Hughes*, 95 F. Supp. 2d 49 (D. Mass. 2000) (judge conducted hearing and denied government access to records); *United States v. Zamora*, 408 F. Supp. 2d 295 (S.D. Tex. 2006) (good cause shown for disclosure of blood alcohol test on night defendant arrested for driving while intoxicated); and *Hurt v. State*, 694 N.E.2d 1212 (Ind. Ct. App. 1998) (defendant's confession to nurse and security guard in hospital was not barred by federal law).

183. Concerning a person's right to sue for a violation of this law, see *Doe v. County of Fairfax*, 225 F.3d 440 (4th Cir. 2000) (no civil liability for obtaining records in violation of federal law, but remand to trial court on issue of liability under Fourth Amendment). A person who violates the law or regulations may be fined up to $500 for a first offense. 42 C.F.R. § 2.4. It appears, however, that evidence illegally obtained in violation of this law is not to be suppressed at a criminal trial. *See* People

v. Jiminez, 217 P.3d 841 (Colo. App. 2008) (adopting majority view on suppression issue).

184. 42 U.S.C. § 2000aa. This law was enacted in response to *Zurcher v. Stanford Daily*, 436 U.S. 547 (1978) (Fourth Amendment does not prohibit search of property with search warrant when owner or possessor of premises to be searched is not reasonably suspected of complicity in crime being investigated— such as the newspaper, an innocent third party in this case).

Cases involving this law include *Guest v. Leis*, 255 F.3d 325 (6th Cir. 2001) (when protected materials are commingled on a criminal suspect's computer with criminal evidence unprotected by law, no liability for seizure of protected materials; court noted, however, that officers may not then search protected materials seized incidentally to seizure of criminal evidence); *Citicasters v. McCaskill*, 89 F.3d 1350 (8th Cir. 1996) (law does not require application for search warrant to describe exception that would permit use of search warrant; plaintiff entitled to remand to have opportunity to establish that prosecutor directed, supervised, or otherwise engaged in execution of search warrant of television station for videotape of crime); *Steve Jackson Games, Inc. v. U.S. Secret Service*, 816 F. Supp. 432 (W.D. Tex. 1993), *aff'd on different issue*, 36 F.3d 457 (5th Cir. 1994) (Secret Service agent's seizure with search warrant of work product materials from premises of operator of computer bulletin board violated law—operator was legitimate publisher of information to public); *Berglund v. City of Maplewood*, 173 F. Supp. 2d 935 (D. Minn. 2001), *aff'd, Zick v. City of Maplewood*, 50 Fed. Appx. 805 (8th Cir. 2002) (warrantless seizure of videotape from hosts of local public access television show was justified by exception that person who possessed videotape had committed crime and also was justified by destruction of evidence exception); *DePugh v. Sutton*, 917 F. Supp. 690 (W.D. Mo. 1996), *aff'd*, 104 F.3d 363 (8th Cir. 1996) (search warrant did not violate law because that plaintiff was criminal suspect); and *United States v. Hunter*, 13 F. Supp. 2d 574 (D. Vt. 1998) (similar ruling).

185. *See* 42 U.S.C. § 2000aa-7 for the definitions of *documentary materials* and *work product materials*.

subpoena must be issued does not apply if any of the following conditions exist:

1. There is probable cause to believe that the person possessing the materials had committed or is committing the criminal offense to which the materials relate
2. The materials sought involve national security or child pornography offenses
3. There is reason to believe that the immediate seizure of such materials is necessary to prevent death or serious bodily injury to a person

Concerning documentary materials, the law also does not apply if (1) there is reason to believe that the giving of notice by a subpoena duces tecum would result in the destruction, alteration, or concealment of the materials, or (2) the materials have not been produced in response to a court order directing compliance with a subpoena duces tecum and all appellate remedies have been exhausted or there is reason to believe that a delay in an investigation or trial occasioned by further proceedings concerning the subpoena would threaten the interests of justice.

Civil liability and exclusionary rules involved with a violation of this federal law are discussed in the accompanying footnote.[186]

Search and Seizure by Valid Consent

(*See page 316 for case summaries on this topic.*)

Although people may have a Fourth Amendment right to privacy in a place or object, they may waive that right if they voluntarily consent to allow law enforcement officers to enter that place or to examine that object. If a person voluntarily consents, officers who may not otherwise have had sufficient justification under the Fourth Amendment to make a search may do so. For example, officers may suspect that a person has a murder weapon in his or her home but lack the probable cause necessary to obtain a search warrant to enter the home and to search. However, the officers may go to the home and ask permission to

enter and to search.[187] If they obtain valid consent, they may enter, look for the weapon, and seize the weapon or any other evidence of a crime they see—if they have probable cause to believe it is evidence of a crime.[188] And they will have obtained the evidence without violating anyone's Fourth Amendment rights.

Issues involving an officer's request for consent after a traffic stop has been completed are discussed on page 49 in Chapter 2.

People Who Are Entitled to Give Valid Consent

(*See page 329 for case summaries on this topic.*)

Generally, officers may obtain a valid consent to search only from a person whose reasonable expectation of privacy may be invaded by the proposed search. Sometimes two or more people—for example, spouses or roommates—share a reasonable expectation of privacy in the same place. Generally, either person may give valid consent to an officer.[189] However, the United States Supreme Court ruled in *Georgia v. Randolph* that if a physically present occupant refuses to consent to a search of a place and a co-occupant consents, the Fourth Amendment prohibits a search based on the co-occupant's consent.[190] The Court made clear that its ruling applies only to a physically present occupant who refuses to consent, as long as officers do not remove a potentially objecting occupant from the entrance to the residence in order to avoid a possible refusal to consent (however, see the discussion of *Fernandez v. California*, below, concerning a legitimate reason to remove an objecting occupant). The Court stated that when officers have obtained consent from a co-occupant, they have no obligation to seek out

---

186. Civil liability for violations of the law is set out in 42 U.S.C. § 2000aa-6. Subsection (e) of this section provides that evidence otherwise admissible (for example, there is no Fourth Amendment violation in seizing the evidence) may not be excluded based on a violation of this law.

187. This procedure is commonly known as "knock and talk." The North Carolina Supreme Court in *State v. Smith*, 346 N.C. 794 (1997), ruled that the knock-and-talk procedure in that case did not violate the defendant's Fourth Amendment rights.

188. While officers are conducting a consent search, the plain view theory allows them to seize an object when they have probable cause to believe it is evidence of a crime. 4 WAYNE R. LaFAVE, SEARCH AND SEIZURE: A TREATISE ON THE FOURTH AMENDMENT § 8.1(c) (5th ed. 2012). Probable cause is required; reasonable suspicion is insufficient. Arizona v. Hicks, 480 U.S. 321 (1987).

189. *Compare* United States v. Matlock, 415 U.S. 164 (1974) (common authority over premises found), *with* Illinois v. Rodriguez, 497 U.S. 177 (1990) (common authority over premises not found).

190. 547 U.S. 103 (2006).

any other occupants to determine if they want to refuse to allow consent. The Court also placed other limits on the scope of its ruling, which are discussed in the accompanying footnote.[191]

The United States Supreme Court in *Fernandez v. California*[192] clarified an issue left open in *Georgia v. Randolph*: the validity of a consent search by a residential occupant after a co-occupant had previously objected to a search but is no longer physically present when the occupant consents. Officers in *Fernandez* saw a man apparently involved in a robbery run into a building.

They heard screams and fighting coming from an apartment there. A woman responded to a knock on the door. She had fresh injuries and admitted that she had been in a fight. Fernandez, a co-occupant, then appeared at the door and objected to officers entering the apartment. Believing that Fernandez had assaulted the woman, the officers arrested him and took him to the police station. An officer returned to the apartment an hour later and obtained the woman's consent to search the apartment. The Court noted that *Randolph* had stressed that its ruling was limited to situations when an objecting occupant was physically present when the co-occupant consented to the search (in which case, officers cannot rely on that consent to enter). The Court ruled that as long as officers have an objectively reasonable basis to remove the defendant (that is, the officers' subjective motive for removal is irrelevant), the co-occupant's later consent is sufficient. In this case, the officers properly removed Fernandez so that they could speak with the alleged assault victim outside of Fernandez's intimidating presence. Also, there was probable cause to arrest Fernandez for assault.

With an objecting occupant's physical presence given prominence in *Fernandez*, it remains to be seen how physical presence will be defined in future cases. Does the objecting occupant need to be present exactly where the co-occupant is consenting, or is it sufficient if he or she is somewhere on or near the premises? The Court appeared to indicate that on or near the premises may be sufficient.[193] But the Court did not definitively decide the issue, and a future Court may decide differently.

When officers are unsure of their authority to search based on one occupant's consent when another occupant is objecting, they may wish to consult with their agency's legal advisor or obtain a search warrant if probable cause exists to search the premises. Sometimes there will be other legal grounds to enter premises without consent or a search warrant, such as an immediate need to protect a victim from harm, seize weapons for self-protection, make a protective sweep of the premises, and so forth.

---

191. The Court noted that the issue of consent is irrelevant when an occupant on his or her own initiative brings evidence from a residence to law enforcement, citing *Coolidge v. New Hampshire*, 403 U.S. 443 (1971). The Court also noted that an occupant can tell law enforcement what he or she knows, which in turn can lead to the issuance of a search warrant. In footnote 6, the Court stated that the exchange of this information in the presence of the nonconsenting occupant may render consent irrelevant by creating an exigency that justifies immediate action. If the occupant cannot be prevented from destroying easily disposable evidence during the time required to get a search warrant, *see* Illinois v. McArthur, 531 U.S. 326 (2001) (preventing suspect's access to residence while law enforcement sought search warrant), a perceived need to act then to preserve evidence may justify entry and search under the exigent circumstances exception to the warrant requirement. The Court also stated that other kinds of exigent circumstances might justify warrantless searches: hot pursuit, protecting officers' safety, imminent destruction to a residence, or likelihood that suspect will imminently flee.

The Court stated that this case had no bearing on the authority of law enforcement to protect domestic violence victims. The issue in this case concerned an entry to search for evidence. The Court stated that no question could reasonably be made about law enforcement authority to enter a residence without consent to protect an occupant from domestic violence, as long as officers have a good reason to believe such a threat exists. Officers could enter without consent to give an alleged victim the opportunity to collect belongings and get out safely or to determine whether violence or a threat of violence has just occurred or is about to (or soon will) occur. And because officers would be lawfully on the premises, they could seize any evidence in plain view or take further action supported by consequent probable cause.

Although the Court did not discuss this issue, when an occupant has a superior privacy interest over another occupant of a residence, as is the case in most living arrangements involving a parent and child, the parent's consent would generally override any expressed refusal to consent by a physically present child. *See generally* 4 WAYNE R. LAFAVE, SEARCH AND SEIZURE: A TREATISE ON THE FOURTH AMENDMENT § 8.4(b) (4th ed. 2012).

192. 134 S. Ct. 1126 (2014).

193. The Court cited *Bailey v. United States*, 133 S. Ct. 1031 (2013) (detaining occupants of premises during search warrant execution is limited to immediate vicinity of premises to be searched).

Spouses

Spouses may consent to a search of property they share, such as a house or car.[194] But one spouse generally may not consent to a search of a particular place within the property where the other spouse clearly has exclusive privacy interests—for example, a locked box for which only one spouse has the key. Generally, for example, one spouse may not consent to a search of the other spouse's separate bedroom. However, some courts have ruled that a spouse may consent to a search of areas or items to which the other spouse has exclusive use but to which the consenting spouse has joint access.[195]

In response to an officer's request, a spouse may voluntarily agree to recover property within the house and turn it over to officers without violating the other spouse's Fourth Amendment rights.[196]

Roommates

The rules about roommates who share property are essentially the same as for spouses. The United States Supreme Court has ruled that roommates implicitly authorize each other to consent to a search of commonly possessed property and they assume the risk that the other may consent.[197]

As with spouses, a roommate generally may not consent to a search of a place where the other roommate clearly has exclusive privacy interests.

Parents and Children

Although a parent's authority to consent to a search of a child's room is not entirely clear, most courts recognize that a parent has the authority to consent.[198] The North Carolina Supreme Court has ruled that a mother properly consented to a search of her 15-year-old son's

bedroom.[199] Generally, a parent has the authority to consent to a search of a child's room (although this authority may be less likely if the child is not a minor—a person under age 18) unless the child has established exclusive use and access to his or her room that would negate a parent's authority to consent to a search there.[200] However, even if a parent may consent to a search of a child's room, the parent may not have the authority to consent to a search of personal possessions there—such as a locked suitcase—if the child has exclusive access and use of those items. A court may review each separate enclosed space or object to determine whether a child has an exclusive privacy interest by considering the totality of circumstances, such as (1) whether the object or space was secured or commonly used for preserving privacy, (2) the child's exclusiveness of use and access to the object or space, and (3) the child's age.[201] If officers are unsure of a parent's authority to consent and they have probable cause to search, they may want to obtain a search warrant unless exigent circumstances exist.

---

194. In *State v. Worsley*, 336 N.C. 268 (1994), the court, overruling *State v. Hall*, 264 N.C. 559 (1965), and other cases, ruled that a wife may consent to a search of the premises she shares with her husband.

195. See the cases cited in 4 Wayne R. LaFave, Search and Seizure: A Treatise on the Fourth Amendment § 8.3(f) n.133 (5th ed. 2012).

196. Coolidge v. New Hampshire, 403 U.S. 443 (1971); Georgia v. Randolph, 547 U.S. 103 (2006) (noting *Coolidge* with approval); State v. Woods, 286 N.C. 612 (1975); State v. Reams, 277 N.C. 391 (1970).

197. United States v. Matlock, 415 U.S. 164 (1974).

198. *See* 4 Wayne R. LaFave, Search and Seizure: A Treatise on the Fourth Amendment § 8.4(b) (5th ed. 2012).

199. State v. Penley, 284 N.C. 247 (1973). *See also* State v. Russell, 92 N.C. App. 639 (1989) (defendant's mother properly gave consent to search of son's bedroom); State v. Washington, 86 N.C. App. 235 (1987) (similar ruling); State v. Braxton, 294 N.C. 446 (1978) (defendant's mother, registered owner of car, properly consented to search of her car, which her son used during rape).

200. United States v. Rith, 164 F.3d 1323 (10th Cir. 1999) (father's consent to search his entire home, including his 18-year-old son's bedroom, was valid despite son's refusal to give consent; son did not pay rent, there was no lock on his bedroom door, and there was no agreement with his parents that they not enter his room without his consent; court stated that there is a rebuttable presumption of control of a child's property when there is a parent–child relationship).

201. *See, e.g.,* United States v. Block, 590 F.2d 535 (4th Cir. 1978) (mother did not have authority to consent to search of 23-year-old son's locked footlocker in his bedroom).

A minor child generally cannot consent to a search of his or her parents' home,[202] although an adult child living there may be able to do so.[203]

Landlords and Tenants

Only tenants of a rented house, apartment, or room may consent to a search of their place, because they alone have a Fourth Amendment privacy interest there. Until tenants permanently leave or otherwise lose their privacy interest in their place, the owner may not give consent.[204] The fact that a lease agreement permits the lessor to enter the lessee's premises for certain reasons—such as maintenance of the property—does not permit the lessor to allow officers to enter as well.[205] On the other hand, officers may enter an owner's property, despite the owner's objections, if the tenants in lawful possession have consented to a search of their leased premises.[206]

Guests in a Home

A person who is an overnight guest in another's home generally has a reasonable expectation of privacy in that home.[207] (It is unclear to what extent, if any, a mere visitor has a reasonable expectation of privacy.)[208] However, the permanent resident of the premises generally may consent to a search anywhere within his or her home, except the guest's bedroom—if the guest has exclusive use of the bedroom—and the guest's personal belongings if they are kept in the guest's luggage or other repository.[209]

Employers and Employees

Employees may consent to a search of their employer's property only if their employment includes authorization to exercise control over the property.[210] For example, a plant supervisor may consent to a search of the employer's property, but a janitor may not.

Employers may consent to a search of their entire property except for any area that they have set aside for the employees' exclusive use in such a way that employees have a reasonable expectation of privacy there—for example, an employee's locker or desk.[211]

---

202. *But see* United States v. Clutter, 914 F.2d 775 (6th Cir. 1990) (children, ages 12 and 14, whose parents left them in exclusive control of house, could give valid consent to officers); United States v. Gutierrez-Hermosillo, 142 F.3d 1225 (10th Cir. 1998) (officers could reasonably believe that defendant's 14-year-old daughter could give consent to search motel room when officers knew she was traveling in company of her father and she answered the door); Lenz v. Winburn, 51 F.3d 1540 (11th Cir. 1995) (nine-year-old could give valid consent to guardian ad litem's entry into residence that child shared with her father and grandparents to retrieve child's personal items; child was being removed from custody of her father); United States v. Sanchez, 608 F.3d 685 (10th Cir. 2010) (15-year-old gave valid consent to search home while she was alone babysitting her younger brother).

203. *See* 4 Wayne R. LaFave, Search and Seizure: A Treatise on the Fourth Amendment § 8.4(c) (5th ed. 2012).

204. Abel v. United States, 362 U.S. 217 (1960).

205. Chapman v. United States, 365 U.S. 610 (1961); United States v. Warner, 843 F.2d 401 (9th Cir. 1988) (landlord's limited right of access to make repairs and to mow lawn did not authorize him to consent for police to enter tenant's property). *See* 4 Wayne R. LaFave, Search and Seizure: A Treatise on the Fourth Amendment § 8.5(a) (5th ed. 2012).

206. *In re* Dwelling of Properties, Inc., 24 N.C. App. 17 (1974).

207. Minnesota v. Olson, 495 U.S. 91 (1990) (overnight guest had reasonable expectation of privacy in apartment to contest officers' warrantless entry to arrest him).

208. *See* Minnesota v. Carter, 525 U.S. 83 (1998) (defendant in apartment a few hours for a business transaction did not have reasonable expectation of privacy there).

209. *See* 4 Wayne R. LaFave, Search and Seizure: A Treatise on the Fourth Amendment § 8.5(d) (5th ed. 2012). *But see* State v. Ray, 274 N.C. 556 (1968) (defendant was permitted to sleep regularly in living room of another's house and was allowed to keep his clothes in homeowner's suitcase in another room; homeowner gave valid consent to officers to seize clothes); State v. Garner, 340 N.C. 573 (1995) (homeowner consented to search by officers to look for pistol involved in shooting; officer found pistol in jacket among pile of clothes (officer was unaware to whom jacket belonged); valid consent found); State v. Barnett, 307 N.C. 608 (1983).

210. *See* 4 Wayne R. LaFave, Search and Seizure: A Treatise on the Fourth Amendment § 8.6(c) (5th ed. 2012).

211. *Id.* at § 8.6(d). For an analysis of the authority to search government employee's offices, lockers, computers, and other digital devices, see *City of Ontario v. Quon*, 560 U.S. 746 (2010) (review of text messages on government-provided pager); *O'Connor v. Ortega*, 480 U.S. 709 (1987) (search of employee's office, desk, and file cabinets); *United States v. Angevine*, 281 F.3d 1130 (10th Cir. 2002) (search of computer); *American Postal Workers Union v. U.S. Postal Service*, 871 F.2d 556 (6th Cir. 1989) (search of postal employees' lockers). *See also* Digital Evidence, *supra* note 140, at 42–45; 5 Wayne R. LaFave, Search and Seizure: A Treatise on the Fourth Amendment § 10.3(d) (5th ed. 2012); Searching and Seizing Computers, *supra* note 101, at 42–56.

Owners and Custodians of Property

When a person is using or has custody of another's property, the authority to consent depends on the degree of control over the property that the owner has given.[212] A parking lot attendant, for example, may not consent to a search of a car the attendant has parked. On the other hand, a car repair facility may have the authority to consent to a search of a car that is left there for repairs—at least to a search of the part of the car to which the owner expected the operator to have general access.[213]

When officers stop a car with several occupants, they should ask the owner for consent to search it.[214] If the owner is not present, they should obtain consent from the occupant who has the owner's permission to use the car. If it appears that two or more occupants equally share the owner's permission, the officer may seek consent from any occupant.

School Administrators and Students

North Carolina courts have not decided whether a school administrator may consent to officers' search of a student's locker. A school administrator's consent, to be valid, would be based on acting in loco parentis—as a substitute parent—or on the student's being informed that the school retains ownership of the lockers and reserves the right to inspect them at any time. Although cases in other states have indicated that a school administrator may consent to a search of a student's locker,[215] officers may not want to rely on that consent, particularly if alternatives exist. For example, a school administrator who has reasonable suspicion that a student's locker or personal possession, such as a pocketbook or book bag, contains evidence of a crime or a violation of school rules may conduct a search with the assistance of law enforcement officers.[216] Cases in other jurisdictions also recog-

nize that a school administrator may search a student's locker without reasonable suspicion when it is reasonable under the Fourth Amendment.[217] Finally, officers on their own may search a student's locker with a search warrant or with consent to search from the student.[218]

University Officials and Students

A university official generally may not consent to a search of a student's dormitory room; only the student may consent.[219]

Officer's Reasonable Mistake of Fact about the Validity of a Person's Authority to Consent

(*See page 333 for case summaries on this topic.*)

If officers reasonably determine that a person is entitled to consent to a search, as outlined above, they may rely on that consent, even though *in fact* they were mistaken about the particular person's authority to consent.[220] For

---

was proper; reasonable suspicion supported search); *In re* Murray, 136 N.C. App. 648 (2000) (assistant principal's search of student's book bag, with assistance of law enforcement officer, was proper; reasonable suspicion supported search). The North Carolina Court of Appeals has also ruled that the reasonable suspicion standard, instead of probable cause, applies when a student resource officer conducts a search of a student in furtherance of school or safety interests. *In re* D.L.D., 203 N.C. App. 434 (2010); *In re* S.W., 171 N.C. App. 335 (2005); *In re* J.F.M., 168 N.C. App. 143 (2005).

217. Commonwealth v. Cass, 709 A.2d 350 (Pa. 1998) (search of all student lockers, with assistance of police officers and a drug dog, was reasonable in light of drug problems in school and students' minimal expectation of privacy in their lockers; students had been given advance notice that their lockers were subject to inspection); *In re* Isiah B., 500 N.W.2d 637 (Wis. 1993) (when school system had notified students in writing that it retained ownership and possession of school lockers and they were subject to inspection as necessary or appropriate, student did not have reasonable expectation of privacy in locker to challenge search by school administrator).

218. Of course, if there was evidence that a bomb was in a locker, then exigent circumstances would allow a search without a search warrant.

219. *See* 4 Wayne R. LaFave, Search and Seizure: A Treatise on the Fourth Amendment § 8.6(e) (5th ed. 2012).

220. Illinois v. Rodriguez, 497 U.S. 177 (1990). Consistent with the *Rodriguez* ruling are G.S. 15A-222(3), which states that consent must be given "[b]y a person who by ownership or otherwise is *reasonably apparently entitled* to give or withhold consent to a search of premises" (emphasis added), and G.S. 15A-222(2), which states that consent to search a vehicle must be given by the registered owner or "by the person in

---

212. 4 Wayne R. LaFave, Search and Seizure: A Treatise on the Fourth Amendment § 8.6(a) (5th ed. 2012).

213. State v. Baker, 65 N.C. App. 430 (1983).

214. If the owner of the car is present and consents to a search of the car, it may be searched despite the passenger's objections. State v. Grant, 279 N.C. 337 (1971); State v. Raynes, 272 N.C. 488 (1968); State v. Hamilton, 264 N.C. 277 (1965).

215. People v. Overton, 229 N.E.2d 596 (N.Y. 1967), *later ruling*, 249 N.E.2d 366 (1969); State v. Stein, 456 P.2d 1 (Kan. 1969). *See also* 4 Wayne R. LaFave, Search and Seizure: A Treatise on the Fourth Amendment § 8.6(e) (5th ed. 2012).

216. *In re* D. D., 146 N.C. App. 309 (2001) (principal's search of student's purse, with assistance of law enforcement officers,

example, if officers ask a person whether she lives with the defendant—to determine whether they may rely on her valid consent to search a jointly possessed home—and she answers yes, the consent search is valid even if it later is determined that she was just a guest. Of course, officers should inquire when they are not sure whether the person in fact is actually authorized to consent. On the other hand, officers' reasonable mistake of law about a person's authority to consent—for example, if officers wrongly believe that a hotel employee may consent to a search of a guest's room—does not validate a consent search[221] (but see the comment in the accompanying footnote).[222]

Content of a Valid Consent

A valid consent to search must be made voluntarily by the person who consents. The following are some issues involved in determining the voluntariness and thus the validity of consent.

Expression of Willingness for a Search to Occur
(*See page 324 for case summaries on this topic.*)

The person who consents must express his or her consent clearly. An expression is not sufficient if what a person says (or writes or does) indicates only that the person is giving in to authority. A person's expression of willingness to consent is not a valid consent if it was made without knowing that it would result in a search. However, deception is permissible under some circumstances. For example, officers may enter in an undercover capacity when they are invited in to conduct illegal business, such as purchasing illegal drugs.[223]

North Carolina law requires that consent must be given in the form of a "statement" to officers,[224] but that statement may be made orally, in writing, or by other means, as long as it communicates the meaning clearly. Although nonverbal conduct intended as an assertion giving consent is sufficient,[225] it may be preferable to obtain a clearer, express statement.

Voluntariness of the Expression
(*See page 316 for case summaries on this topic.*)

A court examines all the circumstances surrounding the giving of consent to search when it decides whether the consent was in fact voluntary or was obtained by duress or coercion, express or implied. In some situations, consent is clearly involuntary: when a person is beaten or threatened with physical force until he or she "consents," or when the person must "consent" to remove a threat to a family member. But consent may be coerced in less obvious ways. For example, a number of officers with drawn guns may make consent a product of coercion rather than of a willingness to permit a search.[226] A court also looks carefully at consent given by a person who is in custody,[227]

---

apparent control of its operation and contents at the time the consent is given" (emphasis added). *See* 4 Wayne R. LaFave, Search and Seizure: A Treatise on the Fourth Amendment § 8.3(g) (5th ed. 2012).

221. United States v. Whitfield, 939 F.2d 1071 (D.C. Cir. 1991); United States v. Salinas-Cano, 959 F.2d 861 (10th Cir. 1992); United States v. Brown, 961 F.2d 1039 (2d Cir. 1992).

222. It is unclear whether the United States Supreme Court's ruling in *Heien v. North Carolina*, 135 S. Ct. 530 (2014), decided after the cases cited in the preceding footnote, that an officer's objectively reasonable mistake of law in making an investigative stop or arrest is reasonable under the Fourth Amendment would apply to a reasonable mistake of law concerning a person's authority to consent.

223. Lewis v. United States, 385 U.S. 206 (1966). *See also* State v. Kuegel, 195 N.C. App. 310 (2009) (consent to search dwelling was voluntarily given, based on totality of circumstances, although officer untruthfully told defendant that he had conducted surveillance of apartment, saw a lot of people

coming and going there, stopped their cars after they left neighborhood, and each time recovered either marijuana or cocaine).

224. G.S. 15A-221(b).

225. State v. Graham, 149 N.C. App. 215 (2002) (nonverbal conduct intended as assertion is a "statement" under G.S. 15A-221(b); when officer asked defendant if she could check his pocket, he stood up and raised his hands away from his body accompanied by gesture that officer understood to mean consent; court ruled that proper consent was obtained); State v. Harper, 158 N.C. App. 595 (2003) (based on an investigation that people in a hotel room were involved with illegal drugs, an officer knocked on the door to the room; the defendant initially opened the door slightly and while continuing to have a conversation with the officer, opened it about halfway; the officer asked the defendant if he could step inside the room to see if George Davis was in; the defendant then stepped back from the officer and the threshold of the door and opened it almost to its full extension; court ruled that the defendant's nonverbal conduct constituted valid consent to enter the hotel room). *See also* United States v. Wilson, 895 F.2d 168 (4th Cir. 1990) (defendant consented to search of his person when officer asked if he could pat him down and defendant responded by shrugging his shoulders and raising his arms).

226. *See* 4 Wayne R. LaFave, Search and Seizure: A Treatise on the Fourth Amendment § 8.2(b) (5th ed. 2012).

227. United States v. Watson, 423 U.S. 411 (1976); State v. Cobb, 295 N.C. 1 (1978).

emotionally disturbed, under the influence of drugs or alcohol, or very young.[228]

Consent may be valid even if officers tell a person that if he or she does not consent they will apply for a search warrant, if officers had the legal authority to obtain the warrant.[229] In such a case, officers may legitimately tell a person that they intend to undertake an action that is legally available to them.[230]

Warning before Asking for Consent

Both the United States Supreme Court[231] and the North Carolina Supreme Court[232] require only that a consent be voluntary. They do not require any specific warning to the person whose property is to be searched (such as the *Miranda* warning required for custodial interrogation, discussed in Chapter 5). For example, officers need not tell the person of the right to refuse to give consent, although the person's knowledge of the right to refuse may be a factor in determining whether consent was voluntary.

Before a person may give valid consent, he or she must know that consent for a search is being sought. Therefore, officers must at a minimum tell the person that they want to search his or her property. To establish the scope of the search to which the person is being asked to consent, officers should tell the person what property they want to search.[233] For example, they should say that they request "permission to search your house and car." Although not necessarily required to do so,[234] officers may want to inform the person of what they are searching for because it would help determine the scope of the consent. For example, if a person gives consent to a request to search a car for drugs, the officers may search every place in the car for which they have an objectively reasonable belief that drugs may be found.[235]

Miranda Assertion of Right to Counsel and Officer's Later Request for Consent

(*See page 334 for case summaries on this topic.*)

As discussed in Chapter 5, when a defendant asserts the *Miranda* right to counsel during custodial interrogation, an officer must immediately stop interrogation. However, because an officer's request for consent is not considered interrogation under *Miranda*, the request after an assertion for counsel does not violate a defendant's *Miranda* rights.[236] Thus, a defendant's voluntary consent to search under these circumstances is valid.

Proof of the Validity of the Consent

Even if officers receive what they believe is valid consent to search, they may later need to prove in court that the consent was properly given. There are at least two ways

---

228. State v. Fincher, 309 N.C. 1 (1983). *See* 4 Wayne R. LaFave, Search and Seizure: A Treatise on the Fourth Amendment § 8.2(e) (5th ed. 2012).

229. *Compare* Bumper v. North Carolina, 391 U.S. 543 (1968); *and* State v. Phillips, 25 N.C. App. 5 (1975); *with* State v. Fincher, 309 N.C. 1 (1983); State v. Raynor, 27 N.C. App. 538 (1975); *and* State v. Paschal, 35 N.C. App. 239 (1974).

230. State v. McMillan, 214 N.C. App. 320 (2011) (court ruled that officers' advising defendant that if he did not consent to giving oral swabs and surrendering certain items of clothing they would detain him until they obtained search warrant did not negate the defendant's voluntary consent to the seizure of those items).

231. Schneckloth v. Bustamonte, 412 U.S. 218 (1973); Ohio v. Robinette, 519 U.S. 33 (1996) (Court rejected a lower court ruling that an officer must advise a lawfully seized defendant that defendant is free to go before a consent to search will be recognized as voluntary); United States v. Watson, 423 U.S. 411 (1976).

232. State v. Powell, 297 N.C. 419 (1979).

233. Officers ordinarily should tell the person where they want to search so that (1) both the person and the officers will understand the scope of the search and (2) the possibility of a misunderstanding will be reduced. North Carolina cases on the scope of a consent search include *State v. Stone*, 362 N.C. 50 (2007); *State v. Belk*, 268 N.C. 320 (1966); *State v. Moore*, 240 N.C. 749 (1954); *State v. Hagin*, 203 N.C. App. 561 (2010); *State v. Neal*, 190 N.C. App. 453 (2008); *State v. Johnson*, 177 N.C. App. 122 (2006); *State v. Jones*, 161 N.C. App. 615 (2003); and *State v. Castellon*, 151 N.C. App. 675 (2002). *See also* 4 Wayne R. LaFave, Search and Seizure: A Treatise on the Fourth Amendment § 8.1(c) (5th ed. 2012).

234. United States v. Snow, 44 F.3d 133 (2d Cir. 1995) (defendant's consent to search of his car included search of duffel bag on backseat; although officer's request for consent to search did not include purpose of search, court noted that it is self-evident that an officer seeking general permission to search a vehicle is looking for evidence of illegal activity and it is obvious that such evidence might be hidden in closed containers).

235. Florida v. Jimeno, 500 U.S. 248 (1991) (defendant's consent to search car for drugs included searching paper bag on floorboard).

236. State v. Cummings, 188 N.C. App. 598 (2008). The *Cummings* court relied on two similar federal appellate court rulings: *United States v. Shlater*, 85 F.3d 1251 (7th Cir. 1996), and *United States v. McCurdy*, 40 F.3d 1111 (10th Cir. 1994). These rulings clearly would also apply when an officer requests consent to search after a defendant has asserted the *Miranda* right to remain silent.

in which officers may improve their chances of proving the validity of a consent search, even though neither is legally required.

One way is to obtain written consent. Although not foolproof—obviously people can say later that they did not know what they were signing or that they were coerced into signing—a written consent shows that officers carefully obtained consent in a more formal manner than a simple oral response.

Another way is to have witnesses, whether consent is given orally or in writing. A court is less likely to believe that consent was coerced or uninformed if witnesses say otherwise, particularly if one of the witnesses is not a law enforcement officer.[237]

Scope of the Search with a Valid Consent

(*See page 324 for case summaries on this topic.*)

Generally, the scope of a consent search is governed by the terms of the consent given to officers. If officers want to increase the likelihood that a court later will rule that a person's consent to search a house included all buildings on the property, they should make it clear that they are requesting consent also to search outbuildings that are on the premises. However, if the person does not object while the officers conduct the search, a court likely will rule that the outbuildings were included in the consent, even if they were not specifically mentioned.[238] If a person has consented without limitation to a search of a car, most courts have ruled that containers within the car also may be searched if the object of the search may be found there.[239] On the other hand, a person's general consent to allow a search for weapons or drugs during a routine traffic stop will ordinarily not permit an intrusive body search, such as moving clothing to see the person's geni-

tals.[240] A more specific request will usually be required.[241] A general consent to search a car does not authorize an officer to intentionally damage the car when conducting the search.[242]

A person who consents may limit that consent in any way he or she wishes. Thus, if the person says, "You may search my house everywhere but in the basement," officers must accept that limitation. And the person may stop a search at any point by revoking consent.[243]

While searching with consent, officers may seize any evidence they see in plain view that they have probable cause to believe is evidence of a crime, even if it is not related to the evidence they were looking for.

Sometimes officers will find evidence during a consent search that gives them probable cause to search further without having to rely on the consent to search justification. A person's revocation of consent thereafter will not bar a further search.[244] For example, suppose officers stop a car to issue a traffic citation and obtain consent to search the interior of the car. If they find cocaine on the

---

237. *See, e.g.,* State v. Brown, 306 N.C. 151 (1982) (defendant's friend and two officers observed defendant give consent).

238. *State v. Hagin,* 203 N.C. App. 561 (2010) (written consent to search personal or real property located at certain address that included description of mobile home also allowed search of small outbuilding on property; occupants were present and never objected to search).

239. *See* Florida v. Jimeno, 500 U.S. 248 (1991); 4 Wayne R. LaFave, Search and Seizure: A Treatise on the Fourth Amendment § 8.1(c) (5th ed. 2012).

240. State v. Stone, 362 N.C. 50 (2007) (scope of consent search for weapons or drugs did not include officer's pulling defendant's sweatpants away from his body and shining flashlight inside defendant's underwear; reasonable person would not have understood that his consent included such an examination).

241. State v. Neal, 190 N.C. App. 453 (2008) (upholding consent strip search when officer informed female defendant that officer wanted to conduct better search to determine what was located in back of her pants, female officer explained she would be conducting a more thorough search, and defendant indicated that she understood).

242. State v. Johnson, 177 N.C. App. 122 (2006), *remanding on another issue,* 360 N.C. 541 (2006) (defendant's general statement of consent to search van could not reasonably have been interpreted to include intentional infliction of damage to van, pulling wall panel inside). *Compare with* State v. Schiro, 219 N.C. App. 105 (2012) (distinguishing *Johnson,* court upheld consent search of vehicle that involved officer's removal of rear quarter panels in trunk that were easily removed).

243. State v. Schiro, 219 N.C. App. 105 (2012) (reasonable person would not have considered defendant's statements that officers were "tearing up" his car to be unequivocal revocation of his consent; defendant should have made revocation of consent in clearer statement); State v. Morocco, 99 N.C. App. 421 (1990) (defendant did not revoke consent to search his vehicle when he made ambiguous statement that tote bag found in car had nude photographs of wife).

244. United States v. Booker, 186 F.3d 1004 (8th Cir. 1999) (officers had probable cause to continue search of truck even after consent to search had been revoked when evidence gathered before revocation had established probable cause).

floorboard, that generally gives them probable cause to search the rest of the car, including the trunk, for more cocaine.[245] In this situation, the person cannot stop the search by revoking consent, because after finding cocaine the officers' justification to search the car no longer rests only on consent.

Consent Searches of Computers and Other Electronic Devices

Officers should be aware that the legality of consent searches of computers and other electronic devices is an evolving issue for which there are no direct United States Supreme Court or North Carolina appellate court rulings. Officers should consider consulting their agency's legal advisor or other legal source for advice. This topic is also discussed in the publication cited in the accompanying footnote.[246]

An officer who wants to request consent to search a computer or other electronic device must first determine (1) the person or persons with a reasonable expectation of privacy in the computer or other device and (2) the scope of a consent to search that may be given to the officer. The determination is generally simple when one person is the sole owner and user of the computer or other device, but it is not as simple if two or more people are involved. If two people jointly own or use a computer and have access to all of its files, then generally either person is authorized to give consent to the seizure and search of the computer.[247] However, if person A has password-protected or encrypted files and the password or encryption key is not shared with person B, then B would ordinarily not have the authority to consent to the search of the password-protected or encrypted files.[248] In such a case, B could consent to the seizure of the computer and the search of all files other than A's password-protected or encrypted files. An officer would need a search warrant to search A's password-protected or encrypted files absent another Fourth Amendment justification, such as probable cause and exigent circumstances.[249]

Another issue is whether the scope of a general consent to search includes a computer and other electronic devices. For example, a consent to search a defendant's "dwelling and personal property" might be sufficient.[250] However, the best way to assure a valid consent search would be to include an explicit consent to seize and search all computers and other electronic devices located in the place to be searched (dwelling, car, etc.). If the officer expects a later offsite search of the computer or other device, the request for consent or the consent form could

---

245. *See, e.g.*, State v. Martin, 97 N.C. App. 19 (1990) (when officer saw empty vials in front passenger area of car that he recognized as being used for cocaine, he had probable cause to search the entire car, including the trunk, without a warrant; *see* United States v. Ross, 456 U.S. 798 (1982) (probable cause to search car for contraband permitted search of entire car, including containers and trunk)). Finding illegal drugs in a car at a minimum supports a fair probability (the standard of probable cause in *Illinois v. Gates*, 462 U.S. 213 (1983)) that more illegal drugs may be secreted elsewhere in the car, including the trunk. The Court in *Michigan v. Thomas*, 458 U.S. 259 (1982), and *Robbins v. California*, 453 U.S. 420 (1981), implicitly recognized that illegal drugs found in a car's glove compartment or other places in the car provide probable cause to search the entire vehicle for more illegal drugs. *See also* United States v. Schecter, 717 F.2d 864 (3d Cir. 1983); United States v. Burnett, 791 F.2d 64 (6th Cir. 1986) (officer's finding two ounces of marijuana on car's floorboard gave probable cause to search without a warrant the entire car, including the trunk and packages in the trunk, based on *United States v. Ross*; small amount found did not adversely affect finding of probable cause for entire car); United States v. Loucks, 806 F.2d 208 (10th Cir. 1986) (similar ruling); State v. Greenwood, 47 N.C. App. 731 (1980), *rev'd on other grounds*, 301 N.C. 705 (1981) (odor of marijuana emanating from car gave officer probable cause to search entire car).

246. DIGITAL EVIDENCE, *supra* note 140, at 57–70.

247. A related issue is whether *Georgia v. Randolph*, 547 U.S. 103 (2006), discussed earlier in the text, applies to personal property, such as a computer. *See* United States v. King, 604 F.3d 125 (3d Cir. 2010) (*Randolph* not applicable to non-password-protected computer that two people shared, A giving consent to seize computer and B being present and objecting to its seizure; B had placed hard drive in computer owned by A and shared by both; court upheld seizure of computer).

248. Trulock v. Freeh, 275 F.3d 391 (4th Cir. 2001). *See also* United States v. Buckner, 473 F.3d 1551 (4th Cir. 2007) (wife did not have actual authority to consent to search of husband's password-protected files; however, officers had objective belief under *Illinois v. Rodriguez*, 497 U.S. 177 (1990) that she had such authority based on available facts, and they had no basis to believe that files were password protected or encrypted).

249. For a discussion of exigent circumstances involving a search of a computer, see SEARCHING AND SEIZING COMPUTERS, *supra* note 101, at 27–31.

250. *See, e.g.*, Guy v. State, 913 A.2d 558 (Del. 2006) (defendant's consent to "complete and thorough search" of apartment included pager when defendant was silent as officer searched it). *But see* United States v. Carey, 172 F.3d 1268 (10th Cir. 1999) (consent to complete search of premises and property did not authorize search of computer files).

also authorize an offsite examination of the items seized to assure a valid consent.[251]

Even if there is explicit or implicit consent to search a computer or other device offsite, an officer should remember that consent may be revoked at any time before or even during the search. Thus, if the offsite search will not be completed soon, an officer may want to obtain a search warrant (assuming probable cause exists) instead of relying solely on consent.

When a person consents to a search for evidence of one criminal offense, that consent may not allow an officer to search for evidence of an unrelated offense—at least not in areas of the computer or other device where evidence of the first offense could not reasonably be found. A request for consent to search a computer or other device that is focused on one criminal offense generally will not include a search for an unrelated offense. To avoid potential legal issues concerning the scope of consent, an officer could explicitly ask consent to search a computer or other device for evidence of a named offense as well as any other criminal offenses. Even if an officer only asks consent to search for one offense but while properly searching for this offense discovers evidence of an unrelated offense, evidence of the unrelated offense will be admissible under the plain view theory.[252] Of course, to avoid all further consent issues, an officer could obtain a search warrant (assuming probable cause exists) to continue searching the computer or other device.

Searches of children's computers with the consent of their parents and searches of employee computers by private and governmental employers will not be discussed here; see the publication cited in the accompanying footnote.[253]

Completion of the Inventory Form after a Search with Consent

North Carolina statutory law requires officers who conduct a consent search to make an inventory of all property they seize and give a copy both to the person who consented and to the owner (if known) of the place searched, if the owner is not the person who consented.[254] The owner's copy may be mailed rather than hand delivered and may be given to the owner's agent—for example, to the resident manager of an apartment complex. Unlike when officers complete an inventory of items seized with a search warrant, officers need not be sworn to the information in the inventory completed after a consent search. Officers also need not give a copy to the clerk, but they may want to do so anyway to ensure that the court file contains a copy.

The Administrative Office of the Courts publishes a form (AOC-CR-206) to use when making an inventory of seized property after a search with consent. It may be obtained from the office of the clerk of superior court or from the AOC's website at www.nccourts.org/Forms/FormSearch.asp.

Invasion of Privacy by a Search or Seizure with Sufficient Reason

The law of search and seizure permits officers to interfere with a person's privacy when they have a justification under the Fourth Amendment to do so. And when that justification exists, they do not need the consent of the person whose privacy is affected, although they sometimes need a search warrant before they may search or seize evidence.

Generally, the four most common justifications that allow officers lawfully to interfere with a person's privacy without consent are the following:

1. Searches for and seizures of evidence with probable cause

---

251. This approach responds to the ruling in *United States v. Carey*, 172 F.3d 1268, 1276 (10th Cir. 1999), which narrowly interpreted a written consent form to permit the seizure of the defendant's computer from his apartment but not the search off-site. For cases that interpret consent more broadly, see SEARCHING AND SEIZING COMPUTERS, *supra* note 101, at 17–18. For an example of a consent form, see *United States v. Long*, 425 F.3d 482 (7th Cir. 2005) (consent form allowed officers to remove "whatever documents, items of property whatsoever, including but not limited to computer hardware, software, and all other external media storage, which they deem pertinent to their investigation and search said items").

252. *See generally* SEARCHING AND SEIZING COMPUTERS, *supra* note 101, at 34–37.

253. SEARCHING AND SEIZING COMPUTERS, *supra* note 101, at 23–24 (parents' consent to search children's computers)

& 42–56 (private- and public-sector workplace computer searches). *See also* City of Ontario v. Quon, 560 U.S. 746 (2010) (court ruled, assuming without deciding that government employee had reasonable expectation of privacy in text messages sent on government-provided page, that government employer's review of text message was reasonable under Fourth Amendment).

254. G.S. 15A-223(b).

2. Searches for and seizures of evidence with reasonable suspicion or some other justification
3. Searches and seizures aimed at protecting people or property
4. General inspections of regulated activities (discussed with administrative inspection warrants in Chapter 4)

Evidence That May Be Searched for and Seized

(*See page 275 for case summaries on this topic.*)

Before discussing the right to search and seize evidence with probable cause, reasonable suspicion, or some other justification, it is important to understand the kinds of evidence officers may search for and seize under the Fourth Amendment.

Generally, officers may search for and seize any evidence that will assist in arresting or prosecuting a person.[255] Such evidence may include the following:[256]

- Instrumentalities of a crime, such as a crowbar used in a burglary or a weapon used in a murder or robbery.
- Fruits of a crime, such as money and property taken during a robbery or burglary.
- Contraband, such as illegal drugs or non-tax-paid liquor, that may not be possessed lawfully. Courts sometimes also describe stolen property—for example, a stolen television set—as contraband or derivative contraband, even though it may otherwise be possessed lawfully.
- Weapons that may present a danger to an officer or others, even though they may not be instrumentalities or fruits of a crime or contraband.[257]
- Evidence, even though it does not fit under any of the first four categories, that is connected (or, as court opinions say, has a nexus) to a crime.[258] Examples of such evidence are (1) clothing worn by the

defendant during a robbery,[259] which is evidence of the identity of a person participating in a crime, or (2) documents—such as letters and photographs—discovered inadvertently in plain view during the execution of a search warrant for drugs that may help to establish the defendant's presence in or possession of the premises where the drugs were found.[260]

Throughout this book, the phrase "evidence of a crime" will be used to include all these kinds of evidence that officers may search for and seize under the Fourth Amendment.

Search and Seizure of Evidence with Probable Cause

(*See page 336 for case summaries on this topic.*)

A search or seizure under some circumstances may be reasonable under the Fourth Amendment without being supported by probable cause.[261] For example, a forcible stop or frisk may be supported by reasonable suspicion, and an inventory search, discussed later in this chapter on page 261, may be reasonable under the Fourth Amendment if conducted for the legitimate purpose of protecting property. But this section discusses only searches and seizures that—to be reasonable under the Fourth Amendment—must be based on probable cause. It also discusses whether a particular search or seizure must be undertaken with a search warrant. Search warrants are discussed in Chapter 4.

The same standard of certainty or quantity of evidence needed in determining probable cause to arrest also applies in determining probable cause to search or seize. Thus, as discussed in Chapter 2, probable cause is a fluid concept that depends on an assessment of probabilities in particular situations; it cannot be reduced readily to a neat set of legal rules. The degree of certainty corresponding to probable cause is a *fair probability*; that is, the amount of proof is *more* than for reasonable suspicion but *less* than for such other legal evidentiary standards as preponderance of evidence, more probable than not,

---

255. Warden v. Hayden, 387 U.S. 294 (1967).

256. G.S. 15A-242 lists the items that may be seized under a search warrant, and all of them would be included in the list set out in the text. Of course, the items also may be seized during a warrantless search and seizure.

257. For example, weapons seized during a frisk. Adams v. Williams, 407 U.S. 143 (1972); Michigan v. Long, 463 U.S. 1112 (1983).

258. Warden v. Hayden, 387 U.S. 294 (1967). *See* 2 Wayne R. LaFave, Search and Seizure: A Treatise on the Fourth Amendment § 3.7(d) (5th ed. 2012).

259. Warden v. Hayden, 387 U.S. 294 (1967).

260. State v. Richards, 294 N.C. 474 (1978); State v. Zimmerman, 23 N.C. App. 396 (1974).

261. *See, e.g.,* New Jersey v. T.L.O., 469 U.S. 325 (1985); New York v. Class, 475 U.S. 106 (1986).

more likely than not, prima facie evidence, clear and convincing evidence, or beyond a reasonable doubt.[262]

Although the standard of certainty—fair probability—is the same whether the subject is probable cause to arrest or probable cause to search or seize, it must be remembered that the inquiries underlying an arrest (was a crime committed and did the defendant commit it?) and a search (is there evidence of a crime in the place or on the person to be searched?) focus on different facts. Thus, probable cause to arrest does not automatically provide probable cause to search—and vice versa.[263] However, there are situations in which officers have reliable information that will support both probable cause to arrest and probable cause to search. For example, as discussed below, reliable information that a person is selling heroin from a car may provide both probable cause to search the car and probable cause to arrest the person for possession and sale of heroin—even before a search for the heroin is conducted.

Because probable cause to search depends on a fair probability that evidence of a crime may be in a certain place or on a specific person, the *timeliness* of information that supports probable cause to search is generally more critical than the timeliness of information that supports probable cause to arrest. Information may become stale and therefore less valuable. Thus, although probable cause may exist at one time to search a car for drugs, there may no longer be probable cause at a later time if there is no longer a *fair probability* that the drugs are still in the car. Probable cause to search also focuses on the *place* where evidence of a crime probably is located. Thus,

even when information is timely, it must provide officers with enough facts to support a fair probability that the evidence may be found where they want to search. Both concepts—that the information must be timely and that it must connect the evidence to be seized with the place to be searched—are discussed in Chapter 4 on search warrants.

Hearsay Evidence

As with the law of arrest, officers and judicial officials are not bound by the rules of evidence that apply to trial proceedings when they determine probable cause to search. Thus, hearsay evidence that otherwise would be inadmissible at a trial is admissible at a suppression hearing.[264] For example, information given to an officer by another officer, a citizen, a confidential informant, or even an anonymous tipster may be considered.[265] Because the law concerning the use of reliable hearsay is the same as for searches with a search warrant, this subject is discussed in Chapter 4 on search warrants and will not be repeated here.

Objective Standard

(*See page 362 for case summaries on this topic.*)

As in the law of arrest, courts use an objective standard in determining whether an officer had the authority to search and to seize evidence. For example: An officer conducts a search of a car's trunk, apparently believing that the inventory search rationale (discussed later in this chapter on page 261) is the only justification to do so. The officer does not believe that probable cause exists to search the trunk. However, a court believes otherwise and upholds the search based on probable cause.[266] A court will uphold a search if the objective facts support

---

262. State v. Crawford, 125 N.C. App. 279 (1997); Illinois v. Gates, 462 U.S. 213 (1983); Texas v. Brown, 460 U.S. 730 (1983); State v. Arrington, 311 N.C. 633 (1984); State v. Zuniga, 312 N.C. 251 (1984); United States v. Adcock, 756 F.2d 346 (5th Cir. 1985); 2 Wayne R. LaFave, Search and Seizure: A Treatise on the Fourth Amendment § 3.2(e) (5th ed. 2012). Although the *Gates* Court discussed the concept of probable cause to support a search warrant, North Carolina appellate courts since that decision have properly used that standard in discussing probable cause for warrantless arrests and searches. State v. Ford, 70 N.C. App. 244 (1984); Steinkrause v. Tatum, 201 N.C. App. 289 (2009), *aff'd*, 364 N.C. 419 (2009). *See also* State v. Davis, 66 N.C. App. 98 (1984) (using *Gates* totality of circumstances analysis to determine reliability of informant's tip that supported reasonable suspicion to stop).

263. See the discussion in 2 Wayne R. LaFave, Search and Seizure: A Treatise on the Fourth Amendment § 3.1(b) (5th ed. 2012).

264. The Fourth Amendment does not bar the use of hearsay evidence in determining reasonable suspicion or probable cause. Brinegar v. United States, 338 U.S. 160 (1949); Draper v. United States, 358 U.S. 307 (1959); Alabama v. White, 496 U.S. 325 (1990); Illinois v. Gates, 462 U.S. 213 (1983). Under Rules 104(a) and 1101(b)(1) of the North Carolina Rules of Evidence in G.S. 8C-1, the rules of evidence do not apply in a hearing that determines the admissibility of evidence, with the exception of rules concerning privileges.

265. State v. Roberts, 276 N.C. 98 (1970); Melton v. Hodges, 114 N.C. App. 795 (1994).

266. United States v. Burnett, 791 F.2d 64 (6th Cir. 1986).

the officer's actions despite the officer's contrary subjective belief.[267]

Advantages of a Search Warrant

As the discussion later in this chapter will indicate, there are many situations in which officers who have probable cause may search for and seize evidence without obtaining a search warrant. And, particularly with vehicle searches, officers often need not obtain a search warrant even when they have the time to get one. The amount of time it takes to obtain a search warrant, when officers could have conducted a warrantless search, is clearly a disadvantage. However, even when officers may legally search and seize without a warrant, there are several advantages in getting one. These advantages include the following:

- Officers' belief that they did not need to obtain a search warrant may later be proven wrong, and the evidence they obtained may be ruled inadmissible at trial. Officers should consider obtaining a warrant when they are uncertain of their legal right to proceed without one and they have the time to obtain a warrant.

- In some cases, the existence of probable cause may be doubtful. In a marginal case, a court may find that probable cause exists if officers acted with a search warrant, but the court may not reach that decision if they acted without a warrant.[268]

- Officers are never legally disadvantaged if they obtain a search warrant. Even if the search warrant is later ruled to be invalid, the officers' search may still be justified by whatever justification properly existed to conduct a warrantless search or seizure.[269]

- Sometimes North Carolina officers' cases are prosecuted in federal court in North Carolina because they involve federal violations such as drug and firearm offenses. There exists in federal court a "good faith" exception to the exclusionary rule when evidence is seized under an invalid search warrant that a reasonably well-trained officer would not have known was invalid (this subject is discussed in Chapter 4). Thus, evidence seized under such a warrant will be admissible at trial.[270] There is not a similar exception for warrantless searches; therefore, officers have an incentive to obtain a search warrant. However, this good faith exception probably does not exist in North Carolina state courts.[271]

- In considering an application for a search warrant, a judicial official may convince officers that they do not have probable cause to search, thereby preventing a possibly illegal search or seizure from taking place. Officers may then investigate further and gather additional information that does supply probable cause.

- If a civil action is brought against officers for allegedly violating a person's Fourth Amendment rights, they may be better protected if they acted with a search warrant than if they did not.[272]

Search and Seizure of Vehicles with Probable Cause

(See page 336 for case summaries on this topic.)

Because officers in their everyday duties often must undertake investigative actions that involve a vehicle, they need to know their authority to search and seize a vehicle—including whether they must have a search war-

---

267. United States v. Swann, 149 F.3d 271 (4th Cir. 1998); State v. Freeman, 307 N.C. 357 (1983); State v. Riggs, 328 N.C. 213 (1991). For United States Supreme Court cases using the objective standard in analyzing Fourth Amendment issues, see *Devenpeck v. Alford*, 543 U.S. 146 (2004), and *Brigham City v. Stuart*, 547 U.S. 398 (2006).

268. United States v. Ventresca, 380 U.S. 102 (1964); Illinois v. Gates, 462 U.S. 213 (1983); United States v. Carlson, 697 F.2d 231 (8th Cir. 1983); United States v. Frietas, 716 F.2d 1216 (9th Cir. 1983).

269. *See, e.g.*, State v. Downes, 57 N.C. App. 102 (1982); State v. Frederick, 31 N.C. App. 503 (1976).

270. United States v. Leon, 468 U.S. 897 (1984); Massachusetts v. Sheppard, 468 U.S. 981 (1984).

271. The North Carolina Supreme Court in *State v. Carter*, 322 N.C. 709 (1988), did not adopt under the Constitution of North Carolina the rulings in *Leon* and *Sheppard*, cited above in note 270, at least based on the facts in *Carter*: "We are not persuaded *on the facts before us* that we should engraft a good faith exception to the exclusionary rule under our state constitution." 322 N.C. at 724 (emphasis added). Note that *State v. Garner*, 331 N.C. 491 (1992), appears to undermine this aspect of the *Carter* ruling. The possible conflict between *Carter* and *Garner* was noted in *State v. Banner*, 207 N.C. App. 729 n.7 (2010). See additional discussion in footnote 1 of Chapter 4.

272. Despite the ruling in *Malley v. Briggs*, 475 U.S. 335 (1986) (officers may be civilly liable for violating a person's constitutional rights if they obtain an arrest warrant and make an arrest when a reasonably well-trained officer in their position would have known that their information failed to establish probable cause to arrest), the use of a search warrant may be a favorable factor when officers seek to persuade a fact finder that they did not violate a person's constitutional rights.

rant to do so. During the past several decades, the United States Supreme Court has clarified the law concerning vehicle searches,[273] and officers now may be more certain about whether they are acting within constitutional limits. Remember that officers need only reasonable suspicion—not probable cause—to make an investigatory stop of a vehicle; see the discussion in Chapter 2 on page 30.

Before discussing an officer's right to conduct searches and seizures of vehicles with probable cause, it is important to note that vehicle searches sometimes may be conducted under other justifications that are discussed later in this chapter. In fact, many times officers may rely on more than one justification in making a search or seizure, although the scope—where and what they may search—may differ depending on the particular justification. Some justifications, other than having probable cause, are the following:

- Evidence found in a warrantless search of the interior of the vehicle, including containers within the interior, incident to the arrest of any occupant of the vehicle
- Evidence in the vehicle seen in plain view and seized without a warrant
- Evidence found during a warrantless inventory search of a vehicle impounded for safekeeping
- The fact that the vehicle itself is evidence of a crime
- The seizure of a vehicle because it is subject to forfeiture
- A warrantless search of a vehicle when an officer is undertaking a community caretaking function
- Reasonable suspicion that a person is dangerous and a weapon that could be used to harm an officer may be in a vehicle

Rulings of the United States Supreme Court and the North Carolina Supreme Court provide that when officers have probable cause to search a vehicle for evidence of a crime and the vehicle is in a public place—that is,

a place where the defendant does not have a reasonable expectation of privacy—they may seize the vehicle without a search warrant, whether the vehicle is moving or parked.[274] And the officers then may search the vehicle without a search warrant at the place where they seized it or may bring it to a law enforcement facility or other place and search it there without a warrant.[275] Thus, a warrantless search may be conducted later at another place even though officers have complete control over the vehicle and could obtain a search warrant without any risk that the vehicle and the evidence inside might disappear.[276]

Officers need exigent circumstances to justify their warrantless seizure of the vehicle only if they enter, without consent, a place where a defendant has a reasonable expectation of privacy, such as the curtilage of the defendant's home.[277] Once the vehicle has been lawfully

---

273. The rules governing vehicle searches often apply to searches of private planes, boats, mobile motor homes, and other property. State v. Russell, 84 N.C. App. 383 (1987) (airplane); California v. Carney, 471 U.S. 386 (1985) (mobile motor home); United States v. Navas, 597 F.3d 492 (2d Cir. 2010) (trailer portion of tractor trailer unhitched from cab; trailer is inherently mobile by having own wheels and could be connected to cab and driven away). *See* 3 WAYNE R. LaFAVE, SEARCH AND SEIZURE: A TREATISE ON THE FOURTH AMENDMENT § 7.2 n.2 (5th ed. 2012).

274. State v. Isleib, 319 N.C. 634 (1987) (this case was decided under both federal and state constitutions); Chambers v. Maroney, 399 U.S. 42 (1970); Texas v. White, 423 U.S. 67 (1975); Michigan v. Thomas, 458 U.S. 259 (1982); United States v. Johns, 469 U.S. 478 (1985); California v. Carney, 471 U.S. 386 (1985); United States v. Bagley, 772 F.2d 482 (9th Cir. 1985). *See generally* 3 WAYNE R. LaFAVE, SEARCH AND SEIZURE: A TREATISE ON THE FOURTH AMENDMENT §§ 7.2(a), (b) (5th ed. 2012).

275. Chambers v. Maroney, 399 U.S. 42 (1970).

276. *Id.*

277. State v. Russell, 92 N.C. App. 639 (1989) (after the defendant was arrested, officers seized the defendant's car from his driveway and searched it without a warrant; although the officers had probable cause to seize and search the car, there were no exigent circumstances and no consent to permit them to act without a search warrant, and their conduct could not be justified under the plain view doctrine set out in *Coolidge v. New Hampshire*, 403 U.S. 443 (1971) (but note that the inadvertence requirement of the plain view doctrine was later overruled in *Horton v. California*, 496 U.S. 128 (1990)). The *Russell* ruling is questionable. *See* Capraro v. Bunt, 44 F.3d 690 (8th Cir. 1995) (warrantless seizure of truck in driveway did not violate Fourth Amendment; truck's position in clear public view on defendant's driveway eliminated any privacy expectation otherwise resulting from its location on private property); United States v. Brookins, 345 F.3d 231 (4th Cir. 2003) (similar ruling); 3 WAYNE R. LaFAVE, SEARCH AND SEIZURE: A TREATISE ON THE FOURTH AMENDMENT § 7.3(a), at 601 (5th ed. 2012) (because officers may enter commonly used area of curtilage, such as a driveway, during course of legitimate investigation, they should be able to seize a vehicle there without a warrant). *See also* United States v. Shepherd, 714 F.2d 316 (4th Cir. 1983) (exigent circumstances existed to search car parked on private property); State v. Mitchell, 300 N.C. 305 (1980) (exigent circumstances existed to seize car parked by house). In both *Shepherd* and *Mitchell*, the defendants did not appear to have a reasonable expectation of privacy where their cars

seized, officers do not need exigent circumstances to justify searching it without a search warrant.[278]

This legal principle, permitting a warrantless vehicle search, is an exception to the general rule that officers may make a warrantless search with probable cause only when exigent circumstances exist to justify a failure to obtain a search warrant—for example, when the evidence might disappear if they took the time to obtain a warrant. The United States Supreme Court and the North Carolina Supreme Court have justified this principle essentially because they have decided that people have a lesser expectation of privacy in their vehicles than in their homes.[279]

What is the permissible scope of a warrantless search of a vehicle? The United States Supreme Court has ruled that it is the same as what a judicial official could authorize with a search warrant.[280] Thus, if there is probable cause to search a car for illegal drugs, officers may make a warrantless search of every place within the car where drugs could be found, including containers such as briefcases, suitcases, and bags located inside.[281] (Cases on searching cell phones under this rationale are summarized in the publication cited in the accompanying footnote.)[282]

Even if probable cause focuses exclusively on the contents of a specific container within a vehicle—that is, there is no probable cause to believe that evidence of a crime is located anywhere else in the vehicle—officers may still seize that container and search it without a search warrant.[283] (There also may be some other justifications for a warrantless search, such as a search incident to the arrest

of an occupant of the vehicle; see the discussion of search incident to arrest later in this chapter on page 249.) For example, if officers are conducting surveillance and see a person put a suitcase in the trunk of a car and they have probable cause to believe that the suitcase contains illegal drugs, they may stop the vehicle and remove the suitcase and search it without a warrant.[284] The Supreme Court has ruled that the legal principles permitting warrantless searches of vehicles apply also to the search of the suitcase, even though it is a repository of personal effects that may deserve a greater degree of privacy than the vehicle itself.[285] Searching suitcases and other containers in other places may require a search warrant; see the discussion on page 242.

It is useful to discuss some significant United States Supreme Court and North Carolina Supreme Court cases to understand the rules governing vehicle searches. The year each case was decided is given in parentheses to show the historical progression of the legal principles.

→ Carroll v. United States (1925)
In *Carroll v. United States*,[286] officers who had probable cause to believe that a car contained contraband liquor properly stopped the car on a highway and searched it there without a search warrant. The United States Supreme Court recognized a constitutional distinction between making a warrantless search of a house and car—the mobility of a car makes it impracticable to secure a search warrant.

→ Chambers v. Maroney (1970)
In *Chambers v. Maroney*,[287] officers stopped a car when they had probable cause to believe that (1) the suspects in the car had just committed an armed robbery and (2) the car contained evidence of that crime. They arrested the suspects, seized the car, and took the car to the police station, where they conducted a thorough warrantless search. The United States Supreme Court upheld the warrantless car search at the police station by extending the ruling in *Carroll v. United States*:

---

were seized, and therefore a finding of exigent circumstances under current prevailing constitutional principles would be unnecessary.

278. *See* cases cited *supra* note 274; United States v. Sinisterra, 77 F.3d 101 (5th Cir. 1996).

279. California v. Carney, 471 U.S. 386 (1985); State v. Isleib, 319 N.C. 634 (1987). Although the United States Supreme Court also has stated that a vehicle's mobility is another reason why a warrantless search is permitted, that reason hardly has much force when the Court permits a warrantless search even after a vehicle and its contents have been immobilized. See the discussion of *United States v. Johns*, 469 U.S. 478 (1985), in 3 Wayne R. LaFave, Search and Seizure: A Treatise on the Fourth Amendment § 7.2(b), at 795 (5th ed. 2012).

280. United States v. Ross, 456 U.S. 798 (1981).

281. *Id.*; State v. Parker, 183 N.C. App. 1 (2007) (searching locked briefcase in vehicle for illegal drugs).

282. Digital Evidence, *supra* note 140.

283. California v. Acevedo, 500 U.S. 565 (1991). *Acevedo* overruled *Arkansas v. Sanders*, 442 U.S. 753 (1979), and

disavowed part of the underlying rationale of *United States v. Chadwick*, 433 U.S. 1 (1977).

284. California v. *Acevedo*, 500 U.S. 565.

285. *Id.*

286. 267 U.S. 132 (1925).

287. 399 U.S. 42 (1970).

When there is probable cause to search a car that is stopped on the highway, the officers may make a warrantless search on the highway or take the car to the police station and conduct a warrantless search there. It is irrelevant that the officers had sufficient time to obtain a search warrant once the car was immobilized at the police station.

— Coolidge v. New Hampshire (1971)

In *Coolidge v. New Hampshire*,[288] officers had probable cause for weeks to search a defendant's car for evidence of a murder. They seized the car without a warrant when it was parked in the defendant's private driveway and took it to the police station, where they searched it without a warrant. When they seized it in the driveway, they had no evidence that the defendant or anyone else was planning to move the car or destroy evidence in the car. The United States Supreme Court ruled that both the warrantless seizure and the later warrantless search of the car were unconstitutional because neither exigent circumstances nor any other justification supported these actions.[289] [Author's note: However, officers may conduct a warrantless search of a car on private premises (1) even if they do not have probable cause to seize and search it before they arrive there but probable cause then develops or (2) if they did have probable cause beforehand but they had insufficient time to obtain a search warrant and exigent circumstances justified a warrantless seizure of the car.][290]

— Cardwell v. Lewis (1974)

In *Cardwell v. Lewis*,[291] officers had probable cause to arrest the defendant for murder and to search his car because it had been used during the murder. At police request, the defendant voluntarily came to the police station. The police then arrested him and seized his car without a search warrant. The car was parked in a nearby parking lot, and it was towed to the police impoundment lot. The next day a police technician removed paint from the car's exterior without a warrant and observed the tread of one of the tires. The United States Supreme Court ruled that the warrantless seizure of the car was proper because it was seized in a public place (contrasting *Coolidge v. New Hampshire*, which involved an entry onto private property to make a warrantless seizure) and because evidence indicated that other persons might remove the car from the parking lot.[292] The Court noted that officers may make a warrantless seizure and later a warrantless search even when they did not obtain a search warrant at the first practicable moment—that is, the officers in this case could have obtained a search warrant earlier in the day.

— Texas v. White (1975)

In *Texas v. White*,[293] the defendant was arrested while attempting to pass fraudulent checks from his car at a bank's drive-in window. Probable cause existed to search the car for checks. One officer drove the defendant to the station house and another drove the defendant's car there. About an hour later, the officers searched the car without a search warrant. The United States Supreme Court ruled that the warrantless search was proper under *Chambers v. Maroney*.

— Colorado v. Bannister (1980)

In *Colorado v. Bannister*,[294] an officer stopped a car he had seen speeding so that he could issue

---

288. 403 U.S. 443 (1971).

289. Although *Coolidge* was a four-Justice plurality opinion, the section stating that there were no exigent circumstances to justify the warrantless seizure of the car in the private driveway is apparently settled law, even though the inadvertence requirement of the plain view doctrine in *Coolidge* was overruled in *Horton v. California*, 496 U.S. 128 (1990). See the discussion of *State v. Russell*, 92 N.C. App. 639 (1989) (neither exigent circumstances nor consent existed when officers improperly seized car in private driveway) and conflicting cases cited *supra* note 277.

290. *See United States v. Shepherd* and *State v. Mitchell*, discussed *supra* note 277.

291. 417 U.S. 583 (1974).

---

292. Although the decision in *Cardwell v. Lewis* was a four-Justice plurality opinion, it is settled law. In *United States v. Bagley*, 772 F.2d 482 (9th Cir. 1985), the United States Court of Appeals for the Ninth Circuit stated that probable cause alone justifies a warrantless seizure and search of a vehicle parked in a public place—at least if the car can move, although the court did not explicitly state this qualification; exigent circumstances are not needed to justify the warrantless seizure or later search of the vehicle. *See also* State v. Isleib, 319 N.C. 634 (1987); United States v. Sinisterra, 77 F.3d 101 (5th Cir. 1996).

293. 423 U.S. 67 (1975).

294. 449 U.S. 1 (1980).

a citation to the driver. When he approached the car, he noticed items in plain view in the car that matched a recently reported theft of motor vehicle parts. The car's two occupants also matched the descriptions of the suspected thieves. The United States Supreme Court ruled that this evidence supported probable cause to arrest the occupants and probable cause to search the car, and the officer's later warrantless search and seizure of the items in the car was proper.

■ United States v. Ross (1982)
In *United States v. Ross,*[295] a confidential and reliable informant gave officers information that the defendant was selling illegal drugs out of the trunk of his car, which was parked on a street. The informant told them that he had just seen the defendant complete a sale and the defendant had told him that additional drugs were in the trunk. After corroborating some of this information, the officers later saw the car traveling in the neighborhood and stopped it. They ordered the defendant out of the car and arrested him. They searched the car without a warrant there and also at the police station. The search included the car's interior and the trunk.[296] Within the trunk officers searched a brown paper bag that contained heroin and a zippered leather pouch that contained $3,200 in cash. The United States Supreme Court ruled that when officers have probable cause to search an entire vehicle for evidence of a crime—in this case, illegal drugs[297]—they may conduct a warrantless search of the entire vehicle, including opening containers within the vehicle, if the object of the search might be found there. The scope of the warrantless search may include all places within the vehicle that a magistrate could authorize with a search warrant.

■ United States v. Johns (1985)
In *United States v. Johns,*[298] federal officers who were investigating a drug-smuggling operation by ground and air surveillance saw two pickup trucks travel to a remote private airstrip where two airplanes arrived and then left. The officers approached the trucks and smelled the odor of marijuana emanating from them. They saw in the back of the trucks packages wrapped in dark green plastic and sealed with tape, a common method of packaging marijuana. They arrested the defendants at the airstrip and took the trucks to agency headquarters, where the packages were removed and placed in a warehouse and later searched without a warrant. The United States Supreme Court ruled that the officers had probable cause to believe that not only the packages but also the trucks themselves contained contraband: the officers had smelled the marijuana odor before they saw the packages in the trucks, and therefore the marijuana could have been anywhere in the trucks.[299] Thus, under *United States v. Ross,* they could search each entire truck, including the packages, without a search warrant.

■ California v. Carney (1985)
In *California v. Carney,*[300] federal officers had information that the defendant was exchanging marijuana for sex with a young man inside the defendant's motor home, which was parked in a lot in downtown San Diego. The officers stopped the youth after he left the motor home. He told the officers that he had received marijuana in return for allowing the defendant to have sexual contact with him. The officers went to the motor home, entered it without consent or an arrest or search warrant, and saw marijuana and other drug implements inside. They then seized the motor home and conducted a warrantless search at the police station. The United States Supreme Court ruled that the officers had probable cause to conduct the searches and could do so without a search warrant. The Court noted that the motor

---

295. 456 U.S. 798 (1982).

296. The Court implicitly recognized that these facts provided probable cause to search the entire vehicle.

297. Although most of the vehicle cases involve a search for contraband, their rationale ordinarily should apply to any search for evidence of a crime, whether contraband or something else. *See* 3 Wayne R. LaFave, Search and Seizure: A Treatise on the Fourth Amendment § 7.2(a), at 723 (5th ed. 2012).

---

298. 469 U.S. 478 (1985).

299. Although the statement in the next sentence of the text about probable cause to search the entire truck was not a ruling in the case, it clearly is a correct statement of existing law.

300. 471 U.S. 386 (1985).

home was readily mobile, even though parked, and an objective observer would conclude that it was being used as a vehicle, not a residence—for example, it was a licensed motor vehicle that was obviously readily mobile by turning the ignition switch.

▶ California v. Acevedo (1991)
In *California v. Acevedo*,[301] law enforcement officers saw the defendant leaving an apartment with a brown paper bag that they had probable cause to believe contained marijuana. The defendant placed the bag in the trunk of a car and drove away. (In this case, the officers did not have probable cause to believe that illegal drugs were located elsewhere in the car other than in the bag.) They stopped the car without a search warrant, opened the trunk and the bag, and found marijuana inside. The United States Supreme Court ruled that law enforcement officers may search without a warrant—under the vehicle exception to the search warrant requirement—a container within a vehicle even when the probable cause to search focuses exclusively on the container and nowhere else in the vehicle. The Court overruled *Arkansas v. Sanders*,[302] which had ruled impermissible an officer's warrantless search for marijuana in a suitcase that had been placed in the trunk of a taxi. The Court also rejected the rationale of *United States v. Chadwick* (1977),[303] which had supported the ruling in the *Sanders* case by implicitly placing a greater expectation of privacy in a container placed in a vehicle than in the vehicle itself.

▶ State v. Isleib (1987)
In *State v. Isleib*,[304] deputy sheriff Midgette learned from a confidential and reliable informant during the afternoon of April 5, 1985, that a woman named Martha would be coming to Hat-

teras Island from the beach area north of Oregon Inlet the following day. Martha would be driving her army-green Dodge or Plymouth station wagon with letters or a decal on the door, she would be accompanied by a white male, and she would be delivering quarter-ounce bags of marijuana. Midgette was familiar with the car described and with Martha—he had known her for seven or eight years, and she lived at the beach north of Oregon Inlet. About 20 hours later, at about 12:35 p.m. on April 6, Midgette was driving north on Hatteras Island when he saw Martha driving a green station wagon in a southerly direction. He telephoned another deputy, who stopped the vehicle. Midgette arrived minutes later and found Martha standing beside the vehicle and a white male still seated on the passenger's side. Midgette then conducted a warrantless search of the vehicle. The North Carolina Supreme Court ruled that there was probable cause to search the vehicle and the search was properly conducted without a search warrant. A search warrant is not required when probable cause exists to search a motor vehicle in a public place—that is, a place other than where a person has a reasonable expectation of privacy, such as the curtilage of a home.[305] The inherent mobility of a vehicle automatically establishes exigent circumstances to make a warrantless search of a vehicle, assuming there is probable cause to search.

In summary, these cases indicate that officers often may seize and search a vehicle and its contents without a warrant. But they need to understand clearly the justification(s) that support their actions so they do not exceed the scope of a permissible warrantless search or seizure.

Seizure of a Vehicle Subject to Forfeiture
(*See page 344 for case summaries on this topic.*)
North Carolina statutes authorize the forfeiture (divesting of ownership) of vehicles and other property used in

---

301. 500 U.S. 565 (1991).

302. 442 U.S. 753 (1979).

303. 433 U.S. 1 (1977).

304. 319 N.C. 634 (1987). The court's ruling was decided under the Constitution of North Carolina as well as under the United States Constitution. For cases consistent with the ruling in *Isleib*, see *United States v. Reis*, 906 F.2d 284 (7th Cir. 1990) (car parked on street in front of residence); *United States v. Nixon*, 918 F.2d 895 (11th Cir. 1990); and *United States v. Wider*, 951 F.2d 1283 (D.C. Cir. 1991).

---

305. See the discussion of *State v. Russell*, 92 N.C. App. 639 (1989) (neither exigent circumstances nor consent existed when officers improperly seized car in private driveway) and conflicting cases discussed *supra* note 277.

certain criminal activities.[306] The most commonly used statute authorizes the forfeiture of a conveyance used to conceal or transport controlled substances during a felonious drug violation.[307] It authorizes officers to seize the conveyance without a warrant when they have probable cause to believe that it is subject to forfeiture if the seizure occurs (1) when a person is being arrested for committing the felony drug violation or (2) when a search warrant is being executed.[308] At all other times, officers must obtain an order from a district or superior court judge to seize a conveyance that is subject to forfeiture.[309] However, they need not obtain such an order if they have another justification to seize the vehicle without a warrant—for example, probable cause to believe that the vehicle contains evidence of a crime.

If officers seize a vehicle because it is subject to forfeiture, they may conduct an inventory search without a search warrant.[310] Inventory searches are discussed later in this chapter on page 261.

Seizure of a Vehicle as Evidence of a Crime or an Instrument of a Crime

Appellate cases authorize officers to seize a vehicle because the vehicle itself is evidence of a crime or an instrument of a crime.[311] For example, officers may seize a vehicle that they have probable cause to believe was used in an armed robbery because it is both evidence of the robbery and an instrument of the robbery. And officers may seize the vehicle without a search warrant if it is located in a public place—that is, a place other than where a person has a reasonable expectation of privacy, such as the curtilage of a home.

Of course, officers often also will be justified in (1) seizing and searching a vehicle because they have probable cause to believe that the vehicle contains evidence of a crime—for example, the proceeds from an armed robbery; or (2) seizing a vehicle because it is subject to forfeiture. These are justifications separate and distinct from seizing a vehicle as evidence of or as an instrument of a crime.

Search and Seizure of Containers with Probable Cause
(See page 345 for case summaries on this topic.)

The United States Supreme Court has recognized that people have a greater expectation of privacy in containers that are repositories of personal effects than they have in their vehicles or when those containers are in their vehicles.[312] The protection accorded containers applies to any objects that might contain personal effects. A paper bag may deserve as much Fourth Amendment protection as a briefcase or luggage.[313]

Generally, officers who have probable cause to believe that a container of personal effects contains evidence of a crime must obtain a search warrant before they may search the container, although they may seize the container without a warrant and keep it in their custody while they apply for a search warrant.[314] But this search warrant requirement is subject to several exceptions:

- When there is probable cause to search without a warrant throughout a vehicle for evidence of a crime, officers may also search containers found in that vehicle without a warrant, if the object of the search might reasonably be found there.[315]
- When there is probable cause to search a container in a vehicle for evidence of a crime, officers may search that container without a warrant.[316]

---

306. Some of North Carolina's vehicle forfeiture statutes include G.S. 14-86.1 (conveyance used in felonious larceny, robbery, etc.); G.S. 18B-504 (conveyance and containers used in alcoholic beverage violations); G.S. 20-28.2 (motor vehicle used in impaired driving offense when driver had impaired driving license revocation); G.S. 20-141.3 (motor vehicle used in prearranged speed competition); G.S. 90-112(a)(4) (conveyance used in felony drug violation); and G.S. 113-137(i) (weapons, equipment, vessels, conveyances, fish, wildlife, etc., used in wildlife and marine fisheries violations).

307. G.S. 90-112. This statute also provides for the forfeiture of other kinds of property used during a felony or misdemeanor drug violation, such as money.

308. G.S. 90-112(b). The subsection also permits a warrantless seizure when the property is subject to a prior judgment for the State in a criminal injunction or forfeiture proceeding under G.S. Chapter 90, Article 5.

309. G.S. 90-112(b). Although the statute does not require that the seizure order be based on a finding that there is probable cause to believe that the property is subject to forfeiture, such a finding is probably constitutionally required, except when a judgment of forfeiture already has been entered.

310. Cooper v. California, 386 U.S. 58 (1967).

311. United States v. Cooper, 949 F.2d 737 (5th Cir. 1991); State v. Mitchell, 300 N.C. 305 (1980).

312. See the discussion in *California v. Acevedo*, 500 U.S. 565 (1991).

313. The Court in *United States v. Ross*, 456 U.S. 798 (1982), clearly rejected a distinction between "worthy" and "unworthy" containers—that is, whether they are worthy or unworthy of Fourth Amendment protection.

314. See the discussion in *United States v. Jacobsen*, 466 U.S. 109 (1984), and *California v. Acevedo*, 500 U.S. 565 (1991).

315. United States v. Ross, 456 U.S. 798 (1982).

316. California v. Acevedo, 500 U.S. 565 (1991).

- Officers may search without a warrant, as incident to arrest, most containers—for example, wallets and pocketbooks—that the arrestee is carrying or that are within the arrestee's immediate control; however, the North Carolina Court of Appeals has ruled that a large, locked suitcase may not be searched incident to arrest (see page 249).[317]
- Officers under certain circumstances may search without a warrant, as incident to the arrest of an occupant of a vehicle, any containers within the vehicle's interior (see page 252).[318]
- Containers sometimes may be searched without a warrant during an inventory search before an arrestee enters a detention facility (see page 257) or during a vehicle inventory search (see page 261).[319]
- A container may be searched without a warrant if there are exigent circumstances—for example, a bomb is in the container[320]—or if there is other evidence that may be destroyed or dissipated during the time needed to obtain a warrant.

The United States Supreme Court has indicated that a person does not have a reasonable expectation of privacy in containers that by their shape (for example, a gun case), transparency (for example, clear plastic wrapping around marijuana), or obvious single purpose (for example, a tied-off balloon that contains white powder and is found with other drug paraphernalia) in effect clearly reveal their contents so that the contents are considered to be in plain view.[321] Officers who have probable cause to believe that evidence of a crime is within these containers are authorized to search them without a warrant.[322] However, officers who are unsure of the legality of a warrantless search based on this justification may want to obtain a search warrant to ensure that they are conducting a lawful search.

Officers who have only reasonable suspicion that evidence of a crime is in a container may seize it briefly for further investigation. This authority is discussed on page 248.

Exigent Circumstances to Enter Home with Probable Cause to Search for Evidence

(*See page 348 for case summaries on this topic.*)

Generally, officers may not enter a home or other place of residence to search for evidence of a crime without a search warrant or consent, unless probable cause to search and exigent circumstances exist. Although the United States Supreme Court has not precisely set out the factors in determining when exigent circumstances permit such a search,[323] some factors[324] are as follows:

- Whether officers had an objectively reasonable belief that destruction or removal of the evidence was imminent, including whether it was likely that people within the house might destroy or remove the evidence because they were aware of the officers' knowledge of the evidence inside the house[325]

---

317. State v. Thomas, 81 N.C. App. 200 (1986).

318. See the discussion of *Arizona v. Gant*, 556 U.S. 332 (2009), on page 252.

319. Illinois v. LaFayette, 462 U.S. 640 (1983); Colorado v. Bertine, 479 U.S. 367 (1987); Florida v. Wells, 495 U.S. 1 (1990).

320. United States v. Sullivan, 544 F. Supp. 701 (D. Maine 1982), aff'd, 711 F.2d 1 (1st Cir. 1983); United States v. Sarkissian, 841 F.2d 959 (9th Cir. 1988).

321. In *United States v. Johns*, 469 U.S. 478 (1985), the Court suggested in dicta that if officers detect an odor of marijuana emanating from a package, they may search the package without a warrant because the odor effectively places the package's contents in plain view (smell), so that a person could no longer have a privacy interest in the package. The Court cited *United States v. Haley*, 669 F.2d 201 (4th Cir. 1982), and *Arkansas v. Sanders*, 442 U.S. 753 n.13 (1979). *See also* Justice Stevens's concurring opinion in *Texas v. Brown*, 460 U.S. 730 (1983); *United States v. Jacobsen*, 466 U.S. 109 (1984); and 3 Wayne R. LaFave, Search and Seizure: A Treatise on the Fourth Amendment § 5.5(f) (5th ed. 2012).

322. *See, e.g.*, United States v. Williams, 41 F.3d 192 (4th Cir. 1994) (it was a "foregone conclusion" that cellophane wrapped packages contained cocaine and were properly searched without a search warrant).

323. See the discussion in 3 Wayne R. LaFave, Search and Seizure: A Treatise on the Fourth Amendment § 6.5(a) (5th ed. 2012); *Segura v. United States*, 468 U.S. 796 (1984); and *Vale v. Louisiana*, 399 U.S. 30 (1970). In *Kentucky v. King*, 563 U.S. 452 (2011), the Court decided the case by assuming, without deciding, that exigent circumstances existed.

324. *See generally* 3 Wayne R. LaFave, Search and Seizure: A Treatise on the Fourth Amendment § 6.5(b) (5th ed. 2012).

325. Cases finding exigent circumstances include *United States v. Moses*, 540 F.3d 263 (4th Cir. 2008); *United States v. Grissett*, 925 F.2d 776 (4th Cir. 1991); *United States v. Tobin*, 923 F.2d 1506 (11th Cir. 1991); *United States v. Sangiento-Miranda*, 859 F.2d 1501 (6th Cir. 1988); and *State v. Prevette*, 43 N.C. App. 450 (1979). Cases not finding exigent circumstances include *Vale v. Louisiana*, 399 U.S. 30 (1970); *State v. Nowell*, 144 N.C. App. 636 (2001), aff'd, 355 N.C. 273 (2002); *United States v. Timberlake*, 896 F.2d 592 (D.C. Cir. 1990); *United States v. Buchanan*, 904 F.2d 349 (6th Cir. 1990); *United States v. Radka*, 904 F.2d 357 (6th Cir. 1990); and *United States*

- The likelihood that violence might be committed against the officers[326]
- The gravity of the offense for which the officers are searching for evidence[327]
- How long it would take to obtain a search warrant[328]

Although the United States Supreme Court has not set out the precise factors that constitute exigent circumstances, it has delineated the scope of the rule that allows officers to enter a residence without a search warrant to search for evidence of a crime when exigent circumstances exist. The Court ruled in *Kentucky v. King*[329] that when exigent circumstances exist, officers may make a warrantless entry if they simply knock on the door of a residence and announce their presence and as a result the occupants attempt to destroy evidence. The Court stated that if officers do not create exigent circumstances by engaging in or threatening to engage in conduct that violates the Fourth Amendment, a warrantless entry to prevent the destruction of evidence is reasonable and thus permissible.[330]

After officers have entered the house and secured it so that the exigent circumstances that permitted their entry and search no longer exist, they must obtain a search warrant—absent consent to search—to conduct any further search of the house. Of course, evidence officers saw in plain view while properly entering and securing the house may be seized without a search warrant.

An alternative to entering and searching a house without a search warrant is impounding the property while an officer applies for a search warrant.[331] Impoundment may be accomplished in either of two ways:

1. Officers may enter the house without a warrant and seize control until another officer obtains a search warrant. However, the warrantless entry to impound the property must be supported by the same exigent circumstances needed to support a warrantless entry and search, discussed above. The basic advantage of this approach over a warrantless entry and a warrantless search is that officers conduct the search with a search warrant.

2. Several officers may surround the house—a perimeter stakeout—while another officer obtains a search warrant. Exigent circumstances probably are not required to justify the stakeout. This approach probably should be used only when officers believe that evidence may be lost or destroyed if they do not limit access to the property. Of course, probable cause must support the warrantless seizure—the stakeout—as well as the search warrant that is obtained later.

---

v. Lynch, 934 F.2d 1226 (11th Cir. 1991). For additional cases, see the case summaries section in this chapter.

326. United States v. Jones, 239 F.3d 716 (5th Cir. 2001); United States v. MacDonald, 916 F.2d 766 (2d Cir. 1990) (en banc) (1991); State v. Taylor, 298 N.C. 405 (1979); State v. Mackins, 47 N.C. App. 168 (1980); State v. Prevette, 43 N.C. App. 450 (1979).

327. Welsh v. Wisconsin, 466 U.S. 740 (1984) (exigent circumstances did not exist to enter home without warrant to arrest for impaired driving, punished as civil sanction under Wisconsin law). Although this case involved a warrantless entry to arrest, its emphasis on the gravity of the offense in determining exigent circumstances would likely apply to a case that involved a warrantless entry to search. *See also* Illinois v. McArthur, 531 U.S. 326 (2001) (court distinguished *Welsh* when it ruled that restraint of defendant outside his trailer was reasonable while another officer went to obtain search warrant to search trailer for evidence of jailable misdemeanors).

328. State v. Prevette, 43 N.C. App. 450 (1979).

329. 563 U.S. 452 (2011). The Court in *King* assumed, without deciding, that exigent circumstances existed.

330. The Court rejected additional requirements for the exigent circumstances rule that would bar officers from entering without a warrant if (1) officers had a bad faith intent to avoid obtaining a search warrant; (2) it was reasonably foreseeable that officers' investigative tactics would create exigent circumstances; (3) after acquiring evidence sufficient to establish probable cause, officers did not seek a search warrant but instead knocked on the door and sought either to speak with an occupant or to obtain consent to search; (4) the officers' investigation was contrary to standard or good law

enforcement practices; and (5) officers impermissibly created an exigency when they engaged in conduct that would cause a reasonable person to believe that entry was imminent and inevitable.

331. *See* 3 Wayne R. LaFave, Search and Seizure: A Treatise on the Fourth Amendment § 6.5(c) (5th ed. 2012); State v. Tripp, 52 N.C. App. 244 (1981) (officers entered trailer with consent; seizure of people in trailer by officer for one hour while another officer went to obtain search warrant was reasonable because they knew of officers' desire to search and some stolen items were readily destructible). *See also* Illinois v. McArthur, 531 U.S. 326 (2001) (court ruled that restraint of defendant outside his trailer was reasonable while another officer went to obtain search warrant to search trailer for evidence of jailable misdemeanors); Segura v. United States, 468 U.S. 796 (1984) (but note that only two Justices joined that part of the opinion that approved the warrantless seizure of the apartment while a search warrant was being sought).

An officer who impounds property under either alternative must obtain a search warrant without unnecessary delay.

Warrantlessly entering a home with exigent circumstances to make an arrest is discussed in Chapter 2 on page 71. Warrantlessly entering a home to save life, prevent injury, or protect property is discussed later in this chapter on page 260.

Search of a Person for Evidence with Probable Cause
(*See page 346 for case summaries on this topic.*)

Probable cause to arrest and to search. Often an officer will have information that establishes both probable cause to arrest and probable cause to search a person. For example, a reliable confidential informant tells an officer at 6 p.m. that several people, including Joe Louis, are selling drugs in a certain area. The officer tells the informant to call if the informant obtains more information. The informant meets the officer at 8:30 p.m. and tells the officer that the informant has just seen Joe Louis Wooten with heroin and Wooten is still in the same area. The informant describes this person in detail. When the officer arrives at the particular location shortly thereafter, the officer sees a person who matches this description and the person admits that he is Joe Louis Wooten. The officer then has both probable cause to arrest Wooten for possession of heroin and probable cause to search him for heroin.[332]

The officer may (1) arrest Wooten and search him incident to arrest or (2) search Wooten first and then arrest him; both actions are justifiable under the search incident to arrest justification (see page 250). Or the officer could search Wooten first based on another justification:

---

332. State v. Wooten, 34 N.C. App. 85 (1977). Although the court recognized that both probable cause to arrest and probable cause to search existed and exigent circumstances existed to support a warrantless search before arrest, it upheld the search that was conducted before the arrest based on the recognized principle that a search incident to arrest may precede an arrest when it is conducted contemporaneously with the arrest. Rawlings v. Kentucky, 448 U.S. 98 (1980); State v. Mills, 104 N.C. App. 724 (1991) (court ruled that officer's warrantless search of defendant–drug seller's pockets for cocaine was supported by two independent grounds: (1) search incident to arrest and (2) probable cause and exigent circumstances). *See also* State v. Chadwick, 149 N.C. App. 200 (2002) (officer's corroboration of informant's information provided both probable cause to arrest defendant and probable cause to search him).

the officer has probable cause to search, and exigent circumstances permit a warrantless search—Wooten would destroy or hide the evidence and leave.[333]

Sometimes officers may have probable cause to arrest and to search a person, but—for investigative or other reasons—they do not want to make the arrest yet. If exigent circumstances permit a warrantless search, officers may search the person without making an arrest—but they cannot then rely on the search incident to arrest justification, because an arrest was not in fact made. In a United States Supreme Court case,[334] the defendant's wife was strangled to death in her home and she had abrasions and lacerations about her throat. There was no evidence of a break-in or robbery. Officers sent a message to her husband that they wanted to speak to him. Shortly after the defendant voluntarily came to the police station, the officers noticed a dark spot under his fingernail. Believing that the spot might be dried blood and knowing that evidence of strangulation is often found under fingernails, they asked the defendant if they could take a scraping of his fingernails. He refused, put his hands behind his back and appeared to rub them together, then put his hands in his pocket—and the officers heard a metallic sound, such as keys or change rattling. They then took fingernail scrapings without a warrant. The defendant was detained only long enough to take the scrapings and was not arrested until a month later.

The Court first determined that, considering other facts in the case, the officers had probable cause to arrest the defendant for murder before they took the scrapings. Because they had not formally arrested him, the officers could not make a full search incident to arrest. However, the Court ruled that the limited detention and search by scraping the defendant's fingernails was permissible to preserve readily destructible evidence.

Note that if an officer has only reasonable suspicion that a person committed a crime and needs to obtain evidence from a suspect, the officer may ask a prosecutor to apply for a nontestimonial identification order; see the discussion in Chapter 4 on page 459.

Obtaining a blood sample when an impaired driver refuses a chemical test. Officers who arrest or charge a

---

333. *See* 3 Wayne R. LaFave, Search and Seizure: A Treatise on the Fourth Amendment § 5.4(b) (5th ed. 2012); State v. Mills, 104 N.C. App. 724 (1991).

334. Cupp v. Murphy, 412 U.S. 291 (1973).

person with an impaired-driving offense may ask that person to take a blood or breath test, or both.[335] If the person refuses to take a designated test, no test may be given under the authority of the statute authorizing officers to make the request. But officers can still test the person's alcohol content under "other applicable procedures of law."[336] Officers may use a search warrant to obtain a blood sample to analyze its alcohol content (see AOC-CR-155, a search warrant form specifically for this purpose).[337]

The United States Supreme Court in *Missouri v. McNeely*[338] ruled that in impaired driving investigations, the natural dissipation of alcohol in the bloodstream does not constitute an exigency in every case sufficient to justify conducting a blood test without a search warrant. The Court noted that under *Schmerber v. California*[339] and the Court's case law, applying the exigent circumstances exception requires consideration of all of the facts and circumstances of the particular case. It then rejected the State's request for a per se rule for blood testing in impaired driving cases, declining to "depart from careful case-by-case assessment of exigency."[340] It concluded that "while the natural dissipation of alcohol in the blood may support a finding of exigency in a specific case, as it did in *Schmerber*, it does not do so categorically. Whether a warrantless blood test of a drunk-driving suspect is reasonable must be determined case by case based on the totality of the circumstances."[341] For an analysis of *McNeely*, see the publication cited in the accompanying footnote.[342]

Searching for evidence on or within a person's body. (See page 358 for case summaries on this topic.) Sometimes officers have probable cause to believe that evidence of a crime is located or hidden on or within a person's body, such as a rape victim's pubic hairs on the defendant's body or drugs concealed in a body cavity. Ordinarily these searches occur after a person is arrested, and they are therefore discussed on page 249, under the search incident to arrest justification.

Search and Seizure of Obscene Materials with Probable Cause

(See page 362 for case summaries on this topic.)

Although obscenity is not protected by the First Amendment, the United States Supreme Court has imposed special rules concerning searches and seizures

---

335. G.S. 20-139.1(b5) provides that a person may be requested to submit to a chemical analysis of his or her blood or other bodily fluid or substance (for example, urine) in addition to or instead of a chemical analysis of the breath, in the officer's discretion. (There are special provisions involving a violation of G.S. 20-141.4, felony and misdemeanor death by vehicle and other offenses.) Thus, for example, an officer may request a person to submit to a breath test and then request a blood test. Under G.S. 20-139.1(c), when an officer requests a blood or urine test, a physician, registered nurse, emergency medical technician, or other qualified person "shall" withdraw the blood sample and obtain the urine sample. That person may refuse to withdraw or obtain the sample if it reasonably appears that the procedure cannot be performed without endangering the safety of the person collecting the sample or the person from whom the sample is being collected.

336. G.S. 20-16.2(c). *See also* G.S. 20-139.1(a) (statute does not limit introduction of other competent evidence concerning person's alcohol concentration or results of other tests showing presence of impairing substance, including other chemical tests); State v. Drdak, 330 N.C. 587 (1992) (hospital's blood test results admissible under "other competent evidence" provision in G.S. 20-139.1(a)). On a related issue, see *Birchfield v. North Dakota*, 136 S. Ct. 2160 (2016) (warrantless breath testing of impaired-driving suspects is permissible under the Fourth Amendment as a search incident to arrest but warrantless blood testing is not permissible as a search incident to arrest), discussed in Shea Denning, *Breath Tests Incident to Arrest Are Reasonable But Prosecution for Refusing a Blood Test Goes Too Far*, NC Crim. L. Blog (June 29, 2016), http://nccriminallaw.sog.unc.edu/breath-tests-incident-arrest-reasonable-prosecution-refusing-blood-test-goes-far/.

337. *See* State v. Davis, 142 N.C. App. 81 (2001), in which the state obtained a search warrant to take blood from an impaired-driving arrestee who had refused to give a blood sample when requested by an officer under the state's implied consent law. The court rejected the defendant's due process argument that because he was told that he had a right to refuse to be tested under the state's implied consent law, no test could thereafter be given.

338. 135 S. Ct. 1552 (2014).

339. 384 U.S. 757 (1966).

340. *McNeely*, 133 S. Ct. at 1554–55.

341. *Id.* at 1563. For a post-*McNeely* case finding exigent circumstances to take blood without a search warrant, see *State v. Dahlquist*, 231 N.C. App. 100 (2013), discussed in Shea Denning, *Four Hour Delay to Obtain Search Warrant an Exigency, At Least for Now*, NC Crim. L. Blog (Dec. 4, 2013), http://nccriminallaw.sog.unc.edu/?p=4556.

342. Shea Riggsbee Denning, The Law of Impaired Driving and Related Implied Consent Offenses in North Carolina 18–19 (UNC School of Government, 2014). In addition to the post-*McNeely* cases of *State v. Dahlquist*, 231 N.C. App. 100 (2013) (exigent circumstances existed), and *State v. Granger*, 235 N.C. App. 157 (2014) (exigent circumstances existed), which were discussed in this publication, a case decided since the publication of this book is *State v. Romano*, ___ N.C. App. ___, 785 S.E.2d 168 (2016).

of books, magazines, motion pictures, and the like so that nonobscene materials—which are protected by the First Amendment's freedom of speech provision—are not improperly seized during officers' efforts to search for and seize allegedly obscene materials. Generally, officers may not search for or seize books, magazines, or motion pictures that they have probable cause to believe are obscene unless they have a search warrant. If they apply for a search warrant after receiving a prosecutor's authorization,[343] it must particularly describe each book, magazine, or motion picture with sufficient detail that the issuing judicial official may make an independent judgment that each item is obscene[344] and officers who execute the search warrant can be sure which item to seize.[345] Search warrants for obscene materials are discussed in Chapter 4.

Certain seizure authority available to officers in an ordinary criminal investigation may be impermissible when they seize books, magazines, and motion pictures. For example, the United States Supreme Court has ruled that officers who arrest a theater manager for allegedly showing an obscene movie may not, without a search warrant, seize the movie from the projection booth.[346] The Court has indicated that exigent circumstances may permit a warrantless seizure of allegedly obscene materials when a now-or-never situation requires an immediate seizure because it would be impossible to seize the materials if officers took the time to obtain a search warrant.[347] Even in such a situation, officers would be wise to seize

the materials briefly to protect them from being removed or destroyed while they applied for a search warrant.

The United States Supreme Court has ruled that undercover officers do not conduct a seizure under the Fourth Amendment when they enter a bookstore and purchase a few allegedly obscene magazines—just as any member of the public could do.[348] Thus, officers may make small purchases without any justification under the Fourth Amendment, although a massive purchase that significantly reduces the stock of publications in the store might be considered a seizure that requires a search warrant.

Reexamination or Testing of Evidence in State's Possession; Second Look Doctrine
(*See page 362 for case summaries on this topic.*)

Sometimes officers need to reexamine evidence in the State's possession or test it to conduct a further investigation or to investigate a new offense. Generally, officers do not need additional legal process to do so, such as a search warrant, because under these circumstances a defendant no longer has a protected privacy interest in the evidence. For example, officers may examine or test evidence that is in their department's evidence room, in a jail's inventory room, or impounded at a garage.[349] Reexamination

---

343. G.S. 14-190.20 requires that a search warrant for certain obscenity offenses may be issued only on a prosecutor's request.

344. Some courts have upheld search warrant descriptions that specifically name allegedly obscene materials to be seized and then also authorize the seizure of additional materials if they contain presentations of specifically named sexual acts. Sequoia Books, Inc. v. McDonald, 725 F.2d 1091 (7th Cir. 1984); United States v. Hurt, 795 F.2d 765 (9th Cir. 1986), *opinion amended*, 808 F.2d 707 (9th Cir. 1987); United States v. Dornhofer, 859 F.2d 1195 (4th Cir. 1988).

345. Lo-Ji Sales, Inc. v. New York, 442 U.S. 319 (1979). The standard of probable cause (fair probability) is the same whether the search warrant authorizes a seizure of obscenity or a seizure of illegal drugs or any other evidence. New York v. P. J. Video, Inc., 475 U.S. 868 (1986).

346. Roaden v. Kentucky, 413 U.S. 496 (1973).

347. *Id.*; 3 Wayne R. LaFave, Search and Seizure: A Treatise on the Fourth Amendment § 6.7(e), at 660 (5th ed. 2012).

348. Maryland v. Macon, 472 U.S. 463 (1985).

349. State v. Nelson, 298 N.C. 573 (1979) (defendants, who were military personnel, were arrested and confined to county jail for state criminal offenses; military personnel's inventory of their military quarters, conducted pursuant to military regulations requiring inventory of quarters of personnel confined by civilian authorities, was reasonable; military officers then looked again at inventoried items when they determined, three days later, that items might be connected with a crime; court ruled that this second look at same items already inventoried, even though it was done for an investigatory purpose, did not violate Fourth Amendment); State v. Warren, 309 N.C. 224 (1983) (chemical tests performed on bloodstains in car while it was impounded at garage—after first search under search warrant had been completed—was justified under *State v. Nelson*, cited above); State v. Steen, 352 N.C. 227 (2000) (defendant was arrested for possession of drug paraphernalia and stolen credit cards and taken to jail on February 29, 1996; his clothing was taken from him, and he was issued standard jail jumpsuit; under jail rules, his clothing would be returned to him when released from jail; on March 6, 1996, an officer who was investigating defendant for a murder went to the jail and, without a search warrant, obtained defendant's clothes to analyze them for blood and glass particles; court ruled, relying on *United States v. Edwards*, 415 U.S. 800 (1974), that the warrantless search and seizure of defendant's clothes did not

of evidence is commonly known as the second look doctrine.[350] Also, a blood sample lawfully taken from a defendant for an investigation of a criminal offense may later be tested for use in an investigation of a different offense.[351]

Search and Seizure of Evidence with Reasonable Suspicion

Just as officers may briefly stop a person when they have reasonable suspicion that the person has committed, is committing, or is about to commit a crime, they are also authorized—under limited circumstances discussed below—to seize property briefly for investigation when they have reasonable suspicion that it is evidence of a crime or contains evidence of a crime.[352] Also, a person who is suspected of committing a crime can be detained briefly with a court order while certain nontestimonial identification procedures are performed, if the procedures may materially assist in determining whether the person committed a criminal offense.[353]

Seizing Luggage or Other Containers of Personal Effects for Brief Investigation

(*See page 345 for case summaries on this topic.*)

The United States Supreme Court has ruled that officers may briefly detain luggage at an airport for further investigation—for example, so that a trained dog can sniff the luggage for drugs—when they have reasonable suspicion that the luggage contains drugs.[354] (Of course, if officers had probable cause to believe that the luggage contained drugs, they could seize the luggage without a warrant and obtain a search warrant to search it.) Although the Court has specifically declined to set a maximum time limit for a detention based on reasonable suspicion,[355] it did rule that 90 minutes was excessive when officers had prior knowledge of the luggage's arrival at the airport and could have had a drug-sniffing dog there earlier. Generally, the permissible detention period depends on whether officers have diligently pursued their investigation of the suspected contents of the luggage.[356]

Detaining a Person Briefly for a Nontestimonial Identification Procedure

Sometimes officers may have a reasonable suspicion—but not probable cause to believe—that a person committed a crime. In that case, they may not arrest the person and then conduct various investigative procedures, such as fingerprinting, that are permitted as a search incident to arrest (discussed below). When only reasonable suspicion exists, however, a prosecutor may obtain a court order that permits a brief detention of a person so that nontestimonial identification procedures can be conducted. These procedures—such as fingerprinting, taking handwriting samples, or having the person appear in a lineup—may

---

violate Fourth Amendment; defendant was in custody under valid arrest, and defendant's clothing had already been administratively taken from his possession); State v. Motley, 153 N.C. App. 701 (2002) (rifle lawfully obtained by one law enforcement agency and transferred for testing by another agency did not constitute illegal search or seizure). *See generally* 3 WAYNE R. LAFAVE, SEARCH AND SEIZURE: A TREATISE ON THE FOURTH AMENDMENT §§ 5.3(b) and 7.5(c) (5th ed. 2012); United States v. Turner, 28 F.3d 981 (9th Cir. 1994) (federal postal inspector could seize without a warrant defendant's cap that was in state jail's lawful custody based on defendant's state charges so inspector could investigate unrelated federal charges—see other cases discussed in court's opinion).

350. State v. Nelson, 298 N.C. 573 (1979).

351. *See* State v. Barkley, 144 N.C. App. 514 (2001) (DNA evidence was introduced at trial that had been obtained from blood sample defendant had voluntarily given to law enforcement officers in investigation of unrelated murder; court ruled that blood sample lawfully obtained in investigation of one crime may be used as evidence in prosecution of unrelated crime without any additional justification under Fourth Amendment; court stated that once the blood was lawfully drawn from defendant's body, he no longer had possessory interest in it). *See also* State v. Motley, 153 N.C. App. 701 (2002) (transfer of rifle from one law enforcement agency to another agency was not a search or seizure).

352. United States v. Place, 462 U.S. 696 (1983).

353. G.S. 15A-271 through -282; Hayes v. Florida, 470 U.S. 811 (1985).

---

354. United States v. Place, 462 U.S. 696 (1983). On the other hand, the United States Supreme Court ruled in *Arizona v. Hicks*, 480 U.S. 321 (1987), that under the plain view doctrine an item may not be searched or seized with less than probable cause. However, the Court's ruling did not affect the validity of the *Place* ruling.

355. See note 10 of the Court's opinion in *United States v. Place*, 462 U.S. 696 (1983).

356. Detention of luggage for 20 to 35 minutes to await a dog sniff was approved in *United States v. West*, 731 F.2d 90 (1st Cir. 1984), and detention of luggage for 75 minutes to await a dog sniff was approved in *United States v. Borys*, 766 F.2d 304 (7th Cir. 1985). *See also* United States v. Sturgis, 238 F.3d 956 (8th Cir. 2001) (two-hour wait for drug dog did not violate Fourth Amendment because officers had probable cause to arrest detained defendant).

materially aid in determining whether that person committed the crime. A nontestimonial identification order may not be used to take blood, however. Probable cause and a search warrant are needed to take blood, unless exigent circumstances permit taking blood without a search warrant.[357] (A nontestimonial identification order for a juvenile may be used to take blood when the order is based on probable cause—see the discussion in Chapter 4 on page 459.)

The United States Supreme Court has ruled that when officers have only reasonable suspicion that a person committed a criminal offense, they may not take the person to another place for fingerprinting during an investigative detention unless they have judicial authorization.[358] In such a situation, therefore, officers should either obtain the person's voluntary consent to be moved to another place for fingerprinting or consult with a prosecutor to determine whether a nontestimonial identification order should be obtained. (Nontestimonial identification orders are discussed in more detail in Chapter 4.)

Search and Seizure to Protect Officers, Other People, or Property

The Fourth Amendment permits various kinds of searches and seizures to protect people and property in circumstances that present particular threats of injury to people and damage to property. Ordinarily, these searches and seizures need not be justified by probable cause or a search warrant. Instead, they are considered reasonable under the Fourth Amendment if the government's legitimate interests in protecting people or property outweigh the intrusion on a person's privacy interests.[359]

Search Incident to Arrest

(*See page 371 for case summaries on this topic.*)

A search incident to arrest is justified by the need to prevent the arrested person from using weapons or destroying evidence. However, when officers arrest a person, a search incident to arrest is legally justified no matter how minor the offense, how harmless the arrestee, and how unlikely it is that the arrestee may have a weapon or may destroy evidence (but see the next paragraph).

The United States Supreme Court clearly has ruled in prior cases that officers *automatically* have the right to search incident to arrest; that is, they need not consider a particular arrestee's dangerousness or the likelihood that the arrestee may destroy evidence before they conduct their search.[360] However, in 2009, the Court in *Arizona v. Gant*[361] (discussed in detail on page 252), significantly restricted an officer's authority to conduct a search of the interior of a vehicle incident to the arrest of an occupant. Because the arrestee in *Gant* could not reasonably access the vehicle when the search was conducted (he was handcuffed in a police car), the Court ruled that the search was not authorized on grounds of dangerousness or evidence destruction. The Court did not address whether the *Gant* ruling affects its prior rulings involving a search incident to arrest in a nonvehicle context, such as a search of an arrestee's person or the area (including personal items) within his or her immediate control. It is unclear whether the Court would modify those rulings in a future case. North Carolina appellate courts had not addressed *Gant*'s possible impact on nonvehicle searches as of the date of this book's publication.[362]

---

357. *See* G.S. 15A-271 through -282; State v. Carter, 322 N.C. 753 (1988) (probable cause is required under state constitution to take blood from suspect; nontestimonial identification order, which is based on reasonable suspicion, is not sufficient legal process to take blood; probable cause and search warrant are required to take blood, unless exigent circumstances allow taking blood without search warrant). G.S. 7B-2105(b) authorizes a nontestimonial identification order to take blood from a juvenile when the order is based on probable cause. This statute does not violate the *Carter* ruling.

358. Hayes v. Florida, 470 U.S. 811 (1985). However, the *Hayes* Court indicated that it might be permissible to detain a suspect where he or she was originally stopped to be fingerprinted—if there is reasonable suspicion to support the detention. *See also* Davis v. Mississippi, 394 U.S. 721 (1969); United States v. Gonzalez, 763 F.2d 1127 (10th Cir. 1985).

359. Illinois v. Lafayette, 462 U.S. 640 (1983).

360. United States v. Robinson, 414 U.S. 218 (1973); Gustafson v. Florida, 414 U.S. 260 (1973).

361. 556 U.S. 332 (2009).

362. However, the North Carolina Court of Appeals in *State v. Banner*, 207 N.C. App. 729 (2010), recognized the distinction between a search of a person under *United States v. Robinson*, 414 U.S. 218 (1973), and a search incident to the arrest of a vehicle occupant in *Arizona v. Gant*, 556 U.S. 332 (2009), although the *Banner* court was not required to decide whether the *Gant* rationale modified Fourth Amendment law concerning a search of an arrestee's person or area within his or her immediate control. Federal appellate courts that have considered this issue include *United States v. Perdoma*, 621 F.3d 745 (8th Cir. 2010) (court upheld search of zipped duffel bag that defendant was carrying when arrested; court recognized that *Gant* rationale may be instructive outside vehicle search context in some cases but not in this case when search occurred in close proximity to handcuffed defendant); and *United States v. Shakir*, 616 F.3d 315 (3d Cir. 2010) (court rejected government's

Need for a valid custodial arrest. A search incident to arrest may be made only if the person to be searched has been arrested or is in the process of being arrested. The search may be made before an actual arrest and still be justified as a search incident to arrest if the arrest is made contemporaneously with the search.[363] Of course, whatever is found during a search incident to arrest that occurs before the formal arrest cannot be used to support probable cause for the arrest.[364] Instead, the arrest must be supported by probable cause that existed before the search incident to arrest began.

If officers decide to issue a citation for a misdemeanor, they may not make a search incident to arrest, because they are not taking the cited person into custody.[365] If the violation is an infraction, officers cannot conduct a search incident to arrest, because they are not authorized to make an arrest. But they may be able to frisk the person, if the person presents a danger to them (see page 257).

A search incident to arrest is only as valid as the arrest itself. Thus, if the arrest is not supported by probable cause, the search incident to that arrest is unconstitutional.

Closeness in time and place to the arrest. Generally, a search incident to arrest is not justified if the search is remote in time or place from the arrest.[366] However, a later search at a law enforcement facility or jail sometimes may be justified as an inventory search or incident to a change in custody, even if the search incident to arrest justification did not support the search.[367] Under the second look doctrine, officers sometimes are authorized to search an arrestee's possessions again without a warrant or probable cause when the arrestee remains in custody.[368]

Scope of search incident to arrest—generally. (See page 371 for case summaries on this topic.) Generally, the scope of a search incident to arrest—other than a search made when an occupant of a vehicle is arrested—is limited to a search of the arrestee's person and the area (and objects in that area) within the arrestee's immediate control. Thus, officers who arrest a person at the front door of a home may not search the rest of the house based on the search incident to arrest justification.[369]

The search of the arrestee and the area and objects within the arrestee's immediate control may be a full search. For example, officers may search the arrestee's wallet, handbag, clothing, or a cigarette pack in a pocket;[370] take the arrestee's clothes when they may be useful as evidence or for some other legitimate purpose;[371] or remove head, arm, or pubic hair samples when the procedure is done in a reasonable manner and the material may be useful as evidence.[372] However, officers may want

---

argument that *Gant* was confined to vehicle searches and stated that *Gant* refocuses attention on suspect's ability or inability to access weapons or destroy evidence when search incident to arrest is conducted; court ruled that officer had authority to search handcuffed defendant's gym bag as incident to arrest).

363. Rawlings v. Kentucky, 448 U.S. 98 (1980); State v. Mills, 104 N.C. App. 724 (1991).

364. Smith v. Ohio, 494 U.S. 541 (1990).

365. Knowles v. Iowa, 525 U.S. 113 (1998); State v. Fisher, 141 N.C. App. 448 (2000).

366. Preston v. United States, 376 U.S. 364 (1964) (at-the-station search of car not justified as search incident to arrest); State v. Jackson, 280 N.C. 122 (1971) (delay of 30 to 45 minutes for female jail employee to search female defendant did not invalidate search as incident to arrest). Even if a later search is not justified as a search incident to arrest, it still may be valid if (1) there was probable cause to search the vehicle or (2) an inventory search was conducted under standard operating procedures. And the inevitable discovery exception to the exclusionary rule may apply if the evidence was seized as a result of an unconstitutional search incident to arrest but the evidence would have been inevitably discovered under a valid inventory search. United State v. Cartwright, 630 F.3d 610 (7th Cir. 2010). *See also* State v. Garner, 331 N.C. 491 (1992) (recognizing inevitable discovery doctrine under state constitution).

367. Illinois v. LaFayette, 462 U.S. 640 (1983); United States v. Edwards, 415 U.S. 800 (1974); State v. Payne, 328 N.C. 377 (1991).

368. State v. Nelson, 298 N.C. 573 (1979); State v. Steen, 352 N.C. 227 (2000). See the discussion of the second look doctrine on page 247.

369. Chimel v. California, 395 U.S. 752 (1969).

370. United States v. Robinson, 414 U.S. 218 (1973); Gustafson v. Florida, 414 U.S. 260 (1973); United States v. Litman, 739 F.2d 137 (4th Cir. 1984); State v. Nesmith, 40 N.C. App. 748 (1979).

371. United States v. Edwards, 415 U.S. 800 (1974); State v. Steen, 352 N.C. 227 (2000); State v. Shedd, 274 N.C. 95 (1968); State v. Lucas, 302 N.C. 342 (1981).

372. State v. Steen, 352 N.C. 227 (2000); State v. Thomas, 329 N.C. 423 (1991); State v. Cobb, 295 N.C. 1 (1978); State v. Norman, 100 N.C. App. 660 (1990). Officers also may use reasonable force to prevent an arrestee from swallowing evidence, such as drugs. *See generally* State v. Williams, 209 N.C. App. 255 (2011); State v. Watson, 119 N.C. App. 395 (1995); *In re* I.R.T., 184 N.C. App. 579 (2007); 3 WAYNE R. LaFAVE, SEARCH AND SEIZURE: A TREATISE ON THE FOURTH AMENDMENT § 5.2(i) (5th ed. 2012). See also *Birchfield v. North Dakota*, 136 S. Ct. 2160 (2016) (warrantless breath testing of impaired-driving suspects is permissible under the Fourth Amendment as a search incident to arrest but warrantless blood testing is not permissible as a search incident to arrest), discussed in Shea

to obtain a search warrant before taking these samples, particularly if the arrestee has already been placed in a detention facility.[373]

Generally, officers may search briefcases, duffel bags, suitcases, and the like that an arrestee is carrying or that are within the arrestee's immediate control when he or she is arrested, if the search is conducted contemporaneously with the arrest.[374] However, the North Carolina

Court of Appeals has ruled that officers did not have the authority to search incident to arrest a large, locked suitcase that a person was carrying when arrested.[375] Thus, at least as to such a suitcase, officers must obtain a search warrant to search it—assuming there is probable cause to search. Of course, if the arrestee is committed to a detention facility, the luggage may be searched without a search warrant under the inventory search justification[376] (see page 257).

When officers arrest a person in a home or other premises, they may as incident to that arrest automatically—that is, without needing probable cause or reasonable suspicion to do so—search closets and other spaces immediately adjoining the place of arrest from which an attack on them from another person could occur.[377] This search is limited to looking for people who may pose a danger; it may not be conducted to discover evidence.

Fingerprinting, photographing, and taking a DNA sample of an arrestee are discussed in Chapter 2 on page 81.

Denning, *Breath Tests Incident to Arrest Are Reasonable But Prosecution for Refusing a Blood Test Goes Too Far*, NC CRIM. L. BLOG (June 29, 2016), http://nccriminallaw.sog.unc.edu/breath-tests-incident-arrest-reasonable-prosecution-refusing-blood-test-goes-far/.

373. The North Carolina Supreme Court ruled in *State v. Welch*, 316 N.C. 578 (1986), that a judge may issue a nontestimonial identification order on the State's motion only when a person (1) has not been arrested (but reasonable suspicion exists that the person committed a crime punishable by more than one year's imprisonment—under current law, a felony or Class A1 or 1 misdemeanor) or (2) has been arrested and released from custody pending trial. The court ruled that a superior court judge erred when he issued such an order when the defendant had been arrested for murder and armed robbery and was in jail awaiting trial. Thus, an officer must obtain a search warrant (or court order; see next paragraph) instead of a nontestimonial identification order if the officer wants to use legal process before taking the samples mentioned in the text. If the officer wants to conduct more intrusive procedures, such as taking a blood sample, the officer must obtain a search warrant unless the defendant consents or probable cause and exigent circumstances exist; *see* State v. Carter, 322 N.C. 753 (1988).

Although the *Welch* court discussed only the use of a search warrant (when a judge had no authority to issue a nontestimonial identification order because the defendant had been arrested and was still in custody), a judge has the inherent authority to issue a court order to compel the defendant to submit to a nontestimonial procedure if the prosecutor makes a sufficient showing—similar to a probable cause statement in an affidavit for a search warrant—to support the order. *Cf. In re Superior Court Order*, 315 N.C. 378 (1986).

374. The impact of *Arizona v. Gant*, 556 U.S. 332 (2009), on the legality of these searches is unclear. Federal appellate cases analyzing searches of containers incident to arrest in light of *Gant* and upholding the searches include *United States v. Shakir*, 616 F.3d 315 (3d Cir. 2010) (gym bag) and *United States v. Perdoma*, 621 F.3d 745 (8th Cir. 2010) (zipped duffel bag). Federal appellate cases decided before *Gant* and upholding searches of containers include *United States v. Tavolacci*, 895 F.2d 1423 (D.C. Cir. 1990) (locked luggage); *United States v. Porter*, 738 F.2d 622 (4th Cir. 1984) (en banc) (carry-on luggage); *United States v. Torres*, 740 F.2d 122 (2d Cir. 1984) (leather bag); *United States v. Johnson*, 846 F.2d 279 (5th Cir. 1988) (briefcase); *United States v. Aguiar*, 825 F.2d 39 (4th Cir. 1987) (luggage); *United States v. Herrera*, 810 F.2d 989 (10th

Cir. 1987) (briefcase); *United States v. Andersson*, 813 F.2d 1450 (9th Cir. 1987) (suitcase); *United States v. Cervantes-Gaitan*, 792 F.2d 770 (9th Cir. 1986) (duffel bag); *United States v. Litman*, 739 F.2d 137 (4th Cir. 1984) (shoulder bag); and *United States v. Morales*, 923 F.2d 621 (8th Cir. 1991) (knapsack and duffel bag). Federal appellate cases decided before *Gant* and ruling invalid searches of containers include *United States v. Myers*, 308 F.3d 251 (3d Cir. 2002) (search of bag of handcuffed arrestee after officer had gone elsewhere in house and then returned); *United States v. Bonitz*, 826 F.2d 954 (10th Cir. 1987) (search of gun case three feet from handcuffed arrestee); and *United States v. $639,558 in U.S. Currency*, 955 F.2d 712 (D.C. Cir. 1992) (search of luggage was not incident to arrest because it was not contemporaneous with arrest).

375. State v. Thomas, 81 N.C. App. 200 (1986).

376. Officers may inventory the defendant's suitcase before the arrestee enters the detention facility even when they have probable cause to obtain a search warrant but decide not to obtain one. The inventory search is a separate and independently sufficient justification to search the suitcase. *See* United States v. Cervantes-Gaitan, 792 F.2d 770 (9th Cir. 1986). Even when a warrantless search of a container violates the Fourth Amendment, the evidence in the container may still be admissible under the inevitable discovery doctrine if the State can prove that it was inevitable that an officer would have conducted an inventory search and discovered the evidence. *See* United States v. Gorski, 852 F.2d 692 (2d Cir. 1988); State v. Garner, 331 N.C. 491 (1992) (recognizing inevitable discovery doctrine under state constitution).

377. Maryland v. Buie, 494 U.S. 325 (1990).

Scope of a search incident to the arrest of an occupant of a vehicle. (See page 375 for case summaries on this topic.) The United States Supreme Court in 2009 issued a ruling in *Arizona v. Gant*[378] that significantly restricted[379] an officer's authority, based on the theory of search incident to arrest, to conduct a search of the passenger compartment of a vehicle after arresting an occupant or recent occupant. The Court ruled that officers may search a vehicle incident to arrest only if (1) the arrestee is unsecured and within reaching distance of the passenger compartment when the search is conducted or (2) it is reasonable to believe that evidence relevant to the crime of arrest might be found in the vehicle.[380] The Court did not define *reasonable to believe*, but it is highly likely that it means less evidence than needed to establish probable cause. The North Carolina Supreme Court after *Gant* ruled that it means reasonable suspicion.[381]

Concerning a search under circumstance (1) above, the Court stated that it will be a rare case in which an officer is unable to fully effectuate an arrest so that an arrestee has a realistic possibility of access to the vehicle. Thus, the typical case in which an officer secures the arrestee with handcuffs and places the arrestee in a patrol vehicle will not satisfy this circumstance. Even if a handcuffed arrestee is not placed in a patrol car, it is not likely that the arrestee has realistic access to the vehicle absent unusual circumstances.

Concerning a search under circumstance (2) above, it would be highly unlikely that this circumstance would exist to permit a search of the vehicle for arrests for motor vehicle criminal offenses such as driving while license revoked, driving without a valid driver's license, misdemeanor speeding, and so forth.[382] For other motor vehicle offenses, such as impaired driving, there may be valid grounds for believing that evidence relevant to the offense may exist in the vehicle (for example, impairing substances or containers used to drink or otherwise ingest them). For arrests based on outstanding arrest warrants, it is highly unlikely that this circumstance would exist to permit a search of the vehicle, unless incriminating facts concerning the offense charged in the warrant exist at the arrest scene or the offense is one for which evidence of the offense likely would still be found in the vehicle.[383] How recently the offense was committed may be an important factor in determining the reasonable to believe standard in this context. Concerning arrests for non-motor-vehicle offenses resulting from information discovered during a vehicle stop, the existing circumstances will determine whether it is reasonable to believe that evidence relevant to the crime of arrest may be found in the vehicle.[384]

---

378. 556 U.S. 332 (2009).

379. The Court's ruling significantly restricted what the Court believed to be overly broad interpretations by lower courts of its ruling in *New York v. Belton*, 453 U.S. 454 (1981), which upheld an officer's search of a jacket in a vehicle's backseat after arresting and removing the occupants.

380. Even if a search is not justified as a search incident to arrest of a vehicle occupant, a search may be justified by probable cause to search. State v. Armstrong, 236 N.C. App. 130 (2014).

381. State v. Mbacke, 365 N.C. 403 (2012).

382. *Gant* involved an arrest for driving with a suspended license, and the Court ruled that there was not a reasonable belief that evidence of this offense might be found in the vehicle. *See also* State v. Johnson, 204 N.C. App. 259 (2010) (search incident to arrest for driving while license suspended was not authorized under *Gant*); State v. Carter, 200 N.C. App. 47 (2009) (search incident to arrest for expired registration tag and failing to notify Division of Motor Vehicles of change of address was not authorized under *Gant*).

383. For example, the sale of illegal drugs. *See, e.g.*, United States v. Hinson, 585 F.3d 1328 (10th Cir. 2009) (proper to search truck for evidence of trafficking offense under *Gant*'s reasonable to believe standard when defendant was arrested for that trafficking offense after stop of same truck from which offense was committed a month ago by selling drug from truck).

384. State v. Mbacke, 365 N.C. 403 (2012) (officer arrested defendant for carrying concealed weapon discovered in defendant's waistband after traffic stop; court ruled, based on *Gant*, that it was reasonable to believe that evidence of offense was in vehicle to permit search of vehicle incident to arrest, based on the circumstances, such as defendant's actions the prior night involving shooting at house and his furtive behavior at arrest scene); State v. Fitzovic, ___ N.C. App. ___, 770 S.E.2d 717 (2015) (officer who arrested defendant for open container offense had reasonable belief that evidence related to that violation might be found in the defendant's vehicle); State v. Foy, 208 N.C. App. 699 (2010) (officer arrested defendant for carrying concealed weapon discovered beneath truck's center console during traffic stop; court ruled, based on *Gant*, that it was reasonable to believe that offense-related evidence, such as another firearm, ammunition, receipt, or gun permit, could exist to permit search incident to arrest). Concerning drug offenses, see *State v. Watkins*, 220 N.C. App. 384 (2012) (after arrest of defendant's passenger for possession of drug paraphernalia, officers had reasonable belief that evidence relevant to that offense might be found in vehicle); *Powell v. Commonwealth*, 701 S.E.2d 831 (Va. App. 2010) (reasonable to believe that vehicle contained evidence related to drug transaction that officer had witnessed and for which officer had arrested defendant); *United States v. Slone*, 636 F.3d 845 (7th Cir. 2011)

A search of a vehicle, when based only on the search incident to arrest justification, does not include the trunk. The trunk may be searched when probable cause exists to search the entire vehicle (discussed above) or when officers conduct an inventory search (discussed on page 261). Although the United States Supreme Court and North Carolina appellate courts have not decided this issue, other courts have ruled that a search incident to the arrest of an occupant of a station wagon, sports utility vehicle (SUV), or hatchback includes searching all areas of the vehicle that could be reached from within the vehicle.[385]

Although the law is not settled, an arrest of an occupant of a vehicle probably does not authorize officers—under the search incident to arrest justification—*automatically* (that is, without reasonable suspicion or other justification) to frisk or to search other people in the vehicle simply because an occupant has been arrested. However, courts will consider the dangerousness of the arrestee as a factor in determining whether officers have the authority to frisk the arrestee's companions in the vehicle.[386]

Search of cell phone incident to arrest. Searching cell phones incident to arrest is discussed on page 213.

Strip searches and body-cavity searches. (See page 354 for case summaries on this topic.) This section discusses a strip search or body-cavity search of a person whom officers have arrested or whom they have probable cause to search. See also the references set out in the accompanying note.[387]

Body-cavity or strip searches of jail and prison inmates are not discussed here; see the legal resources in the accompanying note.[388]

There are relatively few appellate court rulings on these issues,[389] and there are not clear guidelines—the United States Supreme Court has not ruled on these issues. However, strip searches and body-cavity searches are substantial intrusions on a person's privacy, and courts will consider (1) the justification for the search,

---

(arrest of defendant for drug offense while driving truck in tandem with another vehicle transporting marijuana permitted search of truck incident to arrest because it was reasonable to believe that evidence related to the offense would be found in the truck's passenger compartment); *State v. Toledo,* 204 N.C. App. 170 (2010) (court discussed *Gant* in context of search of vehicle for drugs but disclaimed reliance on it to uphold search; in any event, search of tire in undercarriage of vehicle would not be within *Gant*'s ruling because tire was not in vehicle's interior); *State v. Louis,* 199 N.C. App. 319 (2009) (unpublished) (after stop of vehicle and search of occupant's person revealed marijuana for which he was arrested, it was reasonable to believe under *Gant* that evidence of marijuana offense was in vehicle; although not discussed by court, warrantless search of vehicle would also have been justified based on probable cause to search vehicle).

385. United States v. Olguin-Rivera, 168 F.3d 1203 (10th Cir. 1999) (SUV); United States v. Pino, 855 F.2d 357 (6th Cir. 1988), *opinion amended,* 866 F.2d 147 (1989) (station wagon); United States v. Russell, 670 F.2d 323 (D.C. Cir. 1982) (hatchback). See the discussion in 3 Wayne R. LaFave, Search and Seizure: A Treatise on the Fourth Amendment § 7.1(b), at 681 (5th ed. 2012).

386. *Compare* United States v. Bell, 762 F.2d 495 (6th Cir. 1985) *and* United States v. Flett, 806 F.2d 823 (8th Cir. 1986) *with* United States v. DiRe, 332 U.S. 581 (1948). *See generally* 3 Wayne R. LaFave, Search and Seizure: A Treatise on the Fourth Amendment § 9.6(a), at 868–73 (5th ed. 2012).

387. Bob Farb, *Strip Searches by Law Enforcement Officers* (Part I), NC Crim. L. Blog (Sept. 4, 2013), http://nccriminallaw.sog.unc.edu/strip-searches-by-law-enforcement-officers-part-i/; Bob Farb, *Strip Searches by Law Enforcement Officers* (Part II), NC Crim. L. Blog (Sept. 5, 2013), http://nccriminallaw.sog.unc.edu/strip-searches-by-law-enforcement-officers-part-ii/.

388. 3 & 5 Wayne R. LaFave, Search and Seizure: A Treatise on the Fourth Amendment §§ 5.3(c), 10.0(b) (5th ed. 2012); Jamie Markham, *Strip Searches of Arrestees at the Jail,* NC Crim. L. Blog (Feb. 19, 2010), http://nccriminallaw.sog.unc.edu/strip-searches-of-arrestees-at-the-jail/.

389. Cases on these issues other than the North Carolina appellate cases discussed in the text include *United States v. Daniels,* 323 Fed. Appx. 201 (4th Cir. 2009) (unpublished) (strip search of defendant's underwear after drug distribution arrest was authorized when officer had reasonable suspicion drugs were concealed there and search occurred away from public view); *Amaechi v. West,* 237 F.3d 356 (4th Cir. 2001) (search incident to arrest for two-day-old misdemeanor noise violation involved officer's touching and penetrating female genitalia and kneading her buttocks in public; officer offered no security or evidence destruction or concealment justifications for search; court ruled that search violated Fourth Amendment); *United States v. Brack,* 188 F.3d 748 (7th Cir. 1999) (arrestee, suspect in drug investigation, asked for toilet paper at police station so he could relieve himself; officer became suspicious and instructed defendant to undress and turn around; officer saw piece of tissue in crease of defendant's buttocks; at officer's request, defendant removed tissue and two plastic bags; court ruled that search did not violate Fourth Amendment); *United States v. Dorlouis,* 107 F.3d 248 (4th Cir. 1997) (strip search of arrested defendant in police van by pulling down his trousers to search for missing drug money did not violate Fourth Amendment); and *Starks v. City of Minneapolis,* 6 F. Supp. 2d 1084 (D. Minn. 1998) (strip search on public street would violate Fourth Amendment; a ruling on defendant's motion for summary judgment).

(2) the scope of the search, (3) the manner in which the search was conducted, and (4) the place where the search was conducted.[390]

Officers who are unsure of the legality of a proposed strip search or body-cavity search may wish to consult their agency's legal advisor or other legal resource.

A review of terminology, as set out in a federal appellate case, is useful.[391] A strip search generally involves a removal of some or all of a person's clothing, a search of the clothing, and a squat and cough. A visual body-cavity search generally requires a person to expose his anal or her anal and vaginal cavities for visual inspection. A manual body-cavity search generally involves a digital touching or probing of the anal or vaginal cavity by another person.

There have been several North Carolina appellate cases on strip searches or similarly intrusive body searches. In *State v. Smith*,[392] officers had probable cause to believe that the defendant possessed cocaine and specific information that the cocaine would be concealed in or under his crotch. Based on these facts, the court ruled that the officers had authority to make a warrantless search of the defendant, including his crotch area, after the officers had stopped the defendant in his vehicle. While blocking the defendant from being seen by the public, an officer pulled the defendant's underwear down and removed a paper towel that contained cocaine. The court noted that the officer took reasonable precautions to prevent public exposure of the defendant's private areas.

In *State v. David Johnson*,[393] the court ruled that probable cause and exigent circumstances supported an officer's roadside search of the defendant's underwear conducted after a vehicle stop and that the search was conducted in a reasonable manner. After finding nothing in the defendant's outer clothing, the officer placed the defendant on the side of his vehicle, with the vehicle between the defendant and the travelled portion of the

highway. Other troopers stood around the defendant to prevent passers-by from seeing him. The officer pulled out the front waistband of the defendant's pants and looked inside. The defendant was wearing two pairs of underwear—an outer pair of boxer briefs and an inner pair of athletic compression shorts. Between the two pairs of underwear the officer found a cellophane package containing several smaller packages. There was probable cause to search because the defendant smelled of marijuana, officers found a scale of the type used to measure drugs in his car, a drug dog alerted in his car, and during a pat down the officer noticed a blunt object in the inseam of the defendant's pants. Because narcotics can be easily and quickly hidden or destroyed, especially after a defendant has notice of an officer's intent to discover whether the defendant possessed them, exigent circumstances may be sufficient to justify a warrantless search, as was the case here. In addition, the search here was conducted in a reasonable manner. Although the officer did not see the defendant's private parts, the level of the defendant's exposure was relevant in analyzing whether the search was reasonable. The court reasoned that the officer had a sufficient basis to believe that contraband was in the defendant's underwear, including the fact that although the defendant smelled of marijuana, a search of his outer clothing found nothing; the defendant turned away from the officer when the officer frisked his groin and thigh area; and the officer felt a blunt object in the defendant's crotch area during the pat-down. Finally, the court concluded that the officer took reasonable steps to protect the defendant's privacy when conducting the search.

In *State v. William Johnson*,[394] officers had a search warrant to search the defendant and his apartment for crack cocaine. The officers required the defendant to remove his clothes and move his genitals and spread his buttocks to exhibit his anal area. The officers saw a piece of plastic protruding from his anus. The defendant removed the package at their request; it contained individually packaged bags of crack cocaine. The court upheld this law enforcement action as a valid strip search. The court noted that although the necessity for a strip search was not articulated in the application for the search warrant, an officer testified at the suppression hearing that

---

390. United States v. Brack, 188 F.3d 748 (7th Cir. 1999).

391. Leverette v. Bell, 247 F.3d 160 (4th Cir. 2001). Although this case involved a search of a prison employee, the description of different kinds of searches is useful in all contexts.

392. 342 N.C. 407 (1995). The court of appeals in *State v. Smith*, 118 N.C. App. 106 (1995), had ruled that the search was unreasonable under the Fourth Amendment. However, the dissenting opinion disagreed, and the supreme court in a per curiam opinion reversed the court of appeals and adopted the dissenting opinion, thus upholding the search.

393. 225 N.C. App. 440 (2013).

---

394. 143 N.C. App. 307 (2001). The court noted that while some states have required a heightened standard to conduct strip searches, neither the United States Supreme Court nor the North Carolina Supreme Court has done so.

there was a trend toward hiding controlled substances in body cavities. The court also noted that before the strip search took place, a search of the defendant revealed almost $2,000 in small denominations and a search of the premises revealed electronic scales. The court also ruled that the search was conducted in a reasonable manner. Two male officers searched the defendant in his bedroom, and they did not touch him. Note that in this case the defendant was specifically named in the search warrant as a person to be searched; the court's ruling may not have upheld the strip search otherwise.[395]

In *State v. Battle*,[396] officers received a tip from a confidential informant that three named people were driving to another municipality to obtain cocaine and transport it. After stopping the vehicle, officers searched two male passengers and did not find any illegal drugs. The third passenger, a female, was strip searched by a female officer at the roadside between the vehicle's open doors (in daylight hours with pedestrians and vehicles in the immediate vicinity). The search included pulling her underwear out from her body, which resulted in the discovery of a folded $5 bill and a crack pipe. All three judges on the panel of the North Carolina Court of Appeals deciding this case concluded that the defendant's motion to suppress the evidence discovered during the strip search should have been granted, but there was not a majority opinion as to why the search violated the Fourth Amendment.[397]

In *State v. Fowler*,[398] the court ruled that two roadside strip searches of the defendant were reasonable and constitutional. The court first rejected the State's argument that the searches were not strip searches. During both searches the defendant's private areas were observed by an officer, and during the second search the defendant's pants were removed and an officer searched inside the defendant's underwear with his hand. Second, the court ruled that probable cause supported the searches. The officers stopped the defendant's vehicle for speeding after receiving information from another officer and his informant that the defendant would be traveling on a specified road in a silver Kia, carrying 3 grams of crack cocaine. The strip searches occurred after a consensual search of the defendant's vehicle produced marijuana but no cocaine. The court found competent evidence to show that the informant, who was known to the officers and had previously provided reliable information, gave sufficient reliable information, corroborated by an officer, to establish probable cause to believe that the defendant would be carrying a small amount of cocaine in his vehicle. When the consensual search of the defendant's vehicle did not produce the cocaine, the officers had sufficient probable cause, under the totality of the circumstances, to believe that the defendant was hiding the drugs on his person. Third, the court found that exigent circumstances supported the searches. Specifically, the officer knew that the defendant had prior experience with jail intake procedures and that he could reasonably expect that the defendant would attempt to get rid of evidence in order to prevent his going to jail. Fourth, the court found that the searches were reasonable. The trial court had determined that although the searches were intrusive, the most intrusive one occurred in a dark area away from the traveled roadway, with no one other than the defendant and the officers in the immediate vicinity. In

---

395. The court noted the ruling in *State v. Colin*, 809 P.2d 228 (Wash. Ct. App. 1991), that upheld a strip search under similar circumstances when the defendant was specifically named in the warrant as a person to be searched.

396. 204 N.C. App. 170 (2010).

397. The opinion for the court, which was not joined by the two other judges on the three-judge panel, noted that for purposes of this appeal, it was assumed that the officers had probable cause to arrest the defendant and search her incident to arrest. However, the opinion stated that for a roadside strip search to be constitutional, there must be both probable cause and exigent circumstances to show that some significant governmental or public interest would be endangered if law enforcement officers were required to wait until they could conduct the search in a more discreet location, usually at a private location within a law enforcement facility. The opinion, which extensively discussed the facts and case law from North Carolina and other jurisdictions, ruled that the strip search violated the defendant's Fourth Amendment rights. The opinion stated that the trial court's order denying the defendant's motion to suppress did not show that there were exigent circumstances justifying a search more intrusive

than that allowed incident to any arrest. A second judge on the three-judge panel concurred only in the result (granting the defendant's motion to suppress) without an opinion. A third judge concurred with an opinion that noted that the North Carolina Supreme Court in *State v. Stone*, 362 N.C. 50 (2007) (defendant's general consent to search did not include officer's flashlight search of genitals inside defendant's underwear), had ruled that an officer's search with at least questionable consent was not permissible under the Fourth Amendment. And because the search in *Battle* without the defendant's consent was more intrusive than that in *Stone*, it was not permissible under the Fourth Amendment.

398. 220 N.C. App. 263 (2012).

addition, the trial court found that the officer did not pull down the defendant's underwear or otherwise expose his bare buttocks or genitals, and females were not present or within view during the search. The court determined that these findings supported the trial court's conclusion that, although the searches were intrusive, they were conducted in a discreet manner, away from the view of others, and were limited in scope to finding a small amount of cocaine based on the corroborated tip of a known, reliable informant. Sometimes a weapons frisk can supply justification for a later strip search. In *State v. Robinson*,[399] the court ruled that an officer had probable cause to arrest the defendant after he felt something hard between the defendant's buttocks during a weapons frisk. The officer properly inferred that the defendant might be hiding drugs in his buttocks. The officer knew that the defendant was sitting in a car parked in a high crime area, a large machete was seen in the car, and a passenger possessed what appeared to be cocaine. When officers began to speak with the vehicle's occupants, the defendant dropped a large sum of cash on the floor and made a quick movement behind his back. The court also ruled that the searching officer took reasonable steps to protect the defendant's privacy during an intrusive search that discovered a clear plastic baggie of crack cocaine located between the defendant's buttocks. The officer shielded the defendant from public view by opening his patrol car's rear door and stood directly behind the defendant. The patrol car's lights were not turned on. The shining of the officer's flashlight into the defendant's pants was the only illumination in the immediate vicinity, and there were no other people in the search area.

Another issue involving strip searches is whether a consent to search includes an intrusive bodily search. In *State v. Stone*,[400] the court ruled that a defendant who had given a general consent to a search for weapons or drugs during a routine traffic stop did not authorize an officer's pulling the defendant's sweatpants away and shining a flashlight inside his underwear onto the defendant's groin area. The court stated that a reasonable person would not have understood his consent to include such an examination. The scope of a general consent to search does not necessarily include consent for an officer to move cloth-

ing to directly observe the genitals of a clothed person. In *State v. Neal*,[401] the court ruled that the scope of the defendant's consent to search included a strip search. An officer detected a mild odor of marijuana coming from the passenger side of a car in which the defendant was seated. The defendant consented to a pat-down search of her person to check for weapons and also consented to a search of her purse. A drug dog reacted to the passenger side of the car. While the canine search was being conducted, the defendant acted very nervous and often put her hands in and out of the back of the waistband of her pants. An officer noticed a bulge in the back of her pants, and the defendant was instructed to keep her hands away from the waistband. An officer informed the defendant that he wanted to conduct a better search to determine what was located in the back of her pants and that he had contacted a female officer for assistance. The female officer conducted a search of the defendant in the women's bathroom, with another officer standing outside the door to prevent others from coming in. The female officer explained to the defendant that she would be conducting a more thorough search. The defendant indicated that she understood. During the search, the defendant was asked to lower her underwear, and a package containing cocaine fell out. The female officer testified that the defendant was "very cooperative, extremely cooperative" during the search and never expressed any misgivings about the scope of the search.

Although the United States Supreme Court has not decided the Fourth Amendment's requirements for manual searching of body cavities,[402] officers should assume that they need (1) probable cause that evidence of a crime is in a body cavity;[403] (2) a search warrant, unless exigent

---

399. 221 N.C. App. 266 (2012). There was a dissenting opinion in this case, but the defendant later withdrew his appeal to the North Carolina Supreme Court, 366 N.C. 247 (2012).

400. State v. Stone, 362 N.C. 50 (2007).

401. State v. Neal, 190 N.C. App. 453 (2008).

402. United States v. Montoya de Hernandez, 473 U.S. 531 (1985).

403. Although the case was decided in a different context, the United States Supreme Court has rejected a third standard for body-cavity searches, such as a "clear indication" that the evidence sought is in the body cavity. *See* United States v. Montoya de Hernandez, 473 U.S. 531 (1985). In *State v. Fowler*, 89 N.C. App. 10 (1988), the court upheld a body-cavity search conducted with a search warrant in which a male defendant's rectum was searched for drugs. *See also* Rodriques v. Furtado, 950 F.2d 805 (1st Cir. 1991) (manual search of vagina); Fuller v. M. G. Jewelry, 950 F.2d 1437 (9th Cir. 1991) (visual inspection of rectum and vagina); Salinas v. Breier, 695 F.2d 1073 (7th Cir. 1982) (manual and visual inspection of private parts of male and female suspects).

circumstances make it impracticable to obtain a warrant—that is, the evidence would be destroyed or would dissipate while officers sought a warrant; and (3) qualified personnel who will conduct the search in a reasonable manner.[404] A North Carolina appellate case has upheld the use of a search warrant to conduct a body cavity search that was performed by a physician.[405]

Surgical intrusion for evidence. If officers have probable cause to search for and seize evidence that may be obtained only by surgery (for example, to recover a bullet in the defendant's body that allegedly was shot from the robbery victim's gun), the United States Supreme Court has ruled that a court may order the surgery only if the government demonstrates a compelling need for the evidence that outweighs the arrestee's privacy interests—the threat to the arrestee's safety and health by the proposed surgery and the right to protect the integrity of one's body.[406]

Inventory of an Arrestee's Possessions before the Arrestee Enters a Detention Facility

As discussed above, officers may conduct a full search incident to a person's arrest. An arrestee who cannot meet the conditions of pretrial release normally is committed to a detention facility. Before entering the detention facility, the arrestee and his or her possessions may be fully searched and inventoried. This search and inventory is based on a justification under the Fourth Amendment separate from the search incident to arrest justification. The United States Supreme Court has ruled that officers or jailers may examine all of an arrestee's personal possessions while conducting this inventory.[407] Although they could secure an arrestee's possessions by,

for example, merely placing a shoulder bag in a locker without opening it and examining it, they are not constitutionally restricted to doing so. Of course, officers and jailers should follow whatever inventory policy their agency has adopted.

Frisk of a Person for Weapons

(See page 379 for case summaries on this topic.)

Under some circumstances, officers may make a limited search to protect themselves when they confront a person who might be armed and dangerous, even though they do not have grounds to arrest the suspect. This type of limited search is known as a *frisk*.

Determining when a person may be frisked. The United States Supreme Court has ruled that officers may frisk a person when (1) they are confronting the person for a legitimate reason and (2) they have a reasonable suspicion that the person is armed and presents a threat to their safety or the safety of others.[408] If these conditions are satisfied, a frisk may be conducted even if officers do not additionally have cause to believe that the person is involved in criminal activity.[409]

Although a frisk often follows an investigative stop that is supported by reasonable suspicion that a person has committed, is committing, or is about to commit a crime, the grounds for a frisk must be considered independently of the grounds for a stop. Generally, a frisk is not automatically justified solely by the right to stop someone.[410] A stop focuses on the apparent commission or imminent commission of a crime, and a frisk focuses on a person's apparent dangerousness. However, courts permit officers automatically—that is, without reasonable suspicion or other justification—to frisk a person who they reasonably suspect has committed a violent crime (such as robbery, homicide, or assault) or a crime associated with violence and the possession of weapons (such as the sale of drugs).[411]

---

404. *See* State v. Fowler, 89 N.C. App. 10 (1988) (upholding doctor's probing of male's rectum for drugs under search warrant and, on discovering a foreign object, administering an enema to remove it). See the discussion in 3 Wayne R. LaFave, Search and Seizure: A Treatise on the Fourth Amendment § 5.3(c) (5th ed. 2012).

405. State v. Fowler, 89 N.C. App. 10 (1988).

406. Winston v. Lee, 470 U.S. 753 (1985).

407. Illinois v. LaFayette, 462 U.S. 640 (1983). In *Florence v. Board of Chosen Freeholders*, 132 S. Ct. 1510 (2012), the United States Supreme Court ruled that reasonable suspicion is not required for a close visual inspection of arrestees who will be held in the general population of a detention facility. The Court rejected the assertion that certain detainees, such as those arrested for minor offenses, should be exempt from this process unless they give officers a particular reason to suspect them of hiding contraband. *See also* State v. Nesmith, 40 N.C.

App. 748 (1979) (search of wallet was valid as inventory of personal possessions before defendant was placed in jail).

408. Terry v. Ohio, 392 U.S. 1 (1968); Adams v. Williams, 407 U.S. 143 (1972). See the discussion in 4 Wayne R. LaFave, Search and Seizure: A Treatise on the Fourth Amendment § 9.6 (5th ed. 2012).

409. Arizona v. Johnson, 555 U.S. 323 (2009) (proper frisk of vehicle passenger during traffic stop).

410. United States v. Thomas, 863 F.2d 622 (9th Cir. 1988); United States v. Rideau, 969 F.2d 1572 (5th Cir. 1992) (en banc).

411. In *State v. Butler*, 331 N.C. 227 (1992), the court upheld the frisk of a drug suspect—when there were no specific facts

A court may consider the following factors in determining whether officers had reasonable suspicion to frisk a person:

- The kind of crime for which the person was stopped
- Whether officers knew—on their own or based on information received from others, including informants[412]—that the person was armed and dangerous
- The behavior of the person frisked
- Whether there was a bulge in the person's clothing or an observation of an object there
- The person's prior criminal record and history of dangerousness[413]

A court applies an objective test when it determines whether an officer had proper grounds to frisk. An officer's subjective beliefs are not controlling; in fact, a court may find that there were grounds to support a frisk even when the officer cannot articulate them.[414]

Appellate cases disagree as to whether an arrest of a person automatically (that is, without reasonable suspicion) authorizes officers to frisk the arrestee's companions.[415] Even without an automatic frisk rule, a court will consider the arrestee's dangerousness as a factor in determining whether officers had authority to frisk the arrestee's companions.[416]

When officers are lawfully transporting a person in their vehicle, they may frisk the person for weapons before placing him or her in the vehicle even if they do not have reasonable suspicion that the person is armed and dangerous.[417]

Conducting a frisk. A frisk is a patting down of the person's outer clothing to determine whether the person has a weapon. It is not an extensive full search of the type permitted during a search incident to an arrest. During the pat down, officers may search more thoroughly if they believe that a weapon is located in a particular place on a person's body.

Discovering evidence during a frisk; plain touch (feel) doctrine. (See page 390 for case summaries on this topic.) If the frisk indicates that a weapon is present, officers may reach into the suspect's clothing or possessions and seize the weapon to neutralize the danger to themselves or others. If officers find a weapon, they may have probable cause to arrest the person for carrying a concealed weapon,[418] and then they may conduct a full search incident to that arrest.

The United States Supreme Court in *Minnesota v. Dickerson* recognized the sense of touch within plain view sensory perceptions under the Fourth Amendment.[419] The plain touch doctrine often is an issue when a frisk uncovers evidence other than a weapon.

In *Dickerson,* an officer had reasonable suspicion to stop the defendant and to frisk him for weapons. During the frisk the officer felt a lump—a small, hard object wrapped in plastic—in the defendant's jacket pocket that the officer knew was not a weapon. However, after concluding that the lump was not a weapon, the officer determined that the lump was cocaine *only after* "squeezing,

---

indicating the suspect possessed a weapon—and stated that an officer is entitled to formulate "common-sense conclusions" about the "modes or patterns of operation of certain kinds of lawbreakers" in concluding that the suspect, reasonably suspected of drug trafficking, might be armed. *See also* United States v. Sakyi, 160 F.3d 164 (4th Cir. 1998) (when officers have reasonable suspicion that illegal drugs are in a vehicle, they may, in the absence of factors allaying safety concerns, order occupants out of vehicle and pat them down briefly for weapons to ensure their safety and safety of others). *See generally* 4 WAYNE R. LaFAVE, SEARCH AND SEIZURE: A TREATISE ON THE FOURTH AMENDMENT § 9.6(a), at 853–55 (5th ed. 2012).

412. Adams v. Williams, 407 U.S. 143 (1972).

413. *See* 4 WAYNE R. LaFAVE, SEARCH AND SEIZURE: A TREATISE ON THE FOURTH AMENDMENT § 9.6(a), at 860 (5th ed. 2012).

414. State v. Peck, 305 N.C. 734 (1982) (objective evidence supported officer's removal, for safety reasons, of object from defendant's pants pocket when he furtively reached for pocket; officer's subjective belief that the defendant did not have gun when defendant reached in his pocket is immaterial in determining legality of frisk).

415. *Compare* United States v. Berryhill, 445 F.2d 1189 (9th Cir. 1971) (automatic frisk of companions of arrestee is permitted); United States v. Poms, 484 F.2d 919 (4th Cir. 1973) (agreeing with *Berryhill*); *and* United States v. Simmons, 567 F.2d 314 (7th Cir. 1977) (indicating agreement with *Berryhill*); *with* United States v. Bell, 762 F.2d 495 (6th Cir. 1985) (disagreeing

with *Berryhill*); and United States v. Flett, 806 F.2d 823 (8th Cir. 1986) (similar ruling).

416. *See* 4 WAYNE R. LaFAVE, SEARCH AND SEIZURE: A TREATISE ON THE FOURTH AMENDMENT § 9.6(a), at 868–73 (5th ed. 2012).

417. United States v. McCargo, 464 F.3d 192 (2d Cir. 2006); 4 WAYNE R. LaFAVE, SEARCH AND SEIZURE: A TREATISE ON THE FOURTH AMENDMENT § 9.6(a), at 843 (5th ed. 2012).

418. G.S. 14-269. Of course, if the person has a concealed weapon permit under G.S. 14-415.11, then the possession of the weapon may be lawful.

419. 508 U.S. 366 (1993).

sliding and otherwise manipulating the contents of the defendant's pocket."

The Court ruled that the plain view doctrine applies by analogy to cases in which an officer discovers contraband through the sense of touch during an otherwise lawful search. The plain view doctrine provides that an officer may seize an object if all of the following conditions are met:

1. Officers are lawfully in a position in which they view an object
2. The object's incriminating character is immediately apparent—that is, officers have probable cause to seize it[420]
3. The officers have a lawful right of access to the object

The Court ruled that the officer in this case was not justified in seizing the cocaine because he exceeded the search for weapons that is permitted by the Fourth Amendment.[421] Once the officer determined that the lump was not a weapon, his continued exploration of the lump until he developed probable cause to believe it was cocaine was an additional search that was not justified by the Fourth Amendment. Thus, the officer's action would have been permissible only if he had developed probable cause to believe that the lump was cocaine at the time he determined the lump was not a weapon.[422]

North Carolina appellate cases on this issue are summarized in the accompanying footnote.[423]

Frisking during the execution of a search warrant. (See page 504 for case summaries on this topic.) Officers normally may automatically frisk persons present in a private residence when a search warrant is being executed there—at least if their search involves a potentially dangerous activity, such as the sale of illegal drugs.[424] However, the United States Supreme Court has ruled that when officers are executing a search warrant in a public place (for example, a tavern), they may not automatically—that is, without reasonable suspicion—frisk a customer there who was not named in the search warrant as a person to be searched.[425] To frisk such a person, officers must have reasonable suspicion that the person is armed and dangerous.

Protective Search of a Vehicle

Search of a vehicle for a weapon when no arrest is made (car frisk). (See page 379 for case summaries on this topic.) Officers often interact with people in or near a vehicle but do not make an arrest; for example, officers may stop a vehicle to issue a citation. The United States Supreme Court has recognized that officers may search a vehicle

---

420. State v. Williams, 195 N.C. App. 554 (2009) (immediately apparent means probable cause).

421. *Cf.* Terry v. Ohio, 392 U.S. 1 (1968).

422. Sometimes an officer may develop probable cause when feeling a container, considering all the circumstances of an encounter with a person. *See State v. Robinson*, 189 N.C. App. 454 (2008), and *State v. Briggs*, 140 N.C. App. 484 (2000), summarized *infra* note 423.

423. State v. Morton, 204 N.C. App. 578 (2010) (officer knew object in defendant's pocket was digital scale based on his pat down without manipulation of object); State v. Robinson, 189 N.C. App. 454 (2008) (officer's discovery of crack cocaine in film canister during frisk was proper under *Minnesota v. Dickerson* because contents of film canister were immediately identifiable by officer as crack cocaine); State v. Briggs, 140 N.C. App. 484 (2000) (officer had probable cause to seize cigar holder, believing it to contain crack cocaine); State v. Benjamin, 124 N.C. App. 734 (1996) (during frisk officer felt two hard plastic containers customarily used to hold illegal drugs and asked defendant about them; defendant promptly responded that they were "crack"; these and other facts supported seizure

of cocaine); *In re* Whitley, 122 N.C. App. 290 (1996) (incriminating character of seized object was immediately apparent to officer when during frisk it fell from the suspect's buttocks into his pants; seizure of cocaine was proper); State v. Wilson, 112 N.C. App. 777 (1993) (officer during frisk felt lump in the left breast pocket of defendant's jacket and immediately believed that it was crack cocaine; seizure of cocaine was proper); State v. Sanders, 112 N.C. App. 477 (1993) (court ruled, based on *Minnesota v. Dickerson*, that trooper acted properly in conducting frisk by feeling packet in bulge in jacket to determine if it was weapon; court remanded case to trial court to determine, in light of *Dickerson* (decided after case was heard in trial court), whether it was immediately apparent to trooper that what he felt was illegal drugs); State v. Beveridge, 112 N.C. App. 688 (1993), *aff'd per curiam*, 336 N.C. 601 (1994) (once officer concluded that cylindrical-shaped rolled-up plastic bag in defendant's front pocket was not a weapon and it was not immediately apparent that it was an illegal substance, he could not continue the search).

424. State v. Long, 37 N.C. App. 662 (1978). Although *Long* was decided before *Ybarra v. Illinois*, 444 U.S. 85 (1979), its ruling is not inconsistent with that decision. G.S. 15A-255 also authorizes officers to frisk all those present if they reasonably believe that their safety or the safety of others justifies the frisk. The statute does not require an individualized reasonable belief; rather, it requires an assessment of the circumstances that exist in private premises.

425. Ybarra v. Illinois, 444 U.S. 85 (1979). *See also* 2 Wayne R. LaFave, Search and Seizure: A Treatise on the Fourth Amendment § 4.9(d) (5th ed. 2012).

for weapons without a warrant, even when they are not making an arrest, if they have reasonable suspicion that a person is dangerous and a weapon that could be used to harm them may be in the vehicle.[426] This search—sometimes called a car frisk—may be no more intrusive than is necessary to locate weapons.

Search of a vehicle for a weapon when there is a danger to the public: community caretaking function. (See page 398 for case summaries on this topic.) A basic reason for an inventory search of an impounded vehicle, discussed below, is to ascertain the vehicle's contents so that they may be safeguarded. A somewhat different reason—known as the community caretaking function—justifies a warrantless search of an impounded vehicle when officers have infor-

mation that a weapon may be inside. An intruder could remove the weapon and possibly endanger the public.[427]

Search of a vehicle to determine ownership. (See page 344 for case summaries on this topic.) Generally, officers may make a limited warrantless search of a vehicle when they need to determine its ownership.[428] For example, if officers believe that a vehicle has been stolen or vandalized, they may need to determine its ownership so that they can inform the owner about what has happened to his or her vehicle.

Entry or Search of a Home to Render Emergency Assistance or for Self-Protection

(*See page 396 for case summaries on this topic.*)

Officers may enter a home without a warrant when necessary to save life, to render emergency assistance, and to prevent injury to themselves or others.[429] And, while they are undertaking emergency action in good faith, they may seize any evidence of a crime that they see in plain view.

Searches of crime scenes and fire scenes are discussed separately below.

Entering a home to render emergency assistance to injured occupant or to protect occupant from imminent injury. The United States Supreme Court has recognized an emergency aid exception to the Fourth Amendment's warrant requirement to allow officers to enter a home without a warrant to (1) render emergency assistance

---

426. Michigan v. Long, 463 U.S. 1032 (1983). In *State v. Braxton*, 90 N.C. App. 204 (1988), an officer approached a speeding car and saw the defendant-driver, who appeared to be stuffing something under the seat. The defendant pulled over, and then the officer pulled over, parked behind the defendant, and got out of his car. The defendant started moving his car forward and again appeared to be stuffing something under the seat. The officer got back in his car, and the defendant then stopped his car again. As the officer approached the defendant's car, the defendant got out of his car and closed the door. The officer asked the defendant twice what he had stuffed under the seat, but the defendant did not respond. The officer opened the car door, reached under the front seat, and discovered a plastic bag containing marijuana. The court ruled that the officer's action was not justified as a protective search for weapons under *Michigan v. Long*, but the court inadequately explained why the facts did not support the officer's action: the court stated that the "defendant could not obtain any weapon or other item from the car," yet the defendant was not under arrest then and clearly could have reentered after the officer wrote a citation for the speeding infraction. Compare the *Braxton* ruling with *United States v. Nash*, 876 F.2d 1359 (7th Cir. 1989) (search of car for weapon justified under *Michigan v. Long* when officer saw defendant, while still driving, make furtive gesture by appearing to raise himself up from car seat and begin reaching toward floor, and when officer approached car he saw jacket tucked under defendant's lap and stretched out to floor). Other North Carolina cases involving *Michigan v. Long* include *State v. Thomas*, 183 N.C. App. 1 (2007) (detective had reasonable belief that defendant was dangerous and had immediate access to weapon in car and search of drawstring bag was valid part of weapons search); *State v. Edwards*, 164 N.C. App. 130 (2004) (officer had authority to make protective search of defendant's vehicle for weapon when, after defendant's vehicle was stopped by officer, defendant immediately put both hands underneath his seat and jumped out of vehicle).

427. Cady v. Dombrowski, 413 U.S. 433 (1983); 3 WAYNE R. LAFAVE, SEARCH AND SEIZURE: A TREATISE ON THE FOURTH AMENDMENT § 7.4(c) (5th ed. 2012). The community caretaking function sometimes may support the stop of a vehicle when, for example, an officer needs to check the safety and well-being of an occupant. State v. Sawyers, ___ N.C. App. ___, 786 S.E.2d 753 (2016).

428. *Cf.* New York v. Class, 475 U.S. 106 (1986) (after stopping vehicle for traffic violations and after driver left vehicle, officer conducted proper search by entering car to remove papers that obscured vehicle's Vehicle Identification Number). *But see* State v. Green, 103 N.C. App. 38 (1991) (officer lacked authority to search car for license and registration, based on facts in this case; intrusion was not minimal as in *New York v. Class*). *See also* 3 WAYNE R. LAFAVE, SEARCH AND SEIZURE: A TREATISE ON THE FOURTH AMENDMENT § 7.4(d) (5th ed. 2012).

429. Mincey v. Arizona, 437 U.S. 385 (1978); Maryland v. Buie, 494 U.S. 325 (1990); Brigham City v. Stuart, 547 U.S. 398 (2006); Michigan v. Fisher, 558 U.S. 45 (2009); 3 WAYNE R. LAFAVE, SEARCH AND SEIZURE: A TREATISE ON THE FOURTH AMENDMENT § 6.6 (5th ed. 2012).

to an injured occupant or (2) protect an occupant from imminent injury.[430] This exception does not depend on the officers' subjective intent or the seriousness of any crime that they are investigating when the emergency arises. It only requires an objectively reasonable basis for believing that a person within a house is in need of immediate aid.

A North Carolina statute recognizes an officer's authority to enter buildings or premises without a search warrant to save life or to prevent serious bodily harm.[431]

Entering a home to seize weapons for self-protection. Officers may make a warrantless entry into a home when exigent circumstances support their reasonable belief that weapons are present that may be used against them and others.[432] For example, if officers arrest a dangerous fugitive outside a house and believe that the fugitive's weapon is still inside the home but are unsure whether anyone else is inside, they may make a limited protective search of the house to recover the weapon.[433]

Protective sweep when officer is in a home to make an arrest. When officers arrest a person in a home or other premises, they may as incident to that arrest automatically—that is, without needing probable cause or reasonable suspicion to do so—search closets and other spaces immediately adjoining the place of arrest from which an attack on them from another person could occur. This search is limited to looking for people who may pose a danger; its purpose is not to discover evidence. Officers also may make a warrantless sweep of the rest of the premises, but only if there is reasonable suspicion that the place to be searched harbors a person who is a danger to the officers there.[434]

While in a home to make an arrest or immediately after the arrest, officers may make a protective search for weapons if they have a reasonable belief that the search is necessary to protect themselves.[435]

Impoundment and Inventory of Vehicles
(*See page 393 for case summaries on this topic.*)

Impoundments and inventories of vehicles are seizures and searches, respectively, under the Fourth Amendment and, therefore, must be reasonable. However, impoundments and inventories need not be supported with reasonable suspicion, probable cause, or a search warrant because their purpose is not to discover evidence of a crime.[436]

Impounding a vehicle may be justified by a need to protect a vehicle and its contents, a need to prevent the vehicle from becoming a traffic hazard, or some other reason. Inventorying a vehicle may be justified by a need to protect the owner's property while it remains in officers' custody; a need to protect the officers and their agency from claims or disputes about lost, damaged, or stolen property; or a need to protect officers or the public from potential danger from property, such as dangerous weapons, that may be in the vehicle.

Although *written* impound and inventory procedures are not constitutionally required,[437] an impoundment

---

430. Brigham City v. Stuart, 547 U.S. 398 (2006); Michigan v. Fisher, 558 U.S. 45 (2009). The *Fisher* Court noted it was sufficient in that case to invoke the emergency aid exception that it was reasonable to believe the occupant had hurt himself and needed treatment, which in his rage he was unable to provide, or that he was about to hurt, or had already hurt, someone else. *See also* Johnson v. City of Memphis, 617 F.3d 864 (6th Cir. 2010) (officers who received dispatch about 911 hang-up call did not violate Fourth Amendment by making warrantless entry of residence from which call was placed after no one responded to their calls).

North Carolina cases concerning a warrantless entry to render assistance include *State v. Cline*, 205 N.C. App. 676 (2010) (warrantless entry into home was necessary to ascertain whether someone in home needed immediate assistance), and *State v. McKinney*, 361 N.C. 53 (2006) (exigent circumstances did not exist to enter house without warrant to look for possible missing victim). Concerning a related issue, see *State v. Wade*, 198 N.C. App. 257 (2009) (officer did not violate Fourth Amendment when stopping vehicle containing passenger who had been reported missing by his parents).

431. G.S. 15A-285. *See* State v. Braswell, 312 N.C. 553 (1985) (officers' entry into home was justified under G.S. 15A-285 because they believed person might be inside who was injured and needed assistance).

432. Ryburn v. Huff, 132 S. Ct. 987 (2012) (Fourth Amendment permitted officers to enter residence if there was an objectively reasonable basis to fear that violence was imminent; in this case, student who may have threatened to "shoot up" school).

433. State v. Taylor, 298 N.C. 405 (1979); State v. Mackins, 47 N.C. App. 168 (1980).

---

434. Maryland v. Buie, 494 U.S. 325 (1990); 3 Wayne R. LaFave, Search and Seizure: A Treatise on the Fourth Amendment § 6.4(c) (5th ed. 2012).

435. Warden v. Hayden, 387 U.S. 294 (1967).

436. South Dakota v. Opperman, 428 U.S. 364 (1976).

437. *See* United States v. Hawkins, 279 F.3d 83 (1st Cir. 2002); United States v. Lage, 183 F.3d 374 (5th Cir. 1999); United States v. Duguay, 93 F.3d 346 (7th Cir. 1996); United States v. Como, 53 F.3d 87 (5th Cir. 1995); United States v.

or inventory must be conducted under standard operating procedures that are reasonable under the Fourth Amendment. Standard operating procedures reduce the possibility that officers will impound or inventory a vehicle as a pretext to search for evidence. A law enforcement agency should consider adopting written standard operating procedures so that its officers will understand (1) the circumstances under which they should impound a vehicle and (2) the scope of any inventory search they conduct after the vehicle has been placed in a storage facility.

Impounding vehicles. Officers may impound a vehicle according to their agency's standard operating procedures, whether written or informally understood. These procedures may provide for impoundment when (1) a person is arrested and impoundment is necessary to safeguard the vehicle and its contents; (2) a vehicle is illegally parked and towing is permitted, or the illegally parked vehicle is a traffic hazard; or (3) there are circumstances in which it is reasonably necessary to protect the vehicle or other property or people.[438] Officers should be aware of their responsibilities under North Carolina law to notify the registered owner when they authorize a vehicle to be towed under certain circumstances.[439]

Inventorying vehicles and containers within vehicles. Officers may inventory a vehicle and the containers within the vehicle according to their agency's standard operating procedures, whether written or informally understood. The United States Supreme Court has not clearly delineated the permissible scope of an inventory search, but an inventory could include all areas within a vehicle that may contain valuables and weapons—for example, the interior, including glove compartment and console, and the trunk. However, the court has indicated that closed containers within vehicles, such as luggage and briefcases, may not be opened unless an agency's standard operating procedures (1) require officers to

open all closed containers or (2) authorize officers to open closed containers when they are unable to determine their contents by examining the exteriors of the containers.[440] Officers should not ordinarily break open locked containers to inventory them; they should simply state the fact that a container was locked on the inventory form (for example, by writing "one locked, sealed briefcase").

A law enforcement agency may, of course, adopt inventory procedures that are less intrusive of a person's privacy interests than constitutionally permissible procedures.

Abusing impoundment and inventory search authority. Officers must be careful to follow their own agency's standard operating procedures, whether written or informally understood, when they impound and inventory a vehicle. If they do not follow these procedures, a court may rule that their actions were unreasonable under the Fourth Amendment. If the improper impoundment or inventory search is the only justification that supports officers' actions, evidence seized as a result of an improper search may be excluded at trial.[441]

Search of a Crime Scene
(See page 399 for case summaries on this topic.)

As discussed above, officers may enter a home without a warrant when necessary to save life, to render emergency assistance, and to prevent injury to themselves or others. For example, when a crime may have occurred in a home—such as an assault or a homicide—officers may enter without a warrant to determine the victim's condition and to call for appropriate medical assistance. Officers may also search the home without a warrant to

---

Lowe, 9 F.3d 43 (8th Cir. 1993); United States v. Mancera-Londono, 912 F.2d 373 (9th Cir. 1990); United States v. Kordosky, 921 F.2d 722 (7th Cir. 1991); United States v. Walker, 931 F.2d 1066 (5th Cir. 1991); United States v. Griffin, 729 F.2d 475 (7th Cir. 1984).

438. *See* 3 Wayne R. LaFave, Search and Seizure: A Treatise on the Fourth Amendment §§ 7.3(c) through (e) (5th ed. 2012). Some statutory provisions authorizing towing include G.S. 20-137.6 through -137.14, -161, -162; G.S. Chapter 153A, Article 6; and G.S. Chapter 160A, Article 15. These provisions are not the exclusive authority to impound vehicles.

439. G.S. 20-219.9 through -219.14.

440. *See* Florida v. Wells, 495 U.S. 1 (1990) (dicta); Colorado v. Bertine, 479 U.S. 367 (1987); United States v. Como, 53 F.3d 87 (5th Cir. 1995); United States v. Kordosky, 921 F.2d 722 (7th Cir. 1991). Although the court's ruling in *State v. Hall*, 52 N.C. App. 492 (1981), that the inventory search was unconstitutional because it was based on an improper investigatory motive is supportable, the court's alternative ruling that opening the bottle exceeded the permissible scope of the inventory search and its dicta questioning an officer's right to open any closed container during an inventory search must be reconsidered in light of *Colorado v. Bertine* and *Florida v. Wells*.

441. State v. Phifer, 297 N.C. 216 (1979); State v. Vernon, 45 N.C. App. 486 (1980). Although an officer's motive is irrelevant in determining the legality of an officer's search or seizure with probable cause or reasonable suspicion, motive is relevant when conducting inventory searches—which need not be justified by probable cause or reasonable suspicion. *Cf.* City of Indianapolis v. Edmond, 531 U.S. 32 (2000).

determine whether there are other victims or suspects there. While undertaking these actions, they may seize any evidence of a crime they see in plain view.[442] However, the United States Supreme Court has ruled that once officers have completed these actions, they may search further only with a search warrant or with consent.[443] Thus, before laboratory technicians or other officers may enter the home and begin to search for evidence and conduct tests, a search warrant or consent[444] must be obtained.[445] However, if evidence may dissipate or be destroyed while a search warrant is being sought, a warrantless search or seizure of that evidence is permissible.[446]

Chapter 4 discusses how to fill out an application for a search warrant to search a crime scene.

Search of a Fire Scene
(See page 401 for case summaries on this topic.)

The United States Supreme Court has ruled that fire personnel and others may enter a home or business without a warrant and remain there until they have put out the fire and determined the fire's origin so that it will not start again after they leave.[447] Generally, however, once they leave the fire scene,[448] they must obtain an administrative inspection warrant, search warrant, or consent if they want to reenter the home or business to investigate the fire's origin further.[449]

If officers have information that establishes probable cause to believe that the fire was caused by a criminal act, such as arson, they must obtain a search warrant instead of an administrative inspection warrant before they may reenter to search.[450] If during an inspection of the premises with an administrative inspection warrant they determine the fire's origin and find probable cause to believe that the fire was caused by a criminal act, they must obtain a search warrant to search the remainder of the premises.[451]

---

442. *See* Thompson v. Louisiana, 469 U.S. 17 (1984); 3 Wayne R. LaFave, Search and Seizure: A Treatise on the Fourth Amendment § 6.5(e), at 591–92 (5th ed. 2012).

443. Mincey v. Arizona, 437 U.S. 385 (1978); Thompson v. Louisiana, 469 U.S. 17 (1984). Of course, only a person who had a reasonable expectation of privacy in the home could challenge the constitutionality of the search and seizure. Thus, a burglar who entered a home and killed a resident would not have a reasonable expectation of privacy in the home to contest an allegedly unconstitutional search of the home during a criminal investigation.

444. *See* Thompson v. Louisiana, 469 U.S. 17 (1984).

445. In *Thompson v. Louisiana*, 469 U.S. 17 (1984), the Supreme Court ruled unconstitutional the officers' warrantless entry and exploratory search for evidence that began 35 minutes after the homicide victim and injured defendant had been removed and the house had been searched for other victims and suspects. In *State v. Jolley*, 312 N.C. 296 (1984), decided before *Thompson*, the North Carolina Supreme Court ruled that an officer seized a rifle he saw in plain view in a home after he entered to respond to a homicide, even though he did not physically take possession of the rifle then. After removing the emotionally upset defendant and securing the area, he and another officer reentered the home about 10 minutes later and physically took possession of the rifle. The court upheld this action because it believed that the officer had constructively seized the rifle earlier when he secured the crime scene. It is unclear whether this warrantless reentry and seizure is permissible under the *Thompson* reasoning. *See also* State v. Phillips, 151 N.C. App. 185 (2002) (ruling similar to *Jolley*).

446. See Part I of Justice Rehnquist's opinion concurring in part and dissenting in part in *Mincey v. Arizona*, 437 U.S. 385 (1978). The opinion mentions that blood might need to be examined immediately so that the evidence is not dissipated or lost.

447. Michigan v. Tyler, 436 U.S. 499 (1978); Michigan v. Clifford, 464 U.S. 287 (1984). *See generally* 4 Wayne R. LaFave, Search and Seizure: A Treatise on the Fourth Amendment § 10.4 (5th ed. 2012).

448. If smoke or darkness requires that fire officials leave the building for a few hours, a warrantless reentry into the building to continue a determination of the fire's origin is permissible. *See* Michigan v. Tyler, 436 U.S. 499 (1978).

449. In *Michigan v. Clifford*, 464 U.S. 287 (1984), a majority of the Justices said that an administrative inspection warrant is not needed for an inspection to determine the fire's origin when the fire inspector gives or reasonably attempts to give the owner (or other person with privacy interests in the home or business) advance notice of the need to inspect so that the person can be present at the inspection. Nevertheless, a cautious officer should obtain an administrative inspection warrant until the Court (or a federal or North Carolina appellate court) rules that a warrant is unnecessary when advance notice is given or a reasonable attempt is made to give advance notice.

If a home or business is sufficiently damaged so that it is no longer usable, the owner or possessor would not have a reasonable expectation of privacy there and could not successfully challenge a search conducted there. See a statement to that effect in *Clifford*, 464 U.S. at 292.

450. *Id.* at 294.

451. In *Michigan v. Clifford*, 464 U.S. 287 (1984), eight Justices agreed that once officers determined that the fire began in the basement and its cause was arson, they could not search the rest of the home without a search warrant.

Chapter 4 discusses how to fill out an application for an administrative inspection warrant to inspect a fire scene.

Inspection of Mail and Mail Covers
Mail

A first-class domestic letter generally may be opened only with a search warrant.[452]

Federal customs officers may open foreign mail, including first-class mail, without a warrant when they have reasonable suspicion that it contains illegally imported matter.[453]

The legality of intercepting or reading outgoing or incoming mail of prisoners and inmates will not be discussed here; see the appellate cases and legal resources listed in the accompanying note.[454]

---

452. 39 U.S.C. § 404(c). *See* Anuj C. Desai, *Can the President Read Your Mail? A Legal Analysis*, 59 CATH. U. L. REV. 315 (2010). A State search warrant may be used to open first-class domestic mail. State v. Marshall, 586 A.2d 85 (N.J. 1991).

453. 19 U.S.C. § 482; United States v. Ramsey, 431 U.S. 606 (1977).

454. *See* State v. Martin, 322 N.C. 229 (1988) (court applied the ruling of *Hudson v. Palmer*, 468 U.S. 517 (1984) (prisoner has no reasonable expectation of privacy in a prison cell), to a pretrial detainee's jail cell and ruled that a jailer's search of the cell and his reading of the defendant's notebook and discovery of letter to defendant's brother—urging him to commit perjury at trial—did not violate Fourth Amendment; jailer could have read something in notebook that would have enabled him better to maintain order in the jail); State v. Wiley, 355 N.C. 592 (2002) (deputy sheriff, acting pursuant to jail's mail policy provided to inmates when they enter jail, properly scanned outgoing letter not addressed to attorney to determine that there was no contraband, matters concerning jail escape, or possible harm to jail personnel; inmate did not have reasonable expectation of privacy in this letter); State v. Fuller, 166 N.C. App. 548 (2004) (jail personnel's seizure and reading of letters that were outgoing mail to nonattorney did not violate Fourth Amendment, and letters to defendant's wife were not inadmissible under the marital communications privilege); State v. Kennedy, 58 N.C. App. 810 (1982) (defendant, who was not an inmate, wrote and mailed letter to prison inmate; correctional officer, following routine procedure, opened letter and examined it for contraband; officer saw reference to shotgun in letter and read further, and letter revealed defendant's participation in armed robbery; officer gave letter to police officer; court ruled sender of letter had no reasonable expectation of privacy in letter); Altizer v. Deeds, 191 F.3d 540 (4th Cir. 1999) (opening and inspecting inmate's outgoing nonlegal mail is reasonably related to legitimate penological interests and is constitutional); Lavado v. Keohane, 992 F.2d 601 (6th Cir. 1993) (opening incoming prisoner mail

Mail Covers

A *mail cover* records information that appears on the outside of all mail going to and from a particular person.[455] Only designated United States postal inspectors and other employees may order mail covers.[456] State and local law enforcement officers may make a written request for a mail cover, but they must show reasonable grounds for believing that the mail cover would aid in (1) protecting national security, (2) locating a fugitive, (3) obtaining information concerning the commission or attempted commission of a crime punishable by more than one year's imprisonment, or (4) assisting in the identification of property, proceeds, or assets forfeitable under criminal law.[457]

Special Search Authority during Emergencies and Riots

North Carolina law attempts to control public disorders in several ways[458] by

- Defining certain conduct as always being unlawful—for example, rioting and disorderly conduct
- Setting the procedures by which the state and local governments may declare states of emergency
- Stating what other restrictions governments may impose when a state of emergency exists—for example, curfews or limitations on liquor sales
- Granting law enforcement officers certain additional authority when a riot or state of emergency occurs

The additional enforcement authority includes an expanded power to frisk and to use warrants to search vehicles near riots or in other areas for any dangerous weapon or substance. The term "dangerous weapon or substance" includes things that may destroy property as well as those that might cause serious bodily injury; it includes ammunition and parts of weapons as well as complete weapons.[459] The law does not restrict an offi-

---

pursuant to uniform policy is constitutional); Jamie Markham, *Mail Regulation in the Jail*, NC CRIM. L. BLOG (Dec. 7, 2015), http://nccriminallaw.sog.unc.edu/mail-regulation-in-the-jail/; 4 WAYNE R. LAFAVE, SEARCH AND SEIZURE: A TREATISE ON THE FOURTH AMENDMENT § 10.9(c) (5th ed. 2012).

455. 39 C.F.R. § 233.3.

456. *Id.* §§ 233.3(d) & (e).

457. *Id.*

458. G.S. 14-288.1 through -288.20.

459. G.S. 14-288.1(2).

cer's use of any other permissible authority to arrest, frisk, search, or the like.

A riot exists when three or more people assemble and by disorderly or violent conduct—or by the imminent threat of that conduct—injure or damage persons or property or present a clear and present danger that they will do so.[460] A declared state of emergency must be proclaimed by the governor or by an appropriate municipal official (usually, the mayor) or county official (usually, the chairman of the board of county commissioners). This declaration may be made when public authorities are unable to maintain adequate protection for lives or property because of a public crisis, disaster, riot, catastrophe, or similar emergency.[461]

Special Frisk Authority

Law enforcement officers have special powers to frisk people who are found near riots or who are violating a curfew during a state of emergency. The special powers are broader than the general power to frisk discussed earlier in this chapter.

Frisk of people close to existing riots. Officers may frisk a person and inspect personal belongings to discover whether the person has any dangerous weapons or substances if (1) they have reasonable grounds to believe that the person is or may become unlawfully involved in an existing riot and (2) the person is close enough to the riot that he or she could become immediately involved in it.[462] If the person is in a vehicle, officers probably could also inspect the vehicle.

Frisk of curfew violators. Officers may frisk a person and inspect personal belongings to discover whether the person has any dangerous weapons or substances if he or she is violating a curfew proclaimed during a state of emergency or civil disorder.[463] If the person is in a vehicle, officers probably could also inspect the vehicle.

If a dangerous weapon or substance is found as a result of a frisk of a person close to an existing riot or in violation of a curfew, the person may be violating either the concealed weapon law[464] or the law prohibiting possession of a dangerous weapon or substance—whether concealed or not—in the area where a declared state of emergency exists or within the immediate vicinity of a riot.[465]

Special Search Warrants to Search Vehicles

Officers have an inspection power under a special kind of search warrant to check all vehicles entering an area where a civil disorder is occurring to make sure that those vehicles are not bringing in dangerous weapons or substances.

Two kinds of search warrants may be issued:[466]

1. Warrants authorizing inspections for dangerous weapons or substances of all vehicles entering or approaching a municipality where a state of emergency exists
2. Warrants authorizing inspections for dangerous weapons or substances of all vehicles that may be within or approaching the immediate vicinity of a riot

The existence of the state of emergency or riot need not have been proclaimed, but the official who issues the warrant must have found such a condition. The only judicial officials who may issue this kind of warrant are district, superior, or appellate court judges—a magistrate or a clerk of court may not do so.[467] Officers may not seek the warrant on their own initiative; they must have authorization to apply for the warrant from the head of their agency.[468]

When issued, the warrant must state which kind it is—whether for inspection around a municipality under a state of emergency or for inspection in the vicinity of a riot—and give the date and hour of issuance. It also must state that it will automatically expire 24 hours after it was issued. Chapter 4 discusses how to complete this kind of warrant.

---

460. G.S. 14-288.2.

461. See definitions in G.S. 14-288.1 and other pertinent statutes in G.S. Chapter 14, Article 36A.

462. G.S. 14-288.10(a).

463. G.S. 14-288.10(b).

464. G.S. 14-269.

---

465. G.S. 14-288.7.

466. G.S. 14-288.11.

467. G.S. 14-288.11(c).

468. G.S. 14-288.11(d).

Chapter 3 Appendix: Case Summaries

Chapter 3 Appendix: Case Summaries

Search and Seizure Issues

What Is a Search and Seizure and What Evidence May Be Searched for and Seized
Definition of a Search

Grady v. North Carolina, 135 S. Ct. 1368 (2015). The Court ruled that under *United States v. Jones*, 132 S. Ct. 945 (2012), and *Florida v. Jardines*, 133 S. Ct. 1409 (2013), satellite-based monitoring for sex offenders constitutes a search under the Fourth Amendment. The Court stated that "a State . . . conducts a search when it attaches a device to a person's body, without consent, for the purpose of tracking that individual's movements." The Court rejected the reasoning of the North Carolina Court of Appeals, ___ N.C. App. ___, 759 S.E.2d 712 (2014), which had relied on the fact that the monitoring program was "civil in nature" to conclude that no search occurred, explaining: "A building inspector who enters a home simply to ensure compliance with civil safety regulations has undoubtedly conducted a search under the Fourth Amendment." The Court did not decide the "ultimate question of the program's constitutionality" because the state courts had not assessed whether the search was reasonable. The Court remanded for further proceedings. *See* State v. Blue, ___ N.C. App. ___, 783 S.E.2d 524 (2016) (trial court erred under *Grady* in failing to determine, based on the totality of circumstances, whether the satellite-based monitoring program constituted a reasonable search under the Fourth Amendment; court remands case to trial court for hearing, appropriate findings, and ruling, and State at hearing has the burden of proving that the search is reasonable); State v. Morris, ___ N.C. App. ___, 783 S.E.2d 528 (2016) (similar ruling).

Florida v. Jardines, 133 S. Ct. 1409 (2013). The Court ruled that officers' use of a drug-sniffing dog on a homeowner's porch to investigate the contents of the home is a "search" within the meaning of the Fourth Amendment. The Court's reasoning was based on the theory that the officers engaged in a physical intrusion of a constitution-ally protected area. Applying that principle, the Court ruled:

> The officers were gathering information in an area belonging to [the defendant] and immediately surrounding his house—in the curtilage of the house, which we have held enjoys protection as part of the home itself. And they gathered that information by physically entering and occupying the area to engage in conduct not explicitly or implicitly permitted by the homeowner.

The Court did not decide the case on a reasonable expectation of privacy analysis.

United States v. Jones, 132 S. Ct. 945 (2012). The Court ruled that the government's installation of a GPS tracking device on a vehicle and its use of that device to monitor the vehicle's movements on public streets constituted a "search" within the meaning of the Fourth Amendment. Officers who suspected that the defendant was involved in drug trafficking installed a GPS device without a valid search warrant on the undercarriage of a vehicle while it was parked in a public parking lot in Maryland. Over the next 28 days, the government used the device to track the vehicle's movements and once had to replace the device's battery when the vehicle was parked in a different public lot in Maryland. By means of signals from multiple satellites, the device established the vehicle's location within 50 to 100 feet and communicated that location by cellular phone to a government computer. It relayed more than 2,000 pages of data over the four-week period. The defendant was charged with several drug offenses. He unsuccessfully sought to suppress the evidence obtained through the GPS device. The government argued before the United States Supreme Court that a warrant was not required for the GPS device. Concluding that the evidence should have been suppressed, the Court characterized the government's conduct as having "physically occupied private property for the purpose of obtaining information." Thus, the Court had "no doubt that such a physical intrusion would have been considered a 'search' within the meaning of the Fourth Amendment when it was adopted." The Court declined to address whether the defendant had a reasonable expectation of privacy in the undercarriage of his car and in the car's locations on the public roads, concluding that such an analysis was not required when the intrusion—as here—"encroached on a protected area."

Bond v. United States, 529 U.S. 334 (2000). A Border Patrol agent boarded a commercial bus at a permanent Border Patrol checkpoint. While walking from the back of the bus to the front, he squeezed soft luggage that passengers had placed in the overhead storage space above the seats. Above the defendant's seat, he squeezed a green opaque canvas bag and noticed that it contained a brick-like object. The defendant admitted that the bag was his and then consented to allow the agent to open it. The officer discovered a brick of methamphetamine. The Court ruled that the officer's squeeze of the bag was a search under the Fourth Amendment for which the officer did not have appropriate justification. The Court stated that when bus passengers place bags in an overhead bin, they expect that other passengers or bus employees may move them for one reason or another. Thus, passengers clearly expect that their bags may be handled. However, they do not expect that others will, as a matter of course, feel a bag in an exploratory manner, as was done in this case. The Court rejected the government's argument, based on aircraft overflight cases (*California v. Ciraolo*, 476 U.S. 207 (1986), and *Florida v. Riley*, 488 U.S. 445 (1989)), that by exposing his bag to the public, the defendant lost a reasonable expectation of privacy that his bag would not be physically manipulated. Physically invasive inspection is simply more intrusive that purely visual inspection.

Skinner v. Railway Labor Executives' Association, 489 U.S. 602 (1989). Subjecting a person to a breath test and collecting and testing a person's urine and blood are searches under the Fourth Amendment.

United States v. Jacobsen, 466 U.S. 109 (1984). A search under the Fourth Amendment occurs when an expectation of privacy that society is prepared to consider reasonable is infringed. An officer's examination of a package that had been inspected by a private carrier was not a search, when the officer's examination did not exceed the scope of the private carrier's inspection. A field test of a substance to determine whether it is cocaine is not a search.

Illinois v. Andreas, 463 U.S. 765 (1983). Reopening a container after reseizing it was not a search when there was no substantial likelihood that the container's contents had been changed between the time officers sealed it for delivery and when they reseized it from the defendant.

Katz v. United States, 389 U.S. 347 (1967). The government's activities in electronically listening to and recording the defendant's words violated the privacy upon which he justifiably relied while using the telephone booth and thus constituted a search and seizure within the meaning of the Fourth Amendment. The fact that the electronic device employed to achieve that end did not happen to penetrate the wall of the booth can have no constitutional significance. Justice Harlan's concurring opinion stated that (1) an enclosed telephone booth is an area where, like a home, and unlike a field, a person has a constitutionally protected reasonable expectation of privacy; (2) electronic as well as physical intrusion into a place that is in this sense private may constitute a violation of the Fourth Amendment; and (3) the invasion of a constitutionally protected area by government is, as the Court has long held, presumptively unreasonable in the absence of a search warrant.

State v. Miller, 367 N.C. 702 (2014) (citation omitted). The court ruled that a police dog's instinctive action, unguided and undirected by the police, that brings into plain view evidence not otherwise in plain view is not a search under the Fourth Amendment. Responding to a burglar alarm, officers arrived at the defendant's home with a police dog, Jack. The officers deployed Jack to search the premises for intruders. Jack went from room to room until he reached a side bedroom, where he remained. When an officer entered to investigate, Jack was sitting on the bedroom floor staring at a dresser drawer, alerting the officer to the presence of drugs. The officer opened the drawer and found a brick of marijuana. Leaving the drugs there, the officer and Jack continued the protective sweep. Jack stopped in front of a closet and began barking at the closet door, alerting the officer to the presence of a human suspect. Unlike the passive sit and stare alert that Jack used to signal for the presence of narcotics, Jack was trained to bark to signal the presence of human suspects. Officers opened the closet and found two large black trash bags on the closet floor. When Jack nuzzled a bag, marijuana was visible. The officers secured the premises and obtained a search warrant. At issue on appeal was whether Jack's nuzzling of the bags in the closet violated the Fourth Amendment. The court of appeals determined that Jack's nuzzling of the bags was an action unrelated to the objectives of the authorized intrusion, creating a new invasion of the defendant's privacy unjustified by the exigent circumstance that validated the entry. That court viewed Jack as an instrumentality of the police and concluded that "his actions, regardless of whether they are instinctive or not, are no different than those undertaken by an officer." 228 N.C. App. 496 (2013). The North Carolina Supreme Court disagreed, concluding that "Jack's actions are different from the actions of an officer, particularly if the dog's actions were instinctive, undirected, and unguided by the police." It ruled:

> If a police dog is acting without assistance, facilitation, or other intentional action by its handler (. . . acting "instinctively"), it cannot be said that a State or governmental actor intends to do anything. In such a case, the dog is simply being a dog. If, however, police misconduct is present, or if the dog is acting at the direction or guidance of its handler, then it can be readily inferred from the dog's action that there is an intent to find something or to obtain information. . . . In short, we hold that a police dog's instinctive action, unguided and undirected by the police, that brings evidence not otherwise in plain view into plain view is not a search within the meaning of the Fourth Amendment or Article I, Section 20 of the North Carolina Constitution. Therefore, the decision of the Court of Appeals that Jack was an instrumentality of the police, regardless of whether his actions were instinctive, is reversed.

The court remanded for the trial court to decide whether Jack's nuzzling in this case was in fact instinctive, undirected, and unguided by the officers.

State v. Virgil, 276 N.C. 217 (1970). When a car was parked across a sidewalk, a search did not occur when officers inspected the outside chrome bolting below the door and saw blood.

State v. Clyburn, ___ N.C. App. ___, 770 S.E.2d 689 (2015). The court reversed and remanded for further findings of fact concerning the defendant's motion to suppress evidence obtained as a result of a search of the digital contents of a GPS device found on the defendant's person that, as a result of the search, was determined to have been stolen. The court ruled that under *Riley v. California*, 134 S. Ct. 2473 (2014), the search was not justified as a search incident to arrest. As to whether the

defendant had a reasonable expectation of privacy in the GPS device, the court ruled that a defendant may have a legitimate expectation of privacy in a stolen item if he or she acquired it innocently and does not know that the item was stolen. Here, evidence at the suppression hearing would allow the trial court to conclude that the defendant had a legitimate possessory interest in the GPS device. However, because the trial court failed to make a factual determination concerning whether the defendant innocently purchased the GPS device, the court reversed and remanded for further findings of fact.

State v. Borders, 236 N.C. App. 149 (2014) (emphasis in original). In this rape and murder case, the court ruled that a Fourth Amendment violation did not occur when an officer seized a cigarette butt containing the defendant's DNA. The defendant, a suspect in a murder case, refused four requests by the police to provide a DNA sample. Acting with the primary purpose of obtaining a sample of the defendant's DNA to compare to DNA from the victim's rape kit, officers went to his residence to execute an unrelated arrest warrant. After the defendant was handcuffed and taken outside to the driveway, an officer asked him if he wanted to smoke a cigarette. The defendant said yes, and after he took several drags from the cigarette, the officer asked if he could take the cigarette to throw it away for the defendant. The defendant said yes, but instead of throwing away the cigarette, the officer extinguished it and placed it in an evidence bag. The DNA on the cigarette butt came back as a match to the rape kit DNA. The court acknowledged that if the defendant had discarded the cigarette himself within the curtilage of the premises, the officers could not have seized it. However, the defendant voluntarily accepted the officer's offer to throw away the cigarette butt. The court continued, rejecting the defendant's argument that he had a reasonable expectation of privacy in the cigarette butt. When the defendant, while under arrest and handcuffed, placed the cigarette butt in the officer's gloved hand—instead of on the ground or in some other object within the curtilage—the defendant relinquished possession of the butt and any reasonable expectation of privacy in it. Finally, although indicating that it was "troubled" by the officers' trickery, the court concluded that the officers' actions did not require suppression of the DNA evidence. The court reasoned that because "the police did not commit an *illegal* act in effectuating the valid arrest warrant and because the subjective motives of police do not affect the validity of serving the underlying arrest warrant," suppression was not required.

State v. Jones, 231 N.C. App. 123 (2013). The court ruled that the trial court did not err by requiring the defendant to enroll in lifetime satellite-based monitoring (SBM). The court rejected the defendant's argument that SBM was an unreasonable search and seizure under *United States v. Jones*, 132 S. Ct. 945 (2012) (government's installation of a GPS tracking device on a vehicle and its use of that device to monitor the vehicle's movements on public streets constitutes a "search"). The court found *Jones* irrelevant to a civil SBM proceeding.

In re V.C.R., 227 N.C. App. 80 (2013). Although an officer had reasonable suspicion to stop a juvenile, the officer's subsequent conduct of ordering the juvenile to empty her pockets constituted a search, and this search was illegal; it was not incident to an arrest or consensual. The district court thus erred by denying the juvenile's motion to suppress.

State v. Chambers, 203 N.C. App. 373 (2010) (unpublished). The court ruled that a license tag displayed on the back of a vehicle, as required by North Carolina law, does not provide a defendant with a subjective or objective reasonable expectation of privacy in the license tag. Thus, an officer who ran the license tag through the Division of Criminal Information and the Division of Motor Vehicles for violations and warrants did not conduct a search under the Fourth Amendment.

State v. Robinson, 187 N.C. App. 795 (2007). The defendant was convicted of multiple counts of first-degree statutory rape and sex offense with young girls. A videotape of the defendant engaging in the sexual activities was introduced at trial. The court ruled, relying on *United States v. Runyan*, 275 F.3d 449 (5th Cir. 2001), and *United States v. Simpson*, 904 F.2d 607 (11th Cir. 1990), that no Fourth Amendment violation occurred when an officer without a search warrant viewed the videotape supplied by a private person who had viewed it and decided to give it to law enforcement, even though the officer's viewing of the videotape was more thorough than the private person's. The private person's viewing of the videotape did not violate the Fourth Amendment because he was not acting under the authority of the State. The viewing effectively frustrated the defendant's expectation of privacy concerning the videotape's contents, and thus the officer's later viewing did not violate the defendant's Fourth Amendment rights. While the private person stated that he had only viewed portions of the videotape,

his viewing "opened the container" of the videotape, and the later viewing of the entire videotape by the officer was not outside the scope of the private person's viewing.

State v. Fisher, 141 N.C. App. 448 (2000). The court stated that a dog sniff of a vehicle's exterior is not a search under the Fourth Amendment, citing state appellate cases finding that the dog sniffs of the following objects were not searches: a passenger's luggage, *State v. Odum*, 119 N.C. App. 676 (1995); a briefcase, *State v. McDaniels*, 103 N.C. App. 175 (1991); an airplane, *State v. Darack*, 66 N.C. App. 608 (1984); and a safety deposit box, *State v. Rogers*, 43 N.C. App. 475 (1979). The court also noted similar statements in *United States v. Place*, 462 U.S. 696 (1983), and *City of Indianapolis v. Edmond*, 531 U.S. 32 (2000).

State v. Church, 110 N.C. App. 569 (1993). Based on a first-time informant's information that marijuana was being grown near a white frame house, officers went to investigate. They saw a white frame house and a second house with wood siding, about 150 feet west of the white house. The officers walked to the front porch of the white house, knocked on the door, and received no answer. From the porch, they saw two marijuana plants growing along a fence that went from the white house to a third residence east of the white house and a third marijuana plant growing directly behind the second house. After seeing the plants, the officers walked to the second house to determine who lived in the houses. One officer knocked on the front and side doors and then saw the defendant emerge from the garage that was next to the second house. The defendant informed the officers that he owned both houses but lived in the second house. The officers asked the defendant if they could search the houses and garage, but he refused. After arresting the defendant, the officers asked him for a garage door key, which he produced. An officer inserted the key in the lock, found that it fit, and withdrew the key without opening the door.

The court ruled that insertion of the key in the lock was not an unlawful search. [Author's note: Other courts have disagreed about whether inserting a key in a lock is a search; *compare* United States v. Lyons, 898 F.2d 210 (1st Cir. 1990) (inserting key into padlock of storage unit is not a search), *and* United States v. Salgado, 250 F.3d 438 (6th Cir. 2001) (inserting key into apartment lock is not a search), *with* United States v. Concepcion, 942 F.2d 1170 (7th Cir. 1991) (inserting key into apartment lock is a search, but only reasonable suspicion is required to do so).]

United States v. Ryles, 988 F.2d 13 (5th Cir. 1993). An officer conducted a search under the Fourth Amendment when he placed his head into the defendant's van, although his action was reasonable based on the facts in this case.

United States v. George, 971 F.2d 1113 (4th Cir. 1992). A person has no reasonable expectation of privacy in the exterior of a vehicle in a public place, including its tires.

United States v. Williams, 902 F.2d 678 (8th Cir. 1990). After the defendant's arrest, an ultraviolet light examination of his hands detected the presence of fluorescent detection powder that officers had placed in a bag used for a controlled drug delivery. The court ruled that such an examination was not a search under the Fourth Amendment.

Definition of a Seizure

Soldal v. Cook County, 506 U.S. 56 (1992). Officers' involvement with moving a mobile home during an eviction was a seizure under the Fourth Amendment.

United States v. Jacobsen, 466 U.S. 109 (1984). A seizure of property under the Fourth Amendment occurs when there is a meaningful interference with an individual's possessory interests in that property. The destruction of a trace amount of a powdery substance during a field test to determine whether it was cocaine was not a seizure.

United States v. Van Leeuwen, 397 U.S. 249 (1970). Detention of first-class mail so that a search warrant could be obtained was reasonable.

United States v. Letsinger, 93 F.3d 140 (4th Cir. 1996). Drug task force officers were standing outside the defendant's train compartment. The defendant was standing in the doorway, and his bag was behind him inside the compartment. During the conversation between the officers and the defendant, an officer told the defendant that they were going to detain his bag. However, the officers made no effort to take possession of the bag and the defendant did not give the bag to them or otherwise assent to their taking it. Relying on *California v. Hodari D.*, 499 U.S. 621 (1991), the court ruled that the bag was not seized under the Fourth Amendment because the defendant did not acquiesce to the officer's statement that they were going to detain his bag.

United States v. Brown, 884 F.2d 1309 (9th Cir. 1989). The brief detention of checked luggage at an airport while it was moving on a conveyor belt to a cargo hold was not a seizure.

Evidence That May Be Searched for and Seized

(*This topic is discussed on page 234.*)

Zurcher v. Stanford Daily, 436 U.S. 547 (1978). The Fourth Amendment does not prohibit a search of property with a search warrant on the grounds that the owner or possessor of the premises to be searched is not reasonably suspected of complicity in the crime being investigated. [Author's note: But see the limitations on searches by law enforcement officers and others of news media work product materials in 42 U.S.C.A. §§ 2000aa through 2000aa-7, discussed on page 223 in Chapter 3.]

Andresen v. Maryland, 427 U.S. 463 (1976). Documents were properly seized under the *Warden v. Hayden* rationale, even though they were not directly related to the crime that was the basis for issuance of the search warrant. The documents were relevant to prove a similar criminal act committed by the defendant and thus helped prove the intent to defraud element of the crime that was the object of the search warrant.

Warden v. Hayden, 387 U.S. 294 (1967). Officers entered a house looking for an armed-robbery suspect and the weapon used during the robbery. While looking for the weapon in a washing machine, an officer found a jacket and trousers of the type that the robber reportedly wore during the robbery. The Court ruled that an officer may seize not only instrumentalities (for example, a crowbar used during a burglary); fruits (for example, money stolen during a crime); weapons; and contraband (for example, heroin); but also evidence (known as "mere evidence") that will assist in arresting or prosecuting a person. Evidence that is not an instrumentality, fruit of a crime, or contraband may be seized only if there is a nexus (connection) between it and the crime. In this case, the clothes were properly seized because the officer had probable cause to believe that they would assist in identifying the offender.

State v. Lane, 328 N.C. 598 (1991). The defendant voluntarily turned over a weapon to an officer, who properly declined to return it because he had probable cause to believe that it was the murder weapon. Relying on *United States v. Edwards*, 415 U.S. 800 (1974), the court also ruled that there is no constitutional violation in admitting into evidence testing on the weapon that had been lawfully seized without a warrant.

State v. Williams, 299 N.C. 529 (1980). Officers seized some letters and photographs that they inadvertently had seen in plain view during the earlier search with a search warrant for heroin. The court ruled that these materials were properly seized under the plain view doctrine because they were evidence of the identity of those who possessed the heroin. *See also* State v. Zimmerman, 23 N.C. App. 396 (1974) (traffic citation properly was seized because it helped prove that defendant lived where the marijuana had been found during execution of search warrant); State v. Richards, 294 N.C. 474 (1978) (weapons were properly seized, because officers had probable cause to believe that they might be connected with, and used as evidence in, the crime being investigated); State v. Newsom, 284 N.C. 412 (1973) (currency and checks were properly seized during execution of a search warrant for drugs, because the officers had reason to believe that these items were related to purchase or distribution of drugs; defendant had attempted to dispose of the checks before the officers entered the apartment to search); State v. Tate, 58 N.C. App. 494, *aff'd*, 307 N.C. 464 (1983) (search warrant for cocaine; drug apparatus, cash, and defendants' mail and photographs were properly seized).

Observations and Actions That May Not Implicate Fourth Amendment Rights
Private Search or Seizure
(*This topic is discussed on page 195.*)

UNITED STATES SUPREME COURT

Skinner v. Railway Labor Executives' Association, 489 U.S. 602 (1989). Federal government regulations that (1) mandate that railroad companies test the blood and urine of railroad workers after major train accidents and (2) authorize (but do not require) the testing of railroad workers who violate certain safety rules involve sufficient government action to make the testing subject to the Fourth Amendment. *See also* Boesche v. Raleigh-Durham Airport Authority, 111 N.C. App. 149 (1993) (airport authority's drug testing policy requiring testing of maintenance worker was constitutional).

United States v. Jacobsen, 466 U.S. 109 (1984). A private freight carrier's examination of a damaged package is a private action that is not governed by the Fourth Amendment. The federal drug agent's later inspection of the package, at least to the extent that he learned nothing that had not been discovered previously during the private search, did not infringe on the defendant's legitimate expectation of privacy and therefore was not a search under the Fourth Amendment.

Walter v. United States, 447 U.S. 649 (1980). The plurality opinion announcing the judgment of the Court (which clearly represents prevailing law) ruled that an FBI agent's screening of obscene films without a search warrant violated the Fourth Amendment, because the screening exceeded the scope of an earlier search by a private person, and the screening—which was an additional search—was not supported by any justification that would allow a search without a search warrant. *See also* United States v. Runyan, 275 F.3d 449 (5th Cir. 2001) (officers' examination of computer disks exceeded scope of prior private search).

Coolidge v. New Hampshire, 403 U.S. 443 (1971). When the defendant's wife voluntarily and without police coercion took her husband's guns out of a closet and gave them to the officers, her action was private and was not a search under the Fourth Amendment.

Burdeau v. McDowell, 256 U.S. 465 (1921). Actions of private detectives and other private individuals in taking papers from a safe and desk were not governed by the Fourth Amendment.

NORTH CAROLINA SUPREME COURT

State v. Sanders, 327 N.C. 319 (1990). The court adopted a totality of circumstances test to determine whether a private person's search or seizure is attributable to law enforcement so that it would constitute a search or seizure governed by the Fourth Amendment. Factors to consider are (1) the private person's motivation for conducting the search or seizure; (2) the degree of law enforcement involvement, such as advice, encouragement, and knowledge of the nature of the person's activities; and (3) the legality of conduct that was encouraged by law enforcement. The court determined in this case that the private person's (Gardin's) entry by ruse into a home and taking of jewelry from the defendant's bedroom was a private search. While Gardin's actions were based on information shared with him by law enforcement officers and his actions furthered their efforts, his primary purpose in obtaining the jewelry was to console a grieving family and to alleviate community tensions that a murder had caused. Gardin's seizure of jewelry was without the knowledge, encouragement, or acquiescence of law enforcement officers.

State v. Kornegay, 313 N.C. 1 (1985). A private secretary's act of copying her employer's records to protect herself and then voluntarily giving them to law enforcement officers was a private action and not a search under the Fourth Amendment. *See also* United States v. Knoll, 116 F.3d 994 (2d Cir. 1997) (private person's act of burglarizing law office and turning over stolen files was not search under Fourth Amendment, based on facts in this case).

State v. Reams, 277 N.C. 391 (1970). When a detective asked the defendant's wife for her husband's gun and she later voluntarily and without police coercion took the gun from a closet and gave it to an officer, her action was private and not a search under the Fourth Amendment.

NORTH CAROLINA COURT OF APPEALS

State v. Weaver, 231 N.C. App. 473 (2013). The court ruled that the trial court, in granting the defendant's motion to suppress in a DWI case, erred by concluding that a licensed security guard was a state actor when he stopped the defendant's vehicle. Determining whether a private citizen is a state actor requires consideration of the totality of the circumstances, with special consideration of (1) the citizen's motivation for the search or seizure; (2) the degree of governmental involvement, such as advice, encouragement, and knowledge about the nature of the citizen's activities; and (3) the legality of the conduct encouraged by the officer. Importantly, the court noted, once a private search or seizure has been completed, later involvement of government agents does not transform the original intrusion into a governmental search. Alternatively, the court ruled that even if the security guard was a state actor, reasonable suspicion existed for the stop.

State v. McBennett, 191 N.C. App. 734 (2008). A waitress who delivered room service to the defendant's hotel room reported that the room was in disarray. A hotel manager decided to investigate and could not enter the room because the door caught on the interior lock. The defendant told the manager that he did not need housekeeping and did not open the door. The manager called law enforcement. When the defendant refused to open the door, the manager told the defendant that they would bust the door down. The defendant opened the door and an officer who was the first to enter the room saw marijuana and syringes in the room.

(1) The court ruled that hotel personnel have the implied right to enter a hotel room to keep the hotel in a reasonably safe condition and to exercise reasonable care to discover criminal acts that might cause harm to other guests. The entry of hotel personnel for this purpose is not a search under the Fourth Amendment. (2) The court ruled that the officers' entry into the hotel room with the hotel personnel was a search under the Fourth Amendment and the discovery of the evidence in the room was not justified by the plain view theory because the officers' entry was not lawful. There were no exigent circumstances to authorize the entry. Also, the defendant did not voluntarily consent to allow the officers' entry.

State v. Robinson, 187 N.C. App. 795 (2007). The defendant was convicted of multiple counts of first-degree statutory rape and sex offense with young girls. A videotape of the defendant engaging in the sexual activities was introduced at trial. The court ruled, relying on *United States v. Runyan*, 275 F.3d 449 (5th Cir. 2001), and *United States v. Simpson*, 904 F.2d 607 (11th Cir. 1990), that no Fourth Amendment violation occurred when an officer without a search warrant viewed the videotape supplied by a private person who had viewed it and decided to give it to law enforcement, even though the officer's viewing of the videotape was more thorough than the private person's. The private person's viewing of the videotape did not violate the Fourth Amendment because he was not acting under the authority of the state. The private viewing effectively frustrated the defendant's expectation of privacy concerning the videotape's contents, and thus the officer's later viewing did not violate the defendant's Fourth Amendment rights. While the private person stated that he had only viewed portions of the videotape, his viewing "opened the container" of the videotape, and the later viewing of the entire videotape by the officer was not outside the scope of the private person's viewing.

State v. Keadle, 51 N.C. App. 660 (1981). A state university dormitory adviser's inspection of a student's room was a private action and was not a search under the Fourth Amendment.

State v. Morris, 41 N.C. App. 164 (1979). An air freight carrier's opening of a package on his own initiative was not a search under the Fourth Amendment.

State v. Reagan, 35 N.C. App. 140 (1978). A larceny victim's looking into the defendant's locked barn without police involvement was not a search under the Fourth Amendment.

State v. Carr, 20 N.C. App. 619 (1974). A private person's inspection of an impounded car in an attempt to find stolen property was not a search under the Fourth Amendment, because the inspection was done without police involvement.

State v. Peele, 16 N.C. App. 227 (1972). A larceny victim's search of the defendant's attic, made without police involvement, was not a search under the Fourth Amendment.

FEDERAL APPELLATE COURTS

United States v. Dahlstrom, 180 F.3d 677 (5th Cir. 1999). Employees' taking of documents from business office was a private search, when the employees devised a plan to take documents on their own and the presence of the sheriff was solely to keep the peace.

United States v. Shahid, 117 F.3d 322 (7th Cir. 1997). Private mall's security officers, whose primary role was to provide safety and security for all people on mall property, were not government actors under the Fourth Amendment when they detained and searched a shoplifter.

United States v. Leffall, 82 F.3d 343 (10th Cir. 1996). The court stated that the test to determine when a search by a private person becomes government action under the Fourth Amendment is a two-part inquiry: (1) whether the government knew of and acquiesced in the intrusive conduct, and (2) whether the party performing the search intended to assist law enforcement efforts or to further the party's own ends. In this case, the court ruled that an airline employee who independently decided to open a package because he believed it contained contraband conducted a private search even though he asked a law enforcement officer to witness his opening of the package. The officer did not participate in the search nor encourage the airline employee to search the package. *Compare with* United States v. Souza, 223 F.3d 1197 (10th Cir. 2001) (UPS employee's opening package was governmental search because it was orchestrated by law enforcement officers; employee did not have legitimate, independent motivation to open package).

United States v. Cleaveland, 38 F.3d 1092 (9th Cir. 1994). A public power company received an anonymous tip that there was an illegal power diversion and possible marijuana manufacturing at the defendant's residence. Power company employees planned to go to the residence to investigate the power diversion and asked police to be present if danger arose. While the employees investigated the power meter, an officer waited a block away. Based on the information learned by the employees, the officer obtained a search warrant to search the residence for marijuana. The court ruled that the search by the power company employees was a private search because they initiated the plan to inspect the meter. Even though they may have had dual motives to conduct the inspection—to recover money for the company's loss of power and to assist the police in capturing the power thief and uncovering the marijuana manufacturing—the motive to recover for the loss of power was independent of the other motive.

United States v. Koenig, 856 F.2d 843 (7th Cir. 1988). A Federal Express security officer was not acting as a government agent when he opened a package and discovered cocaine. The company's policy of opening suspicious packages was based on its own sound business interests. The fact that the company also maintained good relations with law enforcement agencies and reported discoveries of suspected drugs to them did not convert private searches to those searches governed by the Fourth Amendment. The officer in this case was not an agent of the government. *See also* United States v. Young, 153 F.3d 1079 (9th Cir. 1998) (similar ruling); United States v. Simpson, 904 F.2d 607 (11th Cir. 1990) (mere fact that Federal Express employees receive training from government concerning when to contact government agents after they discover contraband does not make them agents of the government when the searches are initiated by Federal Express employees for normal business purposes).

Abandoned Property and Garbage

(*This topic is discussed on page 198.*)

UNITED STATES SUPREME COURT

Smith v. Ohio, 494 U.S. 541 (1990). A non-uniformed officer approached the defendant as he left a private residence and entered a YMCA parking lot. The defendant was carrying a grocery bag. The officer, without informing the defendant that he was an officer, asked the defendant to come to him. The defendant did not respond and kept walking. When the officer identified himself as an officer, the defendant threw the grocery bag onto the hood of his car and turned to face the approaching officer. The Court ruled that the defendant did not abandon his grocery bag, because he was protecting it from the officer's inspection by placing it on his car.

California v. Greenwood, 486 U.S. 35 (1988). The Court ruled that the Fourth Amendment does not prohibit the warrantless search and seizure of garbage left for collection outside the curtilage of a home. A defendant's asserted expectation of privacy in that garbage is not one that society is prepared to accept as reasonable. Thus, the police did not violate the defendant's Fourth Amendment rights when they obtained (from the regular trash collector) garbage the defendant had left on the curb in front of his house for pickup and then searched it and found evidence of narcotics use. The Court's ruling did not rest on the abandonment justification; instead, the Court stated that the defendant exposed his garbage to the public by placing it by the curb and thus did not have a reasonable expectation of privacy in the garbage.

Abel v. United States, 362 U.S. 217 (1960). After the defendant was arrested in his hotel room, he agreed to check out. He removed all the items he wanted to take and left others. He paid his hotel bill and turned in his key. Officers then received permission from the hotel management and searched the room. The Court ruled that there was no search or seizure, because the room had been abandoned. *See also* United States v. Kitchens, 114 F.3d 29 (4th Cir. 1997) (absent a pattern or practice allowing guests to stay in their hotel rooms past checkout time, a guest does not have a reasonable expectation of privacy in his or her hotel room after checkout time). *But see* United States v. Owens, 782 F.2d 146 (10th Cir. 1986) (motel guest had a reasonable expectation of privacy for a short period past checkout time).

Hester v. United States, 265 U.S. 57 (1924). The defendant and a companion dropped containers of illegal whiskey while law enforcement officers were pursuing them. No search or seizure occurred when the officers examined the contents of the containers, because they had been abandoned.

NORTH CAROLINA SUPREME COURT

State v. Hauser, 342 N.C. 382 (1995). A detective made arrangements with the city sanitation department to collect trash at the defendant's residence and give it to two detectives. A sanitation worker collected the garbage left at the back of the residence for collection. The collection was routine except that the sanitation worker prevented the garbage from commingling with other garbage by depositing the defendant's garbage into a container in the back of the garbage truck instead of into the truck's collection bin. The sanitation worker gave the defendant's garbage to the detectives, who found cocaine residue in it. One of the detectives then obtained a search warrant

based on the cocaine found in the garbage and information received from four informants. One of the informants stated that the defendant had sold him cocaine at the defendant's residence. In addition, the officers provided facts showing the reliability of the informants' information. The officers executed the search warrant, and more than a pound of cocaine was found in the defendant's residence.

The court, disavowing a contrary conclusion in the court of appeals opinion in this case, 115 N.C. App. 431 (1994), ruled that the search of the defendant's garbage did not violate the Fourth Amendment, based on the ruling in *California v. Greenwood*, 486 U.S. 35 (1988) (no reasonable expectation of privacy under the Fourth Amendment in garbage left for collection). The defendant sought to distinguish *Greenwood* by arguing that the garbage was left at the curb in *Greenwood* while the garbage in this case was left for collection within the curtilage of the home, the defendant's backyard. The court rejected the defendant's argument, relying on *United States v. Hedrick*, 922 F.2d 396 (7th Cir. 1991) (no Fourth Amendment violation when officers seized garbage placed for collection 18 to 20 feet within home's curtilage; garbage was placed in view of public passing by on the sidewalk, distance between garbage and sidewalk was short, and there was no fence or other barrier preventing public access to garbage). The court stated that the location of the defendant's garbage within the home's curtilage did not automatically establish that he possessed a reasonable expectation of privacy in it. Relying on *United States v. Biondich*, 652 F.2d 743 (8th Cir. 1981) (no Fourth Amendment violation when officer arranged with regular trash collection service to deliver defendant's garbage to officer, even though there may have been an expectation of privacy in garbage while it remained within the curtilage), and distinguishing *United States v. Certain Real Property Located at 987 Fisher Road*, 719 F. Supp. 1396 (E.D. Mich. 1989) (Fourth Amendment was violated when police went onto defendant's property and seized garbage bags placed against back wall of house), the court ruled that the defendant did not retain a reasonable expectation of privacy in his garbage once it left his yard in the usual manner.

NORTH CAROLINA COURT OF APPEALS

State v. Williford, ___ N.C. App. ___, 767 S.E.2d 139 (2015). The court ruled that the trial court did not err by denying the defendant's motion to suppress DNA evidence obtained from his discarded cigarette butt. When the defendant refused to supply a DNA sample in connection with a rape and murder investigation, officers sought to obtain his DNA by other means. After the defendant discarded a cigarette butt in a parking lot, officers retrieved the butt. The parking lot was located directly in front of the defendant's four-unit apartment building, was uncovered, and included five to seven unassigned parking spaces used by the residents. The area between the road and the parking lot was heavily wooded, but no gate restricted access to the lot and no signs suggested either that access to the parking lot was restricted or that the lot was private. After DNA on the cigarette butt matched DNA found on the victim, the defendant was charged with the crimes. At trial, the defendant unsuccessfully moved to suppress the DNA evidence. On appeal, the court rejected the defendant's argument that the seizure of the cigarette butt violated his constitutional rights because it occurred within the curtilage of his apartment:

> [W]e conclude that the parking lot was not located in the curtilage of defendant's building. While the parking lot was in close proximity to the building, it was not enclosed, was used for parking by both the buildings' residents and the general public, and was only protected in a limited way. Consequently, the parking lot was not a location where defendant possessed "a reasonable and legitimate expectation of privacy that society is prepared to accept."

Next, the court rejected the defendant's argument that even if the parking lot was not considered curtilage, he still maintained a possessory interest in the cigarette butt because he did not put it in a trash can or otherwise convey it to a third party. The court reasoned that the cigarette butt was abandoned property. Finally, the court rejected the defendant's argument that even if officers lawfully obtained the cigarette butt, they still were required to obtain a warrant before testing it for his DNA because he had a legitimate expectation of privacy in his DNA. The court reasoned that the extraction of DNA from an abandoned item does not implicate the Fourth Amendment.

State v. Joe, 222 N.C. App. 206 (2012). The court ruled that the defendant did not voluntarily abandon controlled substances. Noting that the defendant was illegally arrested without probable cause, the court concluded that property abandoned as a result of illegal police activity cannot be held to have been voluntarily abandoned.

State v. Eaton, 210 N.C. App. 142 (2011). The court ruled that because the defendant had not been seized under the Fourth Amendment when he discarded a plastic baggie beside a public road, the baggie was abandoned property in which the defendant no longer retained a reasonable expectation of privacy. Thus, no Fourth Amendment violation occurred when an officer took possession of the baggie.

State v. Reed, 182 N.C. App. 109 (2007). Two detectives investigating a burglary, sexual offense, and robbery arrived at the defendant's apartment to talk with him. The defendant led the detectives to a small patio at the back of his apartment. After the defendant finished a cigarette, he flicked the butt at a pile of trash located in the corner of the concrete patio. The butt struck the pile of trash and rolled between the defendant and one of the detectives, who kicked the butt off the patio into the grassy common area. The conversation ended and the detective, who had kept his eye on the still-burning cigarette butt, retrieved the butt after the other detective and the defendant turned to go back inside the apartment. A DNA test of the cigarette butt resulted in evidence introduced against the defendant at trial. The court ruled, relying on *State v. Rhodes*, 151 N.C. App. 208 (2002) (officer's warrantless search of trash can located immediately by steps to side-entry door of defendant's house violated Fourth Amendment), and other cases, and distinguishing *State v. Hauser*, 342 N.C. 382 (1995), that the seizure of the cigarette butt violated the defendant's Fourth Amendment rights. The court rejected the State's argument that the defendant discarded the cigarette butt and thus lost his reasonable expectation of privacy. The cigarette butt was not abandoned within the curtilage of the defendant's home. [Author's note: The issue of whether the detective had probable cause to seize the cigarette butt was not involved in this case.]

State v. Rhodes, 151 N.C. App. 208 (2002). The court ruled, distinguishing *California v. Greenwood*, 486 U.S. 35 (1988), and *State v. Hauser*, 342 N.C. 382 (1995), that the officers' warrantless search of a trash can located immediately by the steps to the side-entry door of the defendant's house violated the Fourth Amendment. The court noted that the trash can, 50 feet from the road, was within the curtilage of the home. Unlike officers in *Greenwood* and *Hauser*, the officers in this case did not obtain the trash can's contents from a sanitation worker who had obtained the trash in the usual manner (that is, the contents of the trash can were not placed there for collection in the usual and routine manner).

State v. Washington, 134 N.C. App. 479 (1999). An officer received information from an unknown informant that a person known only as D was selling drugs. The informant gave a detailed physical description of D and said that he lived in an apartment at 3903-A Marcom Street in Raleigh. The officer began surveillance of the apartment and saw a person matching the informant's description take two white plastic bags, tied with yellow strips, across the parking lot to the communal apartment dumpster. Shortly thereafter, the officer removed the bags from the dumpster and discovered drugs inside them. Relying on *State v. Hauser*, 342 N.C. 382 (1995), the court ruled that the defendant did not have a reasonable expectation of privacy in his garbage after he placed it in the communal apartment dumpster, and therefore the officer's removal of the garbage did not violate the defendant's Fourth Amendment rights.

State v. Johnson, 98 N.C. App. 290 (1990). After officers, during a bus boarding, had spoken with all the bus passengers about which bags belonged to whom, one bag located in the front of the bus had not been claimed. The officers asked each passenger (including the defendant) whether the bag belonged to him or her. No one claimed it. The officers then removed the bag from the bus, searched it, and found cocaine and a traffic citation issued in Tampa, Florida. The officers reboarded the bus and asked the passengers for identification. The defendant was the only passenger with a Tampa address on his driver's license. The officers requested that the defendant leave the bus, and he did. The officers again asked him if the luggage belonged to him; he denied ownership of the bag. The court ruled that the defendant lost his reasonable expectation of privacy in the bag when he denied that he owned or controlled the bag. *See also* United States v. Flowers, 912 F.2d 707 (4th Cir. 1990) (similar ruling); United States v. Lewis, 921 F.2d 1294 (D.C. Cir. 1990) (similar ruling); United States v. Carrasquillo, 877 F.2d 73 (D.C. Cir. 1989) (similar ruling; defendant on train affirmatively disclaimed ownership of garment bag under his feet). The court also rejected defendant's argument that the officers needed a search warrant to search the bag. The defendant did not have standing to contest the bag he had abandoned.

State v. Williams, 71 N.C. App. 136 (1984). A confidential informant told detectives that the defendant possessed marijuana. When the detectives approached the defendant in his car, he got out and ran. When a deputy sheriff identified himself and told the defendant to halt, he dropped his jacket and continued to run. The court ruled that the jacket was abandoned under the Fourth Amendment.

State v. Teltser, 61 N.C. App. 290 (1983). After being involved in an automobile accident, the defendant took a suitcase from his car and hid it in woods that were not on his property, planning to get it later. The court ruled that the defendant abandoned the suitcase under the Fourth Amendment.

State v. Casey, 59 N.C. App. 99 (1982). The defendant, who was involved in an airport drug investigation encounter with officers, had a plastic bag and a briefcase in his hands. When asked by the officers, the defendant denied that the items were his. The court ruled that the defendant's disclaimer of ownership did not constitute abandonment, because he had the right to exclude all others from the bag and briefcase when he legitimately possessed and controlled them.

State v. Cromartie, 55 N.C. App. 221 (1973). When an officer told the defendant that he was going to arrest him, the defendant threw an aspirin box on the street. He abandoned the box under the Fourth Amendment.

State v. Cooke, 54 N.C. App. 33, *modified and aff'd*, 306 N.C. 132 (1982). A defendant does not abandon property if the defendant discards property as a result of an officer's illegal conduct. *See also* United States v. Garzon, 119 F.3d 1446 (10th Cir. 1997) (defendant did not abandon his backpacks that he left on a bus when he and other passengers had been illegally ordered by officer to leave bus and take personal possessions with them).

FEDERAL APPELLATE COURTS

United States v. Sanders, 196 F.3d 910 (8th Cir. 1999). A defendant's disclaimer of ownership of a bag and a ball of tape constituted abandonment of that property, even if an officer believed the defendant was lying.

United States v. Long, 176 F.3d 1304 (10th Cir. 1999). The defendant placed his garbage bags on top of a trailer for pickup by the garbage collector. The trailer was parked only three feet from a public alleyway. The court ruled that, even if the garbage bags were within the curtilage, the defendant did not have a reasonable expectation of privacy to contest law enforcement officers' taking the bags. The defendant's placement of the bags exposed them not just to the garbage collector but also to anyone traveling down the alleyway.

United States v. Shanks, 97 F.3d 977 (7th Cir. 1996). After receiving an anonymous tip that someone was selling drugs from a residence on the upper floor of a two-story duplex condominium, officers attempted to corroborate the tip by looking for evidence of drug activity in garbage containers located next to a garage that was approximately 20 feet away from the residence. The garbage containers were located on a narrow strip of land occupying the space between the garage and the alley. The officers confiscated the containers in the early hours of the morning and replaced them with identical containers so that no one would notice. They found drug items in opaque bags located in the containers and obtained a search warrant of the defendant's residence based on this information. The court ruled that the containers were not within the curtilage of the residence because they were located adjacent to the alley. The court also ruled that, even assuming the containers were within the curtilage, the defendant did not have a reasonable expectation of privacy in them. The containers were readily accessible to and visible from a public thoroughfare (the alley), and scavengers commonly snoop through garbage containers found in such alleys. The court also ruled that the defendant did not have a reasonable expectation of privacy merely because officers, rather than the regular garbage service, rummaged through his garbage or because his garbage was hidden in opaque bags.

United States v. Leshuk, 65 F.3d 1105 (4th Cir. 1995). The defendant's disclaimer of ownership of a garbage bag and backpacks located near him was a voluntary abandonment of the property. Thus, he was precluded from seeking to suppress evidence found in them.

United States v. Boone, 62 F.3d 323 (10th Cir. 1995). After officers conducted an illegal search of a vehicle and discovered marijuana, the defendant got in the vehicle and a high-speed chase occurred. During the chase, the defendant threw illegal drugs from the vehicle. The court ruled that the defendant abandoned the drugs. Although abandonment does not occur as a direct result of officers' illegal conduct, the defendant's independent and voluntary decision to throw the illegal drugs from the vehicle during the high-speed chase was sufficient intervening conduct to remove the taint from the prior illegal search of the vehicle.

United States v. Washington, 12 F.3d 1128 (D.C. Cir. 1994). Officers in a patrol car were involved in a high-speed chase of a car in which the defendant and others were passengers. The car crashed, and the defendant and the passengers fled the car. The court ruled that the car was abandoned under the Fourth Amendment.

United States v. Scott, 975 F.2d 927 (1st Cir. 1992). The defendant did not have a reasonable expectation of privacy in shredded documents placed in garbage bags and left for collection in front of his house.

United States v. Hedrick, 922 F.2d 396 (7th Cir. 1991). The defendant did not have a reasonable expectation of privacy in garbage cans permanently located in a driveway 18 to 20 feet from the sidewalk, 20 feet from an unattached garage, and 50 feet from the house, even though the cans were within the curtilage. The cans were so readily accessible to the public that they were exposed to the public. *See also* United States v. Redmon, 138 F.3d 1109 (7th Cir. 1998) (en banc) (similar ruling; garbage cans placed for collection outside garage door where they were publicly accessible); United States v. Wilkinson, 926 F.2d 22 (1st Cir. 1991) (proper to search trash left for collection on lawn near curb); United States v. Comeaux, 955 F.2d 586 (8th Cir. 1992) (search of garbage can in alley near garage was proper, even if within curtilage).

United States v. Dunkel, 900 F.2d 105 (7th Cir. 1990). The defendant did not have a reasonable expectation of privacy in a dumpster, located in the parking lot of a commercial building, that was used by tenants of the building and was accessible to the public.

United States v. Thomas, 864 F.2d 843 (D.C. Cir. 1989). The court ruled that the defendant abandoned his gym bag when, after seeing the police, he went into an apartment building and up the stairway to the second floor, left the bag there, and went down the stairway to go outside. The court noted that this case is similar to a case in which a person, during lawful police pursuit, tosses away an object to prevent its discovery. *See also* United States v. Wider, 951 F.2d 1283 (D.C. Cir. 1991) (defendant abandoned paper bag by placing it on steps in public place and walking away).

United States v. Sanders, 719 F.2d 882 (6th Cir. 1983). The act of leaving an airport without claiming one's luggage in itself does not constitute abandonment. The defendant never affirmatively disclaimed ownership of the suitcase, consistently refused to consent to a search of the suitcase, and told officers that she had not claimed the suitcase at the airport because she was not going straight home. *Compare with* United States v. Tolbert, 692 F.2d 1041 (6th Cir. 1982) (defendant abandoned a suitcase when she left the airport without it and specifically disclaimed ownership); United States v. Moskowitz, 883

F.2d 1142 (2d Cir. 1989) (airplane passenger abandoned luggage when he told officers that he did not have any checked luggage; fact that an officer did not believe defendant's denial is irrelevant to determining abandonment, which focuses on defendant's intent).

United States v. Kramer, 711 F.2d 789 (7th Cir. 1983). Garbage in plastic trash bags inside covered garbage containers was located inside a perimeter fence along the street curb 30 feet from a house to be collected by a private garbage removal service. Police picked up the trash bags, took them to the police station, and searched their contents. The court ruled that (1) the garbage was abandoned under the Fourth Amendment, and (2) the alleged police trespass on the property to obtain the garbage did not violate a reasonable expectation of privacy under the Fourth Amendment. For similar cases, see *United States v. Terry*, 702 F.2d 299 (2d Cir. 1983); *United States v. Compton*, 704 F.2d 739 (5th Cir. 1983); *United States v. Dela Espriella*, 781 F.2d 1432 (9th Cir. 1986).

Areas outside the Home: Curtilage and Open Fields
(This topic is discussed on page 200.)

UNITED STATES SUPREME COURT

Florida v. Jardines, 133 S. Ct. 1409 (2013). The Court ruled that officers' use of a drug-sniffing dog on a homeowner's porch to investigate the contents of the home is a "search" within the meaning of the Fourth Amendment. The Court's reasoning was based on the theory that the officers engaged in a physical intrusion of a constitutionally protected area. Applying that principle, the Court ruled:

> The officers were gathering information in an area belonging to [the defendant] and immediately surrounding his house—in the curtilage of the house, which we have held enjoys protection as part of the home itself. And they gathered that information by physically entering and occupying the area to engage in conduct not explicitly or implicitly permitted by the homeowner.

The Court did not decide the case on a reasonable expectation of privacy analysis. The concurring opinion concluded that the conduct was a search based on both property and reasonable expectation of privacy grounds.

Florida v. White, 526 U.S. 559 (1999). Officers developed probable cause to believe that the defendant's car was subject to forfeiture under Florida's drug forfeiture law, but they did not immediately arrest the defendant or seize his car. Several months later, officers arrested the defendant for unrelated charges and, without a search warrant, seized his car from his employer's parking lot; the car was seized for forfeiture, based on the probable cause that had existed months earlier. The court ruled, relying on *G.M. Leasing Corp. v. United States*, 429 U.S. 338 (1977), and other cases, that the officers' warrantless seizure of the defendant's car in a public place did not violate the Fourth Amendment. [Author's note: G.S. 90-112(b) provides that property subject to forfeiture may be seized by a law enforcement officer with court process, except that it may be seized without court process when (1) the seizure is incident to an arrest or search with a search warrant or (2) the property subject to seizure has been the subject of a prior judgment in the State's favor.]

Florida v. Riley, 488 U.S. 445 (1989). The defendant lived in a mobile home located on five acres of rural property. His greenhouse was located 10 to 20 feet behind the mobile home (within its curtilage). Two roofing panels on the greenhouse were missing. An officer, circling twice over the defendant's property in a helicopter at 400 feet, saw with his unaided eye what appeared to be marijuana growing in the greenhouse. He then obtained a search warrant and seized the marijuana. A four-Justice plurality opinion ruled, relying on *California v. Ciraolo*, discussed below, that the defendant did not have a reasonable expectation of privacy from observations from the helicopter, because it was flying in lawful navigable airspace. A fifth Justice's concurring opinion set out a different standard: a defendant does not have a reasonable expectation of privacy if a helicopter is in public airspace at an altitude at which the public travels with sufficient regularity. The defendant has the burden of proving that the aerial observation was unreasonable, and he failed to do so in this case.

United States v. Dunn, 480 U.S. 294 (1987). The Court adopted a four-part test to determine whether property is within a home's curtilage: (1) the proximity of the area to the home, (2) whether the area is within an enclosure surrounding the home, (3) the nature and use to which the area is put, and (4) the steps taken by the resident to protect the area from observations by passersby. The Court stated that these factors are useful analytical tools in determining whether the area in question is so intimately tied to the home itself that it should be placed under the home's Fourth Amendment protection.

Applying these factors, the Court ruled that a barn 60 yards from a home was not within the home's curtilage. The Court noted that the barn was 60 yards from the fence surrounding the house. The barn stood out as a distinct part of the defendant's ranch, quite separate from the house. Officers possessed objective information (a strong smell from the barn of phenylacetic acid, which is used in making illegal drugs) that the barn was not being used for intimate activities of the home. And the defendant did little to protect the barn area from observations by those standing in open fields—other interior fences on the defendant's property were designed and constructed to corral livestock, not to prevent people from observing the enclosed area. (The officers crossed over five fences—not including the fence surrounding the house—before they got to the barn.)

The Court—assuming without deciding that although the barn was not within the curtilage, it was entitled to Fourth Amendment protection and could not be entered without a warrant—ruled that the officers did not violate the defendant's Fourth Amendment rights when they stood next to the barn's locked front gates, shined a flashlight through the opaque netting above the gates (without entering the barn), and looked into the barn. (The officers left, obtained a search warrant, and then searched the barn with the warrant.) *See also* United States v. Pace, 955 F.2d 270 (5th Cir. 1992) (there is no curtilage surrounding a barn in an open field; officers may walk up to edge of structure).

Dow Chemical Co. v. United States, 476 U.S. 227 (1986). Surveillance and photographing by the Environmental Protection Agency (EPA) from an airplane flying in lawful navigable airspace over the buildings and grounds of an enclosed manufacturing plant complex was not a search under the Fourth Amendment. The open areas of the complex (with buildings spread over 2,000 acres) were not analogous to the curtilage of a dwelling for the purpose of aerial surveillance; the complex was more comparable to an open field. The Court noted that the EPA used a conventional commercial camera commonly used in mapmaking. Although the photographs provided more detailed information than a person could see unaided from the airplane, they did not reveal intimate details that might infringe on Fourth Amendment rights.

California v. Ciraolo, 476 U.S. 207 (1986). Officers received an anonymous tip that the defendant was growing marijuana in his backyard, which was within the curtilage of his home. They were unable to see the marijuana from ground level because a tall fence surrounded the yard, with the home providing one side of the perimeter. They flew over the house in a private plane at 1,000 feet—which was within lawful navigable airspace—and readily saw and identified (without any visual device) marijuana plants growing in the yard. They then obtained a search warrant and seized the marijuana. The Court ruled that, although the defendant may have had a subjective expectation of privacy in the area within his yard, his expectation of privacy from all observations was unreasonable under the Fourth Amendment; such an expectation was not one that society was prepared to honor. Thus, the officers' visual observation from the airplane was not a search under the Fourth Amendment. The Court noted that it did not decide in this case whether a search from an airplane may occur if officers use technological devices (sophisticated cameras and the like) that disclose intimate activities within the curtilage that could not be seen by unaided visual observation.

Oliver v. United States, 466 U.S. 170 (1984). A person has no reasonable expectation of privacy in land beyond the curtilage of his home, and therefore an officer's presence there is not a search under the Fourth Amendment. Even if land outside the curtilage is fenced and posted with "No Trespassing" signs, an officer's entry onto and presence on the land (even though the officer may be committing a criminal trespass) is not a Fourth Amendment violation. The Court reaffirmed *Hester v. United States*, 265 U.S. 57 (1924). *See also* United States v. Lewis, 240 F.3d 866 (10th Cir. 2001) (similar ruling); United States v. Rapanos, 115 F.3d 367 (6th Cir. 1997) (similar ruling).

G.M. Leasing Corp. v. United States, 429 U.S. 338 (1977). No search warrant was required to seize cars (with probable cause) to satisfy a tax assessment, because the cars were located on public streets, parking lots, and other open places where there was no intrusion on privacy—that is, officers did not conduct a search before they seized the cars without a warrant.

Air Pollution Variance Board v. Western Alfalfa Corp., 416 U.S. 861 (1974). A state inspector conducted a pollution test of a factory's smoke emissions while standing on the company's property—but not on property from which the public was excluded. The Court ruled that the Fourth Amendment was not violated because the area was within the "open fields" exception.

NORTH CAROLINA SUPREME COURT

State v. Grice, 367 N.C. 753 (2015). (1) Reversing the court of appeals, 223 N.C. App. 460 (2012), the court ruled that officers did not violate the Fourth Amendment by seizing marijuana plants seen in plain view. After receiving a tip that the defendant was growing marijuana at a specified residence, officers went to the residence to conduct a knock and talk. Finding the front door inaccessible, covered with plastic, and obscured by furniture, the officers noticed that the driveway led to a side door, which appeared to be the main entrance. One of the officers knocked on the side door. No one answered. From the door, the officer noticed plants growing in several buckets about 15 yards away. Both officers recognized the plants as marijuana. The officers seized the plants, returned to the sheriff's office, and got a search warrant to search the home. The defendant was charged with manufacturing a controlled substance and moved to suppress evidence of the marijuana plants. The trial court denied the motion and the court of appeals reversed. The supreme court began by finding that the officers observed the plants in plain view. It then explained that a warrantless seizure may be justified as reasonable under the plain view doctrine if the officer did not violate the Fourth Amendment in arriving at the place from where the evidence could be plainly viewed, the evidence's incriminating character was immediately apparent, and the officer had a lawful right of access to the object itself. Additionally, the court noted, "[t]he North Carolina General Assembly has . . . required that the discovery of evidence in plain view be inadvertent." The court noted that the sole point of contention in this case was whether the officers had a lawful right of access from the driveway 15 yards across the defendant's property to the plants' location. Finding against the defendant on this issue, the court stated: "Here, the knock and talk investigation constituted the initial entry onto defendant's property which brought the officers within plain view of the marijuana plants. The presence of the clearly identifiable contraband justified walking further into the curtilage." The court rejected the defendant's argument that the seizure was unlawful because the plants were on the curtilage of his property, stating:

> [W]e conclude that the unfenced portion of the property fifteen yards from the home and bordering a wood line is closer in kind to an open field than it is to the paradigmatic curtilage

which protects "the privacies of life" inside the home. . . . However, even if the property at issue can be considered the curtilage of the home for Fourth Amendment purposes, we disagree with defendant's claim that a justified presence in one portion of the curtilage (the driveway and front porch) does not extend to justify recovery of contraband in plain view located in another portion of the curtilage (the side yard). By analogy, it is difficult to imagine what formulation of the Fourth Amendment would prohibit the officers from seizing the contraband if the plants had been growing on the porch—the paradigmatic curtilage—rather than at a distance, particularly when the officers' initial presence on the curtilage was justified. The plants in question were situated on the periphery of the curtilage, and the protections cannot be greater than if the plants were growing on the porch itself. The officers in this case were, by the custom and tradition of our society, implicitly invited into the curtilage to approach the home. Traveling within the curtilage to seize contraband in plain view within the curtilage did not violate the Fourth Amendment.

(2) The court ruled that the seizure also was justified by exigent circumstances, concluding: "Reviewing the record, it is objectively reasonable to conclude that someone may have been home, that the individual would have been aware of the officers' presence, and that the individual could easily have moved or destroyed the plants if they were left on the property."

State v. Hauser, 342 N.C. 382 (1995). A detective made arrangements with the city sanitation department to collect trash at the defendant's residence and give it to two detectives. A sanitation worker collected the garbage left at the back of the residence for collection. The collection was routine except that the sanitation worker prevented the garbage from commingling with other garbage by depositing the defendant's garbage into a container in the back of the garbage truck instead of into the truck's collection bin. The sanitation worker gave the defendant's garbage to the detectives, who found cocaine residue in it. One of the detectives then obtained a search warrant based on the cocaine found in the garbage and information received from four informants. One of the informants stated that the defendant had sold him cocaine at the defendant's residence. In addition, the officers provided facts showing the reliability of the informants' information. The officers executed the search warrant, and more than a pound of cocaine was found in the defendant's residence.

The court, disavowing a contrary conclusion in the court of appeals opinion in this case, 115 N.C. App. 431 (1994), ruled that the search of the defendant's garbage did not violate the Fourth Amendment, based on the ruling in *California v. Greenwood*, 486 U.S. 35 (1988) (no reasonable expectation of privacy under the Fourth Amendment in garbage left for collection). The defendant sought to distinguish the *Greenwood* ruling by noting that the garbage was left at the curb in *Greenwood* while the garbage in this case was left for collection within the curtilage of the home, the defendant's backyard. The court rejected the defendant's argument, relying on *United States v. Hedrick*, 922 F.2d 396 (7th Cir. 1991) (no Fourth Amendment violation when officers seized garbage placed for collection 18 to 20 feet within home's curtilage; garbage was placed in view of public passing by on the sidewalk, distance between garbage and sidewalk was short, and there was no fence or other barrier preventing public access to garbage). The North Carolina Supreme Court stated that the location of the defendant's garbage within the home's curtilage did not automatically establish that he possessed a reasonable expectation of privacy in the garbage. Relying on the ruling in *United States v. Biondich*, 652 F.2d 743 (8th Cir. 1981) (no Fourth Amendment violation when officer arranged with regular trash collection service to deliver defendant's garbage to officer, even though there may be an expectation of privacy in garbage while it remained within the curtilage), and distinguishing *United States v. Certain Real Property Located at 987 Fisher Road*, 719 F. Supp. 1396 (E.D. Mich. 1989) (Fourth Amendment was violated when police went onto defendant's property and seized garbage bags placed against back wall of house), the court ruled that the defendant did not retain a reasonable expectation of privacy in his garbage once it left his yard in the usual manner, based on the facts in this case. The court also ruled that, even assuming that the search of the defendant's garbage violated the Fourth Amendment, the information supplied by the informants provided a substantial basis for probable cause to support the search warrant for the defendant's house. See also *United States v. Shanks*, 97 F.3d 977 (7th Cir. 1996), discussed above.

State v. Tarantino, 322 N.C. 386 (1988). Distinguishing *United States v. Dunn*, discussed above, the court ruled that the defendant had a reasonable expectation of privacy in a boarded-up store building, and an officer's peering through a quarter-inch crack in the store building's rear wall after entering the enclosed porch there violated the defendant's Fourth Amendment rights. *See also* Siebert v. Severino, 256 F.3d 648 (7th Cir. 2001) (warrantless search of barn with enclosed doors located outside dwelling's curtilage violated Fourth Amendment). *But see* United States v. Pace, 955 F.2d 270 (5th Cir. 1992) (no search occurred when officers pressed their faces against small opening in barn to see inside); United States v. Elkins, 300 F.3d 638 (6th Cir. 2002) (similar ruling); United States v. Taylor, 90 F.3d 903 (4th Cir. 1996) (officers' observation through open blinds while standing at front door did not violate Fourth Amendment); United States v. Fields, 113 F.3d 313 (2d Cir. 1997) (officers' observation through window in which there was five- to six-inch gap plainly visible below blinds, made from side yard of multi-occupant apartment building, did not violate Fourth Amendment).

State v. Boone, 293 N.C. 702 (1977). An open shed and a barn to which it was attached were the only structures within a fenced-in area that was 1.5 miles from the defendant's home. The defendant did not have a reasonable expectation of privacy in that area, and an officer did not violate the defendant's Fourth Amendment rights when he entered the area, looked into an open shed, and obtained the serial number of a stolen tractor inside.

NORTH CAROLINA COURT OF APPEALS

State v. Smith, ___ N.C. App. ___, 783 S.E.2d 504 (2016). The court ruled that no Fourth Amendment violation occurred when officers entered the defendant's driveway to investigate a shooting. When detectives arrived at the defendant's property, they found the gate to his driveway open. The officers did not recall observing a "no trespassing" sign that had been reported the previous day. After a backup deputy arrived, the officers drove both of their vehicles through the open gate and up the defendant's driveway. Once the officers parked, the defendant came out of the house and spoke with the detectives. The defendant denied any knowledge of a shooting and denied owning a rifle. However, the defendant's wife told the officers that there was a rifle inside the residence. The defendant gave verbal consent to search the home. In the course of getting consent, the defendant made incriminating statements. A search of the home found a rifle and shotgun. The rifle was seized, but the defendant was not arrested. After leaving and learning that the defendant had a prior felony conviction from Texas, the officers obtained a search warrant to retrieve the other gun seen in his home and a warrant for the defendant's arrest. When officers returned to the defendant's residence, the driveway gate was closed and a sign on the gate warned, "Trespassers will be shot exclamation!!! Survivors will be shot again!!!" The team entered and found multiple weapons on the premises.

At trial the defendant unsuccessfully moved to suppress all of the evidence obtained during the detectives' first visit to the property and procured by the search warrant the following day. He pled guilty and appealed. The court rejected the defendant's argument that a "no trespassing" sign on his gate expressly removed an implied license to approach his home. While the trial court found that a no trespassing sign was posted on the day of the shooting, there was no evidence that the sign was present on the day the officers first visited the property. Also, there was no evidence that the defendant took consistent steps to physically prevent visitors from entering the property; the open gate suggested otherwise. Finally, the defendant's conduct upon the detectives' arrival belied any notion that their approach was unwelcome. Specifically, when they arrived, he came out and greeted them. For these reasons, the defendant's actions did not reflect a clear demonstration of an intent to revoke the implied license to approach. The court ruled that the officers' actions did not exceed the scope of a lawful knock and talk. Finally, it rejected the defendant's argument that his Fourth Amendment rights were violated because the encounter occurred within the home's curtilage. The court noted that no search of the curtilage occurs when an officer is in a place where the public is allowed to be for purposes of a general inquiry. Here, officers entered the property through an open driveway and did not deviate from the area where their presence was lawful.

State v. Williford, ___ N.C. App. ___, 767 S.E.2d 139 (2015). The court ruled that the trial court did not err by denying the defendant's motion to suppress DNA evidence obtained from his discarded cigarette butt. When the defendant refused to supply a DNA sample in connection with a rape and murder investigation, officers sought to obtain his DNA by other means. After the defendant discarded a cigarette butt in a parking lot, officers retrieved the butt. The parking lot was located directly in front of the defendant's four-unit apartment building, was uncovered, and included five to seven unassigned parking spaces used by the residents. The area between the road and the parking lot was heavily wooded, but no gate restricted access to the lot and no signs suggested either that access to the parking lot was restricted or that the lot was private. After DNA on the cigarette butt matched DNA found on the victim, the defendant was charged with the crimes. At trial, the defendant unsuccessfully moved to suppress the DNA evidence. On appeal, the court rejected the defendant's argument that the seizure of the cigarette butt violated his constitutional rights because it occurred within the curtilage of his apartment:

> [W]e conclude that the parking lot was not located in the curtilage of defendant's building. While the parking lot was in close proximity to the building, it was not enclosed, was used for parking by both the buildings' residents and the general public, and was only protected in a limited way. Consequently, the parking lot was not a location where defendant possessed "a reasonable and legitimate expectation of privacy that society is prepared to accept."

Next, the court rejected the defendant's argument that even if the parking lot was not considered curtilage, he still maintained a possessory interest in the cigarette butt because he did not put it in a trash can or otherwise convey it to a third party. The court reasoned that the cigarette butt was abandoned property. Finally, the court rejected the defendant's argument that even if officers lawfully obtained the cigarette butt, they still were required to obtain a warrant before testing it for his DNA because he had a legitimate expectation of privacy in his DNA. The court reasoned that the extraction of DNA from an abandoned item does not implicate the Fourth Amendment.

State v. Gentile, 237 N.C. App. 304 (2014). The court ruled that a search of the defendant's garage pursuant to a search warrant violated the Fourth Amendment. Following up on a tip that the defendant was growing marijuana on his property, officers went to his residence. They knocked on the front door but received no response. They then went to the back of the house because they heard barking dogs and thought that an occupant might not have heard them knock. Once there they smelled marijuana coming from the garage, and this discovery formed the basis for the search warrant. The court concluded that "the sound of barking dogs, alone, was not sufficient to support the detectives' decision to enter the curtilage of defendant's property by walking into the back yard of the home and the area on the driveway within ten feet of the garage." The court concluded that when the detectives smelled the odor of marijuana, "their purported general inquiry about the information received from the anonymous tip was in fact a trespassory invasion of defendant's curtilage, and they had no legal right to be in that location." The subsequent search—based, in part, on the odor of marijuana—violated the Fourth Amendment.

State v. Borders, 236 N.C. App. 149 (2014) (emphasis in original). In this rape and murder case, the court ruled that the Fourth Amendment was not violated when an officer seized a cigarette butt containing the defendant's DNA. The defendant, a suspect in a murder case, refused four requests by the police to provide a DNA sample. Acting with the primary purpose of obtaining a sample of the defendant's DNA to compare to DNA from the victim's rape kit, officers went to his residence to execute an unrelated arrest warrant. After the defendant was handcuffed and taken outside to the driveway, an officer asked him if he wanted to smoke a cigarette. The defendant said yes, and after he took several drags from the cigarette, the officer asked if he could take the cigarette to throw it away for the defendant. The defendant said yes, but instead of throwing away the cigarette, the officer extinguished it and placed it in an evidence bag. The DNA on the cigarette butt came back as a match to the rape kit DNA. The court acknowledged that if the defendant had discarded the cigarette himself within the curtilage of the premises, the officers could not have seized it. However, the defendant voluntarily accepted the officer's offer to throw away the cigarette butt. The court continued, rejecting the defendant's argument that he had a reasonable expectation of privacy in the cigarette butt. When the defendant, while under arrest and handcuffed, placed the cigarette butt in the officer's gloved hand—instead of on the ground or in some other object within the curtilage—the defendant relinquished possession of the butt and any reasonable expectation of privacy in it. Finally, although indicating that it was "troubled" by the officers' trickery, the court concluded that the officers' actions did not require suppression of the DNA evidence. The court reasoned that because "the police did not commit an *illegal* act in effectuating the valid arrest warrant and because the subjective motives of police do not affect the validity of serving the underlying arrest warrant," suppression was not required.

State v. Pasour, 223 N.C. App. 175 (2012). The court of appeals ruled that the trial court erred by denying the defendant's motion to suppress property seized in a warrantless search. After receiving a tip that a person living at a specified address was growing marijuana, officers went to the address and knocked on the front and side doors. After getting no answer, two officers went to the back of the residence. In the backyard they found and seized marijuana plants. The officers were within the curtilage when they viewed the plants, there was no evidence indicating that the plants were visible from the front of the house or from the road, and a "no trespassing" sign was plainly visible on the side of the house. Even if the officers did not see the sign, it is evidence of the homeowner's intent that the side and back of the home were not open to the public. There was no evidence of a path or anything else to suggest a visitor's use of the rear door. Instead, all visitor traffic appeared to be kept to the front door, and traffic to the rear was discouraged by the posted sign. Further, there was no evidence indicating that the officers had reason to believe that knocking at the back door would produce a response after knocking multiple times at the front and side doors had not. The court concluded that on these facts, "there was no justification for the officers to enter [d]efendant's backyard and so their actions were violative of the Fourth Amendment."

State v. Ballance, 218 N.C. App. 202 (2012). The court of appeals ruled that the trial court did not err by rejecting the defendant's motion to suppress evidence obtained by officers when they entered the property in question. The court concluded that the property constituted an "open field," so that the investigating officers' entry onto the property and the observations made there did not constitute a "search" for Fourth Amendment purposes. The property consisted of 119 acres of wooded land used for hunting and did not contain any buildings or residences.

State v. Nance, 149 N.C. App. 734 (2002). The defendant leased barns and paddocks for her horses. Animal control officers received a telephone call on December 18, 1998, that the horses were being treated cruelly. That same day they viewed the horses from a road. The horses were located in open, accessible areas on the defendant's leased property. They were emaciated and appeared to be starving. On December 21, 1998, the officers entered the property and seized the horses without a search warrant. The court noted that although the officers did not violate the Fourth Amendment when they initially viewed the horses on December 18, 1998, they deprived the defendant of her Fourth Amendment possessory interest in the horses when they removed them three days later. The court then ruled that exigent circumstances did not support the officers' seizure of the horses on the defendant's property without a search warrant. The court stated that the officers had ample time during the three days to secure a search warrant.

[Author's note: The court's ruling is questionable. First, the court's view that the second entry onto the defendant's property without a search warrant or consent violated the Fourth Amendment because it was "private property" is in direct conflict with *Oliver v. United States*, 466 U.S. 170 (1984) (person has no reasonable expectation of privacy in land beyond curtilage of his or her home and, therefore, officer's presence there is not a search under the Fourth Amendment). Because the defendant had no reasonable expectation of privacy in the land on which the horses were located, officers could walk on that land without a search warrant or consent as often as they wanted without violating the defendant's Fourth Amendment rights. Second, the plain view doctrine does not require that the officers' seizure of the horses be supported by exigent circumstances. The plain view doctrine is the basis for upholding a warrantless seizure of evidence when (1) an officer is lawfully in a position to make a plain view observation (or touch, smell, etc.); (2) the officer has a lawful right of access to the object; and (3) the officer has probable cause to believe that the object to be seized is evidence of a crime. Horton v. California, 496 U.S. 128 (1990); United States v. Soussi, 29 F.3d 565 (10th Cir. 1994). There is no additional requirement of exigency to seize evidence of a crime in plain view if an officer's presence on property is lawful; the officer has lawful access to the object to be seized (in this case, the horses in an open, accessible area); and there is probable cause to seize it. *See* G & G Jewelry, Inc. v. City of Oakland, 989 F.2d 1093 (9th Cir. 1993) (upholding warrantless seizure of stolen property at pawn shop under plain view doctrine, which does not require showing of exigent circumstances); United States v. Perry, 95 Fed. Appx. 598 (5th Cir. 2004) (unpublished) (upholding warrantless seizure of marijuana in open field under plain view doctrine); United States v. Paige, 136 F.3d 1012 (5th Cir. 1998). The officers were lawfully on the land on December 21, 1998, when they approached the horses, because the land was not a place where the defendant had a reasonable expectation of privacy. Thus, there was a valid intrusion onto the land where the officers made a plain view observation of the horses. They also had probable cause to believe that the property they seized (the horses) was evidence of the crime of cruelty to animals and that they could seize the horses under the plain view doctrine without a warrant or a showing of exigent circumstances.]

State v. Wooding, 117 N.C. App. 109 (1994). An officer received a radio communication that a person at the Southern Lights Restaurant had seen a black man of a given description get out of a 1980s gray Monte Carlo car and hide behind a dumpster near the restaurant. The person believed that the man lived in one of the apartments at 109 North Cedar Street. While investigating this communication, the officer received another radio communication that a robbery had occurred at the Equinox Restaurant. The description of the robber matched the description of the suspicious person at the Southern Lights Restaurant. The officer went to 109 North Cedar Street. He saw a gray Monte Carlo car parked in front of the building, which contained four apartments—two at ground level and two upstairs. Before leaving his vehicle, the officer saw—through an open window in the side of one of the downstairs apartments—a black male matching the descriptions. After getting out of his vehicle, the officer saw this same person through the open window walking around the apartment and "heard a lot of noise which appeared to [him] to be coins hitting metal." He believed that the noise was definitely change being counted or sifted. The officer went to the back porch of the apartment in which he had seen the black male (there was a partition that separated the porches of the two lower-level apartments). Once on the porch, the officer leaned over a couch next to the window, got close to the window, and looked into the apartment through a three- to four-inch opening in the window curtains. The officer saw two black males sitting on the floor in the hallway counting money. The officer radioed what he had seen to an officer who was in front of the apartment with the robbery victim. Shortly thereafter, the defendant came out onto the front porch and was arrested for the robbery. Then the other person came out of the apartment and was identified as the robber by the victim. Both men thereafter consented to a search of the apartment, and the officers found a handgun and money in the apartment. The court, relying on *State v. Tarantino*, 322 N.C. 386 (1988), ruled that the officer's looking into the apartment window while on the back porch was an unlawful search under the Fourth Amendment.

State v. Church, 110 N.C. App. 569 (1993). Based on a first-time informant's information that marijuana was being grown near a white frame house, officers went to investigate. They saw a white frame house and a second house with wood siding about 150 feet west of the white house. The officers walked to the front porch of the white house, knocked on the door, and received no answer. From the porch, they saw two marijuana plants growing along a fence that went from the white house to a third residence east of the white house and a third marijuana plant growing directly behind the second house. After seeing the plants, the officers walked to the second house to determine who lived in the houses. One officer knocked on the front and side doors and then saw the defendant emerge from the garage that was next to the second house. The defendant informed the officers that he owned both houses but lived in the second house. The officers asked the defendant if they could search the houses and garage, but he refused. After arresting the defendant, the officers asked him for a garage door key, which he produced. An officer inserted the key in the lock, found that it fit, and withdrew the key without opening the door.

The officers learned that the defendant was on probation, contacted his probation officer, and were informed that as a condition of probation, the defendant was obligated to submit to warrantless searches by his probation officer. An officer informed the probation officer of the discovery of marijuana and asked her if she would be interested in conducting a warrantless search under the probation condition. She told the officer that she would be willing to conduct a warrantless search if she saw marijuana growing outside the defendant's house and determined that the plants more than likely belonged to him. She went to the house, saw the plants, determined that they probably belonged to the defendant, and authorized a warrantless search of the defendant's premises. She and nine law enforcement officers conducted the search.

The court ruled that the officers' entry onto the defendant's property by walking to the front and side doors to look for the resident was permissible, based on *State v. Prevette*, 43 N.C. App. 450 (1979). The court also noted that the inadvertence component of the plain view doctrine was deleted in *Horton v. California*, 496 U.S. 128 (1990), and ruled that the plain view doctrine was satisfied in this case. [Author's note: The plain view doctrine must be satisfied *only* when there is a seizure of property, not when only a search takes place. The officer's initial observation of the marijuana, before any seizure took place, did not need to satisfy the plain view doctrine.]

State v. Russell, 92 N.C. App. 639 (1989). After the defendant was arrested, officers seized the defendant's car from his driveway and searched it without a warrant. Although the officers had probable cause to seize and search the car, there were no exigent circumstances and there was no consent to permit them to act without a search warrant, and their conduct could not be justified under the plain view doctrine set out in *Coolidge v. New Hampshire*, 403 U.S. 443 (1971) (but note that the inadvertence requirement of the plain view doctrine was later overruled in *Horton v. California*, 496 U.S. 128 (1990)). The ruling in this case is questionable. *See* Capraro v. Bunt, 44 F.3d 690 (8th Cir. 1995) (warrantless seizure of truck in driveway did not violate Fourth Amendment; truck's position in clear public view on defendant's driveway eliminated any privacy expectation otherwise resulting from its location on private property).

State v. Washington, 86 N.C. App. 235 (1987). Applying the curtilage test of *United States v. Dunn*, discussed above, the court ruled that the tobacco barn, packhouse, and hog shelter that were 50 to 75 feet from the house were not within its curtilage.

State v. Ford, 71 N.C. App. 748 (1984). Officers in the woods beyond a cleared area immediately surrounding a mobile home were not within the curtilage.

State v. Burch, 70 N.C. App. 444 (1984). The court ruled that a brush pile, concealing marijuana plants, was within the curtilage when it was located 84 feet behind a house, because just beyond the brush pile were a small crib, a privy, a cider press, and cider barrels. Beyond the crib was a recreation building that contained a piano, a pool table, and a refrigerator, and beyond the recreation building was a private garage containing junked cars. Sown and mowed grass was around the house, between the house and the marijuana patch, alongside the crib, and between a farm road and the recreation building. Therefore, officers committed an unlawful search by entering (without a warrant) the area where the marijuana was located, which was within the curtilage of the house. The expansive definition of *curtilage* in *Burch* may have been implicitly modified by the later case of *State v. Fields*, 315 N.C. 191 (1985) (toolshed at least 45 feet from dwelling was not within curtilage for second-degree burglary offense).

State v. Perry, 69 N.C. App. 477 (1984). The Fourth Amendment was not violated when officers entered property and found marijuana behind a packhouse that was not near a dwelling and was in a cornfield.

State v. Simmons, 66 N.C. App. 402, *aff'd*, 312 N.C. 78 (1984). The defendant had no reasonable expectation of privacy under the Fourth Amendment in a cornfield in which he was growing marijuana that was one-quarter mile from his home. *See also* State v. Grindstaff, 77 N.C. App. 467 (1985).

State v. Baker, 65 N.C. App. 430 (1983). An officer's entry onto the customer parking area of the defendant's business, which was closed when the officer entered, did not violate the defendant's reasonable expectation of privacy.

State v. Courtright, 60 N.C. App. 247 (1983). The court ruled that the defendant's car, parked on a street in front of a house but with its wheels on the driver's side projecting off the pavement six or seven inches into the yard, was within the curtilage so that it could be searched pursuant to a search warrant that did not describe that car as an object to be searched. This ruling—that the car was within the curtilage—is questionable, because it is highly unlikely that a person would have a reasonable expectation of privacy in a location that is six to seven inches from the street, even though it is on his property. The court could have upheld the search on the ground that the defendant's car was on his premises, even if not on the curtilage, and therefore the car could be searched during the execution of the search warrant; *see, e.g.,* United States v. Asselin, 775 F.2d 445 (1st Cir. 1985).

State v. Prevette, 43 N.C. App. 450 (1979). When officers were making a general inquiry about whether marijuana was on the premises, their entering private property and going to the front door was not a trespass. *See also* United States v. Smith, 783 F.2d 648 (6th Cir. 1986) (entering driveway is generally not a search); United States v. Raines, 243 F.3d 419 (8th Cir. 2001) (no Fourth Amendment violation when officer entered property's backyard under belief that person whom he was attempting to serve with civil process was at residence and that occupants of residence were in backyard and unable to hear officer knocking at front door); United States v. Hammett, 236 F.3d 1054 (9th Cir. 2001) (no Fourth Amendment violation when officers walked across open field where they had landed helicopter to defendant's front door to question defendant about green plants—possibly marijuana— they had seen on the property; officers also acted properly in walking around house to locate someone with whom they could speak); Alvarez v. Montgomery County, 147

F.3d 354 (4th Cir. 1998) (no Fourth Amendment violation when officers, responding to 911 call about underage drinking, entered backyard when circumstances indicated that they might find the homeowner there—even though they did not first knock on front door—in light of sign reading "Party In Back" with an arrow pointing to backyard).

State v. Barbee, 34 N.C. App. 66 (1977). The defendant operated a self-service gas station and a grocery store in a building. An officer's entry into a field behind the building and his walking up to the building's back wall did not violate the defendant's reasonable expectation of privacy. The defendant invited the public to patronize his business, and—by maintaining a parking lot in the back of the building—he invited the public to come to that area.

State v. Jarrell, 24 N.C. App. 610 (1975). An officer, concealed in a public restroom's ceiling, did not violate the defendants' reasonable expectation of privacy under the Fourth Amendment when he observed them engaging in oral sex in the open, public area of the restroom. In this case, the officer did not observe either defendant in an enclosed toilet stall.

State v. Kaplan, 23 N.C. App. 410 (1974). No Fourth Amendment violation occurred when an officer conducted a warrantless search of a tent-like structure that was outside the curtilage of the defendant's dwelling. *See also* United States v. Ruckman, 806 F.2d 1471 (10th Cir. 1986) (warrantless search of cave on government land did not violate Fourth Amendment because defendant did not have reasonable expectation of privacy there). *But see* United States v. Sandoval, 200 F.3d 659 (9th Cir. 2000) (warrantless search of tent located on government land violated Fourth Amendment, even if defendant did not have permission to be there).

FEDERAL APPELLATE COURTS

Freeman v. City of Dallas, 242 F.3d 642 (5th Cir. 2001) (en banc). The seizure and demolition of the owner's apartment buildings without a warrant, after the buildings were condemned under a city ordinance and state law, were reasonable under the Fourth Amendment. See similar rulings in *Hroch v. City of Omaha*, 4 F.3d 693 (8th Cir. 1993), and *Samuels v. Meriwether*, 94 F.3d 1163 (8th Cir. 1996). The court disagreed with the ruling in *Conner v. City of Santa Anna*, 897 F.2d 1487 (9th Cir. 1990) (after hearings, city council declared several old and inoperable cars on plaintiff's property a public nuisance and ordered the nuisance abated; city police called a towing company and city officials broke down a fence surrounding the backyard of the property and removed two of the cars from the property; the court ruled that judicial authorization was necessary to enter the enclosed backyard and seize the cars, where the plaintiff had a reasonable expectation of privacy, because there were no exigent circumstances to justify the city's acting without judicial authorization).

United States v. Reilly, 76 F.3d 1271 (2d Cir. 1996). The court ruled that the curtilage of the defendant's residence included a cottage that was 375 feet from the residence on a 10.71 acre farm. The property was enclosed by a wire fence, hedgerows, and thick woods. There was no interior fencing separating the cottage from the residence. The defendant and his guests used the cottage area for a variety of private activities, including fishing, naked swimming, croquet, cooking, and sexual intercourse. The area's park-like appearance made it readily apparent to observers that the area was private. *See also* United States v. Depew, 8 F.3d 1424 (9th Cir. 1993) (area 6 feet from the defendant's garage and 50 to 60 feet from the defendant's house was within the curtilage; area was not readily visible from the road); Daughenbaugh v. City of Tiffin, 150 F.3d 594 (6th Cir. 1998) (backyard and unattached garage about 50 yards behind house were within the curtilage); United States v. Jenkins, 124 F.3d 768 (6th Cir. 1997) (backyard enclosed on three sides by wire fence was within the curtilage).

United States v. Friend, 50 F.3d 548 (8th Cir. 1995), *vacated on other grounds*, 517 U.S. 1152 (1996). The defendant's residence was located within a locked gate and fence. An officer entered onto the defendant's property with a drug detection dog, which alerted to the defendant's car. The car was parked outside the locked gate and fence, between the garage and a public alley. The court ruled that the car was not located with the curtilage of the defendant's residence, and therefore the officer's entry onto the defendant's property did not violate the Fourth Amendment. *See also* United States v. French, 291 F.3d 945 (7th Cir. 2002) (gravel walkway within 20 feet of defendant's trailer home that connected shed and lean-to on defendant's property was not within curtilage, because defendant did not take steps to protect walkway area from public view).

United States v. Van Damme, 48 F.3d 461 (9th Cir. 1995). The court ruled that the defendant's three greenhouses were not within the curtilage of his home. The greenhouses were over 200 feet from the home. A wire fence surrounding the home and greenhouses was a perimeter fence enclosing several acres, not a fence surrounding only the home and curtilage. A board fence surrounding one of the greenhouses made it a distinct portion of the property quite separate from the home. The greenhouses lacked any indicia of activities commonly associated with domestic life. The cultivation of crops, such as the marijuana involved in this case, is an activity that occurs in open fields, not an intimate activity of the home. Thus, the officers were not within the curtilage when they saw the marijuana through the board fence and the greenhouse doors; nor were any of the greenhouses within the curtilage. *See also* United States v. Wright, 991 F.2d 1182 (4th Cir. 1993) (barn on path from defendant's house was not within curtilage); United States v. Traynor, 990 F.2d 1153 (9th Cir. 1993) (outbuilding about 75 feet away from house was not within curtilage).

United States v. Hall, 47 F.3d 1091 (11th Cir. 1995). An officer entered a commercial company's property and removed a bag of paper shreddings from a garbage dumpster located near the company's offices in a parking area reserved for company employees. The officer drove 40 yards on a private paved road to get to the dumpster. However, there were no signs that indicated that the road was private, and the dumpster was readily accessible to the public. The court noted that the United States Supreme Court has consistently stated that a commercial proprietor has a reasonable expectation of privacy only in those areas where affirmative steps have been taken to exclude the public. The court concluded that the company's subjective expectation of privacy was not one that society was prepared to accept as objectively reasonable. Thus, the officer's search of the dumpster did not violate the Fourth Amendment.

United States v. Hatch, 931 F.2d 1478 (11th Cir. 1991). A marijuana field growing 30 yards or more from the defendant's house was not within the curtilage. The field was separated from the house by a taxidermy building, several fences, stock pens, a tack room, and a drying barn. The fact that the defendant had erected a perimeter fence surrounding his 300-acre tract did not create a protected privacy interest in the open fields on his property. Helicopter flights over the marijuana field also did not violate the defendant's Fourth Amendment rights.

United States v. Cuevas-Sanchez, 821 F.2d 248 (5th Cir. 1987). Officers' placing a video camera on a utility pole to record all activities in the defendant's backyard, when the backyard was surrounded by a 10-foot-high fence, was a search under the Fourth Amendment. The court distinguished *California v. Ciraolo*, discussed above. It also ruled that the search warrant that authorized the installation of the video camera was proper under the Fourth Amendment. *See also* United States v. Koyomejian, 970 F.2d 536 (9th Cir. 1992) (court described legal requirements to conduct nonaural video surveillance); United States v. Williams, 124 F.3d 411 (3d Cir. 1997) (similar ruling); United States v. Falls, 34 F.3d 674 (8th Cir. 1994) (similar ruling).

United States v. Broadhurst, 805 F.2d 849 (9th Cir. 1986). Airplane surveillance of a greenhouse was proper under *California v. Ciraolo* and *Dow Chemical Co. v. United States*, discussed above.

United States v. Whaley, 781 F.2d 417 (5th Cir. 1986). Absent exigent circumstances, an officer's warrantless entry and seizure of marijuana plants within a farm dwelling's curtilage is unconstitutional.

Plain View (Sensory Perception)

(*This topic is discussed on page 203.*)

UNITED STATES SUPREME COURT

Minnesota v. Dickerson, 508 U.S. 366 (1993). An officer had reasonable suspicion to stop the defendant and to frisk him for weapons. During the frisk, the officer felt a lump—a small, hard object wrapped in plastic—in the defendant's jacket pocket that he knew was not a weapon. The officer determined that the lump was cocaine only after "squeezing, sliding and otherwise manipulating the contents of the defendant's pocket." The Court ruled that the plain view doctrine applies by analogy to cases in which an officer discovers contraband through the sense of touch during an otherwise lawful search. (The plain view doctrine provides that if officers are lawfully in a position in which they view an object, if its incriminating character is immediately apparent—that is, they have probable cause to seize it—and if the officers have a lawful right of access to the object, they may seize it without a warrant.) However, the Court also ruled that the officer in this case was not justified in seizing the cocaine because the officer exceeded the search for weapons permitted by *Terry v. Ohio*, 392 U.S. 1 (1968). Once the officer determined that the lump was not a weapon, his continued exploration of the lump until he developed probable cause to believe it was cocaine was an additional search that was not justified by *Terry v. Ohio*. (Thus, the officer's action would have been permissible in this case only if

he had developed probable cause to believe the lump was cocaine at the time he determined that the lump was not a weapon.) *See also* United States v. Ashley, 37 F.3d 678 (D.C. Cir. 1994) (officer felt hard object during initial pat down; based on facts in this case, it was immediately apparent to officer that object was crack cocaine); United States v. Craft, 30 F.3d 1044 (8th Cir. 1994) (officer at airport felt hard, compact packages attached to defendant's ankles; it was immediately apparent to officer that packages contained controlled substances).

Horton v. California, 496 U.S. 128 (1990). A person was robbed of jewelry and cash by two masked men, one armed with a machine gun and the other with a stun gun. An officer developed probable cause to search a home for the weapons and robbery proceeds, but the search warrant issued by the magistrate authorized only a search for the robbery proceeds, not the weapons. While searching for the proceeds, the officer discovered the weapons in plain view and seized them. The Court overruled the part of the opinion in *Coolidge v. New Hampshire*, 403 U.S. 443 (1971), that required (under the plain view doctrine) that the discovery of evidence to be seized must be inadvertent.

The Court then ruled that the seizure in this case was authorized by the plain view doctrine because (1) the weapons were seized during a lawful search for the robbery proceeds, authorized by a valid search warrant; and (2) when the weapons were discovered, it was immediately apparent to the officer that they constituted incriminating evidence (that is, the officer had probable cause to believe that the weapons had been used in the robbery). The search was authorized by a search warrant, and the seizure was authorized by the plain view doctrine. [Author's note: When an officer is executing a search warrant, G.S. 15A-253 permits the seizure of items "inadvertently" discovered. If this statute is violated when an officer does not seize items inadvertently, G.S. 15A-974(a)(2) will govern whether the items should be excluded from a trial.]

Arizona v. Hicks, 480 U.S. 321 (1987). The Court ruled that an officer who conducts a search or seizure of an item under the plain view doctrine must have probable cause to do so; reasonable suspicion is insufficient. In *Hicks* officers properly entered (without a warrant) an apartment where a shooting had occurred to search for the shooter and any victims or weapons. They seized three weapons and a stocking-cap mask. In the squalid apartment, they saw two expensive stereo components. An officer read serial numbers from some of the items without moving them. The Court ruled that this act was neither a search nor a seizure and therefore did not violate the defendant's Fourth Amendment rights. The officer also moved a turntable so that he could read its serial number. The Court ruled that this act constituted a search that required probable cause—probable cause also was necessary to support the later seizure of the turntable from the apartment. Because the State of Arizona had conceded (unwisely, it appears) that only reasonable suspicion existed to move the turntable, the Court ruled that the officer's actions violated the defendant's Fourth Amendment rights.

United States v. Dunn, 480 U.S. 294 (1987). An officer's shining a flashlight into a barn did not violate the defendant's Fourth Amendment rights.

Illinois v. Andreas, 463 U.S. 765 (1983). A customs agent lawfully discovered drugs concealed in a container and notified other law enforcement officers, who arranged a controlled delivery to the defendant. A short time after the container was delivered to the defendant, officers arrested him, reseized the container, and searched it without a warrant. The Court ruled that reopening the container after reseizing it was not a search under the Fourth Amendment, because there was no substantial likelihood that the contents of the container had been changed between the time the officers sealed it for delivery and the time they reseized it from the defendant. No legitimate expectation of privacy remained in the contents of the container once it was lawfully opened by the officers, because privacy interests already had been lawfully invaded and the contraband drugs had been discovered. The Court noted the similarity of these facts to facts covered by the plain view doctrine, because an owner's privacy interest is lost when an officer observes an object. The owner may have retained a privacy interest in title and possession, but the owner did not retain a privacy interest in the container's contents.

United States v. Place, 462 U.S. 696 (1983). Using a drug-sniffing dog to examine the outside of luggage during a temporary seizure in a public place is not a search under the Fourth Amendment. Although a person has a Fourth Amendment privacy interest in the contents of his or her luggage, a dog sniff does not reveal the luggage's contents unless it contains contraband narcotics, and the dog sniff does not require that the luggage be opened.

Texas v. Brown, 460 U.S. 730 (1983). After an officer lawfully stopped a car for a license check, he shined his flashlight into the car and saw a party balloon—tied near its tip—fall from the defendant-driver's hand to the seat beside him. While the defendant looked in the glove compartment for his license, the officer shifted his position and saw small plastic vials, loose white powder, and an open bag of party balloons in the glove compartment. The officer picked up the balloon, which appeared to contain a powdery substance.

A four-Justice plurality ruled that all three elements of the plain view doctrine were satisfied to support the officer's seizure of the balloon: (1) the officer's actions (stopping the vehicle, shining his flashlight, shifting his position) were lawful and properly allowed him to look inside the car; (2) the officer's experience made it "immediately apparent" to him that the balloon contained evidence of a crime (all nine Justices agreed that immediately apparent at most requires probable cause to believe the balloon contained illegal drugs); and (3) the balloon was discovered inadvertently—the officer did not conduct the license check only to discover drugs in plain view. [Author's note: The inadvertence requirement in (3) is no longer a part of the plain view doctrine as a result of the ruling in *Horton v. California*, discussed above.] This case did not present the issue of whether the later warrantless search of the balloon was proper (but see Justice Stevens's concurring opinion).

Washington v. Chrisman, 455 U.S. 1 (1982). An officer accompanied an arrestee back to his college dormitory room so that the arrestee could obtain his identification. While the officer was standing in the doorway to the room, he noticed seeds and a small pipe lying on a desk 8 to 10 feet away. Based on his training and experience, he believed that the seeds were marijuana and that the pipe was used to smoke marijuana. The Court ruled that the officer properly entered the room to seize the marijuana and the pipe that he saw in plain view. An officer, as a matter of routine, may monitor the movements of a person the officer has arrested, including entering a private room if the arrestee goes there.

Colorado v. Bannister, 449 U.S. 1 (1980). An officer saw a speeding car that disappeared before he could stop it. He then heard a radio dispatch that reported a theft of motor vehicle parts, including chrome lug nuts, and described the two suspected thieves. A few minutes later, he saw the car that had been speeding enter a service station. The officer approached the car on foot to issue a speeding citation and began talking with the two occupants. He noticed chrome lug nuts in an open glove compartment and two lug wrenches on the floorboard of the backseat. The occupants matched the radio descriptions of the men suspected of stealing the motor vehicle parts. The Court ruled that the plain view observation of items in the car gave the officer probable cause to seize the parts and probable cause to arrest the occupants. The warrantless seizure of the items was permissible under *Carroll v. United States*, 267 U.S. 132 (1925).

NORTH CAROLINA SUPREME COURT

State v. Grice, 367 N.C. 753 (2015). (1) Reversing the court of appeals, 223 N.C. App. 460 (2012), the court ruled that officers did not violate the Fourth Amendment by seizing marijuana plants seen in plain view. After receiving a tip that the defendant was growing marijuana at a specified residence, officers went to the residence to conduct a knock and talk. Finding the front door inaccessible, covered with plastic, and obscured by furniture, the officers noticed that the driveway led to a side door, which appeared to be the main entrance. One of the officers knocked on the side door. No one answered. From the door, the officer noticed plants growing in several buckets about 15 yards away. Both officers recognized the plants as marijuana. The officers seized the plants, returned to the sheriff's office, and got a search warrant to search the home. The defendant was charged with manufacturing a controlled substance and moved to suppress evidence of the marijuana plants. The trial court denied the motion and the court of appeals reversed. The supreme court began by finding that the officers observed the plants in plain view. It then explained that a warrantless seizure may be justified as reasonable under the plain view doctrine if the officer did not violate the Fourth Amendment in arriving at the place from where the evidence could be plainly viewed, the evidence's incriminating character was immediately apparent, and the officer had a lawful right of access to the object itself. Additionally, the court noted, "[t]he North Carolina General Assembly has . . . required that the discovery of evidence in plain view be inadvertent." The court noted that the sole point of contention in this case was whether the officers had a lawful right of access from the driveway 15 yards across the defendant's property to the plants' location. Finding against the defendant on this issue, the court stated: "Here, the knock and talk investigation constituted the initial entry onto defendant's property which brought the officers within plain view of the marijuana plants. The presence of the clearly identifiable contraband justified walking further into the curtilage." The court rejected the defendant's argument that the seizure was unlawful because the plants were on the curtilage of his property, stating:

> [W]e conclude that the unfenced portion of the property fifteen yards from the home and bordering a wood line is closer in kind to an open field than it is to the paradigmatic curtilage which protects "the privacies of life" inside the home. . . . However, even if the property at issue can be considered the curtilage of the home for Fourth Amendment purposes, we disagree with defendant's claim that a justified presence in one portion of the curtilage (the driveway and front porch) does not extend to justify recovery of contraband in plain view located in another portion of the curtilage (the side yard). By analogy, it is difficult to imagine what formulation of the Fourth Amendment would prohibit the officers from seizing the contraband if the plants had been growing on the porch—the paradigmatic curtilage—rather than at a distance, particularly when the officers' initial presence on the curtilage was justified. The plants in question were situated on the periphery of the curtilage, and the protections cannot be greater than if the plants were growing on the porch itself. The officers in this case were, by the custom and tradition of our society, implicitly invited into the curtilage to approach the home. Traveling within the curtilage to seize contraband in plain view within the curtilage did not violate the Fourth Amendment.

(2) The court ruled that the seizure also was justified by exigent circumstances, concluding: "Reviewing the record, it is objectively reasonable to conclude that someone may have been home, that the individual would have been aware of the officers' presence, and that the individual could easily have moved or destroyed the plants if they were left on the property."

State v. Mickey, 347 N.C. 508 (1998). Officers found the body of a murder victim in a bedroom. The victim's husband was charged with the murder. Among items seized at the scene were a credit card found on the top of a desk located eight feet from the victim's body and several pornographic magazines addressed to someone other than the victim's husband that were discovered under the bed after the bloodstained mattress and the box springs were properly seized and removed. The defendant did not challenge the officers' authority to secure the murder scene or to seize evidence related to the murder, such as the victim's body and the bloodstained mattress. However, the defendant challenged the seizure of the credit card and pornographic magazines. The court ruled, distinguishing *Arizona v. Hicks*, 480 U.S. 321 (1987), that these items were properly seized because they were in plain view and were evidence of the murder. The court noted that it would have been immediately apparent to the officers that these items—bearing names other than the victim's or defendant's—could be evidence of the murder, because they were likely to reveal the identity of the killer or of a material witness.

State v. Brooks, 337 N.C. 132 (1994). The court ruled that the officer's shining his flashlight into a car's interior was not a search, citing *Texas v. Brown*, 460 U.S. 730 (1983), and *State v. Whitley*, 33 N.C. App. 753 (1977).

State v. White, 322 N.C. 770 (1988). Officers executed a search warrant for stolen property and seized stolen items that were not named in the warrant. The court ruled that "inadvertence" under the plain view doctrine means that officers do not have probable cause to believe that evidence will be discovered until they actually observe it during an otherwise justified search. [Author's note: Inadvertence is no longer required under the Fourth Amendment, see *Horton v. California*, 496 U.S. 128 (1990), but it applies under G.S. 15A-253 (1988).] Judicial review involves a two-step inquiry: (1) Before the search, did officers have probable cause to secure a search warrant for the later-seized items that were not named in the search warrant? If the answer is yes, the seizure is illegal. If the answer is no, then the review proceeds to the second inquiry. (2) Did the officers have probable cause to believe that the seized items were evidence of a crime when they seized them without a warrant?

The court ruled that the officers' use of break-in incident reports when they were executing a search warrant did not violate the plain view inadvertence requirement because they did not have probable cause to list the items named in these reports in a search warrant. Therefore, the officers properly seized these items. The court ruled, however, that they did not have probable cause to seize other items, not named in the reports, until after they seized them; therefore, the officers illegally seized these items. *See also* State v. Williams, 315 N.C. 310 (1986) (officer properly seized padlock while executing search warrant for bloody clothing); State v. Sapatch, 34 N.C. App. 197 (1992) (officer did not have probable cause to

search closed film canisters during administrative search for alcohol beverage control violations).

State v. Tarantino, 322 N.C. 386 (1988). The defendant had a reasonable expectation of privacy in a boarded-up store building, and an officer's peering through a quarter-inch crack in the store building's rear wall after entering an enclosed porch there violated the defendant's Fourth Amendment rights. *But see* United States v. Pace, 955 F.2d 270 (5th Cir. 1992) (no search occurred when officers pressed their faces against small opening in barn to see inside); United States v. Taylor, 90 F.3d 903 (4th Cir. 1996) (officers' observation through open blinds while standing at front door did not violate Fourth Amendment).

State v. Peck, 305 N.C. 734 (1982). An officer had probable cause under the plain view doctrine to seize a plastic bag containing white powder as evidence of illegal drugs that were discovered when he frisked the defendant, who was apparently intoxicated and possibly under the influence of drugs as well.

State v. Jackson, 302 N.C. 101 (1981). A mother invited an officer into her house and opened a bag in front of him to find a change of clothes for her arrested son. When the mother opened the bag, a knife fell out. The officer properly seized the knife (used in a rape) under the plain view doctrine.

State v. Williams, 299 N.C. 529 (1980). When executing a search warrant for heroin at a trailer, officers properly seized letters and photographs not listed in the warrant as evidence of the trailer's ownership under the plain view doctrine and under G.S. 15A-253 (setting out the plain view doctrine when executing a search warrant). *See also* State v. Richards, 294 N.C. 474 (1978).

State v. Crews, 286 N.C. 41 (1974). Officers were in a house to serve an order for arrest on the defendant. As the defendant approached the bedroom closet to get his clothing, an officer followed him and noticed on a shelf a clear, brown-tinted, pint-sized bottle that contained several hundred multicolored pills. The officer had received drug detection training, and the pills looked like amphetamines, which he had seen before. In addition, the size of the bottle, the large number of pills, and the lack of a prescription or label on it led him to believe the pills were amphetamines. The court ruled that this evidence was sufficient to establish probable cause to seize the bottle under the plain view doctrine. Although this case was decided before *Texas v. Brown*, discussed above, it is consistent with the finding of probable cause in that case.

State v. Carey, 285 N.C. 509 (1974). The officer, who was in a house to make an arrest for an armed robbery and murder (in which a shotgun was used), properly seized, under the plain view doctrine, shotgun shells that he saw in an open kitchen drawer.

State v. Harvey, 281 N.C. 1 (1972). While serving an arrest warrant in a defendant's home, an officer properly seized, under the plain view doctrine, seeds he saw on top of the freezer that he recognized as marijuana seeds.

NORTH CAROLINA COURT OF APPEALS

State v. Malunda, 230 N.C. App. 355 (2013). The court ruled that the trial court erred by concluding that officers had probable cause to conduct a warrantless search of the defendant, a passenger in a stopped vehicle. After detecting an odor of marijuana on the driver's side of the vehicle, the officers conducted a warrantless search of the vehicle and discovered marijuana in the driver's side door. However, the officers did not detect an odor of marijuana on the vehicle's passenger side or on the defendant. The court found that none of the other circumstances, including the defendant's location in an area known for drug activity, his prior criminal history, his nervousness and failure to immediately produce identification, or his commission of the infraction of possessing an open container of alcohol in a motor vehicle, when considered separately or in combination, established probable cause to search the defendant's person.

State v. Carter, 200 N.C. App. 47 (2009). An officer noticed that a vehicle's temporary tag was old or worn and had an obscured expiration date. He stopped the vehicle, which was being driven by the defendant. The officer saw several whole pieces of paper lying on the passenger seat and noticed that the defendant seemed unusually nervous. The officer investigated the vehicle's registration and then arrested the defendant for an expired registration tag and failure to notify the Division of Motor Vehicles of a change of address. The defendant was removed from the vehicle, handcuffed, and directed to sit on a curb while the vehicle was searched. The officer noticed that the whole pieces of paper had been ripped into smaller pieces. He placed the pieces together and discovered incriminating evidence.

(1) The court ruled that the officer's search of the vehicle incident to the defendant's arrest violated the Fourth Amendment under the ruling in *Arizona v. Gant*, 556 U.S. 332 (2009). First, the defendant was not within reaching distance or otherwise able to access the passenger compartment when the search began. He had been arrested, handcuffed, and was sitting on the curb. Second, there was no evidence that the papers were related to the offenses for which the defendant had been arrested. (2) The court ruled that the officer's seizure and search of the papers were not justified under the plain view doctrine because it was not immediately apparent that the papers were evidence of a crime or contraband. [Author's note: The term "immediately apparent" is synonymous with probable cause. State v. Wilson, 112 N.C. App. 777 (1993).]

State v. Robinson, 189 N.C. App. 454 (2008). An officer was on bicycle patrol in a community known for drug activity. He saw a car speed down a street, cross over the road, and jump the curb onto the grass. The driver then drove the vehicle behind a building and out of the officer's view. The officer was informed by radio that the defendant owned the vehicle, and the officer recalled that his agency had received a tip that named this building as being a drug location and the defendant as selling a large amount of cocaine from it. The officer went to the building and saw the defendant talking to someone inside an apartment. The officer made eye contact with the defendant, who then stopped talking. The defendant straightened up abruptly and had a surprised or frightened look on his face. The officer thought he was going to take off running. When the officer asked him what he was doing, the defendant started to back away. He turned his right side away from the officer and reached into his right pocket. The officer told him to keep his hands out of his pockets. The officer did a pat frisk and felt a cylindrical object that made a rattling sound when moved. The object felt like a film canister. The officer asked the defendant if there was crack in his pocket. He responded "no" and lowered his head and slumped his shoulders. The officer then reached into the pocket, pulled out and opened the canister, and discovered rocks of crack cocaine.

(1) The court ruled that the officer had reasonable suspicion to make an investigative stop and frisk the defendant, based on the facts set out above. (2) The court ruled that the officer's discovery of the crack cocaine in the film canister during the frisk of the defendant did not violate the Fourth Amendment. Under the plain feel doctrine set out in *Minnesota v. Dickerson*, 508 U.S. 366 (1993), there was substantial evidence that the contents of the film canister were immediately identifiable by the officer as crack cocaine, based on the facts set out above.

State v. Harper, 158 N.C. App. 595 (2003). Based on an investigation that indicated people in a hotel room were involved with illegal drugs, an officer knocked on the door to the room. The defendant initially opened the door slightly and then, while continuing to have a conversation with the officer, opened it about halfway. The officer asked the defendant if he could step inside the room to see if George Davis was in. The defendant then stepped back from the officer and the threshold of the door and opened the door almost to its full extension. The officer saw a set of electronic scales on the nightstand between the room's two beds and knew that drug dealers often used such scales to measure illegal drugs. There was another person in the room in addition to the defendant. That person started moving around the room, refused the officer's order to remain seated on a bed, and became increasingly agitated. He was handcuffed. The defendant defied the officer's order to remain seated on a bed and was handcuffed. The officer then searched for weapons in the mattresses and nightstand. The officer and other officers saw illegal drugs and cash in these places. They obtained a search warrant, conducted a search of the hotel room, and seized evidence. The court ruled (after determining that the officer was lawfully in the room with the consent to enter) that the scales were lawfully observed and seized under the plain view doctrine. [Author's note: The court's ruling is clearly correct. However, the court referred to statements in *State v. Bone*, 354 N.C. 1, 9 (2001), that the discovery of evidence under the plain view doctrine must be inadvertent. The statements in *Bone* were incorrect. An inadvertent discovery is not required under the Fourth Amendment; *see* Horton v. California, 496 U.S. 128 (1990). Inadvertence is required by G.S. 15A-253, but only during the execution of a search warrant. The discovery in this case did not occur during the execution of a search warrant.]

State v. Briggs, 140 N.C. App. 484 (2000). Officers were conducting a driver's license check in a high crime area. As one officer returned the defendant's license to the defendant, another officer recognized the defendant as someone whom he had previously arrested for cocaine offenses. The officer knew that the defendant was on probation and had been convicted of drug offenses more than once. Although the defendant denied that he had been drinking or taking drugs, the officer noted that the defendant was chewing gum "real hard" and that his eyes were glassy and bloodshot. Also, the officer smelled the odor of burned cigar tobacco inside the vehicle and

on the defendant's person. When the officer asked about the smell, the defendant stated that he did not smoke cigars but that a female who was in the vehicle earlier had been smoking a cigar. The officer knew from his experience that drug users often smoke cigars to mask the smell of illegal drugs. The defendant declined the officer's request to search the defendant's vehicle. The officer then required the defendant to get out of the vehicle and frisked him for weapons. The officer was aware from his experience that drug dealers frequently carry weapons. The officer testified that during the frisk, "I felt a hard, cylindrical shape in [defendant's] pocket and it felt like a cigar holder; and I'm familiar with these because folks carry these frequently to keep their controlled substances in. It's like a little plastic test tube with a little cap on it; and there's really nothing else that's shaped exactly like that." The officer asked the defendant what that object was, and the defendant stated, "A cigar holder." The officer said, "I thought you didn't smoke cigars," but the defendant did not respond. The officer then removed the cigar holder from the defendant's pocket, and when he shook it, the cigar holder "rattled like it had a number of small hard objects in it." The officer opened the cigar holder, found 10 rocks of crack cocaine inside, and arrested the defendant.

The court ruled, relying on *State v. Butler*, 331 N.C. 227 (1992), and *State v. McGuirt*, 122 N.C. App. 237 (1996), *aff'd*, 345 N.C. 624 (1997), that the officer had reasonable suspicion to conduct the frisk, based on the facts discussed above. (2) The court ruled that the officer had probable cause to seize the cigar holder under the plain feel doctrine set out in *Minnesota v. Dickerson*, 508 U.S. 366 (1993). The court discussed cases from other jurisdictions that have split on the issue of whether the plain feel doctrine may be satisfied when an officer feels a container the shape of which does not itself reveal its identity as contraband. Courts upholding such seizures consider factors in addition to the officer's tactile perception to determine probable cause. Other courts declining to uphold such seizures have determined that touching the containers themselves cannot sustain a probable cause finding. The court adopted the view that it would consider the totality of circumstances in deciding whether an officer had probable cause to seize such a container when the officer felt it, and the court stated that the probable cause determination involves considering the evidence as understood by law enforcement officers. Based on the facts discussed above, the officer in this case had probable cause to seize the cigar holder. *See also* State v. Green, 146

N.C. App. 702 (2001) (during encounter with defendant in area known for drug activity, officer had probable cause to seize plastic baggie protruding from defendant's pocket when officer knew that illegal drugs were customarily packaged in plastic baggies).

State v. Graves, 135 N.C. App. 216 (1999). The defendant was shot in an area known for high drug activity. An officer went to the hospital to learn about the shooting. While speaking to the defendant, who was on a stretcher, the officer noticed wads of brown paper falling from the defendant's shoe or pant leg as a nurse began to remove the defendant's shoes and clothing. The officer picked up the paper wads, unraveled them, and found a crack pipe and crack cocaine. The court ruled that the officer did not have probable cause—the equivalent of "immediately apparent" under the plain view doctrine—to believe that the contents of the wads of paper contained illegal drugs. The court noted, citing *State v. Sanders*, 112 N.C. App. 477 (1993), that the officer was not asked, nor did he testify, about what he suspected was contained in the paper wads before he unwrapped them.

State v. Bartlett, 130 N.C. App. 79 (1998). During a lawful search of a vehicle, an officer searched a book bag within the vehicle and seized (1) a clear plastic bag containing finely chopped vegetable material with many white specks and (2) a piece of black, hard, plastic-like material wrapped in aluminum foil. Because the officer did not recognize the plastic-like material, she asked another officer, who was experienced in drug cases, to examine it. That officer didn't know what it was, so she decided to send it to the SBI laboratory for analysis, which revealed that the substance was bufotenine, a Schedule I controlled substance. The SBI chemist testified at the suppression hearing that he had performed thousands of tests on suspected controlled substances but had only encountered bufotenine three or four times in his career. The State argued that the proximity of the plastic-like substance to a clear plastic bag containing finely chopped vegetable material was sufficient to establish probable cause to seize the plastic-like substance. The court stated, however, that the officers were equally unsure of the identity of the vegetable material—which later laboratory analysis concluded did not contain any controlled substance. The seizing officer testified that the "plastic bag almost looked as if it could have possibly contained some sort of very finely chopped marijuana." The court ruled, citing *State v. Beaver*, 37 N.C. App. 513 (1978), that the officer had a conjecture—but not probable cause—to

seize the plastic-like material, and that therefore the seizure of the bufotenine violated the Fourth Amendment.

State v. Benjamin, 124 N.C. App. 734 (1996). An officer conducted a frisk of the defendant after an investigative stop for a traffic violation. As the officer was patting the defendant, he felt two hard plastic containers in a breast pocket of the defendant's winter jacket. Based on his narcotics training, it was immediately apparent to the officer that these containers were vials of the type customarily used to hold illegal drugs. When the officer felt the containers through the jacket, he asked the defendant, "What is that?" The defendant responded that it was "crack." The officer removed two vials from the coat pocket and found cocaine.

(1) The court ruled that the defendant was not in custody when the officer asked him what the objects were, and therefore *Miranda* warnings were not required. The court noted that the fact that a defendant is not free to leave does not necessarily constitute "custody" under *Miranda*. Instead, the inquiry is whether a reasonable person in the defendant's position would believe that he or she was under arrest or the functional equivalent of arrest; the court cited and discussed *Stansbury v. California*, 511 U.S. 318 (1994), and *Berkemer v. McCarty*, 468 U.S. 420 (1984). The court concluded that a reasonable person would not have believed that he was in custody, based on these facts. (2) The court ruled that the seizure of the cocaine was proper under the plain feel theory of *Minnesota v. Dickerson*, 508 U.S. 366 (1993). The court stated that the officer had probable cause to believe (or, to state it a different way, that it became immediately apparent to the officer) that the objects were contraband based on the officer's experience and narcotics training; the size, shape, and mass of the objects; and the defendant's response to the officer's question. The court also ruled that an officer may ask a suspect the nature of an object in the suspect's pocket during a lawful frisk even after the officer has determined that the object is not a weapon.

In re Whitley, 122 N.C. App. 290 (1996). Two officers responded to a call that drug sales were occurring between two black males on a certain street. The officers saw the respondent and another person under a tree. They approached and told them that they were going to do a weapons search. During the search of the respondent, an officer noticed that his lower body and legs were tight, so he asked him to spread his legs. The officer's hands were outside the respondent's trousers in the bottom crotch area when an item fell from the respondent's buttocks into his pants and onto the officer's hand. When the officer retrieved the item from the respondent's pants, he saw that it was a plastic bag containing a white powdered substance. The officer placed the respondent under arrest.

The court ruled (1) that there was reasonable suspicion that the respondent might be armed, dangerous, and involved in criminal activity to frisk him [Author's note: This ruling—that there was reasonable suspicion—is now questionable in light of the later case of *Florida v. J.L.*, 529 U.S. 266 (1999).] and (2) that the incriminating character of the object seized was immediately apparent to the officer, noting *State v. Wilson*, 112 N.C. App. 777 (1993), and *Minnesota v. Dickerson*, 508 U.S. 366 (1993). The court noted that there was no evidence that the officer improperly manipulated the object to determine if it was an illegal substance.

State v. Wooding, 117 N.C. App. 109 (1994). An officer received a radio communication that a person at the Southern Lights Restaurant had seen a black man of a given description get out of a 1980s gray Monte Carlo car and hide behind a dumpster near the restaurant. The person believed that the man lived in one of the apartments at 109 North Cedar Street. While investigating this communication, the officer received another radio communication that a robbery had occurred at the Equinox Restaurant. The description of the robber matched the description of the suspicious person at the Southern Lights Restaurant. The officer went to 109 North Cedar Street. He saw a gray Monte Carlo car parked in front of the building, which contained four apartments—two at ground level and two upstairs. Before leaving his vehicle, the officer saw—through an open window in the side of one of the downstairs apartments—a black male matching the descriptions. After getting out of his vehicle, the officer saw this same person through the open window walking around the apartment and "heard a lot of noise which appeared to [him] to be coins hitting metal." He believed that the noise was definitely change being counted or sifted through. The officer went to the back porch of the apartment in which he had seen the black male (there was a partition that separated the porches of the two lower-level apartments). Once on the porch, the officer leaned over a couch next to the window, got close to the window, and looked into the apartment through a three- to four-inch opening in the window curtains. The officer saw two black males sitting on the floor in the hallway counting money. The officer radioed what he had seen to an officer who was in front of the apartment with

the robbery victim (the victim heard the officer's communication). Shortly thereafter, the defendant came out onto the front porch and was arrested for the robbery. Then the other person came out of the apartment and was identified as the robber by the victim. Both men thereafter consented to a search of the apartment, and the officers found a handgun and money in the apartment.

The court, relying on *State v. Tarantino*, 322 N.C. 386 (1988) (looking through cracks in building violated Fourth Amendment), ruled that the officer's looking into the apartment window while on the back porch was an unlawful search under the Fourth Amendment. The court rejected the State's argument that the later consent search of the apartment—when a handgun and money were found—was based on lawful activity independent of the officer's initial unlawful observation into the apartment window. The court ruled that (1) the arrest of the defendant was based entirely on the officer's unlawful search and was therefore itself unlawful; (2) the consent to search, given by the defendant after his arrest, was tainted by the unlawful search; and (3) the victim's identification of the second person in the apartment was made only after the victim learned what the officer had seen through the back window—two people counting money in the apartment; thus, the identification and the later consent to search were also tainted by the unlawful search.

State v. Wilson, 112 N.C. App. 777 (1993). A police department received an anonymous phone call that several people were selling drugs in the breezeway of Building 1304 in the Hunter Oaks Apartments. The caller did not provide names or descriptions of the alleged drug dealers. Two officers familiar with the area knew that if a police car entered the parking lot at one end of the breezeway, the suspects would run out the other end. They devised a plan whereby a police car would enter the parking lot and officers would position themselves so that they could stop anyone who ran out of the back of the breezeway. An officer stopped the defendant as he ran out of the back of the breezeway and conducted a frisk. During the frisk, the officer felt a lump in the left breast pocket of the defendant's jacket and immediately believed that it was crack cocaine. The officer then asked the defendant if his coat had an inside pocket. The defendant did not respond verbally but instead opened his jacket so that the inside pocket was visible. The officer saw and removed a small plastic bag that contained crack cocaine.

(1) Distinguishing *State v. Fleming*, 106 N.C. App. 165 (1992), the court ruled that the officer had authority to stop and frisk the defendant, based on the anonymous phone call, the flight of the defendant and others when the police car pulled into the parking lot, and the officer's experience that weapons were frequently involved in drug transactions. (2) Distinguishing *Minnesota v. Dickerson*, 508 U.S. 366 (1993), the court noted that the officer in this case—unlike the officer in *Dickerson*—did not need to manipulate the item in the defendant's pocket to determine that it was cocaine; he immediately believed it was crack cocaine. The court ruled that the requirement in *Dickerson* that it must be "immediately apparent" to the officer that the item is illegal means that the officer must have probable cause to believe that the item is illegal. The court also ruled that the officer's tactile senses, based on his experience and the facts in this case, gave him probable cause to believe that the item was crack cocaine. Thus, the officer did not exceed the scope of a frisk under the *Dickerson* ruling.

State v. Whitted, 112 N.C. App. 640 (1993). A car parked in front of a residence fled at high speed after the driver saw a marked patrol car. The area from which the car fled was known for frequent drug sales, especially crack cocaine. People commonly pulled over to the curbside after being flagged down and purchased drugs. This area had been under surveillance for 30 days, and several arrests had been made based on drug sales at the residence from which the car had fled. After officers stopped the car, they went on each side of the car to investigate. The defendant was sitting in the front passenger seat, and an officer saw that the defendant kept his hand by his front pants pocket and "kept pushing something down." The defendant did not move his hand when the officer asked him to do so, and the officer then frisked the defendant for weapons. During the frisk, the officer felt a "pebble" (that is, a hard substance) in the defendant's pocket that he believed, based on his experience and knowledge of the circumstances, to be crack cocaine. He removed the object and discovered that it was crack cocaine.

The court ruled, based on all the circumstances in this case including the suspicious behavior and flight from the officers, that the officer had probable cause to search the defendant after the officer felt the object in the defendant's pocket. [Author's note: Although the court did not discuss *Minnesota v. Dickerson*, 508 U.S. 366 (1993), its ruling is consistent with that case.]

State v. Sanders, 112 N.C. App. 477 (1993). Two State Highway Patrol officers set up a driver's license check at a ramp off a highway. They did not post signs warning the public that a license check was being conducted. The officers checked every car that approached the checkpoint unless they were busy writing citations. The defendant entered the ramp, and as he approached the checkpoint, he stopped his car 150 feet from one of the troopers. The defendant then drove up to the checkpoint, stopped his car, and rolled down his window. In response to the trooper's request for driver's license and registration, the defendant said that he did not have the registration or any identification and that he was not the owner of the car. The passenger in the car also failed to produce any identification. The trooper asked the defendant to get out of the car. As he stepped out of the car, the trooper saw a bulge about the size of two fists in the right pocket of the defendant's jacket. The trooper then told the defendant to face the car and place his hands on it so that he could pat him down for weapons. As the defendant was following the trooper's instructions, the trooper saw plastic protruding from his right pocket. While frisking the defendant, the trooper touched the bulge and noted that it felt like "hard flour dough." The trooper removed the plastic bag from the defendant's pocket. It contained three smaller bags with cocaine inside.

(1) Distinguishing *Delaware v. Prouse*, 440 U.S. 648 (1979), the court ruled that the stop at the license checkpoint was constitutional. The court noted that the troopers followed their agency's guidelines in selecting the location and time for the license check and detained every car that passed through, except for those that came through while they were issuing citations. (2) Following *State v. Peck*, 305 N.C. 734 (1982), the court ruled that the trooper—based on the facts described above, his testimony that people driving stolen cars often provide officers with false names and insist that they have no identification, and the bulge in the defendant's pocket—had reason to believe that the defendant was armed and dangerous and therefore could frisk him. (3) The court also ruled, based on *Minnesota v. Dickerson*, 508 U.S. 366 (1993), that the trooper acted properly in conducting the frisk by feeling the packet in the bulge in the jacket to determine if it was a weapon. (4) The court remanded the case to the trial court to determine, in light of *Dickerson* (decided after this case was heard in the trial court), whether it was immediately apparent to the trooper that what he felt was illegal drugs.

State v. Church, 110 N.C. App. 569 (1993). Based on a first-time informant's information that marijuana was being grown near a white frame house, officers went to investigate. They saw a white frame house and a second house with wood siding about 150 feet west of the white house. The officers walked to the front porch of the white house, knocked on the door, and received no answer. From the porch, they saw two marijuana plants growing along a fence that went from the white house to a third residence east of the white house and a third marijuana plant growing directly behind the second house. After seeing the plants, the officers walked to the second house to determine who lived in the houses. One officer knocked on the front and side doors and then saw the defendant emerge from the garage that was next to the second house. The defendant informed the officers that he owned both houses but lived in the second house. The officers asked the defendant if they could search the houses and garage, but he refused. After arresting the defendant, the officers asked him for a garage door key, which he produced. An officer inserted the key in the lock, found that it fit, and withdrew the key without opening the door.

The officers learned that the defendant was on probation, contacted his probation officer, and were informed that as a condition of probation, the defendant was obligated to submit to warrantless searches by his probation officer. An officer informed the probation officer of the discovery of marijuana and asked her if she would be interested in conducting a warrantless search under the probation condition. She told the officer that she would be willing to conduct a warrantless search if she saw marijuana growing outside the defendant's house and determined that the plants more than likely belonged to him. She went to the house, saw the plants, determined that they probably belonged to the defendant, and authorized a warrantless search of the defendant's premises. She and nine law enforcement officers conducted the search.

The court ruled that officers' entry onto the defendant's property by walking to the front and side doors to look for the resident was permissible, based on *State v. Prevette*, 43 N.C. App. 450 (1979). The court also noted that the inadvertence component of the plain view doctrine was deleted in *Horton v. California*, 496 U.S. 128 (1990), and ruled that the plain view doctrine was satisfied in this case. [Author's note: The plain view doctrine must be satisfied only when there is a seizure of property, not when only a search takes place. The officer's initial observation of the marijuana, before any seizure took place, did not need to satisfy the plain view doctrine.]

State v. Corpening, 109 N.C. App. 586 (1993). A deputy sheriff responded to a report that the defendant's van had caught fire and was off the highway in the lot of an old store. The fire had been extinguished when a deputy sheriff arrived. The deputy, who had been an officer for 13 years and had smelled "white liquor" many times, detected the odor of that substance coming from the van. The court ruled that the deputy's detection of the odor was sufficient to establish probable cause to search the van (in addition, the defendant had acted very nervous and had placed cardboard over a burned-out window), and thus the warrantless search of the van was constitutional, based on *State v. Isleib*, 319 N.C. 634 (1987).

State v. Trapper, 48 N.C. App. 481 (1980). The officer's detection of the odor of marijuana while standing beside a truck did not violate the defendant's Fourth Amendment rights. For other cases involving the detection of the odor of marijuana and other drugs, see *State v. Greenwood*, 47 N.C. App. 731 (1980), *reversed on other grounds*, 301 N.C. 705 (1981) (odor of marijuana provided probable cause to search vehicle); *State v. Cornelius*, 104 N.C. App. 583 (1991) (similar ruling); *State v. Ford*, 71 N.C. App. 748 (1984) (odor of marijuana provided probable cause to search mobile home); *United States v. McKeever*, 906 F.2d 129 (5th Cir. 1990) (officer's smelling aroma of cooking amphetamine provided probable cause for search warrant).

State v. Beaver, 37 N.C. App. 513 (1978). An officer properly stopped a car with one taillight out. He saw between a passenger's legs a shot glass that had a white powdery substance in it. Although he saw this evidence in plain view, he lacked probable cause to believe that the glass contained an illegal drug, and therefore his seizure of it was unconstitutional. The officer did not have training or familiarity with controlled substances to establish probable cause that the white powder was an illegal drug. *Compare with* State v. Wolfe, 26 N.C. App. 464 (1975) (officer, who saw in the car a transparent plastic bag containing small tinfoil packets, had probable cause to believe that packets contained illegal drugs; although the result probably is correct, the court did not set out facts that supported probable cause); State v. Tillett, 50 N.C. App. 520 (1981) (after shining flashlight in car, officer saw an object that his training and experience gave him probable cause to believe—court used the synonymous term "probability"—was a marijuana cigarette).

State v. Blackwelder, 34 N.C. App. 352 (1977). Because an officer had no legal justification to stop or search a car or to arrest or search the occupants, he had no justification under the plain view doctrine to seize a box of LSD tablets after he stopped the car, took the defendant out of the car, reached under the front seat, and picked up the box.

State v. Absher, 34 N.C. App. 197 (1977). While officers were executing a search warrant to search for marijuana, they seized a ledger book that contained names with dollar signs beside them. The ledger was properly seized under the plain view doctrine because (1) a nexus existed between the item seized and marijuana possession; (2) the item was in plain view; and (3) the discovery of the item was inadvertent (see *State v. White*, discussed above, about the inadvertence requirement) because the officers did not have probable cause to search for the ledger before they executed the search warrant—they only had some information that it might be there. *See also* State v. Zimmerman, 23 N.C. App. 396 (1974); State v. Wynn, 45 N.C. App. 267 (1980) (mere expectation that evidence will be discovered does not negate the inadvertence element).

State v. Whitley, 33 N.C. App. 753 (1977). Shining a flashlight into a car properly may be used to support an officer's observation under the plain view doctrine. *See also* State v. Wynn, 45 N.C. App. 267 (1980).

State v. Spruill, 33 N.C. App. 731 (1977). An officer who looked at a car's wheels and rims did not conduct a search under the Fourth Amendment, because anyone could have seen them by looking at the car.

State v. Young, 21 N.C. App. 369 (1974). Officers went to the defendant's trailer to talk to him about a murder. The defendant was last seen with the murder victim, who had bled profusely from the attack. After the officers discovered that the trailer had burned down, they saw the defendant's car, which appeared to have blood stains on the door, door handles, and bumper. The officers properly seized the car as evidence of murder based on the plain view doctrine. The seizure was inadvertent (see *State v. White*, discussed above, concerning the inadvertence requirement), because the officers had intended to look for the defendant rather than search for evidence.

FEDERAL APPELLATE COURTS

United States v. Taylor, 90 F.3d 903 (4th Cir. 1996). Two law enforcement officers went to the defendant's home to return a handgun pursuant to a court order. As they approached the front door, they could clearly see into a well-lit dining room through unclosed vertical blinds in a picture window. The court ruled, based on these facts, that the defendant did not possess a reasonable expectation of privacy from the officers' observations, and thus their observations were not a search under the Fourth Amendment.

United States v. Williams, 41 F.3d 192 (4th Cir. 1994). An officer properly conducted a warrantless search of five legally seized packages located in lost luggage at an airport because the fact that they contained cocaine was clearly indicated (the court stated that their contents were a "foregone conclusion") based on (1) the manner in which the cocaine was packaged—each package apparently weighed about one kilogram and was heavily wrapped in cellophane with a brown opaque material inside; (2) the officer's firm belief, based on 10 years' experience, that packages appearing in this manner always contained narcotics; (3) an airline baggage agent's belief that the packages contained narcotics; and (4) the fact that the only items found in the suitcase besides the five packages of cocaine were towels, dirty blankets, and a shirt with a cigarette burn.

G & G Jewelry, Inc. v. City of Oakland, 989 F.2d 1093 (9th Cir. 1993). An officer's warrantless seizure of stolen property being held at a pawn shop under a pawn agreement was proper under the plain view theory if the seizure was for investigatory purposes—but not if the stolen property was seized simply to return it to the rightful owner.

United States v. Moreno, 897 F.2d 26 (2d Cir. 1990). An officer with 16 years' experience investigating drug offenses looked into a bag that was opened by the defendant and saw a brick-shaped package wrapped in brown paper and tape, which the officer believed, based on his experience, to contain cocaine. The court ruled that the officer had probable cause to seize the package, considering also that the defendant was extremely nervous and falsely stated that the bag contained food.

United States v. Thompson, 837 F.2d 673 (5th Cir. 1988). The defendant's keys were lawfully taken from him for an inventory when he was jailed. The officer's later examination of these keys was not a search, because once property has been seized with proper justification and is in plain view of government officials, the owner no longer has a reasonable expectation of privacy in that property, and it may be seized without a warrant.

United States v. Williams, 822 F.2d 1174 (D.C. Cir. 1987). An officer's touching a bag to determine if it contained a weapon supplied probable cause to believe that heroin was inside, based on the officer's training and experience. The officer's plain touch revealed its contents.

GPS and Other Tracking Devices

(This topic is discussed on page 207.)

United States v. Jones, 132 S. Ct. 945 (2012). The Court ruled that the government's installation of a GPS tracking device on a vehicle and its use of that device to monitor the vehicle's movements on public streets constitute a "search" within the meaning of the Fourth Amendment. Officers who suspected that the defendant was involved in drug trafficking installed a GPS device without a valid search warrant on the undercarriage of a vehicle while it was parked in a public parking lot in Maryland. Over the next 28 days, the government used the device to track the vehicle's movements and once had to replace the device's battery when the vehicle was parked in a different public lot in Maryland. By means of signals from multiple satellites, the device established the vehicle's location within 50 to 100 feet and communicated that location by cellular phone to a government computer. It relayed more than 2,000 pages of data over the four-week period. The defendant was charged with several drug offenses. He unsuccessfully sought to suppress the evidence obtained through the GPS device. The government argued before the United States Supreme Court that a warrant was not required for the GPS device. Concluding that the evidence should have been suppressed, the Court characterized the government's conduct as having "physically occupied private property for the purpose of obtaining information." Thus, the Court had "no doubt that such a physical intrusion would have been considered a 'search' within the meaning of the Fourth Amendment when it was adopted." The Court declined to address whether the defendant had a reasonable expectation of privacy in the undercarriage of his car and in the car's locations on the public roads, concluding that such an analysis was not required when the intrusion—as here—"encroached on a protected area."

United States v. Karo, 468 U.S. 705 (1984). The warrantless installation of a beeper in a can of ether with the owner's consent and the later transfer of the can with the beeper to the defendant was not a search or seizure under the Fourth Amendment, and therefore it did not violate the defendant's Fourth Amendment rights. However, monitoring a beeper inside a private residence is a search under the Fourth Amendment and requires a search warrant, unless exigent circumstances exist.

United States v. Knotts, 460 U.S. 276 (1983). Monitoring a beeper signal in a container while the automobile in which the container was placed traveled on public highways and then drove up to a cabin was not a search or seizure under the Fourth Amendment, and therefore it did not violate the defendant's Fourth Amendment rights. [Author's note: Three federal appellate courts have either ruled or indicated that *Knotts* applies to GPS devices. United States v. Pineda-Moreno, 591 F.3d 1212 (9th Cir. 2010) (GPS device attached to undercarriage of vehicle and then monitored); United States v. Marquez, 605 F.3d 604 (8th Cir. 2010); United States v. Garcia, 474 F.3d 994 (7th Cir. 2007). However, another federal appellate court ruled in *United States v. Maynard*, 615 F.3d 544 (D.C. Cir. 2010), that "prolonged" GPS tracking (in this case, 24 hours a day for four weeks), even in public places, is a search under the Fourth Amendment and requires justification (which usually means probable cause and judicial authorization—either a search warrant or court order).]

State v. Hendricks, 43 N.C. App. 245 (1979). The court's ruling and statements in its opinion on using beepers must be reconsidered in light of the later United States Supreme Court cases, *United States v. Knotts* and *United States v. Karo*, discussed above, and the definitions of search and seizure in *United States v. Jacobsen*, 466 U.S. 109 (1984).

United States v. McIver, 186 F.3d 1119 (9th Cir. 1999). The placement of a magnetic electronic tracking device on the undercarriage of a vehicle was not a search or seizure under the Fourth Amendment. Also, the entry on the driveway of the defendant's residence to place the device on the vehicle, when the driveway was outside the curtilage and was open to observation by passersby and not enclosed by a fence or gate, was not a search under the Fourth Amendment—even assuming, arguendo, that the officers committed a trespass by entering the driveway.

United States v. Jones, 31 F.3d 1304 (4th Cir. 1994). A postal inspector's use of an electronic tracking device to monitor the movement of a government mail pouch was not a search under the Fourth Amendment when the defendant stole the mail pouch and hid it in his van.

Historical Cell-Site Information

State v. Perry, ___ N.C. App. ___, 776 S.E. 2d 528 (2015). The court ruled that no Fourth Amendment violation occurred when law enforcement officers obtained the defendant's cell-site location information (CSLI) from his service provider, AT&T, without a search warrant based on probable cause. The court noted that while courts have held that "real time" CSLI may be obtained only pursuant to a warrant supported by probable cause, the Stored Communications Act (SCA) allows for access to "historical" information upon a lesser showing. It continued: "The distinguishing characteristic separating historical records from 'real-time' information is the former shows where the cell phone has been located at some point in the past, whereas the latter shows where the phone is presently located through the use of GPS or precision location data." The court concluded that the CSLI at issue was historical information:

> [Officers] followed Defendant's historical travel by entering the coordinates of cell tower "pings" provided by AT&T into a Google Maps search engine to determine the physical location of the last tower "pinged." Defendant's cell phone was never contacted, "pinged," or its precise location directly tracked by the officers. The officers did not interact with Defendant's cell phone, nor was any of the information received either directly from the cell phone or in "real time." All evidence shows the cell tower site location information provided by AT&T was historical stored third-party records and properly disclosed under the court's order as expressly provided in the SCA.

The court found it significant that an officer testified that there was a five- to seven-minute delay in the CSLI that he received from AT&T. The court went on to conclude that retrieval of the "historical" information was not a search under the Fourth Amendment. Noting that the U.S. Supreme Court has not decided whether "historical" CSLI raises a Fourth Amendment issue, the question is one of first impression in North Carolina. The court distinguished the United States Supreme Court's ruling in *United States v. Jones*, 132 S. Ct. 945 (2012) (government's installation of a GPS tracking device on a vehicle and its use of that device to monitor the vehicle's movements on public streets constitutes a "search" within the meaning of the Fourth Amendment) in three respects. First, unlike in *Jones*, here there was no physical trespass on the defendant's property. Second, the tracking in question here was not "real-time"—the court reiterated that "officers only received the coordinates of historical cell tower 'pings' after they had been recorded and stored by AT&T, a third

party." Third, the trespass in *Jones* was not authorized by a warrant or a court order of any kind, whereas here a court order was entered. And, most importantly, *Jones* did not rely on the third-party doctrine. Citing decisions from the Third, Fifth, and Eleventh Circuits, the court held that obtaining the CSLI did not constitute a search under the Fourth Amendment. The court distinguished the recent Fourth Circuit opinion in *United States v. Graham*, 796 F.3d 332 (4th Cir. 2015), *government's petition for rehearing en banc granted*, 624 Fed. Appx. 75 (4th Cir. 2015), on the ground that in that case the government obtained the defendant's historical CSLI for an extended period of time. Here, only two days of information were at issue. The court rejected the *Graham* court's conclusion that the third-party doctrine did not apply to CSLI information because the defendants did not voluntarily disclose it to their service providers. The court continued, concluding that even if it were to find that a search warrant based on probable cause was required, the Fourth Amendment's good faith exception to the exclusionary rule would apply.

Dogs
(This topic is discussed on page 209.)

UNITED STATES SUPREME COURT

Florida v. Harris, 133 S. Ct. 1050 (2013). The Court ruled that the dog sniff in this case provided probable cause to search a vehicle. The Court rejected the ruling of the Florida Supreme Court that would have required the prosecution to present, in every case, an exhaustive set of records, including a log of the dog's performance in the field, to establish the dog's reliability. The Court found this demand "inconsistent with the 'flexible, common-sense standard' of probable cause." It instructed:

> In short, a probable-cause hearing focusing on a dog's alert should proceed much like any other. The court should allow the parties to make their best case, consistent with the usual rules of criminal procedure. And the court should then evaluate the proffered evidence to decide what all the circumstances demonstrate. If the State has produced proof from controlled settings that a dog performs reliably in detecting drugs, and the defendant has not contested that showing, then the court should find probable cause. If, in contrast, the defendant has challenged the State's

case (by disputing the reliability of the dog overall or of a particular alert), then the court should weigh the competing evidence. In all events, the court should not prescribe, as the Florida Supreme Court did, an inflexible set of evidentiary requirements. The question—similar to every inquiry into probable cause—is whether all the facts surrounding a dog's alert, viewed through the lens of common sense, would make a reasonably prudent person think that a search would reveal contraband or evidence of a crime. A sniff is up to snuff when it meets that test.

Applying that test to the drug dog's sniff in the case at hand, the Court found that it had been satisfied and ruled that there was probable cause to search the defendant's vehicle.

Florida v. Jardines, 133 S. Ct. 1409 (2013). The Court ruled that officers' use of a drug-sniffing dog on a homeowner's porch to investigate the contents of the home is a "search" within the meaning of the Fourth Amendment. The Court's reasoning was based on the theory that the officers engaged in a physical intrusion of a constitutionally protected area. Applying that principle, the Court ruled:

> The officers were gathering information in an area belonging to [the defendant] and immediately surrounding his house—in the curtilage of the house, which we have held enjoys protection as part of the home itself. And they gathered that information by physically entering and occupying the area to engage in conduct not explicitly or implicitly permitted by the homeowner.

The Court did not decide the case on a reasonable expectation of privacy analysis.

Illinois v. Caballes, 543 U.S. 405 (2005). The defendant was lawfully stopped for speeding. While the stopping officer was writing a warning ticket, another officer arrived and walked a drug detection dog around the defendant's vehicle. The dog alerted to the trunk and a search discovered marijuana. The entire incident lasted less than 10 minutes. The Court stated that the issue in this case was a narrow one: whether the Fourth Amendment requires reasonable, articulable suspicion to justify using a drug detection dog to sniff a vehicle during a legitimate traffic stop. The Court noted that a seizure justified solely by the interest in issuing a warning ticket

can become unlawful if it is prolonged beyond the time reasonably required to complete that mission. The Court stated that the state court had reviewed the stopping officer's conversations with the defendant and the precise timing of his radio transmissions to the dispatcher to determine whether the officer had improperly extended the duration of the stop to enable the dog sniff to occur. The Court accepted the state court's conclusion that the duration of the stop in this case was entirely justified by the traffic offense and the ordinary inquiries incident to such a stop. The Court noted that the state appellate court had ruled, however, that the use of the drug detection dog converted the encounter from a lawful traffic stop into a drug investigation, and because the shift in purpose was not supported by reasonable suspicion that the defendant possessed illegal drugs, it violated the Fourth Amendment. The Court rejected this analysis and ruling. It stated that conducting a dog sniff would not change the character of a traffic stop that is lawful at its inception and otherwise conducted in a reasonable manner, unless the dog sniff itself violated the defendant's Fourth Amendment right to privacy. The Court ruled that the dog sniff did not do so, relying on *United States v. Jacobsen*, 466 U.S. 109 (1984); *United States v. Place*, 462 U.S. 696 (1983); and *City of Indianapolis v. Edmond*, 531 U.S. 32 (2000); and distinguishing *Kyllo v. United States*, 533 U.S. 27 (2001). The Court stated that a dog sniff conducted during a lawful traffic stop that reveals no information other than the location of a substance that a person had no right to possess does not violate the Fourth Amendment.

[Author's note: (1) The United States Supreme Court in *City of Indianapolis v. Edmond*, 531 U.S. 32 (2000), ruled that a checkpoint for which the primary purpose was drug detection violated the Fourth Amendment. The *Caballes* ruling did not change the *Edmond* ruling. For example, if officers walked a drug dog around all vehicles initially stopped at a DWI or license checkpoint (in contrast to walking a drug dog around a car after the driver had been lawfully detained at the checkpoint for further investigation for a valid reason), then a court would likely rule that the primary purpose of the checkpoint was drug detection, not DWI or license checks. (2) The detention in *Caballes* took about 10 minutes. Absent the driver's consent to remain at the location of the traffic stop or an officer's reasonable suspicion of criminal activity to justify a further detention, the duration of a typical traffic stop would likely become unconstitutionally long if the driver was detained solely because the officer was waiting for a drug dog to arrive, the officer had already completed the necessary actions related to the traffic stop, and the time spent awaiting the drug dog measurably extended the duration of the stop. *See generally* Arizona v. Johnson, 555 U.S. 323 (2009); State v. Brimmer, 187 N.C. App. 451 (2007).]

United States v. Place, 462 U.S. 696 (1983). Using a drug-sniffing dog to examine the outside of luggage during a temporary seizure in a public place is not a search under the Fourth Amendment. Although a person has a Fourth Amendment privacy interest in the contents of his or her luggage, a dog sniff does not reveal its contents unless it contains contraband narcotics, and the dog sniff does not require that the luggage be opened. *See also* City of Indianapolis v. Edmond, 531 U.S. 32 (2000) (exterior sniff of car by a dog is not a search); Jennings v. Joshua Independent School District, 877 F.2d 313 (5th Cir. 1989) (using trained dogs to sniff cars parked in public parking lots was not a search under Fourth Amendment); United States v. Roby, 122 F.3d 1120 (8th Cir. 1997) (use of dog to sniff rooms from hallway of hotel was not a search under Fourth Amendment); United States v. Colyer, 878 F.2d 469 (D.C. Cir. 1989) (dog sniff from public corridor for drugs in train sleeper compartment was not a search under Fourth Amendment); United States v. Vasquez, 909 F.2d 235 (7th Cir. 1990) (using dog to sniff contents of garage while dog was in public alley did not constitute a search under Fourth Amendment); United States v. Morales-Zamora, 914 F.2d 200 (10th Cir. 1990) (walking a drug dog around the exterior of a vehicle while it was lawfully stopped for a license check was not a search under Fourth Amendment); United States v. Rodriguez-Morales, 929 F.2d 780 (1st Cir. 1991) (similar ruling; impounded vehicle); State v. McLamb, 70 N.C. App. 712 (1984) (court indicated that using dogs in open fields and around abandoned vehicles did not violate Fourth Amendment).

NORTH CAROLINA SUPREME COURT

State v. Miller, 367 N.C. 702 (2014) (emphasis in original) (citation omitted). The court ruled that a police dog's instinctive action, unguided and undirected by the police, that brings into plain view evidence not otherwise in plain view is not a search under the Fourth Amendment. Responding to a burglar alarm, officers arrived at the defendant's home with a police dog, Jack. The officers deployed Jack to search the premises for intruders. Jack went from room to room until he reached a side bed-

room, where he remained. When an officer entered to investigate, Jack was sitting on the bedroom floor staring at a dresser drawer, alerting the officer to the presence of drugs. The officer opened the drawer and found a brick of marijuana. Leaving the drugs there, the officer and Jack continued the protective sweep. Jack stopped in front of a closet and began barking at the closet door, alerting the officer to the presence of a human suspect. Unlike the passive sit and stare alert that Jack used to signal for the presence of narcotics, Jack was trained to bark to signal the presence of human suspects. Officers opened the closet and found two large black trash bags on the closet floor. When Jack nuzzled a bag, marijuana was visible. The officers secured the premises and obtained a search warrant. At issue on appeal was whether Jack's nuzzling of the bags in the closet violated the Fourth Amendment. The court of appeals determined that Jack's nuzzling of the bags was an action unrelated to the objectives of the authorized intrusion, creating a new invasion of the defendant's privacy unjustified by the exigent circumstance that validated the entry. That court viewed Jack as an instrumentality of the police and concluded that "his actions, regardless of whether they are instinctive or not, are no different than those undertaken by an officer." 228 N.C. App. 496 (2013). The North Carolina Supreme Court disagreed, concluding that "Jack's actions *are* different from the actions of an officer, particularly if the dog's actions were instinctive, undirected, and unguided by the police." It ruled:

> If a police dog is acting without assistance, facilitation, or other intentional action by its handler (. . . acting "instinctively"), it cannot be said that a State or governmental actor intends to do anything. In such a case, the dog is simply being a dog. If, however, police misconduct is present, or if the dog is acting at the direction or guidance of its handler, then it can be readily inferred from the dog's action that there is an intent to find something or to obtain information. . . . In short, we hold that a police dog's instinctive action, unguided and undirected by the police, that brings evidence not otherwise in plain view into plain view is not a search within the meaning of the Fourth Amendment or Article I, Section 20 of the North Carolina Constitution. Therefore, the decision of the Court of Appeals that Jack was

an instrumentality of the police, regardless of whether his actions were instinctive, is reversed.

The court remanded for the trial court to decide whether Jack's nuzzling in this case was in fact instinctive, undirected, and unguided by the officers.

NORTH CAROLINA COURT OF APPEALS

State v. Smith, 222 N.C. App. 253 (2012). On what it described as an issue of first impression in North Carolina, the court ruled that a drug dog's positive alert at the front side driver's door of a motor vehicle is insufficient evidence to support probable cause to conduct a warrantless search of the person of a recent passenger of the vehicle who was standing outside the vehicle.

State v. Washburn, 201 N.C. App. 93 (2009). An informant told an officer that the defendant kept a large quantity of drugs in a toolbox in his garage and rented a climate-controlled storage unit somewhere within the Kernersville town limits. The informant provided additional details about the defendant, his vehicle, and so forth. Another officer, provided with this information, went to the only climate-controlled storage facility in Kernersville. The officer had confirmed that the defendant rented a unit there as well as other details provided by the informant. With the consent of the facility's manager, a drug dog was permitted to walk the hallway within one of the buildings containing the defendant's unit. The dog alerted to the defendant's unit, and officers then obtained a search warrant and searched it. Cocaine and drug paraphernalia were discovered, and officers then obtained a search warrant for the defendant's residence and searched it. The court ruled, relying on *United States v. Place*, 462 U.S. 696 (1983), and other cases, that the use of the dog to sweep the common area of the storage facility did not violate the defendant's Fourth Amendment rights. The dog sniff revealed only the presence of illegal drugs; that does not compromise any legitimate privacy interest. In addition, the officers were legally in the common hallway of the building with the consent of the facility's manager. The defendant did not possess a reasonable expectation of privacy in the common hallway. The court also rejected the defendant's argument that there was no nexus between the presence of cocaine in the storage unit and the existence of illegal drugs at the defendant's residence to provide probable cause to issue a search warrant for the residence. The court discussed in its opinion the informant's reliability and basis of knowledge

State v. Branch, 177 N.C. App. 104 (2006). Officers were conducting a driver's license checkpoint. They stopped all cars approaching an intersection and quickly assessed whether the registration and license were valid. Officers with a drug dog unit were available for assistance. The defendant was stopped at the checkpoint by an officer who recognized her as someone whom he had previously arrested for drug possession and whose driver's license might be revoked. The defendant presented a duplicate driver's license. The officer testified at the suppression hearing that duplicate licenses are often used by drivers whose originally issued licenses have been taken due to license revocations. Another officer, who was with the drug dog unit, testified that he saw the defendant and recalled previously issuing her a citation for a moving violation for which she had failed to appear in court—an act that would normally result in a license revocation. After the two officers conferred, the defendant was directed to the side of the road so that they could check for outstanding warrants and the status of her license. While that check was being done, an officer took a drug dog for a walk around the defendant's vehicle. The dog alerted. A search resulted in the discovery of illegal drugs and the defendant's conviction. In the defendant's initial appeal to the North Carolina Court of Appeals, 162 N.C. App. 707 (2004), the court ruled that there was reasonable suspicion to detain the defendant in her vehicle while the check was being done based on the interaction of two facts: presentation of a duplicate license and failure to appear in court. However, the court also ruled in the initial appeal that these facts did not support reasonable suspicion to walk the drug dog around the car's exterior. After this ruling was issued, the United States Supreme Court ruled in *Illinois v. Caballes*, 543 U.S. 405 (2005), that walking a drug dog around a vehicle while the driver was lawfully detained as an officer issued a warning ticket for speeding did not violate the Fourth Amendment. The United States Supreme Court granted the State of North Carolina's petition for a writ of certiorari to review the *Branch* ruling, vacated the ruling, and remanded it to the North Carolina Court of Appeals for further consideration in light of *Caballes*. The court of appeals on remand stated that once the lawfulness of a defendant's detention was established, the *Caballes* ruling required no additional justification under the Fourth Amendment to walk the drug dog around the exterior of the defendant's vehicle.

State v. Fisher, 141 N.C. App. 448 (2000). The court stated that a dog sniff of a vehicle's exterior is not a search under the Fourth Amendment, citing prior state appellate cases finding that the dog sniffs of the following objects were not searches: a passenger's luggage, *State v. Odum*, 119 N.C. App. 676 (1995); a briefcase, *State v. McDaniels*, 103 N.C. App. 175 (1991); an airplane, *State v. Darack*, 66 N.C. App. 608 (1984); and a safety deposit box, *State v. Rogers*, 43 N.C. App. 475 (1979). The court also noted similar statements in *United States v. Place*, 462 U.S. 696 110 (1983), and *City of Indianapolis v. Edmond*, 531 U.S. 32 (2000). The court ruled, citing *State v. Falana*, 129 N.C. App. 813 (1998), and *State v. McClendon*, 130 N.C. App. 368 (1998), *aff'd*, 350 N.C. 630 (1999), that the officers in this case lacked reasonable suspicion to detain the defendant beyond the scope of the stop for the driving while license revoked charge; thus the dog sniff occurred during an illegal detention and violated the Fourth Amendment.

State v. McDaniels, 103 N.C. App. 175 (1991), *aff'd*, 331 N.C. 112 (1992). Officers properly stopped a car and obtained from the driver consent to search the car. During the search, an officer picked up a briefcase from the floor and asked both the driver and the defendant-passenger if it was theirs. The defendant-passenger stated that the briefcase belonged to his cousin, and he objected to a search of it without a warrant. The officer placed the briefcase on the backseat and advised the driver that he wished to use a drug detection dog, which had been brought to the scene. Neither the driver nor the defendant-passenger objected. The dog alerted positively to the presence of drugs in the briefcase, and both the driver and defendant-passenger were arrested. The court ruled that the dog's sniffing of the exterior of the briefcase, based on these facts, was not a search under the Fourth Amendment. The court also ruled that the dog's positive alert to the briefcase established probable cause to issue a search warrant to search the briefcase, because the dog was properly trained and certified to alert to cocaine, heroin, marijuana, and hashish. *See also* United States v. Hill, 195 F.3d 258 (6th Cir. 1999) (positive alert by properly trained and reliable drug detection dog provided probable cause to search U-Haul truck).

FEDERAL APPELLATE COURTS

United States v. Sturgis, 238 F.3d 956 (8th Cir. 2001). A two-hour wait for a drug dog did not violate the Fourth Amendment because officers had probable cause to arrest the detained defendant.

B.C. v. Plumas Unified School District, 192 F.3d 1260 (9th Cir. 1999). A dog sniff of a person is a search under the Fourth Amendment, and the suspicionless sniffing of students in this case was unreasonable. *See also* Horton v. Goose Creek Indep. Sch. Dist., 690 F.2d 470 (5th Cir. 1982) (similar ruling). *But see* Doe v. Renfrow, 631 F.2d 91 (7th Cir. 1980) (dog sniff of person is not a search).

Hearn v. Board of Public Education, 191 F.3d 1329 (11th Cir. 1999). A dog sniff of a car in a school parking lot was not a search under the Fourth Amendment. A drug dog's alerting to a car provided probable cause to search the car without a search warrant.

United States v. Sundby, 186 F.3d 873 (8th Cir. 1999). To establish a dog's reliability, an affidavit for a search warrant need only state that the dog has been trained and certified to detect drugs.

United States v. Reed, 141 F.3d 644 (6th Cir. 1998). Even if a drug dog instinctively opened a dresser drawer when alerting to illegal drugs inside and an officer thereby made a plain view observation inside the drawer, the dog's action—absent the officer's misconduct—did not violate the Fourth Amendment.

United States v. Jeffus, 22 F.3d 554 (4th Cir. 1994). The use of a drug dog to walk around the defendant's car while it was lawfully stopped for a traffic offense was not a search under the Fourth Amendment. When the dog alerted positively for the presence of drugs, officers had probable cause to search the car without a search warrant.

United States v. Ludwig, 10 F.3d 1523 (10th Cir. 1993). The use of a drug dog to randomly sniff vehicles in a motel parking lot open to the public was not a search under the Fourth Amendment. The dog's alerting to the defendant's car in the parking lot gave an officer probable cause to conduct a warrantless search of the car.

Thermal Imagers

(This topic is discussed on page 207.)

Kyllo v. United States, 533 U.S. 27 (2001). A law enforcement officer suspected that marijuana was being grown in a person's home. The officer used a thermal imager to scan the home while in his vehicle on a public street. Based on tips from informants, utility bills, and the results of the thermal imaging, a judge issued a search warrant to authorize a search of the home, which revealed more than one hundred marijuana plants. The Court ruled that the use of a thermal imager aimed at a private home from a public street to detect the relative amounts of heat within a home constitutes a search under the Fourth Amendment. The Court stated that obtaining by sense-enhancing technology any information concerning the interior of a home that could not otherwise have been obtained without physical intrusion into a constitutionally protected area constitutes a search—at least when, as in this case, the technology in question is not in general public use. [Author's note: The Court's ruling requires probable cause and a search warrant to conduct thermal imaging of a home, absent exigent circumstances to excuse the requirement of a search warrant.] *See also* United States v. Elkins, 300 F.3d 638 (6th Cir. 2002) (court notes but does not decide issue of whether *Kyllo* ruling applies to use of thermal imager directed at commercial building).

Recording of Conversations When One Party Consents

United States v. White, 401 U.S. 745 (1970). No Fourth Amendment violation occurred when government agents listened to conversations between the defendant and a cooperating informant, who had a radio transmitter concealed on his person. *See also* United States v. Caceres, 440 U.S. 741 n.2 (1979); *On Lee v. United States*, 343 U.S. 747 (1952).

Lopez v. United States, 373 U.S. 427 (1963). No Fourth Amendment violation occurred when an undercover federal agent secretly recorded his conversation with the defendant in the defendant's office.

State v. Levan, 326 N.C. 155 (1990). The court adopted under the North Carolina Constitution various rulings of the United States Supreme Court that permit law enforcement officers to use an agent to secretly record pre-arrest conversations with a defendant—see, for example, *United States v. White*, discussed above.

United States v. Miller, 720 F.2d 227 (1st Cir. 1983). No violation of the Fourth Amendment or the federal wiretapping law occurred when only one party to a telephone conversation consented to the recording of the conversation. *See also* State v. Branch, 288 N.C. 514 (1975); State v. Thompson, 332 N.C. 204 (1992). [Author's note: The state wiretapping law, G.S. 15A-287(a), is the same as the federal wiretapping law on this issue.]

Obtaining a Customer's Bank Records

(*This topic is discussed on page 222.*)

United States v. Miller, 425 U.S. 435 (1976). A depositor has no reasonable expectation of privacy in copies of checks and other bank records that are in the bank's possession.

In re Superior Court Order, 315 N.C. 378 (1986). [Author's note: Since this case was decided, legislation—G.S. 53B-1 through -10—was enacted that now regulates access to a customer's financial records. These statutory provisions must be followed. See the discussion in Chapter 3.] A superior court judge has the inherent power to order a bank to disclose a customer's bank account records if reasonable suspicion exists that a crime was committed and that the records probably will relate to the investigation of that crime (but the court found that the district attorney's petition in this case failed to set out facts to support the order). A judge also may order the bank not to disclose the examination of records to the customer for a specified period if the judge finds that the disclosure could impede the investigation. (Of course, if probable cause existed that a crime had been committed, a search warrant to seize the records could be obtained or—if a criminal charge was pending in court—a subpoena could be issued to the bank to produce the records).

United States v. Kington, 801 F.2d 733 (5th Cir. 1986). Congress did not intend that evidence obtained in violation of the federal Right to Financial Privacy Act be suppressed when it did not authorize that remedy; therefore suppression is inappropriate. The rationale of this ruling would likely apply to a violation of North Carolina's Financial Privacy Act (G.S. 53B-1 through -10, discussed in Chapter 3).

Prison or Jail Cell, Mail, and Telephone Calls

State v. Wiley, 355 N.C. 592 (2002). The defendant, a jail inmate awaiting trial for first-degree murder, asked jail personnel to give an unsealed letter to the defendant's father, who had visited the defendant and was still in the waiting room. Pursuant to jail policy concerning incoming and outgoing mail that does not have the words "legal mail" written on it and is not addressed to an attorney, a deputy sheriff scanned the letter to ascertain that there was no contraband or information concerning a jail break or possible harm to jail personnel and to make sure that inmates were not communicating between cell blocks. (Inmates are informed of the mail policy when they enter the jail and commonly leave their nonlegal mail unsealed because they are aware that it will be examined by jail personnel.) The deputy sheriff noticed information in the letter related to the pending murder trial. He made a copy of the letter, gave the original to the defendant's father, and gave the copy to the state's investigators.

The court ruled, citing *Stroud v. United States*, 251 U.S. 15 (1919), and several other federal and state cases, that the defendant did not have a reasonable expectation of privacy in his nonlegal mail. The court stated that when prisoners or pretrial detainees are made aware that their nonlegal mail will be subject to scrutiny before reaching its intended recipient, pursuant to institutional policies to maintain order and safety, later examination of such mail does not violate their Fourth Amendment rights. Copying and forwarding such mail also does not violate the Fourth Amendment. For an analysis of mail regulation in jails, see Jamie Markham, *Mail Regulation in the Jail*, N.C. Crim. L. Blog (Dec. 7, 2015), http://nccriminallaw.sog.unc.edu/mail-regulation-in-the-jail/.

State v. Martin, 322 N.C. 229 (1988). The court applied the ruling of *Hudson v. Palmer*, 468 U.S. 517 (1984) (prisoner has no reasonable expectation of privacy in a prison cell), to a pretrial detainee's jail cell and ruled that a jailer's search of the cell and his reading of the defendant's notebook and discovery of a letter to the defendant's brother urging him to commit perjury at trial did not violate the Fourth Amendment. The jailer could have read something in the notebook that would have enabled him better to maintain order in the jail.

State v. Troy, 198 N.C. App. 396 (2009). The defendant was being held at a detention center in South Carolina. When the defendant made telephone calls on March 31, 2002, both he and the person he called heard a recorded message that stated, "[t]his call is subject to being monitored and recorded. Thank you for using Evercom." A fellow inmate arranged three-way telephone calls on behalf of the defendant on April 2 and April 4, 2002. The defendant sought to suppress the contents of the recorded April telephone calls because the defendant was not provided with a recorded message that his conversations could be monitored or recorded. The court ruled, relying on *State v. Price*, 170 N.C. App. 57 (2005), that the recordings of the April telephone conversations did not violate federal or state eavesdropping laws because the defendant impliedly consented to the recordings. The defendant was aware from the March 31, 2002, calls that telephone calls from the detention center were subject to being recorded.

State v. Hocutt, 177 N.C. App. 341 (2006). While in jail, the defendant made incriminating statements over the phone to his girlfriend and to his brother, which were recorded pursuant to jail policy. Inmates receive an informational handbook concerning this policy, notices are posted in the cell blocks telling inmates that their telephone calls are monitored, and before being connected, both the caller and the person being called hear a recorded warning that "all calls are subject to monitoring and recording," except for "attorney calls." The court ruled that the defendant's recorded jail telephone conversations were properly obtained under the Fourth, Sixth, and Fourteenth Amendments.

State v. Price, 170 N.C. App. 57 (2005). While in jail awaiting trial, the defendant placed telephone calls to his mother. The jail's phone system played, for all outgoing calls from the jail, a recording heard by both parties to the call that stated in pertinent part: "This call is subject to monitoring and recording." These calls were recorded—as were all inmate calls at the jail—and introduced into evidence at the defendant's trial. The court ruled that the defendant impliedly consented under both federal and state law to the monitoring and recording of the telephone calls.

State v. Fuller, 166 N.C. App. 548 (2004). Jail personnel seized and read the defendant's letters that were not marked "legal," were given to them to be mailed with the outgoing mail, and were not addressed to an attorney. The court ruled, relying on *State v. Wiley*, 355 N.C. 592 (2002), that the defendant did not have a reasonable expectation of privacy in the letters and his Fourth Amendment rights were not violated. The court also ruled, relying on *State v. Wallace*, 162 N.C. 623 (1913), that these letters to the defendant's wife were not inadmissible under the marital communications privilege when a third party—jail personnel lawfully in possession of the letters and authorized to read them—was effectively a party to the communication. See also *State v. Martin*, 322 N.C. 229 (1988), discussed above; *State v. Wiley*, 355 N.C. 592 (2002), discussed above; *State v. Kennedy*, 58 N.C. App. 810 (1982) (the defendant, who was not an inmate, wrote and mailed letter to a prison inmate; a correctional officer following routine procedure opened the letter and examined it for contraband; he saw reference to a shotgun in the letter and read further, and the letter revealed defendant's participation in an armed robbery; the officer gave the letter to a police officer; the court ruled that a sender of the letter had no reasonable expectation of privacy in the letter); *Altizer v. Deeds*, 191 F.3d 540 (4th Cir. 1999) (opening and inspection of an inmate's outgoing nonlegal mail is reasonably related to legitimate penological interests and is constitutional); and *Lavado v. Keohane*, 992 F.2d 601 (6th Cir. 1993) (opening incoming prisoner mail pursuant to uniform policy is constitutional).

Willis v. Artuz, 301 F.3d 65 (2d Cir. 2002). The warrantless search of a convicted prisoner's cell, conducted at the request of officers who were seeking evidence of an uncharged crime, did not violate the prisoner's Fourth Amendment rights, even though the search did not serve any purpose related to prison security. The court distinguished *United States v. Cohen*, 796 F.2d 20 (2d Cir. 1986) (pretrial detainee's Fourth Amendment rights were violated when prosecutor instigated warrantless search of jail to obtain evidence for pending trial).

United States v. Peoples, 250 F.3d 630 (8th Cir. 2001). The recording of conversations between an inmate and visitor made with an internal communication device (physically resembling a telephone handset) and used while the visitor and inmate were separated by a glass partition was not a violation of federal eavesdropping law because neither had a reasonable expectation of privacy.

Angel v. Williams, 12 F.3d 786 (8th Cir. 1993). The tape recording of conversations between law enforcement officers and a prisoner in a jail did not violate federal wiretapping law because the officers and the prisoner did not have a reasonable expectation of privacy that their conversations would not be intercepted.

United States v. Feekes, 879 F.2d 1562 (7th Cir. 1989). The tape recording of all prisoners' telephone calls to people outside the prison (except to their lawyers) under the federal Bureau of Prisons' regulations falls within an exception to the federal wiretapping law, 18 U.S.C.A. § 2510(5)(ii). Therefore, the recording of a prisoner's telephone call to a nonlawyer did not violate the law. For cases discussing the legality of intercepting or recording telephone calls of prisoners and inmates and conversations within prisons and jails, see *United States v. Footman*, 215 F.3d 145 (1st Cir. 2000) (court upholds recording of prisoner's telephone calls based on prisoner's consent to recording, based on prior notice that is given to all prisoners that their calls, except to designated attorneys, will be recorded, and each prisoner having signed a form reflecting that understanding); *United States v. Hammond*, 286 F.3d 189 (4th Cir. 2002); *United States v. Daniels*, 902 F.2d 1238 (7th Cir. 1990); *United States v. Harrelson*, 754 F.2d 1153 (5th Cir. 1985); *United States v. Noriega*, 917 F.2d 1543 (11th Cir. 1990); *United States v. Noriega*, 764 F. Supp. 1480 (S.D. Fla. 1991); *United States v. Willoughby*, 860 F.2d 15 (2d Cir. 1988); *United States v. Amen*, 831 F.2d 373 (2d Cir. 1987); *United States v. Paul*, 614 F.2d 115 (6th Cir. 1980); *United States v. Sababu*, 891 F.2d 1308 (7th Cir. 1989); and *Campiti v. Walonis*, 611 F.2d 387 (1st Cir. 1979).

Use of Lawfully Taken Blood Sample in Unrelated Investigation

State v. Barkley, 144 N.C. App. 514 (2001). The defendant was convicted of first-degree rape. DNA evidence was introduced at trial that had been obtained from a blood sample the defendant had voluntarily given to law enforcement officers in an investigation of an unrelated murder. The court ruled, relying on cases from other jurisdictions, that a blood sample lawfully obtained in the investigation of one crime may be used as evidence in the prosecution of an unrelated crime without any additional justification under the Fourth Amendment. The court stated that once the blood was lawfully drawn from the defendant's body, he no longer had a possessory interest in it. The court also examined the facts surrounding the defendant's consent to give a blood sample in the murder investigation and ruled that a reasonable person would have understood by his conversation with the investigating law enforcement officer that his blood analysis could be used generally for investigative purposes and was not limited to the murder investigation.

Search and Seizure by Valid Consent

(*This topic is discussed on page 224.*)

Voluntariness

(*This topic is discussed on page 229.*)

Generally
UNITED STATES SUPREME COURT

United States v. Drayton, 536 U.S. 194 (2002). Three law enforcement officers—dressed in plain clothes, carrying concealed weapons, and displaying visible badges—boarded a bus while it was stopped at a bus terminal. One officer knelt at the driver's seat (the bus driver was not in the bus) without blocking the aisle or obstructing the bus exit, while two officers went to the rear of the bus. One officer stayed there while the other worked his way toward the front, speaking to passengers as he went. To avoid blocking the aisle, the officer stood next to or just behind each passenger with whom he spoke. He explained that the officers were conducting a bus interdiction to deter drugs and illegal weapons from being transported on the bus. He did not inform passengers of their right to refuse to cooperate. Defendants Drayton and Brown were seated together. Brown consented to a search of a bag in the overhead luggage rack, which revealed no contraband. The officer noted that both defendants were wearing heavy jackets and baggy pants despite the warm weather. Due to his experience, the officer knew that drug traffickers often use baggy clothing to conceal weapons or narcotics. The officer received consent from Brown to search his person after asking, "Do you mind if I check your person?" He found hard objects similar to drug packages that he had detected on other occasions and arrested Brown. The officer then received consent from Drayton after asking, "Mind if I check you?" He discovered the same hard objects, and arrested Drayton.

The Court ruled that (1) the officers did not seize the defendants during this bus boarding procedure—a reasonable person would have felt free to terminate the encounter with the officer; (2) the Fourth Amendment does not require officers to advise bus passengers of their right not to cooperate and to refuse to consent to searches; and (3) the defendants voluntarily consented to the search of their luggage and their bodies.

Ohio v. Robinette, 519 U.S. 33 (1996). An officer stopped the defendant for speeding. The defendant gave his driver's license to the officer, who ran a computer check that revealed that the defendant had no prior violations. The officer then asked the defendant to step out of his car, issued a verbal warning to the defendant, and returned his license. The officer asked the defendant if he had any illegal contraband in his car, and the defendant said "no." The officer then asked the defendant if he could search his car, and the defendant consented.

The Court rejected a lower court ruling that an officer must advise a lawfully seized defendant that the defendant is free to go before a consent to search will be recognized as voluntary. The Court noted that the Fourth Amendment requires that a consent to search must be voluntary, and voluntariness is a question of fact that must be determined from all the circumstances. An officer's warning before obtaining consent to search is not required by the Fourth Amendment for a consent to search to be valid.

Florida v. Bostick, 501 U.S. 429 (1991). Two officers boarded a bus bound from Miami to Atlanta during a stopover in Fort Lauderdale. They asked the defendant-passenger (for whom they did not have reasonable suspicion of criminal activity) for permission to inspect his ticket and identification. He consented. The ticket, from Miami to Atlanta, matched the defendant's identification

and was returned to him. The officers explained that they were narcotics agents looking for illegal drugs, and they requested the defendant's consent to search his luggage. He consented. The Florida Supreme Court ruled that the bus boarding was an illegal seizure of the passengers and thus the defendant's consent to search the luggage was tainted by the illegal seizure of the defendant.

The Court, reversing and remanding, noted two facts: (1) the officers specifically advised the defendant that he had a right to refuse to consent [Author's note: Although this fact may be relevant to the seizure issue in this case, such a warning is not required when obtaining consent to search; see *Schneckloth v. Bustamonte*, discussed below.]; and (2) although one officer carried a zipper pouch containing a pistol, the pistol was never removed from the pouch, pointed at the defendant, or otherwise used in a threatening manner. The Court rejected a *per se* rule adopted by the Florida Supreme Court that bus passengers are seized when officers board a bus because the passengers do not feel free to leave the bus to avoid the officers' questioning. The Court also rejected, in analyzing whether the facts of this case constitute a seizure, the definition of a seizure set forth in *Michigan v. Chesternut*, 486 U.S. 567 (1988), providing that a seizure occurs when a reasonable person would reasonably believe that he or she is not "free to leave." Because the defendant was a passenger on a bus that was scheduled to depart, he would not have felt free to leave the bus even if the officers had not been present. His movements were essentially confined as the natural result of his decision to take the bus—which is not related to the issue of whether the officers' conduct was coercive. The Court ruled that the appropriate inquiry is whether a reasonable person would feel free to decline the officers' requests or otherwise terminate the encounter. It stated that this inquiry applies equally to all encounters that occur on streets, on trains, at airports, and so forth. The Court also rejected defendant's argument that he must have been seized because a reasonable person would not freely consent to a search of luggage that the person knows contains drugs: the Court ruled that the proper "reasonable person" test presupposes an *innocent* person.

United States v. Watson, 423 U.S. 411 (1976). The defendant was arrested in a restaurant and removed to the street, where he gave officers consent to search his nearby car. The fact that the defendant consented while he was in custody and was not informed that he could withhold consent was insufficient to show that consent was involuntary, when no other evidence indicated that it was involuntary.

Schneckloth v. Bustamonte, 412 U.S. 218 (1973). The Court ruled that the defendant consented to a search of his car after an officer validly stopped it. Whether consent to search is voluntarily given is determined by the totality of circumstances. The State need not prove that the person who consented to the search knew of the right to refuse to consent, although such knowledge is a factor that may be considered in determining voluntariness. An officer need not give any warning of rights before obtaining consent.

Amos v. United States, 255 U.S. 313 (1921). The defendant's wife was by implication coerced into giving consent to revenue officers when they told her that they had come to search the store for revenue violations and she simply opened the store to let them in.

NORTH CAROLINA SUPREME COURT

State v. Pearson, 348 N.C. 272 (1998). Officer A stopped a car on an interstate highway that had been drifting back and forth within its lane and traveling below the speed limit. The defendant was the driver of the car, and there was a female passenger. Officer A asked the defendant to leave the vehicle and come to the patrol car. Officer A noticed that the defendant had a slight odor of alcohol about him, acted nervous, and had a rapid heart rate while in the patrol car. Officer A determined, however, that the defendant was tired, not impaired by alcohol. The defendant said that he and his fiancée had left the Charlotte area the day before and had spent the night at his parents' home in Virginia. Officer A then talked to the passenger, who was seated in the defendant's car. She said that the couple had spent the previous night in New York visiting the defendant's parents. Officer A did not see any drugs or weapons in the defendant's car. Officer A then returned to his patrol car and received the defendant's written consent to search his car. Officer B arrived and was asked by Officer A to frisk the defendant while Officer A searched the defendant's car. The officers testified at the suppression hearing that the defendant was frisked because it was standard procedure to do so when a vehicle is searched.

The court ruled that this evidence was insufficient to establish reasonable suspicion to frisk the defendant. The court noted that the defendant was polite and cooperative. The officers were not aware that the defendant had

a criminal record or drug background. The defendant had not made any movement or statement that would indicate that he had a weapon. Neither the defendant's nervousness nor the variance in the statements of the defendant and his fiancée were sufficient to justify the frisk. The court distinguished *State v. McGirt*, 122 N.C. App. 237 (1996), *aff'd*, 345 N.C. 624 (1997). The court also ruled that the defendant did not consent to be frisked. The written consent form authorized a search only of the defendant's vehicle, not a search of his person. Also, the defendant's acquiescence when Officer B told him he would frisk him was not consent, considering the circumstances of this case.

State v. Smith, 346 N.C. 794 (1997). Officers received information that illegal drugs were located in a suitcase in a bedroom in the defendant's house. The source of the information, the defendant's girlfriend who shared a bedroom with the defendant, told the officers that she would consent to a search. Officers decided to seek consent to search the house because they believed that they lacked probable cause to obtain a search warrant—officers referred to the procedure of approaching a house to ask consent to search as "knock and talk." Officers arrived at the house with a drug dog. One of the residents (a person who lived there, but who was not the girlfriend or the defendant) let them into the house. The girlfriend allowed the officers' entry into and search of the bedroom she shared with the defendant. The drug dog alerted, and the officers seized illegal drugs there. The court, relying on *Schneckloth v. Bustamonte*, 412 U.S. 218 (1973), ruled that officers who approach a residence with the intent to obtain consent to conduct a warrantless search do not violate the Fourth Amendment by simply using such a procedure. [Author's note: This ruling would apply whether or not the officers had probable cause to obtain a search warrant; see the court's excerpt from *Schneckloth* included in its opinion.] *See also* United States v. Cephas, 254 F.3d 488 (4th Cir. 2001) (similar ruling). The court also noted that the officers' subjective state of mind in using such a procedure is irrelevant, citing *Whren v. United States*, 517 U.S. 806 (1996). The court remanded the case to superior court so that the judge could make specific factual findings on the voluntariness of the consent given to the officers by the girlfriend.

State v. Williams, 314 N.C. 337 (1985). Considering all the circumstances in this case, an officer's statement to the defendant that the district attorney would be informed of his cooperation was not the factor that induced him to consent to a search of his car. There was no evidence that the defendant believed that he could expect easier treatment if he consented.

State v. Fincher, 309 N.C. 1 (1983). The defendant voluntarily and understandingly consented to a search of his bedroom, although he was 17 years old and had a low IQ and although officers told him that if he refused to give consent they would obtain a search warrant and conduct a search anyway.

State v. Brown, 306 N.C. 151 (1982). The fact that officers obtained a search warrant after the defendant voluntarily consented to a search does not negate the consent originally given, and—assuming the search warrant was valid—the State may justify a search of the defendant's apartment on either ground.

State v. Cobb, 295 N.C. 1 (1978). When a defendant is in custody at the time that he consents to a search, the State has a greater burden to show that consent was voluntary. In this case, evidence—including signed consent forms—proved that consent was voluntarily given.

State v. Long, 293 N.C. 286 (1977). A specific warning about Fourth Amendment rights is not necessary to validate a consent to search, even when the defendant is in custody. *See also* State v. Christie, 96 N.C. App. 178 (1989) (consent to search luggage during bus boarding was valid, even though defendant was not informed of his right to refuse to consent to search).

State v. Woods, 286 N.C. 612 (1975). No search occurred when the defendant's wife voluntarily took her mother and officers to the trailer where she and the defendant lived, took two rings from her blue jeans in her bedroom, and gave them to the officers. *See also* State v. Reams, 277 N.C. 391 (1970) (no search occurred when defendant's wife removed his shotgun from a closet and gave it to an officer); Coolidge v. New Hampshire, 403 U.S. 443 (1971) (similar ruling).

NORTH CAROLINA COURT OF APPEALS

State v. McMillan, 214 N.C. App. 320 (2011). The court ruled that the officers' advising the defendant that if he did not consent to giving oral swabs and surrendering certain items of clothing they would detain him until they obtained a search warrant did not negate the defendant's voluntary consent to the seizure of those items.

State v. Boyd, 207 N.C. App. 632 (2010). The court ruled that the defendant voluntarily consented to allow officers to take a saliva sample for DNA testing. The defendant was told that the sample could be used to exonerate him in ongoing investigations of break-ins and assaults on women that occurred in Charlotte in 1998. The defendant argued that because the detective failed to inform him of all of the charges that were being investigated—specifically, rape and sexual assault—his consent was involuntary. Following *State v. Barkley*, 144 N.C. App. 514 (2001), the court rejected this argument. The court concluded that the consent was voluntary even though the defendant did not know that the assaults were of a sexual nature and that a reasonable person in the defendant's position would have understood that the DNA could be used generally for investigative purposes.

State v. Medina, 205 N.C. App. 683 (2010). A warrantless search of the defendant's car was valid on grounds of consent. The court rejected the defendant's argument that his consent was invalid because the officer who procured it was not fluent in Spanish. The court noted that the defendant was nonresponsive to initial questions posed in English but that he responded when spoken to in Spanish. The officer asked simple questions about weapons or drugs, and when he gestured to the car and asked to "look," the defendant nodded in the affirmative. Although not fluent in Spanish, the officer had Spanish instruction in high school and college and the two conversed entirely in Spanish for periods of up to 30 minutes. The officer asked open-ended questions, which the defendant answered appropriately. The defendant never indicated that he did not understand a question. The court also rejected the defendant's argument that his consent was invalid because the officer wore a sidearm while seeking the consent, concluding that the mere presence of a holstered sidearm does not render consent involuntary.

State v. McLeod, 197 N.C. App. 707 (2009). Officers responded to a disturbance between the defendant and his mother at a residence where both lived. After speaking with and calming both, the officers left. Within 30 minutes, the officers were called to the residence again. The defendant was locked out of the residence and sitting in the garage area. Officer A went into the residence and spoke with the mother. Officer B remained with the defendant. The mother told Officer A that the defendant had a gun in his bedroom. Officer A then went outside to Officer B. The defendant was asked if he had a weapon, and he responded that there was a gun in the house under his bed. After receiving this information, both officers accompanied the defendant inside the residence and went to the defendant's bedroom and seized the gun. The court ruled, relying on *United States v. Hylton*, 349 F.3d 781

(4th Cir. 2003), that the officers had implied consent to enter the house and search for and seize the defendant's gun. The court reasoned that both the defendant and his mother gave consent through their words and actions.

State v. Kuegel, 195 N.C. App. 310 (2009). After receiving information that the defendant was selling marijuana and cocaine from his apartment, an officer decided to go to the apartment to conduct a knock and talk. Two other officers stationed themselves about three houses away. The officer identified himself and told the defendant that he knew the defendant had both marijuana and cocaine in the apartment and wanted his consent to search it without a search warrant. He untruthfully told the defendant that he had conducted surveillance of the apartment, had seen a lot of people coming and going, had stopped people's cars after they left the neighborhood, and had recovered either marijuana or cocaine each time he stopped someone. The defendant said, "What if I give you what I got?" The officer explained that he needed to find all the drugs inside the apartment and said that if the defendant did not feel comfortable giving consent to search, he would leave two officers at the apartment and apply for a search warrant. The defendant asked, "If I cooperate, what will you do for me?" The officer replied that he could not make any promises, but if the defendant did not have a kilo or a dead body in the apartment, he might be able to keep him out of jail for the holiday (it was December 21). The defendant invited the officers in and agreed to show them where everything was.

The defendant argued on appeal that his consent to search was not voluntary because it was the product of the officer's deceptive practices. The court ruled, relying on *State v. Sokolowski*, 344 N.C. 428 (1996) (no coercion when eight officers disarmed defendant before asking consent to search); *State v. Fincher*, 309 N.C. 1 (1983) (no coercion when officers told defendant that if he did not consent officers would get search warrant and search anyway); and *State v. Barnes*, 154 N.C. App. 111 (2002) (officer's deception in telling pedophile that victim was pregnant, in effort to elicit confession, was not sufficient to overcome defendant's will and render confession inadmissible), that the defendant's consent to search was voluntary based on the totality of circumstances.

State v. Jacobs, 162 N.C. App. 251 (2004). The defendant was convicted of several drug offenses. An officer stopped the defendant's vehicle, detained him for about three to five minutes, received consent to search the vehicle, and discovered evidence in the car and on the defendant's person. The court rejected the defendant's argument that the State failed to establish that the officer had reasonable suspicion to request the defendant's consent to search the vehicle. The State only needs to show that a consent to search is voluntary; neither reasonable suspicion nor probable cause is a prerequisite for an officer's asking for consent to search.

State v. Graham, 149 N.C. App. 215 (2002). Officers responded to a tip reporting drug activity at an apartment. They entered with consent and stated their intention to search for drugs and pat down the occupants for weapons. They noticed that the defendant continuously reached into his pants pocket. The defendant responded "no" to an officer's question about whether he had anything in his pocket. When the officer asked the defendant if she could check his pants pocket, he stood up and raised his hands away from his body, making a gesture that the officer understood to mean consent. Shortly thereafter, the defendant allowed the officer to search his pocket. The officer found a folded $20 dollar bill with a lump in it. Based on her training and experience, she knew that to be consistent with the way drugs are packaged or concealed. She unfolded the bill and found crack cocaine. The court ruled that proper consent was obtained because nonverbal conduct intended as an assertion is a "statement" giving consent to search under G.S. 15A-221(b).

State v. Crenshaw, 144 N.C. App. 574 (2001). The defendant's vehicle was stopped for an inoperable taillight and illegal parking in an area known for drug activity. One of the officers involved with the stop of the vehicle knew that the defendant previously had been convicted of possession of a firearm by a felon. The officers checked his license and registration, which were valid. They then ordered the defendant out of his vehicle and frisked him. The court ruled, relying on *State v. Butler*, 331 N.C. 227 (1992), that the duration of the vehicle stop beyond the initial stop was reasonable, based on the officers' familiarity with the defendant, the defendant's presence in an area known for drug activity, and the defendant's having been illegally parked. The officers testified at the suppression hearing that the defendant verbally consented to a search of his vehicle by answering "okay" when one of the officers stated that he wanted to search the vehicle. The defendant did not offer any evidence to refute the voluntariness of his consent. The court ruled that evidence supported the trial judge's ruling that the consent to search was voluntary.

State v. Barkley, 144 N.C. App. 514 (2001). The defendant was convicted of first-degree rape. DNA evidence that had been obtained from a blood sample the defendant had voluntarily given to law enforcement officers in an investigation of an unrelated murder was introduced at trial. The court ruled, relying on cases from other jurisdictions, that a blood sample lawfully obtained in the investigation of one crime may be used as evidence in the prosecution of an unrelated crime without any additional justification under the Fourth Amendment. The court stated that once the blood was lawfully drawn from the defendant's body, he no longer had a possessory interest in it. The court also examined the facts surrounding the defendant's consent to give a blood sample in the murder investigation and ruled that a reasonable person would have understood by his conversation with the investigating law enforcement officer that his blood analysis could be used generally for investigative purposes and was not limited to the murder investigation.

State v. Schiffer, 132 N.C. App. 22 (1999). An officer saw a vehicle with windows and windshield that he believed to be tinted darker than permitted by North Carolina law. Once he pulled behind the vehicle, he saw that it had Florida tags. He then pulled alongside the vehicle to see if the window displayed a sticker indicating that the tinting complied with Florida law. (The officer also saw that the windshield tinting extended about 10 inches from the top of the windshield, about 4 to 5 inches in excess of what is permitted under G.S. 20-127(b).) Finding no such sticker, he stopped the vehicle. After the driver rolled down his window, the scent of unburned marijuana emanated from the vehicle. The officer asked the defendant's consent to search the vehicle. The defendant said that he did not know if he could consent to its search because he did not own the vehicle. The officer explained that the defendant could consent because he was in control of the vehicle. He further explained that he could search the vehicle even without the defendant's consent because he smelled marijuana and that he could obtain a search warrant. The defendant then consented to a search of the vehicle.

The court ruled that the defendant's consent was voluntary. The court stated that the officer's statements to the defendant just before the defendant consented were entirely accurate. The officer did not speak to the defendant in an intimidating manner, and he did not engage in any other conduct designed to coerce the defendant into agreeing to a search. The court noted that the smell of marijuana gave the officer probable cause to justify a warrantless search of the car without the defendant's consent.

State v. James, 118 N.C. App. 221 (1995). An officer saw the defendant nervously pacing until he reboarded a bus. The defendant moved toward the rear of the bus and picked up a duffel-type bag from a seat and put it in the overhead luggage bin. Officers went through the typical bus boarding procedures designed to find illegal drugs. The defendant agreed to allow an officer to look in his bag. The officer removed a portable radio from the bag and noticed that screws on the radio had been unscrewed several times. The officer asked the defendant if he would get off the bus so they could talk privately. The defendant did not respond verbally but left the bus with the officer. They went to a private area of the bus terminal, where the officer again obtained a consent to search. The officer discovered cocaine in the radio.

(1) Relying on *State v. McDowell*, 329 N.C. 363 (1991), and other cases, the court reviewed the facts of the bus boarding and ruled that the defendant's consent to search was voluntarily given, although he had an IQ of 70. (2) Relying on *State v. Christie*, 96 N.C. App. 178 (1989), and *State v. Bromfield*, 332 N.C. 24 (1992), the court ruled that the defendant was not seized when he was on the bus or when he left the bus with the officers.

State v. Wooding, 117 N.C. App. 109 (1994). An officer received a radio communication that a person at the Southern Lights Restaurant had seen a black man of a given description get out of a 1980s gray Monte Carlo car and hide behind a dumpster near the restaurant. The person believed that the man lived in one of the apartments at 109 North Cedar Street. While investigating this communication, the officer received another radio communication that a robbery had occurred at the Equinox Restaurant. The description of the robber matched the description of the suspicious person at the Southern Lights Restaurant. The officer went to 109 North Cedar Street. He saw a gray Monte Carlo car parked in front of the building, which contained four apartments—two at ground level and two upstairs. Before leaving his vehicle, the officer saw—through an open window in the side of one of the downstairs apartments—a black male matching the descriptions. After getting out of his vehicle, the officer saw this same person through the open window walking around the apartment and "heard a lot of noise which appeared to [him] to be coins hitting metal." He believed that the noise was definitely change being counted or sifted through.

The officer went to the back porch of the apartment in which he had seen the black male (there was a partition that separated the porches of the two lower-level apartments). Once on the porch, the officer leaned over a couch next to the window, got close to the window, and looked into the apartment through a three- to four-inch opening in the window curtains. The officer saw two black males sitting on the floor in the hallway counting money. The officer radioed what he had seen to an officer who was in the front of the apartment with the robbery victim (the victim heard the officer's communication). Shortly thereafter, the defendant came out onto the front porch and was arrested for the robbery. Then the other person came out of the apartment and was identified as the robber by the victim. Both men thereafter consented to a search of the apartment, and the officers found a handgun and money in the apartment.

The court, relying on *State v. Tarantino*, 322 N.C. 386 (1988) (looking through cracks in building violated Fourth Amendment), ruled that the officer's looking into the apartment window while on the back porch was an unlawful search under the Fourth Amendment. The court rejected the State's argument that the later consent search of the apartment—when a handgun and money were found—was based on lawful activity independent of the officer's initial unlawful observation into the apartment window. The court ruled that (1) the arrest of the defendant was based entirely on the officer's unlawful search and was therefore itself unlawful; (2) the consent to search, given by the defendant after his arrest, was tainted by the unlawful search; and (3) the victim's identification of the second person in the apartment was made only after the victim learned what the officer had seen through the back window—two people counting money in the apartment; thus, the identification and the later consent to search were also tainted by the unlawful search.

State v. Wise, 117 N.C. 105 (1994). A State Highway Patrol trooper stopped a vehicle for speeding. He saw the defendant-passenger grab his midsection between his stomach and his belt line with both hands. Reaching in from the driver's side of the car, the trooper patted down the defendant and felt a "round cylinder object" in the area that the defendant had grabbed, but he determined that it was not a weapon. The trooper asked the defendant what he had grabbed, which prompted the defendant to reach inside his jacket and hand the trooper a white, non-transparent Bayer aspirin bottle. The trooper shook the bottle and it "rattled lightly," sounding as if it had "BBs in it." He was suspicious because such a bottle normally has cotton in it, so the rattle would not sound the same. The trooper then opened the bottle, shined his flashlight in it, looked inside, and saw what he determined was rock cocaine. The court ruled that the officer unconstitutionally opened the bottle, because (1) there was no evidence that the defendant consented to a search of the bottle; and (2) there was not probable cause to believe, based on these facts, that the bottle contained illegal drugs.

State v. McDaniels, 103 N.C. App. 175 (1991), *aff'd*, 331 N.C. 112 (1992). The defendant-passenger never objected to the driver's consent to a search of the car at the scene, and the defendant-passenger did not assert ownership rights in either the car or its contents. The court ruled that even if the defendant-passenger had ownership rights in the contents of the car, his failure to assert those rights is considered a voluntary consent to search, because he remained silent when he knew that the driver had given verbal consent to search. The court also ruled that a driver was in "apparent control" (see G.S. 15A-222(s)) of a car and its contents, whether the vehicle or its contents belonged to the driver or to others. Although the officers had reason to believe that the driver was not the registered owner, the officers—based on these facts—could rely on the driver's words of consent in assuming that he was lawfully controlling the vehicle.

State v. Davy, 100 N.C. App. 551 (1990). During a rape investigation, the defendant—who was a suspect—agreed to go with a deputy sheriff to the sheriff's office, where he consented to allow his pants to be rolled for hairs and fibers. The court ruled that although the defendant had requested to speak to a lawyer, his consent was freely and voluntarily given because he had been told that he was free to leave the sheriff's office before he was asked to allow his pants to be rolled.

State v. Bogin, 66 N.C. App. 184 (1984). Officers went to the defendant's home with a warrant to arrest a person (Ruff) who did not live there. When the defendant's father answered the door, the officers said that they had an arrest warrant for Ruff. The father let them in, and the defendant-son volunteered that Ruff might be in his (the son's) room. The court ruled that consent to enter was voluntary because the officers announced only their authority to arrest, not search, and therefore their admittance was not a mere acquiescence to lawful authority under *Bumper v. North Carolina*, discussed below.

FEDERAL APPELLATE COURTS

United States v. Purcell, 236 F.3d 1274 (11th Cir. 2001). An officer stopped a vehicle for a traffic violation. While giving the citation to the defendant to sign and still possessing the defendant's driver's license, the officer asked for and received consent to search the vehicle. The court rejected the defendant's argument that the consent was involuntary because the officer possessed the defendant's driver's license when asking for consent. The court ruled that the issue of voluntariness of a consent to search is based on the totality of circumstances—there is no litmus test on this issue. The court ruled that the defendant's consent to search was voluntary.

United States v. Gigley, 207 F.3d 1212 (10th Cir. 2000). The court noted that the detention of the defendant-driver following a traffic stop ended when the officer returned her license and registration and gave her a warning citation, telling her, "That's all I have for you." The consensual encounter began when the defendant gave the officer permission to ask her some questions. The court ruled that the mere fact that the defendant was sitting in the front passenger seat of the officer's patrol car did not make her consent involuntary.

United States v. Shaibu, 920 F.2d 1423 (9th Cir. 1990). When officers arrived, the defendant came out of his apartment and left his door open. The defendant did not respond to an officer's question about whether a particular person was inside but instead walked back into his apartment, leaving the door open. The officers did not ask permission to enter and did not state their intention to do so but simply followed the defendant through the open door. The court ruled that, absent a specific request by the officer for permission to enter the defendant's apartment, the defendant's failure to object to entry did not establish consent to enter. *Compare with* United States v. Garcia, 997 F.2d 1273 (9th Cir. 1993) (distinguishing *United States v. Shaibu*, court upheld defendant's consent to enter apartment when officer grabbed door, flashed badge, and said, "We'd like to talk to you," and defendant said, "Okay," nodded, and stepped back), *and* United States v. Walls, 225 F.3d 858 (7th Cir. 2000) (officer dressed as FedEx employee delivered packages to a residence; later, when officers knocked at the door of the residence, people inside yelled at them and told them to get a search warrant; however, the defendant then came to the door after the officers knocked, and the officers identified themselves and informed her that they were conducting an investigation concerning the two packages that had just been delivered to the residence; court ruled that her actions—opening the door and stepping back to allow their entrance—constituted consent to officers' entry into the house).

United States v. Kon Yu-Leung, 910 F.2d 33 (2d Cir. 1990). The defendant was indicted and arrested. He then gave consent to a search of his house. The court ruled that giving consent to a search after indictment was not a critical stage that entitled the defendant to the Sixth Amendment right to counsel.

United States v. Bosse, 898 F.2d 113 (9th Cir. 1990). An entry by a ruse that occurred when a defendant was informed that the person seeking entry was a government officer, but the defendant was misinformed as to the purpose for which the officer sought entry, could not be justified by consent. In this case, a state government inspector received the permission of the defendant, a licensed semiautomatic firearms dealer, to inspect the defendant's home and premises concerning a pending application to buy and sell automatic machine guns. A federal firearms agent accompanied the state officer, without identifying himself as a federal agent, to investigate federal violations. The court ruled that the federal agent deliberately misrepresented his purpose and his surreptitious entry was illegal.

Officer's Statement about a Search Warrant

Bumper v. North Carolina, 391 U.S. 543 (1968). Consent to enter a home is involuntary if it is given in acquiescence to an officer's assertion that he has a search warrant when in fact he has none or the warrant is invalid. *See* State v. Phillips, 25 N.C. App. 5 (1975) (consent to search was involuntary when made in response to officers' statement that they had a search warrant, which was invalid).

State v. Fincher, 309 N.C. 1 (1983). The defendant, who was 17 years old, had a low IQ, and was told by officers that if he refused to give consent they would obtain a search warrant and conduct a search anyway, voluntarily and understandingly consented to a search of his bedroom.

State v. McMillan, 214 N.C. App. 320 (2011). The court ruled that the officers' advising the defendant that if he did not consent to giving oral swabs and surrendering certain items of clothing they would detain him until they obtained a search warrant did not negate the defendant's voluntary consent to the seizure of those items.

State v. Raynor, 27 N.C. App. 538 (1975). Officers arrested the defendant at his apartment and told him that if he did not give them the stolen stereo they were seeking, they would get a search warrant. The defendant retrieved the stereo from his apartment and gave it to the officers. Nothing improper occurred, because officers had probable cause to obtain a valid search warrant. *See also* State v. Paschal, 35 N.C. App. 239 (1978) (officer, who had probable cause to search car, properly obtained consent to search it after he told defendant that if he refused to consent, the officer would impound the car and go before a magistrate to obtain a search warrant); United States v. Tutino, 883 F.2d 1125 (2d Cir. 1989) (officer's advice that other officers were in the process of obtaining a search warrant did not make resulting homeowner's consent to search involuntary); United States v. Kaplan, 895 F.2d 618 (9th Cir. 1990) (arrestee was informed that he could either give his permission to a search of his desk or he would have to wait for a search warrant; he was also informed that he had a right to refuse; based on these and other facts, consent was voluntarily given); United States v. Tompkins, 130 F.3d 117 (5th Cir. 1997) (fact that officer told defendant that a search warrant would be obtained, not that a search warrant would be sought or applied for, is but one factor in considering totality of circumstances in evaluating defendant's consent; court found consent was voluntary in this case).

Validity of Nonverbal Consent

(This topic is discussed on page 229.)

State v. Harper, 158 N.C. App. 595 (2003). Based on an investigation that indicated people in a hotel room were involved with illegal drugs, an officer knocked on the door to the room. The defendant initially opened the door slightly and then, while continuing to have a conversation with the officer, opened it about halfway. The officer asked the defendant if he could step inside the room to see if George Davis was in. The defendant then stepped back from the officer and the threshold of the door and opened the door almost to its full extension. The officer saw a set of electronic scales on the nightstand between the room's two beds and knew that drug dealers often used such scales to measure illegal drugs. There was another person in the room in addition to the defendant. That person started moving around the room, refused the officer's order to remain seated on a bed, and became increasingly agitated. He was handcuffed. The defendant defied the officer's order to remain seated on a bed and

was handcuffed. The officer then searched for weapons in the mattresses and nightstand. The officer and other officers saw illegal drugs and cash in these places. They obtained a search warrant, conducted a search of the hotel room, and seized evidence. The court ruled, relying on *State v. Graham*, 149 N.C. App. 215 (2002), that the defendant's nonverbal conduct constituted valid consent to enter the hotel room.

Scope of the Search

(This topic is discussed on page 231.)

UNITED STATES SUPREME COURT

Florida v. Jimeno, 500 U.S. 248 (1991). An officer stopped the defendant's car and, after asking for and receiving the defendant's consent to search the car for drugs, found cocaine inside a folded paper bag on the car's floorboard. The Court ruled that the officer's belief that the defendant's consent to search his car included the containers within the car was objectively reasonable, and therefore the search did not violate the Fourth Amendment. The Court noted that the defendant had granted the officer consent to search his car for drugs and did not explicitly limit the scope of the search, and a reasonable person may be expected to know that drugs are generally carried in some type of container. An officer does not need to make a specific request for the defendant's consent to search containers within a car to authorize the officer's searching them.

NORTH CAROLINA SUPREME COURT

State v. Stone, 362 N.C. 50 (2007). The court ruled that a search of a defendant in which an officer shined a flashlight inside the defendant's underwear, when the defendant had given consent to a generic search for weapons or drugs during a routine traffic stop, was not within the scope of the defendant's consent to search and thus violated the Fourth Amendment. An officer stopped a car for speeding. The officer asked the defendant, a passenger, whether he had any drugs or weapons on his person. The defendant said no, which prompted the officer to ask for consent to search. The defendant gave consent. The defendant was wearing a jacket and drawstring sweatpants. During the initial search, the officer found $552 in cash in the lower left pocket of the sweatpants. He again asked the defendant if he had anything on him. Once again, the defendant denied having drugs or weapons and authorized the officer to continue the search. The officer checked the rear of the sweatpants and moved his hands to the front of the defendant's waistband. The officer then pulled the defendant's sweatpants away from his body and trained his flashlight on the defendant's groin area. The defendant objected, but by that time, the officer had already seen the white cap of what appeared to be a pill bottle tucked in between the defendant's inner thigh and testicles. The court concluded that a reasonable person would not have understood that his consent included such an examination. The scope of a general consent to search does not necessarily include consent for an officer to move clothing to directly observe the genitals of a clothed person. The court noted that its ruling is necessarily predicated on the facts and that different actions by the officer could have led to a different result. [Author's note: The only basis on which the State justified the officer's search was consent. Thus, the court did not discuss whether probable cause and exigent circumstances supported the search. See *State v. Smith*, 342 N.C. 407 (1995), reversing the court of appeals for reasons stated in the dissenting opinion, 118 N.C. App. 106 (1995), discussed in the court's opinion.]

State v. Belk, 268 N.C. 320 (1966). When an officer asked the defendant, the owner and operator of the car, for permission to search the car, the defendant replied that he "would get the key and let them [the officers] look in the trunk." The court found that this answer did not limit the officers to searching the trunk; if the defendant made accessible to officers that portion of the car, the trunk, that they could not see and to which they had no ready physical access, he gave consent to search any part of the car. Therefore, the officer's search of a paper bag between the legs of the occupant in the right rear was permissible.

State v. Moore, 240 N.C. 749 (1954). When officers asked for the defendant's consent to search his home and place of business (both in the same building), the defendant replied, "Go ahead, it is not around here but you are welcome to search." The court ruled that this consent to search included the entire building when the defendant never objected during the search.

NORTH CAROLINA COURT OF APPEALS

State v. Ladd, ___ N.C. App. ___, 782 S.E.2d 397 (2016). The defendant was convicted of multiple charges of secretly using a photographic device with the intent to capture images of another person. The court ruled that the trial court erred in denying the defendant's motion to suppress evidence obtained during a warrantless search of the defendant's external hard drives. While the defendant had consented to a search of his laptops and smart phone, the trial court's finding of fact (based on the State's stipulation to the facts set out in defense counsel's affidavit filed with the suppression motion) unambiguously showed that the defendant did not consent to the search of the external hard drives. And the officers' warrantless search of these drives, for which the defendant possessed a Fourth Amendment privacy interest under *Riley v. California*, 134 S. Ct. 2473 (2014), were not justified. They did not pose a safety threat to the officers nor was there any reason to believe that the information in the drives would have been destroyed while the officers obtained a search warrant.

State v. Lopez, 219 N.C. App. 139 (2012). The court ruled that the defendant's voluntary consent to a search of his vehicle extended to the officer's looking under the hood and in the vehicle's air filter compartment.

State v. Schiro, 219 N.C. App. 105 (2012). The court ruled that a consent search of the defendant's vehicle was not invalid because it involved taking off the vehicle's rear quarter panels. The trial court found that both rear quarter panels were fitted with a carpet/cardboard type interior trim and that they "were loose." Additionally, the trial court found that the officer "was easily able to pull back the carpet/cardboard type trim . . . covering the right rear quarter panel where he observed what appeared to be a sock with a pistol handle protruding from the sock."

State v. Hagin, 203 N.C. App. 561 (2010). The defendant was convicted of manufacture of methamphetamine. The defendant and his wife executed a written consent to search that permitted a search of the personal or real property located at an address in Wadesboro and described a single-wide mobile home. The officer informed them that they could withdraw their consent at any time. The defendant accompanied the officer and another officer as they searched the mobile home. They then went outside, and one of the officers saw a small outbuilding located about 15 to 20 feet from the home's back porch. The officers searched the outbuilding, and neither the defendant nor his wife withdrew their consent to search their real property. The court ruled, relying on *State v. Williams*, 67 N.C. App. 519 (1984), and other cases, that the search of the outbuilding was within the scope of the consent given. A reasonable person who believed that his consent did not include the outbuilding would have objected to the search. The defendant's silence was some evidence that he believed the outbuilding to be within the scope of his consent. [Author's note: In preparing a written consent involving a residence, an officer may want to include a specific reference to "all outbuildings on the property, wherever located." A person giving consent would have a better understanding of the scope of the proposed search, and a reviewing court would more likely find that an outbuilding was included in the consent to search.]

State v. Neal, 190 N.C. App. 453 (2008). The defendant was convicted of several cocaine offenses. The court ruled, relying on the standards set out in *Florida v. Jimeno*, 500 U.S. 248 (1991), and *State v. Stone*, 362 N.C. 50 (2007), that the scope of the defendant's consent to search included a strip search. An officer detected a mild odor of marijuana coming from the passenger side of a car in which the defendant was seated. The defendant consented to a pat-down search of her person to check for weapons and also consented to a search of her purse. A drug dog reacted to the passenger side of the car. While the canine search was being conducted, the defendant acted very nervous and often put her hands in and out of the back of the waistband of her pants. An officer noticed a bulge in the back of her pants, and she was instructed to keep her hands away from the waistband. The officer informed the defendant that he wanted to conduct a better search to determine what was located in the back of her pants and that he had contacted a female officer for assistance. The female officer conducted a search of the defendant in the women's bathroom, with another officer standing outside the door to prevent others from entering. The female officer explained to the defendant that she would be conducting a more thorough search. The defendant indicated that she understood. During the search, the defendant was asked to lower her underwear and a package containing cocaine fell out. The female officer testified that the defendant was "very cooperative, extremely cooperative" during the search and never expressed any misgivings about the scope of the search.

State v. Johnson, 177 N.C. App. 122 (2006). An officer stopped a passenger van and issued a warning ticket for a license plate display violation. The officer asked the defendant if he had in the van any illegal guns or drugs or amounts of money exceeding $10,000. The defendant said "no" several times. The defendant then gave consent to a search of the van. The officer discovered a piece of rubber that had been glued in an unusual place on a plastic wall panel inside the van. The officer pulled back the wall panel and discovered cocaine. The court ruled, applying the objective-reasonableness test of *Florida v. Jimeno*, 500 U.S. 248 (1991), and other cases, that the defendant's general statement of consent to search could not reasonably have been interpreted to include the intentional infliction of damage to the van. [Author's note: The North Carolina Supreme Court, 360 N.C. 541 (2006), later ordered that this case be remanded to the trial court for findings of fact and conclusions of law on the issue of whether probable cause supported the officer's search of the van. The court did not, however, vacate the court of appeals ruling on the consent issue.]

State v. Jones, 161 N.C. App. 615 (2003). Officers saw the defendant get into a vehicle and take off his leather jacket and place it on the backseat. He later got out of the vehicle. A drug dog walking outside of the vehicle alerted "very strongly" on the passenger side of the vehicle where the defendant had been located. Another person told the officers that the vehicle belonged to his wife and that he was in charge of the car; he then gave consent to search the vehicle and gave the car keys to the officers. The officers removed the jacket and found illegal drugs in it. The court ruled, relying on *Florida v. Jimeno*, 500 U.S. 248 (1991); *United States v. Matlock*, 415 U.S. 164 (1974); *State v. Garner*, 340 N.C. 573 (1995); and other cases, that the consent to search the vehicle included the jacket and was valid.

State v. Castellon, 151 N.C. App. 675 (2002). Officer A stopped the defendant, who was driving the vehicle, for failing to wear a seat belt. The officer used his mobile data computer to check the defendant's driver's license for outstanding warrants. The computer responded slowly. Officer B arrived and both officers saw several indicators of illegal drug activity. After 25 minutes and a determination that the driver's license was valid and the defendant was not wanted, the defendant was given a warning ticket. As the defendant was leaving the patrol car, Officer A asked the defendant for consent to search his vehicle. The defendant gave consent. During a search of the trunk, Officer B found cocaine in the back of a television set.

(1) The court ruled, citing *State v. Munoz*, 141 N.C. App. 675 (2001), that the length of detention to determine the validity of the driver's license was reasonable under the Fourth Amendment. (2) The court ruled that the search of a television set in the trunk did not exceed the scope of the driver's consent: the television set was lying face down. Officer B saw a package wrapped in saran wrap inside the back panel of the set. The officer

knew that illegal drugs are commonly packaged with saran wrap. Based on this information, the court ruled that the officers were justified under the plain view doctrine in unscrewing the back panel of the television set and seizing the package.

State v. McDaniels, 103 N.C. App. 175 (1991), *aff'd*, 331 N.C. 112 (1992). The court ruled that the driver's consent to a search of the car was not limited. There was no evidence that the driver or defendant-passenger objected to the officers' use of a dog in searching the car and its contents (in this case, a briefcase), and the driver did not at any time attempt to modify or withdraw his initial consent to search.

State v. Aubin, 100 N.C. App. 628 (1990). The officer stopped the defendant for impaired driving. The officer informed the defendant that cars heading north were being searched for weapons and contraband, and he asked the defendant for his consent to search his car. The defendant said "okay." Although the defendant did not sign the consent to search form, he stated, "You're all right to look in the car," and "You can go and check my car. No problem. I don't understand you no way." The defendant stood by the officer as he searched the car. The officer opened the back passenger door and searched the backseat areas, including lifting the bottom portion of the seat up and out of position. He found cocaine and arrested the defendant. The court ruled that the officer's search did not exceed the scope of the defendant's consent to a search, noting that the defendant did not object in any way to what the officer was doing.

State v. Morocco, 99 N.C. App. 421 (1990). The defendant voluntarily signed a consent to search form that permitted a search of his car after the officer had explained to the defendant that he wanted to search his car for illegal weapons, alcohol, and contraband. The court ruled that the officer's search of a tote bag in the backseat of the defendant's car did not exceed the scope of the defendant's consent, because contraband could reasonably be found there. The defendant did not withdraw his consent simply because he told the officer that the tote bag contained some nude photographs of the defendant's wife.

State v. Leonard, 87 N.C. App. 448 (1987). An officer did not exceed the scope of consent given by the defendant to search his house for his fugitive son when the officer lifted a cover over a tub. The evidence supported the trial judge's finding that the officer believed that the covered area was large enough for a person to hide in, and the officer had raised the cover to look for the son.

State v. Lash, 21 N.C. App. 365 (1974). The defendant consented to a search of her entire car, including the trunk, when she gave the officer the ignition key only and asserted that she did not have the trunk key. Officers obtained access to the trunk through the rear seat.

FEDERAL APPELLATE COURTS

United States v. Osage, 235 F.3d 518 (10th Cir. 2000). The court ruled that the defendant's consent to a search of his suitcase did not extend to the officer's opening with a tool a 28-ounce sealed can labeled "tamales in gravy" that was in the suitcase. The court noted that this search destroyed or rendered completely useless the item searched. *Compare with* United States v. Kim, 27 F.3d 947 (3d Cir. 1994) (consent search of handbag permitted officers to open factory-sealed cans with intact lids).

United States v. Melgar, 227 F.3d 1038 (7th Cir. 2000). A female person's granting of consent to search a hotel room, which she had rented, included the consent to search a purse there, because the officers had no reason to know that the purse did not belong to her.

United States v. McSween, 53 F.3d 684 (5th Cir. 1995). The defendant's consent to search his car included a search under the hood. In this case, the officer made a general request for a search without identifying his objective, and the defendant did not attempt to limit the scope of the search. *See also* United States v. Crain, 33 F.3d 480 (5th Cir. 1994) (similar ruling); United States v. Zapata, 180 F.3d 1237 (11th Cir. 1999) (after officer explained that he was concerned about interstate transportation of drugs, weapons, and large sums of money, defendant's consent to search his vehicle authorized search of area behind interior door panels).

United States v. Snow, 44 F.3d 133 (2d Cir. 1995). The defendant's consent to a search of his car included a search of a duffel bag on the backseat. Although the officer's request for consent to search did not include the purpose of the search, the court noted that it is self-evident that an officer seeking general permission to search a vehicle is looking for evidence of illegal activity—and it is obvious that such evidence might be hidden in closed containers. *See also* United States v. Forbes, 181 F.3d 1 (1st Cir. 1999) (consent to search of trunk included a search of duffel bags inside trunk).

United States v. Rich, 992 F.2d 502 (5th Cir. 1993). Officer's request to "look in your truck" included suitcase behind passenger seat.

United States v. Rodney, 956 F.2d 295 (D.C. Cir. 1992). The defendant's consent to a search of his body for drugs included the officer's placing his hands in a continuous sweeping motion over the defendant's crotch area.

United States v. Chaidez, 906 F.2d 377 (8th Cir. 1990). The defendant's consent to allow the officer to look in the car permitted the officer to run his hand in the opening on the side of the raised cushion and underneath the seat when the defendant was present during the search and never objected.

United States v. Strickland, 902 F.2d 937 (11th Cir. 1990). The defendant's consent to a search of the entire contents of a car for drugs authorized the officer to examine the spare tire in the trunk, to remove it to search around the spare tire compartment, and to roll the spare tire on the pavement.

United States v. Smith, 901 F.2d 1116 (D.C. Cir. 1990). The defendant's consent to the search of a tote bag for drugs authorized an officer to search a paper bag within the tote bag. *See also* United States v. Springs, 936 F.2d 1330 (D.C. Cir. 1991) (similar ruling; search of baby powder container within tote bag).

Delay in Conducting a Consent Search

State v. Williams, 67 N.C. App. 519 (1984). The defendant gave written consent to search his car located at the police department. A 23-hour delay between the giving of consent and the search was not unlawful when the written consent did not have a time limitation, the defendant never withdrew his consent, the officers were conducting other investigations during that time, and the result of the search would not have been different if it had been conducted earlier. Moving the car to the impound lot before the search was not unlawful when the written consent did not limit where the search could be conducted and the result of the search would not have been different if it had been made at the police department.

Airport Cases

United States v. Mendenhall, 446 U.S. 544 (1980). The Court ruled that a deplaning passenger at an airport voluntarily consented to accompany officers from the concourse to the drug agency's office and voluntarily consented to remove her clothing so that the officer could search for drugs. *See also* State v. White, 77 N.C. App. 45 (1985).

State v. Porter, 65 N.C. App. 13 (1983). After being lawfully stopped at the airport, the defendant voluntarily consented to a search of her purse. She thought that she had nothing to lose by consenting to the search, but she had forgotten that she had hashish in her purse. *See also* State v. Perkerol, 77 N.C. App. 292 (1985).

State v. Casey, 59 N.C. App. 99 (1982). The defendant, who was being questioned at an airport, voluntarily consented to go with officers to the basement office. The officers specifically told the defendant that he was not under arrest, and they did not threaten or coerce him. In the office, the defendant voluntarily consented to a search of the bags he was holding for another person after officers truthfully told him that the person had consented to a search of the bags and that he, the defendant, could refuse to do so.

Undercover Officers and Informants

Hoffa v. United States, 385 U.S. 293 (1966). A government informant did not enter the defendant's hotel room by force or by stealth but was invited in by the defendant—thus, no Fourth Amendment violation occurred. The Court distinguished *Gouled v. United States*, discussed below.

Lewis v. United States, 385 U.S. 206 (1966). The defendant, who was selling drugs, invited into his home a federal undercover drug agent, who misrepresented his identity and stated that he wanted to purchase drugs. No Fourth Amendment violation occurred, because the defendant's privacy interests were not violated when he voluntarily allowed someone to enter his home to transact illegal business.

Gouled v. United States, 255 U.S. 298 (1921). The defendant's Fourth Amendment rights were violated when the defendant's business acquaintance, acting under orders of federal officers, fraudulently obtained permission to enter an office allegedly for a social visit and then seized papers.

United States v. Akinsanya, 53 F.3d 852 (7th Cir. 1995). An undercover informant agreed to arrange a purchase of heroin from the defendant. The informant went to the defendant's apartment to consummate the purchase. He saw the heroin there and called an officer (pretending that the officer was the buyer) to tell him. The informant then left the apartment, pretending to get the money to buy the heroin. Officers then entered the apartment without a warrant and seized the heroin.

The court ruled that the doctrine of consent once removed justified the entry and seizure. The doctrine applies when an undercover officer or informant (1) enters a place at the express invitation of someone with the authority to consent, (2) establishes then the existence of probable cause to arrest or to search, and (3) immediately summons help from other officers. The court ruled that all three criteria were met and the officers' actions did not violate the Fourth Amendment. *See also* United States v. Diaz, 814 F.2d 454 (7th Cir. 1987); United States v. Pollard, 215 F.3d 643 (6th Cir. 2000); United States v. Bramble, 103 F.3d 1475 (9th Cir. 1996).

Consent to Come to a Law Enforcement Facility

State v. Freeman, 307 N.C. 357 (1983). An officer arrested the defendant (without probable cause) when he went to the suspect's house and told him that he was there to "pick him up" and then took him without his consent to the sheriff's department for questioning; the resulting confession was inadmissible.

State v. Simpson, 303 N.C. 439 (1981). The defendant was not arrested or otherwise seized under the Fourth Amendment when he voluntarily accompanied officers to a law enforcement building at their request; was taken to an unlocked interrogation room; was interviewed throughout the day; but was never arrested, handcuffed, or restrained or otherwise treated as in custody until an arrest warrant was served in the evening. An officer's statement at a court hearing that the defendant was in his "custody" during the day is not dispositive when the evidence showed that the restraint on the defendant's freedom was not sufficient to constitute a seizure under the Fourth Amendment. *See also* State v. Bromfield, 332 N.C. 24 (1992); State v. Johnson, 317 N.C. 343 (1986); State v. Jackson, 308 N.C. 549 (1983), *later appeal*, 317 N.C. 1 (1986); State v. Davis, 305 N.C. 400 (1982); State v. Morgan, 299 N.C. 191 (1980); State v. Reynolds, 298 N.C. 380 (1979); State v. Cass, 55 N.C. App. 291 (1982); State v. Smith, 61 N.C. App. 52 (1983).

Ordering Passenger out of Vehicle When Driver Gives Consent to Search

State v. Pulliam, 139 N.C. App. 437 (2000). Officers were conducting a driver's license checkpoint. The driver gave consent to a search of his vehicle. When the officer asked who his passenger was, the driver asserted that he did not know the defendant's name. The officer ordered the defendant-passenger—whom the officer knew to be a convicted drug trafficker—to get out of the vehicle. The defendant became belligerent, saying that the officer had no right to make him get out. The defendant smelled of alcohol, was loud and argumentative, and used profanity. When the defendant finally got out of the vehicle, he was unsteady on his feet and appeared to be intoxicated. The officer saw a large bulge, one inch wide and six or seven inches long, in the defendant's front pants pocket. He patted that place and discovered a utility razor knife. The court ruled, relying on *Maryland v. Wilson*, 519 U.S. 408 (1997) (officer who has made traffic stop may order passengers as well as driver to exit vehicle), and other cases, that the driver's consent to search his vehicle allowed the officer to order the passenger out of the vehicle without the necessity of showing reasonable suspicion of criminal activity.

Special Relationships

(This topic is discussed on page 224.)

Landlord–Tenant and Hotel–Guest

Stoner v. California, 376 U.S. 483 (1964). A hotel clerk could not give consent to officers to search the hotel room that the defendant was renting. Only the defendant could waive his Fourth Amendment privacy rights.

Chapman v. United States, 365 U.S. 610 (1961). Officers entered the defendant's rented house with the landlord's consent. That consent did not permit the officers to enter the house without a search warrant. *See also* United States v. Brown, 961 F.2d 1039 (2d Cir. 1992).

Abel v. United States, 362 U.S. 217 (1960). The hotel manager could allow officers to search a room after the defendant permanently vacated it.

State v. McBennett, 191 N.C. App. 734 (2008). A waitress who delivered room service to the defendant's hotel room reported that the room was in disarray. A hotel manager decided to investigate and could not enter the room because the door caught on the interior lock. The defendant told the manager that he did not need housekeeping and did not open the door. The manager called law enforcement. When the defendant refused to open the door, the manager told the defendant that they would bust the door down. The defendant opened the door and an officer who was the first to enter the room saw marijuana and syringes in the room.

(1) The court ruled that hotel personnel have the implied right to enter a hotel room to keep the hotel in a reasonably safe condition and to exercise reasonable care to discover criminal acts that might cause harm to other guests. The entry of hotel personnel for this purpose is not a search under the Fourth Amendment. (2) The court

ruled that the officers' entry into the hotel room with the hotel personnel was a search under the Fourth Amendment and the discovery of the evidence in the room was not justified by the plain view theory because the officers' entry was not lawful. There were no exigent circumstances to authorize the entry. Also, the defendant did not voluntarily consent to allow the officers' entry.

State v. Williams, 47 N.C. App. 205 (1980). The landlord's consent to a search of the basement of the apartment house where the defendant lived was valid, because the basement was under the landlord's control.

State v. Reagan, 35 N.C. App. 140 (1978). The tenant's possessory interest in a farm included the barn. The landlord-defendant's temporary use of the barn to store stolen tobacco did not extinguish the permission given the tenant to use the barn, particularly because the landlord locked the barn and gave the tenant a key. The tenant therefore gave valid consent to officers to search the barn.

In re Dwelling of Properties, Inc., 24 N.C. App. 17 (1974). A tenant who is in actual possession and control of premises may consent to a warrantless inspection by the city housing inspector, despite the owner's objection before the inspection took place.

United States v. Kitchens, 114 F.3d 29 (4th Cir. 1997). Absent a pattern or practice of allowing guests to stay in their hotel rooms past checkout time, a guest does not have a reasonable expectation of privacy in his or her hotel room after checkout time.

Spouses and Other Shared Relationships
UNITED STATES SUPREME COURT

Fernandez v. California, 134 S. Ct. 1126 (2014). The Court in this case clarified an issue left open in *Georgia v. Randolph*, 547 U.S. 103 (2006) (discussed on page 224 of the book): the validity of a consent search by a residential occupant after a co-occupant has previously objected to a search but is no longer physically present when the occupant consents. Officers in *Fernandez* saw a man apparently involved in a robbery run into a building. They heard screams and fighting coming from an apartment therein. A woman responded to a knock on the door. She had fresh injuries and admitted that she had been in a fight. Fernandez, a co-occupant, then appeared at the door and objected to officers entering the apartment. Believing that Fernandez had assaulted the woman, the officers arrested him and took him to the police station. An hour later, an officer returned to the apartment and obtained the woman's consent to search the apart-

ment. The Court noted that *Randolph* had stressed that its ruling was limited to situations in which an objecting occupant was physically present when the co-occupant consented to the search (in which case, officers cannot rely on that consent to enter). The Court ruled that as long as officers have an objectively reasonable basis to remove the defendant (that is, the officers' subjective motive for removal is irrelevant), the co-occupant's later consent is sufficient. In this case, the officers properly removed Fernandez so that they could speak with the alleged assault victim outside of Fernandez's intimidating presence. Also, there was probable cause to arrest Fernandez for assault.

Georgia v. Randolph, 547 U.S. 103 (2006). The defendant's wife called law enforcement about a domestic dispute with her husband, the defendant. She told law enforcement about the defendant's drug use and said that there was drug evidence in the house. The defendant, who was physically present, unequivocally refused to consent to a search of the house. The defendant's wife then consented to a search. Officers relied on her consent and entered the house. They found drug evidence that was used to prosecute the defendant. The Court ruled, distinguishing *United States v. Matlock*, 415 U.S. 164 (1974) (valid consent of co-occupant with common authority over premises against absent occupant), and *Illinois v. Rodriguez*, 497 U.S. 177 (1990) (valid consent by person whom officer reasonably, but erroneously, believed to possess shared authority as an occupant), that when a physically present occupant refuses to consent to a search of a dwelling even though another co-occupant has consented to a search, the Fourth Amendment prohibits a search of the dwelling based on the co-occupant's consent. [Author's note: Concerning related post-*Randolph* issues, see *United States v. Henderson*, 536 F.3d 776 (7th Cir. 2008) (valid arrest of nonconsenting domestic violence suspect from home and later consent of victim to search house was valid); *United States v. Hudspeth*, 518 F.3d 954 (8th Cir. 2008) (en banc) (arrest of nonconsenting husband at workplace and later consent by wife to enter and seize computer at home was valid); *United States v. Murphy*, 516 F.3d 1117 (9th Cir. 2008) (when co-tenant objects to search and another party with common authority subsequently gives consent to that search in the absence of the first co-tenant, consent to search is invalid).]

The Court made clear that its ruling applies only to a physically present occupant who refuses to consent, as long as officers do not remove a potentially objecting occupant from the entrance to the residence in order to avoid a possible refusal to consent. The Court stated that when officers have obtained consent from a co-occupant, they have no obligation to seek out any other occupants to determine if they want to refuse to allow consent.

The Court noted that the issue of consent is irrelevant when an occupant on his or her own initiative brings evidence from a residence to law enforcement, citing *Coolidge v. New Hampshire*, 403 U.S. 443 (1971). The Court also noted that an occupant can tell law enforcement what he or she knows, which in turn can lead to the issuance of a search warrant. In footnote 6, the Court stated that the exchange of this information in the presence of the nonconsenting occupant may render consent irrelevant by creating an exigency that justifies immediate action. If the occupant cannot be prevented from destroying easily disposable evidence during the time required to get a search warrant, *see* Illinois v. McArthur, 531 U.S. 326 (2001) (preventing suspect's access to residence while law enforcement sought search warrant), a fairly perceived need to act then to preserve evidence may justify entry and search under the exigent circumstances exception to the warrant requirement. The Court also stated that additional exigent circumstances might justify warrantless searches: hot pursuit, protecting officers' safety, imminent destruction to a residence, or likelihood that suspect will imminently flee.

The Court stated that this case has no bearing on the authority of law enforcement to protect domestic violence victims. The issue in this case is about an entry to search for evidence. The Court stated that no question could reasonably be made about law enforcement authority to enter a residence without consent to protect an occupant from domestic violence: as long as officers have a good reason to believe such a threat exists, officers can enter without consent to give an alleged victim the opportunity to collect belongings and get out safely or to determine whether violence or a threat of violence has just occurred or is about to (or soon will) occur. And because officers would be lawfully on the premises, they could seize any evidence in plain view or take further action supported by consequent probable cause. [Author's note: When an occupant has a superior privacy interest over another occupant of a residence, such as most living arrangements involving a parent and child, the parent's consent would override any expressed refusal to consent by a physically present child.]

Illinois v. Rodriguez, 497 U.S. 177 (1990). The female victim of an assault committed by the male defendant in his apartment gave officers consent to enter his apartment. She unlocked the apartment door with her key. She referred to his apartment as "our" apartment and said that she had clothes and furniture there. Evidence at a court hearing later showed that the victim had lived with the defendant in the apartment with her two small children for about one and one-half years, but she had moved out about a month before the search was conducted. She had taken her and her children's clothing with her, but she had left some furniture and household effects there. After leaving the apartment, she sometimes spent the night there, but she never invited her friends there and never went there herself when the defendant was not there. Her name was not on the lease, and she did not contribute to the rent. She had a key to the apartment, which at the defendant's trial she testified that she had taken without the defendant's knowledge—although at the preliminary hearing she said that the defendant had given her the key.

The Court ruled that the victim did not have joint access to or control of the apartment for most purposes and therefore did not have authority to give consent to search the apartment. However, the Court also ruled that the search may be reasonable under the Fourth Amendment, if the officers reasonably believed that the victim had authority to consent, and the Court remanded to the state appellate court to determine whether the officers had such a reasonable belief in this case. [Author's note: G.S. 15A-222(3), which permits a search by consent when consent is given by "a person who by ownership or otherwise is reasonably apparently entitled to give or withhold consent to a search of premises," is consistent with this ruling.]

United States v. Matlock, 415 U.S. 164 (1974). Officers arrested the defendant outside his house. They received consent to search the house and upstairs bedroom from a woman who lived in the house with the defendant. The consent was valid because the woman had common authority over the bedroom with the defendant. The Court stated that common authority does not necessarily depend on ownership of the property but instead depends on the mutual use of the property by those who have joint access or control for most purposes. Each co-inhabitant has a right to permit inspection in his or her own right, and each assumes the risk that the other might permit a common area to be searched.

Frazier v. Cupp, 394 U.S. 731 (1969). The defendant and Rawls jointly used a duffel bag. Rawls gave officers consent to search the bag, and the officers found evidence to use against the defendant. Responding to the defendant's argument that Rawls had permission to use only one of the bag's compartments and not other compartments, the Court stated that the defendant—in allowing Rawls to use the bag and in leaving it in his house—assumed the risk that Rawls would allow someone else to look inside.

NORTH CAROLINA SUPREME COURT

State v. Garner, 340 N.C. 573 (1995). A homeowner consented to a search of her residence after officers said that they were looking for a pistol involved in a shooting. An officer saw a pile of men's and women's clothes in a room. He picked them up and squeezed them to see if he could find a weapon. He found a weapon in a man's jacket (the officer was unaware to whom the jacket belonged), which later was determined to be the defendant's. The court ruled that the homeowner's consent was valid under *United States v. Matlock*, 415 U.S. 164 (1974).

State v. Weathers, 339 N.C. 441 (1994). The court ruled that the defendant's stepdaughter had the authority to consent to a search of the house and bedroom that she shared with the defendant. (The court did not provide the age of the stepdaughter.)

State v. Worsley, 336 N.C. 268 (1994). Overruling *State v. Hall*, 264 N.C. 559 (1965), and other cases, the court ruled that a wife may consent to a search of the premises she shares with her husband. *See also* State v. Carter, 56 N.C. App. 435 (1982).

State v. Barnett, 307 N.C. 608 (1983). A woman lived in a rented house with her daughter. The defendants slept there only occasionally and did not help pay the rent. The woman had, at a minimum, common authority over the house to permit officers to enter so that they could arrest the defendants.

State v. Braxton, 294 N.C. 446 (1978). The registered owner of a car properly consented to a search of her car, which her defendant-son used during a rape.

State v. Penley, 284 N.C. 247 (1973). The owner of the house, in which her 15-year-old son lived, gave valid consent to a search of the house, including her son's bedroom.

State v. Ray, 274 N.C. 556 (1968). The defendant was permitted to sleep regularly in the living room of another's house and was allowed to keep his clothes in the homeowner's suitcase that was in another room. The homeowner gave valid consent to officers to seize the defendant's clothes. *Compare with* United States v. Salinas-Cano, 959 F.2d 861 (10th Cir. 1992) (girlfriend did not have authority to consent to a search of the suitcase of her boyfriend, who periodically lived in the girlfriend's apartment; the girlfriend had told the officers before giving consent that the suitcase belonged to her boyfriend, and the officers knew that was true).

State v. Hamilton, 264 N.C. 277 (1965). Car passengers cannot validly object to a search made with the consent of the person who has possession and control of car. *See also* State v. Belk, 268 N.C. 320 (1966); State v. Raynes, 272 N.C. 488 (1968); State v. Grant, 279 N.C. 337 (1971).

NORTH CAROLINA COURT OF APPEALS

State v. Russell, 92 N.C. App. 639 (1989). The defendant's mother, who owned the residence in which the defendant lived, gave officers consent to search her defendant-son's bedroom. The defendant was not paying rent, although the mother testified at the suppression hearing that her son was "paying his way." (The court did not give the defendant's age or discuss the mother's extent of access to the defendant's bedroom, which are two factors that should be considered in determining her authority to consent.) The court upheld the trial judge's ruling that the mother had common authority over the premises with her son and was apparently entitled to give or to withhold consent to the search of the premises.

State v. Washington, 86 N.C. App. 235 (1987). (1) The defendant-son, who had lived with his wife and child in his mother's house for four months before the search, had a possessory interest in the premises (the house and curtilage) to contest the search, even though he did not own or lease the house or contribute to its maintenance. (2) The defendant failed to show a possessory interest in the outbuildings located outside the curtilage. Even assuming that he had a possessory interest, he had no reasonable expectation of privacy in outbuildings that were essentially open (the hog shelter was open to exposure and the packhouse had missing boards). (3) Even assuming that the defendant had a privacy interest in the outbuildings, his mother's consent to a search was proper because she retained common authority over the outbuildings; the defendant did not have exclusive control. (4) His mother's consent was valid despite the defendant's physical presence when she gave consent. The defendant did not refuse to give consent or communicate his refusal to his mother. (5) The defendant's mother, as registered owner of the car and in apparent control of the car, properly consented to its search under G.S. 15A-222(2), although she never drove the car (but she had keys and paid the insurance) and the defendant had purchased it.

State v. Kellam, 48 N.C. App. 391 (1980). Homeowners gave a key to their house to a neighbor and asked the neighbor to look after the house and to live there if she desired. The neighbor lived there one winter. The neighbor properly gave officers consent to search the house, even though the son of the homeowners lived there, because the neighbor had joint access to and control of the house for most purposes.

State v. Turgeon, 44 N.C. App. 547 (1980). The defendant gave a briefcase to a friend for safekeeping. The friend's consent to officers to seize the briefcase was valid.

FEDERAL APPELLATE COURTS

United States v. Rith, 164 F.3d 1323 (10th Cir. 1999). A father's consent given to officers to search his entire home, including his 18-year-old son's bedroom, for weapons was valid despite his son's refusal to give consent. The son did not pay rent, there was no lock on his bedroom door, and there was no agreement with his parents that they not enter his room without his consent. The court stated that there is a presumption of control of property when there is a parent-child relationship, although that presumption may be rebutted. The court specifically declined to adopt the analysis used in *United States v. Whitfield*, discussed below.

United States v. Beshore, 961 F.2d 1380 (8th Cir. 1992). The defendant's girlfriend properly gave consent to a search of the defendant's car she was driving (the defendant was not present in the car), because the defendant had given her permission to use the car and had put her license plates on the car.

United States v. Duran, 957 F.2d 499 (7th Cir. 1992). A wife had authority to consent to a search of a farmhouse—on property where she and her husband lived—that she considered her husband's private gym, because she was not denied access to it. It simply was her habit not to enter the building.

United States v. Whitfield, 939 F.2d 1071 (D.C. Cir. 1991). Officers did not have a reasonable belief that the 29-year-old defendant's mother had authority to consent to a search of his bedroom, because (1) the officers' superficial and cursory questioning of the mother did not support such a belief, and (2) although the son's room generally remained unlocked, the mother gave no answers to officers' questions that would have led them to believe that the mother had mutual use of defendant's

room. Compare this ruling with *United States v. Rith*, discussed above.

United States v. Anderson, 859 F.2d 1171 (3d Cir. 1988). The driver of a car gave consent to an officer to search it. The officer searched the defendant-occupant's bag in the trunk. The court ruled that the driver (neither driver nor defendant was the owner of the car) had common authority over the trunk and could validly consent to the search. The court also noted that the defendant watched without objection while the car was searched; that behavior was inconsistent with an expectation of privacy in the bag.

United States v. Trzaska, 859 F.2d 1118 (2d Cir. 1988). The defendant's estranged wife, who had moved from the defendant's apartment two weeks earlier, had authority to consent to a search of the apartment because she still had her key to the apartment and personal belongings there. Compare with *Illinois v. Rodriguez*, discussed above.

Miscellaneous

State v. Mandina, 91 N.C. App. 686 (1988). Although the defendant offered evidence that he had paid a car dealer most of the purchase price of the car, the car was parked on the car dealer's lot for repairs, and title and registration were still in the car dealership's name. The court ruled that the officer properly obtained consent to search the car from the car dealer, who had told the officer that he owned the car.

State v. Baker, 65 N.C. App. 430 (1983). The defendant left his truck at a service station for repairs. The garage operator gave valid consent to the Division of Motor Vehicles inspector to (1) open the truck door to check the plate serial number and (2) walk under the truck while it was on a lift to obtain the manufacturer's frame number.

Reasonable Belief That Person Is Entitled to Give Consent

(*This topic is discussed on page 228.*)

Illinois v. Rodriguez, 497 U.S. 177 (1990). The female victim of an assault committed by the male defendant in his apartment gave officers consent to enter his apartment. She unlocked the apartment door with her key. She referred to his apartment as "our" apartment and said that she had clothes and furniture there. Evidence at a court hearing later showed that the victim had lived with the defendant in the apartment with her two small children for about one and one-half years, but she had moved out about a month before the search was conducted. She had taken her and her children's clothing with her, but she had left some furniture and household effects there. After leaving the apartment, she sometimes spent the night there, but she never invited her friends there and never went there herself when the defendant was not there. Her name was not on the lease, and she did not contribute to the rent. She had a key to the apartment, which at the defendant's trial she testified that she had taken without the defendant's knowledge—although at the preliminary hearing she said that the defendant had given her the key.

The Court ruled that the victim did not have joint access to or control of the apartment for most purposes and therefore did not have authority to give consent to search the apartment. However, the Court also ruled that the search may be reasonable under the Fourth Amendment, if the officers reasonably believed that the victim had authority to consent, and the Court remanded to the state appellate court to determine whether the officers had such a reasonable belief in this case. [Author's note: G.S. 15A-222(3), which permits a search by consent when consent is given by "a person who by ownership or otherwise is reasonably apparently entitled to give or withhold consent to a search of premises," is consistent with this ruling.] *But see* United States v. Whitfield, 939 F.2d 1071 (D.C. Cir. 1991) (court ruled that *Illinois v. Rodriguez* did not apply when officers were mistaken about the law concerning authority to consent); United States v. Salinas-Cano, 959 F.2d 861 (10th Cir. 1992) (similar ruling); United States v. Brown, 961 F.2d 1039 (2d Cir. 1992) (similar ruling).

United States v. Basinski, 226 F.3d 829 (7th Cir. 2000). The court ruled that a friend to whom the defendant had given a locked briefcase did not have apparent authority to consent to a search of the briefcase, and a government agent could not reasonably believe that he did. The friend did not have access to the briefcase's contents (the defendant did not give the friend the combination to the lock) and had been instructed to destroy the briefcase and its contents rather than allow anyone else access to it. The court also rejected the government's argument that the defendant had abandoned the briefcase.

United States v. Jenkins, 92 F.3d 430 (6th Cir. 1996). The court ruled that an officer is justified in believing that the driver of a tractor trailer has the authority to consent to a search of the trailer unless the officer knows or is told other information to the contrary.

United States v. Dearing, 9 F.3d 1428 (9th Cir. 1993). The court ruled that an officer's belief that a person who lived in a house as a caretaker and occasional housekeeper had use of and access to or control over the homeowner's bedroom and thus apparent authority to consent to a search of the bedroom was unreasonable under the Fourth Amendment. Even though the officer knew that the caretaker had been in the bedroom on prior occasions, there was nothing to indicate that the prior access was authorized, the bedroom door was closed at the time of the search, and the officer knew that the caretaker's relationship with the homeowner was nearing an end.

United States v. Welch, 4 F.3d 761 (9th Cir. 1993). A male person's (McGee's) consent to search a vehicle did not give officers the actual or apparent authority to search the female defendant's purse in the rental car's trunk. When the officers decided to search the purse, they knew that she was McGee's girlfriend, that she had traveled with him in the rental car, and that the purse belonged to a woman. The officers did not have a reasonable belief that McGee shared the use of and had joint access to or control over his girlfriend's purse.

Admissibility of Evidence of Refusal to Consent

State v. Jennings, 333 N.C. 579 (1993). The court ruled that the defendant's refusal to give consent to search was not admissible as evidence of the defendant's guilt.

United States v. Dozal, 173 F.3d 787 (10th Cir. 1999). The court ruled that evidence of the defendant's refusal to allow officers to search property under his exclusive control was introduced not to impute the defendant's guilty knowledge but for the proper purpose of establishing the defendant's dominion and control over the premises.

Requesting Consent to Search after Defendant Asserts *Miranda* Right to Silence or Right to Counsel
(*This topic is discussed on page 230.*)

State v. Cummings, 188 N.C. App. 598 (2008). The defendant was advised of his *Miranda* rights and waived them. Shortly after questioning began, he requested a lawyer and questioning stopped. However, an officer then asked for the defendant's consent to search his vehicle, which he granted. The court upheld the trial judge's denial of the defendant's motion to suppress evidence seized as a result of the consent search. The court noted that *State v. Frank*, 284 N.C. 137 (1973), had ruled that *Miranda* warnings are inapplicable to searches and seizures. The court also stated that it found persuasive many federal court cases that have ruled that asking for a consent search is not interrogation under *Miranda*; for example, *United*

States v. Shlater, 85 F.3d 1251 (7th Cir. 1996), and *United States v. McCurdy*, 40 F.3d 1111 (10th Cir. 1994).

United States v. Shlater, 85 F.3d 1251 (7th Cir. 1996). An officer's request that the defendant consent to a search is not a violation of *Miranda* and related rulings even though the request was made after the defendant asserted the right to counsel.

United States v. Hildalgo, 7 F.3d 1566 (11th Cir. 1993). An officer's request that the defendant consent to a search is not a violation of *Miranda* and related rulings even though the request was made after the defendant asserted the right to remain silent. A consent to search is not a self-incriminatory statement—it is neither testimonial nor communicative.

United States v. Gleena, 878 F.2d 967 (7th Cir. 1989). An officer's request that the defendant consent to a search is not an interrogation, because it is not reasonably likely to evoke an incriminating response. Therefore, *Miranda* warnings are not required before asking consent to search. *See also* United States v. McCurdy, 40 F.3d 1111 (10th Cir. 1994).

Consent Given during Investigative Stop

State v. Parker, 183 N.C. App. 1 (2007). The court ruled that although a detective's request for consent to search a vehicle passenger's purse was unrelated to the traffic infraction for which the detective initially stopped the defendant, the request was supported by reasonable suspicion that the purse would contain contraband or evidence of a drug crime. [Author's note: When an officer has lawfully detained a person, an officer's questioning of that person (including a request for consent), even if the questioning is unrelated to the purpose of the detention, is not a seizure under the Fourth Amendment (as long as the questioning does not unnecessarily prolong the detention) and therefore does not need any justification (for example, reasonable suspicion). *See generally* Arizona v. Gant, 556 U.S. 332 (2009); Muehler v. Mena, 544 U.S. 93 (2005); United States v. Mendez, 476 F.3d 1077 (9th Cir. 2007); United States v. Alcarez-Arellano, 441 F.3d 1252 (10th Cir. 2006); United States v. Slater, 411 F.3d 1003 (8th Cir. 2005). In this case, the detective clearly had reasonable suspicion to detain the vehicle's occupants based on the discovery of the contents of a drawstring bag and thus did not need any justification under the Fourth Amendment for asking for consent to search the passenger's purse, even though that request was not related to the purpose of the traffic stop.]

Whether Consent Search Is Tainted by Prior Illegality

Florida v. Royer, 460 U.S. 491 (1983). The defendant's consent to the opening of his luggage was tainted by his unconstitutional arrest, and therefore evidence from the search was inadmissible.

State v. Wooding, 117 N.C. App. 109 (1994). An officer received a radio communication that a person at the Southern Lights Restaurant had seen a black man of a given description get out of a 1980s gray Monte Carlo car and hide behind a dumpster near the restaurant. The person believed that the man lived in one of the apartments at 109 North Cedar Street. While investigating this communication, the officer received another radio communication that a robbery had occurred at the Equinox Restaurant. The description of the robber matched the description of the suspicious person at the Southern Lights Restaurant. The officer went to 109 North Cedar Street. He saw a gray Monte Carlo car parked in front of the building, which contained four apartments—two at ground level and two upstairs. Before leaving his vehicle, the officer saw—through an open window in the side of one of the downstairs apartments—a black male matching the earlier descriptions. After getting out of his vehicle, the officer saw this same person through the open window walking around the apartment and "heard a lot of noise which appeared to [him] to be coins hitting metal." He believed that the noise was definitely change being counted or sifted.

The officer went to the back porch of the apartment in which he had seen the black male (there was a partition that separated the porches of the two lower level apartments). Once on the porch, the officer leaned over a couch next to the window, got close to the window, and looked into the apartment through a three- to four-inch opening in the window curtains. The officer saw two black males sitting on the floor in the hallway counting money. The officer radioed what he had seen to an officer who was in front of the apartment with the robbery victim. Shortly thereafter, the defendant came out onto the front porch and was arrested for the robbery. Then the other person came out of the apartment and was identified as the robber by the victim. Both men thereafter consented to a search of the apartment, and the officers found a handgun and money in the apartment.

The court ruled, relying on *State v. Tarantino*, 322 N.C. 386 (1988), that the officer's looking into the apartment window while on the back porch was an unlawful search under the Fourth Amendment. The court rejected the State's argument that the later consent search of the apartment, when a handgun and money were found, was based on lawful activity independent of the officer's initial unlawful observation into the apartment window. The court ruled that (1) the arrest of the defendant was based entirely on the officer's unlawful search and was therefore itself unlawful; (2) the consent to search, given by the defendant after his arrest, was tainted by the unlawful search; and (3) the victim's identification of the second person in the apartment was made only after the victim learned what the officer had seen through the back window—two people counting money in the apartment; thus, the identification and the later consent to search were also tainted by the unlawful search.

United States v. Boone, 245 F.3d 352 (4th Cir. 2001). The court ruled that the defendant's consent to search was voluntary, even if the investigative stop of the defendant exceeded permissive bounds. The court noted other appellate cases that have ruled that consent may be voluntary even if it is procured during an illegal detention, as long as the totality of circumstances confirms that the consent was not coerced: *United States v. Beason*, 220 F.3d 964 (8th Cir. 2000); *United States v. Guimond*, 116 F.3d 166 (6th Cir. 1997); and *United States v. Thompson*, 106 F.3d 794 (7th Cir. 1997).

United States v. Santa, 236 F.3d 662 (11th Cir. 2000). The defendant consented to a search of his apartment shortly after officers unlawfully entered his apartment without a warrant to arrest him. The court ruled that the consent—even if voluntarily given—was invalid as a product of the unlawful entry into the apartment.

United States v. Jones, 234 F.3d 234 (5th Cir. 2000). The defendant's consent to search his car after a traffic stop was invalid because it was directly a result of his illegal detention during the stop.

United States v. Edwards, 103 F.3d 90 (10th Cir. 1996). The defendant's detention resulted in an arrest because it exceeded the scope of an investigative stop, and the arrest was not supported by probable cause. However, officers then developed probable cause to arrest the defendant from other information not tainted by the illegal arrest. The defendant's later consent search was valid because it was not tainted by the illegal arrest.

Search and Seizure of Evidence with Probable Cause, Reasonable Suspicion, or Other Justification

(*This topic is discussed on page 234.*)

Vehicles, Including Containers within Vehicles

(*This topic is discussed on page 236.*)

Generally

UNITED STATES SUPREME COURT

Maryland v. Dyson, 527 U.S. 465 (1999). Officers developed probable cause to search a vehicle for drugs. About 13 hours later, the officers stopped and searched the vehicle without a search warrant. The Court reaffirmed its prior rulings, *United States v. Ross*, 456 U.S. 798 (1982), and *Pennsylvania v. Labron*, 518 U.S. 938 (1996), that probable cause to search a vehicle permits a warrantless search of the vehicle; a showing of exigent circumstances is not required.

Wyoming v. Houghton, 526 U.S. 295 (1999). An officer stopped a vehicle that was occupied by a male driver and two female passengers—the defendant was one of the female passengers. Thereafter, the officer developed probable cause to search the vehicle for illegal drugs, based on information learned from the driver. After the three occupants had been removed from the car, the officer found a purse on the backseat—which was claimed by one of the female passengers—and searched it without a search warrant. She was prosecuted for illegal drugs found in her purse. Relying on *United States v. Ross*, 456 U.S. 798 (1982), and other cases, the Court ruled that an officer who has probable cause to search a vehicle may search without a search warrant a container in a vehicle that is capable of concealing the object of the search, regardless of the owner of the container.

Pennsylvania v. Labron, 518 U.S. 938 (1996). The Court, per curiam, reaffirmed its prior rulings—*see, e.g.,* California v. Carney, 471 U.S. 386 (1985)—that an officer who has probable cause to search a readily mobile vehicle for contraband may conduct a search of the vehicle without a search warrant. A showing of exigent circumstances to conduct such a warrantless vehicle search is unnecessary.

California v. Acevedo, 500 U.S. 565 (1991). Law enforcement officers saw the defendant leaving an apartment with a brown paper bag; they had information establishing probable cause to believe that the bag contained marijuana. The defendant placed the bag in the trunk of a car and drove away. The officers did not have probable cause to believe that drugs were located elsewhere in the car other than in the bag. The Court ruled that law enforcement officers may, under the vehicle exception to the search warrant requirement, search without a warrant a container within a vehicle even when probable cause to search focuses exclusively on the container and nowhere else in the vehicle. The Court overruled *Arkansas v. Sanders*, 442 U.S. 753 (1979) (a warrantless search for marijuana in a suitcase located in a taxi's trunk was unconstitutional because probable cause focused exclusively on the suitcase's contents), disavowed part of the underlying rationale of *United States v. Chadwick*, 433 U.S. 1 (1977) (a warrantless search for marijuana in a footlocker was unconstitutional because a person has a greater expectation of privacy in containers than in vehicles), and reaffirmed *United States v. Ross*, discussed below (when probable cause exists to search a vehicle, a warrantless search may be conducted anywhere in the vehicle—including containers—where evidence could reasonably be found).

California v. Carney, 471 U.S. 386 (1985). Federal officers had information that the defendant was exchanging marijuana for sex with a young man inside the defendant's motor home, which was parked in a lot in downtown San Diego. The officers stopped the youth after he left the motor home. He told the officers that he had received marijuana in return for allowing the defendant to have sexual contacts with him. The officers went to the motor home, entered it without consent or an arrest or search warrant, and saw marijuana and other drug implements inside. They then seized the motor home and took it to the police station, where they conducted a warrantless search. The Court ruled that the officers had probable cause to conduct the searches and could do so without a search warrant. The Court noted that the motor home was readily mobile, even though parked, and an objective observer would conclude that it was being used as a vehicle, not a residence (for example, it was a licensed motor vehicle that was obviously made readily mobile by turning the ignition switch). *See also* United States v. Albers, 136 F.3d 670 (9th Cir. 1998) (citing *Carney*, court ruled that readily mobile houseboat—that is, not permanently moored—is subject to warrantless search under vehicle exception).

United States v. Johns, 469 U.S. 478 (1985). While investigating a drug-smuggling operation with ground and air surveillance, federal officers saw two pickup trucks travel to a remote private airstrip, where two airplanes arrived and departed. The officers approached the trucks, smelled the odor of marijuana emanating from them, and saw in the back of the trucks packages wrapped in dark green plastic sealed with tape—a common method of packaging marijuana. The defendants were arrested at the airstrip and the trucks were taken to agency headquarters, where the packages were removed and placed in a warehouse. The officers made a warrantless search of the packages three days later and found marijuana.

The Court ruled: (1) Officers had probable cause to believe that not only the packages but also the trucks themselves contained contraband (the officers smelled the marijuana odor before they saw the packages in the truck, and therefore marijuana could be anywhere in the truck), and thus under *United States v. Ross*, discussed below, they had probable cause to search without a warrant the entire truck, including the packages. [Author's note: The later case of *California v. Acevedo*, discussed above, permits a warrantless search of a container in a vehicle whether probable cause exists to search an entire vehicle or focuses exclusively on packages in a vehicle.] (2) A warrantless search of the vehicle and the packages inside could take place where they were seized or later where the vehicle and its contents were taken, as provided in *Florida v. Meyers*, discussed below. (3) The three-day delay in conducting the warrantless search of the packages was not unreasonable in this case because it did not adversely affect a privacy or possessory interest under the Fourth Amendment; the defendants did not challenge the legitimacy of the seizure of the trucks or packages, and they never sought return of the property. *See also* United States v. Albers, 136 F.3d 670 (9th Cir. 1998) (citing *Johns*, court found as reasonable 7- to 10-day delay in viewing videotapes and film legally seized from houseboat).

Florida v. Meyers, 466 U.S. 380 (1984). The defendant was arrested for sexual battery. His car was searched without a warrant when he was arrested, and several items were seized. The car was towed by a private wrecker, which impounded it in a locked, secure area. An officer went there eight hours later, searched the car without a warrant, and seized more evidence. The defendant conceded that the first search was valid but challenged the second warrantless search, because the car was no longer mobile. The Court ruled that the second warrantless search was valid under *Michigan v. Thomas*, discussed below.

Michigan v. Long, 463 U.S. 1032 (1983). Officers saw a car, traveling fast and erratically, leave the road and go into a ditch. The defendant-driver met the officers at the rear of the car. His appearance and conduct indicated that he was under the influence of some substance. The defendant began to walk to the open door of the driver's side of the vehicle, and the officers followed him. They saw a large hunting knife on the floorboard and stopped the defendant and frisked him—but found no weapons. One officer then searched the car for other weapons and eventually found marijuana in an open pouch on the front seat in plain view. The Court ruled that when officers reasonably suspect that a suspect is dangerous and may gain immediate control of weapons, they may search a car's passenger compartment in areas where a weapon may have been placed or hidden. It also ruled that the officers' search was justified and the pouch containing the marijuana was properly searched, because it could have contained a weapon. In this case, the officers had not arrested the defendant for any crime until the discovery of the marijuana. The Court noted that the officers acted reasonably in taking preventive measures to ensure that there were no other weapons within the defendant's grasp before permitting him to reenter his car.

Michigan v. Thomas, 458 U.S. 259 (1982). Once officers found marijuana in the glove compartment during a valid inventory search on the highway, they could conduct a warrantless search (supported with probable cause) of the rest of the car, even though the car was under their control and exigent circumstances did not exist. The officers properly seized a loaded weapon they found during a warrantless search of the air vent under the dashboard.

United States v. Ross, 456 U.S. 798 (1982). A confidential reliable informant gave officers information, some of which they corroborated, that the defendant was selling illegal drugs from the trunk of his car and that he possessed additional drugs. The officers stopped the defendant's car, ordered him out, and arrested him. They searched the car there without a warrant and also at the police station. The search included the car's interior and the trunk. Among the items the officers searched within the trunk were a brown paper bag that contained heroin and a zippered leather pouch that contained $3,200 in cash. The Court ruled that when officers have probable cause to search an entire vehicle, they may conduct a warrantless search of the entire vehicle, including contain-

ers within the vehicle, if the object of the search might be found there. The scope of the warrantless search may include all places within the vehicle for which a magistrate could authorize a search with a search warrant. The Court reaffirmed rulings in *United States v. Chadwick*, 433 U.S. 1 (1977), and *Arkansas v. Sanders*, 442 U.S. 753 (1979). [Author's note: *California v. Acevedo*, discussed above, overruled *Sanders* and disavowed part of the underlying rationale of *Chadwick*.] The Court also overruled *Robbins v. California*, 453 U.S. 420 (1981), which had ruled that although the officer had probable cause to search the entire vehicle for marijuana, he needed a search warrant to open a package found within the vehicle.

Colorado v. Bannister, 449 U.S. 1 (1980). An officer saw a speeding car that disappeared before he could stop it. He then heard a radio dispatch that reported a theft of motor vehicle parts, including chrome lug nuts, and described the suspected thieves. A few minutes later, he saw the car again at a service station. The officer approached the car on foot to issue a speeding citation and began talking with the two occupants. He noticed chrome lug nuts in an open glove compartment and two lug wrenches on the floorboard of the backseat. Both occupants matched the radio description of the man suspected of stealing the motor vehicle parts. The Court ruled that the plain view observation of items in the car gave the officer probable cause to seize them and probable cause to arrest the two occupants. The warrantless seizure of the items was permissible under *Carroll v. United States*.

Texas v. White, 423 U.S. 67 (1975). The defendant was arrested while attempting to pass fraudulent checks from his car at a bank's drive-in window, and there was probable cause to search the car for the checks. One officer drove the defendant to the station house, and another officer drove the defendant's car there. After about an hour, the officers searched the car without a search warrant. The Court ruled that a warrantless search was proper under *Chambers v. Maroney*. *See also* State v. Jones, 295 N.C. 345 (1978).

Cardwell v. Lewis, 417 U.S. 583 (1974). Officers had probable cause to arrest the defendant for murder and to search his car because it had been used to commit a murder. At police request, the defendant voluntarily came to the police station (officers had obtained an arrest warrant earlier in the day but not a search warrant). He was arrested and his car, which was parked in a public commercial parking lot nearby, was seized without a warrant and towed to the police impoundment lot. The next day, without a warrant a police technician removed paint from the car's exterior and observed the tread of one of the tires.

A four-Justice plurality opinion questioned whether a "search" occurred but found the warrantless actions reasonable because there was probable cause. Distinguishing *Coolidge v. New Hampshire*, 403 U.S. 443 (1971), the opinion upheld a warrantless seizure of a car in a public place. [Author's note: *Coolidge* involved a seizure in a private driveway; but see *State v. Mitchell*, 300 N.C. 305 (1980), and *United States v. Shepherd*, 714 F.2d 316 (4th Cir. 1983), in which warrantless seizures on private premises were proper.] The opinion also relied on *Chambers v. Maroney* in upholding a warrantless seizure, because evidence indicated that the car might have been removed from the parking lot by others. Exigent circumstances existed in this case, even though officers might have obtained a search warrant earlier in the day before the defendant arrived with his car. The Court stated that a search warrant need not be obtained at the first practicable moment.

Chambers v. Maroney, 399 U.S. 42 (1970). The defendant and others committed an armed robbery and drove away in a car. Witnesses described both the car and the suspects to officers. Within an hour of the robbery, the officers stopped a car and its occupants that matched the descriptions given earlier. All occupants were arrested and the car was seized and taken to the police station, where a thorough warrantless search was conducted. Evidence of the robbery and another robbery committed a week before was found: weapons, the robbery victim's glove with money inside, and cards bearing the name of an earlier robbery victim. The Court ruled that under *Preston v. United States*, 376 U.S. 364 (1964), the search could not be justified as incident to the arrest, because it was made at another place—a police station—sometime after the arrest. But the Court upheld a warrantless search of the car at the station by extending *Carroll*: if there is probable cause to search a vehicle when it is stopped on the highway, officers may make a warrantless search on the highway or take the car to the police station and conduct a warrantless search there.

Cooper v. California, 386 U.S. 58 (1967). The defendant was arrested for selling heroin and his car was impounded because state law made it subject to forfeiture. The officers searched the car without a warrant one week after its seizure. (The actual forfeiture occurred

about four months after the seizure.) The Court ruled that the warrantless search was reasonable under the Fourth Amendment, noting that the officers had a right to search the car for their own protection. *See also* United States v. Pace, 898 F.2d 1218 (7th Cir. 1990).

Carroll v. United States, 267 U.S. 132 (1925). An officer who has probable cause to believe that a vehicle has contraband liquor may stop the vehicle on the highway and search it there without a warrant. The Court recognized a constitutional distinction between warrantless searches of a house and a car: the mobility of a car makes it impracticable to secure a warrant.

NORTH CAROLINA SUPREME COURT

State v. Isleib, 319 N.C. 634 (1987). An officer received information that established probable cause to believe that the following day the defendant would be driving a car containing marijuana. The next day—about 20 hours after receiving that information—an officer saw that car being driven on a highway, stopped and searched it without a search warrant, and found marijuana and seized it from the car.

The court rejected the defendant's argument that a search warrant was required because the officer had had sufficient time to obtain one before the search. The court, after examining United States Supreme Court decisions, ruled that no exigent circumstances other than the motor vehicle itself are required to make a warrantless search of the vehicle when there is probable cause to believe it contains evidence of a crime and the vehicle is in a public place. The court based its ruling on provisions of both the United States Constitution and the Constitution of North Carolina.

State v. Mitchell, 300 N.C. 305 (1980). Officers had the right to make a warrantless seizure (and search) of a parked car at a private residence, because there was no indication that it could not be moved and the defendant was still at large and could have driven the car away while a warrant was being obtained. *See also* United States v. Shepherd, 714 F.2d 316 (4th Cir. 1983).

NORTH CAROLINA COURT OF APPEALS

State v. Mitchell, 224 N.C. App. 171 (2012). The court ruled that the discovery of marijuana on a passenger provided probable cause to search a vehicle. After an officer stopped the defendant and determined that he had a revoked license, the officer told the defendant that the officer's K-9 dog would walk around the vehicle. At that point, the defendant indicated that his passenger had a marijuana cigarette, which she removed from her pants. The officer then searched the car and found marijuana in the trunk.

State v. Simmons, 201 N.C. App. 698 (2010). An officer stopped a vehicle to issue the driver a seat belt citation. The officer noticed a white plastic grocery bag sticking out of the storage holder on the passenger side of the defendant's vehicle. He was suspicious that the bag contained illegal contraband because he had found illegal contraband in that sort of container on at least three prior occasions. The officer asked the defendant what was in the bag. The defendant responded that the bag contained "cigar guts." The officer took this response to mean that tobacco had been removed from a cigar. He had previously seized marijuana in cigars. Based on his training, he had learned that marijuana was sometimes placed in cigars to be smoked. However, the officer could not see inside the bag nor did he smell any illegal contraband. The officer searched the bag. The court ruled that the defendant's response that the grocery bag contained cigar guts did not, without more information, establish probable cause to search the bag. The officer's training and experience established a link between the presence of hollowed-out cigars and marijuana, not a link between the presence of loose tobacco and marijuana. Furthermore, there was no evidence that the defendant was stopped in a drug area or at an unusual time of day.

State v. Martin, 97 N.C. App. 19 (1990). When an officer stopped a car for a traffic violation, he noticed empty vials in the car, which he recognized as being used for selling cocaine. Relying on *United States v. Ross*, discussed above, the court ruled that the officer had probable cause to search without a warrant the rest of the car, including the trunk, for illegal drugs.

State v. Russell, 92 N.C. App. 639 (1989). After the defendant was arrested, officers seized the defendant's car from his driveway and searched it without a warrant. Although the officers had probable cause to seize and search the car, there were no exigent circumstances and there was no consent to permit them to act without a search warrant, and their conduct could not be justified under the plain view doctrine set out in *Coolidge v. New Hampshire*, 403 U.S. 443 (1971) (but note that the inadvertence requirement of the plain view doctrine was later overruled in *Horton v. California*, 496 U.S. 128 (1990)). The ruling in this case is questionable; *see* Capraro v. Bunt, 44 F.3d 690 (8th Cir. 1995) (warrantless seizure of

truck in driveway did not violate Fourth Amendment; truck's position in clear public view on defendant's driveway eliminated any privacy expectation otherwise resulting from its location on private property); United States v. McIver, 186 F.3d 1119 (9th Cir. 1999) (similar ruling involving entry on driveway to place electronic tracking device under vehicle).

State v. Poczontek, 90 N.C. App. 455 (1988). An informant told an officer that the defendant usually used marijuana while driving away from his store after work. Two weeks later, the officer, after learning that the defendant's car was improperly registered, followed him from the store and stopped his car. The officer neither smelled nor saw anything to indicate that the defendant had consumed alcohol or used marijuana. The court ruled that the officer did not have probable cause to search the vehicle.

State v. Russell, 84 N.C. App. 383 (1987). The court applied the rationale of the vehicle search case, *United States v. Ross*, discussed above, to uphold the warrantless search of an airplane and the containers within it when the officers had probable cause to believe it contained illegal drugs. The officers had seized the airplane and its occupants when the airplane landed at a rural airport late at night.

State v. Bennett, 65 N.C. App. 394 (1983). When the defendant was arrested for driving under the influence, the officer saw on the car floor evidence from a break-in that had occurred about a week earlier. He therefore had probable cause to search without a warrant (under *United States v. Ross*, discussed above) the rest of the car for additional property taken from the break-in.

State v. Schneider, 60 N.C. App. 185 (1982). An undercover agent bought 88 pounds of marijuana from the defendant at his house and agreed to buy more. The defendant told the agent that more was on the way. When the codefendant drove up in his car to the defendant's house, both the defendant and the codefendant were arrested and the car was searched. The court ruled that the officer's initial warrantless search of the car's trunk was proper under *United States v. Ross* and *Michigan v. Thomas*, discussed above.

FEDERAL APPELLATE COURTS

United States v. Gastiaburo, 16 F.3d 582 (4th Cir. 1994). An officer's warrantless search of a hidden compartment of a car that occurred 38 days after the car had been seized and impounded was reasonable under the

Fourth Amendment. The officer conducted the warrantless search on the day he learned that the hidden compartment contained drugs, money, and a handgun. *See also* United States v. Spires, 3 F.3d 1234 (9th Cir. 1993) (warrantless search of truck seven days after it was impounded as a forfeited asset was proper).

United States v. Hatley, 15 F.3d 856 (9th Cir. 1994). The court ruled that the automobile exception to the search warrant requirement applied to a car that appeared to the officer to be mobile, even though it was not actually mobile. An officer is not required to determine the actual functional capacity of a car to satisfy the automobile exception.

Probable Cause to Search a Vehicle

(This topic is discussed on page 236.)

NORTH CAROLINA SUPREME COURT

State v. Mitchell, 300 N.C. 305 (1980). Probable cause existed to search and seize an old white Pinto car when (1) a car matching that description was involved in two recent robberies, (2) the defendant was known to drive such a car, (3) a man whose description matched that of the defendant had been involved in both robberies, and (4) the tire tread on one tire matched the tire impression found at the scene of one of the robberies.

State v. Allen, 282 N.C. 503 (1973). Officers had probable cause to search a car because (1) they had earlier seen near the car two men who had run from the area behind a closed company building in the early morning hours, (2) they saw a bag of money in the car that was wrapped with material bearing the company's name, and (3) one of the defendants fled from the car when the officer commented about the money.

State v. Simmons, 278 N.C. 468 (1971). Officers had probable cause to seize jugs they saw in a car because they knew that jugs like these were commonly used as containers for non-tax-paid liquor.

State v. Shedd, 274 N.C. 95 (1968). The defendants were arrested at the scene of a commercial plant break-in and safecracking, and numerous implements of the crime were found. They showed officers where their car was parked—only 100 yards from the plant. These facts provided probable cause to search the car for evidence of these crimes.

NORTH CAROLINA COURT OF APPEALS

State v. Toledo, 204 N.C. App. 170 (2010). An officer noted the odor of marijuana emanating from a spare tire in the luggage area of a Chevrolet Suburban after the defendant had validly consented to a search of the vehicle. The officer had conducted a "ping" test, pressing the tire valve to release some of the air, and noted a very strong odor of marijuana. The officer arrested the defendant for possession of marijuana. The officer then warrantlessly searched a second spare tire located in the undercarriage of the vehicle and noted the odor of marijuana after conducting a ping test. Marijuana was found in both spare tires. At issue was the validity of the search of the second spare tire. The court ruled, relying on *United States v. Ross*, 456 U.S. 798 (1982), that the officer had probable cause to make a warrantless search for more marijuana in the rest of the vehicle, which included the second spare tire. [Author's note: The court in footnote 4 appeared to suggest a separate justification for the search of the vehicle, including the spare tire in the undercarriage, under *Arizona v. Gant*, 556 U.S. 332 (2009) (court ruled that officers may search vehicle incident to arrest only if (1) arrestee is unsecured and within reaching distance of passenger compartment when search is conducted, or (2) it is reasonable to believe that evidence relevant to crime of arrest might be found in vehicle), because it was reasonable to believe that the vehicle contained evidence of the crime of arrest, possession of marijuana. However, a search of the spare tire in the undercarriage would not be subject to a search of a vehicle incident to arrest because a search under that justification is limited to the vehicle's interior.]

State v. Corpening, 200 N.C. App. 311 (2009). The defendant approached a checkpoint in his vehicle, pulled over, and parked on the side of the road about 100 to 200 feet before the checkpoint. He sat alone in the vehicle for about 30 to 45 seconds. An officer walked to the vehicle and smelled a marijuana odor emanating from it. The court ruled that the officer's "plain smell" of the marijuana provided probable cause to conduct a warrantless search of the vehicle. The court also ruled that the defendant's argument that the checkpoint was unconstitutional was irrelevant because the defendant stopped solely on his own volition (that is, the defendant was not seized under the Fourth Amendment). Also, the officer did not conduct a seizure by simply approaching the vehicle to investigate.

State v. Smith, 192 N.C. App. 690 (2008). An officer stopped a Ford pickup truck for failing to display a proper registration tag. After the stop, the officer smelled the odor of marijuana emanating from the vehicle. Two other officers conducted a warrantless search (the defendant refused to give consent) and recovered a handgun in the bed (cargo area) of the vehicle. The bed was fitted with a lift-up cover. The officers did not find any marijuana. The court ruled, citing *State v. Greenwood*, 301 N.C. 705 (1981), that the odor of marijuana emanating from the vehicle provided probable cause to make a warrantless search of the vehicle.

State v. Nixon, 160 N.C. App. 31 (2003). Officer A received information from an informant he knew to be reliable that the defendant shortly would meet with a named person at a specified restaurant to purchase marijuana and then return to his home driving a specified vehicle. Officer A relayed that information to Officer B, telling him that it came from a CRI (confidential and reliable informant). Officer B relayed the information to Officer C, who conducted a warrantless search of the vehicle for marijuana. Officer A testified at the suppression hearing and established that the informant had given him information several times over the previous two years and the information given had been correct every time and had led to several arrests. The court ruled that this and the other information provided probable cause to search the defendant's vehicle. The court noted, relying on *United States v. Hensley*, 469 U.S. 221 (1985), that an officer who takes a law enforcement action (in this case, the warrantless search) need not know the facts establishing probable cause when directed by another officer who has probable cause and, for the evidence seized to be admissible at trial, those facts are provided at a suppression hearing if they are necessary to support the law enforcement action. The court distinguished *State v. Hughes*, 353 N.C. 200 (2000), because in that case the officer with knowledge of the information about an informant did not testify at the suppression hearing (or supply that information to other officers who testified at the suppression hearing).

State v. Earhart, 134 N.C. App. 130 (1999). The court ruled that the following information established probable cause to search a vehicle for drugs. On April 27, 1999, Deputy Sheriff A received an anonymous telephone call that a white Trans Am would be traveling to a residence on North Spot Road in Powell's Point sometime between April 27 and April 28 and that it might be accompanied by a blue Subaru. The caller stated that the Trans Am would be transporting a pound of marijuana. The caller did not identify himself, and the deputy sheriff did not recognize the voice. The caller telephoned the deputy a few minutes later and told him that the suspects in the vehicle had scanners and that information should not be broadcast over police radio. The deputy notified other deputies (Deputy Sheriff B and Deputy Sheriff C) of this information. Deputy B told Deputy A that he had received information from the SBI about the owner of a white Trans Am who lived on North Spot Road and who was being investigated for drug dealing; also, the suspect was reportedly armed with a Desert Eagle handgun. Deputy C began surveillance along North Spot Road after 6:00 p.m. on April 27, 1997. Deputy B contacted him there and informed him that the white Trans Am would have license number KPA-1083 and would be driven by a person named Earhart, who was known to carry weapons. Shortly thereafter, Deputy C saw a blue Subaru, matching the description given by the anonymous informant, pull into the driveway of a residence along North Spot Road. The deputy pulled behind the car and learned from the female driver that Earhart drove a white Trans Am and was the boyfriend of the woman whom she was visiting at this residence. Later that evening, Deputy C stopped a white Trans Am driven by the defendant (whose last name is Earhart). A warrantless search of the vehicle resulted in the seizure of cocaine. The court concluded that the informant's information, the SBI's information, and the deputies' independent investigation collectively supported probable cause to search the Trans Am.

State v. Holmes, 109 N.C. App. 615 (1993). The court ruled that reasonable suspicion existed to stop a vehicle based on the following facts. A trained drug officer saw the defendant driving slowly into a neighborhood known for violence and illegal drugs. From his car, the defendant engaged two different groups of people in conversation, and he then went inside a house personally known to the officer because he had made drug arrests there. The defendant then returned to the car after a few minutes and lit a cigarette, which he shared with two passengers until it was gone and the car was filled with smoke. Based on his training, the officer believed the cigarette was a marijuana cigarette. The defendant then placed a plastic bag in the trunk of the car and went back into the house alone for about 30 seconds. When the defendant returned to the car, he carefully concealed an object underneath the driver's seat. After the officer stopped the car, he opened a passenger door to question a passenger and saw two needles and syringes in a small compartment on the car door. The officer then arrested the passenger for possession of drug paraphernalia and searched the rest of the car.

The court ruled that the officer had probable cause to search the rest of car, including the area underneath the driver's seat for more contraband, based on *United States v. Ross*, 456 U.S. 798 (1982), and *State v. Martin*, 97 N.C. App. 19 (1990). *See also* State v. Parker, 183 N.C. App. 1 (2007) (officer had probable cause to search vehicle for illegal drugs, including locked briefcase found inside vehicle).

State v. Corpening, 109 N.C. App. 586 (1993). A deputy sheriff responded to a report that the defendant's van had caught fire and was off the highway in the lot of an old store. The fire had been extinguished when a deputy sheriff arrived. The deputy, who had been an officer for 13 years and had smelled "white liquor" many times, detected the odor of that substance coming from the van. The court ruled that the deputy's detection of the odor was sufficient to establish probable cause to search the van (in addition, the defendant had acted very nervous and had placed cardboard over a burned-out window), and thus the warrantless search of the van was constitutional, based on *State v. Isleib*, 319 N.C. 634 (1987).

State v. Mackey, 56 N.C. App. 468 (1982). The court ruled that an officer who made a warrantless search of a van for marijuana did not have probable cause because he did not know, either independently or from fellow officers, that the van was being used to store or transport marijuana. The officer knew only that a search of a house with a warrant had discovered a small amount of marijuana and packaging material for a much larger quantity and that immediately after that search the officer who searched the house broadcast an all-points bulletin for the van. The officer in this case later searched a vehicle that matched the bulletin's description of the van. The court's opinion does not describe the contents of the all-points bulletin. [Author's note: If the bulletin had directed officers to search the van and probable cause had existed for that search, the officer who searched the van did not himself need to know the facts supporting probable cause. *See* United States v. Hensley, 469 U.S. 221 (1985).]

State v. Rogers, 56 N.C. App. 457 (1982). An officer had probable cause to search a car without a warrant when (1) he knew that goods had been stolen from a business a few days earlier, (2) the defendant returned some of the stolen goods when a reward was offered, (3) the defendant ran from the officer at a drive-in when the officer sought to talk to him, and (4) the defendant's car was parked in the drive-in's parking lot.

State v. Greenwood, 47 N.C. App. 731 (1980), *rev'd on other grounds*, 301 N.C. 705 (1981). The odor of marijuana emanating from the vehicle gave the officer probable cause to search the vehicle. The court rejected the analysis in cases from other jurisdictions that distinguished—in determining probable cause—whether the odor was from burning or burned marijuana. *See also* State v. Cornelius, 104 N.C. App. 583 (1991); State v. Trapper, 48 N.C. App. 481 (1980); United States v. Johns, 469 U.S. 478 (1985); United States v. Haley, 669 F.2d 201 (4th Cir. 1982); United States v. Reed, 882 F.2d 147 (5th Cir. 1989).

State v. Vernon, 45 N.C. App. 486 (1980). The codefendant, who had arranged a drug sale at a motel, arrived there in his own car. The defendant, who acted as the lookout or bodyguard, arrived separately. The court ruled that after the codefendant and the defendant were arrested at the motel, there was no probable cause to search the defendant's car. The court's additional observation—that even if probable cause existed to search the codefendant's car, a search warrant was required—is questionable in light of *Chambers v. Maroney*, discussed above, and later cases, such as *California v. Carney*, discussed above.

State v. Chambers, 41 N.C. App. 380 (1979). An officer saw the defendant sell marijuana in a plastic bag to an informant in February 1978. At that sale, the defendant was driving a pickup truck. On April 18, 1978, the officer observed various events that gave him probable cause to search the pickup truck. (1) The defendant met with the codefendant at a gas station but did not buy any gas there; the defendant inspected the codefendant's right hip pocket, and they met again at an auto agency parking lot. (2) The pickup truck then went to the defendant's house and returned to an auto agency lot, where the defendant transferred a large dark bag from the back of his truck to the trunk of the codefendant's vehicle. A search without a warrant of the codefendant's vehicle was upheld under the authority of *Chambers v. Maroney*, discussed above: a warrant was not required even though the vehicle was seized on the auto agency lot and the officer could have seized the car and then obtained a warrant from a magistrate, who was only one and one-half miles away.

State v. Tickle, 37 N.C. App. 416 (1978). Following *Draper v. United States*, 358 U.S. 307 (1959), the court ruled that the officer had probable cause to search a car based on an informant's purchase of drugs from the defendant's car an hour earlier. Furthermore, although the officer did not know then about the informant's reliability, the informant's detailed information was probably reliable, and the officer had corroborated some of it.

FEDERAL APPELLATE COURTS

United States v. Patterson, 150 F.3d 382 (4th Cir. 1998). Two masked men robbed a bank. After being arrested, Greene confessed that he was one of the robbers. He told the officer that the defendant was the other robber. He also gave the officer the defendant's address and a detailed description of his car. The car was later seized. The court ruled, noting a similar ruling in *Craig v. Singletary*, 127 F.3d 1030 (11th Cir. 1997) (en banc), that Greene's information supplied probable cause to seize the car. The court noted that it would be anomalous to permit an accomplice's uncorroborated testimony to convict a defendant but not permit an accomplice's confession to establish probable cause to arrest and search (unless it contains inaccurate information or is incredible).

United States v. Turner, 119 F.3d 18 (D.C. Cir. 1997). The officer's observation of pieces of torn cigar paper arrayed around a driver and a ziplock bag of green weed material on the floor on the driver's side, along with the smell of burnt marijuana emanating from the car, established probable cause to search the trunk for marijuana. The court rejected the defendant's argument that because the officer's observations constituted evidence of nothing more than personal use of marijuana, a person would keep the marijuana within his control and not in the trunk.

United States v. Padro, 52 F.3d 120 (6th Cir. 1995). The court ruled that an anonymous informant's detailed information about a specific vehicle—including its license plate number—bringing cocaine to a particular city was sufficient evidence to establish probable cause to search the vehicle when an officer extensively corroborated the information.

Seizure of a Vehicle Subject to Forfeiture

(*This topic is discussed on page 241.*)

State v. Chisholm, 135 N.C. App. 578 (1999). The court ruled that the vehicle seizure and forfeiture laws involving the offense of driving while impaired did not violate the Fourth, Fifth, and Fourteenth Amendments to the United States Constitution or Article I, Section 19, of the North Carolina Constitution.

State v. Hall, 52 N.C. App. 492 (1981). On March 12, 1979, the defendant opened the door to his station wagon, reached in to pick up a paper sack containing one pound of marijuana, and sold it to an undercover agent for $355. On April 9, 1979, a district court judge issued an order to seize the station wagon for forfeiture under G.S. 90-112 for the act committed on March 12, 1979. The court ruled that G.S. 90-112(f) does not necessarily restrict the time within which a vehicle may be seized after a controlled-substances violation has been observed that makes the vehicle subject to forfeiture if an undercover operation would be jeopardized by an immediate seizure. *See generally* United States v. Pace, 898 F.2d 1218 (7th Cir. 1990) (Fourth Amendment permits warrantless seizure of vehicle for forfeiture).

Search of a Vehicle for Its Identification

(*This topic is discussed on page 260.*)

New York v. Class, 475 U.S. 106 (1986). After stopping a vehicle for traffic violations and after the driver had left the car, an officer conducted a proper search—without needing reasonable suspicion or probable cause—by entering the car to remove papers on the dashboard that prevented the car's Vehicle Identification Number (VIN) from being seen from outside the car. Before entering the car to remove the papers, the officer had opened the driver's door and had unsuccessfully looked on the door-jamb for the VIN. He then properly seized a weapon he saw in plain view.

State v. Green, 103 N.C. App. 38 (1991). An officer stopped the defendant's car to investigate impaired driving. After the officer's investigation, he no longer believed that the defendant had been driving while impaired. However, the officer did not believe the defendant's statements about his name, birth date, and address on his driver's license. The officer then entered the defendant's car to find his license, registration, or identification and found drugs in the glove box. The court ruled that the officer did not have authority to enter the car because (1) he did not have probable cause to search; (2) he had no safety justification, because he had already frisked the defendant and searched the car for weapons; and (3) his intrusion into the car was not justified under *New York v. Class*, discussed above.

State v. Baker, 65 N.C. App. 430 (1983). The defendant left his truck at a garage for servicing. A Division of Motor

Vehicles inspector, with the garage operator's consent, opened the truck door to check the plate serial number and walked under the already lifted truck to obtain the manufacturer's frame number. In addition to upholding the inspector's action based on the garage operator's consent, the court upheld his action as a reasonable search, because he knew that the vehicle was stolen and that a serial number plate was missing on another of the defendant's trucks. The inspector had at least reasonable suspicion under *Terry v. Ohio* to make a search by opening the truck door and looking for the plate serial number.

Containers (Other Than in Vehicles)
Probable Cause
(*This topic is discussed on page 242.*)

United States v. Jacobsen, 466 U.S. 109 (1984). A warrantless seizure of a container is constitutional when there is probable cause to believe it contains contraband. However, a search of such a container—when its outward appearance supports a reasonable expectation of privacy of its contents—must be conducted with a search warrant unless some other justification for a warrantless search exists. See also *United States v. Johns*, 469 U.S. 478 (1985), and cases cited therein, and *United States v. Villarreal*, 963 F.2d 770 (5th Cir. 1992) (defendants had reasonable expectation of privacy in 55-gallon drums being shipped by common carrier; warrantless search was illegal).

State v. Wise, 117 N.C. 105 (1994). A State Highway Patrol trooper stopped a vehicle for speeding. He saw the defendant-passenger grab his midsection between his stomach and his belt line with both hands. Reaching in from the driver's side of the car, the trooper patted down the defendant and felt a "round cylinder object" in the area that the defendant had grabbed, but he determined that it was not a weapon. The trooper asked the defendant what he had grabbed, which prompted the defendant to reach inside his jacket and hand the trooper a white, nontransparent Bayer aspirin bottle. The trooper shook the bottle and it "rattled lightly," sounding as if it had "BBs in it." He was suspicious because such a bottle normally has cotton in it, so the rattle would not sound the same. The trooper then opened the bottle, shined his flashlight in it, looked inside, and saw what he determined was rock cocaine. The court ruled that the officer unconstitutionally opened the bottle, because (1) there was no evidence that the defendant consented to a search of the bottle; and (2) there was not probable cause to believe, based on these facts, that the bottle contained illegal drugs.

State v. Porter, 65 N.C. App. 13 (1983). An officer had probable cause to seize a suitcase at the airport without a search warrant (a later search of the suitcase was conducted with a search warrant) based on the following facts. (1) an informant reported that the defendant and her husband were bringing drugs from New York into the airport, (2) hashish had been found in the defendant's purse, (3) the defendant was traveling under an assumed name, (4) an unclaimed suitcase was tagged with the name Barbara Williams and a passenger with the same name had canceled an earlier flight and had been listed on a later flight on which the defendant arrived, and (5) the defendant's name was not listed on the passenger list of either flight.

United States v. Donnes, 947 F.2d 1430 (10th Cir. 1991). An officer found a syringe and camera lens case inside a glove. The officer's opening of the camera lens case without a search warrant violated the Fourth Amendment.

Reasonable Suspicion
(*This topic is discussed on page 248.*)

United States v. Place, 462 U.S. 696 (1983). Based on *Terry v. Ohio*, officers may briefly seize luggage at an airport when they have reasonable suspicion that it contains drugs. However, in this case the seizure was unreasonably long because the luggage was detained about 90 minutes, and officers could have had a dog sniff the luggage at the airport earlier because they had several hours' advance notice of when the luggage would arrive. *Compare with* United States v. Sturgis, 238 F.3d 956 (8th Cir. 2001) (two-hour wait for drug dog did not violate Fourth Amendment because officers had probable cause to arrest detained defendant).

State v. Odum, 343 N.C. 116 (1996). The court, per curiam and without an opinion, reversed the decision of the court of appeals, 119 N.C. App. 676 (1995), that had affirmed the defendant's conviction. The court stated that the decision was reversed for the reasons stated in the dissenting opinion in the court of appeals.

Officers were working drug interdiction at the Raleigh train station. They had received information from a ticket agent that the defendant had purchased a train ticket with cash, using small bills; had departed Raleigh for New York City on April 27; and was to return on the afternoon of April 29. The officers also learned that the defendant had previously been arrested for attempted robbery in New Jersey, although the charge had been dismissed. When the train arrived in Raleigh on April 29, the defendant left the train carrying a red nylon gym bag and appeared to be headed toward a car in the parking lot in which a female was sitting. The officers approached the defendant, showed him their badges, and asked him to answer a few questions. The defendant agreed to talk to them, and they moved over to the sidewalk. When asked to produce his train ticket, the defendant showed them his ticket stub bearing the name D. Odum (his name was David Odum). When asked for identification, the defendant became visibly nervous when he could not find his identification. When he looked into his gym bag for identification, one of the officers saw that the defendant was apparently trying to conceal the contents of the bag. The defendant finally told the officers that he could not find any identification. Although the defendant objected, the officers then seized his gym bag to await a drug detection dog to sniff it. They told the defendant that he was free to leave and that if he left an address, they would have the bag delivered to him. During this conversation, the defendant informed the officers that the woman sitting in the car was his ride. One officer testified at the suppression hearing that the woman neither spoke nor made eye contact with the defendant during the entire questioning.

The dissenting opinion concluded that reasonable suspicion did not exist to support the seizure of the gym bag. The evidence as a whole could easily be associated with many travelers. Many travelers daily embark on trips similar to the defendant's, and the fact that the defendant paid for his ticket in cash was not remarkable, considering the price was $107. The opinion noted that one officer testified that there was no evidence that the defendant had any prior involvement with drugs, and the prior robbery charge that was later dismissed was not a sufficient reflection of a person's propensity to be involved in drug trafficking. The court also noted that one of the officers testified that the defendant did not give him any false information during the interaction at the train station. The officers never inquired about the nature of the defendant's trip, nor was there evidence of any questions that might have bolstered their suspicions. Although the defendant became visibly nervous when he could not find his identification, the opinion noted that it is not uncommon for a person to appear nervous when approached by a law enforcement officer. Also, the actions of the woman in the car and the defendant's reluctance to let the officers see what was in his bag did not provide reasonable suspicion.

United States v. Cagle, 849 F.2d 924 (5th Cir. 1988). Officers' detention of defendant's suitcase for one and one-half hours to await the arrival of a narcotics dog was unreasonable. *See also* United States v. $191,910 in U.S. Currency, 16 F.3d 1051 (9th Cir. 1994) (two hours' delay to await arrival of narcotics dog to sniff luggage was unreasonable).

United States v. West, 731 F.2d 90 (1st Cir. 1984). Drug agents seized the defendant's luggage with reasonable suspicion that it contained drugs. The defendant was allowed to continue his flight and was told how to contact agents to get his luggage back. The luggage was detained for 20 to 35 minutes until a dog sniffed it and detected drugs. Following *United States v. Place*, the court ruled that the detention of luggage was reasonable. (In this case, the dog was already at the airport when the luggage was seized.) *See also* United States v. Borys, 766 F.2d 304 (7th Cir. 1985) (court upheld a 75-minute detention of luggage to await a dog sniff); United States v. Hooper, 935 F.2d 484 (2d Cir. 1991) (detention of luggage for 30 minutes was proper); United States v. Alpert, 816 F.2d 958 (4th Cir. 1987) (50-minute detention of briefcase for dog sniff was reasonable); United States v. Cooper, 873 F.2d 269 (11th Cir. 1989) (35-minute detention of luggage for dog sniff was reasonable).

Probable Cause to Search a Person
(*This topic is discussed on page 245.*)

State v. Smith, 342 N.C. 407 (1995). The court, per curiam and without an opinion, reversed the decision of the court of appeals, 118 N.C. App. 106 (1995), that had awarded the defendant a new trial. The court stated that the decision was reversed for the reasons stated in the dissenting opinion in the court of appeals. The dissenting opinion concurred without additional comment with the majority opinion on issue (1), discussed below, and disagreed with the majority opinion on issue (2), which is set out below as discussed in the dissenting opinion—except some facts are excerpted from the majority opinion.

(1) An officer had known the defendant for two to three years and had information that he was operating a drug house and selling drugs in a certain area of Fayetteville. The officer received a phone call at 12:15 a.m. on May 12, 1992, from a reliable informant, who told the officer that the defendant would be driving a red Ford Escort with a specific license plate and was going to an unknown location to purchase cocaine. The informant said that the defendant then would go to a particular apartment on

Johnson Street, where he would package the cocaine, and then would go to a house on Buffalo Street, where he would sell it. The informant told the officer that the defendant would have the cocaine concealed in or under his crotch when he left the Johnson Street apartment. The officer and other officers took the informant to Johnson Street, where the informant pointed out the apartment and the Ford Escort. At approximately 1:15 a.m. on May 12, 1992, the defendant left the apartment in the Ford Escort. The officers stopped the defendant's car in the middle of Johnson Street where it intersected with Bragg Boulevard. The time was 1:30 a.m. The officers had probable cause to make a warrantless search of the defendant, including his crotch area.

(2) After stopping the defendant's vehicle, the officer informed the defendant that he was going to search him completely by using his flashlight and his hands. He asked the defendant to step behind the car door of the defendant's vehicle, which was open, and the officer stood between him and the car door on the outside. After the defendant opened his trousers, the officer could not see underneath the defendant's scrotum and testicles and therefore asked the defendant to pull down his underwear. Because the defendant resisted, the officer slid the defendant's underwear down and pointed his flashlight there. He saw the corner of a small paper towel underneath the defendant's scrotum. He pulled the underwear further. The defendant resisted. The officer pushed the defendant into the door, reached underneath the defendant's scrotum, and removed the paper towel that contained cocaine.

Before the search, the officer asked the defendant to step behind the open car door of his vehicle, and the officer positioned himself between the defendant and the car door on the outside. The officer testified that he took these steps because he did not want to embarrass the defendant in public. The defendant did not dispute the officer's testimony. The opinion stated that the officer took reasonable precautions to prevent the public exposure of the defendant's private areas and that "[w]hile there may have been other less intrusive means of conducting the search . . . the availability of those less intrusive means does not automatically transform an otherwise reasonable search into a Fourth Amendment violation." The search did not violate the Fourth Amendment.

State v. Williams, 209 N.C. App. 255 (2011). Probable cause and exigent circumstances supported an officer's warrantless search of the defendant's mouth by grab-bing him around the throat, pushing him onto the hood of a vehicle, and demanding that he spit out whatever he was trying to swallow. Probable cause to believe that the defendant possessed illegal drugs and was attempting to destroy them was supported by information from three reliable informants and the following facts. (1) the defendant's vehicle was covered in talcum powder, which is used to mask the odor of drugs; (2) while the officer was conducting a consent search of the defendant's person, the defendant attempted to swallow something; and (3) other suspects had attempted to swallow drugs in the officer's presence. Exigent circumstances existed because the defendant attempted to swallow four packages of cocaine, which could have endangered his health.

State v. Yates, 162 N.C. App. 118 (2004). An officer conducted a warrantless search of the defendant when he detected the odor of marijuana about his person. The officer was qualified to recognize the odor of marijuana. Relying on cases from other states, the court ruled that the officer's detection of the odor of marijuana about the defendant's person provided probable cause to search him and that exigent circumstances existed to support the warrantless search of the defendant. [Author's note: A warrantless search often may be justified by an additional theory that does not rely on a finding of exigent circumstances. Because an officer has probable cause to arrest a defendant for possession of marijuana based on the detection of the odor, a warrantless search may be conducted before an arrest as a search incident to arrest as long as the search is contemporaneous with the arrest. *See* Rawlings v. Kentucky, 448 U.S. 98 (1973); State v. Mills, 104 N.C. App. 724 (1991).]

State v. Pittman, 111 N.C. App. 808 (1993). Two officers were on patrol at the train station at 1:30 a.m. They saw the female defendant and a man speak and then part company when they saw the officers. Officer Gunn approached the defendant, and Officer Ferrell approached the man. The defendant showed Gunn a train ticket and stated that she was traveling alone and did not know the man with whom she had been seen. Gunn noticed that the defendant was constantly looking over at the man, who was 20 feet away. The defendant consented to a search of her bag; nothing was found. Meanwhile, Ferrell spoke with the man, who said he was traveling alone and did not know the defendant. The man consented to a search of his bag; nothing was found. Later a vehicle pulled up to the train station, and the man put his bag in the trunk. The man then motioned to the defendant to approach the car. He placed her bag in the trunk, and the two of them got in the car and left. The officers compared information they had learned from their encounters with the man and the defendant and had the car stopped by a uniformed officer. A female officer was called to the scene to search the defendant, who refused to consent to a search—instead the defendant was taken to the police station and searched.

(1) The court ruled that Officer Gunn did not seize the defendant at the train station. He merely approached her and asked a few questions, and she voluntarily gave him her train ticket and consented to a search of her bag. The court relied on *Florida v. Bostick*, 501 U.S. 429 (1991). (2) The court ruled that the officers had reasonable suspicion to stop the vehicle in which the defendant was a passenger, based on the facts discussed above. (3) The court ruled that the officers did not have probable cause to search the defendant after the vehicle stop, based on the facts discussed above.

Warrantless Entry with Exigent Circumstances to Search a Place for Evidence or Weapons

(This topic is discussed on pages 243 and 261.)

UNITED STATES SUPREME COURT

Kentucky v. King, 563 U.S. 452 (2011) [Author's note: The Court in this case delineated the scope of the rule that allows officers to enter a residence without a search warrant to search for evidence of a crime when exigent circumstances exist. It assumed without deciding that exigent circumstances existed, and thus the reader should remember that the Court did not decide this issue.] The officers set up a controlled buy of crack cocaine outside an apartment complex. After an undercover officer watched the deal occur, he radioed uniformed officers to move in, telling them that the suspect was moving quickly toward the breezeway of an apartment building and urging them to hurry before the suspect entered an apartment. As the uniformed officers ran into the breezeway, they heard a door shut and detected a strong odor of burnt marijuana. At the end of the breezeway they saw two apartments, one on the left and one on the right; they did not know which apartment the suspect had entered. Because they smelled marijuana coming from the apartment on the left, they approached that door, banged on it as loudly as they could, and announced their presence as the police. They heard people and things moving inside, leading them to believe that drug-related evidence was about to be destroyed. The officers then announced that they were going to enter, kicked in the door, and went in. On these facts, the state appellate court determined that the exigent circumstances rule did not allow a warrantless entry because the officers should have foreseen that their conduct would prompt the occupants to attempt to destroy evidence. The Court rejected this interpretation and stated that "the exigent circumstances rule justifies a warrantless search when the conduct of the police preceding the exigency is reasonable." It concluded: "Where, as here, the police did not create the exigency by engaging or threatening to engage in conduct that violates the Fourth Amendment, warrantless entry to prevent the destruction of evidence is reasonable and thus allowed." The Court ruled that the exigent circumstances rule applied to authorize a warrantless entry when the officers knocked on the door of a residence and announced their presence and as a result the occupants attempted to destroy evidence.

The Court rejected additional requirements for the exigent circumstances rule that would bar officers from entering without a warrant if (1) officers had a bad faith intent to avoid obtaining a search warrant; (2) it was reasonably foreseeable that officers' investigative tactics would create exigent circumstances; (3) after acquiring evidence sufficient to establish probable cause, officers did not seek a search warrant but instead knocked on the door and sought either to speak with an occupant or to obtain consent to search; (4) the officers' investigation was contrary to standard or good law enforcement practices; and (5) officers impermissibly created an exigency when they engaged in conduct that would cause a reasonable person to believe that entry was imminent and inevitable.

Mincey v. Arizona, 437 U.S. 385 (1978). The Court rejected a "murder scene exception" to the Fourth Amendment's requirement that a search warrant is generally necessary to search a house. It ruled that a four-day warrantless search of an apartment where a homicide took place was unconstitutional. There were no exigent circumstances—that is, there was no indication that evidence would be lost, destroyed, or removed during the time required to obtain a search warrant. The Court recognized an officer's authority (1) to enter and search without a warrant when the officer reasonably believes that a person within a home needs immediate aid and (2) to make a prompt warrantless search of the house to determine whether there are other victims or suspects on the premises. (See additional cases below under "Search of a Crime Scene" and "Search of a Fire Scene.")

G.M. Leasing Corp. v. United States, 429 U.S. 338 (1977). A warrantless search of a business office located in private premises was unconstitutional because there were no exigent circumstances to justify a warrantless search. Officers had delayed entry into the office for more than a day after they saw materials being removed from the office.

Vale v. Louisiana, 399 U.S. 30 (1970). Officers arrested the defendant outside his home. A warrantless search of the home for drugs was not justified because there was no emergency: the drugs were not about to be destroyed or removed. *But see* United States v. Turner, 650 F.2d 526 (4th Cir. 1981) (a warrantless entry into an apartment was justified because a person inside might have observed his accomplice's arrest outside and destroyed drugs).

Trupiano v. United States, 334 U.S. 699 (1948). A warrantless search of a building containing an illegal still was unconstitutional because officers had had probable cause to obtain a search warrant for about three weeks; thus, exigent circumstances did not exist to justify a warrantless search.

NORTH CAROLINA SUPREME COURT

State v. McKinney, 361 N.C. 53 (2006). Amy advised law enforcement that her roommate, Aja, had told her that Aja's friend, the defendant, had killed his roommate. The address of the residence where the defendant and victim apparently lived was supplied to law enforcement. Officers arrived at the residence and were advised there that the defendant was reportedly driving the victim's vehicle, which was not in the driveway. The victim's sister arrived and informed officers that the victim lived there. The victim's brother arrived shortly thereafter. Officers learned that neither the brother nor the sister had had any contact with the victim in several days and the victim had not reported for work the prior day, which was very unusual. The officers also learned that the defendant had told Aja that the victim had pulled a knife on the defendant, and that the victim "wouldn't be coming back." The victim's brother then entered the house through a window and officers followed him. The officers saw what appeared to be blood spatter in the front bedroom and other indications of blood elsewhere in the house; they secured the house, obtained a search warrant, and thereafter discovered the victim's body in a large garbage can in the house. The court ruled that the officers did not

have exigent circumstances to enter the house without a search warrant to look for the possible missing victim.

State v. Taylor, 298 N.C. 405 (1979). Even though the defendant had been arrested outside the house, officers had reason to fear for their safety from the possible use of a firearm by someone inside the house. Therefore, exigent circumstances permitted a warrantless search of the house to find the weapon.

NORTH CAROLINA COURT OF APPEALS

State v. Nowell, 144 N.C. App. 636 (2001), *aff'd*, 355 N.C. 273 (2002). The court ruled that officers did not have exigent circumstances to enter a residence to seize marijuana, based on the following facts. A drug courier working with law enforcement officers and wearing a body wire delivered approximately 50 pounds of marijuana to a residence where the purchaser and his accomplice were waiting for the delivery of the marijuana. When an officer heard through a radio transmitter that the purchaser and his accomplice were about to roll a marijuana cigarette from the marijuana and smoke it, law enforcement officers entered the residence without a search warrant.

State v. Frazier, 142 N.C. App. 361 (2001). The defendant and his girlfriend were staying long term in a motel room. The motel owners received an anonymous letter indicating that drugs were being sold in that motel room. When they informed the defendant of the letter, the defendant neither denied nor confirmed that he was selling drugs. After speaking with the motel owners, an officer decided to do a knock and talk. The girlfriend allowed the officer to enter the motel room. As the officer entered, he saw the defendant lying on a bed. The defendant got off the bed and walked toward the bathroom. The officer asked the defendant if the defendant had a problem with the officer coming in and talking with them. The defendant did not respond but continued walking toward the bathroom. The officer repeated what he had said, and the defendant told the officer that he could come into the room. As the defendant continued to walk away from the officer, the defendant looked back with what the officer felt was "a suspicious sort of look." The officer asked the defendant to stop. Instead the defendant continued walking and made a "lunge" behind a wall and shut the bathroom door. The officer feared for his safety and the safety of the officers with him. The officer forced the bathroom door open and found the defendant between the door and the tub with his hands in the ceiling tiles—where the officer later found crack cocaine and other items.

The court ruled that, based on this evidence, that the officer had probable cause and exigent circumstances to follow the defendant into the bathroom to search for illegal drugs. The court noted the following factors, among others, in determining probable cause: the defendant's suspicious behavior, his flight from the officers, and the officer's knowledge of the defendant's past criminal conduct—the court noted that the anonymous letter in this case would have been insufficient by itself to establish probable cause. The court noted the following factors, among others, in determining exigent circumstances: a defendant's fleeing or seeking to escape, the possible destruction of illegal drugs, and the degree of probable cause to believe the defendant committed the crime.

State v. Wallace, 111 N.C. App. 581 (1993). Officers received information that marijuana was being grown in the basement of a residence. However, the officers were unable to corroborate the informant's information. Therefore, they went to the residence to investigate. After the officers knocked on the door, Jolly came out and closed the door behind him. The officers told him why they were there and asked him if there were others in the residence. Jolly told the officers that one of his roommates was asleep inside. The officers then asked for consent to search the residence. Before Jolly could answer, Wallace came out of the residence. The officers then asked for consent to search, which Wallace and Jolly denied. Jolly then stated that "there might be some drug paraphernalia and marijuana seeds in the house" and that he would not consent to a search until he had time to get rid of the contraband. After the officers were denied consent to search, they heard footsteps in the residence and a door shut on the inside. The officers asked Wallace and Jolly who was in the residence, and they said they did not know because they had just arrived. The officers then went inside to execute a protective sweep before leaving the residence to obtain a search warrant. The officers saw what appeared to be marijuana plants while inside. The defendants were detained in the residence while other officers obtained a search warrant, which included information about their observation of marijuana in the house.

The court ruled: (1) Uncorroborated information initially given to the officers was insufficient to establish probable cause to search the residence. (2) The officers did not violate the defendants' rights by going to the residence to investigate. (3) Probable cause existed to search the residence when Jolly made the quoted statement above. (4) The officers did not have exigent circum-

stances to enter the residence without a search warrant. The court stated that the "record is devoid of any evidence that the officers entered the residence with a reasonably objective belief that evidence was about to be removed or destroyed." The court noted that the only purpose of the officers' entry into the residence was to conduct a protective sweep until a search warrant could be obtained, and the officers did not believe that they were in danger at any time. (5) The State could not justify the search of the residence under the independent source exception to the exclusionary rule; *see* Murray v. United States, 487 U.S. 533 (1988); Segura v. United States, 468 U.S. 796 (1984). In this case, the search warrant was prompted by what the officers saw in their unlawful entry, and the information obtained during the illegal entry was presented to the magistrate and affected the decision to issue the search warrant.

State v. Mackins, 47 N.C. App. 168 (1980). Two persons were shot in their car at night by a person in a house. One victim called a law enforcement agency. Officers arrived at the house and called for the defendant to come out. He did so after an hour. The officers handcuffed him on the front porch. The court ruled that a later warrantless entry into the house to find the weapon used in the shooting was justified by exigent circumstances—to protect the officers and others.

State v. Prevette, 43 N.C. App. 450 (1979). Exigent circumstances permitted officers to enter a house without a search warrant when (1) they saw marijuana through the front screen door and also saw persons within and outside the house who presented a danger to their safety and could possibly destroy the evidence, (2) the suspects were aware of the officers' presence, and (3) it would have taken at least one hour to get a search warrant.

State v. Sneed, 36 N.C. App. 341 (1978). Officers obtained a search warrant to search the defendant's motel room for stolen and forged checks used in a professional forgery scheme. When the officers arrived, they learned that the defendant and others had moved to another motel after they saw that the officers were checking car license plates at the first motel. Officers drove to various motels until they recognized several cars at one motel and saw an accomplice enter a particular room. Believing that the accomplice had seen them watching him go into the room, the officers conducted an immediate warrantless search. The court ruled that exigent circumstances permitted a warrantless search, based on these and other facts set out in its opinion.

FEDERAL APPELLATE COURTS

United States v. Limares, 269 F.3d 794 (7th Cir. 2001). Law enforcement officers obtained an anticipatory search warrant for the search of a residence to which a package of drugs, with a radio transmitter placed inside, was being delivered. The recipient left the residence shortly after the delivery, and the radio transmitter told officers that the package had been opened. The recipient walked a few blocks and entered another residence. Fearing that the occupants of this residence would destroy the package and its contents, officers entered it without a search warrant. The court ruled that exigent circumstances supported the officers' warrantless entry.

United States v. Jones, 239 F.3d 716 (5th Cir. 2001). Officers conducted a knock and talk at an apartment based on a complaint that drugs were being sold there. As the officers approached the apartment, the door was open, but the screen door was shut. One of the officers announced his presence and could see into the apartment through the screen door. A handgun was on the kitchen table in the officers' plain view. The defendant was standing with his back to the door near the table. The court ruled that exigent circumstances existed to permit the officers to enter the apartment to protect themselves from the possible use of the weapon against them.

United States v. Tovar-Rico, 61 F.3d 1529 (11th Cir. 1995). Officers did not have exigent circumstances to enter an apartment to seize illegal drugs when the only reason supporting exigent circumstances—that the suspects were aware of the officers' presence and might destroy the drugs—was not supported by the evidence presented at the suppression hearing.

United States v. Reed, 935 F.2d 641 (4th Cir. 1991). Exigent circumstances existed to justify an officer's warrantless entry into a trailer home to seize a sawed-off shotgun he saw resting against the wall near a man sleeping on a couch.

United States v. MacDonald, 916 F.2d 766 (2d Cir. 1990) (en banc). An undercover officer was admitted to an apartment where he purchased marijuana. He noticed a person with a cocked semiautomatic weapon, another person counting a stack of money and within reach of a .357 Magnum revolver, large quantities of marijuana and cocaine, and four other people. He also detected the odor of marijuana smoke. Ten minutes after the controlled purchase, the officer returned to the apartment with several officers. After knocking on the door and identifying

themselves, they heard the sounds of shuffling feet. Officers elsewhere advised them by radio that the occupants of the apartment were attempting to escape through a bathroom window. The officers then used a battering ram to force entry.

The court ruled that the officers had exigent circumstances to enter the apartment, based on these facts: (1) the grave nature of the ongoing crimes; (2) the presence of loaded weapons; (3) a likelihood that the suspects were using drugs; (4) a clear and immediate threat of danger to law enforcement officers and to the public; (5) not just probable cause, but actual knowledge, that the suspect committed the crime; (6) a strong reason to believe that the suspects were in the apartment; (7) a likelihood, that became reality, that a suspect might escape if not quickly arrested; (8) an urgent need to prevent a loss of evidence; (9) the additional time required to obtain a warrant at the late evening hour; and (10) the officers' attempt to enter peacefully. The court also ruled that when officers act in a lawful manner—in this case, knocking on the door—they do not impermissibly create exigent circumstances. *See also* United States v. Medina, 944 F.2d 60 (2d Cir. 1991); United States v. Gorfils, 982 F.2d 64 (2d Cir. 1992).

United States v. Timberlake, 896 F.2d 592 (D.C. Cir. 1990). Exigent circumstances did not exist to justify the officers' warrantless entry into an apartment. Although one of the three non-uniformed officers smelled the odor of PCP, there was no evidence that PCP fumes presented a danger of explosion; thus, there was no danger to people or property. There also was no evidence that those inside the apartment were aware of the officers' presence, and therefore there was no evidence that destruction of evidence was imminent. *See also* United States v. Radka, 904 F.2d 357 (6th Cir. 1990) (no objectively reasonable likelihood that people on premises would have observed law enforcement activity outside premises); United States v. Lynch, 934 F.2d 1226 (11th Cir. 1991) (similar ruling; no evidence that those in home would become suspicious when confederates were arrested away from home).

United States v. Lindsey, 877 F.2d 777 (9th Cir. 1989). Exigent circumstances existed to justify the officers' warrantless entry into a house when, after an arrest of a drug courier who had obtained drugs from the house, officers obtained information that those inside the house possessed guns and bombs and would become suspicious when the drug courier failed to return there after the sale.

United States v. Sangineto-Miranda, 859 F.2d 1501 (6th Cir. 1988). Exigent circumstances existed to justify the officers' entering an apartment without a warrant and securing the apartment while a search warrant was obtained, because the officers had an objectively reasonable belief that destruction of drugs was imminent. The officers could reasonably believe that their arrest of a drug dealer and his continued absence from the apartment would alert his accomplice in the apartment to destroy the drugs there. *See also* United States v. Socey, 846 F.2d 1439 (D.C. Cir. 1988); United States v. Lai, 944 F.2d 1434 (9th Cir. 1991); United States v. Munoz, 894 F.2d 292 (8th Cir. 1990); United States v. Schaper, 903 F.2d 891 (2d Cir. 1990) (reasonable belief existed that evidence might be destroyed if house was not immediately secured); United States v. Halliman, 923 F.2d 873 (D.C. Cir. 1991) (similar ruling; hotel room); United States v. Tobin, 923 F.2d 1506 (11th Cir. 1991) (en banc) (exigent circumstances existed to enter house to prevent destruction of evidence, based on facts occurring before knocking on door and then smelling odor of marijuana after door was opened); United States v. Carr, 939 F.2d 1442 (10th Cir. 1991) (similar ruling; smell of PCP after door was opened); United States v. Grissett, 925 F.2d 776 (4th Cir. 1991) (exigent circumstances permitted warrantless entry into motel room after door was opened and officers smelled odor of marijuana; officers did not create exigency, because person previously arrested elsewhere in motel had directed officers to this room as a place where someone could identify him); United States v. Cephas, 254 F.3d 488 (4th Cir. 2001) (exigent circumstances permitted warrantless entry into apartment when officer, after receiving anonymous information that named person was smoking marijuana with 14-year-old girl in apartment, corroborated that named person lived there, knocked on door, saw young girl in apartment, and smelled odor of marijuana coming from apartment, and person who opened apartment door tried to slam the door shut).

Warrantless Entry for a Nonsearch Purpose

(*This topic is discussed on page 260.*)

Michigan v. Fisher, 558 U.S. 45 (2009). Officers responded to a disturbance call. A couple directed them to a house where a man was "going crazy." Officers saw a pickup truck in the driveway with its front smashed; damaged fence posts along the side of the property; and three broken windows, the glass still on the ground outside. The officers also saw blood on the pickup's hood and on clothes inside the pickup, as well as on one of the doors to the house. Through a window to the house, they could

see the defendant screaming and throwing things. The back door was locked, and a couch had been placed to block the front door. The officers knocked, but the defendant refused to answer. They saw that he had a cut on his hand, and they asked him whether he needed medical attention. The defendant ignored these questions and demanded, with accompanying profanity, that the officers get a search warrant. One of the officers pushed the front door and entered the house. The Court ruled that a straightforward application of the emergency aid exception, as in *Brigham City v. Stuart*, 547 U.S. 398 (2006) (law enforcement officers may enter a home without a search warrant when they have an objectively reasonable basis for believing that an occupant is seriously injured or imminently threatened with such injury), dictates that the officer's entry into the house was reasonable under the Fourth Amendment. The Court stated that the state appellate court in this case erred in replacing the objective injury under *Brigham City* into what appeared to the officers with its hindsight determination that there was in fact no emergency: "It does not meet the needs of law enforcement or the demands of public safety to require officers to walk away from a situation like the one they encountered here. Only when an apparent threat has become an actual harm can officers rule out innocuous explanations for ominous circumstances. . . . It sufficed to invoke the emergency aid exception that it was reasonable to believe that [the defendant] had hurt himself (albeit nonfatally) and needed treatment that in his rage he was unable to provide, or that [the defendant] was about to hurt, or had already hurt, someone else."

Brigham City v. Stuart, 547 U.S. 398 (2006). About 3:00 a.m., four law enforcement officers responded to a call concerning a loud party at a residence. They heard shouting from inside and entered the driveway to investigate. They saw two juveniles drinking beer in the backyard. The officers entered the backyard and saw—through a screen door and windows—four adults attempting with some difficulty to restrain a juvenile. The juvenile eventually broke free, swung a fist, and struck one of the adults in the face. One of the officers saw the victim of the blow spitting blood into a nearby sink. The other adults continued to attempt to restrain the juvenile, pressing him against a refrigerator with such force that the refrigerator began moving across the floor. An officer opened the screen door and announced the officers' presence. Amid the tumult, nobody noticed the officer. The officer entered the kitchen and again spoke, and as the occupants slowly became aware that the officers were there, the altercation stopped.

The Court ruled that law enforcement officers may enter a home without a search warrant when they have an objectively reasonable basis for believing that an occupant is seriously injured or imminently threatened with such injury. The Court found that the officers' entry in this case was reasonable under the Fourth Amendment. The officers had an objectively reasonable basis for believing that the injured adult might need help and that the violence in the kitchen was just beginning. Also, the manner of the officers' entry was reasonable. Once they made an announcement, they were free to enter. They were not required to await a response while those within fought, oblivious to their presence. The Court, relying on its prior Fourth Amendment cases, rejected an inquiry into the officers' subjective motivation in entering the residence. An action is reasonable under the Fourth Amendment, regardless of an officer's state of mind, as long as the circumstances, viewed objectively, justify the action. It did not matter whether the officers entered the kitchen to make an arrest and gather evidence against those inside or to assist the injured and prevent further violence. The circumstances, viewed objectively, supported the entry based on a belief that an occupant was seriously injured or imminently threatened with such injury.

State v. Braswell, 312 N.C. 553 (1985). Two deputy sheriffs went to the defendant–deputy sheriff's house to inform him of his wife's violent death. The defendant's empty patrol car was parked in his driveway with the driver's door open. The officers found an empty revolver and a necktie with a bullet hole through it. These facts justified the officers' warrantless entry into the house, because they had reason to believe that the defendant might be injured and need assistance. *But see* United States v. Moss, 963 F.2d 673 (4th Cir. 1992) (officer did not have objectively reasonable belief that concern for health of cabin's occupants justified warrantless entry into and search of cabin, based on facts in this case).

State v. Jordan, ___ N.C. App. ___, 776 S.E.2d 515 (2015). The court ruled that the trial court erred in denying the defendant's motion to suppress evidence obtained as a result of a warrantless search of her residence. According to the court: "The trial court's findings that the officers observed a broken window, that the front door was unlocked, and that no one responded when the officers knocked on the door are insufficient to show that they had an objectively reasonable belief that a break-ing and entering had *recently* taken place or *was still in progress*, such that there existed an urgent need to enter the property" and that the search was justified under the exigent circumstances exception to the warrant requirement. The court continued:

In this case, the only circumstances justifying the officers' entry into defendant's residence were a broken window, an unlocked door, and the lack of response to the officers' knock at the door. We hold that although these findings may be sufficient to give the officers a reasonable belief that an illegal entry had occurred *at some point*, they are insufficient to give the officers an objectively reasonable belief that a breaking and entering was in progress or had occurred recently.

State v. China, 150 N.C. App. 469 (2002). An officer and two victims of a burglary that had occurred within an hour approached an apartment where they believed that the burglary suspect was located. As they approached, they heard a violent argument emanating from inside the apartment. The officer knocked on the door, the door opened, and the officers walked inside. One person was sitting in the living room with a knife in her hand, and the defendant walked out of the kitchen bleeding profusely from his forearm. The court ruled, citing *State v. Woods*, 136 N.C. App. 386 (2000), and *Mincey v. Arizona*, 437 U.S. 385 (1978), that the officer's warrantless entry into the apartment did not violate the Fourth Amendment because he reasonably believed that someone inside needed immediate assistance.

State v. Woods, 136 N.C. App. 386 (2000). Officers were dispatched to investigate an alarm sounding at the defendant's residence. After arriving at the residence, an officer heard the alarm and saw that the rear door of the residence was open. After announcing his presence and identity, he heard no response from inside the residence. The officer conducted a cursory search of the residence for potential victims or suspects. He found no one but saw evidence of a break-in. He and other officers reentered the residence to conduct a more thorough search, looking again for victims and suspects. In the master bedroom, they opened a drawer in a standing chest that was about 15 to 20 inches deep, 25 to 30 inches long, and 18 inches wide; they discovered a bag of green vegetable material and then radioed drug officers to come to the scene. In the area containing the kitchen and living room, they saw a cabinet that was about 34 inches tall and 48 inches wide.

While attempting to open the doors to the cabinet, an officer moved a chair and heard a noise underneath it. His flashlight revealed a tear on the bottom of the chair and a bag inside that appeared to contain money. He opened the cabinet door but found nothing. Officers later obtained a search warrant and discovered various drugs, money, and drug paraphernalia.

Relying on *United States v. Dart*, 747 F.2d 263 (4th Cir. 1984), and other cases, the court ruled that the officers' warrantless entry into the residence to investigate a possible break-in was justified by exigent circumstances and thus was reasonable under the Fourth Amendment. It was clear that a break-in had occurred, and the officers had reason to believe that the intruders or victims could still be in the residence. The court also ruled, relying on *Mincey v. Arizona*, 437 U.S. 385 (1978), that the officers' search of the chest of drawers, chair, and cabinet exceeded the scope of the permissible search for suspects and victims. It was unreasonable to believe that a small child could have been found in the cabinet, based on the facts in this case. Because the fruits of the illegal searches established probable cause for the search warrant, the evidence seized was inadmissible at trial.

Strip Search of a Person

(This topic is discussed on page 253.)

State v. Stone, 362 N.C. 50 (2007). The court ruled that a search of a defendant in which an officer shined a flashlight inside the defendant's underwear, when the defendant had given consent to a generic search for weapons or drugs during a routine traffic stop, was not within the scope of the defendant's consent to search and thus violated the Fourth Amendment. An officer stopped a car for speeding. The officer asked the defendant, a passenger, whether he had any drugs or weapons on his person. The defendant said no, which prompted the officer to ask for consent to search. The defendant gave consent. The defendant was wearing a jacket and drawstring sweatpants. During the initial search, the officer found $552 in cash in the lower left pocket of the sweatpants. He again asked the defendant if he had anything on him. Once again, the defendant denied having drugs or weapons and authorized the officer to continue the search. The officer checked the rear of the sweatpants and moved his hands to the front of the defendant's waistband. The officer then pulled the defendant's sweatpants away from his body and trained his flashlight on the defendant's groin area. The defendant objected, but by that time, the officer

had already seen the white cap of what appeared to be a pill bottle tucked in between the defendant's inner thigh and testicles. The court concluded that a reasonable person would not have understood that his consent included such an examination. The scope of a general consent to search does not necessarily include consent for an officer to move clothing to directly observe the genitals of a clothed person. The court noted that its ruling is necessarily predicated on the facts and that different actions by the officer could have led to a different result. [Author's note: The only basis on which the State justified the officer's search was consent. Thus, the court did not discuss whether probable cause and exigent circumstances supported the search. See *State v. Smith*, 342 N.C. 407 (1995), reversing the court of appeals for reasons stated in the dissenting opinion, 118 N.C. App. 106 (1995), discussed in the court's opinion.]

State v. Smith, 342 N.C. 407 (1995). The court, per curiam and without an opinion, reversed the decision of the court of appeals, 118 N.C. App. 106 (1995), that had awarded the defendant a new trial. The court stated that the decision was reversed for the reasons stated in the dissenting opinion in the court of appeals. The dissenting opinion concurred without additional comment with the majority opinion on issue (1), discussed below, and disagreed with the majority opinion on issue (2), which is set out below as discussed in the dissenting opinion—except some facts are excerpted from the majority opinion.

(1) An officer had known the defendant for two to three years and had information that he was operating a drug house and selling drugs in a certain area of Fayetteville. The officer received a phone call at 12:15 a.m. on May 12, 1992, from a reliable informant, who told the officer that the defendant would be driving a red Ford Escort with a specific license plate and was going to an unknown location to purchase cocaine. The informant said that the defendant then would go to a particular apartment on Johnson Street, where he would package the cocaine, and then would go to a house on Buffalo Street, where he would sell it. The informant told the officer that the defendant would have the cocaine concealed in or under his crotch when he left the Johnson Street apartment. The officer and other officers took the informant to Johnson Street, where the informant pointed out the apartment and the Ford Escort. At approximately 1:15 a.m. on May 12, 1992, the defendant left the apartment in the Ford Escort. The officers stopped the defendant's car in the middle of Johnson Street where it intersected with Bragg

Boulevard. The time was 1:30 a.m. The officers had probable cause to make a warrantless search of the defendant, including his crotch area.

(2) After stopping the defendant's vehicle, the officer informed the defendant that he was going to search him completely by using his flashlight and his hands. He asked the defendant to step behind the car door of the defendant's vehicle, which was open, and the officer stood between him and the car door on the outside. After the defendant opened his trousers, the officer could not see underneath the defendant's scrotum and testicles and therefore asked the defendant to pull down his underwear. Because the defendant resisted, the officer slid the defendant's underwear down and pointed his flashlight there. He saw the corner of a small paper towel underneath the defendant's scrotum. He pulled the underwear further. The defendant resisted. The officer pushed the defendant into the door, reached underneath the defendant's scrotum, and removed the paper towel that contained cocaine.

Before the search, the officer asked the defendant to step behind the open car door of his vehicle, and the officer positioned himself between the defendant and the car door on the outside. The officer testified that he took these steps because he did not want to embarrass the defendant in public. The defendant did not dispute the officer's testimony. The opinion stated that the officer took reasonable precautions to prevent the public exposure of the defendant's private areas and that "[w]hile there may have been other less intrusive means of conducting the search . . . the availability of those less intrusive means does not automatically transform an otherwise reasonable search into a Fourth Amendment violation." The search did not violate the Fourth Amendment.

State v. Johnson, 225 N.C. App. 440 (2013). The court ruled (1) that probable cause and exigent circumstances supported an officer's roadside search of the defendant's underwear conducted after a vehicle stop and (2) that the search was conducted in a reasonable manner. After finding nothing in the defendant's outer clothing, the officer placed the defendant on the side of his vehicle, with the vehicle between the defendant and the travelled portion of the highway. Other troopers stood around the defendant to prevent passersby from seeing him. The officer pulled out the front waistband of the defendant's pants and looked inside. The defendant was wearing two pairs of underwear—an outer pair of boxer briefs and an inner pair of athletic compression shorts. Between the two

pairs of underwear the officer found a cellophane package containing several smaller packages. There was probable cause to search when the defendant smelled of marijuana, officers found a scale of the type used to measure drugs in his car, a drug dog alerted in his car, and during a pat-down the officer noticed a blunt object in the inseam of the defendant's pants. Because narcotics can be easily and quickly hidden or destroyed, especially after a defendant has notice of an officer's intent to discover whether the defendant possessed them, such exigent circumstances may be sufficient to justify a warrantless search, as was the case here. In addition, the search here was conducted in a reasonable manner. Although the officer did not see the defendant's private parts, the level of the defendant's exposure was relevant to analyze whether the search was reasonable. The court reasoned that the officer had a sufficient basis to believe that contraband was in the defendant's underwear, including the fact that although the defendant smelled of marijuana, a search of his outer clothing found nothing; the defendant turned away from the officer when the officer frisked his groin and thigh area; and the officer felt a blunt object in the defendant's crotch area during the pat down. Finally, the court concluded that the officer took reasonable steps to protect the defendant's privacy when conducting the search.

State v. Robinson, 221 N.C. App. 266 (2012). [Author's note: There was a dissenting opinion in this case, but the defendant later withdrew his appeal to the North Carolina Supreme Court, 366 N.C. 247 (2012).] The court ruled that an officer had probable cause to arrest the defendant after he felt something hard between the defendant's buttocks during a weapons frisk. The officer properly inferred that the defendant may be hiding drugs in his buttocks. The officer knew that the defendant was sitting in a car parked in a high crime area, a large machete was seen in the car, and a passenger possessed what appeared to be cocaine. When officers began to speak with the vehicle's occupants, the defendant dropped a large sum of cash on the floor and made a quick movement behind his back. The court also ruled that the searching officer had a sufficient basis to believe that the defendant had contraband beneath his underwear and that he took reasonable steps to protect the defendant's privacy during an intrusive search that discovered a clear plastic baggie of crack cocaine located between the defendant's buttocks. The officer shielded the defendant from public view by opening his patrol car's rear door and standing directly behind the defendant. The patrol car's lights were not turned on.

The shining of the officer's flashlight into the defendant's pants was the only illumination in the immediate vicinity, and there were no other people in the search area. The officer did not put his hands or his flashlight down the defendant's pants.

State v. Fowler, 220 N.C. App. 263 (2012). The court ruled that two roadside strip searches of the defendant by officers were reasonable and constitutional. The court first rejected the State's argument that the searches were not strip searches. During both searches the defendant's private areas were observed by an officer, and during the second search the defendant's pants were removed and an officer searched inside the defendant's underwear with his hand. Second, the court ruled that probable cause supported the searches. The officers stopped the defendant's vehicle for speeding after receiving information from another officer and his informant that the defendant would be traveling on a specified road in a silver Kia, carrying 3 grams of crack cocaine. The strip searches occurred after a consensual search of the defendant's vehicle produced marijuana but no cocaine. The court found competent evidence to show that the informant, who was known to the officers and had previously provided reliable information, provided sufficient reliable information, corroborated by an officer, to establish probable cause to believe that the defendant would be carrying a small amount of cocaine in his vehicle. When the consensual search of the defendant's vehicle did not produce the cocaine, the officers had sufficient probable cause, under the totality of the circumstances, to believe that the defendant was hiding the drugs on his person. Third, the court found that exigent circumstances supported the searches. Specifically, the officer knew that the defendant had prior experience with jail intake procedures and that he could reasonably expect that the defendant would attempt to get rid of evidence in order to prevent his going to jail. Fourth, the court found that the searches were reasonable. The trial court had determined that although the searches were intrusive, the most intrusive one occurred in a dark area away from the traveled roadway, with no one other than the defendant and the officers in the immediate vicinity. In addition, the trial court found that the officer did not pull down the defendant's underwear or otherwise expose his bare buttocks or genitals, and no females were present or within view during the search.

The court determined that these findings supported the trial court's conclusion that, although the searches were intrusive, they were conducted in a discreet manner, away from the view of others, and they were limited in scope to finding a small amount of cocaine based on the corroborated tip of a known, reliable informant.

State v. Battle, 202 N.C. App. 376 (2010). Officers received a tip from a confidential informant that three named people were going to Durham to obtain cocaine and then transport it back to Granville County, exiting at the Linden Avenue exit off Interstate 95. The officers stopped the vehicle shortly after it exited there. It was daylight (a summer day around 5:00 p.m.). Two male passengers were searched and no illegal drugs were found. The third passenger, a female, was strip searched by a female officer between the open doors of the vehicle at the roadside. The officer conducting the search pulled the female passenger's underwear out from her body and discovered a folded five dollar bill and a crack pipe.

(1) The opinion for the court, which was not joined by the two other judges on the three-judge panel, noted that for purposes of this appeal, it was assumed that the officers had probable cause to arrest the defendant and search her incident to arrest. However, the opinion stated that for a roadside strip search to be constitutional, there must be both probable cause and exigent circumstances to show that some significant government or public interest would be endangered were law enforcement officers to wait until they could conduct the search in a more discreet location, usually at a private location within a law enforcement facility. The opinion, which extensively discussed the facts and case law from North Carolina and other jurisdictions, ruled that the strip search violated the defendant's Fourth Amendment rights. The opinion stated that the trial court's order denying the defendant's motion to suppress did not show that there were exigent circumstances justifying any search more intrusive than that allowed incident to any arrest. (2) A second judge on the three-judge panel concurred only in the result (granting the defendant's motion to suppress) without an opinion. (3) A third judge on the three-judge panel concurred with an opinion that noted that the North Carolina Supreme Court in *State v. Stone*, 362 N.C. 50 (2007) (defendant's general consent to search did not include officer's flashlight search of genitals inside defendant's underwear), had ruled that an officer's search with at least questionable consent was not permissible under the Fourth Amendment. And because the search in *Battle*

without the defendant's consent was more intrusive than that in *Stone*, it was not permissible under the Fourth Amendment. [Author's note: Although a majority of the three-judge panel agreed that the strip search violated the Fourth Amendment, there was not majority agreement as to why the search violated the Fourth Amendment.]

State v. Neal, 190 N.C. App. 453 (2008). The defendant was convicted of several cocaine offenses. The court ruled, relying on the standards set out in *Florida v. Jimeno*, 500 U.S. 248 (1991), and *State v. Stone*, 362 N.C. 50 (2007), that the scope of the defendant's consent to search included a strip search. An officer detected a mild odor of marijuana coming from the passenger side of a car in which the defendant was seated. The defendant consented to a pat-down search of her person to check for weapons and also consented to a search of her purse. A drug dog reacted to the passenger side. While the canine search was being conducted, the defendant acted very nervous and often put her hands in and out of the back of the waistband of her pants. An officer noticed a bulge in the back of the defendant's pants, and she was instructed to keep her hands away from the waistband. The officer informed the defendant that he wanted to conduct a better search to determine what was located in the back of her pants and that he had contacted a female officer for assistance. The female officer conducted a search of the defendant in the women's bathroom, with another officer standing outside the door to prevent others from entering. The female officer explained to the defendant that she would be conducting a more thorough search. The defendant indicated that she understood. During the search, the defendant was asked to lower her underwear and a package containing cocaine fell out. The female officer testified that the defendant was "very cooperative, extremely cooperative" during the search and never expressed any misgivings about the scope of the search.

State v. Johnson, 143 N.C. App. 307 (2001). Officers executed a search warrant authorizing a search of the defendant and his apartment for illegal drugs, based on information that the defendant was selling crack cocaine in his apartment. During the search, the officers seized two shotguns and a pair of electronic scales. An initial search of the defendant revealed almost $2,000 in small denominations. The officers then asked the defendant to remove his clothing and to bend over at the waist. When he did, they saw a piece of plastic protruding from his anus. The defendant complied with the officers' request that he remove the package, which contained seventeen individually packaged bags of crack cocaine.

The court ruled that this strip search was reasonable under the totality of circumstances. The court stated that the strip search was not unreasonable simply because the officer did not articulate specific reasons in the search warrant application as to why a strip search was necessary. [Author's note: The court noted a case that ruled that reasons were not necessary, *State v. Colin*, 809 P.2d 228 (Wash. App. 1991).] Controlled substances could readily be concealed on a person so that they would not be found without a strip search, and an officer testified at the suppression hearing that there is a trend toward hiding controlled substances in body cavities. The court also noted the approval of a strip search in *State v. Smith*, 342 N.C. 407 (1995) (pulling down defendant's pants far enough that officers could see the corner of a towel underneath the defendant's scrotum). The court also ruled that the search was conducted in a reasonable manner. Two male officers searched the defendant in his bedroom, and they did not touch him.

Amaechi v. West, 237 F.3d 356 (4th Cir. 2001). An officer arrested a person (the plaintiff in this civil lawsuit against the officer) with an arrest warrant charging a misdemeanor violation of a town ordinance that had occurred two days earlier. The arrestee was naked under her house dress and did not resist the arrest, but the officer still searched her—in public—by swiping his ungloved hand, palm up, across her bare vagina, at which time the tip of his finger slightly penetrated her genitals. The court ruled that this search incident to arrest was unreasonable under the Fourth Amendment. The officer's search was highly intrusive without any apparent justification. *Compare with* United States v. Daniels, 323 Fed. Appx. 201 (4th Cir. 2009) (unpublished) (strip search of defendant's underwear after drug distribution arrest was authorized when officer had reasonable suspicion drugs were concealed there and search occurred away from public view).

Swain v. Spinney, 117 F.3d 1 (1st Cir. 1997). The defendant was arrested for marijuana and was in a police station jail cell about an hour after she was arrested when she was subjected to a strip search and a visual body cavity search. The court ruled that a strip search and a visual body cavity search must be justified, at the least, by reasonable suspicion that the arrestee was concealing drugs or weapons.

Search and Seizure of Evidence from a Person's Body

(*This topic is discussed on page 246.*)

UNITED STATES SUPREME COURT

Maryland v. King, 133 S. Ct. 1958 (2013). The Court ruled that the defendant's Fourth Amendment rights were not violated by the taking of a DNA cheek swab as part of booking procedures. When the defendant was arrested in April 2009 for menacing a group of people with a shotgun and charged in state court with assault, he was processed for detention in custody at a central booking facility. Booking personnel used a cheek swab to take the DNA sample from him pursuant to the Maryland DNA Collection Act (Maryland Act). His DNA record was uploaded into the Maryland DNA database, and it was discovered that his profile matched a DNA sample from a 2003 unsolved rape case. He was later charged and convicted in the rape case. He challenged the conviction by arguing that the Maryland Act violated the Fourth Amendment. The Maryland appellate court agreed. The Supreme Court reversed. The Court found that using a buccal swab on the inner tissues of a person's cheek to obtain a DNA sample was a search. The Court noted that a determination of the reasonableness of the search requires a weighing of "the promotion of legitimate governmental interests" against "the degree to which [the search] intrudes upon an individual's privacy." It found that "[i]n the balance of reasonableness . . . , the Court must give great weight both to the significant government interest at stake in the identification of arrestees and to the unmatched potential of DNA identification to serve that interest." The Court noted in particular the superiority of DNA identification over fingerprint and photographic identification. Addressing privacy issues, the Court found that "the intrusion of a cheek swab to obtain a DNA sample is a minimal one." It noted that a gentle rub along the inside of the cheek does not break the skin and involves virtually no risk, trauma, or pain. And, distinguishing special needs searches, the Court noted: "Once an individual has been arrested on probable cause for a dangerous offense that may require detention before trial . . . his or her expectations of privacy and freedom from police scrutiny are reduced. DNA identification like that at issue here thus does not require consideration of any unique needs that would be required to justify searching the average citizen." The Court further determined that the processing of the defendant's DNA was not unconstitutional. The information obtained does not reveal genetic traits or private medical information, and testing is solely for the purpose of identification. Additionally, the Maryland Act protects against further invasions of privacy by, for example, limiting use to identification. The Court concluded:

> In light of the context of a valid arrest supported by probable cause respondent's expectations of privacy were not offended by the minor intrusion of a brief swab of his cheeks. By contrast, that same context of arrest gives rise to significant state interests in identifying respondent not only so that the proper name can be attached to his charges but also so that the criminal justice system can make informed decisions concerning pretrial custody. Upon these considerations the Court concludes that DNA identification of arrestees is a reasonable search that can be considered part of a routine booking procedure. When officers make an arrest supported by probable cause to hold for a serious offense and they bring the suspect to the station to be detained in custody, taking and analyzing a cheek swab of the arrestee's DNA is, like fingerprinting and photographing, a legitimate police booking procedure that is reasonable under the Fourth Amendment.

Missouri v. McNeely, 133 S. Ct. 1552 (2013). The Court ruled that in impaired driving investigations, the natural dissipation of alcohol in the bloodstream does not constitute an exigency in every case sufficient to justify conducting a blood test without a warrant. After stopping the defendant's vehicle for speeding and crossing the center line, an officer noticed several signs that the defendant was intoxicated, and the defendant acknowledged that he had consumed "a couple of beers." When the defendant performed poorly on field sobriety tests and declined to use a portable breath-test device, the officer placed him under arrest and began driving to the stationhouse. But when the defendant said that he would again refuse to provide a breath sample, the officer took him to a nearby hospital for blood testing. The officer did not attempt to secure a search warrant for the defendant's blood draw. Test results showed that the defendant's blood alcohol content was above the legal limit. The defendant was charged with impaired driving, and he moved to suppress the blood test. The trial court granted the defendant's motion, concluding that the exigency exception to the search warrant requirement did not apply because, apart from the fact that as in all intoxication cases, the defendant's blood alcohol was being metabolized by his liver, there were no circumstances suggesting that the officer faced an emergency in which he could not practicably obtain a search warrant. The state supreme court affirmed, reasoning that *Schmerber v. California*, 384 U.S. 757 (1966), required lower courts to consider the totality of the circumstances when determining whether exigency permits a nonconsensual, warrantless blood draw. The state court concluded that *Schmerber* "requires more than the mere dissipation of blood-alcohol evidence to support a warrantless blood draw in an alcohol-related case." (*See* State v. McNeely, 358 S.W.3d 65 (2012).) The United States Supreme Court affirmed. The Court noted that under *Schmerber* and the Court's case law, applying the exigent circumstances exception requires consideration of all of the facts and circumstances of the particular case. It then rejected the State's request for a per se rule for blood testing in impaired driving cases, declining to "depart from careful case-by-case assessment of exigency." It concluded: "[W]hile the natural dissipation of alcohol in the blood may support a finding of exigency in a specific case, as it did in *Schmerber*, it does not do so categorically. Whether a warrantless blood test of a drunk-driving suspect is reasonable must be determined case by case based on the totality of the circumstances."

Board of Education of Independent School District No. 92 of Pottawatomie County v. Earls, 536 U.S. 822 (2002). The Court ruled that requiring drug testing of high school students involved in competitive extracurricular activities does not violate the Fourth Amendment, even though there is no reasonable suspicion to believe that the students use illegal drugs.

Vernonia School District 47J v. Acton, 515 U.S. 646 (1995). The Court ruled that random urinalysis testing of public school students participating in interscholastic athletics was reasonable under the Fourth Amendment, based on the facts in this case, even though the testing was not based on reasonable suspicion. *See also* Miller *ex. rel* Miller v. Wilkes, 172 F.3d 574 (8th Cir. 1999) (policy of random urine testing of students for presence of controlled substances and alcohol, with disqualification from extra activities as sanction for refusing to submit to test or for testing positive, did not violate Fourth Amendment).

Hayes v. Florida, 470 U.S. 811 (1985). With neither probable cause to arrest nor judicial authorization, offi-

cers took the defendant without his consent from his home to a police station and took his fingerprints. The Court ruled that the officers' action was an illegal seizure under the Fourth Amendment. It noted that the Fourth Amendment may permit a judicial official to authorize a seizure of a person with less than probable cause and to bring him to a police station for fingerprinting. The Court also noted that the Fourth Amendment may permit an officer to detain briefly a person in the field for fingerprinting when the officer has reasonable suspicion that the person committed a crime and a reasonable belief that fingerprinting will establish or negate the suspect's connection with the crime.

Winston v. Lee, 470 U.S. 753 (1985). A shopkeeper shot an assailant in the left side during an attempted robbery, and he later identified the defendant at a hospital as the assailant. The State sought a court order to compel surgery on the defendant to remove the bullet from his body for evidence. Based on *Schmerber v. California*, discussed below, the Court ruled that surgery in this case would be unreasonable under the Fourth Amendment. The State did not show a compelling need for evidence that outweighed the proposed surgical intrusion into the defendant's body under general anesthesia to retrieve the bullet.

Cupp v. Murphy, 412 U.S. 291 (1973). The defendant appeared voluntarily at the police station for questioning about the strangulation murder of his wife. Abrasions and lacerations had been found on the victim's throat, and there was no sign of a break-in or robbery. Although the defendant was not arrested when he appeared at the station, police had probable cause to arrest him. At the station, officers noticed a dark spot under the defendant's fingernail. Suspecting that it might be dried blood and knowing that evidence of strangulation is often found under fingernails, officers asked him whether they could scrape under his fingernails. The defendant refused and put his hands in his pocket, but the officers took the scrapings anyway. The defendant then left the station. The Court ruled that the limited warrantless intrusion by scraping under the fingernails was reasonable under the Fourth Amendment, because that evidence could readily have been destroyed. Although a full search incident to arrest could not have been conducted because the defendant was not arrested, the scraping of fingernails was a limited permissible search under the facts in this case.

Davis v. Mississippi, 394 U.S. 721 (1969). Officers took the defendant without his consent to police headquarters and took his fingerprints. They had neither probable cause to arrest him nor judicial authorization to take his fingerprints. The Court ruled that detention for fingerprinting was an illegal seizure under the Fourth Amendment and the fingerprint evidence was inadmissible at trial. It noted that it need not determine whether the Fourth Amendment would permit—under narrowly circumscribed procedures—fingerprinting of a person for whom an officer does not have probable cause to arrest.

Schmerber v. California, 384 U.S. 757 (1966). The defendant, while receiving treatment at a hospital for injuries suffered in a car accident, was arrested for driving under the influence of intoxicating liquor. An officer directed a doctor, over the defendant's objection—which was based on the advice of counsel—to take blood for analysis of its alcohol content.

The Court ruled that the taking of blood did not violate the defendant's Fourth, Fifth, or Sixth Amendment rights. It also ruled that exigent circumstances permitted taking the blood without a search warrant, because alcohol in the blood begins to dissipate shortly after the drinking stops. The Court also noted that the taking of blood was performed in a reasonable manner—by a doctor in a hospital according to accepted medical practices. *See also* State v. Welch, 316 N.C. 578 (1986), State v. Hollingsworth, 77 N.C. App. 36 (1985); United States v. Edmo, 140 F.3d 1289 (9th Cir. 1998) (taking urine sample from impaired driving defendant to test for marijuana did not violate his Fourth, Fifth, or Sixth Amendment rights, based on *Schmerber*).

NORTH CAROLINA SUPREME COURT

State v. Carter, 322 N.C. 709 (1988). An officer's use of a nontestimonial identification order to obtain a blood sample for blood-typing from an in-custody defendant was unlawful, based on prior court rulings—for example, *State v. Welch*, 316 N.C. 578 (1986), discussed in Chapter 4. The court ruled that the taking of the blood sample without the defendant's consent violated the North Carolina Constitution because probable cause and a search warrant are required unless exigent circumstances exist, and there were no exigent circumstances in this case because the blood was needed for blood-typing. Reasonable suspicion is an insufficient evidentiary standard to take a blood sample from a defendant.

State v. Sharpe, 284 N.C. 157 (1973). The defendant was arrested for murder and was in police custody. A warrantless seizure of the defendant's arm hairs and head hairs was reasonable under the Fourth Amendment, when the means used to obtain the hairs were reasonable. In this case, the defendant pulled out his head hair and gave it to the technician; the record does not reveal how arm hair was removed. *See also* State v. Downes, 57 N.C. App. 102 (1982); State v. Reynolds, 298 N.C. 380 (1979); State v. Payne, 328 N.C. 377 (1991).

NORTH CAROLINA COURT OF APPEALS

State v. Romano, ___ N.C. App. ___, 785 S.E.2d 168 (2016). In this DWI case, the court ruled that the trial court did not err by suppressing blood draw evidence that an officer collected from a nurse who was treating the defendant. The trial court had found that no exigency existed justifying the warrantless search and that G.S. 20-16.2, as applied in this case, violated *Missouri v. McNeely*, 133 S. Ct. 1552 (2013). The court noted that in *McNeely*, the United States Supreme Court ruled that "the natural metabolization of alcohol in the bloodstream" does not present a "per se exigency that justifies an exception to the Fourth Amendment's warrant requirement for nonconsensual blood testing in all drunk-driving cases." Rather, it ruled that exigency must be determined based on the totality of the circumstances. Here, the officer never advised the defendant of his rights according to G.S. 20-16.2 and did not obtain his written or oral consent to the blood test. Rather, she waited until an excess of blood was drawn, beyond the amount needed for medical treatment, and procured it from the attending nurse. The officer testified that she believed her actions were reasonable under G.S. 20-16.2(b), which allows the testing of an unconscious person in certain circumstances. Noting that it had affirmed the use of the statute to justify warrantless blood draws of unconscious DWI defendants, the court further noted that all of those decisions were decided before *McNeely*. Here, under the totality of the circumstances and considering the alleged exigencies, the warrantless blood draw was not objectively reasonable. The court rejected the State's argument that the blood should be admitted under the independent source doctrine, noting that the evidence was never obtained independently from lawful activities untainted by the initial illegality. It likewise rejected the State's argument that the blood should be admitted under the good faith exception. That exception allows officers to objectively and reasonably rely on a warrant later found to be invalid. Here, however, the officers never obtained a search warrant.

State v. Granger, 235 N.C. App. 157 (2014). In this DWI case, the court ruled that under *Missouri v. McNeely*, 133 S. Ct. 1552 (2013) (the natural dissipation of alcohol in the bloodstream does not constitute an exigency in every case sufficient to justify conducting a blood test without a warrant), exigent circumstances justified the warrantless blood draw. The officer was concerned about the dissipation of alcohol from the defendant's blood because it took more than an hour for the officer to establish probable cause to make his request for the defendant's blood. The delay occurred because the defendant's injuries and need for medical care prevented the officer from investigating the matter until he arrived at the hospital, where the defendant was taken after his accident. The officer was concerned about the delay in getting a warrant (about 40 minutes), including the need to wait for another officer to come to the hospital and stay with the defendant while he left to get the warrant. Additionally, the officer was concerned that if he waited for a warrant, the defendant would receive pain medication for his injuries, contaminating his blood sample.

State v. Dahlquist, 231 N.C. App. 491 (2013). The court in this DWI case ruled that the trial court properly denied the defendant's motion to suppress evidence obtained from blood samples taken at a hospital without a search warrant when probable cause and exigent circumstances supported the warrantless blood draw. Noting the United States Supreme Court's ruling in *Missouri v. McNeely*, 133 S. Ct. 1552 (2013) (natural dissipation of alcohol in the bloodstream does not constitute an exigency in every case sufficient to justify conducting a blood test without a warrant), the court found that the totality of the circumstances supported the warrantless blood draw. Specifically, when the defendant pulled up to a checkpoint, an officer noticed the odor of alcohol and the defendant admitted to drinking five beers. After the defendant failed field sobriety tests, he refused to take an Intoxilyzer test. The officer then took the defendant to the hospital to have a blood sample taken without first obtaining a search warrant. The officer did this because it would have taken four to five hours to get the sample if he first had to travel to a magistrate for a warrant. The court noted however that the "'video transmission' option that has been allowed by [G.S.] 15A-245(a)(3) [for communicating with a magistrate] . . . is a method that should be considered by arresting officers in cases such as this where the technology is available." It also advised: "[W]e believe the better practice in such cases might be for an arresting officer, where practical, to call the hospital and the [magistrate's office] to obtain information regarding the wait times on that specific night, rather than relying on previous experiences."

State v. Williams, 209 N.C. App. 255 (2011). Probable cause and exigent circumstances supported an officer's warrantless search of the defendant's mouth by grabbing him around the throat, pushing him onto the hood of a vehicle, and demanding that he spit out whatever he was trying to swallow. Probable cause to believe that the defendant possessed illegal drugs and was attempting to destroy them was supported by information from three reliable informants and the following facts: (1) the defendant's vehicle was covered in talcum powder, which is used to mask the odor of drugs; (2) while the officer was conducting a consent search of the defendant's person, the defendant attempted to swallow something; and (3) other suspects had attempted to swallow drugs in the officer's presence. Exigent circumstances existed because the defendant attempted to swallow four packages of cocaine, which could have endangered his health.

State v. Fletcher, 202 N.C. App. 107 (2010). The defendant was arrested at a checkpoint for DWI and taken to a police station for Intoximeter breath testing, which the defendant refused. An officer then transported the defendant to a hospital to compel a blood test. The defendant's blood was drawn, and the blood test result was 0.10. The court ruled that the officer reasonably believed under G.S. 20-139.1(d1) that the delay necessary to obtain a court order would result in the dissipation of alcohol in the defendant's blood. The officer testified that the entire process of driving to the magistrate's office, standing in line, completing the required forms, returning to the hospital, and having the defendant's blood drawn would have taken from two to three hours. The court also ruled that probable cause and exigent circumstances supported the warrantless compelling of the blood sample and did not violate the Fourth Amendment or various provisions of the North Carolina Constitution.

Jones v. Graham County Board of Education, 197 N.C. App. 279 (2009). The court ruled, distinguishing Boesche v. Raleigh-Durham Airport Authority, 111 N.C. App. 149 (1993), that a local school board's policy of random, suspicionless drug and alcohol testing of all employees violated Article I, Section 20, of the North Carolina Constitution prohibiting unreasonable searches.

State v. Watson, 119 N.C. App. 395 (1995). Three officers approached a convenience store at night. Officer A had made 50 or more arrests for possession of cocaine in this area. Officer A knew that the defendant had previously been arrested for drug charges. The defendant, on seeing the officers, put items in his mouth and started to go back into the store. Officer A grabbed the defendant's jacket, and the defendant then attempted to drink a soft drink. The officer took the drink away, ordered the defendant to spit out the objects in his mouth, and applied pressure to the defendant's throat so that he would spit out the items. The defendant spit out three baggies containing crack cocaine.

Based on this and other evidence—for example, officers testified at the suppression hearing that drug dealers will attempt to conceal or to swallow drugs when they see officers—the court ruled that the officers had reasonable suspicion to stop the defendant; the court cited *State v. Butler*, 331 N.C. 227 (1992). The court also ruled that exigent circumstances supported the reasonableness of the officer's actions in applying pressure to the defendant's throat so that he would not swallow the drugs he had placed in his mouth (the court considered the officers' training and experience, their familiarity with the area, the defendant, and the practice of drug dealers of hiding drugs in their mouths to elude detection).

Second Look Doctrine

(*This topic is discussed on page 247.*)

State v. Nelson, 298 N.C. 573 (1979). Defendants, who were military personnel, were arrested and confined to a county jail for state criminal offenses. The military's inventory of the defendant's military quarters, conducted pursuant to military regulations requiring inventory of quarters of personnel confined by civilian authorities, was reasonable. Military officers then looked again at the inventoried items when they determined, three days later, that the items might be connected with a crime.

The court ruled that this "second look" at the same items already inventoried—even though it was done for an investigatory purpose—did not violate the Fourth Amendment. *See also* State v. Warren, 309 N.C. 224 (1983) (chemical tests performed on bloodstains in car while it was impounded at garage—after first search under search warrant had been completed—was justified under *State v. Nelson*, cited above). *See generally* United States v. Turner, 28 F.3d 981 (9th Cir. 1994) (federal postal inspector could seize without a warrant defendant's cap that was in state jail's lawful custody); United States v. Burnette, 698 F.2d

1038 (9th Cir. 1983); United States v. Grill, 484 F.2d 990 (5th Cir. 1973).

Search and Seizure of Obscene Materials

(*This topic is discussed on page 246.*)

Maryland v. Macon, 472 U.S. 463 (1985). An undercover detective's purchase of two allegedly obscene magazines in an adult bookstore open to the public is not a search or seizure under the Fourth Amendment.

Roaden v. Kentucky, 413 U.S. 496 (1973). A sheriff watched a movie at a commercial drive-in and decided that it was obscene (no prior judicial determination of obscenity had been made). After the movie ended, he arrested the theater manager without a warrant and seized without a warrant one copy of the movie incident to the arrest. The Court ruled that the sheriff's warrantless seizure of the movie was unreasonable under the Fourth Amendment because it was a form of prior restraint of freedom of expression of material allegedly within the protection of the First Amendment. The Court noted that this was not a "now or never" situation in which exigent circumstances may permit a warrantless seizure. It explained that when movies are scheduled for exhibition in a commercial theater open to the public, obtaining a search warrant based on a prior judicial determination of obscenity does not risk a loss of evidence. (See page 497 for cases on search warrants for obscene materials.)

Objective Standard in Determining Probable Cause or Reasonable Suspicion

(*This topic is discussed on page 235.*)

United States v. Swann, 149 F.3d 271 (4th Cir. 1998). An officer stopped and frisked two suspects. The officer felt something hard and unusual in the defendant's sock. He did not testify that he believed it to be a weapon or that he knew it was not a weapon; rather, he stated only that he did not know what it was. The court ruled that even though the officer did not testify that he believed the item in the defendant's sock to be a weapon when he removed it, a reasonable officer in these circumstances could have believed that the item was a weapon—specifically, a box cutter with a sharp blade. Thus, the frisk was constitutional.

United States v. Burnett, 791 F.2d 64 (6th Cir. 1986). An officer's subjective belief that he did not have probable cause to search a car's trunk after finding drugs in the passenger area is irrelevant in determining the legality of the search. The court upheld a warrantless search of the car's trunk because the objective facts (marijuana found on the car's floorboard) supported the officer's actions, despite his contrary subjective belief. *See also* State v. Riggs, 328 N.C. 213 (1991) (officer's belief about what constitutes legal requirements to determine reliability of an informant, when the informant's information is used to support probable cause to search, is irrelevant).

Search of a Government Employee's Office or Electronic Devices

City of Ontario v. Quon, 560 U.S. 746 (2010). A California police department provided pagers to some of its officers to assist the SWAT team in responding to emergencies. Under the department's contract with a private wireless service provider, each pager was allotted a limited number of characters sent or received each month. Usage in excess of that amount would result in an additional fee. When two officers (Quon, the plaintiff in this case, and another officer) consistently exceeded the character limit, the police chief ordered a supervisor to request transcripts of text messages for two consecutive months. The chief wanted to determine whether the existing character limit was too low or if the overages were for personal messages. The supervisor reviewed the transcripts and discovered that many of the messages sent and received on Quon's pager were not work related, and some were sexually explicit. After further investigation, Quon was allegedly disciplined. He then sued the city and several officers, alleging that his Fourth Amendment rights were violated.

The Court stated that it would decide this case on narrow grounds and assumed, without deciding, that (1) Quon had a reasonable expectation of privacy in the text messages sent on the city-provided pager, (2) the city officials' review of the transcripts constituted a search under the Fourth Amendment, and (3) the principles applicable to a government employer's search of an employee's physical office also apply when the employer intrudes on the employee's privacy interest in electronic communications. The Court ruled that under the standards set out by either the plurality opinion or the concurring opinion in *O'Connor v. Ortega*, 480 U.S. 709 (1987), the search of the text messages did not violate the Fourth Amendment. The search was justified at its inception because there were reasonable grounds for suspecting that the search was necessary for a noninvestigatory work-related purpose (checking whether the character limit was sufficient). Reviewing the transcripts was reasonable because it was an efficient and expedient way to determine whether Quon's overages were the result of work-related messaging or personal use. A reasonable employee would be aware that sound management principles might require the audit of messages to determine whether the pager was being appropriately used. The search was permissible in scope; that the search revealed intimate details of Quon's life did not make it unreasonable, because under the circumstances, a reasonable employer would not expect that such a review would intrude on these details.

O'Connor v. Ortega, 480 U.S. 709 (1987). State hospital officials conducted a warrantless search of a state employee's office and seized items from the employee's desk and his file cabinets. Five Justices (one concurring and four dissenting) concluded that the employee had a reasonable expectation of privacy in his office. All nine Justices concluded that the employee had a reasonable expectation of privacy in his desk and file cabinets. The Court ruled that reasonable suspicion is the standard to determine the constitutionality of an employer's warrantless search for noninvestigatory, work-related purposes or investigations of work-related misconduct. *See also* Ortega v. O'Connor, 146 F.3d 1149 (9th Cir. 1998) (later case upholding jury verdict that search of state employee's office and seizure of items violated Fourth Amendment).

United States v. Simons, 206 F.3d 392 (4th Cir. 2000). (1) A government employer's remote search and seizure of computer files that defendant-employee downloaded from the Internet did not violate the Fourth Amendment. The employee did not have a reasonable expectation of privacy concerning his Internet use in light of the employer's policy notifying employees that their use of the Internet was subject to auditing. (2) The employer's warrantless entry into the employee's office where the employee had a reasonable expectation of privacy to retrieve the employee's computer hard drive was reasonable under *O'Connor v. Ortega*, discussed above, because the entry and seizure concerned the investigation of work-related misconduct and was supported by reasonable suspicion. The court noted that the employer had an interest in fully investigating the employee's misconduct, even if the misconduct was criminal—in this case, possessing child pornography. *See also* United States v. Slanina, 283 F.3d 670 (5th Cir. 2002) (although defendant had reasonable expectation of privacy in his office and office computer equipment, search of computer for work-related misconduct—using computer to access child pornography—was reasonable under Fourth Amendment, even though supervisor was also a law enforcement officer).

United States v. Taketa, 923 F.2d 665 (9th Cir. 1991). The court ruled that a law enforcement officer had a reasonable expectation of privacy in his office, which was not open to the public and was not regularly inspected by his employer, who did not have a key to open it. The fact that three other officers had regular access to the office did not defeat the officer's privacy right. The court ruled that while a warrantless initial search of the office was justified by an investigation of work-related employee misconduct, the later videotaping of the office occurred during a criminal investigation and required probable cause and a search warrant.

Court Order to Obtain Corporate Records

In re Computer Technology Corp., 80 N.C. App. 709 (1986). A superior court judge's order that directed corporate officials to provide corporate records of transactions with two other corporations and the City of Charlotte was supported by the district attorney's petition and police investigator's affidavit that met the standards set out in *In re Superior Court Order*, 315 N.C. 378 (1986). The affidavit supported reasonable grounds to suspect that a violation of criminal law had occurred and that the records sought were likely connected to the investigation of a crime.

Probation or Parole Officer's Search of Home

Samson v. California, 547 U.S. 843 (2006). A California law requires every prisoner eligible for release on parole to agree in writing to be subject to a search or seizure by a parole officer or law enforcement officer without a search warrant and with or without cause. The Court ruled that the Fourth Amendment did not prohibit a law enforcement officer from conducting a suspicionless search of a parolee as permitted under this California law. The Court noted that California law prohibits such a search if it is arbitrary, capricious, or harassing. [Author's note: There is not a North Carolina law similar to California's law.]

United States v. Knights, 534 U.S. 112 (2001). The defendant was on probation, which included a condition that he submit to a search at any time, with or without a search or arrest warrant or reasonable cause, by any probation officer or law enforcement officer. An officer who was aware of this probation condition and who had reasonable suspicion that evidence of a crime was in the

defendant's apartment searched the apartment without a search warrant. The Court ruled that no more than reasonable suspicion was required to search the defendant's home and thus the officer's warrantless search was reasonable under the Fourth Amendment. [Author's note: G.S. 15A-1343(b1)(7), a special condition of probation, requires that a probationer submit to a warrantless search by a probation officer under the circumstances set out in the statute. It does not authorize a search by a law enforcement officer.] *See also* United States v. Reyes, 283 F.3d 446 (2d Cir. 2002) (no Fourth Amendment violation when probation officer conducted home visit after law enforcement officers provided information to probation officer that probationer was growing marijuana at his home).

Griffin v. Wisconsin, 483 U.S. 868 (1987). A Wisconsin regulation that permitted a probation officer to make a warrantless search of a probationer's home when "reasonable grounds" existed to search was constitutional. A search warrant was not required. *See also* United States v. Giannetta, 909 F.2d 571 (1st Cir. 1990) (probation condition permitted probation officer to search defendant's residence; court upheld probation officer's warrantless search of residence based on reasonable suspicion of alleged probation violations); United States v. Payne, 181 F.3d 781 (6th Cir. 1999) (reasonable suspicion standard for parole officer's search of parolee or his or her property is constitutional, but insufficient evidence of reasonable suspicion in this case); United States v. Davis, 932 F.2d 752 (9th Cir. 1991) (officer properly searched safe in probationer's apartment, which was shared with another person, without a warrant, based on reasonable suspicion that it was owned, possessed, or controlled by the probationer).

State v. Robinson, 148 N.C. App. 422 (2002). A law enforcement officer received anonymous information that the defendant was growing marijuana in his house. About 15 months earlier, an officer had searched the defendant's residence and found marijuana. An officer spoke with the defendant's probation officer, who said that the defendant was on probation from the earlier drug offense that included a condition consenting to warrantless searches of his person and residence. The probation officer went to the defendant's house, where he attempted to enforce the warrantless search condition. The defendant refused to allow the search, and the probation officer arrested him. The law enforcement officers were informed of the defendant's arrest and went to the house. No one answered the door, although the officers had learned from the probation officer that the defendant's girlfriend was there. While the other officers were knocking on the door, one of the officers, who was on the driveway, smelled a strong odor of marijuana emanating from the house and saw movement in the house. The officers left. They then telephoned the defendant's girlfriend, who refused to consent to a search of the house. They returned to the house, knocked on the door and received no answer, and then broke into the house. They conducted a security sweep and restrained the girlfriend. One officer obtained a search warrant, and they then searched the house, finding marijuana. The court ruled that the law enforcement officers properly interacted with the probation officer, who later sought to enforce the warrantless search condition of the drug defendant's probation—the court cited *State v. Church*, 110 N.C. App. 569 (1993), and *United States v. Knights*, 534 U.S. 112 (2001).

State v. Church, 110 N.C. App. 569 (1993). Based on a first-time informant's information that marijuana was being grown near a white frame house, officers went to investigate. They saw a white frame house and a second house with wood siding, about 150 feet west of the white house. The officers walked to the front porch of the white house, knocked on the door, and received no answer. From the porch, they saw two marijuana plants growing along a fence that went from the white house to a third residence east of the white house and a third marijuana plant growing directly behind the second house. After seeing the plants, the officers walked to the second house to determine who lived in the houses. One officer knocked on the front and side doors and then saw the defendant emerge from the garage that was next to the second house. The defendant informed the officers that he owned both houses but lived in the second house. The officers asked the defendant if they could search the houses and garage, but he refused. After arresting the defendant, the officers asked him for a garage door key, which he produced. An officer inserted the key in the lock, found that it fit, and withdrew the key without opening the door.

The officers learned that the defendant was on probation, contacted his probation officer, and were informed that as a condition of probation, the defendant was obligated to submit to warrantless searches by his probation officer. An officer informed the probation officer of the discovery of marijuana and asked her if she would be interested in conducting a warrantless search under the probation condition. She told the officer that she would be willing to conduct a warrantless search if she saw marijuana growing outside the defendant's house and determined that the plants more than likely belonged to him. She went to the house, saw the plants, determined that they probably belonged to the defendant, and authorized a warrantless search of the defendant's premises. She and nine law enforcement officers conducted the search.

The court ruled that officers' entry onto the defendant's property by walking to the front and side doors to look for the resident was permissible, based on *State v. Prevette*, 43 N.C. App. 450 (1979). The court also noted that the inadvertence component of the plain view doctrine was deleted in *Horton v. California*, 496 U.S. 128 (1990), and ruled that the plain view doctrine was satisfied in this case. [Author's note: The plain view doctrine must be satisfied only when there is a seizure of property, not when only a search takes place. The officer's initial observation of the marijuana, before any seizure took place, did not need to satisfy the plain view doctrine.]

United States v. Cardona, 903 F.2d 60 (1st Cir. 1990). A parolee may be arrested in his or her own home by a law enforcement officer who does not possess an arrest warrant (although, in this case, such a warrant had been issued) when the officer acts in good faith at the request of parole authorities who, in accordance with parole regulations, have reasonable cause to order the parolee's arrest as a parole violator. *See also* United States v. Harper, 928 F.2d 894 (9th Cir. 1991) (warrantless search of parolee's house to arrest parolee was constitutional when parole board had issued arrest warrant for parole violations).

Wiretapping, Eavesdropping, Digital Evidence, and Video Surveillance
(*This topic is discussed on page 210.*)

UNITED STATES SUPREME COURT
Riley v. California, 134 S. Ct. 2473 (2014). The Court ruled that the search incident to arrest exception to the search warrant requirement did not apply to a search of a cell phone. The Court stated that searches incident to arrest generally are justified (1) to ensure that the arrestee does not have a weapon and (2) to prevent the arrestee from destroying evidence. Cell phone searches do not implicate those concerns. "[O]fficers remain free to examine the physical aspects of a phone to ensure that it will not be used as a weapon," but the data on the phone does

not pose a risk of physical harm. And there is little risk that the data on a phone will be destroyed by the arrestee.

The government had argued that even seized phones could be locked or remotely wiped if not inspected immediately, but the Court found little reason to believe that these practices were prevalent or could be remedied by a search incident to arrest. Further, the risk of such practices can be managed by using Faraday bags (which block the radio waves that cell phones use to communicate) and other tools. Thus, the Court found little justification for allowing phones to be searched incident to arrest.

The Court also found a strong privacy interest militating against such warrantless searches. It noted that phones often contain vast quantities of data, making a search intrusive far beyond the mere fact of arrest itself and far beyond the level of intrusion associated with more traditional searches of pockets, wallets, and purses incident to arrest. Many phones can access data stored on remote servers, making a search extend beyond the immediate area of the arrestee. Emphasizing the need to establish a clear and workable rule, the Court therefore categorically exempted cell phones from the search incident to arrest doctrine.

City of Ontario v. Quon, 560 U.S. 746 (2010). A California police department provided pagers to some of its officers to assist the SWAT team in responding to emergencies. Under the department's contract with a private wireless service provider, each pager was allotted a limited number of characters sent or received each month. Usage in excess of that amount would result in an additional fee. When two officers (Quon, the plaintiff in this case, and another officer) consistently exceeded the character limit, the police chief ordered a supervisor to request transcripts of text messages for two consecutive months. The chief wanted to determine whether the existing character limit was too low or if the overages were for personal messages. The supervisor reviewed the transcripts and discovered that many of the messages sent and received on Quon's pager were not work related and some were sexually explicit. After further investigation, Quon was allegedly disciplined. He then sued the city and several officers, alleging that his Fourth Amendment rights were violated.

The Court stated that it would decide this case on narrow grounds and assumed, without deciding that (1) Quon had a reasonable expectation of privacy in the text messages sent on the city-provided pager, (2) the city officials' review of the transcripts constituted a search under the Fourth Amendment, and (3) the principles applicable to a government employer's search of an employee's physical office also apply when the employer intrudes on the employee's privacy interest in electronic communications. The Court ruled that under the standards set out by either the plurality opinion or the concurring opinion in *O'Connor v. Ortega*, 480 U.S. 709 (1987), the search of the text messages did not violate the Fourth Amendment. The search was justified at its inception because there were reasonable grounds for suspecting that the search was necessary for a noninvestigatory work-related purpose (checking whether the character limit was sufficient). Reviewing the transcripts was reasonable because it was an efficient and expedient way to determine whether Quon's overages were the result of work-related messaging or personal use. A reasonable employee would be aware that sound management principles might require the audit of messages to determine whether the pager was being used appropriately. The search was permissible in scope; that the search revealed intimate details of Quon's life did not make it unreasonable, because under the circumstances, a reasonable employer would not expect that such a review would intrude on these details.

Bartnicki v. Vopper, 532 U.S. 514 (2001). The Court ruled that the First Amendment bars a civil action against radio broadcasters who intentionally disclosed the contents of an illegally taped cellular telephone conversation involving matters of public concern when the radio broadcasters did not participate in the illegal taping.

NORTH CAROLINA COURT OF APPEALS

State v. Ladd, ___ N.C. App. ___, 782 S.E.2d 397 (2016). The defendant was convicted of multiple charges of secretly using a photographic device with the intent to capture images of another person. The court ruled that the trial court erred in denying the defendant's motion to suppress evidence obtained during a warrantless search of the defendant's external hard drives. While the defendant had consented to a search of his laptops and smart phone, the trial court's finding of fact (based on the State's stipulation to the facts set out in defense counsel's affidavit filed with the suppression motion) unambiguously showed that the defendant did not consent to the search of the external hard drives. And the officers' warrantless search of these drives, for which the defendant possessed a Fourth Amendment privacy interest under *Riley v. California*, 134 S. Ct. 2473 (2014), were not justified. They did not pose a safety threat to the officers nor was there any reason to believe that the information in the drives would have been destroyed while the officers obtained a search warrant.

Wright v. Town of Zebulon, 202 N.C. App. 540 (2010). The plaintiff, a police officer, sued his department, the city, and various officers and others for allegedly violating the North Carolina Electronic Surveillance Act (G.S. 15A-286 through -298) by intercepting his oral communications in his vehicle. The police chief and others intercepted these communications to check, based on information from an informant and others, whether the officer was tipping off drug dealers about confidential police department information. The trial court granted summary judgment for the various defendants (the police chief and others), and the plaintiff appealed to the North Carolina Court of Appeals. The court ruled that the defendants did not violate the act because they did not act "willfully" (see G.S. 15A-287(a)(1)) as that term has been interpreted by federal case law involving the federal electronic surveillance law, on which the North Carolina law was modeled. Based on the police chief's purpose in conducting the interception as an integrity check to ensure public safety (to determine if officers, informants, and the general public were in danger of harm), the defendants did not act with a bad purpose or without a justifiable excuse.

State v. Stitt, 201 N.C. App. 233 (2009). The defendant was convicted of first-degree murder of one victim, second-degree murder of another victim, and armed robbery. After the killings, the defendant used two cell phones belonging to one of the victims. The cell phones were seized from the defendant when he was arrested in New York. The defendant made a motion to suppress cellular telephone records obtained by the State. The court affirmed the trial court's ruling that the defendant failed to meet his burden to show that he had a Fourth Amendment privacy interest in the cell phones to have standing to contest the records obtained by the State. [Author's note: In any event, a person does not have a Fourth Amendment right to privacy in his or her telephone records. Smith v. Maryland, 442 U.S. 735 (1979).] The court also ruled, assuming arguendo that the State did not fully comply with federal law (18 U.S.C. § 2703(d)) in obtaining the telephone records, that federal law does not authorize the suppression of evidence as a remedy for a violation of this federal law. It only provides civil remedies and criminal punishment. The court cited *United States v. Ferguson*, 508 F. Supp. 2d 7 (D.D.C. 2007), and *United States v. Smith*, 155 F.3d 1051 (9th Cir. 1998).

Kroh v. Kroh, 152 N.C. App. 347 (2002). The plaintiff-husband sued the defendant-wife for violations of North Carolina's Electronic Surveillance Act. Without her husband's knowledge, the wife placed voice-activated tape recorders and a video camera in the family home. The tape recorders picked up conversations between the husband and others when the wife was not a party to the communications. There was no evidence that the video camera recorded conversations.

(1) The court ruled that the wife's nonconsensual interception of oral communications between the husband and others in the family home violated North Carolina's Electronic Surveillance Act. *See* G.S. 15A-287(a)(1). Because the wife was not a party to the intercepted communications, she could not escape liability under G.S. 15A-287(a), which effectively permits the interception if one party to the communication consents to the interception. [Author's note: This ruling is also consistent with interpretations of similar federal law.] (2) The wife contended that she vicariously consented, on behalf of her minor children, to the interception of any oral communications between her husband and her sons. The court adopted the vicarious consent doctrine set out in several federal cases. This doctrine permits a custodial parent to vicariously consent to the recording of a minor child's conversations as long as the parent has a good faith, objectively reasonable belief that the interception of the conversation is necessary for the child's best interests (for example, to uncover child abuse). (3) The court ruled that nonconsensual videotaping without aural acquisition of oral communications does not violate North Carolina's Electronic Surveillance Act. [Author's note: This ruling is also consistent with interpretations of similar federal law. However, law enforcement officers should remember that there are Fourth Amendment issues involved when officers videotape people in places where they have a reasonable expectation of privacy.]

State v. McGriff, 151 N.C. App. 631 (2002). A person was using her cordless telephone when she inadvertently intercepted a call between two people she recognized. The conversation was about a prior commission of a sex crime that one caller, the defendant, had committed against the other caller, who was a minor. She listened to the conversation and testified about it at trial. The court ruled, relying on *Adams v. Sumner*, 39 F.3d 933 (9th Cir. 1994) (hotel switchboard operator inadvertently overheard hotel guest refer to guns and remained on line for several minutes; interception not willful because operator remained on line because of concern for other hotel guests after hearing reference to guns), that the interception was not willful and therefore was not unlawful under G.S. 15A-287(a)(1) and 18 U.S.C. § 2511(1)(a). The person continued to listen because of her concern for the minor. Evidence of the conversation was properly admitted at trial. The court also noted, citing *In re Askin*, 47 F.3d 100 (4th Cir. 1995), and other cases, that the defendant did not have a reasonable expectation of privacy in his cordless telephone conversation.

State v. Shaw, 103 N.C. App. 268 (1991). A mother attached a microcassette tape recorder to a telephone extension line in her house. She tape recorded a telephone conversation between her son, who was using that line, and another young man about their drug activities. Neither the son nor the other man consented to the recording of their conversation. The mother played the tape recording for a detective, who used information from the tape to obtain a search warrant. Relying on *Rickenbaker v. Rickenbaker*, 290 N.C. 373 (1976) (husband violated federal wiretapping law by tape recording his wife's telephone conversations without her consent), the court ruled that the mother violated federal wiretapping law in making the tape recording and that federal law barred the use of the contents of the conversation in the affidavit for the search warrant.

FEDERAL APPELLATE COURTS

Guest v. Leis, 255 F.3d 325 (6th Cir. 2001). This civil lawsuit involved seizures of two bulletin board systems, A and B. Officers, acting with a search warrant in both situations, seized computers, servers, and associated equipment concerning these bulletin board systems. Evidence showed that obscenity was available on both systems.

(1) Because bulletin board system A posted a disclaimer that personal communications were not private, users of this system did not have a reasonable expectation of privacy under the Fourth Amendment. (2) Users of bulletin board system B did not have a reasonable expectation of privacy in materials intended for publication or public posting or in an email message that had already reached its recipient. (3) Because of the technical difficulties of conducting computer searches in the suspects' homes, it was reasonable to allow the officers to take the computers off-site and separate relevant files from unrelated files. (4) Users did not have a reasonable expectation of privacy in their subscriber information because they communicated it to system operators, third parties.

The court relied on *United States v. Miller*, 425 U.S. 435 (1976). (5) The search warrants were sufficiently specific concerning the things to be seized by requiring that the communications and computer records pertain to the criminal offenses listed in the warrant. (6) The officers did not violate the users' First Amendment rights by seizing and shutting down the bulletin board systems. (7) The officers did not violate the federal Electronic Communications Privacy Act because they acted with a search warrant as provided under 18 U.S.C.A. §§ 2703(a) and (b). (8) The officers were not civilly liable under the federal Privacy Protection Act (PPA), 42 U.S.C.A. § 2000aa, which protects work product materials intended for publication that are possessed by innocent third parties. The seizure of PPA-protected materials occurred incidentally to the seizures of criminal evidence under valid search warrants, and the plaintiffs did not show that the protected materials were searched.

Adams v. City of Battle Creek, 250 F.3d 980 (6th Cir. 2001). A police department supplied a pager to an officer for use in his official duties. The department suspected that the officer was assisting drug dealers, so it intercepted messages from the officer's pager with the use of a clone pager. The court ruled that the department's use of the clone pager was not authorized by the business or law enforcement exceptions under 18 U.S.C. § 2510(5) and thus its use was illegal. The court noted that the department did not routinely monitor officers' pagers or give them notice that random monitoring of these department-issued pagers might occur. The court rejected the department's argument that the officer impliedly consented to the interception of his messages on his pager simply because he accepted and used a department-issued pager.

Kee v. City of Rowlett, 247 F.3d 206 (5th Cir. 2001). The plaintiffs failed to show that they had a subjective expectation of privacy necessary to prove a violation of federal eavesdropping law when law enforcement officers placed an electronic surveillance microphone in a funeral urn during a public accessible gravesite service attended by news media and other third parties.

Abraham v. County of Greenville, 237 F.3d 386 (4th Cir. 2001). A county's recording of judges' telephone calls from their offices in a county detention center was not within the federal wiretapping statute's law enforcement exception. Monitoring the judges' calls was not part of the "ordinary course" of the county's law enforcement duties, even if the county installed the recording device in the detention center for a legitimate law enforcement purpose.

United States v. Nerber, 222 F.3d 597 (9th Cir. 2000). A drug deal was set up in a hotel room in which informants acting on behalf of law enforcement officers were to sell cocaine to the defendants. With the consent of the informants, officers set up video surveillance to watch the transaction. However, when the informants left the room, the video surveillance of the defendants continued for about three hours. The court ruled that the defendants had a reasonable expectation of privacy once the informants left the room, and the officers violated the Fourth Amendment by failing to obtain a search warrant to conduct the video surveillance. *Compare with* United States v. Chavez, 328 F.3d 974 (8th Cir. 2003) (defendant was not videotaped while alone (or alone with a codefendant) in hotel room but only while meeting with cooperating accomplice, who had consented to the taping; no Fourth Amendment violation).

United States v. Jackson, 213 F.3d 1269 (10th Cir. 2000). Officers, without obtaining a search warrant, installed silent video cameras on telephone poles outside the defendant's residence that viewed activities occurring outside the residence that were visible to people who passed by. The court ruled that the cameras did not violate the Fourth Amendment because the defendant did not have a reasonable expectation of privacy in the areas viewed by the cameras. The use of the silent video cameras also did not violate federal wiretapping or eavesdropping laws. *See also* United States v. McIver, 186 F.3d 1119 (9th Cir. 1999) (placement of motion-activated still and video cameras near marijuana plants in national forest did not violate Fourth Amendment; defendants did not have reasonable expectation of privacy in their cultivation of marijuana in area open to public); Vega-Rodriguez v. Puerto Rico Tel. Co., 110 F.3d 174 (1st Cir. 1997) (employees lacked reasonable expectation of privacy to contest disclosed, nonaural video surveillance while working in open and undifferentiated work area).

Arias v. Mutual Central Alarm Service, Inc., 202 F.3d 553 (2d Cir. 2000). An alarm services company, which monitored the burglar and fire alarms of its customers and notified police and fire departments as appropriate, recorded on a 24-hour basis all incoming and outgoing telephone calls involving its employees. The recording practice is routine among central station alarm companies and is recommended or even mandated by various standard-setting and regulatory bodies in the industry. The court ruled that the recording practice was permissible under the "ordinary course of . . . business" exception in 18 U.S.C. § 2510(5).

Dorris v. Absher, 179 F.3d 420 (6th Cir. 1999). The civil defendant and four plaintiffs worked together at a government office that consisted of one large room, which all employees shared, and an adjoining bathroom that was also used for storage. The defendant placed a tape recorder in the storage room/bathroom and secretly recorded the conversations of the four plaintiff-employees. No one other than the four employees was present during the conversations, and the conversations stopped whenever a car pulled into the building's driveway or the telephone was being used. The court ruled that the plaintiff-employees had a reasonable expectation of privacy in their conversations to support a cause of action against the defendant under the federal wiretapping law. The court also ruled that the passive act of listening to an illegally intercepted communication—in this case, listening to the tape-recorded communication—is not an illegal "use" of that communication as that term is used in the federal wiretapping law.

Amati v. City of Woodstock, 176 F.3d 952 (7th Cir. 1999). The law enforcement "ordinary course of . . . duties" exception under 18 U.S.C. § 2510(5)(a)(ii) permitted taping of all telephone calls to and from a police department, even if there was no express notice to the people whose conversations were taped.

Culbertson v. Culbertson, 143 F.3d 825 (4th Cir. 1998). Evidence obtained through illegal wiretapping is admissible for impeachment purposes. *See also* United States v. Baftiri, 263 F.3d 856 (8th Cir. 2001) (similar ruling).

Chandler v. United States Army, 125 F.3d 1296 (9th Cir. 1997). Law enforcement officers under 18 U.S.C. §§ 2517(1) and (2) may not share with other law enforcement officers the contents of wiretapping they know or have reason to know to be illegally obtained.

United States v. Ortiz, 84 F.3d 977 (7th Cir. 1996). Officers seized an electronic pager incident to the defendant's arrest. They pushed a button on the pager that revealed the numeric messages previously transmitted to the pager. The court ruled, relying on *United States v. Meriwether*, 917 F.2d 955 (6th Cir. 1990), that the officers' actions were proper as a search incident to arrest.

Brown v. Waddell, 50 F.3d 285 (4th Cir. 1995). Officers used pager clones to receive and record numeric messages being simultaneously received by a person's digital display pager. The court rejected the officers' argument that their use of pager clones was effectively a pen register and therefore they did not need an appropriate court order under Title III of the Omnibus Crime Control and Safe Roads Act of 1968 and the Electronic Communications Privacy Act of 1986 (ECPA). The court ruled that using pager clones without an appropriate court order was an unauthorized interception of an electronic communication under the ECPA.

Adams v. Sumner, 39 F.3d 933 (9th Cir. 1994). The court ruled that a hotel telephone operator did not violate federal wiretapping law by staying on the line after inadvertently hearing an occupant of the hotel refer to guns when the operator was concerned that there might be a danger to people in the hotel.

United States v. Clark, 22 F.3d 799 (8th Cir. 1994). Before an officer left his patrol car to conduct a search, he surreptitiously activated a tape recorder while two suspects sat in the patrol car's backseat. Their conversations were recorded, and the officer played the tape and heard incriminating remarks by one of the suspects. The court ruled that the suspects did not have a reasonable expectation of privacy in the backseat of the patrol car, and the recording of their conversations did not violate the Fourth Amendment or federal wiretapping law. *See also* United States v. McKinnon, 985 F.2d 525 (11th Cir. 1993) (similar ruling); United States v. Turner, 209 F.3d 1198 (10th Cir. 2000).

United States v. Taketa, 923 F.2d 665 (9th Cir. 1991). The court ruled that a law enforcement officer had a reasonable expectation of privacy in his office, which was not open to the public and was not regularly inspected by his employer, who did not have a key to open it. The fact that three other officers had regular access to the office did not defeat his privacy right. The court ruled that while a warrantless initial search of the office was justified by an investigation of work-related employee misconduct, the later videotaping of the office occurred during a criminal investigation and required probable cause and a search warrant.

United States v. Meriwether, 917 F.2d 955 (6th Cir. 1990). Officers who were executing a search warrant for drugs and other evidence seized an electronic digital display-type pager in the "on" position. The officers monitored the pager as it recorded 40 incoming phone numbers. They used one of the telephone numbers to make a drug sale to the defendant.

The court ruled that (1) the pager was among items to be seized as described in the warrant as "telephone numbers of customers, suppliers, couriers" and (2) the defendant did not have a reasonable expectation of privacy in his telephone number, which he had transmitted to the pager. The court also ruled that the officers' seizure of the defendant's telephone number (by seeing it displayed on the pager) did not violate federal law that makes illegal the interception of a digital pager communication. Congress made illegal only the interception of a "transmission." Once the officer heard the pager emit a signal, the transmission over the system had ceased; the later retrieval of the message was not an interception. An officer lawfully possessed the paging device, and by pressing the digital display button, the officer became a party to the communication. Therefore, the officer did not intercept it. In addition, the officer did not violate federal law because he did not use an "electronic, mechanical or other device" to intercept; he simply used the pager that he had lawfully acquired. The court also noted that Congress did not provide for the statutory remedy of suppression of evidence for the interception of electronic communications like the interception involved in this case. *See also* State v. Harris, 145 N.C. App. 570 (2001) (officer's accessing telephone numbers stored in pager's memory after pager had been seized incident to defendant's arrest did not violate Fourth Amendment when officer had probable cause to believe that pager contained information that would assist in investigation of drug offenses).

United States v. Cuevas-Sanchez, 821 F.2d 248 (5th Cir. 1987). Officers' placing a video camera on a utility pole to record all activities in the defendant's backyard, when his backyard was surrounded by a 10-foot-high fence, was a search under the Fourth Amendment. The court distinguished *California v. Ciraolo*, 476 U.S. 207 (1986). It also ruled that the search warrant that authorized the installation of the video camera was proper under the Fourth Amendment. *See also* United States v. Koyomejian, 970 F.2d 536 (9th Cir. 1992) (court described legal requirements to conduct nonaural video surveillance); United States v. Falls, 34 F.3d 674 (8th Cir. 1994) (similar ruling).

United States v. Vest, 813 F.2d 477 (1st Cir. 1987). Statutory exclusionary rule in 18 U.S.C. § 2515 for a Title III violation applies not only when the government obtains evidence from a violation of Title III but also when the government with "clean hands" (government was not involved in or did not procure the violation) receives evidence obtained by a private person in violation of Title III. *See also* United States v. Crabtree, 565 F.3d 887 (4th

Cir. 2009); *In re* Grand Jury, 111 F.3d 1066 (3d Cir. 1997); Chandler v. United States Army, 125 F.3d 1296 (9th Cir. 1997); Berry v. Funk, 146 F.3d 1003 (D.C. Cir. 1998). *But see* United States v. Murdock, 63 F.3d 1391 (6th Cir. 1995) (disagreeing with *United States v. Vest*, cited above, court ruled that statutory exclusionary rule in 18 U.S.C. § 2515 for a Title III violation does not apply to evidence that the government with "clean hands" receives from a private person who obtained the evidence in violation of Title III).

Fraser v. Nationwide Mutual Insurance Co., 135 F. Supp. 2d 623 (E.D. Pa. 2001). The court ruled that an employer's acquisition of an employee's electronic mail (email) from post-transmission storage did not violate federal wiretapping law or the federal law prohibiting unauthorized access to electronic communications.

United States v. Monroe, 52 M.J. 326 (2000). The defendant, an Air Force sergeant, did not have a reasonable expectation of privacy in his email messages or email box in an electronic mail host (EMH) residing on a computer owned by the Air Force, at least from personnel charged with maintaining the EMH system, when users received specific notice that by logging onto the system, they consented to monitoring. Thus, it was not a search under the Fourth Amendment when maintenance personnel opened the defendant's email messages and later opened his email box while investigating a problem with the system.

Commonwealth v. Proetto, 771 A.2d 823 (Pa. Super. 2001). After the victim received an email message from the defendant, the victim forwarded it to law enforcement officers. Because the victim had received the email message and could forward it to anyone, the defendant did not have a reasonable expectation of privacy in the message. The court also ruled that a person does not have a reasonable expectation of privacy in chat room electronic conversations because he or she has no way of verifying to whom he or she is speaking—thus, the defendant could not challenge the conversations he had in a chat room with a law enforcement officer who was impersonating a young girl. *See also* United States v. Charbonneau, 979 F. Supp. 1177 (S.D. Ohio 1997) (similar ruling); United States v. Maxwell, 45 M.J. 406 (1996) (similar ruling).

Protective Searches
Scope of Search Incident to Arrest
(This topic is discussed on page 249.)

Generally
UNITED STATES SUPREME COURT

Riley v. California, 134 S. Ct. 2473 (2014). The Court ruled that the search incident to arrest exception to the search warrant requirement did not apply to a search of a cell phone. The Court stated that searches incident to arrest generally are justified (1) to ensure that the arrestee does not have a weapon and (2) to prevent the arrestee from destroying evidence. Cell phone searches do not implicate those concerns. "[O]fficers remain free to examine the physical aspects of a phone to ensure that it will not be used as a weapon," but the data on the phone does not pose a risk of physical harm. And there is little risk that the data on a phone will be destroyed by the arrestee.

The government had argued that even seized phones could be locked or remotely wiped if not inspected immediately, but the Court found little reason to believe that these practices were prevalent or could be remedied by a search incident to arrest. Further, the risk of such practices can be managed by using Faraday bags (which block the radio waves that cell phones use to communicate) and other tools. Thus, the Court found little justification for allowing phones to be searched incident to arrest.

The Court also found a strong privacy interest militating against such warrantless searches. It noted that phones often contain vast quantities of data, making a search intrusive far beyond the mere fact of arrest itself and far beyond the level of intrusion associated with more traditional searches of pockets, wallets, and purses incident to arrest. Many phones can access data stored on remote servers, making a search extend beyond the immediate area of the arrestee. Emphasizing the need to establish a clear and workable rule, the Court therefore categorically exempted cell phones from the search incident to arrest doctrine.

Birchfield v. North Dakota, 136 S. Ct. 2160 (2016). The Court held in three consolidated cases that while a warrantless breath test of a motorist lawfully arrested for drunk driving is permissible as a search incident to arrest, a warrantless blood draw is not. It concluded: "Because breath tests are significantly less intrusive than blood tests and in most cases amply serve law enforcement interests, we conclude that a breath test, but not a blood test, may be administered as a search incident to a lawful arrest for drunk driving. As in all cases involving reasonable searches incident to arrest, a warrant is not needed in this situation." Having found that the search incident to arrest doctrine does not justify the warrantless taking of a blood sample, the Court turned to the argument that blood tests are justified based on the driver's legally implied consent to submit to them. In this respect, it concluded, "motorists cannot be deemed to have consented to submit to a blood test on pain of committing a criminal offense."

Arizona v. Gant, 556 U.S. 332 (2009). The Court ruled that officers may search a vehicle incident to arrest only if (1) the arrestee is unsecured and within reaching distance of the passenger compartment when the search is conducted or (2) it is reasonable to believe that evidence relevant to the crime of arrest might be found in the vehicle. For a discussion of this ruling, see page 252. *See also* Robert L. Farb, *The United States Supreme Court's Ruling in* Arizona v. Gant (UNC School of Government, 2009), www.sog.unc.edu/sites/www.sog.unc.edu/files/reports/arizonagantbyfarb.pdf.

Virginia v. Moore, 553 U.S. 164 (2008). The Court ruled that a search incident to the arrest for an arrest that was valid under the Fourth Amendment, although the arrest was not valid under state law, did not violate the Fourth Amendment. The Court noted that the arrest rules that the officers violated were those of state law alone, and it is not the province of the Fourth Amendment to enforce state law.

Smith v. Ohio, 494 U.S. 541 (1990). Officers illegally searched the defendant's paper bag without a warrant and found drug paraphernalia. This illegal search then provided probable cause to arrest the defendant. The Court ruled that this search may not be justified as a search incident to arrest.

Maryland v. Buie, 494 U.S. 325 (1990). When officers arrest a person in a home or similar kind of premise, they may as incident to that arrest automatically (that is, without needing probable cause or reasonable suspicion to do so) search closets and other spaces immediately adjoining the place of arrest from which an attack on them from another person could be immediately launched. They also may make a warrantless sweep of the rest of the premises, but only if they have reasonable suspicion that the place to be searched harbors a person who is a danger to the officers.

Rawlings v. Kentucky, 448 U.S. 98 (1980). When probable cause exists to arrest a person, a search of the person incident to the arrest may occur before the actual arrest if the arrest occurs contemporaneously with the search. *See also* State v. Walden, 52 N.C. App. 125 (1981); State v. Wooten, 34 N.C. App. 85 (1977); State v. Gilliam, 71 N.C. App. 83 (1984); State v. Mills, 104 N.C. App. 724 (1991).

United States v. Edwards, 415 U.S. 800 (1974). The defendant, arrested for breaking into a post office that night, was placed in jail. A later investigation revealed that entry had been made through a wooden window, leaving paint chips on the windowsill. The next morning the defendant's clothing was taken from him without a warrant and examined. The Court ruled that the warrantless seizure of the defendant's clothes was constitutional. The officers did no more by taking the clothes the following morning than they could have done incident to the defendant's arrest or initial incarceration.

Gustafson v. Florida, 414 U.S. 260 (1973). The custodial arrest of a defendant for a traffic offense permitted a full search of his person, including a cigarette box in his coat pocket.

United States v. Robinson, 414 U.S. 218 (1973). An officer who has probable cause to arrest and takes the defendant into custody may make a full search incident to that arrest, even if the arrest is for only a traffic violation. A search of a crumpled cigarette package found in the left breast pocket of the defendant's coat was constitutionally permissible as incident to the arrest. A custodial arrest provides the automatic authority to search; justification for the search does not depend on an officer's fear for his or her safety or need to search for evidence of a crime.

Chimel v. California, 395 U.S. 752 (1969). The defendant was arrested in his home. A search of the entire home incident to his arrest was unconstitutional. A search incident to an arrest is limited to the person of the arrestee and the area within the arrestee's immediate control.

Preston v. United States, 376 U.S. 364 (1964). Three men were arrested in their car for vagrancy. The car was taken to the police station, where it was searched without a warrant. The Court ruled that when a car search is based on the search incident to arrest justification and the arrestee is in custody, a warrantless search of the car at another place is not justified as incident to that arrest. [Author's note: In this case probable cause to search did not exist, and therefore the later ruling in *Chambers v. Maroney*, 399 U.S. 42 (1970), would not apply to these facts.] *See also* Dyke v. Taylor Implement Mfg. Co., 391 U.S. 216 (1968).

NORTH CAROLINA SUPREME COURT

State v. Steen, 352 N.C. 227 (2000). (1) The defendant was arrested for possession of drug paraphernalia and stolen credit cards and taken to jail on February 29, 1996. His clothing was taken from him, and he was issued a standard jail jumpsuit. Under jail rules, his clothing would be returned to him when he was released from jail. On March 6, 1996, an officer who was investigating the defendant for a murder went to the jail and, without a search warrant, obtained the defendant's clothes to analyze them for blood and glass particles. Relying on *United States v. Edwards*, 415 U.S. 800 (1974), the court ruled that the warrantless search and seizure of the defendant's clothes did not violate the Fourth Amendment. The defendant was in custody under a valid arrest, and the defendant's clothing had already been administratively taken from his possession. (2) The defendant was released from custody on March 14, 1996. He was arrested on March 16, 1996, for murder, and an officer took hair and saliva samples incident to the arrest. Relying on *State v. Thomas*, 329 N.C. 423 (1991), the court ruled that neither a court order nor a search warrant was necessary to take the hair and saliva samples.

State v. Brooks, 337 N.C. 132 (1994). The court upheld a search of a nylon pouch as a proper search incident to the arrest of the defendant for carrying a concealed weapon. The agent had probable cause to arrest the defendant; the search may be made before the actual arrest and still be justified as a search incident to arrest when, as here, the agent made the search contemporaneously with the arrest; *see* Rawlings v. Kentucky, 448 U.S. 98 (1980).

State v. Thomas, 329 N.C. 423 (1991). The day after the defendant's arrest for murder, law enforcement officers obtained (by using the services of a medical examiner) the following evidence from the defendant without a warrant: samples of the defendant's blood; head and pubic hair; saliva; fingernails; and molds of his teeth, lips, and fingernails. [Author's note: They had obtained a nontestimonial identification order to obtain this evidence, but it was invalid under *State v. Welch*, 316 N.C. 578 (1986), because the defendant was in custody.] The defendant moved to suppress all this evidence by arguing that the federal and state constitutions required the officers to obtain a search warrant based on probable cause before taking blood and other personal identification samples of a defendant already in custody. The court ruled that blood was taken improperly, based on *State v. Carter*, 322 N.C. 709 (1988). However, the court ruled as admissible evidence the defendant's fingerprints, pubic hair, teeth, saliva, and lips, because that evidence was properly obtained while defendant was in police custody.

State v. Payne, 328 N.C. 377 (1991). Relying on *United States v. Edwards*, 415 U.S. 800 (1974), the court upheld the warrantless seizure of the arrested defendant's clothing that occurred five hours after his arrest and while he remained in lawful custody.

State v. Cherry, 298 N.C. 86 (1979). Officers arrested the defendant at his motel room door, handcuffed him, and sat him in a chair in the room. Officers had been informed earlier that the defendant had a gun. One officer saw a lump in the rug and seized a weapon there. The court ruled that the search was proper as incident to the arrest and under the plain view justification. The area was within the defendant's immediate control under the search incident to arrest justification, and the fact that the defendant was handcuffed did not affect the lawfulness of the seizure incident to arrest.

State v. Hopkins, 296 N.C. 673 (1979). A female defendant was arrested in Tennessee and placed in jail but only visually searched. A North Carolina officer, who believed that she might have a gun, requested that she be searched more thoroughly. During a full search conducted six or seven hours after the arrest, a gun was found in the defendant's blouse. The court ruled that the full search was not too remote in time and therefore could be justified as incident to her arrest.

State v. Cobb, 295 N.C. 1 (1978). The defendant was arrested for rape. It was proper, as a search incident to the arrest, to take a pubic hair sample from the defendant and his clothes. *See also* State v. Norman, 100 N.C. App. 660 (1990) (defendant arrested for sex offenses was properly strip searched and his pubic area combed).

State v. Richards, 294 N.C. 474 (1978). An officer who accompanied the defendant to her bedroom after her arrest had the right to seize a weapon he saw in the top dresser drawer as a search incident to her arrest. Justification for the seizure does not depend on showing with "mathematical precision that the defendant could have reached the weapon moments before the seizure." The area was one within which the defendant might have gained possession of the weapon. *See also* State v. Parker, 315 N.C. 222 (1985).

State v. Jackson, 280 N.C. 122 (1971). An officer had information that the defendant, arrested for a drug offense, might have drugs concealed in her bra. Neither the removal of the defendant to jail nor a 30- to 45-minute wait for a matron to arrive to search her made the search too remote in time or place to be invalid as a search incident to a lawful arrest.

State v. Shedd, 274 N.C. 95 (1968). The defendant's clothes were properly seized incident to his arrest. *See also* State v. Lucas, 302 N.C. 342 (1981).

NORTH CAROLINA COURT OF APPEALS

State v. Clyburn, ___ N.C. App. ___, 770 S.E.2d 689 (2015). The court reversed and remanded for further findings of fact concerning the defendant's motion to suppress evidence obtained as a result of a search of the digital contents of a GPS device found on the defendant's person that, as a result of the search, was determined to have been stolen. The court ruled that under *Riley v. California*, 134 S. Ct. 2473 (2014), the search was not justified as a search incident to arrest. As to whether the defendant had a reasonable expectation of privacy in the GPS device, the court ruled that a defendant may have a legitimate expectation of privacy in a stolen item if he or she acquired it innocently and does not know that the item was stolen. Here, evidence at the suppression hearing would allow the trial court to conclude that the defendant had a legitimate possessory interest in the GPS device. However, because the trial court failed to make a factual determination concerning whether the defendant innocently purchased the GPS device, the court reversed and remanded for further findings of fact, providing additional guidance for the trial court in its decision.

State v. Taylor, 117 N.C. App. 644 (1995). Officer A knew that the defendant had been previously arrested for drugs and had a reputation in the community as a drug dealer. Officer A and other officers saw the defendant with others in an area known for drug trafficking. As officers approached the area in their marked car, the defendant left. The officers saw him at a nearby intersection. The defendant stopped as the police car approached him. As Officer A got out of the car, the defendant walked toward him and dropped something on the ground. The officer approached the defendant and brought him over to the police car. He determined that the dropped item was marijuana and arrested the defendant. He then noticed that the defendant was talking "funny" and ordered him to spit out whatever was in his mouth. The defendant spit out individually wrapped pieces of crack cocaine. The court ruled that (1) the defendant was not seized until after he dropped the item to the ground, because he had not yielded to a show of authority before then; *see* California v. Hodari D., 499 U.S. 621 (1991); (2) after the defendant dropped the item, Officer A had reasonable suspicion to detain the defendant, considering everything the officer knew; (3) Officer A had probable cause to arrest the defendant when he determined that the item was marijuana; and (4) even if the defendant did not voluntarily spit out the cocaine, it was admissible as a search incident to arrest.

State v. Thomas, 81 N.C. App. 200 (1986). The court ruled that a large, locked suitcase that the defendant was carrying when he was arrested could not be searched without a warrant incident to the defendant's arrest. The court stated that the suitcase was not immediately associated with the defendant's person, the defendant was in custody and could not have reached its contents, and the suitcase had been effectively reduced to the officers' exclusive control.

State v. Mack, 57 N.C. App. 163 (1982). An arrestee's pants pocket may be searched incident to his arrest.

State v. Booker, 44 N.C. App. 492 (1980). A purse attached to the arrestee's belt may be searched incident to an arrest.

State v. Nesmith, 40 N.C. App. 748 (1979). A search and inspection of the contents of an arrestee's wallet was valid as a search incident to the arrest. A search of the wallet was also valid as an inventory of personal possessions before the defendant was placed in jail. *See also* State v. Willis, 61 N.C. App. 23, *modified and aff'd*, 309 N.C. 451 (1983) (wallet).

State v. Ervin, 38 N.C. App. 261 (1978). An arrestee's socks may be searched incident to his arrest.

FEDERAL APPELLATE COURTS

United States v. Perdoma, 621 F.3d 745 (8th Cir. 2010). The court upheld a search of a zipped duffel bag that the defendant was carrying when he was arrested. The court recognized that the rationale of *Arizona v. Gant*, 556 U.S. 332 (2009), may be instructive outside the vehicle search context in some cases—but not in this case when the search occurred in close proximity to the handcuffed defendant.

United States v. Shakir, 616 F.3d 315 (3d Cir. 2010). The court rejected the government's argument that *Arizona v. Gant*, 556 U.S. 332 (2009), was confined to vehicle searches and stated that *Gant* refocuses attention on a suspect's ability or inability to access weapons or destroy evidence when a search incident to arrest is conducted. The court ruled that the officer had the authority to search the handcuffed defendant's gym bag as incident to arrest.

United States v. Nelson, 102 F.3d 1344 (4th Cir. 1996). A search of a shoulder bag incident to arrest of the defendant was constitutional although the search occurred a few minutes after the defendant had been taken to another room in a house.

United States v. Han, 74 F.3d 537 (4th Cir. 1996). A travel bag was next to the feet of the defendant, who was inside a residence. An officer moved the bag for safety purposes and conducted a safety sweep of the residence. The officer interviewed a witness in the back room and then searched the bag. The court ruled that a search of the bag was proper incident to the defendant's arrest although there was a few minutes' delay between the search and the arrest. A reasonable delay in conducting a search incident to arrest is permitted so that any danger to the officers can be eliminated.

United States v. Savage, 889 F.2d 1113 (D.C. Cir. 1989). A search of a cardboard box in the defendant's train roomette after the defendant's arrest there was permissible because the box was within his immediate grasp.

Arrest of an Occupant of a Vehicle

(*This topic is discussed on page 252.*)

Arizona v. Gant, 556 U.S. 332 (2009). The Court ruled that officers may search a vehicle incident to arrest only if (1) the arrestee is unsecured and within reaching distance of the passenger compartment when the search is conducted or (2) it is reasonable to believe that evidence relevant to the crime of arrest might be found in the vehicle. The search of the vehicle incident to the defendant's arrest was not justified, because he was handcuffed in the backseat of a patrol car when the search was conducted and it was not reasonable to believe that evidence relevant to the crime of arrest (driving with a suspended license) might be found in the vehicle. For a discussion of this ruling, see page 252 in Chapter 3. *See also* Robert L. Farb, *The United States Supreme Court's Ruling in* Arizona v. Gant (UNC School of Government, 2009), www.sog.unc.edu/sites/www.sog.unc.edu/files/reports/arizonagantbyfarb.pdf.

Knowles v. Iowa, 525 U.S. 113 (1998). An officer stopped a vehicle for speeding and issued a citation to the driver, even though the officer could have arrested him under Iowa state law. The officer—without consent or probable cause to search—then conducted a full search of the vehicle. The Court ruled that the officer's search violated the Fourth Amendment, rejecting the theory of a search incident to the issuance of a citation.

State v. Mbacke, 365 N.C. 403 (2012). The state supreme court reversed the court of appeals and determined that a search of the defendant's vehicle incident to his arrest for carrying a concealed gun did not violate the Fourth Amendment. The defendant was indicted for, among other things, trafficking in cocaine and carrying a concealed gun. Officers were dispatched to a specific street address in response to a 911 caller's report that a black male armed with a black handgun, wearing a yellow shirt, and driving a red Ford Escape was parked in his driveway and that the male had "shot up" his house the previous night. Officers Walley and Horsley arrived at the scene less than six minutes after the 911 call. They observed a black male (later identified as the defendant) wearing a yellow shirt and backing a red or maroon Ford Escape out of the driveway. The officers exited their vehicles, drew their weapons, and moved toward the defendant while ordering him to stop and put his hands in the air. Officer Woods then arrived and blocked the driveway to prevent escape. The defendant initially rested his hands on his steering wheel but then lowered them towards his waist. Officers then began shouting at the defendant to keep his hands in sight and to exit his vehicle. The defendant raised his hands and stepped out of his car, kicking or bumping the driver's door shut as he did so. Officers ordered the defendant to lie on the ground and then handcuffed him, advising him that he was being detained because they had received a report that a person matching his description was carrying a weapon. After the defendant said that he had a gun in his waistband and officers found the gun, the defendant was arrested for carrying a concealed gun. The officers secured the defendant in the back of a patrol car, returned to his vehicle, and opened the driver's side door. Officer Horsley immediately saw a white brick wrapped in green plastic protruding from beneath the driver's seat. As Officer Horsley was showing this to Officer Walley, the defendant attempted to escape from the patrol car. After re-securing the defendant, the officers searched his vehicle incident to the arrest but found no other contraband. The white brick turned out to be 993.8 grams of cocaine. The court noted that the case required it to apply *Arizona v. Gant*, 556 U.S. 332 (2009) (officers may search a vehicle incident to arrest only if (1) the arrestee is unsecured and within reaching distance of the passenger compartment when the search is conducted or (2) it is reasonable to believe that evidence relevant to the crime of arrest might be found in the vehicle). It began its analysis by concluding that, as used in the second prong of the *Gant* test, the term "reasonable to believe" establishes a threshold lower than probable cause that "parallels the objective 'reasonable suspicion' standard sufficient to justify a *Terry* stop." Thus, it held that "when investigators have a reasonable and articulable basis to believe that evidence of the offense of arrest might be found in a suspect's vehicle after the occupants have been removed and secured, the investigators are permitted to conduct a search of that vehicle." Applying that standard, the court concluded:

> [D]efendant was arrested for . . . carrying a concealed gun. The arrest was based upon defendant's disclosure that the weapon was under his shirt. Other circumstances . . . such as the report of defendant's actions the night before and defendant's furtive behavior when confronted by officers, support a finding that it was reasonable to believe additional evidence of the offense of arrest could be found in defendant's vehicle. Accordingly, the search was permissible under *Gant* . . . .

The court concluded by noting that it "[was] not holding that an arrest for carrying a concealed weapon is *ipso facto* an occasion that justifies the search of a vehicle." It expressed the belief that "the 'reasonable to believe' standard required by *Gant* will not routinely be based on the nature or type of the offense of arrest and that the circumstances of each case ordinarily will determine the propriety of any vehicular searches conducted incident to an arrest."

State v. Fizovic, ___ N.C. App. ___, 770 S.E.2d 717 (2015). The court ruled that a search of the defendant's vehicle was properly conducted incident to the defendant's arrest for an open container offense when the officer had probable cause to arrest before the search even though the formal arrest did not occur until after the search was completed. The court noted that under *Arizona v. Gant*, 556 U.S. 332 (2009), "[a]n officer may conduct a warrantless search of a suspect's vehicle incident to his arrest if he has a reasonable belief that evidence related to the offense of arrest may be found inside the vehicle." The trial court's unchallenged findings of fact that it is common to find alcohol in vehicles of individuals stopped for alcohol violations and that the center console in the defendant's car was large enough to hold beer cans support the conclusion that the arresting officer had a reasonable belief that evidence related to the open container violation might be found in the defendant's vehicle. The court rejected the defendant's argument that the search was an unconstitutional "search incident to citation," noting that the defendant was arrested, not issued a citation.

State v. Watkins, 220 N.C. App. 384 (2012). The court ruled that the search of a vehicle driven by the defendant was valid under *Arizona v. Gant*, 556 U.S. 332 (2009), as incident to the arrest of the defendant's passenger for possession of drug paraphernalia. Officers had a reasonable belief that evidence relevant to the passenger's possession of drug paraphernalia might be found in the vehicle. Additionally, the objective circumstances provided the officers with probable cause for a warrantless search of the vehicle, including the fact that drug paraphernalia was found on the passenger, there was an anonymous tip that the vehicle would be transporting drugs, there were outstanding arrest warrants for the car's owner, the defendant behaved nervously while driving and upon exiting the vehicle, and there was an alert by a drug-sniffing dog.

State v. Foy, 208 N.C. App. 562 (2010). The trial court erred by suppressing evidence obtained pursuant to a search incident to arrest. After stopping the defendant's vehicle, an officer decided not to charge him with impaired driving but to allow the defendant to have someone pick him up. The defendant consented to the officer's retrieving a cell phone from the vehicle. While doing that, the officer saw a weapon and charged the defendant with carrying a concealed weapon. Following the arrest, officers searched the defendant's vehicle and found additional contraband, which was suppressed by the trial court. The court noted that under *Arizona v. Gant*, 556 U.S. 332 (2009), officers may search a vehicle incident to arrest only if the arrestee is within reaching distance of the passenger compartment at the time of the search or if it is reasonable to believe that the vehicle contains evidence of the offense of arrest. When these justifications are absent, a search of the vehicle will be unreasonable unless police obtain a warrant or show that another exception to the warrant requirement applies. Citing *State v. Toledo*, 204 N.C. App. 170 (2010), the court held that after having arrested the defendant for carrying a concealed weapon, it was reasonable for the officer to believe that the vehicle contained additional offense-related contraband within the meaning of the second *Gant* exception.

State v. Johnson, 204 N.C. App. 259 (2010). Officers saw a blue Mitsubishi with a license plate of WT 3453 being driven by a black male wearing a white T-shirt. An officer entered the license plate information into his computer, which revealed that the vehicle was registered to a Kelvin Johnson, black male, date of birth August 5, 1964. It also showed that Johnson's driver's license was suspended. Officers stopped the vehicle, arrested the defendant for driving while license revoked, placed him in the back of a patrol car, and searched the defendant's vehicle incident to his arrest. The court ruled that the ruling in *Arizona v. Gant*, 556 U.S. 332 (2009), applied to the defendant's case because it was on direct appeal and not yet final. The court also ruled that the search incident to arrest of the defendant's vehicle violated the Fourth Amendment because it did not satisfy the *Gant* ruling. The defendant was secured in a patrol car, and it was not reasonable to believe that evidence of the offense of driving while license revoked might be found in the vehicle.

State v. Carter, 200 N.C. App. 47 (2009). An officer noticed that a vehicle's temporary tag was old or worn and had an obscured expiration date. He stopped the vehicle, which was being driven by the defendant. The officer saw several whole pieces of paper lying on the passenger seat and noticed that the defendant seemed unusually nervous. The officer investigated the vehicle's registration and then arrested the defendant for an expired registration tag and failure to notify the Division of Motor Vehicles of a change of address. The defendant was removed from the vehicle, handcuffed, and directed to sit on a curb while the vehicle was searched. The officer noticed that the whole pieces of paper had been ripped into smaller pieces. He placed the pieces together and discovered incriminating evidence.

(1) The court ruled that the officer's search of the vehicle incident to the defendant's arrest violated the Fourth Amendment under the ruling in *Arizona v. Gant*, 556 U.S. 332 (2009). First, the defendant was not within reaching distance or otherwise able to access the passenger compartment when the search began. He had been arrested, handcuffed, and was sitting on the curb. Second, there was no evidence that the papers were related to the offenses for which the defendant had been arrested.

United States v. Slone, 636 F.3d 845 (7th Cir. 2011). The defendant was arrested for a drug offense because he was driving his truck in tandem with another vehicle that was transporting a large amount of marijuana (there were other incriminating facts as well). The court ruled, relying on *Arizona v. Gant*, 556 U.S. 332 (2009), that the officers could search the defendant's truck incident to arrest because it was reasonable to believe that evidence related to the offense would be found in the truck's passenger compartment. Officers could have reasonably expected to find money, cell phones, maps, drawings, or other evidence linking the occupants of the truck to the offense.

Protective Sweep of Premises

(This topic is discussed on page 261.)

Maryland v. Buie, 494 U.S. 325 (1990). When officers arrest a person in a home or similar kind of premise, they may as incident to that arrest automatically (that is, without needing probable cause or reasonable suspicion to do so) search closets and other spaces immediately adjoining the place of arrest from which an attack on them from another person could be immediately launched. They also may make a warrantless sweep of the rest of the premises, but only if they have reasonable suspicion that the place to be searched harbors a person who is a danger to the officers there. *See also* United States v. Delgado, 903 F.2d 1495 (11th Cir. 1990) (protective sweep of warehouse for additional suspects was proper); United States v. Oguns, 921 F.2d 442 (2d Cir. 1990) (arrest of defendant outside apartment with open door permitted security sweep of apartment, based on facts in this case); United States v. Tisdale, 921 F.2d 1095 (10th Cir. 1990) (similar ruling). *But see* United States v. Akrawi, 920 F.2d 418 (6th Cir. 1990) (protective sweep of second floor of house after arresting defendant at front door was not justified by reasonable suspicion; court also noted that officers inexplicably remained in house for 45 minutes).

State v. Taylor, 298 N.C. 405 (1979). Even though the defendant had been arrested outside the house, officers had reason to fear for their safety from the possible use of a firearm by someone inside the house. Therefore, exigent circumstances permitted a warrantless search of the house to find the weapon.

State v. Dial, 228 N.C. App. 83 (2013). The court of appeals ruled that the trial court did not err by denying the defendant's motion to suppress evidence discovered as a result of a protective sweep of his residence when officers had a reasonable belief based on specific and articulable facts that the residence harbored an individual who posed a danger to the officers' safety. Officers were at the defendant's residence to serve an order for arrest. Although the defendant on prior encounters had answered his door promptly, this time he did not respond for 10 to 15 minutes after an officer knocked and announced his presence. The officer heard shuffling on the other side of the front door. When two other officers arrived, the first officer briefed them on the situation, showed them the order for arrest, and explained his belief based on past experience that weapons were normally inside. When the deputies again approached the residence, "the front door flew open" and the defendant exited. The officers then issued verbal commands to the defendant, but he walked down the front steps with his hands raised, failing to comply with the officers' instructions. As soon as the first officer reached the defendant, the other officers entered the home and performed a protective sweep, lasting about 30 seconds. Evidence supporting the protective sweep included the fact that the officers viewed the open door to the residence as a "fatal funnel" that could provide someone inside with a clear shot at the officers, the defendant's unusually long response time and resistance, the known potential threat of weapons inside the residence, shuffling noises that could have indicated more than one person inside the residence, the defendant's alarming exit from the residence, and the defendant's own actions that led to his arrest in the open doorway.

State v. Bullin, 150 N.C. App. 631 (2002). Officers entered the defendant's residence with an arrest warrant for illegal drugs and arrested him. They then made a protective search of the home to ensure that another person who could harm them was not present. The officers seized drug items that they saw in plain view in the master bedroom closet. They then obtained a search warrant to search the residence. The court, relying on *Maryland v. Buie*, 494 U.S. 325 (1990), ruled that the protective search was valid; the court noted that the officers limited their search to obvious hiding places. Before conducting the protective search, the officers knew that the defendant (1) had a history of drug dealing, (2) was currently involved in drug dealing, (3) was a current suspect in a drug trafficking investigation involving many people, and (4) resisted arrest when informed of the arrest warrant. The court also stated that drug trafficking was dangerous.

State v. Wallace, 111 N.C. App. 581 (1993). Officers received information that marijuana was being grown in the basement of a residence. However, the officers were unable to corroborate the informant's information. Therefore, they went to the residence to investigate. After the officers knocked on the door, Jolly came out and

closed the door behind him. The officers told him why they were there and asked him if there were others in the residence. Jolly told the officers that one of his roommates was asleep inside. The officers then asked for consent to search the residence. Before Jolly could answer, Wallace came out of the residence. The officers then asked for consent to search, which Wallace and Jolly denied. Jolly then stated that "there might be some drug paraphernalia and marijuana seeds in the house" and that he would not consent to a search until he had time to get rid of the contraband. After the officers were denied consent to search, they heard footsteps in the residence and a door shut on the inside. The officers asked Wallace and Jolly who was in the residence, and they said they did not know because they had just arrived. The officers then went inside to execute a protective sweep before leaving the residence to obtain a search warrant. The officers saw what appeared to be marijuana plants while inside. The defendants were detained in the residence while other officers obtained a search warrant, which included information about their observation of marijuana in the house.

The court ruled: (1) Uncorroborated information initially given to the officers was insufficient to establish probable cause to search the residence. (2) The officers did not violate the defendants' rights by going to the residence to investigate. (3) Probable cause existed to search the residence when Jolly made the quoted statement above. (4) The officers did not have exigent circumstances to enter the residence without a search warrant. The court stated that the "record is devoid of any evidence that the officers entered the residence with a reasonably objective belief that evidence was about to be removed or destroyed." The court noted that the only purpose of the officers' entry into the residence was to conduct a protective sweep until a search warrant could be obtained, and the officers did not believe that they were in danger at any time. (5) The State could not justify the search of the residence under the independent source exception to the exclusionary rule; see *Murray v. United States*, 487 U.S. 533 (1988); *Segura v. United States*, 468 U.S. 796 (1984). In this case, the search warrant was prompted by what the officers saw in their unlawful entry, and the information obtained during the illegal entry was presented to the magistrate and affected the decision to issue the search warrant.

United States v. Ford, 56 F.3d 265 (D.C. Cir. 1995). An officer conducting a protective sweep of premises could not lift a mattress or look behind a window shade when the officer knew that a person could not be found there.

United States v. Henry, 48 F.3d 1282 (D.C. Cir. 1995). The mere fact that an arrest occurs outside a residence does not bar officers from conducting a protective sweep of the residence under *Maryland v. Buie*, 494 U.S. 325 (1990), if there is a reasonable belief that a sweep is necessary to protect the safety of the arresting officers. The court found that the protective sweep was proper in this case. *Compare with* United States v. Colbert, 76 F.3d 773 (6th Cir. 1996) (court ruled that facts in this case did not justify search of residence after defendant was arrested outside residence).

Frisk

(This topic is discussed on page 257.)

Generally
UNITED STATES SUPREME COURT

Arizona v. Johnson, 555 U.S. 323 (2009). Three officers, members of a gang task force, were on patrol near a neighborhood associated with the Crips gang. They stopped a vehicle after a license plate check revealed that the vehicle's registration had been suspended for an insurance-related violation, which under Arizona state law was a civil infraction warranting a citation. There were three occupants in the vehicle: the driver, a front-seat passenger, and the defendant (a backseat passenger). When making the stop, the officers had no reason to suspect anyone of criminal activity. Each officer dealt with one of the occupants. The officer involved with the defendant had noticed on the officers' approach to the vehicle that the defendant had looked back and kept his eyes on the officers. She observed that the defendant was wearing clothing that was consistent with Crips membership. She also noticed a scanner in the defendant's back pocket, which she believed that most people would not carry in that manner unless they were involved in criminal activity or trying to evade law enforcement. The defendant answered the officer's questions (he provided his name and date of birth but had no identification; he said that he had served time in prison for burglary) and also volunteered that he was from an Arizona town that the officer knew was home to a Crips gang. The defendant complied with the officer's request to get out of the car. Based on her observations and the defendant's answers to her questions, the officer suspected that he might have a weapon and frisked him and discovered a gun.

The Court reviewed its case law on stop and frisk beginning with *Terry v. Ohio*, 392 U.S. 1 (1968), particularly noting *Pennsylvania v. Mimms*, 434 U.S. 106 (1977) (officer may automatically order driver out of lawfully stopped vehicle); *Maryland v. Wilson*, 519 U.S. 408 (1997) (applying *Mimms* to passengers); and *Brendlin v. California*, 551 U.S. 249 (2007) (when vehicle is stopped, passengers as well as driver are seized). The Court stated that the combined thrust of these three cases is that an officer who conducts a routine traffic stop may frisk the driver and any passenger the officer reasonably suspects to be armed and dangerous. The officer need not additionally have cause to believe that any vehicle occupant is involved in criminal activity.

Michigan v. Long, 463 U.S. 1032 (1983). An officer properly protected himself by conducting a search for weapons in the passenger compartment of a motor vehicle when (1) he stopped the vehicle, (2) the defendant was removed, and (3) the officer had a reasonable belief that the suspect was potentially dangerous and could obtain a weapon when he reentered the vehicle. In this case, the officers already had seen a large knife in the vehicle's interior when they removed the suspect, who was intoxicated. *See also* United States v. Stanfield, 109 F.3d 976 (4th Cir. 1997) (officers conducting traffic stop of vehicle with windows so heavily tinted that they are unable to view interior may open door of vehicle and visually inspect its interior); United States v. Brown, 133 F.3d 993 (7th Cir. 1998) (officer properly searched car for weapons when two men inside vehicle had been stopped for investigation of their prowling in high crime area); United States v. Holifield, 956 F.2d 665 (7th Cir. 1992).

Ybarra v. Illinois, 444 U.S. 85 (1979). When executing a search warrant that authorized a search for drugs in a public tavern and on the person of the bartender, officers were not entitled to frisk the defendant—a bar patron who was present at the time of the search—without reasonable suspicion that he was armed and dangerous.

Pennsylvania v. Mimms, 434 U.S. 106 (1977). An officer had the right to frisk the defendant when he saw a bulge that he believed might be a weapon under the defendant's jacket when he got out of his car.

Adams v. Williams, 407 U.S. 143 (1972). An officer had the authority to forcibly stop the defendant, who was sitting in a car in a high crime area late at night when a person whom the officer knew told him that the defendant was carrying narcotics and had a gun at his waist. After the officer approached the car, the defendant rolled down his window rather than complying with the officer's request to step out of the car. Under these circumstances, the officer had a right to frisk the occupant by reaching toward his waist for the gun in order to protect himself.

Sibron v. New York, 392 U.S. 40 (1968). An officer had no authority to frisk the defendant when the defendant put his hand in his pocket. The officer did not fear that the defendant was reaching for a weapon; instead, he thought that the defendant had narcotics in his pockets.

Terry v. Ohio, 392 U.S. 1 (1968). The Court recognized the authority of law enforcement officers to stop and frisk, although the opinion narrowly focused on the officer's frisk of the defendant for weapons, based on evidence that he and an accomplice were about to rob a store. Justice Harlan's concurring opinion discussed the officer's right to make a forcible stop with articulable suspicion, a standard that requires less evidence than probable cause.

NORTH CAROLINA SUPREME COURT

State v. Morton, 363 N.C. 737 (2009), *rev'g* 198 N.C. App. 206 (2009). The court, per curiam and without an opinion, reversed the ruling of the North Carolina Court of Appeals for reasons stated in Section I of the dissenting opinion, which concluded that officers had reasonable suspicion to conduct a frisk of the defendant. The dissenting opinion stated that under the totality of circumstances, the officers were aware of the following: (1) at least one confidential informant who had provided information in the past had implicated the defendant in a recent drive-by shooting; (2) several informants and anonymous tipsters had reported that the defendant sold drugs in the area; (3) the defendant was traveling in a path from a food mart to his grandmother's house as the informants and tipsters had claimed he would; (4) the defendant picked up his pace when he saw the officers looking in his direction; (5) the defendant was visibly nervous when the officers attempted to question him; and (6) the defendant was wearing red pants, which indicated to one of the officers, a gang analyst, that the defendant might be affiliated with a local gang. (See the complete analysis of the frisk issue in the dissenting opinion.)

State v. Pearson, 348 N.C. 272 (1998). Officer A stopped a car that had been drifting back and forth within its lane on an interstate highway and traveling below the speed limit. The defendant was the driver of the car, and there was a female passenger. Officer A asked the defendant to leave the vehicle and come to the patrol car. Officer A noticed that the defendant had a slight odor of

alcohol about him, acted nervous, and had a rapid heart rate while in the patrol car. Officer A determined, however, that the defendant was tired, not impaired by alcohol. The defendant said that he and his fiancée had left the Charlotte area the day before and had spent the night at his parents' home in Virginia. Officer A then talked to the passenger, who was seated in the defendant's car. She said that the couple had spent the previous night in New York visiting the defendant's parents. Officer A did not see any drugs or weapons in the defendant's car. Officer A then returned to his patrol car and received the defendant's written consent to search his car. Officer B arrived and was asked by Officer A to frisk the defendant while Officer A searched the defendant's car. The officers testified at the suppression hearing that the defendant was frisked because it was standard procedure to do so when a vehicle is searched.

The court ruled that this evidence was insufficient to establish reasonable suspicion to frisk the defendant. The court noted that the defendant was polite and cooperative. The officers were not aware that the defendant had a criminal record or drug background. The defendant had not made any movement or statement that would indicate that he had a weapon. Neither the defendant's nervousness nor the variance in the statements of the defendant and his fiancée was sufficient to justify the frisk. The court distinguished *State v. McGirt*, 122 N.C. App. 237 (1996), *aff'd*, 345 N.C. 624 (1997). The court also ruled that the defendant did not consent to be frisked. The written consent form authorized only a search of the defendant's vehicle, not a search of his person. Also, the defendant's acquiescence when Officer B told him he would frisk him was not consent, considering the circumstances of this case.

State v. Butler, 331 N.C. 227 (1992). The court upheld an officer's stop and frisk of a drug suspect, citing these factors: (1) the officer saw the defendant in the midst of a group of people congregated on a corner known as a "drug hole"; (2) the officer had watched the corner daily for several months; (3) the officer knew that the corner was a center of drug activity because he had made four to six drug-related arrests there in the past six months; (4) the officer was aware of other arrests there; (5) the defendant was a stranger to the officer; (6) when the defendant made eye contact with the uniformed officers, he immediately left the corner and walked away, behavior that is evidence of flight; and (7) the officer's experience was that people involved in drug trafficking are often armed. The court stated that, in considering the legality of the frisk, the officer was entitled to formulate "common-sense conclusions" about "the modes or patterns of operation of certain kinds of lawbreakers" (citing *United States v. Cortez*, 449 U.S. 411 (1981)) in concluding that the defendant, reasonably suspected of drug trafficking, might be armed.

State v. Peck, 305 N.C. 734 (1982). An officer's subjective belief that the defendant did not have a gun when the defendant reached in his pocket is immaterial in determining the legality of a frisk. Objective facts supported the officer's frisk because he needed to protect himself from a dangerous weapon that may have been in the defendant's pocket.

NORTH CAROLINA COURT OF APPEALS

State v. Johnson, ___ N.C. App. ___, 784 S.E.2d 633 (2016). In this drug trafficking case, the court ruled that an officer had reasonable suspicion to extend a traffic stop. After Officer Ward initiated a traffic stop and asked the driver for his license and registration, the driver produced his license but was unable to produce a registration. The driver's license listed his address as Raleigh, but he could not give a clear answer as to whether he resided in Brunswick County or Raleigh. Throughout the conversation, the driver changed his story about where he resided. The driver was speaking into one cell phone and had two other cell phones on the center console of his vehicle. The officer saw a vehicle power control (VPC) module on the floor of the vehicle, an unusual item that might be associated with criminal activity. When Ward attempted to question the defendant, a passenger, the defendant mumbled answers and appeared very nervous. Ward then determined that the driver's license was inactive, issued the driver a citation, and told him that he was free to go. However, Ward asked the driver if he would mind exiting the vehicle to answer a few questions. Ward also asked the driver if he could pat him down, and the driver agreed. Meanwhile, Deputy Arnold, who was assisting, observed a rectangular shaped bulge underneath the defendant's shorts, in his crotch area. When he asked the defendant to identify the item, the defendant responded that it was his male anatomy. Arnold asked the defendant to step out of the vehicle so that he could do a pat down; before this could be completed, a ziplock bag containing heroin fell from the defendant's shorts. The extension of the traffic stop was justified: the driver could not answer basic questions, such as where he was coming from and where he lived; the driver changed his story; the driver could not explain why he did not have his registration; the presence of the VPC was unusual; and the defendant was extremely nervous and gave vague answers to the officer's questions. The court ruled that the officer properly frisked the defendant. The defendant's nervousness, evasiveness, and failure to identify what was in his shorts, coupled with the size and nature of the object, supported a reasonable suspicion that the defendant was armed and dangerous.

State v. Hargett, ___ N.C. App. ___, 772 S.E.2d 115 (2015). In the course of rejecting the defendant's ineffective assistance of counsel claim related to preserving a denial of a motion to suppress, the court ruled that no prejudice occurred because the trial court properly denied the motion. The officer received a report from an identified tipster that a window at a residence appeared to have been tampered with and that the owner of the residence was incarcerated. After the officer confirmed that a window screen had been pushed aside and the window was open, he repeatedly knocked on the door. Initially there was no response. Finally, an individual inside asked, "Who's there?" The officer responded, "It's the police." The individual said, "Okay," came to the door, and opened it. When the officer asked the person's identity, the individual gave a very long, slow response, finally gave his name, but either would not or could not provide any ID. When asked who owned the house, he gave no answer. Although the individual was asked repeatedly to keep his hands visible, he continued to put them in his pockets. These facts were sufficient to create reasonable suspicion that the defendant might have broken into the home and also justified a frisk of the defendant. During the lawful frisk, the officer discovered and identified baggies of marijuana in the defendant's sock by plain feel.

State v. Henry, 237 N.C. App. 311 (2014). The court ruled that even if the defendant had properly preserved the issue, a frisk conducted during a valid traffic stop was lawful when the officer knew that the defendant had prior drug convictions, the defendant appeared nervous, the defendant deliberately concealed his right hand and refused to open it despite repeated requests, and the officer knew from his training and experience that people who deal drugs frequently carry weapons and that weapons can be concealed in a hand.

State v. Sutton, 232 N.C. App. 667 (2014). The court ruled that an officer had reasonable suspicion to stop and frisk the defendant when the defendant was in a high crime area and made movements that the officer found suspicious. The defendant was in a public housing area patrolled by a Special Response Unit of the United States Marshals Service and the Drug Enforcement Administration concentrating on violent crimes and gun crimes. The officer in question had 10 years of experience and was assigned to the Special Response Unit. Many people were banned from the public housing area—in fact, the banned list was nine pages long. On a prior occasion the officer had heard shots fired near the area. In the present case, the officer saw the defendant walking normally while swinging his arms. When the defendant turned and "used his right hand to grab his waistband to clinch an item" after looking directly at the officer, the officer believed that the defendant was trying to hide something on his body. The officer then stopped the defendant to identify him, frisked him, and found a gun in the defendant's waistband.

State v. Phifer, 226 N.C. App. 359 (2013). The court ruled that the trial court improperly denied the defendant's motion to suppress. An officer saw the defendant walking in the middle of the street. The officer stopped the defendant to warn him about impeding the flow of street traffic. After issuing this warning, the officer frisked the defendant because of his "suspicious behavior"—specifically, that he "appeared to be nervous and kept moving back and forth." The court found that "the nervous pacing of a suspect, temporarily detained by an officer to warn him not to walk in the street, is insufficient to warrant further detention and search."

State v. Hemphill, 219 N.C. App. 50 (2012). The court of appeals ruled that an officer, after feeling a screwdriver and wrench on the defendant's person during a pat down, was justified in removing the tools because they both constituted a potential danger to the officer and were suggestive of criminal activity at a closed business late at night.

In re D.B., 214 N.C. App. 489 (2011). The court of appeals ruled that the trial court erred by admitting evidence obtained by an officer who exceeded the proper scope of a *Terry* frisk. After the officer stopped the juvenile, he conducted a weapons frisk and found nothing. When the officer asked the juvenile to identify himself, the juvenile did not respond. Because the officer thought that he felt an identification card in the juvenile's pocket during the frisk, he retrieved it. It turned out to be a stolen credit card, which was admitted into evidence. Although officers who lawfully stop a person may ask a moderate number of questions to determine the person's identity and gain information confirming or dispelling the suspicions that prompted the stop, no authority suggests that an officer may physically search a person for evidence of his or her identity in connection with a *Terry* stop.

State v. King, 206 N.C. App. 585 (2010). The court ruled that an officer had reasonable suspicion to believe that the defendant was armed and dangerous, justifying a pat-down frisk. Around midnight, the officer stopped the defendant's vehicle after determining that the tag was registered to a different car; before the stop, the defendant and his passenger had looked oddly at the officer. After the stop, the defendant held his hands out the window; volunteered that he had a gun, which was loaded; and when exiting the vehicle removed his coat, even though it was cold outside. At this point, the pat down occurred. The court rejected the defendant's argument that his efforts to show that he did not pose a threat obviated the need for the pat down. It also rejected the defendant's argument that the discovery of the gun could not support a reasonable suspicion that he still might be armed and dangerous; instead, the court concluded that the confirmed presence of a weapon was a compelling factor justifying a frisk, even when that weapon was secured and out of the defendant's reach. Additionally, the officer was entitled to formulate "common-sense conclusions"—based upon an observed pattern that one weapon often signals the presence of other weapons—in believing that the defendant, who had already called the officer's attention to one readily visible weapon, might be armed.

State v. Campbell, 188 N.C. App. 701 (2008). At approximately 3:40 a.m., Officer A responded to a report of a breaking and entering in progress at a residence. While driving to the residence (he arrived within three minutes of the report), the officer saw the defendant riding a bicycle on a road that was near the reported break-in (about a quarter-mile away). The officer did not see anyone else in the vicinity. The officer continued on to the dwelling without making any contact with the bicyclist. He saw that a window had been opened with a small, flathead screwdriver or a pry tool and he notified other officers of that information. Officer B, aware of Officer A's report about the bicyclist and the break-in—including the type of instrument that may have been used—eventually stopped the defendant, who had a backpack and was playing with something inside it. Officer C arrived and recognized the defendant as having an extensive history of breaking and entering as well as being a substance abuser. Officer B handcuffed the defendant and frisked him. A small flashlight and a Swiss Army–type knife were found in the defendant's pockets. The defendant was then arrested. The court ruled that Officer B had reasonable suspicion to stop the defendant, noting the defendant's proximity to the break-in, the time of day, and the absence of other people in the area. The court also ruled that the officer did not violate the Fourth Amendment by handcuffing and frisking the defendant during the investigative stop. Handcuffing was supported by the knowledge of one of the officers that the defendant was a flight risk based on prior history. The frisk for weapons was justified by the late hour and the nature of the crime committed. The defendant could have been carrying anything from a pen that had an enclosed knife to a small handgun.

State v. Parker, 183 N.C. App. 1 (2007). A narcotics detective was conducting surveillance of the defendant in response to a citizen's complaint that the defendant was trafficking in methamphetamine. He stopped a vehicle that the defendant was driving because it was going approximately 60 m.p.h. in a 45 m.p.h. zone and then passed another vehicle at approximately 80 m.p.h. in a 55 m.p.h. zone. The defendant stepped out of his vehicle and approached the detective's vehicle. The detective ordered the defendant to return to his vehicle, but he refused to do so. The detective then secured the defendant in the backseat of the defendant's vehicle. Two passengers (A and B) were also seated in the vehicle. The defendant told the detective that there was a gun in the vehicle. The detective opened the door to the front passenger seat where A was sitting and saw a 12-gauge shotgun located between the seat and door. As he assisted A and B out of the vehicle, he saw a piece of newspaper fall to the ground. The detective then conducted a weapons frisk of the vehicle for his own safety to make sure there were no other weapons there. He examined the piece of newspaper and saw that it was covering a drawstring bag. Inside the bag he found a substance he believed to be methamphetamine and a smoking device. He found a pistol under the front passenger seat. The court ruled that the officer conducted a valid "vehicle frisk" for weapons inside the defendant's vehicle under *Michigan v. Long*, 463 U.S. 1032 (1983). The detective had a reasonable belief that the defendant was dangerous and had immediate access to a weapon in the car. And the search of the drawstring bag was a valid part of the weapons search.

State v. Edwards, 164 N.C. App. 130 (2004). Suspecting that the defendant had committed sexual assaults on females on December 23, 2000, and December 26, 2000, based on information gathered from the victims, officers placed him under surveillance. On January 9, 2001, evidence from surveillance at about 2:50 a.m. indicated that the defendant's car had left his residence and was traveling toward a nearby town. At about 4:00 a.m., officers heard an alert from that town's police that a female had been sexually assaulted with a handgun by a person whose general description matched the defendant's. Officers saw no vehicles on the road that night other than patrol cars (it was snowing). The defendant's vehicle then passed an officer's vehicle; it was coming from the other town and heading to the defendant's residence. The officers stopped the defendant's vehicle. The defendant immediately put both of his hands underneath his seat and jumped out of the vehicle. Officers had to draw their weapons on the defendant because he failed to comply with their orders. After handcuffing the defendant, one of the officers searched under the front seat of the defendant's vehicle for a weapon and found a handgun. (1) The court ruled that the officers had reasonable suspicion to stop the defendant to investigate the recent sexual assault. The court noted that the officers also had authority to stop the vehicle because it had an expired Illinois license plate. (2) The court ruled that the officer had the authority to make a protective search of the defendant's vehicle for a weapon under *Michigan v. Long*, 463 U.S. 1032 (1983).

State v. Harper, 158 N.C. App. 595 (2003). Based on an investigation that indicated people in a hotel room were involved with illegal drugs, an officer knocked on the door to the room. The defendant initially opened the door slightly and then, while continuing to have a conversation with the officer, opened it about halfway. The officer asked the defendant if he could step inside the room to see if George Davis was in. The defendant then stepped back from the officer and the threshold of the door and opened the door almost to its full extension. The officer saw a set of electronic scales on the nightstand between the room's two beds and knew that drug dealers often used such scales to measure illegal drugs. There was another person in the room in addition to the defendant. That person started moving around the room, refused the officer's order to remain seated on a bed, and became increasingly agitated. He was handcuffed. The defendant defied the officer's order to remain seated on a bed and was handcuffed. The officer then searched for weapons in the mattresses and nightstand. The officer and other officers saw illegal drugs and cash in these places. They obtained a search warrant, conducted a search of the hotel room, and seized evidence. The court ruled that the warrantless search for weapons of the mattresses and nightstand drawer (where the defendant and the other person had repeatedly moved) was justified for the officers' self-protection.

State v. Martinez, 158 N.C. App. 105 (2003). The court ruled that reasonable suspicion supported an officer's investigative stop of a vehicle for possible criminal activity. At 2:00 a.m., Officer A was on routine patrol in a marked vehicle when he saw and drove past a male pedestrian. The officer immediately turned around and pulled over on the side of the road behind the pedestrian; on seeing the officer, the pedestrian ran toward the woods in the direction of a mobile home park. About four minutes later, while the officer was driving through the mobile home park in an unsuccessful attempt to locate the pedestrian, Officer B contacted Officer A by radio and informed him that there was a motor vehicle parked on the right shoulder of the road near the mobile home park. Officer A then drove out of the mobile home park and saw a white vehicle leaving the right shoulder of the road near the mobile home park. This vehicle was located about 50 yards from the place where the officer had seen the pedestrian flee from him earlier. The officer then stopped the vehicle. The court stated that it was reasonable for the officer to infer that the person who had fled from him was in some way related to the stopped vehicle located a mere 50 yards from the fleeing pedestrian. The fact that the stop occurred around 2:00 a.m., when there was generally no foot traffic and there were no vehicles on the road except this vehicle and the patrol vehicles, contributed to the officer's suspicion. The court also ruled that the frisk of the driver of the stopped vehicle was proper. After presenting the officer with a Maryland driver's license, the defendant began digging in the glove compartment and then reaching around to several areas in the vehicle's interior, including behind the passenger seat toward the floorboard. The defendant exhibited a significant degree of nervousness. Concerned for his safety, the officer asked the defendant to exit the vehicle. The defendant did not respond when asked if he had any weapons. During the pat down for weapons, the officer felt a large bulge in the defendant's right front pants pocket and asked the defendant what the object was. The defendant responded, "Dope." The officer retrieved a large amount of currency and two bags of cocaine from the pocket. The court ruled

that the defendant's nonresponse to the question about weapons and the nervous digging in the vehicle supported the frisk. Relying on *State v. Benjamin*, 124 N.C. App. 734 (1996) (*Miranda* warnings not required before question asked during frisk), the court also ruled that the officer's brief inquiry during the frisk was not improper.

State v. Summey, 150 N.C. App. 662 (2002). Officers were conducting surveillance in a known drug area. An officer watched a residence that had been the subject of a nuisance-abatement proceeding for drug-related activities. A group of men were standing in the residence's front yard. The officer saw a pickup truck stop at the residence. One man in the yard approached the truck and appeared to converse with the driver. A few moments later, the man returned to the yard and the truck drove away. Believing he had witnessed a drug transaction, the officer radioed other officers, who stopped the vehicle. The defendant was seated in the passenger seat with her left hand hidden underneath a fabric material. An officer recognized her from prior investigative stops. Concerned about small weapons in her hand, the officer asked her to show her hands. She lifted her hands but kept her left hand closed in a fist. The officer noticed a rock-like substance, which he believed to be crack cocaine, wedged in a gap between the defendant's fingers. She refused to open her left hand. The officer applied pressure to the back of her hand and forced it open. The officer recognized one piece of crack cocaine that fell from her hand while another piece remained stuck to her palm.

(1) The court ruled that reasonable suspicion existed to make an investigative stop of the vehicle for illegal drugs. (2) The court ruled that reasonable suspicion existed to search the defendant's closed hand for weapons. The court noted that at the suppression hearing, the officers testified that they had been trained that a small knife or razor blade could be concealed in a clenched fist. Also, the search of the defendant's hand was justified by the officer's having seen crack cocaine wedged in her fingers. (3) The court ruled that reasonable force was used to open the defendant's closed hand to search for weapons and to prevent the destruction of evidence.

State v. Briggs, 140 N.C. App. 484 (2000). Officers were conducting a driver's license check in a high crime area. As one officer returned the defendant's license to the defendant, another officer recognized the defendant as someone whom he had previously arrested for cocaine offenses. The officer knew that the defendant was on probation and had been convicted of drug offenses more than once. Although the defendant denied that he had been drinking or taking drugs, the officer noted that the defendant was chewing gum "real hard" and that his eyes were glassy and bloodshot. Also, the officer smelled the odor of burned cigar tobacco inside the vehicle and on the defendant's person. When the officer asked about the smell, the defendant stated that he did not smoke cigars but that a female who was in the vehicle earlier had been smoking a cigar. The officer knew from his experience that drug users often smoke cigars to mask the smell of illegal drugs. The defendant declined the officer's request to search the vehicle. The officer then required the defendant to get out of the vehicle and frisked him for weapons. The officer was aware from his experience that drug dealers frequently carry weapons. The officer testified that during the frisk, "I felt a hard, cylindrical shape in [defendant's] pocket and it felt like a cigar holder; and I'm familiar with these because folks carry these frequently to keep their controlled substances in. It's like a little plastic test tube with a little cap on it; and there's really nothing else that's shaped exactly like that." The officer asked the defendant what that object was, and the defendant stated, "A cigar holder." The officer said, "I thought you didn't smoke cigars," but the defendant did not respond. The officer then removed the cigar holder from the defendant's pocket, and when he shook it, the cigar holder "rattled like it had a number of small hard objects in it." The officer opened the cigar holder, found 10 rocks of crack cocaine inside, and arrested the defendant.

The court ruled, relying on *State v. Butler*, 331 N.C. 227 (1992), and *State v. McGuirt*, 122 N.C. App. 237 (1996), *aff'd*, 345 N.C. 624 (1997), that the officer had reasonable suspicion to conduct the frisk, based on the facts discussed above. (2) The court ruled that the officer had probable cause to seize the cigar holder under the plain feel doctrine set out in *Minnesota v. Dickerson*, 508 U.S. 366 (1993). The court discussed cases from other jurisdictions that have split on the issue of whether the plain feel doctrine may be satisfied when an officer feels a container the shape of which does not itself reveal its identity as contraband. Courts upholding such seizures consider factors in addition to the officer's tactile perception to determine probable cause. Other courts declining to uphold such seizures have determined that touching the containers themselves cannot sustain a probable cause finding. The court adopted the view that it would consider the totality of circumstances in deciding whether an officer had probable cause to seize such a container when

the officer felt it, and the court stated that the probable cause determination involves considering the evidence as understood by law enforcement officers. Based on the facts discussed above, the officer in this case had probable cause to seize the cigar holder.

State v. Minor, 132 N.C. App. 478 (1999). Two officers stopped a car because its temporary tag was smeared and illegible. Before stopping the car, Officer A had seen the defendant-passenger move his hand toward the center console of the car after the police car's blue lights had been activated. Officer A removed the driver, frisked him, and talked with him while Officer B stood at the passenger side of the car. Officer B saw the defendant rub his hand on his thigh as though feeling his pocket. The defendant then put his hand on the door handle as if to emerge from the car but dropped his hand and remained in the car when he saw Officer B beside the car. After determining that the driver had no weapons, Officer A ordered the passengers—the defendant and one other passenger—out of the car. Both men were frisked, and no contraband or weapons were discovered. Officer A then searched the interior of the car and found a jacket with a .32 caliber handgun in the pocket where the defendant had been sitting.

Distinguishing *Michigan v. Long*, 463 U.S. 1032 (1983) (officer may search vehicle for weapon when reasonable suspicion that occupant is dangerous and may gain access to weapon), and relying on *State v. Braxton*, 90 N.C. App. 204 (1988), the court ruled that the officer's search of the car was not justified under *Michigan v. Long*. The court stated that the defendant's motions were not "clearly furtive." Because the officers did not have any specific knowledge linking the defendant to criminal activity or any reasonable belief that he was armed or dangerous, the search of the vehicle violated the Fourth Amendment.

State v. Willis, 125 N.C. App. 537 (1997). Officers were conducting surveillance of a residence while a search warrant was being sought to search it for drugs. The defendant, whom the officers did not recognize, left the residence on foot. Concerned that he might be involved in drug activity occurring in the residence, they decided to follow him. When the defendant realized that he was being followed, he took evasive action by cutting through a parking lot. A detective then asked a uniformed officer to stop the defendant and ask him for identification. That officer approached the defendant on foot, told him he was conducting an investigative stop, and asked him for identification and for consent to a pat down for drugs and weapons. The defendant consented to the pat down. The officer began to pat down the exterior and then the interior of the defendant's leather jacket. Just as the officer began to check the jacket's interior pocket, the defendant lunged into the jacket with his hand. The officer, believing that the defendant might be reaching for a weapon and fearing for his safety, immediately locked his hands around the defendant's jacket, effectively locking the defendant's hand inside the pocket. Another officer arrived and assisted the officer. When the two officers managed to get the defendant's hand out of his pocket, they put the defendant's hands behind him and reached into the defendant's interior jacket pocket and emptied it, revealing several baggies of crack cocaine.

Relying on *State v. Butler*, 331 N.C. 227 (1992), the court ruled that the officer's investigative stop was supported by reasonable suspicion. The court noted that the defendant left a suspected drug house just before the search warrant was to be executed. He took evasive action when he knew that he was being followed, and he exhibited nervous behavior. The court also ruled that the frisk and resulting search of the defendant's jacket pocket was proper. The court noted that the officers reasonably feared for their personal safety based on (1) their knowledge that people involved with drugs often carry weapons; (2) the defendant's exit from the suspected drug house; (3) the defendant's later furtive, evasive behavior; and (4) the defendant's sudden lunge of his hand into the interior of his jacket.

State v. Hamilton, 125 N.C. App. 396 (1997). An officer involved in drug surveillance stopped a vehicle because the driver and front-seat passenger were not wearing seat belts as required by law. As the officer approached the front passenger side of the vehicle and informed the defendant (the front-seat passenger) that he was a police officer, the defendant began to reach his hand toward his left side. The officer believed that the defendant was reaching for a weapon. The officer then asked the defendant to step outside the vehicle and told him that he was going to frisk him. The court ruled that the officer was justified in conducting the frisk.

State v. Rhyne, 124 N.C. App. 84 (1996). An officer received an anonymous report that people were selling drugs in the breezeway of a building. The court ruled that the officer did not have reasonable suspicion to frisk the defendant, who was sitting in the breezeway, because (1) the anonymous tip was not specific to the defendant; (2) although the area was known for drug activity, the

defendant lived there; and (3) the defendant was cooperative when questioned and did not flee.

State v. Artis, 123 N.C. App. 114 (1996). An officer who was part of a drug interdiction task force at an airport saw the defendant operating a video game in the airport game room, a location that had a reputation for drug activity. The game room could be accessed without going through the airport's metal detectors. The officer approached the defendant, identified himself, and learned that the defendant intended to take a departing flight. The officer saw a large crescent-shaped bulge in the defendant's left front pocket that appeared to be either brass knuckles or a weapon's handgrip. The officer asked the defendant several times if he was carrying any weapons or drugs, and the defendant responded each time by asking, "Why would I carry weapons or drugs?" The officer then told the defendant that he thought he was carrying a weapon in his left front pocket and that he wanted to pat the area down to satisfy himself that the object was not a weapon. As he made this statement, the officer reached for the pocket. The defendant, however, turned away from the officer and attempted to take a step backward. As the defendant stepped back, the officer placed his hand inside the defendant's pants pocket and on the object. The officer thought the object was brass knuckles. The defendant attempted to reach into the pocket despite the officer's request not to do so. The officer reached into the pocket to get control of the suspected weapon and removed a clear plastic bag that contained crack cocaine.

The court ruled that the officer's frisk violated the Fourth Amendment. The court stated that the officer had only a generalized suspicion to conduct the frisk, and it was not reasonable to infer that the bulge in the defendant's pants pocket was a weapon simply because the defendant had not yet passed through the airport's metal detectors. Also, the officer had no apparent need to check whether the defendant was armed with a weapon that could be used against him or others. When the officer approached, the defendant was merely operating a video game machine.

State v. McGirt, 122 N.C. App. 237 (1996), *aff'd*, 345 N.C. 624 (1997). An officer stopped a vehicle because the defendant-driver was not wearing his seat belt. The officer had been looking for the defendant's vehicle the prior night and was investigating the defendant for cocaine trafficking. The officer knew that the defendant had prior felony drug convictions and in his experience knew that cocaine traffickers normally carry weapons. After stopping the vehicle, the defendant complied with the officer's request to exit the vehicle. When the officer asked the defendant if he had anything on him, the defendant said "no" and raised his hands. The officer then frisked the defendant and felt a hard object, which the officer believed was a gun. When the officer asked the defendant to identify the object, the defendant said that it was a pistol and handed it to the officer.

The court ruled that the officer, based on this evidence, had reasonable suspicion to frisk the defendant. The court noted that (1) the officer knew that the defendant was a convicted felon, (2) the defendant was under investigation by the officer for cocaine trafficking, and (3) it was the officer's experience that cocaine traffickers normally carry weapons. The court stated that the totality of circumstances, even in the face of a cooperative defendant who presents no obvious signs of carrying a weapon, supports the legality of the frisk for weapons.

State v. Clyburn, 120 N.C. App. 377 (1995). Officers were conducting surveillance at night at a place that had a reputation for drug activity and where officers had previously made drug arrests. Officers saw three males in front of a vacant duplex. Individuals would approach one of the males, who would disappear behind the duplex with each individual. The other two males remained in front of the duplex as if acting as lookouts. Each time the defendant reappeared, the other two males conferred with him. Based on the officers' training and experience with similar activity, they believed that drug transactions were being conducted. After one such activity, one of the males and a female got into a car and drove away. Officers stopped the car and frisked the male (the defendant) and female. An officer searched the passenger area of the car and found a .357 Magnum in the glove compartment. The male was arrested for carrying a concealed weapon. Following the arrest, officers searched the car and found crack cocaine in an ashtray.

The court ruled that (1) the officers had reasonable suspicion to stop the car to investigate drug activity and (2) the search of the car for weapons was proper under *Michigan v. Long*, 463 U.S. 1032 (1983); after the defendant had been frisked, he became belligerent and the officers could reasonably believe that the defendant was potentially dangerous and might be armed because of his involvement in drug trafficking. The court also cited *State v. Butler*, 331 N.C. 227 (1992).

State v. Fleming, 106 N.C. App. 165 (1992). At 12:10 a.m. officers were in a housing project area where illegal drug activity was common. An officer saw the defendant and a companion, strangers to the area, standing in an open area between two apartment buildings. The two men watched the officer for a few minutes and began walking on a sidewalk away from him. The officer drove around to where the men were walking, got out of his car, and commanded them to come to him. They hesitated a minute and then approached him. The defendant acted "real nervous." As the officer was questioning the defendant about why he was in the area, to which the defendant responded that a friend had dropped him off and he was walking through, the officer frisked him and found crack cocaine. The court ruled, relying on *Brown v. Texas*, 443 U.S. 47 (1979), that the officer's stop and frisk of the defendant was not supported by reasonable suspicion of criminal activity.

State v. Hudson, 103 N.C. App. 708 (1991). An officer went to a car that was stopped for a motor vehicle violation to get the VIN and saw a passenger sitting in the front seat with an open newspaper across her lap. The officer feared that there might be a weapon under the newspaper, because it was not at an angle appropriate for reading and there was not sufficient light to read—the dome light was not on. When the officer asked the passenger if she had identification, she said "no." He asked her to step out of the vehicle, which she did, carrying a briefcase. The officer then saw in plain view another briefcase on the vehicle's floorboard with the butt of a gun protruding from it. He opened it and found two handguns and money. The officer then searched the briefcase in the passenger's possession and found cocaine and a revolver. The court ruled that the officer had authority to order the passenger out of the vehicle based on reasonable suspicion that she may have been trying to hide a weapon, and the officer had authority to search the briefcase on the vehicle's floorboard with a gun protruding from it for his self-protection.

State v. Harris, 95 N.C. App. 691 (1989), *aff'd per curiam*, 326 N.C. 588 (1990). Officers were outside a motel room planning to execute a search warrant for the room the next time the door to the room opened. The officers were looking for a person named Bernard Hobson, who was wanted on drug charges. When the defendant left the room, some officers went into the room to execute the warrant while other officers frisked the defendant for a weapon. The court ruled that the frisk was proper because (1) the officers had reasonable suspicion that people in the room were armed because Hobson was wanted on drug charges and the officers knew that there had been significant traffic in and out of the room that may have been related to drug dealing; (2) the officers believed that weapons would be found on people in this drug setting, based on their previous experience that weapons were found in at least 85 percent of similar situations; and (3) the officers were involved in a swiftly developing situation. Even if the officers knew that the defendant was not Hobson, they acted properly, because they did not know whether the defendant would leave the premises or perhaps turn around and begin shooting.

State v. Adkerson, 90 N.C. App. 333 (1988). An officer arrested the driver of a vehicle for impaired driving and placed him in his patrol car. He returned to the vehicle and found marijuana on the front seat. The defendant was sitting in the backseat with his feet on a jacket, and a brown paper bag was on the floor. The officer ordered the defendant out of the car and frisked him for weapons before conducting a search of the backseat. The court ruled that the frisk was justified because of the late hour, the rural surroundings, and the officer's vulnerable position if he leaned over toward the floor of the car with someone standing behind him.

State v. Braxton, 90 N.C. App. 204 (1988). An officer activated his blue light in an effort to stop a speeding car and later turned on his siren when the defendant failed to stop. He saw the defendant appear to stuff something under the seat, and then the defendant stopped his car. The officer pulled over, parked behind the defendant, and got out of his car. The defendant started moving his car forward and again appeared to be stuffing something under the seat. The officer got back in his car and followed the defendant. The defendant then stopped his car again. As the officer approached the defendant's car, the defendant got out of his car and closed the door. The officer asked the defendant twice what he had stuffed under the seat; the defendant did not answer either time. The officer opened the car door, reached under the front seat, and discovered a plastic bag containing marijuana.

The court ruled that the officer's action was not justified as a protective search for weapons under *Michigan v. Long*, discussed above. [Author's note: The court inadequately explained why the facts did not support the officer's action; it stated that the "defendant could not obtain any weapon or other item from the car," yet the defendant was not under arrest then and clearly could have reentered his car if the officer had decided to write a citation for the speeding violation.] *Compare with* United

States v. Nash, 876 F.2d 1359 (7th Cir. 1989) (1990) (search of car for weapon justified under *Michigan v. Long*, discussed above, when officer saw defendant—while still driving—make furtive gesture by appearing to raise himself up from car seat and begin reaching toward floor, and when officer approached car he saw jacket tucked under defendant's lap and stretched out to floor); United States v. Colin, 928 F.2d 676 (5th Cir. 1991) (car passenger stooping down and moving from side to side in front seat justified frisk); United States v. Woodall, 938 F.2d 834 (8th Cir. 1991) (passenger's reaching down to floorboard twice and officer's knowledge of passenger and driver as drug traffickers permitted frisk of both); United States v. Moorefield, 111 F.3d 10 (3d Cir. 1997) (car passenger's furtive hand movements and refusal to obey officers' orders that he remain in vehicle and keep his hands in air while officers conducted traffic stop permitted frisk).

State v. Collins, 38 N.C. App. 617 (1978). As an intoxicated passenger stepped out of a car, the officer saw a bulge in his pants pocket that appeared to be a knife. The officer properly frisked the defendant and seized a key chain and the plastic bag containing marijuana that was twined around it. *See also* United States v. Rideau, 969 F.2d 1572 (5th Cir. 1992) (en banc) (proper frisk of intoxicated person standing in the road at night in high crime area).

State v. Long, 37 N.C. App. 662 (1978). In a case decided before *Ybarra v. Illinois*, 444 U.S. 85 (1979), but not necessarily inconsistent with its rationale, the court ruled that an officer properly frisked for weapons the boot of a person who was present in private premises when a search warrant for drugs was being executed. Drugs found in the boot were properly seized. The court stated that a frisk for weapons automatically may be made of all persons present in a private residence when it is searched with a search warrant, at least when probable cause exists that it is a place where drugs are bought and sold.

State v. Stanfield, 19 N.C. App. 622 (1973). An officer received a phone call from an informant (apparently from an informant the officer knew, but that fact is not clear from the court's opinion) that the defendant had a pistol in his coat at a shopping mall. The officer knew about the defendant's prior criminal background, went to the mall, noticed a bulge in his coat pocket, and frisked him. His action was proper under *Terry v. Ohio*, 392 U.S. 1 (1968), and *Adams v. Williams*, 407 U.S. 143 (1972).

FEDERAL APPELLATE COURTS

United States v. Burton, 228 F.3d 524 (4th Cir. 2000). An officer did not have reasonable suspicion to conduct a frisk of the defendant during a voluntary encounter with him when the defendant declined to answer the officer's questions, had his hand in his coat pocket, and refused the officer's request to remove his hand from the pocket.

United States v. Sakyi, 160 F.3d 164 (4th Cir. 1998). The court ruled that during a lawful traffic stop of a vehicle when an officer has a reasonable suspicion that illegal drugs are in the vehicle, the officer may, in the absence of factors allaying his or her safety concerns, order the occupants out of the vehicle and pat them down briefly for weapons to ensure the officer's safety and the safety of others.

United States v. Swann, 149 F.3d 271 (4th Cir. 1998). An officer stopped and frisked two suspects. The officer felt something hard and unusual in the defendant's sock. He did not testify that he believed it to be a weapon or that he knew it was not a weapon; rather, he stated only that he did not know what it was. The court ruled that even though the officer did not testify that he believed the item in the defendant's sock to be a weapon when he removed it, a reasonable officer in these circumstances could have believed that the item was a weapon—specifically, a box cutter with a sharp blade. Thus, the frisk was constitutional.

United States v. Menard, 95 F.3d 9 (8th Cir. 1996). An officer stopped a vehicle with a driver and two passengers (Walker and the defendant) at 2:00 a.m. on a relatively deserted highway. Upon finding a weapon on Walker after frisking him, the officer arrested Walker for carrying a concealed weapon. Walker was also suspected of being a drug trafficker. The officer then frisked the defendant and found a weapon. The court upheld the frisk of the defendant, noting that Walker's arrest heightened the threat to the officer's safety because an armed associate of Walker might use force to free him.

United States v. Baker, 78 F.3d 135 (4th Cir. 1996). An officer lawfully stopped a car that was involved in evasive driving and traffic violations with three other cars. The officer saw a triangular-shaped bulge underneath the front of the driver's shirt, near the waistband of his pants. The officer ordered the defendant to raise his shirt so that the officer could see what was underneath it. The court ruled that, based on these facts, the officer had reasonable suspicion to frisk the driver for weapons and the method of conducting the frisk was reasonable. The court rejected the defendant's argument that the officer was limited to conducting a pat-down frisk.

United States v. Michelletti, 13 F.3d 838 (5th Cir. 1994) (en banc). The court ruled that a law enforcement officer had reasonable suspicion of criminal activity and that the defendant might be armed to justify frisking him when (1) the officer was on routine patrol in a high crime area at the closing time for bars; (2) the officer saw the defendant drinking beer as he was leaving a bar, a possible alcoholic beverage offense; (3) the officer saw the defendant approach a group of people acting suspiciously outside the bar; and (4) the defendant had his right hand in his pocket at all times, leading the officer to believe that the defendant might have a gun.

United States v. Mitchell, 951 F.2d 1291 (D.C. Cir. 1991). As an officer with 18 years' experience approached a lawfully stopped car from the front and went around to the passenger side of the car, he saw the passenger moving both his hands inside his coat as he leaned forward. The court ruled that the officer had authority to order the passenger out of the car and frisk him.

United States v. Hernandez, 941 F.2d 133 (2d Cir. 1991). After handcuffing a person during a security sweep of premises, officers properly searched the area near the person for weapons—in this case, between the bed's box spring and mattress.

United States v. Cruz, 909 F.2d 422 (11th Cir. 1989). When an officer had reasonable suspicion to make an investigative stop of the defendant for drugs in an area known for heavy drug trafficking, the officer also had the right to make a limited search of the defendant's shoulder bag for weapons, based on the facts in this case. The court noted judicial recognition that those involved in drug trafficking are often armed.

United States v. Chaidez, 906 F.2d 377 (8th Cir. 1990). When the officer developed reasonable suspicion that the defendant was smuggling drugs in his car, he also had reasonable suspicion that the car contained weapons, because guns are considered essential tools of the drug trade. *See also* United States v. Coleman, 969 F.2d 126 (5th Cir. 1992) (proper to search for gun in leather pouch found in car during stop); United States v. Hishaw, 235 F.3d 565 (10th Cir. 2000) (frisk proper when reasonable suspicion defendant was distributing drugs); United States v. Perrin, 45 F.3d 869 (4th Cir. 1995) (similar ruling).

United States v. Flett, 806 F.2d 823 (8th Cir. 1986). Although the court rejected the rule in other federal circuits that companions of an arrestee are automatically subject to frisk, it ruled that the frisk of a companion of the arrestee was proper under the totality of circumstances in this case, even though the companion did not make a threatening move or have a bulge in his clothing: the companion was a member of the same motorcycle gang as the arrestee, the arrestee was charged with a drug violation, the arrest was made in a home, etc.

Plain Feel or Touch Doctrine
(*This topic is discussed on page 258.*)

UNITED STATES SUPREME COURT

Minnesota v. Dickerson, 508 U.S. 366 (1993). An officer had reasonable suspicion to stop the defendant and to frisk him for weapons. During the frisk, the officer felt a lump—a small, hard object wrapped in plastic—in the defendant's jacket pocket that he knew was not a weapon. The officer determined that the lump was cocaine only *after* "squeezing, sliding and otherwise manipulating the contents of the defendant's pocket."

The Court ruled that the plain view doctrine applies by analogy to cases in which an officer discovers contraband through the sense of touch during an otherwise lawful search. (The plain view doctrine provides that if officers are lawfully in a position in which they view an object, if its incriminating character is immediately apparent—that is, they have probable cause to seize it—and if the officers have a lawful right of access to the object, they may seize it without a warrant.) However, the Court also ruled that the officer in this case was not justified in seizing the cocaine, because the officer exceeded the search for weapons permitted by *Terry v. Ohio*, 392 U.S. 1 (1968). Once the officer determined that the lump was not a weapon, his continued exploration of the lump until he developed probable cause to believe it was cocaine was an additional search that was not justified by *Terry*. [Author's note: Thus, the officer's action would have been permissible in this case only if he had developed probable cause to believe that the lump was cocaine at the time he determined that the lump was not a weapon.] *See also* United States v. Ashley, 37 F.3d 678 (D.C. Cir. 1994) (officer felt hard object during initial pat down; based on facts in this case, it was immediately apparent to officer that object was crack cocaine); United States v. Craft, 30 F.3d 1044 (8th Cir. 1994) (officer at airport felt hard, compact packages attached to defendant's ankles; it was immediately apparent to officer that packages contained controlled substances).

NORTH CAROLINA COURT OF APPEALS

State v. Reid, 224 N.C. App. 181 (2012). The court ruled that a seizure of cocaine was justified under the plain feel doctrine. While searching the defendant, the officer "felt a large bulge" in his pocket and immediately knew based on its packing that it was narcotics.

State v. Richmond, 215 N.C. App. 475 (2011). An officer was present at a location to execute a search warrant in connection with drug offenses. The court of appeals ruled that evidence supported the trial court's finding that the officer, based on his training and experience, immediately formed the opinion during a pat down that a bulge in the defendant's pants contained a controlled substance. Although the officer testified that he felt a "knot" in the defendant's pants that he could not "describe with any specificity," the officer also testified that he had discovered similar knots before in his six years of experience and had previously discovered "[b]ags of marijuana, bags of cocaine, bags of crack."

State v. Morton, 204 N.C. App. 578 (2010). The court ruled, relying on *Minnesota v. Dickerson*, 508 U.S. 366 (1993), that an officer conducting a frisk of a drug suspect lawfully seized a digital scale from his pocket because its identity was immediately apparent without manipulating it. [Author's note: "Immediately apparent" means the same as probable cause.] The officer testified that scales are often used to weigh controlled substances before distribution.

State v. Briggs, 140 N.C. App. 484 (2000). Officers were conducting a driver's license check in a high crime area. As one officer returned the defendant's license to the defendant, another officer recognized the defendant as someone whom he had previously arrested for cocaine offenses. The officer knew that the defendant was on probation and had been convicted of drug offenses more than once. Although the defendant denied that he had been drinking or taking drugs, the officer noted that the defendant was chewing gum "real hard" and that his eyes were glassy and bloodshot. Also, the officer smelled the odor of burned cigar tobacco inside the vehicle and on the defendant's person. When the officer asked about the smell, the defendant stated that he did not smoke cigars but that a female who was in the vehicle earlier had been smoking a cigar. The officer knew from his experience that drug users often smoked cigars to mask the smell of illegal drugs. The defendant declined the officer's request to search the defendant's vehicle. The officer then required the defendant to get out of the vehicle and frisked him for weapons. The officer was aware from his experience that drug dealers frequently carry weapons. The officer testified that during the frisk, "I felt a hard, cylindrical shape in [defendant's] pocket and it felt like a cigar holder; and I'm familiar with these because folks carry these frequently to keep their controlled substances in. It's like a little plastic test tube with a little cap on it; and there's really nothing else that's shaped exactly like that." The officer asked the defendant what that object was, and the defendant stated, "A cigar holder." The officer said, "I thought you didn't smoke cigars," but the defendant did not respond. The officer then removed the cigar holder from the defendant's pocket, and when he shook it, the cigar holder "rattled like it had a number of small hard objects in it." The officer opened the cigar holder, found 10 rocks of crack cocaine inside, and arrested the defendant.

The court ruled, relying on *State v. Butler*, 331 N.C. 227 (1992), and *State v. McGuirt*, 122 N.C. App. 237 (1996), *aff'd*, 345 N.C. 624 (1997), that the officer had reasonable suspicion to conduct the frisk, based on the facts discussed above. The court also ruled that the officer had probable cause to seize the cigar holder under the plain feel doctrine set out in *Minnesota v. Dickerson*, 508 U.S. 366 (1993). The court discussed cases from other jurisdictions that have split on the issue of whether the plain feel doctrine may be satisfied when an officer feels a container the shape of which does not itself reveal its identity as contraband. Courts upholding such seizures consider factors in addition to the officer's tactile perception to determine probable cause. Other courts declining to uphold such seizures have determined that touching the containers themselves cannot sustain a probable cause finding. The court adopted the view that it would consider the totality of circumstances in deciding whether an officer had probable cause to seize such a container when the officer felt it, and the court stated that the probable cause determination involves considering the evidence as understood by law enforcement officers. Based on the facts discussed above, the officer in this case had probable cause to seize the cigar holder.

State v. Pulliam, 139 N.C. App. 437 (2000). Officers were conducting a driver's license checkpoint. The driver gave consent to a search of his vehicle. When the officer asked who his passenger was, the driver asserted that he did not know the defendant's name. The officer recognized the defendant-passenger as a convicted drug trafficker and ordered him out of the vehicle. The defendant became belligerent, saying that the officer had no right to make him get out. The defendant smelled of alcohol, was loud and argumentative, and used profanity. When the defendant finally got out, he was unsteady on his feet and appeared to be intoxicated. When the officer saw a large bulge, one inch wide and six or seven inches long, in the defendant's front pants pocket, he patted that place and discovered a utility razor knife.

(1) The court ruled, relying on *Maryland v. Wilson*, 519 U.S. 408 (1997) (officer who has made traffic stop may order passengers and driver to exit vehicle), and other cases, that the driver's consent to search his vehicle allowed the officer to order the defendant-passenger out of vehicle without the necessity of showing reasonable suspicion of criminal activity. (2) Based on the facts set out above, the court ruled that the officer had reasonable suspicion that the defendant was armed and dangerous to justify the frisk.

State v. Benjamin, 124 N.C. App. 734 (1996). An officer conducted a frisk of the defendant after an investigative stop for a traffic violation. As the officer was patting the defendant, he felt two hard plastic containers in a breast pocket of the defendant's winter jacket. Based on his narcotics training, it was immediately apparent that these containers were vials of the type customarily used to hold illegal drugs. When the officer felt the container through the jacket, he asked the defendant, "What is that?" The defendant responded that it was "crack." The officer removed two vials from the coat pocket and found cocaine.

The court ruled that the defendant was not in custody when the officer asked him what the objects were, and therefore *Miranda* warnings were not required. The court noted that the fact that a defendant is not free to leave does not necessarily constitute "custody" under *Miranda*. Instead, the inquiry is whether a reasonable person in the defendant's position would believe that he or she was under arrest or the functional equivalent of arrest; the court cited and discussed *Stansbury v. California*, 511 U.S. 318 (1994), and *Berkemer v. McCarty*, 468 U.S. 420 (1984). The court concluded that a reasonable person would not have believed that he was in custody, based on these facts. The court also ruled that the seizure of the cocaine was proper under the plain feel theory of *Minnesota v. Dickerson*, 508 U.S. 366 (1993). The court stated that the officer had probable cause to believe (or, to state it a different way, it became immediately apparent to the officer) that the objects were contraband based on the officer's experience and narcotics training; the size, shape, and mass of the objects; and the defendant's response to the officer's question. The court also ruled that an officer may ask a suspect the nature of an object in the suspect's pocket during a lawful frisk even after the officer has determined that the object is not a weapon.

In re Whitley, 122 N.C. App. 290 (1996). Two officers responded to a call that drug sales were occurring between two black males on a certain street. The officers saw the respondent and another person under a tree. They approached and told them that they were going to do a weapons search. During the search of the respondent, an officer noticed that his lower body and legs were tight, so he asked him to spread his legs. The officer's hands were outside the respondent's trousers in the bottom crotch area when an item fell from the respondent's buttocks into his pants and onto the officer's hand. When the officer retrieved the item from the respondent's pants, he saw that it was a plastic bag containing a white powdered substance. The officer placed the respondent under arrest.

The court ruled (1) that there was reasonable suspicion that the respondent might be armed, dangerous, and involved in criminal activity to frisk him [Author's note: This ruling—that there was reasonable suspicion—is now questionable in light of the later case of *Florida v. J.L.*, 529 U.S. 266 (1999).] and (2) that the incriminating character of the object seized was immediately apparent to the officer, noting *State v. Wilson*, 112 N.C. App. 777 (1993), and *Minnesota v. Dickerson*, 508 U.S. 366 (1993). The court noted that there was no evidence that the officer improperly manipulated the object to determine if it was an illegal substance.

State v. Wilson, 112 N.C. App. 777 (1993). A police department received an anonymous phone call that several people were selling drugs in the breezeway of Building 1304 in the Hunter Oaks Apartments. The caller did not provide names or descriptions of the alleged drug dealers. Two officers familiar with the area knew that if a police car entered the parking lot at one end of the breezeway, the suspects would run out the other end. They devised a plan whereby a police car would enter the parking lot and officers would position themselves so that they could stop anyone who ran out of the back of the breezeway. An officer stopped the defendant as he ran out of the back of the breezeway and conducted a frisk. During the frisk, the officer felt a lump in the left breast pocket of the defendant's jacket and immediately believed that it was crack cocaine. The officer then asked the defendant if his coat had an inside pocket. The defendant

did not respond verbally but instead opened his jacket so that the inside pocket was visible. The officer saw and removed a small plastic bag that contained crack cocaine.

(1) Distinguishing *State v. Fleming*, 106 N.C. App. 165 (1992), the court ruled that the officer had authority to stop and frisk the defendant, based on the anonymous phone call, the flight of the defendant and others when the police car pulled into the parking lot, and the officer's experience that weapons were frequently involved in drug transactions. (2) Distinguishing *Minnesota v. Dickerson*, 508 U.S. 366 (1993), the court noted that the officer in this case—unlike the officer in *Dickerson*—did not need to manipulate the item in the defendant's pocket to determine that it was cocaine; he immediately believed it was crack cocaine. The court ruled that the requirement in *Dickerson* that it must be "immediately apparent" to the officer that the item is illegal means that the officer must have probable cause to believe that the item is illegal. The court also ruled that the officer's tactile senses, based on his experience and the facts in this case, gave him probable cause to believe that the item was crack cocaine. Thus, the officer did not exceed the scope of a frisk under the *Dickerson* ruling.

State v. Beveridge, 112 N.C. App. 688 (1993), *aff'd*, 336 N.C. 601 (1994). While Officer Johnson was arresting a driver for impaired driving, Officer Gregory secured the car and asked the defendant, a passenger, to get out. Officer Gregory noticed a strong odor of alcohol about the defendant, who also was acting "giddy." The officer believed, based on the facts in this case, that the defendant was under the influence of alcohol and a controlled substance. He told the defendant that he was going to pat him down for weapons. During the pat down, the officer noticed that there was a cylindrical-shaped, rolled-up plastic bag in the defendant's front pocket. The officer asked him what it was, and the defendant started laughing and pulled out some money. However, the officer could still see the long cylindrical bulge in his pocket. He again asked the defendant what it was. The defendant then stuck his hand in his pocket and tried to palm what he had. The officer asked him what he was trying to hide, and the defendant rolled open his hand and showed the officer a white plastic bag with a white powdery substance in it. The officer believed that the substance was cocaine and arrested the defendant for possession of cocaine.

The court ruled that Officer Gregory was justified in conducting a limited pat down of the defendant to determine whether the defendant was armed, but once he concluded that there was no weapon, he could not continue to search "or question" the defendant to determine whether the bag contained illegal drugs. [Author's note: The part of the court's ruling in quotation marks in the preceding sentence does not appear consistent with prevailing federal constitutional law because a person is ordinarily not in "custody" under *Miranda* when seized during an investigative stop. *See, e.g.,* State v. Benjamin, 124 N.C. App. 734 (1996).] The court ruled that the search exceeded the scope of the frisk under *Minnesota v. Dickerson*, 508 U.S. 366 (1993), because it was not immediately apparent that the item in the defendant's pocket was an illegal substance.

State v. Whitted, 112 N.C. App. 640 (1993). A car parked in front of a residence fled at high speed after the driver saw a marked patrol car. The area from which the car fled was known for frequent drug sales, especially crack cocaine. People commonly pulled over to the curbside after being flagged down and purchased drugs. This area had been under surveillance for 30 days, and several arrests had been made based on drug sales at the residence from which the car had fled. After officers stopped the car, they went on each side of the car to investigate. The defendant was sitting in the front passenger seat, and an officer saw that the defendant kept his hand by his front pants pocket and "kept pushing something down." The defendant did not move his hand when the officer asked him to do so, and the officer then frisked the defendant for weapons. During the frisk, the officer felt a "pebble" (that is, a hard substance) in the defendant's pocket that he believed, based on his experience and knowledge of the circumstances, to be crack cocaine. He removed the object and discovered that it was crack cocaine.

The court ruled, based on all the circumstances in this case including the suspicious behavior and flight from the officers, that the officer had probable cause to search the defendant after the officer felt the object in the defendant's pocket. [Author's note: Although the court did not discuss *Minnesota v. Dickerson*, 508 U.S. 366 (1993), its ruling is consistent with that case.]

State v. Sanders, 112 N.C. App. 477 (1993). Two State Highway Patrol officers set up a driver's license check at a ramp off a highway. They did not post signs warning the public that a license check was being conducted. The officers checked every car that approached the checkpoint unless they were busy writing citations. The defendant entered the ramp, and as he approached the checkpoint, he stopped his car 150 feet from one of the troopers.

The defendant then drove up to the checkpoint, stopped his car, and rolled down his window. In response to the trooper's request for driver's license and registration, the defendant said that he did not have the registration or any identification and that he was not the owner of the car. The passenger in the car also failed to produce any identification. The trooper asked the defendant to get out of the car. As he stepped out of the car, the trooper saw a bulge about the size of two fists in the right pocket of the defendant's jacket. The trooper then told the defendant to face the car and place his hands on it so that he could pat him down for weapons. As the defendant was following the trooper's instructions, the trooper saw plastic protruding from his right pocket. While frisking the defendant, the trooper touched the bulge and noted that it felt like "hard flour dough." The trooper removed the plastic bag from the defendant's pocket. It contained three smaller bags with cocaine inside.

(1) Distinguishing *Delaware v. Prouse*, 440 U.S. 648 (1979), the court ruled that the stop at the license checkpoint was constitutional. The court noted that the troopers followed their agency's guidelines in selecting the location and time for the license check and detained every car that passed through, except for those that came through while they were issuing citations. (2) Following *State v. Peck*, 305 N.C. 734 (1982), the court ruled that the trooper—based on the facts described above, his testimony that people driving stolen cars often provide officers with false names and insist they have no identification, and the bulge in the defendant's pocket—had reason to believe that the defendant was armed and dangerous and therefore could frisk him. (3) The court also ruled, based on *Minnesota v. Dickerson*, 508 U.S. 366 (1993), that the trooper acted properly in conducting the frisk by feeling the packet in the bulge in the jacket to determine if it was a weapon. (4) The court remanded the case to the trial court to determine, in light of *Dickerson* (decided after this case was heard in the trial court), whether it was immediately apparent to the trooper that what he felt was illegal drugs.

Inventory

(This topic is discussed on page 261.)

Vehicles

Florida v. Wells, 495 U.S. 1 (1990). A Florida highway patrol officer arrested the defendant for impaired driving, impounded his car, and conducted an inventory search—which included prying open a locked suitcase in the trunk. The Court affirmed the judgment of the Florida Supreme Court, which ruled that the inventory search was unconstitutional because the Florida Highway Patrol did not have a policy that authorized the opening of closed containers found during inventory searches. In dicta, the Court clarified *Colorado v. Bertine*, discussed below, by stating that a constitutionally valid inventory policy need not require the opening of all containers found during an inventory. For example, a policy could allow officers some discretion in opening containers, such as authorizing officers to open a closed container when they are unable to determine its contents by examining its exterior.

Colorado v. Bertine, 479 U.S. 367 (1987). After an officer arrested the defendant for impaired driving, he conducted an inventory of the defendant's van before it was towed to the impoundment lot. The department's standardized inventory procedure required an officer to open containers found within a vehicle and to list their contents. The officer opened a backpack, saw a nylon bag containing metal canisters, opened the canisters, and found drugs inside. The Court upheld the inventory search, because the officer followed the department's standardized procedure and did not act in bad faith or for an investigative purpose.

South Dakota v. Opperman, 428 U.S. 364 (1976). Police lawfully impounded a car for violating a municipal parking ordinance. Using a standard inventory form and following standard police procedures, an officer inventoried the car's contents, including the unlocked glove compartment, in which he found marijuana. The Court ruled that the inventory procedure and the scope of the inventory were reasonable under the Fourth Amendment and noted that there was no evidence that the inventory was a pretext concealing an investigatory police motive. The Court stated that an inventory procedure serves three purposes: (1) to protect officers and the public from dangerous weapons and the like, (2) to protect officers against claims or disputes over lost or stolen property, and (3) to protect the owner's property while it remains in a law enforcement agency's custody.

Harris v. United States, 390 U.S. 234 (1968). The defendant's car had been seen leaving the scene of an armed robbery. The defendant was arrested as he was entering his car near his home. An officer took him to the police station and had the car towed to an impound lot as evidence. Pursuant to department regulation, the officer went to the lot to search the car, placed a property tag on it, rolled up the windows, and locked the doors. While doing this, he seized evidence that he saw in plain view. The Court upheld the seizure because the Fourth Amendment allows an officer to take measures to protect a car while it is in police custody.

State v. Phifer, 297 N.C. 216 (1979). A search of an arrestee's car based on the inventory search justification was invalid because (1) the officers had no authority under the department's standard procedures to impound, tow, or inventory the car; and (2) the officers had conducted the inventory as a pretext when the defendant was known as a drug dealer and the officers conducted the inventory search to look for contraband. *See also* United States v. Ibarra, 955 F.2d 1405 (10th Cir. 1992).

State v. Peaten, 110 N.C. App. 749 (1993). Officers executed a search warrant to search a nightclub to determine if tax-paid alcoholic beverages were being illegally sold there. An executing officer decided to impound and to conduct an inventory of a BMW parked in the club's parking lot, because he believed it would have been vandalized if left there. The court ruled, relying on *State v. Phifer*, 297 N.C. 216 (1979), that the impoundment and inventory search were unlawful because the stated reason for the impoundment and inventory—the vehicle would be vandalized—was not a ground authorized by departmental policy. The court noted that the defendant was not present to make a disposition about the car, the car was not a hazard to traffic because it was parked in the club parking lot, and towing the car was not necessary concerning any arrest.

State v. Hall, 52 N.C. App. 492 (1981). Officers lawfully seized a car subject to forfeiture under G.S. 90-112. A later inventory search was unconstitutional because the inventory procedure was a pretext: evidence showed that the officers were investigating drugs and did not appear to be conducting the inventory for the legitimate purpose of safeguarding the defendant's property. For example, they opened a brown opaque bottle to examine the pills inside. The court's ruling was supportable, but its alternative ruling that opening the bottle exceeded permissible scope of the inventory search and its dicta that questioned an officer's right to open any closed container during an inventory search must be reconsidered in light of *Colorado v. Bertine* and *Florida v. Wells*, discussed above.

State v. Vernon, 45 N.C. App. 486 (1980). After the defendant was arrested for a drug transaction at a motel, an officer impounded the defendant's car because he did not want to be responsible for any damage to it if it was left in a motel parking lot. The officer admitted that his impoundment was contrary to the police department's written policy, because (1) the defendant was capable of deciding what to do about his car, (2) the car did not present a traffic hazard, and (3) the car was not being seized for evidence or for any other reason relating to the drug charge. Thus, the inventory search was improper.

State v. Spruill, 33 N.C. App. 731 (1977). An officer seized a car without a warrant as evidence of a crime because the rims and tires on the car were stolen. An inventory search of the contents of a car was properly conducted pursuant to department procedure.

United States v. Duguay, 93 F.3d 346 (7th Cir. 1996). Although a written impoundment is not required under the Fourth Amendment, the court ruled that the facts in this case showed that the law enforcement agency did not have a standardized impoundment procedure to guide officers as to when they could impound a vehicle. In addition, the officers failed to articulate a legitimate rationale for impounding the defendant's vehicle, and impounding it without regard to whether the defendant could have provided for its removal was unreasonable under the Fourth Amendment.

United States v. Hahn, 922 F.2d 243 (5th Cir. 1991). IRS agents searched an unlocked briefcase found in a vehicle without standardized inventory procedures regulating the opening of closed containers. The court ruled that the inventory search was unreasonable, based on *Florida v. Wells*, 495 U.S. 1 (1990). *See also* United States v. Salmon, 944 F.2d 1106 (3d Cir. 1991) (similar ruling); United States v. Lugo, 978 F.2d 631 (10th Cir. 1992).

United States v. Mancera-Londono, 912 F.2d 373 (9th Cir. 1990). Standardized inventory procedures need not be written. *See also* United States v. Kordosky, 921 F.2d 722 (7th Cir. 1991) (because unwritten policy required opening containers found in vehicle, opening paper bag in trunk was proper); United States v. Walker, 931 F.2d 1066 (5th Cir. 1991).

United States v. Welling, 758 F.2d 318 (8th Cir. 1985). An inventory of a car's trunk under standard department procedure was constitutional. *See also* United States v. Wilson, 758 F.2d 304 (8th Cir. 1985); United States v. Duncan, 763 F.2d 220 (6th. Cir. 1984); United States v. Penn, 233 F.3d 1111 (9th Cir. 2000).

United States v. Griffin, 729 F.2d 475 (7th Cir. 1984). An inventory of a car conducted under standard department policy properly included looking in an unlocked storage compartment within the car's passenger area, opening a brown paper bag inside the compartment, and—when an unusual odor emanated from the bag—removing the unsecured end of a tape-wrapped package that was in the bag in order to see what was inside.

Personal Effects

Florida v. Wells, 495 U.S. 1 (1990). A Florida highway patrol officer arrested the defendant for impaired driving, impounded his car, and conducted an inventory search—which included prying open a locked suitcase in the trunk. The Court affirmed the judgment of the Florida Supreme Court, which ruled that the inventory search was unconstitutional because the Florida Highway Patrol did not have a policy that authorized the opening of closed containers found during inventory searches. In dicta, the Court clarified *Colorado v. Bertine*, discussed above, by stating that a constitutionally valid inventory policy need not require the opening of all containers found during an inventory. For example, a policy could allow officers some discretion in opening containers, such as authorizing officers to open a closed container when they are unable to determine its contents by examining its exterior.

Colorado v. Bertine, 479 U.S. 367 (1987). After an officer arrested the defendant for impaired driving, he conducted an inventory of the defendant's van before it was towed to the impoundment lot. The department's standardized inventory procedure required an officer to open containers found within a vehicle and to list their contents. The officer opened a backpack, saw a nylon bag containing metal canisters, opened the canisters, and found drugs inside. The Court upheld the inventory search because the officer followed the department's standardized procedure and did not act in bad faith or for an investigative purpose.

Illinois v. Lafayette, 462 U.S. 640 (1983). The defendant was arrested and taken to the police station. While he was being booked and jailed, his shoulder bag was searched and drugs were found inside a cigarette package in the bag. The Court ruled that the routine inventory search was reasonable under the Fourth Amendment.

The Court noted that an inventory deters false claims of theft, inhibits theft or careless handling of articles taken from the arrestee, and protects against dangerous instrumentalities, and thus examining all items in an arrestee's possession is a reasonable administrative procedure. The Court rejected the argument that officers could have used a less intrusive means of safeguarding the contents by simply locking the shoulder bag in a safe place, ruling that the fact that less intrusive means may be available does not necessarily make a full inventory unreasonable under the Fourth Amendment.

State v. Jones, 63 N.C. App. 411 (1983). An officer was investigating an accident involving a bus and a car. He entered the bus after the bus company told him that he should not allow anyone to remove baggage without proper identification. The officer opened an untagged and unmarked briefcase lying beside the bus driver's seat. The court ruled that the officer properly searched the briefcase to determine its owner so that he could safeguard its contents.

State v. Nesmith, 40 N.C. App. 748 (1979). A search and inspection of the contents of the arrestee's wallet was a valid inventory search of personal possessions before the defendant was placed in jail.

State v. Francum, 39 N.C. App. 429 (1979). An officer arrived at an accident scene as the defendant was being taken to the hospital in an ambulance. He noticed a brown paper bag lying near the damaged car and looked inside. The search was reasonable because the officer needed to secure any personal effects in the car before it was towed. The court's statement that if the officer had found a briefcase or suitcase, he could not have examined it, is not consistent with the rationale of later inventory cases, such as *Illinois v. Lafayette*, discussed above, and the rejection of a worthy/unworthy-container distinction in *United States v. Ross*, 456 U.S. 798 (1982).

State v. Brandon, 18 N.C. App. 483 (1973). A defendant in the county jail asked the jailer to bring his coat from his car. The jailer unlocked the car and got the coat, searched it, and found drugs. This search was reasonable under the Fourth Amendment.

United States v. Sumlin, 909 F.2d 1218 (8th Cir. 1990). An officer recovered the robbery victim's purse. He opened a leather cigarette case in the purse because he believed it likely would contain a driver's license or credit cards. The court ruled that the officer's actions were reasonable under the circumstances because the officer was seeking identification and recovering stolen property.

United States v. Khoury, 901 F.2d 948 (11th Cir. 1990). During an inventory search of the contents of a briefcase found in a car's trunk, an officer properly flipped through a notebook to determine if it contained items of value; the officer determined that it did not. However, the officer exceeded the scope of an inventory when he then inspected the notebook further.

United States v. Trullo, 790 F.2d 205 (1st Cir. 1986). The defendant was arrested, and during an inventory search of the defendant's car at the station house, an officer picked up an oil can that by its light weight indicated it did not contain oil. On discovering that the top pulled out, the officer removed the top and found cocaine. The court noted that an easily opened can could have contained paper currency and ruled that if a container may be searched for an inventory purpose, a court should not inquire about an officer's subjective thoughts (that is, the officer's expecting to find drugs).

Entering Premises for Public Safety Reasons

(This topic is discussed on page 260.)

Ryburn v. Huff, 132 S. Ct. 987 (2012). The United States Supreme Court reversed a federal appellate court ruling that officers were not entitled to qualified immunity in a Section 1983 federal civil rights action that arose after the officers entered a home without a warrant. When officers responded to a call from a high school, the principal informed them that a student, Vincent Huff, was rumored to have written a letter threatening to "shoot up" the school. The officers learned that Vincent had been absent two days, that he was a victim of bullying, and that a classmate believed him to be capable of carrying out the alleged threat. Officers found these facts troubling in light of training suggesting that these characteristics are common among perpetrators of school shootings. When the officers went to Vincent's home and knocked at the door, no one answered. They then called the home phone and no one answered. When they called Vincent's mother's cell phone, she reported that she and Vincent were inside. Vincent and Mrs. Huff then came outside to talk with the officers. Mrs. Huff declined an officer's request to continue the discussion inside. When an officer asked Mrs. Huff if there were any guns in the house, she immediately turned around and ran inside. The officers followed and eventually determined the threat to be unfounded. The Huffs filed a Section 1983 action against the officers for violating their Fourth Amendment rights by entering their home without a search warrant. The federal district court ruled for the officers, concluding that they were entitled to qualified immunity because Mrs. Huff's odd behavior, combined with the information that the officers gathered at the school, could have led reasonable officers to believe that there could be weapons inside the house and that family members or the officers themselves were in danger. A divided panel of a federal appellate court disagreed with the conclusion that the officers were entitled to qualified immunity. The United States Supreme Court reversed, determining that reasonable officers could have come to the conclusion that the Fourth Amendment permitted them to enter the residence if there was an objectively reasonable basis to fear that violence was imminent. It further determined that a reasonable officer could have come to such a conclusion based on the facts as found by the trial court.

Michigan v. Fisher, 558 U.S. 45 (2009). Officers responded to a disturbance call. A couple directed them to a house where a man was "going crazy." Officers saw a pickup truck in the driveway with its front smashed; damaged fence posts along the side of the property; and three broken windows, the glass still on the ground outside. The officers also saw blood on the pickup's hood and on clothes inside the pickup, as well as on one of the doors to the house. Through a window to the house, they could see the defendant screaming and throwing things. The back door was locked, and a couch had been placed to block the front door. The officers knocked, but the defendant refused to answer. They saw that he had a cut on his hand, and they asked him whether he needed medical attention. The defendant ignored these questions and demanded, with accompanying profanity, that the officers get a search warrant. One of the officers pushed the front door and entered the house. The Court ruled that a straightforward application of the emergency aid exception, as in *Brigham City v. Stuart*, 547 U.S. 398 (2006) (law enforcement officers may enter a home without a search warrant when they have an objectively reasonable basis for believing that an occupant is seriously injured or imminently threatened with such injury), dictates that the officer's entry into the house was reasonable under the Fourth Amendment. The Court stated that the state appellate court in this case erred in replacing the objective injury under *Brigham City* into what appeared to the officers with its hindsight determination that there was in fact no emergency: "It does not meet the needs of law enforcement or the demands of public safety to require officers to walk away from a situation like the one they encountered here. Only when an apparent threat has become an actual harm can officers rule out innocuous explanations for ominous circumstances.... It sufficed to invoke the emergency aid exception that it was reasonable to believe that [the defendant] had hurt himself (albeit nonfatally) and needed treatment that in his rage he was unable to provide, or that [the defendant] was about to hurt, or had already hurt, someone else."

Brigham City v. Stuart, 547 U.S. 398 (2006). About 3:00 a.m., four law enforcement officers responded to a call concerning a loud party at a residence. They heard shouting from inside and entered the driveway to investigate. They saw two juveniles drinking beer in the backyard. The officers entered the backyard and saw—through a screen door and windows—four adults attempting with some difficulty to restrain a juvenile. The juvenile eventually broke free, swung a fist, and struck one of the adults in the face. One of the officers saw the victim of the blow spitting blood into a nearby sink. The other adults continued to attempt to restrain the juvenile, pressing him against a refrigerator with such force that the refrigerator began moving across the floor. An officer opened the screen door and announced the officers' presence. Amid the tumult, nobody noticed the officer. The officer entered the kitchen and again spoke, and as the occupants slowly became aware that the officers were there, the altercation stopped.

The Court ruled that law enforcement officers may enter a home without a search warrant when they have an objectively reasonable basis for believing that an occupant is seriously injured or imminently threatened with such injury. The Court found that the officers' entry in this case was reasonable under the Fourth Amendment. The officers had an objectively reasonable basis for believing that the injured adult might need help and that the violence in the kitchen was just beginning. Also, the manner of the officers' entry was reasonable. Once they made an announcement, they were free to enter. They were not required to await a response while those within fought, oblivious to their presence. The Court, relying on its prior Fourth Amendment cases, rejected an inquiry into the officers' subjective motivation in entering the residence. An action is reasonable under the Fourth Amendment, regardless of an officer's state of mind, as long as the circumstances, viewed objectively, justify the action. It did not matter whether the officers entered the kitchen to make an arrest and gather evidence against those inside or to assist the injured and prevent further violence. The circumstances, viewed objectively, supported the entry based on a belief that an occupant was seriously injured or imminently threatened with such injury.

State v. McKinney, 361 N.C. 53 (2006). The defendant was convicted of first-degree murder. Amy advised law enforcement that her roommate, Aja, had told her that Aja's friend, the defendant, had killed his roommate. The address of the residence where the defendant and victim apparently lived was supplied to law enforcement. Officers arrived at the residence and were advised there that the defendant was reportedly driving the victim's vehicle, which was not in the driveway. The victim's sister arrived and informed officers that the victim lived there. The victim's brother arrived shortly thereafter. Officers learned that neither the brother nor the sister had had any contact with the victim in several days and the victim had not reported for work the prior day, which was very unusual. The officers also learned that the defendant had told Aja that the victim had pulled a knife on the defendant, and that the victim "wouldn't be coming back." The victim's brother then entered the house through a window and officers followed him. The officers saw what appeared to be blood spatter in the front bedroom and other indications of blood elsewhere in the house; they secured the house, obtained a search warrant, and thereafter discovered the victim's body in a large garbage can in the house.

(1) The court ruled that the officers did not have exigent circumstances to enter the house without a search warrant to look for the possible missing victim. (2) The court remanded to the trial court for a determination of whether the defendant had a reasonable expectation of privacy in the house to contest the officers' entry into the house (had the defendant permanently abandoned the house?). (3) The court remanded to the trial court for a determination of whether the independent source exception to the Fourth Amendment's exclusionary rule (*Murray v. United States*, 487 U.S. 533 (1988)) would support finding probable cause for the search warrant with the exclusion of illegally obtained information (the apparent blood spatter and other indications of blood in the house) that had been included in search warrant's affidavit.

State v. Cline, 205 N.C. App. 696 (2010). The court ruled that exigent circumstances existed for an officer to make a warrantless entry into the defendant's home to ascertain whether someone inside was in need of immediate assistance or under threat of serious injury. The officer was summoned after motorists discovered a young, naked, unattended toddler on the side of a major highway. The officer was able to determine with reasonable certainty that the child was the defendant's son and that the defendant resided at the premises in question. When the officer knocked and banged on the front door, he received no response. The officer found the back door ajar. The court concluded that an immediate warrantless entry was necessary to ascertain whether someone in the home needed immediate assistance or was under the threat of serious injury. It would have taken the officer approximately two hours to get a search warrant for the premises.

Protection of the Public from Dangerous Weapons: The Community Caretaking Function

(*This topic is discussed on page 260.*)

Cady v. Dombrowski, 413 U.S. 433 (1973). The defendant, a Chicago police officer, was involved in a one-car accident in another state while off duty. His car was disabled, and it was towed and stored at a private lot. While the defendant was hospitalized and formally arrested for drunken driving, an officer searched the car for the defendant's weapon, believing that Chicago police officers were required to carry a weapon at all times. The officer's effort to find the revolver was standard department procedure to protect the public from the possibility that an unauthorized person might remove the weapon. The Court ruled that the officer's warrantless search throughout the car's interior and locked trunk to find the weapon was reasonable under the Fourth Amendment to protect the public safety because the officer was properly performing a community caretaking function. *See also* United States v. Lugo, 978 F.2d 631 (10th Cir. 1992) (search in the door panel's interior exceeded community caretaking justification).

United States v. York, 895 F.2d 1026 (5th Cir. 1990). The officer's entry into the defendant's home to enable live-in guests to remove themselves and their possessions, after the defendant had become intoxicated and threatened them, was a proper community caretaking function. (Although the court ruled that no search occurred, the more appropriate analysis is that the officer's action was a reasonable search under the Fourth Amendment.)

Wilkinson v. Forst, 832 F.2d 1330 (2d Cir. 1987). The court ruled that, based on prior experiences of officers finding weapons at Ku Klux Klan rallies in Connecticut, general magnetometer screening may be conducted at future Ku Klux Klan rallies to screen people or packages without reasonable suspicion or probable cause that weapons may be found. A frisk may be conducted when the magnetometer indicates the presence of metal and the situation cannot be resolved by using only the magnetometer. However, the court ruled that mass pat-down searches that had been conducted at prior Ku Klux Klan rallies without reasonable suspicion or probable cause had violated the Fourth Amendment. The court noted that more intrusive measures than magnetometer screening might be justified by future events. For a later ruling in this case, see *Wilkinson v. Forst*, 717 F. Supp. 49 (D. Conn. 1989).

Search of a Crime Scene

(This topic is discussed on page 262.)

Flippo v. West Virginia, 528 U.S. 11 (1999). The defendant was tried and convicted of the murder of his wife. The defendant and his wife were vacationing at a cabin in a state park. The defendant called 911 to report that he and his wife had been attacked. Officers arrived and found the defendant, who had bodily injuries, outside the cabin. After questioning the defendant, the officers entered the cabin and found his wife with fatal head wounds. They closed off the area, took the defendant to the hospital, and searched the exterior and environs of the cabin for footprints or signs of forced entry. When a police photographer later arrived, the officers reentered the cabin without a search warrant and processed the crime scene for more than 16 hours. During this prolonged search, the officers found photographs in a briefcase in the cabin that were introduced into evidence against the defendant. The trial judge upheld the warrantless search because it was a "homicide crime scene." The Court ruled that the trial judge's ruling was inconsistent with *Mincey v. Arizona*, 437 U.S. 385 (1978), which rejected a "homicide scene exception" to the Warrant Clause of the Fourth Amendment. The Court specifically did not decide other possible Fourth Amendment justifications, such as a consent search.

Thompson v. Louisiana, 469 U.S. 17 (1984). A warrantless search of a homicide defendant's home, 35 minutes after she was taken from her home and transported to the hospital, was unconstitutional. Investigating officers who initially arrived at the homicide scene already had searched the home for other victims and suspects. The later warrantless search was simply an exploratory search for evidence and was not justified by exigent circumstances.

Mincey v. Arizona, 437 U.S. 385 (1978). The Court rejected a "murder scene exception" to the Fourth Amendment's requirement that a search warrant is generally necessary to search a house. It ruled that a four-day warrantless search of an apartment where a homicide took place was unconstitutional when there were no exigent circumstances. The Court recognized an officer's authority to (1) enter and search without a warrant when the officer reasonably believes that a person within a home needs immediate aid and (2) make a prompt warrantless search of the house to determine whether there are other victims or suspects on the premises.

State v. Scott, 343 N.C. 313 (1996). An officer, responding to a report of a missing person, went to the defendant's home, where the missing person lived. Two vehicles were in the driveway, but no one responded to the officer's knock on the front door. The officer noticed large green flies flying under the house through an air vent. He had previously seen this kind of flies on dead animals and people. He then went to the rear of the house, where he saw the flies at the access door to the crawl space under the house, smelled the odor of decaying flesh, and saw a green carpet lying against the access door. When he moved the carpet, he saw that the grass under it was green, indicating that it had been placed there recently. He then opened the access door, shined his flashlight in the crawl space, and saw the body of a dead female there. After a warrantless search of the home for other possible victims or suspects, a search warrant was obtained and a thorough search of the home was made pursuant to the search warrant. The defendant argued that the warrantless search of the crawl space and home was unconstitutional. The court ruled, citing *Mincey v. Arizona*, 437 U.S. 385 (1978), that the warrantless search of the crawl space and the home was reasonable under the Fourth Amendment.

State v. Jolley, 312 N.C. 296 (1984). In a case decided before *Thompson v. Louisiana*, 469 U.S. 17 (1984), discussed above, the court ruled that an officer seized a rifle he saw in plain view in a home that he had entered in response to a homicide, even though he did not then physically take possession of the rifle. After removing the emotionally upset defendant and securing the area, he and another officer reentered the home about 10 minutes later and took possession of the rifle. The court ruled that the warrantless reentry was permissible because the officer had constructively seized the rifle when he secured the crime scene earlier. [Author's note: It is unclear whether this warrantless reentry and seizure is consistent with *Thompson. See also* State v. Phillips, 151 N.C. App. 185 (2002) (similar ruling).]

State v. Jordan, ___ N.C. App. ___, 776 S.E.2d 515 (2015). The court ruled that the trial court erred in denying the defendant's motion to suppress evidence obtained as a result of a warrantless search of her residence. According to the court: "The trial court's findings that the officers observed a broken window, that the front door was unlocked, and that no one responded when the officers knocked on the door are insufficient to show that they had an objectively reasonable belief that a breaking and entering had *recently* taken place or *was still in progress*, such that there existed an urgent need to enter the property" and that the search was justified under the exigent circumstances exception to the warrant requirement. It continued:

> In this case, the only circumstances justifying the officers' entry into defendant's residence were a broken window, an unlocked door, and the lack of response to the officers' knock at the door. We hold that although these findings may be sufficient to give the officers a reasonable belief that an illegal entry had occurred *at some point*, they are insufficient to give the officers an objectively reasonable belief that a breaking and entering was in progress or had occurred recently.

State v. Woods, 136 N.C. App. 386 (2000). Officers were dispatched to investigate an alarm sounding at the defendant's residence. After arriving at the residence, an officer heard the alarm and saw that the rear door of the residence was open. After announcing his presence and identity, he heard no response from inside the residence. The officer conducted a cursory search of the residence for potential victims or suspects. He found no one but saw evidence of a break-in. He and other officers reentered the residence to conduct a more thorough search, looking again for victims and suspects. In the master bedroom, they opened a drawer in a standing chest that was about 15 to 20 inches deep, 25 to 30 inches long, and 18 inches wide; they discovered a bag of green vegetable material and then radioed drug officers to come to the scene. In the area containing the kitchen and living room, they saw a cabinet that was about 34 inches tall and 48 inches wide. While attempting to open the doors to the cabinet, an officer moved a chair and heard a noise underneath it. His flashlight revealed a tear on the bottom of the chair and a

bag inside that appeared to contain money. He opened the cabinet door but found nothing. Officers later obtained a search warrant and discovered various drugs, money, and drug paraphernalia.

Relying on *United States v. Dart*, 747 F.2d 263 (4th Cir. 1984), and other cases, the court ruled that the officers' warrantless entry into the residence to investigate a possible break-in was justified by exigent circumstances and thus was reasonable under the Fourth Amendment. It was clear that a break-in had occurred, and the officers had reason to believe that the intruders or victims could still be in the residence. The court also ruled, relying on *Mincey v. Arizona*, 437 U.S. 385 (1978), that the officers' search of the chest of drawers, chair, and cabinet exceeded the scope of the permissible search for suspects and victims. It was unreasonable to believe that a small child could have been found in the cabinet, based on the facts in this case. Because the fruits of the illegal searches established probable cause for the search warrant, the evidence seized was inadmissible at trial.

State v. Williams, 116 N.C. App. 225 (1994). Officers responded to an emergency call directing them to the defendant's residence. They found the defendant pacing in the front yard and another male person lying wounded in the doorway of the residence. The defendant told the officers that a man had shot his wife and was fleeing through the woods. The officers radioed for emergency personnel and then entered the residence to check for other victims or suspects. They found the defendant's wife lying dead on a couch in the den, with a gunshot wound above her left ear. They conducted a sweep of the residence. They found a pistol near the kitchen and ammunition casings and a white, rock-like substance on a stereo in the den. Having conducted this initial 30-second sweep, the officers then left the house and secured it against intruders. No one was allowed to enter the residence until investigators arrived 15 minutes after the first officers had arrived. The investigators entered the house without consent or a search warrant and continued to search the premises. Distinguishing *Thompson v. Louisiana*, 469 U.S. 17 (1984), the court ruled that the search by investigators was constitutional. Here, the investigators arrived shortly after the initial 30-second sweep by the first responding officers. Responding to the ongoing emergency, the investigators conducted a more complete search of the premises that could have revealed additional victims or hiding suspects. In *Thompson*, the investigators arrived 35 minutes after the first officers on the scene had already searched the home, secured the scene, and sent the defendant to the hospital for medical treatment. The court stated that if it ruled that the search in this case was unconstitutional, it would mean that "once any law enforcement officer makes an initial sweep through a home no matter how hurried or brief it may be, no other officers may search the home until a search warrant is obtained. Such a rule ignores the fact that the first responding officers making a quick initial search of a home may overlook a victim or suspect located in less obvious places." [Author's note: Although the warrantless search by the investigators in this case may have been consistent with the Fourth Amendment, law enforcement officers should consider obtaining a search warrant or consent to search before conducting a similar search.]

Search of a Fire Scene

(This topic is discussed on page 263.)

Michigan v. Clifford, 464 U.S. 287 (1984) (Four-Justice opinion announcing the Court's judgment, but the opinion states current law.) A residential fire occurred at about 5:00 a.m. Fire officers arrived, extinguished the fire, and left the scene at about 7:00 a.m. At 1:30 p.m. that same day, fire officials entered the house without a warrant to investigate the cause of the fire. They found evidence of arson in the basement and then searched the rest of the house, where they found that most valuables apparently had been removed before the fire began. Although the home was uninhabitable after the fire, the Court ruled that because personal belongings remained and the defendant had arranged after the fire to have his house secured, he retained a sufficient Fourth Amendment privacy interest in his home to require that post-fire investigations be conducted with a warrant, absent exigent circumstances. This case differed from *Michigan v. Tyler*, discussed below, because the investigator's entry at 1:30 p.m. was not a continuation of an earlier entry. An administrative warrant or consent was necessary to reenter the house in this case. (However, five Justices expressed the view that if advance notice to the owner had been given or if a reasonable attempt to do so had been made, the search could have been conducted without a warrant.) Once evidence of arson was found in the basement, a search warrant was required to search the rest of the house. The Court excluded all evidence found during these unconstitutional searches but ruled admissible a fuel can that fire personnel saw in the basement when they were fighting the fire and placed in the driveway of the residence.

Michigan v. Tyler, 436 U.S. 499 (1978). Fire officers properly entered a burning furniture store without a warrant to fight a fire and properly remained there for a reasonable time after the fire was extinguished to investigate its cause, to prevent its recurrence, and to preserve property from intentional or accidental destruction. They left at 4:00 a.m. after the fire had been extinguished. A warrantless reentry at 8:00 a.m. was justified in this case because the investigation of the fire's cause had been hindered by smoke and darkness, and the reentry was merely a continuation of a legitimate determination of the fire's cause. However, warrantless reentries at 9 a.m. that same day and weeks later were unconstitutional, because there were no longer exigent circumstances that excused obtaining a warrant. These additional entries to investigate the cause of the fire must be made with an administrative inspection warrant. If probable cause exists to search for evidence of a crime, such as arson, a search warrant must be obtained. *See also* United States v. Martin, 781 F.2d 671 (9th Cir. 1985) (second warrantless entry and search was permissible to look for injured persons and source of fire and explosion in an apartment); United States v. Loos, 165 F.3d 504 (7th Cir. 1998) (drug agent's gathering of evidence from fire caused by illegal methamphetamine lab while firefighters stood by to prevent smoldering ashes from rekindling did not violate ruling in *Michigan v. Tyler*).

State v. Langley, 64 N.C. App. 674 (1983). The court ruled that a fire marshal who was investigating the cause and origin of a fire properly conducted a warrantless search for accelerants on fire-damaged premises (it is unclear from the opinion when the search was conducted).

United States v. Boettger, 71 F.3d 1410 (8th Cir. 1995). An explosion occurred in an apartment. Exigent circumstances existed because of a continuing danger to public safety presented by explosive chemicals and destructive devices found in the defendant's apartment and thus justified warrantless entries into the apartment over a period of one and one-half days to determine the cause of the explosion and to prevent another explosion.

Collective Knowledge of Officers

(*See discussion of this topic on page 31 and summaries of other cases on this topic on page 181.*)

State v. Bowman, 193 N.C. App. 104 (2008). A team of officers was positioned near a bank where they had probable cause to believe that one person was about to make a drug sale to another person. The seller arrived at the bank in a Pontiac and left the vehicle to make the drug sale. The Pontiac's driver, the defendant, remained in the vehicle. An officer confronted the seller and seized 100 Oxycodone pills. One officer radioed the other officers to block the Pontiac from leaving the bank's parking lot. An officer searched the vehicle even though he was not specifically instructed to do so. Although some of the officers testified at the suppression hearing, the searching officer and the officer who had ordered the Pontiac to be blocked did not. The court ruled that the collective knowledge of the officers investigating the drug sale, which had established probable cause to search the vehicle, was imputed to the officer who searched the vehicle. The fact that some officers did not testify at the suppression hearing did not bar application of the collective knowledge theory.

Motions to Suppress, Suppression Hearings, and Exclusionary Rules

(*See page 534 for cases on this topic.*)

Chapter 4

Search Warrants, Administrative Inspection Warrants, and Nontestimonial Identification Orders

Chapter 4

Search Warrants, Administrative Inspection Warrants, and Nontestimonial Identification Orders

The right of the people to be secure in their persons, houses, papers, and effects, against unreasonable searches and seizures, shall not be violated, and no Warrants shall issue, but upon probable cause, supported by Oath or affirmation and particularly describing the place to be searched, and the persons or things to be seized.

—United States Constitution, Amendment IV

This chapter discusses how to prepare and execute search warrants, administrative inspection warrants, and nontestimonial identification orders. Sometimes stricter standards are recommended than are legally required so that law enforcement officers and issuing officials may be more confident that a court will rule that they complied with all federal and state constitutional[1] and statutory

requirements. However, the reader should be aware that a legally sufficient statement of probable cause in a search warrant often may consist of only one or two paragraphs.

---

1. Section 20 of Article I of the North Carolina Constitution prohibits the use of general warrants: "General warrants, whereby any officer or other person may be commanded to search suspected places without evidence of the act committed, or to seize any person or persons not named, whose offense is not particularly described and supported by evidence, are dangerous to liberty and shall not be granted." In *State v. Garner*, 331 N.C. 491 (1992), the court rejected the defendant's contention that this constitutional provision should not include an "inevitable discovery exception" to the exclusionary rule. The court stated:

> While this Court has held that Article I, Section 20 of our Constitution, like the Fourth Amendment to the United States Constitution, prohibits unreasonable searches and seizures, e.g., *State v. Arrington*, 311 N.C. 633, 319 S.E.2d 254; *State v. Ellington*, 284 N.C. 198, 200 S.E.2d 177 (1973), and requires the exclusion of evidence obtained by unreasonable search and seizure, e.g., *State v. Carter*, 322 N.C. 709, 370 S.E.2d 553, there is nothing to indicate anywhere in the text of Article I, Section 20 any enlargement or expansion of rights beyond those afforded in the Fourth Amendment as applied to the states by the Fourteenth Amendment. 331 N.C. at 506, 417 S.E.2d at 510.

The court later stated, "We therefore hold the defendant's contention that Article I, Section 20 of our Constitution should be read as an extension of rights beyond those afforded in the Fourth Amendment is misplaced." 331 N.C. at 506–07 (1992). The court's general statements indicate that in other cases it may not interpret this constitutional section more broadly in favor of the defendant's rights than the Fourth Amendment. It appears that *Garner* may undermine the court's ruling in *State v. Carter*, 322 N.C. 709 (1988), which had rejected under this constitutional section the good faith exception to the exclusionary rule under the Fourth Amendment as set out in *United States v. Leon*, 468 U.S. 897 (1984), and *Massachusetts v. Sheppard*, 468 U.S. 981 (1984). The possible conflict between *Carter* and *Garner* was noted in *State v. Banner*, 207 N.C. App. 729 n.7 (2010).

The North Carolina General Assembly in S.L. 2011-6 (1) requested the North Carolina Supreme Court to reconsider and overrule the *Carter* ruling and (2) imported the Fourth Amendment's good faith exception into the statutory exclusionary rule contained in Section 15A-974 of the North Carolina General Statutes (hereafter, G.S.). For a discussion of this legislation, see Bob Farb, *New North Carolina Legislation on Good Faith Exception to Exclusionary Rules*, NC Crim. L. Blog (Mar. 21, 2011), http://nccriminallaw.sog.unc.edu/new-north-carolina-legislation-on-good-faith-exception-to-exclusionary-rules/.

Part I. Search Warrants

Introduction

Advantages of a Search Warrant

As Chapter 3 indicated, officers in many situations may—with probable cause—search for and seize evidence without obtaining a search warrant. And, particularly with vehicle searches, officers often are not required to obtain a search warrant even when they clearly have the time to get one. There are several advantages, however, in having a search warrant:

- Officers' belief that they did not need to obtain a search warrant may later be proven wrong, and the evidence they obtained may be ruled inadmissible at trial. Officers should consider obtaining a warrant when they are uncertain of their legal right to proceed without one and they have the time to obtain a warrant.

- In some cases, the existence of probable cause may be doubtful. In a marginal case, a court may find that probable cause exists if officers acted with a search warrant, but the court may not do so if they acted without a warrant.[2]

- Officers are never legally disadvantaged if they obtain a search warrant. Even if the search warrant is later ruled to be invalid, the officers' search may still be justified by whatever justification properly existed to conduct a warrantless search or seizure.[3]

- Some cases (particularly drug and firearm violations) investigated by North Carolina officers are prosecuted in federal court in North Carolina because they involve federal violations. There exists in federal court a "good faith" exception to the exclusionary rule: that is, evidence seized under an invalid search warrant is admissible at trial if a reasonably well-trained officer would not have known that the warrant was invalid.[4] (This good faith exception probably does not exist in North

Carolina state courts—see the discussion below.)[5] There is not a similar exception for warrantless searches. Therefore, officers have an incentive to obtain a search warrant.

- In considering an application for a search warrant, a judicial official may convince officers that they do not have probable cause to search, thereby preventing a possibly illegal search or seizure from taking place. Officers may then investigate further and gather additional information that establishes probable cause.

- If a civil lawsuit is brought against officers for allegedly violating a person's Fourth Amendment rights, they may be better protected if they acted with a search warrant than without one.[6]

Consequences of an Unlawful Search or Seizure

Generally

An unlawful search or seizure may result in several undesirable consequences, including (1) the exclusion of evidence from criminal proceedings,[7] (2) a civil lawsuit for money damages against the officers who made the illegal

---

2. United States v. Ventresca, 380 U.S. 102 (1964); Illinois v. Gates, 462 U.S. 213 (1983); United States v. Carlson, 697 F.2d 231 (8th Cir. 1983); United States v. Frietas, 716 F.2d 1216 (9th Cir. 1983).

3. *See, e.g.,* State v. Downes, 57 N.C. App. 102 (1982); State v. Frederick, 31 N.C. App. 503 (1976).

4. United States v. Leon, 468 U.S. 897 (1984); Massachusetts v. Sheppard, 468 U.S. 981 (1984).

5. The North Carolina Supreme Court in *State v. Carter,* 322 N.C. 709 (1988), did not adopt under the Constitution of North Carolina the rulings in *Leon* and *Sheppard* (cited *supra* note 4), at least based on the facts in *Carter:* "[W]e are not persuaded *on the facts before us* that we should engraft a good faith exception to the exclusionary rule under our state constitution." 322 N.C. at 724 (emphasis added). See the discussion of *Carter* and *State v. Garner,* 331 N.C. 491 (1992), *supra* note 1.

6. Despite the ruling in *Malley v. Briggs,* 475 U.S. 335 (1986) (court ruled that officers may be civilly liable for violating a person's constitutional rights if they obtain an arrest warrant and make an arrest when a reasonably well-trained officer in their position would have known that their information failed to establish probable cause to arrest), the use of a warrant may be a favorable factor when officers seek to persuade a fact finder that they did not violate a person's constitutional rights. *See also* Messerschmidt v. Millender, 132 S. Ct. 1235 (2012) (Court ruled that officer had qualified immunity in civil rights lawsuit against him because it was not entirely unreasonable to believe that he had probable cause to support issuance of search warrant for all firearms, firearm-related materials, and gang paraphernalia; the fact that the officer sought and obtained approval of the search warrant application from a superior law enforcement officer and a prosecutor provided further support for the conclusion that he could reasonably believe the search warrant was supported by probable cause).

7. Mapp v. Ohio, 367 U.S. 643 (1961); G.S. 15A-974.

search or seizure,[8] (3) a criminal prosecution against the officers,[9] and (4) disciplinary action against the officers by their employing agency.

Exclusionary Rules

(*See page 534 for case summaries on this topic.*)

North Carolina law provides that evidence may not be admitted in court when either the United States Constitution or the North Carolina Constitution requires that it be excluded.[10] The United States Supreme Court has ruled that the United States Constitution generally does not allow evidence that an officer obtains by violating a person's Fourth Amendment rights to be used in court.[11] This principle of law is commonly known as the Fourth Amendment exclusionary rule. For example, it bars the introduction of illegal drugs as evidence at trial if the illegal drugs were seized during an unconstitutional search of a person's car. It also sometimes bars the use of a confession obtained after an unconstitutional arrest. (Exclusionary rules concerning confessions and lineups are discussed in Chapter 5.)

Good faith exception under the United States Constitution. The United States Supreme Court has stated that the exclusionary rule is intended to deter officers from committing Fourth Amendment violations—that is, they are not likely to violate a person's Fourth Amendment rights by making an unlawful search or seizure when they know that evidence they obtain will be inadmissible in court.[12] However, the Court has adopted a good faith exception to the exclusionary rule.[13] If an officer searches with a search warrant that a court later rules to be invalid, evidence seized with the warrant still will be admissible if a reasonably well-trained officer (an objective standard that generally does not consider the training of the particular officer involved) would not have known that the warrant was invalid. For example, if a court rules that a search warrant was invalid because its statement of probable cause was insufficient, but a reasonably well-trained officer would not have known that it was insufficient, then evidence obtained with that warrant is admissible even though a Fourth Amendment violation has occurred.[14] The Court does not apply the exclusionary rule in such a case because the rule has no deterrent effect if a reasonably well-trained officer objectively believed that he or she was complying with the Fourth Amendment.

The Court has not yet decided whether a good faith exception to the exclusionary rule should apply to warrantless searches and seizures.

Exclusionary rules under the North Carolina Constitution. In the context of law enforcement officers' authority,

---

8. The most often used statute under which a person may sue a law enforcement officer is Section 1983 of Title 42 of the United States Code (hereafter, U.S.C.) (dates are omitted from U.S.C. cites), which provides for a civil remedy against state and local government officials for deprivations of citizens' constitutional rights. *See, e.g.,* Malley v. Briggs, 475 U.S. 335 (1986); Graham v. Connor, 490 U.S. 386 (1989); Anderson v. Creighton, 483 U.S. 635 (1987) (court ruled that test set out in *Harlow v. Fitzgerald,* 457 U.S. 800 (1982), applied to officer who conducted warrantless search of third party's home: objective test is used to determine whether officer could have believed that search was lawful in light of clearly established law and searching officer's information). Officers may also be sued under other federal and state statutes and for torts (civil wrongs) recognized by state law, such as false imprisonment and assault. *See* Myrick v. Cooley, 91 N.C. App. 209 (1988). Under certain circumstances, an officer's supervisors and the local government unit that employs the officer also may be held responsible for the officer's unconstitutional acts.

9. Two commonly used federal criminal statutes for prosecuting criminal violations of constitutional rights are 18 U.S.C. §§ 241 and 242. An officer may also be prosecuted under such state criminal laws as assault and battery.

10. G.S. 15A-974(1). The supreme court in *State v. Garner,* 331 N.C. 491 (1992), incorrectly stated that this statute "provides in relevant part that evidence seized in violation of the federal or state constitution must be suppressed." The statute does not say that; it provides that evidence must be suppressed if its exclusion is required by the federal or state constitution. *See* Official Commentary to G.S. 15A-974. Thus, for example, the statute would not require evidence to be suppressed if the federal and state constitutions were interpreted as not requiring suppression of evidence.

11. Mapp v. Ohio, 367 U.S. 643 (1961); Herring v. United States, 555 U.S. 135 (2009). For summaries of cases on various applications of and exceptions to exclusionary rules, see page 534.

12. United States v. Leon, 468 U.S. 897 (1984). The Court recast the Fourth Amendment's exclusionary rule in *Herring v. United States,* 555 U.S. 135 (2009) (exclusionary rule did not bar admission of evidence seized after arrest that was based on officer's reasonable belief that there was outstanding arrest warrant, although law enforcement agency had negligently failed to enter warrant's recall in computer database).

13. United States v. Leon, 468 U.S. 897 (1984); Massachusetts v. Sheppard, 468 U.S. 981 (1984). The objective good faith test of *Leon* and *Sheppard* also applies to the sufficiency of the descriptions of the place to be searched and things to be seized. *See* 2 WAYNE R. LaFAVE, SEARCH AND SEIZURE: A TREATISE ON THE FOURTH AMENDMENT § 4.5, at 710, and § 4.6, at 764 (5th ed. 2012).

14. United States v. Leon, 468 U.S. 897 (1984).

North Carolina courts generally have not interpreted the state's constitutional provisions as imposing greater restrictions on their authority than the federal constitution.[15] However, the North Carolina Supreme Court strongly indicated that there is no good faith exception to the exclusionary rule for a violation of the North Carolina Constitution like the "good faith" exception to the Fourth Amendment exclusionary rule, discussed in the preceding section.[16] Thus, the good faith exception is probably unavailable in North Carolina state courts to admit evidence that was seized under an invalid search warrant, but it is available in federal courts in North Carolina, where cases (for example, drug and firearm violations) of North Carolina law enforcement officers are sometimes tried.

North Carolina statutory exclusionary rule. North Carolina law also provides that evidence may not be admitted at trial under certain circumstances if it was obtained by a violation of Chapter 15A of the North Carolina General Statutes (hereafter, G.S.),[17] which contains the statutory rules governing arrest, search and seizure, search warrants, and nontestimonial identification orders. Evidence is to be excluded only in the following circumstances:

1. It is obtained as a result of a "substantial" violation of Chapter 15A
2. The officer committing the violation did not act under an objectively reasonable, good faith belief that his or her actions were lawful[18]

Thus, evidence may be excluded when officers obtain it as a result of a violation of one of these statutes, even if their actions do not violate a person's constitutional rights. In determining whether a violation is substantial under issue 1, above, a court considers how a person's privacy has been violated, the extent of the violation and whether it was deliberate, and whether the evidence should be excluded to deter future violations.[19] Thus, for example, a court might not exclude evidence seized by officers who executed a search warrant and merely did not satisfy the statutory requirement that they swear to the inventory of seized items.[20] On the other hand, a court might exclude evidence seized with a search warrant when officers deliberately violated the statutory requirement of giving notice before they entered a home.[21] In determining the ground under issue 2, above, a court essentially considers whether or not a reasonably well-trained officer would have known that his or her conduct violated a statute.[22]

Defendant's Standing to Exclude Evidence

(*See page 542 for case summaries on this topic.*)

Even if officers violated a constitutional provision when they conducted a search or made an arrest, a defendant cannot successfully move to exclude evidence that was obtained as a result of that constitutional violation unless *his* or *her* constitutional rights were violated. In the context of Fourth Amendment violations, a defendant has the burden of proving that officers violated the defendant's reasonable expectation of privacy. A violation of another person's Fourth Amendment rights generally does not result in the suppression of evidence at the defendant's trial.[23] Thus, evidence generally is not suppressed if officers unconstitutionally search a place in which a defendant cannot reasonably expect privacy—for

---

15. In *State v. Garner*, 331 N.C. 491 (1992), the court's general statements indicated that the state constitution does not provide a defendant with more rights than those provided by the Fourth Amendment. The *Garner* ruling appears to undermine the ruling in *State v. Carter*, discussed *supra* notes 1 and 5.

16. *See supra* notes 1 and 5.

17. G.S. 15A-974 (a)(2).

18. Issue 2 was added by S.L. 2011-6 and was intended to import into G.S. 15A-974 the Fourth Amendment's good faith exception. For a discussion of this legislation, see Bob Farb, *New North Carolina Legislation on Good Faith Exception to Exclusionary Rules*, NC CRIM. L. BLOG (Mar. 21, 2011), http://nccriminallaw.sog.unc.edu/new-north-carolina-legislation-on-good-faith-exception-to-exclusionary-rules.

19. *See* State v. Richardson, 295 N.C. 309 (1978); State v. Fruitt, 35 N.C. App. 177 (1978); State v. Brown, 35 N.C. App. 634 (1978); State v. Gwyn, 103 N.C. App. 369 (1991).

20. State v. Dobbins, 306 N.C. 342 (1982).

21. State v. Brown, 35 N.C. App. 634 (1978). *See also* State v. Hyleman, 324 N.C. 506 (1989) (substantial violation occurred when search warrant's affidavit failed to establish probable cause). Of course, the Fourth Amendment may be violated as well when officers fail to give notice before entering a home. Wilson v. Arkansas, 514 U.S. 927 (1995); Richards v. Wisconsin, 520 U.S. 385 (1997). However, the Fourth Amendment's exclusionary rule would not apply to bar evidence seized from such a violation. Hudson v. Michigan, 547 U.S. 586 (2006).

22. For a discussion of issue 2, see Bob Farb, *New North Carolina Legislation on Good Faith Exception to Exclusionary Rules*, NC CRIM. L. BLOG (Mar. 21, 2011), http://nccriminallaw.sog.unc.edu/new-north-carolina-legislation-on-good-faith-exception-to-exclusionary-rules.

23. Rakas v. Illinois, 439 U.S. 128 (1978); Rawlings v. Kentucky, 448 U.S. 98 (1980); State v. Jones, 299 N.C. 298 (1980).

example, in many instances a defendant has no privacy interests in another's home, car, and other personal property, such as another's pocketbook.[24] In legal language, the fact that a defendant must prove that his or her constitutional rights were violated means that the defendant must have "standing" to contest a constitutional violation.[25] The same standing principle also applies to a violation of a North Carolina statute.[26]

Procedure for Excluding Evidence: Suppression Motions and Hearings

(*See page 534 for case summaries on this topic.*)

Defendants who want to object to evidence that they believe was found as a result of an unconstitutional search or seizure or a substantial statutory violation must make a motion to suppress in court.

When a misdemeanor case is tried in district court, defendants may make their suppression motions before or during trial, except for impaired driving cases, when the motion ordinarily must be made before trial.[27] If defendants are convicted and appeal for a trial de novo in superior court, they must make their suppression motions before trial or lose their right to do so.[28]

When felony cases are tried in superior court, defendants often must make their suppression motions before trial. If a search was made with a search warrant and a defendant was present during the search, the defendant must make a suppression motion before trial.[29] If a search was made without a search warrant or if the defendant was not present when it was made with a search warrant, a prosecutor can require the defendant to make a suppression motion before trial by giving the defendant notice of the prosecutor's intention to use the evidence gained in the search. Officers need to alert a prosecutor about such evidence so that he or she can give the proper notice to the defendant. If the prosecutor gives notice 20 working days or more before the trial begins, the defendant must make a suppression motion at least 10 working days before trial or lose the right to do so.[30] If the prosecutor does not give timely notice, the defendant may make a suppression motion during trial.[31] If the defendant's suppression motion is made before trial, a hearing normally will be conducted before trial. If the evidence is ruled inadmissible at a pretrial hearing, a prosecutor may appeal the ruling to an appellate court before the trial starts.[32] If an appellate court reverses the trial judge's ruling, the evidence will be admissible when the trial is conducted.

If a suppression motion is heard during a trial and the judge rules that the evidence is inadmissible, the prosecutor may not appeal and must try the case without the evidence. The importance of having suppression motions heard before trial—and therefore the importance of officers timely informing a prosecutor about evidence—is readily apparent.

The Issuing Official

The best way for an officer to ensure that there is a justification to make a search is to use a search warrant. A search warrant helps protect a person's right to privacy because it is issued by an independent, disinterested judicial official who has reviewed the officer's judgment that there is probable cause to justify a search in the place proposed to be searched.[33] A judicial official, who has no

24. Rakas v. Illinois, 439 U.S. 128 (1978) (mere presence in another's car was insufficient by itself to show reasonable expectation of privacy); Rawlings v. Kentucky, 448 U.S. 98 (1980) (defendant failed to show reasonable expectation of privacy in female companion's purse); State v. Jones, 229 N.C. 298 (1980) (defendant had no standing to contest search of his parents' garage when he did not assert any property or possessory interest there); State v. Crews, 296 N.C. 607 (1979) (defendant had no standing to contest search of stolen vehicle). *But see* Minnesota v. Olson, 495 U.S. 91 (1990) (overnight guest in home has reasonable expectation of privacy there). See other cases on standing in the case summaries section of this chapter on page 542.

25. Although the United States Supreme Court in *Rakas v. Illinois*, 439 U.S. 128 (1978), subsumed "standing" into substantive Fourth Amendment law, the issue is easier to understand and to analyze when it is discussed separately.

26. A motion to suppress, whether based on a constitutional or statutory violation, may only be made by a defendant who is "aggrieved." G.S. 15A-972; State v. Taylor, 298 N.C. 405 (1979).

27. G.S. 15A-973; 20-38.6.

28. G.S. 15A-975; State v. Simmons, 59 N.C. App. 287 (1982).

29. G.S. 15A-975.

30. G.S. 15A-975(b), -976(b); State v. Hill, 294 N.C. 320 (1978).

31. A defendant who is properly permitted to make a suppression motion during trial may make the motion orally or in writing, and an affidavit is not required to be filed with the motion. State v. Roper, 328 N.C. 337 (1991).

32. G.S. 15A-979(c).

33. See, for example, the discussion in *Johnson v. United States*, 333 U.S. 10 (1948); *Lo-Ji Sales, Inc. v. New York*, 442

interest or stake in the investigation, may be more likely than the officer to determine correctly whether the available information justifies the proposed search.

Who May Issue a Search Warrant

In North Carolina, only the following judicial officials may issue search warrants: appellate justices and judges, superior court and district court judges, clerks of superior court and assistant and deputy clerks, and magistrates.[34] Because most search warrants are issued by magistrates, the term "magistrate" will be used exclusively throughout this chapter.

Unlike arrest warrants, search warrants are not always valid statewide. Clerks of superior court, assistant and deputy clerks, and magistrates generally may issue warrants to search only places located within their county;[35] a search warrant issued to search a place located in another county is invalid. District court judges may issue a search warrant to search anywhere in their district.[36] Appellate court justices and judges and superior court judges may issue warrants to search anywhere in the state.[37]

Examination of the Applicant

When an officer[38] applies for a search warrant, a magistrate must examine the officer under oath or affirmation to determine whether probable cause exists to issue the warrant.[39] Although the examination is normally done in person, state law allows oral testimony by a sworn officer by means of an audio and video transmission in which the magistrate and officer can see and hear each other. Before using this method, the procedures and type of equipment for audio and video transmission must be submitted to the Administrative Office of the Courts (AOC) by the senior resident superior court judge and the chief district court judge for a judicial district and approved by the AOC.[40]

An officer typically prepares the application for the warrant, which includes the officer's affidavit. The magistrate should read the application and ask clarifying questions. Whatever information may be necessary to establish or to help establish probable cause should be added to the application.[41] The application should accurately reflect the officer's knowledge so that the officer can sign it as a statement of his or her belief that there is probable cause to search. In a complicated case, an officer may want to ask a prosecutor or his or her agency's legal advisor to assist in writing the application.

Officers need not state all they know about the investigation in the application, but they must provide enough information to establish probable cause. As discussed later in this chapter, an informant's identity need not be given if probable cause can be established without doing so.

Even though a magistrate's primary function is to make an independent determination of whether probable cause exists, a magistrate's careful examination of the applicant serves another important purpose. Officers may become so familiar with an investigation, having worked

---

U.S. 319 (1979); and *State v. Woods*, 26 N.C. App. 584 (1975). For case summaries on a neutral and detached magistrate, see page 498.

34. G.S. 15A-243.

35. G.S. 15A-243(b)(3); 7A-273(4) (magistrates); 15A-243(b)(2); 7A-180(5) (clerk of superior court); 7A-181(2) (assistant and deputy clerks). *See also* G.S. 7A-293 (special authority of magistrates assigned to municipality whose boundaries lie in more than one county of a district court district or whose boundaries lie in two district court districts; these provisions extend these magistrates' authority to issue a search warrant beyond their county); State v. Pennington, 327 N.C. 89 (1990) (court ruled that superior court clerks may issue search warrants when underlying investigation is for felony or misdemeanor violation).

36. G.S. 15A-243(b)(1); 7A-291(5).

37. G.S. 15A-243(a).

38. Although law enforcement officers normally apply for search warrants, any person or entity may apply for one. *In re* 1990 Red Cherokee Jeep, 131 N.C. App. 108 (1998) (Town of Waynesville had authority to apply for search warrant). Thus, for example, animal control officers and animal cruelty investigators may apply for search warrants even if they are not law enforcement officers. However, only a law enforcement officer may execute a search warrant. G.S. 15A-247.

39. G.S. 15A-244, -245(a). *See* State v. Upchurch, 267 N.C. 417 (1966) (search warrant invalid because clerk who issued warrant merely witnessed officer's signature on affidavit without examining him under oath); State v. McCord, 140 N.C. App. 634 (2000) (application for search warrant did not state on its face that it was sworn to; however, applicant attached sworn affidavit to her application, and she testified that she signed application in issuing judicial official's presence after being sworn by the judicial official; court ruled that this evidence was sufficient to show that application was sworn to in compliance with G.S. 15A-244).

40. G.S. 15A-245(a)(3).

41. United States v. Ramirez, 63 F.3d 937 (10th Cir. 1995) (issuing judge's commonsense alterations of affidavit for search warrant and search warrant itself did not violate judge's duty to be a neutral and detached magistrate; judge altered the person and items to be seized, but alteration was based on narrative portion of affidavit that provided probable cause to do so).

on it so long, that they state their conclusions about the investigation rather than the facts that led to those conclusions. If magistrates are to make independent determinations, they must know the facts that support officers' conclusions so that they can decide on their own whether they would reach the same conclusions. When a magistrate who is unfamiliar with the investigation examines the application critically, the magistrate's questions often elicit information that the investigating officer knows but has simply not included in the application. That information can then be added to strengthen the statement of probable cause in the application so that the search warrant is more likely to be ruled valid if it is challenged in court.

Court Review of a Search Warrant's Legality

As stated above, a magistrate's primary function is to determine independently whether there is probable cause to search. Thus, the magistrate is a check on the officer's judgment concerning probable cause. The magistrate's decision to issue a search warrant also is subject to review if a defendant challenges its legality in court. A judge must decide whether the magistrate had a "substantial basis" for concluding that probable cause existed to issue the search warrant.[42]

When reviewing a magistrate's decision to issue a search warrant, a North Carolina judge may consider only information that was written in the application or, if the facts were given orally, information that was recorded or summarized in writing when the search warrant was issued.[43] And, of course, all this information must be given under oath or affirmation.[44] Thus, if information is not written in the application, it is critical that the magistrate and officer make sure that the magistrate makes a record—written or tape-recorded—of all the information the magistrate considered in determining probable cause.

The Form and Content of the Application and Warrant

Two basic documents are used in obtaining a search warrant—the application for the warrant and the warrant form itself. The application must be supported with one or more affidavits by those who have information establishing probable cause to search.[45] The AOC prepares a two-sided form (AOC-CR-119) that contains the application—with an affidavit within the application—on one side and the search warrant on the other side. This form is available from the AOC's website at www.nccourts.org/Forms/FormSearch.asp. The AOC also prepares a special search warrant to seize blood or urine in impaired driving cases, AOC-CR-155, also available on the website. Both forms can be completed and printed at the website.[46] (For a list of forms available on the AOC website, see the sidebar on page 412.)

Three copies of a search warrant must be prepared, although an officer may want an additional copy for his or her investigative file. After issuing the search warrant, the magistrate sends one copy—the clerk's copy of record—to the clerk's office. Two copies are given to the officer. After the warrant is executed, or if it is never executed, the officer returns one copy—commonly known as the original copy—to the clerk of court's office (or the magistrate's office, for forwarding to the clerk's office). The officer who executes the search warrant gives a copy to the person whose premises are searched. (See the discussion on execution of search warrants on page 437.)

If the information does not all fit on the form, additional sheets may be attached. A satisfactory procedure is to staple the additional sheets to the form with

---

42. Illinois v. Gates, 462 U.S. 213 (1983); State v. Arrington, 311 N.C. 633 (1984); State v. Tuggle, 99 N.C. App. 164 (1990).

43. G.S. 15A-245(a) (1988); State v. Hicks, 60 N.C. App. 116 (1982) (magistrate made handwritten notes of information officer gave her under oath and considered this information in determining probable cause—in addition to information in affidavit; notes were not attached to search warrant so that informant's identity could be protected; court ruled that under G.S. 15A-245(a), notes could be considered in determining whether probable cause supported search warrant); State v. Teasley, 82 N.C. App. 150 (1986) (officer's oral testimony given to magistrate when he applied for a search warrant could not be considered by the trial judge in determining the sufficiency of the warrant because the magistrate did not record the oral testimony or contemporaneously summarize it in the record); State v. Brown, ___ N.C. App. ___, ___ S.E.2d ___ (June 21, 2016) (officer testified at suppression hearing that what he meant to state in search warrant affidavit was that the informant had obtained information within the last 48 hours; court ruled that

trial court erred in considering this testimony, which was not included in affidavit).

44. State v. Heath, 73 N.C. App. 391 (1985) (court ruled that in determining probable cause, magistrate may not consider unsworn written statements submitted in addition to affidavit).

45. G.S. 15A-244.

46. Paper copies of these forms are printed and shipped to a county when requested by the clerk's office.

The following forms are available on the AOC website at www.nccourts.org/Forms/FormSearch.asp:

AOC-CR-119	SEARCH WARRANT
AOC-CR-155	SEARCH WARRANT FOR BLOOD OR URINE IN DWI CASES
AOC-CR-206	INVENTORY OF ITEMS SEIZED PURSUANT TO SEARCH
AOC-CR-913M	AFFIDAVIT TO OBTAIN ADMINISTRATIVE INSPECTION WARRANT FOR PARTICULAR CONDITION OR ACTIVITY
AOC-CR-914M	AFFIDAVIT TO OBTAIN ADMINISTRATIVE INSPECTION WARRANT FOR PERIODIC INSPECTION
AOC-CR-204	APPLICATION FOR NONTESTIMONIAL IDENTIFICATION ORDER (ADULT SUSPECT)
AOC-CR-205	NONTESTIMONIAL IDENTIFICATION ORDER (ADULT SUSPECT)
AOC-J-204	APPLICATION FOR NONTESTIMONIAL IDENTIFICATION ORDER (JUVENILE SUSPECT)
AOC-J-205	NONTESTIMONIAL IDENTIFICATION ORDER (JUVENILE SUSPECT)

---

a reference in the appropriate place on the form, such as "see attached"; date the attachment; and include on it the name of the search warrant (for example, "In the Matter of Howard Smith") and the signatures of both the applicant and the issuing official. This procedure clearly identifies all attachments and helps prove that they were not added after the search warrant was issued.

As discussed above, if information other than what is written in the application is given to the magistrate when the magistrate is determining probable cause and does not appear in writing on the application, that information must be either recorded or summarized separately when the warrant is issued. Sometimes this is done so that a suspect will not learn of a confidential informant's information when the suspect is served with his or her copy and be able to determine the informant's identity from that information. The magistrate also should check the block on the application to indicate that sworn testimony was reduced to writing or tape recorded—if that information is not included in the application. In whatever form the information is recorded, a magistrate should give a copy of it to the clerk of court along with the copy of the application and search warrant.[47]

The officer who is applying for the search warrant must state the facts and sign the application under oath or affirmation.[48] North Carolina law does not specify the exact wording of this oath or affirmation. It is sufficient if the applicant simply swears or affirms that the information in the application is true to the best of the applicant's knowledge.[49] The officer must sign the application, and the magistrate must sign and date the block in the form indicating that the applicant signed the application before the magistrate and swore to or affirmed the information contained within it.

The search warrant must be directed to officers authorized to execute it; the AOC form supplies that language. The magistrate must sign the search warrant and give the date and time of issuance. The date and time are important because the officer has only 48 hours to execute a search warrant after it is issued.[50]

The most important requirements of the application and warrant are the description of the items to be searched for, the description of the place to be searched, and the statement of facts showing probable cause for the search. The substance of these three requirements is discussed later in this chapter.

---

47. *But see* State v. Hicks, 60 N.C. App. 116 (1982) (magistrate made notes contemporaneously from information supplied by search warrant's affiant under oath and kept them in magistrate's office drawer; court ruled that these notes were not required to be filed with the clerk's office). Despite the *Hicks* ruling, it is a good practice to file the information with the clerk's office to reduce the likelihood that it will be lost and to refute a later allegation that the information was not contemporaneously reduced to writing or tape recorded.

48. G.S. 15A-245(a).

49. Provisions for oaths are contained in G.S. Chapter 11.

50. G.S. 15A-248. The time limitation is discussed later in this chapter.

Preparation of the Search Warrant Worksheet

Before officers write an application for a search warrant, they should consider organizing the pertinent investigative information in a written worksheet. This practice will be useful in writing a well-organized and coherent application and will make it more likely that all the necessary information will be included. In addition, the worksheet may alert officers that more information is needed to establish probable cause. The sample worksheet on page 415 asks for information that officers should consider for inclusion in the application. Not all of the information is necessarily legally required, however. (The legal requirements are discussed later in this chapter.) The worksheet is organized in the same order as the application for a search warrant.

Description of the Property to Be Seized

(*See page 494 for case summaries on this topic.*)

In applying for a search warrant, an officer must describe the property to be seized. The purpose of this requirement is twofold:

1. To avoid the possibility that the search warrant might be used to search for and seize items for which there is no probable cause to believe a connection with criminal activity exists—in other words, to prevent a general search for evidence
2. To prevent the seizure of objects by mistake—for example, the description "a stolen watch" could result in an officer's seizing many "innocent" watches in a house

Generally, an officer should try to identify the property clearly enough so that another officer, unfamiliar with the case, can read the description and know which items should be seized. When the property to be seized—for example, a television set—can be possessed lawfully, greater detail is required than when the property—for example, heroin—can never be possessed lawfully, because a greater possibility exists of wrongfully seizing lawfully possessed property.

Although there are no clearly defined rules on what constitutes an adequate description, it is helpful to discuss the subject by category.

Stolen Goods

If a search warrant authorizes an officer to seize a stolen television set, a description stating "a color TV" will probably not be sufficient, because the executing officer who sees a television set will probably not be able to determine from the description whether the set the officer sees is the one that was stolen. With no further instruction than to seize "a color TV," an officer may well seize a television set that is not connected with a crime.

The description of stolen goods should be as accurate as possible. Serial numbers should be given if they are available—or, if serial numbers are not available, a physical description of the goods, including make, color, size, and any scratches or other unique damage should be provided.[51] If the officer has an inventory of the stolen items prepared by the victim or investigating officer, it can be used to describe the items or can be attached to the application and incorporated by reference in the space provided for the property description of the property—for example, "See attached list of property to be seized."

Weapons and Other Instruments Used during Crimes

The same rules governing the description of stolen goods apply to descriptions of weapons and other instruments used in committing crimes—such as burglary tools, a knife used in an assault, and a shotgun used in a murder. Officers should try to be as accurate as possible with the information they have collected. For example, they should not simply state "weapon used in felonious assault" when they know the kind of weapon—a revolver—and perhaps the weapon's make, model, and serial number.[52]

---

51. *See generally* 2 Wayne R. LaFave, Search and Seizure: A Treatise on the Fourth Amendment § 4.6(c) (5th ed. 2012); State v. Connard, 81 N.C. App. 327 (1986), *aff'd*, 319 N.C. 392 (1987) (description "stolen goods" was invalid); United States v. Fuccillo, 808 F.2d 173 (1st Cir. 1987) (although general descriptions of items to be seized are not always invalid, general descriptions of clothes to be seized in this case were invalid because officers had available information to provide more specific descriptions).

52. *See generally* 2 Wayne R. LaFave, Search and Seizure: A Treatise on the Fourth Amendment § 4.6(d) (5th ed. 2012).

General Evidence

An object that is usually lawfully possessed may be so clearly connected with a crime that a general description may be acceptable when no greater specificity can be given—for example, "blood-stained clothes."[53] Of course, more detail should be given, if known—for example, a "blood-stained blue jacket."

Documents Associated with White Collar Crimes

When investigating complex white collar crimes, officers need not describe in the search warrant application each individual paper to be seized, although they should be as specific as the circumstances of the investigated activity permit. Officers should describe the specific documents they have probable cause to seize and then should list the types of items—checkbooks, canceled checks, deposit slips—that pertain to the crime under investigation and any other similar evidence related to the crime.[54]

Evidence of Ownership or Possession of Premises

Officers who are executing a search warrant to seize illegal drugs also may seize items not named in the warrant—such as letters and photographs—that they see inadvertently in plain view, if the items help prove who owns or lives in the premises where the drugs have been found.[55] However, officers also may list these kinds of items in the search warrant so that they need not rely on the plain view doctrine to justify their seizure; that is, the search warrant will specifically authorize the seizure.

One way to describe them in the application is "items or articles of personal property tending to show ownership, dominion, or control of the premises."[56]

Evidence at a Crime Scene

As discussed in Chapter 3, officers who enter a home when responding to a report of a crime may search without a warrant throughout the home for victims or suspects, but they generally need a search warrant or consent to search for evidence once they have completed their initial search. Of course, officers may not be sure exactly what they may be looking for when they apply for a search warrant. For example, they may have discovered a dead body with multiple gunshot wounds during their initial search for victims and suspects. They clearly could name, as objects of the search, a weapon and the scientific evidence that is normally sought in a homicide investigation. For example, they could state "fingerprints, bloodstains, fired and unfired bullets and casings, footwear impressions, trace hair and clothing fibers, physical layout of the premises," and then they could add "any and all evidence that may relate to the suspected murder."[57]

Evidence in Computers and Other Electronic Devices

(*See page 495 for cases summaries on this topic.*)

An extensive discussion of this topic is contained in *Digital Evidence*, a 2015 School of Government publication by Jeffrey B. Welty. Below is a brief review of some of the issues.

- Because adequate and appropriate descriptions in search warrants to seize and search computers or other electronic device (hereafter, "computer" will be used to refer to all devices) and evidence in them may involve constantly evolving technology, detailed examples of descriptions will not be set out here. Officers who are unsure how to write these descriptions should consult the publication noted above or seek expert advice; for example, the State Bureau of Investigation is available to provide

---

53. State v. Seefeldt, 242 A.2d 322 (N.J. 1968).

54. Andresen v. Maryland, 427 U.S. 463 (1976); State v. Kornegay, 313 N.C. 1 (1985) (court ruled as a sufficient description all checkbooks, canceled checks, deposit slips, bank statements, trust account receipts, check stubs, books and papers, etc., that would tend to show a fraudulent intent or any elements of the crimes of false pretenses or embezzlement); United States v. Rude, 88 F.3d 1538 (9th Cir. 1996) (business permeated with fraud justified broad description of documents to be seized); United States v. Cantu, 774 F.2d 1305 (5th Cir. 1985); United States v. Bentley, 825 F.2d 1104 (7th Cir. 1987) (court ruled that, when fraud infects entire business, description may properly include seizure of all business documents); *In re* Impounded Case (Law Firm), 840 F.2d 196 (3d Cir. 1988), *later appeal*, 879 F.2d 1211 (3d Cir. 1989) (search warrant to seize law office files that was limited to seizure of a designated group of files, all of which the affidavit alleged contained evidence of fraudulent claims, was sufficiently specific). *See generally* 2 Wayne R. LaFave, Search and Seizure: A Treatise on the Fourth Amendment § 4.6(d) (5th ed. 2012).

55. State v. Williams, 299 N.C. 529 (1980).

56. *See, e.g.*, United States v. Alexander, 761 F.2d 1294 (9th Cir. 1985); United States v. Tabares, 951 F.2d 405 (1st Cir. 1991).

57. *See generally* State v. Hodges, 603 P.2d 1205 (Or. App. 1979); Commonwealth v. Freiberg, 540 N.E.2d 1289 (Mass. 1989); 3 Wayne R. LaFave, Search and Seizure: A Treatise on the Fourth Amendment § 6.5(e), at 594 (5th ed. 2012).

Search Warrant Worksheet

Information for an Application Other Than the Statement of Probable Cause

1. Give the name of the officer who will apply for a search warrant.
2. Describe the items to be seized with particularity or, if the warrant is to be used to search for a person to be arrested, describe the person.
3. Name the crime(s) that is connected with the items to be seized.
4. Describe the premises to be searched by giving the address and apartment number (if applicable), tell how to get there (if necessary to find the premises), state the type of structure, and (if known) name any outbuildings on the premises—such as an unattached garage, barn, or storage shed—in which items to be seized may be located.
5. Describe the person(s) to be searched by giving his or her name, sex, date of birth, hair, race, height, and other identifying features—when the person's name is unknown.
6. Describe the vehicle(s) to be searched by giving the year, make, color, registration, license, identification number, and any unusual features—when the car has not otherwise been adequately described.
7. Describe any other place or item to be searched if it is not in premises, on a person, or in a vehicle. For example, if a search warrant is to be used to search a suitcase seized at an airport terminal, describe the suitcase and where it is now located.

Information to Complete the Statement of Probable Cause

1. The affiant-officer's personal observations and information.
   a. The officer's experience and expertise concerning investigation of crimes that are the subject of the search warrant.
   b. The officer's observations—including when (date and time) and where they were made—and details of the observations, including details that may be significant only to an experienced investigator.
   c. The officer's own information (detailed as above) that substantiates the information given by the informant, victims, and witnesses.
   d. The officer's knowledge of the suspect's prior arrests, convictions, and criminal activity related to the criminal acts under current investigation.
2. Other officers' observations and information (detailed as above for the affiant-officer).
3. The victim's observations and information.
   a. The victim's name, address, and occupation.
   b. The date and time when the victim reported the observations to the officer, and the name of the officer.
   c. The victim's observations, including the date and time of observations and the facts indicating that the victim personally made the observations or, if not, from whom the victim received the information.
   d. The officer's corroboration of the victim's observations and information.
4. Witnesses' observations and information (detailed as above for the victim's observations).
5. A confidential informant's observations and information.
   a. The date (or approximate date, if necessary to protect the informant's identity) when the informant reported observations to the officer and the name of the officer.
   b. The informant's observations, including the date or approximate date of the observations and facts indicating that the informant personally made the observations or, if not, from whom the informant received the information and whether that source personally made the observations.
   c. Reliability of the informant or his or her observations and information.
      (1) Prior information from the informant that has led to arrests and convictions (give details), whether that information has been accurate or inaccurate (give details), and to whom that information was given.
      (2) The informant's background—for example, does the informant recognize drugs because the informant uses them, or has the officer seen the informant correctly identify drugs?
      (3) The informant's motive for giving information.
      (4) The informant's admission of participation in crime(s) under investigation.
   d. Corroboration of the informant's observations and information.
      (1) Reports from other informants (detailed as above for this informant).
      (2) The officer's observations or investigation that substantiates the informant's observations and information.
         (a) The officer's prior knowledge showing the informant to be accurate.
         (b) The officer's investigation showing the informant to be accurate.
         (c) The facts indicating that the suspect probably is involved in the kind of criminal activity reported by the informant.

assistance to law enforcement officers.[58] A United States Department of Justice publication cited in the accompanying footnote[59] offers advice (although not necessarily legally required steps), including the following: If the computer hardware is itself contraband or an instrumentality or fruit of a crime (for example, a computer used to download child pornography), describe the hardware and indicate that the hardware will be seized.

- When the computer and its files will be removed from the place of seizure and searched later at a law enforcement or forensic facility, explain that in the search warrant's affidavit.[60]
- When probable cause to search relates in whole or in part to information stored in the computer, rather than to the computer itself, focus primarily on describing the content of the relevant files rather than the storage devices that may contain them. (A wide range of computer devices and storage media may be subject to search because digital files are easily moved or copied.)
- Officers should be particularly careful when seeking authority to seize a broad class of information—for example, searching computers at a business. One technique is to identify records concerning a particular crime and to specify the types of records that are likely to be found.

A few more issues concerning other aspects of computer searches are discussed below.

Officers who are executing a search warrant for records in a computer concerning one crime, such as a drug offense, and discover evidence in plain view of an unrelated crime (for example, child pornography) may want under some circumstances to obtain another search warrant to continue searching the computer for evidence of child pornography.[61]

If a search warrant authorizes a search of premises for a particularized list of records (for example, records of drug transactions), then the warrant ordinarily authorizes officers to seize a computer not named in the warrant that they discover in the premises if they reasonably believe the described records may be stored on a computer.[62] However, it is unclear under these circumstances whether the computer may be searched without obtaining another search warrant.[63] Of course, if an officer applying for an

---

58. Officers may contact the Computer Crimes Unit of the State Bureau of Investigation by calling the main telephone number (919.662.4500) and asking to be transferred to the unit.

59. SEARCHING AND SEIZING COMPUTERS AND OBTAINING ELECTRONIC EVIDENCE IN CRIMINAL INVESTIGATIONS 61–83 (United States Department of Justice, 2009), www.justice.gov/criminal-ccips/ccips-documents-and-reports. *See also* Jeffrey B. Welty, DIGITAL EVIDENCE 2–40 (UNC School of Government, 2015) (hereafter, DIGITAL EVIDENCE).

60. Federal appellate courts recognize the necessity of off-site computer searches. See, for example, *United States v. Stabile*, 633 F.3d 219 (3d Cir. 2011) ("practical realities of computer investigations preclude on-site searches") and the discussion in DIGITAL EVIDENCE, *supra* note 59, at 30–36. North Carolina appellate courts would likely agree with *Stabile* and similar cases.

61. There is conflicting case law on this issue. *See* the following cases as well as the cases summarized in DIGITAL EVIDENCE, *supra* note 59, at 30–32: United States v. Carey, 172 F.3d 1268 (10th Cir. 1999) (seizure of images from computer of child pornography beyond initial discovery of images was not authorized by search warrant for evidence concerning sale of controlled substances). However, compare the *Carey* ruling with *United States v. Williams*, 592 F.3d 511 (4th Cir. 2010) (criticizing *Carey* ruling that improperly focused on officer's subjective motivation for continuing to search computer files instead of whether search warrant's terms objectively permitted continuation of search; warrant authorized a search of defendant's computers and digital media for evidence relating to Virginia crimes of making threats and computer harassment; to conduct that search, warrant impliedly authorized officers to open each file on the computer and view its contents, at least cursorily, to determine whether the file fell within the scope of the warrant's authorization—that is, whether it related to the Virginia crimes; discovery of child pornography was upheld under plain view doctrine). *See also* United States v. Giberson, 527 F.3d 882 (9th Cir. 2008) (search warrant for "documents" without mentioning computers allowed search of computers because documents may be found in computers); United States v. Payton, 573 F.3d 859 (9th Cir. 2009) (distinguishing *Giberson*, search of computer when computer was not explicitly named in search warrant exceeded scope of warrant to search for financial transactions or other records related to drug sales); United States v. Hudspeth, 459 F.3d 922 (8th Cir. 2006) (search warrant for business records authorized search of computer, although computer was not explicitly named as object of search), *rev'd in part on other grounds*, 518 F.3d 954 (8th Cir. 2006) (en banc). Neither the United States Supreme Court nor North Carolina appellate courts have ruled on this issue.

62. *See generally* United States v. Giberson, 527 F.3d 882 (9th Cir. 2008); People v. Gall, 30 P.3d 145 (Colo. 2001); Commonwealth v. McDermott, 864 N.E.2d 471 (Mass. 2007).

63. United States v. Payton, 573 F.3d 859 (9th Cir. 2009) (search of computer pursuant to search warrant authorizing search of residence to seize evidence of drug sales and financial transactions violated Fourth Amendment when warrant did

initial search warrant for records has probable cause to believe that the premises may contain a computer or computers that may store records, computers should be specifically named as objects to be seized and searched.

Consent to search computers differs from other consent searches, such as consent to search a vehicle, and poses unique issues. See the discussion of computer consent issues on page 232 of Chapter 3 as well as the publication cited in the accompanying footnote.[64]

Officers who are searching computers need to be aware of federal laws that restrict access to stored email and documents in the possession of the news media, writers, and publishers. These issues are discussed on page 218 in Chapter 3 and in the publication cited in the accompanying footnote[65]

North Carolina cases that analyze probable cause to search computers are summarized in the accompanying footnote.[66]

Evidence at the Scene of a Fire

As discussed in Chapter 3, fire personnel and others may enter a home or business without a warrant and remain there until they have put out the fire and have determined its origin so that it does not start again after they leave. Generally, however, once they leave the fire scene, they must obtain an administrative inspection warrant or consent if they want to reenter the home or business to investigate the fire's origin further. If they have information that establishes probable cause to believe that the fire was caused by a criminal act, such as arson, they must obtain a search warrant instead of an administrative inspection warrant before they reenter to search. Just as with a search warrant to search a crime scene, officers may not be sure exactly what they may be looking for when they apply for a search warrant to search a fire scene. They clearly could name whatever items—for example, fuel cans—gave them reason to believe that arson was committed, but they also could list evidence that is normally sought in an arson investigation, such as ashes, fuses, fuse trails, adhesive tape, burned furniture, fibers, hairs, accelerants, patterns of burning, physical layout of the premises, fire alarms and extinguishers, and other evidence tending to show how the fire started and spread.

Illegal Drugs and Drug-Related Items

It is preferable to state the illegal drug to be seized specifically—for example, "marijuana"—rather than to state "controlled substances," although that description is probably sufficient, particularly when the affidavit's statement of probable cause names the specific drug that is to be seized.[67] It is unnecessary to state the quantity of illegal drugs being sought, as possession of any amount is illegal.

---

not explicitly authorize search of computer and officers did not find any evidence of drug sales before searching computer). It is unclear whether the United States Supreme Court or North Carolina appellate courts would agree with the *Payton* ruling, which rests in part on the rationale that under some circumstances computers are an exception to the rule permitting searches of containers to find objects specified in a search warrant (because unlike other containers, they are capable of storing enormous amounts of data). In the context of vehicle searches, the United States Supreme Court in *United States v. Ross*, 456 U.S. 798 (1982), rejected a distinction between "worthy" and "unworthy" containers (that is, worthy or unworthy of Fourth Amendment protection) in permitting a search of containers in a vehicle without a search warrant when probable cause existed to search the vehicle.

64. Digital Evidence, *supra* note 59, at 57–70.

65. *Id.* at 87–137.

66. In addition to the following cases, see the cases summarized in Digital Evidence, *supra* note 59, at 3–17: State v. Peterson, 179 N.C. App. 437, *aff'd*, 361 N.C. 587 (2007) (affidavit for search warrant to seize computers at defendant's home where homicide investigation was ongoing did not provide probable cause when affidavit did not include substance of conversations or discoveries in 36-hour investigation that might lead one to check computers in home and did not include any indication, other than the amount of blood, that would suggest search of computers would lead to information about possible homicide); State v. Pickard, 178 N.C. App. 330 (2006) (upholding a search warrant to seize a computer and other items involving sexual exploitation of minors; the search warrant's information was not stale because the affidavit showed the defendant's commission of ongoing sex crimes with children, and the items to be seized were of continuing utility to the defendant); State v. Dexter, 186 N.C. App. 587 (2007) (probable

---

cause supported search warrant for defendant's home and his computer for child pornography); State v. Ellis, 188 N.C. App. 820 (2008) (probable cause supported search warrant for computer in defendant's home based on instant messages between defendant and law enforcement officers posing as 12-year-old girl).

67. State v. Foye, 14 N.C. App. 200 (1972) (search warrant authorizing search for "narcotic drugs, the possession of which is a crime" sufficient); State v. Ledbetter, 120 N.C. App. 117 (1995) (affidavit for search warrant described informant's controlled buy of cocaine under officer's supervision; application for search warrant referred to the seizure of the "Schedule II controlled substance marijuana" when it should have stated "cocaine"; court ruled that because affidavit referred to cocaine, this error did not invalidate search warrant).

Often an affidavit that establishes that a residence is a place for drug trafficking will support a search for items that are associated with drug trafficking—for example, an officer's experience that drug traffickers keep records of transactions in their homes will support a seizure of such records.[68] In addition to the warrant giving specific authority to seize evidence of ownership or possession of premises—discussed in the section on evidence of ownership, above—the warrant may specifically authorize officers to seize records of illegal drug activities, documents, photographs, letters, drug paraphernalia, money, beepers, firearms, telephone records, and other evidence of drug trafficking.[69] Although officers generally will be authorized to seize these items under the plain view doctrine,[70] it is helpful to name them in the search warrant so that the warrant will specifically authorize their seizure.

Obscene Materials, Including Child Pornography

(*See page 497 for case summaries on this topic.*)

Because books, magazines, and movies are presumptively protected by the First Amendment's freedom of speech provisions, the United States Supreme Court has imposed stricter rules governing the search and seizure of allegedly obscene materials than those governing the search and seizure of criminal evidence such as contraband, stolen goods, and so forth.[71] Thus, merely stating that "obscene materials" are to be seized is clearly inadequate.[72] Instead, the allegedly obscene materials should be described by title and other identifying information so that only the allegedly obscene materials will be seized. Federal cases also have approved search warrant descriptions that specifically name the allegedly obscene materials to be seized and then also authorize the seizure of additional materials if they contain presentations of specifically named sexual acts.[73]

The issues involved in search warrants for child pornography are discussed in the publication cited in the accompanying footnote.[74]

Description of the Person to Be Arrested

As discussed in Chapter 2, officers need a search warrant to enter a third party's home to arrest a defendant unless they have obtained consent to enter or exigent circumstances permit a warrantless entry. When a search warrant is used for this purpose, the person to be arrested must be described in the application in the place where the property to be seized is normally described. Usually the person's name is sufficient; a complete description, although not necessarily legally required, would also include the person's sex, date of birth, hair, race, height, and any other identifying features. A detailed description is required when the person's name is unknown.

---

68. United States v. Peters, 92 F.3d 768 (8th Cir. 1996) (drug search warrant authorized the seizure of, among other things, "records . . . associated with cocaine distribution. . . ."; court, distinguishing *Walter v. United States*, 447 U.S. 649 (1980), ruled that search warrant authorized seizure of three unmarked audiocassettes that were intermingled with notes and letters from drug co-conspirator who was incarcerated; thus, seizing officer was authorized to listen to audiocassettes before deciding whether to seize them); United States v. Wylie, 919 F.2d 969 (5th Cir. 1990); United States v. Riley, 906 F.2d 841 (2d Cir. 1990).

69. *See* United States v. Rey, 923 F.2d 1217 (6th Cir. 1991); United States v. Martin, 920 F.2d 393 (6th Cir. 1990); United States v. Sullivan, 919 F.2d 1403 (10th Cir. 1991); United States v. Wylie, 919 F.2d 969 (5th Cir. 1990); United States v. Smith, 918 F.2d 1501 (11th Cir. 1990); United States v. Riley, 906 F.2d 841 (2d Cir. 1990); United States v. Harris, 903 F.2d 770 (10th Cir. 1990); United States v. Hinds, 856 F.2d 438 (1st Cir. 1988). *See generally* 2 WAYNE R. LaFAVE, SEARCH AND SEIZURE: A TREATISE ON THE FOURTH AMENDMENT § 3.7(d), at 534–45 (5th ed. 2012).

70. United States v. Smith, 918 F.2d 1501 (11th Cir. 1990) (although not named in search warrant, officers properly seized firearms in plain view because they are tools of drug trade); United States v. Wayne, 903 F.2d 1188 (8th Cir. 1990) (weapons, communication equipment, and grinder were properly seized under plain view doctrine).

71. See the discussions in *Lo-Ji Sales, Inc. v. New York*, 442 U.S. 319 (1979), and *Maryland v. Macon*, 472 U.S. 463 (1985). However, the probable cause standard is the same, whether searching for obscene materials or drugs. New York v. P.J. Video, Inc., 475 U.S. 868 (1986).

72. *See* Marcus v. Search Warrant, 367 U.S. 717 (1961); Lo-Ji Sales, Inc. v. New York, 442 U.S. 319 (1979); United States v. Espinosa, 641 F.2d 153 (4th Cir. 1981).

73. *See* Sequoia Books, Inc. v. McDonald, 725 F.2d 1091 (7th Cir. 1984); United States v. Hurt, 795 F.2d 765 (9th Cir. 1986), *opinion amended*, 808 F.2d 707 (1987) (distinguishing *United States v. Hale*, 784 F.2d 1465 (9th Cir. 1986), court upheld description in search warrant that authorized seizure of three named films and seizure of books, magazines, films, etc., depicting minors under age 16 engaged in sexually explicit conduct and correspondence ordering and paying for child pornography); United States v. Dornhofer, 859 F.2d 1195 (4th Cir. 1988) (similar ruling); United States v. Peden, 891 F.2d 514 (5th Cir. 1989) (similar ruling); United States v. Layne, 43 F.3d 127 (5th Cir. 1995) (description "child pornography" sufficient). *But see* United States v. Guarino, 729 F.2d 864 (1st Cir. 1984).

74. DIGITAL EVIDENCE, *supra* note 59, at 5–17.

Relation of the Property to a Crime

After describing the property to be searched for and seized, the officer who fills out the search warrant application will notice that the words printed on the form state that the property "constitutes evidence of a crime and the identity of a person participating in a crime." The first phrase ("constitutes evidence of a crime") describes circumstances when the property being sought is stolen (for example, a stolen television set) or contraband (for example, illegal drugs) or was used to commit a crime (for example, a gun used in a robbery). The second phrase ("[constitutes evidence of] the identity of a person participating in a crime") describes circumstances when the property being sought does not fall into these categories but helps identify the defendant (for example, the shirt or hat that was worn during a robbery). The officer does not have to choose the appropriate phrase—both are alleged. If one of them does not apply, the additional language does not affect the warrant's validity.

Next is the space where the kind of crime must be stated. Because the application is for a search warrant, not an arrest warrant, the crime may be stated summarily. The easiest way to state the crime is to cite the General Statutes section that has been violated, the common term for that crime, and the date and location—for example, "G.S. 14-87, armed robbery of Phil's Quick-Service, Sunshine, N.C., on May 14, 2011." If the property being sought is contraband and thus evidence of an ongoing possession offense, the location and date of the offense might be omitted. For example, "G.S. 90-95, possession of heroin, a Schedule I controlled substance" is sufficient. Also, the exact date and location of an already completed offense may not be known when the search warrant is issued—for example, a murder weapon is being sought but the officers are not yet sure when and where the killing took place. In that case, officers may omit the date and location of the crime, because they must only establish that the property being searched for has some connection with the crime.[75]

Description of the Premises, the Person to Be Searched, or the Vehicle

(See page 494 for case summaries on this topic.)

Officers must describe in the application the premises, person, or vehicle to be searched. A separate space is provided for each description. In addition, a fourth space is provided for describing any other place or item to be searched that does not fit within any of the first three categories—for example, luggage that is already in an officer's possession.

The purpose of describing the person or place to be searched is to avoid the possibility that officers might use the warrant to search a person or place for which probable cause has not been established. The description should be specific enough that someone unfamiliar with the case could accurately locate the place and distinguish it from any other place with which it might be confused.[76] However, a court will be more likely to decide that a description is sufficient if an executing officer personally knows the place that was intended to be searched with the warrant.[77]

The Premises

Usually the best way to describe a place is to give the street address, because two places should not have the same address. If the address is correct, it is an adequate description,[78] but a physical description of the premises may save a search warrant that may otherwise be invalid because it gave the wrong address. For example, the place to be searched may be described as "412 Elm Street, Smithville, N.C." If that is the correct address, then the address alone is a satisfactory description. But what if officers who went to make the search with that warrant found 402 Elm Street and 422 Elm Street, but not 412? The warrant description might be invalid, and any search made at either 402 or 422 Elm Street may be unlawful.[79] Suppose, however, that the description said

---

75. Even if officers omitted the name of a crime in this space, the search warrant would not be invalid if the statement of probable cause in the affidavit connects the evidence being sought with a crime.

76. Both the Fourth Amendment and G.S. 15A-246(4) require that the premises to be searched be particularly described.

77. *See, e.g.*, State v. Cloninger, 37 N.C. App. 22 (1978); United States v. Turner, 770 F.2d 1508 (9th Cir. 1985); 2 WAYNE R. LAFAVE, SEARCH AND SEIZURE: A TREATISE ON THE FOURTH AMENDMENT § 4.5(a), at 714–15 (5th ed. 2012).

78. Steele v. United States, 267 U.S. 498 (1925); United States v. Dancy, 947 F.2d 1232 (5th Cir. 1991).

79. *But see* United States v. Vega-Figueroa, 234 F.3d 744 (1st Cir. 2000) (search warrant provided incorrect address

"412 Elm Street, Smithville, N.C., a two-story white frame residence with red shutters," and the residence at 422 Elm Street was the only one on Elm Street that met that physical description. Although there was no residence at 412 Elm Street, the warrant would likely be valid. Thus, an incorrect street number need not invalidate a warrant if enough other information is given to identify the premises to be searched.[80]

Another useful piece of information is the name of the possessor of the premises—for example, "412 Elm Street, Smithville, N.C., a two-story white frame house with red shutters, occupied by Allen Greeby." If that name appears on a mailbox in front of the house or by the front door, it will help officers determine which house is to be searched, or which part of the building is to be searched if it is a duplex or apartment building.[81] Although the possessor's name helps a description, that information is not required and by itself is not sufficient. Describing the premises simply as "the home of Fred Johnson" without giving an address or any other information normally would be inadequate.

If the place to be searched is in a rural area and has no street address, the building or its location must be described in more detail than if it had a number. The description might be supplemented by information about the building's distance from other structures and roads and directions on how to get there from a named highway or building.

If the place to be searched is a business, the address might be supplemented by information about signs on the premises—for example, "5580 Main Boulevard, a one-story building with a sign reading 'Smithville Hardware.'"

Vehicles on the Premises

Generally, a warrant to search premises gives executing officers the authority to search a vehicle on the premises,[82] even though the vehicle is not specifically named in the warrant as a place to be searched, if both of the following exist:

1. The evidence to be seized may reasonably be found there
2. The vehicle is owned or under the control of an occupant of the premises[83] or officers have a reasonable basis for believing that the vehicle is so owned or controlled[84]

If a vehicle may not be searched under this authority, it may be searched without a warrant under certain

---

(building 44, apartment 446, instead of building 45, apartment 446) as place to be searched; however, officer who made observations that led to issuance of search warrant was executing officer and member of search team; he correctly directed searching officers to defendant's apartment; court ruled that search warrant was properly issued and executed).

80. *See, e.g.,* State v. Hunter, 208 N.C. App. 506 (2010) (although numerical portion of street address was incorrect, warrant was sufficient because it contained correct description of residence); State v. Walsh, 19 N.C. App. 420 (1973); United States v. Valentine, 984 F.2d 906 (8th Cir. 1993); United States v. Garza, 980 F.2d 546 (9th Cir. 1992); United States v. Turner, 770 F.2d 1508 (9th Cir. 1985); Lyons v. Robinson, 783 F.2d 737 (8th Cir. 1985); 2 Wayne R. LaFave, Search and Seizure: A Treatise on the Fourth Amendment § 4.5(a), at 722 (5th ed. 2012).

81. In *People v. Estrada*, 44 Cal. Rptr. 165 (Cal. App. 1965), the warrant gave the correct street address but did not indicate which apartment was to be searched. However, the warrant was valid because the description indicated the name of the occupant and, with this information, the officers were able to determine which apartment to search. *See generally* 2 Wayne R. LaFave, Search and Seizure: A Treatise on the Fourth Amendment § 4.5(a) (5th ed. 2012).

82. When officers have a warrant to search the premises, their authority to search the vehicles should not depend on the vehicles being on the curtilage, although some appellate cases appear to require that the vehicles be on the curtilage. The vehicles simply must be somewhere on the property where the residence is located. *See* United States v. Patterson, 278 F.3d 315 (4th Cir. 2002) (officers had objectively reasonable but mistaken belief that vehicle not named in search warrant was on premises; court ruled that vehicle was subject to search under search warrant).

83. State v. Reid, 286 N.C. 323 (1974); State v. Logan, 27 N.C. App. 430 (1975); State v. Courtright, 60 N.C. App. 247 (1983) (although court questionably concluded that a car parked on the street with its front wheels six to seven inches into the yard was sufficiently within the curtilage to permit a search of the vehicle under the search warrant, the result of that decision was correct because the car was on the premises, even if not within the curtilage)—*see supra* note 82; State v. McLamb, 70 N.C. App. 712 (1984) (court questionably upheld search of car under search warrant when car was across a road 15 feet beyond the property line because car "appeared to be connected to" premises to be searched; court's alternative ruling upholding the search on the ground that the defendant had no reasonable expectation of privacy in car appeared to be more soundly based).

84. United States v. Gottschalk, 915 F.2d 1459 (10th Cir. 1990) (sufficient if vehicles appear, based on objectively reasonable indicia, to be controlled by owner of premises).

circumstances if there is probable cause to search it, as discussed in Chapter 3.[85]

If officers know that a vehicle may contain evidence that they are searching for, they should describe it specifically in the search warrant as an object to be searched so that (1) they need not rely on the implicit authority to search it if it is on the premises when they execute the warrant, and (2) they may search the vehicle under the authority of the warrant even if it is not on the premises but is parked nearby (on a public street, for example).[86]

The description "all vehicles present on the premises" is generally invalid unless there is probable cause to believe that all vehicles on the premises would contain the items to be seized.[87] However, if the description is invalid, it would not affect the legality of a search of those vehicles under the occupant's control because, as discussed above, they may be searched without being specifically described in the warrant.

Outbuildings on the Premises

Generally, a search warrant to search premises authorizes the executing officers to search all outbuildings (unattached garage, storage building, and so forth) within the curtilage of the premises, even though they are not specifically named in the warrant as places to be searched, if the evidence to be seized may reasonably be found there.[88] Officers who know that outbuildings are on the premises may want to name them specifically in the application as places to be searched—or at least mention them gener-

ally as "outbuildings"—so that the officers have explicit authority to search them, particularly if the outbuildings are on the premises but beyond the curtilage.[89]

Multiple Occupants in the Structure(s)

A search warrant for an apartment, duplex, or other structure in which separate living units are maintained must particularly describe the unit within the structure for which there is probable cause to search—unless, of course, there is probable cause to search the entire structure.[90] The description should include the street address and apartment number or other means of identifying the particular unit to be searched—for example, "880 Davis Drive, Bellow, N.C., Apartment 2, the front right apartment occupied by Clarence and Patrice Mantle."

A search warrant for a home of a named owner does not authorize a search of a separate rented room within the home or a separate rented building on the property that the renter exclusively occupies and uses.[91] Thus, if there is probable cause to search the entire home and separate buildings, the search warrant should specifically name them and their possessors—or separate search warrants could be issued for each. But if the possessor of a separate room or building did not have exclusive control of it, or if the affiant or executing officers did not reasonably know about the multiple occupancy, a search warrant that describes the entire premises would be valid.[92]

---

85. *See* 2 Wayne R. LaFave, Search and Seizure: A Treatise on the Fourth Amendment § 4.10(c), at 958 (5th ed. 2012).

86. State v. Ward, 712 A.2d 534 (Md. 1998) (single search warrant for premises and car in custody of law enforcement was valid); 2 Wayne R. LaFave, Search and Seizure: A Treatise on the Fourth Amendment § 4.5(c), at 745 (5th ed. 2012).

87. *See* 2 Wayne R. LaFave, Search and Seizure: A Treatise on the Fourth Amendment § 4.5(d), at 750–52 (5th ed. 2012).

88. State v. Trapper, 48 N.C. App. 481 (1980); State v. Travatello, 24 N.C. App. 511 (1975); United States v. Griffin, 827 F.2d 1108 (7th Cir. 1987) (search warrant's description of "premises" at specific address authorized the search of tool shed and yard there, including digging in yard, when the object of search—drugs, chemicals and chemical equipment, and notes and formulas—could reasonably be found there); United States v. Bertrand, 926 F.2d 838 (9th Cir. 1991) (search warrant supported search of outlying real property, based on information in affidavit).

89. United States v. Alexander, 761 F.2d 1294 (9th Cir. 1985) (search warrant for all buildings on 40-acre ranch to search for cocaine included unspecified small trailer, when all buildings on ranch were under common control).

90. *See generally* 2 Wayne R. LaFave, Search and Seizure: A Treatise on the Fourth Amendment § 4.5(b) (5th ed. 2012). *But see* Maryland v. Garrison, 480 U.S. 79 (1987) (search warrant's description and its execution did not violate defendant's Fourth Amendment rights because it was objectively reasonable that officers failed to realize the warrant's overbroad description of the third floor apartment—officers reasonably did not know that third floor contained two apartments, not just one).

91. State v. Mills, 246 N.C. 237 (1957). This requirement does not apply when there is joint occupancy of areas within the premises; *see* State v. Woodard, 35 N.C. App. 605 (1978). Also note that a search warrant's description and execution may still be reasonable under the Fourth Amendment based on the ruling in *Maryland v. Garrison*, summarized *supra* note 90, when officers make a reasonable mistake in believing the house is entirely occupied by one person or family. See State v. Woodard, *supra*, decided before *Garrison* but consistent with it.

92. Maryland v. Garrison, 480 U.S. 79 (1987); State v. Woodard, 35 N.C. App. 605 (1978). *See generally* 2 Wayne R.

Multiple Structures on Separate Property

A search warrant to search premises occupied by a person does not authorize officers to search other separate premises. For example, if Fred Jones is selling drugs from his home and from his private business located several miles away, a search warrant that names only his home would not authorize a search of the business. If the facts in the affidavit establish probable cause to search both places, one search warrant could be used to search both if it particularly described them both.[93] Or a separate search warrant could be obtained for each place.

The Person

If the facts establishing probable cause indicate that (1) a particular person is involved in the crime being investigated, (2) the person may be on the premises when they are searched, and (3) the evidence may be hidden on the person, the application block should be checked to request authority to search for the evidence "on the following person(s)" as well as in the premises. The person should be particularly described. The easiest way to distinguish one person from another is by a name. If a person is using an alias, the alias may be used if it will help officers distinguish who is to be searched. If the name is questionable or completely unknown, a physical description of the person should be given—approximate age, sex, height, weight, race, and the like. If officers who have been investigating the case can identify the unknown person and will assist in executing the warrant, a conditional description might be used—for example, "a white male, approximately age 40, 6 ft., 170 lbs., to be identified by Detective Sylvia Goode when the officers enter the premises." Because this is a search warrant and not an arrest warrant, the description need not be quite as specific. It only needs to be sufficiently specific to allow officers to be reasonably certain in identifying the person to be searched.

If a warrant specifically authorizes a search of a person in addition to the premises, the person may be searched on or off the premises, as discussed above for vehicles. For example, if a warrant authorizes the search of a house, a vehicle, and a person, and the officers see the vehicle and the person two blocks before they reach the house, they can search the vehicle and the person there under the authority of the warrant and then search the house.[94]

The description "all persons present" in the premises to be searched generally is not justified, unless the facts in the affidavit provide probable cause to believe that anyone in the premises would have on his or her person the evidence that is being sought.[95]

Even when a person is not named to be searched in a warrant, executing officers have authority, under certain circumstances, to detain, frisk, or search persons present during a search of the premises and other structures. And sometimes officers will have probable cause to arrest a person there, which will allow them to make a full search of that person incident to the arrest. This subject is discussed later in this chapter.

The Vehicle

If a warrant authorizes the search of a vehicle, either alone or in connection with a search of premises (see discussion above), the vehicle must be particularly described. The description should contain the license plate number or vehicle identification number, if known, and any other information that will enable executing officers to identify the car to be searched. This information may include the owner, year, model, color, and any unique characteristics.

See page 420 for a discussion of the description "all vehicles present."

Other Places or Items to Be Searched

The blank space in the application that is located below the description of vehicles may be used when the place or item to be searched is not on the premises, on a person, or in a vehicle. For example, officers may seize luggage during a drug investigation and may need—or simply desire—the authority of a search warrant to search it.

LaFave, Search and Seizure: A Treatise on the Fourth Amendment § 4.5(b) (5th ed. 2012).

93. *See generally* 2 Wayne R. LaFave, Search and Seizure: A Treatise on the Fourth Amendment § 4.5(c) (5th ed. 2012).

94. *See generally id.* § 4.5(c), at 745.

95. *See generally id.* § 4.5(e), at 758–62. *Compare* State v. Jackson, 616 N.W.2d 412 (S.D. 2000) (search warrant permitting search of "all persons present" was valid as to defendant who was searched; affidavit provided sufficient evidence to show that there was good reason to believe that anyone present would probably be participant in illegal drug activities in house), *and* United States v. Abbott, 574 F.3d 203 (3d Cir. 2009), *aff'd on other issue*, 562 U.S. 8 (2010) (probable cause supported search of all persons present), *with* Marks v. Clarke, 102 F.3d 1012 (9th Cir. 1996) (search warrant's authorization to search "any persons on the premises" was not supported by probable cause).

They could describe the luggage as follows: "Dark brown, Samsonite luggage, initials 'Q' and 'R' on top, American Airlines identification tag 'Quincy Reynolds, 413 East Main Street, Muncey, N.C.' Luggage now in possession of Detective Arthur Betters of the Muncey Police Department."

Statement of Facts Showing Probable Cause to Search
Definition

Probable cause is the legal phrase describing the state of facts or amount of information that must exist before a search warrant may be issued. The application for a search warrant must contain a written statement of facts showing that there is probable cause to believe that the evidence being sought is in the place to be searched.

Probable cause is a fluid concept that depends on an assessment of probabilities in particular situations, and it cannot be readily reduced to a neat set of legal rules. The degree of certainty corresponding to probable cause is *fair probability,* which means that more proof is required than reasonable suspicion but *less* proof than such legal evidentiary standards as preponderance of evidence, more probable than not, more likely than not, prima facie evidence, clear and convincing evidence, or beyond a reasonable doubt.[96] A magistrate's duty is to make a practical, commonsense decision on whether, given all the circumstances set forth in the affidavit—including hearsay information—there is a "fair probability" that evidence of a crime will be found in a particular place.[97] In considering whether information establishes probable cause, courts place great weight on officers' observations and conclusions about criminal activity that are based on their training and experience.[98]

Because probable cause to search depends on the probability that evidence of a crime may be in a certain place, the *timeliness* of the information that supports prob-

able cause is critical. Information may become stale and therefore less valuable. Thus, although probable cause may exist at a particular time to search a house for illegal drugs, there may no longer be probable cause at a later time if it is no longer *probable* that the drugs are still in the house. Probable cause to search also focuses on the *place* where evidence of a crime probably is located. Even when information is timely, it must give a magistrate enough facts to support a fair probability that the evidence will be found where the officer wants to search. For example, the fact that a person is selling drugs from his or her house does not automatically provide probable cause to believe that drugs may be found at the person's place of business—in some cases, however, evidence may support a finding that there is probable cause to search the business. Both concepts—that the information must be timely and that it must connect the evidence to be seized with the place to be searched—are discussed in more detail later in this chapter.

It is worth repeating here that North Carolina law requires that all the information used to establish probable cause must be either stated in the application or summarized in writing or recorded when the warrant is issued.[99] If the officer who is applying for the warrant gives the magistrate information that is not written in the application or is not recorded or summarized when the warrant is issued, the information will not be considered at a later court proceeding to determine whether there was probable cause to search.

Sources of Information to Establish Probable Cause
(*See page 487 for case summaries on this topic.*)

Probable cause may be established with information from several sources:

- Personal observations of the officer-affiant who applies for the warrant, considered in light of the officer's training and experience
- Hearsay information from people who may or may not be named in the officer's affidavit
- Information from records

These sources of information, or any particular combination of them, need not all be present in each statement of probable cause. It is the total effect of whatever combination is used that must establish probable cause.

---

96. State v. Crawford, 125 N.C. App. 279 (1997); United States v. Garcia, 179 F.3d 265 (5th Cir. 1999).

97. Illinois v. Gates, 462 U.S. 213 (1983).

98. *See, e.g.,* Illinois v. Gates, 462 U.S. 213 (1983); United States v. Martin, 920 F.2d 393 (6th Cir. 1990); United States v. Wylie, 919 F.2d 969 (5th Cir. 1990). *See generally* 2 WAYNE R. LaFave, SEARCH AND SEIZURE: A TREATISE ON THE FOURTH AMENDMENT § 3.2(c) (5th ed. 2012).

---

99. G.S. 15A-245(a); State v. Hicks, 60 N.C. App. 116 (1982).

Affiant's Personal Observations

Generally. The easiest way for an officer-affiant to establish probable cause is to use facts the officer knows from personal observations. These facts may directly establish probable cause—for example, if the officer makes an undercover purchase of illegal drugs at a suspect's home and learns that the suspect has more drugs available for sale. Or the officer's observations may indirectly help establish probable cause—for example, if the officer partially corroborates an informant's information that the suspect is selling stolen goods from a motel room by going there and seeing the suspect's car parked near the room.

An officer should clearly indicate in the application that he or she personally made the observation. The officer should provide enough detail to show that he or she carefully observed the particular activity and should state when the observations were made. For example, in a search warrant for illegal drugs, the statement of probable cause might include a sentence like this:

> The suspect, Ronald Jones, has been observed on several occasions carrying from his automobile into the house clear plastic bags containing a green vegetable matter that appeared to be marijuana.

However, a better way of phrasing the same information would be like this:

> On December 26, 2010, at about 4 p.m., and on December 27, 2010, at about 8 p.m., with the aid of binoculars, I saw the suspect, Ronald Jones, carrying clear plastic bags containing a green vegetable matter that appeared to be marijuana from the automobile in his driveway into his house.

The second statement takes a little more time to write than the first, but it is preferable for several reasons:

1. It makes clear that the officer personally made the observations and is not simply passing along information the officer heard from someone else
2. The dates indicate that the observations were made recently, and it is therefore more likely that the evidence is still in the place to be searched
3. The second statement establishes better than the first that the officer was a careful observer

An officer's statement of probable cause should be detailed so that a magistrate may determine probable cause independently and need not rely on the officer's conclusions. Thus. the magistrate should be informed of the officer's observations, not just the officer's conclusions from his or her observations. In both versions above, the officer described seeing the suspect carrying plastic bags containing a green vegetable matter. The officer supplied facts and not just an opinion that the suspect was carrying marijuana. The officer also could add that from training and experience, the officer knows that plastic bags are commonly used to carry marijuana, and he or she can correctly identify marijuana. The United States Supreme Court has clearly stated that evidence considered for probable cause determinations must be understood in light of a law enforcement officer's training and experience.[100]

With all this information—along with any other information the officer might have—a magistrate can decide whether it is fairly probable that marijuana will be found in that house. The magistrate can assess the value of the facts independently rather than simply rely on the officer's conclusions.

Each time officers apply for a search warrant, they should try to record the following information:

- Who made the observation
- When the observation was made
- How the observation was made
- The facts of the observation, not just a conclusion
- In light of the officer's training and experience, how the observation helps reveal evidence of criminal activity

Officers should follow this procedure for recording the information they receive from others as well as for their own observations.

Unconstitutionally obtained or false information. Officers should be aware that they may not use information they have obtained as a direct result of a constitutional violation. For example, if officers enter the curtilage of a dwelling without appropriate constitutional justification and obtain information that they use to establish probable cause, a later reviewing court will not consider that information in determining whether the search warrant

---

100. Illinois v. Gates, 462 U.S. 213 (1983). *See generally* 2 Wayne R. LaFave, Search and Seizure: A Treatise on the Fourth Amendment § 3.2(c) (5th ed. 2012).

was supported by probable cause.[101] Officers also should be aware that if they knowingly or recklessly provide false information in an affidavit, not only are they subject to a prosecution for perjury, but the false information also cannot be considered in establishing probable cause.[102]

Affiant's Use of Hearsay Information

There is little difficulty when an officer's personal observations alone are used to establish probable cause, because the magistrate may question the officer if the magistrate has any doubt about the officer's observations. Problems may arise, however, when hearsay information (information from another person) is used, although hearsay information is clearly admissible in determining probable cause.[103] The report passes through at least one person before it reaches the magistrate, and the possibility that some of the information will be conveyed inaccurately is therefore increased. Because the person who made the observation is not present, the magistrate cannot ask questions about any ambiguities or assess the person's truthfulness by observing the person's demeanor.

Whether or not officers name the person who gave them hearsay information, they should make clear who gave them the particular information described in the affidavit, and they should say when they received that information. Of course, officers also should provide the other information discussed above, such as when the person made the observation, how the observation was made, and the like.

Information from other officers. An officer applying for a search warrant may state information in the affidavit that the officer has received from another officer without establishing that officer's reliability, because an officer is automatically considered to be reliable.[104] But if the other officer's information includes, for example, a report from a confidential informant, the applying officer usually needs to show why the informant or the informant's information is reliable and how the informant obtained the information (see the discussion on page 426 on using an informant's information).

Although not legally required, the other officer could appear before the magistrate and complete his or her own affidavit, which would then be attached to the application.[105]

Information from victims, witnesses, and other citizen-informants. When officers use information they have received from a confidential informant—someone who is involved in criminal activity or is associated with the criminal environment—they have a greater burden to show that the person is credible or the person's information is reliable than when they receive information from a crime victim, witness, or other citizen-informant.[106]

Generally, officers applying for a search warrant may state information in the affidavit that they have received from a crime victim, witness, or other citizen-informant without indicating that person's credibility or reliability, unless the person has a motive to falsify information or unless other circumstances indicate that the person's credibility or information is questionable.[107] However, officers can strengthen a statement in an affidavit by

---

101. *See generally* 6 Wayne R. LaFave, Search and Seizure: A Treatise on the Fourth Amendment § 11.4(f) (5th ed. 2012); United States v. Karo, 468 U.S. 705 (1984); State v. Lombardo, 306 N.C. 594 (1982), *later appeal,* 74 N.C. App. 460 (1985); State v. Barbee, 34 N.C. App. 66 (1977).

102. Franks v. Delaware, 438 U.S. 154 (1978); State v. Severn, 130 N.C. App. 319 (1998) (officer's false information used in search warrant); State v. Vick, 130 N.C. App. 207 (1998) (officer's information used in search warrant was not false); United States v. Kirk, 781 F.2d 1498 (11th Cir. 1986).

103. Jones v. United States, 362 U.S. 257 (1960); Draper v. United States, 358 U.S. 327 (1960); Illinois v. Gates, 462 U.S. 213 (1983). *See also* State v. Roberts, 276 N.C. 98 (1970); Melton v. Hodges, 114 N.C. App. 795 (1994); 2 Wayne R. LaFave, Search and Seizure: A Treatise on the Fourth Amendment § 3.2(d), at 69 (5th ed. 2012). Under Rules 104(a) and 1101(b)(1) of the North Carolina Rules of Evidence set out in G.S. 8C-1, the rules of evidence do not apply in a hearing that determines the admissibility of evidence, except rules concerning privileges.

104. United States v. Ventresca, 380 U.S. 102 (1965); State v. Vestal, 278 N.C. 561 (1971); State v. Horner, 310 N.C. 274 (1984); State v. Crawford, 104 N.C. App. 591 (1991).

105. G.S. 15A-244(3) & -246(3).

106. State v. Sanders, 327 N.C. 319 (1990) (court, in analyzing information from a citizen-informant to establish probable cause, stated that law does not demand of private citizens who voluntarily assist law enforcement same standards of reliability applicable to paid informants; citizen-informant may be entitled to greater degree of credibility than habitual informant); State v. Martin, 315 N.C. 667 (1986); United States v. Fooladi, 703 F.2d 180 (5th Cir. 1983), *later appeal,* 746 F.2d 1027 (5th Cir. 1984). *See generally* 2 Wayne R. LaFave, Search and Seizure: A Treatise on the Fourth Amendment § 3.4(a) (5th ed. 2012).

107. *See supra* note 106. *But see* Hale v. Fish, 899 F.2d 390 (5th Cir. 1990) (victim who was eyewitness had motive to lie; no automatic reliability).

showing why the person who gave the information is truthful and why the information is reliable. Although officers need not reveal the person's name (they may want to state the reason—for example, the person fears for his or her personal safety), the information may be more valuable if they do.[108] If officers do not reveal the person's name, they ordinarily must provide more corroboration of that person's truthfulness or the reliability of the information.[109] The fact that the person is willing to give his or her name is usually considered to increase the likelihood that the information is true. If the person's identity is revealed, the magistrate may know the person or the person's reputation and be better able to judge the reliability of the information. Even if the magistrate does not know the person, revealing something about the person's standing in the community can help back up the information. When information is used from such a person, the same rules should be followed as when officers describe their own observations—when the observation was made, how it was made, and the like. For example, an application for a search warrant might include a summary statement like this:

> Last weekend a witness told me that suspect Robert Graham had stolen goods in his possession, which included a television set and a DVD player.

However, a better way to state the same information would be like this:

> On October 22, 2016, Raymond Price, the manager of Ray's Grocery Store, was approached near his store by suspect Robert Graham, who offered to sell him a 19-inch SONY television set for $75 and a DVD player for $20.

Including the kind of detail in the second statement has several advantages. Identifying the person and his position in the community strengthens the information because it provides a basis for judging trustworthiness. Also, the detail clearly shows that the person made the observation and is not just passing on a rumor heard from

someone else; third-hand information is less reliable. Giving the date and describing the goods indicates that the person carefully remembered his interaction with the suspect, and it makes the information more believable. These details also indicate that officers investigated the case carefully and that they listened closely to what the witness said and recorded it precisely. If officers were that careful about this part of their investigation, they probably were as careful about the rest of their information, and it is probably reliable. Finally, using detail about the suspect's goods may make it possible to corroborate the report. Perhaps a house near the grocery store was burglarized that Saturday and these kinds of goods were stolen. Corroborating a detail that may be unimportant by itself (for example, that the television set had a 19-inch screen) makes it more likely that the other parts of the account are also true. This example gives more detail than officers ordinarily will want to include or will have time to write down in an application, but it illustrates the benefits of recording information precisely.

Although not legally required, a witness could appear before the magistrate and complete an affidavit, which would then be attached to the application.[110]

Information from confidential informants. Information from any source may be used to help establish probable cause to search, whether or not the person's name is revealed.[111] However, information from a confidential informant generally has less value unless an officer corroborates all or part of the information.

The two-pronged test for informants. In the 1960s, the United States Supreme Court established a test, commonly known as the "two-pronged test," to determine the sufficiency of an affidavit that is based on information from a confidential informant.[112] The test required that the affidavit (1) establish the informant's *basis of knowledge*—the particular means by which the informant obtained his or her information—and (2) provide facts establishing either the informant's *credibility* or the specific *reliability* of the information.

In the 1980s, the Court abandoned the two-pronged test because it had become too technical and complex and had not applied a commonsense judgment about

---

108. State v. Eason, 328 N.C. 409 (1991) (court ruled that the fact that citizen-informant—who was the mother of the defendant—was named in search warrant's affidavit provided magistrate with sufficient information to determine that citizen-informant was reliable).

109. *See generally* 2 Wayne R. LaFave, Search and Seizure: A Treatise on the Fourth Amendment § 3.4(a) (5th ed. 2012).

110. G.S. 15A-244(3) & -246(3).

111. Jones v. United States, 362 U.S. 257 (1960).

112. Spinelli v. United States, 393 U.S. 410 (1969); Aguilar v. Texas, 378 U.S. 108 (1964).

the value of an informant's information.[113] Instead, the Court adopted a totality of the circumstances analysis of probable cause that examines the entire affidavit, gives appropriate weight to each relevant piece of information, and assesses the various indications of reliability or unreliability in an informant's report. Essentially, the Court made it easier to establish probable cause under this new standard than under the two-pronged test.

Although officers no longer have to satisfy the two-pronged test, they should still attempt to comply with it when they prepare their affidavits. By satisfying the test, they can be more confident that the informant's information (1) will be given the weight it deserves and (2) adequately establishes probable cause by itself or contributes to a finding of probable cause when it is considered with the other information in the affidavit.

Informant's credibility or the reliability of the informant's information. Officers can support a confidential informant's information in several ways when they attempt to show that the informant is credible or that the information is reliable.[114] One way is to show that the informant has previously given correct information: if the informant told the truth before, it is somewhat more likely that the informant is telling the truth now. (This factor is discussed in more detail below.)

Another way to support a confidential informant is to prove that part of his or her information is true: if part of the information can be corroborated, it is more likely that the rest of the information is true. For example, if the informant said that Joseph Liske is selling drugs from his house at 123 E. Main Street, officers help corroborate that information if they state that they went to the house and saw the name "Liske" on the mailbox. Still another way to enhance credibility is to show that the informant is making a statement against his or her penal interest—that is, the informant is admitting involvement in the crime being investigated or some other crime. Court cases recognize that a person does not lightly admit a crime and give incriminating evidence to law enforcement officers;

thus, an informant's admission of involvement in a crime gives credibility to his or her information.[115] Finally, the way an informant's information is given can by itself enhance its credibility. Detailed information can show that the informant personally made the observation, the information is recent, and the observation was made carefully.[116]

The most common way to support a confidential informant's information is to show that the informant previously has given information that was reliable—whether it was simply investigative information about drug activity in the community or information that led to arrests or convictions.[117] Whether or not the informant has previously supplied information, his or her information can be used to help establish probable cause[118]—but an officer's lack of experience with a first-time informant generally means that the rest of the statement of probable cause will need to be stronger than if the person has been used many times before. If the informant has previously given information, officers should state something about the use of that information rather than simply stating that the informant is "reliable" and "has given good information in the past." Some indication should be given of the kinds of cases for which the informant gave information, when those took place, and what the results were—although this amount of detail is not normally legally required.

One way to keep an informant's track record readily available is to maintain records that show each informant's code name or an identifying number, the dates on which the informant gave information, the cases in which the information was used, whether the information was accurate, and any other relevant data about the informant. By keeping such records current, officers will

---

113. *Illinois v. Gates*, 462 U.S. 213 (1983); *Massachusetts v. Upton*, 466 U.S. 727 (1984). In *State v. Arrington*, 311 N.C. 633 (1984), the North Carolina Supreme Court adopted the reasoning of these two cases for determining probable cause under Article I, Section 20, of the Constitution of North Carolina.

114. *See, e.g.,* State v. Riggs, 328 N.C. 213 (1991). An officer could also bring the informant before the issuing judicial official to submit to questioning by that official. United States v. Lloyd, 71 F.3d 1256 (7th Cir. 1995).

115. United States v. Harris, 403 U.S. 573 (1971); State v. Arrington, 311 N.C. 633 (1984); State v. Beam, 325 N.C. 217 (1989); State v. Milloway, 94 N.C. App. 579 (1989).

116. Under the technical rules of the two-pronged test, self-verifying detail in an informant's report could not satisfy the "credibility" prong. See footnote 4 in the majority opinion in *Illinois v. Gates*, 462 U.S. 213 (1983). Now that these technical rules have been abandoned, a court may consider a detailed report for whatever value it adds under a totality of circumstances analysis.

117. An informant's past information that led to arrests—even if no convictions followed—may be sufficient to establish an informant's reliability. State v. Arrington, 311 N.C. 633 (1984); State v. Hayes, 291 N.C. 293 (1976).

118. United States v. Delario, 912 F.2d 766 (5th Cir. 1990) (use of first-time informant's information).

have a readily accessible means of establishing their informants' reliability. When a warrant application requires the use of a particular informant's report, officers can check these records to assist in completing the application and to enhance its accuracy.

Informant's basis of knowledge. After showing why an informant is credible or why his or her information is reliable, officers should show how the informant obtained the information—that is, the basis of the informant's knowledge. It is important to state not only how the informant obtained the information ("the informant saw the drugs in the house") but also when the informant obtained it ("the informant saw the drugs in the house within the past 48 hours") and when the informant told the officer about it ("the informant told me this morning, December 24, 2001, that the informant saw the drugs in the house within the past 48 hours"). One way to describe an informant's basis of knowledge would be like this:

> A confidential informant told me that Peter Jones has marijuana at his mobile home and is selling it there. The informant advised me that the informant had purchased marijuana from Peter Jones.

However, a better way would be like this:

> A confidential informant told me this morning, December 24, 2011, that Peter Jones has marijuana at his mobile home and is selling it there. The informant advised me that the informant had purchased marijuana within the past 48 hours from Peter Jones at his mobile home, and Jones indicated to the informant that he was willing to sell more.

Note that the second statement is more detailed than the first because it tells when the informant gave the officer the information, when the informant purchased the marijuana, and where the marijuana was purchased, and it then indicates that Jones has more marijuana in the mobile home. The second statement's greater detail makes it more valuable in showing probable cause to search the mobile home, and it supports the informant's conclusion that marijuana is in the mobile home. Although the first statement may help establish probable cause when considered with additional information,[119] its lack of detail reduces its value.

When an informant's identity is revealed. North Carolina law provides that a defendant is not entitled to learn of an informant's identity if an officer used the informant's information to support a probable cause statement in a search warrant.[120] However, some evidence of an informant's existence (other than from the officer who used the informant) must be given when the information is used to justify a warrantless search.[121] This may be accomplished by asking an officer—other than the officer who received the information from the informant—to talk with the informant before the suppression hearing to verify that the informant in fact is the person who gave the officer the information that led to the warrantless search. Or the other officer may have listened to the conversation between the officer and the informant when the person gave the information that led to the search.

Although probable cause can be established without revealing the confidential informant's name, in some cases the prosecution may be forced either to reveal an informant's name at trial or to dismiss the case. That may occur when the defendant needs to know the informant's identity to assist in the defense at trial—as, for example, when the informant is a material witness to a drug transaction for which the defendant is being tried.[122]

Information from records. Records are a final source of information that may be used to establish probable cause. The records most often used are those showing prior convictions.[123] Although a prior conviction by itself does not establish probable cause, the fact that a person has been convicted of the same or a similar offense increases the likelihood of involvement in the offense being investi-

---

119. *See* State v. Arrington, 311 N.C. 633 (1984).

120. G.S. 15A-978(b)(1); State v. Creason, 313 N.C. 122 (1985); State v. Carver, 70 N.C. App. 555 (1984); State v. Caldwell, 53 N.C. App. 1 (1981); State v. Roseboro, 55 N.C. App. 205 (1981). *See generally* McCray v. Illinois, 386 U.S. 300 (1967).

121. G.S. 15A-978(b)(2); State v. Ellis, 50 N.C. App. 181 (1980); State v. Bunn, 36 N.C. App. 114 (1978); State v. Collins, 44 N.C. App. 141, *aff'd*, 300 N.C. 142 (1980). An alternative approach consists of the judge conducting an in camera hearing with only the judge, prosecutor, and informant present. *See* 2 WAYNE R. LaFAVE, SEARCH AND SEIZURE: A TREATISE ON THE FOURTH AMENDMENT § 3.3(g), at 262–63 (5th ed. 2012).

122. State v. Jackson, 103 N.C. App. 239 (1991), *aff'd*, 331 N.C. 113 (1992); State v. Cameron, 283 N.C. 191 (1973); State v. Johnson, 81 N.C. App. 454 (1986); State v. Hodges, 51 N.C. App. 229 (1981); State v. Ketchie, 286 N.C. 387 (1975). *See generally* Rovario v. United States, 353 U.S. 53 (1957).

123. *See generally* 2 WAYNE R. LaFAVE, SEARCH AND SEIZURE: A TREATISE ON THE FOURTH AMENDMENT § 3.2(d) (5th ed. 2012).

gated. If that fact assists in supporting probable cause, the suspect's specific convictions should be stated rather than a vague phrase such as "known drug dealer" or "known thief." One way this information may be stated is as follows: "Suspect David Lyle has, in the last four years, been convicted of possessing stolen goods and felonious larceny." The dates of the convictions may also be given. Information about prior arrests that did not result in convictions or have not yet come to trial may be used, but it has less value than conviction information.[124]

Other information from records could include law enforcement data on a suspect's activities that have not resulted in criminal charges. For example, an officer who is seeking a warrant to search a suspect's house for drugs may know from other law enforcement officers that the suspect has often been present where drug transactions frequently take place. Even though the officer who is completing the application does not personally know this information, it can be used. Obviously, this secondhand information of noncriminal activity may not by itself establish probable cause, but it may help somewhat in establishing probable cause under the totality of circumstances analysis.

Although a suspect's reputation for involvement in criminal activity may be considered in establishing probable cause, its vagueness makes it less valuable than the information discussed above.[125]

Finally, records from sources not associated with criminal activity may also be useful. For example, information from a telephone company or the city water department may be useful in showing that the suspect lives at the place to be searched.

Timeliness or Staleness of Information

(See page 484 for case summaries on this topic.)

Because probable cause to search focuses on the probability, when a search warrant is issued, that certain evidence will be found at a particular place, the timeliness (or staleness) of the information allegedly establishing probable cause is important. For example, if an officer receives information on December 20 that a certain car contains money taken from an armed robbery committed on December 19, probable cause to search that car will not exist one year later—absent unusual circumstances—because it is then no longer likely that the money is still in the car.

There are no simple rules for determining whether information has become too stale to support a finding of probable cause. The probability that evidence will still be found in a particular place cannot be measured by a particular number of days or weeks. How recently the information was observed is obviously important. Other factors[126] to consider are the following:

- The nature of the criminal activity: Is it a continuing activity, like the sale of drugs, or one isolated event?[127]

---

124. *Id.*; Brinegar v. United States, 407 U.S. 143 (1949); State v. Arrington, 311 N.C. 633 (1984); State v. Hayes, 291 N.C. 293 (1976).

125. *Compare* United States v. Harris, 403 U.S. 573 (1971) (court ruled that reputation evidence may be considered), *with* Spinelli v. United States, 394 U.S. 410 (1969) (court ruled that reputation evidence was entitled to no weight). In light of the totality of circumstances analysis set out in *Illinois v. Gates*, 462 U.S. 213 (1983), *Harris* represents the prevailing view.

126. *See generally* 2 WAYNE R. LaFave, SEARCH AND SEIZURE: A TREATISE ON THE FOURTH AMENDMENT § 3.7(a), (b) (5th ed. 2012).

127. United States v. Harris, 403 U.S. 573 (1971) (reliable informant said that he had purchased illegal liquor from house for two years and most recently within past two weeks; information not stale); State v. Beam, 325 N.C. 217 (1989) (evidence of defendant's having one pound of marijuana a week before search warrant issued provided probable cause because either (1) it was for personal use and would not be consumed in one week or (2) it was for sale, which indicated ongoing drug activity); State v. Pickard, 178 N.C. App. 330 (2006) (information was not stale when it showed defendant's commission of ongoing sex crimes with children, and items to be seized were of continuing utility to defendant); State v. King, 44 N.C. App. 31 (1979) (pattern of drug sales at residence, last sale within two weeks of issuance of search warrant; information not stale); United States v. Rhynes, 206 F.3d 349 (4th Cir. 1999) (information in search warrant was not stale even though most recent drug trafficking or money laundering activities alleged in search warrant affidavit were over two years old; criminal enterprise had been ongoing for more than 20 years); United States v. Reyes, 798 F.2d 380 (10th Cir. 1986) (although search warrant for residence was issued five months after last drug transaction there, probable cause existed because there was ongoing drug conspiracy); United States v. Dozier, 844 F.2d 701 (9th Cir. 1988) (similar ruling); United States v. McNeese, 901 F.2d 585 (7th Cir. 1990) (similar ruling).

In *State v. Witherspoon*, 110 N.C. App. 413 (1993), the court ruled that a search warrant for the defendant's home was based on probable cause. The search warrant included the following information: A concerned citizen told officers that he had been in the defendant's home within the past 30 days and had seen

- The type of evidence to be seized: Is it perishable, easily transferable, useful for other purposes,[128] likely to be retained for long periods of time,[129] or highly incriminating and likely to be destroyed or removed?
- The place to be searched: Is it used for criminal activity? Is it a common storage area for the evidence or a convenient but transitory place to hide the evidence? What is the suspect's relationship to the place?

Essentially, a commonsense judgment must be made on whether the facts in a particular case support a fair probability that the evidence will be found in the place for which the search warrant is sought.[130]

It is helpful if the affidavit states when the officer's and others' observations were made, so that the issuing magistrate and a later reviewing court can more easily determine the weight to give them in determin-

ing probable cause.[131] A recurring issue is the timeliness of information to support a search of a home for drugs. A North Carolina case approved a search warrant for a home when the last reported sale of drugs occurred as long as two weeks before the date of the search warrant and a pattern of drug sales had taken place there.[132] Federal cases have approved search warrants for residences when drug transactions occurred several months before the warrants were issued, when the affidavits detailed the suspects' continuing drug trafficking activities up to the date the warrants were issued.[133] On the other hand, a North Carolina case disapproved a search warrant when it determined that drugs had last been seen in the home about a year before the search warrant was issued.[134] Each case is unique, and officers should not assume that these cases set either minimum or maximum time limits in determining the existence of probable cause.

The Connection between a Crime, the Evidence to Be Seized, and the Place to Be Searched

Even when information is timely, it must also link the crime, the evidence to be seized, and the place to be searched. The easiest way to connect them is by direct observation. For example, if an officer's confidential informant has recently observed drugs being sold in a particular house, the crime (possession of drugs), the evidence (drugs) to be seized, and the place (the house) to be searched have been sufficiently connected to authorize a search of the house. Normally, a sale of drugs at

---

about 100 marijuana plants in the home's crawl space that were growing with the use of a lighting system and automatic timers. The concerned citizen had spoken with the defendant often about the defendant's growing these plants, and the concerned citizen had used marijuana and had previously seen it growing. Officers corroborated the concerned citizen's information about the defendant's car that was parked in the defendant's driveway, and officers also checked power company's records that showed the defendant's paying the power bill for the house in the past six months. The court, relying on several cases, including *State v. Beam, supra*, rejected the defendant's argument that the information was stale because a concerned citizen had seen marijuana plants in the defendant's home within the last 30 days. The court noted that, based on the facts set out in the affidavit, the magistrate who issued the search warrant could reasonably infer that the marijuana would likely remain in the defendant's home for 30 days.

128. State v. Jones, 299 N.C. 298 (1980) (murder committed with hatchet and pipe and defendant was wearing welder's gloves when he committed the murder; information was not too stale to search house five months later because items were not incriminating by themselves and had general utility, and reasonably prudent magistrate could conclude that they were probably located where accomplice had said they were located).

129. Andresen v. Maryland, 427 U.S. 463 (1976) (business records prepared in ordinary course of business; three-month time period from completion of transactions to search of office with warrant was not too long); State v. Louchheim, 296 N.C. 314 (1979) (corporate documents kept in the course of business; 14 months since documents were seen in office until search of office with warrant was not too long).

130. State v. Riggs, 328 N.C. 213 (1991); State v. Crawford, 104 N.C. App. 591 (1991); State v. McCoy, 100 N.C. App. 574 (1990); State v. Jones, 299 N.C. 298 (1980).

131. State v. Cobb, 21 N.C. App. 66 (1974) (affidavit did not specify or imply when informant saw heroin in home, yet court stated that magistrate could "reasonably and realistically conclude" that informant observed heroin so recently that probable cause existed when warrant was issued).

132. State v. King, 44 N.C. App. 31 (1979).

133. United States v. McNeese, 901 F.2d 585 (7th Cir. 1990); United States v. Reyes, 798 F.2d 380 (10th Cir. 1986); United States v. Dozier, 844 F.2d 701 (9th Cir. 1988).

134. State v. Lindsey, 58 N.C. App. 564 (1982). The court, however, appeared to give little weight to some other pertinent facts in the case. This case was decided before *Illinois v. Gates*, 462 U.S. 213 (1983); it is unclear whether the decision would be the same under the *Gates* test.

a place supports an inference that more drugs may be found there.[135]

Direct observation is not the only way to connect the place with the crime and evidence to be seized. For example, assuming that the information is timely, court cases recognize that the proceeds from a burglary, breaking or entering, or robbery will likely be found in (1) the suspect's home or other place where the suspect is residing or from which the suspect may sell the proceeds, such as a business, and (2) under certain circumstances, the suspect's car.[136]

Court cases recognize that if a person is selling drugs on the street or other similar place, more drugs will be found at the place from which the person is operating— whether that place is a house, motel, or car—if that place is sufficiently implicated by showing, for example, that the seller went to the place before the sale, that a sale occurred in or near the place, or that other information supports an inference that drugs will be found there.[137]

Court cases recognize that drug traffickers may keep cash and records of their transactions at their residences, even if they are selling the drugs elsewhere, and, therefore, search warrants may be issued for their residences.[138] Each case will present a unique set of facts, but the essential question in every case is whether it is fairly probable, judging from the totality of the circumstances, that the evidence will be found in the place sought to be searched.

It is often helpful to state in the affidavit that a residence is the likely repository of one's personal possessions and—if factually appropriate—that the defendant is not known to keep any other residence, office, or storage facility. Thus, the issuing official may properly infer that the residence is the probable storage place for the evidence to be seized.

Future Events: Anticipatory Search Warrants

(See page 491 for case summaries on this topic.)

Sometimes officers may not have enough information to establish probable cause to search a place unless a particular event occurs. In such a case, officers may want to obtain what is commonly known as an anticipatory search warrant—that is, a search warrant that may be executed only if the event occurs.[139]

Officers may want to obtain an anticipatory search warrant (1) when they have intercepted a drug courier

---

135. *See* State v. Riggs, 328 N.C. 213 (1991); 2 Wayne R. LaFave, Search and Seizure: A Treatise on the Fourth Amendment § 3.7(d), at 530–31 (5th ed. 2012).

136. *See generally* 2 Wayne R. LaFave, Search and Seizure: A Treatise on the Fourth Amendment §3.7(d) (5th ed. 2012). *See also* State v. Whitely, 58 N.C. App. 539 (1982); State v. McKinnon, 306 N.C. 288 (1982); United States v. Laury, 985 F.2d 1293 (5th Cir. 1993); United States v. Jones, 994 F.2d 1051 (3d Cir. 1993); United States v. Jenkins, 901 F.2d 1075 (11th Cir. 1990); United States v. Grandstaff, 813 F.2d 1353 (9th Cir. 1987); United States v. Thomas, 973 F.2d 1152 (5th Cir. 1992).

137. *See generally* 2 Wayne R. LaFave, Search and Seizure: A Treatise on the Fourth Amendment § 3.7(d) (5th ed. 2012). *See also* State v. Riggs, 328 N.C. 213 (1991) (drug sales at driveway of residence supported search of residence); State v. McCoy, 100 N.C. App. 574 (1990) (drug sales at two other motel rooms within 10-day period supported search of another motel room); State v. Mavroganis, 57 N.C. App. 178 (1982) (although informant saw drugs only in college dormitory room, reasonable inference that drugs were also in defendant's car parked 100 yards from dorm); State v. Byrd, 60 N.C. App. 740 (1983) (premises sufficiently connected as storage place for drugs); United States v. Hodge, 246 F.3d 301 (1st Cir. 2001) (evidence of defendant's sale of drugs in same city in which he lived and that he was involved in the drug trade supplied probable cause to support search warrant of his home). *But see* State v. Campbell, 282 N.C. 125 (1972) (premises not sufficiently connected by affiant's conclusory statements); State v. Armstrong, 33 N.C. App. 52 (1977) (premises not sufficiently connected as place where drugs were located when sale of drugs occurred elsewhere); United States v. Lalor, 996 F.2d 1578 (4th Cir. 1993) (no evidence offered to link drugs sold on

street to support probable cause to believe drugs located in house).

138. United States v. Fanin, 817 F.2d 1379 (9th Cir. 1987) (search warrant was properly issued to search defendant's home for evidence of drug trafficking, even though defendant's only participation in drug transaction that occurred elsewhere was to supply money for it; magistrate may find probable cause to search home based on experienced drug agent's statement that drug traffickers keep records of transactions in their homes—even though there was no specific evidence in this case that defendant did so); United States v. Thomas, 989 F.2d 1252 (D.C. Cir. 1993); United States v. Suarez, 906 F.2d 977 (4th Cir. 1990); United States v. Pace, 955 F.2d 270 (5th Cir. 1992); United States v. Feliz, 182 F.3d 82 (1st Cir. 1999).

139. United States Supreme Court and North Carolina cases involving the use of anticipatory search warrants include *United States v. Grubbs*, 547 U.S. 90 (2006); *State v. Stallings*, 189 N.C. App. 376 (2008); *State v. Carrillo*, 164 N.C. App. 204 (2004); *State v. Baldwin*, 161 N.C. App. 382 (2003); *State v. Phillips*, 160 N.C. App. 549 (2003); *State v. Smith*, 124 N.C. App. 565 (1996).

who is about to deliver a package of illegal drugs to a residence and now want to control the delivery of the illegal drugs there, or (2) when a common carrier, such as Federal Express, has informed them that a package of illegal drugs has been discovered, and the common carrier will cooperate with law enforcement officers in making a delivery—or an undercover officer will make the delivery. The officers may allow the package or a substitute package to be delivered and then conduct a search of the premises with their anticipatory search warrant, which is to be executed only if the delivery takes place.

The North Carolina Court of Appeals in *State v. Smith* set out the requirements for the issuance of an anticipatory search warrant:[140]

1. An anticipatory search warrant must set out explicit, clear, and narrowly drawn triggering events that must occur before execution of the warrant may take place.
2. These triggering events, from which probable cause arises, must be ascertainable and preordained—that is, the property is on a sure and irreversible course to its destination (for example, an undercover officer will deliver the cocaine to the house to be searched).
3. A search may not occur unless and until the property does, in fact, arrive at that destination.

The court stated that these three conditions ensure that the required nexus between the criminal act, the evidence to be seized, and the identity of the place to be searched is achieved.

An example of what might be contained in an affidavit for an anticipatory search warrant to search premises, in addition to the statement establishing probable cause, is as follows:

I request that a search warrant for the premises described above be issued with its execution contingent on the following events having occurred: On August 14, 2016, an officer with the Smithville Police Department will pose as a Super Express employee and will deliver the package described above to the premises described above. The package—which is addressed to the premises described above—will contain a powdery substance containing a small amount of cocaine, with most of the cocaine having been removed when the package was previously intercepted as described in this affidavit. After the package is delivered to the above-described premises and is taken inside, this search warrant will be executed.

The United States Supreme Court and the North Carolina Court of Appeals have ruled that an anticipatory search warrant is sufficient when the affidavit instead of the warrant itself contains the contingency language if the warrant incorporates the affidavit by reference (which the AOC search warrant does).[141]

Restrictions on Issuing Search Warrants for Obscenity Offenses

North Carolina law provides that a search warrant may be issued to search for evidence of obscenity offenses set out in G.S. 14-190.1 (disseminating obscenity and other offenses), G.S. 14-190.4 (coercing acceptance of obscene materials), and G.S. 14-190.5 (preparing obscene materials) only on the request of a district attorney or an assistant district attorney.[142]

Examples of Statements of Probable Cause

The following summaries of statements of probable cause in search warrants should provide a better understanding of the information that is necessary to satisfy constitutional requirements.

---

140. 124 N.C. App. 565 (1996). The court ruled that anticipatory search warrants must meet the requirements set out in the text to satisfy the North Carolina Constitution (these requirements would also satisfy the Fourth Amendment under *United States v. Grubbs*, 547 U.S. 90 (2006)). The court also ruled that the search warrant in the case before it was not a valid anticipatory search warrant, based on the requirements for such a warrant. The court noted that the search warrant's most glaring deficiency was the absence of any language denoting it as anticipatory. For a discussion of anticipatory search warrants, see 2 Wayne R. LaFave, Search and Seizure: A Treatise on the Fourth Amendment § 3.7(c) (5th ed. 2012).

---

141. United States v. Grubbs, 547 U.S. 90 (2006); State v. Carrillo, 164 N.C. App. 204 (2004).

142. G.S. 14-190.20.

▬◀ Illinois v. Gates

On May 3, 1978, the police department in Bloomingdale, Illinois, received by mail an anonymous handwritten letter that said that the defendants (husband and wife), who lived in Bloomingdale, made their living by selling drugs. The letter stated that the wife, Sue Gates, regularly drove their car to Florida, loaded the car with drugs, and left it there. Then Lance Gates, the husband, flew down and drove it back, while his wife flew back. The letter then said that on May 3 she would drive to Florida and he would fly down a few days later to drive the car back. The letter stated that they had drugs worth over $100,000 in their basement. The police confirmed that the Gateses lived at the address identified in the letter and that L. Gates had reservations for a flight on May 5 from Chicago to West Palm Beach, Florida. Officers watched Gates board that flight, arrive in West Palm Beach, and check into a motel room registered to Susan Gates. The following day he and an unidentified woman left the motel in a car bearing Illinois license plates registered to Gates and drove north on an interstate highway that travelers frequently use in driving to the Chicago area. A judge issued a warrant for a search of the car and the Gateses' home.

The United States Supreme Court in *Illinois v. Gates*[143] ruled that this information established probable cause to search the car and the home. The officers' independent corroboration of the major portions of the anonymous letter's predictions established a fair probability that the writer of the anonymous letter had obtained information from the Gateses or someone they trusted. Responding to the argument that the officers simply corroborated innocent activity, the Court noted that the relevant inquiry is not whether the particular conduct is "innocent" or "guilty" but the degree of suspicion that surrounds particular kinds of noncriminal acts. The Court also noted that the one inaccuracy in the letter—that Sue Gates would fly back, when in fact she drove with her husband—did not undermine the letter as a whole. Informants need not be infallible. The Court concluded that there was a "substantial basis" to support the judge's decision to issue the search warrant.

▬◀ Massachusetts v. Upton

At noon on September 11, 1980, Lt. Beland of the police department in Yarmouth, Massachusetts, executed a search warrant for a motel room registered to Richard Kelleher. The search uncovered several items that belonged to people whose homes had been recently burglarized, but the stolen jewelry from the burglaries was not found. At 3:20 p.m. on the same day, Beland received a telephone call from an unidentified woman who told him that there was "a motor home full of stolen stuff," including jewelry, parked behind the home of the defendant and his mother. She said that the defendant (naming him) was soon going to move the motor home because Kelleher's motel room had been raided and the defendant had purchased these stolen items from him. The woman said that she had seen the stolen items, but she refused to identify herself because she believed that the defendant would kill her. Beland told her that he knew she was the defendant's girlfriend (giving her name), and she expressed surprise that he knew who she was. She said that she had broken up with the defendant and "wanted to burn him." Beland went to the defendant's house and verified that a motor home was parked on the property. A magistrate issued a search warrant to search the motor home.

The United States Supreme Court in *Massachusetts v. Upton*[144] ruled that this statement established probable cause to search the motor home. Although no single fact was conclusive, the pieces of information fit neatly together to support the magistrate's determination that there was a fair probability that evidence of a crime would be found in the motor home. The informant knew details about the earlier search and who had been in that motel room, had seen the stolen goods and described them, and explained the connection between the goods in the motel room and those in the defendant's motor home. She provided a motive for both her attempt to be anonymous (fear of the defendant) and her furnishing of information (her recent breakup with the defendant and desire to get even with him). The court also noted that Beland's inference that the informant was the defendant's girlfriend was reasonable and conformed with the other pieces of

---

143. 462 U.S. 213 (1983).

144. 466 U.S. 727 (1984).

information in his investigation. The magistrate had a "substantial basis" for issuing the search warrant.

State v. Arrington

On March 14, 1982, a county ABC enforcement officer applied for a search warrant to search the defendant's (Charles Arrington's) mobile home and truck for drugs. His affidavit stated the following:

> I received from a confidential source within the last forty-eight (48) hours that Charles Arrington had in his possession at his mobile home marijuana for sale. Confidential source advised that they had purchased marijuana from Charles Arrington. Source also advised that Arrington was growing marijuana in his home. A second confidential source advised that within the last twenty-four hours that there had been a steady flow of traffic to the Arrington home and also a steady flow of traffic for the past 2 months. The traffic is known to source as people that use drugs. The first source and second source has proven reliable in the past in that the first source has given information on numerous occasions in the past that has led to arrests. The second source has proven to be reliable in that I have known this source for many years and that they have furnished information not only to me but to other law enforcement officers that has proven to be reliable and arrests have been made.

The North Carolina Supreme Court ruled in *State v. Arrington*[145] that this statement established probable cause to issue the search warrant under the totality of circumstances analysis of *Illinois v. Gates* and *Massachusetts v. Upton*, discussed above. The first informant stated, against his penal interest, that he had purchased marijuana from the defendant, and in addition he said that the defendant was growing marijuana in his home. The court stated that these facts support the probability that the informant spoke with personal knowledge and that the marijuana would be found at the defendant's home. (Note that the officer could have improved the statement of probable cause by specifically indicating when and how the informant had obtained his information: when and where he had purchased the marijuana and how he

knew the defendant was growing marijuana in his home.) The court stated that the second informant's tip created a strong inference that the illegal activity was continuing and had occurred within the last 24 hours. (Note that the officer could have improved the statement if the officer had specifically indicated how the second informant had obtained his information and perhaps provided more details about the "traffic" going to the defendant's home.) The court also noted that both informants' reliability had been sufficiently shown, and it concluded that a "common sense reading of the information supplied by both informants provides a substantial basis for the *probability* that the defendant had sold marijuana, had grown it in his own home, and was continuing to sell it from his home to a steady flow of drug users within the last 24 hours. No more is required under the Fourth Amendment."

State v. Riggs

On March 25, 1987, an officer used a confidential informant to purchase marijuana from an unwitting middleman trusted by the defendants. The officer searched the informant to be sure the informant did not possess drugs and gave the informant $45 to make the purchase. The informant met with the unwitting middleman, and they both went by vehicle to the driveway of the defendants' residence. The informant then gave the middleman the $45, and the middleman "walked down the driveway" to the residence. The middleman returned to the vehicle and gave the informant marijuana, which was later turned over to the officer. On February 27, 1987, a similar purchase had been made by a different confidential informant. On that date, the informant had gone to the middleman's residence and given him $45. Officers watched as the middleman went to the defendants' residence and then returned to the middleman's residence, where the marijuana was given to the informant.

The officers obtained a search warrant on March 27, 1987, and searched the defendants' residence.

The North Carolina Supreme Court in *State v. Riggs*[146] ruled that the information established probable cause

---

145. 311 N.C. 633 (1984).

146. 328 N.C. 213 (1991). The court also ruled that it was irrelevant that the officer-affiant believed that one of his informants was not reliable because the informant had only made one prior controlled drug purchase—the officer thought

to search the defendants' residence, based on *Illinois v. Gates* and *State v. Arrington*. The defendants contended that probable cause to search the residence did not exist because the illegal drug transactions had occurred on the driveway; thus, there was no direct evidence that there were illegal drugs in the residence. The court rejected the defendants' contentions. A magistrate may draw reasonable inferences from available observations, particularly coupled with common or specialized experience. The court stated: "Where, as here, information before a magistrate indicates that suspects are operating, in essence, a short-order marijuana drive-through on their premises, the logical inference is that a cache of marijuana is located somewhere on those premises; that inference, in turn, establishes probable cause for a warrant to search the premises, including the residence."

➤ State v. Hyleman

The officer-affiant stated on July 25, 1986, that he purchased with marked money two ounces of cocaine from three people, who were arrested when they delivered the cocaine. (Although not stated in the application, the officer made a partial payment at 7:00 p.m., surveillance of the three people continued while they apparently looked for their cocaine supplier, and officers arrested them when they returned at 10:50 p.m. to complete the transaction.) The officer stated that from the time of the purchase to the time of the arrest the three people were kept under surveillance by officers, and that "from the movement of the suspects during, and before the purchase, and information received during the purchase, and information from two confidential sources of information after the purchase" the applicant has reason to believe that the marked money is in the residence of one of the defendants.

The North Carolina Supreme Court in *State v. Hyleman*[147] ruled that the statement was insufficient to establish probable cause. The court noted that the officer-

---

that two prior purchases were required to constitute reliability. The court noted that establishing the reliability of information is not limited to narrowly defined categories, and the officer's belief was a misunderstanding of the law.

147. 324 N.C. 506 (1989). The court ruled that the search warrant lacked probable cause under the requirements of G.S. 15A-244(3), which is the same standard as under the Fourth Amendment.

affiant failed to state what information he had received from the informants during and after the purchase of cocaine. The affidavit also failed to disclose any facts that would lead the officer or the magistrate to believe that the identified currency and cocaine were at the defendant's residence. The court also noted that evidence offered in court at the suppression hearing showed that, contrary to the affidavit's implication that the three drug sellers were under continuous surveillance, the officers had lost track of them for more than two hours.

➤ State v. Beam

The affidavit stated:

> A reliable informant who has provided accurate and reliable information in the past and whose information in the past has led to arrest and convictions under N.C. Controlled Substances Act has told the undersigned [officer] that [approximately] one week ago the informant saw Lilly Ann Beam with [approximately] one pound of marijuana at her home on Ridge Road. Another informant told the undersigned [officer] that Lilly Ann Beam sold marijuana to them on 02/07/87. Lilly Ann Beam is on probation for violation of [the] Controlled Substance[s] Act.

The officer obtained a search warrant on February 7, 1987, to search Lilly Ann Beam's residence.

The North Carolina Supreme Court in *State v. Beam*[148] ruled that this information was sufficient to establish probable cause to issue a search warrant, based on *Illinois v. Gates* and *State v. Arrington*. The court stated that the reliability of both informants was shown by (1) the first informant's having provided prior reliable information and (2) the second informant's statement against penal interest admitting that the informant purchased marijuana. (Note that the affidavit could have been improved by stating more about the second informant's reliability and specifying where Lilly Ann Beam sold the marijuana to the informant.) The court noted that a reliable informant saw the defendant with approximately one pound of marijuana at her home one week before the search warrant was issued. It stated:

> If the marijuana was for personal use, it is unlikely that she would consume such a large quantity

---

148. 325 N.C. 217 (1989).

in a week's time. Therefore, at least a portion of it would likely remain in her home a week later. On the other hand, if the marijuana was kept in defendant's home for purposes of sale, then the informants' tips, taken together, indicate that defendant was engaged in the ongoing criminal activity of selling marijuana. Under either scenario there was a substantial basis for the magistrate to conclude that there was a fair probability that marijuana would be found at defendant's residence on the date the warrant was issued.

— Aquilar v. Texas
The affidavit stated:

> *Affiants have received reliable information from a credible person and do believe that heroin, marijuana, barbiturates and other narcotics and narcotic paraphernalia are being kept at the [defendant's house] for the purpose of sale and use contrary to the provisions of law.*

The Houston, Texas, officers obtained a search warrant to search the defendant's house for narcotics.

The United States Supreme Court in *Aguilar v. Texas*[149] ruled—and, as to the finding of no probable cause in this case, reaffirmed in *Illinois v. Gates*—that this statement was insufficient to establish probable cause. It merely makes conclusory statements without providing facts that allow a magistrate to determine independently whether probable cause exists. A magistrate cannot simply ratify the officer's conclusions about facts. Instead, the officer must provide in the affidavit some of the underlying facts that support a conclusion that the evidence is in the place to be searched.

— State v. Heath
The affidavit stated:

> *The affiant has received information from concerned citizens who state that in the past week and the past 48 hours, they have seen and know that drugs are being sold at Apt. 3219-OE Will-O-Wisp Apartment and the concerned citizens want to remain anonymous. The concerned citizens reported that there is a large amount of traffic goin[g] and coming from the apartment*

> *and that the visitors stay only a few minutes at each and one given time.*

The statement then recited surveillance of the apartment by officers contained in an attached "affidavit," but in fact there were two attachments that were unsworn statements of officers that could not be considered in determining probable cause. In addition, at the suppression hearing the officer-affiant testified that the support for the first statement above was a telephone call from an anonymous informant in which she did not mention the 48-hour time frame or state that drugs were being sold at the location named in the affidavit. Rather, she said, "I know where there's a place in Kinston and a lot of drugs in there . . . I went over there one time but I didn't know it was that kind of place. . . ."

The North Carolina Court of Appeals in *State v. Heath*[150] ruled that the statement given above, considered with the officer-affiant's testimony at the suppression hearing, did not establish probable cause to issue a warrant to search the apartment under *Illinois v. Gates*. The statement was essentially a conclusion of "concerned citizens" without any underlying facts to support their conclusion or corroboration by law enforcement officers.

— State v. Walker
The officer-affiant received information from a reliable informant that the defendant possessed approximately three pounds of marijuana located in a house at 4501 Denver Avenue, Charlotte. The informant had been in the house in the past 48 hours and had seen the marijuana. The officer had known the informant for five months. During this time the informant had made drug buys under the officer's supervision. He had given information about drug dealers that the officer had verified through investigation.

The North Carolina Court of Appeals in *State v. Walker*[151] ruled that this information established probable cause to search the house under *Illinois v. Gates*. Note that this statement of probable cause was sufficient even though it was based solely on an informant's report.

---

149. 378 U.S. 108 (1964).

150. 73 N.C. App. 391 (1985).

151. 70 N.C. App. 403 (1984). Cases similar to *Walker* include *State v. Graham*, 90 N.C. App. 564 (1988); *State v. King*, 92 N.C. App. 75 (1988); and *State v. Marshall*, 94 N.C. App. 20 (1989).

State v. McCoy

After an informant made a controlled purchase of cocaine from the defendant at room 203 of the Econo Lodge in Winston-Salem on or after August 15, 1988, a search warrant was issued on August 18, 1988, for that room, but the defendant had vacated the premises by then. The same informant made a controlled purchase of cocaine from the defendant at room 209 of the same Econo Lodge on or after August 21, 1988; a search warrant was issued on August 23, 1988, for that room, but the defendant had vacated the premises by then. Registrations for room 209 showed that the defendant and a female had given Winston-Salem addresses as their home addresses. On August 25, 1988, officers confirmed information that the defendant was occupying room 406 of the Innkeeper Motel in Winston-Salem and the defendant was operating the same female's car, which was parked in the motel lot. The search warrant's affidavit stated that the defendant had previously been convicted of selling drugs.

The North Carolina Court of Appeals in *State v. McCoy*[152] ruled that this information was sufficient to establish probable cause under *Illinois v. Gates*. The court stated that the facts showed that the defendant, previously convicted of selling drugs, had within a 10-day period rented three different motel rooms, each time for several days, in a city in which he had a local address, and that at two of those locations he had sold cocaine. The court ruled that circumstances of the two prior sales of cocaine in other motel rooms within a 10-day period reasonably led to an inference that cocaine could be found in room 406 of the Innkeeper Motel, despite the absence of any direct evidence that cocaine was there.

Execution and Return of the Search Warrant

Before officers attempt to execute a search warrant, they should make sure that it has been properly filled out. They should particularly check that the magistrate has signed the warrant and given the date and time it was issued.

Jurisdiction to Execute a Search Warrant

A search authorized by a search warrant may be made by officers who have jurisdiction over the crime (subject-matter jurisdiction) and are acting within their territorial jurisdiction.[153] Generally, only certain state officers (State Bureau of Investigation agents, State Highway Patrol officers, wildlife law enforcement officers, marine fisheries enforcement officers, and others) need to be concerned about having jurisdiction over the crime. Local officers need to be concerned about their territorial jurisdiction. For example, city law enforcement officers generally can execute or assist in executing a search warrant only for a place in their city or within one mile beyond its limits.[154]

The officer who makes the search need not be the same officer who applied for the warrant.[155]

Officers should remember that certain judicial officials can issue search warrants only for limited areas. As discussed earlier in this chapter, magistrates, clerks of superior court, and assistant or deputy clerks of superior court generally may issue warrants to search only places within their county.[156] District court judges may issue warrants to search anywhere within their district. A warrant issued by these officials for a search outside their areas is invalid. Superior court judges and appellate court justices and judges may issue warrants to search anywhere in the state.

Time of Execution

North Carolina law requires that a search with a search warrant must be made within 48 hours after the warrant is issued.[157] (It is unclear whether the search must only begin within 48 hours or whether it must also end

---

152. 100 N.C. App. 574 (1990).

153. G.S. 15A-247.

154. State v. Proctor, 62 N.C. App. 233 (1983); State v. Treants, 60 N.C. App. 203 (1982). City law enforcement officers also may execute search warrants on property owned or leased by the city, wherever the property is located. G.S. 160A-286.

155. State v. Jones, 97 N.C. App. 189 (1990).

156. *But see supra* note 35, on extension of magistrates' authority beyond their counties.

157. G.S. 15A-248. Because the search warrant is void if it is not executed within 48 hours, the search would be treated as one made without a search warrant and would have to be justified, if possible, as a warrantless search. It should be noted that North Carolina's 48-hour time limitation is not constitutionally required, at least not when probable cause still exists after 48 hours have elapsed. *See generally* 2 Wayne R. LaFave, Search and Seizure: A Treatise on the Fourth Amendment § 4.7(a) (5th ed. 2012).

within that period. Although it appears that the search must only begin within 48 hours, cautious officers may want to obtain a second search warrant if the search extends beyond 48 hours.) If a search is not begun within 48 hours, the warrant must be marked "not executed" and returned to the clerk of court. Any evidence found as a result of a search executed after more than 48 hours is not justified by the warrant, because the warrant is void after that time (but see the next paragraph concerning a computer search that is conducted after the 48-hour period when the computer had been timely seized under the search warrant).

Often after a computer is seized with a search warrant and within 48 hours of issuance of the search warrant, a forensic or other comprehensive examination of the computer may take weeks or months. It would not appear that the later examination is a violation of the time limitation, based on cases from other jurisdictions involving their statutes or rules.[158] North Carolina appellate courts would likely agree with these cases.

Although officers must return an unexecuted warrant after 48 hours have elapsed, they may use the same information to obtain another warrant if the facts still indicate that the evidence will probably be found in the place designated. But if they searched and did not find any evidence, no other search may be made with that warrant. The failure to find evidence destroys the probable cause, and additional facts must be presented before another warrant may be issued.

In an unusual case, a warrant could become invalid before the end of the 48-hour period. That would occur if the facts establishing probable cause clearly indicate that the evidence will be in the place only briefly—for some period less than 48 hours. For example, officers might have an informant's report that a person with stolen goods is in a local motel room and will leave the next morning. A warrant to search that motel room might become invalid after about 24 hours because the facts clearly indicate that the evidence is not likely to be found there after that time has passed—unless information showed that the person was still there.

Unlike some jurisdictions, North Carolina does not restrict when a search with a search warrant may be conducted. The search may be made at any time of day or night, whether or not anyone is home—although a search when someone is present helps establish the occupant's possession of the evidence. However, the North Carolina Court of Appeals has indicated that the Fourth Amendment requires that a search conducted at night must be justified by a legitimate law enforcement purpose.[159] For example, a nighttime search may be justified because occupants will be less aware of the search than during the daylight, and therefore they will be less able to destroy incriminating evidence.

Notice and Entry

(See page 498 for case summaries on this topic.)

North Carolina law requires that officers, before they enter premises to search with a warrant, give notice of their identity and purpose.[160] This is usually satisfied by knocking on the door or ringing the doorbell and stating that they are officers with a search warrant. If they have reasonable grounds to believe that giving notice would endanger their lives or the life of someone else, they need not give notice before entering, and they may use deception or a ruse to gain entry.[161] Officers who do not give notice must be able to articulate specific facts that made them fear for their lives, such as an informant's report that the occupants were drug dealers who had threatened

---

158. Commonwealth v. Kaupp, 899 N.E.2d 809 (Mass. 2009); United States v. Syphers, 426 F.3d 461 (1st Cir. 2005). See also the case summaries and text on this issue in DIGITAL EVIDENCE, *supra* note 59, at 32–33.

159. State v. Edwards, 70 N.C. App. 317 (1984), *rev'd on other grounds*, 315 N.C. 304 (1985). *See also* Gooding v. United States, 416 U.S. 430 (1974); 2 WAYNE R. LaFAVE, SEARCH AND SEIZURE: A TREATISE ON THE FOURTH AMENDMENT § 4.7(b) (5th ed. 2012).

160. G.S. 15A-249. The Fourth Amendment requires that an unannounced entry into a home must be reasonable, which will often require that officers give notice of their identity and purpose. Wilson v. Arkansas, 514 U.S. 927 (1995) (knock and announce is subject to reasonableness provision of Fourth Amendment); Richards v. Wisconsin, 520 U.S. 385 (1997) (officers are not required to knock and announce their presence before entering home if they have reasonable suspicion that doing so would be dangerous or futile or that it would inhibit effective investigation of crime by, for example, allowing destruction of evidence). For the application of Fourth Amendment and state statutory exclusionary rules with knock-and-announce violations, see the summary of *Hudson v. Michigan*, 547 U.S. 1096 (2006), on page 498.

161. G.S. 15A-251(2). Clearly, if officers are not required to give notice, then using deception to enter is permissible. *See generally* 2 WAYNE R. LaFAVE, SEARCH AND SEIZURE: A TREATISE ON THE FOURTH AMENDMENT § 4.8(b) (5th ed. 2012).

to kill law enforcement officers and had weapons in the house to be searched.[162]

Notice before entry must be given—with the single exception noted above—even if it would increase the likelihood that evidence might be destroyed before officers can enter. Thus, an entry without notice by using deception or a ruse, such as by creating a traffic accident to draw the suspect out of the house and rushing in without notice, is not permissible.[163] If officers have information that evidence will likely be destroyed, they may make a quick entry after giving notice.[164] For example, officers with a search warrant for drugs would be justified in entering immediately after knocking and stating their purpose if they noticed that someone saw them from the window and immediately ran away toward the rear of the house.[165] If it appears that no one is home and officers still want to enter to make the search, they must announce their authority loudly enough that someone inside could hear them.[166] Officers may use force to enter a home if one of the following conditions exists:

1. The officers have previously announced their identity and purpose and reasonably believe either that their admittance is being denied or unreasonably delayed or that the home is unoccupied.
2. The officers have probable cause to believe that the giving of notice would endanger the life or safety of any person.[167]

North Carolina law requires that if someone is present, officers must read the search warrant to that person before beginning their search.[168] They need only read the warrant side of the form—not the side on which the application was filled out. If a person inside the premises is using or is likely to use the time while the warrant is being read to destroy evidence, officers may secure the premises before continuing to read it. In addition to reading the warrant, officers must leave a copy of the warrant and application and any affidavits with the person in charge of the premises. If no one is present, the copies should be left in a conspicuous place so that they will be found when the occupant returns. If someone is present and there is no danger to the officers or no likelihood that evidence will be destroyed, officers may want to give that person a few minutes to look over the warrant and application before the search begins.

Anyone who willfully interferes with officers when they enter the premises or make the search is guilty of resisting, delaying, or obstructing public officers in performing their duties—a Class 2 misdemeanor.[169] Generally, verbal

---

162. State v. Lyons, 340 N.C. 646 (1995) (although officers announced their identity and purpose before executing search warrant, court stated that they were not required to do so—officers believed that firearm was inside defendant's apartment; defendant would not cooperate; area outside defendant's door was so small that even though officers felt situation was dangerous, their weapons were not drawn because of fear of harming other officers and bystanders; and one officer heard two people arguing within apartment).

163. State v. Brown, 35 N.C. App. 634 (1978).

164. State v. Gaines, 33 N.C. App. 66 (1977); State v. Edwards, 70 N.C. App. 317 (1984), *rev'd on other grounds*, 315 N.C. 304 (1985).

165. State v. Marshall, 94 N.C. App. 20 (1989).

166. G.S. 15A-249. *See also* United States v. Banks, 540 U.S. 31 (2003) (forcible entry did not violate Fourth Amendment when officers with search warrant for cocaine at premises where it was being sold gave notice, waited 15 to 20 seconds with no answer, and broke open front door with battering ram).

167. G.S. 15A-251; State v. Lyons, 340 N.C. 646 (1995) (court noted that the following evidence supported a forcible entry under G.S. 15A-251(2): officers believed that a firearm was inside defendant's apartment; defendant would not cooperate;

area outside defendant's door was so small that even though officers felt situation was dangerous, their weapons were not drawn because of fear of harming other officers and bystanders; and one officer heard two people arguing within the apartment); State v. Knight, 340 N.C. 531 (1995) (forced entry upheld for safety reasons); State v. Vick, 130 N.C. App. 207 (1998) (forced entry upheld when entry was being denied or unreasonably delayed); State v. Jones, 97 N.C. App. 189 (1990) (similar ruling); State v. Marshall, 94 N.C. App. 20 (1989) (similar ruling).

The statutory standard of probable cause in G.S. 15A-251(2) is a greater burden on officers to meet than the standard required by the Fourth Amendment. Richards v. Wisconsin, 520 U.S. 385 (1997) (officers are not required to knock and announce their presence before entering home if they have reasonable suspicion that doing so would be dangerous or futile or that it would inhibit effective investigation of crime by, for example, allowing destruction of evidence); United States v. Ramirez, 523 U.S. 65 (1998) (court rejected defendant's argument that higher standard than set out in *Richards v. Wisconsin* should apply when officers must destroy property to enter home). There may be cases in which an officer violates the North Carolina statutory standard but not the Fourth Amendment. If so, then only the statutory exclusionary rule in G.S. 15A-974 would apply in determining if evidence should be suppressed. Note also that under *Hudson v. Michigan*, 547 U.S. 586 (2006), the Fourth Amendment exclusionary rule does not bar the admission of evidence for knock-and-announce violations.

168. G.S. 15A-252.

169. G.S. 14-223.

abuse alone is not considered a violation unless it is so severe that it keeps the officers from talking to witnesses or otherwise carrying out their investigation.[170]

Scope of the Search

(See page 508 for case summaries on this topic.)

Some of what is discussed here has already been discussed earlier in this chapter, but it is worth repeating so that all the information about the scope of a search with a warrant is together.

Outbuildings

Generally, a search warrant to search premises authorizes the executing officers to search all outbuildings (unattached garage, storage building, and the like) within the curtilage of the premises, even though they are not specifically named in the warrant as places to be searched, if the evidence to be seized may reasonably be found there.[171] In other words, a warrant to search the "premises" at 345 Oak Street, Bovine, North Carolina, for stolen television sets would authorize a search of the dwelling house at that address, the garage attached to the side of the house, and the storage shed about 20 yards behind the house. However, that warrant would not authorize a search of a garage apartment rented to another person or a search of another house a block away that is owned and occupied by the person who owns the house specified in the warrant.

Although not legally required to do so, officers who are aware of outbuildings on the premises may want to name them specifically in the search warrant as places to be searched so that they have explicit authority to search them.

Where Officers May Search

Where officers may search is determined by what they are looking for. A warrant authorizes the search of only those places on the premises that are large enough to contain the object of the search. A warrant to search for a stolen automobile authorizes a search of the garage but not of the kitchen or any other part of the house where the car could not reasonably be found. A warrant to search for a large stolen television set authorizes a search of the garage, the kitchen, and the bedroom, but not the dresser drawers in the bedroom. A warrant to search for heroin

authorizes a search of all those places. If officers search unauthorized places, the search may be unlawful and the evidence found in the unauthorized places may be excluded from use at trial.

Assistance from Private People and Dogs

Court cases have authorized officers to bring private people with them to assist in executing a search warrant when it is reasonable to do so.[172] For example, officers may take a burglary victim with them to help identify the victim's stolen goods. Of course, officers should consider whether the execution of the search warrant may involve danger to private people they take with them.

Officers also may take dogs with them if they are useful in discovering drugs, accelerants, or other substances.[173] Although not legally required, officers may want to request in the search warrant application the authority to take a private person or a dog with them when they execute the warrant.

News Media Presence during Search

Officers violate the Fourth Amendment rights of homeowners when they allow the news media to accompany them during the execution of search warrants (or arrest warrants) in a person's home or other similar place where a person has a reasonable expectation of privacy.[174]

Seizure of Items in Plain View

While searching for a particular item named in the warrant to be seized, officers may search everywhere they reasonably may find the objects the warrant permits them

---

170. State v. Leigh, 278 N.C. 243 (1971).

171. *See supra* note 88.

172. *See* 2 WAYNE R. LaFAVE, SEARCH AND SEIZURE: A TREATISE ON THE FOURTH AMENDMENT § 4.10(d) (5th ed. 2012). Allowing private people to assist officers was explicitly recognized as permissible in *Wilson v. Layne*, 526 U.S. 603 (1999). *See also* Bills v. Aseltine, 958 F.2d 697 (6th Cir. 1992), *later appeal*, 52 F.3d 596 (6th Cir. 1995).

173. 2 WAYNE R. LaFAVE, SEARCH AND SEIZURE: A TREATISE ON THE FOURTH AMENDMENT § 4.10(d), at 763 (5th ed. 2012).

174. Hanlon v. Berger, 526 U.S. 808 (1999) (search warrants); Wilson v. Layne, 526 U.S. 603 (1999) (arrest warrants). Although officers may be civilly liable for bringing news media during the execution of arrest and search warrants, the exclusionary rule probably does not apply. United States v. Hendrixson, 234 F.3d 494 (11th Cir. 2000) (exclusionary rule does not apply to evidence seized by law enforcement officers during execution of search warrant when news media are present in violation of *Wilson v. Layne*).

to seize. Officers also may seize other property that they find "inadvertently"[175] in plain view, if they have probable cause[176] to believe it is evidence of a crime,[177] even if it is not related to the crime under investigation.[178] For example, while searching for stolen television sets, officers may seize illegal drugs they see in plain view. Officers find and seize an object inadvertently if, before the warrant was issued, they did not have probable cause to seize it and did not specifically intend to search for and seize it.[179]

Officers' authority to seize objects in plain view under these circumstances is known as the *plain view doctrine.*

Officers also may seize evidence that bears a reasonable relationship (connection or nexus) to the crime for which the named object is evidence. For example, a search warrant for marijuana would allow officers to seize cigarette papers, scales, envelopes, and plastic bags—items well known for their connection with distributing marijuana.[180] Large sums of money on the premises also may be seized when they are likely to be connected to gambling or drug offenses[181] for which the search warrant was issued. Likewise, if possession of the premises may be necessary to prove an offense (for example, possession of illegal drugs) for which the search is made, evidence of possession or use of the premises—such as a checkbook, an electric bill, or a traffic citation issued to that address—may be seized.[182] However, officers may want to describe these kinds of items in the search warrant so that they will not need to rely on the plain view doctrine to justify their seizure—that is, the search warrant will specifically authorize the seizure. One way to describe them in the application is as "items or articles of personal property tending to show ownership, dominion, or control of the premises."[183]

---

175. In *Horton v. California*, 496 U.S. 128 (1990), the Court overruled *Coolidge v. New Hampshire*, 403 U.S. 443 (1971), and ruled that the plain view doctrine does not require that an officer inadvertently discover the object to be seized. However, G.S. 15A-253 requires that a discovery of evidence during the execution of a search warrant must be inadvertent. Because inadvertence is only a statutory requirement, only the statutory exclusionary rule in G.S. 15A-974 would apply in determining whether the evidence is admissible.

176. In *Arizona v. Hicks*, 480 U.S. 321 (1988), the Court ruled that officers who conduct a search or seizure under the plain view doctrine must have probable cause to do so; reasonable suspicion is insufficient. Officers in *Hicks* properly entered an apartment where a shooting had occurred to search for the shooter and any victims or weapons. They seized three weapons and a stocking-cap mask. In this squalid apartment, they noticed two sets of expensive stereo components. An officer read serial numbers from some of the items without moving them; the Court ruled that this act was neither a search nor a seizure and therefore did not violate the defendant's Fourth Amendment rights. However, the officer moved a turntable so that he could read its serial number. This act constituted a search that required probable cause (probable cause also was necessary to support the later seizure of the turntable from the apartment). Because the State had conceded (unwisely, it appears) that only reasonable suspicion existed to move the turntable, the Court ruled that the officer's actions violated the defendant's Fourth Amendment rights.

177. Officers who are executing a search warrant may seize evidence of federal crimes as well as state crimes. United States v. Smith, 899 F.2d 116 (1st Cir. 1990).

178. State v. Cummings, 113 N.C. App. 368 (1994) (officers executing search warrant for drugs, drug records, and the like discovered and seized 94 photographs of nude women; seizure was proper under plain view justification because photographs could have been evidence of obscenity offense).

179. State v. White, 322 N.C. 770 (1988). Officers in *White* executed a search warrant for stolen property and seized stolen items that were not named in the warrant. The court ruled that "inadvertence" (which no longer is required under the Fourth Amendment, Horton v. California, 496 U.S. 128 (1990), but is required under G.S. 15A-253 (1988)) under the plain view doctrine means that officers do not have probable cause to believe that evidence will be discovered until they actually observe it during an otherwise justified search. Judicial review

involves a two-step inquiry: Before the search, did officers have probable cause to secure a search warrant for the later-seized items that were not named in the search warrant? If the answer is yes, the seizure is illegal. If the answer is no, then the review proceeds to the second inquiry: Did the officers have probable cause to believe that the seized items were evidence of a crime when they seized them without a warrant? The court ruled that the officers' use of break-in incident reports when they were executing a search warrant did not violate the "inadvertence" standard because they did not have probable cause to seize the items named in these reports and could not have listed them in a search warrant. Therefore, the officers properly seized these items. The court ruled, however, that they did not have probable cause to seize some items not named in the reports until after they seized them; therefore, the officers illegally seized them.

180. State v. Zimmerman, 23 N.C. App. 396 (1974).

181. State v. Newsom, 284 N.C. 412 (1973).

182. State v. Williams, 299 N.C. 529 (1980).

183. *See, e.g.*, United States v. Alexander, 761 F.2d 1294 (9th Cir. 1985); United States v. Tabares, 951 F.2d 405 (1st Cir. 1991); 2 Wayne R. LaFave, Search and Seizure: A Treatise on the Fourth Amendment § 4.6(d) (5th ed. 2012).

Vehicles on the Premises

Generally, a warrant to search premises gives executing officers the authority to search a vehicle on the premises,[184] even though the vehicle is not specifically named in the warrant as a place to be searched, if both of the following exist:

1. The evidence to be seized may reasonably be found there

2. The vehicle is owned or under the control of an occupant of the premises[185] or officers have a reasonable basis for believing the vehicle is so owned or controlled[186]

(If a vehicle may not be searched under this authority, it may be searched without a warrant under certain circumstances if there is probable cause, as discussed in Chapter 3.)[187] If officers know that a vehicle may contain evidence that they are searching for, they should describe it specifically in the search warrant as an object to be searched so that (1) they need not rely on the implicit authority to search it if it is on the premises when they execute the warrant and (2) they may search that vehicle under the authority of the warrant even if it is not on the premises but parked nearby (on a public street, for example).[188]

Length of Time to Search

There are no set time limits for a search with a warrant. (However, as discussed above, it is not clear whether the search must only *begin* within 48 hours after the warrant is issued or whether it must *end* within 48 hours.) Officers may search as long as reasonably necessary to find what they are authorized to look for, but if they continue longer than that, the search may become unlawful and the evidence may be excluded. The length of time required will depend on the place being searched and what is being looked for. It will probably take longer to search a 12-room house than a 3-room apartment. A search for a stolen refrigerator, which cannot easily be hidden, does not usually take as long as a search for drugs, which can be secreted in many more places.

People on the Premises

(See page 502 for case summaries on this topic.)

If a person is named in the warrant as someone to be searched or if officers have an arrest warrant or other justification for arresting the person, an immediate, thorough search of that person may be made.[189] Otherwise, there are limitations on handling persons who are present when officers enter to search a place.

Public Place

When officers enter a public place to make a search, they generally may not detain people there unless those people are named in the warrant to be searched or unless there is some other justification for detaining them. In addition, the officers may not automatically—that is, without reasonable suspicion—frisk a person there.[190] Instead, they must have reasonable suspicion that a person is armed and dangerous before they may frisk that person—although knowledge that a place may contain weapons is a factor in determining dangerousness.[191]

Nonpublic Place

Detaining and frisking. When officers enter a nonpublic place to make a search, they may detain—when they enter and while they conduct the search—anyone who is on the premises.[192] However, there are limitations to this detention authority. The United States Supreme Court ruled in *Bailey v. United States*[193] that its prior ruling in *Michigan v. Summers*[194] did not authorize officers, who saw the defendant, Bailey, leaving in a vehicle from the premises where a search warrant was about to be executed for a gun involved in a drug purchase, to delay making a detention until the defendant was about a mile away. The Court

---

184. *See supra* note 82.

185. *See supra* note 83.

186. *See supra* note 84.

187. *See supra* note 85.

188. *See supra* note 86.

189. State v. Johnson, 143 N.C. App. 307 (2001) (officers executing search warrant authorizing search of defendant and his apartment for illegal drugs properly strip-searched him, based on totality of circumstances).

190. Ybarra v. Illinois, 444 U.S. 85 (1979). *See generally* 2 Wayne R. LaFave, Search and Seizure: A Treatise on the Fourth Amendment § 4.9(d) (5th ed. 2012).

191. State v. Davis, 94 N.C. App. 358 (1989) (frisk in lounge was justified based on patron's actions and officer's knowledge from prior searches involving the lounge that its patrons often carried weapons).

192. G.S. 15A-256. *See* Michigan v. Summers, 452 U.S. 692 (1981) (this case involved a detention of a resident of the premises); State v. Guy, 54 N.C. App. 208 (1981).

193. 133 S. Ct. 1031 (2013).

194. 452 U.S. 692 (1981).

stated that the *Summers* ruling and its reasoning was limited to people in the immediate vicinity[195] of the premises to be searched, which clearly did not include where Bailey was stopped.

The authority to detain should not be abused; clearly innocent people (who have no connection with the crime under investigation) should not be inconvenienced. If a person tries to obstruct an officer or to frustrate the search in some other significant way, the person may be arrested for obstructing an officer, as discussed on page 439.

If there is reasonable suspicion that a person is armed and poses a threat, the person may be frisked for weapons. To justify the frisk, the officers generally must be able to articulate specific facts as to why the person was dangerous, such as hostility combined with a bulge on the person's body where a weapon might be kept. However, officers normally may automatically—that is, without reasonable suspicion—frisk people present in a private residence, at least when their search involves a potentially dangerous activity, such as selling illegal drugs.[196]

If the frisk indicates an object that might be a weapon, officers may remove it. If the object is not a weapon but the officer's training and experience provide probable cause to believe that the object being touched is a package containing illegal drugs, such as crack cocaine, the officer may remove the object from the person.[197] If the object is a weapon, officers must remember that while the offense of carrying a concealed weapon does not apply when a person is on his or her own premises,[198] the possession of a firearm by a convicted felon does apply on one's own premises.[199]

Searching people present for evidence. In one specific circumstance, officers may search people on the premises who are not named in the search warrant and are not otherwise subject to arrest or frisk. Officers may search those who were present on the premises when they entered to search if the following three conditions exist:

1. The place is not open to the public
2. The evidence that is the object of the search is small enough that it can be hidden on a person
3. The search of the premises fails to uncover that evidence[200]

If the evidence or evidence of a like kind—for example, all drugs are considered the same kind of evidence—is found on a person, it may be used at trial. If evidence of a different kind—for example, a stolen firearm discovered during a search for drugs—is found, it may be seized,[201] but it may not be used at trial.

This limitation on using evidence applies only when the evidence has been seized under the limited statutory authority to search those on the premises not named in the warrant. Thus, if a person is named to be searched in

---

195. The Court declined to precisely define the term "immediate vicinity," leaving it to the lower courts to make this determination based on "the lawful limits of the premises, whether the occupant was within the line of sight of his dwelling, the ease of reentry from the occupant's location, and other relevant factors." *Bailey*, 133 S. Ct. at 1042.

196. State v. Long, 37 N.C. App. 662 (1978). Although *Long* was decided before *Ybarra v. Illinois*, 444 U.S. 85 (1979), its ruling is not inconsistent with that decision. 2 WAYNE R. LaFAVE, SEARCH AND SEIZURE: A TREATISE ON THE FOURTH AMENDMENT § 4.9(d) (5th ed. 2012). G.S. 15A-255 also authorizes officers to frisk all those present if they reasonably believe their safety or the safety of others justifies the frisk. The statute does not necessarily require an individualized reasonable belief; rather, it requires an assessment of all the circumstances that exist in the private premises. *See generally* State v. Harris, 95 N.C. App. 691 (1989), *aff'd*, 326 N.C. 588 (1990).

197. Minnesota v. Dickerson, 508 U.S. 366 (1993). See the discussion of the plain touch doctrine in Chapter 3.

198. G.S. 14-269.

199. G.S. 14-415.1. The person may be violating federal firearm laws, which also do not contain exemptions for possessing a firearm on one's own premises. *See, e.g.*, 18 U.S.C. § 922(g) (possessing firearm when person has specified prior conviction or other disability). *See also* 18 U.S.C. § 924(c)(1) (sentence enhancement for using or carrying firearm during federal drug trafficking offense or crime of violence).

200. G.S. 15A-256; State v. Cutshall, 136 N.C. App. 756 (2000) (court rejected State's argument that evidence found in outbuildings is not to be considered in applying G.S. 15A-256, stating that the statute does not distinguish between different units on the premises); State v. Brooks, 51 N.C. App. 90 (1981) (search of person present permitted because object of search warrant, ready-to-sell hashish, had not been found); State v. Watlington, 30 N.C. App. 101 (1976) (search of car with search warrant failed to find heroin; court upheld search of passenger under authority of G.S. 15A-256).

201. Although G.S. 15A-256 in effect states that property of a different type may not be seized, this statute should not prevent officers from seizing property that a person may not lawfully possess, such as a stolen firearm—the example given in the text. If officers told a person that the watch was stolen, and the person still wanted to possess it, officers should not be required to return the watch to that person. Of course, if the person continues to possess the watch after being told that it was stolen, that person is committing the offense of possessing stolen goods; see G.S. 14-71.1.

a search warrant for stolen firearms and is searched under the authority of the warrant, illegal drugs found on that person will be admissible as evidence. The same is true if the person is arrested under an arrest warrant for larceny of firearms and drugs are found during a search incident to that arrest. Also, the drugs would be admissible if inadvertently found in plain view in the dresser drawer during the search of the house for the firearms. There is one situation in which the drugs would be inadmissible, however. If the search warrant is to search only the "premises," the person is not under arrest, and the search of the person is made after the search of the house did not reveal any firearms (or the search revealed only some of the firearms present), the drugs would not be admissible as evidence. This limitation emphasizes the advisability of naming in the search warrant any suspects whom the statement of probable cause connects with the evidence being sought and who may be present when the search is made.

Inventory of Seized Property

(*See page 506 for case summaries on this topic.*)

North Carolina law requires that officers write and sign a receipt (inventory) of all objects seized in the search.[202] The AOC prepares form AOC-CR-206 (inventory of items seized pursuant to search) that officers may use for this purpose. This form is available from the AOC's website at www.nccourts.org/Forms/FormSearch.asp, where it also may be completed and printed.[203] (For a list of forms available on the AOC website, see the sidebar on page 412.)

If officers seize evidence from a person, they must give the person a copy of the completed inventory form. If immediate delivery of the form is not practical, they may deliver it within a reasonable time thereafter. If they seize evidence from a building or vehicle, they must give a copy of the completed form to the owner or person in apparent control. If no one was present during the search, they must leave the form in a conspicuous place on the premises or vehicle searched.

The completed inventory form must be returned with the search warrant. The officer who fills out the form must swear or affirm to its contents.[204] If the clerk's office is not open, an officer may swear or affirm to the inventory before a magistrate (the AOC form provides for a

magistrate's signature), who will forward it to the clerk's office.

For a discussion of special issues involved with the return of an inventory when a computer is searched off-site, see the publication cited in the accompanying footnote.[205]

Return of the Search Warrant

After the search is made, whether evidence was found or not, the officer must return the warrant to the clerk of the court who issued it.[206] There is no time limit for returning the warrant, but it should be done without unreasonable delay. If the search is made on a weekend, the warrant may be returned when the clerk's office opens on Monday. The officer may return the warrant to a magistrate if the magistrate is willing to forward it to the clerk's office when it opens.

An officer who returns the warrant must complete the "Return of Service" section of the search warrant form. For a discussion of special issues involved with the return of a search warrant when a computer is searched off-site, see the publication cited in the accompanying footnote.[207]

An officer may be subject to prosecution for a misdemeanor for not returning the warrant, but possible prosecution is remote and is not the most important reason for returning the warrant. If the search is unsuccessful, the warrant cannot be used again, and it should be returned to make certain that it is not inadvertently served by another officer. Also, the warrant will be needed to prove the legality of the search if a civil suit is brought against the officer. If the search is successful, the warrant should be returned so that it will be available at trial to show that the search was lawful. Before returning the document to the clerk or magistrate, the officer may want to make a photocopy of the application and warrant, because a photocopy is admissible at trial if the original is lost.[208]

---

202. G.S. 15A-254; State v. Fruitt, 35 N.C. App. 177 (1978).

203. Paper copies of these forms are printed and shipped to a county when requested by a county's clerk's office.

204. G.S. 15A-257.

205. Digital Evidence, *supra* note 59, at 36–37.

206. G.S. 15A-257.

207. Digital Evidence, *supra* note 59, at 36–37.

208. State v. Edwards, 286 N.C. 162 (1974); G.S. 8C-1, Rules 1001, 1003.

Sealing Search Warrant from Public Inspection

A search warrant becomes available for public inspection when an officer returns it to the clerk's office.[209] A North Carolina Court of Appeals case has recognized that a court may issue an order sealing a search warrant from public inspection under certain circumstances.[210]

Disposition of Seized Property Pending Trial

North Carolina law[211] requires that the seized property be held by one of the following: (1) the person who applied for the warrant, (2) the officer who executed the warrant or the officer's employing agency, or (3) any other law enforcement agency or person who may evaluate or analyze it.[212] A court is authorized to retain the seized items or to order them delivered to another court.

As few people as possible should handle the evidence so that the chain of custody may easily be established at trial if it becomes necessary to do so. (See Chapter 6 for a discussion of chain of custody.)

Whether officers may immediately destroy hazardous chemicals and other dangerous items (for example, meth-amphetamine laboratories) before a defendant has had a chance to examine and test them is discussed in the blog post cited in the accompanying footnote.[213]

Search Warrants in Areas of Riot or State of Emergency

North Carolina law attempts to control public disorders in several ways[214] by

- Defining certain conduct as always being unlawful—for example, rioting and disorderly conduct
- Setting the procedures by which the state and local governments may declare states of emergency
- Stating what other restrictions governments may impose when a state of emergency exists—for example, curfews or limitations on liquor sales
- Granting law enforcement officers certain additional authority when a riot or state of emergency occurs

The additional enforcement authority includes an expanded power to frisk and use warrants to search vehicles near riots for any dangerous weapon or substance. "Dangerous weapon or substance" includes things that may destroy property as well as those that might cause serious bodily injury; the term includes ammunition and parts of weapons as well as complete weapons.[215] This law does not restrict officers' use of any other permissible authority to arrest, frisk, search, or the like.

A riot exists when three or more people assemble and by disorderly or violent conduct, or the imminent threat of that conduct, injure or damage persons or property or present a clear and present danger that they will do so.[216] A declared state of emergency must be proclaimed by the governor or an appropriate municipal official (usually, the mayor) or county official (usually, the chairman of the board of county commissioners). This declaration may be made when public authorities are unable to maintain adequate protection for lives or property because

---

209. The wording of G.S. 132-1.4(k) appears to recognize that a search warrant does not become available for public inspection until it is returned—by implicitly recognizing that it may be sealed thereafter.

210. *In re* Cooper, 200 N.C. App. 180 (2009) (court ruled that trial court properly sealed from public inspection search warrants involving the ongoing investigation of a murder); *In re* Baker, 220 N.C. App. 108 (2012) (when search warrants were unsealed in accordance with procedures set forth in senior resident superior court judge's administrative order, and State failed to make timely motion to extend period for which documents were sealed, trial judge did not err by unsealing documents). See the criteria for sealing a search warrant set out in *Cooper*.

211. G.S. 15A-258.

212. State v. Jones, 97 N.C. App. 189 (1990) (court ruled that officers did not violate G.S. 15A-258 when before trial they released to federal Drug Enforcement Administration currency seized during execution of search warrant for drugs; court reasoned that statute expressly authorized property to be held by any law enforcement agency); State v. Hill, 153 N.C. App. 716 (2002) (neither G.S. 15-11.1 nor G.S. 90-112 bars North Carolina state or local law enforcement officers from delivering evidence to federal authorities, including illegal drug-related currency to be forfeited under federal law); *In re* Beck, 109 N.C. App. 539 (1993) (after criminal charges had been dismissed, sheriff's department did not act illegally in transferring sexually explicit materials—which had been seized pursuant to a search warrant—to county department of social services for its use in parental termination hearing).

---

213. Jeff Welty, *Search Warrants for Meth Labs*, NC Crim. L. Blog (Feb. 6, 2014), http://nccriminallaw.sog.unc.edu/?p=4625. The analysis is contained in a PDF file; a link to the PDF is provided in the blog post.

214. G.S. 14-288.1 through -288.20.

215. G.S. 14-288.1(2).

216. G.S. 14-288.2.

of a public crisis, disaster, riot, catastrophe, or similar emergency.[217]

Special Frisk Authority

Law enforcement officers have special powers to frisk people found near riots or violating a curfew during a state of emergency. These powers are broader than the general power to frisk discussed in Chapter 3.

Frisking People Close to Existing Riots

Officers may frisk a person and inspect personal belongings to discover whether the person has any dangerous weapons or substances if (1) they have reasonable grounds to believe that the person is or may become unlawfully involved in an existing riot and (2) the person is close enough to the riot that the person could become immediately involved in it.[218] If the person is in a vehicle, it probably also may be inspected.

Frisking Curfew Violators

Officers may frisk a person and inspect personal belongings to discover whether he or she has any dangerous weapons or substances if the person is violating a curfew proclaimed during a state of emergency or civil disorder.[219] If the person is in a vehicle, it probably also may be inspected.

If a dangerous weapon or substance is found as a result of a frisk of a curfew violator or a person close to an existing riot, the person may be violating either the concealed weapon law[220] or the law prohibiting possession of a dangerous weapon or substance—whether concealed or not—in the area where a declared state of emergency exists or within the immediate vicinity of a riot.[221]

Special Search Warrants to Search Vehicles

Officers have an inspection power under a special kind of search warrant to check all vehicles entering an area where a civil disorder is occurring to make sure that those vehicles are not bringing in dangerous weapons or substances.

Two kinds of search warrants may be issued: (1) warrants authorizing inspections for dangerous weapons or substances of all vehicles entering or approaching a municipality where a state of emergency exists, and (2) warrants authorizing inspections for dangerous weapons or substances of all vehicles that may be within or approaching the immediate vicinity of a riot.[222] The existence of the state of emergency or riot need not have been proclaimed, but the official who issues the warrant must have found such a condition. The only judicial officials who may issue these kinds of warrants are district, superior, or appellate court justices or judges—a magistrate or clerk of court may not do so.[223] Officers may not seek the warrant on their own initiative; they must have authorization to apply for the warrant from the head of their agency.[224]

When issued, the warrant must state which kind it is—whether for an inspection around a municipality under a state of emergency or for an inspection in the vicinity of a riot—and give the date and hour of issuance. It must also state that it will automatically expire 24 hours after it is issued.

The law does not specify the area where the warrant may be used, but the issuing official must place territorial limitations in the warrant because the law requires that the area be set out with "reasonable precision." In this way the search will be restricted to only places where it is necessary to halt the transportation of weapons into the area of violence. When officers apply for the warrant, they should be prepared to state the area where the riot or state of emergency exists and in which streets or in which area they want to exercise their inspection authority. A marked city street map attached to the application is the easiest way to meet this requirement.

The law does not specify how to execute the warrant. Because executing the warrant will undoubtedly mean that different vehicles must be inspected at different intersections at the same time, it would be a good practice to make multiple copies of the warrant so that a copy may be shown to each driver who is stopped.

The law authorizes the search of vehicles for dangerous weapons or substances, and thus the search may be as thorough as is necessary to find them. If a dangerous weapon or substance is found, the driver may be violating

---

217. See the definitions in G.S. 14-288.1 and other pertinent statutes in G.S. Chapter 14, Article 36A (G.S. 14-288.1 through -288.20).

218. G.S. 14-288.10(a).

219. G.S. 14-288.10(b).

220. G.S. 14-269.

221. G.S. 14-288.7.

---

222. G.S. 14-288.11.

223. G.S. 14-288.11(c).

224. G.S. 14-288.11(d).

either the concealed weapon law[225] or the law prohibiting possession of a dangerous weapon or substance—whether concealed or not—in the area where a declared state of emergency exists or within the immediate vicinity of a riot.[226] The roadblock where the vehicle was searched and the weapon discovered may be located outside those areas. If so, officers should then determine whether the concealed weapon law applies; if so, an arrest and search may be made for that offense. If the weapon is not concealed, a violation has not occurred and nothing may be seized. Officers may want to inform the driver that going to the area where a state of emergency has been declared or a riot is occurring may violate the law and may result in the driver's arrest.

The most important things to remember about these kinds of search warrants are as follows: (1) only certain judicial officials may issue them, (2) officers may apply for the warrant only if the head of their agency has authorized them to do so, (3) the warrant authorizes only a search of vehicles for dangerous weapons or substances, (4) the warrant is restricted to legally defined emergencies or riots, and (5) the warrant automatically expires after 24 hours.

There are no printed forms available for these kinds of warrants. Some sample forms are reproduced on pages 453 through 458.

Magistrate's Order to Seize Cruelly Treated Animal

North Carolina law authorizes an animal cruelty investigator to file a sworn complaint requesting an order to take custody of a cruelly treated animal[227] and provide care for it. To issue an order, a magistrate[228] must find probable cause to believe that the animal is being cruelly treated and it is necessary for the investigator to take immediate custody. The order is valid for only 24 hours after it is issued.[229] The investigator may request a law enforcement officer or animal control officer to assist in seizing the animal and must give notice of his or her identity and purpose before entering the premises. The investigator may use force to enter premises or a vehicle to execute the order only if (1) a district court judge issues an order authorizing forcible entry, (2) the investigator reasonably believes the premises or vehicle is unoccupied and that the animal is there, (3) the investigator is accompanied by a law enforcement officer, and (4) the forcible entry occurs during daylight hours.[230]

The investigator who seizes the animal must leave a copy of the magistrate's order with the owner, if known, or affixed to the premises or vehicle. He or she must also leave a written notice with a description of the animal, the place where it will be taken, the reason for taking the animal, and the investigator's intent to file a complaint in district court requesting custody of the animal.[231]

After executing the order, the investigator must return it with a written inventory of the animal or animals seized to the clerk of court in the county where the order was issued.

There is another way in which a cruelly treated animal may be seized, which is unrelated to the legal provisions discussed above. An animal cruelty investigator could apply for a search warrant—or seek the cooperation of a law enforcement officer to apply for one—to seize an animal that is evidence of a crime, such as cruelty to animals.[232] However, although any person may apply for a search warrant, only a law enforcement officer may execute a search warrant (animal cruelty investigators are usually not law enforcement officers).[233]

---

225. G.S. 14-269.

226. G.S. 14-288.7.

227. Definitions of "cruelty" and "cruel treatment" are provided in G.S. 19A-1(2), which include acts, omissions, or neglect that cause or permit unjustifiable physical pain, suffering, or death.

228. A magistrate is the only judicial official mentioned in G.S. 19A-46(a) who may issue the order. However, G.S. 19A-46(e) requires a district court judge to issue an order authorizing forcible entry.

229. G.S. 19A-46(a).

230. G.S. 19A-46(b), (e).

231. G.S. 19A-46(c).

232. G.S. 14-360.

233. Although law enforcement officers normally apply for search warrants, any person or entity may apply for one. *In re 1990 Red Cherokee Jeep*, 131 N.C. App. 108 (1998) (Town of Waynesville had authority to apply for search warrant). Thus, for example, animal cruelty investigators and animal control officers may apply for search warrants even if they are not law enforcement officers. However, only a law enforcement officer may execute a search warrant. G.S. 15A-247.

Part II. Administrative Inspection Warrants

Many state and local laws authorize public officials or employees to inspect certain places or records. For example, wildlife law enforcement officers and marine fisheries enforcement officers may inspect hunting and fishing equipment and game to see whether those who have used the equipment have complied with the game and fish laws.[234] Housing inspectors may inspect houses to determine whether they comply with the building code.[235] Division of Motor Vehicles (DMV) license and theft inspectors may inspect automobile dealers' records.[236] These inspections are almost always conducted without any objection by the person who is subject to the inspection. (Remember that the person who must consent to an inspection of a rented apartment is the tenant, not the landlord.)[237] However, those who make these kinds of inspections must know what to do if someone refuses to allow the inspection.

Authority for Issuing Administrative Inspection Warrants

North Carolina law authorizes the issuance of an administrative inspection warrant.[238] This warrant may be issued to state or local officials or employees who have been designated to carry out a legally authorized program of inspection. (The terms "officer" and "inspector" will be used throughout this section to refer to all those authorized to conduct inspections and execute warrants.) The statute, ordinance, or administrative regulation must specify the circumstances under which an inspection is authorized—for example, housing inspections will be required once every two years. If the inspection authorization exists, the warrant may be issued for either of two reasons:

1. The property is naturally part of a program of inspection; the general plan for enforcement of the statute, ordinance, or regulation is based on reasonable standards; and these standards are applied neutrally to a particular business or place.[239]

2. There is probable cause to believe that a condition, object, activity, or circumstance exists that justifies the inspection.[240]

Reason 1, above, exists when a program of inspection has been authorized in an area where the property is located. For example, a town might decide to inspect all the houses in town to see whether they comply with the local housing code. A certain area of town is designated for inspection in May, but the owner of one house refuses to admit the inspector. The warrant could be issued in that case by showing that (1) the town's ordinances authorize housing inspections, (2) the housing office has set a schedule for making the inspections, (3) the schedule is reasonable and is applied neutrally to all houses, (4) this house is within the area of inspection this month, and (5) the owner has refused to allow the inspection.

Legislation enacted in 2011[241] placed limitations on periodic inspections by counties and cities of residential buildings and structures. Such an inspection may be conducted, with limited exceptions,[242] only when there is "reasonable cause," which means when

- the landlord or owner has a history of more than two verified violations of the housing ordinances or codes within a 12-month period;
- there has been a complaint that substandard conditions exist within the building or there has been a request that the building be inspected;
- the inspection department has actual knowledge of an unsafe condition within the building; or

---

234. G.S. 113-136, -302.1. *See generally* State v. Nobles, 107 N.C. App. 627 (1992), *aff'd*, 333 N.C. 787 (1993).

235. G.S. 153A-364; 160A-424. Note that there are some limitations on an officer's inspection authority in G.S. 113-136(k).

236. G.S. 20-49(9).

237. *In re* Dwelling of Properties, Inc., 24 N.C. App. 17 (1974).

238. G.S. 15-27.2.

239. G.S. 15-27.2(c)(1); Brooks, Comm'r of Labor v. Butler, 70 N.C. App. 681 (1984).

240. G.S. 15-27.2(c)(1); South Blvd. Video & News v. Charlotte Zoning Bd. of Adjustment, 129 N.C. App. 282 (1998) (probable cause supported issuance of warrant to determine if business was adult bookstore or adult mini motion-picture theater being operated in violation of city ordinance); Durham Video v. Durham Bd. of Adjustment, 144 N.C. App. 236 (2001) (similar ruling).

241. S.L. 2011-281, which amended G.S. 153A-364 (periodic inspections by counties); G.S. 160A-424 (periodic inspections by cities).

242. Periodic inspections may be conducted in accordance with the state fire prevention code (or when otherwise required by state law) or as part of a targeted effort within a geographic area that has been designated by the county commissioners or city council.

- violations of local ordinances or codes are visible from the outside of the property.[243]

For an extensive analysis of this legislation, see the publication cited in the accompanying footnote.[244]

Occupational Safety and Health Act (OSHA) inspections of businesses involve complex issues that will not be discussed in this book.[245]

Reason 2, above, exists when the inspection occurs for a reason other than a periodic inspection of an area. For example, an inspection may be made when (1) a housing inspector receives information that rats have been seen near an apartment building, (2) the inspector sees rat feces by the building, and (3) a tenant complains about rats running throughout the apartment's hallways.

Note that neither justification for obtaining an administrative inspection warrant requires a probability that a crime is being committed on the premises.[246] If there is probable cause to believe that a crime is being committed, that information is a particularly persuasive version of reason 2. It could also be used to obtain a regular search warrant.

Usually an administrative inspection warrant is not sought until the owner has refused to allow a voluntary inspection, but a refusal is not a prerequisite to issuing a warrant.[247] If inspectors believe that their inspection might be resisted, they might want to obtain a warrant before they attempt to make the inspection.

Issuing an Administrative Inspection Warrant

(*See page 522 for case summaries on this topic.*)

The Judicial Official's Territorial Jurisdiction

Only a judicial official may issue an administrative inspection warrant. Like search warrants, administrative inspection warrants do not always have statewide validity.[248] Magistrates, clerks of court, and assistant or deputy clerks generally may issue warrants to inspect only places within their county.[249] District court judges may issue warrants to inspect anywhere within their district. Superior court judges and appellate justices and judges may issue warrants to inspect anywhere within the state.

Warrant Forms

The AOC has prepared two forms that may be used for issuing administrative inspection warrants. AOC-CR-913M provides an affidavit and a warrant for inspections based on a particular condition or activity—reason 2, discussed above. AOC-CR-914M provides an affidavit and a warrant for periodic inspections—reason 1, discussed above. These are model forms; that is, they are not printed for distribution but are available from the office of the clerk of superior court for photocopying as necessary. They are also available from the AOC's website at www.nccourts.org/Forms/FormSearch.asp, where they may be completed and printed. (For a list of forms available on the AOC website, see the sidebar on page 412.)

Completing Warrant Forms

When inspectors apply for a warrant, they must complete an affidavit—which must be signed under oath or affirmation—stating the reason for the inspection. The judicial official may examine the inspector about the contents of the affidavit. The premises to be inspected must be described with the same particularity as is required for a search warrant.

---

243. G.S. 153A-364(a) (counties); 160A-424(a) (cities).

244. C. Tyler Mulligan, *Residential Rental Property Inspections, Permits, and Registration: Questions and Answers*, Community & Econ. Dev. Bull. No. 8 (Nov. 2011), http://sogpubs.unc.edu/electronicversions/pdfs/cedb8.pdf.

245. For OSHA publications that are available from the North Carolina Department of Labor, see www.nclabor.com/pubs.htm. *See also* Brooks, Comm'r of Labor v. Butler, 70 N.C. App. 681 (1984).

246. G.S. 15-27.2 reflects the probable cause standard set out in *Camara v. Municipal Court*, 387 U.S. 523 (1967).

247. Brooks, Comm'r of Labor v. Butler, 70 N.C. App. 681 (1984).

248. G.S. 15-27.2(b) states that a judicial official may issue an administrative inspection warrant when the official's "territorial jurisdiction encompasses the property to be inspected." There are no North Carolina appellate cases on this issue, but the most reasonable way to interpret this language is to define a judicial official's territorial jurisdiction as being the same as the official's territorial jurisdiction to issue a search warrant.

249. *But see supra* note 35, on extension of some magistrates' authority beyond their county.

The warrant must bear the date and hour of issuance. This is important because a warrant must be executed within certain time limitations, discussed below.

Although not legally required, at least two copies of the original warrant and affidavit should be made. The issuing official should keep one copy, to be filed in the clerk's office. The second copy should be given to the person whose property is to be inspected. The executing officer will return the original warrant and affidavit to the clerk's or magistrate's office after it is executed. The executing officer may want to make a third copy for his or her files. Remember that the affidavit and warrant should be attached to each other if they are not on a single sheet of paper.

Periodic Inspection Warrant

The affidavit for an administrative inspection warrant based on a periodic inspection must indicate the condition, object, activity, or circumstance for which the inspection is being made, but sometimes a general statement may be sufficient. What follows is a fictitious example:

> I, N. Spector, Livingston housing inspector, being duly sworn and examined under oath, state under oath that there is a program of inspection authorized by G.S. 160A-424 and the Livingston City Ordinance § 18.4 and that is part of a targeted effort within a geographic area designated by the city council that naturally includes the property owned or possessed by Harold R. Day and described as follows: a one-story yellow frame residence at 140 Jones Street, Livingston, North Carolina. The program of inspection referred to covers the area of the city of Livingston, specifically all residences on Jones Street and Main Street, and is being conducted for the purpose of checking or revealing the following: unsafe, unsanitary, and hazardous conditions. This is part of a periodic 10-year inspection of plumbing and electrical facilities. Ten-year periodic plumbing and electrical inspections of residences are justified by the National Building Code. All residences on Jones Street and Main Street are being checked at this time. This inspection program is a legal function of the Livingston Housing Department and is under the supervision of George Hollings, director of the Livingston Housing Department.

> Mr. Day has refused to allow me to inspect his house.

Warrant Based on a Particular Condition or Activity

Generally. An administrative inspection warrant based on a particular condition or activity should provide the facts—not just conclusions—that establish probable cause to believe that a reason exists to inspect a particular place. What follows is a fictitious example:

> I, N. Spector, Livingston housing inspector, being duly sworn and examined under oath, state under oath that there is probable cause for believing that there are unsafe, unsanitary, and hazardous conditions (see description below) at the property owned or possessed by Frank W. Brown and described as follows: a brick apartment building at 135 Jones Street, Livingston, North Carolina. The facts that establish probable cause to believe this are as follows: Two days ago Sam and Sylvia Wilson, who live on the street on which the above-described apartment building is located, told me that the plumbing in the apartment building does not work. They know about the plumbing because they both have been in the building in the past week, specifically Apartments 1 and 5, and sought to use the bathrooms there. The toilets did not work and were leaking. Yesterday Edward Duncan told me that he had visited Apartment 4 in the above-described building that day so he could consider whether to rent it. He saw water on the floor, broken windows, and rat holes. He also smelled the odor of urine and excrement. Mr. Frank W. Brown, the owner of the apartment building, has refused to allow me to inspect the building.

Inspection of a fire scene. As discussed in Chapter 3, the United States Supreme Court has ruled that fire personnel and others may enter a home or business without a warrant and remain there until they have put out the fire and have determined its origin, so that it will not start again after they leave.[250] Generally, however, once they

---

250. Michigan v. Tyler, 436 U.S. 499 (1978); Michigan v. Clifford, 464 U.S. 287 (1984). *See generally* 5 WAYNE R. LAFAVE, SEARCH AND SEIZURE: A TREATISE ON THE FOURTH AMENDMENT § 10.4 (5th ed. 2012).

leave the fire scene,[251] they must obtain an administrative inspection warrant or consent if they want to reenter the home or business to investigate the fire's origin further.[252] If they have information that establishes probable cause to believe that the fire was caused by a criminal act, such as arson, they must obtain a search warrant instead of an administrative inspection warrant before they reenter to search.[253] If, while they are inspecting the premises with an administrative inspection warrant, they determine the fire's origin and develop probable cause to believe that the fire was caused by a criminal act, they must obtain a search warrant to search the rest of the premises.[254]

The following fictitious example shows how an officer might complete an affidavit to obtain an administrative inspection warrant for a particular condition or activity to inspect a fire scene:

> I, Robert Montjoy, fire chief of the Millburn Fire Department, being duly sworn and examined under oath, state under oath that there is probable cause for believing that there is real and personal property that has been damaged or destroyed by fire at the property owned or possessed by Mr. and Mrs. J. K. Lamp, Jr., and described as follows: a two-story brick residence with blue trim and red shutters located at 919 Simmons Lane, Millburn, North Carolina, and occupied by Mr. and Mrs. J. K. Lamp, Jr. The facts that establish probable cause to believe this are as follows: The residence described above was partially destroyed by fire three nights ago on September 21, 2016. A preliminary investigation by Fire Inspector James Rhodes immediately after the fire was extinguished indicated that fire may have begun from a kerosene heater in a bedroom located on the second floor. However, additional investigation is necessary to determine the cause of the fire because Rhodes and other fire officials had to leave the Lamp residence shortly after the fire was extinguished to handle a major warehouse fire elsewhere in Millburn. I intend to inspect the kerosene heater, all electrical wiring in the house, and any other evidence that would help to establish the cause of the fire. Mr. and Mrs. Lamp, who were shopping when the fire began, have refused to allow my entry for the inspection.

G.S. 58-79-1 authorizes inspections to determine the cause of fires in which property has been damaged or destroyed.

Execution of an Administrative Inspection Warrant

An administrative inspection warrant is valid for only 24 hours from the time it is issued. It must be personally served on the owner or possessor of the property and executed between 8:00 a.m. and 8:00 p.m., and it must be returned to the clerk's or magistrate's office within 48 hours—whether or not it is executed. But if the warrant is issued to inspect the cause of a fire under G.S. 58-79-1, it may be executed at any hour. It is valid for 48 hours after its issuance, and it must be returned to the clerk's or magistrate's office without unnecessary delay after its execution or after the 48-hour period if it is not used.[255]

---

251. If smoke or darkness requires the fire officials to leave the building for a few hours, a warrantless reentry into the building to continue a determination of the fire's origin is permissible. *See* Michigan v. Tyler, 436 U.S. 499 (1978).

252. In *Michigan v. Clifford*, 464 U.S. 287 (1984), a majority of the Justices expressed the view that an administrative inspection warrant is not needed for an inspection to determine the fire's origin when the fire inspector gives or reasonably attempts to give the owner (or other person with privacy interests in the home or business) advance notice of the need to inspect so that the owner may be present at the inspection. Still, an officer should obtain an administrative inspection warrant until the Court (or a federal or North Carolina appellate court) rules that a warrant is unnecessary when advance notice is given or a reasonable attempt is made to give such notice.

If the home or business is damaged so much that it is no longer usable, the owner or possessor would not have a reasonable expectation of privacy there and could not successfully challenge a search conducted there. See the statement to that effect in *Clifford*, 464 U.S. at 292.

253. *Id.*

254. In *Michigan v. Clifford*, 464 U.S. 287 (1984), eight Justices agreed that once officers determined that the fire began in the basement and arson was the cause, they could not search the rest of the home without a search warrant.

255. G.S. 15-27.2(e). The statute does not literally require execution between 8:00 a.m. and 8:00 p.m. Rather, it requires only personal service on the owner between 8:00 a.m. and 8:00 p.m. It also does not literally require that personal service occur at the place to be inspected. However, the most reasonable interpretation of the statute requires that the warrant be

The warrant need not be personally served on the owner or possessor if the executing officer cannot find that person after a reasonable effort to do so. The officer may inspect the premises in the owner's or possessor's absence—still between 8:00 a.m. and 8:00 p.m., except for fire inspections—but the officer must leave a copy of the warrant in a conspicuous place so the owner or possessor may see it later.[256]

Anyone who willfully interferes with officers in entering the premises or making the inspection is guilty of resisting, delaying, or obstructing public officers in performing their duties, a Class 2 misdemeanor.[257] Generally, verbal abuse alone is not considered a violation unless it is so severe that it keeps officers from talking to witnesses or otherwise carrying out their inspection.[258] Reasonable force may be used to accomplish the inspection, if necessary. Officers may inspect the premises as extensively as is reasonably necessary to carry out the purposes of the inspection.

If, during the inspection with a warrant, an officer discovers evidence of a crime not related to the purpose of the inspection, North Carolina law prohibits the use of the evidence in any civil, criminal, or administrative proceeding or as a basis for obtaining any warrant.[259] For example, if a housing inspector saw marijuana while inspecting a house with a warrant for housing code violations, a law enforcement officer could not use that information later to obtain a search warrant to search that house. This prohibition does not apply, however, if the inspection was conducted with consent or if the inspection could have been made constitutionally without a warrant—for example, an emergency inspection—even though a warrant was used.[260]

Emergency Inspection without a Warrant

(See page 523 for case summaries on this topic.)

Sometimes an inspection may be made without a warrant in an emergency when officers have the authority to inspect but they reasonably believe that if they took the time to obtain a warrant, the condition or object for which they are making the inspection would likely disappear. For example, wildlife law enforcement officers and marine fisheries enforcement officers would have authority with some of their inspection powers[261] to inspect without a warrant if the evidence (wildlife, seafood products, and the like) would probably disappear if they took the time to obtain a warrant. These officers, whose duties include looking for unlawfully possessed things that can be disposed of easily, will sometimes encounter situations when an emergency inspection is justified. But building inspectors and others whose jobs are to inspect relatively permanent conditions will rarely be justified in conducting an emergency inspection, particularly an inspection of a home—a place entitled to the greatest protection of privacy under the Fourth Amendment.

Wildlife law enforcement officers and marine fisheries enforcement officers also are authorized to arrest for the misdemeanor offense of refusing to exhibit a license or under certain circumstances to allow inspection of weapons, equipment, fish, or wildlife.[262] A person who refuses to allow an inspection and is told that he or she will be arrested for that refusal may reconsider and permit the inspection.

---

executed during that time and personally served at the place to be inspected. As noted in the next paragraph of the text, the statute permits the warrant to be executed without personal service when the executing officer has made reasonable efforts at service.

256. *Id.*

257. G.S. 14-223.

258. State v. Leigh, 278 N.C. 243 (1971).

259. G.S. 15-27.2(f).

260. *Id.*

261. G.S. 113-136(g) permits marine fisheries enforcement officers to inspect a conveyance they reasonably believe is transporting seafood products. This statute would permit an emergency warrantless inspection under appropriate circumstances. G.S. 113-302.1(a) permits wildlife law enforcement officers to enter and inspect certain premises for wildlife. G.S. 113-302.1(c) would permit an emergency warrantless inspection under appropriate circumstances.

262. G.S. 113-136(k). This statute merely creates a misdemeanor offense and does not authorize an inspection when a person refuses. (There are limitations to the misdemeanor offense concerning the inspection of weapons and equipment.) But if the person is arrested for this offense, the search incident to arrest justification would permit a warrantless search of the arrestee's person and the area and objects within the arrestee's immediate control. If the person to be arrested is an occupant of a vehicle, the entire interior of the vehicle (including containers there) may under some circumstances be searched incident to the arrest. See the discussion of search incident to arrest in Chapter 3.

AUTHORIZATION TO SEEK WARRANT TO INSPECT ALL VEHICLES ENTERING OR APPROACHING A MUNICIPALITY IN WHICH A STATE OF EMERGENCY EXISTS

Note: This certificate should be attached to the affidavit.

As head of _____ ,
(Name and location of law enforcement agency)

I authorize _____
(Name and rank of officer who is to apply for warrant)

to seek a warrant for the inspection of all vehicles entering or approaching the municipality

of _____ , North Carolina.
(Name of municipality where state of emergency exists)

The warrant is being sought based on the belief that a state of emergency (as defined in G.S. 14-288.1) exists in the named municipality, and that the warrant is necessary to discover any dangerous weapons or substances likely to be used by a person who is or may become unlawfully involved in a riot.

Date:_____ , _____   _____
(Signature of head of agency)

Time: _____ (A.M.)(P.M.)   _____
(Printed name and title of head of agency)

AUTHORIZATION TO SEEK WARRANT TO INSPECT ALL VEHICLES WITHIN OR APPROACHING THE IMMEDIATE VICINITY OF A RIOT

Note: This certificate should be attached to the affidavit.

As head of _____ ,
(Name and location of law enforcement agency)

I authorize _____ to seek
(Name and rank of officer who is to apply for warrant)

a warrant for the inspection of all vehicles within or approaching the immediate vicinity of a riot, which exists

in the following area: _____
(Description of the area where riot is
occurring, with attached map if appropriate)

The warrant is being sought based on the belief that a riot (as defined in G.S. 14-288.2) exists in that area, and

in the belief that the warrant is necessary to discover any dangerous weapons or substances likely to be used

by a person who is or may become unlawfully involved in a riot.

Date: _____ , _____   _____
(Signature of head of agency)

Time: _____ (A.M.)(P.M.)   _____
(Printed name and title of head of agency)

STATE OF NORTH CAROLINA

AFFIDAVIT TO OBTAIN A WARRANT TO INSPECT ALL VEHICLES ENTERING OR APPROACHING A MUNICIPALITY IN WHICH A STATE OF EMERGENCY EXISTS

COUNTY OF _____

In the General Court of Justice

District/Superior Court Division

I,_____ , being duly sworn and examined
               (Applicant's name, rank, and department)

under oath, state under oath that I have been authorized by _____

_____ [see attached authorization certificate]
        (Name and rank of head of officer's agency)

to seek a warrant for the inspection of all vehicles entering or approaching the municipality of

_____ , North Carolina,
        (Name of municipality where state of emergency exists)

for the purpose of discovering any dangerous weapon or substance likely to be used by a person who is or

may become unlawfully involved in a riot. In support of that warrant, I state under oath that I believe that a

state of emergency (as defined in G.S. 14-288.1) exists in the named municipality. The facts that establish the

existence of a state of emergency are as follows:

_____

_____

_____

_____ (continue on additional sheets if necessary).

_____
             (Signature of applicant)

Subscribed and sworn to before me this _____ day of, _____ .

_____
            District/Superior Court Judge

STATE OF NORTH CAROLINA

WARRANT TO INSPECT ALL VEHICLES ENTERING OR APPROACHING A MUNICIPALITY WHERE A STATE OF EMERGENCY EXISTS

COUNTY OF _____

In the General Court of Justice

District/Superior Court Division

To any officer with jurisdiction to conduct inspection authorized by this warrant:

_____ ,

(Applicant's name, rank, and department)

being duly sworn, has stated to me that the applicant has been authorized by _____

_____ to seek this warrant to

(Name and rank of head of officer's agency)

inspect all vehicles entering or approaching the municipality of _____

_____ , North Carolina.

(Name of municipality where state of emergency exists)

I have examined this applicant under oath or affirmation and have determined that the applicant is so

authorized, and that a state of emergency (as defined in G.S. 14-288.1) does exist in this municipality.

Therefore, you are commanded to inspect such vehicles to discover any dangerous weapons or substances

likely to be used by a person who is or may become unlawfully involved in a riot.

THIS WARRANT MAY BE EXECUTED ONLY WHERE NECESSARY TO HALT THE TRANSPORTATION OF DANGEROUS

WEAPONS AND SUBSTANCES INTO THE MUNICIPALITY; NAMELY, ONLY WITHIN THE FOLLOWING AREA:

_____

_____

_____

_____ .

(Specify the area with reasonable precision, attaching map if appropriate)

NOTE: THIS WARRANT MAY BE EXECUTED ONLY WITHIN TWENTY-FOUR (24) HOURS FOLLOWING ITS ISSUANCE.

Issued this _____ day of _____, _____, at _____ (A.M.)(P.M.)

_____

District/Superior Court Judge

STATE OF NORTH CAROLINA

COUNTY OF _____

AFFIDAVIT TO OBTAIN A WARRANT TO INSPECT ALL VEHICLES WITHIN OR APPROACHING THE IMMEDIATE VICINITY OF A RIOT

In the General Court of Justice

District/Superior Court Division

I, _____ , being duly sworn and examined under oath,

(Applicant's name, rank, and department)

state under oath that I have been authorized by _____

_____ [see attached authorization certificate]

(Name and rank of head of officer's agency)

to seek a warrant for the inspection of all vehicles within or approaching the immediate vicinity of a riot, which

exists in the following area:

_____

(Description of area where riot is occurring, with attached map if appropriate)

_____

_____ (continue on additional sheets if necessary).

This warrant is for the purpose of discovering any dangerous weapon or substance likely to be used by a

person who is or may become unlawfully involved in a riot. In support of that warrant, I state under oath that I

believe that a riot (as defined in G.S. 14-288.2) exists in the area. The facts that establish the existence of a riot

in that area are as follows:

_____

_____

_____

_____ (continue on additional sheets if necessary).

_____

(Signature of applicant)

Subscribed and sworn to before me this _____ day of _____, _____.

_____

District/Superior Court Judge

STATE OF NORTH CAROLINA

COUNTY OF _____

WARRANT TO INSPECT ALL VEHICLES WITHIN OR APPROACHING THE IMMEDIATE VICINITY OF RIOT

In the General Court of Justice

District/Superior Court Division

To any officer with jurisdiction to conduct inspection authorized by this warrant:

_____ ,

(Applicant's name, rank, and department)

being duly sworn, has stated to me that the applicant has been authorized by

_____ to seek this warrant to

(Name and rank of head of officer's agency)

inspect all vehicles within or approaching the immediate vicinity of a riot, which exists in the following area:

_____

_____

_____ .

(Description of the area where the riot is occurring, with attached map if appropriate)

I have examined this applicant under oath or affirmation and have determined that the applicant is so authorized, and that a riot (as defined in G.S. 14-288.2) does exist in that area. Therefore, you are commanded to inspect such vehicles to discover any dangerous weapons or substances likely to be used by a person who is or may become unlawfully involved in the riot.

THIS WARRANT MAY BE EXECUTED ONLY WHERE NECESSARY TO HALT THE TRANSPORTATION OF DANGEROUS WEAPONS AND SUBSTANCES INTO THE VICINITY OF THE RIOT; NAMELY, ONLY WITHIN THE FOLLOWING AREA:

_____

_____

_____ .

(Specify the area with reasonable precision, attaching map if appropriate)

NOTE: THIS WARRANT MAY BE EXECUTED ONLY WITHIN TWENTY-FOUR (24) HOURS FOLLOWING ITS ISSUANCE.

Issued this _____ day of _____, _____, at _____ (A.M.)(P.M.)

_____

District/Superior Court Judge

Warrantless Inspections of Pervasively Regulated Industries

(*See page 522 for case summaries on this topic.*)

The United States Supreme Court has recognized the constitutionality of legislation that authorizes warrantless administrative inspections—or criminal prosecution or a civil penalty for not permitting a warrantless inspection—of commercial property of certain industries or enterprises (for example, mining, gun dealers, or liquor dealers) that are subject to pervasive regulation.[263] This subject will not be discussed further in this book.[264]

Part III. Nontestimonial Identification Orders

Readers should carefully note the special limitations concerning juveniles and nontestimonial identification orders, discussed in the last section of this part.

Introduction

As discussed in Chapters 2 and 3, officers may fully search an arrestee and any area or objects within that person's immediate control without a search warrant. They also may fingerprint and photograph the person, place him or her in a lineup, scrape under fingernails, take hair samples, wipe hands for a gunshot residue test, and the like.[265] Their authority to do these things flows automatically from an arrest based on probable cause,

probable cause to search, or both. But officers usually need probable cause and a search warrant or court order for more intrusive searches such as body-cavity probes or surgical intrusions. And to take a blood sample from a person, they need a search warrant supported by probable cause, unless exigent circumstances and probable cause exist that would allow taking a blood sample without a search warrant—for example, taking a blood sample to determine the alcohol concentration of a person who has committed a vehicular homicide.[266]

Sometimes an investigation clearly establishes probable cause that a crime was committed but only reasonable suspicion that a particular person or persons committed the crime. As discussed in Chapter 2, reasonable suspicion ordinarily allows officers only to detain a person briefly. If probable cause to arrest does not develop, they must release the person. Without that person's consent, officers may not take the person for interrogation elsewhere—for example, to their agency's headquarters—or conduct various searches and seizures that are permitted incident to arrest.[267]

What may officers do when they have only reasonable suspicion that a person committed a crime, but they need to obtain that person's fingerprints, conduct a lineup, or the like and the person will not consent? North Carolina law authorizes the use of a *nontestimonial identification order* to require that person to submit to certain identification tests that may possibly connect the person with a crime, even though there is not yet probable cause to arrest the person.[268] For example, a drug dealer has been murdered, and fingerprints and hair samples have been found at the scene. The crime scene indicates that robbery

---

263. *See generally* Donovan v. Dewey, 452 U.S. 594 (1981). For summaries of pertinent cases, see the case summaries section at the end of this chapter.

264. See the discussion of inspections of businesses in 5 Wayne R. LaFave, Search and Seizure: A Treatise on the Fourth Amendment § 10.2 (5th ed. 2012).

265. State v. Coplen, 138 N.C. App. 48 (2000) (court stated that although gunshot residue test is a nontestimonial identification procedure under G.S. 15A-271, that statute does not set out exclusive procedures for performing that test; court ruled that detective had probable cause and exigent circumstances to perform the test). *See also* State v. Page, 169 N.C. App. 127 (2005) (similar ruling). Although the *Coplen* ruling is based on a finding of probable cause and exigent circumstances, an officer clearly could take a hand wiping from a defendant for a gunshot residue test as a proper search incident to arrest.

266. State v. Carter, 322 N.C. 709 (1988); Schmerber v. California, 384 U.S. 757 (1966). However, a blood sample may be taken from a juvenile with a nontestimonial identification order, as discussed in the text on page 465.

267. Dunaway v. New York, 442 U.S. 200 (1979); Davis v. Mississippi, 394 U.S. 721 (1969). In *Hayes v. Florida*, 470 U.S. 811 (1985), the United States Supreme Court noted that the Fourth Amendment may permit officers to detain a person briefly in the field (without a court order) to fingerprint the person when they have reasonable suspicion that the person committed a crime and a reasonable belief that fingerprinting will establish or negate the suspect's connection with the crime.

268. G.S. 15A-271 through -282; 7B-2103 through -2106. Dicta in *Davis v. Mississippi*, 394 U.S. 721 (1969), and *Hayes v. Florida*, 470 U.S. 811 (1985), are the constitutional underpinnings for using a nontestimonial identification order against a person for whom probable cause to arrest does not exist.

was the motive. Several people immediately become prime suspects because of their close connection with the victim, their involvement in drug trafficking, their probable match with the hair sample, and their lack of an alibi for the time of the murder. Probable cause may not yet exist to arrest any of the suspects, but a hair sample and fingerprints taken from each would clearly help establish whether one or more of them committed the crime. A district attorney or an assistant district attorney may request a nontestimonial identification order from a district or superior court judge that would require each suspect to provide hair samples and submit to fingerprinting. A suspect who does not comply with the order may be held in contempt of court, discussed later in this chapter.

A judge also may issue a nontestimonial identification order to require a person who has been arrested with probable cause and has been released from custody pending trial to submit to a nontestimonial identification procedure, even if the procedure could have been conducted automatically incident to arrest without a nontestimonial identification order. However, if the arrestee is still in custody, a judge has no authority (on the State's motion) to issue a nontestimonial identification order. Instead, the officer should obtain a search warrant or a court order.[269] (See also the discussion of nontestimonial identification

orders in Part II, "Lineups and Other Identification Procedures," in Chapter 5.)

Authority to Conduct Nontestimonial Identification Procedures

(See page 531 for case summaries on this topic.)

The nontestimonial identification order may be used only for a nontestimonial identification, which means that it may not be used to bring a suspect in for interrogation. The kinds of tests or procedures that might be required include fingerprints, palm prints, footprints, measurements, urine specimens, saliva samples, hair samples, handwriting samples, voice samples, photographs, lineups or similar identification procedures requiring the presence of a suspect, hand wiping for gunshot residue, and the like.[270] Although the statute involving adult suspects also permits taking a blood sample with a nontestimonial identification order based on reasonable suspicion, the North Carolina Supreme Court has ruled that the North Carolina Constitution requires probable cause and a search warrant to take a blood sample unless exigent circumstances permit taking the blood sample without a search warrant (of course, probable cause must also exist when acting without a search warrant).[271] The statute involving juvenile suspects, discussed later in this chapter, permits taking a blood sample with a nontestimonial identification order based on probable cause and thus effectively complies with the North Carolina Supreme Court ruling.

A nontestimonial identification order may be used only to determine whether the suspect committed the offense. For example, a North Carolina case ruled that a judge did not have authority to issue a nontestimonial identification order to require a defendant charged with automobile manslaughter to take a visual-acuity test to determine whether the defendant was grossly negligent in driving his car, because the test did not help identify the defendant as the driver who committed the offense.[272]

---

269. The North Carolina Supreme Court ruled in *State v. Welch*, 316 N.C. 578 (1986), relying on *State v. Irick*, 291 N.C. 480 (1977), that a judge may issue a nontestimonial identification order on the State's motion only when a person (1) has not been arrested (but reasonable suspicion exists that the person committed a crime punishable by more than one year's imprisonment—now, a felony or Class A1 or 1 misdemeanor) or (2) has been arrested and released from custody pending trial. The court ruled that a superior court judge erred when he issued such an order when the defendant had been arrested for murder and armed robbery and was in jail awaiting trial. Thus, an officer must obtain a search warrant (or court order; see the next paragraph) instead of a nontestimonial identification order if the officer wants to use legal process before taking the samples mentioned in the text. If the officer wants to conduct more intrusive procedures, such as taking a blood sample, the officer must obtain a search warrant unless the defendant consents or probable cause and exigent circumstances exist; see *State v. Carter*, 322 N.C. 709 (1988).

Although the *Welch* court discussed only the use of a search warrant (when a judge had no authority to issue a nontestimonial identification order because the defendant had been arrested and was still in custody), a judge has the inherent authority to issue a court order to compel the defendant to submit to a nontestimonial procedure if the prosecutor makes a sufficient showing (similar to a probable cause statement in

an affidavit for a search warrant) to support the order. *Cf. In re Superior Court Order*, 315 N.C. 378 (1986).

270. G.S. 15A-271; 7B-2103.

271. *State v. Carter*, 322 N.C. 709 (1988).

272. *State v. Whaley*, 58 N.C. App. 233 (1982). It would appear that a judge would have authority to issue such an order (but not as a nontestimonial identification order) if a reasonable basis supported it, because the defendant has no

Application for the Order and Issuance of the Order; Adult and Juvenile Suspect Forms

The AOC prepares four forms that may be used to apply for and obtain a nontestimonial identification order. Two forms involving adult suspects are AOC-CR-204 (prosecutor's application, with an affidavit to support it) and AOC-CR-205 (nontestimonial identification order). These forms should be used with a person who is charged with a crime committed on or after his or her 16th birthday, a juvenile charged as an adult,[273] or a juvenile whose case has been transferred to superior court for trial as an adult. Two forms involving juvenile suspects are AOC-J-204 (prosecutor's application, with an affidavit to support it) and AOC-J-205 (nontestimonial identification order). These forms should be used with a person who is charged with a crime committed before his or her 16th birthday, who is *not* charged as an adult,[274] and whose case has *not* been transferred to superior court for trial as an adult.[275] All four forms are available from the AOC's website at www.nccourts.org/Forms/FormSearch.asp, where they also may be completed and printed. (For a list of forms available on the AOC website, see the sidebar on page 412.)

A nontestimonial identification order may be issued only by a judge, not by a magistrate or clerk, and only a district attorney or assistant district attorney may apply for the order.[276] An affidavit—ordinarily filled out by the investigating officer—must be submitted with the prosecutor's application, which must establish that (1) a felony or Class A1 or Class 1 misdemeanor has been committed (for juveniles, a felony only); (2) there are reasonable grounds to suspect that the person to be tested has committed the offense; and (3) the results of the nontestimonial identification procedure would materially aid in determining whether the suspect committed the offense.[277] The same kind of information that may establish probable cause to issue a search warrant (discussed earlier in this chapter) or arrest warrant may be used to establish reasonable grounds to suspect that the person committed the offense—and the same rules about confidentiality of informants apply.

"Reasonable grounds to suspect" is the same as reasonable suspicion, which is discussed in Chapter 2. Reasonable suspicion is something less than probable cause, but the reasons for suspicion must be specifically stated. The prosecutor's application with its supporting affidavit must provide facts to show why the person is suspected of committing the crime. It is not enough that the suspect has a bad reputation, the prosecutor has a hunch that the suspect committed the robbery, or that the suspect is "known" to be involved in this kind of crime. For example, some relevant factors in a robbery case would include whether the suspect matched an eyewitness's description, had a prior history of similar crimes, had been seen near the crime scene, recently threatened the victim, owned a gun like the one used in the robbery, or had distinctive clothes similar to those seen on the robber; whether there were reports from informants of the suspect's involvement; and whether there were any specific facts that point to the suspect (not all of these would be necessary to establish reasonable suspicion).

The North Carolina Supreme Court in *State v. Pearson*[278] ruled that reasonable suspicion supported the issuance of a nontestimonial identification order to require a rape suspect to supply head and pubic hair samples and a saliva sample. The suspect met the physical description of the perpetrator given by two rape victims. A peeping tom was reported at the location of one of the rapes—about eight months before the rape occurred at that location. An officer saw a man, wearing a light gray or

---

recognizable Fourth or Fifth Amendment objections to such a test.

273. G.S. 7B-1604(a) provides that a juvenile who is emancipated (for example, is married) must be prosecuted as an adult. G.S. 7B-1604(b) provides that a juvenile who is transferred to and convicted in superior court must be prosecuted as an adult for any criminal offense committed after the superior court conviction.

274. *See supra* note 273.

275. The title of G.S. 7B-2103, "Authority to issue nontestimonial identification order where juvenile *alleged to be delinquent*" (emphasis added), clearly shows the legislative intent that a nontestimonial identification order under that section applies only to a juvenile who commits an offense before his or her 16th birthday and is not charged as an adult. Also, the section's text specifically excepts from its coverage a nontestimonial identification order for a juvenile charged as an adult or whose case has been transferred to superior court for trial as an adult. See also note 439 of Chapter 2.

276. G.S. 15A-271; 7B-2103.

277. G.S. 15A-273; 7B-2105(a). *See* State v. Pearson, 356 N.C. 22 (2001) (court ruled that there was reasonable suspicion to support issuance of nontestimonial identification order to require rape suspect to supply head and pubic hair samples and a saliva sample).

278. 356 N.C. 22 (2002).

blue windbreaker and blue jeans, squatting near an air-conditioning unit directly behind an apartment building. The man ran when he saw the officer. Shortly thereafter, the defendant—wearing blue jeans and a light blue windbreaker—was stopped by an officer.

In applying for a nontestimonial identification order, prosecutors must state what specific procedures they are requesting and why the procedures will materially aid in determining whether the suspect committed the offense.

If the judge issues the order, the order must tell the person when and where to appear, what procedures will be used and how long they will take, the reasons for suspecting the person, and the consequences of not appearing—being found in contempt of court. The order also must state that the person will not be subject to interrogation and is entitled to be represented by counsel, that counsel will be appointed if the person cannot afford to pay for counsel, and that the person may request a change in the time and place of appearance.[279] This information is printed on both AOC-CR-204 and AOC-J-205.

Service of the Order and Modification of the Order

The nontestimonial identification order must be served on the suspect personally. Officers should obtain a search warrant to enter private premises to serve the order if they do not obtain consent to enter. Generally, service must be made at least 72 hours before the suspect's appearance is required. However, if the judge who issues the order determines that delay would probably adversely affect the probative value (usefulness in establishing proof) of the evidence being sought, the judge may set it earlier or dispense with notice altogether.[280] Abandoning the 72-hour notice might be justified, for example, if there was evidence that a male suspect might substantially alter his appearance by shaving off his beard to reduce the likelihood of identification at a lineup, or if the suspect might flee the jurisdiction.

The person who is ordered to appear may ask the judge who issued the order to change the time or place of appearance. For example, the person may ask that a procedure, other than a lineup, take place at his or her residence.[281] Although the statute does not say so, the person probably could also request a change in the nature of the procedure if it is more intrusive than necessary to achieve its purpose.

The Nontestimonial Identification Procedure

(*See page 533 for case summaries on this topic.*)

A person who is ordered to submit to an identification procedure may be found in contempt for either willfully not appearing or not cooperating, and the person's noncompliance with the order may be considered with other evidence in determining whether there is probable cause to arrest the person for the crime.[282] The procedure may be conducted by any law enforcement officer or other person designated by the judge who issued the order. Any extraction of bodily fluid must be done by a qualified health professional, such as a doctor, nurse, or medical technician. The judge can order medical supervision of any other kind of test.[283]

The person is entitled to have counsel present—and counsel appointed if the person is indigent—and must be told about this right before the test takes place.[284] If the person makes any statement during the identification procedure—other than that required by a procedure, such as a voice identification—the statement is not admissible as evidence against the person unless counsel was present.[285]

---

281. G.S. 15A-275, -278(7); 7B-2106.

282. G.S. 15A-279(g); 7B-2106.

283. G.S. 15A-279(a); 7B-2106.

284. G.S. 15A-279(d); 7B-2106. Although there is a statutory right to counsel provided by these statutes, there generally is no Sixth Amendment right to counsel when nontestimonial identification procedures are conducted, such as taking handwriting samples (Gilbert v. California, 388 U.S. 263 (1967)); taking blood (Schmerber v. California, 384 U.S. 757 (1966)); taking hair and fingerprints (United States v. Wade, 388 U.S. 218 (1967)); and the administration of a gunshot residue test (State v. Odom, 303 N.C. 163 (1981)). Thus, if these procedures are lawfully conducted (for example, as a search incident to arrest or based on probable cause), other than under the nontestimonial identification procedures provided by these statutes, a person does not have a right to counsel. But note that there is a Sixth Amendment right to counsel at an in-person lineup after the state has initiated adversary judicial proceedings (Kirby v. Illinois, 406 U.S. 682 (1972)).

285. G.S. 15A-279(d); 7B-2106.

---

279. G.S. 15A-278; 7B-2106.

280. G.S. 15A-277; 7B-2106.

A person may be held only long enough for the test to be conducted—no more than six hours, unless the person is arrested. No unreasonable or unnecessary force may be used in conducting the identification procedure.[286]

Criminal and Civil Contempt

If the person willfully fails to appear or refuses to cooperate, the prosecutor may inform the judge who issued the order. The judge may then order the suspect to appear in court and show why he or she should not be held in civil[287] or criminal[288] contempt. But the suspect may not be found in both civil and criminal contempt for the same conduct.[289]

The purpose of civil contempt is to compel compliance with a court order. If the judge finds the suspect in civil contempt, the judge may order the person imprisoned for up to 90 days, unless the suspect had been arrested before the nontestimonial identification order was issued.[290] A suspect who had been arrested may be imprisoned for successive 90-day periods, up to 12 months, as long as he or she continues to refuse to comply with the nontestimonial identification order.[291]

The purpose of criminal contempt is to punish contemptuous conduct. If the judge finds the suspect in criminal contempt, the judge may order the suspect imprisoned for up to 90 days and fined up to $500.[292]

A procedure that might be done without a suspect's cooperation, such as taking a hair sample or fingerprints, can be accomplished with reasonable force. But if a procedure, such as the taking of a handwriting or voice sample, requires the suspect's cooperation, the only apparent option would be to seek a recommitment for an additional 90 days when a civil contempt term expires (assuming the defendant had been arrested based on probable cause) and try again to conduct the procedure.[293]

A person's refusal to submit to a nontestimonial identification procedure may be admissible at trial.[294]

Return of the Order and the Inventory of Results

The suspect or his or her counsel must be given a copy of the report of the test results as soon as it becomes available.[295] Within 90 days after the procedure for an adult suspect, an inventory of the results must be returned to the judge who issued the order or another judge designated by the issuing judge. If probable cause to arrest has not been established then, the person who was tested may move for the destruction of copies of products and test results from the procedure. The motion must be granted unless the prosecutor can show good reason for not doing so.[296]

Detailed procedures for the destruction or retention of records of a nontestimonial identification procedure conducted with a juvenile are set out in G.S. 7B-2108.

Defendant's Request for a Nontestimonial Identification Order

(*See page 533 for case summaries on this topic.*)

An adult arrested for or charged with a felony or a Class A1 or Class 1 misdemeanor or a juvenile in custody or charged with a felony may request that nontestimonial

---

286. G.S. 15A-279(b), (c); 7B-2106. *See generally* United States v. Bullock, 71 F.3d 171 (5th Cir. 1995) (use of force in executing search warrant to take blood was reasonable under Fourth Amendment); Rendleman v. Scott, 378 Fed. Appx. 309 (4th Cir. 2010) (unpublished) (proper to threaten force to take DNA sample from prisoner).

287. G.S. 15A-279(e); 5A-21(a), -21(b), & -21(b1).

288. G.S. 15A-279(e); 5A-11(a)(3), -11(a)(10), -12(a).

289. G.S. 5A-12(d), -21(c), -23(g).

290. G.S. 5A-21(b1).

291. G.S. 5A-21(b2). The North Carolina Supreme Court ruled in *State v. Welch*, 316 N.C. 578 (1986), relying on *State v. Irick*, 291 N.C. 480 (1977), that a judge has no authority to issue a nontestimonial identification order when a defendant has been arrested and is in custody, but the court stated that such an order could be used when the arrestee has been released from custody pending trial. *See supra* note 269. If a prosecutor or officer obtained a court order, issued under the court's inherent authority, directing the defendant to give a handwriting sample when a nontestimonial identification order was not authorized because the defendant was in custody, the defendant's refusal to comply with the court order also could subject the defendant to criminal or civil contempt.

292. G.S. 5A-12(a).

293. *See* G.S. 5A-21(b1), (b2).

294. See note 167 in Chapter 5.

295. G.S. 15A-282; 7B-2106.

296. G.S. 15A-280.

identification procedures be conducted on him or her.[297] For example, the person may request that a lineup be conducted to determine whether the robbery victim can identify the person. Just as with the prosecutor's request, however, before a judge must order the State to conduct the procedure, the person must show that the procedure will materially aid in determining whether the person committed the offense.[298]

Other Lawful Identification Procedures

North Carolina law specifically provides that the nontestimonial identification order provisions do not prohibit the use of other lawful identification procedures.[299] Thus, a search warrant, a court order, the authority flowing automatically from arrest, and reasonable force when appropriate (see the discussions in Chapters 2 and 3) may be used instead of a nontestimonial identification order.

Juveniles and Nontestimonial Identification Procedures

(*See page 532 for case summaries on this topic.*)

North Carolina law generally prohibits officers from conducting any nontestimonial identification procedure on a juvenile unless a superior or district court judge issues a nontestimonial identification order.[300] However, there are exceptions for fingerprinting or photographing a juvenile. First, a law enforcement officer or agency must fingerprint and photograph a juvenile who was 10 years old or older when the juvenile allegedly committed a nondivertible offense: first-degree and second-degree murder, rape, sexual offense, and arson; first-degree

burglary; crime against nature; felony drug violation; and any felony involving the willful infliction of serious bodily injury or committed with a deadly weapon.[301] The duty to fingerprint occurs when a complaint has been prepared for filing as a petition and the juvenile is in the physical custody of law enforcement or the Division of Juvenile Justice (formerly, Department of Juvenile Justice and Delinquency Prevention).[302] Second, a juvenile may be fingerprinted and photographed if the juvenile has been charged as an adult[303] or the juvenile's case has been transferred to superior court for trial as an adult.[304] Third, a law enforcement officer or agency must fingerprint and photograph a juvenile who has been adjudicated delinquent if the juvenile was 10 years old or older when the juvenile committed a felony.[305]

Unlike the situation with adults, a nontestimonial identification order may be used when a juvenile is in custody.[306] Also, unlike with adults, an officer may not conduct a nontestimonial identification procedure on a juvenile (for example, photographing the juvenile) even if the juvenile consents to the procedure.[307]

An officer who willfully violates the laws concerning nontestimonial identification procedures on juveniles is guilty of a Class 1 misdemeanor.[308]

---

297. G.S. 15A-281; 7B-2107.

298. G.S. 15A-281; G.S. 7B-2107; State v. Abdullah, 66 N.C. App. 173 (1984); State v. Jackson, 306 N.C. 642 (1982). *See* State v. Tucker, 329 N.C. 709 (1991) (defendant sought nontestimonial identification order to require a State's witness to provide hair sample for analysis; court ruled that there is no statutory or other authorization for such an order); State v. Ryals, 179 N.C. App. 733 (2006) (similar ruling; defendant sought nontestimonial identification order to require State's witness to provide DNA sample).

299. G.S. 15A-272; State v. Page, 169 N.C. App. 127 (2005); State v. Coplen, 138 N.C. App. 48 (2000); State v. McLean, 47 N.C. App. 672 (1982).

300. G.S. 7B-2103 through -2109; 15A-502(c).

301. G.S. 7B-2102(a). A nondivertible offense is defined in G.S. 7B-1701.

302. The Department of Juvenile Justice and Delinquency Prevention was renamed the Division of Juvenile Justice when several state departments were consolidated into a new Department of Public Safety by S.L. 2011-145.

303. Under G.S. 7B-1604, a juvenile who is emancipated must be prosecuted as an adult and a juvenile who has been convicted of an offense in superior court must be prosecuted as an adult for offenses committed thereafter. Also, G.S. 7B-2103 excepts from its provisions requiring a nontestimonial identification order a "juvenile [who] has been charged as an adult."

304. G.S. 7B-2103.

305. G.S. 7B-2102(b).

306. The language in G.S. 7B-2103 clearly applies to all custodial and noncustodial situations involving juveniles, unlike the language in G.S. 15A-272 ("prior to the arrest of a suspect or after arrest and prior to trial") that was the basis of the rulings in *State v. Welch*, 316 N.C. 578 (1986), and *State v. Irick*, 291 N.C. 480 (1977), that a nontestimonial identification order may not be used when an adult suspect is in custody.

307. State v. Green, 124 N.C. App. 269 (1996).

308. G.S. 7B-2109.

Blood Samples

As discussed earlier, the North Carolina Supreme Court has ruled that under the North Carolina Constitution, blood may not be taken from a person unless probable cause exists, and blood may not be taken without a search warrant unless probable cause *and* exigent circumstances exist.[309] Thus, a nontestimonial identification order for adult suspects, which is based on reasonable suspicion, may not be used to take blood. On the other hand, the law dealing with juvenile suspects specifically authorizes the use of a nontestimonial identification order to take blood from a juvenile suspect when a judge finds *probable cause* to do so.[310] This law effectively complies with the North Carolina Supreme Court ruling.[311]

Juvenile's Age

Although there is some uncertainty about what age constitutes a juvenile for the purpose of conducting nontestimonial identification procedures, clearly the more persuasive view is that a juvenile is a person under 16 years old—not a person under 18 years old.[312] (See the discussion on page 461 of circumstances under which the adult or the juvenile suspect form should be used.) Officers may wish to consult their agency's legal advisor or their district attorney to determine how they should handle nontestimonial identification procedures for 16- and 17-year-olds.

Showup Identification Conducted Shortly after Crime without Nontestimonial Identification Order

The North Carolina Supreme Court in *In re Stallings*[313] ruled that shortly after a crime occurred an officer properly conducted, without obtaining a nontestimonial identification order, a one-on-one showup with a victim and juvenile suspects (see the discussion of showups in Chapter 5). The court reasoned that the legislature did not intend to prohibit this law enforcement technique. If officers had to take the time to obtain a court order, they would never be able to conduct a showup immediately after a crime occurred.[314] The court also ruled that the showup between the victim of a housebreaking and two juvenile suspects that occurred about an hour after the crime had been committed did not violate constitutional due process: the victim's identification was sufficiently reliable, based on her observation of the suspects running from her house and her later identification of them at the crime scene.

Transfer of Juvenile's Case to Adult Court

As discussed above, officers may fingerprint and photograph a juvenile without a nontestimonial identification order when the juvenile's case has been transferred to superior court for trial as an adult. The other nontestimonial identification procedures applicable to adults, discussed earlier in this chapter, also then apply to the juvenile.[315]

---

309. State v. Carter, 322 N.C. 709 (1988).

310. G.S. 7B-2105(b).

311. Although the court in *State v. Carter*, 322 N.C. 709 (1988), spoke of probable cause and a search warrant to take blood, it clearly would approve of the use of a nontestimonial identification order based on probable cause. A nontestimonial identification order is issued by a judicial official, as is a search warrant, and thus there is no substantive difference between them under the court's constitutionally based ruling.

312. *See supra* note 275.

313. 318 N.C. 565 (1986). The court's ruling reversed the opinion of the North Carolina Court of Appeals, 77 N.C. App. 592 (1985), and effectively reversed the ruling in *State v. Norris*, 77 N.C. App. 525 (1985), that a one-on-one showup cannot be conducted with a juvenile without a nontestimonial identification order.

314. This ruling may permit, for example, the administration of an alcohol breath test on a juvenile in an impaired driving case without a nontestimonial identification order, because alcohol in the body would dissipate while an officer attempted to obtain an order.

315. G.S. 7B-2103.

Chapter 4 Appendix: Case Summaries

Chapter 4 Appendix: Case Summaries

I. Search Warrants

Probable Cause
Generally
(*This topic is discussed on page 423.*)

UNITED STATES SUPREME COURT

Massachusetts v. Upton, 466 U.S. 727 (1984). The Court reaffirmed its abandonment in *Illinois v. Gates* of the two-pronged test and again made clear that a reviewing court must not conduct a de novo determination of probable cause but rather must merely decide whether the evidence viewed as a whole provided a "substantial basis" for the issuing official's finding of probable cause. The Court determined that the warrant to search a motor home in this case was supported by probable cause. An officer received a telephone call from a person he reasonably believed was the suspect's girlfriend, who told him that she saw stolen items in a motor home. He also corroborated some of her information, including verifying that the motor home was where she said it was.

Illinois v. Gates, 462 U.S. 213 (1983). The Court abandoned the two-pronged test of *Aguilar v. Texas*, 378 U.S. 108 (1964), and *Spinelli v. United States*, 393 U.S. 410 (1969), which had been used for determining probable cause based on information supplied by informants. Instead, the two prongs (the informant's veracity or the reliability of the information and the informant's basis of knowledge) are simply relevant factors when considering the totality of circumstances that guides probable cause determinations. The warrant-issuing official's task is to make a practical commonsense decision whether—given all the circumstances set out in the affidavit, including the veracity and basis of knowledge of persons who supply hearsay information—there is a "fair probability" that evidence of a crime will be found in a particular place. A reviewing court's duty in evaluating the official's determination of probable cause is simply to ensure that the official had a substantial basis for concluding that prob-

able cause existed; a court is not to make a de novo determination of probable cause.

The Court determined that the warrant to search a home and car in this case was supported by probable cause. The police received an anonymous letter describing how an Illinois couple planned to go to Florida and drive back with drugs, and officers corroborated a major part of the letter's predictions. One inaccuracy in the letter did not undermine the probable cause finding. The Court stated that police informants need not be infallible. *See also* United States v. Walker, 237 F.3d 845 (7th Cir. 2001) (anonymous tip plus police corroboration provided probable cause to issue search warrant).

United States v. Harris, 403 U.S. 573 (1971). If the informant has made a statement against his or her penal interest (that is, an admission that he or she has committed a crime), that statement may be considered in crediting the information the informant gave an officer in an affidavit for a search warrant. The Court ruled that probable cause existed when the informant told the officer-affiant that (1) he had purchased illegal liquor in a residence for more than two years and most recently within the last two weeks and (2) he had personal knowledge that purchasers consumed illegal liquor on the premises.

United States v. Ventresca, 380 U.S. 102 (1965). Other officers' observations that are included in the applying officer's affidavit are considered reliable for purposes of determining probable cause to issue a search warrant. The Court ruled that the affiant's and a fellow officer's observations (including the smell of fermenting mash that they detected outside a house from the sidewalk) detailed in an affidavit established probable cause to search the house for an illegal distillery. The Court stated that reviewing courts should interpret affidavits in "commonsense and realistic fashion. They are normally drafted by nonlawyers in the midst and haste of a criminal investigation. Technical requirements of elaborate specificity once exacted under common law pleadings have no proper place in this area. A grudging or negative attitude by reviewing courts toward warrants will tend to discourage police officers from submitting their evidence to a judicial officer before acting."

Aguilar v. Texas, 378 U.S. 108 (1964). An affidavit failed to supply probable cause when it merely provided a conclusory statement—that is, without any underlying facts—that the affiant "received information from a credible person and [believed] that heroin, marijuana, barbiturates and other narcotic paraphernalia [were] being kept at the above described premises for the purpose of sale and use contrary to the provisions of the law."

Rugendorf v. United States, 376 U.S. 528 (1964). The Court ruled that probable cause existed for a search warrant when a reliable informant had seen stolen furs (the informant's description of furs closely matched an officer's description of furs recently stolen in the area) in a home within the past week, and other information indicated that the defendant fenced stolen goods.

Jones v. United States, 362 U.S. 257 (1960). Probable cause for a search warrant may be based essentially on hearsay information supplied by a reliable informant, when there is a substantial basis for crediting the hearsay. The Court ruled that probable cause existed when the officer-affiant established the informant's reliability and provided the underlying facts—for example, that the informant had recently purchased drugs from the defendant's apartment—to support a belief that illegal drugs were in the place to be searched.

Nathanson v. United States, 290 U.S. 41 (1933). An affidavit failed to supply probable cause when it merely provided a conclusory statement—that is, without any underlying facts—that the affiant believed that certain liquor had been brought illegally into the United States and was located in certain described premises.

NORTH CAROLINA SUPREME COURT

State v. McKinney, 368 N.C. 1 (2015). Reversing the court of appeals, 231 N.C. App. 594 (2014), the court ruled that the trial court properly denied the defendant's motion to suppress, finding that probable cause existed to justify issuance of a search warrant authorizing a search of the defendant's apartment. The application was based on the following evidence: an anonymous citizen reported observing suspected drug-related activity at and around the apartment; the officer then saw an individual named Foushee come to the apartment and leave after six minutes; Foushee was searched and, after he was found with marijuana and a large amount of cash, arrested; and a search of Foushee's phone revealed text messages between Foushee and an individual named Chad proposing a drug transaction. The court rejected the defendant's argument that the citizen's complaint was unreliable because it gave no indication when the citizen observed the events, that the complaint was only a "naked assertion" that the observed activities were narcotics related, and that the State failed to establish a nexus between Foushee's vehicle and the defendant's apartment, finding none of these arguments persuasive, individually or collectively. The court held that "under the totality of circumstances, all the evidence described in the affidavit both established a substantial nexus between the marijuana remnants recovered from Foushee's vehicle and defendant's residence, and also was sufficient to support the magistrate's finding of probable cause to search defendant's apartment."

State v. Elder, 368 N.C. 70 (2015). Modifying and affirming the court of appeals, 232 N.C. App. 80 (2014), the court ruled that the district court exceeded its statutory authority under G.S. 50B-3 by ordering a search of the defendant's person, vehicle, and residence pursuant to an ex parte civil Domestic Violence Order of Protection (DVPO) and that the ensuing search violated the defendant's constitutional rights. Relying on G.S. 50B-3(a)(13) (authorizing the court to order "any additional prohibitions or requirements the court deems necessary to protect any party or any minor child"), the district court included in the DVPO a provision stating, "[a]ny Law Enforcement officer serving this Order shall search the Defendant's person, vehicle and residence and seize any and all weapons found." The district court made no findings or conclusions that probable cause existed to search the defendant's property or that the defendant even owned or possessed a weapon. Following this mandate, the officer who served the order conducted a search as instructed. As a result of evidence found, the defendant was charged with drug crimes. The defendant unsuccessfully moved to suppress, was convicted, and appealed. The supreme court concluded that the catchall provision in G.S. 50B-3 "does not authorize the court to order law enforcement, which is not a party to the civil DVPO, to proactively search defendant's person, vehicle, or residence." The court further concluded that "by requiring officers to conduct a search of defendant's home under sole authority of a civil DVPO without a warrant or probable cause, the district court's order violated defendant's constitutional rights" under the Fourth Amendment.

State v. Benters, 367 N.C. 660 (2014). The court ruled that an affidavit supporting a search warrant failed to provide a substantial basis for the magistrate to conclude that probable cause existed. In the affidavit, the affiant officer stated that another officer conveyed to him a tip from a confidential informant that the suspect was growing marijuana at a specified premises. The affiant then recounted certain corroboration done by officers. The court first held that the tipster would be treated as anonymous, not as one who is confidential and reliable. It explained: "It is clear from the affidavit that the information provided does not contain a statement against the source's penal interest. Nor does the affidavit indicate that the source previously provided reliable information so as to have an established 'track record.' Thus, the source cannot be treated as a confidential and reliable informant on these two bases." The court rejected the State's argument that because an officer met "face-to-face" with the source, the source should be considered more reliable, reasoning: "The affidavit does not suggest [the affiant] was acquainted with or knew anything about [the] source or could rely on anything other than [the other officer's] statement that the source was confidential and reliable." Treating the source as an anonymous tipster, the court found that the tip was supported by insufficient corroboration. The State argued that the following corroboration supported the tip: the affiant's knowledge of the defendant and his property resulting "from a criminal case involving a stolen flatbed trailer"; subpoenaed utility records indicating that the defendant was the current subscriber and that the kilowatt usage hours are indicative of a marijuana growing operation; and officers' observations of items at the premises indicative of an indoor marijuana growing operation, including potting soil, starting fertilizer, seed starting trays, plastic cups, metal storage racks, and portable pump-type sprayers. Considering the novel issue of utility records offered in support of probable cause, the court noted that "[t]he weight given to power records increases when meaningful comparisons are made between a suspect's current electricity consumption and prior consumption, or between a suspect's consumption and that of nearby, similar properties." It continued: "By contrast, little to no value should be accorded to wholly conclusory, non-comparative allegations regarding energy usage records." Here, the affidavit summarily concluded that kilowatt usage was indicative of a marijuana growing operation and that "the absence of any comparative analysis severely limits the potentially significant value of defendant's utility records." Thus, the court concluded: "[T]hese unsupported allegations do little to establish probable cause independently or by corroborating the anonymous tip." The court was similarly unimpressed by the officers' observation of plant growing items, noting:

> The affidavit does not state whether or when the gardening supplies were, or appeared to have been, used, or whether the supplies appeared to be new, or old and in disrepair. Thus, amid a field of speculative possibilities, the affidavit impermissibly requires the magistrate to make what otherwise might be reasonable inferences based on conclusory allegations rather than sufficient underlying circumstances. This we cannot abide.

As to the affidavit's extensive recounting of the officers' experience, the court ruled:

> We are not convinced that these officers' training and experience are sufficient to balance the quantitative and qualitative deficit left by an anonymous tip amounting to little more than a rumor, limited corroboration of facts, non-comparative utility records, observations of innocuous gardening supplies, and a compilation of conclusory allegations.

State v. Dickens, 346 N.C. 26 (1997). An officer's affidavit provided probable cause to take blood samples from the defendant. The affidavit contained (1) a description of the murder (the female victim was beaten to death with a hammer); (2) an accomplice's statement that the defendant struck the victim several times but the accomplice was uncertain whether the defendant sexually assaulted the victim; (3) the defendant's assertion that he did not actually see his accomplice sexually assault the victim, although she was on the floor and the mattress was partially off the bed when the defendant entered the bedroom; (4) the accomplice's description of the clothes the defendant was wearing when the murder was committed; (5) confirmation that the defendant's clothes were submitted to the SBI serology laboratory; (6) an officer's advice concerning the advantages of obtaining a DNA profile from a suspect; and (7) the defendant's admission that he struck the victim on the head multiple times with a hammer. The court concluded that the cumulative effect of this information established that the blood samples to be seized from the defendant would provide evidence of the murder and the identity of the person participating in the murder.

State v. Riggs, 328 N.C. 213 (1991). On February 26, 1987, and March 25, 1987, officers used different informants to purchase marijuana. On each occasion, the officers gave money to the informant to purchase marijuana from an unwitting middleman of the defendants. After the informant worked out a deal for marijuana with the middleman, the middleman walked to the defendants' residence and returned to conduct the transaction on the defendants' driveway. On March 27, 1987, the officer received a warrant to search the defendants and their home. The court ruled that probable cause existed to search the defendants' residence, even though there was no direct evidence that marijuana was located there. The information in the search warrant's affidavit indicated that the defendants were operating a marijuana business on their premises, and this information supported an inference that the marijuana was somewhere on the premises, which included the residence.

During the suppression hearing, an officer testified that the informant he used during one of the marijuana transactions was not reliable, contrary to what the officer had stated in the search warrant's affidavit. However, the officer incorrectly believed that by law an informant was not reliable until the informant had made at least two prior controlled drug purchases—the informant in this case had made only one such purchase. The court ruled that the officer's subjective belief of the law's requirements was irrelevant. The court also ruled that the officer's statement in the affidavit—that the source was reliable because he knew what marijuana looked like and his information had always been true and exact—was an accurate statement, even if it was based on only one prior controlled purchase, and was sufficient evidence of the informant's reliability.

State v. Beam, 325 N.C. 217 (1989). The search warrant's affidavit supported probable cause to search the defendant's home when it stated that (1) a reliable informant, who had previously provided accurate and reliable information that led to drug arrests and convictions, told the officer-affiant that about one week earlier the informant had seen the defendant with about one pound of marijuana at her home; (2) another informant told the officer-affiant that the defendant had sold marijuana to "them" [*sic*] on February 7, 1987, the day the search warrant was issued; and (3) the defendant was on probation for a drug-law conviction. The court ruled that the first

informant's veracity was sufficiently shown and that the second informant's credibility was supported by the statement against penal interest—that is, an admission that the informant had committed a crime, the purchase of an illegal drug. The court noted that if the defendant's one pound of marijuana was for personal use, it is unlikely it would be consumed in a week. On the other hand, if it was kept for sale, then both informants' information indicated that the defendant was selling marijuana as an ongoing criminal activity. Either scenario provided a substantial basis to support the magistrate's conclusion that there was a fair probability that marijuana would be found at the defendant's home on the day the search warrant was issued.

State v. Hyleman, 324 N.C. 506 (1989). The officer-affiant stated in the search warrant application that he purchased two ounces of cocaine from three people, who were arrested when they delivered the cocaine. The officer-affiant had paid $1,650 in marked currency for the cocaine—the money had been paid a few hours before the actual delivery, but that information was not included in the affidavit. The officer-affiant then stated that, based on "the movement of the suspects during, and before the purchase, and information received during the purchase, and information from two confidential sources of information after the purchase," he had reason to believe that the marked currency was located in the defendant's residence.

Instead of analyzing the search warrant under the United States or North Carolina constitution, the court determined that the search warrant violated G.S. 15A-244(3), which restates the Fourth Amendment's command that there must be facts in the affidavit setting forth probable cause to believe that the items to be seized are in the places or in the possession of the people to be searched. The affidavit failed to state what information the officer had received from the informants and failed to disclose facts to link the items to be seized, the marked currency, to the residence to be searched. The affidavit contained mere conclusory statements. The court then ruled that the affidavit's failure to comply with G.S. 15A-244(3) was a substantial violation that required exclusion under G.S. 15A-974(2) (now, G.S. 15A-974(a)(2)) because (1) the "bare bones" conclusory affidavit was totally inadequate to establish probable cause, (2) the affiant's statement about the extent of surveillance of the suspects was willfully inaccurate, (3) the defendant had a fundamental constitutional and statutory right in North Carolina to be free from unlawful searches and seizures, and (4) the exclusion of illegally seized evidence is the greatest deterrent to future similar violations.

State v. Greene, 324 N.C. 1 (1989). A search warrant for the defendant's home was supported by probable cause when the officer-affiant stated that (1) the murder victim—the defendant's father—appeared to have been beaten to death, resulting in a large amount of blood at the scene; (2) a confidential informant, described in the accompanying affidavit as a "reliable citizen," told the officer-affiant that on the day of the murder she saw the defendant, who lived in a trailer behind his father's house, wearing clothing apparently covered with blood and carrying what appeared to be the barrel of a long gun; and (3) officers had found the splintered stock of a long gun at the home of the murder victim, who had been beaten to death there. The court ruled that although it was later determined, after the search warrant was issued, that the splintered stock of the long gun was unrelated to the murder, that fact did not adversely affect the finding of probable cause, because a reviewing court must view the evidence as it was presented to the magistrate when the warrant was issued. The court also ruled that the officer did not deliberately withhold information about the informant's veracity, because there was no evidence that the officer-affiant knew when he applied for the search warrant that the informant had been indicted 11 times for obtaining property by false pretenses.

State v. Kornegay, 313 N.C. 1 (1985). There was probable cause to support a warrant to search the law firm's and the defendant-attorney's records when information and records supplied by the law firm's secretary and the defendant's law partners demonstrated that the defendant had criminally mishandled the law firm's and clients' funds.

State v. Arrington, 311 N.C. 633 (1984). The court adopted the totality of circumstances test set out in *Illinois v. Gates* and *Massachusetts v. Upton* to determine whether probable cause exists for issuance of a search warrant under Article I, Section 20, of the North Carolina Constitution. The court ruled that information in the officer's affidavit from two informants supplied probable cause. Although the first informant did not specify when he obtained his information or the basis of his knowledge, he did state that he had bought marijuana from the defendant—a statement against his penal interest—and that the defendant was growing marijuana in his home. The court noted that this information supported a prob-

ability that the informant spoke with personal knowledge and that the marijuana would be found at the defendant's home. The second informant told the officer-affiant that within the last 24 hours—as well as over the past two months—there had been a steady flow of drug traffic to the defendant's home. The court noted that this information supports a strong inference that the illegal activity was continuing and had occurred within the last 24 hours. The affidavit also supplied sufficient information to show reliability; for example, that the informants had supplied previous information leading to arrests.

NORTH CAROLINA COURT OF APPEALS

State v. Bernard, 236 N.C. App. 134 (2014). In a case involving unlawful access to computers and identity theft, the court ruled that a search warrant authorizing a search of the defendant and her home and vehicle was supported by probable cause. The court rejected the defendant's argument that hearsay evidence was improperly considered in the probable cause determination. It went on to conclude that the warrant was supported by probable cause where the defendant's home was connected to an IP address used to unlawfully access an email account of a North Carolina A & T University employee.

State v. Rayfield, 231 N.C. App. 632 (2014). The court in a child sex case ruled that the trial court did not err by denying the defendant's motion to suppress evidence obtained pursuant to a search warrant authorizing a search of his house. The victim told officers about various incidents occurring in several locations (the defendant's home, a motel, etc.) from the time that she was 8 years old until she was 11. The affidavit alleged that the defendant had shown the victim pornographic videos and images in his home. The affidavit noted that the defendant is a registered sex offender and requested a search warrant to search his home for magazines, videos, computers, cell phones, and thumb drives.

The court rejected the defendant's argument that the victim's information to the officers was stale, given the lengthy gap of time between when the defendant allegedly showed the victim the images and the actual search. It concluded: "Although [the victim] was generally unable to provide dates to the attesting officers . . . her allegations of inappropriate sexual touching by Defendant over a sustained period of time allowed the magistrate to reasonably conclude that probable cause was present to justify the search of Defendant's residence." It noted that "when items to be searched are not inherently incriminating [as here] and have enduring utility for the person to be searched, a reasonably prudent magistrate could conclude that the items can be found in the area to be searched." The court concluded:

> There was no reason for the magistrate in this case to conclude that Defendant would have felt the need to dispose of the evidence sought even though acts associated with that evidence were committed years earlier. Indeed, a practical assessment of the information contained in the warrant would lead a reasonably prudent magistrate to conclude that the computers, cameras, accessories, and photographs were likely located in Defendant's home even though certain allegations made in the affidavit referred to acts committed years before.

State v. Oates, 224 N.C. App. 634 (2012). Reversing the trial court, the court of appeals ruled that probable cause supported the issuance of a search warrant to search the defendant's residence. Although the affidavit supporting the warrant was based on information from anonymous callers, law enforcement corroborated specific information provided by a certain caller so that the tip had sufficient indicia of reliability. In addition, the affidavit provided a sufficient nexus between the items sought and the residence to be searched. Finally, the court ruled that the information was not stale.

State v. McCain, 212 N.C. App. 159 (2011). The court ruled that a search warrant in a drug investigation was supported by probable cause. The affidavit of the officer applying for the search warrant stated that he had received information within the past 30 days from confidential reliable informants (CRIs) that the defendant was selling narcotics from his residence. During June and July of 2008, the sheriff's department had received information from anonymous callers and CRIs that drugs were being sold at the defendant's residence. In July 2008, the officer met with a "concerned citizen" who stated that the defendant was supplying drugs to his sister who was addicted to "crack" cocaine. The defendant's residence had been "synonymous with the constant sale and delivery of illegally [sic] controlled substances" as the defendant had been the subject of past charges and arrests for possession with intent to sell and deliver illegal controlled substances. The defendant's criminal background check revealed a prior history of possession of narcotics. Given the specific information from multiple sources that there

was ongoing drug activity at the defendant's residence, combined with the defendant's past criminal involvement with illegal drugs, the court concluded that the affidavit presented sufficient probable cause. The court stated that the informants' information was properly considered, noting that (1) the CRIs had been "certified" because their information had resulted in arrests and convictions in the past; (2) they were familiar with the appearance, packaging, and effects of cocaine; (3) they provided statements against penal interest; (4) the officer had met personally with the concerned citizen; and (5) the CRIs, callers, and the concerned citizen had all given consistent information that during the months of June and July 2008 illegal drugs were being sold at the defendant's residence.

State v. Hinson, 203 N.C. App. 172, *rev'd on other grounds*, 364 N.C. 414 (2010). The court ruled that an informant's observations of methamphetamine production and materials at a location and an officer's opinion that, based on his experience, there was an ongoing drug production operation at the location supplied probable cause supporting the issuance of a search warrant.

State v. Taylor, 191 N.C. App. 587 (2008). Between August 2, 2006, and September 27, 2006, a reliable, confidential informant made six controlled purchases of cocaine at 3095 Brewer Road in Faison, North Carolina, under the supervision of a law enforcement officer. The search warrant application described two dwellings on the property to be searched: a mobile home and a wood frame house located directly behind the mobile home. The application did not identify the owner or occupant of either dwelling. The affidavit was silent concerning where specifically on the property and from whom the informant made the controlled purchases. The affidavit lacked any facts concerning whether the officer saw the informant enter either the mobile home or the wood frame house to make the purchases. Distinguishing *State v. Riggs*, 328 N.C. 213 (1991), the court ruled that the magistrate did not have a substantial basis for finding probable cause to issue the search warrant.

State v. Ellis, 188 N.C. App. 820 (2008). The court ruled that probable cause existed to issue a search warrant to search a computer in the defendant's home based on instant messages between the defendant and law enforcement officers posing as a 12-year-old girl. The search warrant affidavit contained many sexually explicit instant message conversations in which the defendant asked to meet the "children" to engage in sexual conduct and stated that he transmitted a video of himself masturbating. Other conversations included his statements to a "mother" of young girls involving sexual contact with the girls. In other conversations the defendant admitted that he had penetrated children with his penis.

State v. Dexter, 186 N.C. App. 587 (2007). Officers received an email tip from a person they later verified as the defendant's housemate. The email reported the defendant's having child pornography on his home computer. The court noted that although the housemate later recanted her email tip, the officers confirmed the easily verified information from the tip, which increased her credibility. The court reviewed the officers' additional corroboration of the tip (see the facts set out in its opinion) and ruled that probable cause supported the issuance of a search warrant for the defendant's home and computer for child pornography.

State v. Edwards, 185 N.C. App. 701 (2007). The trial judge granted the defendant's pretrial motion to suppress evidence on the ground that probable cause did not exist to issue a search warrant to search the defendant's home for illegal drugs. The judge then dismissed the indictments against the defendant. The State appealed. The court ruled that the magistrate had a substantial basis for concluding that there was probable cause to issue a search warrant to search the defendant's home for illegal drugs. The officer's affidavit stated that he had received information from a confidential and reliable informant who had seen hydrocodone (without a prescription) inside the defendant's home within the past 48 hours. He had known the informant for nine years, during which time the informant had provided "confidential and reliable" information that had proven true through independent investigations. The informant was familiar with hydrocodone and its uses. The officer had 24 years' experience with his law enforcement agency, including 7 years of street level drug interdiction. The court stated that even though the officer did not set out in exact detail the connection between the informant and the prior drug investigations, the magistrate could properly infer that the informant had provided reliable information to the officer in these situations.

State v. Reid, 151 N.C. App. 379 (2002). The court ruled that probable cause supported a search warrant to search an apartment for cocaine. A confidential informant told officers that a white female named Thomasina and an unknown black male were in the business of selling cocaine from the apartment, and the informant had seen them possessing cocaine within the past six days. In addition, the informant, at the direction of the officers, had made a controlled buy from the apartment within the past six days. The court rejected as immaterial the search warrant's failure to specify the person from whom the informant had purchased the cocaine during the controlled buy.

State v. Ledbetter, 120 N.C. App. 117 (1995). The affidavit for a search warrant described an informant's controlled buy of cocaine under an officer's supervision from a house on 25 Monmouth Street, Winston-Salem. The controlled buy was made within six days of the application for the search warrant to search the house for cocaine. The court ruled that this information provided a substantial basis for concluding that probable cause existed to search the house for cocaine. The court noted that the reliability of the informant was irrelevant in this case because the focus of the information was the controlled buy made under the officer's supervision. The court also rejected the defendant's argument that the passage of six days from the controlled buy made the information too stale to establish probable cause. The court noted that drug selling is ordinarily a continuing activity.

Barnett v. Karpinos, 119 N.C. App. 719 (1995). The court reversed the trial judge's grant of summary judgment for the civil defendants. (Thus, for purposes of this appeal, the plaintiffs' allegations are assumed to be true.) A search warrant authorized a search for cocaine, drug paraphernalia, currency, and drug transaction records in buildings at 107 and 115 Graham Street and of people congregating in the block of Graham Street between W. Franklin and W. Rosemary streets in Chapel Hill. The court ruled that, based on the facts in this case, the search warrant was invalid because it was a general warrant that was not supported by probable cause. The court also ruled that the defendants' decision to detain and frisk all people found within the block was not supported, based on the facts in this case, by individualized justification under the Fourth Amendment.

State v. Waterfield, 117 N.C. App. 295 (1994). On May 13, 1993, officers went to the defendant's residence without a search warrant. The defendant refused to consent to a search of his residence. One officer told the defendant that he would stay with the defendant while the other officers obtained a search warrant. When the officers insisted that the defendant remain in their view at all times, the defendant shut and locked the door. One officer kicked the door down and forced the defendant to sit in a chair. About one and one-half hours later, officers returned with a search warrant and conducted a search.

No information obtained during the initial entry was used in the affidavit for the search warrant. The affidavit stated that on April 1, 1993, three people gave an officer about 3 grams of marijuana that they said the defendant had given them. They stated that the defendant had shown them marijuana kept in a padlocked cabinet in his bedroom at his residence. On April 2, 1993, a confidential informant told an officer that he had seen marijuana in the defendant's residence and stated that the defendant kept the marijuana in a padlocked cabinet in his bedroom. On April 5, 1993, officers visited the defendant's residence and confirmed that he lived there. On May 12, 1993, another confidential informant reported to an officer that within the last 24 hours the informant had seen about a half pound of marijuana at the defendant's residence and had seen the defendant sell marijuana from his home; the informant also stated that the defendant kept marijuana in a padlocked cabinet in his bedroom. The court ruled that the affidavit supplied probable cause to support the search warrant. Although the affidavit did not mention the reliability of the officers' sources of information, it did provide information about the presence and sale of marijuana at the defendant's residence within 24 hours of the warrant application. It further provided information about the location and manner of the defendant's storage of the marijuana that matched information supplied by other sources. Relying on *Segura v. United States*, 468 U.S. 796 (1984), the court also ruled that the search pursuant to the search warrant was valid because the information used to obtain the search warrant was obtained entirely independent of the allegedly illegal initial entry to secure the residence.

State v. Styles, 116 N.C. App. 479 (1994). The court ruled that the following affidavit did not support a search warrant, dated September 11, 1992, to search the defendant's home:

> I [name of officer] being first duly sworn, do hereby swear the following to be true to the best of my knowledge and based upon personal knowledge and upon information I received from a confidential informant. That [defendant] is a known felon with a large criminal record. He has been convicted of possession of marijuana in the past two years and [has] been reported to me before on many occasions for selling controlled substances.

> In addition to this I received information today that [defendant] has a large quantity of marijuana in his possession today. This was relayed to me by a confidential reliable informant who stated that two other men had been to the apartment on 9-10-92 and saw large quantities of marijuana in the apartment. This informant has given me reliable information in the past which led to arrests.

The court concluded that the affiant did not adequately explain why the double hearsay was credible: "[T]he deputy only states that the informant has given the deputy reliable information in the past. The magistrate had no way of knowing whether the informant was with the two men, if he observed the two men, or if the two men told the informant what happened."

State v. Tuggle, 99 N.C. App. 164 (1990). The court ruled that the trial court's findings of fact, which supported its ruling that probable cause did not exist to issue a search warrant, was characteristic of the two-pronged test rejected by *Illinois v. Gates*, discussed above, and was a de novo review of the affidavit's sufficiency, which is inconsistent with *Illinois v. Gates*, 462 U.S. 213 (1983), *Massachusetts v. Upton*, 466 U.S. 727 (1984), and *State v. Arrington*, 311 N.C. 633 (1984). The court then analyzed the information supplied by three confidential informants and found that the magistrate had a substantial basis for concluding that probable cause existed.

State v. Rosario, 93 N.C. App. 627 (1989). Officers in Florida intercepted a package of cocaine that was being carried by a drug courier for delivery to the defendant's house in Fayetteville. The courier then agreed to cooperate with the officers by carrying a similar-looking substitute package that contained cocaine supplied by the SBI laboratory in Raleigh. After the courier delivered the package to the house, the officers obtained a search warrant to search the house. The court rejected the defendant's argument that this law enforcement activity could not support the search warrant because the officers created the probable cause to justify the search. The officers did not materially alter the drug transaction. They simply allowed the original plan to be carried out.

State v. King, 92 N.C. App. 75 (1988). A search warrant was supported by probable cause when the affidavit stated that an informant familiar with cocaine and how it is packaged for street use was in the house to be searched within the past 48 hours and saw the defendant with cocaine, and the reliability of the informant was shown. *See also* State v. Marshall, 94 N.C. App. 20 (1989).

State v. Barnhardt, 92 N.C. App. 94 (1988). A search warrant was supported by probable cause when the affidavit stated that a confidential informant, who had not given the officer information before, had seen a large amount of cocaine in the defendant's house (the house to be searched) in the past 24 hours. The informant was familiar with cocaine because he had used and bought it. The officer verified the informant's description and the location of the house by going there and calling the Division of Motor Vehicles to determine that the defendant owned the vehicle that the officer saw parked there.

State v. Graham, 90 N.C. App. 564 (1988). A search warrant was supported by probable cause when the affidavit revealed that officers received information from an informant who (1) admitted the prior use of cocaine and (2) had previously given information that led to the arrests of six people for drug violations. It also showed that the informant had been in the home within the past 48 hours and had seen cocaine inside the home and being sold.

State v. Leonard, 87 N.C. App. 448 (1987). The officer's statement that he saw "a green vegetable matter" that appeared to be marijuana in a house was sufficient to establish probable cause that marijuana was in the house.

State v. Newcomb, 84 N.C. App. 92 (1987). A search warrant was not supported by probable cause when the affidavit contained only an informant's statement that he saw marijuana in the house and did not state when he saw it. Also, the affidavit did not contain a statement that the informant was reliable.

State v. Roark, 83 N.C. App. 425 (1986). A search warrant was not supported by probable cause when the affidavit stated only that a confidential informant told the officer that the stolen property was in the house to be searched.

State v. Heath, 73 N.C. App. 391 (1985). Probable cause was not provided by an affidavit stating that the officer-affiant received information from anonymous concerned citizens in the past 48 hours who "have seen and know" that drugs were being sold in a particular apartment and who also reported that there was much traffic going to and from that apartment and that visitors stayed only a few minutes each time. The affidavit also stated that officers conducted surveillance of the apartment and that the pattern of traffic was similar to traffic in other areas where drug arrests had been made. The

court ruled that the *Gates* standard was not satisfied by the affidavit's conclusory statements. It also noted that (1) the officer-affiant testified at the suppression hearing that he had no reason to believe that the "concerned citizens" were reliable and (2) the statement in the affidavit was incorrect when it said that in the past 48 hours concerned citizens had seen and known that drugs were being sold in the apartment. Instead, a concerned citizen had merely stated that she knew that the apartment had a lot of drugs and she went there once but "didn't know it was that kind of place." The court also ruled that the magistrate who issued the warrant could not consider, in determining probable cause, unsworn statements by others that were attached to the affidavit.

State v. Walker, 70 N.C. App. 403 (1984). There was probable cause to support a warrant to search the defendant's house when the informant had told the officer-affiant that he had been in the house within the past 48 hours and had seen three pounds of marijuana in the defendant's possession. The officer had known the informant for five months, during which time the informant had made controlled drug buys under his supervision. The informant also had given the officer information about drug dealers that the officer had verified by investigation.

FEDERAL APPELLATE COURTS

United States v. Tuter, 240 F.3d 1292 (10th Cir. 2001). An anonymous tip that the defendant makes pipe bombs in his garage and has weapons in his home, without any significant corroboration by law enforcement, was insufficient to establish probable cause for a search warrant to search the home and garage.

United States v. Berry, 90 F.3d 148 (6th Cir. 1996). An affidavit for a search warrant to search a car stated that a drug detection dog alerted to the car, indicating the probable presence of drugs. It also stated that the dog was trained and qualified to conduct drug investigations. The court ruled that these statements sufficiently established the dog's training and reliability. The court rejected the defendant's argument that the affidavit had to also describe the details of the dog's training. *See also* United States v. Sundby, 186 F.3d 873 (8th Cir. 1999) (similar ruling); United States v. Delaney, 52 F.3d 182 (8th Cir. 1995) (description of drug detection dog in affidavit for search warrant was sufficient).

United States v. Wilhelm, 80 F.3d 116 (4th Cir. 1996). The court ruled that an anonymous person's information was insufficient to establish probable cause to support a search warrant to search a residence for illegal drugs. Although the person said that he or she saw residents selling marijuana at the house within the last 48 hours, there was no specific information in the search warrant's affidavit concerning the person's reliability or truthfulness. In addition, the only corroboration offered by law enforcement was that the person's directions to the residence were correct. *See also* United States v. Clark, 31 F.3d 831 (9th Cir. 1994) (similar ruling); United States v. Leake, 998 F.2d 1359 (1993) (similar ruling).

Timeliness or Staleness of Information

(*This topic is discussed on page 429.*)

UNITED STATES SUPREME COURT

Andresen v. Maryland, 427 U.S. 463 (1976). A three-month delay between completion of real estate transactions on which the search warrants were based and the searches conducted under the search warrants did not preclude a determination that there was probable cause that the business office contained records that were evidence of the crime. These records were prepared in the ordinary course of business, and it would be reasonable to expect that they would be kept there for a period of time.

United States v. Harris, 403 U.S. 573 (1971). A reliable informant said that he had purchased illegal liquor from a house for two years and most recently within the past two weeks. The Court stated that the informant's observations were not too stale to establish probable cause to search the house for illegal liquor. The reported purchase within the last two weeks could well have included purchases up to the date of the affidavit.

Sgro v. United States, 287 U.S. 206 (1932). A warrant was issued on July 6, 1926, to search a hotel for intoxicating liquor, based on the affiant's information that he had purchased beer there. After the search warrant became invalid because it was not executed within 10 days (as required by federal law), an official reissued it by changing the date of the search warrant to July 26, 1926, without hearing any new evidence. The Court ruled that the second warrant was invalid, because there was no evidence of probable cause to search when it was issued.

NORTH CAROLINA SUPREME COURT

State v. McKinnon, 306 N.C. 288 (1982). Stolen items were placed in a car that was used to commit a robbery and other crimes on December 15, 1980. Seeing the car in the yard of a residence on December 28, 1980, officers learned that (1) the car was locked, the keys had apparently been lost, and the motor had blown up, and (2) the car had become inoperative sometime before Christmas. The court ruled that the magistrate who issued the warrant was not unreasonable in concluding that there was probable cause to believe that some of the stolen items remained in the car.

State v. Jones, 299 N.C. 298 (1980). A murder was committed on March 30, 1978, with a hatchet and a pipe, and officers knew that the offender had worn welder's gloves during the murder. An accomplice told officers almost five months later (August 23, 1978) where the defendant had hidden the hatchet and gloves. The court ruled that this information was not stale and supported probable cause to issue a search warrant. The court noted that the items sought—a hatchet and welder's gloves—were not incriminating by themselves and had a useful value and that a reasonably prudent magistrate could conclude that they were probably located in the places where the accomplice had said they were located. *See also* United States v. Shomo, 786 F.2d 981 (10th Cir. 1986).

State v. Louchheim, 296 N.C. 314 (1979). A warrant was issued to search a business office for various documents concerning numerous false-pretenses charges. Although it had been fourteen months since anyone had seen the incriminating documents in the office, (1) the alleged crime was complex and took place over a number of years, (2) the affidavit alleged that the invoices were kept in the office in compliance with the state advertising contract, and (3) other documents sought were corporate documents kept in the course of business. The court ruled that the magistrate had a substantial basis for concluding that the business records were probably located at the defendant's business offices.

NORTH CAROLINA COURT OF APPEALS

State v. Hinson, 203 N.C. App. 172, *rev'd on other grounds*, 364 N.C. 414 (2010). The court rejected the defendant's argument that information relied upon by officers to establish probable cause for a search warrant was stale. Although certain information provided by an informant was three weeks old, other information pertained to the informant's observations that were made only one day before the application for the warrant was submitted. Also, an officer opined, based on his experience, that an ongoing drug production operation was present at the location.

State v. Pickard, 178 N.C. App. 330 (2006). The search warrant for the defendant's home authorized the seizure of computers, computer equipment and accessories, cassette videos and DVDs, video cameras, digital cameras, film cameras and accessories, and photographs and printed materials that could be consistent with the exploitation of a minor. The affidavit described the defendant's sexual and other inappropriate activity with four children under 9 years old and with a 14-year-old. The victims described the defendant's taking photographs and his use of video cameras and computers. The activity with the 14-year-old had taken place about 18 months before the issuance of the search warrant. [Author's note: The affidavit apparently did not contain specific dates concerning the defendant's sexual activity with the younger children, but the affidavit stated that the officer's interviews with the younger children occurred the day before the officer applied for the search warrant.] The court ruled, relying on *State v. Jones*, 299 N.C. 298 (1980), and cases from other jurisdictions, that the search warrant's information was not stale, because the affidavit showed the defendant's commission of ongoing sex crimes with the children and the items to be seized were of continuing utility to the defendant.

State v. Witherspoon, 110 N.C. App. 413 (1993). The court ruled that a search warrant for the defendant's home was based on probable cause. The search warrant affidavit included the following information. A concerned citizen told officers that he had been in the defendant's home within the past 30 days and had seen about 100 marijuana plants growing in the home's crawl space with the use of a lighting system and automatic timers. The concerned citizen had spoken with the defendant often about the defendant's growing these plants, and the concerned citizen had used marijuana and had seen it growing in the past. Officers corroborated the concerned citizen's information about the defendant's car that was parked in the defendant's driveway, and officers also checked the power company's records, which showed that the defendant had been paying the power bill for the house in the past six months. The court, relying on several cases, including *State v. Beam*, 325 N.C. 217 (1989), rejected the defendant's argument that the information was stale. The court noted that, based on the facts set out in the affidavit, the magistrate who issued the search warrant could reasonably infer that the marijuana would likely remain in the defendant's home for 30 days.

State v. Goforth, 65 N.C. App. 302 (1983). The court ruled that an affidavit failed to establish probable cause to search premises for drugs when its information consisted of surveillance of movements by persons to and from the premises, a conclusory statement about persons involved in drug smuggling, and a six-year-old drug indictment of one defendant and a four-year-old drug conviction (the court erroneously noted it as only an arrest) of another defendant. However, the court apparently failed to consider as relevant to a determination of probable cause that on the day the search warrant was issued, a confidential informant told the affiant that (1) two named individuals were coming to the town in which the premises were located to purchase marijuana, (2) officers conducting surveillance stopped the car with the named individuals inside after they left the premises and smelled the odor of marijuana in the trunk (although no marijuana was found), and (3) one of the named individuals had $5,000 to $6,000 in cash. This ruling does not appear to be consistent with the totality of circumstances analysis of *Illinois v. Gates* (the court did not discuss *Gates*).

State v. Lindsey, 58 N.C. App. 564 (1982). A warrant was issued to search the defendant's home for marijuana. The affidavit stated that a confidential informant told the affiant that he had seen drugs in the defendant's home about one year ago. An undercover officer told the affiant that three weeks before the search warrant was issued, the defendant and another man sold the officer more than 10 pounds of marijuana and 377 doses of phenobarbital. A month before this sale, the defendant had attempted to sell 2 pounds of marijuana to the undercover officer. This officer had purchased drugs in the defendant's presence at his service station. He also had seen the defendant at a friend's apartment several times when drugs were being sold. The court ruled that the year-old information was the only evidence that drugs were in the defendant's residence and that the undercover officer's recent information did not provide a reasonable inference that the defendant continued to possess drugs in his home when the search warrant was issued. The dissenting opinion concluded that the facts supplied probable cause that marijuana was in the defendant's home. [Author's note: This case was decided before *Illinois v. Gates*, and it is likely that the dissenting opinion would reflect the result under a *Gates* totality of circumstances analysis.]

State v. Windham, 57 N.C. App. 571 (1982). Information about drugs in a home within the past 24 hours was not stale when drug sales at the home had been made regularly for months. *See also* State v. King, 44 N.C. App. 31 (1979) (pattern of drug sales at residence and last sale was within two weeks of issuance of warrant; information was not stale); State v. Caldwell, 53 N.C. App. 1 (1981) (large amount of cocaine was seen in house within five days of issuance of search warrant; information was not stale); State v. Singleton, 33 N.C. App. 390 (1977) (informant saw marijuana and LSD in home within last 48 hours; information was not stale); State v. Cobb, 21 N.C. App. 66 (1974) (affidavit did not specify or imply when informant saw heroin in home, yet court stated that magistrate could "reasonably and realistically conclude" that informant saw heroin so recently that probable cause existed when the warrant was issued); State v. Williams, 49 N.C. App. 184 (1980) (ruling similar to *Cobb*).

FEDERAL APPELLATE COURTS

United States v. Rhynes, 196 F.3d 207 (4th Cir. 1999). The information in a search warrant was not stale even though the most recent drug trafficking or money laundering activities alleged in the search warrant affidavit were more than two years old. The criminal enterprise had been ongoing for more than 20 years. The drug trafficking and money laundering were supported and aided by the operation of seemingly legitimate businesses through which the defendant laundered proceeds and facilitated the distribution of illegal drugs. Also, the property to be seized included various documents that are not ordinarily destroyed or moved from one place to another.

United States v. Grandstaff, 813 F.2d 1353 (9th Cir. 1987). When a federal bank robbery fugitive had stolen $3.3 million in cash, less than a third of which had been recovered, it was proper to infer that he might have some part of it with him in a hotel room five months after the robbery; thus, probable cause existed to issue a search warrant for the room.

United States v. Reyes, 798 F.2d 380 (10th Cir. 1986). Although a search warrant for the residence was issued five months after the last drug transaction there, probable cause still existed because the search warrant's affidavit showed an ongoing drug conspiracy. *See also* United States v. Dozier, 844 F.2d 701 (9th Cir. 1988) (information that was five and one-half months old was sufficient to support probable cause, because marijuana cultivation is a long-term crime); United States v. Feliz, 182 F.3d 82 (1st Cir. 1999) (because informant had been purchasing drugs from defendant for about 12 years, the fact that drug transactions described in affidavit took place about

three months before issuing search warrant did not render them stale).

Information from a Confidential Informant

(*This topic is discussed on page 426.*)

Informant's Credibility or the Reliability of the Informant's Information

(*See other cases under "Probable Cause," "Generally," on page 427.*)

State v. Rosario, 93 N.C. App. 627 (1989). Information in a search warrant's affidavit from a confidential informant that was provided to the officer-affiant by another officer was properly considered by the officer-affiant when the other officer provided a basis for that informant's reliability.

State v. Atwell, 62 N.C. App. 643 (1983). The reliability of a confidential informant's information was sufficiently established by (1) an officer-affiant's statement that the informant was "reliable" and (2) the affidavit's description of the informant's detailed report about criminal activity. *See also* State v. Chapman, 24 N.C. App. 462 (1975).

State v. Windham, 57 N.C. App. 571 (1982). An officer-affiant's statement that the informant had provided information that led to arrests and convictions on at least 10 previous occasions sufficiently showed the informant's credibility. The officer's statement at the suppression hearing that the informant had been incorrect at least once did not undermine the finding of credibility.

State v. Akel, 21 N.C. App. 415 (1974). The court stated that an informant's credibility may be established by an affiant's statement that his information has led to arrests.

State v. Staley, 7 N.C. App. 345 (1970). An officer-affiant's statement that he knows the confidential informant well, that the informant has given him and other members of the vice division information that was highly reliable and accurate, and that the informant has been most dependable in all his dealings with the vice division sufficiently established that informant's credibility.

Informant's Basis of Knowledge

(*See other cases under "Probable Cause," "Generally" on page 428.*)

State v. Edwards, 286 N.C. 162 (1974). An affidavit stating that "a confidential and reliable informant who has given reliable information says that there is non-tax-paid whiskey at above location at this time" was insufficient to establish probable cause because it did not provide underlying circumstances from which the informant concluded that the non-tax-paid whiskey was where he said it was.

State v. Weatherford, 60 N.C. App. 196 (1982). An officer-affiant established the basis-of-knowledge prong by stating that the confidential informant had seen the stolen item on the premises to be searched.

State v. Windham, 57 N.C. App. 571 (1982). An officer-affiant established the basis-of-knowledge prong by stating that the confidential informant provided the following information: (1) the defendant lived at the address given in the search warrant, (2) the informant purchased marijuana and other drugs from the defendant at that address, and (3) the informant had been in contact with the defendant within 24 hours before the search warrant was issued and had learned that the defendant had drugs at that address.

State v. Phillips, 25 N.C. App. 5 (1975). The affidavit failed to provide probable cause that a stolen pistol was in the defendant's car when it merely alleged that a reliable informant said that the defendant took the pistol during an armed robbery. The affidavit lacked any information that supported the informant's belief that the pistol was in the defendant's car.

State v. Graves, 16 N.C. App. 389 (1972). The affidavit did not provide probable cause that LSD was in the defendant's home, because it merely alleged that the affiant received information from a reliable confidential informant that the defendant had LSD in his home. The affidavit lacked any information that supported the informant's belief that drugs were in the defendant's home.

State v. Staley, 7 N.C. App. 345 (1970). Although the affidavit failed to state explicitly that a confidential informant personally obtained his information, the informant described the defendant's sale and use of marijuana in his room with sufficient detail so that the issuing magistrate could know that the informant's information was based on personal knowledge, rather than on rumor or other unsubstantiated belief.

Information from a Citizen Informant

(*This topic is discussed on page 425.*)

State v. Eason, 328 N.C. 409 (1991). The court ruled that the fact that the citizen-informant (who was the mother of the defendant) was named in the search warrant's affidavit provided the magistrate with sufficient information to determine that the citizen-informant was reliable.

State v. Sanders, 327 N.C. 319 (1990). The court, in analyzing information from a citizen-informant to establish probable cause, stated that the law does not demand of private citizens who voluntarily assist law enforcement the same standards of reliability applicable to paid informants. A citizen-informant may be entitled to a greater degree of credibility than a habitual informant. *See also* State v. Martin, 315 N.C. 667 (1986).

United States v. Fooladi, 703 F.2d 180 (5th Cir. 1983). Officer-affiant stated that an unnamed employee of a named glass manufacturer told him that the firm had shipped some glassware and laboratory equipment to a particular company. Because a nonprofessional informant—a disinterested businessman—gave detailed information that the officer corroborated, the reliability of the information and informant was satisfied.

Probable Cause for Premises to Be Searched

(*This topic is discussed on page 430. See other cases under "Probable Cause," "Generally," on page 475.*)

NORTH CAROLINA SUPREME COURT

State v. Sinapi, 359 N.C. 394 (2005). Law enforcement officers were investigating a heroin overdose in which the defendant was implicated as the seller of the heroin. A criminal records check revealed that the defendant had been previously arrested twice for drug offenses. Division of Motor Vehicle records showed that the defendant resided at 3300 Pinecrest Drive. Officers went to that address and performed a trash pickup on the normal trash day during the normal time. They recovered a single, white plastic garbage bag from the front yard/curb line beside the driveway. Inside the garbage bag were eight marijuana plants, although there were no items in the bag that specifically connected the contents to the residence at that address (such as documents or mail). The court ruled that this information was sufficient to establish probable cause to issue a search warrant to search the residence. The court stated that the issuing magistrate was entitled to infer that the garbage bag came from the defendant's residence and the items inside were probably also associated with that residence. This inference was bolstered by the location of the garbage bag and the officers' retrieval of it from the defendant's yard on the regularly scheduled garbage collection day. The marijuana plants in the garbage bag, taken in conjunction with the defendant's drug-related criminal history and the information linking the defendant to a heroin sale and overdose, established a fair probability that contraband and evidence of a crime would be found in the residence. The affidavit constituted a substantial basis for the magistrate's finding probable cause to issue the search warrant.

State v. Riggs, 328 N.C. 213 (1991). On February 26, 1987, and March 25, 1987, officers used different informants to purchase marijuana. On each occasion, the officers gave money to the informant to purchase marijuana from an unwitting middleman trusted by the defendants. After the informant worked out a deal for marijuana with the middleman, the middleman walked to the defendants' residence and returned to conduct the transaction on the defendants' driveway. On March 27, 1987, the officer received a search warrant to search the defendants and their home. The court ruled that probable cause existed to search the defendants' residence, even though there was no direct evidence that marijuana was located there. The information in the search warrant's affidavit indicated that the defendants were operating a marijuana business on their premises, and this information supported an inference that the marijuana was located somewhere on the premises, which included the residence.

State v. Rook, 304 N.C. 201 (1981). The affidavit supplied probable cause to believe that the murder weapon and bloody clothing would be found in the defendant's trailer because after the murder, the defendant returned a borrowed car to a witness who said that the defendant then went to his trailer.

State v. Silhan, 302 N.C. 223 (1981). The affidavit stated that a light blue van was seen parked at the scene of a murder and rape and that a tire print was in the mud. When the defendant was arrested for these crimes, he was operating a blue 1976 Chevrolet van. The court ruled that probable cause existed to link the van to these crimes.

State v. Campbell, 282 N.C. 125 (1972). The affidavit for a warrant to search the defendant's house for drugs stated that the affiant had arrest warrants for several persons, including the defendant, who had sold drugs to an SBI agent as well as to many college students. The court ruled that the affidavit failed to implicate the house in illegal possession or sale of drugs and thus did not establish probable cause to search the house.

NORTH CAROLINA COURT OF APPEALS

State v. Rodgers, 161 N.C. App. 345 (2003). The defendant was convicted of trafficking in cocaine. The court ruled that probable cause supported a search warrant to search the defendant's home for cocaine. The affida-

vit recited information from a confidential informant, supported by facts setting out the informant's reliability, that the defendant would be transporting a large quantity of cocaine from his home. The informant described the defendant, gave the defendant's home address, and described his car (the car description was substantially but not completely corroborated later by the officer). On the same day that the officer received that information, the officer conducted surveillance at the defendant's home and eventually stopped the defendant's car and discovered marijuana and $1,500 in U.S. currency in the possession of another vehicle occupant. The court noted that the officer could reasonably believe that finding marijuana and a large sum of money indicated that the defendant was involved in drug activities. Not finding cocaine in the vehicle, as reported by the informant, provided probable cause to believe that cocaine was still in the defendant's home.

State v. Hunt, 150 N.C. App. 101 (2002). The court ruled, relying on *State v. Crisp*, 19 N.C. App. 456 (1973), and *State v. Ford*, 71 N.C. App. 748 (1985), and distinguishing *State v. Barnhardt*, 92 N.C. App. 94 (1988), that probable cause did not exist to support a search warrant for a residence when it was based on (1) anonymous citizen complaints asserting suspicions of drug activity based on heavy vehicular traffic with short visits and (2) an officer's conclusion that there was illegal drug activity based on his observation of heavy vehicular traffic. The court noted that no one ever saw drugs on the premises.

State v. Crawford, 104 N.C. App. 591 (1991). The court ruled that probable cause existed on May 10, 1990, to issue a warrant to search an apartment based on (1) the ongoing surveillance by a veteran drug officer (Stanton) in February 1990 of a four-block area, including the apartment that was the object of the search warrant, and the officer's observation of people in and around the apartment; (2) the arrest on April 19, 1990, of five people with cocaine in their possession after they left the apartment and Stanton's observation of other activities that day, consistent with drug activities, including seeing the defendant in that apartment; (3) Stanton's record as an experienced drug officer who had made 60 drug arrests in the area in the preceding three and one-half months; (4) Stanton's continuing surveillance of the apartment between April 19 and April 30, 1990, and his observation that people arriving by car at a rate of eight every two or three hours were leaving the apartment after staying there only two or three minutes (defendant answered the door each time); and (5) Stanton's continued surveillance until May 8, 1990. The court rejected the defendant's contention that probable cause exists only if facts in the search warrant's affidavit show that drugs were seen in the premises, stating: "The law does not require absolute certainty, it requires only that probable cause exists to believe there are drugs on the premises."

State v. McCoy, 100 N.C. App. 574 (1990). After an informant made a controlled purchase of cocaine from the defendant at room 203 of an Econo Lodge in Winston-Salem on or after August 15, 1988, a search warrant was issued on August 18, 1988, for that room. The defendant had vacated the premises by then. After the same informant made a controlled purchase of cocaine from the defendant at room 209 of the same Econo Lodge on or after August 21, 1988, a search warrant was issued on August 23, 1988, for that room. Again, the defendant had vacated the premises by then. Registrations for room 209 showed that the defendant and a female had given Winston-Salem addresses as their home addresses. On August 25, 1988, officers confirmed information that the defendant was occupying room 406 of the Innkeeper Motel in Winston-Salem and the defendant was operating the same female's car, which was parked in the motel lot.

The court stated that the facts showed that the defendant, previously convicted of selling drugs, had within a 10-day period rented three different motel rooms, each time for several days, in a city in which he had a local address, and that at two of those locations he had sold cocaine. The court ruled that circumstances of the two prior sales of cocaine in other motel rooms within a 10-day period reasonably leads to an inference that cocaine could be found in room 406 of the Innkeeper Motel, despite there being no direct evidence that cocaine was there.

State v. O'Kelly, 98 N.C. App. 265 (1990). Officers executed a search warrant for the defendant's residence in Kitty Hawk (the court ruled that probable cause supported this search warrant) and found methamphetamine and the remnants of a clandestine laboratory used in the manufacture of that illegal drug. They also found a lease for a storage unit at a self-storage facility in Nags Head. Based on these discoveries and information that was supplied in the search warrant for the residence, the officers obtained a search warrant to search the storage unit.

The court ruled that the search warrant for the storage unit was based on probable cause: discovery of remnants of a clandestine laboratory in the defendant's premises and information that the defendant had been seen putting part of his laboratory into his car would justify a reasonable belief that a storage unit rented by the defendant would hold other parts of the laboratory, the chemicals used in producing the drugs, or the drugs themselves.

State v. Ford, 71 N.C. App. 748 (1984). The officers' detection of a strong odor of marijuana emanating from a mobile home, along with unusual traffic there, provided probable cause to issue a warrant to search that home. *See also* State v. Robinson, 148 N.C. App. 422 (2002) (strong odor of marijuana emanating from house, along with other facts, supplied probable cause to issue search warrant).

State v. Goforth, 65 N.C. App. 302 (1983). The court ruled that an affidavit failed to implicate premises to be searched when the only statements concerning the premises were (1) a conclusory statement that the premises were being used for storing drugs and an illegal drug operation and (2) the fact that at the premises were two persons who a confidential informant said were going to purchase marijuana. However, the court apparently failed to consider as relevant to a determination of probable cause the fact that on the day the search warrant was issued, a confidential informant told the affiant that (1) Roach and Robinson were coming to the town where the premises were located to purchase marijuana, (2) officers conducting surveillance stopped the car with Roach and Robinson inside after they left the premises and smelled an odor of marijuana in the trunk (although no marijuana was found), and (3) Robinson had $5,000 to $6,000 in cash. [Author's note: This ruling does not appear to be consistent with the totality of circumstances analysis of *Illinois v. Gates*, although the court did not discuss *Gates*.]

State v. Byrd, 60 N.C. App. 740 (1983). An affidavit for a warrant to search a home sufficiently implicated the home as a storage place for drugs when evidence showed that an undercover officer bought cocaine four times over a seven-week period from a person who traveled to the home and then brought drugs to the officer. Although the drug seller was seen only once actually entering the home and returning with drugs, the court stated that common sense supported a reasonable belief that drugs were in the home, particularly when a drug transaction had been only partially completed on the date the search warrant was issued, and it was reasonable to expect that the remainder of the order would be at the home. *See also*

State v. Willis, 58 N.C. App. 617 (1982), *aff'd*, 307 N.C. 461 (1983) (affiant received information from an informant on the day that he applied for a search warrant (1) that the defendant had heroin in the residence and (2) that the informant had seen heroin in the residence and had seen the defendant sell heroin in the past 72 hours; the court ruled that this information provided probable cause that the defendant had heroin in the residence); State v. Armstrong, 33 N.C. App. 52 (1977) (affidavit failed to establish probable cause to search trailer for drugs when information merely showed that on the day before, the drug seller had gone to trailer, met with defendant, and left with him in defendant's car; no connection was shown between either person and the trailer); State v. Dailey, 33 N.C. App. 600 (1977) (probable cause existed to issue a warrant to search an apartment when (1) officers watched a person deliver a bag to the apartment after stopping at a house; (2) the person went back to the house, came out with a suitcase, and was stopped; (3) a search of the suitcase revealed marijuana; and (4) marijuana was also found in a later search of the house); State v. Crisp, 19 N.C. App. 456 (1973) (probable cause did not exist to search the defendants' home based on (1) the officer's stopping a vehicle on a highway and finding 5 grams of marijuana and (2) the officer's allegation in affidavit that he had seen "heavy traffic" entering and leaving the defendant's home); State v. Eutsler, 41 N.C. App. 182 (1979) (probable cause existed to search a house for marijuana when (1) officers found a marijuana patch growing across the road from house, (2) a path went directly from the patch to the house, (3) footprints went directly from the patch to the house, (4) a plant fertilizer box with a military store price tag was found by the patch and the house was the only one in the area where military personnel lived, and (5) there was no other house within a quarter-mile of the patch).

State v. Whitley, 58 N.C. App. 539 (1982). Although a confidential informant stated only that stolen items were in the defendant's possession, not specifically that they were in the defendant's home, his detailed information concerning the recent sale of some of the stolen items after a break-in supported an inference that the stolen goods were in the defendant's home and not likely to be stored only on the defendant's person.

State v. Mavroganis, 57 N.C. App. 178 (1982). An affidavit for a warrant to search the defendant's college dorm room and his car was based on an informant's information that (1) the defendant possessed marijuana and was selling it, (2) the informant had seen marijuana in the defendant's room, and (3) the defendant owned and possessed a described Ford Mustang. The court ruled that probable cause supported a search of the car, which was parked about 100 yards from the dorm (not in the dormitory's parking lot), because there was a reasonable belief that a college student living on campus who possessed and sold drugs would have drugs in both his room and his car, even though the informant saw drugs only in his room. The student's car would be a convenient instrumentality for receiving, storing, and delivering drugs.

State v. May, 41 N.C. App. 370 (1979). An affidavit established probable cause to search a grocery store when the officers saw two persons loading stolen meat into their car from the closed grocery store at night and a quantity of meat with the same distinguishing wrapping (and other items) had been taken in a break-in earlier the same day.

FEDERAL APPELLATE COURTS

United States v. Anderson, 851 F.2d 727 (4th Cir. 1988). The affidavit for a warrant to search the defendant's home for a weapon and silencer attachment contained no direct evidence that the weapon was there. However, the court ruled that the issuing magistrate could reasonably have believed that the defendant likely would keep these items there. The affidavit revealed that the defendant attempted to sell them to three different people and that they had been used to kill the victim of the murder under investigation. *See also* United States v. Thomas, 973 F.2d 1152 (5th Cir. 1992) (because dies that were illegally used to stamp VIN plates were not found at defendant's business, it was reasonable to believe that they were at his home).

United States v. Fannin, 817 F.2d 1379 (9th Cir. 1987). A warrant was properly issued to search the defendant's home for evidence of drug trafficking, even though the defendant's only participation in a drug transaction (which occurred elsewhere) was to supply money for it. A magistrate may find probable cause to search a home based on an experienced drug agent's statement that drug traffickers keep records of transactions in their homes, even though there was no specific evidence in this case that the defendant did so. *See also* United States v. Feliz, 182 F.3d 82 (1st Cir. 1999) (similar ruling); United States v. Pace, 955 F.2d 270 (5th Cir. 1992) (after discovery of marijuana plants in barn, probable cause existed to search suspects' residences for drug transaction records, based on law enforcement officer's experience that records would be found there); United States v. Hodge, 246 F.3d 301 (1st Cir. 2001) (evidence of defendant's sale of drugs in same city in which he lived and that he was involved in the drug trade supplied probable cause to support search warrant of his home). *But see* United States v. Lalor, 996 F.2d 1578 (4th Cir. 1993) (no evidence offered to link drugs sold on street to support probable cause to believe drugs located in house).

Probable Cause for Property to Be Seized

State v. Kornegay, 313 N.C. 1 (1985). The affidavit supplied probable cause to seize a law firm's savings account passbook when evidence showed that the defendant had fraudulently converted or embezzled interest on money transferred from a trust account to the savings account, and therefore the seizure of the passbook would aid in convicting the defendant.

State v. Adams, 159 N.C. App. 676 (2003). Officers executed a search warrant for the defendant's mobile home to search for marijuana. The warrant also authorized the seizure of "articles of personal property tending to establish and document sales of marijuana . . . plus articles of personal property tending to establish the identity of persons in control of the premises . . . ." Four people in addition to the defendant lived in the defendant's mobile home. Officers found in the defendant's bedroom marijuana, drug paraphernalia, a concealed video camera positioned to videotape the bed area, and a box of homemade videotapes located in a closet. There were no markings or labels on the videotapes. An officer briefly viewed two of the videotapes while in the bedroom and saw sexual activity between a male and female in the defendant's bedroom. Another officer arrived later and, not knowing what the other officer had seen on the videotapes, questioned the defendant about them. The defendant admitted that they depicted his having sex with women in his bedroom. The officer seized the videotapes to establish who was in control of the bedroom in which the marijuana had been found. Based on the evidence from the videotapes, the defendant was convicted of first-degree sexual exploitation of a minor and participating in the prostitution of a minor. The court ruled that the videotapes were properly seized under G.S. 15A-242(4) because there was probable cause to believe they constituted evidence of the identity of a person participating in an offense.

Probable Cause for Body-Cavity Search

State v. Fowler, 89 N.C. App. 10 (1988). An officer with a valid search warrant was searching the defendant for drugs when he noticed an excessive amount of a lubricant near his anal cavity. This information, supplied to a magistrate in an additional affidavit and together with the information in the original search warrant, provided probable cause for a doctor to conduct a body-cavity search of the defendant's rectum.

Objective Standard in Considering an Officer's Information

(*This topic is discussed on page 235.*)

State v. Riggs, 328 N.C. 213 (1991). On February 26, 1987, and March 25, 1987, officers used different informants to purchase marijuana. On each occasion, the officers gave money to the informant to purchase marijuana from an unwitting middleman trusted by the defendants. After the informant worked out a deal for marijuana with the middleman, the middleman walked to the defendants' residence and returned to conduct the transaction on the defendants' driveway. On March 27, 1987, the officers received a warrant to search the defendants and their home.

During the suppression hearing, an officer testified that the informant he used during one of the marijuana transactions was not reliable, contrary to what the officer had stated in the search warrant's affidavit. However, the officer incorrectly believed that by law an informant was not reliable until the informant had made at least two prior controlled drug purchases—the informant in this case had made only one such purchase. The court ruled that the officer's subjective belief of the law's requirements was irrelevant. The court also ruled that the officer's statement in the affidavit—that the source was reliable because he knew what marijuana looked like and his information had always been true and exact—was an accurate statement, even if it was based on only one prior controlled purchase, and was sufficient evidence of the informant's reliability.

Anticipatory Search Warrants

(*This topic is discussed on page 431.*)

United States v. Grubbs, 547 U.S. 90 (2006). Federal postal inspectors planned a controlled delivery of a child pornography videotape purchased by the defendant for delivery at his home. They obtained a search warrant to search the defendant's home contingent on the delivery of the videotape and its being taken into the residence. The contingency language was contained in the affidavit to the search warrant, but the affidavit was not incorporated into the search warrant. [Author's note: North Carolina's search warrant form, AOC-CR-119, incorporates the application for a search warrant, which includes the affidavit. *See* State v. Carrillo, 164 N.C. App. 204 (2004) (anticipatory search warrant was valid under Fourth Amendment when contingency language for executing the search warrant was set out in affidavit and warrant incorporated the affidavit by reference).]

(1) The Court ruled that anticipatory search warrants do not categorically violate the Fourth Amendment. Two prerequisites must be satisfied, however. There must be a fair probability (probable cause) that contraband or evidence of a crime will be found in a particular place, and there must be probable cause to believe that the triggering condition will occur. (2) The Court also ruled that the Fourth Amendment does not require that the conditions precedent to the execution of an anticipatory search warrant must be set out in the warrant itself. In this case, the conditions precedent to the warrant's execution were set out in the affidavit to the search warrant.

State v. Stallings, 189 N.C. App. 376 (2008). The court, relying on *State v. Falbo*, 526 N.W.2d 814 (Wisc. Ct. App. 1994), and *State v. Smith*, 124 N.C. App. 565 (1996), upheld an anticipatory search warrant the execution of which was contingent on a confidential informant, who was working under officers' directions, giving a prearranged signal to the officers after the informant entered a residence and purchased marijuana there. During a prior one-year period, the confidential informant had purchased marijuana from the defendant at his residence. Based on the *Falbo* and *Smith* rulings, the court set out a test to consider the legality of this anticipatory search warrant and concluded that the warrant satisfied the test.

State v. Carrillo, 164 N.C. App. 204 (2004). The court ruled, relying on *Groh v. Ramirez*, 540 U.S. 551 (2004), and *State v. Flowers*, 12 N.C. App. 487 (1971), that an anticipatory search warrant was valid under the Fourth Amendment when the contingency language for executing the search warrant was set out in an affidavit and the warrant incorporated the affidavit by reference.

State v. Baldwin, 161 N.C. App. 382 (2003). A U.S. Postal Inspector intercepted a package and found a trafficking amount of cocaine in it; the package was addressed to Sean Smith. Officers obtained an antici-

patory search warrant for the house at the address on the package, and the execution of the search warrant was conditioned on the delivery of the package there. The inspector, in an undercover capacity, delivered the package at the address. The defendant (Eddie Baldwin) indicated that he was Sean Smith and took the package inside the house. Within a few minutes, the defendant took the package out of the house and placed it in a Pontiac. About an hour later, the defendant came out of the house, removed the package from the Pontiac, and placed it in a Toyota. Another person (the defendant's housemate) drove away in the Toyota. Officers then executed the search warrant for the house, where they found guns, 414.5 grams of marijuana, surveillance equipment, and plastic bags containing traces of cocaine. The court ruled that because the search warrant met the requirements for an anticipatory search warrant set out in *State v. Smith*, 124 N.C. App. 565 (1996), once the package arrived at the residence the nexus between the package and the residence was established. Even though the package was no longer on the premises, delivery of the package linked the house to the criminal activity inside, establishing probable cause to search the house. In addition, because the warrant specifically allowed the officers to search the premises at this address to find and seize cocaine generally and to identify the participants of the crime, the officers' thorough search of the premises was within the scope of the warrant.

State v. Phillips, 160 N.C. App. 549 (2003). Approximately 1,000 grams of cocaine were found in a package at a Federal Express facility in Greensboro. A detective obtained a search warrant for the residence at the address to which the package was to be delivered and arranged a controlled delivery of the resealed package. The package was addressed to Sonya Moore, 1412 Hamlet Pl., Greensboro, North Carolina. The pertinent part of the search warrant stated:

> On this date, the applicant and other officers will attempt to make a controlled delivery of the Federal Express Package addressed to Sonya Moore, 1412 Hamlet Pl., Greensboro, North Carolina. If this Federal Express Package is delivered to said residence within forty eight hours of the Issuance of this Warrant, this search warrant will be executed shortly thereafter.

The controlled delivery took place the same day the search warrant was obtained. Because there was no answer at the residence and the mailing label indicated a signature release, allowing the package to be left if no one was home, the officer attempting delivery left the package on the porch. A few minutes later, the defendant opened the front door from inside the residence and retrieved the package. About 20 minutes later, the detective executed the search warrant and forced entry into the defendant's residence when no one answered the door. The court ruled that this anticipatory warrant was valid under the standards set out in *State v. Smith*, 124 N.C. App. 565 (1996). First, the warrant set out "explicit, clear, and narrowly drawn triggering events" authorizing the execution of the warrant. The triggering event was the successful controlled delivery of the package to the listed address. The court rejected the defendant's argument that 48 hours was too long for law enforcement to be entitled to execute the anticipatory search warrant and that the phrase "shortly thereafter" concerning the timing of the execution after delivery was ambiguous. The court stated that *Smith* requires only that the execution of the search warrant occur after the triggering event, and the triggering event must be appropriately articulated, as it was in this case. Second, the search warrant satisfied the *Smith* requirement that the contraband must be on a sure, irreversible course to the place of the intended search, and any future search of the place must be made expressly contingent on the contraband's arrival there. In this case, the execution of the search warrant was made contingent on the delivery of the package to the listed address after a controlled delivery. Third, the search under the search warrant was contingent upon the arrival of the contraband to the place listed in the search warrant, which happened in this case.

State v. Smith, 124 N.C. App. 565 (1996). Officers planned to use a cooperating informant to sell cocaine to the defendant and his accomplice on February 15, 1993. On February 14, 1993, they obtained a search warrant to search the defendant's home for cocaine (apparently anticipating that the cocaine would be sold the next day and would then be located in the defendant's home). The affidavit for the search warrant stated, among other things, that on February 15, 1993 (a date that had not yet occurred), the affiant received information from a confidential informant who, within the past 72 hours, had seen cocaine in the defendant's residence. The court ruled that this search warrant was not a valid anticipatory search warrant, based on the requirements for such a warrant as set out in its opinion (see below). The court noted that the

search warrant's most glaring deficiency was the absence of any language denoting it as anticipatory.

The court ruled that the Constitution of North Carolina does not require that the object of a search be in the place searched when a search warrant is issued; it only requires probable cause to believe that contraband presently in transit will be at the place to be searched when the search warrant is executed. Thus, an anticipatory search warrant is permitted, as long as a judicial official who issues such a warrant carefully eliminates the opportunity for officers to exercise unfettered discretion in executing it. The state constitution requires the following conditions. (1) An anticipatory search warrant must set out explicit, clear, and narrowly drawn triggering events that must occur before execution of the warrant may take place. (2) These triggering events, from which probable cause arises, must be both ascertainable and preordained (that is, the property is on a sure and irreversible course to its destination; for example, an undercover officer will deliver the cocaine to the house to be searched). (3) A search may not occur unless and until the property does, in fact, arrive at that destination. The court stated that these three conditions ensure that the required nexus between the criminal act, the evidence to be seized, and the identity of the place to be searched is achieved.

[Author's note: An example of what might be contained in an affidavit for an anticipatory search warrant to search premises, in addition to the statement establishing probable cause, is as follows:

> I request that a search warrant for the premises described above be issued with its execution contingent on the following procedures having occurred: On August 14, 2001, an officer with the Smithville Police Department will pose as a Super Express employee and will deliver the package described above to the premises described above. The package—which is addressed to the premises described above—will contain a powdery substance containing a small amount of cocaine, with most of the cocaine having been removed when the package was previously intercepted as described in this affidavit. After the package is delivered to the above-described premises and is taken inside, this search warrant will be executed.

A later North Carolina case, *State v. Carrillo*, 164 N.C. App. 204 (2004), ruled that an anticipatory search warrant was valid under the Fourth Amendment when the contingency language for executing the search warrant was set out in affidavit and the warrant incorporated the affidavit by reference.]

United States v. Limares, 269 F.3d 794 (7th Cir. 2001). Law enforcement officers obtained an anticipatory search warrant for the search of a residence to which a package of drugs, with a radio transmitter placed inside, was being delivered. The recipient left the residence shortly after the delivery, and the radio transmitter told the officers that the package had been opened. The recipient walked a few blocks and entered another residence. Fearing that the occupants of this residence would destroy the package and its contents, officers entered it without a search warrant. The court ruled that exigent circumstances supported the officers' warrantless entry.

Descriptions in a Search Warrant

(This topic is discussed on page 419.)

Description of the Premises to Be Searched

Maryland v. Garrison, 480 U.S. 79 (1987). Officers executed a search warrant that described the place to be searched as the "third floor apartment" of the premises at a certain address when they reasonably believed that there was only one apartment on the third floor. However, there were actually two apartments on the third floor. The officers found drugs in the other apartment on that floor, which was not the object of the search, before they realized their mistake. The Court ruled that (1) the search warrant was valid when it was issued, considering the officers' information then, and (2) the execution of the warrant did not violate the defendant's Fourth Amendment rights, because the officers' failure to realize the warrant's overbroad description of the third floor apartment was objectively reasonable.

State v. Hunter, 208 N.C. App. 506 (2010). The court rejected the defendant's argument that a search warrant executed at a residence was invalid because the application and warrant referenced an incorrect street address. Although the numerical portion of the street address was incorrect, the warrant was sufficient because it contained a correct description of the residence.

State v. Cloninger, 37 N.C. App. 22 (1978). A search warrant sufficiently described the mobile home to be searched by stating who owned and occupied it and describing its location at the end of a dirt road approxi-

mately 100 yards behind a specified truck stop. Furthermore, the executing officer knew the trailer and had seen the defendant there several times. An executing officer's prior knowledge about the place to be searched is relevant in determining whether the description is adequate. *See also* State v. Woods, 26 N.C. App. 584 (1975) (error in stating who owned mobile home was not fatal).

State v. Walsh, 19 N.C. App. 420 (1973). Any error in the address of premises to be searched was not fatal when the premises were described with reasonable certainty and the executing officer was familiar with the premises.

Description of the Property to Be Seized

Groh v. Ramirez, 540 U.S. 551 (2004). An officer with the Bureau of Alcohol, Tobacco, and Firearms prepared and signed an application for a search warrant to search a ranch for specified weapons, explosives, and records. The application was accompanied by a detailed affidavit setting out the basis for believing that the items were on the ranch and by a warrant form that the officer completed. The magistrate signed the warrant form even though it did not describe the things to be seized; instead, the space on the warrant for listing those items merely described the house on the ranch. The warrant did not incorporate by reference the application's list of the items to be seized.

(1) The Court ruled that the search warrant was invalid under the Fourth Amendment because it did not describe the things to be seized and did not incorporate by reference the application's description of the things to be seized. [Author's note: This ruling does not affect the validity of AOC-CR-119 (Search Warrant), because the warrant language specifically incorporates by reference the items to be seized that are described on the accompanying application.] (2) The Court ruled that the officer was not entitled to qualified immunity because no reasonable officer could believe that the search warrant complied with the Fourth Amendment.

Andresen v. Maryland, 427 U.S. 463 (1976). A search warrant was sufficiently specific under the Fourth Amendment when it described a set of documents and then used the phrase "together with other fruits, instrumentalities and evidence of crime at this [time] unknown"; it was clear from the context that the word "crime" referred only to the crime under investigation, a fraudulent real estate transaction. *See also* United States v. Cantu, 774 F.2d 1305 (9th Cir. 1985) (sufficient description of financial records involving tax fraud); United States v. Holzman, 871 F.2d 1496 (9th Cir. 1989) (sufficient description of credit cards and credit card drafts); United States v. Bentley, 825 F.2d 1104 (7th Cir. 1987) (when fraud infects entire business, description may properly include seizure of all business documents); United States v. Rude, 88 F.3d 1538 (9th Cir. 1996) (business permeated with fraud justified broad description of documents to be seized); *In re* Impounded Case (Law Firm), 840 F.2d 196 (3rd Cir. 1988) (search warrant to seize law office files that was limited to seizure of a designated group of files, all of which the affidavit alleged contained evidence of fraudulent claims, was sufficiently specific).

State v. Kornegay, 313 N.C. 1 (1985). The court stated that Article I, Section 20, of the North Carolina Constitution did not require more particularity in search warrants in describing items to be seized than did the Fourth Amendment. A search warrant need not describe each individual paper to be seized, particularly in cases involving complex white-collar crimes. A description of property is sufficient when it is as specific as the circumstances and the nature of the activity being investigated permit. The court ruled as a sufficient description in this case all checkbooks, canceled checks, deposit slips, bank statements, trust account receipts, check stubs, books and papers, and so forth that would tend to show a fraudulent intent or any elements of the crimes of false pretenses or embezzlement.

State v. Connard, 81 N.C. App. 327 (1986), *aff'd*, 319 N.C. 392 (1987). A search warrant authorized the seizure of Dilaudid, Valium, and stolen goods—with no description of the goods. The court ruled that the description "stolen goods" was insufficient, although the descriptions "Dilaudid" and "Valium" were sufficient. The warrant's provisions were severable. Thus, the officers constitutionally could search for the named drugs or those of the same class, but they could not make a general exploratory search of the defendant's home and van and make an inventory of their contents to discover stolen goods.

State v. Foye, 14 N.C. App. 200 (1972). A description that read "narcotic drugs, the possession of which is a crime" sufficiently described the items to be seized.

United States v. Peters, 92 F.3d 768 (8th Cir. 1996). A drug search warrant authorized the seizure of, among other things, "records . . . associated with cocaine distribution. . . ." The court, distinguishing *Walter v. United States*, 447 U.S. 649 (1980), ruled that the search warrant authorized the seizure of three unmarked audiocassettes that were intermingled with notes and letters from a drug co-conspirator who was incarcerated. Thus, the seizing

officer was authorized to listen to the audiotapes before deciding whether to seize them.

United States v. Rey, 923 F.2d 1217 (6th Cir. 1991). Probable cause existed to support a search warrant's authorization to seize "controlled substances, records of narcotics activities, documents, paraphernalia and other evidence of drug dealing and importation." *See also* United States v. Martin, 920 F.2d 393 (6th Cir. 1990); United States v. Sullivan, 919 F.2d 1403 (10th Cir. 1991); United States v. Wylie, 919 F.2d 969 (5th Cir. 1990); United States v. Smith, 918 F.2d 1501 (11th Cir. 1990); United States v. Riley, 906 F.2d 841 (2d Cir. 1990); United States v. Harris, 903 F.2d 770 (10th Cir. 1990); United States v. Hinds, 856 F.2d 438 (1st Cir. 1988).

United States v. Calisto, 838 F.2d 711 (3d Cir. 1988). A search warrant authorized the seizure of illegal drugs and "items used in the manufacture, sale, use, etc. of controlled substances." The court ruled that this description authorized the seizure of two firearms in the bedroom where drugs were found, because firearms may be considered items used in connection with illegal drugs.

Description Incorporated by Reference to Affidavit

State v. Fowler, 89 N.C. App. 10 (1988). A search warrant that failed to list specifically the defendant's body cavity as a place to be searched was not defective when the application for the search warrant specifically referred to the attached affidavit, which requested that the search include the defendant's body cavity. The language in the warrant and application incorporated the affidavit by reference.

Search Warrants for Computers

(*This topic is discussed on page 414.*)

State v. Ellis, 188 N.C. App. 820 (2008). The court ruled that probable cause existed to issue a search warrant to search a computer in the defendant's home based on instant messages between the defendant and law enforcement officers posing as a 12-year-old girl. The search warrant affidavit contained many sexually explicit instant message conversations in which the defendant asked to meet the "children" to engage in sexual conduct and stated that he transmitted a video of himself masturbating. Other conversations included his statements to a "mother" of young girls involving sexual contact with the girls. In other conversations the defendant admitted that he had penetrated children with his penis.

State v. Dexter, 186 N.C. App. 587 (2007). Officers received an email tip from a person they later verified as the defendant's housemate. The email reported the defendant's having child pornography on his home computer. The court noted that although the housemate later recanted her email tip, the officers confirmed the easily verified information from the tip, which increased her credibility. The court reviewed the officers' additional corroboration of the tip (see the facts set out in its opinion) and ruled that probable cause supported the issuance of a search warrant for the defendant's home and computer for child pornography.

State v. Peterson, 179 N.C. App. 437 (2006), *aff'd*, 361 N.C. 587 (2007). The court ruled that the affidavit for a search warrant to seize computers at the defendant's home where a homicide investigation was ongoing did not provide probable cause when the affidavit (1) did not include the substance of conversations or discoveries in the 36-hour investigation that might lead one to check computers in the home and (2) did not include any indication, other than the amount of blood, to suggest that a search of computers would lead to information about the possible homicide.

State v. Pickard, 178 N.C. App. 330 (2006). The search warrant for the defendant's home authorized the seizure of computers, computer equipment and accessories, cassette videos and DVDs, video cameras, digital cameras, film cameras and accessories, and photographs and printed materials that could be consistent with the exploitation of a minor. The affidavit described the defendant's sexual and other inappropriate activity with four children under 9 years old and with a 14-year-old. The victims described the defendant's taking photographs and his use of video cameras and computers. The activity with the 14-year-old had taken place about 18 months before the issuance of the search warrant. [Author's note: The affidavit apparently did not contain specific dates concerning the defendant's sexual activity with the younger children, but the affidavit stated that the officer's interviews with the younger children occurred the day before the officer applied for the search warrant.] The court ruled, relying on *State v. Jones*, 299 N.C. 298 (1980), and cases from other jurisdictions, that the search warrant's information was not stale, because the affidavit showed the defendant's commission of ongoing sex crimes with

the children and the items to be seized were of continuing utility to the defendant.

United States v. Williams, 592 F.3d 511 (4th Cir. 2010). A search warrant authorized a search of the defendant's computers and digital media for evidence relating to the designated Virginia crimes of making threats and computer harassment. The court stated that (1) to conduct that search, the warrant impliedly authorized officers to open each file on the computer and view its contents, at least cursorily, to determine whether the file fell within the scope of the warrant's authorization—that is, whether it related to the designated Virginia crimes of making threats or computer harassment; (2) to be effective, such a search could not be limited to reviewing only the files' designation or labeling, because the designation or labeling of files on a computer can easily be manipulated to hide their substance; and (3) if the owner of a computer is engaged in criminal conduct on that computer, he or she will not label the files to indicate their criminality. The court criticized the ruling in *United States v. Carey*, 172 F.3d 1268 (10th Cir. 1999), as improperly focusing on the officer's subjective motivation for continuing to search computer files instead of on whether the warrant's terms objectively permitted continuing to search.

United States v. Hay, 231 F.3d 630 (9th Cir. 2000). The court ruled that there was probable cause to support a search warrant for the defendant's computer based on evidence that a computer in Canada had transmitted to the defendant's computer nineteen files of child pornography and on other facts set out in the officer's affidavit. The court also ruled that the information was not too stale even though the transmission occurred six months before the application for the search warrant. The court also upheld the defendant's entire computer system having been seized and taken off site because of the time, expertise, and controlled environment required for a proper analysis. *See also* United States v. Lacy, 119 F.3d 742 (9th Cir. 1997) (similar ruling).

United States v. Carey, 172 F.3d 1268 (10th Cir. 1999). Officers obtained a search warrant to search the files on the defendant's computers for "names, telephone numbers, ledger receipts, addresses, and other documentary evidence pertaining to the sale and distribution of controlled substances." Upon opening a file labeled "JPG," the officer discovered child pornography. The officer then opened many more files with that label and discovered more child pornography. The court ruled that the child pornography files seized were not authorized by the search warrant. After opening the first child pornography file, the officer was aware what the label meant. When he opened the additional files with that label, he knew that he was not going to find items related to drug activity as specified in the search warrant.

United States v. Upham, 168 F.3d 532 (1st Cir. 1999). The court ruled that in a search warrant to seize child pornography on a computer in a home, the following descriptions of items to be seized were not overly broad: (1) "Any and all computer software and hardware, . . . computer disks, disk drives . . ."; and (2) "Any and all visual depictions, in any format or media, of minors engaging in sexually explicit conduct [as defined by the statute]." The court also ruled that the search warrant permitted the recovery of deleted material on the hard disk. *See also* United States v. Hall, 142 F.3d 988 (7th Cir. 1998) (items to be seized were sufficiently particular because they were qualified by phrases emphasizing that items sought were those related to child pornography); United States v. Campos, 221 F.3d 1143 (10th Cir. 2000) (similar ruling).

Search Warrants for Obscene Materials

(This topic is discussed on page 418. See also case summaries in prior section, "Search Warrants for Computers.")

Fort Wayne Books, Inc. v. Indiana, 489 U.S. 46 (1989). Following past precedents, such as *Marcus v. Search Warrant*, 367 U.S. 717 (1961), the Court ruled that it is unconstitutional to make mass seizures of allegedly obscene materials without a court conducting a prior adversary hearing to determine whether they were obscene.

New York v. P. J. Video, Inc., 475 U.S. 868 (1986). A magistrate need not personally view allegedly obscene materials before issuing a warrant to seize them; a reasonably specific affidavit describing the content of the materials is generally sufficient. The same standard of probable cause ("fair probability") to issue a search warrant under *Illinois v. Gates*, 462 U.S. 213 (1983), applied to a search warrant to seize obscene materials. The Court ruled that probable cause existed to issue the search warrant in this case when the affidavits summarized the theme of, and sexual conduct depicted in, each movie to be seized. *See also* United States v. Espinoza, 641 F.2d 153 (4th Cir. 1981); Sequoia Books, Inc. v. McDonald, 725 F.2d 1091 (7th Cir. 1984).

Lo-Ji Sales, Inc. v. New York, 442 U.S. 319 (1979). A New York officer purchased two allegedly obscene films from an adult bookstore and took them to a town justice, who viewed them and concluded that they were obscene. He issued a search warrant to search the bookstore and to seize other copies of the two films. In addition, based on the officer's affidavit that "similar" films and printed matter were in the bookstore, the justice authorized in the search warrant the seizure of the "following items that the Court independently [on examination] has determined to be possessed in violation of" New York law. However, when the justice signed the search warrant, no items were listed or described following this statement. Instead, he accompanied the officers to the bookstore and participated in the search and ordered the seizure of various items, which were then described in the warrant after they were seized. The Court ruled that such an open-ended search warrant was unconstitutional, because it did not particularly describe the things to be seized. In addition, by becoming a member of the search party, the town justice did not act as a "neutral and detached" magistrate; he acted as an adjunct law enforcement officer. The Court distinguished this case from *Heller v. New York*, 413 U.S. 483 (1973), discussed below, where a judge viewed a film in a theater as a paying patron and then issued a search warrant to seize the allegedly obscene film.

Roaden v. Kentucky, 413 U.S. 496 (1973). After viewing a movie at a drive-in theater and determining that it was obscene, an officer arrested the theater manager without an arrest warrant and seized a copy of the film without a search warrant. The Court ruled that a seizure of the film without a search warrant was unconstitutional because it was a prior restraint on freedom of expression. It noted that in this case there was no risk that evidence might have been lost if the officer had taken the time to obtain a search warrant; the film was being commercially exhibited to the public at scheduled times.

Heller v. New York, 413 U.S. 483 (1973). A judge viewed a film in a theater as a paying patron and then issued a search warrant to seize the allegedly obscene film. Officers seized a single copy of the film. No pretrial motion was made for return of the film, nor was there a pretrial assertion that seizing the film prevented its exhibition because it was the only copy. The Court ruled that when a single copy of a film is seized pursuant to a search warrant for the bona fide purpose of preserving it as evidence in a criminal proceeding, the seizure is constitutional if a prompt judicial determination (an adversary hearing) of the obscenity issue is available after the seizure at the request of any interested party. If the exhibitor of the seized film has no other available copies, a court must permit the seized film to be copied so that it may be shown pending the judicial determination at the adversary proceeding. Otherwise, the film must be returned. Therefore, with such safeguards, an adversary hearing before a seizure pursuant to a search warrant is not constitutionally required.

The Court distinguished this case from *A Quantity of Books v. Kansas*, 378 U.S. 205 (1964), and *Marcus v. Search Warrant*, 367 U.S. 717 (1961), noting that both involved seizures of large quantities of books for the purpose of destroying them. In those circumstances, a prior judicial determination of obscenity in an adversary proceeding is constitutionally required to avoid a prior restraint of materials presumptively protected under the First Amendment.

Lee Art Theatre v. Virginia, 392 U.S. 636 (1968). A justice of the peace issued a search warrant to seize motion pictures based on an officer's affidavit that gave only the titles of the motion pictures and stated that the officer had determined that they were obscene from having viewed them personally and having seen the contents of a billboard in front of the theater that was exhibiting them. The Court ruled that the search warrant was constitutionally defective, because the determination of obscenity was based solely on the officer's conclusory assertions without any independent inquiry by a justice of the peace as to whether they were obscene. The Court stated that it need not decide whether the justice of the peace should have viewed the motion pictures before he issued the search warrant.

A Neutral and Detached Magistrate

Lo-Ji Sales, Inc. v. New York, 442 U.S. 319 (1979). A town justice was not a neutral and detached magistrate when he issued a search warrant to search a bookstore and to seize allegedly obscene films and then accompanied officers as a member of the searching party. He acted as an adjunct law enforcement officer. *See also* People v. Lowenstein, 325 N.W.2d 462 (Mich. Ct. App. 1982) (magistrate who issued arrest warrant was not neutral and detached when he had previously prosecuted defendant and had been sued by defendant; court indicates that new arrest warrant issued by neutral and detached magistrate would be permissible).

State v. Long, 37 N.C. App. 662 (1978). A military base commanding officer qualified as a neutral and detached magistrate when a search of a home was made pursuant to the authority to do so issued by the commanding officer.

State v. Woods, 26 N.C. App. 584 (1975). When an officer brought before him a person arrested for drug violations, the magistrate heard the arrestee say that another person possessed a large quantity of drugs. The magistrate knew that the arrestee was a police informant and advised the officer to call a police chief who knew him. The officer called the police chief and determined that the arrestee was reliable. The magistrate then issued a search warrant based on the officer's affidavit. The court ruled that the magistrate's actions did not violate his role as a neutral and detached magistrate, because he properly informed the officer of information that might support a finding of probable cause.

United States v. Ramirez, 63 F.3d 937 (10th Cir. 1995). An issuing judge's commonsense alterations of an affidavit for a search warrant and the search warrant itself did not violate the judge's duty to be a neutral and detached magistrate, based on the facts in this case. The judge altered the person and items to be seized, but the alteration was based on the narrative portion of the affidavit that provided probable cause to do so.

United States v. McKeever, 906 F.2d 129 (5th Cir. 1990). The magistrate's former position as a reserve deputy, her husband's current position as a reserve deputy (he was not involved in obtaining or executing the search warrant), and her visiting the site of the search as a mere observer after the premises were secured and arrests were made did not affect her objectivity such that she was no longer neutral and detached.

Executing a Search Warrant
Notice and Entry
(*This topic is discussed on page 438.*)

UNITED STATES SUPREME COURT

Hudson v. Michigan, 547 U.S. 1096 (2006). Officers with a valid search warrant entered the defendant's home in violation of the Fourth Amendment's knock-and-announce requirement. The officers seized drugs and a firearm. The Court ruled that the Fourth Amendment's exclusionary rule did not apply to bar the admission of the seized evidence even though the officers violated the knock-and-announce requirement. The Court reasoned that because the privacy interests violated in this case had nothing to do with the seizure of the evidence, the exclusionary rule was inapplicable. The Court rejected the defendant's argument that there would be no deterrence without suppression of the seized evidence. The Court noted that misconduct by law enforcement officers is subject to a civil lawsuit under 42 U.S.C. § 1983 and to discipline of officers by their law enforcement agencies. [Author's note: A violation of North Carolina law that requires notice of identity and purpose before executing a search warrant (G.S. 15A-249, with an exception in G.S. 15A-251(2)) may subject the seized evidence to suppression under North Carolina's statutory exclusionary rule set out in G.S. 15A-974(a)(2).] *See also* United States v. Hector, 474 F.3d 1150 (9th Cir. 2007) (court ruled under rationale of *Hudson v. Michigan* that exclusionary rule did not apply to seizure of evidence pursuant to search warrant when copy of search warrant was not served on defendant); United States v. Pelletier, 469 F.3d 194 (1st Cir. 2006) (*Hudson v. Michigan* ruling applies to execution of arrest warrants).

United States v. Banks, 540 U.S. 31 (2003). Officers with knowledge that the defendant was selling cocaine at his residence obtained a search warrant to search his two-bedroom apartment. As soon as they arrived there in the afternoon, officers at the front door called out "police search warrant" and rapped hard enough on the door to be heard by officers at the back door. There was no indication whether anyone was at home, and after waiting 15 to 20 seconds without receiving an answer, they broke open the front door with a battering ram. The Court ruled that the forcible entry into the apartment under these circumstances did not violate the Fourth Amendment. [Author's note: This ruling did not set 15 to 20 seconds as a Fourth Amendment required minimum waiting time before using force to enter a residence with a search warrant. The Court in its opinion stressed that each case must be decided on the totality of circumstances presented to the officers as they attempt to execute a search warrant.]

United States v. Ramirez, 523 U.S. 65 (1998). In *Richards v. Wisconsin*, 520 U.S. 385 (1997), discussed below, the Court ruled that under the Fourth Amendment officers are not required to knock and announce their presence before entering a home if they have reasonable suspicion that doing so would be dangerous or futile or that it would inhibit the effective investigation of crime.

The Court in this case rejected the defendant's argument that a higher standard should apply when officers must destroy property to enter a home—for example, if they must break a window. Instead, the Court ruled that the *Richards* standard applies in such a case. The Court then examined the facts in this case, in which officers broke a window in a garage where they suspected weapons were located that could be used against them, and determined that the officers' "no knock" entry was reasonable under the Fourth Amendment.

Richards v. Wisconsin, 520 U.S. 385 (1997). After obtaining a search warrant to search a hotel room for drugs, several officers went to the hotel room to execute the warrant. One officer, dressed as a maintenance man, was the lead officer. Among the other officers was at least one uniformed officer. The lead officer knocked on the hotel room door and, responding to a query from inside the room, stated that he was a maintenance man. The defendant cracked open the door with the chain still attached. The defendant saw a uniformed officer among the officers outside the door and quickly slammed the door shut. After waiting two or three seconds, the officers began kicking and ramming the door to gain entry. The officers identified themselves as officers while they were kicking in the door.

(1) The Court rejected a lower court ruling in this case that officers executing a search warrant involving felony drug crimes are never required to comply with the knock-and-announce rule under the Fourth Amendment. The Court stated that *Wilson v. Arkansas*, 514 U.S. 927 (1995), did not support the lower court's ruling. (2) The Court ruled that officers are not required to knock and announce their presence before entering a home if they have reasonable suspicion that doing so would be dangerous or futile or that it would inhibit the effective investigation of crime by, for example, allowing the destruction of evidence. The Court stated that this standard—as opposed to probable cause—strikes the appropriate balance between legitimate law enforcement concerns in executing a search warrant and the individual privacy interests affected by no-knock entries. (3) The Court ruled that in this case, based on the defendant's apparent recognition of the officers and the easily disposable nature of drugs, the officers were justified in entering the hotel room without first announcing their presence and authority.

[Author's note: G.S. 15A-251 requires an officer, before executing a search warrant and entering premises without giving notice, to have probable cause to believe that giving notice would endanger the life or safety of any person. Thus, this statute imposes a more stringent standard on officers than the Fourth Amendment. See also G.S. 15A-401(e)c, which requires an officer, before entering premises to make an arrest without giving notice of the officer's authority and purpose, to have reasonable cause to believe that the giving of such notice would present a clear danger to human life.]

Wilson v. Arkansas, 514 U.S. 927 (1995). Officers made an unannounced entry into a home to execute a search warrant. The Arkansas Supreme Court ruled that the Fourth Amendment does not require officers to knock and announce before entering a home. The Court, rejecting that ruling, ruled that an officer's unannounced entry into a home must be reasonable under the Fourth Amendment. Whether an officer announced his or her presence and authority before entering a home is among the factors to be considered in determining whether the entry was reasonable (along with the threat of physical harm to the officer, the pursuit of a recently escaped arrestee, and the likely destruction of evidence if advance notice was given). The Court specifically stated that it will leave to lower courts the task of determining whether an unannounced entry was reasonable and remanded this case to the Arkansas Supreme Court for that purpose. *See also* United States v. Conley, 92 F.3d 157 (3d Cir. 1996) (execution of search warrant was reasonable when the officers entered during daylight and business hours, they entered through an unlocked door, an occupant witnessed the officers' approach, the officers announced their presence soon after entry, and the entry occurred at a commercial establishment); United States v. Moore, 91 F.3d 96 (10th Cir. 1996) (mere statement by officers that firearms were present inside the dwelling to be searched was insufficient to excuse notice when executing search warrant); United States v. Bates, 84 F.3d 790 (6th Cir. 1996) (mere presence of firearm in apartment and barricaded door were insufficient to excuse notice when executing search warrant).

[Author's note: G.S. 15A-249 sets standards in entering private premises to execute a search warrant, and G.S. 15A-401(e) sets standards in entering private premises to arrest. See the discussion above in *Richards v. Wisconsin*.]

NORTH CAROLINA SUPREME COURT

State v. Lyons, 340 N.C. 646 (1995). Officers executing a search warrant of an apartment to search for drugs announced their identity and purpose while using a battering ram to enter the apartment, even though—based on the facts in this case—they did not need to make such an announcement under G.S. 15A-251(2) (forcible breaking and entering to execute a warrant is authorized if the officer has probable cause to believe that the giving of notice would endanger life). The court ruled that the fact that officers announced their identity and purpose did not mean that entry by force could not be justified under G.S. 15A-251(2). In this case, the court noted that the following evidence supported a forcible entry under G.S. 15A-251(2): the officers believed that a firearm was inside the defendant's apartment; the defendant would not cooperate; the area outside the defendant's door was so small that even though officers felt the situation was dangerous, their weapons were not drawn because of the fear of harming other officers and bystanders; and one officer heard two arguing voices within the apartment.

State v. Knight, 340 N.C. 531 (1995). The murder victim was stabbed 27 times, was castrated, and his penis was inserted in his mouth. Officers went to the defendant's home to execute arrest and search warrants for this murder. They knocked on the front door several times and announced, "Police! Search warrant!" at least two or three times. After waiting 30 to 60 seconds and hearing no response from inside the residence, the officers used a battering ram to open the door. They entered the residence, conducted a quick sweep for weapons, and arrested the defendant. The defendant was taken to the police station, where he confessed to his participation in the murder and also told the officers where one of the knives used in the murder was located in the residence officers had entered. The court ruled that the officers' forcible entry into the premises was reasonable under the Fourth Amendment (*see* Wilson v. Arkansas, 514 U.S. 927 (1995)) and that it complied with the provisions of G.S. Chapter 15A. They had probable cause to believe that further delay in entering the residence or the giving of more specific notice would endanger their own safety or that of other occupants of the residence. They knew that the defendant was dangerous, armed with a hunting knife and possibly firearms; there was at least one other suspect who had not been arrested; they were concerned about the safety of a woman and her children inside the residence, who might become hostages; and if the entry was not forced, it would not be safe.

NORTH CAROLINA COURT OF APPEALS

State v. Terry, 207 N.C. App. 311 (2010). In a search warrant for marijuana based on sales in the residence, officers entered through an unlocked door shortly after knocking and announcing that they were from the sheriff's department and had a search warrant. The court ruled that the brief delay between notice and entry was reasonable because the search warrant was based on marijuana being sold there, and marijuana could be easily and quickly disposed of.

State v. Reid, 151 N.C. App. 379 (2002). In executing a search warrant for cocaine, officers knocked three times on the door of the apartment, announced, "Sheriff's Office, search warrant," then knocked three more times and repeated the announcement. After waiting six to eight seconds, the officers forcibly entered the apartment by breaking down the door with a battering ram. The court ruled that the delay of six to eight seconds before the officers made a forcible entry into the apartment did not violate the defendant's Fourth Amendment rights or G.S. 15A-251.

State v. Vick, 130 N.C. App. 207 (1998). Officers executing a search warrant for drugs were aware that the defendant was inside his apartment. They also were aware that the defendant had sold large amounts of cocaine to informants on at least two prior occasions, and they believed that he was dangerous. They knocked loudly on the door and announced their purpose and identity, waited at least two to three seconds, and then knocked and announced a second time. Approximately 10 to 15 seconds elapsed between the first knock and announcement and the officers' forcible entry. Before their entry, they did not hear any sound from inside the apartment, and they assumed that entry was being denied or unreasonably delayed. The court ruled that the officers' assumption was reasonable and the forced entry was proper.

State v. Jones, 97 N.C. App. 189 (1990). Officers acted properly in executing a search warrant when they knocked on the door of the premises and announced their identity and purpose loudly and, after waiting approximately one minute and receiving no response, forcibly entered the premises.

State v. Marshall, 94 N.C. App. 20 (1989). Officers acted properly in executing a search warrant for drugs when they gave proper notice, heard the word "police" and the sound of people running inside the house, and then forced their way in. The officers reasonably believed that they were being denied access and that evidence could be destroyed.

State v. Edwards, 70 N.C. App. 317 (1984), *rev'd on other grounds*, 315 N.C. 304 (1985). A warrant to search an apartment for cocaine was executed at about 10:45 p.m. An officer knocked on a locked storm door and announced in a loud, authoritative voice, "Police have a search warrant, open the door." After about 30 seconds elapsed without an answer, officers forced open the storm door and the wooden front door and entered the apartment. The court ruled that the announcement and forcible entry complied with G.S. 15A-249 and G.S. 15A-251. Because the object of the search was powdery cocaine that can be instantly disposed of, the 30-second wait between notice and forcible entry was reasonable. The court also ruled that the fact that the search was conducted at night did not make the search unreasonable. Traffic in and out of the apartment was heavier at night, and officers needed the cover of darkness in approaching the apartment so that the defendant and others could not interfere with the execution of the search warrant.

State v. Willis, 58 N.C. App. 617 (1982), *aff'd*, 307 N.C. 461 (1983). An officer did not give proper notice as he entered a house to execute a search warrant when he merely shouted "police" but failed to state his purpose for entering. The officer did not have probable cause to believe that giving notice would endanger the life or safety of any person. However, the court ruled that the violation was not so substantial as to exclude the evidence under G.S. 15A-974, because it was not willful, and officers feared that someone inside the house might destroy contraband they were searching for—although this latter fact did not excuse the officers from giving proper notice. [Author's note: Legislation enacted in 2011 (S.L. 2011-6) added a good faith exception to the application of G.S. 15A-974.]

State v. Brown, 35 N.C. App. 634 (1978). Officers had a search warrant to search the defendant's home for marijuana. They devised a plan to enter the home quickly so that the defendant could not destroy any drugs he possessed (the trial judge later found that a confidential informant had told the officers that the drugs might be destroyed). Officers staged a mock chase in front of the defendant's house. The defendant opened his door and stepped outside the door to investigate the commotion, and one non-uniformed officer, without identifying himself, asked whether he could use the phone. When the defendant refused, the officer pushed his way inside the house, and the search began. The court ruled that officers violated notice provisions of G.S. 15A-249. Notice may not be dispensed with even when destruction of contraband is probable. Unannounced, forcible entries are permitted only when a person's life or safety may be endangered by giving notice. The court also ruled that the violation was substantial under G.S. 15A-974, so that evidence found during the search was inadmissible: the violation was willful, privacy interests were violated, the officers completely failed to follow the provisions of G.S. 15A-249, and the exclusion of evidence would tend to deter future violations. [Author's note: Legislation enacted in 2011 (S.L. 2011-6) added a good faith exception to the application of G.S. 15A-974.]

State v. Fruitt, 35 N.C. App. 177 (1978). An officer was executing a search warrant for a dwelling and an outbuilding. He gave notice at the dwelling, and no one responded. His failure to give a second notice before entering the outbuilding was not a substantial violation of G.S. 15A-249.

State v. Gaines, 33 N.C. App. 66 (1977). When approaching a residence to execute a search warrant, officers saw a man run out of the house and speed away in a car. An officer went to the front of the residence, where a screen door was closed but unlocked and the inside door was open about a foot. The officer announced, "Police officer, search warrant." He then immediately opened the screen door and entered. The court stated that the amount of time required between notice and entry depends on the particular circumstances, and it ruled that notice and entry were proper in this case.

People Present during the Execution of a Search Warrant

(*This topic is discussed on page 442.*)

Detaining People Present

Bailey v. United States, 133 S. Ct. 1031 (2013). The United States Supreme Court ruled that *Michigan v. Summers*, 452 U.S. 692 (1981) (officers executing a search warrant may detain occupants on the premises while the search is conducted), does not justify the detention of occupants beyond the immediate vicinity of the premises covered by a search warrant. In this case, the defendant left the premises before the search began and officers waited to detain him until he had driven about one mile away. The Court reasoned that none of the rationales supporting the *Summers* decision—officer safety, facilitating the completion of the search, and preventing flight—apply with the same or similar force to the detention of recent occupants beyond the immediate vicinity of the premises. It further concluded that "[a]ny of the individual interests is also insufficient, on its own, to justify an expansion of the rule in *Summers* to permit the detention of a former occupant, wherever he may be found away from the scene of the search." It stated: "The categorical authority to detain incident to the execution of a search warrant must be limited to the immediate vicinity of the premises to be searched." The Court continued, noting that *Summers* also relied on the limited intrusion on personal liberty involved with detaining occupants incident to the execution of a search warrant. It concluded that where officers arrest an individual away from his or her home, there is an additional level of intrusiveness. The Court declined to precisely define the term "immediate vicinity," leaving it to the lower courts to make this determination based on "the lawful limits of the premises, whether the occupant was within the line of sight of his dwelling, the ease of reentry from the occupant's location, and other relevant factors."

Los Angeles County v. Rettele, 550 U.S. 609 (2007). The plaintiffs (a male and a female) sued law enforcement officers and others for allegedly violating their Fourth Amendment rights during an execution of a search warrant authorizing a search of their residence. From September to December 2001, officers investigated a fraud and identity theft crime ring involving four suspects, all of whom were known to be African Americans. One had registered a 9 millimeter Glock handgun. On December 11, 2001, an officer obtained a search warrant for two houses where he believed he could find the suspects. (The plaintiffs did not challenge the validity of the search warrant or the means by which it was obtained.) Six officers were involved with the execution of the search warrant and were informed that the suspects were African Americans, one of whom owned a registered handgun. The officers, with guns drawn, entered the house and then a bedroom in which the plaintiffs were in bed under bed sheets. The plaintiffs, who were white, were ordered to get out of bed and show their hands. They protested that they were not wearing clothes. They were held at gunpoint for one to two minutes before being allowed to get dressed. The officers apologized to the plaintiffs, thanked them for not becoming upset, and left within minutes. The Court ruled that the officers did not act unreasonably under the Fourth Amendment in executing the search warrant. Concerning the plaintiffs' race, the Court noted that when the officers ordered them from their bed, they had no way of knowing whether the African American suspects were elsewhere in the house. The officers, who were searching a house where they believed a suspect was armed, could secure the premises before deciding whether to continue the search. The Court stated that the Constitution does not require an officer to ignore the possibility that an armed suspect may sleep with a weapon within reach. The officers were not required to turn their backs to allow the plaintiffs to retrieve clothing or to cover themselves with the bed sheets. And there was no allegation that the officers prevented the plaintiffs from dressing longer than necessary to protect their safety.

Muehler v. Mena, 544 U.S. 93 (2005). Officers obtained a search warrant for a house and premises to search for deadly weapons and evidence of gang membership related to an investigation of a gang-related drive-by shooting. A SWAT team and other officers (a total of 18 officers altogether) executed the warrant. Aware that the gang was composed primarily of illegal immigrants, an INS officer accompanied the officers. One or two officers guarded four occupants detained at the scene, who were handcuffed for about two to three hours while the warrant was executed. In addition, an INS officer questioned the occupants about their immigration status while the warrant was executed. One of the occupants (the plaintiff in this case) sued the officers for allegedly violating her Fourth Amendment rights during the execution of the search warrant. The Court ruled that the detention of the plaintiff in handcuffs was reasonable under the Fourth Amendment. The two-to-three-hour detention in handcuffs in this case did not outweigh the officers' continuing safety interests.

Illinois v. McArthur, 531 U.S. 326 (2001). Officers accompanied the defendant's wife to a trailer, where she lived with the defendant, so that she could peacefully remove her belongings. After collecting her belongings and leaving the trailer, she told the officers that she had seen the defendant slide some marijuana under the couch. An officer knocked on the door, told the defendant what his wife had said, and asked consent to search the trailer. The defendant refused. The officer then told another officer to get a search warrant and told the defendant (who was now outside the trailer) that he could not reenter the trailer without an officer accompanying him. A search warrant was obtained within two hours. The Court ruled that the officers' action in preventing the defendant from reentering the trailer was reasonable under the Fourth Amendment. First, the officers had probable cause to believe that the trailer contained illegal drugs. Second, they had good reason to fear that the defendant, unless restrained, would destroy the drugs before they could return with a search warrant. Third, the officers imposed a significantly less restrictive restraint than arresting the defendant or searching the trailer without a warrant. Fourth, they imposed the restraint for a limited period of time, two hours.

Michigan v. Summers, 452 U.S. 692 (1981). As officers were arriving at a house to execute a search warrant for drugs, they saw the defendant go out the front door of the house and walk across the porch and down the steps. They asked his help in gaining entry and detained him while they searched the house. He later was arrested when officers found drugs in the house and determined that he owned the house. The Court ruled that a search warrant for contraband implicitly authorizes executing officers to detain occupants of premises while a search is conducted. *See also* State v. Guy, 54 N.C. App. 208 (1981), and G.S. 15A-256, which authorizes the detention of all persons present, not just occupants, during a search of premises not generally open to the public or of a vehicle other than a common carrier; United States v. Pace, 898 F.2d 1218 (7th Cir. 1990) (detaining visitors in condominium being searched with search warrant was proper, based on facts in this case); Baker v. Monroe Township, 50 F.3d 1186 (3d Cir. 1995) (detaining people who were walking up to door of house in which officers were about to execute a search warrant for illegal drugs was reasonable; detention is permissible to determine if people live there).

State v. Crabtree, 126 N.C. App. 729 (1997). While executing search warrants of a bingo hall to seize evidence being used to operate illegal gambling, officers asked questions of detained bingo hall employees. The court ruled that the officers acted within their authority under G.S. 15A-256 and the manner in which they executed the search warrants did not convert them into general search warrants.

State v. Patrick, 88 N.C. App. 582 (1988). An officer approached a private residence to investigate a report that illegal drugs were being used there. He saw the defendant outside the residence using a bong, a device commonly used to smoke an illegal drug. The officer returned 30 minutes later with a search warrant to search the residence. The defendant arrived at the residence while the officer was executing the search warrant. The court ruled that the officer had authority to detain the defendant under G.S. 15A-256.

United States v. Edwards, 103 F.3d 90 (10th Cir. 1996). The defendant, a nonresident of a house to be searched with a search warrant, left the house in a car and was stopped three blocks from the house. The court ruled that the detention of the defendant was not supported by *Michigan v. Summers*, 452 U.S. 692 (1981), because his detention did not play any part in facilitating the execution of the search warrant.

United States v. Fountain, 2 F.3d 656 (6th Cir. 1993). The detention of a nonresident occupant during officers' execution of a search warrant to search a home for drugs was reasonable and justified by legitimate interests in preventing flight on discovery of any incriminating evidence and in minimizing the risk of harm to the officers. The officers entered a confined, unfamiliar environment that was likely to be dangerous in light of the nature of the drug investigation and the fact that weapons had been seized from the home one month before the search.

United States v. Young, 909 F.2d 442 (11th Cir. 1990). An occupant fled from a house as officers were approaching to execute a search warrant for drugs. The court ruled that officers had authority to detain the occupant and search her bulging purse, based on probable cause and exigent circumstances.

Searching People Present

State v. Cutshall, 136 N.C. App. 756 (2000). Officers executed a search warrant that authorized a search for (1) crack cocaine and other controlled substances at a mobile home and all outbuildings at 5516 Cross Street and (2) a search of a specific person, who was not the defendant. The officers secured the mobile home and several people there, including the defendant. The officers found crack cocaine in an outbuilding but not in the mobile home. An officer searched the defendant and found crack cocaine and crack pipes in his jacket pocket. G.S. 15A-256 did not authorize the search of the defendant. The statute authorizes a search of a person who is not named in a search warrant and who is found on private premises when the search warrant is executed only if a search of the premises does not reveal the items sought in the search warrant. The court rejected the State's argument that evidence found in outbuildings is not to be considered in applying G.S. 15A-256, stating that the statute does not distinguish between different units on the premises. The court also noted that the record in this case did not support probable cause to search the defendant.

State v. Brooks, 51 N.C. App. 90 (1981). When a search of the residence found some hashish but not the specific 100 grams of ready-to-sell hashish being sought (and apparently described in the warrant's affidavit), an officer then had authority under G.S. 15A-256 to search the defendant at the residence. The court alternatively ruled that the officers had probable cause to believe that the defendant may have had the hashish on his person. *See also* State v. Watlington, 30 N.C. App. 101 (1976) (search of car with search warrant failed to find heroin; the court upheld search of passenger under authority of G.S. 15A-256).

Frisking People Present

Los Angeles County v. Rettele, 550 U.S. 609 (2007). The plaintiffs (a male and a female) sued law enforcement officers and others for allegedly violating their Fourth Amendment rights during an execution of a search warrant authorizing a search of their residence. From September to December 2001, officers investigated a fraud and identity theft crime ring involving four suspects, all of whom were known to be African Americans. One had registered a 9 millimeter Glock handgun. On December 11, 2001, an officer obtained a search warrant for two houses where he believed he could find the suspects. (The plaintiffs did not challenge the validity of the search warrant or the means by which it was obtained.) Six officers were involved with the execution of the search warrant and were informed that the suspects were African Americans, one of whom owned a registered handgun. The officers, with guns drawn, entered the house and then a bedroom in which the plaintiffs were in bed under bed sheets. The plaintiffs, who were white, were ordered to get out of bed and show their hands. They protested that they were not wearing clothes. They were held at gunpoint for one to two minutes before being allowed to get dressed. The officers apologized to the plaintiffs, thanked them for not becoming upset, and left within minutes. The Court ruled that the officers did not act unreasonably under the Fourth Amendment in executing the search warrant. Concerning the plaintiffs' race, the Court noted that when the officers ordered them from their bed, they had no way of knowing whether the African American suspects were elsewhere in the house. The officers, who were searching a house where they believed a suspect was armed, could secure the premises before deciding whether to continue the search. The Court stated that the Constitution does not require an officer to ignore the possibility that an armed suspect may sleep with a weapon within reach. The officers were not required to turn their backs to allow the plaintiffs to retrieve clothing or to cover themselves with the bed sheets. And there was no allegation that the officers prevented the plaintiffs from dressing longer than necessary to protect their safety.

Ybarra v. Illinois, 444 U.S. 85 (1979). When executing a warrant that authorized a search for drugs in a public tavern and on the person of the bartender, officers could not frisk the defendant—a bar patron who was present at the time of the search—without reasonable suspicion that he was armed and dangerous.

State v. Richmond, 215 N.C. App. 475 (2011). An officer was present at a location to execute a search warrant in connection with drug offenses. The court of appeals ruled that evidence supported the trial court's finding that the officer, based on his training and experience, immediately formed the opinion during a pat down that a bulge in the defendant's pants contained a controlled substance. Although the officer testified that he felt a "knot" in the defendant's pants that he could not "describe with any specificity," the officer also testified that he had discovered similar knots before in his six years of experience and had previously discovered "[b]ags of marijuana, bags of cocaine, bags of crack."

State v. Harris, 95 N.C. App. 691 (1989), *aff'd per curiam*, 326 N.C. 588 (1990). Officers had a warrant to search a motel room to arrest a person for drug charges. The officers were outside the motel room planning to execute the warrant the next time the door to the room opened. When the defendant (who was not the person to be arrested) exited the room into the hallway, some officers went into the room to execute the warrant while other officers frisked the defendant for a weapon. The court upheld the frisk because the officers had a reasonable suspicion that the defendant had a weapon, based on their professional experience that weapons are found on people or premises in at least 85 percent of the searches they conduct when drugs are involved (and the activity in the motel room indicated that a drug transaction might have occurred there).

State v. Davis, 94 N.C. App. 358 (1989). Officers entered a lounge with a search warrant to search it and two proprietors of the lounge. The officers knew from prior searches of the lounge that its patrons often carried weapons. An officer told all the people in the lounge to raise their hands above their heads and announced that they all would be frisked for weapons. The defendant raised his hands as instructed, but he attempted three times to lower one hand. Each time he lowered his hand, the officer told him to keep his hands up. After the third attempt, the officer frisked the defendant and felt an object in his coat. The officer reached into the coat pocket and found a revolver. The court ruled that the officer had a factual basis for the frisk under G.S. 15A-255.

State v. Long, 37 N.C. App. 662 (1978). In a case decided before *Ybarra v. Illinois*, 444 U.S. 85 (1979), discussed above, but not necessarily inconsistent with its rationale, the court ruled that an officer properly frisked for weapons the boot of a person who was present in private premises when a search warrant for drugs was being executed. The court stated that a frisk for weapons automatically may be made of all persons present in a private residence when it is searched under a search warrant, if there is probable cause to believe that it is a place where drugs are bought and sold.

Strip Search of Person Named in Search Warrant to Be Searched

State v. Johnson, 143 N.C. App. 307 (2001). Officers executed a search warrant authorizing a search of the defendant and his apartment for illegal drugs, based on information that the defendant was selling crack cocaine in his apartment. During the search, the officers seized two shotguns and a pair of electronic scales. An initial search of the defendant revealed almost $2,000 in small denominations. The officers then asked the defendant to remove his clothing and to bend over at the waist. When he did, they saw a piece of plastic protruding from his anus. The defendant complied with their request to remove the package, which contained seventeen individually packaged bags of crack cocaine.

The court ruled that this strip search was reasonable under the totality of the circumstances. The court stated that the strip search was not unreasonable simply because the officer did not articulate specific reasons in the search warrant application as to why a strip search was necessary, citing a case that ruled that reasons were not necessary, *see* State v. Colin, 809 P.2d 228 (Wash. App. 1991). Controlled substances could readily be concealed on a person so that they would not be found without a strip search, and an officer testified at the suppression hearing that there is a trend toward hiding controlled substances in body cavities. The court noted the approval of a strip search in *State v. Smith*, 342 N.C. 407 (1995) (pulling down defendant's pants far enough that officers could see the corner of a towel underneath the defendant's scrotum). The court also ruled that the search was conducted in a reasonable manner. Two male officers searched the defendant in his bedroom, and they did not touch him.

Territorial Jurisdiction to Execute a Search Warrant

(*This topic is discussed on page 410.*)

State v. Proctor, 62 N.C. App. 233 (1983). A city law enforcement officer in this case had no authority to execute a search warrant more than one mile beyond the city limits.

State v. Treants, 60 N.C. App. 203 (1982). A city law enforcement officer had authority to execute a search warrant outside the city limits when he executed it within one mile of the city limits.

Motive in Executing a Search Warrant

United States v. Van Dreel, 155 F.3d 902 (7th Cir. 1998). The court ruled that the ruling in *Whren v. United States*, 517 U.S. 806 (1996) (officer's motive for making traffic stop is irrelevant under Fourth Amendment when probable cause existed for traffic violation), foreclosed inquiry into the defendant's assertion that a drug officer participating in the execution of a valid search warrant for hunting violations subjectively intended to search for illegal drugs rather than hunting violations.

Second Entry under Same Search Warrant

United States v. Kaplan, 895 F.2d 618 (9th Cir. 1990). An officer executing a warrant to search the defendant-doctor's office could properly return to the office two hours later to obtain remaining files listed to be seized in the warrant, which had not been given to the officer earlier. The second entry was a proper continuation of the first entry under the search warrant. *Compare with* United States v. Keszthelyi, 308 F.3d 557 (6th Cir. 2002) (circumstances did not justify second entry under same search warrant).

Service of a Search Warrant and Completion of an Inventory

(*This topic is discussed on pages 437 and 444.*)

City of West Covina v. Perkins, 525 U.S. 234 (1999). The Court ruled that the Due Process Clause does not require law enforcement officers who have seized property to provide the property owner with notice of state law remedies for the return of the property.

State v. Knight, 340 N.C. 531 (1995). The murder victim was stabbed 27 times, was castrated, and his penis was inserted in his mouth. Officers went to the defendant's home to execute arrest and search warrants for this murder. They knocked on the front door several times and announced, "Police! Search warrant!" at least two or three times. After waiting 30 to 60 seconds and hearing no response from inside the residence, the officers used a battering ram to open the door. They entered the residence, conducted a quick sweep for weapons, and arrested the defendant. The search warrant was read to the defendant about 10 minutes after the entry into the residence and the initial sweep but before any search was undertaken. Execution of the search warrant complied with the provisions of G.S. Chapter 15A.

State v. Vick, 130 N.C. App. 207 (1998). The court ruled that the officers violated G.S. 15A-252 by failing to give the defendant a copy of the search warrant and affidavit before executing the warrant (they left it in the apartment at the conclusion of their search), but the violation was not substantial under G.S. 15A-974 to require exclusion of the seized evidence. [Author's note: Legislation enacted in 2011 (S.L. 2011-6) added a good faith exception to the application of G.S. 15A-974.]

In re Beck, 109 N.C. App. 539 (1993). After criminal charges had been dismissed, the sheriff's department did not act illegally in transferring sexually explicit materials (which had been seized pursuant to a search warrant) to the county department of social services for their use in a parental termination hearing.

State v. Moose, 101 N.C. App. 59 (1990). As an officer walked into the defendant's office with a search warrant, the defendant said to the officer, "You don't need that," and told the officer where the cocaine was located. The officer followed the defendant's direction to locate a metal box and then read the search warrant to him. The defendant prevented immediate compliance with G.S. 15A-252 by volunteering the information.

State v. Jones, 97 N.C. App. 189 (1990). (1) Although G.S. 15A-252 requires that a search warrant must be served before an officer conducts a search or seizure, an officer may locate, detain, and frisk individuals on the premises before serving the warrant. (2) An officer who executes a search warrant need not be the same officer to whom the warrant was issued. (3) Officers did not violate G.S. 15A-258 by releasing currency seized during the execution of a search warrant to federal law enforcement officers. The statute does not require that a court order must be obtained before the release of seized property, and it expressly authorizes property to be held by any law enforcement agency. *See also* State v. Hill, 153 N.C. App. 716 (2002) (neither G.S. 15-11.1 nor G.S. 90-112 bars North Carolina state or local law enforcement officers from delivering evidence to federal authorities, including illegal drug-related currency to be forfeited under federal law).

State v. Copeland, 64 N.C. App. 612 (1983). The officer who executed the warrant gave the defendant an illegible copy of the search warrant affidavit and application, although the copy of the search warrant was legible. The court noted that there was no evidence that the violation was willful and concluded that it was not a substantial violation under G.S. 15A-974 that required exclusion of evidence seized during the execution of the search warrant. [Author's note: Legislation enacted in 2011 (S.L. 2011-6) added a good faith exception to the application of G.S. 15A-974.]

State v. Fruitt, 35 N.C. App. 177 (1978). The officer violated G.S. 15A-252 by not leaving a copy of the search warrant affixed to the premises and G.S. 15A-254 by not leaving an itemized receipt of items taken. However, these were not substantial violations under G.S. 15A-974, because the officer returned to the premises hours later and gave the defendant an itemized receipt (and apparently gave him a copy of the search warrant). In addition, the violations were not willful, and they occurred after the search had been completed. [Author's note: Legislation enacted in 2011 (S.L. 2011-6) added a good faith exception to the application of G.S. 15A-974.]

Lathon v. City of St. Louis, 242 F.3d 841 (8th Cir. 2001). A police department refused to return weapons and ammunition seized under a search warrant after it was determined that these items were not contraband and were not required as evidence in a court proceeding. The department's refusal was based on the belief that a court order was necessary to return the items. The court ruled that the owner properly alleged a due process violation and that the adequacy of a post-deprivation remedy is irrelevant to whether the owner may maintain that claim.

United States v. Simons, 206 F.3d 392 (4th Cir. 2000). An officer's failure to leave a copy of a search warrant or a receipt for the items taken does not render the search unreasonable under the Fourth Amendment.

Objectively Reasonable Conduct in Executing a Search Warrant

Maryland v. Garrison, 480 U.S. 79 (1987). Officers executed a search warrant that described the place to be searched as the "third floor apartment" of the premises at a certain address when they reasonably believed that there was only one apartment on the third floor. However, there were actually two apartments on the third floor. The officers found drugs in the other apartment on that floor, which was not the object of the search, before they realized their mistake. The Court ruled that (1) the search warrant was valid when it was issued, considering the officers' information then, and (2) the execution of the warrant did not violate the defendant's Fourth Amendment rights, because the officers' failure to realize the warrant's overbroad description of the third floor apartment was objectively reasonable. *See also* United States v. Williams, 917 F.2d 1088 (8th Cir. 1990).

Using a Search Warrant to Take Blood

State v. Chavez, 237 N.C. App. 475 (2014). The court rejected the defendant's argument that the right to have a witness present for blood alcohol testing performed under G.S. 20-16.2 applies to blood draws taken pursuant to a search warrant. The court also rejected the defendant's argument that failure to allow a witness to be present for the blood draw violated his constitutional rights, ruling that the defendant had no constitutional right to have a witness present for the execution of the search warrant.

State v. Davis, 142 N.C. App. 81 (2001). The defendant drove through a red light and struck another vehicle. He was convicted of DWI and running a red light. An officer arrested the defendant and took him to a hospital for a blood test. A chemical analyst advised him of his rights under North Carolina's implied consent law, but the defendant refused to take a blood test. When a search warrant was then obtained, the defendant submitted to blood and urine testing. Evidence of the test results was admitted at trial.

(1) The court ruled, relying on *State v. Drdak*, 330 N.C. 587 (1992), that the test results were admissible under G.S. 20-16.2(c) (refusal under implied consent law does not preclude testing under "other applicable procedures of law"); *see also* G.S. 20-139.1(a). The court also rejected the defendant's due process argument that because he was told he had a right to refuse to be tested, no test can thereafter be given. (2) The court ruled that evidence of the

defendant's refusal to submit to blood testing under the implied consent law was admissible at trial even though the officer later obtained a search warrant for blood and urine. The officer's failure to warn the defendant that the officer could seek alternative methods of testing does not render inadmissible the defendant's refusal under the implied consent law. [Author's note: Based on the ruling in *Schmerber v. California*, 384 U.S. 757 (1966), an officer is not required to obtain a search warrant to take blood when probable cause and exigent circumstances exist; the dissipation of alcohol in the bloodstream constitutes exigent circumstances.]

United States v. Bullock, 71 F.3d 171 (5th Cir. 1995). Officers obtained a search warrant to take blood from the defendant. Knowing that the defendant had threatened to resist the execution of the search warrant, the officers sought and received judicial approval to use physical force. A seven-member "control team" was used to subdue him. The defendant was handcuffed and shackled between two cots that were strapped together. He physically resisted by kicking, hitting, and attempting to bite the officers. A towel was placed on the defendant's face because he was spitting on the officers. A nurse took blood from the defendant's hand.

The court ruled, based on these facts, that the use of force to execute the search warrant was reasonable under the Fourth Amendment. Citing *United States v. Wade*, 388 U.S. 218 (1967), the court also rejected the defendant's argument that his Sixth Amendment right to counsel was violated because his attorney was not present during the procedures. *See also* Hammer v. Gross, 932 F.2d 842 (9th Cir. 1991) (officers entitled to qualified immunity in civil lawsuit against them that alleged excessive use of force to obtain blood from defendant who had been arrested for impaired driving); State v. Clary, 2 P.3d 1255 (Ariz. App. 2000) (use of force to obtain blood from DWI defendant pursuant to search warrant was reasonable).

Bringing News Media or Third Parties during Execution of a Search Warrant

(*This topic is discussed on page 440.*)

Wilson v. Layne, 526 U.S. 603 (1999). Law enforcement officers invited news media representatives to accompany them during the execution of an arrest warrant in a home. The Court ruled that officers violate the Fourth Amendment when they bring news media or other third parties into a home during the execution of a warrant when the third parties' presence is not aiding the warrant's execution. The news media clearly were not aiding the execution of the arrest warrant in this case. The Court noted that third parties may properly aid the execution of a search warrant by, for example, identifying stolen property. The Court also ruled that the officers in this case were entitled to qualified immunity because the Fourth Amendment right set out in this opinion was not clearly established when the violation occurred in 1992. The Court issued a similar ruling in *Hanlon v. Berger*, 526 U.S. 808 (1999), which involved officers allowing the news media to accompany them during the execution of a search warrant for a ranch and its outbuildings.

United States v. Hendrixson, 234 F.3d 494 (11th Cir. 2000). The exclusionary rule does not apply to evidence seized by law enforcement officers during the execution of a search warrant when news media are present in violation of *Wilson v. Layne*, discussed above.

Buonocore v. Harris, 65 F.3d 347 (4th Cir. 1995), *later appeal*, 134 F.3d 245 (4th Cir. 1998). The Fourth Amendment prohibits government agents from allowing a search warrant to be used to facilitate a private individual's independent search of another's home for items unrelated to those specified in the warrant.

Scope of the Search and Seizure with a Search Warrant
Seizing Items in Plain View
(*This topic is discussed on page 440.*)

UNITED STATES SUPREME COURT

Horton v. California, 496 U.S. 128 (1990). A person was robbed of jewelry and cash by two masked men, one armed with a machine gun and the other with a stun gun. An officer developed probable cause to search a home for the weapons and robbery proceeds, but the search warrant issued by the magistrate authorized a search only for the proceeds, not the weapons. While searching for the proceeds, the officer discovered the weapons in plain view and seized them.

The Court overruled that part of the opinion in *Coolidge v. New Hampshire*, 403 U.S. 443 (1971), that required, under the plain view doctrine, that the discovery of evidence to be seized must be inadvertent. The Court then ruled that the seizure in this case was authorized by the plain view doctrine because (1) the weapons were seized during a lawful search for the robbery proceeds that was authorized by a valid search warrant and (2) when the weapons were discovered, it was immediately apparent to the officer that they constituted incriminating evidence (i.e., the officer had probable cause to believe that the weapons had been used in the robbery). The search was authorized by a search warrant, and the seizure was authorized by the plain view doctrine. [Author's note: When an officer is executing a search warrant, G.S. 15A-253 permits the seizure of items "inadvertently" discovered. If this statute is considered to have been violated because an officer does not seize items inadvertently, G.S. 15A-974(a)(2) will govern whether the items should be excluded from a trial. See the discussion of G.S. 15A-253 in *State v. Mickey*, 347 N.C. 508 (1998). Unfortunately, North Carolina appellate courts continue to assert erroneously that the plain view doctrine requires that the evidence must be discovered inadvertently during a warrantless seizure in which G.S. 15A-253 is inapplicable. *See, e.g.*, State v. Bone, 354 N.C. 1 (2001); State v. Castellon, 151 N.C. App. 675 (2002).]

Arizona v. Hicks, 480 U.S. 321 (1987). The Court ruled that an officer who conducts a search or seizure under the plain view doctrine must have probable cause to do so; reasonable suspicion is insufficient. In *Hicks*, officers without a warrant properly entered an apartment where a shooting had occurred to search for the shooter and any victims or weapons. They seized three weapons and a stocking-cap mask. In this squalid apartment, they saw two expensive stereo components. An officer read serial numbers from some items without moving them; the Court ruled that this act was neither a search nor a seizure and therefore did not violate the defendant's Fourth Amendment rights. However, the officer moved a turntable so that he could read its serial number. This act constituted a search that required probable cause—probable cause also was necessary to support the later seizure of the turntable from the apartment. Because the State had conceded (unwisely, it appears) that only reasonable suspicion existed to move the turntable, the Court ruled that the officer's actions violated the defendant's Fourth Amendment rights.

NORTH CAROLINA SUPREME COURT

State v. White, 322 N.C. 770 (1988). Officers executed a search warrant for stolen property and seized stolen items that were not named in the warrant. The court ruled that "inadvertence" (which no longer is required

under the Fourth Amendment—see *Horton v. California*, discussed above—but applies under G.S. 15A-253) under the plain view doctrine means that officers do not have probable cause to believe that evidence will be discovered until they actually observe it during an otherwise justified search. Judicial review involves a two-step inquiry: (1) Before the search, did officers have probable cause to secure a search warrant for the later-seized items that were not named in the search warrant? If the answer is yes, the seizure is illegal. If the answer is no, then the review proceeds to the second inquiry. (2) Did the officers have probable cause to believe that the seized items were evidence of a crime when they seized them without a warrant?

The court ruled that the officers' use of break-in incident reports when they were executing a search warrant did not violate the plain view inadvertence requirement, because they did not have probable cause to list the items named in these reports in a search warrant. Therefore, the officers properly seized these items. The court ruled, however, that they did not have probable cause to seize other items, not named in the reports, until after they seized them; therefore, the officers illegally seized these items.

State v. Williams, 315 N.C. 310 (1986). When executing a search warrant to seize bloody clothing, an officer acted reasonably when he lifted a telephone book to look for the clothing, because it could be hidden under, behind, or even inside a book. Also, an officer properly seized a missing padlock. The discovery of the padlock was inadvertent (but see *Horton v. California*, 496 U.S. 128 (1990), discussed above, about the inadvertence requirement), because the officers did not intend to search for and seize it when they were searching for the clothing.

State v. Williams, 299 N.C. 529 (1980). When executing a search warrant for heroin, officers properly seized letters and photographs (although they were not listed in the warrant as objects to be seized) as evidence of who owned the trailer under the plain view doctrine and under G.S. 15A-253 (which sets out the plain view doctrine when executing a search warrant).

State v. Richards, 294 N.C. 474 (1978). Officers who were executing a search warrant for a .25 caliber pistol discovered and seized a .38 caliber revolver and a .22 caliber sawed-off rifle. The court ruled that these weapons were discovered inadvertently (but see *Horton v. California*, 496 U.S. 128 (1990), discussed above, about the inadvertence requirement) while the officers were searching for the .25 caliber pistol. Although the officers knew that other weapons might have been involved in the murder, they could not describe them and did not have any information as to where they were located. A nexus existed between criminal activity and these weapons because the officers had information linking a hired killer and the other handguns, and they had taken a weapon from the defendant when he was arrested the day before this search. *See also* State v. Riddick, 291 N.C. 399 (1976) (proper seizure of tennis shoes worn during murder); State v. Rigsbee, 285 N.C. 708 (1974) (proper seizure of marked money used during drug transaction); State v. Newsom, 284 N.C. 412 (1973) (proper seizure of currency commingled with illegal drugs); State v. Armstrong, 45 N.C. App. 40 (1980) (proper seizure of stolen television set while search warrant for items from a different break-in was being executed); State v. Estep, 61 N.C. App. 495 (1983) (proper seizure of stolen cars while search warrant for illegal drugs was being executed).

NORTH CAROLINA COURT OF APPEALS

State v. Cummings, 113 N.C. App. 368 (1994). Officers executing a search warrant for drugs, drug records, and the like discovered and seized 94 photographs of nude women. The seizure was proper under the plain view justification because the photographs could have been evidence of an obscenity offense.

State v. Connard, 81 N.C. App. 327 (1986), *aff'd*, 319 N.C. 392 (1987). A search warrant authorized the seizure of Dilaudid, Valium, and stolen goods—with no description of the goods. The court ruled that the description "stolen goods" was insufficient, although the descriptions "Dilaudid" and "Valium" were sufficient. Because the warrant's provisions were severable, the officers could search for the named drugs or those of the same class, but they could not conduct a general exploratory search of the defendant's home and van and could not inventory their contents to discover stolen goods. The court ruled the officers' seizure of all but one stolen item unconstitutional because the officers did not determine that these items were stolen until they inventoried the goods in the house and van and checked police files. This case was decided before the ruling in *Arizona v. Hicks*, 480 U.S. 321 (1987), discussed above. Assuming that the officers conducted a search or a seizure of each item, as those terms are defined in *Arizona v. Hicks*, the court's ruling is consistent with that decision.

The court upheld under the plain view theory the seizure of a television set that was missing its outside serial number. The court ruled that a missing serial number, when other suspicious circumstances exist, is sufficient to authorize a seizure under the plain view theory. Assuming that the officers did not move the television to see that the serial number was missing, the ruling in this case is consistent with *Arizona v. Hicks*.

State v. Absher, 34 N.C. App. 197 (1977). While executing a warrant to search for marijuana, officers seized a ledger book showing names with dollar signs beside them. The ledger was properly seized under the plain view doctrine because (1) a nexus existed between the item seized and marijuana possession; (2) the item was in plain view; and (3) discovery of the item was inadvertent (but see *Horton v. California*, 496 U.S. 128 (1990), discussed above, about the inadvertence requirement) because before they executed the search warrant, officers had only some information that the ledger might be in a particular place, not probable cause to justify a specific search. *See also* State v. Zimmerman, 23 N.C. App. 396 (1974); State v. Tate, 58 N.C. App. 494, *aff'd*, 307 N.C. 464 (1983).

State v. Cumber, 32 N.C. App. 329 (1977). An officer's seizure of stolen furniture while he was executing a warrant to search for stolen liquor was inadvertent (but see *Horton v. California*, 496 U.S. 128 (1990), discussed above, about the inadvertence requirement) because, although the officer had some information that stolen furniture was on the premises, he did not have probable cause until he went there to help execute the warrant to search for liquor.

FEDERAL APPELLATE COURTS

United States v. Soussi, 29 F.3d 565 (10th Cir. 1994). Even if part of a search warrant is invalid, law enforcement officers may properly seize evidence in plain view listed in the invalid part of the warrant if the redacted warrant justifies the officers' presence in the place to be searched.

United States v. Simpson, 10 F.3d 645 (9th Cir. 1993), *vacated on other grounds*, 513 U.S. 983 (1994). The seizure of a rifle during the execution of a search warrant to search for illegal drugs was proper under the plain view doctrine because of the close relationship between drugs and firearms in the narcotics business.

United States v. Barnes, 909 F.2d 1059 (7th Cir. 1990). Officers who were executing a search warrant for cocaine had authority to look through a spiral notebook that might conceal cocaine. The fact that the notebook contained calculations of weights and lists of individuals, with notations of "paid" and "owe" and numbers after those notations, gave officers probable cause to seize the notebook.

United States v. Caggiano, 899 F.2d 99 (1st Cir. 1990). While executing a search warrant for illegal drugs, officers seized weapons. The court ruled that weapons, like glassine bags, scales, and cutting equipment, are an expected and usual accessory of the drug trade and therefore have evidentiary use at trial. Therefore, officers properly seized them under the plain view doctrine. *See also* United States v. Smith, 918 F.2d 1501 (11th Cir. 1990) (similar ruling); United States v. Matthews, 942 F.2d 779 (10th Cir. 1991) (similar ruling).

United States v. Meyer, 827 F.2d 943 (3d Cir. 1987). During the execution of a search warrant for stolen items, officers discovered (in a crawl space under a partially concealed trap door in the premises of a known fence) four packages of merchandise. Three of the packages contained stolen goods (jewelry) named in the warrant. Based on these and other facts, the officers had probable cause to believe that the 47 wrist watches found in the fourth package were stolen goods. The watches were properly seized under the plain view doctrine. *But see* United States v. Rutkowski, 877 F.2d 139 (1st Cir. 1989) (distinguishing *Meyer*, court ruled that officer executing search warrant did not have probable cause to seize platinum that was not named as object to be seized; the fact that the metal was stolen was not determined until days after the seizure, and there was no evidence at the time of the seizure that the resident of the house that was searched had been involved in a theft of platinum).

Searching Buildings Not Named in the Warrant
(*This topic is discussed on page 440.*)

State v. Trapper, 48 N.C. App. 481 (1980). A warrant that authorized a search of a house trailer for marijuana included a storage shed 30 feet away that was connected to the house by a concrete walkway. *See also* State v. Travatello, 24 N.C. App. 511 (1975).

United States v. Griffin, 827 F.2d 1108 (7th Cir. 1987). A search warrant's description of "premises" at a specific address authorized the search of the tool shed and yard there (including digging in the yard) when the objects of the search—drugs, chemicals and chemical equipment, and notes and formulas—could reasonably be found there.

Searching Vehicles Not Named in the Warrant
(*This topic is discussed on page 442.*)

State v. Reid, 286 N.C. 323 (1974). A warrant authorized a search of the defendant's gasoline station to seize alcoholic beverages. Officers searched the defendant's car, which was parked on the station's lot, even though the warrant did not name the car as an object to be searched. The court ruled that a search warrant for specifically described premises authorizes a search of the owner's vehicle parked there if the evidence reasonably could be found in the vehicle. Here, the officers were justified in concluding that alcoholic beverages might be in the car. *See also* State v. Marshall, 94 N.C. App. 20 (1989) (warrant to search defendant's house for drugs included car that was registered in name of woman who lived with defendant and parked within house's curtilage); State v. Logan, 27 N.C. App. 150 (1975) (warrant to search defendant's house for drugs allowed search of his car in driveway); State v. Bell, 24 N.C. App. 430 (1975) (same; car parked under house built on pilings); State v. Courtright, 60 N.C. App. 247 (1983) (warrant to search defendant's house for drugs allowed search of defendant's car parked on street in front of house with its front wheels six to seven inches into his yard; court reached questionable conclusion that car was parked on curtilage of house, and thus search of car was permitted; court could have ruled that search was permitted because car was parked on the premises, even if not on curtilage—*see* United States v. Asselin, 775 F.2d 445 (1st Cir. 1985)).

State v. McLamb, 70 N.C. App. 712 (1984). A search warrant authorized a search of a residence on a six-acre tract. The court ruled that the affidavit established probable cause to believe that a drug business was taking place on the entire tract. It also ruled that a search of a car across a road 15 feet beyond the property line was proper because it "appeared to be connected to" the property and no other residences were in the vicinity. The court alternatively ruled that even if the car was not within the curtilage, the car appeared to be abandoned and therefore the defendant had no reasonable expectation of privacy in it. [Author's note: It appeared that the car clearly was not within the curtilage, because it was not even on the defendant's property.]

United States v. Gottschalk, 915 F.2d 1459 (10th Cir. 1990). The court ruled that a search warrant for premises permitted a search of vehicles either actually owned or controlled by the owner or possessor of the premises, or alternatively, of those vehicles that appear to be so controlled, based on objectively reasonable indicia that existed when the search was conducted.

Challenging the Validity of a Search Warrant
Truthfulness of the Information
UNITED STATES SUPREME COURT

Franks v. Delaware, 438 U.S. 154 (1978). When a defendant makes a substantial preliminary showing that (1) an affiant, when applying for a search warrant, made a false statement and knew it was false or acted in reckless disregard of its falsity and (2) probable cause would not have been found except for the allegedly false statement, the Fourth Amendment requires that a hearing be held. If the defendant proves both points by a preponderance of evidence at the hearing, the false information must be disregarded in determining whether probable cause exists. If the remaining portion of the affidavit is insufficient to establish probable cause, then the search warrant is invalid and evidence seized under it must be suppressed. *See also* United States v. Fawole, 785 F.2d 1141 (4th Cir. 1986); United States v. Kirk, 781 F.2d 1498 (11th Cir. 1986); United States v. McNeese, 901 F.2d 585 (7th Cir. 1990) (omission of facts from search warrant affidavit is material and voids warrant only if it involves a deliberate falsehood or reckless disregard for the truth).

NORTH CAROLINA SUPREME COURT

State v. Barnes, 333 N.C. 666 (1993). The court examined the officer's statements in a search warrant affidavit and determined, based on the facts in this case, that they were not deliberately false or made in reckless disregard of the truth under *Franks v. Delaware*, 438 U.S. 154 (1978).

State v. Creason, 313 N.C. 122 (1985). The court ruled that by the express terms of G.S. 15A-978(b)(1), a defendant is not entitled, on statutory grounds, to the disclosure of an informant's identity when attacking the information in a search warrant affidavit. The court also ruled that the defendant in this case waived his right to appellate review, on constitutional grounds, of the failure to disclose the informant's identity when he failed to raise the issue at trial.

State v. Louchheim, 296 N.C. 314 (1979). Probable cause supported the search warrant in this case, even if the allegedly false information was disregarded. *See also*

State v. Montserrate, 125 N.C. App. 22 (1997); State v. Reddick, 55 N.C. App. 646 (1982); United States v. Cummins, 912 F.2d 98 (6th Cir. 1990).

NORTH CAROLINA COURT OF APPEALS

State v. Severn, 130 N.C. App. 319 (1998). In an affidavit for a search warrant to search a residence for drugs, the officer stated that he had "been able to recover both marijuana and cocaine from inside of [the defendant's] residence, using investigative means." In fact, the officer had obtained the drugs from a trash can next to the side of the house. The officer testified at the suppression hearing that he had deduced that the drugs had been used inside the residence. He explained that he "just used common sense" in believing that items in the trash probably came from inside the house, and he did not intend to mislead the magistrate. He used the term "investigative means" because he did not want the defendant to know that a trash pickup was the method used. The court ruled that the officer's statement in the affidavit was false and made in bad faith, and therefore it could not be used in establishing probable cause to issue the search warrant. *See* Franks v. Delaware, 438 U.S. 154 (1978). The court stated that it was undisputed that no one entered the defendant's residence in obtaining the drugs; the statement to the contrary in the affidavit was false and the officer knew it was false. The officer's use of the words "investigative means" supported the ruling that the affidavit was prepared in bad faith, because the officer admitted that he wanted to conceal from the defendant how the evidence was obtained.

State v. Vick, 130 N.C. App. 207 (1998). Officers saw the defendant leave his apartment in his vehicle and make a sale of $1,500 worth of cocaine to an informant working for the officers and under their surveillance. An officer in an affidavit for a search warrant to search the defendant's apartment for drugs stated: "After [the defendant] left his residence he drove directly to the location and met the informant *therefore the cocaine came out of [the defendant's apartment]*." The defendant argued that the italicized part of this statement was false and should be excluded from the search warrant in determining probable cause. The court disagreed, stating that the statement makes clear that the officer inferred from the surrounding circumstances that the cocaine was in the defendant's apartment. Therefore, the officer's statement was not false and did not mislead the magistrate.

State v. Elliott, 69 N.C. App. 89 (1984). A search warrant cannot be successfully challenged by merely showing that the affidavit contained a false statement. The defendant must also show that the affiant knew that the statement was false or acted in reckless disregard of its falsity; in effect, the defendant must show that the affiant acted in bad faith when including the false statement in the affidavit. *See also* State v. Winfrey, 40 N.C. App. 266 (1979); State v. Kramer, 45 N.C. App. 291 (1980); United States v. Owens, 882 F.2d 1493 (10th Cir. 1989).

FEDERAL APPELLATE COURTS

Simmons v. Poe, 47 F.3d 1370 (4th Cir. 1995). The court ruled that a defendant is entitled to a hearing under *Franks v. Delaware,* 438 U.S. 154 (1978), if the defendant shows that omissions from an affidavit to a search warrant were (1) designed to mislead or made with reckless disregard of whether they mislead the issuing judicial official and (2) material to the determination of probable cause. In this case, the defendant failed to meet his burden on either of the two issues.

Use of Unconstitutionally Obtained Evidence

United States v. Karo, 468 U.S. 705 (1984). The Court analyzed a search warrant affidavit and determined that it was not so tainted by illegal beeper monitoring that it would not support probable cause to issue a search warrant.

State v. Miller, 137 N.C. App. 450 (2000). Officers used statements of a third party in establishing probable cause to issue a search warrant. The defendant argued that the statements were taken in violation of the third party's Fifth Amendment rights. The court ruled, relying on *State v. Greenwood,* 301 N.C. 705 (1981), that the defendant had no standing to object to the use of the third party's statements in establishing probable cause for the search warrant.

Revelation of a Confidential Informant's Identity at a Suppression Hearing or Trial
UNITED STATES SUPREME COURT

McCray v. Illinois, 386 U.S. 300 (1967). At a hearing to determine whether probable cause existed to arrest the defendant, officers testified that a reliable confidential informant gave them information that led to the arrest. The trial judge refused to require the officers to reveal their confidential informant's name. The Court ruled that the judge's decision did not violate the defendant's

constitutional rights. Each state may recognize an evidentiary informant's privilege. The Court noted that it has recognized federal officers' right to withhold an informant's identity when they apply for an arrest or search warrant. The Court distinguished this case from *Roviaro v. United States,* 353 U.S. 53 (1957), discussed below. *See also* G.S. 15A-978 (defendant is entitled to informant's identity under certain circumstances, but not when evidence sought to be suppressed was seized under authority of search warrant or incident to an arrest with arrest warrant).

Roviaro v. United States, 353 U.S. 53 (1957). The Court ruled that when an informant is a material witness to the crime being tried, his identity must be disclosed to the defendant under certain circumstances when that knowledge would be helpful in preparing the defendant's defense.

NORTH CAROLINA SUPREME COURT

State v. Creason, 313 N.C. 122 (1985). By the express terms of G.S. 15A-978(b)(1), a defendant is not entitled to the disclosure of an informant's identity when challenging the information in a search warrant affidavit. The court also ruled that the defendant in this case waived his right to appellate review, on constitutional grounds, of the failure to disclose the informant's identity when he did not raise the constitutional issue at trial.

NORTH CAROLINA COURT OF APPEALS

State v. Avent, 222 N.C. App. 147 (2012). The trial court did not err by denying the defendant's motion to compel disclosure of the identity of a confidential informant who provided the defendant's cell phone number to the police. Applying *Roviaro v. United States,* 353 U.S. 53 (1957), the court noted that the defendant failed to show or allege that the informant participated in the crime, and the evidence did not contradict material facts that the informant could clarify. Although the State asserted that the defendant was the shooter in the murder being tried and the defendant asserted that he was not at the scene, the defendant failed to show how the informant's identity would be relevant to this issue. Additionally, evidence independent of the informant's testimony established the defendant's guilt, including an eyewitness to the murder.

State v. Mack, 214 N.C. App. 169 (2011). The trial court did not err by denying the defendant's motion to disclose the identity of a confidential informant in a drug case when the defendant failed to show that the circumstances of his case required disclosure. The informant was not a participant in the crime—he introduced the defendant to the undercover police officer and then stood aside while they haggled about the price of the drugs. The defendant did not need the informant's testimony at trial, despite his argument that (1) the informant could have testified that he (the defendant) was not the person who sold the drugs to the officer because other people were present in the house when the drug sale occurred and (2) the informant also could have testified about the officer's allegedly mistaken identification of the defendant. The officer had clearly identified the defendant as the person who sold him the drugs.

State v. Ellison, 213 N.C. App. 300 (2011), *aff'd on other grounds,* 366 N.C. 439 (2013). The trial court did not err by denying the defendant's motion for disclosure of an informant's identity when the informant's existence was sufficiently corroborated under G.S. 15A-978(b). A second officer testified that the principal investigating officer had told her about information that he had gained from a "tipster" concerning an illegal drug transaction, and she confirmed the truth of the information through her own investigation.

State v. Dark, 204 N.C. App. 591 (2010). The defendant was convicted of cocaine offenses involving a sale to an undercover officer set up with the assistance of a confidential informant. The defendant told the informant to come to a specific parking place at an apartment complex. The undercover officer drove there with the informant. The officer paid the defendant for crack cocaine and marijuana. The officer later identified the defendant in a photo lineup. The defendant did not offer evidence at trial. The court ruled that the trial court did not err in denying the defendant's motion to require the State to disclose the confidential informant's identity. Although the informant's presence and role in arranging the purchase was a factor favoring disclosure, the court agreed with the trial court's finding that the defendant did not show how the informant's identity could provide useful information for the defendant to clarify any contradiction between the State's evidence and the defendant's denial that he committed the offenses. Moreover, the informant's testimony was not admitted at trial. The testimony of the undercover officer and another officer established the defendant's guilt.

State v. Moctezuma, 141 N.C. App. 90 (2000). The defendant in a drug prosecution made a motion to disclose the identity of a confidential informant because the informant was a necessary witness in the case. The court stated that the judge erred in closing the hearing on this issue to the defendant, the defense counsel, and the public without making findings supporting the need to do so. (The judge apparently closed the hearing to be informed of the identity of the confidential informant.) See the discussion in the court's opinion on how a judge should handle this issue.

State v. McEachern, 114 N.C. App. 218 (1994). The State's evidence at a pretrial hearing showed that on March 7, 1991, a confidential informant told an officer that he saw cocaine in the defendant's trailer home and identified the man selling it as Toney (defendant's first name). On March 8, 1991, the informant made a controlled buy, set up by the officer, from the same person at the trailer home. Later that day, the officer obtained a search warrant for the trailer home. The defendant was backing out of his yard when they arrived. The officers entered the trailer home and found marijuana and cocaine. The defendant testified that he gave permission to his nephew to use his trailer home for a party and was out of town from March 7, 1991, until just before the officers arrived on March 8, 1991. He said that there were no illegal drugs in his home when he left on March 7, 1991, and he did not know who was in his home during his absence. The defendant argued that the informant, if called as a witness, could testify that the defendant was not in fact the person who was selling drugs; the informant could also testify as to who sold the drugs to him and that the drugs belonged to a third party.

The trial judge found that the informant was a material and necessary witness for the defense to corroborate the defendant's alibi and the informant's testimony could point to the guilt of a third party and show that the defendant did not exclusively occupy the premises. The judge granted the defendant's motion to require the State to disclose the informant's identity. When the State refused to do so, the judge dismissed the charges against the defendant. The court, relying on *Brady v. Maryland,* 373 U.S. 83 (1963); *Roviaro v. United States,* 353 U.S. 53 (1957); and G.S. 15A-910(3b); upheld the trial judge's rulings that required disclosure of the informant's identity and the dismissal of all charges when the State failed to disclose.

State v. Jackson, 103 N.C. App. 239 (1991), *aff'd,* 331 N.C. 113 (1992). An undercover officer, with the assistance of a confidential informant, set up a drug deal with Allison. The informant had two separate conversations with Allison (outside the officer's presence) to set up the deal. Allison returned later in a car driven by the defendant. Allison walked to the informant's car and placed drugs inside. The court upheld the trial judge's denial of the defendant's motion to disclose the informant's identity. Although the informant's presence and role in arranging the drug deal favored disclosure, the following factors outweighed disclosure: (1) the defendant did not offer evidence in his defense at trial, so there was no contradiction between the State's evidence and the defendant's evidence that the informant could clarify; (2) the informant's statements were not admitted at trial; and (3) the State asserted that the disclosure of the informant's identity would jeopardize pending investigations. *See also* State v. Cameron, 283 N.C. 191 (1973) (defendant was not entitled to know identity of confidential informant who was not present in room of house where sale of heroin took place).

State v. Locklear, 84 N.C. App. 637 (1987). The defendant's affidavit, filed with his motion to suppress evidence seized with a search warrant, merely denied the existence of the confidential informant who had supplied information to the affiant-officer. Based on this information, the trial judge properly denied summarily (1) the defendant's request for an evidentiary hearing on the good faith of the officer's search warrant affidavit and (2) the defendant's request that the judge conduct an in camera hearing with the State's confidential informant.

State v. Johnson, 81 N.C. App. 454 (1986). The defendant had a right to be informed of the confidential informant's identity, because the informant had participated with an undercover officer during the drug sale being tried and could possibly testify that the defendant was not the person who sold drugs to the undercover officer.

State v. Roseboro, 55 N.C. App. 205 (1981). When an informant's information only supplied probable cause to issue a search warrant and the informant did not participate in the drug activities for which the defendant was being tried, the defendant was not entitled to know his identity. For cases involving a defendant's right to an informant's identity (1) at a suppression motion involving a warrantless search or (2) in preparation of the defendant's defense at trial, see *State v. Ketchie*, 286 N.C. 387 (1975) (informant was not participant or witness; disclosure not required); *State v. Moose*, 101 N.C. App. 59 (1990) (informant's information provided probable cause to issue search warrant; defendant failed to offer reason for revealing identity of informant, who was not a partici-

pant in the offense); *State v. Marshall*, 94 N.C. App. 20 (1989) (defendant was not entitled to identity of informant who did not participate in the offense); *State v. Grainger*, 60 N.C. App. 188 (1982) (informant merely supplied information that led to defendant's warrantless arrest and search incident to that arrest; defendant failed to show need for informant's identity for defense at trial); *State v. Hodges*, 51 N.C. App. 229 (1981) (informant was present when defendant sold marijuana to undercover agent; disclosure required); *State v. Ellis*, 50 N.C. App. 181 (1980) (defendant was not entitled to informant's identity during suppression motion concerning warrantless search when another officer corroborated informant's existence under G.S. 15A-978(b)(2)); *State v. Bunn*, 36 N.C. App. 114 (1978) (same); and *State v. Collins*, 44 N.C. App. 141, aff'd, 300 N.C. 142 (1980) (same, but defendant should be allowed to offer evidence of informant's nonexistence).

FEDERAL APPELLATE COURTS

United States v. Martinez, 922 F.2d 914 (1st Cir. 1991). The defendant's assertion that the informant could have provided exculpatory evidence for his defense did not entitle him to disclosure of the informant's identity when the defendant did not offer facts to support the assertion. The informant was a mere tipster and was not present when the offense was committed.

Possible Defects in a Search Warrant or the Procedure in Issuing a Search Warrant
Generally

State v. Pennington, 327 N.C. 89 (1990). The court ruled that superior court clerks may issue search warrants involving both felonies and misdemeanors, rejecting the defendant's argument that clerks were limited to issuing search warrants involving misdemeanors because the titles of G.S. 7A-180 and G.S. 7A-181 refer to the functions of clerks in district court matters.

State v. Norwood, 303 N.C. 473 (1981). A magistrate's clerical errors concerning dates on a warrant or affidavit may be corrected. *See also* State v. Beddard, 35 N.C. App. 212 (1978).

State v. Edwards, 286 N.C. 162 (1974). When the original search warrant was lost, the trial judge properly considered a photocopy of the warrant in ruling on its validity. *See also* State v. McMilliam, 243 N.C. 771 (1956) (court indicated that if search warrant was lost, State could prove its existence with oral testimony).

State v. Upchurch, 267 N.C. 417 (1966). When evidence at the suppression hearing showed that the clerk who issued the search warrant merely witnessed the officer's signature on the affidavit, without examining him under oath, the search warrant was invalid.

State v. Brown, ___ N.C. App. ___, 787 S.E.2d 81 (2016). The court ruled that because an affidavit for a search warrant failed to specify when an informant witnessed the defendant's allegedly criminal activities, there was insufficient evidence establishing probable cause to support issuance of a search warrant. The applying officer stated in the affidavit that he received a counterfeit $100 bill from an informant who claimed it had been obtained from the defendant's home. At the suppression hearing, the officer testified that what he meant to state in the affidavit was that the informant had obtained the bill within the last 48 hours. It was error under G.S. 15A-245(a) for the trial court to consider this additional testimony from the officer that was outside of the facts recited in the affidavit. Considering the content of the affidavit, the court held that without any indication of when the informant received the bill, the affidavit failed on grounds of staleness.

State v. Rayfield, 231 N.C. App. 632 (2014). The court ruled in a child sex case that although the magistrate violated G.S. 15A-245 by considering an officer's sworn testimony when determining whether probable cause supported a search warrant but failing to record that testimony as required by the statute, this violation was not a sufficient basis to grant the defendant's suppression motion. The trial court had based its ruling solely on the filed affidavit, not the sworn testimony, and the affidavit was sufficient to establish probable cause.

State v. Hunter, 208 N.C. App. 506 (2010). The court rejected the defendant's argument that a search warrant executed at a residence was invalid because the application and warrant referenced an incorrect street address. Although the numerical portion of the street address was incorrect, the warrant was sufficient because it contained a correct description of the residence.

State v. Moore, 152 N.C. App. 156 (2002). There were two mobile homes in a driveway with separate addresses, 996 Camp Ground Road and 995 Camp Ground Road. Probable cause existed to search the defendant's mobile home at 995 Camp Ground Road but not the mobile home at 996 Camp Ground Road, the address listed in the search warrant. However, a map to the defendant's mobile home was attached to the search warrant, and the defendant's home was correctly described as being white with brown trim. Based on these and other facts, the court ruled that the error reciting the address did not require the suppression of evidence seized from the defendant's mobile home. The executing officer's prior knowledge of the place to be searched was relevant in this case.

State v. McCord, 140 N.C. App. 634 (2000). The application for a search warrant did not state on its face that it was sworn. However, the applicant attached a sworn affidavit to her application, and she testified that she signed the application in the issuing judicial official's presence after being sworn by the judicial official. The court ruled that this evidence was sufficient to show that the application was sworn to in compliance with G.S. 15A-244.

State v. Ledbetter, 120 N.C. App. 117 (1995). The affidavit for a search warrant described an informant's controlled buy of cocaine under an officer's supervision. The application for the search warrant referred to the seizure of the "Schedule II controlled substance marijuana" when it should have stated "cocaine." The court ruled that because the affidavit referred to cocaine, this error was not fatal to the validity of the search warrant.

State v. Marshall, 94 N.C. App. 20 (1989). G.S. 15A-244 does not require that a search warrant be accompanied by a separate sworn writing labeled "affidavit" in addition to the sworn application.

State v. Hyleman, 89 N.C. App. 424 (1988), *rev'd on other grounds*, 324 N.C. 506 (1989). The notation of the time of issuance of the search warrant was missing in its location above the magistrate's signature as required by G.S. 15A-246(1). The court ruled that this error was not prejudicial because the time was noted elsewhere on the face of the warrant.

State v. Teasley, 82 N.C. App. 150 (1986). When ruling on the sufficiency of a search warrant, a trial judge could not consider an officer's oral testimony before a magistrate when he applied for the warrant, because the magistrate did not record the oral testimony or contemporaneously summarize it in the record as required by G.S. 15A-245.

State v. Heath, 73 N.C. App. 391 (1985). In determining probable cause, a magistrate may not consider unsworn written statements submitted in addition to the affidavit.

State v. Hicks, 60 N.C. App. 116 (1982). The magistrate made handwritten notes of the information the officer had given her under oath and considered the information in determining probable cause, in addition to information in the affidavit. The magistrate's failure to check the box on the application indicating that she had received additional information was not fatal. She kept the notes in a desk drawer and testified at the suppression hearing that they were in the same condition when she issued the search warrant. She did not attach the notes to the search warrant, so that the informant's identity could be protected. The court ruled that under G.S. 15A-245(a), the notes could be considered in determining whether probable cause supported the search warrant.

State v. Caldwell, 53 N.C. App. 1 (1981). After a magistrate refused to issue a search warrant because he believed that the affidavit did not supply probable cause, the officer applied for a search warrant before a different magistrate. The affidavit supplied with the second application contained additional information concerning the informant's reliability. The court ruled that the second magistrate could issue the search warrant based on these facts.

State v. Flynn, 33 N.C. App. 492 (1977). An inadvertent omission of the magistrate's signature on an affidavit in an application for a search warrant did not make the search warrant invalid, when both the magistrate and the officer testified at the suppression hearing that the magistrate swore the officer to the information he gave in the affidavit. The search warrant was valid on its face. *See also* United States v. Smith, 63 F.3d 766 (8th Cir. 1995) (similar ruling).

State v. Sorrell, 26 N.C. App. 325 (1975). An error in naming the father rather than the son as the owner of the premises to be searched was not fatal.

State v. Brannon, 25 N.C. App. 635 (1975). The search warrant was not invalid when the magistrate had signed at the place where the affiant should sign and vice versa.

United States v. Pace, 898 F.2d 1218 (7th Cir. 1990). The Fourth Amendment did not prohibit the government from seeking a second magistrate's approval to issue a search warrant when another magistrate refused to issue a search warrant, even though the same affidavit that had been presented to the first magistrate was presented to the second magistrate.

An Officer's Civil Liability

Hunter v. Bryant, 502 U.S. 224 (1991). The Court ruled that Secret Service agents were entitled to qualified immunity for the arrest of a person because a reasonable officer could have believed that probable cause existed to make an arrest, based on facts in this case.

Malley v. Briggs, 475 U.S. 335 (1986). An officer may be civilly liable under federal law for violating a person's constitutional rights if the officer obtains an arrest warrant (and makes an arrest with it) when a reasonably well-trained officer in that position would have known that the information failed to establish probable cause to arrest. The Court clearly indicated that this standard of civil liability also applies to search warrants.

Exclusionary Rules Particularly Applicable to Search Warrants
Exclusionary Rules under United States Constitution

Hudson v. Michigan, 547 U.S. 1096 (2006). Officers with a valid search warrant entered the defendant's home in violation of the Fourth Amendment's knock-and-announce requirement. The officers seized drugs and a firearm. The Court ruled that the Fourth Amendment's exclusionary rule did not apply to bar the admission of the seized evidence even though the officers violated the knock-and-announce requirement. The Court reasoned that because the privacy interests violated in this case had nothing to do with the seizure of the evidence, the exclusionary rule was inapplicable. The Court rejected the defendant's argument that there would be no deterrence without suppression of the seized evidence. The Court noted that misconduct by law enforcement officers is subject to a civil lawsuit under 42 U.S.C. § 1983 and to discipline of officers by their law enforcement agencies. [Author's note: A substantial violation of North Carolina law that requires notice of identity and purpose before executing a search warrant (G.S. 15A-249, with an exception in G.S. 15A-251(2)) may subject the seized evidence to suppression under North Carolina's statutory exclusionary rule set out in G.S. 15A-974(a)(2).] *See also* United States v. Hector, 474 F.3d 1150 (9th Cir. 2007) (court ruled under rationale of *Hudson v. Michigan* that exclusionary rule did not apply to seizure of evidence pursuant to search warrant when copy of search warrant was not served on defendant); United States v. Pelletier, 469 F.3d 194 (1st Cir. 2006) (*Hudson v. Michigan* ruling applies to execution of arrest warrants).

Massachusetts v. Sheppard, 468 U.S. 981 (1984). This was a companion case with *United States v. Leon*, discussed below. The Court determined that the officer was objectively reasonable in relying on the issuing judge's assurances to him that the search warrant adequately described the evidence to be seized.

United States v. Leon, 468 U.S. 897 (1984). The Fourth Amendment's exclusionary rule does not apply when a law enforcement officer conducts a search in objectively reasonable reliance on a search warrant that is issued by a detached and neutral magistrate but is later determined to be invalid. "Objectively reasonable reliance" means that a reasonably well-trained officer would not have known that the search was unconstitutional. The Court determined in this case that the officer's reliance on the magistrate's determination of probable cause was objectively reasonable (that is, the affidavit contained more than a "bare bones" statement of probable cause).

The Court stated that the exclusionary rule still would apply in the following kinds of cases: (1) when the issuing official is misled by information in the affidavit that the affiant knew was false or would have known was false except for the affiant's reckless disregard of the truth; (2) when the issuing official totally abandons a neutral and detached role; (3) when the affidavit is so lacking in facts to establish probable cause that an officer's belief that probable cause exists is entirely unreasonable; and (4) when the search warrant is so facially deficient (in not specifying the place to be searched or the things to be seized) that the officer who executed it could not have reasonably presumed it to be valid (but see *Massachusetts v. Sheppard*, 468 U.S. 981 (1984), discussed above).

[Author's note: The five North Carolina appellate cases discussed below may no longer be pertinent to the application of the exclusionary rule in North Carolina courts because *State v. Carter*, 322 N.C. 709 (1988), discussed below, strongly indicated that there is no good faith exception under the North Carolina Constitution—although see the discussion of the post-*Carter* case of *State v. Garner*, 331 N.C. 491 (1992), discussed below. Even if there is no good faith exception in North Carolina state courts, the good faith exception will still be applied to searches by North Carolina law enforcement officers that result in evidence being offered in prosecutions (for example, for drug and firearm violations) in federal courts in North Carolina. *See* United States v. Pforzheimer, 826 F.2d 200 (2d Cir. 1987) (in federal prosecution involving a search by state officers, federal instead of state exclusionary rules apply).]

State v. Welch, 316 N.C. 578 (1986). The defendant was arrested for murder and armed robbery. While he was in jail, a superior court judge issued, on the prosecutor's motion, a nontestimonial identification order to compel the defendant to give a blood sample for blood-typing. The court ruled, citing *State v. Irick*, 291 N.C. 480 (1977), that a judge may issue a nontestimonial identification order on the prosecutor's motion only when (1) a person has not been arrested and reasonable suspicion exists that the person committed a crime punishable by more than one year's imprisonment (under current law, a felony or Class A1 or A misdemeanor) or (2) a person has been arrested and released from custody pending trial. Thus, the judge erred in issuing the order.

The court stated that the Fourth Amendment requires an officer to obtain a search warrant to compel a defendant, without his or her consent, to give a blood sample unless probable cause and exigent circumstances exist. The court strongly indicated that a nontestimonial identification order may not constitutionally be issued to compel a blood sample when only reasonable suspicion exists that the defendant committed a crime (see the later case of *State v. Carter*, 322 N.C. 709 (1988), discussed below). Because exigent circumstances did not exist in this case—a person's blood type does not change, unlike the quantity of alcohol in one's blood—the defendant's Fourth Amendment rights were violated when his blood was drawn without a search warrant.

The court discussed the good faith exception to the exclusionary rule of *United States v. Leon* and *Massachusetts v. Sheppard* and ruled that the exclusionary rule should not apply. The officer reasonably relied on the nontestimonial identification order issued by the superior court judge; he took every reasonable step to comply with the Fourth Amendment. But see the later case of *State v. Carter*, 322 N.C. 709 (1988), discussed below, which strongly indicated that there is no good faith exception to the exclusionary rule under the North Carolina Constitution, an issue not raised in this case. *See also* State v. Banner, 207 N.C. App. 729 n.7 (2010) (noting possible conflict between *Carter* and *Garner*).

State v. Leonard, 87 N.C. App. 448 (1987). Even if the facts in the search warrant's affidavit could have been stated with greater precision, the officers reasonably relied on the warrant in conducting a search under the good faith exception to the exclusionary rule discussed in *United States v. Leon.*

State v. Newcomb, 84 N.C. App. 92 (1987). Probable cause did not exist to support a search warrant when the affidavit only contained an informant's statement that he saw marijuana in the house and did not state when he saw it. Also, the officer did not state that the informant was reliable. The good faith exception to the exclusionary rule cannot be applied to this search warrant, because the officer did not take reasonable steps to comply with the Fourth Amendment.

State v. Roark, 83 N.C. App. 425 (1986). Probable cause did not exist to support a search warrant when the affidavit stated only that a confidential informant told the officer that the stolen property was in the house to be searched. The exception to the exclusionary rule in *United States v. Leon* does not apply to this "bare bones" statement of probable cause, because a reasonably well-trained officer would have known that probable cause did not exist.

State v. Connard, 81 N.C. App. 327 (1986), *aff'd*, 319 N.C. 392 (1987). The good faith exception to the exclusionary rule under *United States v. Leon* did not apply to an unconstitutional seizure of stolen items, because the executing officers could not reasonably believe that the search warrant's description, "stolen goods," was valid.

Exclusionary Rules under the North Carolina Constitution

State v. Garner, 331 N.C. 491 (1992). The court rejected the defendant's contention that it should not recognize the inevitable discovery exception under Article I, Section 20, of the North Carolina Constitution. The court stated: "While this Court has held that Article I, Section 20 of our Constitution, like the Fourth Amendment to the United States Constitution, prohibits unreasonable searches and seizures, *e.g.*, State v. Arrington, 311 N.C. 633 (1984); State v. Ellington, 284 N.C. 198 (1973), and requires the exclusion of evidence obtained by unreasonable search and seizure, *e.g.*, State v. Carter, 322 N.C. 709 (1988), there is nothing to indicate anywhere in the text of Article I, Section 20 any enlargement or expansion of rights beyond those afforded in the Fourth Amendment as applied to the states by the Fourteenth Amendment." The court later stated: "We therefore hold the defendant's contention that Article I, Section 20 of our Constitution should be read as an extension of rights beyond those afforded in the Fourth Amendment is misplaced."

[Author's note: The court's general statements indicate that in other cases it may not interpret Article I, Section 20, more broadly than the Fourth Amendment. It appears that *Garner* may undermine *State v. Carter*, discussed below, which had rejected under this constitutional section the good faith exception to the exclusionary rule under the Fourth Amendment, as set out in *United States v. Leon* and *Massachusetts v. Sheppard*, discussed above.] *See also* State v. Banner, 207 N.C. App. 729 n.7 (2010) (noting possible conflict between *Carter* and *Garner*).

State v. Carter, 322 N.C. 709 (1988). An officer obtained a blood sample for blood-typing from an in-custody defendant with a nontestimonial identification order. The use of the nontestimonial identification order to obtain evidence from an in-custody defendant was unlawful based on prior court rulings—for example, *State v. Welch*, discussed above. The court ruled as follows: (1) The taking of the blood sample violated the North Carolina Constitution, because probable cause and a search warrant are required unless exigent circumstances exist (there were no exigent circumstances in this case because the blood was needed for blood-typing). Reasonable suspicion is an insufficient evidentiary standard on the basis of which to take a defendant's blood. (2) Since 1937, the expressed legislative policy of North Carolina has been to exclude evidence obtained in violation of constitutional rights against unreasonable searches and seizures. The dual purposes of deterrence and judicial integrity called for a rejection of a good faith exception to the exclusionary rule under the North Carolina Constitution in this case, which involved the most intrusive type of search—the invasion of the defendant's body to draw blood. Although the court appeared to have rejected a good faith exception in all cases, the court stated later in its opinion that "[w]e are not persuaded *on the facts before us* that we should engraft a good faith exception to the exclusionary rule under our state constitution" (emphasis added).

North Carolina's Statutory Exclusionary Rule

State v. Hyleman, 324 N.C. 506 (1989). The officer-affiant stated in the search warrant application that he purchased two ounces of cocaine from three people, who were arrested when they delivered the cocaine. The officer-affiant also stated that he paid $1,650 in marked currency for the cocaine (the money had been paid a few hours before the actual delivery, but that information was not included in the affidavit). The officer-affiant stated that, based on "the movements of the suspects during, and before the purchase, and information received from two confidential sources of information after the purchase," he had reason to believe that the marked currency was located in the defendant's residence.

Instead of analyzing the search warrant under the United States or North Carolina constitutions, the court determined that the search warrant violated G.S. 15A-244(3), which restates the Fourth Amendment's command that there must be facts in the affidavit setting forth probable cause to believe that the items to be seized are in the places or in the possession of the people to be searched. The affidavit failed to disclose facts to link the items to be seized—the marked currency—to the residence to be searched. The affidavit contained mere conclusory statements. The court then ruled that the affidavit's failure to comply with G.S. 15A-244(3) was a substantial violation that required exclusion under G.S. 15A-974(2) (now, G.S. 15A-974(a)(2)) because (1) the "bare bones" conclusory affidavit was totally inadequate to establish probable cause, (2) the affiant's statement about the extent of surveillance of the suspects was willfully inaccurate, (3) the defendant has a fundamental constitutional and statutory right in North Carolina to be free from unlawful searches and seizures, and (4) the exclusion of illegally seized evidence is the greatest deterrent to future similar violations. [Author's note: Legislation enacted in 2011 (S.L. 2011-6) added a good faith exception to the application of G.S. 15A-974.]

State v. Dobbins, 306 N.C. 342 (1982). An officer's failure to swear to an inventory of items seized under a search warrant was not a sufficient violation to require that evidence be excluded under G.S. 15A-974. [Author's note: Legislation enacted in 2011 (S.L. 2011-6) added a good faith exception to the application of G.S. 15A-974.]

State v. White, 184 N.C. App. 519 (2007). Officers executed a search warrant for illegal drugs. The trial court ruled that the officers' forcible entry into the residence violated the Fourth Amendment and was a substantial violation of G.S. 15A-251, and the substantial violation required suppression of the evidence seized in the residence as a fruit of the poisonous tree. The State on its appeal of the trial court's ruling did not contest that the officers' entry into the residence violated the Fourth Amendment and was a substantial violation of G.S. 15A-251. The court ruled, relying on *State v. Richardson*, 295 N.C. 309 (1978), that the evidence seized in the residence was not subject to suppression because there was no causal relationship between the violation and the seizure of the evidence. The search was conducted sometime after the forced entry and only after the occupants were secured and the defendant was read a copy of the search warrant. The cocaine would likely have been located even in the absence of the forced entry. [Author's note: The Fourth Amendment's exclusionary rule was not applicable based on the ruling in *Hudson v. Michigan*, 547 U.S. 586 (2006).]

State v. Sumpter, 150 N.C. App. 431 (2002). An officer executed a search warrant for illegal drugs at a residence. As the officer pushed open an unlocked exterior door, he announced his identity and purpose ("police officer, search warrant"). The court noted that the officer violated G.S. 15A-249 by not announcing his identity and purpose before opening the door and entering the residence. However, the court ruled that this violation was not substantial enough to require the exclusion of evidence found in the search (G.S. 15A-974(2); now G.S. 15A-974(a)(2)). An immediate entry could prevent the destruction of illegal drugs, the door was unlocked, no one objected to the officer's entry into the residence, several people had been seen entering the residence without knocking or receiving an invitation to enter, and people who use crack cocaine usually carry weapons. [Author's note: Legislation enacted in 2011 (S.L. 2011-6) added a good faith exception to the application of G.S. 15A-974.]

State v. Davidson, 131 N.C. App. 276 (1998). A search warrant for bank records was served and returned within the 48-hour statutory period, but a delay beyond 48 hours in receiving the records resulted from the bank's need to locate the records to be seized. The court ruled, relying on *State v. Dobbins*, 306 N.C. 342 (1982), and *State v. Fruitt*, 35 N.C. App. 177 (1978), that this delay was not a substantial violation within G.S. 15A-974 to require that the records be suppressed. [Author's note: Legislation enacted in 2011 (S.L. 2011-6) added a good faith exception to the application of G.S. 15A-974.]

State v. Vick, 130 N.C. App. 207 (1998). The court ruled that the officers violated G.S. 15A-252 by failing to give the defendant a copy of the search warrant and affidavit before executing the warrant (they left it in the apartment at the conclusion of their search), but the violation was not substantial under G.S. 15A-974 to require exclusion of the seized evidence. [Author's note: Legislation enacted in 2011 (S.L. 2011-6) added a good faith exception to the application of G.S. 15A-974.]

State v. Gwyn, 103 N.C. App. 369 (1991). An officer arrested the defendant for impaired driving just inside the boundary of the state of Virginia after he had seen the defendant driving in North Carolina. However, the officer did not know that he was in Virginia when he arrested the defendant. The court ruled that although the arrest was illegal, it was constitutionally valid because it was supported by probable cause. Evidence seized as a result of the arrest—the officer's detection of alcohol on the defendant's breath and the Breathalyzer test reading—was admissible under the balancing test of G.S. 15A-974(2) (now, G.S. 15A-974(a)(2)). The interest of the defendant from being illegally arrested was outweighed by the defendant's driving, which was a menace to public safety, and the officer's violation was neither extensive nor willful—because he did not know the defendant was in Virginia. *See generally* State v. Eubanks, 283 N.C. 556 (1973) (illegal, although constitutional, arrest for impaired driving did not require suppression of evidence found after the arrest). [Author's note: G.S. 15A-974 did not exist when *Eubanks* was decided.] [Author's note: Legislation enacted in 2011 (S.L. 2011-6) added a good faith exception to the application of G.S. 15A-974.]

State v. Marshall, 94 N.C. App. 20 (1989). The failure to file the search warrant and its application promptly with the clerk under G.S. 15A-245(b) did not require suppression under G.S. 15A-974. [Author's note: Legislation enacted in 2011 (S.L. 2011-6) added a good faith exception to the application of G.S. 15A-974.]

State v. Edwards, 70 N.C. App. 317 (1984), *rev'd on other grounds*, 315 N.C. 304 (1985). A search warrant to search an apartment for cocaine was executed at about 10:45 p.m. An officer knocked on the locked storm door and announced in a loud, authoritative voice, "Police have a search warrant, open the door." After about 30 seconds elapsed without an answer, officers forced open the storm door and wooden front door and entered the apartment. The court ruled that the announcement and forcible entry complied with G.S. 15A-249 and G.S. 15A-251. Because the object of the search was powdery cocaine that can be instantly disposed of, the 30-second wait between notice and the forcible entry was reasonable. The court also ruled that the fact that the search was made at night did not make it unreasonable. Traffic in and out of the apartment was heavier at night, and officers needed the cover of darkness in approaching the apartment so that the defendant and others could not interfere with the execution of the search warrant.

State v. Copeland, 64 N.C. App. 612 (1983). The officer who executed the warrant gave the defendant an illegible copy of the search warrant affidavit and application, although the copy of the search warrant was legible. The court noted that there was no evidence that the violation was willful and concluded that it was not a substantial violation under G.S. 15A-974 that required exclusion of evidence seized during the execution of the search warrant. [Author's note: Legislation enacted in 2011 (S.L. 2011-6) added a good faith exception to the application of G.S. 15A-974.]

State v. Willis, 58 N.C. App. 617 (1982), *aff'd*, 307 N.C. 461 (1983). An officer did not give proper notice as he entered a house to execute a search warrant when he merely shouted "police" but failed to state his purpose for entering. The officer did not have probable cause to believe that giving notice would endanger the life or safety of any person. However, the court ruled that the violation was not sufficiently substantial to require the exclusion of evidence under G.S. 15A-974, because it was not willful, and officers had feared that someone inside the house might destroy contraband they were to search for—although this latter fact did not excuse the need to give proper notice. [Author's note: Legislation enacted in 2011 (S.L. 2011-6) added a good faith exception to the application of G.S. 15A-974.]

State v. Brown, 35 N.C. App. 634 (1978). Officers had a warrant to search the defendant's home for marijuana. They devised a plan to enter the home quickly so that the defendant could not destroy any drugs (the trial court later determined that a confidential informant had told the officers that the drugs might be destroyed). The officers staged a mock chase in front of the defendant's house. The defendant opened his door and stepped outside to investigate the commotion, and one non-uniformed officer, without identifying himself, asked whether he could use the phone. When the defendant refused, the officer pushed his way inside the house and began the search. The court ruled that officers violated notice provisions of G.S. 15A-249. Notice may not be dispensed with when destruction of contraband is probable. Unannounced, forcible entries are permitted only when a person's life or safety may be endangered by giving notice. The court also ruled that the violation was substantial under G.S. 15A-974, so that evidence found during the search was inadmissible: the violation was willful, privacy interests were violated, the officers completely failed to follow the provisions of G.S. 15A-249, and the exclusion of evidence would tend to deter future violations. [Author's note: Legislation enacted in 2011 (S.L. 2011-6) added a good faith exception to the application of G.S. 15A-974.]

State v. Fruitt, 35 N.C. App. 177 (1978). (1) An officer was executing a search warrant for a dwelling and outbuilding. He gave notice at the dwelling and no one responded. His failure to give notice again before entering the outbuilding was not a substantial violation of G.S. 15A-249. (2) The officer violated G.S. 15A-252 by not leaving a copy of the search warrant affixed to the premises, and he violated G.S. 15A-254 by not leaving an itemized inventory receipt of the items taken. However, these were not substantial violations under G.S. 15A-974, because the officer returned to the premises hours later and gave the defendant an itemized receipt and apparently gave him a copy of the search warrant. In addition, the violations were not willful, and they occurred after the search had been completed. [Author's note: Legislation enacted in 2011 (S.L. 2011-6) added a good faith exception to the application of G.S. 15A-974.]

Fifth Amendment Issues When Personal or Business Records Are Seized

Doe v. United States, 487 U.S. 201 (1988). A federal district court order required the defendant to execute a consent directive authorizing foreign banks to disclose records of any accounts over which the defendant had a right of withdrawal, without identifying or acknowledging the existence of any account. The Court ruled that the consent directive did not violate the defendant's Fifth Amendment rights, because it was not testimonial. A defendant's oral or written communication or act is "testimonial" when it explicitly or implicitly relates a factual assertion or discloses information. The consent directive in this case did not involve the defendant's revealing that an account existed or, if there was an account, that records were there, and the execution of the defendant's consent directive would reveal only the bank's implicit declaration, by its act of producing records, that it believes that the account is the defendant's account.

Braswell v. United States, 487 U.S. 99 (1988). The custodian of corporate records may not resist a subpoena for records on the ground that the act of production will incriminate the custodian. However, the government may not make evidentiary use of the "individual act" of production against the individual.

Andresen v. Maryland, 427 U.S. 463 (1976). An execution of a search warrant of the defendant's office for business records did not violate his Fifth Amendment rights, because he was not required to aid in the discovery, production, or authentication of the evidence that was seized. *See also* State v. Downing, 31 N.C. App. 743 (1976). For a discussion of the Fifth Amendment issues involved when the State issues a subpoena for records, see *Doe v. United States*, discussed above, and *Fisher v. United States*, 425 U.S. 391 (1976). For a related issue, involving whether a mother-custodian of a child may assert her Fifth Amendment privilege to resist a court order to produce the child, see *Baltimore City Department of Social Services v. Bouknight*, 493 U.S. 549 (1990).

II. Administrative Inspections

Probable Cause

(This topic is discussed on page 448.)

Camara v. Municipal Court, 387 U.S. 523 (1967). The Court in this case adopted the "probable cause" standard for administrative inspections that is reflected in current G.S. 15-27.2.

South Boulevard Video & News v. Charlotte Zoning Board of Adjustment, 129 N.C. App. 282 (1998). A zoning enforcement officer conducted an inspection of a business with an administrative inspection warrant to determine if it was an adult bookstore or adult mini motion-picture theater being operated in violation of a city ordinance. The court ruled that probable cause supported the issuance of the warrant. The officer's affidavit stated that he had seen videotapes and magazines that appeared to be distinguished by their emphasis on depicting or describing sexual activities and human genitals, pubic regions, buttocks, and female breasts. In addition, merchandise such as artificial genitals and other sexual paraphernalia was displayed. There were also booths for viewing adult videotapes and movies. *See* Durham Video v. Durham Bd. of Adjustment, 144 N.C. App. 236 (2001) (similar ruling).

Brooks, Commissioner of Labor v. Butler, 70 N.C. App. 681 (1984). An affidavit in support of an administrative inspection warrant of a business under the Occupational Safety and Health Act (OSHA) sufficiently supported an inspection as part of a legally authorized inspection program that naturally included the property to be inspected.

Gooden v. Brooks, Commissioner of Labor, 39 N.C. App. 519 (1979). The court ruled (1) that G.S. 15-27.2(c)(1) is constitutional under *Marshall v. Barlow's, Inc.*, 436 U.S. 307 (1978), because it requires a showing that the property to be inspected is part of a legally authorized program of inspection that naturally includes the property, the general administrative plan for enforcement is based on reasonable legislative or administrative standards (as the court interpreted the statute), and the administrative standards are applied neutrally to a particular business; and (2) that the administrative inspection warrant in this case was invalid because the affidavit contained no underlying facts to support the warrant.

Warrantless Administrative Inspections

(*This topic is discussed on page 459.*)

Generally

City of Los Angeles v. Patel, 135 S. Ct. 2443 (2015) (citations omitted). A group of motel owners and a lodging association (respondents) challenged a provision of the Los Angeles Municipal Code (LAMC) requiring motel owners to turn over to the police hotel registry information. Concerning the relevant LAMC provisions, Section 41.49 requires hotel operators to record information about their guests, including the guest's name and address; the number of people in each guest's party; the make, model, and license plate number of any guest's vehicle parked on hotel property; the guest's date and time of arrival and scheduled departure date; the room number assigned to the guest; the rate charged and amount collected for the room; and the method of payment. Under this provision, guests without reservations, those who pay for their rooms with cash, and any guests who rent a room for less than 12 hours must present photographic identification at the time of check-in, and hotel operators are required to record the number and expiration date of that document. For those guests who check in using an electronic kiosk, the hotel's records must also contain the guest's credit card information. This information can be maintained in either electronic or paper form, but it must be "kept on the hotel premises in the guest reception or guest check-in area or in an office adjacent"

thereto for a period of 90 days. LAMC Section 41.49(3)(a) states, in pertinent part, that hotel guest records "shall be made available to any officer of the Los Angeles Police Department for inspection," provided that "[w]henever possible, the inspection shall be conducted at a time and in a manner that minimizes any interference with the operation of the business." A hotel operator's failure to make his or her guest records available for police inspection is a misdemeanor punishable by up to six months in jail and a $1,000 fine.

The respondents brought a facial challenge to Section 41.49(3)(a) on Fourth Amendment grounds, seeking declaratory and injunctive relief. The United States Supreme Court ruled that facial challenges under the Fourth Amendment are not categorically barred. Turning to the merits of the claim, the Court ruled that the challenged portion of the LAMC is facially unconstitutional because it fails to provide hotel operators with an opportunity for precompliance review. The Court reasoned, in part:

> [A]bsent consent, exigent circumstances, or the like, in order for an administrative search to be constitutional, the subject of the search must be afforded an opportunity to obtain precompliance review before a neutral decisionmaker. . . . And, we see no reason why this minimal requirement is inapplicable here. While the Court has never attempted to prescribe the exact form an opportunity for precompliance review must take, the City does not even attempt to argue that § 41.49(3)(a) affords hotel operators any opportunity whatsoever. Section 41.49(3)(a) is, therefore, facially invalid.

Clarifying the scope of its ruling, the Court continued: "As they often do, hotel operators remain free to consent to searches of their registries and police can compel them to turn them over if they have a proper administrative warrant—including one that was issued *ex parte*—or if some other exception to the warrant requirement applies, including exigent circumstances." The Court rejected a suggestion that hotels are "closely regulated" and that the ordinance is facially valid under the more relaxed standard that applies to searches of that category of businesses.

New York v. Burger, 482 U.S. 691 (1987). A New York statute authorizing a warrantless administrative search of an auto junkyard was constitutional (a junkyard fits within a "closely regulated" business). Because the regulatory scheme is administrative, the fact that the statute permitted law enforcement officers to conduct an administrative search was irrelevant in determining the statute's constitutionality. An administrative inspection statute may serve both administrative and penal goals. *See also* United States v. Thomas, 973 F.2d 1152 (5th Cir. 1992).

Illinois v. Krull, 480 U.S. 340 (1987). The Fourth Amendment's exclusionary rule does not apply to exclude evidence obtained by a warrantless administrative search conducted by an officer in the objective reasonable reliance on a statute authorizing such a search—even though the statute is later declared unconstitutional. See the discussion of this case in *State v. Carter*, 322 N.C. 753 (1988).

State v. Pike, 139 N.C. App. 96 (2000). Wildlife law enforcement officers were patrolling Badin Lake at night and were stopping every vessel for a safety inspection. They saw a pontoon boat on the lake and signaled the operator to stop, which the defendant did immediately. The officers activated their take-down lights, announced their presence, and informed the defendant that they were going to conduct a safety check of the vessel. They did so without boarding the vessel. After the safety inspection, the defendant was arrested for operating a motor vessel while impaired in violation of G.S. 75A-10(b1)(2). Relying on *Schenekl v. State*, 996 S.W.2d 305 (Tex. Ct. App. 1999), the court ruled that the officers did not violate the Fourth Amendment by stopping the vessel, even though they did not have reasonable suspicion to conduct the stop. The court found that the government's interest in maintaining, for its citizens, safety on its lakes and rivers substantially outweighed this defendant's reasonable expectation of privacy in his vessel. [Author's note: The court did not decide whether the officers could have boarded the motor vessel without reasonable suspicion or probable cause; *see* Klutz v. Beam, 374 F. Supp. 1129 (W.D.N.C. 1973) (warrantless boarding for inspection in landlocked lake of private boat used as a home and without consent or without basis for believing there was a law violation was unconstitutional).]

State v. Nobles, 107 N.C. App. 627 (1992), *aff'd*, 333 N.C. 787 (1993). The court ruled that G.S. 113-136(k), which permits warrantless administrative inspections of licensed fish dealerships, among other places, is not unconstitutional on its face.

Gooden v. Brooks, Commissioner of Labor, 39 N.C. App. 519 (1979). G.S. 95-136(a) is unconstitutional to the extent that it authorizes warrantless OSHA searches of business establishments. *See also* Marshall v. Barlow's, Inc., 436 U.S. 307 (1978) (warrantless OSHA searches of business premises are unconstitutional); Donovan v. Dewey, 452 U.S. 594 (1981) (warrantless inspections of mines under federal law are constitutional); United States v. Biswell, 406 U.S. 311 (1972) (warrantless inspections of gun dealers' premises under federal law are constitutional); Colonnade Catering Corp. v. United States, 397 U.S. 72 (1970) (warrantless inspections of liquor dealers' premises under federal law are constitutional, but Congress did not authorize the warrantless inspection in this case); Camara v. Mun. Court, 387 U.S. 523 (1967) (building inspector must obtain inspection warrant to inspect residence when occupant objects; Court adopted "probable cause" standard that is reflected in current G.S. 15-27.2); See v. Seattle, 387 U.S. 541 (1967) (fire inspector must obtain inspection warrant to inspect commercial premises); Rush v. Obledo, 756 F.2d 713 (9th Cir. 1985) (limited warrantless inspection of day care homes was proper); Gallaher v. City of Huntington, 759 F.2d 1155 (4th Cir. 1985) (warrantless inspection of records of precious-metals dealers was proper); Peterman v. Coleman, 764 F.2d 1416 (11th Cir. 1985) (warrantless inspection of registers of dealers in secondhand goods was proper); S & S Pawn Shop, Inc. v. City of Del City, 947 F.2d 432 (10th Cir. 1991) (statute permitting warrantless inspections of pawnshop books, records, and property was not unconstitutionally broad); Tart v. Commonwealth of Mass., 949 F.2d 490 (1st Cir. 1991) (warrantless request for fishing license of commercial fishing vessel was valid administrative inspection); United States v. Argent Chem. Labs., Inc., 93 F.3d 572 (9th Cir. 1996) (manufacturer of veterinary drugs is a closely regulated industry under *United States v. Biswell* and therefore is subject to warrantless administrative inspections under the Fourth Amendment); Lesser v. Espy, 34 F.3d 1301 (7th Cir. 1994) (similar ruling involving regulation of rabbitry—selling rabbits for research); United States v. V-1 Oil Co., 63 F.3d 909 (9th Cir. 1995) (warrantless, unannounced inspections—authorized by federal law—of a company involved in the transportation and sale of hazardous materials did not violate the Fourth Amendment); United States v. Fort, 248 F.3d 475 (5th Cir. 2001) (warrantless and suspicionless stopping of commercial vehicles for regulatory inspection is constitutional); United States v. Vasquez-Castillo, 258 F.3d 1207 (10th Cir. 2001) (warrantless inspection of commercial truck at state's border with another state was constitutional).

Elks Lodge v. Board of Alcohol Control, 27 N.C. App. 594 (1976). A warrantless entry of ABC permittee's premises was constitutional.

Freeman v. City of Dallas, 242 F.3d 642 (5th Cir. 2001) (en banc). The seizure and demolition of the owner's apartment buildings without a warrant, after the buildings were condemned under a city ordinance and state law, were reasonable under the Fourth Amendment. *See* Hroch v. City of Omaha, 4 F.3d 693 (8th Cir. 1993) (similar ruling); Samuels v. Meriwether, 94 F.3d 1163 (8th Cir. 1996) (same). The court disagreed with the ruling in *Conner v. City of Santa Anna*, 897 F.2d 1487 (9th Cir. 1990) (after hearings, city council declared several old and inoperable cars on plaintiff's property a public nuisance and ordered the nuisance abated; city police called a towing company, and city officials broke down a fence surrounding the backyard of the property and removed two of the cars from the property; the court ruled that judicial authorization was necessary to enter the enclosed backyard (and to seize the cars), where the plaintiff had a reasonable expectation of privacy, because there were no exigent circumstances to justify the city's acting without judicial authorization).

Calabretta v. Floyd, 189 F.3d 808 (9th Cir. 1999). Based on the facts in this case, exigent circumstances did not exist to permit a social worker to enter a house without consent to conduct a child welfare investigation.

Inspection of a Fire Scene

Michigan v. Clifford, 464 U.S. 287 (1984) (four-Justice opinion announcing the judgment of the Court). A residential fire occurred about 5 a.m. Fire officers arrived, extinguished the fire, and left the scene about 7 a.m. At 1:30 p.m. that same day, fire officials entered the house without a warrant to investigate the cause of the fire. They found evidence of arson in the basement and then searched the rest of the house, where they found that most valuables apparently had been removed before the fire began. Although the home was uninhabitable after the fire, the Court ruled that because personal belongings remained and the defendant had arranged after the fire to have his house secured, the defendant retained a sufficient Fourth Amendment privacy interest in his home to require that post-fire investigations be conducted with a warrant, absent exigent circumstances. This case differed from *Michigan v. Tyler*, 436 U.S. 499 (1978), discussed below, because the investigator's entry at 1:30 p.m. was not a continuation of an earlier entry. An administrative warrant or consent was necessary to reenter the house in this case. (However, five Justices expressed the view that if advance notice of the search had been given to the owner, or if a reasonable attempt had been made to give advance notice, the search could have been conducted without a warrant.) Once evidence of arson was found in the basement, a warrant was required to search the rest of the house. The Court excluded all evidence found during these unconstitutional searches, but it ruled admissible a fuel can that fire personnel had seen in the basement—when they were fighting the fire—and that they later had placed in the driveway of the residence.

Michigan v. Tyler, 436 U.S. 499 (1978). Fire officers properly entered a burning furniture store without a warrant to fight a fire and properly remained there for a reasonable time after the fire was extinguished so that they could investigate its cause to prevent its recurrence and to preserve property from intentional or accidental destruction. The officers left at 4:00 a.m. after the fire had been extinguished. A warrantless reentry at 8:00 a.m. was justified in this case because the investigation of the fire's cause had been hindered by smoke and darkness, and the reentry was merely a continuation of a legitimate determination of the fire's cause. However, warrantless reentries at 9:00 a.m. that same day and weeks later were unconstitutional, because there were no longer exigent circumstances to excuse the failure to obtain a warrant. To be lawful, these additional entries to investigate the cause of the fire must be made with an administrative inspection warrant. If probable cause exists to search for evidence of a crime, such as arson, a search warrant must be obtained. *See also* United States v. Martin, 781 F.2d 671 (9th Cir. 1985) (second warrantless entry and search was permissible to look for injured persons and for the source of fire and explosion in the apartment).

State v. Langley, 64 N.C. App. 674 (1983). The court ruled that a fire marshal investigating the cause and origin of a fire properly conducted a warrantless search for accelerants on fire-damaged premises (it is unclear from the opinion when the search was made).

Descriptions in Administrative Inspection Warrants

(This topic is discussed on page 449.)

Brooks, Commissioner of Labor v. Enterprises, Inc., 298 N.C. 759 (1979). An administrative inspection warrant was invalid (in violation of G.S. 15-27.2(d)) because the warrant itself did not indicate the conditions, objects, activities, or circumstances that the inspection was intended to check or reveal, and the supporting affidavit was not specifically incorporated into the warrant.

Brooks, Commissioner of Labor v. Butler, 70 N.C. App. 681 (1984). An administrative inspection warrant that authorized the inspection of "all pertinent conditions, structures, machines, apparatus, devices, equipment, and materials, and all other things . . ." was not overbroad.

Consent to Authorize Inspections

In re Dwelling of Properties, Inc., 24 N.C. App. 17 (1974). A tenant who was in actual possession and control of premises may consent to a warrantless inspection by the city housing inspector, despite the owner's objection before the inspection took place.

Procedure in Issuing or Executing Administrative Inspection Warrants

In re Glavan Industries, Inc., 122 N.C. App. 628 (1996). A superior court judge issued an administrative inspection warrant to conduct an inspection authorized by the Occupational Safety and Health Act (OSHA) of North Carolina. On the same day the warrant was issued, Glavan Industries made a motion to quash the warrant. The motion was denied. Glavan Industries then gave notice of appeal to the North Carolina Court of Appeals. The court ruled that the appeal is dismissed as interlocutory because no final order had been entered and Glavan did not show that any substantial right was affected.

Brooks, Commissioner of Labor v. Butler, 70 N.C. App. 681 (1984). OSHA administrative inspection warrants may properly be issued ex parte. The owner or possessor of the place to be inspected was not entitled to be given notice and an opportunity to be heard before the warrant was issued.

III. Nontestimonial Identification Procedures and Orders

Constitutional Issues

UNITED STATES SUPREME COURT

Ferguson v. City of Charleston, 532 U.S. 67 (2001). A Charleston, South Carolina, prosecutor set up a joint program with a state hospital concerning pregnant patients who were suspected of using cocaine. Selected pregnant patients would be tested for cocaine through a urine screen. A chain of custody would be followed, presumably to make sure that test results could be used in a criminal prosecution against the patients for child neglect or drug offenses. The threat of law enforcement involvement and prosecution was set forth in two protocols, the first dealing with the identification of cocaine use during pregnancy and the second dealing with the identification of cocaine use after labor. The plaintiffs—women who were patients and arrested after testing positive for cocaine—sued various public officials for Fourth Amendment and other constitutional violations. The case before the United States Supreme Court was decided under the following assumed facts: (1) that the patients had not consented to the urine screen for cocaine and (2) that there was no reasonable suspicion, probable cause, or a search warrant used to obtain the urine or to conduct the urine screen. The Court ruled, distinguishing *Skinner v. Railway Labor Executives' Association*, 489 U.S. 602 (1989), and other "special needs" cases upholding suspicionless searches divorced from general law enforcement interests, that a state hospital's testing, without a search warrant, of patients' urine for cocaine to obtain evidence for law enforcement purposes violated the Fourth Amendment. The Court rejected the State's argument that the searches of the patients' urine were justified by non–law enforcement purposes, based on the facts in this case. The Court stated that while the program's ultimate goal may have been to get the patients into substance treatment and off of drugs, the immediate objective of the searches was to generate evidence for law enforcement purposes to reach that goal.

[Author's note: The Court indicated that its ruling does not adversely affect laws or ethics requiring medical personnel to report to law enforcement agencies child abuse, gunshot wounds, or patients' threats to themselves or others. This ruling also would not make it unconstitutional when medical personnel take a vial of blood from a patient and give it to law enforcement officers at their request when there is probable cause and exigent circumstances exist—for example, the patient was injured in a car accident in which there was evidence of the patient's impaired driving.]

Chandler v. Miller, 520 U.S. 305 (1997). The Court ruled that a Georgia statute requiring candidates for designated state offices to certify that they had taken a urinalysis drug test and that the test result was negative violated the Fourth Amendment. The urinalysis drug test required by this statute, which was not based on reasonable suspicion or any other standard, is an unreasonable search under the Fourth Amendment.

Skinner v. Railway Labor Executives' Association, 489 U.S. 602 (1989). (1) Subjecting a person to a Breathalyzer test and collecting and testing urine are searches under the Fourth Amendment. (2) The Fourth Amendment was not violated when the urine and blood of railway employees involved in train accidents were tested, even though the testing was conducted without a warrant, probable cause, or reasonable suspicion. *See also* Nat'l Treasury Emps. Union v. Von Raab, 489 U.S. 656 (1989) (urinalysis drug testing of United States Customs Service employees seeking promotion or transfer to jobs involving drug interdiction or requiring the possession of firearms does not violate the Fourth Amendment, even though the testing is conducted without a warrant, probable cause, or reasonable suspicion).

Hayes v. Florida, 470 U.S. 811 (1985). Officers took the defendant without his consent from his home to the police station and took his fingerprints. They had neither probable cause to arrest nor judicial authorization to take fingerprints. The Court ruled that the officers' action was an illegal seizure under the Fourth Amendment. It noted that the Fourth Amendment may permit a judicial official to authorize seizure of a person with less than probable cause and to bring the person to the police station for fingerprinting. The Court also noted that the Fourth Amendment may permit officers to briefly detain a person in the field for fingerprinting when they have reasonable suspicion that the person committed a crime and a reasonable belief that fingerprinting will establish or negate the suspect's connection with the crime.

Winston v. Lee, 470 U.S. 753 (1985). A shopkeeper shot an assailant in the left side during an attempted robbery, and he later identified the defendant at a hospital as the assailant. The State sought a court order to compel surgery on the defendant to remove the bullet from his body for evidence. The Court ruled that surgery in this case would be unreasonable under the Fourth Amendment, based on *Schmerber v. California*, discussed below. The State did not show a compelling need for evidence that outweighed the proposed surgical intrusion into the defendant's body under general anesthesia to retrieve the bullet.

Cupp v. Murphy, 412 U.S. 291 (1973). The defendant appeared voluntarily at the police station for questioning about the strangulation murder of his wife. Abrasions and lacerations were found on the victim's throat, and there was no sign of a break-in or robbery. Although the defendant was not arrested when he appeared at the station, police had probable cause to arrest him. While the defendant was at the station, officers noticed a dark spot under his fingernail. Suspecting that it might be dried blood and knowing that evidence of strangulation is often found under fingernails, they asked whether they could scrape under his fingernail. The defendant refused and put his hands in his pocket, but the officers took scrapings anyway. The defendant then left the station. The Court ruled that the limited warrantless intrusion by scraping under the fingernails was reasonable under the Fourth Amendment, because that evidence could readily have been destroyed. Although a full search incident to arrest could not have been conducted because the defendant was not arrested, the scraping of fingernails was a limited permissible search under the facts in this case.

Davis v. Mississippi, 394 U.S. 721 (1969). Officers took the defendant without his consent to police headquarters and took his fingerprints. Officers had neither probable cause to arrest him nor judicial authorization to take his fingerprints. The Court ruled that the detention for fingerprinting was an illegal seizure under the Fourth Amendment and the fingerprint evidence was inadmissible at trial. It noted that it need not determine whether the Fourth Amendment would permit—under narrowly circumscribed procedures—fingerprinting of a person whom an officer does not have probable cause to arrest.

United States v. Wade, 388 U.S. 218 (1967). A defendant has no Fifth Amendment right to refuse to appear in a lineup and speak the words allegedly spoken by the offender during the crime. *See also* Gilbert v. California, 388 U.S. 263 (1967) (no Fifth Amendment right to refuse to give handwriting exemplars); United States v. Dionisio, 410 U.S. 1 (1973) (no Fifth Amendment right to give voice exemplars).

Schmerber v. California, 384 U.S. 757 (1966). The defendant, while receiving treatment at a hospital for injuries suffered in a car accident, was arrested for driving under the influence of intoxicating liquor. An officer directed a doctor, over the defendant's objection—which was based on the advice of counsel—to take blood to analyze it for its alcohol content. The Court ruled that the taking of blood did not violate the defendant's Fourth, Fifth, or Sixth Amendment rights. The Court also ruled that exigent circumstances permitted taking the blood without a search warrant, because alcohol in the blood begins to diminish shortly after the drinking stops. The Court also noted that the taking of blood was performed in a reasonable manner—by the doctor in the hospital according to accepted medical practices. *See also* State v. Welch, 316 N.C. 578 (1986); State v. Hollingworth, 77 N.C. App. 36 (1985).

NORTH CAROLINA SUPREME COURT

State v. Pearson, 356 N.C. 22 (2002). The defendant was convicted of two counts of second-degree rape. (1) The court ruled that there was reasonable suspicion to support the issuance of a nontestimonial identification order to require the suspect—the defendant—to supply head and pubic hair samples and a saliva sample. [Author's note: The nontestimonial identification order also ordered the defendant to supply a blood sample, but note that probable cause is needed to do so. *See* State v. Carter, 322 N.C. 709 (1988).] The defendant met the physical description of the perpetrator given by two rape victims. A peeping tom was reported at the location of one of the rapes—about eight months before the rape occurred at that location. An officer saw a man, wearing a light gray or blue windbreaker and blue jeans, squatting near an air-conditioning unit directly behind an apartment building. The man ran when he saw the officer. Shortly thereafter, the defendant—wearing blue jeans and a light blue windbreaker—was stopped by an officer. (2) The court ruled that an officer did not intentionally provide false information in his affidavit for a nontestimonial identification order. The officer had sufficient evidence to conclude in the affidavit that the suspect—the defendant—was caught secretly peeping at the apartment complex. (3) The court ruled that statutory violations did not require suppression of evidence obtained from the nontestimonial identification order. (See the discussion of the violations and the court's analysis in its opinion.)

State v. Thomas, 329 N.C. 423 (1991). The day after the defendant's arrest for murder, law enforcement officers obtained (by using the services of a medical examiner) the following evidence from the defendant without a warrant (they had obtained a nontestimonial identification order to obtain this evidence, but it was invalid under *State v. Welch*, 316 N.C. 578 (1986), because he was in custody): samples of the defendant's blood; head and pubic hair; saliva; fingernails; and molds of his teeth, lips, and fingernails. The defendant moved to suppress all this evidence on grounds that federal and state constitutions required the officers to obtain a search warrant based on probable cause before taking blood and other personal identification samples of a defendant already in custody. The court ruled that blood was improperly taken, based on *State v. Carter*, 322 N.C. 709 (1988). However, the court ruled admissible evidence of the defendant's fingerprints, pubic hair, teeth, saliva, and lips, because that evidence was properly obtained while the defendant was in police custody.

State v. Carter, 322 N.C. 709 (1988). An officer obtained a blood sample for blood-typing from an in-custody defendant with a nontestimonial identification order. [Author's note: The use of the nontestimonial identification order to obtain evidence from an in-custody defendant was unlawful based on prior court rulings—for example, *State v. Welch*, 316 N.C. 578 (1986).] The court ruled as follows: (1) The taking of the blood sample violated the North Carolina Constitution because probable cause and a search warrant are required unless exigent circumstances exist (there were no exigent circumstances in this case, because the blood was needed for blood-typing). Reasonable suspicion is an insufficient evidentiary standard on the basis of which to take a defendant's blood. (2) Since 1937, the expressed legislative policy of North Carolina has been to exclude evidence obtained in violation of constitutional rights against unreasonable searches and seizures. The dual purposes of deterrence and judicial integrity called for a rejection of a good faith exception to the exclusionary rule under the North Carolina Constitution in this case, which involved the most intrusive type of search—the invasion of the defendant's body to withdraw blood. [Author's note: Although the court appears to have rejected a good faith exception in all cases, the court stated later in its opinion that "[w]e are not persuaded *on the facts before us* that we should engraft a good faith exception to the exclusionary rule under our state constitution" (emphasis added). *But see*

State v. Garner, 331 N.C. 491 (1992) (court's general statements may have undermined *Carter*, to the extent that *Carter* indicated that the good faith exception does not exist under the state constitution). The possible conflict between *Carter* and *Garner* was noted in *State v. Banner*, 207 N.C. App. 729 n.7 (2010).]

State v. Odom, 303 N.C. 163 (1981). The defendant was arrested for a felonious assault and was given her *Miranda* warnings. She waived those rights and answered some questions but later told the officers that she wanted to consult with her attorney, and the officers then stopped their questioning. They asked her to take a gunshot residue test, but she refused to do so until she had talked with her lawyer. At trial, evidence of her refusal was admitted.

State v. Sharpe, 284 N.C. 157 (1973). The defendant was arrested for murder and was in police custody. A warrantless seizure of arm and head hairs from the defendant was reasonable under the Fourth Amendment, when the means used to obtain the hairs were reasonable. In this case, the defendant pulled out his head hair and gave it to the technician; the opinion does not reveal how arm hair was removed. *See also* State v. Downes, 57 N.C. App. 102 (1982); State v. Reynolds, 298 N.C. 380 (1979); State v. Payne, 328 N.C. 377 (1991). The court ruled that (1) the defendant did not have a constitutional right to counsel for the gunshot residue test and (2) her due process rights were not violated by the admission of evidence of her refusal to take the test. [Author's note: The court commented in a footnote that the defendant may have had a statutory right to counsel under G.S. 15A-279(d), but she clearly did not, because the officer was attempting to conduct the procedure without a nontestimonial identification order, as he had a legal right to do.]

NORTH CAROLINA COURT OF APPEALS

State v. Fletcher, 202 N.C. App. 107 (2010). The defendant was arrested at a checkpoint for DWI and taken to a police station for Intoximeter breath testing, which the defendant refused. An officer then transported the defendant to a hospital to compel a blood test. The defendant's blood was drawn, and the blood test result was 0.10. The court ruled that the officer reasonably believed under G.S. 20-139.1(d1) that the delay necessary to obtain a court order would result in the dissipation of alcohol in the defendant's blood. The officer testified that the entire process of driving to the magistrate's office, standing in line, completing the required forms, returning to the hospital, and having the defendant's blood drawn would have

taken from two to three hours. The court also ruled that probable cause and exigent circumstances supported the warrantless compelling of the blood sample and did not violate the Fourth Amendment or various provisions of the Constitution of North Carolina.

State v. Page, 169 N.C. App. 127 (2005). The State introduced at the defendant's murder trial the results of a gunshot residue test administered on the defendant shortly after the homicide had occurred. (1) The court ruled, relying on *State v. Coplen*, 138 N.C. App. 48 (2000), that probable cause and exigent circumstances supported the administration of the test on the defendant without the necessity of a search warrant or a nontestimonial identification order. The defendant was the last person to have seen the victim before the shooting. Witnesses arriving at the crime scene found the defendant to be the only person present. The defendant offered inconsistent statements to investigating officers concerning his whereabouts during the shooting. The gunshot residue test must be conducted within three to four hours of suspected firearm use, and evidence of firing a weapon could be destroyed by wiping or washing hands. (2) The court ruled that the trial judge's finding of facts supported the judge's ruling that the defendant consented to the gunshot residue test. (3) The court ruled that there was no error in admitting the results of the gunshot residue test even though the defendant was not advised of his right to counsel under G.S. 15A-279(d) when the test was administered. Only statements made by the defendant would be suppressed, not the results of the test. [Author's note: Statements in *State v. Odom*, 303 N.C. 163 (1981) (no Sixth Amendment right to counsel at gunshot residue test), and *State v. Coplen*, cited above, that a defendant is statutorily entitled to counsel under G.S. 15A-279(d) during the administration of a gunshot residue test are highly questionable when an officer is not administering the test under Article 14 of Chapter 15A of the General Statutes. The statutory right to counsel in G.S. 15A-279(d) would appear to be required only when the State is conducting a procedure with the use of a nontestimonial identification order, and not when the State is properly conducting a procedure without such an order because there is probable cause and exigent circumstances exist, there is consent, or there is a search warrant.]

State v. Trull, 153 N.C. App. 630 (2002). Responding to a report that the defendant was involved in a shooting, officers handcuffed the defendant to frisk him for weapons and then removed the handcuffs. They asked him if he would voluntarily accompany them to the police station so that they could continue their investigation, and he agreed to go with them. The officers asked the defendant to submit to a gunshot residue test, but he refused. The State was permitted to introduce evidence of this refusal at trial. The court ruled, citing *State v. Coplen*, 138 N.C. App. 48 (2000), that the officers had probable cause and there were exigent circumstances that permitted them to conduct the gunshot residue test without a search warrant. Information from witnesses to the shooting provided probable cause. Testimony by an officer that a gunshot residue test must be conducted within three or four hours of a shooting provided exigent circumstances. The court noted appellate cases that have ruled that evidence of a defendant's refusal to submit to a lawful testing or identification procedure is circumstantial evidence of guilt, and it ruled that the admission of the defendant's refusal to submit to the gunshot residue test was not error.

The Sixth Amendment Right to Counsel and Statutory Right to Counsel

Gilbert v. California, 388 U.S. 263 (1967). A defendant does not have a Sixth Amendment right to counsel at the taking of a handwriting sample.

United States v. Wade, 388 U.S. 218 (1967). A defendant does not have a Sixth Amendment right to counsel at the taking of hair, blood, and fingerprints.

Schmerber v. California, 384 U.S. 757 (1966). A defendant does not have a Sixth Amendment right to counsel at the taking of blood. *See also* United States v. Bullock, 71 F.3d 171 (5th Cir. 1995) (similar ruling).

State v. Grooms, 353 N.C. 50 (2000). The court ruled that a search warrant to seize the defendant's blood, saliva, and hair was supported by probable cause and the State was not required to obtain a nontestimonial identification order so that the defendant would have the statutory right to counsel under G.S. 15A-279(d). The court noted that a constitutional right to counsel does not apply to Fourth Amendment searches and seizures.

State v. Odom, 303 N.C. 163 (1981). A defendant does not have a Sixth Amendment right to counsel at the administration of a gunshot residue test.

State v. Page, 169 N.C. App. 127 (2005). The State introduced at the defendant's murder trial the results of a gunshot residue test administered on the defendant shortly after the homicide had occurred. (1) The court ruled, relying on *State v. Coplen*, 138 N.C. App. 48 (2000), that probable cause and exigent circumstances supported the administration of the test on the defendant without the necessity of a search warrant or a nontestimonial identification order. The defendant was the last person to have seen the victim before the shooting. Witnesses arriving at the crime scene found the defendant to be the only person present. The defendant offered inconsistent statements to investigating officers concerning his whereabouts during the shooting. The gunshot residue test must be conducted within three to four hours of suspected firearm use, and evidence of firing a weapon could be destroyed by wiping or washing hands. (2) The court ruled that the trial judge's finding of facts supported the judge's ruling that the defendant consented to the gunshot residue test. (3) The court ruled that there was no error in admitting the results of the gunshot residue test even though the defendant was not advised of his right to counsel under G.S. 15A-279(d) when the test was administered. Only statements made by the defendant would be suppressed, not the results of the test. [Author's note: Statements in *State v. Odom*, 303 N.C. 163 (1981) (no Sixth Amendment right to counsel at gunshot residue test), and *State v. Coplen*, cited above, that a defendant is statutorily entitled to counsel under G.S. 15A-279(d) during the administration of a gunshot residue test are highly questionable when an officer is not administering the test under Article 14 of Chapter 15A of the General Statutes. The statutory right to counsel in G.S. 15A-279(d) would appear to be required only when the State is conducting a procedure with the use of a nontestimonial identification order, and not when the State is properly conducting a procedure without such an order because there is probable cause and exigent circumstances exist, there is consent, or there is a search warrant.]

State v. Coplen, 138 N.C. App. 48 (2000). The defendant was convicted of murder. Shortly after the shooting, a detective informed the defendant that he was going to perform a gunshot residue test on her hands. The defendant initially refused and asked, "Don't I have the right to counsel?" A few minutes later, the defendant submitted to the test. The court stated that although a gunshot residue test is a nontestimonial identification procedure under G.S. 15A-271, that statute does not set out the exclusive procedures for performing that test. Based on the facts in this case, the court ruled that the detective had probable cause and exigent circumstances existed to perform the test. The court also ruled, citing *State v. Odom*, 303 N.C. 163 (1981), that there is no Sixth Amendment constitutional right to counsel at the test.

Requiring Defendant to Undergo Nontestimonial Identification Procedure before Jury

State v. Perry, 291 N.C. 284 (1976). The defendant's Fifth Amendment rights were not violated when he was required to put on, before the jury, an orange stocking mask found at the scene of the armed robbery. *See also* State v. Suddreth, 105 N.C. App. 122 (1992) (similar ruling; mask worn during sexual assault); *State v. Summers*, 105 N.C. App. 420 (1992) (similar ruling; defendant displaying his teeth—victim had described assailant as a man with missing teeth).

State v. Locklear, 117 N.C. App. 255 (1994). During the trial the trial judge ordered the defendant to speak the exact words of the robber so that a State's witness could attempt to make a voice identification. The court ruled, relying on *State v. Perry*, 291 N.C. 284 (1976), and other cases, that the defendant's Fifth Amendment privilege against compelled self-incrimination was not violated by the judge's order. *See also* State v. Thompson, 129 N.C. App. 13 (1998) (similar ruling).

Authority to Conduct Nontestimonial Identification Procedures

(This topic is discussed on page 460.)

Mandatory and Permissive Use by the State

State v. Carter, 322 N.C. 709 (1988). An officer obtained a blood sample for blood-typing from an in-custody defendant with a nontestimonial identification order. [Author's note: The use of the nontestimonial identification order to obtain evidence from an in-custody defendant was unlawful based on prior court rulings—for example, *State v. Welch*, discussed below.] The court ruled as follows: (1) The taking of the blood sample violated the North Carolina Constitution because probable cause and a search warrant are required unless exigent circumstances exist (there were no exigent circumstances

in this case, because the blood was needed for blood-typing). Reasonable suspicion is an insufficient evidentiary standard on the basis of which to take a defendant's blood. (2) Since 1937, the expressed legislative policy of North Carolina has been to exclude evidence obtained in violation of constitutional rights against unreasonable searches and seizures. The dual purposes of deterrence and judicial integrity called for a rejection of a good faith exception to the exclusionary rule under the North Carolina Constitution in this case, which involved the most intrusive type of search—the invasion of the defendant's body to withdraw blood. Although the court appears to have rejected a good faith exception in all cases, the court stated later in its opinion that "[w]e are not persuaded *on the facts before us* that we should engraft a good faith exception to the exclusionary rule under our state constitution" (emphasis added). *But see* State v. Garner, 331 N.C. 491 (1992) (court's general statements may have undermined *Carter* to the extent that *Carter* indicated that the good faith exception does not exist under the state constitution); State v. Banner, 207 N.C. App. 729 n.7 (2010) (noting possible conflict between *Carter* and *Garner*).

State v. Welch, 316 N.C. 578 (1986). The defendant was arrested for murder and armed robbery. While he was in jail, a superior court judge issued (on the State's motion) a nontestimonial identification order to compel the defendant to give a blood sample for blood-typing. The court ruled—citing *State v. Irick*, 291 N.C. 480 (1977)—that a judge may issue a nontestimonial identification order on the State's motion only when (1) a person has not been arrested (but when reasonable suspicion exists that the person committed a crime punishable by more than one year's imprisonment) or (2) a person has been arrested and released from custody pending trial. Thus, the judge erred in issuing the order. The court stated that the Fourth Amendment requires an officer to obtain a search warrant to compel a defendant (without the defendant's consent) to give a blood sample—unless probable cause and exigent circumstances exist; see the later case of *State v. Carter*, discussed above. Because exigent circumstances did not exist in this case (because a person's blood type does not change, unlike the quantity of alcohol in one's blood), the defendant's Fourth Amendment rights were violated when his blood was withdrawn without a search warrant.

The court discussed the good faith exception to the exclusionary rule of *United States v. Leon*, 468 U.S. 897 (1984), and *Massachusetts v. Sheppard*, 468 U.S. 981

(1984), and ruled that the exclusionary rule should not apply. The officer reasonably relied on the nontestimonial identification order issued by the superior court judge; he took every reasonable step to comply with the Fourth Amendment. But see the later case of *State v. Carter*, discussed above, concerning whether the good faith exception exists under the state constitution.

State v. Page, 169 N.C. App. 127 (2005). The State introduced at the defendant's murder trial the results of a gunshot residue test administered on the defendant shortly after the homicide had occurred. (1) The court ruled, relying on *State v. Coplen*, 138 N.C. App. 48 (2000), that probable cause and exigent circumstances supported the administration of the test on the defendant without the necessity of a search warrant or a nontestimonial identification order. The defendant was the last person to have seen the victim before the shooting. Witnesses arriving at the crime scene found the defendant to be the only person present. The defendant offered inconsistent statements to investigating officers concerning his whereabouts during the shooting. The gunshot residue test must be conducted within three to four hours of suspected firearm use, and evidence of firing a weapon could be destroyed by wiping or washing hands. (2) The court ruled that the trial judge's finding of facts supported the judge's ruling that the defendant consented to the gunshot residue test. (3) The court ruled that there was no error in admitting the results of the gunshot residue test even though the defendant was not advised of his right to counsel under G.S. 15A-279(d) when the test was administered. Only statements made by the defendant would be suppressed, not the results of the test. [Author's note: Statements in *State v. Odom*, 303 N.C. 163 (1981) (no Sixth Amendment right to counsel at gunshot residue test), and *State v. Coplen*, cited above, that a defendant is statutorily entitled to counsel under G.S. 15A-279(d) during the administration of a gunshot residue test are highly questionable when an officer is not administering the test under Article 14 of Chapter 15A of the General Statutes. The statutory right to counsel in G.S. 15A-279(d) would appear to be required only when the State is conducting a procedure with the use of a nontestimonial identification order, and not when the State is properly conducting a procedure without such an order because there is probable cause and exigent circumstances exist, there is consent, or there is a search warrant.]

State v. Whaley, 58 N.C. App. 233 (1982). The defendant was charged with involuntary manslaughter in connection with an auto accident. The court ruled that the judge erred in issuing a nontestimonial identification order that the defendant be examined by a doctor to determine his "visual acuity." It ruled that a nontestimonial identification order may be used to determine whether the suspect committed the charged offense, not whether the offense had been committed. While the visual acuity test may have helped to determine whether the defendant was grossly negligent in operating his vehicle, it did not materially aid in identifying him as the driver of the motor vehicle that caused the victim's death.

State v. McDonald, 32 N.C. App. 457 (1977). The State need not obtain a nontestimonial identification order to conduct a lineup after the defendant has been arrested.

Using Force to Take Blood

United States v. Bullock, 71 F.3d 171 (5th Cir. 1995). Officers obtained a search warrant to take blood from the defendant. Knowing that the defendant had threatened to resist the execution of the search warrant, the officers sought and received judicial approval to use physical force. A seven-member "control team" was used to subdue the defendant. He was handcuffed and shackled between two cots that were strapped together. He physically resisted by kicking, hitting, and attempting to bite the officers. A towel was placed on the defendant's face because he was spitting on the officers. A nurse took blood from the defendant's hand.

The court ruled, based on these facts, that the use of force to execute the search warrant was reasonable under the Fourth Amendment. The court, citing *United States v. Wade*, 388 U.S. 218 (1967), also rejected the defendant's argument that his Sixth Amendment right to counsel was violated because his attorney was not present during the procedures. *See also* Hammer v. Gross, 932 F.2d 842 (9th Cir. 1991); State v. Clary, 2 P.3d 1255 (Ariz. App. 2000) (use of force to obtain blood from DWI defendant pursuant to search warrant was reasonable).

Juveniles

(This topic is discussed on page 464.)

In re Stallings, 318 N.C. 565 (1986). A one-on-one showup between a victim and a juvenile suspect may be conducted without a juvenile nontestimonial identification order (G.S. 7A-596; now, G.S. 7B-2103) when the showup does not violate due process. In this case the showup was conducted within about an hour after the crime occurred and, based on the totality of circumstances, was constitutionally permissible. The court's ruling reversed the opinion of the North Carolina Court of Appeals, 77 N.C. App. 592 (1985). [Author's note: The *Stallings* ruling effectively reversed the ruling in *State v. Norris*, 77 N.C. App. 525 (1985) (one-on-one showup cannot be conducted with a juvenile without a nontestimonial identification order).]

State v. Green, 124 N.C. App. 269 (1996). A law enforcement officer took a photograph of a 13-year-old juvenile suspect with his consent but without a nontestimonial identification order. The court noted that the detective's action violated G.S. 7A-596 because a nontestimonial identification order had not been obtained (that is, the juvenile's consent did not alleviate the obligation to obtain the order).

Alternative of Using a Search Warrant

State v. McLean, 47 N.C. App. 672 (1980). An officer may elect to obtain a search warrant, rather than a nontestimonial identification order, to obtain blood samples and pubic hairs from a defendant. [Author's note: The later case of *State v. Carter*, 322 N.C. 709 (1988), discussed above, requires a search warrant to obtain a blood sample.] A magistrate properly issued a search warrant when the affidavit showed probable cause to believe that a rape was committed and evidence of that crime might be obtained by taking blood samples and pubic hairs from the defendant and comparing them with semen and pubic hair found on the bed linen.

Defendant's Request for a Nontestimonial Identification Order

(*This topic is discussed on page 463.*)

State v. Tucker, 329 N.C. 709 (1991). The defendant sought a nontestimonial identification order to require a State's witness to provide a hair sample for analysis. The court ruled that there is no statutory or other authorization for such an order.

State v. Jackson, 306 N.C. 642 (1982). A district court judge ordered a lineup to be held at the defendant's request under G.S. 15A-281. The judge rescinded his order when the State voluntarily dismissed the case before the lineup was held. The State later recharged the defendant with the same crime, and a lineup was held thereafter at the defendant's request. The court ruled that the defendant had no statutory right to demand a lineup when the first charges were no longer pending against him.

State v. Ryals, 179 N.C. App. 733 (2006). The defendant was convicted of second-degree murder. State's witness Lee testified that she saw the defendant beat the victim with his fists and kick and stomp him. State's witness Winstead also testified about the defendant's beating of the victim. A police department crime technician recovered a black knit cap and other items from the crime scene. Negroid hair was found on the cap, but a State's witness testified that it was not suitable for further analysis. A defense expert witness compared a DNA sample from the hair on the cap with the defendant's DNA sample and concluded that it could not have originated from the defendant. Before trial, a judge denied the defendant's motion for a nontestimonial identification order to collect a DNA sample from Winstead to compare it with DNA from the hair on the cap; the defendant contended that Winstead had a motive to commit the murder, was present at the scene, and could have committed the murder. The court ruled, relying on *State v. Tucker*, 329 N.C. 709 (1991), that the trial judge lacked the authority to issue a defense-requested nontestimonial identification order to require the State to obtain a DNA sample from State's witness Winstead to conduct comparison testing with DNA from the hair on the cap.

State v. Abdullah, 66 N.C. App. 173 (1984). The defendant filed a motion just before his armed robbery trial (about nine months after his arrest) for a pretrial lineup procedure under G.S. 15A-281. The trial judge denied the motion, concluding that the defendant had not shown that a lineup would materially aid the jury in determining whether he committed the robbery. The court upheld the trial judge's ruling, because there was substantial identification evidence (that is, there were many other witnesses) in addition to the victim's identification of the defendant. *See also* State v. Yancey, 58 N.C. App. 52 (1982).

The Nontestimonial Identification Procedure

State v. Temple, 302 N.C. 1 (1981). Although G.S. 15A-279(d) requires that a defendant be informed of the right to counsel (as well as the right of appointment of counsel for an indigent defendant) at a nontestimonial identification procedure, it does not require an express waiver of that right.

Suppression Motions

See other pertinent cases below under "IV. Suppression Motions and Hearings; Exclusionary Rules."

State v. Pearson, 356 N.C. 22 (2002). The court ruled that violations of nontestimonial identification procedure statutes did not require suppression of evidence obtained from the nontestimonial identification order. (See the discussion of the violations and the court's analysis in its opinion.)

State v. Maccia, 311 N.C. 222 (1984). The defendant waived his right to contest on constitutional grounds the admissibility of evidence obtained by a nontestimonial identification order when he failed to make his suppression motion before trial as required by G.S. 15A-975 and there was no exception to permit his making the motion during trial. *See also* State v. Satterfield, 300 N.C. 621 (1980).

IV. Suppression Motions and Hearings; Exclusionary Rules

Contents of Suppression Motion

State v. Pearson, 131 N.C. App. 315 (1998). An officer arrested the defendant for DWI. When an Intoxilyzer malfunctioned, the officer took the defendant outside the officer's territorial jurisdiction to take the Intoxilyzer test there. The court ruled, relying on *State v. Satterfield*, 300 N.C. 621 (1980), that the defendant's failure to file an affidavit with his motion to suppress the chemical test result, based on an allegation of a substantial statutory violation, was a ground to deny the motion.

State v. Chance, 130 N.C. App. 107 (1998). The court ruled that an affidavit submitted with a suppression motion under G.S. 15A-977 may be attested to by the defendant's attorney on information and belief. The defendant is not required to sign the affidavit.

State v. Williams, 98 N.C. App. 405 (1990). The trial judge properly summarily denied the defendant's suppression motion when the affidavit did not support the ground alleged in the motion. The motion challenged the warrantless search of an area outside the defendant's house, but the affidavit stated that the defendant did not exercise dominion over the area where the matchbox

was found; thus, the defendant did not have a reasonable expectation of privacy there.

State v. Langdon, 94 N.C. App. 354 (1989). (1) The defendant's first suppression motion asserted that the "warrant was illegally issued because it does not show probable cause" and that "the information contained in the warrant was stale at the time the warrant was issued." The motion was unverified and was not accompanied by an affidavit. Under G.S. 15A-977, the trial judge did not abuse his discretion in summarily denying the motion. (2) The defendant's second suppression motion was filed on the day the defendant's case was calendared for trial but before jury selection. This motion was timely under G.S. 15A-976, based on the facts in this case. It was accompanied by an affidavit and contained an additional allegation for suppression. The trial judge erred in denying the motion on the ground that one trial judge cannot overrule another. However, the trial judge could have summarily denied the motion, because the affidavit accompanying the motion failed to support the ground alleged. It alleged only factual errors in the officers' application for a search warrant and did not contain any facts to support the motion's allegations that the officers acted in bad faith in supplying information establishing probable cause.

State v. Hall, 73 N.C. App. 101 (1985). The trial court could have summarily denied the defendant's suppression motion, because its stated grounds were so vague that they were no grounds at all.

State v. Harris, 71 N.C. App. 141 (1984). The trial judge properly summarily dismissed the defendant's pretrial motion to suppress identification testimony because it was not accompanied by an affidavit containing facts supporting the motion. The trial judge properly refused to hear the suppression motion during trial because an exception did not exist in G.S. 15A-975 to excuse the failure to make a pretrial motion.

State v. Blackwood, 60 N.C. App. 150 (1982). The trial judge properly summarily denied the defendant's suppression motion when the affidavit did not contain facts supporting the ground alleged in the affidavit.

Timing of Suppression Motion

State v. Fisher, 321 N.C. 19 (1987). The defendant did not waive his right under G.S. 15A-975(b)(2) to make a suppression motion during trial when the State provided laboratory reports to the defendant before trial but failed to notify him that it intended to use the evidence that was the subject of the reports.

State v. Maccia, 311 N.C. 222 (1984). The defendant waived his right to contest on constitutional grounds the admissibility of evidence obtained by a nontestimonial identification order when he failed to make his suppression motion before trial as required by G.S. 15A-975 and an exception did not exist to permit the motion to be made during trial. *See also* State v. Satterfield, 300 N.C. 621 (1980).

State v. Hill, 294 N.C. 320 (1978). When the State gave proper pretrial notice under G.S. 15A-975(b) of its intention to introduce evidence of a warrantless search, and the defendant failed to file a motion to suppress within the required 10 working days, the trial judge properly summarily denied the tardy suppression motion.

State v. Speight, 166 N.C. App. 106 (2004). The defendant filed a motion to suppress during trial, alleging that evidence was improperly seized as a result of a consent search. The court ruled, relying on *State v. Fisher*, 321 N.C. 19 (1987), that the motion was timely filed during trial because the State failed to give proper notice under G.S. 15A-975(b) (State must notify defense counsel 20 working days before trial of intention to use certain evidence) that would have otherwise required the motion to be made before trial.

State v. Davis, 97 N.C. App. 259, *aff'd per curiam*, 327 N.C. 467 (1990). The defendant filed a motion to suppress within the required ten working days under G.S. 15A-976(b), but the trial judge dismissed the motion without prejudice and granted the defendant the opportunity to refile the motion in a form that satisfied procedural requirements under Article 53 of Chapter 15A. The defendant filed the second motion more than two months later. The court ruled that the second motion must be filed within 10 days of the date of the dismissal of the first motion, and therefore the second motion was not timely filed.

State v. Langdon, 94 N.C. App. 354 (1989). (1) The defendant's first suppression motion asserted that the "warrant was illegally issued because it does not show probable cause" and that "the information contained in the warrant was stale at the time the warrant was issued." The motion was unverified and was not accompanied by an affidavit. Under G.S. 15A-977, the trial judge did not abuse his discretion in summarily denying the motion. (2) The defendant's second suppression motion was filed on the day the defendant's case was calendared for trial but before jury selection. This motion was timely under G.S. 15A-976, based on the facts in this case. It was accompanied by an affidavit and contained an additional allegation for suppression. The trial judge erred in denying the motion on the ground that one trial judge cannot overrule another. However, the trial judge could have summarily denied the motion when the affidavit accompanying the motion failed to support the ground alleged. It alleged only factual errors in the officers' application for a search warrant and did not contain any facts to support the motion's allegations that the officers acted in bad faith in supplying information establishing probable cause.

State v. Marshall, 92 N.C. App. 398 (1988). (1) The defendant's motion during the trial to suppress his statements was timely under G.S. 15A-975 when he established that the State had not notified him within 20 working days of the trial of its intention to introduce the statements at the trial. (2) Although the trial judge could have summarily denied the defendant's suppression motion on the ground that it did not state the legal grounds for the motion, the judge did not deny the motion but instead conducted a hearing on the motion and made a ruling on the merits. [Author's note: This ruling—as well as the ruling in *State v. Harvey*, 78 N.C. App. 235 (1985)—appears to be inconsistent with the ruling in *State v. Holloway*, 311 N.C. 573 (1984).]

State v. Simmons, 59 N.C. App. 287 (1982). The trial judge properly summarily denied a suppression motion at a trial de novo in superior court when the defendant failed to make a motion before trial in superior court, as required by G.S. 15A-975. *See also* State v. Golden, 96 N.C. App. 249 (1989).

Suppression Motion Made during Trial

State v. Jaynes, 342 N.C. 249 (1995). Before trial, a suppression hearing was held on the defendant's motion to suppress two letters written by the defendant. The trial court denied the motion. During trial, the defendant moved to suppress a third letter written by him based on the same legal grounds asserted in the pretrial motion. The trial court refused to conduct another suppression hearing. The court ruled that the trial court did not err because there was no reason for another hearing.

State v. Roper, 328 N.C. 337 (1991). When a defendant is permitted to make a suppression motion during trial, the defendant must make the motion orally or in writing, and an affidavit is not required to be filed with the motion (the court disapproved contrary language about an affidavit being required in *State v. Satterfield*, 300 N.C. 621 (1980), and *State v. Simmons*, 59 N.C. App. 287 (1982)). However, a defendant during trial must make a motion to suppress (a general objection is insufficient), request a voir dire, and state the legal grounds for the motion.

State v. Fisher, 321 N.C. 19 (1987). The defendant did not waive his right under G.S. 15A-975(b)(2) to make a suppression motion during trial when the State provided laboratory reports to the defendant before trial but failed to notify him that it intended to use the evidence that was the subject of the reports.

State v. Harris, 71 N.C. App. 141 (1984). The trial court properly summarily dismissed the defendant's pretrial motion to suppress identification testimony because it was not accompanied by an affidavit containing facts supporting the motion. The trial court properly refused to hear the suppression motion during trial because an exception did not exist in G.S. 15A-975 to excuse the failure to make a pretrial motion.

Suppression Motion Based on Newly Discovered Evidence

State v. Watkins, 120 N.C. App. 804 (1995). An officer stopped a vehicle for impaired driving. A prior appeal of this case determined that anonymous information and the officer's observations provided reasonable suspicion for the stop; *see* State v. Watkins, 337 N.C. 437 (1994). The defendant then filed a supplemental suppression motion based on newly discovered evidence that the anonymous information had been supplied to the stopping officer by another officer and the other officer had fabricated the information (there was no evidence that the stopping officer knew that the information was fabricated). The court ruled that the defendant had the authority to file a supplemental suppression motion based on newly discovered evidence; *see* G.S. 15A-975(c).

Trial Court's Ruling on Suppression Motion
When Trial Court's Ruling Must Be Made

State v. Bartlett, 368 N.C. 309 (2015). The court, reversing the court of appeals, 231 N.C. App. 417 (2013), ruled that a new suppression hearing was required. At the close of the suppression hearing, the superior court judge orally granted the defendant's motion and asked counsel to prepare a written order. However, that judge did not sign the proposed order before his term ended. The defendant presented the proposed order to a second superior court judge, who signed it, over the State's objection and without conducting a hearing. The order specifically found that the defendant's expert was credible, gave weight to the expert's testimony, and used the expert's testimony to conclude that no probable cause existed to support the defendant's arrest. The State appealed, contending that the second judge was without authority to sign the order. The court of appeals found it unnecessary to reach the State's contention because that court considered the first judge's oral ruling to be sufficient. Reviewing the law, the supreme court clarified, "our cases require findings of fact only when there is a material conflict in the evidence and allow the trial court to make these findings either orally or in writing." It added that to the extent that cases such as *State v. Williams*, 195 N.C. App. 554 (2009), "suggest otherwise, they are disavowed." Turning to the case before it, the court concluded that at the suppression hearing in this case, disagreement between the parties' expert witnesses created a material conflict in the evidence. Thus, a finding of fact, whether written or oral, was required. Here, however, the first judge made no such finding. The court noted that while he did attempt to explain his rationale for granting the motion, "we cannot construe any of his statements as a definitive finding of fact that resolved the material conflict in the evidence." Having found that the oral ruling was inadequate, the court considered whether the second judge had authority to resolve the evidentiary conflict in his written order even though he did not conduct the suppression hearing. It held that he did not, reasoning that G.S. 15A-977 contemplates that the same trial judge who hears the evidence must also find the facts. The court rejected the defendant's argument that G.S. 15A-1224(b) authorized the second judge to sign the order, concluding that the provision applies only to criminal trials, not suppression hearings.

State v. Trent, 359 N.C. 583 (2005). The defendant filed motions to suppress evidence. After hearing evidence and arguments of counsel on January 17, 2002, the trial court stated that it would announce a ruling later. On August 26, 2002, the trial court announced its ruling that the motions to suppress were denied. The court ruled that the trial court's ruling on the suppression motions was void because it was not announced in open court or entered during the session in which motions were heard, and the trial court did not have explicit consent of both parties to enter the ruling after the session had ended. The defendant was entitled to a new trial without consideration as to whether the defendant was prejudiced by the admission of evidence that was subject to the suppression motions. *See also* State v. Branch, 177 N.C. App. 104 (2006) (entry of ruling on suppression motion made out of term was nullity; defendant had consented to trial court's request to take motion under advisement and issue later order, but defendant did not explicitly consent to order's entry out of term). *See generally* Michael Crowell, *Out-of-Term, Out-of-Session, Out-of-County*, Admin. of Just. Bull. 2008/05 (Nov. 2008), www.sog.unc.edu/sites/www.sog.unc.edu/files/reports/aojb0805.pdf.

State v. Palmer, 334 N.C. 104 (1993). An order denying a motion to suppress was valid, even though the written order was filed after the superior court term had concluded and 57 days after the notice of appeal had been entered, when the trial court had verbally denied the motion in open court after the suppression hearing was held. *See also* State v. Smith, 320 N.C. 404 (1987).

State v. Boone, 310 N.C. 284 (1984). An order denying a pretrial motion to suppress was a nullity because it was entered and signed after the end of the session at which the motion was heard. A trial court must announce the ruling in open court during the session, or the order containing the ruling must be signed and filed with the clerk during the session. *See also* State v. Horner, 310 N.C. 274 (1984) (no error when trial court ruled on motion to suppress during trial but filed written order with clerk out of session and out of county; *Boone* distinguished).

Trial Court's Findings of Fact and Conclusions of Law

State v. Morgan, 225 N.C. App. 784 (2013). The trial court erred by failing to issue a written order denying the defendant's motion to suppress. A written order is necessary unless the court announces its rationale from the bench and there are no material conflicts in the evidence. Although the trial court announced its ruling from the bench, there was a material conflict in the evidence. The court remanded for the entry of a written order.

State v. O'Connor, 222 N.C. App. 235, 243 (2012). In granting the defendant's motion to suppress, the trial court erred by failing to make findings of fact resolving material conflicts in the evidence. The court of appeals rejected the defendant's argument that the trial court "indirectly provided a rationale from the bench" by stating that the motion was granted for the reasons in the defendant's memorandum.

State v. Salinas, 366 N.C. 119 (2012). Modifying and affirming *State v. Salinas*, 214 N.C. App. 408 (2011) (trial court incorrectly applied a probable cause standard instead of a reasonable suspicion standard to a vehicle stop), the state supreme court ruled that the trial court may not rely on allegations contained in a defendant's G.S. 15A-977(a) affidavit when making findings of fact in connection with a motion to suppress.

State v. Baker, 208 N.C. App. 376 (2010). The court stated that when a trial court's failure to make findings of fact and conclusions of law is assigned as error on appeal, the trial court's ruling on a motion to suppress is fully reviewable to determine (1) whether the trial court provided the rationale for its ruling from the bench and (2) whether there was a material conflict in the evidence presented at the suppression hearing. If a reviewing court concludes that both criteria are met (that is, the trial court provided the ruling's rationale from the bench and there was no material conflict in the evidence presented at the suppression hearing), then the findings of fact are implied by the trial court's denial of the motion to suppress and will be binding on appeal, if supported by competent evidence. If a reviewing court concludes that either of the criteria is not met, then a trial court's failure to make findings of fact and conclusions of law is reversible error. A material conflict in the evidence exists when evidence presented by one party controverts evidence presented by an opposing party such that the outcome of the matter is likely to be affected. The court ruled in this case that the defendant had presented evidence that controverts the State's evidence as to whether a seizure occurred. Because there was a material conflict in the evidence, the trial court's failure to make findings of fact and conclusions of law was fatal to its ruling's validity. The court reversed and remanded for findings of fact and conclusions of law. The court noted that even when there is no material conflict in the evidence, the better practice is for the trial court to make findings of fact.

Whether Another Jurisdiction's Ruling Is Binding on North Carolina Courts

State v. Brooks, 337 N.C. 132 (1994). The defendant had previously been prosecuted in federal court on federal drug charges arising from the same search. A federal judge had ruled that the search violated the Fourth Amendment and suppressed the cocaine that had been seized. The North Carolina Supreme Court ruled that the federal court's ruling did not collaterally estop the State from introducing the same evidence in state court. Collateral estoppel does not apply, under either federal or state constitutions, to criminal cases in which separate sovereigns are involved in separate proceedings and there is no privity between the two sovereigns in the first proceeding. The State was not in privity with the federal government concerning federal charges simply because it may have deferred to having federal prosecution begin first.

State v. Myers, 266 N.C. 581 (1966). A Virginia state court's ruling that a search warrant was invalid is not binding on North Carolina courts.

State v. Hernandez, 208 N.C. App. 591 (2010). Any alleged violation of the New Jersey Constitution in connection with a stop in that state leading to charges in North Carolina provided no basis for the suppression of evidence in a North Carolina court.

Law of the Case

State v. Lewis, 365 N.C. 488 (2012). Affirming the court of appeals, the state supreme court ruled that on a retrial the trial court erred by applying the law of the case and denying the defendant's motion to suppress. At the defendant's first trial, he unsuccessfully moved to suppress the victim's identification as unduly suggestive. That issue was affirmed on appeal. At the retrial, the defense filed new motions to suppress on the same grounds. However, at the pretrial hearings on these motions, the defense introduced new evidence relevant to the reliability of the identification. The State successfully argued that the law of the case governed and that the defendant's motions must be denied. After the defendant was again convicted, he appealed, and the court of appeals reversed on this issue. Affirming that ruling, the supreme court noted that "the law of the case doctrine does not apply when the evidence presented at a subsequent proceeding is different from that presented on a former appeal." It then affirmed the court of appeals' ruling that the trial court erred in applying the doctrine of the law of the case to the defendant's motion to suppress at the retrial.

Trial Court Modifying Its Own Suppression Ruling

State v. McNeill, 170 N.C. App. 574 (2005). The trial court granted the defendant's pretrial motion to suppress evidence. However, the trial court during trial changed its ruling and allowed the evidence to be admitted. The court ruled that the trial court did not err in admitting the evidence. The court noted that a pretrial motion to suppress is a type of motion in limine, and such a motion is a preliminary or interlocutory decision that the trial court can change. The court noted that the State has two options when a defendant's pretrial suppression motion is granted. It can appeal the ruling to the appellate courts. Or, the State may proceed to trial, attempt to introduce the evidence subject to suppression, and allow the trial court to either change the pretrial ruling or make the defendant object to the admission of the evidence.

Trial Court Modifying Another Trial Court's Suppression Ruling

State v. Woolridge, 357 N.C. 544 (2003). The court ruled, citing *State v. Hilliard*, 120 N.C. 479 (1997), and other cases, that a trial judge had no authority to rule on the State's motion to reconsider another trial judge's order granting the defendant's motion to suppress when the State did not make a sufficient showing of a substantial change of circumstances since the first judge's order. The court stated that superior court judges must remain mindful that the power of one judge of the superior court is equal and coordinate with that of another. *See generally* Michael Crowell, *One Trial Judge Overruling Another*, ADMIN. OF JUST. BULL. 2008/02 (May 2008), sogpubs.unc.edu/electronicversions/pdfs/aojb0802.pdf.

Suppression Hearings

Simmons v. United States, 390 U.S. 377 (1968). The government may not use a defendant's testimony at a suppression hearing as evidence of guilt at the subsequent prosecution. [Author's note: Although the Court has not decided whether a defendant's testimony may be used for impeachment, *see* United States v. Salvucci, 448 U.S. 83 (1980), it probably would permit the testimony for that limited purpose. For a North Carolina appellate court ruling on this issue, see *State v. Bracey*, 303 N.C. 112 (1981), below.

State v. Bracey, 303 N.C. 112 (1981). The State properly impeached the defendant during cross-examination at trial with testimony he had given during a hearing to suppress his confession.

State v. Edwards, 286 N.C. 162 (1974). A photocopy of a search warrant is admissible at a suppression hearing when the original has been lost.

State v. Williams, 225 N.C. App. 636 (2013). The court of appeals ruled that the trial court did not impermissibly place the burden of proof on the defendant at a suppression hearing. Initially, the burden is on the defendant to show that a suppression motion is timely and in proper form. The burden then is on the State to demonstrate the admissibility of the challenged evidence. The party that bears the burden of proof typically presents evidence first. In this case, the fact that the defendant presented evidence first at the suppression hearing does not by itself establish that the burden of proof was shifted to the defendant.

State v. Cohen, 117 N.C. App. 265 (1994). Officers obtained the consent of the defendant's wife to search her car. The officers searched its contents, including an unlocked briefcase. The defendant made a motion to suppress evidence discovered during the search of the briefcase on the ground that his wife did not have the authority to consent to its search. The trial judge refused to accept the wife's affidavit at the suppression hearing because she was available as a witness; the defendant declined the judge's offer of additional time to produce his wife as a witness. The court ruled that the judge properly refused to admit the affidavit, based on these facts. The court also ruled that the defendant's suppression motion was properly denied because the defendant failed to present evidence that he had an ownership or possessory interest in the briefcase.

State v. Piland, 58 N.C. App. 95 (1982). The defendant's counsel may waive the defendant's right to appear at the pretrial suppression hearing. No prejudice to the defendant was shown in this case by his absence.

State v. Lay, 56 N.C. App. 796 (1982). The State was not collaterally estopped from asserting the validity of a search warrant in a felony case when a district court judge had previously ruled that the warrant was invalid in a related misdemeanor case.

State v. Williams, 42 N.C. App. 662 (1979), *rev'd on other grounds*, 299 N.C. 529 (1980). The State has the burden of proving the legality under the Fourth Amendment of an officer's conduct when the officer acted without a warrant. *See also* State v. Breeden, 306 N.C. 533 (1982) (defendant has burden of going forward by filing motion to suppress out-of-court identification, but State had burden of proving by preponderance of evidence that evidence was admissible).

State v. Gibson, 32 N.C. App. 584 (1977). A defendant has the burden of going forward by filing a motion to suppress evidence seized under a search warrant, but the State has the burden of proof to show that the evidence was lawfully obtained. [Author's note: The defendant has the burden of proving standing to contest a Fourth Amendment violation. *See* Rakas v. Illinois, 439 U.S. 128 (1978).]

State v. Brown, 20 N.C. App. 413 (1974). There is no constitutional or statutory prohibition that prevents a judge from ruling on the validity of a search warrant issued by that judge (although it is better not to do so). *See also* State v. Montserrate, 125 N.C. App. 22 (1997) (similar ruling).

Admissibility of Hearsay at Suppression Hearing

State v. Ingram, ___ N.C. App. ___, 774 S.E.2d 433 (2015). The court rejected the State's argument that the trial court erred by considering hearsay evidence in the defendant's suppression hearing and by relying on the evidence in making its findings of fact. The court noted that the trial court has "great discretion" to admit any evidence relevant to the suppression hearing.

State v. Villeda, 165 N.C. App. 431 (2004). An officer stopped a vehicle driven by a Hispanic male for a seat belt violation. He was later arrested for DWI and convicted in district court, and he appealed for trial de novo in superior court. The defendant moved to suppress evidence seized as a result of the traffic stop. A suppression hearing was conducted, and the trial judge granted the defendant's motion to suppress evidence related to the traffic stop and dismissed the DWI charge. At the suppression hearing, the defendant presented testimony of three attorneys who had represented defendants in other cases involving this officer to show that the officer had stopped Hispanic males based on impermissible ethnic bias. The trial judge admitted their out-of-court conversations with the officer. The State argued on appeal that the attorneys' testimony concerning the officer's statements was inadmissible hearsay. The court ruled, relying on cases from other jurisdictions, that the officer's statements were admissible under Rule 801(d)(D) (a statement offered against a party and made by the party's agent or servant concerning a matter within the scope of the agency or employment, made during the existence of the relationship, is admissible). [Author's note: Rule 104(a) provides, in pertinent part, that preliminary questions concerning the admissibility of evidence shall be determined by the court, and in making its determination the court is not bound by the rules of evidence except those with respect to privileges. Thus, hearsay is admissible at suppression hearings.] *Cf.* Gibson v. Faulkner, 132 N.C. App. 728 (1999) (court ruled, relying on *Melton v. Hodges*, 114 N.C. App. 795 (1994), that trial judge properly could rely on hearsay evidence (information an officer gave the arresting officer) in concluding that the arresting officer had reasonable grounds to believe that a person had committed an implied consent offense (in this case, DWI)).

State v. Melvin, 32 N.C. App. 772 (1977). Hearsay statements by an officer about what a joint occupant said in consenting to a search of the premises is admissible at a voir dire hearing to determine the validity of consent; the court cited *United States v. Matlock*, 415 U.S. 164 (1974). *See also* G.S. 8C-1, Rule 104 (court is not bound by rules of evidence in determining admissibility of evidence, except with respect to privileges).

Appellate Review of Suppression Motions and Rulings

State v. Oates, 366 N.C. 264 (2012). The state supreme court reversed the decision below, 215 N.C. App. 491 (2011), and ruled that the State's notice of appeal of a trial court ruling on a suppression motion was timely. The State's notice was filed seven days after the trial judge in open court orally granted the defendant's pretrial motion to suppress, but three months before the trial judge issued his corresponding written order of suppression. The supreme court ruled that the window for filing a written notice of appeal in a criminal case opens on the date of rendition of the judgment or order and closes 14 days after entry of the judgment or order. The court clarified that rendering a judgment or an order means to pronounce, state, declare, or announce the judgment or order and is "the judicial act of the court in pronouncing the sentence

of the law upon the facts in controversy." Entering a judgment or an order is "a ministerial act which consists in spreading it upon the record." The court continued:

> For the purposes of entering notice of appeal in a criminal case . . . a judgment or an order is rendered when the judge decides the issue before him or her and advises the necessary individuals of the decision; a judgment or an order is entered under that Rule when the clerk of court records or files the judge's decision regarding the judgment or order.

State v. Golphin, 352 N.C. 364 (2000). The court ruled that because a pretrial motion to suppress is a type of motion in limine, a pretrial motion to suppress is insufficient to preserve for appeal the admissibility of evidence if a defendant did not object when the evidence was offered at trial.

State v. Bunnell, 340 N.C. 74 (1995). The defendant's motion to suppress at trial challenged the voluntariness of his statement to a law enforcement officer. The court ruled that the defendant could not assert for the first time on appeal a challenge to his statement on the ground that it was obtained in violation of his Sixth Amendment right to counsel, because he did not assert this ground in his suppression motion at trial.

State v. Benson, 323 N.C. 318 (1988). The defendant argued on appeal that his confession should have been suppressed because it was obtained as the result of an unlawful arrest. However, the defendant's pretrial written suppression motion did not rely on that ground (neither did he argue that ground during the suppression hearing). The court ruled that the defendant could not argue that ground on appeal. *See also* State v. Hunter, 305 N.C. 106 (1982) (similar ruling).

State v. Zuniga, 320 N.C. 233 (1987). A prior appellate ruling in this case upheld the trial judge's denial of the defendant's suppression motion. The court ruled on the second appeal that unless additional evidence was offered after the first appeal, or a new theory of exclusion was raised, courts were bound by "law of the case" on the issue in the suppression motion.

State v. Holloway, 311 N.C. 573 (1984). The defendant waived his right to appeal on constitutional and statutory grounds the issue of a deputy clerk's neutrality in issuing a search warrant when he failed to file an affidavit with his motion to suppress as required by G.S. 15A-977(a) and when his unverified motion failed to specify his source of information or the basis of his belief that the deputy clerk was not neutral and detached. It was irrelevant (concerning the defendant's waiver of appellate review) that the State failed to object to the sufficiency of the motion to suppress at trial or at the evidentiary hearing that was held on the motion. *But see* Holloway v. Woodard, 655 F. Supp. 1245 (W.D.N.C. 1987) (court ruled that the North Carolina Supreme Court's procedural ruling in *State v. Holloway* effectively barred the defendant from a full and fair opportunity to litigate his Fourth Amendment claim in state court under *Stone v. Powell*, 428 U.S. 465 (1976); court remanded the case to state court for a hearing to determine the defendant's Fourth Amendment claim).

State v. Cooke, 306 N.C. 132 (1982). The State may not assert on appeal a ground for upholding a search that it did not raise at the suppression hearing at the trial division. *See also* State v. Green, 103 N.C. App. 38 (1991).

State v. Turner, 305 N.C. 356 (1982). (1) A prosecutor's certificate under G.S. 15A-979(c) (when the State is appealing the granting of a defendant's pretrial motion to suppress) is timely when it is filed before certification of the record on appeal to the appellate division. (2) A defendant may not appeal the denial of a pretrial motion to suppress until after the defendant is convicted.

State v. Reynolds, 298 N.C. 380 (1979). A defendant who intends to appeal from a trial judge's denial of a suppression motion under G.S. 15A-979(b) must give notice of that intention to the prosecutor and the judge before plea negotiations are completed or else waive the right to appellate review of the motion. *See also* State v. McBride, 120 N.C. App. 623 (1995), *aff'd*, 344 N.C. 623 (1996).

State v. Silhan, 295 N.C. 636 (1980). The State's appeal of a ruling at a pretrial suppression motion goes directly to the North Carolina Supreme Court if the punishment for the charge is death or life imprisonment. [Author's note: G.S. 7A-27 was amended after the *Silhan* ruling to permit direct appellate review by the supreme court only when a sentence of death is imposed for a conviction of first-degree murder; therefore, a State's appeal of a pretrial suppression motion would go directly to the supreme court only when the death penalty may be imposed for a first-degree murder conviction.]

State v. Brown, 217 N.C. App. 566 (2011). The court of appeals ruled that the defendant gave sufficient notice of his intent to appeal the denial of his motion to suppress to preserve his right to appeal. The State had argued that defense counsel's language was not specific enough to place the trial court and prosecution on notice of his intention to appeal the adverse ruling. Immediately following an attempt to make a renewed motion to suppress at the end of the State's evidence, defense counsel stated "that [the defendant] would like to preserve any appellate issues that may stem from the motions in this trial." The court of appeals noted that the defendant had only made five motions during trial, two of which were motions to suppress, and that following defense counsel's request, the trial court reentered substantially similar facts to the ones it entered when initially denying the pretrial motion to suppress. Clearly, the court concluded, the trial court understood which motion the defendant intended to appeal and decided to make its findings of fact as clear as possible for the record.

State v. Hudson, 206 N.C. App. 482 (2010). When the defendant's motion to suppress in the trial court raised only a lack of reasonable suspicion for the stop, the defendant failed to preserve other grounds for suppression raised on appeal.

State v. Phillips, 151 N.C. App. 185 (2002). The State at a suppression hearing raised the argument that the defendant did not have standing to contest a Fourth Amendment issue, but later the State explicitly abandoned the argument. As a result, the trial judge made no findings of fact or conclusions of law on the issue. The court ruled, citing *State v. Cooke*, 54 N.C. App. 33 (1981), that the State waived appellate review of this issue.

State v. Seagle, 96 N.C. App. 318 (1989). The court ruled that the State's failure to object to a defendant's oral motion to suppress precludes the State from raising on appeal that the defendant's motion was not timely or properly filed.

State v. Russell, 92 N.C. App. 639 (1989). The defendant pled guilty and properly appealed to the appellate court the denial of his motion to suppress. Although the court ruled that the trial court erred in denying the defendant's suppression motion, the court also ruled that the error was harmless beyond a reasonable doubt. The failure to suppress the evidence could not have affected the defendant's decision to plead guilty, based on the overwhelming evidence of his guilt.

Standing to Contest Fourth Amendment Violations

UNITED STATES SUPREME COURT

Brendlin v. California, 551 U.S. 249 (2007). Officers stopped a car in which the defendant was a passenger. The defendant remained in the vehicle and was eventually arrested. The Court ruled, reviewing its prior cases defining the seizure of a person under the Fourth Amendment, that the passenger was seized and therefore could contest the validity of the stop of the vehicle. The Court stated that any reasonable passenger in the defendant's position would have understood the officers to be exercising control to the extent that no one in the car was free to depart without their permission.

Minnesota v. Carter, 525 U.S. 83 (1998). The defendants came to an apartment, with the lessee's consent, for the sole purpose of packaging cocaine. They had never been to the apartment before and were only in the apartment for about two and one-half hours. The defendants made a motion to suppress evidence based on an officer's allegedly illegal search of the apartment by looking through a gap in the closed blind of the apartment's window.

The Court ruled, distinguishing *Minnesota v. Olson*, 495 U.S. 91 (1990) (overnight guest in house had reasonable expectation of privacy there), that the defendants did not have a reasonable expectation of privacy in the apartment to challenge the officer's alleged illegal search. The Court stated that the defendants were obviously not overnight guests but were in the home essentially for a business transaction that lasted a few hours. They did not have a prior relationship with the lessee nor any other purpose for their visit. There was nothing similar to the overnight guest relationship in *Olson* to suggest a degree of acceptance into the household. While the apartment was a dwelling place for the lessee, it was simply a place to do business for the defendants. [Author's note: The Court did not decide whether the officer's observation was a search under the Fourth Amendment.]

United States v. Padilla, 508 U.S. 77 (1993). An Arizona law enforcement officer stopped a vehicle driven by Arciniega, the sole occupant. He consented to a search of the vehicle, and the officer found cocaine. A federal appellate court ruled that various drug codefendants had standing to contest the search of the vehicle, because a co-conspirator has a legitimate expectation of privacy under the Fourth Amendment if a co-conspirator's par-ticipation in an operation or arrangement indicates joint control and supervision of the place searched. The Court rejected the federal appellate court ruling and remanded the case for consideration of standing under principles set out in *Alderman v. United States*, 394 U.S. 165 (1969); *Rakas v. Illinois*, 439 U.S. 128 (1978); *Rawlings v. Kentucky*, 448 U.S. 98 (1980); and *Soldal v. Cook County*, 506 U.S. 56 (1992).

Minnesota v. Olson, 495 U.S. 91 (1990). An overnight guest in a home has a reasonable expectation of privacy there. Thus, the officers' warrantless entry into the home to arrest the guest violated the Fourth Amendment when they did not have consent to enter and exigent circumstances did not exist. *See also* United States v. Osorio, 949 F.2d 38 (2d Cir. 1991) (overnight guest had reasonable expectation of privacy to contest search of areas within apartment that were not off limits to the guest); United States v. Gamez-Orduno, 235 F.3d 453 (9th Cir. 2000) (marijuana smugglers, overnight guests of person living in trailer and staying there for food and rest, had reasonable expectation of privacy in trailer under *Minnesota v. Olson*; court distinguished *Minnesota v. Carter*); United States v. Fields, 113 F.3d 313 (2d Cir. 1997) (defendant A, who had key from tenant, paid $125 per week for privilege of using apartment, made use of it on 40 to 50 occasions to cook and cut crack cocaine, could bring guests, and could go and come as he pleased had reasonable expectation of privacy in apartment; defendant B, who visited apartment solely as A's guest although he did not spend time overnight, had reasonable expectation of privacy in apartment).

Rawlings v. Kentucky, 448 U.S. 98 (1980). The defendant failed to show a reasonable expectation of privacy in a female companion's purse. He knew others had access to it. His precipitous action in putting his illegal drugs there did not support a careful effort to maintain privacy, and he testified at the suppression hearing that he had no subjective expectation that the purse would be free from government intrusion. His assertion of ownership of the drugs does not by itself allow him to challenge the search of the purse; it is only a factor to be considered. *See* United States v. Salvucci, 448 U.S. 83 (1980) (defendant charged with a possession offense—possession of stolen mail—did not have "automatic standing" to challenge the legality of a search that produced evidence against him; the issue, instead, is whether the defendant had a reasonable expectation of privacy in the place searched). *See* *also* United States v. Karo, 468 U.S. 705 (1984) (analysis of standing of various defendants in a beeper case).

Rakas v. Illinois, 439 U.S. 128 (1978). A defendant who makes a motion to suppress has the burden of proving that his or her own Fourth Amendment rights were violated by the challenged search or seizure. A violation of a third party's Fourth Amendment rights does not result in the suppression of evidence at the defendant's trial. In this case, an officer stopped the apparent getaway car used in a robbery. The four occupants—the two male defendants and two females—were ordered out of the car. Officers discovered a box of rifle shells in the locked glove compartment and a sawed-off rifle under the front passenger seat. When the two defendants made a motion to suppress the evidence, they both conceded that they did not own the car (one of the women was the owner and driver) and were simply passengers. They did not assert that they owned the rifle or shells that were seized.

The Court ruled that presence in the car was not by itself sufficient to show a reasonable expectation of privacy under the Fourth Amendment. And the defendants failed to show that they had a reasonable expectation of privacy in the places searched—the glove compartment and the area under the seat, which are places in which a mere passenger normally does not have a privacy interest. The Court clarified that "standing" is not a separate concept apart from the legality of the search; the two issues merge when determining whether the government violated a person's reasonable expectation of privacy. *See also* State v. Jordan, 40 N.C. App. 412 (1979) (defendant had no reasonable expectation of privacy in the contents of his female passenger's pocketbook).

United States v. Miller, 425 U.S. 435 (1976). A depositor has no reasonable expectation of privacy in copies of checks and other bank records that are in the bank's possession. *See also* State v. Whitted, 99 N.C. App. 502 (1990), and *In re* Superior Court Order, 315 N.C. 378 (1986) (superior court judge has the inherent power to order a bank to disclose a customer's bank account records on a showing that reasonable suspicion exists that a crime was committed and that the records likely will relate to the investigation of that crime). [Author's note: After the decision in *In re Superior Court Order*, the legislature enacted legislation (see G.S. 53B-1 through 53B-10) that governs an officer's authority to obtain bank records. See the discussion of this authority in Chapter 3.]

NORTH CAROLINA SUPREME COURT

State v. Howell, 343 N.C. 229 (1996). The defendant lived in a converted school bus located in a used car junkyard. Before leaving North Carolina, the defendant told an employee that he could have the bus and its contents. The employee sold the bus to the junkyard owner. The court ruled, based on these facts, that the defendant did not have standing under the Fourth Amendment to contest a search of the bus.

State v. Mlo, 335 N.C. 353 (1994). The defendant was on trial for first-degree murder. The defendant sought to suppress evidence obtained from a search of the murder victim's car. The court ruled that the defendant's unsubstantiated and self-serving statements that the victim had loaned his car to him were insufficient to satisfy his burden of showing a legitimate possessory interest in the car; thus, the defendant did not have standing to contest the search of the car. The victim's best friend provided evidence that he had never known the victim to loan his car to anyone.

State v. Austin, 320 N.C. 276 (1987). The male defendant, who lived for five or six years in premises with a female adult (to whom he was not married) and her children, had a reasonable expectation of privacy in the premises to contest a search there.

State v. Greenwood, 301 N.C. 705 (1981). The defendant had no standing to contest a search of a stolen pocketbook found in the rear seat of his car. *See also* State v. Crews, 296 N.C. 607 (1979) (no standing to contest search of stolen vehicle); State v. White, 311 N.C. 238 (1984) (same). The issue of standing to contest a seizure of stolen goods was noted, but not decided, in *State v. Sturkie*, 325 N.C. 225 (1989).

State v. Jones, 299 N.C. 298 (1980). The defendant had no standing to contest a search of his parents' garage. He did not assert any property or possessory interest or any other basis to have a reasonable expectation of privacy there. *See also* State v. Alford, 298 N.C. 465 (1979) (defendant had no standing to contest a search of a metal outbuilding behind his rented house; owner used it to store materials, it was not part of lease agreement, and defendant never sought permission to use it); State v. Taylor, 298 N.C. 405 (1979) (defendant had no standing to contest a search of a room in a "shot house" when evidence showed he was only a customer and hid weapon and ammunition there); State v. Eppley, 282 N.C. 249 (1972) (defendants had no standing to contest search of a house that they occupied as trespassers); State v. Ford, 71 N.C. App. 748 (1984) (defendant had no standing to contest a search of a mobile home when he did not assert a property or possessory interest there and was not on the premises when it was searched; at most, the evidence showed that he was there at some time before the search).

NORTH CAROLINA COURT OF APPEALS

State v. Clyburn, ___ N.C. App. ___, 770 S.E.2d 689 (2015). The court reversed and remanded for further findings of fact concerning the defendant's motion to suppress evidence obtained as a result of a search of the digital contents of a GPS device found on the defendant's person which, as a result of the search, was determined to have been stolen. The court ruled that under *Riley v. California*, 134 S. Ct. 2473 (2014), the search was not justified as a search incident to arrest. As to whether the defendant had a reasonable expectation of privacy in the GPS device, the court ruled that a defendant may have a legitimate expectation of privacy in a stolen item if he or she acquired it innocently and does not know that the item was stolen. Here, evidence at the suppression hearing would allow the trial court to conclude that the defendant had a legitimate possessory interest in the GPS device. However, because the trial court failed to make a factual determination regarding whether the defendant innocently purchased the GPS device, the court reversed and remanded for further findings of fact, providing additional guidance for the trial court in its decision.

State v. Mackey, 207 N.C. App. 116 (2011). The defendant had no standing to challenge a search of a vehicle when he was a passenger, did not own the vehicle, and asserted no possessory interest in it or its contents.

State v. Hernandez, 208 N.C. App. 591 (2010). As a passenger in a vehicle that was stopped, the defendant had standing to challenge the stop.

State v. Boyd, 169 N.C. App. 204 (2005). The court ruled that the defendant did not have a reasonable expectation of privacy in a vehicle to contest its search when the defendant did not own, rent, or lease the vehicle and fled from law enforcement officers after leaving the vehicle open at the scene of an assault. The court stated that even if the defendant had permission to use the vehicle, he relinquished possession and control when he fled from the officers.

State v. VanCamp, 150 N.C. App. 347 (2002). The defendant was a passenger in a vehicle that failed to stop at a driver's license checkpoint but eventually stopped 60 feet beyond the checkpoint in response to an officer's command to stop. The officer looked inside the vehicle with his flashlight and saw the corner of a plastic bag sticking out from the passenger seat occupied by the defendant. The officer knew that plastic bags are often used to transport illegal drugs. When the defendant rolled down the window, the officer smelled the odor of alcohol coming from the vehicle. The officer asked the defendant to get out of the vehicle, frisked him for weapons, felt what he recognized to be a pair of brass knuckles in the defendant's front pants pocket, and arrested him for carrying a concealed weapon. The officer then searched the vehicle and found crack cocaine in the center console. The court ruled that the defendant did not assert an ownership or possessory interest in the vehicle and therefore did not have a reasonable expectation of privacy to challenge the search of the center console.

State v. McMillian, 147 N.C. App. 707 (2001). The court ruled, relying on *United States v. Grandstaff*, 813 F.2d 1353 (9th Cir. 1987), and *United States v. Maddox*, 944 F.2d 1223 (6th Cir. 1991), that a visitor to a motel room did not have a reasonable expectation of privacy to challenge a search there. The evidence showed that the room was rented to another person, the defendant did not have any luggage there, and the defendant had neither spent the night there nor planned to do so.

State v. Sanchez, 147 N.C. App. 619 (2001). The defendant was temporarily residing in a living area of another's house. The living area was located in the basement, which was connected to the garage and laundry room. A door separated the laundry room from the basement and garage area. Cocaine was found under the stairwell located in the laundry room. The court ruled, distinguishing *Minnesota v. Olson*, 495 U.S. 91 (1990), that the defendant did not prove that he had a reasonable expectation of privacy concerning the search and discovery of cocaine under the stairwell, which was a common area of the house.

State v. Phillips, 132 N.C. App. 765 (1999). While the defendant was driving his van and was being pursued by law enforcement officers, he threw a package of crack cocaine on a passenger's lap and told her to put it in his apartment. She got out of the van and went to the defendant's apartment. She put the package in his mailbox because his apartment door was locked. After the passenger told an officer where she had put the package, an officer went to the mailbox, lifted the lid, and looked inside. He seized the package, which appeared to have crack cocaine inside. The court ruled, relying on *State v. Jordan*, 40 N.C. App. 412 (1979), and other cases, that the defendant relinquished his reasonable expectation of privacy in the drugs when he gave them to the passenger, because he no longer had control over them.

State v. Smith, 117 N.C. App. 671 (1995). Officers stopped a cab in which the defendant and Campbell were passengers. The defendant consented to a search of his luggage and Campbell consented to a search of his luggage; cocaine was found in both. The defendant was charged with a trafficking offense. A judge granted the defendant's motion to suppress evidence seized from the defendant's luggage because the stop of the cab was unconstitutional. The defendant was charged with a drug trafficking conspiracy offense. The defendant then moved to suppress the cocaine found in Campbell's luggage and to suppress proposed testimony by Campbell. The court ruled that a judge (who was a different judge than the one who had ruled on the first motion) properly denied that motion because the defendant did not have a reasonable expectation of privacy in Campbell's luggage and did not have standing to object to the proposed testimony of Campbell, even if it was the fruit of the illegal stop of the cab.

State v. Cohen, 117 N.C. App. 265 (1994). Officers obtained the consent of the defendant's wife to search her car. The officers searched the car's contents, including an unlocked briefcase. The defendant made a motion to suppress the search of the briefcase on the ground that his wife did not have the authority to consent to its search by the officers. The trial judge refused to accept the wife's affidavit at the suppression hearing because she was available as a witness; the defendant declined the judge's offer of additional time to produce his wife as a witness. The court ruled that the judge properly refused to admit the affidavit, based on these facts. The court also ruled that the defendant's suppression motion was properly denied because the defendant failed to present evidence that he had an ownership or possessory interest in the briefcase.

State v. Swift, 105 N.C. App. 550 (1992). The defendant's friend picked up the defendant in the friend's car, and they drove to a convenience store. The friend went into the store, leaving the defendant to guard the car. The defendant later fled from law enforcement officers and was arrested. The officers searched the car. The court ruled, based on these facts, that the defendant did not have a reasonable expectation of privacy in the vehicle to contest the officers' search.

State v. Hudson, 103 N.C. App. 708 (1991). The defendant-driver failed to show any ownership or possessory interest in a briefcase in the passenger's possession to contest the officer's search of the briefcase. The passenger had told the officer that the briefcase was hers.

State v. Johnson, 98 N.C. App. 290 (1990). After officers, during a bus boarding, had spoken with all the bus passengers about which bags belonged to whom, one bag located in the front of the bus had not been claimed. The officers asked each passenger (including the defendant) whether the bag belonged to him or her. No one claimed it. The officers then removed the bag from the bus, searched it, and found cocaine and a traffic citation issued in Tampa, Florida. The officers reboarded the bus and asked the passengers for identification. The defendant was the only passenger with a Tampa address on his driver's license. The officers requested that the defendant leave the bus, and he did. The officers again asked him if the luggage belonged to him; he denied ownership of the bag. The court ruled that the defendant lost his reasonable expectation of privacy in the bag when he denied that he owned or controlled the bag. The court also rejected the defendant's argument that the officers needed a search warrant to search the bag. The defendant did not have standing to contest the bag he had abandoned.

State v. Banks, 88 N.C. App. 737 (1988). Distinguishing *State v. Austin*, 320 N.C. 276 (1987), the court ruled that the defendant did not have standing to contest the search of a rented house, except for his bedroom. The defendant's name was not listed on the lease agreement or utility bills. Although he had a key to the entire house, he disclaimed any property or possessory interest there when he was arrested. The evidence at the suppression hearing failed to make clear the arrangements by which the defendant resided in the house and by what authority he remained there. The defendant's use of the bedroom did not automatically confer standing to contest a search of other parts of the house, based on the evidence in this case.

State v. Washington, 86 N.C. App. 235 (1987). (1) The defendant-son, who had lived with his wife and child in his mother's house for four months before the search, had a possessory interest in the premises (house and curtilage) to contest the search, even though he did not own or lease the house or contribute to its maintenance. (2) The defendant failed to show a possessory interest in the outbuildings located outside the curtilage. Even assuming that he had a possessory interest, he had no reasonable expectation of privacy in outbuildings that were essentially open (the hog shelter was open and the packhouse had boards missing). (3) Even assuming that the defendant had a privacy interest in the outbuildings, his mother's consent to a search was proper because she retained common authority over the outbuildings: the defendant did not have exclusive control.

State v. Thompson, 73 N.C. App. 60 (1985). The defendant failed to demonstrate a reasonable expectation of privacy sufficient to give standing to contest a search of a van when he denied ownership of the van and any items inside and did not know what items were there. The mere fact that the search warrant listed him as the van's owner does not convey standing. *See also* State v. Warren, 309 N.C. 224 (1983) (defendant failed to show a reasonable expectation of privacy in a car when he specifically declined to present evidence of ownership or possession of the car).

State v. Joe'l, 67 N.C. App. 177 (1984). Although the defendants possessed a cylindrical container, they had no reasonable expectation of privacy to provide standing to contest a search of the container when they placed it in a hole on the grounds of a building and there was no evidence that they had any possessory or ownership interest in the building. *See also* State v. Telster, 61 N.C. App. 290 (1983) (defendant had no reasonable expectation of privacy in luggage that he buried in the woods; he had no ownership or possessory interest in the woods).

State v. Casey, 59 N.C. App. 99 (1982). The defendant had a reasonable expectation of privacy in the bag he was holding, even though he told the officers that it belonged to someone else. He had lawful possession of the bag, and he had the right to exclude all others from the bag during his encounter with the officers. *See also* United States v. Benitz-Arreguin, 973 F.2d 823 (10th Cir. 1992).

State v. Melvin, 53 N.C. App. 421 (1981). The defendant was a passenger in a car in which incriminating evidence was found. He denied any ownership or possessory interest in the evidence seized. He had no standing under *Rakas v. Illinois*, discussed above, to contest a search of the items seized. *See also* State v. Hunter, 107 N.C. App. 402 (1992) (defendant denied any possessory or proprietary interest in a radio found in a car and therefore did not have standing to contest a search of the radio).

State v. Jordan, 40 N.C. App. 412 (1979). The defendant had no reasonable expectation of privacy in the contents of his female passenger's pocketbook.

FEDERAL APPELLATE COURTS

United States v. Angevine, 281 F.3d 1130 (10th Cir. 2001). The defendant, a university professor, did not have a reasonable expectation of privacy in the university computer he used at work. The university's policies and procedures reserved the right to audit and to monitor Internet use and warned that information flowing through the university network was not confidential. *See also* United States v. Simons, 206 F.3d 392 (4th Cir. 2000) (government employee did not have legitimate expectation of privacy in Internet use when employer's known policy allowed monitoring of "all file transfers, all websites visited, and all e-mail messages").

Leventhal v. Knapek, 266 F.3d 64 (2d Cir. 2001). A state agency employee had a reasonable expectation of privacy in the contents of his office computer because the employee occupied a private office with a door and had exclusive use of the computer. The agency did not routinely conduct searches of office computers, nor had it adopted a policy against mere storage of personal files— although the agency had a policy prohibiting the use of agency time for personal business.

United States v. Henderson, 241 F.3d 638 (9th Cir. 2000). The defendant had a reasonable expectation of privacy in a rental car even though the lease had expired because the rental company had not attempted to repossess the car. A representative of the rental car company stated that it was not unusual for customers to keep the rental cars beyond the terms of their rental agreements; in such cases, the company simply charged the customer for a late return.

United States v. Walker, 237 F.3d 845 (7th Cir. 2001). The court ruled that a person listed on a car rental agreement as an authorized driver has a reasonable expectation of privacy in the car to challenge a search of the car.

Doe v. Broderick, 225 F.3d 440 (4th Cir. 2000). This case involved a civil lawsuit for Fourth Amendment and other violations. A detective entered the file room of a substance abuse treatment clinic and searched many patients' confidential treatment records, including the plaintiff's. The court ruled, distinguishing *United States v. Miller*, 425 U.S. 435 (1976), that the patient had a reasonable expectation of privacy in his records. [Author's note: Federal law also protects a patient's drug treatment records: 42 U.S.C.A. § 290dd-2.]

United States v. Sarkisian, 197 F.3d 966 (9th Cir. 1999). Defendants who merely possessed the authority to access a rental storage room but did not use it did not have a reasonable expectation of privacy to challenge a search of that area. In this case, neither defendant claimed any interest in any of the items seized during the search.

United States v. McRae, 156 F.3d 708 (6th Cir. 1998). The defendant did not have a reasonable expectation of privacy in a vacant house in which he had stayed a week when he did not own or rent the house.

United States v. Kitchens, 114 F.3d 29 (4th Cir. 1997). Absent a pattern or practice of allowing guests to stay in their hotel rooms past checkout time, a guest does not have a reasonable expectation of privacy in his or her hotel room after checkout time.

United States v. Riazco, 91 F.3d 752 (5th Cir. 1996). The court ruled that the driver of a rental car did not have standing to contest the search of the car (in this case, the speaker cavities where drugs were found) when he was not authorized by the rental agreement to drive it and did not have permission from the renter of the car to drive the car. It also was irrelevant that the driver had the permission of the passenger to drive the car, because the passenger was not authorized to drive the car, either. *See also* United States v. Muhammad, 58 F.3d 353 (8th Cir. 1995) (similar ruling).

Bonner v. Anderson, 81 F.3d 472 (4th Cir. 1996). Officers executed a search warrant at a residence while the plaintiff was inside. The plaintiff asserted in a civil lawsuit against the officers that they violated the Fourth Amendment in failing to appropriately knock and announce before entering the residence. The plaintiff did not live in the residence. However, the court, noting *Minnesota v. Olson*, 495 U.S. 91 (1990), ruled that the plaintiff had a reasonable expectation of privacy in the residence because she frequently visited there and often ran errands for an elderly person who lived there.

Bond v. United States, 77 F.3d 1009 (7th Cir. 1996). The defendant told an officer that he did not own a suitcase that was in a hotel room (even though the officer noticed that the suitcase had the defendant's name on it). The officer searched the suitcase and found $128,000 inside. The defendant then admitted that the suitcase was his but denied owning the money inside. The court ruled that the defendant's denial of ownership of the suitcase and his leaving the suitcase in another person's hotel room (the defendant did not have a key to the room and was not registered there) was an abandonment of the suitcase. The defendant therefore did not have a reasonable expectation of privacy in the suitcase to contest its search.

United States v. Austin, 66 F.3d 1115 (10th Cir. 1995). A person (the defendant) at an airport who entrusted his bag to a stranger, by asking him if he would watch the bag while he was gone for "a few minutes," did not retain a reasonable expectation of privacy in the bag. By leaving the bag in the stranger's possession and control, the defendant assumed the risk that the stranger would allow airport authorities access to the bag.

United States v. King, 55 F.3d 1193 (6th Cir. 1995). The defendant mailed some letters to his wife, who later gave them to another person. Law enforcement officers later seized the letters from the other person. The court ruled that the defendant had no standing to contest the seizure of the letters. If a letter is sent to another, the sender's expectation of privacy ordinarily terminates on delivery, even if the sender instructs the recipient to keep the letters private.

United States v. Kopp, 45 F.3d 1450 (10th Cir. 1995). The defendant was driving a pickup truck that was pulling a U-Haul trailer. The court noted that it must consider separately the defendant's reasonable expectation of privacy in the pickup truck and in the trailer. Although the defendant owned the pickup truck, he neither owned nor rented the trailer. Rather, a passenger in his pickup truck rented the trailer and carried the key to it. Based on these facts, the court ruled that the defendant did not have a reasonable expectation of privacy in the trailer and could not contest the legality of the officer's search of the trailer.

United States v. Poulsen, 41 F.3d 1330 (9th Cir. 1994). A person did not have a reasonable expectation of privacy in the contents of his storage locker when the manager of the self-service storage locker had seized the contents pursuant to a valid state law lien after the person failed to pay overdue rent.

United States v. Wellons, 32 F.3d 117 (4th Cir. 1994). The defendant did not have a reasonable expectation of privacy to contest the search of a rental car and the defendant's luggage inside the car when the rental agreement did not authorize the defendant to drive the car, even if the authorized driver gave the defendant permission to drive the car. *Compare with* United States v. Edwards, 242 F.3d 928 (2001) (although defendant did not have a reasonable expectation of privacy to contest search of rental car because he did not rent the car and was not an authorized driver, he did have a reasonable expectation of privacy in his luggage in the car's trunk to contest the search of the luggage).

United States v. Stallings, 28 F.3d 58 (8th Cir. 1994). The defendant did not have a reasonable expectation of privacy in a tote bag he left in an open field owned by another person. There was no indication of ownership on the bag.

United States v. Perea, 986 F.2d 633 (2d Cir. 1993). The bailee of a duffel bag had a reasonable expectation of privacy in the bag to contest its search by law enforcement officers.

United States v. Mohney, 949 F.2d 1397 (6th Cir. 1991). The documents seized during a search were regular corporate records, not records personally prepared by the defendant, and the records were not taken from the defendant's personal office, desk, or files. The defendant did not have a reasonable expectation of privacy to challenge the search when it was not directed at him personally. *See also* United States v. Williams, 976 F.2d 1148 (8th Cir. 1992) (defendant did not have reasonable expectation of privacy in company records). *But see* Mancusi v. DeForte, 392 U.S. 364 (1968) (defendant had reasonable expectation of privacy to contest search of union office he shared with others).

United States v. Sweeting, 933 F.2d 962 (11th Cir. 1991). The defendants denied to officers that they owned or resided at a particular house and maintained that they lived elsewhere. The fact that they had temporary access to the house (as did several family members) and had some personal effects there did not establish a reasonable expectation of privacy there when considered with their explicit disclaimer of ownership or other interest. *See also* United States v. Ibarra, 948 F.2d 903 (5th Cir. 1991) (defendants who denied any knowledge of a house and did not own, lease, or live in the house did not have reasonable expectation of privacy there).

United States v. Davis, 932 F.2d 752 (9th Cir. 1991). The defendant had a reasonable expectation of privacy in an apartment to contest the search of a safe there when he had previously lived there, paid a part of the rent, had a key to the apartment and was free to come and go, stored things there, and took the precaution of storing items in a locked safe to ensure privacy.

United States v. Rascon, 922 F.2d 584 (10th Cir. 1990). The defendant failed to satisfy his burden of showing that he had a reasonable expectation of privacy in the car he was driving when he said that a friend loaned the car to him, the car was registered in another person's name, and there was no evidence offered as to how the friend came to possess the car.

United States v. Arango, 912 F.2d 441 (10th Cir. 1990). The defendant's mere physical possession of the truck he was driving did not confer standing to contest a search of it. In this case, the defendant failed to show that he lawfully possessed the truck, and the court therefore ruled that he did not have a reasonable expectation of privacy in the truck.

United States v. Dunkley, 911 F.2d 522 (11th Cir. 1990). The driver of a car had authority to consent to a search of at least the passenger compartment when the spouse of the lessee of the car, who was a passenger, heard the driver give consent and did not object.

United States v. Reyes, 908 F.2d 281 (8th Cir. 1990). The defendant did not have a reasonable expectation of privacy in a rental locker at a bus terminal when he had rented it for 24 hours and the officer conducted a warrantless search of the locker several days later. Because the rent was overdue, the bus company had already plugged the lock, so the defendant would not have had access to it. It was irrelevant that the defendant was unable to renew the rental of the locker because he was confined as the result of a lawful arrest when his own illegal conduct caused his arrest.

United States v. Monie, 907 F.2d 793 (8th Cir. 1990). The defendant was hired to drive a rented car across the country, knowing that the trunk contained two locked suitcases to which he did not have the keys. When officers stopped the car and asked about the suitcases, the defendant stated that they were not his, the contents belonged to someone else, and he had no access to the contents. He did not attempt to protect the suitcases when the officers forced the zippers. The court ruled that the defendant did not have a reasonable expectation of privacy in the suitcases.

United States v. Kye Soo Lee, 898 F.2d 1034 (5th Cir. 1990). The driver and passenger of a rental truck, to whom the renter had given the keys and had entrusted the truck and its contents, had standing to contest the search of the truck's cargo hold. The renter of the truck, who was not present when the cargo hold of the truck was searched, had standing to contest the search of the cargo hold, because the renter had placed a padlock on it and had given the keys to the driver and passenger. *See also* United States v. Rusher, 966 F.2d 868 (4th Cir. 1992) (defendant-passenger had no standing to contest a search of the bed of a pickup truck, based on the facts in this case).

United States v. Clark, 891 F.2d 501 (4th Cir. 1989). The defendant denied three times that the suitcase officers retrieved from an airport carousel belonged to him, even though it matched the claim stub found in his shoulder bag. Under these circumstances, the defendant did not have a reasonable expectation of privacy in the suitcase.

United States v. Rush, 890 F.2d 45 (7th Cir. 1989). The defendant did not have a reasonable expectation of privacy in a suitcase he was carrying when he told officers, referring to an accomplice, "It's his. It's not mine." The accomplice consented to a search of the luggage and gave an officer the key to open it.

United States v. Judd, 889 F.2d 1410 (5th Cir. 1989). The defendants had no standing to contest a search of corporate records from the corporate bookkeeping office (they did not work in that office).

United States v. McBean, 861 F.2d 1570 (11th Cir. 1988). The defendant told an officer that two pieces of luggage in his car trunk were not his and he did not know what they contained. The court ruled that the defendant had no reasonable expectation of privacy in the luggage to challenge the officer's search of the luggage.

United States v. Paulino, 850 F.2d 93 (2d Cir. 1988). After an officer approached the car in which the defendant was a backseat passenger, the defendant hurriedly placed counterfeit money under the rubber floor mat at his feet. The officer lifted the mat and seized the money. The defendant asserted at the suppression hearing that the money was his. The court ruled that the defendant did not have a reasonable expectation of privacy in the area searched: the defendant had known the car owner for one week, did not have the right to exclude others from the car, and secreted the money in a hurried and furtive manner while the officer questioned the driver.

United States v. Roman, 849 F.2d 920 (5th Cir. 1988). Officers saw the defendant check two suitcases at the airport ticket counter in preparing to board a flight. When officers later approached the defendant, he told them that he had not checked any luggage and denied that he had any luggage on the plane. The court ruled that the defendant abandoned the suitcases and lacked standing to contest the officers' later search of the luggage and seizure of marijuana inside. *See also* United States v. Karman, 849 F.2d 928 (5th Cir. 1988); United States v. Gutierrez, 849 F.2d 940 (5th Cir. 1988).

United States v. One 1986 Mercedes Benz, 846 F.2d 2 (2d Cir. 1988). The defendant, who owned a car, often loaned the car to a friend without any restrictions on its use. Officers stopped the car when the friend was driving it and searched the ashtray in the rear of the car on the driver's side. The defendant did not have a reasonable expectation of privacy to contest the search, because the officers intruded into an area where the defendant's friend could have invited any stranger.

United States v. Blanco, 844 F.2d 344 (6th Cir. 1988). Codefendant Spinola had no reasonable expectation of privacy in his rented car when he did not retain possession of it—having given his only set of car keys to codefendant Fresnada—and had no access to the car thereafter. Codefendant Fresnada had a reasonable expectation of privacy in the rented car, including its door panels in which he stored cocaine. *See also* United States v. Boruff, 909 F.2d 111 (5th Cir. 1990) (defendant had no standing to contest search of the rental car he was driving when his girlfriend had rented it and the rental agreement's express terms provided that only she could operate it).

United States v. Miller, 821 F.2d 546 (11th Cir. 1987). The defendant, who had permission from a friend to use his car, had a legitimate expectation of privacy in the car to challenge a search of the car.

United States v. Dotson, 817 F.2d 1127, *opinion revised*, 821 F.2d 1034 (5th Cir. 1987). The defendant, a lawful possessor of a car even though not its owner, loaned his car to a friend so that he could wash and clean it. The defendant did not lose his reasonable expectation of privacy in his car and thus had standing to challenge a search of the car's trunk.

United States v. McKennon, 814 F.2d 1539 (11th Cir. 1987). The defendant had no reasonable expectation of privacy in a carry-on bag in which he placed some personal items and cocaine. He had transferred possession of the bag to an accomplice, refused to publicly associate with her on her journey, and instructed her that he would go to Kansas City without her if she was detained.

Standing to Contest Fifth Amendment Violations

State v. Weakley, 176 N.C. App. 642 (2006). The defendant argued on appeal that the State was improperly permitted to cross-examine a defense witness concerning her failure to give a statement to a law enforcement officer because the cross-examination violated the witness's Fifth Amendment rights. The court ruled, relying on *State v. Lipford*, 81 N.C. App. 464 (1986), and other cases, that the defendant had no standing to assert the witness's constitutional right against self-incrimination.

State v. Lipford, 81 N.C. App. 464 (1986). The defendant had no standing to contest the admission of her codefendant's statement on the ground that it had been obtained in violation of the codefendant's Fifth Amendment rights.

General Exclusionary Rules
Scope of Fourth Amendment Exclusionary Rule

Davis v. United States, 564 U.S. 229 (2011). The court ruled that the exclusionary rule does not apply when officers conduct a search in compliance with binding precedent that is later overruled. Officers conducted a routine traffic stop that eventually resulted in the arrests of the driver for driving while intoxicated and the passenger (Davis) for giving a false name to the officers. The officers handcuffed both the driver and Davis and placed them in the back of separate patrol cars. The officers then searched the vehicle's interior and found a revolver inside Davis's jacket pocket. The search was conducted in reliance on then existing case law in the officers' jurisdiction that had interpreted *New York v. Belton*, 453 U.S. 454 (1981), to authorize vehicle searches incident to arrests of recent occupants, regardless of whether the arrestee was within reaching distance of the vehicle at the time of the search. Davis was indicted on a weapons charge and unsuccessfully moved to suppress the revolver from being admitted at his trial. He was convicted, and while his case was on appeal, the United States Supreme Court in *Arizona v. Gant*, 556 U.S. 332 (2009), adopted a new, two-part rule under which a vehicle search incident to a recent occupant's arrest is constitutional (1) if the arrestee is within reaching distance of the vehicle during the search or (2) if officers have reason to believe that the vehicle contains evidence relevant to the crime of arrest. Under the *Gant* ruling, which was retroactively applicable to the vehicle search resulting in the discovery of Davis's revolver, the search violated the Fourth Amendment. Analyzing whether to apply the exclusionary rule to the search at issue, the Court determined that the "acknowledged absence of police culpability dooms Davis's claim." The Court stated: "Because suppression would do nothing to deter police misconduct in these circumstances, and because it would come at a high cost to both the truth and the public safety, we hold that searches conducted in objectively reasonable reliance on binding appellate precedent are not subject to the exclusionary rule." The Court relied on its prior exclusionary rule cases, including *Herring v. United States*, 555 U.S. 135 (2009).

Herring v. United States, 555 U.S. 135 (2009). An officer arrested the defendant based on an outstanding arrest warrant listed in a sheriff's computer database in a neighboring county. A search incident to arrest discovered drugs and a gun, which formed the basis for criminal charges. However, there was a mistake about the arrest warrant. A court had recalled the arrest warrant, but a law enforcement official had negligently failed to record that fact, although the official did not act recklessly or deliberately in doing so. For the purpose of deciding this case, the Court accepted the parties' assumption that a Fourth Amendment violation had occurred. The Court reviewed its prior case law on the Fourth Amendment's exclusionary rule and recast it in the context of this case as follows: (1) The exclusionary rule is not an individual right and applies only when it results in appreciable deterrence. The benefits of deterrence must outweigh the costs. (2) The extent to which the exclusionary rule is justified by deterrence principles varies with the culpability of law enforcement conduct. The abuses that gave rise to the exclusionary rule featured intentional conduct that was patently unconstitutional. An error that arises from nonrecurring and attenuated negligence is thus far removed from the core concerns that led the Court to initially adopt the rule. And since *United States v. Leon*, 468 U.S. 897 (1984), the Court has never applied the rule to exclude evidence obtained in violation of the Fourth Amendment when law enforcement conduct was no more intentional or culpable than involved in this case. (3) To trigger the exclusionary rule, law enforcement conduct must be sufficiently deliberate that exclusion can meaningfully deter it and sufficiently culpable that such deterrence is worth the price paid by the criminal justice system. The rule serves to deter deliberate, reckless, or grossly negligent conduct or, in some circumstances, recurring or systemic negligence. The error in this case did not rise to that level. The pertinent analysis of deterrence and culpability is an objective analysis, not an inquiry into the subjective awareness of law enforcement officers. (4) The Court stated that it did not suggest that all recordkeeping errors by law enforcement are immune from the exclusionary rule. If law enforcement has been reckless in maintaining a warrant system or has knowingly made false entries to lay the groundwork for future false arrests, exclusion would certainly be justified should such misconduct cause a Fourth Amendment violation. But there was no evidence in this case that errors in the computer database were routine or widespread. (5) The Court, in light of its repeated prior rulings that the deterrent effect of suppression must be substantial and must outweigh any harm to the justice system, concluded that when law enforcement mistakes are the result of negligence (rather than systemic error or reckless disregard of constitutional requirements), as occurred in this case, any marginal deterrence does not require application of the exclusionary rule.

Direct Evidence

Mapp v. Ohio, 367 U.S. 643 (1961). The Court ruled that evidence obtained in violation of the Fourth Amendment is inadmissible in state court, as it is in federal court. Evidence obtained directly as a result of an officer's unconstitutional search of a home is inadmissible.

Derivative Evidence: Fruit of the Poisonous Tree

United States v. Ceccolini, 435 U.S. 268 (1978). The connection between the illegal search in this case and the discovery of a witness who testified at trial against the defendant was so attenuated as to dissipate the taint of the illegal search. Therefore, the testimony of the witness was admissible. *See also* United States v. Terzado-Madruga, 897 F.2d 1099 (11th Cir. 1990) (no causal connection shown between illegal interrogation of defendant and witness's willingness to testify); United States v. McKinnon, 92 F.3d 244 (4th Cir. 1996) (sufficient attenuation of defendant's mention of his brother after defendant was illegally arrested so that brother's testimony for government at defendant's trial was admissible).

Utah v. Strieff, 136 S. Ct. 2056 (2016). An anonymous tip to the police department reported "narcotics activity" at a particular residence. An officer investigated and saw visitors who left a few minutes after arriving at the house. These visits were sufficiently frequent to raise his suspicion that the occupants were dealing drugs. One visitor was the defendant. After observing the defendant leave the house and walk toward a nearby store, the officer detained the defendant and asked for his identification. The defendant complied, and the officer relayed the defendant's information to a police dispatcher, who reported that the defendant had an outstanding arrest warrant for a traffic violation. The officer then arrested

the defendant pursuant to the warrant. When a search incident to arrest revealed methamphetamine and drug paraphernalia, the defendant was charged.

The defendant unsuccessfully moved to suppress, arguing that the evidence was inadmissible because it was derived from an unlawful investigatory stop, which the State had conceded lacked reasonable suspicion. He was convicted and appealed. The Utah Supreme Court ruled that the evidence was inadmissible.

The United States Supreme Court reversed. The Court noted that it has recognized several exceptions to the exclusionary rule, three of which involve the causal relationship between the unconstitutional act and the discovery of evidence: the independent source doctrine, the inevitable discovery doctrine, and—at issue here—the attenuation doctrine. Under the latter doctrine, "Evidence is admissible when the connection between unconstitutional police conduct and the evidence is remote or has been interrupted by some intervening circumstance, so that the interest protected by the constitutional guarantee that has been violated would not be served by suppression of the evidence obtained." Turning to the application of the attenuation doctrine, the Court first held that the doctrine applies where—as here—the intervening circumstance that the State relies on is the discovery of a valid, preexisting, and untainted arrest warrant. It then concluded that the discovery of a valid arrest warrant was a sufficient intervening event to break the causal chain between the unlawful stop and the discovery of drug-related evidence on the defendant's person. In this respect, the Court applied the three factors articulated in *Brown v. Illinois*, 422 U.S. 590 (1975): the temporal proximity between the unconstitutional conduct and the discovery of evidence to determine how closely the discovery of evidence followed the unconstitutional search, the presence of intervening circumstances, and the purpose and flagrancy of the official misconduct. The Court stated:

> Applying these factors, we hold that the evidence discovered . . . was admissible because the unlawful stop was sufficiently attenuated by the preexisting arrest warrant. Although the illegal stop was close in time to [the] arrest, that consideration is outweighed by two factors supporting the State. The outstanding arrest warrant . . . is a critical intervening circumstance that is wholly independent of the illegal stop. The discovery

of that warrant broke the causal chain between the unconstitutional stop and the discovery of evidence by compelling [the] Officer . . . to arrest [the defendant]. And, it is especially significant that there is no evidence that [the] Officer['s] . . . illegal stop reflected flagrantly unlawful police misconduct.

Wong Sun v. United States, 371 U.S. 471 (1963). (1) Defendant Toy's statement made immediately after his unconstitutional arrest was inadmissible; his statement was not an act of free will so as to purge the primary taint of the arrest. (2) Defendant Toy's statement gave officers knowledge of heroin in defendant Yee's house; they went there and seized the heroin. The Court stated that the question is whether, considering the illegality in obtaining Toy's statement, the heroin was obtained by exploiting that illegality or by means sufficiently distinguishable to purge its taint. The Court noted that officers did not learn of the heroin from an independent source (that is, other than from Toy), nor was their discovery of the heroin so attenuated from the illegality as to dissipate its taint (because the officers went directly to Yee's house after hearing Toy's statement). Therefore, the exclusionary rule barred the use of the discovery of heroin at Toy's trial. (3) Defendant Wong Sun was arrested without probable cause, was released after a lawful arraignment, and returned several days later to make a voluntary statement. The court ruled that the connection between the illegal arrest and the statement had become so attenuated that the taint of the illegal arrest had been dissipated. Therefore, Wong Sun's statement was admissible against him.

Many applications of the derivative evidence rule are set out in this case. For a further discussion of *Wong Sun* in later Supreme Court cases, see *Segura v. United States*, 468 U.S. 796 (1984), and *Nix v. Williams*, 467 U.S. 431 (1984).

State v. Guevara, 349 N.C. 243 (1998). The defendant was convicted of the first-degree murder of Officer A and the felonious assault of Officer B. Officers A and B went to the defendant's home with information that there were outstanding felony arrest warrants for him. They saw the defendant, accompanied by a young boy, standing outside his mobile home's back door. Although he denied being the person who was the subject of the arrest warrants, the officers believed otherwise. After confirmation from a dispatcher that the defendant was still wanted, Officer B stated that they would arrest him. The defendant, hav-

ing heard Officer B's words, retreated into his home and slammed the door. Officer A pushed the door open and entered the home, where he was shot and killed by the defendant. Officer B was shot and seriously injured by the defendant while outside the mobile home. The court, relying on *State v. Miller*, 282 N.C. 633 (1973), ruled that even if Officer A violated the Fourth Amendment in entering the defendant's home to arrest him, the exclusionary rule did not bar the testimony of Officer B about the killing of Officer A.

State v. Friend, 237 N.C. App. 490 (2014). In an assault on an officer case, the court rejected the defendant's argument that evidence of his two assaults on law enforcement officers should be excluded as fruits of the poisonous tree because his initial arrest for resisting an officer was unlawful. The doctrine does not exclude evidence of attacks on police officers when those attacks occur while the officers are engaging in conduct that violates a defendant's Fourth Amendment rights; "[a]pplication of the exclusionary rule in such fashion would in effect give the victims of illegal searches a license to assault and murder the officers involved[.]" Thus, the court held that even if the initial stop and arrest violated the defendant's Fourth Amendment rights, evidence of his subsequent assaults on officers were not "fruits" under the relevant doctrine.

State v. Barron, 202 N.C. App. 686 (2010). The defendant was convicted of identity theft. Upon arrest, the defendant falsely gave his brother's name and birth date as his and falsely confirmed in response to an officer's question the last four digits of the defendant's Social Security number (which were his brother's). The court ruled that the defendant's false confirmation of the last four digits of his Social Security number was sufficient evidence to convict him of identity theft. It was "identifying information" under G.S. 14-113.20(b)(1). The court rejected the defendant's argument that the trial court erred in denying his motion to suppress his post-arrest statements concerning his false name, date of birth, and Social Security number. The court ruled, even assuming that the defendant was arrested without probable cause under the Fourth Amendment, that the exclusionary rule did not bar evidence of the defendant's false statements that supported his identity theft conviction. Relying on *State v. Miller*, 282 N.C. 633 (1973), and *In re J.L.B.M.*, 176 N.C. App. 613 (2006), the court stated that the exclusionary rule does not exclude evidence of crimes committed after an illegal search or seizure. The false statements were not fruits of the poisonous tree.

State v. Graves, 135 N.C. App. 216 (1999). The court noted that statements obtained as a result of an illegal search must be suppressed. However, the officer in this case obtained statements from the defendant without mentioning his discovery of the illegal drugs and drug paraphernalia (pursuant to an illegal search). Thus, the defendant's statements that must be suppressed are only those statements obtained after the officer told the defendant about what he had found.

The Independent Source Exception
UNITED STATES SUPREME COURT

Murray v. United States, 487 U.S. 533 (1988). (This was a four-Justice opinion, but it clearly states existing constitutional law.) After surveillance of a warehouse, officers lawfully seized the vehicles as they left the warehouse and discovered marijuana in them. The officers then unlawfully entered the warehouse without a warrant, saw in plain view numerous burlap-wrapped bales, and left—without handling the bales—to obtain a search warrant. In applying for the search warrant, the officers did not mention their unlawful entry. After the search warrant was issued, the officers returned to the warehouse and seized the bales of marijuana and other evidence.

The Court ruled that the bales properly could be admitted at trial under the independent source exception to the Fourth Amendment exclusionary rule (but the Court remanded for additional fact-finding by the trial court). This exception permits the introduction of evidence that was initially discovered during or as a result of an unlawful search but was later obtained independently by lawful conduct that was untainted by the initial illegality. The exception applies to both intangible evidence (in this case, knowledge of the bales of marijuana) and tangible evidence (in this case, the bales of marijuana) discovered during the initial unlawful search. If the later acquisition of evidence is not the result of the earlier entry, the independent source exception allows the admission of both tangible and intangible evidence. The Court remanded this case to the trial court so that it could determine (1) whether the officers' decision to obtain a search warrant was prompted by what they had seen during the initial unlawful entry and (2) whether information obtained during the unlawful entry was presented to the magistrate or affected his decision to issue the warrant. If the answer to both inquiries is no, then the

evidence found pursuant to the search warrant is admissible under the independent source exception. *See also* United States v. Salas, 879 F.2d 530 (9th Cir. 1989) (officers had probable cause for search warrant for motel room before their illegal entry; although tainted information from their illegal entry was presented to the magistrate, the magistrate's decision to issue search warrant was not affected by that information); United States v. Herrold, 962 F.2d 1131 (3d Cir. 1992) (similar ruling); United States v. Terzado-Madruga, 897 F.2d 1099 (11th Cir. 1990) (identity of witness was known before illegal interrogation of defendant and thus was derived from a lawful source independent of officer's misconduct); United States v. Mithun, 933 F.2d 631 (8th Cir. 1991) (officer's decision to seek search warrant was not prompted by alleged illegal search, and information obtained during alleged illegal search was not presented to magistrate who issued search warrant); United States v. Restrepo, 966 F.2d 964 (5th Cir. 1992) (*Murray v. United States* did not require inquiry in this case as to whether tainted information affected magistrate's decision to issue search warrant).

Segura v. United States, 468 U.S. 796 (1984). Drug agents entered an apartment and secured it pending the issuance of a search warrant. The warrant was eventually issued, and evidence was seized. Assuming without deciding that the drug agents illegally entered the apartment, the Court ruled that the evidence later seized pursuant to the search warrant was admissible: the evidence was not a fruit of the illegal entry, because all of the information that supported the issuance of the search warrant was known by the officers before they entered the apartment. That is, justification for the search with the search warrant came from a source independent of the illegal entry. See the other independent source cases cited and discussed in this opinion.

NORTH CAROLINA SUPREME COURT

In re Stedman, 305 N.C. 92 (1982). Fingerprints were taken unlawfully from a juvenile because he had been indicted and arrested instead of first being tried in juvenile court (he was under 16 years old when the offense was committed). After juvenile petitions were then brought, a judge issued a nontestimonial identification order under G.S. 7A-598 (now, G.S. 7B-2105) to take the juvenile's fingerprints. The court ruled that the fingerprint evidence obtained under G.S. 7A-598 was admissible under the independent source exception, because the order was issued based on information obtained independently of, and not tainted by, the evidence of the unlawful fingerprinting. *See also* State v. Phifer, 297 N.C. 216 (1979) (evidence from glove compartment was obtained lawfully because officers had probable cause to search the vehicle, and thus evidence was not obtained through illegal inventory search); State v. Maness, 321 N.C. 454 (1988) (testimony of witnesses was properly admitted because it was not related to illegal seizure of property); State v. Sanders, 327 N.C. 319 (1990) (evidence that was obtained independently of invalid search supported probable cause to arrest).

NORTH CAROLINA COURT OF APPEALS

State v. Lemonds, 160 N.C. App. 172 (2003). During the course of an investigation into the defendant's drug activities, law enforcement officers conducted two thermal imaging scans of the defendant's residence that revealed a heat signature consistent with a marijuana growing operation. This information was included in the affidavit for a search warrant to search the residence. After the execution of the search warrant, the United States Supreme Court in *Kyllo v. United States*, 533 U.S. 27 (2001), ruled that the warrantless use of a thermal imager to detect heat emanating from a private home violated the Fourth Amendment. The court ruled that even without the thermal imaging results, there was sufficient information in the search warrant's affidavit to support a finding of probable cause to search the residence, including police surveillance, an anonymous tip, and electric bills showing a dramatic increase in electricity usage. (See the 14 factors recited by the court in its opinion.)

State v. Robinson, 148 N.C. App. 422 (2002). A law enforcement officer received anonymous information that the defendant was growing marijuana in his house. About 15 months earlier, an officer had searched the defendant's residence and found marijuana. An officer then spoke with the defendant's probation officer, who said that the defendant was on probation from the earlier drug offense that included a condition consenting to warrantless searches of his person and residence. The probation officer went to the defendant's house, where he attempted to enforce the warrantless search condition. The defendant refused to allow the search, and the probation officer arrested him. The law enforcement officers were informed of the defendant's arrest and went to the house. No one answered the door, although the officers had learned from the probation officer that the defendant's girlfriend was there. While the other officers were

knocking on the door, one of the officers, who was on the driveway, smelled a strong odor of marijuana emanating from the house and saw movement in the house. The officers left. They then telephoned the defendant's girlfriend, who refused to consent to a search of the house. They returned to the house, knocked on the door, received no answer, and then broke into the house. They conducted a security sweep and restrained the girlfriend. One officer obtained a search warrant, and they then searched the house, finding marijuana.

The court ruled that (1) the independent source doctrine (Segura v. United States, 468 U.S. 796 (1984); State v. Wallace, 111 N.C. App. 581 (1993)) supported the seizure of the marijuana with a search warrant even if it is assumed that the officers had previously made an illegal warrantless entry of the house—no evidence from the assumed illegal entry was used in the search warrant, and (2) all the information described above supplied probable cause to support the search warrant.

State v. Treece, 129 N.C. App. 93 (1998). An officer entered a house without a warrant to secure it while a search warrant was obtained. Illegal drugs were later seized with a search warrant. The court noted that the affidavit for the search warrant did not contain any information gained from the officer's entry. Relying on *Segura v. United States*, 468 U.S. 796 (1984), the court ruled that the information supplying probable cause for the search warrant was obtained independently from any possible illegal entry, and thus the illegal drugs were properly seized.

State v. McLean, 120 N.C. App. 838 (1995). Exterminators and apartment managers discovered marijuana in an apartment as a result of the exterminating work performed there. The apartment managers then contacted a local law enforcement agency. An officer entered the apartment with the managers and saw the marijuana. The officer, without seizing any evidence, left the apartment to await a detective. The detective gathered information from the exterminators, the apartment managers, and the law enforcement officer. He provided this information in an affidavit for a search warrant, obtained a search warrant, searched the apartment, and seized the marijuana. The court ruled, assuming without deciding that the officer's entry with the managers was unconstitutional, that the seizure of the marijuana should not be suppressed, based on the independent source exception to the exclusionary rule; see Murray v. United States, 487 U.S. 533 (1988). [Author's note: The entry, apparently without the tenant's consent or exigent circumstances, would have been unconstitutional.] There was sufficient probable cause, independent of the illegal entry by the officer and his corroborative observations of the marijuana, to support the search warrant. The finding of probable cause was unconnected with the illegal entry. The court also noted that the detective who applied for the search warrant did not participate in the illegal entry.

State v. Waterfield, 117 N.C. App. 295 (1994). On May 13, 1993, officers went to the defendant's residence without a search warrant. The defendant refused to consent to a search of his residence. One officer told the defendant that he would stay with the defendant while the other officers obtained a search warrant. When the officers insisted that the defendant remain in their view at all times, the defendant shut and locked the door. One officer kicked the door down and forced the defendant to sit in a chair. About one and one-half hours later, officers returned with a search warrant and conducted a search.

No information obtained during the initial entry was used in the affidavit for the search warrant. The affidavit stated that on April 1, 1993, three people gave an officer about 3 grams of marijuana that they said the defendant had given them. They stated that the defendant had shown them marijuana kept in a padlocked cabinet in his bedroom at his residence. On April 2, 1993, a confidential informant told an officer that he had seen marijuana in the defendant's residence and stated that the defendant kept the marijuana in a padlocked cabinet in his bedroom. On April 5, 1993, officers visited the defendant's residence and confirmed that he lived there. On May 12, 1993, another confidential informant reported to an officer that within the last 24 hours the informant had seen about a half pound of marijuana at the defendant's residence and had seen the defendant sell marijuana from his home; the informant also stated that the defendant kept marijuana in a padlocked cabinet in his bedroom.

The court ruled that the affidavit supplied probable cause to support the search warrant. Although the affidavit did not mention the reliability of the officers' sources of information, it did provide information about the presence and sale of marijuana at the defendant's residence within 24 hours of the warrant application. It also provided information about the location and manner of the defendant's storage of the marijuana that matched information supplied by other sources. Relying on *Segura v. United States*, 468 U.S. 796 (1984), the court also ruled that the search pursuant to the search warrant was valid because the information used to obtain the search warrant was obtained entirely independent of the allegedly illegal initial entry to secure the residence.

State v. Wallace, 111 N.C. App. 581 (1993). Officers received information that marijuana was being grown in the basement of a residence. However, the officers were unable to corroborate the informant's information. Therefore, they went to the residence to investigate. After the officers knocked on the door, Jolly came out and closed the door behind him. The officers told him why they were there and asked him if there were others in the residence. Jolly told the officers that one of his roommates was asleep inside. The officers then asked for consent to search the residence. Before Jolly could answer, Wallace came out of the residence. The officers then asked for consent to search, which Wallace and Jolly denied. The court's opinion stated that "Jolly then stated that 'there might be some drug paraphernalia and marijuana seeds in the house,' and that he would not consent to a search until he had time to get rid of the contraband." After the officers were denied consent to search, they heard footsteps in the residence and a door shut on the inside. The officers asked Wallace and Jolly who was in the residence, and they said they did not know because they had just arrived. The officers then went inside to execute a protective sweep before leaving the residence to obtain a search warrant. The officers saw what appeared to be marijuana plants while inside. The defendants were detained in the residence while other officers obtained a search warrant, which included information about their observation of marijuana in the house.

The court ruled: (1) Uncorroborated information initially given to the officers was insufficient to establish probable cause to search the residence. (2) The officers did not violate the defendants' rights by going to the residence to investigate the information they had received. (3) Probable cause existed to search the residence when Jolly made the statement quoted above. (4) The officers did not have exigent circumstances to enter the residence without a search warrant. The court stated that the "record is devoid of any evidence that the officers entered the residence with a reasonably objective belief that evidence was about to be removed or destroyed." The court noted that the only purpose of officers' entry into the residence was to conduct a protective sweep until a search warrant could be obtained, and the officers did not believe they were in danger at any time. (5) The State could not justify the search of the residence under the independent source exception to the exclusionary rule, *Murray v. United States*, 487 U.S. 533 (1988), and *Segura v. United States*, 468 U.S. 796 (1984). In this case, the search warrant was prompted by what the officers saw in their unlawful entry, and the information obtained during the illegal entry was presented to the magistrate and affected the decision to issue the search warrant.

FEDERAL APPELLATE COURTS

United States v. Grosenheider, 200 F.3d 321 (8th Cir. 2000). Even if an officer conducted an illegal search in viewing child pornography on the defendant's computer, the child pornography evidence was nonetheless admissible under both independent source and inevitable discovery exceptions. The customs agent, who was contacted by the officer, obtained a search warrant based solely on statements made by a computer repairman—who had seen the child pornography before the officer's allegedly illegal search. The seizure of the computer by the customs agent was thus properly based on a valid search warrant. *See also* United States v. Stabile, 633 F.3d 219 (3d Cir. 2011) (similar ruling involving child pornography).

United States v. Johnson, 994 F.2d 980 (2d Cir. 1993). Officers arrested the defendant for felonious assaults and properly seized audiocassette tapes in his pockets. Six months later, the officers listened to the tapes without obtaining a search warrant. The defendant filed a motion to suppress the contents of the tapes, and a judge expressed concern that the officers' warrantless listening to the tapes could not be justified as a search incident to arrest. The government then applied for a search warrant to listen to the tapes again. The court ruled that the affidavit for the search warrant revealed probable cause independent of the information learned from listening to the tapes. Two tapes were labeled with the names of witnesses who had heard that the defendant had taped conversations due to his problems with one of the assault victims. The court also ruled that the officers would have applied for a search warrant had they not listened to the tapes beforehand. Thus, the evidence from the tapes was properly admitted under the independent source exception.

United States v. Miller, 822 F.2d 828 (9th Cir. 1987). A search warrant was supported by probable cause, based on independently obtained information separate from the information that had been obtained by an illegal search. *See also* United States v. Curtis, 931 F.2d 1011 (4th Cir. 1991) (search warrant was based solely on information known by officers before they allegedly made improper warrantless entry).

The Inevitable Discovery Exception
UNITED STATES SUPREME COURT

Nix v. Williams, 467 U.S. 431 (1984). Although a defendant's statements are inadmissible at trial when they are obtained in violation of the defendant's Sixth Amendment rights, other evidence is admissible if the State proves by a preponderance of evidence that the other evidence would have been inevitably discovered by lawful means without using the defendant's illegally obtained statements. The Court ruled in this case that the State satisfied its burden of proving that the victim's body would have been discovered by a searching party even if the defendant's illegally obtained statements had not been used to find it. The Court rejected the proposed requirement that, as part of the inevitable discovery rule, the State must prove that the officer committed the Sixth Amendment violation in a good faith belief that he was acting lawfully. [Author's note: The inevitable discovery rule also may apply—under appropriate circumstances—to other constitutional violations, including Fourth Amendment violations. *See* United States v. Souza, 223 F.3d 1197 (10th Cir. 2000); United States v. Merriweather, 777 F.2d 503 (9th Cir. 1985); United States v. Andrade, 784 F.2d 1431 (9th Cir. 1986); United States v. McConnell, 903 F.2d 566 (8th Cir. 1990) (although search of briefcase was not justified as a search incident to arrest, contents would have been inevitably discovered by inventory search).]

NORTH CAROLINA SUPREME COURT

State v. Garner, 331 N.C. 491 (1992). After the arrest of the defendant for murder and the recovery of a .25 caliber Beretta pistol (the alleged murder weapon), officers obtained a search warrant to search the defendant's residence and seized (1) a Beretta box showing model 950BS, serial number BR88945V from Jim's Pawn Shop; (2) a receipt from Jim's Pawn Shop showing a purchase on December 20, 1986, of a Beretta PPGGG Model 950BS with the same serial number; and (3) five .25 caliber bullets. As a result of the seizure of this evidence, officers went to Jim's Pawn Shop and obtained (1) a copy of the Beretta pistol purchase receipt that they had seized under the search warrant and (2) the defendant's ATF (federal Alcohol, Tobacco, and Firearms Bureau) application to purchase the Beretta weapon.

The trial judge ruled that the search warrant was invalid because probable cause did not exist to search the residence; therefore, the evidence found at the residence was inadmissible at trial. However, the judge ruled that the evidence obtained from Jim's Pawn Shop was admissible under the inevitable discovery exception to the Fourth Amendment's exclusionary rule: the judge found by a preponderance of evidence that (1) it is routine procedure in firearms cases to check PIN (Police Information Network) and ATF documents and (2) "but for" the fact that the information was readily ascertainable by the pawn receipt officers found in the illegal search of the defendant's home with the invalid search warrant, the officers would have conducted a routine check and discovered at Jim's Pawn Shop by lawful means the duplicate Beretta pistol purchase receipt and the defendant's ATF application to purchase the weapon.

The court adopted under the state constitution the inevitable discovery exception to the Fourth Amendment's exclusionary rule, which was recognized in *Nix v. Williams*, 467 U.S. 431 (1984). The court rejected the defendant's contention that the State always must show that an independent investigation (that would have inevitably discovered the evidence by lawful means) must have been ongoing when the illegality occurred that resulted in the discovery of the evidence. Instead, the court adopted a case-by-case approach, "recognizing that the particular facts of any given case will determine whether, absent other means, proof of an ongoing, independent investigation is necessary to show inevitability." The court also ruled that (1) the State's standard of proof in proving the inevitable discovery is preponderance of evidence, rejecting the clear and convincing evidence standard; (2) the officer's bad faith in conducting the illegal search was irrelevant in applying the inevitable discovery exception; and (3) the court's suppression of the primary evidence (evidence seized under the invalid search warrant) was not necessary in applying the inevitable discovery exception. The court reviewed the evidence in this case and affirmed the trial judge's ruling that the inevitable discovery exception applied to admit the evidence found at Jim's Pawn Shop.

The court rejected the defendant's contention that the court should not recognize the inevitable discovery exception under Article I, Section 20, of the North Carolina Constitution. The court stated: "While this Court has held that Article I, Section 20 of our Constitution, like the Fourth Amendment to the United States Constitution, prohibits unreasonable searches and seizures, *e.g.*, State v. Arrington, 311 N.C. 633, 319 S.E.2d 254; State v. Ellington, 284 N.C. 198, 200 S.E.2d 177 (1973), and requires the exclusion of evidence obtained by unreasonable search and seizure, *e.g.*, State v. Carter, 322 N.C. 709, 370 S.E.2d 553, there is nothing to indicate anywhere in the text of Article I, Section 20 any enlargement or expansion of rights beyond those afforded in the Fourth Amendment as applied to the states by the Fourteenth Amendment." The court later stated: "We therefore hold the defendant's contention that Article I, Section 20 of our Constitution should be read as an extension of rights beyond those afforded in the Fourth Amendment is misplaced." [Author's note: The court's general statements indicate that in other cases it may not interpret this constitutional section more broadly than the Fourth Amendment in favor of a defendant's rights. It appears that *Garner* may undermine the court's ruling in *State v. Carter*, 322 N.C. 709 (1988), which had rejected under this constitutional section the good faith exception to the exclusionary rule under the Fourth Amendment, as set out in *United States v. Leon*, 468 U.S. 897 (1984), and *Massachusetts v. Sheppard*, 468 U.S. 981 (1984). *See also* State v. Banner, 207 N.C. App. 729 n.7 (2010) (noting possible conflict between *Carter* and *Garner*).]

State v. Pope, 333 N.C. 106 (1992). Although the defendant's admissions, obtained in violation of *Arizona v. Roberson*, 486 U.S. 675 (1988), led to the discovery of the handgun used in a murder, the court ruled that the handgun and the tests performed on it were admissible under the inevitable discovery exception; *see* State v. Garner, 331 N.C. 491 (1992). Although the handgun was found as a result of the unlawful interrogation, the following facts show that the handgun would have been inevitably discovered by lawful means. The handgun was found under the seat of a 1953 model Ford truck owned by Alan Estridge. Estridge later sold the truck, and he testified at the suppression hearing that when he sells something, he looks in "every crack and crevice of the truck—car or anything—to make sure there's nothing valuable in there or anything left, or even change." He also testified that if he had found a handgun, he would have delivered it to the detectives.

NORTH CAROLINA COURT OF APPEALS

State v. Wells, 225 N.C. App. 487 (2013). In a case in which the defendant was convicted of soliciting a child by computer and attempted indecent liberties on a child, the court of appeals ruled that the trial court erred by concluding that the defendant's laptop would have been inevitably discovered. The trial court ordered suppressed statements that the defendant made to officers during questioning. In those statements, the defendant told officers that he owned a laptop that was located on his bed at the fire station. The trial court denied the defendant's motion to suppress evidence retrieved from his laptop, concluding that it would have been inevitably discovered. The court of appeals found that the State had not presented any evidence—from the investigating officers or anyone else—supporting this conclusion.

State v. Harris, 157 N.C. App. 647 (2003). An officer was executing a search warrant for drugs, which named to be searched a dwelling and the person of the defendant. The officer obtained keys to a truck after the officer asked the defendant if he had any keys and the defendant acknowledged that he had keys in his pocket. The keys were then used to open a locked toolbox on the side of the truck that contained cocaine. The court ruled that the inevitable discovery doctrine supported the officer's seizure of the keys from the defendant's pocket and cocaine from the truck even if the officer's knowledge of the keys resulted from a statement obtained through a *Miranda* violation. Because the search warrant authorized the search of the person of the defendant, the officer would have inevitably located the keys even without the defendant's acknowledgment that the keys were in his pocket

State v. Vick, 130 N.C. App. 207 (1998). Officers entered an apartment to execute a search warrant to seize cocaine. The defendant's statement to the officers during the execution of the search warrant that cocaine was in a refrigerator was obtained in violation of his *Miranda* rights and thus was inadmissible. However, the cocaine seized in the refrigerator was admissible under the inevitable discovery doctrine (*see* State v. Garner, 331 N.C. 491 (1992)) because the officers would have inevitably found it during the execution of the search warrant. The court affirmed the trial judge's ruling. [Author's note: Physical evidence seized as a result of a *Miranda* violation is admissible, State v. May, 334 N.C. 609 (1993), so the court's analysis of the inevitable discovery rule was unnecessary.]

FEDERAL APPELLATE COURTS

United States v. Grosenheider, 200 F.3d 321 (8th Cir. 2000). Even if an officer conducted an illegal search in viewing child pornography on the defendant's computer, evidence was nonetheless admissible under both independent source and inevitable discovery exceptions. The customs agent, who was contacted by the officer, obtained a search warrant based solely on statements made by the computer repairman—who had seen child pornography before the officer's allegedly illegal search. The seizure of the computer by the customs agent was thus properly based on a valid search warrant. *See also* United States v. Stabile, 633 F.3d 219 (3d Cir. 2011) (similar ruling involving child pornography).

United States v. Allen, 159 F.3d 832 (4th Cir. 1998). The inevitable discovery exception did not apply, because there was no evidence that an officer would have used a drug dog to sniff a bag if the bag had not been illegally searched. In addition, there was no evidence that the officer would have obtained a search warrant absent the illegal search.

United States v. Hammons, 152 F.3d 1025 (8th Cir. 1998). Cocaine inside an envelope found during a valid search of the defendant's garment bag was admissible despite the officer's illegally opening the bag after obtaining the defendant's involuntary consent to do so. The officer would have summoned a drug canine unit if the defendant had not consented to the search of the garment bag, as he had informed the defendant he would do. The dog would have alerted to the presence of drugs, and the drugs would have been inevitably discovered through lawful means.

United States v. Procopio, 88 F.3d 21 (1st Cir. 1996). A local police department's search of a briefcase exceeded the scope of its inventory search policy and was unconstitutional under the Fourth Amendment. However, the court ruled, based on the facts in this case, that the contents of the briefcase would have been inevitably discovered by federal law enforcement officers. Local officers would have alerted federal officers to the briefcase because the local officers knew of a pending federal robbery investigation of the defendant, and the federal officers would have obtained a search warrant to search it.

United States v. Eylicio-Montoya, 70 F.3d 1158 (10th Cir. 1993). An officer lawfully stopped a vehicle to investigate marijuana trafficking but then unlawfully arrested the defendant-passenger. The officer then saw burlap bags in the vehicle, which gave him probable cause to search the vehicle for marijuana. The court ruled that the marijuana was admissible because the officer would have inevitably discovered it during the lawful investigative stop, despite the unlawful arrest of the defendant.

United States v. Cabassa, 62 F.3d 470 (2d Cir. 1995). The government failed to prove by a preponderance of evidence that drugs would have inevitably been discovered by means of a search warrant after officers entered an apartment illegally. Officers had prepared a search warrant but never presented it to a judicial official for its issuance.

United States v. Kennedy, 61 F.3d 494 (6th Cir. 1995). Officers discovered illegal drugs after unlawfully searching lost luggage at the airport without a search warrant. However, the court ruled that the drugs would inevitably have been discovered by lawful means because the airline company, following its policy of opening lost luggage to determine its owner, would have opened it, found the cocaine, and then turned it over to the officers.

United States v. Ibarra, 955 F.2d 1405 (10th Cir. 1992). The inevitable discovery exception did not apply because an inventory of the defendant's vehicle could not have been conducted but for the officers' unlawful impoundment of the vehicle.

United States v. Buchanan, 904 F.2d 349 (6th Cir. 1990). Officers made an unlawful warrantless entry into a home, and exigent circumstances did not exist. The inevitable discovery exception did not apply in this case, because the officers simply planned to get a search warrant after their unlawful entry.

United States v. Arango, 879 F.2d 1501 (7th Cir. 1989). Even if the search of the vehicle after the defendant's arrest could not have been justified as a search incident to arrest, the evidence seized would have been admissible under the inevitable discovery doctrine, because a later search at the Drug Enforcement Agency garage was permissible as an inventory search as the vehicle had been lawfully impounded.

United States v. Gorski, 852 F.2d 692 (11th Cir. 1988). The warrantless search of the defendant's bag when he was arrested violated the Fourth Amendment, but the cocaine found in the bag would be admissible under the inevitable discovery doctrine if it was inevitable that an inventory search would have been conducted and cocaine would have been discovered in the bag.

United States v. Namer, 835 F.2d 1084 (5th Cir. 1988). The inevitable discovery exception requires that the government offer a theory about the manner in which officers "would" (not "might" or "could") have made their discovery of the evidence.

United States v. Boatwright, 822 F.2d 862 (9th Cir. 1987). The existence of two independent investigations, one of which was lawful and would have uncovered the information, is not a necessary predicate to the inevitable discovery exception. Generally, however, the exception requires that the fact or likelihood that makes the discovery inevitable must evolve from circumstances other than those disclosed by the illegal search itself. In this case an independent search was not under way, as in *Nix v. Williams*, 467 U.S. 431 (1984). Neither would a search have occurred as a routine procedure, as in *United States v. Andrade*, 784 F.2d 1431 (9th Cir. 1986), or *United States v. Martinez-Gallegos*, 807 F.2d 868 (9th Cir. 1987). There was nothing other than the unlawful search itself that supported the inevitable discovery of the weapons. *See also* United States v. Thomas, 955 F.2d 207 (4th Cir. 1992) (similar ruling).

United States v. Drosten, 819 F.2d 1067 (11th Cir. 1987). The court ruled that two witnesses would have been inevitably discovered (and thus their testimony was properly admitted at trial) despite an illegal, warrantless entry into an apartment. Another witness would not have been inevitably discovered, and thus his testimony was improperly admitted. *See also* United States v. Terzado-Madruga, 897 F.2d 1099 (11th Cir. 1990) (identity of witness would have been inevitably discovered, despite discovery of identity through illegal interrogation in violation of defendant's Sixth Amendment right to counsel).

United States v. Whitehorn, 813 F.2d 646 (4th Cir. 1987). Officers lawfully entered an apartment to execute an arrest warrant for a person other than the defendant. After removing the defendant, officers closed the door to the apartment and undertook to obtain a warrant to search the apartment. Meanwhile, a warrantless unconstitutional search of the apartment was conducted to perform a bomb sweep, and an officer saw many items, including a submachine gun, that were later named in the search warrant's affidavit. The search warrant was then executed and many items seized, including those seen during the unconstitutional search. The court ruled that the inevitable discovery exception authorized the admission into evidence of the items seen during the unconstitutional search, because they inevitably would have been discovered with a lawful search warrant. *See also* United States v. Whitehorn, 829 F.2d 1225 (2d Cir. 1987).

United States v. Pimentel, 810 F.2d 366 (2d Cir. 1987). The inevitable discovery exception applies to direct as well as indirect fruits of an illegal seizure. In this case illegally seized letters would have been inevitably discovered in the course of an audit.

United States v. Hernandez-Cano, 808 F.2d 779 (11th Cir. 1987). The inevitable discovery exception allows the admission in evidence of drugs found in luggage through an officer's illegal search, because a private person (in this case, an airline employee) would have inevitably discovered the drugs when examining the luggage had the officer not interrupted the examination and conducted an illegal search.

United States v. Martinez-Gallegos, 807 F.2d 868 (9th Cir. 1987). The inevitable discovery exception applies to Fifth Amendment violations (immigration officials would have consulted the defendant's immigration file even if they had not unlawfully obtained statements from the defendant in violation of the *Miranda* rule).

Impeachment with Unconstitutionally Obtained Evidence

James v. Illinois, 493 U.S. 307 (1990). Officers unconstitutionally obtained statements from the defendant because they obtained them as a result of an arrest without probable cause. At trial, a prosecutor used these statements to cross-examine a defense witness to impeach her credibility. The Court noted that its prior cases permit the government to impeach a defendant with illegally obtained evidence; see *United States v. Havens*, discussed below. However, the Court ruled that it is not permissible to impeach a defense witness with such evidence. The Court stated that a contrary ruling would significantly weaken the deterrent impact of the exclusionary rule on law enforcement officers. *But see* Wilkes v. United States, 631 A.2d 880 (D.C. App. 1993) (distinguishing *James v. Illinois*, court ruled that when defendant offered testimony of expert on insanity defense and expert's opinion was based largely on statements made to expert by defendant, government could offer evidence of defendant's *Miranda*-tainted statements during impeachment of expert and on rebuttal); State v. DeGraw, 470 S.E.2d 215 (W.Va. 1996) (similar ruling).

United States v. Havens, 446 U.S. 620 (1980). Unconstitutionally seized evidence may be used to impeach a defendant's allegedly false testimony given on direct examination or initially given on the government's cross-examination when the cross-examination is reasonably suggested by the defendant's direct examination. See the Court's discussion of *Agnello v. United States*, 269 U.S. 205 (1925), and *Walder v. United States*, 347 U.S. 623 (1954). For related cases, see "Use of Evidence Obtained as the Result of a *Miranda* Violation" on page 680.

Other Exclusionary Rule Exceptions

(See also "Exclusionary Rules Particularly Applicable to Search Warrants" on page 517.)

UNITED STATES SUPREME COURT

Pennsylvania Board of Probation and Parole v. Scott, 524 U.S. 357 (1998). The Court ruled that the Fourth Amendment's exclusionary rule does not bar the introduction at parole revocation hearings of evidence seized in violation of a parolee's Fourth Amendment rights, even when the searching officer knows that the person is a parolee.

Arizona v. Evans, 514 U.S. 1 (1995). An officer stopped the defendant for a traffic violation. The officer was informed by a computer message that there was an outstanding arrest warrant for the defendant, which—unknown to the officer—was incorrect because the warrant had already been dismissed. The officer arrested the defendant based on the information about the warrant, discovered marijuana, and charged the defendant with possession of marijuana. The defendant moved to suppress the marijuana evidence. The Arizona Supreme Court ruled that the evidence should be suppressed regardless of whether the error about the arrest warrant was the fault of court employees or law enforcement personnel.

The United States Supreme Court ruled that if the error was the fault of court employees, then the exclusionary rule should not bar the admission of the marijuana evidence. Relying on its rulings in *United States v. Leon*, 468 U.S. 897 (1984), *Massachusetts v. Sheppard*, 468 U.S. 981 (1984), and *Illinois v. Krull*, 480 U.S. 340 (1987), the Court noted that the exclusionary rule was historically designed to deter law enforcement misconduct, not errors by court employees. There was no evidence that court employees are inclined to violate the Fourth Amendment to require that the exclusionary rule be invoked. Most importantly, there is no basis for believing that the application of the exclusionary rule would have a significant deterrent effect on court employees who are responsible for informing law enforcement when a warrant has been dismissed.

[Author's note: Because the North Carolina Supreme Court strongly indicated in *State v. Carter*, 322 N.C. 709 (1988), that a good faith exception to the exclusionary rule did not exist under the North Carolina Constitution, thereby not adopting the *Leon* and *Sheppard* rulings that were decided under the United States Constitution, it is unclear whether this ruling would apply in North Carolina state courts. However, for a later case that appeared to express reasoning that differs from *Carter*, see *State v. Garner*, 331 N.C. 491 (1992). *See also* State v. Banner, 207 N.C. App. 729 n.7 (2010) (noting possible conflict between *Carter* and *Garner*).]

Withrow v. Williams, 507 U.S. 680 (1993). The Court ruled that *Miranda* violations must be considered in federal habeas corpus review of state convictions. The Court rejected an extension to *Miranda* violations of the ruling in *Stone v. Powell*, 428 U.S. 465 (1976) (if state provided full and fair review of Fourth Amendment claim, federal habeas review of that claim is unavailable).

United States v. Verdugo-Urquidez, 494 U.S. 259 (1990). The Fourth Amendment does not apply to a search of a nonresident alien's property in a foreign country.

Illinois v. Krull, 480 U.S. 340 (1987). The Fourth Amendment's exclusionary rule does not apply to exclude evidence obtained by a warrantless administrative search conducted by an officer in the objectively reasonable reliance on a statute authorizing such a search—even though the statute is later declared unconstitutional. See the discussion of this case in *State v. Carter*, 322 N.C. 753 (1988).

Kimmelman v. Morrison, 477 U.S. 365 (1986). The ruling in *Stone v. Powell*, 428 U.S. 465 (1976), discussed below, does not apply to a Sixth Amendment ineffective assistance of counsel claim that is based on incompetent representation of a Fourth Amendment issue. The Court ruled that the defense lawyer's complete failure to seek pretrial discovery, which resulted in the failure to file a timely motion to suppress evidence, did not meet the minimum standard of effectiveness of counsel under the Sixth Amendment.

Immigration & Naturalization Service v. Lopez-Mendoza, 468 U.S. 1032 (1984). The exclusionary rule does not apply to bar the use of evidence in a deportation proceeding when the evidence was obtained as a result of an unconstitutional arrest.

Michigan v. DeFillippo, 443 U.S. 31 (1979). The exclusionary rule does not apply to bar the use of evidence seized after an officer made an arrest with probable cause and with a good faith reliance on an ordinance that a court later declared to be unconstitutional.

Stone v. Powell, 428 U.S. 465 (1976). When state courts have provided a defendant with a full and fair opportunity to litigate a Fourth Amendment issue, the defendant cannot raise the issue in a federal habeas corpus proceeding.

United States v. Janis, 428 U.S. 433 (1976). The exclusionary rule does not apply to bar the use of evidence in a federal civil tax proceeding when the evidence was seized unconstitutionally by a state law enforcement officer.

United States v. Calandra, 414 U.S. 338 (1974). The Fourth Amendment's exclusionary rule does not apply to evidence used in grand jury proceedings.

One 1958 Plymouth Sedan v. Pennsylvania, 380 U.S. 693 (1965). The exclusionary rule applies to bar evidence (in this case, a car) in a proceeding to forfeit the evidence when that evidence was seized unconstitutionally. However, the exclusionary rule does not apply if the seized evidence is contraband per se (for example, illegal drugs). And, if the government can prove by lawfully obtained evidence the contraband character of the object to be forfeited, it is irrelevant that the government obtained the object as the result of an illegal search or seizure.

NORTH CAROLINA SUPREME COURT

State v. Lombardo, 306 N.C. 594 (1982), *later appeal*, 74 N.C. App. 460 (1985). The Fourth Amendment's exclusionary rule does not apply to evidence used in a probation hearing.

State v. Sanders, 303 N.C. 608 (1981). The exclusionary rule does not apply to evidence obtained in violation of the Posse Comitatus Act, 18 U.S.C.A. § 1385 (prohibiting the use of the federal military in executing civilian laws).

NORTH CAROLINA COURT OF APPEALS

Combs v. Robertson, 202 N.C. App. 296 (2015). The court ruled that the Fourth Amendment's exclusionary rule does not apply in civil driver's license revocation proceedings. The evidence used in the proceeding here was obtained as a result of an unconstitutional stop; after the same evidence previously had been used to support criminal charges, it was suppressed and the criminal charges were dismissed. The court ruled that while the evidence was subject to the exclusionary rule in a criminal proceeding, that rule did not apply in this civil proceeding, even if it could be viewed as "quasi-criminal in nature."

Hartman v. Robertson, 208 N.C. App. 692 (2010). The exclusionary rule does not apply in a Division of Motor Vehicles civil license revocation proceeding.

State v. Banner, 207 N.C. App. 729 (2010). On February 22, 2007, the defendant was cited to appear in Wilkes County Court for various motor vehicle offenses (hereafter, Wilkes County charges). On June 7, 2007, he was convicted in Caldwell County of unrelated charges (hereafter, unrelated charges) and sent to prison. When a court date was set on the Wilkes County charges, the defendant failed to appear because he was still in prison on the unrelated charges and no writ was issued to secure his presence. The court issued an order for arrest (OFA) for the failure to appear. When the defendant was scheduled to be released from prison on the unrelated charges, Department of Correction employees asked the Wilkes County clerk's office to recall the OFA, explaining that the defendant had been incarcerated when it was issued. However, the OFA was not recalled, and on October 1, 2007, the defendant was arrested pursuant to that order, having previously been released from prison. When he was searched incident to arrest, officers found marijuana and cocaine on his person. The court rejected the defendant's argument that the OFA was invalid because the Wilkes County clerk failed to recall it as requested, concluding that because the underlying charges had not been resolved at the time of arrest, no automatic recall occurred. The court further noted that even if good cause to recall existed, recall was not mandatory and therefore failure to recall did not nullify the OFA. Thus, the officers were entitled to rely on the OFA, and no independent probable cause was required to arrest the defendant. The court declined to resolve the issue of whether there is a good faith exception to Article I, Section 20, of the North Carolina Constitution.

FEDERAL APPELLATE COURTS

United States v. Kington, 801 F.2d 733 (5th Cir. 1986). Congress did not intend that evidence obtained in violation of the federal Right to Financial Privacy Act must be suppressed when the act did not authorize that remedy; therefore, suppression is inappropriate. [Author's note: The rationale of this ruling would apply to a violation of North Carolina's Financial Privacy Act (G.S. 53B-1 through 53B-10, discussed in Chapter 3).]

North Carolina's Statutory Exclusionary Rule

State v. Simpson, 320 N.C. 313 (1987). The magistrate's failure to set bail, assuming it was an error under G.S. 15A-511(e), did not render a later-obtained voluntary confession inadmissible. The assumed violation of Chapter 15A was not a "substantial violation" under G.S. 15A-974(2) (now, G.S. 15A-974(a)(2)). [Author's note: Legislation enacted in 2011 (S.L. 2011-6) added a good faith exception to the application of G.S. 15A-974.]

State v. Richardson, 295 N.C. 309 (1978). Assuming without deciding that the four and one-half hour delay between the defendant's arrest and his being taken before a magistrate was a violation of G.S. 15A-501(2), and assuming without deciding that the officers' failure to comply with this statute was a "substantial violation," the court ruled that the defendant's confession (obtained during the interval between arrest and appearance before a magistrate) was not obtained "as a result of" the alleged substantial violation, as required to suppress evidence under G.S. 15A-974(2) (now, G.S. 15A-974(a)(2)). The statutory exclusionary rule requires, at a minimum, a causal connection between the violation and the resulting evidence. After reviewing the evidence, the court concluded that the defendant's confession was not causally related to the delay in bringing him before a magistrate. [Author's note: Legislation enacted in 2011 (S.L. 2011-6) added a good faith exception to the application of G.S. 15A-974.] *See also* State v. Hunter, 305 N.C. 106 (1982); State v. Jones, 112 N.C. App. 337 (1993).

See other cases on the application of the statutory exclusionary rule on pages 97 and 700.

Interrogation and Confessions, Lineups and Other Identification Procedures, and Undercover Officers and Informants

Chapter 5

Interrogation and Confessions,
Lineups and Other Identification Procedures,
and Undercover Officers and Informants

Thus far this book has discussed how the Fourth Amendment and related statutes affect an officer's authority to make an investigative stop, arrest, and search. This chapter discusses other constitutional provisions and related statutes that affect an officer's authority to investigate crime—specifically interrogation and confessions, lineups and other identification procedures, and the use of undercover officers and informants.

Part I. Interrogation and Confessions

Introduction

A defendant's confession (full acknowledgment of guilt) or admission (partial acknowledgment of guilt) obviously is important evidence in a criminal case. Sometimes even a statement apparently favorable to a defendant—for example, a defendant's statement that he or she acted in self-defense—may be valuable to the prosecution when other evidence disproves it.

Officers must understand some of the basic rules of interrogation so that they do not violate a person's constitutional rights and make the person's statements inadmissible at trial. The rules are sometimes complex: a motion to suppress a defendant's statement at trial may require the court to consider separately whether the defendant's rights have been violated under the Fourth, Fifth, Sixth, or Fourteenth Amendments to the United States Constitution or under the North Carolina Constitution or statutes.

When officers attempt to take a statement from a defendant, they must be aware of at least six constitutional and statutory issues that may affect the statement's admissibility in court:

1. The effect of an unconstitutional seizure under the Fourth Amendment, such as an illegal arrest or investigative stop, that results in a later-obtained statement
2. The effect of an officer's substantial violation of a defendant's statutory rights under North Carolina law that results in a later-obtained statement
3. The requirement under the Fourteenth Amendment that a statement must be given voluntarily
4. Compliance with *Miranda* rules—designed to protect a defendant's Fifth Amendment right not to be compelled to give testimonial evidence— when officers conduct *custodial interrogation* of a defendant
5. Compliance with a defendant's Sixth Amendment right to counsel, which is present at each critical stage of a criminal case at the time or after the right to counsel attaches (begins)
6. Compliance with North Carolina statutory law requiring the electronic recording of a custodial

interrogation at a place of detention when officers are investigating certain offenses or conducting a custodial interrogation of a juvenile

A statement that results from a violation of any one of these rights may be inadmissible as evidence. These issues are discussed below.

An additional issue that arises when a foreign national is arrested is informing that person of the right to have a consular official notified. This issue is discussed on page 80 of Chapter 2.

Unconstitutional Seizure and the Resulting Statement

(*See page 699 for case summaries on this topic.*)

When officers arrest a defendant with probable cause, they may take the defendant into custody, remove the defendant from the scene of arrest to another place, and attempt to interrogate the defendant. And, of course, the officers must take the defendant before a magistrate without unnecessary delay. When officers have reasonable suspicion that a person has committed a crime, they may briefly stop the person to investigate further. However, as discussed in Chapter 2, officers usually exceed the scope of an investigative stop if they take a person without his or her consent from the scene of an investigative stop to a law enforcement facility for interrogation.[1] Thus, if officers do not have probable cause to arrest, they must be able to show in court that the person voluntarily came with them after they made an investigative stop. Officers may want to inform the person that he or she is not under arrest, although such a statement is not legally required to prove that the person voluntarily consented to come with them.

Officers often want to question a person because their investigation indicates that the person is a suspect but there is insufficient evidence to establish probable cause to arrest. Officers may go to the person's home and question the person there if, by their words or conduct, they do not seize the person under the Fourth Amendment[2]

(see the discussion in Chapter 2). If the officers want to question the person at their law enforcement facility, they must receive the person's voluntary consent to come with them—assuming, of course, that they still do not have probable cause to arrest the person. Sometimes officers may leave a note at the person's home that simply mentions that they would like to speak with the person. If the person voluntarily comes to a law enforcement facility in response to that kind of note—or an officer's similar oral request to a member of the person's family—the person usually has not been seized under the Fourth Amendment.[3] Officers may want to inform the person that he or she is not under arrest and is free to leave at any time before they begin their questioning, although such a statement is not legally required to prove that the person is there voluntarily. A signed statement by the person stating that he or she is there voluntarily is also not required, although such a statement is useful in proving that fact in court.[4]

In any of the situations described above, if the person who is with the officers voluntarily gives an incriminating statement that by itself or with other information establishes probable cause, the officer may then arrest the person.

If officers obtain a statement from a person after they have unconstitutionally seized the person under the Fourth Amendment—that is, they exceeded the scope of an investigative stop based on reasonable suspicion or they arrested the person without probable cause—the State has the burden of showing that intervening events occurred between the unconstitutional seizure and the later statement to break the connection between them. The fact that officers properly gave *Miranda* warnings and obtained a valid waiver will not by itself satisfy the State's burden of disproving that the statement directly

---

1. Dunaway v. New York, 442 U.S. 200 (1979); State v. Freeman, 307 N.C. 357 (1983).

2. If officers had reasonable suspicion but did not have probable cause to arrest, they could detain the person briefly there and ask the person questions—and *Miranda* warnings ordinarily would not be required. *See, e.g.*, State v. Benjamin,

124 N.C. App. 734 (1996) (*Miranda* warnings not required during investigative stop); United States v. Striefel, 781 F.2d 953 (1st Cir. 1986), *later ruling sub nom.*, United States v. Quinn, 815 F.2d 153 (1st Cir. 1987); United States v. Bengivenga, 845 F.2d 593 (5th Cir.) (en banc) (1988).

3. *See, e.g.*, State v. Simpson, 303 N.C. 439 (1981) (defendant voluntarily accompanied officers to law enforcement building at their request); State v. Bromfield, 332 N.C. 24 (1992) (similar ruling).

4. See the use of such a form in *State v. Bromfield*, 332 N.C. 24 (1992).

resulted from the officers' violation of the defendant's Fourth Amendment rights.[5]

Consequences of Violating North Carolina's Statutes

(*See page 700 for case summaries on this topic.*)

Even if officers do not violate a person's constitutional rights, a statement may be inadmissible at trial if it was obtained as a result of a substantial violation of a person's statutory rights under North Carolina law.[6] For example, North Carolina law requires that officers take an arrestee to a magistrate without unnecessary delay,[7] although they may delay the arrestee's appearance before the magistrate for various investigative purposes, including interrogation[8] (see the discussion in Chapter 2). If officers substantially violated the arrestee's statutory rights[9] and the unnecessary delay caused the statement to be given, the statement may be inadmissible at trial.[10]

---

5. Taylor v. Alabama, 457 U.S. 687 (1982); Brown v. Illinois, 422 U.S. 590 (1975); Lanier v. South Carolina, 474 U.S. 25 (1985); State v. Allen, 332 N.C. 123 (1992).

6. State v. Richardson, 295 N.C. 309 (1978); State v. Hunter, 305 N.C. 106 (1982); State v. Simpson, 320 N.C. 313 (1987).

7. N.C. GEN. STAT. § 15A-501(2) (hereafter, G.S.).

8. *See* State v. Chapman, 343 N.C. 495 (1996) (court ruled that delay of 11½ hours in taking defendant to magistrate was not unlawful because officers were interrogating defendant about several crimes); State v. Jones, 112 N.C. App. 337 (1993) (trial judge ruled that officers violated G.S. 15A-501(2) (taking the defendant to magistrate without unnecessary delay) and G.S. 15A-501(5) (advising the defendant without unnecessary delay of right to communicate with counsel and friends), but these violations had not proximately caused defendant's incriminating statements); State v. Sings, 35 N.C. App. 1 (1978); State v. Martin, 315 N.C. 667 (1986).

9. The North Carolina Supreme Court in *State v. Richardson*, 295 N.C. 309 (1978), ruled that a defendant did not have a federal constitutional right to be taken before a magistrate without unnecessary delay.

10. The North Carolina Supreme Court in *State v. Richardson*, cited *supra* note 9, stated that, at a minimum, proof of a causal connection between the violation and the statement was required to exclude evidence under the statutory exclusionary rule provided in G.S. 15A-974(2) (now, G.S. 15A-974(a)(2)). The court indicated that more than a causal connection must be shown before evidence may be excluded under this provision. *See also* State v. Hunter, 305 N.C. 106 (1982); State v. Jones, 112 N.C. App. 337 (1993). Legislation enacted in 2011 (S.L. 2011-6) added a good faith exception to the application of G.S. 15A-974.

Recording Custodial Interrogations at a Place of Detention

North Carolina legislation requires that certain custodial interrogations be electronically recorded.[11] Section 15A-211 of the North Carolina General Statutes (hereafter, G.S.), applies to "custodial interrogations" at "any place of detention." These phrases impose four preconditions for the recording requirement:

1. The person must be in "custody," presumably within the meaning of the constitutional definition of *custody* (arrest or its functional equivalent).

2. The person must be "interrogated," again presumably within the meaning of the constitutional definition of *interrogation* (for example, routine booking questions ordinarily would not constitute interrogation).

3. There are two separate categories to which the recording requirement applies. First, all custodial interrogations of juveniles are included.[12] (Although the term "juveniles" is undefined and thus its meaning is unclear, it apparently includes those under 16 years old.)[13] Second, for

---

11. S.L. 2007-434; 2011-329. The 2007 legislation applied only to homicide investigations and became effective for interrogations conducted on or after March 1, 2008. The 2011 legislation completely revised the offenses for which a recording was required, applied the recording requirement to all custodial interrogations of juveniles, and became effective for offenses committed on or after December 1, 2011. The text integrates the requirements of both legislative acts.

12. Of course, the recording requirement is not triggered unless the custodial interrogation is conducted at a "place of detention," as discussed on page 568.

13. The statute makes the recording requirement applicable to "all custodial interrogations of juveniles in criminal investigations conducted at any place of detention." The term "juveniles," as used in G.S. 15A-211, is defined neither in the statute nor elsewhere in Chapter 15A of the General Statutes, although G.S. 7B-1501(17) in the Juvenile Code defines the term "juvenile" to generally include any person who has not reached his or her 18th birthday. It is possible that the legislature intended to make the recording requirement applicable when a criminal defendant is under 18 years old. However, Chapter 15A generally does not use the term "juvenile" or "juveniles"; instead it states a defendant's age or an age range when referring to a person in the criminal justice system who is younger than 18. The use of the term "juveniles" suggests that it is possible, if not likely, that the recording requirement was intended to apply when an investigation involves an offense committed before a juvenile reaches his or her 16th

adults (generally, those 16 years old or older),[14] the recording requirement applies only to the investigation of a Class A, B1, or B2 felony, or any Class C felony of rape, sex offense, or assault with a deadly weapon with intent to kill inflicting serious injury. Thus, the offenses include (1) first- or second-degree murder,[15] (2) first- or second-degree forcible or statutory rape or sexual offense,[16] (3) statutory rape of or sexual offense with a child by an adult,[17] (4) statutory rape or sexual offense of a person who is 15 years old or younger,[18] (5) assault with a deadly weapon with intent to kill inflicting serious injury,[19] (6) certain incest offenses with a child,[20] (7) offenses involving a weapon of mass destruction,[21] and (8) a conspiracy or attempt to commit a Class A or B1 felony.[22]

4. The interrogation must take place at a "place of detention," defined in G.S. 15A-211(c) as a jail, police or sheriff's station, correctional or detention facility, holding facility for prisoners, or other facility a person is held in connection with criminal charges. In light of this requirement, an interrogation at a person's home or other location that does not constitute a place of detention would not be subject to the electronic recording requirement even if the person was under arrest or otherwise in custody.

If an interrogation of a suspect meets the above criteria, an electronic recording must be made of the entire interrogation. An electronic recording must be a simultaneous audio and visual recording whenever reasonably feasible.[23] If the recording is visual, the camera must be placed so that it films both the interrogator and the suspect. The recording must begin with the officer's advice of the person's constitutional rights and must end only when the interview has completely finished. Brief recesses requested by the person in custody or the officer need not be recorded, but the recording must reflect the starting time of the recess and of the resumption of interrogation.

G.S. 15A-211 contains several provisions on the effect of compliance or noncompliance with the recording requirements.[24] First, the statute describes the effect on the admissibility of statements that were not recorded. A failure to comply "shall be considered" by the court in adjudicating a motion to suppress a statement made by the defendant.[25] Also, a failure to comply is admissible in support of a claim that the defendant's statement was involuntary or unreliable if the evidence is otherwise admissible. When evidence of compliance or noncompliance has been presented at trial, the jury must be instructed that it may consider credible evidence of compliance or noncompliance in determining whether the defendant's statement was voluntary and reliable. (This last provision probably does not mean that the jury decides whether the statement was "voluntary" within the meaning of the Fourteenth Amendment requirement of voluntariness, which is a question of law for the court to determine in ruling on a motion to suppress.)

Second, the statute describes the effect of noncompliance on subsequent statements. It states that if the court finds that the defendant was subjected to a custodial interrogation that was not electronically recorded as required, any statements later made by the defendant that are recorded may be questioned concerning their voluntariness and reliability.

---

birthday (that is, to delinquency cases, not criminal cases involving young people).

14. The recording requirement for the offenses set out in the text applies to everyone who is 16 years old or older, except that all custodial interrogations must be recorded for a person who is 16 years old or older and is being investigated or is charged with a delinquent act allegedly committed when the person was under 16 years old.

15. G.S. 14-17.

16. G.S. 14-27.21, -27.22, -27.24, -27.26, -27.27, -27.29.

17. G.S. 14-27.23, -27.28.

18. G.S. 14-27.25, -27.30.

19. G.S. 14-32(a).

20. G.S. 14-178(b)(1)(a) (incest with a child under 13 years old and defendant is at least 12 years old and at least four years older than the child); G.S. 14-178(b)(1)(b) (incest with a child who is 13, 14, or 15 years old and defendant is at least six years older than the child).

21. G.S. 14-288.21, -288.22.

22. A conspiracy or attempt to commit a Class A or B1 felony is a Class B2 felony. G.S. 14-2.4(a), -2.5.

---

23. G.S. 15A-211(c)(1). However, the statute provides that a failure to produce a simultaneous audio and video recording is not a ground for suppression of evidence. Thus, although an audio-only recording may violate the statutory mandate if a video and audio recording was feasible, suppression of evidence is not a remedy.

24. These are in addition to the provision set out in note 23, *supra*.

25. Thus, the court must take a violation into account, but a violation does not necessarily require suppression of the statement. The court would consider whether a violation requires suppression under G.S. 15A-974, the exclusionary rule for violations of Chapter 15A of the North Carolina General Statutes.

Third, the statute provides that the State may present as evidence against the defendant a statement that was recorded as required if the statement is otherwise admissible. It is not clear how this provision adds to the State's right to introduce statements of the defendant that are otherwise admissible.

Fourth, the statute provides that if the State failed to comply with the recording requirements, it may show by clear and convincing evidence that the statement was voluntary and reliable and that the officer had good cause for not electronically recording the interrogation in its entirety. Good cause includes, among other things, the suspect's refusal to have the interrogation recorded and unforeseeable equipment failures.

Fifth, the statute provides that it does not preclude the admission of certain listed statements, such as spontaneous statements not made in response to questioning, statements made during arrest processing in response to routine questions, statements made during custodial interrogation conducted in another state by officers of that state, and statements obtained by a federal law enforcement officer.

The State must retain the electronic recording of a defendant convicted of an offense related to the interrogation until one year after the completion of all appeals of the conviction, including the exhaustion of any appeal of any motion for appropriate relief under state law or habeas corpus proceeding under federal law.[26]

Voluntariness of the Defendant's Statement

(*See page 609 for case summaries on this topic.*)

A defendant's statement is not admissible at trial for any purpose unless it was made voluntarily and with understanding.[27] There are no simple rules for determining whether a statement is voluntary. A court looks at the totality of the circumstances surrounding the statement to determine whether the statement was improperly induced by hope or fear and, therefore, was involuntary, or whether it was made voluntarily and with understanding.[28] Some important factors include the following:

- The officers' conduct before and during the interrogation
- The defendant's physical and mental condition before and during the interrogation[29]
- The defendant's prior history of involvement with law enforcement officers[30]
- The environment in which the questioning took place
- Whether officers made promises or threats to the defendant or used deception

Officers may not use physical threats or other kinds of conduct that might induce a defendant to make a statement in fear of what might happen if the defendant does not do so. Officers also may not make promises to induce the defendant to talk—for example, promises about what will happen to the criminal charge or what the officer will do for the defendant if he or she talks.[31]

It is difficult to generalize about what officers may and may not do or say before and during interrogation because appellate review of their conduct focuses on the total circumstances surrounding the giving of the statement—not just isolated comments or acts.[32] However, officers should avoid making statements that (1) promise a reduced charge or sentence or better treatment if the

---

26. This provision may not establish a definite time limit on retention, because under G.S. 15A-1415, some claims may be raised in a motion for appropriate relief at any time.

27. *Mincey v. Arizona*, 437 U.S. 385 (1978); *Arizona v. Fulminante*, 499 U.S. 279 (1991). However, coercive law enforcement activity is a necessary predicate to a finding that a confession is involuntary under the Due Process Clause. *Colorado v. Connelly*, 479 U.S. 157 (1986).

28. *State v. Corley*, 310 N.C. 40 (1984). Cases that have applied the *Corley* totality of circumstances test include *State v. McCullers*, 341 N.C. 19 (1995); *State v. Smith*, 328 N.C. 99 (1991); *State v. Thomas*, 310 N.C. 369 (1984); *State v. Williams*, 67 N.C. App. 144 (1984); *State v. Parrish*, 73 N.C. App. 662 (1985); and *State v. Durham*, 74 N.C. App. 121 (1985). For United States Supreme Court cases on the voluntariness of confessions, see *Schneckloth v. Bustamonte*, 412 U.S. 218 (1973), and *Arizona v. Fulminante*, 499 U.S. 279 (1991).

29. *State v. McKoy*, 323 N.C. 1 (1988).

30. *State v. Richardson*, 316 N.C. 594 (1986).

31. *Bobby v. Dixon*, 132 S. Ct. 26 (2011) (officers' urging defendant to "cut a deal" before his accomplice did so did not cause resulting confession to be involuntary); *State v. Corley*, 310 N.C. 400 (1984); *State v. Branch*, 306 N.C. 101 (1982) (court upheld confession although officer told defendant that "we would talk with the District Attorney if he made a statement which admitted his involvement"; however, court stated that officers should not speculate about what will happen if the defendant confesses); *State v. Pruitt*, 286 N.C. 442 (1975).

32. *State v. Corley*, 310 N.C. 40 (1984); *State v. McCullers*, 341 N.C. 19 (1995).

defendant will give a statement,[33] (2) inform the defendant that the officers will testify in court for the defendant if he or she gives a statement,[34] or (3) inform the defendant that it will be harder on the defendant if he or she does not cooperate with the officers.[35]

On the other hand, officers may request that the defendant tell the truth.[36] They also may truthfully tell the defendant about or present evidence that they have against the defendant, but they should do so in a non-threatening way so that they do not improperly induce or coerce the defendant to make an incriminating statement.[37]

If officers lie to or deceive the defendant about the evidence against him or her, a resulting incriminating statement is not necessarily considered involuntary.[38] However, a court may rule that the statement is involuntary if all the circumstances surrounding the statement show unacceptable coercion, particularly if the defendant

was in custody or if the officers also made any promises or threats before or during the interrogation.

The fact that officers properly gave *Miranda* warnings and obtained a valid waiver does not, by itself, guarantee that a court will determine that a defendant's statement was in fact made voluntarily and with understanding, if other circumstances show that it was improperly induced by hope or fear.[39]

The *Miranda* Rule and Additional Statutory Rights
Overview

In 1966, the United States Supreme Court decided in *Miranda v. Arizona*[40] that it was necessary to establish procedures during custodial interrogation to protect the Fifth Amendment right not to be compelled to incriminate oneself—in addition to the requirement that a statement be voluntary under the Fourteenth Amendment. The Court ruled that a statement—which includes any statement, whether or not it is a confession or admission[41]—is not admissible unless

- Before officers begin custodial interrogation, they give the following warnings:[42]

    1. You have a right to remain silent.
    2. What you say may be used in court against you.
    3. You have a right to have a lawyer present during interrogation.
    4. You have a right to an appointed lawyer during the interrogation if you cannot afford to hire one.

---

33. State v. Martin, 228 N.C. App. 689 (2013) (officer improperly suggested that he was in a position to offer plea arrangement on defendant's behalf); State v. Fox, 274 N.C. 277 (1968); State v. Sturgill, 121 N.C. App. 629 (1996) (defendant asked "what would be in it" for him if he provided information about certain break-ins; detective told him he would not seek to indict him for habitual felon status; defendant then confessed; based on these and other facts, court ruled that defendant's confession was inadmissible).

34. State v. Fuqua, 269 N.C. 223 (1967); State v. Williams, 33 N.C. App. 624 (1977); State v. Richardson, 316 N.C. 594 (1986).

35. State v. Pruitt, 286 N.C. 442 (1975). See the discussion of *Pruitt* in *State v. Corley*, 310 N.C. 40 (1984).

36. State v. Thomas, 241 N.C. 337 (1955).

37. State v. Booker, 306 N.C. 302 (1982), *later appeal*, 309 N.C. 446 (1983); State v. Chamberlain, 307 N.C. 130 (1982).

38. Frazier v. Cupp, 394 U.S. 731 (1969) (police misrepresentation of accomplice's statements, while relevant, did not make defendant's otherwise voluntary confession inadmissible); State v. Chapman, 343 N.C. 495 (1996) (detective's deceit about the defendant's handwriting and fingerprints being on note found near victim's body did not make confession inadmissible); State v. Hardy, 339 N.C. 207 (1994) (confession was voluntary, even though one officer lied about witness having identified defendant); State v. Jackson, 308 N.C. 549 (1983), *later appeal*, 317 N.C. 1 (1986) (officer's use of deceptive methods or false statements during interrogation did not, by itself, make a confession involuntary); State v. Bordeaux, 207 N.C. App. 645 (2010) (the interviewing officers suggested during custodial interrogation that defendant was involved in ongoing murder investigation, knowing that to be untrue; confession was involuntary based on these and other facts); State v. Barnes, 154 N.C. App. 111 (2002) (officer falsely told defendant, investigated for sexual assault of daughter, that his daughter was pregnant; confession was voluntary).

---

39. State v. Pruitt, 286 N.C. 442 (1975).

40. 384 U.S. 436 (1966). The Court reaffirmed this ruling and its constitutional underpinnings in *Dickerson v. United States*, 530 U.S. 428 (2000).

41. Miranda v. Arizona, 437 U.S. 385 (1966); State v. Siler, 292 N.C. 543 (1977).

42. The United States Supreme Court has upheld warnings that did not precisely follow those set out in *Miranda*. *See, e.g.,* Florida v. Powell, 559 U.S. 50 (2010).

Most, but not all, courts that have considered the issue of whether *Miranda* warnings must be given when a suspect is being questioned with an attorney present have ruled that the warnings are not required, at least when the suspect has had an opportunity to consult with the attorney before the questioning. *See, e.g.* Commonwealth v. Simon, 923 N.E.2d 58 (Mass. 2010).

- After receiving these warnings, the person either has a lawyer present or knowingly and voluntarily waives these rights.

Another part of the *Miranda* ruling must be followed even though officers need not advise the person of it: if, at any time while being questioned, the person expresses an unwillingness to continue with the questioning or asserts the right to counsel, officers must immediately stop the questioning.

The Public Safety Exception

(*See page 625 for case summaries on this topic.*)

The United States Supreme Court has recognized a narrow "public safety" exception to the *Miranda* rule.[43] A person's statement during custodial interrogation that was given without *Miranda* warnings is admissible when officers have an objectively reasonable need—that is, their subjective belief or motivation is not controlling—to protect themselves or the public from an immediate danger associated with a weapon. For example: An officer responds to a report that a woman has been raped by a man with a gun who has just entered a grocery store. The officer arrests and frisks the man and discovers that the arrestee is wearing an empty shoulder holster. After handcuffing him, the officer asks the arrestee where the gun is located. In such a case, the officer may need to determine immediately the whereabouts of the gun that the officer reasonably believes the arrestee has just removed from his holster and discarded in the store. The gun may be dangerous to any person (such as an employee or a customer) who finds it, or an unknown accomplice may use it. The arrestee's answer to the officer's question would be admissible even though he or she had not been given *Miranda* warnings and waived his or her rights.[44] However, once an officer has obtained the necessary information or when the danger is over, the officer must give the arrestee *Miranda* warnings if the officer intends to continue questioning.

The Booking Questions Exception

(*See page 627 for case summaries on this topic.*)

The United States Supreme Court has recognized that routine booking questions may be asked and answered without giving *Miranda* warnings, if the questions are not designed to elicit incriminating statements.[45] Thus, officers may ask an arrestee for such information as name, address, height, weight, eye color, date of birth, current age, employment, and the like without giving *Miranda* warnings—even if the arrestee has already asserted the right to counsel or the right to remain silent—and the information may later be used in prosecuting the arrestee.[46] However, if an arresting officer is a detective investigating a first-degree statutory rape (in which the defendant's age is an element of the crime), the defendant's answer to the detective's question about the defendant's age would not be admissible at trial if a court ruled that the question was designed to elicit an incriminating response.[47]

---

43. New York v. Quarles, 467 U.S. 649 (1984).
44. *Id.*

45. Pennsylvania v. Muniz, 496 U.S. 582 (1990). Although a four-Justice plurality opinion, *Muniz* clearly represents current law. The North Carolina Supreme Court has consistently recognized that routine booking questions are not interrogation under the *Miranda* ruling if they are not intended to elicit an incriminating response. *See* State v. Ladd, 308 N.C. 272 (1983); State v. Banks, 322 N.C. 753 (1988).
46. State v. Brewington, 352 N.C. 489 (2000); United States v. Webster, 769 F.2d 487 (8th Cir. 1985).
47. State v. Locklear, 138 N.C. App. 549 (2000). The defendant in *Locklear* was arrested for statutory rape and was not given *Miranda* warnings. During the booking process, the officer used a form that, among other things, required the entry of the defendant's date of birth. The officer asked the defendant his date of birth, and he stated that it was August 2, 1976. At trial, the officer testified—over the defendant's objection on *Miranda* grounds—about the defendant's date of birth based on the defendant's statement during the booking process. This testimony was the only evidence of the defendant's age, which was an element of statutory rape. The court noted that although *Miranda* does not apply to the gathering of biographical data necessary to complete the booking process, it applies if the questions are designed to elicit a response that the officer knows or should know is reasonably likely to be incriminating. The court stated that the officer, in addition to booking the defendant, was also the investigating officer. The court then ruled that "[s]ince defendant's age was an essential element of the crime charged, . . . [the officer] . . . knew or should have known her question regarding defendant's date of birth would elicit an incriminating response," and therefore the defendant's rights under *Miranda* were violated and the defendant's response was inadmissible. [Author's note: In *State v. Banks*, 322 N.C. 753 (1988), the court ruled that the defendant's date of birth given during the booking process was routine information and was admissible without *Miranda* warnings, even if his age was an essential element of the crimes for which he was being booked. Citing *Banks* but not discussing it, the court in *Locklear* apparently would distinguish that ruling because the officer in this case was also the investigating officer. However,

A Young Arrestee's Additional Statutory Warnings and Rights

(*See page 684 for case summaries on this topic.*)

North Carolina law provides additional statutory warnings and rights to a young person before custodial interrogation may begin.[48] If officers arrest a person who is 14, 15, 16, or 17 years old and who is not a member of the armed forces or emancipated (a person under age 18 is emancipated if the person is married or has been released from parental control by court order), they must advise the person of the right to have a parent, guardian, or custodian present during questioning—in addition to giving *Miranda* warnings. If officers take into custody a person less than 16 years old,[49] a statement obtained during custodial interrogation is not admissible in court unless the youngster's parent, guardian, custodian, or attorney is present during the interrogation.[50] If an attorney is not present, the officers must inform the parent, guardian, or

custodian of the youngster's rights, although that person may not waive those rights on the youngster's behalf.

Whether Miranda Warnings Must Be Repeated If There Is a Lapse in Interrogation

(*See page 621 for case summaries on this topic.*)

The North Carolina Supreme Court has ruled[51] that when a break occurs between an initial interrogation and a later resumption of interrogation, five factors must be considered in determining whether the initial *Miranda* warnings given to the defendant have become so stale that the warnings must be repeated before the second interrogation begins:

1. The length of time between the warnings and the second interrogation
2. Whether the warnings and the later interrogation were given in the same or different places
3. Whether the same or different officers gave the warnings and conducted the later interrogation
4. The extent to which the defendant's later statement differed from prior statements (but note that this is an after-the-fact judgment that officers cannot make when they decide whether to repeat *Miranda* warnings before the later interrogation)
5. The defendant's apparent intellectual or emotional status

It is difficult to derive a general rule from these factors. Although there will be other occasions when officers will not need to repeat *Miranda* warnings, officers may safely forego them if they conducted the first custodial interrogation, if both interrogations occur in the same place, if the time between interrogations is only a few hours, and if they have no reason to believe that the defendant is unaware of the *Miranda* rights given before the first custodial interrogation.[52]

Even when officers do not repeat *Miranda* warnings after a break in questioning, as a matter of caution they

---

a defendant's date of birth is routine information that officers seek to obtain after every arrest.]

48. The North Carolina Supreme Court ruled in *State v. Fincher*, 309 N.C. 1 (1983), that the custodial interrogation warnings listed in G.S. 7A-595 (now, G.S. 7B-2101) must be given to a person *under 18* (who is unemancipated, unmarried, and not in the armed forces) because the court interpreted the word "juvenile" in the statute to mean the same as *juvenile* as defined in G.S. 7A-517(20) (now, G.S. 7B-1501(17)). The court noted that the preface to G.S. 7A-517 states, "Unless the context *clearly* requires otherwise, the following words have the listed meanings . . ." (emphasis added by court). It then concluded that the term "juvenile" in G.S. 7A-595 must be given the definition in G.S. 7A-517(20) because its context does not require or suggest a different interpretation. See the discussion of this case in footnote 439 of Chapter 2.

49. S.L. 2015-58, effective for offenses committed on or after December 1, 2015, amended G.S. 7B-2101(b) to increase the person's age from less than 14 years old to less than 16 years old.

50. State v. Miller, 344 N.C. 658 (1996) (juvenile warnings were sufficient); State v. Oglesby, 361 N.C. 550 (2007) (although aunt testified that she was a "mother figure" to the defendant, court ruled that this evidence did not constitute the legal authority inherent in a guardian or custodial relationship; thus, aunt was not a guardian under G.S. 7B-2101(a)(3) to require the officers to stop their questioning of the defendant); State v. Jones, 147 N.C. App. 527 (2001) (aunt was juvenile's guardian for purposes of G.S. 7A-595(b) (now, G.S. 7B-2101(b)); court noted that term "guardian" is not defined in juvenile code and rejected defendant's argument that guardian means only someone who is court appointed; court ruled that guardian under G.S. 7A-595(b) means a person upon whom government has conferred any authority over juvenile).

---

51. State v. McZorn, 288 N.C. 417 (1975).

52. Cases that discuss the necessity for repeating *Miranda* warnings include *State v. Harris*, 338 N.C. 129 (1994); *State v. Smith*, 328 N.C. 99 (1991); *State v. McZorn*, 288 N.C. 417 (1975); *State v. Branch*, 306 N.C. 101 (1982); *State v. White*, 291 N.C. 118 (1976); *State v. Simpson*, 297 N.C. 399 (1979); *State v. Westmoreland*, 314 N.C. 442 (1983); *State v. Artis*, 304 N.C. 378 (1981); *State v. Cole*, 293 N.C. 328 (1977); *State v. Garrison*, 294 N.C. 270 (1978); *State v. Flowers*, 121 N.C. App. 299 (1996); and *State v. Leak*, 90 N.C. App. 351 (1988).

may want to ask the defendant whether he or she remembers and understands the *Miranda* warnings given earlier. This reminder may be favorable evidence for the State if a court is unclear about whether *Miranda* warnings should have been repeated before the second interrogation.

Deliberate Technique of Question Arrestee First, Give Miranda Warnings Later

(*See page 680 for case summaries on this topic.*)

In *Missouri v. Seibert*,[53] an officer arrested the defendant for her involvement with an unlawful burning of a mobile home and the resulting death of a person inside. As part of an interrogation technique, the officer deliberately failed to give the defendant *Miranda* warnings, interrogated the defendant for 30 to 40 minutes, and obtained a confession. The defendant was then given a 20-minute break. The same officer then gave *Miranda* warnings to the defendant, obtained a waiver, interrogated her again (referring in this second interrogation to statements she had made in the first interrogation), and obtained another confession. The trial judge suppressed the first confession but admitted the second confession. The issue before the United States Supreme Court was the admissibility of the second confession.

The United States Supreme Court ruled that when an officer as part of an interrogation technique deliberately fails to give required *Miranda* warnings and obtains a confession, then later gives *Miranda* warnings and obtains another confession, neither the first nor second confession is admissible absent special circumstances.[54]

---

53. 542 U.S. 600 (2004).

54. The Court's opinion was a four-Justice plurality. A fifth Justice's opinion concurring in the judgment is recognized as the prevailing law by all but one of the federal appellate courts that have ruled on the issue. *See* United States v. Capers, 627 F.3d 470 (2d Cir. 2010). The fifth Justice's opinion disagreed with the reasoning of the plurality opinion. It stated that the admissibility of post-*Miranda* warning statements should continue to be governed by *Oregon v. Elstad*, 470 U.S. 298 (1985) (second voluntary incriminating statement obtained with *Miranda* warnings and waiver at police station was admissible even though it occurred after the defendant had made voluntary incriminating statement at his house that was inadmissible under *Miranda* because warnings had not been given), except when the second statement is obtained in the two-step interrogation technique deliberately used in this case to undermine the *Miranda* warning. In such a case, post-*Miranda* warning statements that are related to the substance of the pre-*Miranda* warning statements must be excluded unless curative measures are taken before the post-*Miranda*

Clearly, officers should not engage in this interrogation technique.

When the *Miranda* Rule Applies: Custody and Interrogation

As discussed above, the *Miranda* requirements—warnings and a waiver of rights—apply only before officers begin a custodial interrogation. Thus, without facts showing both "custody" and "interrogation" as courts have interpreted these terms, the *Miranda* rule is inapplicable. Of course, any statement made with or without the *Miranda* protections still must be made voluntarily, as discussed above.

The Meaning of "Custody"

(*See page 630 for case summaries on this topic.*)

The United States Supreme Court has ruled that a person is in custody under the *Miranda* rule when officers have formally arrested the person—for any offense, whether a felony or misdemeanor—or have restrained a person's movement to a degree associated with a formal arrest.[55]

---

warning statement is made. The curative measures discussed in this opinion were not taken in this case, so the opinion concluded that the second confession was inadmissible. For a North Carolina case since *Seibert*, see State v. Hartley, 212 N.C. App. 1 (2011) (court distinguished *Seibert* by noting that both confessions in *Seibert* were obtained while the defendant was in custody while the defendant in *Hartley* was not in custody when the first confession was obtained).

In *Bobby v. Dixon*, 132 S. Ct. 26 (2011), the Court determined that there was no *Seibert* violation. The nature of the interrogation in the case was different than in *Seibert*. Here, the Court explained, the defendant denied involvement in the murder and then, after *Miranda* warnings were given, changed his mind and confessed; in *Seibert* the defendant confessed both times. Additionally, the Court noted, in contrast to *Seibert*, the two interrogations at issue here did not occur in one continuum. To read more about the case, see the summary of *Bobby v. Dixon* in the case summaries appendix to this chapter.

55. Oregon v. Mathiason, 429 U.S. 492 (1977); California v. Beheler, 463 U.S. 1121 (1983); Berkemer v. McCarty, 468 U.S. 420 (1984); Stansbury v. California, 511 U.S. 318 (1994). Although the Court in *Miranda v. Arizona*, 384 U.S. 436 (1966), used the broad phrase "a person [who] has been taken into custody or otherwise deprived of his freedom of action in any significant way" in defining custody, 384 U.S. at 444, it clearly narrowed the concept of custody in *Berkemer* to situations where a person has been formally arrested or the officer's actions are the functional equivalent of arrest. The North Carolina Supreme Court in *State v. Buchanan*, 353 N.C. 332 (2001), *later ruling*, 355 N.C. 264 (2002), made clear that it

The mere giving of *Miranda* warnings when they are not required (because the defendant is not in custody) does not by itself transform noncustodial questioning into custodial interrogation.[56]

The seizure of a person under the Fourth Amendment. Custody is not the same as a seizure under the Fourth Amendment. For example, officers need not give *Miranda* warnings during an investigative stop unless and until they formally arrest the suspect or act in a manner that is functionally equivalent to a formal arrest.[57] They also need not give *Miranda* warnings when they merely stop a person to issue a citation and then let the person go. Although in both situations (investigative stop and stop to issue a citation) officers may have seized people under the Fourth Amendment, they did not take them into "custody" as the term is used in the *Miranda* decision. To understand the concept of custody better, the following paragraph summarizes the facts from a United States Supreme Court case, *Berkemer v. McCarty*:[58]

An Ohio law enforcement officer saw the defendant's car weaving in and out of a lane on an interstate highway. After following the car for two miles, the officer forced the defendant to stop and asked him to get out of the car. When the defendant got out, the officer noticed that he had difficulty standing. At this time, the officer apparently decided to arrest and charge the defendant, but he did not communicate his intention to the defendant. He asked the defendant to perform a field sobriety test, which the defendant could not do without falling. When the officer asked him whether he had been using intoxicants, the defendant replied that he had drunk some beers and had smoked some marijuana a short time before; his speech was slurred. The officer then formally arrested him and took him to jail.

The Court ruled that the defendant was not in custody under the *Miranda* ruling until the officer formally arrested him and transported him in the patrol car to the county jail. Therefore, the officer did not have to give the *Miranda* warnings until then. The Court stated that (1) the initial stop of the car did not, by itself, render the defendant in custody; (2) at no time between the initial stop and the arrest was the defendant subjected to restraints comparable with those of a formal arrest; (3) only a short time elapsed between the stop and the arrest; and (4) the officer's unarticulated intention to arrest the defendant after he stepped out of the car is irrelevant in considering whether the defendant was in custody. The only relevant inquiry is the objective test of "how a reasonable man in the [defendant's] position would have understood his situation." The officer's later questioning of the defendant beside his car and his request that the defendant perform a simple balancing test were not acts that are the functional equivalent of a formal arrest. However, once the officer formally arrested the defendant and transported him in his patrol car to the county jail, any statements by the defendant that the officer obtained by interrogation—for example, when asking questions in filling out an alcohol-influence report— would be inadmissible unless the officer gave *Miranda* warnings and obtained a waiver of rights.[59]

Functional equivalent of custody. As discussed above, the *Miranda* rule applies to interrogation not only after a formal arrest but also when a person's freedom is restrained in a manner that is similar to the restrictions imposed by a formal arrest. For example, the United States Supreme Court ruled that when four officers went

---

follows the United States Supreme Court rulings on the meaning of custody. It disavowed statements in prior rulings that were inconsistent with its opinion.

56. State v. Davis, 305 N.C. 400 (1982); Davis v. Allsbrook, 778 F.2d 168 (4th Cir. 1985).

57. Several cases provide an excellent analysis of the distinction between a seizure during an investigative stop and custody for *Miranda* purposes; *see* State v. Benjamin, 124 N.C. App. 734 (1996); United States v. Striefel, 781 F.2d 953 (1st Cir. 1986), *later ruling sub nom.* United States v. Quinn, 815 F.2d 153 (1st Cir. 1987); United States v. Bengivenga, 845 F.2d 593 (5th Cir. 1988) (en banc). *See also* State v. Buchanan, 353 N.C. 332 (2001), *later ruling*, 355 N.C. 264 (2002) (court noted that seizure standard under Fourth Amendment is different than custody standard under *Miranda*).

58. 468 U.S. 420 (1984). *See also* State v. Benjamin, 124 N.C. App. 734 (1996); United States v. Ventura, 85 F.3d 713 (1st Cir. 1996); United States v. Striefel, 781 F.2d 953 (1st Cir. 1986), *later ruling sub nom.* United States v. Quinn, 815 F.2d 153 (1st Cir. 1987); United States v. Bengivenga, 845 F.2d 593 (5th Cir. 1988) (en banc).

59. Note, however, that certain actions of a defendant after arrest may not be testimonial under the Fifth Amendment and therefore are admissible without the giving of *Miranda* warnings. *See* Pennsylvania v. Muniz, 496 U.S. 582 (1990) (defendant's slurred speech while being booked for driving under the influence was not testimonial and therefore not protected under the Fifth Amendment).

to a person's home in the middle of the night, entered a bedroom where the person was sleeping, surrounded him, and began to question him about a murder, he was in custody under the *Miranda* ruling even though the officers had not formally arrested him.[60] The person would reasonably perceive the officers' conduct as the beginning of a custodial arrest.

The focus of the investigation. The fact that officers have focused their investigation on a person does not mean that the person is in custody under the *Miranda* ruling.[61] For example, an officer may investigate a suspect for criminally fraudulent conduct, arrange a mutually agreeable meeting with the person at his or her home or at a law enforcement facility, and ask questions without giving *Miranda* warnings, as long as a reasonable person in the suspect's position would not have believed that he or she was under arrest or its functional equivalent.[62]

The officer's unarticulated knowledge or beliefs. As discussed above, the United States Supreme Court in *Berkemer v. McCarty* ruled that an officer's unarticulated

intention to arrest a person is irrelevant in determining whether a person is in custody, because the determination of custody focuses on what a reasonable person in the suspect's position would believe. An officer's knowledge or beliefs that are not communicated to or known by the suspect are therefore irrelevant. For example, the fact that an officer had probable cause to arrest the suspect or that an officer would not have let the suspect leave the officer's presence if the suspect had asked to leave or attempted to leave is irrelevant.[63] On the other hand, if officers tell a suspect that he or she is not under arrest and is free to leave,[64] even though they are not legally required to do so,[65] a suspect normally could not reasonably believe that he or she is in custody—and, therefore, a court likely will rule that the suspect was not in custody.

General on-the-scene questioning. When officers arrive at a crime scene—such as the scene of a homicide—or they are investigating whether a crime has occurred—such as a possible crime[66] arising from a car accident[67]—they may question people there without giving *Miranda* warnings and obtaining a waiver, even if they believe that a particular person with whom they are talking committed a crime. The *Miranda* rule would apply only when the officers formally arrested that person or by their words or conduct restricted the person's freedom in a way that a reasonable person would normally associate with a formal arrest.

Inmate in jail or prison. (See page 645 for case summaries on this topic.) An inmate in a jail or prison is not always in custody for the purposes of the *Miranda* requirement.[68] However, an inmate is considered to be in

---

60. *Orozco v. Texas*, 394 U.S. 324 (1969). Although the finding of custody in *Orozco* is consistent with the discussion of custody in *Berkemer v. McCarty*, 468 U.S. 420 (1984), *Orozco* is now inconsistent with *Berkemer* when it implies that an officer's unarticulated belief that the defendant was under arrest is a factor in determining custody. For other cases finding custody, see *State v. Torres*, 330 N.C. 517 (1992); *State v. Washington*, 330 N.C. 188 (1991); *State v. Johnston*, 154 N.C. App. 500 (2002); *State v. Beckham*, 105 N.C. App. 214 (1992); *State v. Harvey*, 78 N.C. App. 235 (1985); and *United States v. Wauneka*, 770 F.2d 1434 (9th Cir. 1985), *later appeal*, 842 F.2d 1083 (9th Cir. 1988).

61. *Stansbury v. California*, 511 U.S. 318 (1994) (Court rejected focus of investigation as factor in determining custody); *Beckwith v. United States*, 425 U.S. 341 (1976); *Minnesota v. Murphy*, 465 U.S. 420 (1984). The concept of focus of investigation first appeared in the pre-*Miranda* case of *Escobedo v. Illinois*, 378 U.S. 478 (1964), and reappeared in note 4 of the Court's opinion in *Miranda v. Arizona*, 384 U.S. 436 (1966). However, the Court in *Beckwith* and *Murphy* explicitly disavowed the focus of an investigation as the factor constituting custody to require *Miranda* warnings. Unfortunately, the term "focus of investigation" still sometimes appears in appellate decisions that are otherwise correctly decided; *see* State v. West, 317 N.C. 219 (1986). The fact that an officer's investigation has focused on a suspect would be relevant in determining custody only in the rare instance in which (1) the suspect was aware that he or she was the focus of an investigation and (2) that factor along with other evidence would lead a reasonable person in the suspect's position to believe that he or she was in custody or the functional equivalent of custody.

62. *Beckwith v. United States*, 425 U.S. 341 (1976).

63. State v. Buchanan, 353 N.C. 332 (2001), *later ruling*, 355 N.C. 264 (2002); United States v. Feather, 801 F.2d 157 (4th Cir. 1986); United States v. Bengivenga, 845 F.2d 593 (5th Cir. 1988) (en banc).

64. *See, e.g.*, Oregon v. Mathiason, 429 U.S. 492 (1977); State v. Allen, 322 N.C. 176 (1988); United States v. Jones, 818 F.2d 1119 (4th Cir. 1987).

65. *See, e.g.*, State v. Davis, 305 N.C. 400 (1982) (officer's failure to advise defendant that he was free to go at will did not adversely affect the finding that the defendant was not in custody).

66. State v. Chappell, 24 N.C. App. 656 (1975).

67. State v. Hayes, 273 N.C. 712 (1968).

68. Howes v. Field, 132 S. Ct. 1181 (2012) (Court ruled that a federal appellate court erroneously concluded that a prisoner was in custody under *Miranda* when the prisoner was taken aside and questioned about events that occurred outside the prison); State v. Briggs, 137 N.C. App. 125 (2000); United States v. Conley, 779 F.2d 970 (4th Cir. 1985). The court in *Conley*

custody if the inmate is not free to depart from the place of interrogation or if other factors establish that his or her freedom of movement is being restricted beyond the usual restraint of being in a jail or prison.[69]

Age of a juvenile. (See page 647 for case summaries on this topic.) The United States Supreme Court in *J.D.B. v. North Carolina* ruled that the age of a juvenile (a person under 18 years old) is a factor that must be considered in making the objective determination as to whether the juvenile is in custody, as long as the juvenile's age is known or reasonably apparent to an officer.[70] The Court reasoned that a juvenile will often feel bound to submit to law enforcement questioning when an adult in the same circumstances would not. The Court also clearly indicated that the actual age of the juvenile must be considered, because a young juvenile may be more susceptible than an older juvenile; the Court stated that officers and judges "simply need the common sense to know that a 7-year-old is not a 13-year-old and neither is an adult."[71]

The Meaning of "Interrogation"

(See page 650 for case summaries on this topic.)

The United States Supreme Court in *Rhode Island v. Innis*[72] ruled that "interrogation" under the *Miranda* rule includes not only express questioning but also any functional equivalent of questioning; that is, an officer's words or actions—other than those normally associated with arrest and custody—that the officer should know are reasonably likely to elicit an incriminating response from the defendant, as those words or actions are perceived by that particular defendant. The following paragraph summarizes the facts in *Innis*[73] and the Court's analysis of the concept of *functional equivalent of questioning*:

> The defendant was arrested within hours after robbing a taxicab driver with a sawed-off shotgun. He was unarmed when he was arrested. After he was given *Miranda* warnings, he said he wanted to speak with a lawyer. A supervisor then instructed three officers to take him to the police station and told them not to question him in any way. While en route, two officers talked with each other about the missing shotgun and their concern that children from a nearby school for the handicapped might find it and harm themselves. The defendant then volunteered that he would show them where the weapon was located. The Court ruled that the officers' conversation was

---

distinguished the ruling in *Mathis v. United States*, 391 U.S. 1 (1968) (prisoner was in custody when questioned about a crime unrelated to the crime for which he was imprisoned). *See also* Maryland v. Shatzer, 559 U.S. 98 (2010) (Court noted that no one questioned that prisoner serving sentence was in custody during questioning by detective about another crime, based on facts in this case).

69. State v. Briggs, 137 N.C. App. 125 (2000) (inmate is not, because of his incarceration, automatically in custody under *Miranda*; rather, whether inmate is in custody must be determined by considering his freedom to depart from place of his interrogation); State v. Fisher, 158 N.C. App. 133 (2003) (defendant inmate not in custody under *Miranda*); State v. Wright, 184 N.C. App. 464 (2007) (defendant in military brig was not in custody under *Miranda*); United States v. Conley, 779 F.2d 970 (4th Cir. 1985) (prisoner was not in custody when he was questioned about murder while awaiting medical treatment); United States v. Cooper, 800 F.2d 412 (4th Cir. 1986); United States v. Willoughby, 860 F.2d 15 (2d Cir. 1988); United States v. Scalf, 725 F.2d 1272 (10th Cir. 1984); Leviston v. Black, 843 F.2d 302 (8th Cir. 1988); Cervantes v. Walker, 589 F.2d 424 (9th Cir. 1978).

70. 564 U.S. 261 (2011). The Court cautioned, however, that a juvenile's age will not necessarily be a determinative, or even significant, factor in every case. For North Carolina cases, see *In re A.N.C., Jr.*, 225 N.C. App. 315 (2013) (court ruled that a 13-year-old juvenile was not in custody within the meaning of G.S. 7B-2101 or *Miranda* during a roadside questioning by an officer; noting that under *J.D.B. v. North Carolina*, a reviewing court must, when determining whether a suspect has been placed in custody, take into account a juvenile's age if it was known to an officer or would have been objectively apparent to a reasonable officer; the court nevertheless concluded that the juvenile was not in custody); *State v. Yancey*, 221 N.C. App. 397 (2012) (court ruled that the juvenile defendant was not in custody under *Miranda* when questioned in an unmarked law enforcement vehicle by two detectives dressed in plain clothes; the juvenile was 17 years and 10 months old; considering the totality of the circumstances—including the defendant's age— the court concluded that the defendant was not in custody; the court rejected the argument that *J.D.B. v. North Carolina* required a different conclusion).

---

71. 564 U.S. 261, 280.

72. 446 U.S. 291 (1980).

73. *See also* Arizona v. Mauro, 481 U.S. 520 (1987) (defendant was arrested for murder of his son and asserted his right to counsel after being given *Miranda* warnings; defendant's wife insisted on seeing her husband, who was being held in police captain's office; officers allowed meeting, but only if an officer could be present and conversation could be tape recorded; conversation between defendant and his wife was later admitted at defendant's trial; Court ruled that officer did not engage in interrogation as defined in *Rhode Island v. Innis*—it stated: "Officers do not interrogate a suspect simply by hoping that he will incriminate himself.").

not interrogation. There was nothing to suggest that the two officers should have known that their conversation between themselves was reasonably likely to elicit an incriminating response from the defendant. They had no reason to believe that the defendant was peculiarly susceptible to an appeal to his conscience about the handicapped children's safety. Nor did they know that he was unusually disoriented or upset when he was arrested. The Court also noted that the officers did not have a lengthy conversation in the defendant's presence, nor were their remarks particularly evocative.

The North Carolina Court of Appeals ruled that an officer's remarks were the functional equivalent of questioning as set forth in *Rhode Island v. Innis* when an officer held a pocketbook (which he believed the defendant had secreted in a car) in front of the in-custody defendant and twice said to him, "I wonder whose this is?" and then said that it belonged to either the defendant or another named person.[74] The court concluded that the officer should have known that his remarks were likely to elicit an incriminating response.

Volunteered statements. (See page 655 for case summaries on this topic.) An in-custody defendant's voluntary statement is admissible, even if *Miranda* warnings have not been given, if it is not made as a result of interrogation. For example, if a defendant makes a statement while an officer is simply serving an arrest warrant or transporting the defendant, it is a volunteered statement not made in response to interrogation. The statement is admissible at trial even though the officer had not yet given *Miranda* warnings to the defendant.[75] An officer's

questions that are asked in order to clarify a defendant's volunteered statement also are not interrogation.[76]

Questions by undercover law enforcement officers or by non–law enforcement officers. The United States Supreme Court ruled in *Illinois v. Perkins*[77] that *Miranda* warnings are not required when the defendant is not aware that he or she is speaking to a law enforcement officer—even if the defendant is in custody. Thus, if an officer goes into a jail in an undercover capacity and asks questions as if he or she is an inmate, *Miranda* warnings are not required. However, an officer may violate the defendant's Sixth Amendment right to counsel by questioning the defendant about a charge for which he or she already has a Sixth Amendment right to counsel—see the discussion later in this chapter.

Based on the Court's ruling in *Perkins*, *Miranda* warnings also are not required when a defendant is questioned by a private person, even when that person is acting under an officer's direction—unless the defendant knows that the person is acting under the officer's direction.[78]

---

74. State v. Young, 65 N.C. App. 346 (1983). *See also* State v. Washington, 330 N.C. 188 (1991) (similar ruling). Cases in which an officer's remarks were not the functional equivalent of interrogation include *State v. Vick*, 341 N.C. 569 (1995); *State v. DeCastro*, 342 N.C. 667 (1996); *State v. Clark*, 324 N.C. 146 (1989); *State v. Forney*, 310 N.C. 126 (1984); *State v. Ladd*, 308 N.C. 272 (1983); *State v. Porter*, 303 N.C. 680 (1980); and *State v. Crawford*, 58 N.C. App. 160 (1982).

75. State v. Herring, 284 N.C. 398 (1973). *See also* State v. Coffey, 345 N.C. 389 (1997); State v. Walls, 342 N.C. 1 (1995); State v. Edgerton, 328 N.C. 319 (1991); State v. Porter, 303 N.C. 680 (1980); State v. Thomas, 284 N.C. 212 (1973); State v. Muse, 280 N.C. 31 (1971).

76. State v. Porter, 303 N.C. 680 (1980); State v. Moose, 101 N.C. App. 59 (1990); United States v. Gonzales, 121 F.3d 928 (5th Cir. 1997); Anderson v. Thieret, 903 F.2d 526 (7th Cir. 1990).

77. 496 U.S. 292 (1990). An issue unanswered by *Perkins* is whether an officer may act in an undercover capacity after the defendant has asserted the right to counsel under the *Miranda* ruling. Courts have upheld such activity. *See* Salkil v. Delo, 990 F.2d 386 (8th Cir. 1993) (defendant invoked right to counsel for offense A; cellmate acting on behalf of officers questioned defendant about offense B, for which defendant had not yet been charged; no Fifth or Sixth Amendment violation); Alexander v. Connecticut, 917 F.2d 747 (2d Cir. 1990) (similar ruling). However, questioning a defendant may violate a defendant's Sixth Amendment right to counsel under some circumstances. *But see* United States v. Ingle, 157 F.3d 1147 (8th Cir. 1998) (although lawyer had been appointed to represent defendant who was target of grand jury about murder for which defendant had not yet been charged, defendant did not have Sixth Amendment right to counsel when officers used jail inmate to solicit statements from defendant).

78. Salkil v. Delo, 990 F.2d 386 (8th Cir. 1993); Alexander v. Connecticut, 917 F.2d 747 (2d Cir. 1990). The following cases were decided before *Illinois v. Perkins, supra* note 77. The results in these cases are correct, but it is no longer necessary to analyze whether the private people were acting on behalf of law enforcement officers: State v. Holcomb, 295 N.C. 608 (1978) (conversation between defendant and his uncles at sheriff's office was not custodial interrogation when there was no evidence that the uncles were acting as agents of law enforcement officers); State v. Powell, 340 N.C. 674 (1995) (similar ruling); State v. Johnson, 29 N.C. App. 141 (1976) (police radio

(However, an officer may be violating a defendant's Sixth Amendment right to counsel when a non–law enforcement officer acts under the officer's direction, as discussed later in this chapter.) Even if *Miranda* warnings are not required, the defendant's statement still must have been made voluntarily.[79]

Request for consent to search. (See page 655 for case summaries on this topic.) The North Carolina Court of

Appeals has ruled that an officer's request of a defendant for consent to search is not interrogation and, therefore, an officer may approach a defendant—even if the defendant has asserted the right to remain silent or the right to counsel—and ask for consent to search.[80] Of course, officers generally may not reinitiate custodial interrogation when a defendant has asserted the right to remain silent or the right to counsel, as discussed below. Officers also may not conduct interrogation when requesting consent to search if a defendant has asserted those rights.[81]

Waiver of *Miranda* Rights

(See page 621 for case summaries on this topic.)

Before officers undertake custodial interrogation, they must inform the defendant of *Miranda* rights and any applicable North Carolina statutory rights, as discussed above. Officers also must be sure that the defendant understands these rights. The State has the burden of proving by a preponderance of the evidence that the defendant knowingly and voluntarily waived these rights.[82]

The United States Supreme Court has ruled that a court may find a legally sufficient waiver of *Miranda* rights following the giving of warnings without an officer's explicitly discussing a waiver with the defendant if other factors show an implied waiver.[83] Despite this ruling, cautious officers may want to continue to obtain an

---

dispatcher was not a law enforcement officer and was not acting as one); State v. Perry, 50 N.C. App. 540 (1981) (bail bondsman taking defendant into custody as bail jumper was not a law enforcement officer); State v. Conrad, 55 N.C. App. 63 (1981) (magistrate was not acting as law enforcement officer when she talked to defendant). For a post-*Perkins* case that did not discuss *Perkins* but in which the result is correct in any event, see *State v. Clodfelter*, 203 N.C. App. 60 (2010) (mother not agent of law enforcement when all officers asked her to do, and all she in fact did do, was ask her son to tell the truth about his involvement in a murder).

Another issue is whether a government official who is not a law enforcement officer may under some circumstances be required to give *Miranda* warnings. In *State v. Morrell*, 108 N.C. App. 465 (1993), the defendant was arrested for a federal charge of child abduction and was committed to a county jail. A social worker in the county child protective services unit identified herself and told the defendant that she was conducting an investigation of alleged sexual abuse and neglect of a boy with whom the defendant had had a relationship. The defendant confessed to the social worker. Two days later, a deputy sheriff talked with the defendant in the jail after giving her *Miranda* warnings and obtaining a proper waiver. The defendant again confessed. Based on evidence that the social worker was working with the sheriff's department on the case before interviewing the defendant in jail, the court ruled that the social worker was an agent of the State and thus was required to give *Miranda* warnings when that interview occurred. The court upheld the admissibility of the defendant's confession to the deputy sheriff because the confession to the social worker was not coerced. *See* Oregon v. Elstad, 470 U.S. 298 (1985); State v. Barlow, 330 N.C. 133 (1991). However, the court did not discuss *Illinois v. Perkins*, 496 U.S. 292 (1990). If the defendant did not know that the social worker was acting on behalf of the deputy sheriff or was a government official involved in investigating or reporting criminal offenses, then the ruling in *Perkins* may not have required the social worker to give *Miranda* warnings. However, one can argue that the *Morrell* facts clearly establish that the defendant knew the social worker was a government official and that her duties included the investigation or reporting of crimes. *See* Mathis v. United States, 391 U.S. 1 (1968); Cates v. State, 776 S.W.2d 170 (Tex. Crim. App. 1989); State v. Nason, 981 P.2d 866 (Wash. Ct. App. 1999).

79. *See* Arizona v. Fulminante, 499 U.S. 279 (1991); State v. Alston, 295 N.C. 629 (1978); United States v. Ingle, 157 F.3d 1147 (8th Cir. 1998).

80. State v. Cummings, 188 N.C. App. 598 (2008). For similar rulings, see *United States v. Hildalgo*, 7 F.3d 1566 (11th Cir. 1993); *United States v. Shlater*, 85 F.3d 1251 (7th Cir. 1996); *United States v. Gleena*, 878 F.2d 967 (7th Cir. 1989); and *United States v. McCurdy*, 40 F.3d 1111 (10th Cir. 1994). *See also* United States v. Kon Yu-Leung, 910 F.2d 33 (2d Cir. 1990) (post indictment request of defendant to consent to search is not a critical stage); United States v. Edmo, 140 F.3d 1289 (9th Cir. 1998) (request of defendant to give urine sample was not interrogation even though request was made after defendant asserted right to counsel).

81. Of course, if the defendant reinitiates communication with the officer or volunteers statements when the officer requests consent to search, the defendant's statements would be admissible.

82. Colorado v. Connelly, 479 U.S. 157 (1986). A valid waiver focuses on the defendant's state of mind, not on the lawyer who may be representing the defendant. *See* Moran v. Burbine, 475 U.S. 412 (1986); State v. Reese, 319 N.C. 110 (1987).

83. Berghuis v. Thompkins, 560 U.S. 370 (2010). For an analysis of *Berghuis*, see Robert L. Farb, *The United States Supreme Court's Ruling in Berghuis v. Thompkins* (UNC School of Government, June 2010), www.sog.unc.edu/resources/legal-summaries/berghuis-v-thompkins-and-waiver-miranda-rights.

explicit waiver as reflected in many *Miranda* forms. A properly obtained explicit waiver will increase the like-lihood—compared to an impaired waiver—that a court will find a valid waiver. And even if there are deficiencies in obtaining an explicit waiver, there still may be suffi-cient evidence that a court will find a legally sufficient implied waiver.

Both the *Miranda* and statutory warnings and the defendant's waiver may be accomplished orally. Although it is not legally required, officers may want to use a writ-ten form to increase the likelihood of proving the validity of the warnings and waiver, and they may want to orally repeat what is contained in the form to make sure that the defendant fully understands its content.

The discussion below states that an officer is not required to clarify a defendant's equivocal assertion of the right to remain silent or the right to counsel. However, that legal principle may not apply at the waiver stage. (This issue has not been decided by the United States Supreme Court or North Carolina appellate courts.) For example, a court might not find a valid waiver of *Miranda* rights if the defendant was unclear at the waiver stage whether he or she wanted to assert the right to remain silent or the right to counsel. An officer may need to clarify whether the defendant is willing to waive the right to remain silent and the right to counsel before obtaining a valid waiver.[84]

A Defendant's Assertion of the Right to Remain Silent and the Right to Counsel

When an in-custody defendant clearly asserts the right to remain silent or the right to counsel while *Miranda* warnings are being given or after custodial interrogation has begun, officers may not begin interrogation or must immediately stop interrogation if it has already begun.

Asserting the Right to Remain Silent
(*See page 657 for case summaries on this topic.*)

The United States Supreme Court ruled in *Berghuis v. Thompkins* that a defendant must unequivocally assert the right to remain silent to require an officer to stop cus-todial interrogation.[85] Generally, a defendant's statement

that he or she does not want to talk is an unequivocal assertion of the right to remain silent, including a state-ment, "I got nothing to say."[86] On the other hand, a defen-dant's simply remaining silent or failing to answer some questions, while continuing to answer others, generally is not considered an unequivocal assertion of the right to remain silent.[87]

What if a defendant merely expresses uncertainty about talking—that is, he or she does not make an unam-biguous assertion of the right to remain silent? The *Ber-ghuis* ruling provides that an officer is not required to clarify a defendant's equivocal (uncertain) request to remain silent and thus may continue to interrogate the defendant.[88] For example, a defendant's statement, "I'm not sure I want to answer any more questions," would not require clarification by an officer. However, a prudent offi-cer who is unsure whether a defendant's request is clear or equivocal may want to clarify whether the defendant wants to remain silent.

Asserting the Right to Counsel
(*See page 661 for case summaries on this topic.*)

When assertion of right to counsel may be made. A defendant may assert the right to counsel during custo-dial interrogation—for example, when *Miranda* warn-ings are being given or during actual interrogation.[89] In addition, an in-custody defendant may properly assert the right to counsel before impending custodial interroga-tion; that is, the defendant makes the assertion shortly before the officers have given *Miranda* warnings.[90]

A defendant's request for counsel *before* the defendant is in custody is not a proper request for counsel under

---

84. *See* State v. Leyva, 951 P.2d 738 (Utah 1997); State v. Galli, 967 P.2d 930 (Utah 1998). It is unclear whether the rul-ings in these cases, decided before *Berghuis v. Thompkins*, 560 U.S. 370 (2010), are adversely affected by the waiver analysis in *Berghuis*.

85. 560 U.S. 370 (2010). Before the *Berghuis* ruling, the North Carolina Supreme Court had ruled similarly in *State*

v. Golphin, 352 N.C. 364 (2000). Concerning a related issue, a defendant's assertion of the right to remain silent before he or she is in custody—like the assertion of the right to counsel under similar circumstances—is likely not a proper assertion. *Bobby v. Dixon*, 132 S. Ct. 26 (2011) (Court stated that it had never ruled that a person can invoke *Miranda* rights anticipa-torily in a context other than custodial interrogation).

86. State v. Murphy, 342 N.C. 813 (1996).

87. Berghuis v. Thompkins, 560 U.S. 370 (2010); State v. Westmoreland, 314 N.C. 442 (1985). *See also* State v. Robbins, 319 N.C. 465 (1987); United States v. Mikell, 102 F.3d 470 (11th Cir. 1996).

88. 560 U.S. 370 (2010).

89. McNeil v. Wisconsin, 501 U.S. 171 (1991). The Court did not decide in *McNeil* whether a person may assert the right to counsel other than during custodial interrogation. See note 3 of the Court's opinion.

90. State v. Torres, 330 N.C. 517 (1992).

Miranda.[91] Thus, such a request does not bar an officer from interrogating the defendant. Of course, if the defendant requests counsel again after being taken into custody, the officer is barred from conducting interrogation. A prudent officer who is unsure whether the defendant was in custody when the defendant requested counsel may decide not to attempt to interrogate the defendant or seek clarification of the defendant's custodial status before attempting to interrogate the defendant.

A defendant's in-court assertion that he or she wants a lawyer for a pending charge is not considered an assertion of the right to counsel under the Fifth Amendment.[92] However, that in-court assertion clearly qualifies as an assertion of the Sixth Amendment right to counsel for the pending charge; see the discussion later in this chapter.

Equivocal and unequivocal requests for counsel. The United States Supreme Court ruled in *Smith v. Illinois*[93] that when a defendant makes an unequivocal (clear) request for counsel, questioning must stop, and a defendant's responses to additional interrogation conducted after the defendant made a clear request may not be used to cast doubt on the initial request for counsel. The Court ruled in *Smith* that when a defendant said, "Uh, yeah. I'd like to do that," after being told of the right to counsel, that statement was a clear request for counsel—particularly because the defendant had mentioned earlier to the officers that a woman had told him to get a lawyer because they would railroad him.

On the other hand, the United States Supreme Court ruled in *Davis v. United States*[94] that if a defendant makes an equivocal reference to an attorney, an officer is not required to stop the interrogation if a reasonable officer under the circumstances only would have understood that the defendant might be invoking the right to counsel. An officer must stop an interrogation only when the defendant makes an unequivocal assertion of the right to counsel.

The investigators in *Davis* gave the in-custody defendant *Miranda* warnings and received a proper waiver of his rights. About an hour and a half into the interrogation, the defendant said, "Maybe I should talk to a lawyer." The investigators told the defendant that they did not want to violate his rights, that they would stop questioning him if he wanted a lawyer, and that they would not pursue the matter unless it was clarified whether he was asking for a lawyer or was just making a comment about a lawyer. The defendant said, "No, I'm not asking for a lawyer." He then said, "No, I don't want a lawyer." After a short break, the investigators reminded the defendant of his rights to remain silent and to counsel. The defendant then made incriminating statements that he later sought to suppress at trial, arguing that the investigators violated their duty to stop the interrogation once the defendant had asserted the right to counsel. Based on these facts, the Court ruled that the defendant did not make an unequivocal request for counsel and, therefore, the investigators did not violate the defendant's constitutional rights.[95] The Court noted that when a defendant makes an ambiguous or equivocal request for counsel, it often will be good law enforcement practice for officers to clarify whether or not the defendant wants a lawyer. Clarifying questions protect the defendant's rights by ensuring that the defendant gets a lawyer if he or she wants one and minimize the risk of a confession being suppressed by later judicial second-guessing of the meaning of the defendant's statement about counsel. But the Court reiterated that if the defendant's statement is not an unequivocal request for counsel, officers are not obligated to stop interrogation.

As discussed on page 579 concerning waiver of *Miranda* rights, if a defendant makes an equivocal request for counsel when an officer is giving *Miranda* warnings or obtaining a waiver of rights, the officer should clarify whether or not the defendant wants a lawyer.

Partial assertion of right to counsel. Sometimes a defendant makes only a partial assertion of the right to counsel. For example, a United States Supreme Court case involved a defendant who was properly given *Miranda* warnings and waived his rights. He said that he would not give a written statement without the presence of a lawyer, but he was willing to talk about the alleged crime.

---

91. State v. Daughtry, 340 N.C. 488 (1995); State v. Medlin, 333 N.C. 280 (1993); State v. Willis, 109 N.C. App. 184 (1993); Burket v. Angelone, 208 F.3d 172 (4th Cir. 2000). *See also* Bobby v. Dixon, 132 S. Ct. 26 (2011) (Court stated that it had never ruled that a person can invoke *Miranda* rights anticipatorily in a context other than custodial interrogation).

92. McNeil v. Wisconsin, 501 U.S. 171 (1991); State v. Tucker, 331 N.C. 12 (1992).

93. 469 U.S. 91 (1984).

94. 512 U.S. 452 (1994).

95. The Court's *Davis* ruling now casts doubt on the validity of a ruling in *State v. Torres*, 330 N.C. 517 (1992), that the defendant unequivocally invoked her right to counsel when she asked law enforcement officers whether she needed a lawyer.

He then orally confessed. The Court ruled that the defendant's invocation of the right to counsel was limited only to making written statements and did not prohibit further oral discussions with the officers.[96]

Request to speak to a person who is not a lawyer. A defendant's request to speak to someone other than a lawyer is generally not considered an assertion of the right to counsel or the right to remain silent.[97] In such a case, however, officers should be particularly careful when obtaining a waiver of rights to assure that the defendant is willing to talk to them without a lawyer being present. Remember that a person under 18 who asserts the right to have a parent, guardian, or custodian present during custodial interrogation must have that request honored before questioning may begin or continue.[98]

Resumption of Interrogation after the Defendant's Assertion of Rights

When, if ever, may officers attempt to resume interrogation after there has been an assertion of rights? The rules differ, depending upon whether the defendant has asserted the right to remain silent or the right to counsel.[99] Therefore, they will be discussed separately. If the

---

96. Connecticut v. Barrett, 479 U.S. 523 (1987).

97. Fare v. Michael C., 442 U.S. 707 (1979).

98. State v. Smith, 317 N.C. 100 (1986).

99. The United States Supreme Court ruled in *Edwards v. Arizona*, 451 U.S. 477 (1981), that when a defendant has asserted the *right to counsel*, an officer may not question the defendant until a lawyer is made available or unless the defendant "initiates further communication, exchanges, or conversations" with the officer. (The Court recently modified *Edwards* in *Maryland v. Shatzer*, 559 U.S. 98 (2010), to permit reinitiation of interrogation under certain circumstances, as discussed later in the text.)

However, when a defendant has asserted only the *right to remain silent*, the officer's duty is to "scrupulously honor" that assertion. This means, as the United States Supreme Court ruled in *Michigan v. Mosley*, 423 U.S. 96 (1975), that an officer may, under certain circumstances, question the defendant after a period of time even though the defendant has not initiated further communication, exchanges, or conversations with the officer and has not had access to a lawyer.

The North Carolina Supreme Court clearly recognized in *State v. Murphy*, 342 N.C. 813 (1996), that the standard for reinterrogation after a defendant asserts the right to remain silent differs from the standard for reinterrogation when a defendant asserts the right to counsel. Thus, the court implicitly disavowed contrary statements in *State v. Bragg*, 67 N.C. App. 759 (1984) and *State v. Crawford*, 83 N.C. App. 135 (1986), discussed in the next paragraph.

Both *Bragg* and *Crawford* ruled that when a defendant asserts the right to remain silent, the rule of *Edwards v. Arizona* applies. Thus, an officer may not question the defendant until a lawyer is made available or unless the defendant initiates further communication, exchanges, or conversations with the officer. (In both cases, the court's rulings would have been the same if it had applied the standard set out in the *Mosley* case. In *Bragg*, the officer clearly did not "scrupulously honor" the defendant's assertion of his right to remain silent when he interrogated the defendant shortly after he asserted his right to remain silent and continued to interrogate him even when he again stated that he did not want to talk to anyone. In *Crawford*, the officer's conduct did not violate either the *Mosley* or *Edwards* standard. Neither opinion in *Bragg* or *Crawford* discussed the *Mosley* case.) These cases are in direct conflict with *Michigan v. Mosley* and the later case of *State v. Murphy*, 342 N.C. 813 (1996), discussed above, and therefore are not correct statements of federal constitutional law.

After the *Bragg* and *Crawford* cases were decided, the North Carolina Court of Appeals decided *State v. Fortner*, 93 N.C. App. 753 (1989), which was consistent with *Michigan v. Mosley* because it used the "scrupulously honor" test, described above. In *Fortner*, the defendant was arrested for murder and committed to jail. He made an incriminating statement after officers had properly given him *Miranda* warnings and obtained a waiver. He then told them that he did not want to answer any more questions, and the officers immediately stopped the interrogation. Several hours later, an SBI agent questioned the defendant after properly giving him *Miranda* warnings and obtaining a waiver. The court ruled that the SBI agent did not violate the defendant's *Miranda* rights, based on *Michigan v. Mosley*.

The Court's opinion in *Edwards v. Arizona* implicitly recognized the distinction between the "procedural safeguards triggered by a request to remain silent and a request for an attorney." 451 U.S. at 485. All the Justices of the United States Supreme Court recognized in both the majority and dissenting opinions in *Solem v. Stumes*, 465 U.S. 638 (1984), that *Mosley* and *Edwards* had set different standards for reinterrogation depending on whether the defendant had asserted the right to remain silent or the right to counsel. *See* 465 U.S. at 648 (majority opinion) and 465 U.S. at 658 (dissenting opinion). The Court reaffirmed the distinction in *Arizona v. Roberson*, 486 U.S. 465 (1988). *See also* McNeil v. Wisconsin, 501 U.S. 171 (1991); State v. Morris, 332 N.C. 600 (1992).

Although the United States Supreme Court has not directly decided whether the *Mosley* standard also applies when an officer initiates questioning of the defendant about the same crime after the defendant had asserted the right to remain silent, other courts—in addition to the North Carolina appellate courts in *State v. Temple*, 302 N.C. 1 (1981), *State v. Hill*, 294 N.C. 320 (1978), and *State v. Fortner*, cited above—have uniformly applied the *Mosley* standard to that situation as well. *See* Brown v. Caspari, 186 F.3d 1011 (8th Cir. 1999) (court upheld questioning about same crime three hours after defendant asserted the right to remain silent); Kelly v. Lynaugh,

defendant has asserted both rights, the more restrictive rule that applies to assertions of the right to counsel governs both.

The Right to Remain Silent

(*See page 657 for case summaries on this topic.*)

The United States Supreme Court in *Michigan v. Mosley*[100] discussed an officer's authority to resume questioning after a defendant's assertion of the right to remain silent:

> A robbery detective arrested the defendant for two robberies, properly gave him *Miranda* warnings, and properly obtained a waiver of rights. When the defendant said that he did not want to answer any questions about the robberies (he did not assert his right to counsel, however), the detective immediately stopped his questioning. About two hours later, a homicide detective sought to question the defendant about an unrelated murder. He properly gave him *Miranda* warnings and properly obtained a waiver of rights. The defendant did not ask for a lawyer or assert his right to remain silent. He then confessed to the murder.

The Court ruled that the admissibility of a defendant's statements after the defendant has exercised the right to remain silent depends on whether that right is "scrupulously honored"—as it was in this case. The Court noted that the robbery detective immediately stopped his questioning after the defendant said that he did not want to discuss the robberies. He did not attempt to resume questioning or in any way try to persuade the defendant to reconsider his refusal to talk. After questioning had been suspended for a "significant period of time" (in this case, about two hours), the homicide detective—after giving the *Miranda* rights and obtaining a waiver—did not question the defendant about the robberies but instead focused exclusively on a completely unrelated crime.

It is difficult to set out a general rule as to when an officer may resume questioning after a defendant has asserted the right to remain silent. An officer should remember that *Michigan v. Mosley* did not involve a resumption of questioning by the same officer for the same crime. The United States Supreme Court would not necessarily have approved of further questioning under identical circumstances after only two hours. The critical question is whether the officer scrupulously honored the defendant's assertion of the right to remain silent by waiting a significant period of time before attempting a second interrogation.

Federal and state cases have upheld a second interrogation, with new *Miranda* warnings and a waiver, for the same crime after a defendant asserted the right to remain silent.[101] In these cases, officers immediately stopped interrogation when a defendant asserted the right to remain silent during the first interrogation, and they waited for time periods ranging from a few hours to a day before reinterrogating the defendant. On the other hand, the North Carolina Supreme Court ruled that an officer did not scrupulously honor a defendant's assertion of the right to remain silent when the officer initiated interrogation about a different crime 15 minutes after the assertion.[102]

If a defendant asserts the right to remain silent and then changes that decision on his or her own initiative and wants to talk with officers, they may talk with the defendant immediately. However, officers should consider giving *Miranda* rights to the defendant again and obtain-

---

862 F.2d 1126 (5th Cir. 1988) (court upheld officer's resumption of questioning between 8:30 p.m. and 10:00 p.m. about same crime after defendant had asserted right to remain silent during two prior attempts to interrogate him, the first at about 11:00 a.m. and the second at about 4:00 p.m.); Jackson v. Dugger, 837 F.2d 1469 (11th Cir. 1988) (court upheld officer's resumption of questioning about same crime when significant period of time—more than six hours—had elapsed between original assertion of right to remain silent and reinterrogation); Jackson v. Wyrick, 730 F.2d 1177 (8th Cir. 1984) (court upheld officers' resumption of questioning about same crime after assertion of right to remain silent—officers waited 24 hours before resuming questioning); Hatley v. State, 709 S.W.2d 812 (Ark. 1986) (questioning about same crime two hours after assertion of right to silence was permissible); Hatley v. Lockhart, 990 F.2d 1070 (8th Cir. 1993) (effectively affirming Arkansas Supreme Court ruling on federal habeas); People v. Quezada, 731 P.2d 730 (Colo. 1987) (questioning about the same crime one hour after assertion of right to silence was permissible); State v. Turner, 401 N.W.2d 827 (Wis. 1987) (questioning about the same crime 24 hours after assertion of right to silence was permissible).

100. 423 U.S. 96 (1975).

101. *See* cases cited *supra* note 99.

102. State v. Murphy, 342 N.C. 813 (1996).

ing a waiver before resuming interrogation, even though they may not legally be required to do so in all cases.[103]

The Right to Counsel

(*See page 661 for case summaries on this topic.*)

As explained earlier, the rules concerning when an officer may resume interrogation after a defendant has asserted the right to counsel are more restrictive than if the defendant has only asserted the right to remain silent. Four United States Supreme Court cases (*Edwards v. Arizona, Arizona v. Roberson, Minnick v. Mississippi,* and *Maryland v. Shatzer*) are particularly significant and are discussed below in chronological order.

Edwards v. Arizona and prohibiting interrogation after assertion of right to counsel. In *Edwards v. Arizona,*[104] decided in 1981, the United States Supreme Court discussed an officer's authority to resume questioning after a defendant had asserted the right to counsel under *Miranda*:

> The defendant was arrested for murder, robbery, and burglary and was taken to a police station. He was properly given *Miranda* warnings and properly waived his rights, and he began to answer questions. However, he later told the officers, "I want an attorney before making a deal." Questioning then stopped, and the defendant was taken to the county jail. The next morning, two detectives—colleagues of the officer who interrogated the defendant the night before—came to the jail to question the defendant. When the jailer told the defendant that the detectives wanted to speak with him, he said that he did not want to talk with anyone. The jailer told him he "had" to talk and then took him to meet with the detectives. After being given his *Miranda* rights, the defendant agreed to talk and confessed to the crimes.

The Court ruled that once a defendant has asserted the right to counsel, officers may not question the defendant until a lawyer is made available to the defendant or until the "[defendant] himself initiates further communication, exchanges, or conversations" with an officer. The State may not show a valid waiver of the right to counsel after the defendant has asserted that right by merely establishing that the defendant waived that right later after being given another set of *Miranda* warnings. The Court further ruled that in this case the defendant's rights were violated when the officers returned the following day to interrogate him. It noted, however, that if the defendant had initiated that meeting, he could have properly waived his right to counsel that he had asserted the day before.

Arizona v. Roberson and prohibiting interrogation about unrelated crimes while defendant remains in continuous custody. The United States Supreme Court in 1988 ruled in *Arizona v. Roberson*[105] that when a defendant asserts the right to counsel during custodial interrogation, the rule of *Edwards v. Arizona* also applies to custodial interrogation about crimes unrelated to the crime for which the defendant had been arrested. Therefore, for example, when a defendant has asserted the right to counsel during custodial interrogation after being arrested for murder, the defendant may not be questioned about the murder or any other unrelated crime while remaining in continuous custody[106] until counsel has been made available during interrogation (see *Minnick v. Mississippi,* below) or unless the defendant has initiated further communication, exchanges, or conversations with an officer.

The Court also ruled in *Roberson* that the prohibition against interrogation about unrelated crimes applies even if the interrogating officer is from a different law enforcement agency and is unaware of the defendant's assertion of the right to counsel (of course, this ruling applies to interrogation about the same crime as well).[107]

---

103. The North Carolina Supreme Court in *State v. Murphy,* 342 N.C. 813 (1996), clearly rejected a rule that would always require an officer to give new *Miranda* warnings as a prerequisite to reinterrogation after a defendant had asserted the right to remain silent. The court stated that whether or not the defendant had been given new *Miranda* warnings was just one factor in considering whether the defendant's rights had been scrupulously honored under the ruling in *Michigan v. Mosley,* 423 U.S. 96 (1975). *See also* Weeks v. Angelone, 176 F.3d 249 (4th Cir. 1999).

104. 451 U.S. 477 (1981).

105. 486 U.S. 675 (1988).

106. The term "continuous custody" in the text is subject to the later ruling in *Maryland v. Shatzer,* 559 U.S. 98 (2010), in which the Court allowed the reinitiation of interrogation of a prisoner serving a prison sentence because the Court determined that there was a break in custody between the initial prison interrogation (when the prisoner had asserted the right to counsel) and a later prison interrogation.

107. The *Roberson* ruling effectively reversed a contrary ruling in *State v. Dampier,* 314 N.C. 292 (1985).

A federal appellate court has ruled that an assertion of the right to counsel does not bar interrogation about other crimes after a defendant is convicted and begins serving a sentence

Minnick v. Mississippi **and defendant's consultation with a lawyer after asserting the right to counsel.** In the 1990 case of *Minnick v. Mississippi*,[108] the defendant was arrested for murder and asserted his right to counsel during interrogation by federal law enforcement officers. He then communicated with counsel two or three times. A state law enforcement officer then initiated interrogation with the defendant, properly executed *Miranda* warnings and a waiver, and obtained a statement from him. The United States Supreme Court ruled that when a defendant requests counsel under *Miranda*, interrogation must stop, and officers may not reinitiate interrogation (assuming the defendant has remained in continuous custody)[109] without counsel being present, whether or not the defendant has consulted with counsel. Thus, the officer in this case violated the defendant's *Miranda* rights by reinitiating interrogation.

Maryland v. Shatzer **and break in custody permitting reinterrogation.** In 2010 the United States Supreme Court decided *Maryland v. Shatzer*,[110] which modified the rulings in *Edwards, Roberson*, and *Minnick*, discussed above. The Court ruled that when a prisoner serving a sentence asserted the right to counsel during custodial interrogation in prison, (1) an officer had the authority to reinitiate custodial interrogation with *Miranda* warnings and a waiver of rights after there had been a break in custody for 14 days or more, and (2) the prisoner's return to the general prison population after he had asserted the right to counsel was a break in custody that began the running of the 14 days. For an extensive analysis of *Shatzer*, see the publication cited in the accompanying footnote.[111]

A detective went to a Maryland prison in 2003 to question the defendant about his alleged sexual abuse of his son, for which he was not then charged. The defendant was serving a prison sentence for a conviction of a differ-

ent offense. The defendant asserted his right to counsel under *Miranda*, and the detective terminated the custodial interrogation. The defendant was released back to the general prison population to continue serving his sentence, and the child abuse investigation was closed. Another detective reopened the investigation in 2006 and went to another prison where the defendant had been transferred and was still serving his sentence. The detective gave *Miranda* warnings to the defendant, who waived his *Miranda* rights and gave a statement that was introduced at his child sexual abuse trial.

Unlike the defendants in *Edwards, Roberson*, and *Minnick*, who had not been released from custody before being reinterrogated, the defendant in this case had been released from custody and returned to what was for him normal life (during the serving of his sentence). The Court noted that when a defendant has been released from custody and returned to normal life for some time before a later attempted interrogation, there is little reason to believe that the defendant's change of heart concerning interrogation without counsel has been coerced. The defendant likely has been able to seek advice from an attorney, family, and friends. The defendant also knows from the earlier experience that a demand for counsel stops any interrogation and that investigative custody does not last indefinitely. A change of mind to allow questioning is likely attributable not to "badgering" but to a belief after further deliberation that cooperating with the investigation is in the defendant's best interest. The Court in *Shatzer* concluded that an uncritical extension of *Edwards* to the facts presented in this case would not significantly increase the number of genuinely coerced confessions that should be inadmissible, as long as a break in custody is of sufficient duration to dissipate its coercive effects.

The Court adopted a 14-day break in custody as sufficient to deal with potential law enforcement abuse that could occur by releasing the defendant and promptly bringing him or her back into custody for reinterrogation.[112] The Court noted that under *Edwards*, courts had to determine whether the defendant was in custody when he or she requested counsel and when the defendant later made the statements he or she sought to suppress. With

---

for the offense in which he had asserted the right to counsel during custodial interrogation. Thus, the rule in *Arizona v. Roberson* no longer applies. United States v. Arrington, 215 F.3d 855 (8th Cir. 2000). *See also* Isaacs v. Head, 300 F.3d 1232 (11th Cir. 2002). North Carolina appellate courts have not ruled on this issue.

108. 498 U.S. 146 (1990).

109. *See supra* note 106.

110. 559 U.S. 98 (2010).

111. Robert L. Farb, *The United States Supreme Court's Ruling in Maryland v. Shatzer* (UNC School of Government, 2010), www.sog.unc.edu/sites/www.sog.unc.edu/files/reports/marylandshatzer2010.pdf. This memorandum contains various examples not mentioned in the text.

---

112. The Court explained that 14 days provide sufficient time for a defendant to get reacclimated to normal life, to consult with counsel and friends, and to "shake off any residual coercive effects of his prior custody."

the new 14-day break in custody rule, courts simply need to repeat the inquiry for the time between the initial assertion of the right to counsel and reinterrogation. And when it is determined that the defendant has been out of custody for two weeks before the contested reinterrogation, a court is spared the fact-intensive inquiry as to whether he or she ever, anywhere, asserted the *Miranda* right to counsel.

The Court noted that there is no dispute that (1) Shatzer was in custody under *Miranda* during the interrogations in both 2003 and 2006, and (2) he asserted the right to counsel in 2003 when he stated that "he would not talk about the case without having an attorney present." The issue before the Court was whether Shatzer's subsequent release back into the general prison population where he was serving an unrelated sentence constituted a break in *Miranda* custody. The Court ruled that a break in custody occurred because that period of release into the general prison population did not create the coercive pressures identified in *Miranda*. The Court reasoned that when prisoners are released back into the general prison population, they return to their accustomed surroundings and daily routine—they regain the degree of control over their lives that existed before the interrogation. Sentenced prisoners are not isolated with their accusers.[113] They live among other inmates, guards, and workers and often can receive visitors and communicate with people on the outside by mail or telephone.

The Court ruled that because Shatzer experienced a break in *Miranda* custody lasting more than two weeks between the first and second attempts at interrogation, *Edwards* did not require suppression of his 2006 statements.

The *Shatzer* ruling also would apply to a defendant who asserts the right to counsel during custodial interrogation, is charged with an offense, satisfies conditions of pretrial release, and remains on pretrial release for at least 14 days. However, if the reinitiation of interrogation is about the charge for which the defendant was on pretrial release, the defendant would then have a Sixth Amendment right to counsel.[114] Therefore, an officer would be required to give *Miranda* warnings and obtain a waiver of rights before questioning the defendant,[115] even if the defendant was not in custody, because the Sixth Amendment right to counsel exists whether or not a defendant is in custody.[116] As discussed later in this chapter, *Miranda* warnings and waiver are generally sufficient to waive the Sixth Amendment right to counsel.

It is unclear whether an appellate court would apply or extend the *Shatzer* ruling to a defendant who asserts the right to counsel during custodial interrogation and remains in a jail under pretrial detention for more than 14 days.[117]

Defendant's initiation of communication with officers. In *Oregon v. Bradshaw*[118] the United States Supreme Court discussed whether a defendant had initiated further communication about the investigation after he asserted the right to counsel:

> After being arrested and given *Miranda* rights, the defendant talked with an officer for a while but then stated, "I do want an attorney before it goes very much further." The officer immediately stopped his questioning. Sometime before or during a trip to the county jail, the defendant asked an officer, "Well, what is going to happen to me now?" The officer reminded the defendant that he did not have to talk with the officer because he had requested an attorney and said that he did not want the defendant talking to him unless he wanted to. In the discussion that followed, the officer suggested a polygraph examination, and

---

113. The Court's term "accusers" refers to officers when they are conducting custodial interrogation.

114. As discussed later in this chapter, the Sixth Amendment right to counsel begins with a defendant's initial appearance before a magistrate for the charged offense or when the defendant is indicted, whichever occurs first.

115. One can argue that a complete recitation of *Miranda* warnings is not required to waive the Sixth Amendment right to counsel, such as the advice concerning the right to remain silent. However, absent an appellate case on point, the text takes the conservative approach and effectively encourages officers to give the entire warnings.

116. See the discussion of this issue in Robert L. Farb, *The United States Supreme Court's Ruling in Maryland v. Shatzer* 7–8 (UNC School of Government, 2010), www.sog.unc.edu/sites/www.sog.unc.edu/files/reports/marylandshatzer2010.pdf. In addition, the court in *United States v. Ellison*, 632 F.3d 727 (1st Cir. 2010), noted that *Shatzer* left open the question of whether its ruling applied to a defendant in pretrial custody for other charges.

117. See the discussion of this issue in Farb, *supra* note 116, at 6–7.

118. 462 U.S. 1039 (1983). Although a four-Justice plurality opinion, the decision in *Oregon v. Bradshaw* clearly states prevailing law.

the defendant agreed to take one. The next day, after being given *Miranda* warnings, the defendant took a polygraph examination and eventually gave an incriminating statement.

The Court ruled that a two-part test applies when determining the admissibility of statements after a defendant asserts a right to counsel. First, did the defendant initiate further conversation? The Court ruled that in this case the defendant's statement showed a willingness to discuss the investigation. It was not simply a question about the custodial relationship, such as a request for water or to use a telephone. Second, did the defendant validly waive the right to counsel that he had previously asserted? The Court ruled that the State in this case had satisfied its burden of showing that the defendant had done so.

In *State v. Reese*[119] the defendant was arrested for murder, he asserted his right to counsel during custodial interrogation, and interrogation stopped. The defendant was appointed counsel at his first appearance in district court. His lawyer instructed officers not to question his client, the defendant. However, the defendant—in his lawyer's absence—sought out an officer to make a statement. The officer reminded the defendant that he had appointed counsel, truthfully told him that his lawyer was unavailable because he was out of town, and asked the defendant if he still wanted to talk with him. The defendant stated that he still wanted to make a statement. He then voluntarily, knowingly, and intelligently waived his Fifth and Sixth Amendment rights to counsel before he gave a statement. The officer specifically had reminded the defendant that he had an appointed lawyer. The North Carolina Supreme Court ruled that the defendant's waiver was valid despite the fact that the officer did not inform the defendant of his lawyer's instruction to the officers. His lawyer's instruction was irrelevant in determining the validity of the defendant's waiver of counsel. The Fifth and Sixth Amendment right to counsel belongs to the defendant; the defendant's attorney cannot control the defendant's own voluntary exercise of his or her constitutional rights or otherwise prohibit lawful interrogation.

Officers should remember that the State has the burden of showing that the defendant (1) initiated the conversation and (2) then validly waived the right to counsel. Officers should consider giving *Miranda* rights

to the defendant again and obtaining a waiver before they resume interrogation, even though they may not legally be required to do so in all cases.[120]

A Defendant's Sixth Amendment Right to Counsel

(See page 686 for case summaries on this topic.)

As discussed above, a defendant's right to counsel under *Miranda* is based on the Fifth Amendment right not to be compelled to incriminate oneself during custodial interrogation. Thus, this right to counsel is limited.

There is also a right to counsel guaranteed by the Sixth Amendment, which provides a defendant with the right to the presence of counsel at certain pretrial events as well as at the trial itself. An officer's authority to obtain a statement when a defendant has a Sixth Amendment right to counsel presents complex legal issues. Officers need to understand some of the basic principles to avoid violating a defendant's Sixth Amendment rights and to ensure that any statement they obtain will be admissible at trial.

There are two separate issues with the Sixth Amendment right to counsel: (1) when the right attaches (begins), and (2) when a defendant has the right to the presence of counsel.[121]

The United States Supreme Court has ruled that the Sixth Amendment right to counsel attaches (begins) at the initial appearance after arrest that is conducted by a

---

120. In *State v. Harris*, 338 N.C. 129 (1994), North Carolina law enforcement officers went to Georgia to return the defendant to North Carolina for a first-degree murder charge pending in North Carolina. After properly being advised of his *Miranda* rights, the defendant asserted his right to counsel. No interrogation was conducted. After his return to North Carolina 12 hours later, the defendant—through his brother, who was visiting the defendant in jail—asked to talk to the sheriff. The court ruled that (1) the defendant initiated communication with the sheriff by telling his brother to inform the sheriff that he wanted to speak with him, and (2) the sheriff was not required to give *Miranda* warnings again before interrogating the defendant. The court stated that there was no reason to believe that the defendant, having been properly advised of his *Miranda* rights 12 hours earlier, had forgotten them. For example, he should have known of his right to an attorney, because he had exercised that right 12 hours earlier.

121. The two separate issues are noted in *Rothgery v. Gillespie County*, 554 U.S. 191 (2008).

---

119. 319 N.C. 110 (1987).

judicial official (in North Carolina, usually a magistrate) or when the defendant is indicted or an information has been filed,[122] whichever occurs *first* in a particular case.[123] The initial appearance before a judicial official after arrest and the issuance of an indictment or information are triggering events; when they occur, the State is considered to have committed itself to prosecute.[124]

The fact that a defendant has hired a lawyer does not, by itself, necessarily mean that the defendant has the Sixth Amendment protections of the right to the presence of counsel.[125] The determining factor is whether a critical stage of a prosecution is taking place at or after the time when the Sixth Amendment right to counsel has attached (begun).[126]

The Sixth Amendment provides a defendant with the right to the presence of counsel at any critical stage of a criminal case at or after the time when the right to counsel has attached (begun).[127] And officers' deliberate efforts—by themselves or through an informant acting at their direction—to elicit information from a defendant by interrogation or conversation about the pending charge at or after the time that the right to counsel has attached (begun) is always a critical stage (but see the discussion of *Patterson v. Illinois* and *Montejo v. Louisiana* later in this chapter).

Separate Determination for Each Criminal Charge

The time when the Sixth Amendment right to counsel attaches (begins) must be determined for each criminal charge. For example, if a defendant has been charged with crime A for which the Sixth Amendment right to counsel had attached (begun), an undercover informant acting at the officer's direction may not question the defendant about crime A without violating the defendant's Sixth Amendment rights. However, an officer generally may question the defendant about crime B if the right to counsel has not attached (begun) for that crime[128] (see the discussion of *Maine v. Moulton*, below).

---

122. An *information* is a written accusation by a prosecutor, filed with superior court, charging a person represented by counsel with one or more criminal offenses. G.S. 15A-641. An information may not be used to charge a capital offense, such as first-degree murder, and may not be used when a defendant is not represented by counsel.

123. Rothgery v. Gillespie Cty., 554 U.S. 191 (2008); United States v. Gouveia, 467 U.S. 180 (1984); Kirby v. Illinois, 406 U.S. 682 (1972). To the extent that pre-*Rothegary* North Carolina cases had ruled that the defendant's Sixth Amendment right to counsel did not begin until the first appearance in district court for a felony, they have been effectively overruled by *Rothgery*. *See, e.g.*, State v. Tucker, 331 N.C. 12 (1992); State v. Nations, 319 N.C. 318 (1987); State v. Phipps, 331 N.C. 427 (1992).

The United States Supreme Court has yet to rule whether the Sixth Amendment right to counsel begins when an arrest warrant is issued before the defendant's arrest or appearance before a judicial official. In a pre-*Rothgery* case, the North Carolina Supreme Court ruled in *State v. Taylor*, 354 N.C. 28 (2001), that the Sixth Amendment right to counsel did not begin with the issuance of an arrest warrant.

124. The Sixth Amendment right to counsel generally does not begin with an extradition hearing in another state to return a defendant to North Carolina. State v. Taylor, 354 N.C. 28 (2001) (Sixth Amendment right to counsel did not begin with appointment of counsel for Florida extradition hearing to decide whether to return defendant to North Carolina, when only criminal process issued in North Carolina had been an arrest warrant).

125. Moran v. Burbine, 475 U.S. 412 (1986); United States v. Ingle, 157 F.3d 1147 (9th Cir. 1998) (appointment of lawyer for grand jury appearance did not begin Sixth Amendment right to counsel).

126. Moran v. Burbine, 475 U.S. 412 (1986); United States v. Ingle, 157 F.3d 1147 (9th Cir. 1998).

127. Kirby v. Illinois, 406 U.S. 682 (1972). Although *Kirby* was a plurality opinion, it clearly is the prevailing law. *See* United States v. Gouveia, 467 U.S. 180 (1984) (Court also noted that *Escobedo v. Illinois*, 378 U.S. 478 (1964), is now considered to rest on the right to counsel under the Fifth Amendment, not the right to counsel under the Sixth Amendment); Moran v. Burbine, 475 U.S. 412 (1986).

128. In *Texas v. Cobb*, 532 U.S. 167 (2001), a home was burglarized and a mother and daughter living there were missing. The defendant confessed to the burglary but denied any knowledge of the missing mother and daughter. He was indicted for the burglary, and a lawyer was appointed to represent him. Officers later received information that the defendant had murdered the mother and daughter, obtained arrest warrants for the murders, and arrested the defendant. They then gave him *Miranda* warnings and received a proper waiver, and the defendant confessed to the murders. The defendant argued, relying on *Michigan v. Jackson*, 475 U.S. 625 (1986) (since overruled by *Montejo v. Louisiana*, 556 U.S. 778 (2009), discussed later in this chapter), that his Sixth Amendment right to counsel had been violated because officers interrogated him about the murders that were closely related factually to the burglary. Thus, his Sixth Amendment right to counsel attached for the murders when he was indicted for the burglary, even though he had not yet been charged with those murders. The Court rejected the defendant's argument, although it noted that some lower federal courts and state courts had adopted it.

The Court noted, citing its ruling in *McNeil v. Wisconsin*, 501 U.S. 171 (1991), that the Sixth Amendment right to counsel is offense-specific. The Court ruled that the term "offense" in its double jeopardy jurisprudence (see *Blockburger v. United*

Assertion of the Sixth Amendment Right to Counsel
Patterson v. Illinois

The United States Supreme Court in *Patterson v. Illinois*[129] clarified when officers may question a defendant who has been indicted. The defendant was arrested and indicted for murder. Before the defendant's initial court appearance and while he was in custody, an officer and a prosecutor interrogated him about the murder after he had been given *Miranda* warnings and had properly waived his *Miranda* rights. The defendant argued that because he had a Sixth Amendment right to counsel from the time he was indicted for murder, both the officer and the prosecutor had violated that right when they initiated the interrogation about the murder. The Court disagreed and stated that the defendant's Sixth Amendment right to counsel had begun with his murder indictment, but it ruled that this right had not been violated because the defendant had not requested counsel before or during the interrogation. Thus, the defendant's failure to request counsel allowed the initiation of interrogation about the murder.

The Court made clear in *Patterson* that its ruling does not permit undercover officers or those acting at their direction (for example, informants) surreptitiously to question the defendant after an indictment (or after the initial appearance before a judicial official after arrest) about the crime for which the defendant has a Sixth Amendment right to counsel.[130] That is, a defendant's request for counsel is not necessary to bar such surreptitious questioning.

Montejo v. Louisiana

The United States Supreme Court in *Montejo v. Louisiana*[131] overruled one of its prior cases, *Michigan v. Jackson*,[132] and effectively changed law enforcement authority to interrogate a defendant who has a Sixth Amendment right to counsel. *Jackson* had ruled that when a defendant requests counsel at an arraignment or similar court proceeding that takes place at or after the beginning of the Sixth Amendment right to counsel, an officer is thereafter prohibited under the Sixth Amendment from initiating interrogation of the defendant.

The defendant in *Montejo v. Louisiana* was arrested for murder, waived his *Miranda* rights, and gave statements in response to officers' interrogation. He was brought before a judge for a preliminary hearing and was ordered to be held without bond, and the Office of Indigent Defender was appointed to represent him. Later that day, two officers visited the defendant in prison and requested that he accompany them to locate the murder weapon. He was read his *Miranda* rights again and agreed to go with the officers. During the trip, the defendant wrote an inculpatory letter of apology to the murder victim's widow. Only on his return did the defendant finally meet his court-appointed attorney. The issue in this case was whether the letter of apology was erroneously admitted in the defendant's trial based on a violation of his Sixth Amendment right to counsel.

Instead of deciding whether *Jackson* barred the officers from initiating interrogation of Montejo after a lawyer had been appointed for him, the Court overruled *Jackson*.

The Court's overruling of *Jackson* now allows the interrogation barred by *Jackson*, provided an officer advises the defendant of his or her rights and the defendant knowingly and voluntarily waives his or her Sixth Amendment right to counsel (see the discussion below for the content of warnings and waiver). A defendant may

---

States, 284 U.S. 299 (1932)) applies to the determination of whether the Sixth Amendment right to counsel applies to related offenses. Thus, a defendant has a Sixth Amendment right to counsel for an uncharged offense only if it is the same offense under the *Blockburger* test: offenses are not the same if each has an element that is not in the other. The Court ruled that murder and burglary were not the same offense under the *Blockburger* test. Therefore, the defendant in this case did not have a Sixth Amendment right to counsel for the murder charges as a result of the burglary indictment, and the officers did not violate that right when they interrogated the defendant about the murders. *See also* United States v. Avants, 278 F.3d 510 (5th Cir. 2002) (under dual sovereignty doctrine, assertion of Sixth Amendment right to counsel for state murder charge did not bar later interrogation for federal murder charge, even though murder offenses were identical).

Note that this case only involved the Sixth Amendment right to counsel. Under the Fifth Amendment right to counsel, as set out in *Arizona v. Roberson*, 486 U.S. 675 (1988), discussed earlier in this chapter, officers may not initiate interrogation of a defendant about the same or unrelated offenses when the defendant had asserted his right to counsel during custodial interrogation and remains in continuous custody. However, the *Roberson* ruling was modified by *Maryland v. Shatzer*, 559 U.S. 98 (2010), also discussed earlier in this chapter.

129. 487 U.S. 285 (1988).

---

130. See footnote 9 of the Court's opinion in *Patterson v. Illinois*, 487 U.S. 285 (1988).

131. 556 U.S. 778 (2009).

132. 475 U.S. 625 (1986).

execute a waiver of counsel without the presence of his or her attorney.[133]

Although an officer may not be prohibited from initiating interrogation under the Sixth Amendment right to counsel, the officer may still be prohibited from interrogating a defendant by the Fifth Amendment under *Edwards v. Arizona* and *Arizona v. Roberson*, as discussed on page 583. For example: A defendant is arrested for armed robbery and requests counsel during custodial interrogation. Under *Edwards* and *Roberson*, officers are prohibited from continuing or later initiating interrogation about the armed robbery or any other offense, whether related or not to the armed robbery, as long as the defendant remains in continuous custody.[134] If the defendant did not request counsel but asserted the right to remain silent, that assertion bars continuing interrogation or reinitiating interrogation except under limited circumstances, as discussed on page 582.

If there is no Fifth Amendment issue because, for example, the defendant is not in custody, an officer may initiate interrogation of a defendant who has a Sixth Amendment right to counsel if the officer advises the defendant of his or her rights and obtains a valid waiver of those rights (see the discussion below for the content of warnings and waiver).

Assuming the defendant has not asserted the right to counsel during custodial interrogation that would bar interrogation of an in-custody defendant under the Fifth Amendment, the overruling of *Jackson* raises the issue of the extent to which an officer may initiate interrogation under the Sixth Amendment. If an officer sought to interrogate a defendant but the defendant refused to waive his or her Sixth Amendment right to counsel, could the officer try again later? The Court in *Montejo* did not address this issue. However, the Court did discuss in a different context the improper badgering of a defendant to obtain a waiver of counsel. Thus, it would appear that a second attempt to initiate interrogation after a refusal to waive counsel would be questionable.

The overruling of *Jackson* does not change case law that prohibits an officer from surreptitiously questioning a defendant who has a Sixth Amendment right to counsel through the use of an informant or undercover officer.

Sixth Amendment Right to Counsel and the Defendant's Custody Status

Unlike the *Miranda* ruling, which is based on the Fifth Amendment, the Sixth Amendment right to counsel protects a defendant at all times, whether in custody or not in custody, because the amendment protects a defendant when the State has committed itself to prosecute and the assistance of counsel is needed.[135] Thus, an officer may violate a defendant's Sixth Amendment right to counsel when the officer or an informant acting at the officer's direction obtains a statement from a defendant who is not in custody (for example, if the officer conducts noncustodial interrogation of, or deliberately elicits information from,[136] an indicted defendant about the charged offense and fails to give warnings and obtain a waiver of the defendant's Sixth Amendment right to counsel).

Waiver of the Sixth Amendment Right to Counsel

What constitutes a valid waiver of the Sixth Amendment right to counsel? The United States Supreme Court has clearly stated[137] and the North Carolina Supreme Court has ruled[138] that a defendant may validly waive the Sixth Amendment right to counsel even in the absence of the lawyer who is representing the defendant for the charge. Also, *Miranda* warnings and a waiver are usually sufficient to waive the Sixth Amendment right to counsel.[139]

---

133. Montejo v. Louisiana, 556 U.S. 778 (2009).

134. Of course, as discussed on page 584, an officer may have the authority to interrogate a defendant who has asserted the Fifth Amendment right to counsel under the 14-day break in custody rule established in *Maryland v. Shatzer*, 559 U.S. 98 (2010).

135. Massiah v. United States, 377 U.S. 201 (1964).

136. Fellers v. United States, 540 U.S. 519 (2004) (Court ruled that officer "deliberately elicited" statements from indicted defendant about charged offense).

137. Montejo v. Louisiana, 556 U.S. 778 (2009).

138. State v. Reese, 319 N.C. 110 (1987).

139. Montejo v. Louisiana, 556 U.S. 778 (2009) (Court stated: "And when a defendant is read his *Miranda* rights (which include the right to have counsel present during interrogation) and agrees to waive those rights, that typically does the trick, even though the *Miranda* rights purportedly have their source in the *Fifth* Amendment . . . ." and then quoted from *Patterson v. Illinois*, 487 U.S. 285 (1988)); Patterson v. Illinois, 487 U.S. 285 (1988) (court ruled that *Miranda* warnings and waiver were sufficient in this case for waiver of Sixth Amendment right to counsel, but Court did not decide whether officer must also inform defendant that he or she has been indicted—see footnote 8 of the Court's opinion; it is the author's belief that the Court would not impose such a requirement); State v. Palmer, 334 N.C. 104 (1993) (*Miranda* warnings were sufficient); State v. Wynne, 329 N.C. 507 (1991) (assuming

However, because it has not been definitively established by the United States Supreme Court that *Miranda* warnings and a waiver are sufficient in all kinds of Sixth Amendment right to counsel cases, a cautious officer may want to (1) add to the *Miranda* warnings a specific mention of the charge pending against the defendant (for example, "Do you understand that you have been indicted for the murder of Harold Jones?") and of the lawyer or organization (for example, the public defender's office), if any, representing the defendant ("Do you understand that Susan Underwood is your attorney for the murder charge against you?"); and (2) add to the *Miranda* waiver an explicit waiver of the right to counsel who is representing the defendant (for example, "Are you willing to waive your right to have counsel present, including Susan Underwood, your attorney?").

Warnings and a waiver must be executed whether or not the defendant is in custody because the Sixth Amendment right to counsel exists under either circumstance.

The Sixth Amendment Right to Counsel and the Use of Informants to Obtain Statements

(*See page 696 for case summaries on this topic.*)

Although a variety of factual situations may present possible Sixth Amendment violations when an officer deliberately attempts to elicit a statement about the pending charge from a defendant, particularly through the use of informants, it is worth discussing five United States Supreme Court cases that represent some common issues.

— United States v. Henry

United States v. Henry[140] involved an officer's use of an informant to deliberately elicit statements from a jailed defendant after he had a Sixth Amendment right to counsel.

> *The defendant was indicted for armed robbery—thus he had a Sixth Amendment*

right to counsel—and was in jail awaiting trial. A federal officer, who was investigating the robbery, asked a paid government informant who was incarcerated in the same jail (he eventually shared a cell with the defendant) to be alert to any statements made by federal prisoners there. He told the informant that he was not to initiate any conversations with the defendant or any other prisoner but should pay attention to any information they might volunteer. However, the informant engaged the defendant in conversations, and the defendant eventually revealed information to the informant about his participation in the robbery.

The United States Supreme Court stated that the issue is whether the informant, a government agent, "deliberately elicited" statements from the defendant. It ruled that the informant did so and therefore violated the defendant's Sixth Amendment right to counsel. First, the defendant was unaware that the informant was acting as a government agent. Second, the informant had an incentive to produce useful information. He was paid only if he produced useful information. Third, the fact that the informant and the defendant were confined together made the defendant particularly susceptible to the informant's ploys.

Although the federal officer had instructed the informant not to question the defendant, the informant was not a passive listener. Rather, he engaged the defendant in conversations, and the statements resulted from these conversations. Even if the federal agent did not intend that the informant take affirmative steps to secure information from the defendant, he must have known that the proximity of the two would probably lead to that result. This was not a case of a passive listener or a passive listening device that overhears statements—see *Kuhlmann v. Wilson*, discussed below. The Court noted that it did not question its prior rulings concerning the permitted use of undercover agents in obtaining statements from persons not in custody and before they had a Sixth Amendment right to counsel—as in *Hoffa v. United States*[141] (the defendant's incriminating statements made to a secret government informant during the course of a labor-racketeering trial were admissible at a later jury-

---

without deciding that defendant had a Sixth Amendment right to counsel, which he clearly did not, *Miranda* warnings were sufficient to waive Sixth Amendment right to counsel). *See also* United States v. Muca, 945 F.2d 88 (4th Cir. 1991) (*Miranda* warnings were sufficient); United States v. Charria, 919 F.2d 842 (2d Cir. 1990) (similar ruling); United States v. Chadwick, 999 F.2d 1282 (8th Cir. 1993) (*Miranda* warnings were sufficient to waive Sixth Amendment right to counsel; officer is not required to inform defendant that he or she has been indicted).
140. 447 U.S. 264 (1980).

---

141. 385 U.S. 293 (1966). *See also* State v. Thompson, 332 N.C. 204 (1992).

tampering trial because he made them before he had a Sixth Amendment right to counsel for the jury-tampering charge) and *United States v. White*[142] (no Fourth Amendment violation occurred when a government agent was wired so as to transmit to officers his conversations about drug transactions with the defendant because conversations took place before the defendant had a Sixth Amendment right to counsel for the drug charges).

━┫ Kuhlmann v. Wilson
Kuhlmann v. Wilson[143] involved a detective who placed a police informant in a jail cell with the defendant so that the informant could listen to any incriminating statements the defendant might make.

> *The defendant was arrested for robbery and murder. He told officers that he witnessed the robbery but denied being involved. He was arraigned before a judge and committed to jail. A detective placed a police informant in the defendant's cell (the defendant did not know that he was an informant). The detective instructed the informant not to ask the defendant any questions but simply to "keep [his] ear open" for the names of accomplices in the robbery and murder. At first the defendant told the informant the same story he had told the officers, although the informant told the defendant that his explanation "didn't sound too good." A few days later, the defendant's brother visited him and told him that his family was upset because they believed that the defendant was involved in the crimes. After the visit, the defendant essentially confessed to the informant. The*

> *informant told the detective about the confession and gave the detective notes about it that the informant had written in the cell.*

Distinguishing *United States v. Henry*, discussed above, and *Maine v. Moulton*, discussed below, the United States Supreme Court ruled that the defendant's confession was not taken in violation of his Sixth Amendment right to counsel. The Court stated that a defendant's right to counsel is not violated by the sole fact that an informant, either voluntarily or by prior agreement, reports the defendant's incriminating statements to a law enforcement officer. Instead, some evidence must exist that an officer and the informant deliberately intended to elicit incriminating statements—not merely to listen for information. In this case, the detective instructed the informant only to listen to the defendant to determine the identities of other participants in the robbery and murder (solid evidence already linked the defendant to these crimes). The informant never asked the defendant about the pending charges. He only listened to the defendant's spontaneous and unsolicited statements. The mere fact that the informant commented unfavorably to the defendant about his initial version of noninvolvement in the crimes did not support a finding in this case that the informant deliberately elicited the defendant's incriminating statements.

━┫ Massiah v. United States
Massiah v. United States[144] involved a federal agent's use of an accomplice to deliberately elicit statements from a defendant who had been released on bail after he had been indicted.

> *The defendant was indicted for importing drugs into the United States, retained a lawyer, pled not guilty, and was released on bail. A federal agent wired an accomplice's car (with the accomplice's permission but without the defendant's knowledge) with a radio transmitter. Then, while the accomplice and the defendant sat in the car and talked about the case, the agent listened to their conversations and heard the defendant make incriminating statements about the drug charges.*

The United States Supreme Court ruled that the defendant's right to counsel had been violated because

---

142. 401 U.S. 745 (1971). *See also* State v. Thompson, 332 N.C. 204 (1992).

143. 477 U.S. 436 (1986). See also *Thomas v. Cox*, 708 F.2d 132 (4th Cir. 1983) and *State v. Payne*, 312 N.C. 647 (1985), cases decided before *Kuhlmann v. Wilson* but consistent with its reasoning. For cases decided after *Kuhlmann v. Wilson*, see *United States v. York*, 933 F.2d 1343 (7th Cir. 1991) (although inmate was government agent, he did not deliberately elicit information from defendant) and *United States v. Stubbs*, 944 F.2d 828 (11th Cir. 1991) (similar ruling). Of course, when inmates act completely on their own and obtain incriminating statements through deliberate conversations, this does not raise any Sixth Amendment issues because the inmates are not government agents; see State v. Taylor, 332 N.C. 372 (1992) (inmate was not a government agent).

---

144. 377 U.S. 201 (1964).

the government deliberately elicited statements from the defendant after he had a Sixth Amendment right to counsel.

→ Maine v. Moulton

Maine v. Moulton[145] involved an officer's use of a codefendant to deliberately elicit statements from a defendant who had been released on bail after he had been indicted.

> *The defendant was indicted for theft charges with his codefendant, Colson. He retained a lawyer, pled not guilty, and was released on bail. Later the defendant met with Colson and suggested the possibility of killing one of the state's witnesses, and they discussed how to commit the murder. Colson eventually confessed to officers about his involvement with the thefts and some other crimes, and he told them about the plan to kill the witness. The officers offered Colson a deal: they would bring no further charges if he would testify against the defendant and cooperate with them. Colson also agreed to have his telephone conversations recorded to pick up conversations with the defendant and any anonymous threats (Colson had told the officers of threatening calls). The defendant—unaware that Colson was cooperating with the officers—asked Colson to meet him to discuss their defense at their impending theft trial. The officers wired Colson for this meeting but told him not to question the defendant—he was just to have a conversation. During this meeting, the defendant made incriminating statements that were used at his theft trial.*

The United States Supreme Court ruled that the officers deliberately elicited these incriminating statements in violation of the defendant's Sixth Amendment right to counsel. The officers' instructions to Colson were not sufficient to assure that Colson would not discuss the pending theft charges with the defendant, especially as they knew that the defendant had set up the meeting for that purpose. Although the State argued that it had a legitimate reason to record the conversations—the proposed killing of a State's witness—the Court stated that the officers had a second purpose: the continued investigation of the theft charges. Note, however, that the Court clearly stated that the defendant's incriminating statements about the proposed murder would be admissible because he did not have a Sixth Amendment right to counsel when he made statements about the uncharged crime of solicitation to commit murder.

→ Brewer v. Williams

Brewer v. Williams[146] involved an officer's deliberate attempt to elicit information from a defendant after he had a Sixth Amendment right to counsel and after his lawyer had told the officer not to talk to the defendant.

> *The defendant was arraigned before a judge under a warrant charging him with the murder of a young girl whose body had not yet been found, and he was committed to jail. The defendant's lawyer specifically told the officers who were about to transport the defendant to another jail that they were not to question the defendant about the girl's disappearance during the trip. While the defendant was being transported, the detective—who knew that the defendant was a former mental patient and deeply religious—spoke to him about the need to find the girl's body to give her a decent Christian burial and how the falling snow might mean that her body would never be found. The defendant then led the detective to the body.*

The United States Supreme Court ruled that the defendant's Sixth Amendment right to counsel, which existed because he had been arraigned before a judge and committed to jail, was violated by the detective's deliberate attempt during the trip to elicit information from him in the absence of counsel. The Court noted that although the defendant could have waived his right to counsel without notice to his lawyer, the State failed to satisfy its heavy burden of showing a waiver of counsel under the facts of this case.

---

145. 474 U.S. 159 (1985). The Court made it clear in *Moulton* in footnote 11 that the "deliberately elicited" test for a Sixth Amendment right to counsel violation does not require affirmative interrogation. A conversation designed to elicit incriminating statements may constitute a violation. *But see* Kuhlmann v. Wilson, 477 U.S. 436 (1986).

---

146. 430 U.S. 387 (1977).

Comparing the Right to Counsel under the Fifth and Sixth Amendments

Note: A defendant sometimes may simultaneously have both a Fifth and Sixth Amendment right to counsel, and questioning that would be permitted under one amendment may not be permitted under the other amendment.

	Fifth Amendment	Sixth Amendment
When does the right to counsel exist?	During custodial interrogation by a person known by the defendant to be a law enforcement officer or an agent of a law enforcement officer. See page 577.	At each critical stage after Sixth Amendment right to counsel has begun (attached), which occurs with (1) an initial appearance before a judicial official after arrest, or (2) an indictment, whichever occurs first. See page 586.
Does the right to counsel exist whether or not the defendant is in custody?	It exists only when the defendant is in custody. See page 573.	It exists whether or not the defendant is in custody. See page 589.
What warnings and waivers of the right to counsel are required?	*Miranda* warnings and waiver are sufficient. See page 578.	*Miranda* warnings and waiver are usually sufficient. See page 589.
What if the defendant clearly asserts the right to counsel?	Interrogation may not begin or must stop if it already has begun. Officers may not initiate interrogation for *any* offense (not just the offense for which the defendant is in custody) while the defendant remains in continuous custody, *unless* the defendant's lawyer is present or the defendant initiates communication with the officer. However, under certain circumstances an officer may initiate interrogation after 14 days have elapsed if there has been a break in custody. See pages 579 and 584.	Interrogation may not begin or must stop if it already has begun. Officers may not initiate interrogation about the offense for which the defendant has the right to counsel, *unless* the defendant's lawyer is present or the defendant initiates communication with the officers. However, officers may initiate interrogation about other offenses for which the defendant does not have the right to counsel. See page 587.
What if the defendant clearly asserts only the right to remain silent?	Interrogation may not begin or must stop if it already has begun. Officers must scrupulously honor the assertion of the right to remain silent, but they may initiate interrogation after a period of time. See pages 579 and 582.	Not applicable.

Part II. Lineups and Other Identification Procedures

Introduction

Procedures to identify a defendant may be used under several circumstances, including (1) after a defendant's arrest; (2) after the defendant has consented to an identification procedure, even if the defendant has not been arrested; (3) after a brief detention with reasonable suspicion, limited to an identification at or near the scene of the stop;[147] and (4) after the defendant has been served with a nontestimonial identification order. The nontestimonial identification order is discussed in Chapter 4. It is worth repeating here that an officer may use a nontestimonial identification order even when the officer is not legally required to do so—such as when the defendant has been arrested and has been released from custody. However, if the arrestee is in custody, a nontestimonial identification order may not be used. In such a case, an officer should seek a court order that directs a person to appear in a lineup if the person will not consent to participate.[148]

Legal Requirements

Procedures for a witness's identification of a defendant must meet certain legal requirements if the evidence of the identification procedure and the witness's later identification of the defendant are to be admissible in court. Officers must comply with constitutional and, in some cases, statutory provisions, as follows:

1. They must conduct the identification procedure so that it does not violate the defendant's due process rights under the Fourteenth Amendment. That is, the procedure must not be so unnecessarily suggestive that it creates a substantial risk of misidentification.[149]

2. In some cases, the defendant has a Sixth Amendment right to counsel at an identification procedure unless the defendant waives that right. And a defendant has a statutory right to counsel during an identification procedure conducted with a nontestimonial identification order.

3. A North Carolina statute requires certain identification procedures to be followed that may exceed constitutional requirements.

Three identification procedures are discussed below. A *live lineup* is when a witness views in person a number of people together in an attempt to identify the offender. A *showup* is when a witness views just one person. A *photo lineup* is when a witness attempts to identify the perpetrator of a crime by viewing photographs of possible suspects.

Juveniles

(See page 716 for case summaries on this topic.)

Officers must remember that they may not conduct an identification procedure, including a live lineup, involving a juvenile without a nontestimonial identification order. However, the North Carolina Supreme Court has ruled that officers may conduct a showup involving a juvenile suspect shortly after the commission of a crime without a nontestimonial identification order.[150] The court upheld a showup between the victim of a housebreaking and two juvenile suspects that occurred about an hour after the crime had been committed. The court ruled that the showup did not violate constitutional due process, because the victim's identification was sufficiently

---

147. See 4 Wayne R. LaFave, Search and Seizure: A Treatise on the Fourth Amendment § 9.2(g) (5th ed. 2012). *See also* United States v. McCargo, 464 F.3d 192 (2d Cir. 2006); United States v. Martinez, 462 F.3d 903 (8th Cir. 2006); Gallegos v. City of Los Angeles, 462 F.3d 903 (9th Cir. 2002); United States v. Vanichromanee, 742 F.2d 340 (7th Cir. 1984). *Florida v. Royer*, 460 U.S. 491 (1983), does not affect the validity of these cases because unlike the officers in *Royer*, the officers in these cases had a legitimate law enforcement justification to move the suspects.

148. See the discussion of *State v. Welch*, 316 N.C. 578 (1986), in note 373 of Chapter 3. When a nontestimonial identification order cannot be used for a lineup because the defendant is in custody, a judge has the inherent power to issue a court order to compel the defendant to appear in a lineup if the State presents facts to show the need for such an appearance. *Cf. In re* Superior Court Order, 315 N.C. 378 (1986). A court order appears more appropriate than a search warrant in such a case.

149. This is the test for the admissibility of the out-of-court identification. The test for the admissibility of the in-court identification is the same, except that the word "irreparable" is added before "misidentification." *See* Neil v. Biggers, 409 U.S. 188 (1972).

150. *In re* Stallings, 318 N.C. 565 (1986). The court's ruling reversed the opinion of the North Carolina Court of Appeals, 77 N.C. App. 592 (1985), and effectively reversed the ruling in *State v. Norris*, 77 N.C. App. 525 (1985), that a one-on-one showup cannot be conducted with a juvenile without a nontestimonial identification order.

reliable—based on her observation of the suspects running from her house and her later identification of them at the crime scene.

For a discussion about what age constitutes a juvenile for conducting nontestimonial identification procedures, see page 464 of Chapter 4.

Nonsuggestiveness of the Identification Procedure under Due Process Clause

(*See page 710 for case summaries on this topic.*)

Courts use complex tests to determine the admissibility of evidence under the Due Process Clause concerning (1) an out-of-court identification procedure, including a witness's identification of the defendant during that procedure; and (2) a witness's later identification of a defendant in court. These tests are discussed in the accompanying note.[151] Essentially, however, they require various factors to be considered in determining whether a

witness's identification is reliable. To avoid a court ruling that evidence gathered in an identification procedure is inadmissible, officers should conduct the procedure in a manner that does not suggest to the witness who should be identified as the offender. Complying with North Carolina statutory requirements, discussed later in this chapter, will almost always satisfy the Due Process Clause as well.

Presenting only one person to a witness for possible identification is a suggestive identification procedure that normally should be avoided. However, a showup is not always considered *unnecessarily* suggestive if it is used in an emergency or soon after the crime was committed. For example, a showup is permissible when (1) a witness is in the hospital and an immediate identification is needed[152] or (2) shortly after the crime was committed and an immediate identification is justified by the need to solve a crime quickly and to release possibly innocent suspects.[153] North Carolina statutory standards for showups, which are additional to Due Process Clause requirements, are discussed later in this chapter.

Although evidence obtained in showups and later in-court identifications has been ruled admissible under other circumstances than these,[154] officers should consider conducting a lineup or photo lineup to decrease the risk that evidence will be ruled inadmissible.

---

151. *See generally* Neil v. Biggers, 409 U.S. 188 (1972). The due process test for determining whether an in-court identification is admissible at trial is whether the out-of-court identification procedure was so impermissibly suggestive as to give rise to a very substantial likelihood of *irreparable* misidentification. The due process test for determining whether evidence of the out-of-court identification procedure is admissible at trial is whether it was so impermissibly suggestive as to give rise to a very substantial likelihood of misidentification. Note that the test is the same as for the in-court identification except for the deletion of the word "irreparable."

The central issue concerning the admissibility of identification evidence is whether—considering the totality of circumstances—the identification was reliable even though the confrontation procedure may have been suggestive. The factors to consider in evaluating the likelihood of misidentification include the witness's opportunity to view the suspect when the offense was committed, the degree of attention, the accuracy of a prior description of the suspect, the degree of certainty at the identification procedure, and the length of time between the crime and the identification procedure.

In *Perry v. New Hampshire*, 132 S. Ct. 716 (2012), the Court ruled that the Due Process Clause does not require a preliminary judicial inquiry into the reliability of an eyewitness identification when the identification was not procured under unnecessarily suggestive circumstances arranged by law enforcement. The Court stated: "When no improper law enforcement activity is involved . . . it suffices to test reliability through the rights and opportunities generally designed for that purpose, notably, the presence of counsel at postindictment lineups, vigorous cross-examination, protective rules of evidence, and jury instructions on both the fallibility of

eyewitness identification and the requirement that guilt be proved beyond a reasonable doubt." 132 S. Ct. at 721.

152. Stovall v. Denno, 388 U.S. 293 (1967); State v. Sharratt, 29 N.C. App. 199 (1976).

153. *In re* Stallings, 318 N.C. 565 (1986) (court ruled that one-on-one showup between victim and a juvenile suspect may be conducted without juvenile nontestimonial identification order (G.S. 7A-596, now G.S. 7B-2103) when the showup does not violate due process; in this case, the showup was conducted within about an hour after crime occurred and was constitutionally permissible); Stanley v. Cox, 486 F.2d 48 (4th Cir. 1973); Willis v. Garrison, 624 F.2d 491 (4th Cir. 1980). See also the cases *infra* note 154, which provide that even an unnecessarily suggestive showup may be admissible if a resulting identification is reliable.

154. In *Neil v. Biggers*, 409 U.S. 188 (1972), the Court ruled admissible evidence of a showup at a police station that was conducted seven months after the crime was committed. *See also* State v. Oliver, 302 N.C. 28 (1980) (court ruled that evidence of an unnecessarily suggestive showup was admissible because the witness's identification was reliable); State v. Flowers, 318 N.C. 208 (1986) (similar ruling); State v. Capps, 114 N.C. App. 156 (1994) (similar ruling). *But see* State v. Pinchback, 140 N.C. App. 512 (2000).

The Sixth Amendment Right to Counsel at Identification Procedures

Sixth Amendment Right to Presence of Counsel at Lineups or Showups

(See page 709 for case summaries on this topic.)

The United States Supreme Court has ruled that a defendant has a Sixth Amendment right to the presence of counsel when the defendant personally appears in a lineup or showup at or after the right to counsel has attached (begun).[155] A lawyer's basic role is to observe the identification procedure so that he or she may cross-examine witnesses and officers at trial about the procedure and any identifications made there.

The United States Supreme Court has ruled that the Sixth Amendment right to counsel attaches (begins) at the initial appearance after arrest that is conducted by a judicial official (in North Carolina, usually a magistrate) or when an indictment or information has been filed, whichever occurs *first* in a particular case.[156] The initial appearance before a judicial official after arrest and the issuance of an indictment or information are triggering events; when they occur, the State is considered to have committed itself to prosecute.

The fact that a defendant has hired a lawyer does not, by itself, necessarily mean that the defendant has the Sixth Amendment protections of the right to the presence of counsel.[157] The determining factor is still whether a critical stage of a prosecution is taking place at or after the time when the Sixth Amendment right to counsel has begun.[158]

If officers are unsure whether a defendant has a right to counsel, they should *always* make sure either that counsel is provided or that a waiver of the right to counsel is obtained, because a violation of a defendant's Sixth Amendment right to counsel has severe consequences: All evidence of the identification procedure—including any identification of the defendant—is automatically excluded at trial. In addition, if a witness makes an in-court identification, the State must prove by clear and convincing evidence that the identification was based on the witness's observations of the defendant during the crime and was not tainted by the illegal out-of-court identification.[159]

Separate Determination for Each Criminal Charge

The time when the right to counsel has attached (begun) must be determined for each criminal charge. For example, even though a defendant has a Sixth Amendment right to counsel for one crime, if the identification procedure involves another crime for which the right to counsel has not begun, then the defendant has no Sixth Amendment right to the presence of counsel at an identification procedure for the unrelated crime.[160]

Photo Lineup

(See page 709 for case summaries on this topic.)

The defendant does not have a Sixth Amendment right to the presence of counsel or the right to be present when a witness attempts to identify an offender from photographs at a photo lineup, even if the procedure is conducted after the right to counsel has attached (begun), because a photo lineup is not a critical stage of a prosecution when the assistance of counsel is constitutionally necessary.[161] Of course, a photo lineup must still be conducted in a nonsuggestive manner, as discussed above for an in-person lineup, and must follow North Carolina statutory procedures, as discussed below.

---

155. Kirby v. Illinois, 406 U.S. 682 (1972).

156. Rothgery v. Gillespie Cty., 554 U.S. 191 (2008); United States v. Gouveia, 467 U.S. 180 (1984); Kirby v. Illinois, 406 U.S. 682 (1972). To the extent that pre-*Rothgery* North Carolina cases had ruled that the defendant's Sixth Amendment right to counsel did not begin until the first appearance in district court for a felony, they have been effectively overruled. *See, e.g.,* State v. Tucker, 331 N.C. 12 (1992); State v. Nations, 319 N.C. 318 (1987); State v. Phipps, 331 N.C. 427 (1992).

The United States Supreme Court has yet to rule whether the Sixth Amendment right to counsel begins with the mere issuance of an arrest warrant that occurs before the defendant's arrest or appearance before a judicial official. In a pre-*Rothgery* case, the North Carolina Supreme Court ruled in *State v. Taylor,* 354 N.C. 28 (2001), that the Sixth Amendment right to counsel did not begin with the issuance of an arrest warrant.

157. Moran v. Burbine, 475 U.S. 412 (1986); United States v. Ingle, 157 F.3d 1147 (9th Cir. 1998) (appointment of lawyer for grand jury appearance did not begin Sixth Amendment right to counsel).

158. Moran v. Burbine, 475 U.S. 412 (1986); United States v. Ingle, 157 F.3d 1147 (9th Cir. 1998).

159. United States v. Wade, 388 U.S. 218 (1967).

160. State v. Leggett, 305 N.C. 213 (1982).

161. United States v. Ash, 413 U.S. 300 (1973); State v. Miller, 288 N.C. 582 (1975).

Waiver of the Right to Counsel

A defendant may waive the Sixth Amendment right to counsel at a lineup or showup (assuming the right to counsel exists) orally or in writing.[162] The State must prove that the defendant did so knowingly and voluntarily. An officer's request for a waiver of counsel might include the following statements:

1. You are going to be placed in a lineup [*or name another identification procedure*] so that a witness to a crime may attempt to make an identification. [*If the defendant does not understand what a lineup or identification procedure is, explain it.*]
2. You have the right to have an attorney represent you during this lineup if you wish.
3. If you cannot afford to hire an attorney for this purpose, one will be appointed for you before the lineup is conducted.
4. Do you understand the rights I have just explained to you?
5. Do you wish to have an attorney represent you during this lineup?

Proving that a defendant waived the right to counsel sometimes may be difficult. Although an oral waiver can be legally sufficient, a written statement may be more helpful in proving the waiver's validity.

A Defendant's Refusal to Participate

A defendant does not have a Fifth Amendment right to refuse to participate in a lineup, to speak the words allegedly said by the offender during the crime, or to submit to other identification procedures, because the Fifth Amendment protects a person only from being compelled to give testimonial evidence.[163] (The Fifth Amendment also does not protect a person from having to give fingerprints, handwriting samples, voice samples, blood samples, and the like.)[164]

If the defendant refuses to participate in a lineup, officers may consider several alternatives:

- Use reasonable force to require the defendant's participation, although the identification procedure might become suggestive if the defendant continues to protest[165]
- Obtain a nontestimonial identification order (if the defendant has been arrested, a nontestimonial identification order may be used only if the defendant has been released pending trial) or a court order directing the defendant to participate, so that the defendant's continuing refusal would be punishable by criminal or civil contempt[166]
- Use other identification procedures that do not require the defendant's participation, such as a photo lineup

The fact that the defendant refused to participate in an identification or other procedure—whether it is a lineup, procurement of a blood sample, or the like—is admissible at trial.[167]

---

samples); Schmerber v. California, 384 U.S. 757 (1966) (blood sample); United States v. Wade, 388 U.S. 218 (1967) (lineup, speak for identification, and fingerprinting).

165. *See generally* G.S. 5A-11(a)(3), -21.

166. A court order and a subsequent refusal would be a prerequisite for a contempt of court citation when the identification procedure was being conducted without using a nontestimonial identification order. A violation of a court order may be punished by civil or criminal contempt, but not both. See the discussion on page 463 of Chapter 4 on using contempt of court when a defendant refuses to comply with a nontestimonial identification order.

167. United States v. Parhms, 424 F.2d 152 (9th Cir. 1970) (refusal to participate in lineup); Higgins v. Wainwright, 424 F.2d 177 (5th Cir. 1970) (refusal to speak for identification purposes in lineup); United States v. Nix, 465 F.2d 90 (5th Cir. 1972) (refusal to give handwriting sample); South Dakota v. Neville, 459 U.S. 553 (1983) (refusal to give blood sample). Relevant North Carolina cases include *State v. Trull*, 153 N.C. App. 630 (2002) (evidence of defendant's refusal to submit to gunshot residue test was admissible); *State v. Odom*, 303 N.C. 163 (1981) (defendant refused to submit to gunshot residue test until she talked with her lawyer; evidence of her refusal was admissible because she did not have a constitutional right to counsel when the test was scheduled and State did not induce her into believing that she did; court commented in a footnote that she may have had a statutory right to counsel under G.S. 15A-279(d), but she clearly did not, because the officer was attempting to conduct the procedure without a nontestimonial identification order, which he legally had a right to do); *State v. Perry*, 291 N.C. 284 (1976) (defendant required during trial

---

162. United States v. Wade, 388 U.S. 218 (1967); State v. Harris, 279 N.C. 177 (1971); State v. Hill, 278 N.C. 365 (1971); State v. Wright, 274 N.C. 84 (1968), *later appeal*, 275 N.C. 242 (1969).

163. United States v. Wade, 388 U.S. 218 (1967). *See also* Barnett v. Collins, 982 F.2d 922 (5th Cir. 1993) (defendant was required to utter robber's words before jury; no Fifth Amendment violation).

164. Gilbert v. California, 388 U.S. 263 (1967) (handwriting samples); United States v. Dionisio, 410 U.S. 1 (1973) (voice

Under some circumstances, a defendant whose appearance has changed from the time of arrest or commission of the crime to the time of the identification procedure may be required to alter his or her appearance—for example, a male defendant may be required to wear a false beard or to shave his own beard.[168]

North Carolina Statutory Procedures for Live Lineups and Photo Lineups

(*See page 714 for case summaries on this topic.*)

North Carolina legislation enacted in 2007 and 2015 (the main provision is codified in G.S. 15A-284.52) requires law enforcement officers to follow certain procedures when conducting lineups and showups.[169]

The term "lineup" in G.S. 15A-284.52 includes live lineups and photo lineups. A *live lineup* is defined as a procedure in which a group of people is displayed to an eyewitness for the purpose of determining whether the eyewitness is able to identify the perpetrator of a crime. A *photo lineup* is defined as a procedure in which an array of photographs is displayed to an eyewitness for the same purpose.

The principal provisions for lineups are as follows:

- A lineup must be conducted by an *independent administrator*, defined as a person who is not participating in the investigation of the criminal offense and who is unaware of which person in the lineup is a suspect. This procedure is known as a double-blind lineup because neither the witness nor the officer conducting the lineup knows who the suspect is. For photo lineups, certain alternative methods may be used instead of an independent administrator, such as an automated computer program.

- Individuals or photos in a lineup must be presented to witnesses sequentially, with each individual or photo presented to the witness separately and then removed before the next individual or photo is presented. A sequential lineup may reduce the possibility, present in lineups in which a group of people is shown at the same time, that the witness will compare the people in the lineup and pick the person who most closely matches the suspect. The combination of an independent administrator and sequential presentation is known as a double-blind, sequential lineup.

- Before a lineup is conducted, the eyewitness must receive certain instructions, including that the perpetrator may or may not be present in the lineup and that the investigation will continue whether or not an identification is made. The eyewitness must acknowledge receipt of the instructions in writing and, if the eyewitness refuses to sign, the lineup administrator must note the refusal.

- At least five fillers (nonsuspects) must be included in lineups and, if the eyewitness has previously viewed a photo or live lineup in connection with the identification of another suspect in the case, the fillers in the lineup containing the current suspect must be different from the fillers in prior lineups.

- If the eyewitness identifies a person in the lineup as the perpetrator, the lineup administrator must seek and document a clear statement from the eyewitness about the eyewitness's confidence level that the person is the perpetrator. The eyewitness may not be provided any information concerning the person before the lineup administrator obtains the eyewitness's confidence statement.

- Unless it is not practical, a video record of live identification procedures must be made. If a video record is not practical, the reasons must be documented, and an audio record must be made. If an audio record also is not practical, the reasons must be documented, and the lineup administrator must make a written record of the lineup.

- Whether the record is by video, audio, or writing, the record must include specified information, including the identification or nonidentification results, the eyewitness's confidence statement, the

---

to don stocking mask used in robbery); *State v. Suddreth*, 105 N.C. App. 122 (1992) (similar ruling); and *State v. Summers*, 105 N.C. App. 420 (1992) (defendant required during trial to display teeth).

168. United States v. Valenzuela, 722 F.2d 1431 (9th Cir. 1983) (requiring defendant to shave beard for in-court identification).

169. S.L. 2007-434; 2015-212. The 2007 session law was effective for lineups conducted on or after March 1, 2008. The 2015 session law was effective for showups conducted on or after December 1, 2015.

The text in this section is largely adopted from John Rubin, *2007 Legislation Affecting Criminal Law and Procedure*, ADMIN. OF JUST. BULL. 2008/01, 3–4 (Jan. 2008), http://sog-pubs.unc.edu/electronicversions/pdfs/aojb0801.pdf.

names of everyone present at the lineup, and the words used by the eyewitness in any identification.

The term "showup" is defined as a procedure in which an eyewitness, including a law enforcement officer, is presented with a single live suspect to determine whether the eyewitness is able to identify the perpetrator of a crime. It requires all officers who conduct a showup to meet all of the following requirements:

- A showup may only be conducted when a suspect matching the perpetrator's description is located in close proximity in time and place to the crime or when there is a reasonable belief that the perpetrator has changed his or her appearance close in time to the crime, and only if there are circumstances that require the immediate display of a suspect to an eyewitness.
- A showup may only be performed using a live suspect and may not be conducted with a photograph.
- Investigators must photograph a suspect at the time and place of the showup to preserve a record of the suspect's appearance when the showup procedure was conducted.

The legislation setting out the showup requirements also required the North Carolina Criminal Justice Education and Training Standards Commission to develop a policy concerning standard procedures to conduct showups, which applied to all law enforcement agencies beginning August 1, 2016, and addressed all of the following, in addition to the new statutory provisions:

- Standard instructions for an eyewitness
- Confidence statements by the eyewitness, including information concerning the eyewitness's vision, the circumstances of the events witnessed, and communications with other eyewitnesses, if any
- Training officers on how to conduct show-ups
- Any other matters the commission considers appropriate

G.S. 15A-284.52 sets forth the remedies for a violation of its provisions. First, failure to comply with any of the requirements "shall be considered by the court in adjudicating motions to suppress eyewitness identification." Thus, the court must take a violation into account, but a violation does not necessarily require suppression.[170] It appears that the court is to consider whether a violation constitutes a substantial statutory violation, requiring suppression under G.S. 15A-974. The court also may consider whether a failure to follow the specified procedures affects the reliability of the identification, requiring suppression under the Due Process Clause's totality of circumstances test. The statute does not explicitly address the question, but presumably the court also may consider whether a failure to follow the lineup or showup requirements tainted a subsequent identification, rendering that identification inadmissible.

Second, the failure to comply with any requirement is admissible in support of any claim of eyewitness misidentification as long as the evidence is otherwise admissible. Thus, as part of the case at trial, a defendant may offer evidence of a failure to follow the requirements to show that an eyewitness's identification is unreliable.

Third, when evidence of compliance or noncompliance has been presented at trial, the jury must be instructed that it may consider credible evidence of compliance or noncompliance to determine the reliability of an eyewitness identification. This provision suggests that, in support of an eyewitness identification, the State may present evidence at trial that it complied with the eyewitness identification procedures (if the evidence is otherwise admissible under the Confrontation Clause and the North Carolina Rules of Evidence).

Part III. Undercover Officers and Informants

Investigating and detecting some kinds of crimes—especially those with no direct victims, such as drug

---

170. In *State v. Stowes*, 220 N.C. App. 330 (2012), the court ruled that the trial court did not commit plain error by granting the defendant relief under the Eyewitness Identification Reform Act (EIRA), while not excluding evidence of a pretrial identification. The trial court found that an EIRA violation occurred because one of the officers administering the identification procedure was involved in the investigation. The court concluded: "We are not persuaded that the trial court committed plain error by granting Defendant all other available remedies under EIRA, rather than excluding the evidence." 220 N.C. App. at 341.

and liquor offenses—often require using undercover law enforcement officers and informants who associate with defendants without revealing that they are working for or on behalf of a law enforcement agency. Officers need to understand some of the legal issues involved with undercover work and informants.

Constitutional Issues

Fourth Amendment Issues

The United States Supreme Court has recognized that undercover officers and informants are necessary to investigate and detect crimes, but it has had to reconcile that need with the Fourth Amendment right to privacy.[171]

The United States Supreme Court has ruled that a defendant does not have a reasonable expectation of privacy under the Fourth Amendment when the defendant invites or permits an entry into his or her home by an undercover officer or an informant acting under an officer's direction to transact illegal business, such as selling drugs. Any evidence discovered or observations made during these activities are admissible at trial.[172]

The Court also has ruled that an undercover officer or informant (with the informant's consent) may be wired so that conversations with the defendant can be recorded and transmitted.[173] A defendant has no constitutional protection in a misplaced belief that a person to whom the defendant confides wrongdoing will not reveal it— subject to the Fifth and Sixth Amendment limitations discussed below.

There are, of course, Fourth Amendment limitations on actions by undercover officers or informants acting under their directions. For example, officers and informants may not obtain entry into a home by misrepresenting their identities and then search and seize without the defendant's consent throughout the home without a search warrant or other appropriate justification under the Fourth Amendment.[174]

Fifth Amendment Issues

As discussed earlier in this chapter, the *Miranda* ruling does not apply to custodial interrogation of a defendant by an undercover officer or a person acting at an officer's direction if the defendant is unaware that he or she is talking with an officer or a person acting at the officer's direction. However, the State still must prove that a defendant's statement was voluntarily made—for example, not coerced.[175]

If a defendant is not in custody and does not have a Sixth Amendment right to counsel, an undercover officer or an informant acting at an officer's direction may converse with the defendant without violating the defendant's Fifth Amendment right against compelled self-incrimination.[176]

Sixth Amendment Issues

As discussed earlier in this chapter, if a defendant has a Sixth Amendment right to counsel, officers or their informants acting at their direction may not deliberately elicit statements from the defendant, whether or not the defendant is in custody.[177] However, a defendant's right to counsel is not violated when officers or their agents merely listen while the defendant makes incriminating statements—or when a person who is not acting under an officer's direction converses with the defendant and reports that information to officers.[178]

---

171. Lewis v. United States, 385 U.S. 206 (1966).

172. *Id.*

173. United States v. White, 401 U.S. 745 (1971); United States v. Caceres, 440 U.S. 741 (1979); Lopez v. United States, 373 U.S. 427 (1963); On Lee v. United States, 343 U.S. 747 (1952). *See also* Hoffa v. United States, 385 U.S. 293 (1966); Osborn v. United States, 385 U.S. 323 (1966). Federal and state wiretapping and eavesdropping laws are discussed in Chapter 3.

174. Gouled v. United States, 255 U.S. 298 (1921).

175. Arizona v. Fulminante, 499 U.S. 279 (1991).

176. Hoffa v. United States, 385 U.S. 293 (1966); United States v. Burton, 724 F.2d 1283 (7th Cir. 1984). The Fifth Amendment is not violated even if the defendant has retained counsel and invoked the right to remain silent. The fact that a defendant had retained counsel before the Sixth Amendment right to counsel had attached does not, by itself, create a Sixth Amendment violation. *See* Moran v. Burbine, 475 U.S. 412 (1986); United States v. Craig, 573 F.2d 455 (7th Cir. 1977).

177. Massiah v. United States, 377 U.S. 201 (1984); United States v. Henry, 447 U.S. 264 (1980); Brewer v. Williams, 430 U.S. 387 (1977); Maine v. Mouton, 474 U.S. 159 (1985).

178. Kuhlmann v. Wilson, 477 U.S. 436 (1986); Thomas v. Cox, 708 F.2d 132 (4th Cir. 1983); State v. Payne, 312 N.C. 647 (1985).

Entrapment

Entrapment[179] occurs when

1. Officers or an informant acting at their direction induce the defendant to commit a crime by acts of persuasion, trickery, or fraud; and
2. The criminal intent to commit the crime originates with the officers or informant rather than with the innocent defendant, so that the crime is created by the officers or informant.

The second element is often stated another way: a defendant who was predisposed to commit the charged crime cannot successfully prove the entrapment defense. Undercover officers or an informant acting at their direction may give the defendant an opportunity to commit a crime and may even participate with the defendant in committing the crime, but the defendant has not been entrapped if the defendant was predisposed to commit the crime.[180] Thus, undercover officers may ask for and offer to buy drugs or stolen goods from a defendant, but they do not commit entrapment unless they induce or persuade the defendant to do so under circumstances in which the defendant had no prior criminal intent to commit these crimes.[181]

Entrapment is a complete defense to a crime, but the defendant must prove this defense to a jury's satisfaction at trial.[182] A defendant may not present an entrapment defense unless the defendant admits that he or she committed the acts that constitute the charged crime.[183]

Confidentiality of Informants

A major problem with using informants is that their identities often must be kept secret so that they may be used again and are safe from retaliation. There are two common circumstances in which a defendant may try to have a confidential informant's identity revealed:

1. When the defendant makes a motion to suppress evidence because it was seized after a search or arrest that lacked probable cause[184]
2. When the defendant may want to use the informant as a witness or to use the informant's information to defend himself or herself at trial

Challenge of Probable Cause

(*See page 513 for case summaries on this topic.*)

North Carolina law provides that when a defendant makes a motion to suppress evidence that contests the truthfulness of an officer's testimony about probable cause, and the testimony includes information furnished by a confidential informant, the defendant is entitled to be informed of the informant's identity[185] unless

1. The evidence sought to be suppressed was seized with a search warrant[186] or incident to an arrest with an arrest warrant, or

---

179. For a comprehensive analysis of entrapment issues, see JOHN RUBIN, THE ENTRAPMENT DEFENSE IN NORTH CAROLINA (UNC School of Government, 2001).

180. North Carolina cases on entrapment, in addition to those mentioned *infra* notes 181–83, include *State v. Stanley*, 288 N.C. 19 (1975); *State v. Walker*, 295 N.C. 510 (1978); *State v. Coleman*, 270 N.C. 357 (1967); *State v. Salame*, 24 N.C. App. 1 (1974); *State v. Wilkins*, 34 N.C. App. 392 (1977); *State v. Braun*, 31 N.C. App. 101 (1976); *State v. Whisnant*, 36 N.C. App. 252 (1978); *State v. Grier*, 51 N.C. App. 209 (1981); *State v. Pevia*, 56 N.C. App. 384 (1982); and *State v. Jamerson*, 64 N.C. App. 301 (1983).

181. For a case that ruled that an officer committed entrapment as a matter of law—that is, entrapment was sufficiently established so that a jury's determination was unnecessary— see *State v. Stanley*, 288 N.C. 19 (1975). *See also* Jacobsen v. United States, 503 U.S. 540 (1992) (note, however, that this case interpreted federal entrapment law, and the ruling is not binding on North Carolina courts).

182. State v. Hageman, 307 N.C. 1 (1982); State v. Luster, 306 N.C. 566 (1982) (entrapment defense was not available when entrapper was not acting under officer's directions). The defense of entrapment is an issue of state law, although the United States Supreme Court may recognize particularly outrageous

government conduct as violating a defendant's due process rights. *See* Hampton v. United States, 425 U.S. 484 (1976).

183. State v. Neville, 302 N.C. 623 (1981) (defendant was not entitled to jury instruction on defense of entrapment to charges of possessing and selling LSD when his defense was that he merely pretended to possess and sell LSD); State v. Luster, 306 N.C. 566 (1982). *But see* Mathews v. United States, 485 U.S. 58 (1988) (in federal criminal case, defendant was entitled to jury instruction on entrapment defense even though defendant denied committing one or more elements of the criminal offense; this ruling is not binding on North Carolina courts).

184. Although the text refers only to probable cause, the same legal principles also should apply when a confidential informant gives information that helps to establish reasonable suspicion to stop a person or seize evidence.

185. G.S. 15A-978. This statute clearly complies with whatever constitutional requirements may exist in revealing an informant's identity at a suppression hearing. *See* McCray v. Illinois, 386 U.S. 306 (1967).

186. State v. Carver, 70 N.C. App. 555 (1984); State v. Caldwell, 53 N.C. App. 1 (1981).

2. The informant's existence is corroborated by evidence independent of the officer's testimony.

Corroboration means that there must be some evidence—other than the word of the officer who is testifying about probable cause—that the informant actually exists. It does not mean that the truth of the informant's information must be corroborated. Most frequently, evidence of corroboration comes from the testimony of a second officer who knows the informant. For example, the second officer may have talked with the informant before the suppression hearing to determine that the informant in fact was the person who gave the officer the information that led to a warrantless search, or the second officer may have listened to the original conversation between the informant and the officer who used the informant's information.[187]

Defense at Trial

A defendant generally is entitled to know the identity of a confidential informant if the informant directly participated in the offense being tried (for example, by actually buying the drugs or watching an undercover officer buy the drugs)[188] or if the informant is a material witness to

the facts about the defendant's guilt or innocence.[189] The defendant has the burden of showing the need to know the informant's identity.[190]

On the other hand, a defendant generally is not entitled to know an informant's identity when

- The informant did not directly participate in the offense being tried—for example, although present at the scene, the informant did not actually participate in or witness the sale of drugs
- The informant only participated in another offense that is not being tried[191]

---

187. State v. Ellis, 50 N.C. App. 181 (1980); State v. Bunn, 36 N.C. App. 114 (1978); State v. Collins, 44 N.C. App. 141, *aff'd*, 300 N.C. 142 (1980).

188. Roviaro v. United States, 353 U.S. 1 (1957). North Carolina cases that have ruled on the necessity to reveal an informant's identity to assist a defendant at trial include *State*

v. Ketchie, 286 N.C. 387 (1975); *State v. McEachern*, 114 N.C. App. 218 (1994); *State v. Jackson*, 103 N.C. App. 239, *aff'd*, 331 N.C. 113 (1992); *State v. Moose*, 101 N.C. App. 59 (1990); *State v. Marshall*, 94 N.C. App. 20 (1989); *State v. Hodges*, 51 N.C. App. 229 (1981); *State v. Cameron*, 283 N.C. 191 (1973); *State v. Vinson*, 31 N.C. App. 318 (1976); *State v. Ingram*, 23 N.C. App. 186 (1974); *State v. Grainger*, 60 N.C. App. 188 (1982); *State v. Brown*, 29 N.C. App. 409 (1976); *State v. Parks*, 28 N.C. App. 20 (1975); and *State v. Orr*, 28 N.C. App. 317 (1976).

189. State v. Watson, 303 N.C. 533 (1981); State v. Shields, 61 N.C. App. 462 (1983).

190. State v. Hodges, 51 N.C. App. 229 (1981); State v. Orr, 28 N.C. App. 317 (1976); State v. Johnson, 81 N.C. App. 454 (1986).

191. State v. Cameron, 283 N.C. 191 (1973); State v. Jackson, 103 N.C. App. 239, *aff'd*, 331 N.C. 113 (1992); State v. Vinson, 31 N.C. App. 318 (1976); State v. Ingram, 23 N.C. App. 186 (1974); State v. Brown, 29 N.C. App. 409 (1976); State v. Parks, 28 N.C. App. 20 (1975).

Chapter 5 Appendix: Case Summaries

Chapter 5 Appendix: Case Summaries

I. Interrogation and Confessions

Voluntariness of the Defendant's Statement

(This topic is discussed on page 609.)

Generally

UNITED STATES SUPREME COURT

Arizona v. Fulminante, 499 U.S. 279 (1991). The inmate-defendant confessed to a fellow inmate, a government agent, about a murder he committed. The defendant confessed because the government agent had offered to protect the defendant from physical attacks from other inmates in return for the confession. The Court ruled, based on these and other facts, that the totality of circumstances showed that the confession was involuntary because a credible threat of physical violence motivated the defendant to confess. However, the Court rejected statements in *Bram v. United States*, 168 U.S. 532 (1897), that a confession may not be obtained by any direct or implied promises, however slight, or by the exertion of any improper influence. *See also* United States v. McCullah, 76 F.3d 1087 (10th Cir. 1996) (similar ruling to *Arizona v. Fulminante*).

Colorado v. Connelly, 479 U.S. 157 (1986). An apparently mentally ill defendant turned himself in to a law enforcement officer and confessed to a murder. The Court ruled that coercive law enforcement activity is a necessary predicate to a finding that a confession is involuntary under the Due Process Clause. The fact that the defendant's mental condition may have motivated him to confess in this case, absent law enforcement wrongdoing, does not make a confession involuntary. *See also* Snethen v. Nix, 885 F.2d 456 (8th Cir. 1989) (mother's prodding of son to confess, without involvement of law enforcement officers, was not a constitutional violation). *But see* United States v. D.F., 115 F.3d 413 (7th Cir. 1996) (county mental health workers, who believed that prosecution of juvenile patient was one of their roles, violated due process by eliciting involuntary confession).

Mincey v. Arizona, 437 U.S. 385 (1978). A defendant's involuntary statements may not be used in any way at trial (for example, for impeachment, as well as during the State's case in chief). The Court ruled that the defendant's statements were involuntarily made when the detective questioned him in the hospital. The defendant, under arrest for the murder of a policeman, was in the hospital's emergency room because he had been shot and seriously wounded. He had tubes in his throat and had to answer questions by writing on pieces of paper. Although he asked repeatedly that interrogation stop until he could obtain a lawyer, the detective continued to question him. He complained several times that he was confused or unable to think clearly, but the detective stopped his interrogation only during intervals when the defendant lost consciousness or received medical treatment.

The Court noted that the defendant's statements resulted from virtually continuous questioning of a seriously and painfully wounded man on the edge of consciousness. Voluntariness requires a careful evaluation of all the circumstances of an interrogation. The Court ruled that the defendant's statements were involuntary; they were not "the product of his free and rational choice." *Compare with* United States v. Martin, 781 F.2d 671 (9th Cir. 1985) (medicated hospital patient was sufficiently rational to make a voluntary statement).

Rogers v. Richmond, 365 U.S. 534 (1961). The Due Process Clause of the Fourteenth Amendment prohibits the introduction into evidence of a confession that is involuntary—that is, the product of coercion, either physical or psychological. The probable truthfulness or falsity of a confession may not be considered in determining whether it was voluntary. Instead, the question is whether the law enforcement officers' behavior overcame a defendant's will to resist and brought about a confession that was not freely self-determined. For a discussion of Supreme Court cases on voluntariness, see *Schneckloth v. Bustamonte*, 412 U.S. 218 (1973).

NORTH CAROLINA SUPREME COURT

State v. Wallace, 351 N.C. 481 (2000). The court ruled that the officer's promise to allow the defendant to see his girlfriend and daughter did not result in an involuntary confession. The court noted that the defendant made the request, and the officers did not use the request to induce his confession.

State v. Chapman, 343 N.C. 495 (1996). On August 23, 1993, about 9:30 a.m., the defendant was arrested at a bank for attempting to cash a forged check. He waived his *Miranda* rights and admitted that he had attempted to cash a check that he had forged after taking it in a robbery. Officers took the defendant to a school to search for a purse that had been taken in the robbery. They then returned the defendant to the police station, where he confessed to forgery and uttering charges. A detective procured arrest warrants for these charges at 12:15 p.m. and served them on the defendant. The defendant then was questioned by another detective who was investigating the robbery in which the checks were taken, and the defendant confessed to the robbery at 1:27 p.m. Officers prepared an arrest warrant to charge the robbery, but it was not presented to the magistrate then.

The defendant then was interviewed by another detective about a robbery and murder not related to the crimes discussed previously. The detective put nine photos of the murder victim on the walls of the interrogation room and one photo of the victim on the floor directly in front of the chair in which the defendant sat during the interrogation. Thus, the defendant saw a photo of the victim in every direction he turned. During the interview, the detective falsely implied to the defendant that a note found next to the victim's body had been the subject of handwriting analysis that showed it was the defendant's handwriting and that the defendant's fingerprints were on the note. The defendant confessed to the murder at about 7:05 p.m. and was taken to the magistrate about 8:00 p.m.

The court ruled that the defendant's confession was not involuntary. The placement of the photos did not cause his free will to be overcome. Relying on *State v. Jackson*, 308 N.C. 549 (1983), the court stated that the detective's deceit about the defendant's handwriting and fingerprints on the note did not require the trial judge to find that the confession was not of the defendant's own free will, that it was the product of fear or hope of reward, or that the deceit was calculated to produce an untrue statement.

State v. McCullers, 341 N.C. 19 (1995). Officers were investigating a murder in which several people beat, killed, and robbed the victim. The defendant, who was 18 years old and was working toward his GED, agreed to come to the police station for questioning. He was given his *Miranda* warnings and waived them. The defendant was alert and not under the influence of drugs or alcohol. One officer stated to the defendant that it would be better for the defendant if he said that he did not mean to kill the man than for him to keep denying that he did it. He also swore at the defendant on two occasions. Two other officers then took a statement from the defendant, who stated that no one had threatened him or made him say anything he did not want to say.

The court, distinguishing *State v. Pruitt*, 286 N.C. 442 (1975); *State v. Fuqua*, 269 N.C. 223 (1967); and *State v. Stevenson*, 212 N.C. 648 (1937); and relying on *State v. Smith*, 328 N.C. 99 (1991), and *State v. Jackson*, 308 N.C. 549 (1983), upheld the trial judge's ruling that the defendant's confession was voluntary. The court noted that the officer did not accuse the defendant of lying but rather informed him of the crime and urged him to tell the truth and think about what would be better for him. The court also noted that the defendant's contention that he was intimidated or coerced by the officer's profanity was not persuasive in light of the defendant's own use of profanity during the interrogation. Under the totality of circumstances, the officer's isolated statements did not support the defendant's contention that his statement was made involuntarily based on fear or hope.

State v. Wilson, 322 N.C. 91 (1988). An officer arrested the defendant, properly gave *Miranda* warnings and obtained a waiver, and then questioned the defendant about an alleged rape of a young girl. After the defendant answered "yes" to the officer's question as to whether he had sexually assaulted the girl, the officer asked the defendant to look into the officer's eyes and then said, "You're going to have to tell us what happened." The defendant made further incriminating statements. The court ruled, based on the totality of circumstances surrounding the defendant's statements, that the confession was voluntarily made. The officer did not frighten the defendant, overcome his will, or promise him anything as a reward for giving a statement.

State v. Perdue, 320 N.C. 51 (1987). Although the defendant took a tranquilizer before she confessed, her confession was voluntary because her will was not overborne by the tranquilizer.

State v. Richardson, 316 N.C. 594 (1986). Promises or other statements indicating to a defendant that the defendant will receive some benefit if he or she confesses do not make the confession involuntary when they are made in response to a defendant's solicitation. Even assuming that the detective offered to testify about the defendant's cooperation before the defendant asked what would happen if he cooperated, his confession was not involuntary, because he had considerable experience with the criminal justice system and was clearly engaged in bargaining with Tennessee authorities to obtain leniency and to avoid prosecution. *See also* State v. Bailey, 145 N.C. App. 13 (2001) (similar ruling).

State v. Corley, 310 N.C. 40 (1984). In determining whether a defendant's statement was voluntarily and understandingly made, a court must consider the totality of the circumstances and may not rely on any one circumstance by itself or in isolation. The court rejected an absolute rule that would automatically require a finding that a confession was involuntary when an officer told a defendant that "things would be a lot easier" on him if he "went ahead and told the truth" or harder for him if he did not. It ruled, based on the totality of circumstances, that the State had proved by a preponderance of evidence that the defendant's statement was voluntarily made without any suggestion, hope, or fear resulting from the officers' conduct—despite the officer's statement, quoted above. See the court's discussion and citation of prior decisions, including *State v. Pruitt*, 286 N.C. 442 (1975) (the confession was involuntary when an officer told the defendant that "things would be a lot easier on him if he went ahead and told the truth" or harder on him if he did not, and other circumstances showed that the officer frightened the defendant and overcame his will). Cases that have applied the *Corley* test include *State v. Bone*, 354 N.C. 1 (2001); *State v. Smith*, 328 N.C. 99 (1991); *State v. Thomas*, 310 N.C. 369 (1984); *State v. Williams*, 67 N.C. App. 144 (1984); *State v. Parrish*, 73 N.C. App. 662 (1985); and *State v. Durham*, 74 N.C. App. 121 (1985). Other cases upholding confessions as voluntary are *State v. Branch*, 306 N.C. 101 (1982); *State v. Edwards*, 78 N.C. App. 605 (1985); and *State v. Stephenson*, 144 N.C. App. 465 (2001).

State v. Chamberlain, 307 N.C. 130 (1982). Officers may truthfully tell a defendant during the interrogation about the evidence they have against the defendant. Explaining that information does not, by itself, make a later confession involuntary. *See also* State v. Booker, 306 N.C. 302 (1982), *later appeal*, 309 N.C. 446 (1983).

State v. Schneider, 306 N.C. 351 (1982). An officer's failure to advise a defendant during an interrogation of the charge about which the defendant is being questioned does not make the confession involuntary.

NORTH CAROLINA COURT OF APPEALS

State v. Flood, 237 N.C. App. 287 (2014). In a child sexual assault case, the court ruled that the trial court erred by finding that the defendant's statements during an interview were made involuntarily. Although the court found that an officer made improper promises to the defendant, it ruled, based on the totality of the circumstances, that the statements were voluntarily made. Regarding the improper promises, Agent Oaks suggested to the defendant during the interview that she would work with and help him if he confessed and that she "would recommend . . . that [the defendant] get treatment" instead of jail time. She also asserted that Detective Schwab "can ask for, you know, leniency, give you this, do this. He can ask the District Attorney's Office for certain things. It's totally up to them [what] they do with that but they're going to look for recommendations[.]" Oaks told the defendant that if he "admit[s] to what happened here," Schwab is "going to probably talk to the District Attorney and say, 'hey, this is my recommendation. Hey, this guy was honest with us. This guy has done everything we've asked him to do. What can we do?' and talk about it." Because it was clear that the purpose of Oaks's statements "was to improperly induce in Defendant a belief that he might obtain some kind of relief from criminal charges if he confessed," they were improper promises. However, viewing the totality of the circumstances (length of the interview, defendant's extensive experience with the criminal justice system given his prior service as a law enforcement officer, etc.), the court found his statements to be voluntarily made.

State v. Davis, 237 N.C. App. 22 (2014). The court ruled that the trial court did not err by finding that the defendant's statements were given freely and voluntarily. The court rejected the defendant's argument that they were coerced by fear and hope. The court ruled that an officer's promise that the defendant would "walk out" of the interview regardless of what she said did not render her confession involuntary. Without more, the officer's statement could not have led the defendant to believe that she would be treated more favorably if she confessed to her involvement in her child's disappearance and death. Next, the court rejected—as a factual matter—the defendant's argument that officers lied about information provided to them by a third party. Finally, the court rejected the defendant's argument that her mental state rendered her confession involuntary and coerced, when the evidence indicated that the defendant understood what was happening, was coherent, and did not appear to be impaired.

State v. Martin, 228 N.C. App. 687 (2013). The court ruled that the defendant's confession was involuntary. The defendant first made a confession before *Miranda* warnings were given. The officer then gave the defendant *Miranda* warnings and had the defendant repeat his confession. The trial court suppressed the defendant's pre-*Miranda* confession but ruled that the post-*Miranda* confession was admissible. The appeals court disagreed, concluding that the circumstances and tactics used by the officer to induce the first confession must be imputed to the post-*Miranda* confession. The court found the first confession involuntary, noting that the defendant was in custody; the officer made misrepresentations and/or deceptive statements, as well as promises to induce the confession; and the defendant may have had an impaired mental condition.

State v. Rollins, 226 N.C. App. 129 (2013). The court of appeals ruled that the trial court did not err by finding that the defendant's statements to his wife regarding his participation in a murder were voluntary. The defendant's wife spoke with him five times while he was in prison (on charges not connected to the murder) and while wearing a recording device provided by the police. While the wife did not threaten the defendant, she did make up evidence that she claimed law enforcement had recovered and told the defendant that officers suspected that she was involved in the murder. In response, the defendant made incriminating statements in which he corrected the wife's lies concerning the evidence and admitted details of the murder. The court rejected the defendant's argument that his statements were involuntary because of his wife's deception and her emotional appeals to him based on this deception.

State v. Graham, 223 N.C. App. 150 (2012). The court ruled in this child sexual abuse trial that the defendant's confession was not involuntary. After briefly speaking to the defendant at his home about an allegation of child sexual abuse against him, an officer asked him to come to the police station to answer questions. The court rejected the defendant's argument that his subsequent confession was involuntary because he was given a false hope of leniency if he were to confess and because he was told that

additional charges would stem from continued investigation of other children. The officers' offers to "help" the defendant "deal with" his "problem" did not constitute a direct promise that the defendant would receive a lesser charge—or even no charge—should he confess. The court also rejected the defendant's argument that the confession was involuntary because one of the officers relied on his friendship with the defendant and their shared racial background and because another officer asked questions about whether the defendant went to church or believed in God. Finally, the court rejected the defendant's argument that his confession was involuntarily obtained through deception.

State v. Cornelius, 219 N.C. App. 329 (2012). The court of appeals ruled that the trial court did not err by denying the defendant's motion to suppress three statements made while he was in the hospital. The defendant had argued that medication he received rendered the statements involuntary. Based on testimony of the detective who conducted the interview, hospital records, and the recorded statements, the trial court made extensive findings that the defendant was alert and oriented. Those findings supported the trial court's conclusion that the statements were voluntary.

State v. Cooper, 219 N.C. App. 390 (2012). The court of appeals rejected the defendant's argument that his confession was involuntary because it was obtained through police threats. Although the defendant argued that the police threatened to imprison his father unless he confessed, the trial court's findings of fact were more than sufficient to support its conclusion that the confession was not coerced. The trial court found, in part, that the defendant never was promised or told that his father would benefit from any statements that he himself made.

State v. Bordeaux, 207 N.C. App. 645 (2010). The court ruled that the trial court properly suppressed the defendant's confession on the grounds that it was involuntary. Although the defendant received *Miranda* warnings, interviewing officers during custodial interrogation suggested that the defendant was involved in an ongoing murder investigation, knowing that to be untrue. The officers promised to testify on the defendant's behalf, and these promises aroused in the defendant a hope of more lenient punishment. The officers also promised that if the defendant confessed, he might be able to pursue his plans to attend community college.

State v. Clodfelter, 203 N.C. App. 60 (2010). The court ruled, distinguishing *State v. Morrell*, 108 N.C. App. 465

(1993), and *State v. Hauser*, 115 N.C. App. 431 (1994), that the defendant's mother was not acting as an agent of law enforcement and it was therefore not required that *Miranda* warnings be given to the defendant. The mother testified that all the officers asked her to do, and all she in fact did do, was ask her son to tell the truth about his involvement in the murder.

State v. Shelly, 181 N.C. App. 196 (2007). The court ruled that the defendant's confession was not involuntary based on the officer's statements to the defendant. The officer told the defendant that a person who cooperates and shows remorse and who is honest and has no criminal background has the best chance of obtaining leniency because he cooperated. The court upheld the trial judge's findings that no improper promises were made to the defendant. The officer did not promise the defendant any different or preferential treatment as a result of the defendant's cooperation. The officer did not create a hope of leniency that induced the defendant to confess to the murder.

State v. Houston, 169 N.C. App. 367 (2005). Officers arrested the defendant in a parking lot, did not give him *Miranda* warnings, and took him to an apartment where he consented to a search, including a search of a safe to which the defendant gave officers the combination. Cocaine, cash, and a handgun were found in the safe. The officers transported the defendant to the police station, where they advised him of his *Miranda* rights and took a statement. None of the defendant's pre-*Miranda* warning statements were admitted at the defendant's trial. However, the evidence in the safe was admitted into evidence, as well as the defendant's statements at the police station. The court ruled that the defendant's statements at the police station were not involuntary. The court noted that the officers made general statements that they would advise the district attorney and judge of the defendant's cooperation and did not make any representations concerning what, if any, benefit the defendant's cooperation would bring.

State v. Bailey, 163 N.C. App. 84 (2004). The court ruled that the defendant was not coerced into giving a confession. The court noted that although the defendant's statements were taken over a six-hour time span, during which the defendant was secured to a chair by a single handcuff, the evidence also showed that law enforcement officers provided the defendant with food and drink, asked about his comfort at regular intervals, and allowed him several bathroom breaks.

State v. Thompson, 149 N.C. App. 276 (2002). The defendant voluntarily came to the police station and spoke with a detective about a robbery. The court ruled that the detective's repeated assertions that the defendant would not be arrested that day regardless of what he said was not an improper inducement that led the defendant to confess. The court noted that the defendant was familiar with the criminal justice system (he had seven prior convictions) and had doubtless been questioned often by law enforcement officers before the questioning that occurred in this case.

State v. Cabe, 136 N.C. App. 510 (2000). The defendant confessed to law enforcement officers about his sexual assault of his son. The court ruled that the officers did not make any improper promises to the defendant to induce an involuntary confession. The defendant was not under arrest during the questioning, and he was advised of and knowingly waived his constitutional rights. The interview lasted about 45 minutes, and the defendant was allowed to go home. Any of the officer's statements concerning the defendant's employment, possession of his car, and right to visit his son were in response to specific questions asked by the defendant. For example, an officer's statement that she could not see why the defendant would lose his job cannot be construed as a promise to let him keep his job if he cooperated with the officers. Further, any improper promises that may have been made concerned collateral matters, not the sexual assaults.

State v. Sturgill, 121 N.C. App. 629 (1996). Officers arrested the defendant for a felony breaking or entering and larceny. During custodial interrogation, a detective told the defendant that he would be charged with several other break-ins. The defendant then indicated that the only statement he wanted to make was that he did not commit any of the break-ins. The detective stopped the questioning and began to leave the interrogation room. The defendant then asked "what would be in it" for him if he provided information about the break-ins. The detective told him that he would not seek to indict him for habitual felon status. The defendant then confessed.

The court ruled that the officers' statement about the charge of habitual felon status violated the defendant's substantive due process rights (that is, the defendant detrimentally relied on the officer's promise). The statement also violated his statutory rights under G.S. 15A-1021, which bars improper pressure to induce a defendant to plead guilty, and G.S. 15A-974, the statutory exclusionary rule; thus, the confession was inadmissible. [Author's note: Legislation enacted in 2011 (S.L. 2011-6) added a good faith exception to the application of G.S. 15A-974.]

State v. Annadale, 95 N.C. App. 734 (1989). An officer informed the defendant, who had been arrested for several armed robberies, that he had evidence linking the defendant's girlfriend with the robberies. He told the defendant that he would discuss her case with the district attorney, although he advised the defendant that he had no authority to make any deals or bargains. The defendant later confessed. The court ruled that the fact that the defendant may have confessed with the hope of leniency for his girlfriend did not make his statement involuntary. The officer's statement about the defendant's girlfriend was not related to the defendant's charge against him but involved only a collateral advantage.

State v. Moore, 94 N.C. App. 55 (1989). The defendant's confession was not involuntarily obtained when officers confronted him with the evidence against him and told him that his previous statement was "a bunch of crap."

State v. Blackman, 93 N.C. App. 207 (1989). The fact that the officers ingratiated themselves with the defendant and presented themselves as his friends did not render his later confession involuntary, because the officers did not force the defendant to submit to an ordeal traditionally associated with coercive interrogations. *See also* State v. Greene, 332 N.C. 565 (1992) (although officers told defendant that they were his only friends and would help him with any problems, they did not intimate that by confessing he would avoid prosecution or obtain a lesser sentence).

State v. Marshall, 92 N.C. App. 398 (1988). An officer's alleged promise of a bond reduction if the defendant confessed was not related to the possible charge or punishment and therefore did not affect the admissibility of the confession. *See also* State v. Booker, 306 N.C. 302 (1982), *later appeal*, 309 N.C. 446 (1983).

State v. Adams, 85 N.C. App. 200 (1987). A mentally ill defendant who initiated contact with an officer and confessed in a noncustodial setting had no federal or state grounds for having his confession excluded.

State v. Sings, 35 N.C. App. 1 (1978). Showing that a defendant illegally seized evidence before the defendant confessed does not, by itself, make the confession involuntary. *See also* State v. McCloud, 276 N.C. 518 (1970). *But see* State v. Hall, 264 N.C. 559 (1965); State v. Silva, 304 N.C. 122 (1981).

FEDERAL APPELLATE COURTS

United States v. Braxton, 112 F.3d 777 (4th Cir. 1997) (en banc). The court ruled that, considering the totality of circumstances, an officer's statement that the defendant could face five years in jail was not an implied promise and did not make the defendant's confession involuntary. *See also* Rose v. Lee, 252 F.3d 676 (4th Cir. 2001) (officer's comment that things would go easier on the defendant if he told them the location of the body did not make confession involuntary).

United States v. Walton, 10 F.3d 1024 (3d Cir. 1993). The court ruled, based on the totality of circumstances, that an officer's promise to a defendant that what he told the officer would not be used against him coerced the defendant to give a statement. Thus, the defendant's statement was involuntary and inadmissible.

Use of Deception

State v. Hardy, 339 N.C. 207 (1994). The court examined all the evidence surrounding the defendant's confession to law enforcement officers and ruled that the confession was voluntary, even though one officer lied about a witness having identified the defendant and some of the officers' statements could be interpreted as implicit promises or threats. The court concluded, citing *State v. Jackson*, 308 N.C. 549 (1983), that the defendant's independent will was not overcome by mental or psychological coercion or pressure to induce a confession that he was not otherwise disposed to make. See also *State v. Chapman*, 343 N.C. 495 (1996), discussed above.

State v. Jackson, 308 N.C. 549 (1983), *later appeal*, 317 N.C. 1 (1986). An officer's use of deceptive methods or false statements during an interrogation does not, by itself, make a confession involuntary. The admissibility of a confession is determined by the totality of circumstances, one of which is whether an officer's conduct was calculated to procure an untrue confession. *See also* Frazier v. Cupp, 394 U.S. 731 (1969); State v. Barnes, 154 N.C. App. 111 (2002); State v. Chambers, 92 N.C. App. 230 (1988).

State v. Rollins, 226 N.C. App. 129 (2013). The court of appeals ruled that the trial court did not err by finding that the defendant's statements to his wife regarding his participation in a murder were voluntary. The defendant's wife spoke with him five times while he was in prison (on charges not connected to the murder) and while wearing a recording device provided by the police. While the wife did not threaten the defendant, she did make up evidence that she claimed law enforcement had recovered and told the defendant that officers suspected that she was involved in the murder. In response, the defendant made incriminating statements in which he corrected the wife's lies concerning the evidence and admitted details of the murder. The court rejected the defendant's argument that his statements were involuntary because of his wife's deception and her emotional appeals to him based on this deception.

State v. Barnes, 154 N.C. App. 111 (2002). The defendant voluntarily came to the sheriff's department to discuss an investigation against him concerning his alleged sexual assault of his daughter. The investigating officer falsely told the defendant that his daughter was pregnant. The court noted, citing *State v. Jackson*, 308 N.C. 549 (1983), that deception is only one factor in examining the totality of circumstances surrounding the voluntariness of a confession. The court stated that the defendant was not tricked about the nature of the crime or the possible punishment. The officer did not subject the defendant to threats of harm, rewards for a confession, or deprivation of freedom of action. There was not an oppressive environment during the officer's questioning of the defendant. The court ruled that the confession was voluntary.

Mental Capacity to Confess

State v. McKoy, 323 N.C. 1 (1988). The court ruled, based on the totality of circumstances, that the defendant gave a voluntary confession and properly waived his *Miranda* rights although he was mildly intoxicated, had subnormal mental capacity, and had been injured when arrested. *See also* State v. Allen, 322 N.C. 176 (1988); State v. Jones, 153 N.C. App. 358 (2002).

State v. Misenheimer, 304 N.C. 108 (1981). The defendant must have sufficient mental capacity to confess competently and voluntarily when officers question him. *See also* State v. Ross, 297 N.C. 137 (1979); State v. Thompson, 287 N.C. 303 (1975); State v. Spence, 36 N.C. App. 627 (1978).

Intoxication

State v. McKoy, 323 N.C. 1 (1988). The court ruled that the defendant gave a voluntary confession and properly waived his *Miranda* rights although he was mildly intoxicated, had a subnormal mental capacity, and had been injured when arrested. The totality of circumstances supported the trial judge's conclusion that the defen-

dant knowingly, intelligently, and voluntarily waived his *Miranda* rights and that his statements were made freely, understandingly, and voluntarily.

State v. Oxendine, 303 N.C. 235 (1981). A defendant's statement is admissible unless the defendant was so intoxicated that the defendant was not conscious of the meaning of his or her words. *See also* State v. Parton, 303 N.C. 55 (1981).

Confession Made after an Involuntary Confession

State v. Jones, 327 N.C. 439 (1990). The defendant was interrogated by officers for two hours beginning at 12:25 a.m., March 8, 1987. He was interrogated again for about one hour beginning at 4:00 a.m., March 8, 1987, and for about one-half hour beginning at 8:15 a.m. the same morning. The State did not seek to introduce statements of the defendant from any of these interrogations. At 11:25 a.m., March 9, 1987, the defendant was interrogated by officers who were not involved in the prior interrogations, and the State was permitted to introduce his statement from this interrogation, which the trial judge found not to be unconstitutionally coerced.

The court, assuming that the defendant's statements from the March 8, 1987, interrogations were unconstitutionally coerced, upheld the admissibility of the defendant's statement from the March 9, 1987, interrogation, because the coercion of the March 8, 1987, interrogations did not impermissibly taint the March 9 interrogation. [Author's note: The court did not utilize more stringent tests imposed on the State in *State v. Edwards* and *State v. Silver*, discussed below.] The court noted that the following intervening factors between the March 8 interrogations and the March 9 interrogation were sufficient to purge any taint left by the threats and promises of the March 8 interrogations: (1) two different officers conducted the last interrogation, which was held at a different site than the prior interrogations; (2) the defendant had 26 hours between the earlier interrogations and the last interrogation to reconsider his statements; and (3) the defendant, a person of average intelligence, was advised of his rights and knowingly and intelligently waived his rights at the March 9 interrogation. *See also* Leon v. Wainwright, 734 F.2d 770 (11th Cir. 1984) (test is whether the coercion surrounding the first statement had been sufficiently dissipated so that the second statement was voluntary); United States v. Daniel, 932 F.2d 522 (6th Cir. 1991) (similar ruling; court also analyzed United

States Supreme Court rulings); United States v. Jenkins, 938 F.2d 934 (9th Cir. 1991); Holland v. McGinnis, 963 F.2d 1044 (7th Cir. 1992).

State v. Edwards, 284 N.C. 76 (1973). Officers obtained a confession two months after they took an involuntary confession. The court appeared to impose a requirement that the admissibility of the second confession depended on whether the defendant was told before he confessed again that the first confession was invalid and could not be used against him. *See also* State v. Silver, 286 N.C. 709 (1975) (State must disprove by clear and convincing evidence the "presumption" that imputes the same improper influence on the second confession that caused the first confession to be considered involuntary). [Author's note: The tests set out in *Edwards* and *Silver* may now be supplanted by the test set out in *State v. Jones*, discussed above, which is the test used by federal courts.]

State v. Martin, 228 N.C. App. 687 (2013). The court ruled that the defendant's confession was involuntary. The defendant first made a confession before *Miranda* warnings were given. The officer then gave the defendant *Miranda* warnings and had the defendant repeat his confession. The trial court suppressed the defendant's pre-*Miranda* confession but ruled that the post-*Miranda* confession was admissible. The appeals court disagreed, concluding that the circumstances and tactics used by the officer to induce the first confession must be imputed to the post-*Miranda* confession. The court found the first confession involuntary, noting that the defendant was in custody, the officer made misrepresentations or deceptive statements as well as promises to induce the confession, and the defendant may have had an impaired mental condition.

Defendant's Statements: *Miranda* Warnings and Waiver

(This topic is discussed on page 570.)

Generally

UNITED STATES SUPREME COURT

Berghuis v. Thompkins, 560 U.S. 370 (2010). The Court ruled that the defendant impliedly waived his rights under *Miranda v. Arizona*, 384 U.S. 436 (1966).

Officers were investigating a murder. Before beginning a custodial interrogation, one of the officers presented the defendant with a *Miranda* form. The form included the four warnings required by *Miranda v. Arizona*, 384 U.S. 436 (1966) (right to remain silent, use of statements in court, right to have lawyer present, right to have appointed lawyer if indigent), and an additional warning not required by *Miranda*: "You have the right to decide at any time before or during questioning to use your right to remain silent and your right to talk with a lawyer while you are being questioned." The officer asked the defendant to read the fifth warning aloud so that he could ensure that the defendant understood English, which he did. The officer then read the other four *Miranda* warnings aloud and asked the defendant to sign the form to demonstrate that he understood his rights. The defendant declined to sign the form. There was conflicting evidence as to whether the officer verbally confirmed that the defendant understood the rights listed on the form. The officer did not discuss a waiver of *Miranda* rights with the defendant or obtain one from him.

During the interrogation, the defendant never stated that he wanted to remain silent, that he did not want to talk with the officers, or that he wanted a lawyer. About two hours and 45 minutes into the interrogation, during which the defendant was mostly silent, an officer asked the defendant, "Do you believe in God?" The defendant said "yes." The officer asked, "Do you pray to God?" The defendant said "yes." The officer then asked, "Do you pray to God to forgive you for shooting that boy down?" The defendant said "yes" and looked away, and the interview ended shortly thereafter. At trial, the defendant moved to suppress these statements. The issue before the United States Supreme Court was the admissibility of these statements under *Miranda v. Arizona* and later *Miranda*-related cases.

The Court noted that some language in *Miranda v. Arizona* could be read to indicate that a waiver of *Miranda* rights is difficult to establish absent an explicit written waiver or a formal, explicit oral statement. However, the Court discussed its rulings since *Miranda*, particularly *North Carolina v. Butler*, 441 U.S. 369 (1979) (valid waiver when defendant read *Miranda* rights form, said he understood his rights, refused to sign waiver at bottom of form, but said, "I will talk to you but I am not signing any form"), indicating that its later decisions made clear that a waiver of *Miranda* rights may be implied through the defendant's silence, coupled with an understanding of his or her rights and a course of conduct indicating waiver. The Court in effect disavowed the language in *Miranda* suggesting that it is difficult to establish a *Miranda* waiver without an explicit written waiver or a formal, explicit oral statement.

The Court concluded that if the prosecution shows that a defendant was given *Miranda* warnings and understood them, a defendant's uncoerced statements establish an implied waiver of *Miranda* rights. A defendant's explicit waiver need not precede custodial interrogation. Any waiver, explicit or implied, may be withdrawn by a defendant's invocation at any time of the right to counsel or the right to remain silent. Turning to the case before it, the Court ruled that the defendant waived his right to remain silent, and his statements were admissible at trial. The Court found that there was no basis to conclude that the defendant did not understand his *Miranda* rights, and the defendant chose not to invoke or rely on those rights when he made his uncoerced statements.

Dickerson v. United States, 530 U.S. 428 (2000). The Court ruled that its ruling in *Miranda v. Arizona*, 384 U.S. 436 (1966), was constitutionally based and may not be modified by a legislative act, such as 18 U.S.C. § 3501. [Author's note: The Court strongly indicated that the *Dickerson* ruling did not adversely affect its ruling in *Oregon v. Elstad*, 470 U.S. 298 (1985); *see* United States v. Sterling, 283 F.3d 216 (4th Cir. 2002); United States v. DeSumma, 272 F.3d 176 (3d Cir. 2001).]

Pennsylvania v. Muniz, 496 U.S. 582 (1990). An officer arrested the defendant for driving under the influence and took him to the booking center. The officer did not give *Miranda* warnings to the defendant. The officer asked the defendant booking questions, including the date of the defendant's sixth birthday. The officer also had the defendant perform physical sobriety tests, and he asked the defendant to take a Breathalyzer test. All these events were videotaped and introduced into evidence at trial.

(1) The Court ruled that the defendant's slurred speech in answering booking questions was not testimonial, was not protected by the Fifth Amendment, and thus was admissible without the giving of *Miranda* warnings. (2) The Court ruled that the defendant's incriminating answer (showing his mentally confused condition), "No, I don't," to the question, "When you turned six years old, do you remember what the date was?" was testimonial, protected by the Fifth Amendment, and therefore inadmissible in the absence of *Miranda* warnings. (3) A four-Justice plurality ruled that routine booking questions may be asked and answered without *Miranda* warnings

if the questions are not designed to elicit incriminating statements (the questions in this case concerned the defendant's name, address, height, weight, eye color, date of birth, and current age). (4) The Court ruled that the defendant's voluntary utterances (including his questions to the officer and his slurred speech) when he performed the physical sobriety test and during preliminaries of the Breathalyzer testing were not the result of interrogation and therefore were admissible.

Illinois v. Perkins, 496 U.S. 292 (1990). Officers were investigating the defendant as a homicide suspect. While the defendant was in jail on unrelated charges, an officer—acting undercover—was admitted to jail as an inmate. The defendant stated during conversations with the officer that he committed the homicide. The defendant did not know that he was speaking to an officer. The Court ruled that the requirements of the *Miranda* ruling, which include giving *Miranda* warnings, did not apply to these facts. The Court stated that a "police-dominated atmosphere" and compulsion, which underlay the *Miranda* ruling, do not exist when an incarcerated person speaks voluntarily with someone he or she believes to be a fellow inmate. The Court also noted that the defendant's Sixth Amendment right to counsel was not implicated in this case, because the defendant had not yet been charged with the homicide when the undercover officer talked with him in jail. The Court did not discuss whether the officer's conduct would have been permissible if the defendant had asserted his right to counsel under the Fifth Amendment for the unrelated charges for which he had been jailed.

Berkemer v. McCarty, 468 U.S. 420 (1984). The *Miranda* rule applies to all offenses, whether felonies or misdemeanors, for which a person is subject to custodial interrogation.

Miranda v. Arizona, 384 U.S. 436 (1966). The Court stated that it is necessary to establish procedures to protect a person's right not to be compelled to incriminate himself or herself under the Fifth Amendment. It ruled that a person's statements are not admissible unless, before an officer begins custodial interrogation, the officer warns a person that (1) the person has a right to remain silent, (2) what the person says may be used in court against him or her, (3) the person has a right to have a lawyer present during interrogation, and (4) the person has a right to an appointed lawyer during interrogation if he or she cannot afford to hire one. Once the officer has given the person these warnings and the opportunity to exercise these rights, the person may knowingly and intelligently waive them and agree to answer questions or make a statement. If, at any time while the person is being questioned, the person expresses an unwillingness to go on with the questioning or asserts the right to counsel, the officer must stop the questioning.

NORTH CAROLINA SUPREME COURT

State v. Leary, 344 N.C. 109 (1996). The court rejected the defendant's argument that the North Carolina Constitution requires law enforcement officers to give *Miranda*-style warnings to defendants even though they are not in custody.

NORTH CAROLINA COURT OF APPEALS

State v. Quick, 226 N.C. App. 541 (2013). The court of appeals rejected the State's argument that the defendant initiated contact with the police following his initial request for counsel and thus waived his right to counsel. After the defendant asserted his right to counsel, the police returned him to the interrogation room and again asked if he wanted counsel; he said yes. Then, on the way from the interrogation room back to the jail, a detective told the defendant that an attorney would not be able to help him and that he would be served with warrants regardless of whether an attorney was there. The police knew or should have known that telling the defendant that an attorney could not help him with the warrants would be reasonably likely to elicit an incriminating response. It was only after this statement by police that the defendant agreed to talk. Therefore, the court of appeals concluded, the defendant did not initiate the communication. The court also concluded that even if the defendant had initiated communication with police, his waiver was not knowing and intelligent. The trial court had found that the prosecution failed to meet its burden of showing that the defendant made a knowing and intelligent waiver, relying on the facts that the defendant was 18 years old and had limited experience with the criminal justice system. There was a period of time between 12:39 and 12:54 p.m. on the day the defendant was questioned when there was no evidence as to what occurred and no audio or video recording of the interview. The court found that the defendant's age and inexperience, when combined with the circumstances of his interrogation, supported the trial court's conclusion that the State failed to prove the defendant's waiver was knowing and intelligent.

State v. Cureton, 223 N.C. App. 274 (2012). The court ruled that the defendant knowingly and intelligently waived his right to counsel after being read his *Miranda* rights. The court rejected the defendant's argument that the fact that he never signed the waiver of rights form had established that a valid waiver was not made. The court also rejected the defendant's argument that he was incapable of knowingly and intelligently waiving his rights because his borderline mental capacity prevented him from fully understanding those rights. The court relied in part on a psychological evaluation diagnosing the defendant as malingering and finding him competent to stand trial.

State v. Hunter, 208 N.C. App. 506 (2010). The court rejected the defendant's argument that due to being under the influence of cocaine, he did not knowingly, intelligently, and understandingly waive his *Miranda* rights or make a statement to the police. Because the defendant was not under the influence of any impairing substance and answered questions appropriately, the fact that he had ingested crack cocaine several hours earlier was not sufficient to invalidate the trial court's finding that his statements were freely and voluntarily made.

At 11:40 p.m., unarmed agents woke the defendant in his cell and brought him to an interrogation room, where the defendant was not restrained. The defendant was responsive to instructions and was fully advised of his *Miranda* rights; he nodded affirmatively to each right, and at 11:46 p.m. he signed a *Miranda* rights form. When asked whether he was under the influence of any alcohol or drugs, the defendant indicated that he was not but that he had used crack cocaine at around 1:00 p.m. or 2:00 p.m. that day. He responded to questions appropriately. An agent compiled a written summary, which the defendant was given to read and to which he could make changes if desired. Both the defendant and the agent signed the document at around 2:41 a.m. The agents thanked the defendant for cooperating, and the defendant indicated that he was glad to "get all of this off [his] chest." Based on these facts, the defendant's statements were free and voluntary; no promises were made to him, and he was not coerced in any way. He was knowledgeable of his circumstances and cognizant of the meaning of his words.

State v. Nguyen, 178 N.C. App. 447 (2006). The court ruled that the *Miranda* waiver by the Vietnamese-speaking defendant was understandingly, voluntarily, and knowingly made when a Vietnamese-speaking law enforcement officer acted as the translator for the interrogating law enforcement officer. There was no evidence that the officer-translator was deceitful or acted in an otherwise improper manner during his dealings with the defendant. The court rejected the defendant's argument that the officer-translator was not a neutral translator because he was a law enforcement officer.

State v. Ortez, 178 N.C. App. 236 (2006). A law enforcement officer fluent in Spanish read the defendant his *Miranda* rights in Spanish from a preprinted *Miranda* rights and waiver form. The defendant signed the waiver form.

(1) The defendant on appeal challenged the adequacy of the *Miranda* warnings, specifically the use of "corte de ley" for "court of law" and "interrogatorio" for "questioning." The defendant also challenged the Spanish translation of the *Miranda* right to counsel for an indigent person. The court discussed these issues and ruled that the *Miranda* warnings given in Spanish reasonably conveyed to the defendant his *Miranda* rights and were therefore adequate. (2) The defendant's testing showed that he had an IQ ranging from 55 to 77, classifying him as mildly mentally retarded to borderline intellectual or low average functioning. The court noted that a defendant's IQ alone does not mean that the defendant could not make a voluntary, knowing, and intelligent waiver of his *Miranda* rights. The court discussed the facts in this case and ruled that the defendant's waiver was valid based on the totality of circumstances.

In re Pittman, 149 N.C. App. 951 (2002). The court ruled, citing *State v. Adams*, 345 N.C. 745 (1997), and a legal treatise, that the *Miranda* ruling does not apply to a statement made to a law enforcement officer offered into evidence in a civil abuse and neglect proceeding. The *Miranda* ruling only applies to a statement offered into evidence in a criminal proceeding.

In re Phillips, 128 N.C. App. 732 (1998). An assistant school principal questioned a student about stolen school property. No law enforcement officer was involved with the questioning. The assistant principal was not required to give *Miranda* warnings before questioning the student.

State v. Morrell, 108 N.C. App. 465 (1993). The defendant was arrested on a federal charge of child abduction and was committed to the county jail. A social worker in the county child protective services unit identified herself and told the defendant that she was conducting an investigation of alleged sexual abuse and neglect of a boy with whom the defendant had had a relationship. The defendant confessed to the social worker. Two days later, a deputy sheriff talked with the defendant in the jail after giving her *Miranda* warnings and obtaining a proper waiver. The defendant again confessed.

Based on evidence that the social worker was working with the sheriff's department on the case before interviewing the defendant in jail, the court ruled that the social worker was an agent of the State and thus was required to give *Miranda* warnings when that interview occurred. The court upheld the admissibility of the defendant's confession to the deputy sheriff because the confession to the social worker was not coerced; *see* Oregon v. Elstad, 470 U.S. 298 (1985); State v. Barlow, 330 N.C. 133 (1991). [Author's note: The court did not discuss *Illinois v. Perkins*, 496 U.S. 292 (1990). If the defendant did not know that the social worker was acting on behalf of the deputy sheriff or was a government official involved in investigating or reporting criminal offenses, then the ruling in *Illinois v. Perkins* may not have required the social worker to give *Miranda* warnings. However, one can argue that the facts in *Morrell* clearly establish that the defendant knew that the social worker was a government official and her duties included the investigation or reporting of crimes. *See* Mathis v. United States, 391 U.S. 1 (1968); Cates v. State, 776 S.W.2d 170 (Tex. Crim. App. 1989); State v. Nason, 981 P.2d 866 (Wash. Ct. App. 1999).]

FEDERAL APPELLATE COURTS

Alexander v. Connecticut, 917 F.2d 747 (2d Cir. 1990). The defendant was in jail awaiting trial for arson. He had requested a lawyer for the arson charge at arraignment, and the court appointed a lawyer to represent him. The lawyer told officers that the defendant did not want to be questioned further without his lawyer present. The officers suspected that the defendant had committed a murder, for which the defendant had not been charged. A friend of the defendant, acting at the officers' instigation, visited the defendant in jail and obtained incriminating statements that were later used in the defendant's murder trial. Relying on *Illinois v. Perkins*, discussed above, the court ruled that regardless of whether the defendant properly invoked his Fifth Amendment right to counsel, the officers did not violate that right because their conduct was not prohibited by the *Miranda* ruling (that is, there was no interrogation by a law enforcement officer in this case; the defendant simply had a noncoercive conversation with a friend). There also was no violation of the defendant's Sixth Amendment right to counsel, because the defendant had not been charged with the murder when the conversation occurred. *See also* Salkil v. Delo, 990 F.2d 386 (8th Cir. 1993) (similar ruling); United States v. Ingle, 157 F.3d 1147 (8th Cir. 1998) (no *Miranda* warnings required when government encouraged defendant's fellow jail inmates to elicit incriminating statements from defendant).

Adequacy of *Miranda* Warnings

(This topic is discussed on page 570.)

Generally

Florida v. Powell, 559 U.S. 50 (2010). A Florida law enforcement officer, when advising a defendant of his *Miranda* rights, told the defendant, "You have the right to remain silent. If you give up the right to remain silent, anything you say can be used against you in court. You have the right to talk to a lawyer before answering any of our questions. If you cannot afford to hire a lawyer, one will be appointed for you without cost and before any questioning. You have the right to use any of these rights at any time you want during this interview." The Court stated, noting its rulings in *California v. Prysock*, 453 U.S. 355 (1981), and *Duckworth v. Eagan*, 492 U.S. 195 (1989), that it has not dictated the words in which the essential information of a *Miranda* warning must be conveyed. Although the officer's warning concerning the presence of a lawyer during interrogation did not track the language in the *Miranda* ruling, the Court ruled that the warning satisfied the requirement that a defendant must be clearly informed that he has the right to consult with a lawyer and to have the lawyer with him during interrogation. Thus, the warning complied with the *Miranda* ruling.

Duckworth v. Eagan, 492 U.S. 195 (1989). *Miranda* warnings need not be given in the precise form set out in the *Miranda* ruling. The *Miranda* form's warning in this case stated—after advising the defendant that he had a right to a lawyer before questions were asked and to have the lawyer present during questioning—that the officers had no way to give him a lawyer, but that one would be appointed for him if and when he went to court. The court ruled that this form sufficiently complied with the *Miranda* ruling. *But see* United States v. Tillman, 963 F.2d 137 (6th Cir. 1992) (*Miranda* warnings were deficient because defendant was not told that any statements he might make could be used against him, and he was not informed of his right to counsel during questioning).

California v. Prysock, 453 U.S. 355 (1981). *Miranda* warnings need not be a verbatim recitation of the language in that case. Although the officer in this case did not explicitly state that the defendant had a right to have a lawyer appointed before questioning, he clearly told him that he had a right to have a lawyer present before and during questioning and he had a right to have a lawyer appointed at no cost if he could not afford one.

State v. Cummings, 346 N.C. 291 (1997). While advising the defendant of his *Miranda* rights, an officer marked out the words "at no cost" in a sentence that read, "If you want a lawyer before or during questioning but cannot afford to hire one, one will be appointed to represent you at no cost before any questioning." The officer explained to the defendant, "I don't know why they put in this 'at no cost'. If you are found innocent, it is no cost, but if you are found guilty, there is a chance the state will require you to reimburse them for the attorney fees." The officer then explained that he was going to cross it off and initial it because he didn't want to mislead the defendant. The court ruled that the officer gave the defendant a fully effective equivalent of *Miranda* rights. The court noted that the officer's additional information about the cost of an attorney was accurate.

State v. Strobel, 164 N.C. App. 310 (2004). Three people were involved in an armed robbery. The defendant was arrested for conspiracy to commit the armed robbery, appeared in district court, and requested and was appointed an attorney in December 2001. Based on additional information implicating the defendant as a participant in the robbery, in January 2002 an officer arrested her for armed robbery. The officer did not orally advise the defendant of her *Miranda* rights. Instead, he gave her a written form and asked her to read it. She signed each page of the statement that acknowledged that she had read it. During her interrogation, the defendant mentioned that she had a court-appointed attorney representing her on the conspiracy charge. The officer told the defendant that she could use the telephone and telephone book located in the room to call her attorney. He also told her that he would stop interrogation until she had the opportunity to talk to her lawyer. The court ruled, relying on federal appellate cases, that giving the defendant her *Miranda* warnings only in writing did not violate the defendant's *Miranda* rights. The court noted, however, that it is better practice to give a defendant an oral recitation of *Miranda* warnings.

Warnings in Foreign Languages

State v. Ortez, 178 N.C. App. 236 (2006). A law enforcement officer fluent in Spanish read the defendant his *Miranda* rights in Spanish from a preprinted *Miranda* rights and waiver form. The defendant signed the waiver form. The defendant on appeal challenged the adequacy of the *Miranda* warnings, specifically the use of "corte de ley" for "court of law" and "interrogatorio" for "questioning." The defendant also challenged the Spanish translation of the *Miranda* right to counsel for an indigent person. The court discussed these issues and ruled that the *Miranda* warnings given in Spanish reasonably conveyed to the defendant his *Miranda* rights and were therefore adequate.

Necessity to Repeat Warnings

(This topic is discussed on page 572.)

State v. Harris, 338 N.C. 129 (1994). North Carolina law enforcement officers went to Georgia to return the defendant to North Carolina for a first-degree murder charge pending in North Carolina. After properly being advised of his *Miranda* rights, the defendant asserted his right to counsel. No interrogation was conducted. After his return to North Carolina 12 hours later, the defendant, through his brother (who was visiting the defendant in jail), asked to talk to the sheriff.

The court ruled that (1) the defendant initiated communication with the sheriff by telling his brother to inform the sheriff that he wanted to speak with him, and (2) the sheriff was not required to give *Miranda* warnings again before interrogating the defendant. *See generally* State v. McZorn, 288 N.C. 417 (1975). The court stated that there was no reason to believe that the defendant, having been properly advised of his *Miranda* rights 12 hours earlier, had forgotten them. For example, he should have known of his right to an attorney, because he had exercised that right 12 hours earlier.

State v. McZorn, 288 N.C. 417 (1975). When interrogation is broken off and resumed later, there are five factors to consider in deciding whether the initial *Miranda* warnings that were given to the defendant have become so stale that the defendant must be given new warnings before the later interrogation begins: (1) the length of time between the first warnings and the subsequent interrogation; (2) whether the warnings and subsequent interrogation were given in different places; (3) whether different officers gave the warnings and conducted the subsequent interrogation; (4) the extent to which the defendant's subsequent statement differed from prior statements [Author's note: This is an after-the-fact judgment that officers cannot make when they must decide whether to repeat *Miranda* warnings before the subsequent interrogation.]; and (5) the defendant's apparent intellectual or emotional status. *See also* State v. Smith, 328 N.C. 99 (1991); State v. Branch, 306 N.C. 101 (1982); State v. White, 291 N.C. 118 (1976); State v. Simpson, 297 N.C. 399 (1979); State v. Westmoreland, 314 N.C. 442 (1983); State v. Artis, 304 N.C. 378 (1981); State v. Cole, 293 N.C. 328 (1977); State v. Garrison, 294 N.C. 270 (1978); State v. Leak, 90 N.C. App. 351 (1988).

State v. Flowers, 121 N.C. App. 299 (1996). The defendant was not entitled to a repetition of *Miranda* warnings when the evidence showed that she was properly advised of and waived her *Miranda* rights at about 7:38 p.m.; repeated her confession while being tape recorded at 8:30 p.m. that same night, while affirming that she had been advised of her constitutional rights; and the next morning at 10:02 a.m. read and signed a transcript of her recorded statement, affirming the transcript to be her entire statement. The initial *Miranda* warnings were not stale at the time of her later confession the same evening or the time of her affirmation of the transcript the next morning.

Guam v. Dela Pena, 72 F.3d 767 (9th Cir. 1995). Statements made by a defendant during custodial interrogation are not inadmissible simply because officers failed to repeat *Miranda* warnings previously given to the defendant when he was not in custody. In this case, officers gave *Miranda* warnings to the defendant when he was not in custody. Fifteen hours later, the officers reminded him of his previously given *Miranda* warnings before questioning him while he was in custody. Based on these and other facts, the court ruled that the defendant had properly received his *Miranda* warnings.

Waiver of *Miranda* Rights

(This topic is discussed on page 578.)

Generally

UNITED STATES SUPREME COURT

Berghuis v. Thompkins, 560 U.S. 370 (2010). The Court ruled that (1) the defendant impliedly waived his rights under *Miranda v. Arizona*, 384 U.S. 436 (1966), and (2) a defendant must make an unambiguous assertion of the right to remain silent to require an officer to stop custodial interrogation.

Officers were investigating a murder. Before beginning a custodial interrogation, one of the officers presented the defendant with a *Miranda* form. The form included the four warnings required by *Miranda v. Arizona*, 384 U.S. 436 (1966) (right to remain silent, use of statements in court, right to have lawyer present, right to have appointed lawyer if indigent), and an additional warning not required by *Miranda*: "You have the right to decide at any time before or during questioning to use your right to remain silent and your right to talk with a lawyer while you are being questioned." The officer asked the defendant to read the fifth warning aloud so that he could ensure that the defendant understood English, which the defendant did. The officer then read the other four *Miranda* warnings aloud and asked the defendant to sign the form to demonstrate that he understood his rights. The defendant declined to sign the form. There was conflicting evidence as to whether the officer verbally confirmed that the defendant understood the rights listed on the form. The officer did not discuss a waiver of *Miranda* rights with the defendant or obtain one from him.

During the interrogation, the defendant never stated that he wanted to remain silent, that he did not want to talk with the officers, or that he wanted a lawyer. About two hours and 45 minutes into the interrogation, during which the defendant was mostly silent, an officer asked the defendant, "Do you believe in God?" The defendant said "yes." The officer asked, "Do you pray to God?" The defendant said "yes." The officer then asked, "Do you pray to God to forgive you for shooting that boy down?" The defendant said "yes" and looked away, and the interview ended shortly thereafter. At trial, the defendant moved to suppress these statements. The issue before the United States Supreme Court was the admissibility of these statements under *Miranda v. Arizona* and later *Miranda*-related cases.

The Court noted that some language in *Miranda v. Arizona* could be read to indicate that a waiver of *Miranda* rights is difficult to establish absent an explicit written waiver or a formal, explicit oral statement. However, the Court discussed its rulings since *Miranda*, particularly *North Carolina v. Butler*, 441 U.S. 369 (1979) (valid waiver when defendant read *Miranda* rights form, said he understood his rights, refused to sign waiver at bottom of form, but said, "I will talk to you but I am not signing any form"), indicating that its later decisions made clear that a waiver of *Miranda* rights may be implied through the defendant's silence, coupled with an understand-

ing of his or her rights and a course of conduct indicating waiver. The Court in effect disavowed the language in *Miranda* suggesting that it is difficult to establish a *Miranda* waiver without an explicit written waiver or a formal, explicit oral statement.

The Court concluded that if the prosecution shows that a defendant was given *Miranda* warnings and understood them, a defendant's uncoerced statements establish an implied waiver of *Miranda* rights. A defendant's explicit waiver need not precede custodial interrogation. Any waiver, explicit or implied, may be withdrawn by a defendant's invocation at any time of the right to counsel or the right to remain silent.

Turning to the case before it, the Court ruled that the defendant waived his right to remain silent, and his statements were admissible at trial. The Court found that there was no basis to conclude that the defendant did not understand his *Miranda* rights, and the defendant chose not to invoke or rely on those rights when he made his uncoerced statements.

Colorado v. Spring, 479 U.S. 564 (1987). The defendant was arrested for federal firearms violations and was properly given *Miranda* warnings and waived his rights. The officers then asked him about an unrelated murder. The Court ruled that a defendant may validly waive *Miranda* rights without being informed of the subject matter of the ensuing interrogation.

Colorado v. Connelly, 479 U.S. 157 (1986). An apparently mentally ill defendant turned himself in to a law enforcement officer and confessed to a murder. The court ruled: (1) Coercive law enforcement activity is a necessary predicate to a finding that a confession is involuntary under the Due Process Clause; the fact that the defendant's mental condition may have motivated him to confess, absent law enforcement wrongdoing, did not make a confession involuntary. (2) Absent law enforcement coercion, the defendant's waiver of *Miranda* rights was valid despite the fact that the defendant may have felt compelled by his mental condition to waive his rights. (3) The State must prove a valid waiver of *Miranda* rights by the "preponderance of evidence" standard. *But see* United States v. Bradshaw, 935 F.2d 295 (D.C. Cir. 1991) (distinguishing *Colorado v. Connelly*, court ruled that the trial judge must determine whether defendant had the mental capacity to make knowing and intelligent waiver of *Miranda* rights); State v. Sanchez, 328 N.C. 247 (1991) (defendant had right to have expert testify about his lack of mental capacity to understand and waive *Miranda* rights).

Moran v. Burbine, 475 U.S. 412 (1986). A defendant validly waived his *Miranda* rights even though officers did not inform him of his attorney's efforts to contact him. [Author's note: The defendant's Sixth Amendment right to counsel had not attached when his attorney was trying to contact him.] The attorney's efforts to contact him, unknown by the defendant, did not affect the defendant's capacity to waive his *Miranda* rights. The Court also ruled that the officers' conduct was not so outrageous as to constitute a due process violation.

Tague v. Louisiana, 444 U.S. 469 (1980). The defendant's statement was inadmissible because the State did not introduce any evidence to show that the defendant knowingly and intelligently waived his *Miranda* rights before he made his statement. The arresting officer testified that he read the *Miranda* rights from a card, could not remember what those rights were, could not recall whether he asked the defendant if he understood those rights, and could not remember whether the defendant was literate or otherwise capable of understanding his rights.

North Carolina v. Butler, 441 U.S. 369 (1979). A defendant's waiver, after receiving *Miranda* warnings, of the right to counsel or the right to remain silent need not be explicit. Although the State has the burden of showing a waiver of *Miranda* rights, a knowing and voluntary waiver may be shown by the defendant's silence, coupled with an understanding of the rights and a course of conduct that indicates that the defendant implicitly has waived these rights. In this case, the defendant read the *Miranda* rights form, said that he understood his rights, refused to sign the waiver at the bottom of the form, but said, "I will talk to you but I am not signing any form." *See also* State v. Connley, 297 N.C. 584 (1979) (defendant implicitly waived his *Miranda* rights when, after refusing to sign a waiver form, he freely and voluntarily talked with the officer). *But see* State v. Steptoe, 296 N.C. 711 (1979) (defendant did not knowingly, voluntarily, and understandingly waive his right to counsel under *Miranda* when he requested a lawyer, but the officer discouraged the appointment of counsel by telling defendant that he would be brought before a judge and "if the judge saw fit to appoint [him] a lawyer that is where [his] lawyer would come from").

NORTH CAROLINA SUPREME COURT

State v. Daniels, 337 N.C. 243 (1994). During a suppression hearing challenging the defendant's mental capacity to waive *Miranda* rights, the defense called a law enforcement officer who observed the defendant immediately after the defendant's interrogation by other officers. The defense asked the officer whether the defendant "could have waived" his *Miranda* rights and whether the defendant understood the *Miranda* waiver form. The court ruled that the trial judge properly sustained the State's objections to these questions, because they called for a legal conclusion as to whether the defendant had the capacity to waive his rights. The court noted that the defense did not ask whether the defendant had the capacity to understand key words used (such as "right," "attorney," "waiver," and so forth), implying that such questions would be permissible.

State v. Williams, 334 N.C. 440 (1993). An officer gave *Miranda* rights to the defendant. When the officer asked him if he understood the rights, the defendant said "yes." The defendant remained silent when the officer asked him first, whether he wished to waive his right to remain silent, and second, whether he wished to waive his right to have counsel present during questioning. Soon thereafter, someone else asked the defendant whether anything in the room belonged to him. The defendant responded that he owned the boxes. An officer then asked if he would consent to a search of the boxes, to which the defendant responded "yes."

Relying on *North Carolina v. Butler*, 441 U.S. 369 (1979), the court ruled that the defendant properly waived his rights. The court noted that although defendant remained silent when asked if he would waive his rights, he had previously affirmatively stated that he understood his rights. He appeared coherent then and capable of understanding his rights. Also, the officers did not pressure him in any way to answer their questions. Thus, the defendant impliedly waived his right to remain silent and his right to counsel by answering the officers' questions after expressly acknowledging that he understood his right not to do so in the absence of counsel.

State v. McKoy, 332 N.C. 639 (1992). An in-custody defendant indicated to officers that he wanted to waive his *Miranda* rights. The defendant was given a waiver form, but he signed at the place on the form that indicated that he did not waive his rights. The officers then asked the defendant whether he had made a mistake. The defendant indicated that he still desired to answer questions and did not want a lawyer, and he scratched his signature from the form and signed in the appropriate place to waive his rights. The court ruled that officers properly may ask questions to clarify the apparently mistaken way in which the defendant answered their questions.

State v. McKoy, 323 N.C. 1 (1988). The defendant gave a voluntary confession and a proper waiver of his *Miranda* rights although he was mildly intoxicated, had a subnormal mental capacity, and had been injured when arrested. The totality of circumstances supported the trial judge's conclusion that the defendant knowingly, intelligently, and voluntarily waived his *Miranda* rights and that his statements were made freely, understandingly, and voluntarily.

State v. Fincher, 309 N.C. 1 (1983). The court ruled that a mentally retarded 17-year-old defendant had the mental capacity to waive *Miranda* rights, based on the facts in this case. *See also* State v. Brown, 112 N.C. App. 390 (1993), *aff'd per curiam*, 339 N.C. 606 (1995) (similar ruling); State v. Jones, 153 N.C. App. 358 (2002).

State v. Jenkins, 300 N.C. 578 (1980). A mildly mentally retarded defendant had sufficient mental capacity to understand and waive his *Miranda* rights.

State v. Carter, 296 N.C. 344 (1979). It is not necessary that a defendant be informed of the crime that officers are investigating before the defendant may waive his *Miranda* rights, although whether the defendant had been so informed may be a factor in determining the sufficiency of the waiver.

NORTH CAROLINA COURT OF APPEALS

State v. Flowers, 128 N.C. App. 697 (1998). When the mother of the defendant, who was 13 years old, learned that the police were looking for him, she brought him to the police department. Before asking any questions, an officer read the defendant his juvenile rights in the mother's presence. After each right was read, the officer asked the defendant and his mother if they understood, and they answered "yes" each time. The defendant did not make any affirmative statement as to whether he would agree to talk with officers or whether he wanted a lawyer to be present. The officer interrogated the defendant in his mother's presence for about two hours.

(1) The defendant argued that he never expressly waived his right to remain silent and his right to counsel. The court, citing *North Carolina v. Butler*, 441 U.S. 369 (1979), noted that an express waiver of *Miranda* rights is not required and ruled that a juvenile need not make an express waiver of juvenile rights. (2) The defendant argued that he lacked the capacity to understand his rights because of his youth and low mental ability (a psychologist testified that the defendant was mildly retarded with a full scale IQ of 56 and a verbal IQ of 48). The court ruled that the defendant knowingly, intelligently, and voluntarily waived his rights. The court stated, citing *State v. Fincher*, 309 N.C. 1 (1995), that a defendant's youth or subnormal mental capacity does not necessarily make him incapable of waiving his rights knowingly and voluntarily.

Waiver When There Are Foreign Language Issues

State v. Mlo, 335 N.C. 353 (1994). A detective anticipated potential language difficulties in questioning the defendant. Believing that the defendant spoke Vietnamese, the detective obtained a Vietnamese interpreter. However, the defendant, a native of Vietnam's Montagnard region, spoke Dega as well as some English and Vietnamese. On those occasions when the interpreter assisted the defendant, the defendant was able to continue the interview in English and gave logical responses to the questions asked. During the interview, the defendant appeared to understand the questions and responded most of the time in English without the interpreter's assistance. The defendant knowingly, intelligently, and voluntarily waived his *Miranda* rights.

State v. Medina, 205 N.C. App. 683 (2010). The court ruled that the defendant's waiver of *Miranda* rights was valid when *Miranda* warnings were given by an officer who was not fluent in Spanish. The officer communicated effectively with the defendant in Spanish, despite the lack of fluency. The defendant gave clear, logical, and appropriate responses to questions. Also, when the officer informed the defendant of his *Miranda* rights, he did not translate English to Spanish but rather read aloud the Spanish version of the waiver of rights form. Even if the defendant did not understand the officer, the defendant read each right, written in Spanish, initialed next to each right, and signed the form indicating that he understood his rights. The court noted that officers are not required to orally apprise a defendant of *Miranda* rights to effectuate a valid waiver.

State v. Mohamed, 205 N.C. App. 470 (2010). The court ruled that the trial court did not commit plain error by failing to exclude the defendant's statements to investigating officers after his arrest. The defendant had argued that because of his limited command of English, the *Miranda* warnings were inadequate and he did not freely and voluntarily waive his *Miranda* rights. The court determined that there was ample evidence to support a conclusion that the defendant's English skills sufficiently enabled him to understand the *Miranda* warnings that were read to him. Among other things, the court referenced the defendant's ability to comply with an officer's instructions and the fact that he wrote his confession in English. The court also concluded that the evidence was sufficient to permit a finding that the defendant's command of English was sufficient to permit him to knowingly and intelligently waive his *Miranda* rights, referencing, among other things, his command of conversational English and the fact that he never asked for an interpreter.

State v. Nguyen, 178 N.C. App. 447 (2006). The court ruled that a *Miranda* waiver by a Vietnamese-speaking defendant was understandingly, voluntarily, and knowingly made when a Vietnamese-speaking law enforcement officer acted as the translator for the interrogating law enforcement officer. There was no evidence that the officer-translator was deceitful or acted in an otherwise improper manner during his dealings with the defendant. The court rejected the defendant's argument that the officer-translator was not a neutral translator because he was a law enforcement officer.

State v. Ortez, 178 N.C. App. 236 (2006). A law enforcement officer fluent in Spanish read the defendant his *Miranda* rights in Spanish from a preprinted *Miranda* rights and waiver form. The defendant signed the waiver form. The defendant's testing showed that he had an IQ ranging from 55 to 77, classifying him as mildly mentally retarded to borderline intellectual or low average functioning. The court noted that a defendant's IQ alone does not mean that the defendant could not make a voluntary, knowing, and intelligent waiver of his *Miranda* rights. The court discussed the facts in this case and ruled that the defendant's waiver was valid based on the totality of circumstances.

The Public Safety Exception

(*This topic is discussed on page 571.*)

UNITED STATES SUPREME COURT

New York v. Quarles, 467 U.S. 649 (1984). The Court recognized a narrow "public safety" exception to the *Miranda* rule. Responding to a report that a woman had been raped by a man with a gun who had just entered a grocery store, an officer took the defendant into custody. He frisked him and discovered that he was wearing a shoulder holster that was empty. After handcuffing the defendant, the officer asked him where the gun was. The defendant responded, "The gun is over there." The Court ruled that the *Miranda* rule does not apply to custodial interrogation when an officer has an objectively reasonable need (that is, the officer's subjective belief or motivation is not controlling) to protect the officer or the public from an immediate danger associated with a weapon. In this case, officers needed to determine immediately the location of a gun that they had reason to believe the defendant had just removed from his holster and discarded in the grocery store. The discarded gun posed a danger to public safety by anyone who might find it, such as an employee, a customer, or an unknown accomplice.

NORTH CAROLINA SUPREME COURT

State v. Al-Bayyinah, 359 N.C. 644 (2005). The defendant robbed a grocery store owner with a knife. Law enforcement officers responded to a 911 call from the owner and began searching the area around the store for the person matching the description given by the owner. When an officer made eye contact with the defendant, he ran into the woods. Officers secured the perimeter and apprehended the defendant after about an hour of searching. An officer with a tracking dog made the first contact with the defendant and asked him where the knife was. The defendant responded that he did not have a knife. A knife was later found nearby. The court ruled that the defendant's statement was admissible under the public safety exception to the *Miranda* ruling as set out in *New York v. Quarles*, 467 U.S. 649 (1984). The officer was alone and unarmed when he discovered the defendant. He knew that the crime involved a stabbing and the defendant could possess a knife. His question was limited to determining the location of the knife and was necessary to secure the officer's safety.

State v. Brooks, 337 N.C. 132 (1994). An SBI agent accompanied other law enforcement officers in executing a search warrant for a nightclub to search for illegal drugs. On arriving at the nightclub, the agent saw a vehicle parked in the parking lot with the defendant sitting in the driver's seat. The agent walked over to the driver's side of the vehicle and shined his flashlight into the car's interior. He saw on the passenger side of the bucket seats an empty unsnapped holster within the defendant's reach.

The agent asked the defendant, "Where is your gun?" The defendant replied, "I'm sitting on it." The agent was unable to see the gun although he shined his light all about the vehicle. He asked the defendant to get out of the vehicle; the defendant reached under his right thigh and handed the gun to the agent. The agent did not place the defendant under arrest for carrying a concealed weapon but eventually obtained permission to search the vehicle and found cocaine in a nylon pouch.

The court ruled that the defendant was not in custody when the agent asked him where his gun was, and therefore *Miranda* warnings were not required. Even if the defendant had been in custody, *Miranda* warnings were not required because the agent was permitted to ask that question for his own safety; *see* New York v. Quarles, 467 U.S. 649 (1984).

State v. McQueen, 324 N.C. 118 (1989). Officers were conducting an extensive manhunt for the defendant, who had just murdered a highway patrolman and was suspected of having two guns and ammunition. When the officers arrested the defendant, one officer, without giving *Miranda* warnings, asked him several times where the guns were. The defendant replied each time, "No comment." The trial court suppressed the questions and answers, and the court affirmed, stating that the officer's questions about the guns were clearly designed to elicit incriminating responses. [Author's note: It is questionable whether this ruling is consistent with *New York v. Quarles*, discussed above.]

NORTH CAROLINA COURT OF APPEALS

State v. Crook, ___ N.C. App. ___, 785 S.E.2d 771 (2016). The court rejected the State's argument that the public safety exception established in *New York v. Quarles*, 467 U.S. 649 (1984), applied. The court found the facts of this case "noticeably distinguishable" from those in *Quarles*, noting that the defendant was not suspected of carrying a gun or other weapon; rather, he was sitting on the ground in handcuffs and already had been patted down.

State v. Hewson, 182 N.C. App. 196 (2007). Officers went to a home in response to a 911 call by the victim of a shooting, while she was inside her home, reporting that she had been shot by her husband. They saw the defendant outside the house and ordered him to lie face down on the ground. After handcuffing him, an officer asked him, without giving *Miranda* warnings, "Is there anyone else in the house, where is she?" The court ruled that the

defendant's statement in response to the officer's question was admissible under the public safety exception to *Miranda* in *New York v. Quarles*, 467 U.S. 649 (1984).

State v. Garcia-Lorenzo, 110 N.C. App. 319 (1993). The defendant was involved in a vehicular accident by running off a road and was injured. Officers transported the defendant to a hospital, where officers and doctors had to restrain him when he became violent. Because an officer wanted to know whether to look for other victims of the accident, the officer and then a doctor asked the defendant whether he was alone in the car. The defendant responded several times, "No, alone." The court affirmed the trial judge's conclusions of law that this questioning was permissible for the following reasons: (1) It was within *Miranda*'s public safety exception, recognized in *New York v. Quarles*, discussed above, because officers were concerned that someone else may have been injured and lying undiscovered at the scene. (2) The defendant was not subjected to "interrogation" as defined in *Rhode Island v. Innis*, 446 U.S. 291 (1980).

State v. Harris, 95 N.C. App. 691 (1989), *aff'd per curiam*, 326 N.C. 588 (1990). An officer's asking a defendant being frisked if he had a weapon was proper without *Miranda* warnings under *New York v. Quarles*, discussed above.

FEDERAL APPELLATE COURTS

United States v. Mobley, 40 F.3d 688 (4th Cir. 1994). Officers began the execution of a search warrant for drugs at the defendant's apartment by arresting the defendant and conducting a security sweep that revealed that no one else was there. They gave *Miranda* warnings to the defendant, and he asserted his right to counsel. One officer then asked the defendant if there was anything in the apartment that could be of danger to the officers while they executed the search warrant. The court recognized that the public safety exception under *New York v. Quarles*, discussed above, applied even after a defendant's assertion of the right to counsel, but it ruled that the officer's question did not qualify under the exception because there was no apparent danger to the officers. The officers had the defendant in custody and had already conducted a security sweep before an officer asked the question.

Fleming v. Collins, 954 F.2d 1109 (5th Cir. 1992) (en banc). Officers, with guns drawn, approached a bank robber being held by a private citizen, who also had a gun drawn on the robber. The court ruled that the officers' questions to the robber, without giving *Miranda* warnings, about where his gun was located, who had shot him, and whether he had been involved in the bank robbery were proper under *New York v. Quarles*, discussed above.

United States v. Lawrence, 952 F.2d 1034 (8th Cir. 1992). After the defendant volunteered that he had thrown away a gun when he was running from an officer, his responses to an officer's question about the location of the gun and the map the defendant drew at the police station fell within the public safety exception.

United States v. DeSantis, 870 F.2d 536 (9th Cir. 1989). Officers arrested the defendant in his home and gave him *Miranda* warnings. The defendant asserted his right to speak with a lawyer. When the defendant asked to change his clothes in his bedroom, the officers asked if there were any weapons there. The court ruled that the defendant's incriminating response was admissible under *New York v. Quarles*, discussed above.

United States v. Padilla, 819 F.2d 952 (10th Cir. 1987). The defendant was arrested in front of his residence by officers who had responded to a call about a man firing a weapon. After seeing three bullet holes in a window of the residence, an officer asked the defendant if he was okay and the defendant said he was. The officer then asked, "How about inside the house?" The defendant responded, "I shot someone inside the house." The court ruled that the officer's question (asked before he gave *Miranda* warnings) was proper under *New York v. Quarles*, discussed above.

The Booking Questions Exception

(This topic is discussed on page 571.)

UNITED STATES SUPREME COURT

Pennsylvania v. Muniz, 496 U.S. 582 (1990). A four-Justice plurality ruled that routine booking questions may be asked and answered without *Miranda* warnings if the questions are not designed to elicit incriminating statements. The questions in this case concerned the defendant's name, address, height, weight, eye color, date of birth, and current age. [Author's note: This opinion clearly represents current law.]

NORTH CAROLINA SUPREME COURT

State v. Brewington, 352 N.C. 489 (2000). While investigating officers were giving the defendant *Miranda* warnings, he stated, "I believe I need to talk to a lawyer." An officer responded, "I believe you do, too." An officer then asked the defendant for information to complete the

defendant's personal history arrest form, including date of birth, Social Security number, address, height, and weight. During this process, the defendant asked the officers, "What if I know who did it?" One officer informed the defendant that he could not talk to him because he had not waived his rights. He stated that he could not say anything to the defendant and the defendant should say nothing to him. The officer further stated that if the defendant wanted to talk to him, he had to initiate it, and then the officer would be required to readvise the defendant of his *Miranda* rights and obtain a waiver stating that the defendant did not wish to have an attorney. As the defendant continued to ask questions of the officers about the case, an officer again explained that the defendant had invoked his right to counsel and they could not talk with him. The defendant then indicated that he had changed his mind and wanted to talk with them. An officer again informed the defendant that he had invoked his right to counsel and any decision to talk had to be his. Again, the defendant stated that he wanted to talk. He was then given *Miranda* warnings and waived them.

The court ruled, citing *Rhode Island v. Innis*, 446 U.S. 291 (1980), and *State v. Ladd*, 308 N.C. 272 (1983), that the officer's questions to complete the arrest form were not a custodial interrogation in violation of the defendant's assertion of his right to counsel under *Edwards v. Arizona*, 451 U.S. 477 (1981). The court also ruled that the defendant reinitiated interrogation after his assertion of the right to counsel.

State v. Golphin, 352 N.C. 364 (2000). The defendants were charged with several offenses, including the murders of two law enforcement officers. After being advised of his *Miranda* rights, one of the defendants invoked his right to counsel. An officer told the defendant that he could not talk with him about the offenses because the defendant had asserted his right to counsel, but he needed to obtain biographical information and background information for the arrest report. After a conversation about biographical information and other matters, the defendant, erroneously believing that there was a video camera recording of his killing of the law enforcement officers, asked why the officers wanted to talk about the offenses, because they should have been videotaped. An officer responded that they still needed to know what happened—the officers knew that there was no videotape, but they never indicated that fact to the defendant. The defendant then stated that he would tell the officers what had happened.

The court ruled that the defendant's *Miranda* rights were not violated. Citing *State v. Ladd*, 308 N.C. 272 (1983), and other cases, the court noted that questions concerning biographical information necessary to complete the booking process that are not reasonably likely to elicit an incriminating response are not interrogation under *Miranda*. In addition, the defendant initiated further discussion when he asked about the videotape, and the officer should not have believed that his answer to the question would elicit an incriminating response.

State v. Banks, 322 N.C. 753 (1988). An officer's routine booking question to the defendant about his age was not interrogation under *Miranda*. The officer's question was not designed to elicit incriminating information. In determining whether a booking question was interrogation, the focus is when and under what circumstances the question was asked, not how the information obtained by the question is used at trial.

State v. Ladd, 308 N.C. 272 (1983). An officer's routine questions concerning booking information that are not intended to elicit an incriminating response are not interrogation. However, when the officer who asked the booking questions already knew that the defendant's license was in law enforcement custody, his question about its location was asked only to elicit an incriminating response and therefore constituted interrogation.

NORTH CAROLINA COURT OF APPEALS

State v. Boyd, 177 N.C. App. 165 (2006). The defendant was arrested for drug trafficking and other drug offenses. Before *Miranda* warnings were administered, an officer asked booking questions, including the location of the defendant's residence. The defendant gave as his address the place where officers had seized illegal drugs. One of the issues in the case was the defendant's relationship to the dwelling where the illegal drugs had been seized. The court ruled, relying on the *Miranda* bookings question exception discussed in *State v. Golphin*, 352 N.C. 364 (2000), that the exception did not apply to this question because it was reasonably likely to elicit an incriminating response.

State v. Locklear, 138 N.C. App. 549 (2000). The defendant was arrested for statutory rape. He was not given *Miranda* warnings. During the booking process, the officer used a form that, among other things, required the entry of the defendant's date of birth. The officer asked the defendant his date of birth, and the defendant stated that it was August 2, 1976. At trial the officer

testified—over the defendant's objection on *Miranda* grounds—about the defendant's date of birth based on the defendant's statement during the booking process. This testimony was the only evidence of the defendant's age, which is an element of statutory rape.

The court noted that although *Miranda* does not apply to the gathering of biographical data necessary to complete the booking process, it applies if the questions are designed to elicit a response that the officer knows or should know is reasonably likely to be incriminating. The court stated that the officer, in addition to booking the defendant, was also the investigating officer. The court then ruled that "[s]ince defendant's age was an essential element of the crime charged, . . . [the officer] . . . knew or should have known her question regarding defendant's date of birth would elicit an incriminating response," and therefore the defendant's rights under *Miranda* were violated and the defendant's response was inadmissible. [Author's note: In *State v. Banks*, 322 N.C. 753 (1988), the North Carolina Supreme Court ruled that the defendant's date of birth given during the booking process was routine information and was admissible without *Miranda* warnings, even if his age was an essential element of the crimes for which he was being booked. Citing *Banks* but not discussing it, the court in this case apparently would distinguish that ruling because the officer in this case was also the investigating officer. However, a defendant's date of birth is routine information that officers seek to obtain after every arrest.]

State v. Harris, 67 N.C. App. 97 (1984). An officer's questioning of the defendant about his address when completing a waiver of rights form was not interrogation. The question was not asked to elicit an incriminating response nor was it reasonably likely to elicit an incriminating response.

State v. Sellars, 58 N.C. App. 43 (1982). An officer's routine questions about the defendant's name, address, and date of birth after the defendant refused to waive his *Miranda* rights were proper.

FEDERAL APPELLATE COURTS

United States v. Webster, 769 F.2d 487 (8th Cir. 1985). Asking booking questions after assertion of right to remain silent was proper. *See also* United States v. Taylor, 799 F.2d 126 (4th Cir. 1986) (asking defendant his name for booking purposes after his assertion of right to counsel was proper); United States v. Dougall, 919 F.2d 932 (5th

Cir. 1990) (asking booking questions after defendant's assertion of right to remain silent was proper).

Questioning by Non–Law Enforcement Officers

(This topic is discussed on page 577.)

Illinois v. Perkins, 496 U.S. 292 (1990). Officers were investigating the defendant as a homicide suspect. While the defendant was in jail on unrelated charges, an officer—acting undercover—was admitted to jail as an inmate. The defendant stated during conversations with the officer that he committed the homicide. The defendant did not know that he was speaking to an officer. The Court ruled that the requirements of the *Miranda* ruling, which include giving *Miranda* warnings, did not apply to these facts. The Court stated that a "police-dominated atmosphere" and compulsion, which underlay the *Miranda* ruling, do not exist when an incarcerated person speaks voluntarily with someone he or she believes to be a fellow inmate. The Court also noted that the defendant's Sixth Amendment right to counsel was not implicated in this case, because the defendant had not yet been charged with the homicide when the undercover officer talked with him in jail. The Court did not discuss whether the officer's conduct would have been permissible if the defendant had asserted his right to counsel under the Fifth Amendment for the unrelated charges for which he had been jailed.

State v. Powell, 340 N.C. 674 (1995). The defendant was arrested for murder and asserted his right to counsel during custodial interrogation. He was placed in jail. Later the defendant made a telephone call to two people (Weathers and Yelton), who recorded the conversation and gave the recording to the police. Weathers testified that they recorded the conversation for "personal reasons." He also testified that no officer had requested them to record conversations with the defendant, although they had been told that any information they had concerning the murder would help the police. The court ruled that the defendant's Fifth Amendment rights were not violated because Weathers and Yelton did not make the recording as agents of the police.

State v. Massey, 316 N.C. 558 (1986). Questioning by the defendant's father in the jail's conference room with an officer present was not custodial interrogation under the *Miranda* ruling. *See also* State v. Etheridge, 319 N.C. 34 (1987) (defendant's interview with a nurse was not custodial interrogation under the *Miranda* ruling). [Author's note: Although the results in *Massey* and *Etheridge* would

still be correct after the ruling in *Illinois v. Perkins*, 496 U.S. 292 (1990), the analysis would be different. See the comment in the note below under *State v. Morrell*.]

State v. Alston, 295 N.C. 629 (1978). Incriminating statements made to non–law enforcement officers are admissible if they were made freely and voluntarily. *See also* State v. Cooper, 286 N.C. 549 (1975).

State v. Holcomb, 295 N.C. 608 (1978). A conversation between the defendant and his uncles at the sheriff's office was not custodial interrogation when there was no evidence that the uncles were acting as agents of law enforcement officers. *See also* State v. Johnson, 29 N.C. App. 141 (1976) (police radio dispatcher was not a law enforcement officer or acting as one); State v. Perry, 50 N.C. App. 540 (1981) (bail bondsman taking defendant into custody as bail jumper was not a law enforcement officer); State v. Conrad, 55 N.C. App. 63 (1981) (magistrate was not acting as law enforcement officer when she talked to defendant). [Author's note: Although the results in *Holcomb* and the other cases cited in this paragraph would still be correct after the ruling in *Illinois v. Perkins*, 496 U.S. 292 (1990), the analysis would be different. See the comment in the note below under *State v. Morrell*.]

State v. Rollins, 226 N.C. App. 129 (2013). The court ruled that the trial court did not err by finding that the defendant's statements to his wife regarding his participation in a murder were voluntary. The defendant's wife spoke with him five times while he was in prison (on charges not connected to the murder) and while wearing a recording device provided by the police. While the wife did not threaten the defendant, she did make up evidence that she claimed law enforcement had recovered and told the defendant that officers suspected that she was involved in the murder. In response, the defendant made incriminating statements in which he corrected the wife's lies concerning the evidence and admitted details of the murder. The court rejected the defendant's argument that his statements were involuntary because of his wife's deception and her emotional appeals to him based on this deception.

State v. Pittman, 174 N.C. App. 745 (2005). The defendant was convicted of various offenses involving a six-week-old infant, including attempted first-degree murder. While in custody awaiting trial, the mother of the infant wrote letters to the defendant asking him why he had committed the crimes. The mother testified at trial that although the defendant replied to the letters, he never answered her questions. The court ruled that the admission of the mother's testimony did not violate *Doyle v. Ohio*, 426 U.S. 610 (1976) (impermissible use of defendant's post-arrest silence after giving *Miranda* warnings), because any silence of the defendant was not in response to questioning by law enforcement officers. Nor was the mother acting as the agent of officers in writing these letters. [Author's note: It is questionable whether North Carolina rulings applying the *Miranda* ruling to agents of law enforcement officers are still valid after the ruling in *Illinois v. Perkins*, 496 U.S. 292 (1990). See the discussion of *Perkins* and *Alexander v. Connecticut*, 917 F.2d 747 (2d Cir. 1990), on page 617.] The court ruled, alternatively, that even if *Miranda* was applicable, the defendant did not choose to remain silent. Instead, he voluntarily wrote back to the mother, and the State may inquire about the defendant's failure to disclose certain information in the reply letters.

State v. Morrell, 108 N.C. App. 465 (1993). The defendant was arrested on a federal charge of child abduction and was committed to the county jail. A social worker in the county child protective services unit identified herself and told the defendant that she was conducting an investigation of alleged sexual abuse and neglect of a boy with whom the defendant had had a relationship. The defendant confessed to the social worker. Two days later, a deputy sheriff talked with the defendant in the jail after giving her *Miranda* warnings and obtaining a proper waiver. The defendant again confessed.

Based on evidence that the social worker was working with the sheriff's department on the case before interviewing the defendant in jail, the court ruled that the social worker was an agent of the State and thus was required to give *Miranda* warnings when that interview occurred. The court upheld the admissibility of the defendant's confession to the deputy sheriff because the confession to the social worker was not coerced; *see* Oregon v. Elstad, 470 U.S. 298 (1985); State v. Barlow, 330 N.C. 133 (1991). [Author's note: The court did not discuss *Illinois v. Perkins*, 496 U.S. 292 (1990). If the defendant did not know that the social worker was acting on behalf of the deputy sheriff or was a government official involved in investigating or reporting criminal offenses, then the ruling in *Illinois v. Perkins* may not have required the social worker to give *Miranda* warnings. However, one can argue that the facts in *Morrell* clearly establish that the defendant knew that the social worker was a government official and her duties included the investigation or reporting of crimes. See Mathis v. United States, 391 U.S.

1 (1968); Cates v. State, 776 S.W.2d 170 (Tex. Crim. App. 1989); State v. Nason, 981 P.2d 866 (Wash. Ct. App. 1999).]

Alexander v. Connecticut, 917 F.2d 747 (2d Cir. 1990). The defendant was in jail awaiting trial for arson. He had requested a lawyer for the arson charge at arraignment, and the court appointed a lawyer to represent him. The lawyer told officers that the defendant did not want to be questioned further without his lawyer present. The officers suspected that the defendant had committed a murder, for which the defendant had not been charged. A friend of the defendant, acting at the officers' instigation, visited the defendant in jail and obtained incriminating statements that were later used in the defendant's murder trial. Relying on *Illinois v. Perkins*, discussed above, the court ruled that regardless of whether the defendant properly invoked his Fifth Amendment right to counsel, the officers did not violate that right because their conduct was not prohibited by the *Miranda* ruling (that is, there was no interrogation by a law enforcement officer in this case; the defendant simply had a noncoercive conversation with a friend). There also was no violation of the defendant's Sixth Amendment right to counsel, because the defendant had not been charged with the murder when the conversation occurred. *See also* Salkil v. Delo, 990 F.2d 386 (8th Cir. 1993) (similar ruling); United States v. Ingle, 157 F.3d 1147 (8th Cir. 1998) (no *Miranda* warnings required when government encouraged defendant's fellow jail inmates to elicit incriminating statements from defendant); United States v. Cook, 599 F.3d 1208 (10th Cir. 2010) (no Fifth Amendment *Miranda* violation when defendant in detention facility asserted right to counsel and right to remain silent and later a cellmate at instigation of government had conversation with defendant, who was unaware that cellmate was government agent; defendant was not subject to custodial interrogation).

The Meaning of "Custody" under *Miranda*

(*This topic is discussed on page 573.*)

Generally

UNITED STATES SUPREME COURT

J.D.B. v. North Carolina, 564 U.S. 261 (2011). A 13-year-old juvenile, a seventh grade student in middle school, was a suspect in two house break-ins. An officer went to the juvenile's school, where the school resource officer removed the juvenile from class and brought him to a conference room. The officer questioned the juvenile in the presence of the school resource officer, an assistant principal, and an administrative intern. Before being questioned, the juvenile was not given *Miranda* warnings, nor was he informed that he was free to leave the room. Based on these and other facts, the North Carolina Supreme Court ruled that the juvenile was not in custody to require *Miranda* warnings. The court declined to consider the juvenile's age in making the custody determination.

The United States Supreme Court disagreed with the North Carolina Supreme Court's view on the age issue. It ruled that the age of a juvenile (a person under 18 years old) is a factor that must be considered in making the objective determination as to whether the juvenile is in custody, as long as the juvenile's age is known or reasonably apparent to the officer. (The Court cautioned, however, that a juvenile's age will not necessarily be a determinative, or even significant, factor in every case.) The Court reasoned that a juvenile will often feel bound to submit to law enforcement questioning when an adult in the same circumstances would not. The Court also clearly indicated that the actual age of the juvenile must be considered, because a young juvenile may be more susceptible than an older juvenile; the Court stated that officers and judges "simply need the common sense to know that a 7-year-old is not a 13-year-old and neither is an adult." The Court did not determine whether the juvenile in this case was in custody. Instead, it remanded the case to the North Carolina Supreme Court to make that determination.

[Author's note: The Court distinguished a contrary statement on the juvenile age issue in *Yarborough v. Alvarado*, 541 U.S. 652 (2004). However, the Court effectively reaffirmed *Yarborough* to the extent that *Yarborough* ruled that a suspect's prior interrogation history with law enforcement is irrelevant in determining custody under *Miranda*.]

Thompson v. Keohane, 516 U.S. 99 (1995). A state court's ruling on whether a defendant was in custody under *Miranda* is not entitled to a presumption of correctness under federal habeas corpus review. Such a ruling resolves mixed questions of law and fact and therefore warrants de novo review by a federal habeas court.

Stansbury v. California, 511 U.S. 318 (1994). In determining whether a suspect was in custody so that an officer must give *Miranda* warnings before conducting an interrogation, the California Supreme Court considered

as a factor whether the officer's investigation had focused on the suspect. Relying on its prior rulings—including *Beckwith v. United States*, 425 U.S. 341 (1976); *Berkemer v. McCarty*, 468 U.S. 420 (1984); *California v. Beheler*, 463 U.S. 1121 (1983); and *Minnesota v. Murphy*, 465 U.S. 420 (1984)—the Court rejected that factor in determining custody. The Court noted that the determination of custody depends on the objective circumstances of the interview, not on the subjective views of the interrogating officers or the person being questioned. An officer's views concerning the nature of an interrogation or beliefs concerning the potential culpability of the person being questioned may be one of many factors in determining the custody issue, but only if the officer's views or beliefs are somehow manifested to the person and would have affected how a reasonable person in that position would perceive his or her freedom to leave.

The Court noted that even a clear statement from an officer that the person is a prime suspect is not itself dispositive of the custody issue, because some suspects are free to come and go until an officer decides to make an arrest. The Court also noted that an officer's undisclosed views may be relevant in testing the credibility of the officer's account of what happened during an interrogation, but it is the objective surroundings, not any undisclosed views, that control the custody issue.

Pennsylvania v. Bruder, 488 U.S. 9 (1988). An officer stopped the defendant for a red light violation, smelled alcohol on the defendant's breath, and saw him stumble. The officer administered field sobriety tests, asked the defendant to recite the alphabet, and then asked him about his use of alcohol—to which the defendant answered that he had been drinking and was returning home. The officer then arrested him, placed him in his police car, and gave him *Miranda* warnings. Following *Berkemer v. McCarty*, the Court ruled that the defendant was not in custody until he was arrested.

Berkemer v. McCarty, 468 U.S. 420 (1984). The *Miranda* rule does not apply to roadside questioning of a motorist who is stopped for a routine traffic stop, because the motorist is not in custody. If a motorist later is subjected to actions that cause him or her to be in custody, then the *Miranda* rule applies. In this case, a law enforcement officer saw the defendant's car weaving in and out of a lane on an interstate highway. After following the car for two miles, the officer forced the defendant to stop and asked him to get out of the car. When the defendant got out, the officer noticed that he had difficulty standing.

The officer then apparently decided to arrest and charge the defendant, but he did not communicate his intention to the defendant. Instead, he asked the defendant to perform a field sobriety test, which the defendant could not do without falling. When the officer asked him whether he had been using intoxicants, the defendant replied that he had drunk some beers and had smoked some marijuana a short time before. The defendant's speech was slurred. The officer then formally arrested him and took him to jail.

The Court ruled that the defendant was not in custody under *Miranda* until the officer formally arrested him. Therefore, the officer did not have to give the *Miranda* warnings until then. The Court stated that (1) the initial stop of the car did not, by itself, render the defendant in custody; (2) at no time between the initial stop and the arrest was the defendant subjected to restraints comparable to a formal arrest; (3) only a short time elapsed between the stop and the arrest; and (4) the officer's unarticulated intention to arrest the defendant after he stepped out of the car was irrelevant in considering whether the defendant was in custody—the only relevant inquiry is "how a reasonable [person] in the [defendant's] position would have understood [the] situation"; that is, whether a "reasonable person" would have understood that his or her freedom of movement was restrained to a degree associated with a formal arrest. The officer's later questioning of the defendant beside his car and his request that the defendant perform a simple balancing test were not acts functionally equivalent to a formal arrest.

[Author's note: Several cases provide an excellent analysis of the distinction between a seizure under the Fourth Amendment for an investigatory stop and custody under the Fifth Amendment for *Miranda* purposes; *see* United States v. Streifel, 781 F.2d 953 (1st Cir. 1986), *later ruling sub nom.* United States v. Quinn, 815 F.2d 153 (1st Cir. 1987); United States v. Bengivenga, 845 F.2d 593 (5th Cir. 1988) (en banc); United States v. Ventura, 85 F.3d 708 (1st Cir. 1996), *later appeal*, 132 F.3d 844 (1st Cir. 1998). *See also* United States v. Gale, 952 F.2d 1412 (D.C. Cir. 1992) (asking a few brief questions during an investigatory stop was proper without giving *Miranda* warnings); State v. Sykes, 285 N.C. 202 (1974), and State v. Hayes, 273 N.C. 712 (1968) (motor vehicle cases decided before *Berkemer v. McCarty* but consistent with it); State v. Braswell, 312 N.C. 553 (1985) (officers' subjective intent to arrest defendant is irrelevant in determining custody); United States v. Boucher, 909 F.2d 1170 (8th Cir. 1990) (defendant was not in custody while sitting in an officer's car while the officer wrote a speeding citation; the fact that the officer had probable cause to arrest him for carrying a concealed weapon, when the defendant did not know of the officer's intention to arrest, did not constitute custody so as to require *Miranda* warnings); United States v. McDowell, 918 F.2d 1004 (1st Cir. 1990) (defendant, who unknowingly was talking to undercover officer with an arrest warrant for the defendant in his pocket, was not in custody); United States v. Randle, 966 F.2d 1209 (7th Cir. 1992) (defendant's subjective beliefs whether he was in custody were insufficient to establish that he was in custody).]

Minnesota v. Murphy, 465 U.S. 420 (1984). A probationer was not in custody under the *Miranda* rule when he met with his probation officer in her office. *See also* United States v. Davis, 919 F.2d 1181 (6th Cir. 1990) (defendant was not entitled to *Miranda* warnings during pre-sentence interview with probation officer); United States v. Rogers, 921 F.2d 975 (10th Cir. 1990) (similar ruling); United States v. Nieblas, 115 F.3d 703 (9th Cir. 1997) (alleged *Miranda* violation does not bar admission of statement to probation officer that is admitted in probation revocation hearing); United States v. Howard, 115 F.3d 1151 (4th Cir. 1997) (defendant was not in custody while being interviewed by law enforcement officers in probation office after defendant had voluntarily surrendered to probation officer for violation of probation terms).

California v. Beheler, 463 U.S. 1121 (1983). The defendant voluntarily agreed to accompany officers to the station house, and they told him that he was not under arrest. After about 30 minutes of questioning, the officers permitted the defendant to go home. The Court ruled that the defendant was not in custody under the *Miranda* rule, and therefore his statements to the officers were admissible even though he did not receive *Miranda* warnings.

Oregon v. Mathiason, 429 U.S. 492 (1977). In determining whether a person is in custody under the *Miranda* rule, the question is whether the person has been formally arrested or restrained in his or her freedom of movement to a degree associated with a formal arrest. In this case, an officer suspected that the defendant had committed a burglary. He left a note at the defendant's apartment asking him to call him. When the defendant phoned, the officer asked him whether he would come to the State Patrol office to discuss something. When the defendant arrived, the officer told him that he was not under arrest and then questioned him about the burglary for about 30 minutes. The defendant confessed, and the officer then allowed him to leave the station. The Court ruled that the defendant was not in custody. The fact that questioning takes place in a police station or that an officer believes that the person being questioned committed an offense does not automatically trigger the need for *Miranda* warnings. *See also* State v. Jeffries, 55 N.C. App. 269 (1982); State v. Jackson, 308 N.C. 549 (1983), *later appeal*, 317 N.C. 1 (1986).

Beckwith v. United States, 425 U.S. 341 (1976). Two Internal Revenue Service agents, who were investigating the defendant for possible criminal tax fraud, met with him at a private residence and interviewed him. The conversation was friendly and relaxed. The Court ruled that the defendant was not in custody under the *Miranda* rule. The fact that the defendant was the focus of a criminal investigation is irrelevant. The issue is whether the defendant was questioned after he had been taken into custody or its equivalent. *See also* State v. Parrish, 32 N.C. App. 636 (1977).

Orozco v. Texas, 394 U.S. 324 (1969). The defendant argued with a person outside a cafe and shot and killed him. He then left the scene and returned to his boardinghouse. At about 4:00 a.m., four officers arrived there, were admitted by an unidentified woman, and were told that the defendant was asleep in the bedroom. All four officers entered the bedroom and began to question the defendant about the murder. The Court ruled that the defendant was in custody under the *Miranda* rule because the defendant would reasonably perceive the officers' conduct as the beginning of a custodial arrest. [Author's note: However, part of *Orozco* is now inconsistent with *Berkemer v. McCarty*; *Orozco* implied that an officer's unarticulated belief that the defendant was under arrest is a factor in determining custody. *See also* United States v. Wauneka, 770 F.2d 1434 (9th Cir. 1985).]

Mathis v. United States, 391 U.S. 1 (1968). The defendant was in custody under the *Miranda* rule when a government agent questioned him while he was serving a sentence in a state prison. It was irrelevant that the defendant was in custody for an offense different from the one under investigation. *But see* United States v. Conley, 779 F.2d 970 (4th Cir. 1985) (prisoner was not in custody when he was questioned about a murder while awaiting medical treatment); United States v. Cooper, 800 F.2d 412 (4th Cir. 1986) (prisoners were not in custody under *Miranda* when they were questioned by a correctional treatment specialist at their request); Leviston v. Black, 843 F.2d 302 (8th Cir. 1988) (defendant, a jail inmate, was not in custody under *Miranda* when he requested that the officer interview him, he voluntarily went to the jail interview room to talk with the officer, and he remained free to end the conversation at any time); United States v. Willoughby, 860 F.2d 15 (2d Cir. 1988); United States v. Scalf, 725 F.2d 1272 (10th Cir. 1984); United States v. Menzer, 29 F.3d 1223 (7th Cir. 1994); Garcia v. Singletary, 13 F.3d 1487 (11th Cir. 1994).

NORTH CAROLINA SUPREME COURT

State v. Waring, 364 N.C. 443 (2010). The court ruled that, considering the totality of the circumstances, the defendant was not in custody when he admitted that he stabbed the victim. The defendant was an adult with prior criminal justice system experience. The officer who first approached the defendant told him that he was being detained until detectives arrived but that he was not under arrest. When the detectives arrived and told him that he was not under arrest, the defendant voluntarily agreed to go to the police station. The defendant was never restrained and was left alone in the interview room with the door unlocked and no guard. He was given several bathroom breaks and offered food and drink. The defendant was cooperative. The detectives did not raise their voices, use threats, or make promises; the defendant was never misled, deceived, or confronted with false evidence. Once the defendant admitted his involvement in the killing, the interview ended and he was given his *Miranda* rights. Although the first officer told the defendant that he was "detained," he also told the defendant that he was not under arrest. Any custody associated with the detention ended when the defendant voluntarily accompanied detectives, who confirmed that he was not under arrest. The defendant's inability to leave the interview room without supervision or escort did not suggest custody; the defendant was in a nonpublic area of the station and prevention of unsupervised roaming in such a space would not cause a reasonable person to think that a formal arrest had occurred.

State v. Garcia, 358 N.C. 382 (2004). Law enforcement officers responded to an apartment complex clubhouse where a person had just been beaten to death. A short time later, the defendant agreed to be transported to a police station because he wanted to be there while his girlfriend was being questioned as a witness to the murder. He agreed to be patted down for weapons before he was placed in a police vehicle. Officers knew that there was an outstanding arrest warrant for the defendant (which they intended to serve on the defendant if he attempted to leave) and suspected his involvement in the murder, but they did not communicate this information to the defendant. They told him he was not under arrest. The officers found a room in the police station where the defendant could wait. A detective, not in uniform and unarmed, walked into the room, introduced himself, and thanked the defendant for coming. He asked the defendant about his recent activities and about a cut on his finger. The defendant responded to the detective's questions. The detective told the defendant that the defendant's information was different from information that other witnesses were providing. The defendant responded that he was telling the truth, but the detective told him that his girlfriend had "given him up." The defendant requested a drink and a cigarette lighter and said that he had a story for the detective. The detective left the defendant alone in the room and got a lighter and a beverage for him. When the detective returned, the defendant lit a cigarette. Without receiving *Miranda* warnings, he then gave a detailed confession to the murder. The court ruled, distinguishing *State v. Buchanan*, 355 N.C. 264 (2002) (defendant was in custody after he confessed to murder when two officers accompanied him to the bathroom and one officer was in uniform and armed), that the defendant was not in custody under *Miranda* so as to require *Miranda* warnings before he confessed. The court noted, citing *Stansbury v. California*, 511 U.S. 318 (1994), that information that is not communicated to a defendant is not relevant to the issue of whether the defendant was in custody.

State v. Buchanan, 355 N.C. 264 (2002). On remand to determine whether the defendant was in custody and thus required *Miranda* warnings under the appropriate standard for custody (see *State v. Buchanan*, 353 N.C. 332 (2001), discussed below), the trial judge ruled that the defendant was in custody when, after admitting to officers that he had participated in a murder, he was accompanied to the bathroom by the interrogating officers and an officer stayed with him at all times. The court, per curiam, affirmed the trial judge's ruling. [Author's note: The court's opinion did not articulate why the trial judge's legal finding of custody was correct. It is unclear how the officers' mere act of accompanying the defendant to the bathroom, without any restraint of the defendant beyond their presence, constituted custody under the *Miranda* ruling.]

State v. Buchanan, 353 N.C. 332 (2001), *later ruling*, 355 N.C. 264 (2002). The defendant was charged with two counts of first-degree murder. The trial judge granted the defendant's pretrial motion to suppress his confession on the ground that the defendant was in custody and was not given his *Miranda* warnings. The State appealed the judge's ruling. The relevant facts were that an officer contacted the defendant at his job, the defendant went with him to the police station, the interrogation was conducted there, and the defendant eventually confessed. The State argued on appeal that the trial judge had applied, in determining custody under *Miranda*, an incorrect standard—whether a reasonable person in the defendant's position, based on the totality of circumstances, would have felt "free to leave." The State argued that the correct standard is whether a reasonable person would have believed there was a "formal arrest or restraint on freedom of movement of the degree associated with a formal arrest."

The court ruled that the trial judge applied the incorrect standard. The court reviewed the history of *Miranda* cases in the United States Supreme Court and the North Carolina Supreme Court. The court then ruled that the "appropriate inquiry in determining whether a defendant is 'in custody' for purposes of *Miranda* is, based on the totality of circumstances, whether there was a 'formal arrest or restraint on freedom of movement of the degree associated with a formal arrest.'" The court noted that the "free to leave" standard is appropriate for determining whether a person has been seized under the Fourth Amendment, not for determining custody under the *Miranda* ruling, which is based on the Fifth Amendment. The court disavowed statements inconsistent with its ruling that have appeared in its prior cases, specifically citing *State v. Jackson*, 348 N.C. 52 (1998); *State v. Rose*, 335 N.C. 301 (1994); *State v. Hicks*, 333 N.C. 467 (1994); and *State v. Smith*, 317 N.C. 100 (1986).

The court then noted that the trial judge referred to the fact that although a law enforcement officer told the defendant that he was not under arrest and was free to leave, the officer subjectively did not intend to let the defendant leave the station after the defendant verbally confessed to the murders. The trial judge's findings also indicated that the reason the officers did not read the defendant his *Miranda* warnings was because they did not want the defendant to invoke his rights, and the interrogation was intended to elicit an incriminating response from the defendant. Although it was unclear whether the trial judge's conclusion that the defendant was in custody was based on these findings of fact, the court decided to clarify the law on these matters.

Relying on *Stansbury v. California*, 511 U.S. 318 (1994), and *Berkemer v. McCarty*, 468 U.S. 420 (1985), the court clarified that the fact that a law enforcement officer "had decided during the interview that he was not going to allow defendant to leave and was going to arrest defendant at the end of the interview was irrelevant to the custody inquiry, unless those intentions were somehow manifested to defendant. The subjective unspoken intent of a law enforcement officer, provided it is not communicated or manifested to the defendant in any way, and subjective interpretation of a defendant are not relevant to the objective determination whether the totality of the circumstances support the conclusion that defendant was 'in custody.'"

Concerning the officer's intention to obtain a confession without giving *Miranda* warnings because the officer did not want the defendant to invoke his rights and the interrogation was intended to elicit an incriminating response, the court noted, citing *Moran v. Burbine*, 475 U.S. 412 (1986), that the purpose of *Miranda* is to protect against coerced confessions, not to suppress voluntary confessions. Thus, the fact that the officer intended to elicit incriminating responses from the defendant through means other than coercion is irrelevant to the determination as to whether the defendant was in custody. *See also* United States v. Parker, 262 F.3d 415 (4th Cir. 2001) (fact that officer likely would have arrested defendant had she attempted to end interview and leave house, when officer's view was unarticulated to defendant, was irrelevant to the determination as to whether defendant was in custody).

State v. Hipps, 348 N.C. 377 (1998). Officers had been searching all morning for Shelia Wall, pursuant to a missing person report. Later that day, an officer who was involved in the search responded to a disturbance at a store, which was not related to the missing person report. Before the officer said anything, the defendant came up and put his hands on the police car, saying, "Go ahead and take me. I did it." The officer responded, "What's going on? What are you talking about?" The defendant then said, "I did it. Me and Rock." The officers asked, "What are you talking about?" The officer then heard the defendant mumble something about "Shelia." Wanting to clear up the matter, the officer asked the defendant, "[W]hat about

Shelia, where's she at?" The defendant then responded, "[W]e killed her. She's under the bridge."

The court ruled, citing *State v. Meadows*, 272 N.C. 327 (1968), that a reasonable person in the defendant's position would not have thought he was in custody at the time he made the incriminating statement. The court also rejected the defendant's argument that it should consider what occurred after the defendant made the incriminating statement in determining whether the encounter was custodial; the court stated that what occurred afterward did not affect the noncustodial and voluntary nature of the encounter before and while the statement was being made.

State v. Jackson, 348 N.C. 52 (1998). Two detectives went to the defendant's workplace and, after telling him he was not under arrest, requested that he accompany them to the sheriff's office to answer some questions. The defendant agreed. He was told at the sheriff's office that he was a suspect in the murder of Karen Styles. He denied involvement. He was given *Miranda* rights and was again told that he was not under arrest. The defendant consented to a search of his person and the taking of fingerprints and blood and hair samples. He was again told that he was not under arrest. After the defendant had been questioned for about three hours, the sheriff entered the interrogation room and asked the defendant, "What did you do with the rifle that Karen Styles was shot with?" The defendant replied, "I think I need a lawyer present." (A detective's handwritten notes, taken during the interview, read, "2:04 p.m. on 12-20-94, wants a lawyer present.") In response to the defendant's statement, the sheriff told the defendant that he did not want the defendant to answer any more questions, but he wanted to tell him something. The sheriff then stated, "Son, I know you bought the rifle and the duct tape at K-Mart on the 28th of October. I know you were in Bent Creek on the day she was killed, and that's fine, but you need help." The defendant then began crying and stated, "But I didn't mean to kill nobody. I didn't." He continued crying and said, "I'm sorry; I didn't mean to kill her."

The court ruled that the defendant was in custody under *Miranda* when he inquired about an attorney. The court stated that a reasonable person in the defendant's position who had been interrogated for about three hours and thought the sheriff believed that he had committed murder would have believed that the sheriff intended to hold him to be prosecuted for murder. [Author's note: The North Carolina Supreme Court in the later case of *State v. Buchanan*, 353 N.C. 332 (2001), expressly disavowed the "free to leave" test used in this case to determine custody under *Miranda*. Thus, it is unclear whether the court would now reach a different result on the custody issue.]

State v. Gaines, 345 N.C. 647 (1997). The lead investigator in a murder case instructed the other investigators that any suspect interviews were to be conducted as noncustodial interviews. Suspects were not to be placed under arrest and would be free to leave, and any contact with suspects would be on a voluntary basis. The court ruled that both of the defendants in this case were not in custody to require *Miranda* warnings when both suspects (1) voluntarily agreed to come to the law enforcement facility from their respective homes, (2) were repeatedly told that they were not under arrest and were free to leave at any time, and (3) were provided food at the facility and were not handcuffed or restrained.

State v. Daughtry, 340 N.C. 488 (1995). The defendant voluntarily went with two officers to the police station to be questioned about a murder. The officers advised the defendant that he was not under arrest and could leave at any time. One officer advised the defendant of his *Miranda* rights as a precaution. The defendant waived those rights. After some conversation between the officers and the defendant, the defendant said, "I think I need to speak to a lawyer." One officer handed the defendant the telephone directory opened to the yellow pages with attorney listings. As he did so, the officer told the defendant that he could talk to a lawyer and continue to talk to the officers if he wished. The defendant briefly looked at the yellow pages and then told the officers that he was willing to talk to them. One officer reminded the defendant of his right to remain silent and his right to an attorney; the defendant indicated that he understood his rights. The defendant was not placed under arrest. He then confessed.

The court ruled that because the defendant was not in custody when he requested an attorney, his rights under *Miranda* and *Edwards v. Arizona*, 451 U.S. 477 (1981), were inapplicable. Therefore, the court did not need to decide whether the trial judge had erred in concluding that the defendant had voluntarily reinitiated interrogation after requesting an attorney. *See also* United States v. Muick, 167 F.3d 1162 (7th Cir. 1999) (defendant may not invoke right to counsel under *Miranda* unless defendant is being interrogated or interrogation is imminent; attorney may not invoke a defendant's right to counsel under *Miranda*).

State v. Corbett, 339 N.C. 313 (1994). The court ruled that the defendant was not in custody so as to require officers to give *Miranda* warnings for three interviews on three separate days. The first two interviews took place in an officer's car at the defendant's home. The third interview took place in the yard of the defendant's home. The defendant then offered to take the officers to the crime scene. An officer told the defendant's wife that the defendant was not under arrest at this time. At the crime scene, the defendant confessed to the murder. The defendant repeatedly had been told that he was not under arrest and that he would be taken home any time he so requested.

State v. Sweatt, 333 N.C. 407 (1993). The defendant was at a hospital being treated for injuries sustained in an automobile accident. An officer who had responded to the accident but who had not yet talked with the defendant went to the hospital. After a doctor alerted the officer—who by then had been informed that the defendant might have been involved in a homicide before the accident had occurred—that the defendant was saying things the officer might be interested in, the officer walked to where the defendant was being treated and asked him questions. The defendant was not in custody to require the officer to give the defendant *Miranda* warnings before questioning him. *See also* State v. Clark, 324 N.C. 146 (1989) (defendant in a hospital for medical treatment was not in custody to require *Miranda* warnings when evidence showed that defendant afterward voluntarily came to police station to talk and officer made it clear that no one was forcing her to stay).

State v. Medlin, 333 N.C. 280 (1993). Atlantic Beach officers arrested the defendant in a breezeway outside a motel room in Atlantic Beach for a murder and robbery committed in Wake County, based on a mistaken belief that an arrest warrant had been issued in Wake County for these offenses. The court determined, however, that the Atlantic Beach officers had sufficient information to establish probable cause to arrest, based on the facts in this case. Therefore, the warrantless arrest was proper. When the Atlantic Beach officers learned, after they had brought the defendant to the police station, that there were no arrest warrants for him, they told him that he was not under arrest and was free to leave. They also told him that investigators were coming from Wake County and wanted to talk to him, that he could stay and move around the police station at will, and that he should let them know if he needed anything. The defendant indicated that he wanted to stay and in fact remained there and later gave statements to the officers.

Based on these and other facts, the court concluded that the defendant was no longer in custody and therefore he was not entitled to *Miranda* rights, including the right to counsel under *Edwards v. Arizona*, 451 U.S. 477 (1981). Therefore, the court ruled that it was unnecessary to decide whether the defendant properly waived his right to counsel.

State v. Torres, 330 N.C. 517 (1992). The defendant shot and killed her husband in their home in the early evening. Deputy sheriffs arrived to investigate the shooting. A deputy sheriff transported the defendant and her close friend to the sheriff's department. From 7:00 p.m. to 10:00 p.m., she was in the department's conference room with that deputy sheriff, and during that time she was informed that her husband had died. Sometime during that period, the sheriff came into the room. The defendant asked him whether she needed a lawyer and was told that she did not need a lawyer right now. About 10:00 p.m., the defendant was taken to the sheriff's office, where she was told that she would be interviewed by two other officers. Although she was never informed that she was under arrest, she also was never told that she was free to leave. The court ruled that a reasonable person in the defendant's position—knowing that she had just shot her spouse and having been brought to the sheriff's department by a deputy, kept under constant supervision there, and never informed that she was free to leave—would feel compelled to stay and was therefore in custody under *Miranda*.

State v. Hoyle, 325 N.C. 232 (1989). When officers went to the defendant's home to investigate the defendant's involvement in a homicide, he agreed to go with them to police headquarters. When the defendant went to his closet to get his coat, the officers stopped him and got his coat for him. One officer seized a pistol that was on a nearby shelf. The defendant then asked if the officers had a warrant, and they said that they did not. [Author's note: Although it is unclear from the court's opinion, the officers were apparently referring to an arrest warrant.] One officer told the defendant that he would obtain a warrant and that he would leave an officer at the home until it could be obtained. The defendant then went with the officers. At that point the defendant was in custody to require *Miranda* warnings. *See also* State v. Greene, 332 N.C. 565 (1992) (defendant was in custody in sheriff's office when officer handcuffed him and told him he could not leave room; defendant was no longer in custody later when officers told him that he was not under arrest and was free to leave).

State v. Allen, 322 N.C. 176 (1988). The defendant was not in custody to require an officer to give her *Miranda* warnings when the defendant agreed with the officer's request to talk at the sheriff's department; the defendant's minister asked to speak with the defendant and was allowed to do so; and the officer drove the defendant, her husband, and her sister-in-law to the sheriff's department. At the sheriff's department, the officers first interviewed the defendant's husband for 30 minutes, while the defendant and her sister-in-law waited. The defendant was then informed that she did not have to talk to the officers, was twice informed that she was free to go, and was then interviewed alone for one hour and 35 minutes in a comfortable room.

State v. Davis, 305 N.C. 400 (1982). The defendant was not in custody under the *Miranda* rule when he came to the detectives' office voluntarily, answered questions, and left. The defendant came voluntarily a second time at the officers' request and then confessed. At all times a reasonable person in the defendant's position would have believed that he was free to go. The court stated that, based on the facts in this case, the officer's failure to advise the defendant that he was free to go did not adversely affect the finding that the defendant was not in custody. The court noted that the *Miranda* rule does not apply if an officer has given *Miranda* warnings unnecessarily—that is, if the warnings were given when the defendant was not subjected to custodial interrogation. *See also* State v. Phipps, 331 N.C. 427 (1992).

State v. Perry, 298 N.C. 502 (1979). The defendant was not in custody for purposes of the *Miranda* rule when a detective, who was investigating a missing person report, went to the gas station where the defendant worked and asked him to sit inside the detective's car and talk and the defendant voluntarily entered the car and answered questions.

NORTH CAROLINA COURT OF APPEALS

State v. Portillo, ___ N.C. App. ___, 787 S.E.2d 822 (2016). The court ruled that the defendant was not in custody when he gave statements to officers at a hospital. The victim was killed in a robbery committed by the defendant and his accomplice. The defendant was shot during the incident and brought to the hospital. He sought to suppress statements made to law enforcement officers at the hospital, arguing that they were elicited during a custodial interrogation for which he had not been given *Miranda* warnings. The court cited the following factors as to why the defendant was not in custody: (1) there was no evidence that the defendant knew a guard was present when the interview was conducted; (2) the defendant was interrogated in an open area of the ICU where other patients, nurses, and doctors were located, and he had no legitimate reason to believe that he was in law enforcement custody; (3) none of the officers who were guarding him spoke with him about the case before the interview; (4) the officers who questioned him wore plain clothes; and (5) there was no evidence that the defendant's movements were restricted by anything other than the injuries he had sustained and the medical equipment connected to him.

The court rejected the defendant's argument that the interrogation was custodial because he was under the influence of pain and other medication that could have affected his comprehension. It also rejected the defendant's argument that he was in custody because the officers arrived at the hospital with the intention of arresting him. Although they may have had this intention, it was not made known to the defendant and thus has no bearing on whether the interview was custodial.

State v. Crook, ___ N.C. App. ___, 785 S.E.2d 771 (2016). The court ruled that because the defendant was handcuffed and placed under arrest, the trial court erred when it concluded that the defendant was not in custody when he made a statement to a law enforcement officer.

State v. Davis, 237 N.C. App. 22 (2014). The court rejected the defendant's argument that she was in custody within the meaning of *Miranda* during the last of four interviews at the police station about her missing child. It stated that the trial court properly used an objective test to determine whether the interview was custodial. Competent evidence supported the trial court's findings of fact that the defendant was not threatened or restrained, she voluntarily went to the station, she was allowed to leave at the end of the first three interviews, the interview room door was closed but unlocked, the defendant was allowed to take multiple bathroom and cigarette breaks and was given food and drink, and the defendant was offered the opportunity to leave the fourth interview but refused.

State v. Price, 233 N.C. App. 386 (2014). The court ruled that the trial court erred by granting the defendant's motion to suppress. A wildlife officer on patrol in a pine forest approached the defendant, who was dressed in full camouflage and carrying a hunting rifle, and asked to see his hunting license. After the defendant showed his license, the officer asked how he got to the location; he replied that his wife transported him there. The officer then asked him whether he was a convicted felon. The defendant admitted that he was. The officer seized the weapon, and the defendant was later charged with being a felon in possession of a firearm. The court ruled that the defendant was neither seized under the Fourth Amendment nor in custody under *Miranda* when the officer asked about his criminal history, and therefore the trial court erred by granting the motion to suppress.

In re A.N.C., Jr., 225 N.C. App. 315 (2013). The court ruled that a 13-year-old juvenile was not in custody within the meaning of G.S. 7B-2101 or *Miranda* during a roadside questioning by an officer. Responding to a report of a vehicle accident, the officer saw the wrecked vehicle, which had crashed into a utility pole, and three people walking from the scene. When the officer questioned all three, the juvenile admitted that he had been driving the wrecked vehicle. Noting that under *J.D.B. v. North Carolina*, 561 U.S. 261 (2011), a reviewing court must, when determining whether a suspect has been placed in custody, take into account a juvenile's age if it was known to an officer or would have been objectively apparent to a reasonable officer, the court nevertheless concluded that the juvenile here was not in custody.

State v. Yancey, 221 N.C. App. 397 (2012). The court ruled that the juvenile defendant was not in custody for purposes of *Miranda*. After the defendant had been identified as a possible suspect in several breaking or entering cases, two detectives dressed in plain clothes and driving an unmarked vehicle went to the defendant's home and asked to speak with him. Because the defendant had friends visiting his home, the detectives asked the defendant to take a ride in their car with them. The detectives told the defendant that he was free to leave at any time, and they did not touch him. The defendant sat in the front seat of the vehicle while it was driven approximately two miles from his home. When the vehicle stopped, one of the detectives showed the defendant reports of the break-ins. The detectives told the defendant that if he was cooperative, they would not arrest him that day. The defendant admitted to committing the break-ins. The juvenile was 17 years and 10 months old. Considering the totality of the circumstances—including the defendant's age—the court concluded that the defendant was not in custody.

The court rejected the argument that *J.D.B. v. North Carolina*, 564 U.S. 261 (2011), required a different conclusion.

***State v. Hemphill*,** 219 N.C. App. 50 (2012). The court ruled that the defendant's response to an officer's questioning while on the ground and being restrained with handcuffs should have been suppressed because the defendant had not been given *Miranda* warnings. The officer's questioning constituted an interrogation, and a reasonable person in the defendant's position—having been forced to the ground by an officer with a Taser drawn and in the process of being handcuffed—would have felt that his or her freedom of movement had been restrained to a degree associated with formal arrest. Thus, there was a custodial interrogation.

***State v. Hartley*,** 208 N.C. App. 174 (2011). The court ruled that the defendant was not in custody when he confessed to three homicides. Officers approached the defendant as he was walking on a road, confirmed his identity and that he was okay, told him that three people had been injured at his residence, and asked him if he knew anything about the situation. After the defendant stated that he did not know about it, an officer conducted a pat down of the defendant. The defendant's clothes were damp and his hands were shaking. An officer told the defendant that he would like to talk to him about what happened and asked if the defendant would come to the fire department, which was being used as an investigation command post. The officer did not handcuff the defendant, and he told him that he was not under arrest. The defendant agreed to go with the officers, riding in the front passenger seat of the police car. The officers entered a code to access the fire department and the defendant followed them to a classroom, where he sat at one table while two officers sat across from him at a different table. Officers asked the defendant if he wanted anything to eat or drink or to use the restroom and informed him that he was not under arrest. An officer noticed cuts on the defendant's hands, and when asked about them, the defendant stated that he did not know how he got them. Although the officer decided that she would not allow the defendant to leave, she did not tell the defendant that; rather, she said that forensic evidence would likely lead to apprehension of the perpetrator. When she asked the defendant if there was anything else that he wanted to tell her, he confessed to the murders. Due to a concern for public safety, the officer asked where the murder weapon was located, and the defendant told her where it was. The officer then left the room to inform others about the confession while

another officer remained with the defendant. The defendant then was arrested and given *Miranda* warnings. He was not handcuffed and he remained seated at the same table. He waived his rights and restated his confession.

The court concluded that the defendant was not in custody when he gave his initial confession, noting that (1) he was twice told that he was not under arrest, and he voluntarily went to the fire department; (2) he was never handcuffed; (3) he rode in the front of the vehicle; (4) officers asked him if he needed food, water, or use of the restroom; (5) he was never misled or deceived; (6) he was not questioned for a long period of time; and (7) the officers kept their distance during the interview and did not use physical intimidation. The court rejected the defendant's argument that the pat down and the officer's subjective intent to detain him created a custodial situation. The court also rejected the defendant's argument that the interrogation was an impermissible two-stage interrogation under *Missouri v. Seibert*, 542 U.S. 600 (2004), concluding that the case was distinguishable from *Seibert* because the defendant was not in custody when he made his first confession.

***State v. Clark*,** 211 N.C. App. 60 (2011). The court ruled that a reasonable person in the defendant's position would not have believed that he or she was under arrest or restrained in such a way as to necessitate *Miranda* warnings. Key factors in the *Miranda* custody determination include whether a suspect is told he or she is free to leave, whether he or she is handcuffed, whether he or she is in the presence of uniformed officers, and the nature of any security around the suspect. There was no evidence that officers ever explicitly told the defendant that he was being detained. The court rejected the defendant's argument that he was functionally arrested and thus entitled to *Miranda* warnings because he was moved to a patrol car and instructed to remain there when he came in contact with the victim's father, and he was told to "come back and stay" when he attempted to talk to his girlfriend (the victim's sister). The court concluded that the officers' actions were nothing more than an attempt to control the scene and prevent emotional encounters between a suspect and members of the victim's family. Moreover, even if the defendant was detained at the scene, his statements were untainted because the detective expressly told him that he was not under arrest, the defendant repeatedly asked to speak with the detective, and the defendant voluntarily accompanied the detective to the sheriff's department.

State v. Little, 203 N.C. App. 684 (2010). The defendant voluntarily drove to the police station about six hours after a shooting. There was no warrant for the defendant's arrest and the police had not attempted to contact him or request his presence for an interview. A detective who knew the defendant met him in the public lobby and invited him into a secure area that required a passkey for entry, but anyone could leave the secure area without a key. The detective patted him down for weapons (the defendant did not object to the frisk) and told him that a detective wanted to speak with him. The other detective arrived and told the defendant that he was not under arrest and was free to leave. The defendant voluntarily accompanied the detective and another officer upstairs. The defendant was later told on two different occasions that he was not under arrest and was free to leave. Unbeknownst to the defendant, the other officer entered an adjacent room and took notes on the interview. Also, a detective stayed in the hallway to keep the defendant from leaving, but the defendant was unaware of the detective's intentions. The detective began to question the defendant about his actions during the day and about the shooting. At one point, the defendant asked if he needed an attorney. The detective replied, "I don't know, I can't answer that for you, are you asking for one?" The defendant did not reply to this question and continued talking with the detective. At another point the defendant stood up and said, "I'm trying to leave, I didn't do it." The detective did not restrain the defendant, who then sat back down and continued talking. The defendant made inculpatory statements that he sought to suppress. The court ruled that the defendant was not in custody to require *Miranda* warnings. The facts did not show the indicia of an arrest. The court relied on *State v. Gaines*, 345 N.C. 647 (1997), and other cases. Also, the presence of a note-taking officer and an officer's unarticulated determination not to let the defendant leave had no bearing on whether the defendant was in custody, because the defendant was unaware of these facts.

State v. Allen, 200 N.C. App. 709 (2009). The defendant was involved in a knife fight in which the victim was killed and the defendant was also stabbed. The defendant went to a hospital for treatment for his wounds (the victim was also taken to the hospital). Officers arrived there and sought to determine what had occurred. An officer spoke to the defendant intermittently for about 40 minutes. The defendant was not handcuffed, nor was he told that he could not leave or that he was under arrest.

The court ruled that the defendant was not in custody when the officer questioned him at the hospital, and thus *Miranda* warnings were not required. The court noted that any restraint in movement that the defendant may have experienced at the hospital was due to his medical treatment and not the action of law enforcement officers.

State v. Wright, 184 N.C. App. 464 (2007). The defendant, a military officer, was convicted of first-degree murder for the killing of his girlfriend's husband. Based on the defendant's request to see the sheriff, the sheriff and a detective went to the military brig where the defendant was being held on military charges, but those charges did not include murder. The defendant also was not then charged in state court with murder. A guard escorted the defendant—without handcuffs or shackles—to a room. The room contained a table, chairs, and a couch. The defendant sat on the couch while the sheriff and the detective sat at the table. The sheriff explained to the defendant that he was not there to question him but simply to inform him of the status of the murder investigation. The sheriff advised the defendant that if he asked a question, the defendant should not answer it. The defendant was free to leave the room at any time. The court ruled, relying on *State v. Fisher*, 158 N.C. App. 133 (2003), and other cases, that the defendant was not in custody to require *Miranda* warnings.

State v. Smith, 180 N.C. App. 86 (2006). The court ruled that the defendant was not in custody under *Miranda* when he was questioned in the sheriff's department. An officer went to the defendant's house and asked him to come to the department for questioning. The defendant came in a separate vehicle. He waited there about an hour while his wife was questioned, and he could have left at any time. He was told he was not in custody and was offered something to drink. As the questioning began, the defendant did indicate that he wanted to speak to an attorney, but he did not stop making statements. He stood up, became very upset, and made some incriminating statements.

State v. Sutton, 167 N.C. App. 242 (2004). An officer received information from a pharmacist that the pharmacist had just filled a prescription for Oxycontin under suspicious circumstances. An officer arrived at the pharmacy's parking lot, conducted surveillance, and observed an apparent drug sale by the defendant to another person. He then made an investigative stop of the defendant, which the court ruled was supported by reasonable suspicion. The defendant consented to a frisk and told the officer that he had two knives. The officer found two pocket knives but no contraband. When asked if he had any narcotics, the defendant said that he had just filled a prescription. The officer took a pill bottle containing tablets from the defendant and asked how many pills were in the bottle. The defendant said he had filled a prescription for 180 tablets. The officer asked again how many pills were in the bottle. The defendant responded that he had given 45 tablets to a person in the parking lot. The court ruled, relying on *State v. Benjamin*, 124 N.C. App. 734 (1996), that the defendant was not in custody under *Miranda* to require the officer to give *Miranda* warnings when questioning the defendant during this investigative stop. *See also* State v. Martinez, 158 N.C. App. 105 (officer's brief inquiry during frisk was not improper).

State v. Clark, 161 N.C. App. 316 (2003). The court ruled that the defendant was not in custody to require *Miranda* warnings when an officer questioned the defendant in his home, the defendant was told that he was not under arrest or in custody, and the defendant was not restrained in any way.

State v. Crudup, 157 N.C. App. 657 (2003). In response to a reported break-in at a house, Officer A and five or six other officers went there to investigate. As Officer A prepared to enter, the defendant exited the front door. Three officers handcuffed the defendant and detained him as a burglary suspect. Thereafter, Officer A and another officer searched the house and found cocaine but no other suspects. Officer A then asked the defendant, without giving *Miranda* warnings, if he resided in the house, was the only resident, and owned the possessions found on the premises. The court ruled, using the definition of "custody" in *State v. Buchanan*, 353 N.C. 332 (2001), that the defendant was in custody to require *Miranda* warnings before the officer's questioning of the defendant. The handcuffed defendant was questioned while four officers surrounded him. The defendant's freedom of movement was restrained to the degree associated with a formal arrest. A reasonable person under these circumstances would believe he was under arrest. The court ruled that the defendant's responses to the questions must be suppressed.

State v. Cockerham, 155 N.C. App. 729 (2003). Officers were investigating the discharge of a firearm from the defendant's apartment that resulted in a shotgun round going through the common wall and into the adjoining apartment. The defendant let an officer into his apartment. The defendant (who was not patted down, searched, or handcuffed) sat in his living room while two officers observed holes in the walls of both apartments and found a shotgun in the defendant's apartment. One officer then asked the defendant what had happened. The defendant replied that some people had tried to break into his apartment. The officer then asked the defendant why he had shot at the wall. The court ruled, relying on the definition of "custody" in *State v. Buchanan*, 353 N.C. 332 (2001), that the defendant was not in custody to require *Miranda* warnings when the officer asked these two questions. There was no formal arrest of the defendant or restraint on his freedom of movement to the degree associated with a formal arrest.

State v. Johnston, 154 N.C. App. 500 (2002). A sheriff's department received a 911 call that a male, driving a gray car, had fired shots into an occupied vehicle with a sawed-off shotgun. A few hours later, at the place where the shooting occurred, officers saw a gray car driving along the side of the road. With guns drawn, the officers stopped the car, asked the defendant to step out of the car, handcuffed him, and placed him in the back seat of a patrol car. The officers informed the defendant that he was not under arrest but only in "secure custody" for the defendant's safety and the safety of others. The court ruled that the defendant was in custody under *Miranda*—his freedom of movement was restrained to the degree associated with a formal arrest (*see* State v. Buchanan, 353 N.C. 332 (2001)), and a reasonable person under these circumstances would believe he was under arrest.

State v. Hall, 131 N.C. App. 427 (1998), *aff'd*, 350 N.C. 303 (1999). The defendant voluntarily accompanied detectives to the police station after they had asked him if he would come to talk about a robbery. Although the detectives did not specifically indicate to the defendant that he was not under arrest, they did advise him that he didn't have to stay there, telling him that they just needed him to talk to them.

The court noted that it appears that the defendant was free to leave at any time. Citing a statement in *Stansbury v. California*, 511 U.S. 318 (1994) (even a clear statement by an officer that person under interrogation is prime suspect is not, by itself, dispositive of custody issue, because some suspects are free to come and to go until officers decide to make an arrest), the court rejected the defendant's argument that a reasonable person in the defendant's position would not feel free to leave when the detectives confronted him with a statement by a witness implicating him in the robbery. The court, citing and discussing statements from *Oregon v. Mathiason*, 429 U.S. 492 (1977), also rejected the defendant's argument that he was in custody because he was interrogated in a coercive, police-dominated atmosphere. The court acknowledged that any time an officer interviews a suspect, there undoubtedly will be coercive aspects present. The court noted that the interrogation lasted between one and two hours. The defendant was alert and sober. He was not restrained in any way, the door to the interrogation room was left open, and there were no threats or shows of violence or promises of leniency. The court concluded that the defendant was not in custody, and therefore *Miranda* warnings were not required.

State v. Green, 129 N.C. App. 539 (1998), *aff'd*, 350 N.C. 59 (1999). The defendant voluntarily left his home and went with several officers to the sheriff's department to be interrogated about a murder. The officers told him that he was not under arrest. During seven hours of interrogation, the defendant was allowed breaks, used the restroom without being accompanied by an officer, was not handcuffed or restrained in any way, was provided or offered food several times, and was allowed to call his mother. The officers conducted a vigorous interrogation, including telling him that he was lying to them. The court, distinguishing *State v. Jackson*, 348 N.C. 52 (1998), ruled that the defendant was not in custody and therefore *Miranda* warnings were not required.

State v. Benjamin, 124 N.C. App. 734 (1996). An officer conducted a frisk of the defendant after an investigative stop for a traffic violation. As the officer was patting the defendant, he felt two hard plastic containers in a breast pocket of the defendant's winter jacket. Based on the officer's narcotics training, it was immediately apparent that these containers were vials of the type customarily used to hold illegal drugs. When the officer felt the container through the jacket, he asked the defendant, "What is that?" The defendant responded that it was "crack." The officer removed two vials from the coat pocket and found cocaine.

The court ruled that the defendant was not in custody to require *Miranda* warnings when the officer asked the question while conducting the frisk. The court noted that the fact that a defendant is not free to leave does not necessarily constitute custody under *Miranda*. Instead, the inquiry is whether a reasonable person in the defendant's position would believe that he or she was under arrest or the functional equivalent of arrest; the court cited and discussed *Stansbury v. California*, 511 U.S. 318

(1994), and *Berkemer v. McCarty*, 468 U.S. 420 (1984). The court concluded that a reasonable person would not have believed that he was in custody based on these facts.

State v. Sanders, 122 N.C. App. 691 (1996). The court ruled that the following evidence supported the trial judge's ruling that the defendant was not in custody to require officers to give *Miranda* warnings. The defendant agreed to accompany the officers to the police station. Two officers were in the interview room with the defendant during the entire period of the interview, which lasted about two hours, and they were joined briefly by a third officer. The defendant was never threatened or promised that he would not be prosecuted or would obtain a lesser sentence by cooperating with the officers. He was allowed to go to the bathroom on request and was allowed a 20-minute smoking break outside the room. The defendant was told he was free to leave. He asked to call his wife and was told that he could do so later. The officers confronted the defendant with physical evidence that in fact had been found at the crime scene. The officers falsely told him that the victim had identified him as the person who beat and robbed him. The defendant admitted robbing and beating the victim but consistently denied that he had used a weapon. *See also* State v. Jones, 153 N.C. App. 358 (2002) (defendant with limited mental capacity who agreed to leave school and go to police department for questioning was not in custody to require *Miranda* warnings).

State v. Soles, 119 N.C. App. 375 (1995). Officers took the defendant, with his consent, for questioning. The defendant was not handcuffed during a four-hour interview, was left alone, and was allowed to use the vending machines. The defendant conceded on appeal that he was free to leave and voluntarily gave a statement to the officers. The court ruled that the defendant was not in custody to require *Miranda* warnings. At a second interview six days later, a polygraph examiner confronted the defendant about patterns of deception and questioned him in addition to the polygraph testing. The operator had given *Miranda* warnings to the defendant and obtained a waiver before the testing. In any event, the court ruled that the defendant was not in custody to require *Miranda* warnings, because the defendant had voluntarily come to the police station for the polygraph and was free to leave at any time. The court also ruled, based on the facts in this case, that the defendant's second statement was voluntarily given.

State v. Dukes, 110 N.C. App. 695 (1993). Officer Moore arrived at a trailer park to investigate the murder of the defendant's wife. Both the defendant and a baby he was holding had blood on their clothing. Officer Moore accompanied the defendant and the baby to the defendant's trailer (the defendant lived in a different trailer than his wife). Officer Moore instructed Officer Thompson to guard the defendant, not allow him to leave his trailer, not allow any other person to enter the trailer, and not allow the defendant to wash or to change his clothes. Officer Thompson allowed the defendant to make telephone calls after he asked permission from the officer to do so. Officer Thompson accompanied the defendant to the bathroom to ensure that he did not wash or change his clothes. Officer Thompson later asked the defendant, "Do you know what happened?"

(1) The court ruled that the defendant was in custody to require *Miranda* warnings while he was at his trailer with Officer Thompson. A reasonable person who knew that his wife had just been killed and who was being kept under constant police supervision, had been told not to wash or change his clothing, and was never informed that he was free to leave his own home would not feel free to get up and go. The court also ruled that the officer's question constituted interrogation under the *Miranda* ruling. (2) The defendant was later arrested and taken to a law enforcement center. While the officer was advising the defendant of his *Miranda* rights, the defendant said, "I stabbed her." The court ruled that this statement was voluntary and not the result of custodial interrogation.

State v. Beckham, 105 N.C. App. 214 (1992). During the execution of a drug search warrant for a house, officers pushed the defendant to the floor and handcuffed him. The officers read the search warrant to the defendant and gave him a copy of the warrant. An officer began questioning the defendant without giving *Miranda* warnings. The court ruled that the defendant was in custody to require *Miranda* warnings before questioning could begin.

State v. Chappell, 24 N.C. App. 656 (1975). An officer arrived at a home to investigate a reported shooting. The defendant allowed the officer inside. In responding to the officer's question about who was shot, the defendant pointed toward the deceased's body. The officer then asked, "Where is the gun?" The defendant directed him to a bedroom dresser drawer, where the officer found a pistol. The officer then asked what had happened, and the defendant replied, "I shot the son of a bitch. He deserved

what he got and I would do it again." The defendant was not in custody when the officer asked these questions. *See also* State v. Bacon, 326 N.C. 404 (1990) (defendant was not in custody when he invited officers into his home and the conversation between defendant and officers was cordial); State v. Holsclaw, 42 N.C. App. 696 (1979).

FEDERAL APPELLATE COURTS

Booker v. Ward, 94 F.3d 1052 (7th Cir. 1996). The mere giving of *Miranda* warnings when they are not required does not transform noncustodial questioning into nonconsensual custodial interrogation. *See also* State v. Davis, 305 N.C. 400 (1982) (similar ruling); Davis v. Allsbrooks, 778 F.2d 168 (4th Cir. 1985) (similar ruling); Sprosty v. Buchler, 79 F.3d 635 (7th Cir. 1996).

United States v. Ritchie, 35 F.3d 1477 (10th Cir. 1994). The defendant was not in custody to require officers to give him *Miranda* warnings when officers detained him during the execution of a search warrant of his residence. Officers did not draw their guns, use handcuffs, or otherwise use force or the threat of force during questioning.

United States v. Perdue, 8 F.3d 1455 (10th Cir. 1993). The intrusiveness of the investigative stop required officers to give the defendant *Miranda* warnings before questioning him. Officers had forced the defendant out of his car at gunpoint, required him to lie on the ground, and then interrogated him without giving *Miranda* warnings.

United States v. Sylvester, 848 F.2d 520 (5th Cir. 1988). Officers' questioning of defendants-hunters in an open field while issuing them citations for hunting violations did not require *Miranda* warnings, because the defendants were not in custody. The mere fact that the defendants were requested to gather together to discuss the reason for the citations and their vehicles were blocked by the officers' vehicles did not make their detention comparable to a formal arrest or its functional equivalent.

Traffic Cases
UNITED STATES SUPREME COURT

Pennsylvania v. Bruder, 488 U.S. 9 (1988). An officer stopped the defendant for a red light violation, smelled alcohol on the defendant's breath, and saw him stumble. The officer administered field sobriety tests, asked the defendant to recite the alphabet, and then asked him about his use of alcohol—to which the defendant answered that he had been drinking and was returning home. The officer then arrested him, placed him in his police car, and gave him *Miranda* warnings. Following

Berkemer v. McCarty, the Court ruled that the defendant was not in custody until he was arrested.

Berkemer v. McCarty, 468 U.S. 420 (1984). The *Miranda* rule does not apply to roadside questioning of a motorist who is stopped for a routine traffic stop, because the motorist is not in custody. If a motorist later is subjected to actions that cause him or her to be in custody, then the *Miranda* rule applies. In this case, a law enforcement officer saw the defendant's car weaving in and out of a lane on an interstate highway. After following the car for two miles, the officer forced the defendant to stop and asked him to get out of the car. When the defendant got out, the officer noticed that he had difficulty standing. The officer then apparently decided to arrest and charge the defendant, but he did not communicate his intention to the defendant. Instead, he asked the defendant to perform a field sobriety test, which the defendant could not do without falling. When the officer asked him whether he had been using intoxicants, the defendant replied that he had drunk some beers and had smoked some marijuana a short time before. The defendant's speech was slurred. The officer then formally arrested him and took him to jail.

The Court ruled that the defendant was not in custody under *Miranda* until the officer formally arrested him. Therefore, the officer did not have to give the *Miranda* warnings until then. The Court stated that (1) the initial stop of the car did not, by itself, render the defendant in custody; (2) at no time between the initial stop and the arrest was the defendant subjected to restraints comparable to a formal arrest; (3) only a short time elapsed between the stop and the arrest; and (4) the officer's unarticulated intention to arrest the defendant after he stepped out of the car was irrelevant in considering whether the defendant was in custody—the only relevant inquiry is "how a reasonable [person] in the [defendant's] position would have understood [the] situation"; that is, whether a "reasonable person" would have understood that his or her freedom of movement was restrained to a degree associated with a formal arrest. The officer's later questioning of the defendant beside his car and his request that the defendant perform a simple balancing test were not acts functionally equivalent to a formal arrest.

[Author's note: Several cases provide excellent analysis of the distinction between a seizure under the Fourth Amendment for an investigatory stop and custody under the Fifth Amendment for *Miranda* purposes; *see* United States v. Streifel, 781 F.2d 953 (1st Cir. 1986), *later ruling sub nom.* United States v. Quinn, 815 F.2d 153 (1st Cir. 1987); United States v. Bengivenga, 845 F.2d 593 (5th Cir. 1988) (en banc); United States v. Ventura, 85 F.3d 708 (1st Cir. 1996), *later appeal*, 132 F.3d 844 (1st Cir. 1998). *See also* United States v. Gale, 952 F.2d 1412 (D.C. Cir. 1992) (asking a few brief questions during an investigatory stop was proper without giving *Miranda* warnings); State v. Sykes, 285 N.C. 202 (1974) and State v. Hayes, 273 N.C. 712 (1968) (motor vehicle cases decided before *Berkemer v. McCarty* but consistent with it); State v. Braswell, 312 N.C. 553 (1985) (officers' subjective intent to arrest defendant is irrelevant in determining custody); United States v. Boucher, 909 F.2d 1170 (8th Cir. 1990) (defendant was not in custody while sitting in an officer's car while the officer wrote a speeding citation; the fact that the officer had probable cause to arrest him for carrying a concealed weapon, when the defendant did not know of the officer's intention to arrest, did not constitute custody so as to require *Miranda* warnings); United States v. McDowell, 918 F.2d 1004 (1st Cir. 1990) (defendant, who unknowingly was talking to undercover officer with an arrest warrant for the defendant in his pocket, was not in custody); United States v. Randle, 966 F.2d 1209 (7th Cir. 1992) (defendant's subjective beliefs whether he was in custody were insufficient to establish that he was in custody).]

NORTH CAROLINA SUPREME COURT

State v. Washington, 330 N.C. 188 (1991). The court, per curiam and without opinion, reversed the majority opinion of the North Carolina Court of Appeals, 102 N.C. App. 535 (1991) (ruling that defendant was not in custody to require *Miranda* warnings), for the reasons stated in the dissenting opinion. An officer saw the defendant driving a car with a broken headlight and other damage that indicated that it had recently been involved in an accident. The officer suspected that the car had been involved in a hit-and-run accident and therefore stopped it. The defendant got out of the car and met the officer in front of the patrol car. The defendant did not have a driver's license, and the officer placed him in the backseat of the patrol car while he checked his identity with the Division of Motor Vehicles. When he returned to the defendant's car, the officer saw a bullet on the floorboard. The officer then returned to the patrol car and asked the defendant, who was still sitting inside, where the gun was located. [Author's note: Neither the majority nor dissenting opinion provided the elapsed time from the defendant's placement in the back of the patrol car to the officer's asking the defendant a question.] After the defendant denied that there was a gun in the car and that the car was his, he also told the officer that he could search the car. The officer then searched the car and found a bag with smaller bags inside that contained a white powdery substance, which later was determined to be cocaine. The officer showed the bag to defendant and then said, "Look what I've got." The defendant responded that it was only baking soda that he and a friend had been flaking. The officer asked the defendant what "flaking" meant, and the defendant responded that he had bagged up baking soda to look like cocaine in order to sell it and make a profit. The officer then placed the defendant under arrest.

The dissenting opinion, adopted by the North Carolina Supreme Court, stated that the facts of this case differ significantly from routine traffic stop cases in which custody did not exist, citing *Pennsylvania v. Bruder*, 488 U.S. 9 (1988), and *State v. Seagle*, 96 N.C. App. 318 (1989). When the defendant in this case was stopped and placed in the backseat of the patrol car, he was not free to leave at will because the inside door handles of the backseat doors did not work. He was "in effect, incarcerated on the side of the road" and therefore was in custody when he made statements to the officer. Also, the officer's act of showing defendant the bag and his words, "Look what I've got," were "interrogation" under the test set out in *Rhode Island v. Innis*, 446 U.S. 291 (1980). Thus, the officer was required to give *Miranda* warnings before questioning the defendant.

NORTH CAROLINA COURT OF APPEALS

State v. Beasley, 104 N.C. App. 529 (1991). A trooper stopped a speeding car. When the defendant-driver stepped out of the car, the trooper noticed a strong odor of alcohol on his breath and also saw three or four empty beer cans on the car's floorboard. The defendant swayed as he stood, and his eyes appeared red and glassy. The trooper told the defendant to have a seat in the patrol car and informed him why he had been stopped. He asked the defendant how much he had been drinking, and the defendant replied that he had had one drink. The trooper then told the defendant that he was under arrest for impaired driving.

The court ruled that the defendant was not in custody under *Miranda* until he was informed that he was under arrest. It was not reasonable to believe that he was deprived of his freedom of movement in any significant way. The court stated that during a traffic stop, a driver is not in custody when the driver is asked a moderate number of questions and is not informed that the detention will be other than temporary.

State v. Seagle, 96 N.C. App. 318 (1989). Relying on *Berkemer v. McCarty*, 468 U.S. 420 (1984), the court ruled that the defendant was not in custody so as to require *Miranda* warnings when the officer stopped him near the scene of a one-car accident and asked him questions, including whether the defendant was the driver of the car involved in the accident. The defendant had been detained only for a few minutes and had not been placed under arrest. *See also* State v. Kincaid, 147 N.C. App. 94 (2001) (defendant who was detained during traffic stop was not in custody to require *Miranda* warnings).

FEDERAL APPELLATE COURTS

United States v. Sullivan, 138 F.3d 126 (4th Cir. 1998). Following a traffic stop and after its purpose had been served (checking license and registration and returning them to the defendant), an officer asked the defendant whether he had anything illegal in the car. When the defendant did not directly answer, the officer repeated the question several times. During this dialogue, which lasted less than a minute, the officer advised the defendant that it would be better "to tell me now" and that he "would be cool" with the defendant. The questions culminated with the defendant's admission that he had a gun under the front seat. The court ruled that the defendant was not in custody under *Miranda*. The court stated that the mere fact that the officer did not affirmatively advise the defendant that he could refuse to answer the officer's questions or that he was free to leave did not transform the encounter into a custodial interrogation.

Prisoners and Jail Inmates

Howes v. Fields, 132 S. Ct. 1181 (2012). The United States Supreme Court ruled that a federal appellate court erroneously concluded that a prisoner was in custody under *Miranda* when the prisoner was taken aside and questioned about events that occurred outside the prison. The prisoner (Fields) was escorted by a correction officer to a conference room where two sheriff's deputies questioned him about allegations that, before he came to prison, he had engaged in sexual conduct with a 12-year-old boy. To get to the conference room, Fields had to go down one floor and pass through a locked door that separated two sections of the facility. Fields arrived at the conference room between 7:00 and 9:00 p.m. and was questioned for about five to seven hours. At the beginning of the interview, Fields was told that he was free to leave and return to his cell. Later, he was again told that he could leave whenever he wanted. The interviewing deputies were armed, but Fields remained free of handcuffs and other restraints. The door to the conference room was sometimes open and sometimes shut. About halfway through the interview, after Fields had been confronted with the allegations of abuse, he became agitated and began to yell. One of the deputies, using an expletive, told Fields to sit down and said that "if [he] didn't want to cooperate, [he] could leave." Fields eventually confessed to engaging in sex acts with the boy. Fields asserted that he said several times during the interview that he no longer wanted to talk to the deputies but that he did not ask to go back to his cell before the interview ended. When he was eventually ready to leave, he had to wait an additional 20 minutes or so because an officer had to be called to escort him back to his cell, and he did not return to his cell until well after the time he generally went to bed. Fields was never given *Miranda* warnings or advised that he did not have to speak with the deputies. Fields was charged with criminal sexual conduct. He unsuccessfully moved to suppress his confession, and the jury convicted him of criminal sexual conduct. After an unsuccessful direct appeal, Fields filed for federal habeas relief. The federal district court granted relief and the Sixth Circuit affirmed, ruling that the interview was a custodial interrogation because isolation from the general prison population, combined with questioning about conduct occurring outside the prison, made any interrogation automatically custodial. Reversing, the Supreme Court stated: "[I]t is abundantly clear that our precedents do not clearly establish the categorical rule on which the Court of Appeals relied, *i.e.*, that the questioning of a prisoner is always custodial when the prisoner is removed from the general prison population and questioned about events that occurred outside the prison." "On the contrary," the Court stated, "we have repeatedly declined to adopt any categorical rule with respect to whether the questioning of a prison inmate is custodial." The Court ruled that based on the facts presented, Fields was not in custody under *Miranda*.

Mathis v. United States, 391 U.S. 1 (1968). The defendant was in custody under the *Miranda* rule when a government agent questioned him while he was serv-ing a sentence in a state prison. It was irrelevant that the defendant was in custody for an offense different from the one under investigation. *But see* United States v. Conley, 779 F.2d 970 (4th Cir. 1985) (prisoner was not in custody when he was questioned about a murder while awaiting medical treatment); United States v. Cooper, 800 F.2d 412 (4th Cir. 1986) (prisoners were not in custody under *Miranda* when they were questioned by a correctional treatment specialist at their request); Leviston v. Black, 843 F.2d 302 (8th Cir. 1988) (defendant, a jail inmate, was not in custody under *Miranda* when he requested that the officer interview him, he voluntarily went to the jail interview room to talk with the officer, and he remained free to end the conversation at any time); United States v. Willoughby, 860 F.2d 15 (2d Cir. 1988); United States v. Scalf, 725 F.2d 1272 (10th Cir. 1984); United States v. Menzer, 29 F.3d 1223 (7th Cir. 1994); Garcia v. Singletary, 13 F.3d 1487 (11th Cir. 1994).

State v. Briggs, 137 N.C. App. 125 (2000). The defendant, a prisoner, was placed in segregation lockup pending the investigation of a rule violation for allegedly sending a threatening letter to a person outside the prison. The defendant was required to go from his cell to a correctional unit manager's office for questioning about the matter. He was escorted by another correctional officer and wore waist chains and handcuffs. Once inside the office, the defendant denied writing the letter. The manager told him that he believed that the defendant had written the letter and would proceed administratively. The defendant stood up and said that he did not have anything else to say. He then got up to leave the office. When he reached the open door, he asked the manager if he could close it. After the manager said that he could, the defendant closed the door, sat back down, and admitted that he wrote the letter. He then got up and was escorted back to his cell.

The court ruled, citing *United States v. Conley*, 779 F.2d 970 (4th Cir. 1985), that an inmate is not, because of his incarceration, automatically in custody under *Miranda*; rather, whether an inmate is in custody must be determined by considering his freedom to depart from the place of his interrogation. Based on these facts, the court ruled that the defendant was not in custody to require *Miranda* warnings. The court noted that the defendant remained free not to talk and could leave the office and return to his cell at any time. [Author's note: The State had conceded at trial that the defendant's statements were the result of interrogation, so the court did not address that issue.]

Juveniles

J.D.B. v. North Carolina, 564 U.S. 261 (2011). A 13-year-old juvenile, a seventh grade student in middle school, was a suspect in two house break-ins. An officer went to the juvenile's school, where the school resource officer removed the juvenile from class and brought him to a conference room. The officer questioned the juvenile in the presence of the school resource officer, an assistant principal, and an administrative intern. Before being questioned, the juvenile was not given *Miranda* warnings, nor was he informed that he was free to leave the room. Based on these and other facts, the North Carolina Supreme Court ruled that the juvenile was not in custody to require *Miranda* warnings. The court declined to consider the juvenile's age in making the custody determination.

The United States Supreme Court disagreed with the North Carolina Supreme Court's view on the age issue. It ruled that the age of a juvenile (a person under 18 years old) is a factor that must be considered in making the objective determination as to whether the juvenile is in custody, as long as the juvenile's age is known or reasonably apparent to the officer. (The Court cautioned, however, that a juvenile's age will not necessarily be a determinative, or even significant, factor in every case.) The Court reasoned that a juvenile will often feel bound to submit to law enforcement questioning when an adult in the same circumstances would not. The Court also clearly indicated that the actual age of the juvenile must be considered, because a young juvenile may be more susceptible than an older juvenile; the Court stated that officers and judges "simply need the common sense to know that a 7-year-old is not a 13-year-old and neither is an adult." The Court did not determine whether the juvenile in this case was in custody. Instead, it remanded the case to the North Carolina Supreme Court to make that determination.

[Author's note: The Court distinguished a contrary statement on the juvenile age issue in *Yarborough v. Alvarado*, 541 U.S. 652 (2004). However, the Court effectively reaffirmed Yarborough to the extent that *Yarborough* ruled that a suspect's prior interrogation history with law enforcement is irrelevant in determining custody under *Miranda*.]

In re A.N.C., Jr., 225 N.C. App. 315 (2013). The court ruled that a 13-year-old juvenile was not in custody within the meaning of G.S. 7B-2101 or *Miranda* during a roadside questioning by an officer. Responding to a report of a vehicle accident, the officer saw the wrecked vehicle, which had crashed into a utility pole, and three people walking from the scene. When the officer questioned all three, the juvenile admitted that he had been driving the wrecked vehicle. Noting that under *J.D.B. v. North Carolina*, 564 U.S. 261 (2011), a reviewing court must, when determining whether a suspect has been placed in custody, take into account a juvenile's age if it was known to an officer or would have been objectively apparent to a reasonable officer, the court nevertheless concluded that the juvenile here was not in custody.

State v. Yancey, 221 N.C. App. 397 (2012). The juvenile defendant was not in custody for purposes of *Miranda*. After the defendant had been identified as a possible suspect in several breaking or entering cases, two detectives dressed in plain clothes and driving an unmarked vehicle went to the defendant's home and asked to speak with him. Because the defendant had friends visiting his home, the detectives asked the defendant to take a ride in their car with them. The detectives told the defendant that he was free to leave at any time, and they did not touch him. The defendant sat in the front seat of the vehicle while it was driven approximately two miles from his home. When the vehicle stopped, one of the detectives showed the defendant reports of the break-ins. The detectives told the defendant that if he was cooperative, they would not arrest him that day. The defendant admitted to committing the break-ins. The juvenile was 17 years and 10 months old. Considering the totality of the circumstances—including the defendant's age—the court concluded that the defendant was not in custody. The court rejected the argument that *J.D.B. v. North Carolina*, 564 U.S. 261 (2011), required a different conclusion.

In re K.D.L., 207 N.C. App. 453 (2010). The court ruled that the trial court erred by denying a juvenile's motion to suppress when the juvenile's confession was made in the course of custodial interrogation but without the warnings required by *Miranda* and G.S. 7B-2101(a) and without his being informed of and afforded his right to have a parent present. The court found that the juvenile was in custody, noting that he knew that he was suspected of a crime; he was questioned by a school official for about six hours, mostly in the presence of an armed police officer; and he was frisked by the officer and transported in the officer's vehicle to the principal's office where he remained alone with the officer until the principal arrived. Although the officer was not with the juvenile at all times, the juvenile was never told that he was free to leave. Furthermore, the court ruled that although the principal, not the officer, asked the questions, an interrogation occurred, noting that the officer's conduct significantly increased the likelihood that the juvenile would produce an incriminating response to the principal's questioning. The court concluded that the officer's near-constant supervision of the juvenile's interrogation and "active listening" could cause a reasonable person to believe that the principal's interrogation was done in concert with the officer or that the person would endure harsher criminal punishment for failing to answer.

In re L.I., 205 N.C. App. 155 (2010). The juvenile was a passenger in a vehicle stopped by an officer. When the officer ordered the juvenile out of the vehicle, he asked, "[Where is] the marijuana I know you have[?]" The juvenile turned away and appeared to reach into her pants. When the officer tried to see what the juvenile was reaching for, she told him that he could not look in her pants. After handcuffing and placing the juvenile in the back of the patrol car, the officer—without giving *Miranda* and juvenile statutory warnings—told her that he was going to "take her downtown" and that "if [she] t[ook] drugs into the jail it[] [would be] an additional charge." The juvenile shortly thereafter told the officer that she had marijuana and that it was in her coat pocket. The Court ruled, relying on *State v. Johnston*, 154 N.C. App. 500 (2002), that the juvenile was in custody when the officer spoke to her. The officer had placed her in investigative detention, handcuffed her, and placed her in the backseat of his vehicle.

In re W.R., 179 N.C. App. 642 (2006). As a result of information that the juvenile, a 14-year-old middle school student, might have brought a knife to school, an assistant principal took the juvenile out of his classroom and to her office. The principal and assistant principal questioned him for a while and then a law enforcement officer (a school resource officer) joined in the questioning. The officer also conducted a search of the juvenile's pockets for weapons. None were found. The questioning took about 30 minutes and then the juvenile admitted possessing a knife at school on the prior day. The juvenile was never left unsupervised during that time, and the officer was there for most of that time period, with the juvenile under his supervision while the principal and assistant

principal left the office to conduct the investigation. The court ruled, distinguishing *In re Phillips*, 128 N.C. App. 732 (1998) (juvenile was not in custody when questioned by school officials in school office and no law enforcement officers were present), that the juvenile was in custody to require *Miranda* and juvenile statutory warnings. Given the totality of circumstances, a reasonable person in the juvenile's position would have believed that he was restrained to a degree associated with a formal arrest.

In re Hodge, 153 N.C. App. 102 (2002). A juvenile was not in custody to require juvenile interrogation rights when a detective spoke to the juvenile, his mother, and the juvenile's brother in the living room of their home as a result of an allegation made by the brother. The detective prefaced her interview with the juvenile by telling him that he did not have to talk to her and she was not going to arrest him.

State v. Harvey, 78 N.C. App. 235 (1985). Two officers went to the defendant's home around 9:00 a.m. and asked his mother if her son, who was a 17-year-old with limited mental capacity (IQ of 78), could ride with them. The officers took the defendant directly to the police department and interrogated him for an hour about two break-ins of the home of the defendant's uncle. The defendant repeatedly denied his involvement in the crimes despite the officers' vigorous interrogation. The court ruled that the defendant was in custody to require *Miranda* warnings before interrogation began. The defendant, who was young and had limited mental capacity, was taken far from his home, placed in a closed office with two officers, subjected to lengthy interrogation, and never told that he was not under arrest, that he was free to leave, or that he could end the questioning at any time.

Military Personnel

State v. Walker, 167 N.C. App. 110 (2004). The defendant, a U.S. Marine, was given *Miranda* warnings by a deputy sheriff and military investigator before questioning about a robbery. The next day, the defendant's military superior, a master gunnery sergeant, asked the defendant why he had been questioned the prior day, if he had anything to do with "this mess," and if he was carrying a weapon during the incident involving the robbery. The questioning took place in the sergeant's office. There was no evidence that the defendant felt that he could not leave or that he had to answer the sergeant's questions. The court ruled that the defendant was not in custody under *Miranda* based on the ruling in *State v. Davis*, 158 N.C. 1

(2003) (discussing custody standard when military member gives statement to superior).

State v. Davis, 158 N.C. App. 1 (2003). The defendant was serving in the Marine Corps and was stationed in California. While on leave in North Carolina, he committed a murder, but he was not arrested then. The defendant returned to his Marine Corps base in California. He told his sergeant that he needed to telephone a lawyer. The sergeant asked why, but the defendant refused to talk about it. The sergeant took the defendant to his platoon sergeant, who then took the defendant to the platoon commander. The platoon sergeant told the commander that the defendant had received a phone call indicating that the sheriff's department was on the way to arrest him and that the commander would want to hear what the defendant had to say. The defendant confirmed to the commander that his mother had called and warned him that a detective from North Carolina was coming to California because the defendant was a suspect in a murder case. The commander asked the defendant if he was involved in the murder and the defendant replied, "Sort of." The commander then said, "Well, are you involved or not involved? Yes or no question." The defendant replied, "Yes, I am involved." The defendant explained that he did not know the murdered man, but that he had been told that the man raped his wife in North Carolina while he was in California. The defendant was then allowed to make a telephone call. The court ruled, citing cases from other jurisdictions, that the commander was conducting custodial interrogation, and the defendant's statements were inadmissible because *Miranda* warnings had not been given and waived.

Polygraph Cases

State v. Brewington, 352 N.C. 489 (2000). The defendant drove himself to the sheriff's department, where he agreed to a polygraph examination by an SBI agent. The agent told him that the test was voluntary and that he could leave at any time. The defendant signed a polygraph examination consent form that reaffirmed that he was not in custody and was taking the examination voluntarily. The defendant was not handcuffed or restrained at any time. At the conclusion of the examination, the agent told the defendant that she did not believe he was telling the whole truth. The defendant stated that he had been present when the fire started, but he blamed the fire on his nephew. The agent left the room and reported this statement to investigating officers. When the agent

returned to the room, the defendant made an additional incriminating statement.

The court noted, citing *Stansbury v. California,* 511 U.S. 318 (1994), that the definitive inquiry concerning custody under *Miranda* is whether there was a formal arrest or restraint on the defendant's freedom of movement of the degree associated with a formal arrest. The court ruled that the defendant was not in custody during the entire interview with the agent.

State v. Hicks, 333 N.C. 467 (1993). An officer told the defendant that he was a suspect in a murder because he and the victim had broken up just before she was murdered. Officers then asked the defendant to take a polygraph test to "clear his name." They transported the defendant, with his consent, to the SBI office—over an hour's drive from the defendant's home—for the purpose of taking the test. Although he refused to take the polygraph test three separate times during two hours of questioning, the defendant was never taken home or offered transportation home. Although the polygraph operator informed the defendant during his explanation of the polygraph procedure that he was not under arrest, the defendant never was told that he was free to leave. After the third refusal to take the test, the defendant told the polygraph operator that he wanted to go outside with him. During a conversation in the parking lot, the defendant told the operator that he wanted to take responsibility for the murder. They came back into the building, and the operator informed two investigating officers that the defendant wanted to confess. When the defendant refused to elaborate on the details of the crime, the officers told him that he would have to tell them what had happened, including any details. The defendant then gave them the details and demonstrated how he shot the victim. After the defendant explained the details of the murder, the officers advised the defendant of his *Miranda* rights and obtained a valid waiver. The defendant then gave a second confession.

The court ruled that a reasonable person in the defendant's position, knowing that he was a suspect in a murder case and having just stated to an officer that he wanted to take responsibility for a murder, would feel that he was compelled to stay; therefore, the defendant was in custody under *Miranda* immediately following that statement. [Author's note: The North Carolina Supreme Court in the later case of *State v. Buchanan*, 353 N.C. 332 (2001), expressly disavowed the "free to leave" test used in this case to determine custody under *Miranda*. Therefore, it is unclear whether the court would now reach the same result on the custody issue.] Thus, the first confession that was taken without *Miranda* warnings should have been ruled inadmissible. However, the court ruled that the second confession, taken after *Miranda* warnings had been properly given and waived, was admissible under the ruling in *Oregon v. Elstad*, 470 U.S. 298 (1985) (fact that voluntary confession is inadmissible because of *Miranda* violation does not prohibit admission of later voluntary confession given after proper *Miranda* warnings and waiver). The court adopted the *Oregon v. Elstad* ruling to determine alleged constitutional violations under Article I, Sections 19 and 23, of the North Carolina Constitution.

The Meaning of "Interrogation" under *Miranda*

(*This topic is discussed on page 576.*)

Generally

UNITED STATES SUPREME COURT

Pennsylvania v. Muniz, 496 U.S. 582 (1990). The Court ruled that the defendant's voluntary utterances (including his questions to the officer and his slurred speech) when he performed the physical sobriety test and during preliminaries of the Breathalyzer testing were not the result of interrogation and therefore were admissible.

Arizona v. Mauro, 481 U.S. 520 (1987). The defendant was arrested for the murder of his son and asserted his right to counsel after being given *Miranda* warnings. The defendant's wife insisted on seeing her husband, who was being held in a police captain's office. The officers allowed the meeting, but only on the condition that an officer could be present and the conversation could be tape recorded. The conversation between the defendant and his wife was later admitted at the defendant's trial. The Court ruled that the officer did not engage in "interrogation" as defined in *Rhode Island v. Innis*, discussed below. The Court stated, "Officers do not interrogate a suspect simply by hoping that he will incriminate himself."

Rhode Island v. Innis, 446 U.S. 291 (1980). Interrogation, under the *Miranda* rule, includes not only express questioning but also the functional equivalent of questioning—that is, any words or actions by an officer (other than those normally associated with arrest and custody) that the officer should know are reasonably likely to elicit an incriminating response from the particular defendant in custody as those words or acts are perceived by that defendant. In this case, the defendant was arrested within hours after robbing a taxicab driver with a sawed-off shotgun. He was unarmed when he was arrested. After he was given *Miranda* warnings, he said that he wanted to speak with a lawyer. A supervisor then instructed three officers to take him to the police station and told them not to question him in any way. While en route, two officers talked with each other about the missing shotgun and their concern that children from a nearby school for the handicapped might find it and harm themselves. The defendant then volunteered to show them where the gun was.

The Court ruled that the officers' conversation was not interrogation. There was nothing to suggest that the two officers should have known that their conversation between themselves was reasonably likely to elicit an incriminating response from the defendant. They had no reason to believe that the defendant was peculiarly susceptible to an appeal to his conscience about the handicapped children's safety. Nor did they know that he was unusually disoriented or upset when he was arrested. The Court also noted that the officers did not have a lengthy conversation in the defendant's presence, nor were their remarks particularly evocative.

NORTH CAROLINA SUPREME COURT

State v. Brewington, 352 N.C. 489 (2000). While investigating officers were giving the defendant *Miranda* warnings, he stated, "I believe I need to talk to a lawyer." An officer responded, "I believe you do, too." An officer then asked the defendant for information to complete the defendant's personal history arrest form, including date of birth, Social Security number, address, height, and weight. During this process, the defendant asked the officers, "What if I know who did it?" One officer informed the defendant that he could not talk to him because he had not waived his rights. He stated that he could not say anything to the defendant and the defendant should say nothing to him. The officer further stated that if the defendant wanted to talk to him, he had to initiate it, and then the officer would be required to readvise the defendant of his *Miranda* rights and obtain a waiver stating that the defendant did not wish to have an attorney. As the defendant continued to ask questions of the officers about the case, an officer again explained that the defendant had invoked his right to counsel and they could not talk with him. The defendant then indicated that he had changed his mind and wanted to talk with them. An officer again informed the defendant that he had invoked his right to counsel and any decision to talk had to be his. Again, the defendant stated that he wanted to talk. He was then given *Miranda* warnings and waived them.

The court ruled, citing *Rhode Island v. Innis*, 446 U.S. 291 (1980), and *State v. Ladd*, 308 N.C. 272 (1983), that the officer's questions to complete the arrest form were not a custodial interrogation in violation of the defendant's assertion of his right to counsel under *Edwards v. Arizona*, 451 U.S. 477 (1981). The court also ruled that the defendant reinitiated interrogation after his assertion of the right to counsel.

State v. DeCastro, 342 N.C. 667 (1996). The defendant was arrested for two murders and a robbery committed during the murders in which money was taken. He requested a lawyer during custodial interrogation. He was then taken to the jail area so that his clothing could be collected as evidence. When instructed to empty his pockets, the defendant placed $13 on a bench. Officer A asked Officer B "if it was okay for [the defendant] to keep the money." Officer B turned toward the defendant and saw some more money in the defendant's top pocket. Before Officer B could say anything, the defendant said, "I had some of my own money, too, now."

The court ruled, relying on *Rhode Island v. Innis*, discussed above, that the defendant's answer was not the result of interrogation. The question by Officer A was directed toward Officer B. Furthermore, the defendant made his statement during a general conversation while turning over his clothing and property in exchange for an inmate jumpsuit. The officer's question was not an initiation of questioning in violation of the defendant's assertion of the right to counsel, because the question was not reasonably likely to elicit an incriminating response from the defendant.

State v. Vick, 341 N.C. 569 (1995). The defendant was arrested for murder. Before *Miranda* warnings had been given and while he was being fingerprinted, an officer approached the defendant and told him that he would like to talk to him after the fingerprinting was complete and that he would answer any of the defendant's questions then. The defendant indicated that he needed to talk to someone and said, "I don't understand. Why isn't Collette here? She was there that night with me." The court ruled that the officer's comments were not interrogation under *Rhode Island v. Innis*, discussed above.

State v. Washington, 330 N.C. 188 (1991). The court, per curiam and without its own opinion, reversed the majority opinion, 102 N.C. App. 535 (1991), of the court of appeals for the reasons stated in the dissenting opinion of the court of appeals. The dissenting opinion concluded that the officer's act of showing the defendant (who was in custody in the officer's vehicle) a bag containing a white powdery substance and the officer's words, "Look what I've got," were interrogation under *Rhode v. Innis*, discussed above.

State v. Edgerton, 328 N.C. 319 (1991). As an officer attempted to advise the defendant of his *Miranda* rights, the defendant spontaneously began to make a statement. The court ruled that the statement was admissible, because it was not made as a result of interrogation.

State v. Clark, 324 N.C. 146 (1989). The defendant expressed reservations as to whether she should talk with the officers without first contacting an attorney, because she did not know what to do. She indicated that she wanted to talk with them, yet she hesitated to sign the waiver form. The officers told her repeatedly that she could use the telephone, which was less than six feet away, and, specifically, that she could call a lawyer immediately if she wanted. She eventually signed the waiver form. Although the officers spoke between themselves within her hearing range about the evidence against her, and one of them urged her to tell her side of the story, the officers did not initiate questioning before she signed the form or so badger her that their conduct was the functional equivalent of interrogation under *Rhode Island v. Innis*, discussed above. Encouraging a defendant to tell the truth, even after he or she has asked for a lawyer, does not constitute interrogation or its functional equivalent. The court ruled that the defendant's *Miranda* rights were not violated.

State v. Allen, 323 N.C. 208 (1988). When a defendant who was in custody asserted his right to counsel, officers stopped interrogating him. One officer told the defendant that all he wanted was the truth, that the defendant would be returned to his jail cell, and that there would be no further interviews with him. He informed the defendant that if he wished to have a further conversation, he should call an officer. Another officer told the defendant the name of the specific officer he should contact if he decided to call an officer. The defendant then said, "Okay," and added, "I want to talk to you now, man." The court ruled that the officers' statements after the defendant's assertion of the right to counsel did not violate the ruling in *Edwards* *v. Arizona*, 451 U.S. 477 (1981), because they were not interrogation.

State v. Forney, 310 N.C. 126 (1984). A sheriff was taking the defendant from the jail to the courthouse when they passed by a holding cell. When the sheriff asked the defendant, "Do you know these two fellows?" the defendant responded that they had broken into a house with him. No further conversation took place. The court ruled that "this casual question" under these circumstances was not interrogation under *Rhode Island v. Innis*, discussed above.

State v. Ladd, 308 N.C. 272 (1983). An officer's statement, "You know why," to a defendant when the defendant asked why he was being arrested was not interrogation. The officer had no reason to anticipate that the defendant would make an incriminating response to this "offhand remark." *See also* State v. Porter, 303 N.C. 680 (1980); State v. Crawford, 58 N.C. App. 160 (1982).

NORTH CAROLINA COURT OF APPEALS

State v. Hogan, 234 N.C. App. 218 (2014). The court ruled that the defendant's statements, made while a law enforcement officer who had responded to a domestic violence call questioned the defendant's girlfriend in his presence (the officer asked how she got marks that were visible on her neck), were spontaneous and not in response to interrogation. The State conceded that the defendant was in custody at the time. The court rejected the defendant's argument that asking his girlfriend what happened in front of him was a coercive technique designed to elicit an incriminating statement. Acknowledging that the "case is a close one," the court concluded that the officer's question to the girlfriend did not constitute the functional equivalent of questioning the defendant; the officer's question did not call for a response from the defendant, and therefore it was not reasonably likely to elicit an incriminating response from him.

In re L.I., 205 N.C. App. 155 (2010). The juvenile was a passenger in a vehicle stopped by an officer. When the officer ordered the juvenile out of the vehicle, he asked, "[Where is] the marijuana I know you have[?]" The juvenile turned away and appeared to reach into her pants. When the officer tried to see what the juvenile was reaching for, she told him that he could not look in her pants. After handcuffing and placing the juvenile in the back of the patrol car, the officer—without giving *Miranda* and juvenile statutory warnings—told her that he was going to "take her downtown" and that "if [she] t[ook] drugs into

the jail it[] [would be] an additional charge." The juvenile shortly thereafter told the officer that she had marijuana and that it was in her coat pocket.

(1) The Court ruled, relying on *State v. Johnston*, 154 N.C. App. 500 (2002), that the juvenile was in custody when the officer spoke to her. She had been detained, handcuffed, and placed in the backseat of the officer's vehicle. (2) The court ruled, relying on *State v. Phelps*, 156 N.C. App. 119 (2003), that the officer's statements to the juvenile constituted interrogation under *Rhode Island v. Innis*, 446 U.S. 291 (1980), because the officer knew or should have known that the statements were reasonably likely to elicit an incriminating response from her. The officer's objective purpose was to obtain the juvenile's admission that she possessed the marijuana that he knew she had. The trial court erred in admitting the juvenile's statements made in response to the officer's custodial interrogation.

In re D.L.D., 203 N.C. App. 434 (2010). The juvenile was adjudicated delinquent of possession of marijuana with the intent to sell or deliver. An officer was assigned to a high school as a resource officer and had made many arrests for controlled substances at one of the school's bathrooms. The officer and an assistant principal (hereafter, principal) noticed on monitoring cameras that two male juveniles were entering the bathroom and one was standing outside. The principal told the officer that the situation "looked kind of fishy" and suggested they check it. As they approached the bathroom, they saw one male student outside the men's bathroom and another male student outside the women's bathroom, and both students stared at the officer and principal. They then saw the juvenile and two other male students leave the bathroom. When the juvenile saw the officer and the principal, he ran back into the bathroom, and they followed him. When the officer said that he saw the juvenile put something in his pants, the principal replied, "We need to check it." The officer frisked the juvenile and found a container used to hold BB gun pellets. Inside the container were three individually wrapped bags of marijuana worth $20 each. The officer handcuffed the juvenile and took him to a school office. The principal told the officer that they needed to check the juvenile to make sure that he did not have anything else. The officer searched the juvenile and discovered $59 in his pocket. The juvenile immediately stated that "the money was not from selling drugs" but was his mother's rent money. The court ruled that although the juvenile was in custody and had not been given *Miranda* and statutory warnings, his statement in the school office was admissible because it was unsolicited and spontaneous and not a result of interrogation. The court cited *State v. Hall*, 131 N.C. App. 427 (1998), and other cases.

State v. Hensley, 201 N.C. App. 607 (2010). The court ruled that an officer's conduct and his statements to the defendant after his arrest constituted interrogation to require *Miranda* warnings. The officer should have known that his conduct and statements were reasonably likely to elicit an incriminating response from the defendant; see the definition of "interrogation" in *State v. Golphin*, 352 N.C. 364 (2000), and *Rhode Island v. Innis*, 446 U.S. 291 (1980). The defendant took a drug overdose and was taken to a hospital. The following day, upon being informed that the defendant was about to be released, the officer arrested him at the hospital. The officer told the defendant (whom he knew from a prior investigation) that he hoped the defendant would continue to cooperate even though he had been arrested. The officer inquired as to whether the defendant would agree to talk with him the next day if the officer came to work on overtime to obtain a statement from him. The defendant then made an incriminating statement.

State v. Rollins, 189 N.C. App. 248 (2008). The court ruled that a correctional officer's statements to a prisoner during transport from one correctional facility to another constituted interrogation under *Rhode Island v. Innis*, 446 U.S. 291 (1980), and thus the prisoner's response was inadmissible because *Miranda* warnings had not been given. The officer initiated questioning related to a murder. By doing so, the officer steered the conversation to a topic that, if discussed by the defendant, was likely to elicit an incriminating statement.

State v. Dent, 174 N.C. App. 459 (2005). An officer arrested the defendant for driving while license revoked. He did not administer *Miranda* warnings to the defendant. While searching him, the officer noted the smell of burnt marijuana but did not find any marijuana. When the officer asked the defendant several times whether he had any marijuana, the defendant said "no." Before taking the defendant inside the detention facility, the officer asked the defendant whether he had any controlled substances. The defendant said "no." Once in the detention center and inside a search room, the officer informed the defendant that he would be strip searched. The defendant then stated that he had "residue" in his right sock. Distinguishing *State v. Phelps*, 156 N.C. App. 119 (2003),

rev'd on other grounds, 358 N.C. 142 (2004), and relying on *Rhode Island v. Innis*, 446 U.S. 291 (1980), and *State v. Golphin*, 352 N.C. 364 (2000), the court ruled that the officer's statement before the strip search (that the defendant would be strip searched) was not intended or reasonably expected to elicit an incriminating response from the defendant and therefore did not constitute interrogation under *Miranda*. The officer was merely informing the defendant of the extent of the impending search. [Author's note: The officer's questions to the defendant as to whether he had any marijuana or controlled substances clearly constituted interrogation, although the admissibility of the defendant's responses was not an issue in this case.]

State v. Jackson, 165 N.C. App. 763 (2004). A 15-year-old juvenile was charged with felonies. Two officers were with him during a juvenile court hearing. After the hearing, the juvenile was talkative. When the juvenile saw a cap that had been introduced into evidence, he spontaneously stated that he knew where the cap came from. One of the officers responded, "So do I." The juvenile then talked about a robbery. The officer never initiated a conversation at any point other than to ask the juvenile for clarification at times. The court ruled that the officer's response and requests for clarification were not interrogation under *Miranda* and also did not violate the juvenile's Sixth Amendment right to counsel.

State v. Gantt, 161 N.C. App. 265 (2003). Officers arrested the defendant for a sexual offense but did not give him *Miranda* warnings. On the drive to the magistrate's office, the defendant—in the midst of making threats of suicide and self-destructive behavior—said, "I didn't do nothing." An officer responded, "She says differently." Shortly thereafter, the defendant again talked about killing himself. The officer stated, "You broke into the lady's apartment. You were hiding in her closet." The defendant then stated, "I got four fingers in her pussy." The court ruled, relying on *State v. Young*, 317 N.C. 396 (1986), that the officer's statements were not interrogation, and thus the defendant's statements were not taken in violation of the *Miranda* ruling. The officer's statements did not call for a response from the defendant and thus were not the functional equivalent of interrogation.

State v. Smith, 160 N.C. App. 107 (2003). While being held in the county jail awaiting trial for several felonies, the defendant was served in the holding area of the magistrate's office with an order involving another case. The defendant questioned a detective about whether his mother would be arrested as an accessory after the fact involving the pending felony cases. When the detective responded affirmatively, the defendant became angry and said, "Look, man, my mom is innocent. Just because I attacked two innocent people in Greensboro doesn't mean you have to charge innocent people." The court ruled, relying on *State v. Young*, 317 N.C. 396 (1986), that the detective's factually correct response to the defendant's question called for no response from the defendant; it was neither express questioning nor was it likely to elicit an incriminating response from the defendant under the standard set out in *Rhode Island v. Innis*, 446 U.S. 291 (1980). Thus, the defendant's statement was admissible at trial even though he had not been given *Miranda* warnings.

State v. Phelps, 156 N.C. App. 119 (2003), *rev'd on other grounds*, 358 N.C. 142 (2004). A law enforcement officer arrested the defendant based on two outstanding arrest warrants. The officer did not administer *Miranda* warnings. In the parking lot of the county jail, before taking the defendant into the building for processing, the officer told the defendant that he needed to inform the officer if he possessed any illegal substance or weapons because it was an automatic felony to possess them in jail. The court ruled that this statement was interrogation under *Miranda* because the officer knew or should have known that his statement to the defendant was reasonably likely to elicit an incriminating response; the court cited *Rhode Island v. Innis*, 446 U.S. 291 (1980).

State v. Jordan, 128 N.C. App. 469 (1998). After several hours of interrogation, the defendant indicated that he might need an attorney. An officer stopped the interrogation, left the interview room, and informed his sergeant, who asked the defendant if he needed a lawyer. The defendant responded, "Yes, I've told them the truth." The sergeant replied, "No, you did not, that's bullshit, you're lying, and you're going to jail for murder." The officers left the defendant alone for 20 minutes while an officer located the proper booking forms. Sometime during the booking process the defendant stated, "I told you I had something else to say if I was going to be charged." The officers then left him alone, conferred among themselves, and concluded that he was attempting to initiate further conversation. They then reapproached him, verified that he wanted to speak with them without a lawyer, and elicited incriminating statements from him.

(1) The court ruled that the sergeant's remarks to the defendant after he asserted his right to counsel were not interrogation or the functional equivalent of interrogation. The exchange was very brief and was not reasonably likely to evoke an incriminating response. *See* Rhode Island v. Innis, 446 U.S. 291 (1980). Also, the 20-minute period during which the defendant was left alone was not reasonably likely to evoke an incriminating response. (2) The court ruled that the defendant's statement, "I told you I had something else to say if I was going to be charged," was a reinitiation of communication after his prior assertion of the right to counsel. Therefore, the officers did not violate his *Miranda* rights by reapproaching him and eliciting incriminating statements.

State v. Jones, 112 N.C. App. 337 (1993). The defendant was arrested for breaking and entering and larceny about 1:05 p.m. and taken to the police department. He waived his *Miranda* rights and talked to officers for a while and then asserted his right to counsel. The officers stopped the interrogation and left the defendant in the interrogation room until about 7:00 p.m., when they obtained a search warrant for his apartment. The officers took the defendant with them to execute the search warrant. The defendant and an officer had a general conversation there, including the officer's responding to the defendant's request for a cigarette (the trial judge found that the conversation was not calculated to induce the defendant to make incriminating statements, and the defendant made none). The defendant's live-in girlfriend became upset during the officers' questioning of her about which items in the apartment were hers. The defendant then decided to initiate a conversation with the officers so that they would not bother his girlfriend about these items, and he showed the officers which items were stolen. When the officers took him back to the police station, the defendant was advised of his *Miranda* rights, waived those rights, and confessed.

The court ruled, following *Rhode Island v. Innis*, 446 U.S. 291 (1980), that the evidence did not show that the officers should have known that their actions (taking the defendant for execution of the search warrant, questioning his girlfriend, etc.) would elicit an incriminating response.

State v. Garcia-Lorenzo, 110 N.C. App. 319 (1993). The defendant was involved in a vehicular accident by running off a road and was injured. Officers transported the defendant to a hospital, where officers and doctors had to restrain him when he became violent. Because an officer wanted to know whether to look for other victims of the accident, the officer and then a doctor asked the defendant whether he was alone in the car. The defendant responded several times, "No, alone."

The court affirmed the trial judge's conclusions of law that this questioning was permissible for the following reasons: (1) It was within *Miranda*'s public safety exception, recognized in *New York v. Quarles*, 467 U.S. 649 (1984), because officers were concerned that someone else may have been injured and lying undiscovered at the scene. (2) The defendant was not subjected to "interrogation" as defined in *Rhode Island v. Innis*, 446 U.S. 291 (1980).

State v. Moose, 101 N.C. App. 59 (1990). Before the officer could read the search warrant to the defendant, the defendant said, "You don't need that; it's in there." When the officer asked what the defendant meant, he replied, "The cocaine you're looking for is in there." The court ruled that the defendant's statement was not made in response to interrogation, because the officer simply asked the defendant to clarify a statement that he had made voluntarily.

State v. Young, 65 N.C. App. 346 (1983). While the defendant was in custody, an officer held a pocketbook (which he believed the defendant had secreted in a car) in his hand in front of the defendant. Twice he said, "I wonder whose this is," and then he said that the pocketbook belonged to either the defendant or another named person. The court ruled that the officer's remarks were interrogation under *Rhode Island v. Innis*, discussed above, because he should have known that they were likely to elicit an incriminating response.

FEDERAL APPELLATE COURTS

United States v. Dougall, 919 F.2d 932 (5th Cir. 1990). The defendant was arrested for rape. He was given *Miranda* warnings and requested a lawyer. Officers then requested minimal personal data from the defendant. They also requested a hair sample, informing the defendant that they would obtain a court order if he failed to comply voluntarily. The defendant then began to talk about the charge and signed a waiver of his *Miranda* rights. When he again requested a lawyer and became silent, the officers sat in the room in silence for a short time. The defendant then resumed talking and confessed.

The court ruled that the routine booking questions were not interrogation (*see* Pennsylvania v. Muniz, 496 U.S. 582 (1990)) and that the officers' request for hair samples did not violate the defendant's Fifth or Sixth Amendment rights. Compulsion to submit to hair samples does

not violate the Fifth Amendment, and the request for the hair samples did not occur at a critical stage of the proceedings for purposes of the Sixth Amendment right to counsel. The court also ruled that the moment of silence after the defendant's second request for counsel was not designed to elicit incriminating responses and therefore did not violate the defendant's Fifth or Sixth Amendment rights.

Request for Consent to Search
(*This topic is discussed on page 578.*)

State v. Cummings, 188 N.C. App. 598 (2008). The defendant was advised of his *Miranda* rights and waived them. Shortly after questioning began, the defendant requested a lawyer and questioning stopped. However, an officer then asked for the defendant's consent to search his vehicle, which he granted. The court upheld the trial judge's denial of the defendant's motion to suppress evidence seized as a result of the consent search. The court noted that *State v. Frank*, 284 N.C. 137 (1973), had ruled that *Miranda* warnings are inapplicable to searches and seizures. The court also stated that it found persuasive many federal court cases that have ruled that asking for a consent search is not interrogation under *Miranda*; for example, *United States v. Shlater*, 85 F.3d 1251 (7th Cir. 1996), and *United States v. McCurdy*, 40 F.3d 1111 (10th Cir. 1994).

Volunteered Statements
(*This topic is discussed on page 577.*)

Pennsylvania v. Muniz, 496 U.S. 582 (1990). The Court ruled that the defendant's voluntary utterances (including his questions to the officer and his slurred speech) when he performed the physical sobriety test and during preliminaries of the Breathalyzer testing were not the result of interrogation and therefore were admissible.

State v. Coffey, 345 N.C. 389 (1997). The defendant was arrested for murder, and two attorneys were appointed to represent him. The attorneys requested that the district attorney have a polygraph examination conducted on the defendant but did not express any desire to accompany their client to the polygraph site. When the defendant was being removed from his cell for the polygraph examination, he told a deputy sheriff that he wanted to call his attorney. The deputy declined to allow the defendant to do so, because the policy of the sheriff's office did not permit a prisoner to make a telephone call while being transported from one facility to another.

Later, when the polygraph operator was explaining the polygraph procedures to the defendant, the defendant stated that he did not tell the investigating officers the truth about the money taken from the murder victim. The operator asked him what he did not tell the truth about. The defendant said that he was handed the money by his accomplice and the accomplice "went off." The operator did not ask any further questions; instead, he conducted the polygraph examination. After the examination, the operator informed the defendant that he had not passed the polygraph about the murder and robbery. The defendant then made an incriminating statement. The operator asked the defendant if he would be willing to talk to one of the investigating officers. The defendant named a particular officer and later repeated the same incriminating statement to that officer.

The court ruled that the defendant was not being interrogated in violation of *Edwards v. Arizona*, 451 U.S. 477 (1981) (interrogation is not permitted after defendant has asserted right to counsel), when he made his statements to the polygraph operator and the investigating officer. These statements were volunteered by the defendant. Thus, neither his Fifth nor Sixth Amendment rights to counsel were violated. The court alternatively ruled, assuming that the defendant was being interrogated, that the defendant initiated the communication with the polygraph operator and investigating officer. *See, e.g.,* Oregon v. Bradshaw, 462 U.S. 1039 (1983).

State v. Walls, 342 N.C. 1 (1995). The defendant was arrested, was orally informed of his *Miranda* rights, and orally waived them. At the sheriff's department, a detective took the defendant to the fingerprinting room and asked him if he remembered his rights; the defendant said that he did. Nevertheless, the detective read him his *Miranda* rights again, provided him with a written copy, and obtained a written waiver. After being told of the two assaults for which he was charged, the defendant denied any knowledge of them and signed a writing that he no longer wished to make a statement. The detective did not ask any questions and began to fingerprint the defendant. When the detective took his right hand, the defendant exclaimed, "Ouch, take it easy." The detective noticed that the defendant's hand was badly swollen and cut, so he asked him, "What happened to your hand?" The defendant answered, "I hit an oak tree." The detective asked, "[W]hat did you hit a tree for? A tree had never hurt anybody." The defendant replied, "I should have hit her a little harder so I could really hurt my hand." The court ruled

that the defendant's remarks were volunteered statements, and the detective's questions did not convert the conversation into an interrogation under *Miranda. See also* State v. Coffey, 345 N.C. 389 (1997).

State v. Lambert, 341 N.C. 36 (1995). The defendant was in jail and requested that an officer come and speak to her. After the defendant spoke with her father, she approached the officer and told him that she had "blacked out" and could not remember anything. The court ruled that her statement was admissible under *Miranda* because (1) it was not made as a result of interrogation and (2) it was not an invocation of the right to silence—her specific request to speak to the officer and her statement indicated a desire not to remain silent.

State v. Edgerton, 328 N.C. 319 (1991). As an officer attempted to advise the defendant of his *Miranda* rights, the defendant spontaneously began to make a statement. The court ruled that the statement was admissible, because it was not made as a result of interrogation.

State v. Porter, 303 N.C. 680 (1980). While in custody for armed robbery, a defendant heard (over the radio) an officer ask the arresting officer whether the bank bag had been found. The defendant responded, "The bank bag is in the car." The defendant's response was a volunteered statement that was not prohibited by the *Miranda* ruling, because the radio question was not addressed to the defendant. *See also* State v. Herring, 284 N.C. 398 (1973); State v. Thomas, 284 N.C. 212 (1973); State v. Muse, 280 N.C. 31 (1971).

In re D.L.D., 203 N.C. App. 434 (2010). The juvenile was adjudicated delinquent of possession of marijuana with the intent to sell or deliver. An officer was assigned to a high school as a resource officer and had made many arrests for controlled substances at one of the school's bathrooms. The officer and an assistant principal (hereafter, principal) noticed on monitoring cameras that two male juveniles were entering the bathroom and one was standing outside. The principal told the officer that the situation "looked kind of fishy" and suggested they check it. As they approached the bathroom, they saw one male student outside the men's bathroom and another male student outside the women's bathroom, and both students stared at the officer and principal. They then saw the juvenile and two other male students leave the bathroom. When the juvenile saw the officer and the principal, he ran back into the bathroom, and they followed him. When the officer said that he saw the juvenile put something in his pants, the principal replied, "We need to check it." The officer frisked the juvenile and found a container used to hold BB gun pellets. Inside the container were three individually wrapped bags of marijuana worth $20 each. The officer handcuffed the juvenile and took him to a school office. The principal told the officer that they needed to check the juvenile to make sure that he did not have anything else. The officer searched the juvenile and discovered $59 in his pocket. The juvenile immediately stated that "the money was not from selling drugs" but was his mother's rent money. The court ruled that although the juvenile was in custody and had not been given *Miranda* and statutory warnings, his statement in the school office was admissible because it was unsolicited and spontaneous and not a result of interrogation. The court cited *State v. Hall*, 131 N.C. App. 427 (1998), and other cases.

State v. Dukes, 110 N.C. App. 695 (1993). Officer Moore arrived at a trailer park to investigate the murder of the defendant's wife. Both the defendant and a baby he was holding had blood on their clothing. Officer Moore accompanied the defendant and the baby to the defendant's trailer (the defendant lived in a different trailer than his wife). Officer Moore instructed Officer Thompson to guard the defendant, not allow him to leave his trailer, not allow any other person to enter the trailer, and not allow the defendant to wash or to change his clothes. Officer Thompson allowed the defendant to make telephone calls after he asked permission from the officer to do so. Officer Thompson accompanied the defendant to the bathroom to ensure that he did not wash or change his clothes. Officer Thompson later asked the defendant, "Do you know what happened?"

(1) The court ruled that the defendant was in custody to require Miranda warnings while he was at his trailer with Officer Thompson. A reasonable person who knew that his wife had just been killed and who was being kept under constant police supervision, had been told not to wash or change his clothing, and was never informed that he was free to leave his own home would not feel free to get up and go. The court also ruled that the officer's question constituted interrogation under the *Miranda* ruling. (2) The defendant was later arrested and taken to a law enforcement center. While the officer was advising the defendant of his *Miranda* rights, the defendant said, "I stabbed her." The court ruled that this statement was voluntary and not the result of custodial interrogation.

Assertion of *Miranda* Rights
Assertion of the Right to Remain Silent
(*This topic is discussed on page 579.*)

UNITED STATES SUPREME COURT

Berghuis v. Thompkins, 560 U.S. 370 (2010). The Court ruled that a defendant must make an unambiguous assertion of the right to remain silent to require an officer to stop custodial interrogation.

Officers were investigating a murder. Before beginning a custodial interrogation, one of the officers presented the defendant with a *Miranda* form. The form included the four warnings required by *Miranda v. Arizona*, 384 U.S. 436 (1966) (right to remain silent, use of statements in court, right to have lawyer present, right to have appointed lawyer if indigent), and an additional warning not required by *Miranda*: "You have the right to decide at any time before or during questioning to use your right to remain silent and your right to talk with a lawyer while you are being questioned." The officer asked the defendant to read the fifth warning aloud so that he could ensure that the defendant understood English, which he did. The officer then read the other four *Miranda* warnings aloud and asked the defendant to sign the form to demonstrate that he understood his rights. The defendant declined to sign the form. There was conflicting evidence as to whether the officer verbally confirmed that the defendant understood the rights listed on the form. The officer did not discuss a waiver of *Miranda* rights with the defendant or obtain one from him.

During the interrogation, the defendant never stated that he wanted to remain silent, that he did not want to talk with the officers, or that he wanted a lawyer. About two hours and 45 minutes into the interrogation, during which the defendant was mostly silent, an officer asked the defendant, "Do you believe in God?" The defendant said "yes." The officer asked, "Do you pray to God?" The defendant said "yes." The officer then asked, "Do you pray to God to forgive you for shooting that boy down?" The defendant said "yes" and looked away, and the interview ended shortly thereafter. At trial, the defendant moved to suppress these statements. The issue before the United States Supreme Court was the admissibility of these statements under *Miranda v. Arizona* and later *Miranda*-related cases.

The Court rejected the defendant's argument that he invoked his right to remain silent by not saying anything for a sufficient time period during the interrogation. The Court noted that it had ruled in *Davis v. United States*, 512 U.S. 452 (1994), that in the context of invoking the *Miranda* right to counsel, a defendant must do so unambiguously. If a defendant makes a statement concerning the right to counsel that is ambiguous or equivocal or makes no statement, officers are not required to end the interrogation or to ask questions as to whether the defendant wants to invoke his or her *Miranda* rights. The Court concluded that there was no principled reason to adopt different standards for determining when a defendant has invoked the *Miranda* right to remain silent and the *Miranda* right to counsel. The Court noted that the defendant did not say that he wanted to remain silent or that he did not want to talk with the officers, and therefore the Court ruled that the defendant did not invoke the right to remain silent so as to require the officers to stop their interrogation.

Michigan v. Mosley, 423 U.S. 96 (1975). A Detroit robbery detective arrested the defendant for two robberies, properly gave him the *Miranda* warnings, and properly obtained a waiver of rights. When the defendant said that he did not want to answer any questions about the robberies (he did not assert his right to counsel, however), the detective immediately stopped his questioning. About two hours later, a Detroit homicide detective sought to question the defendant about an unrelated murder. He properly gave him the *Miranda* warnings and properly obtained a waiver of rights. The defendant did not ask for a lawyer or assert his right to remain silent. He then confessed to the murder.

The Court ruled that the admissibility of statements that a defendant makes after he has exercised his right to remain silent depends on whether that right is "scrupulously honored"; the officers did so in this case. The Court noted that the robbery detective immediately stopped his questioning after the defendant said that he did not want to discuss the robberies, and he did not attempt to resume questioning or in any way attempt to persuade the defendant to reconsider his refusal to talk. After questioning had been suspended for a "significant period of time" (in this case, about two hours), the homicide detective—after giving the *Miranda* warnings and obtaining a waiver—did not question the defendant about the robberies but instead focused exclusively on a completely separate, unrelated crime.

See also State v. Temple, 302 N.C. 1 (1981); State v. Hill, 294 N.C. 320 (1978); State v. Riddick, 291 N.C. 399 (1976);

Jackson v. Wyrick, 730 F.2d 1177 (8th Cir. 1984) (court upheld officers' resumption of questioning about same crime after assertion of right to remain silent—officers waited 24 hours before resuming questioning); Kelly v. Lynaugh, 862 F.2d 1126 (5th Cir. 1988) (court upheld officer's resumption of questioning between 8:30 p.m. and 10:00 p.m. about same crime after defendant had asserted right to remain silent in two prior attempts to interrogate him, the first about 11:00 a.m. and the second about 4:00 p.m.); Jackson v. Dugger, 837 F.2d 1469 (11th Cir. 1988) (court upheld officer's resumption of questioning about same crime when a significant period of time, more than six hours, elapsed between original assertion of the right to remain silent and reinterrogation); United States v. Udey, 748 F.2d 1231 (8th Cir. 1984) (questioning about same crime six hours after defendant asserted the right to remain silent was proper); Brown v. Caspari, 186 F.3d 1011 (8th Cir. 1999) (questioning about same crime three hours after defendant asserted the right to remain silent was proper).

NORTH CAROLINA SUPREME COURT

State v. Waring, 364 N.C. 443 (2010). The court rejected the defendant's argument that by telling officers that he did not want to snitch on anyone and declining to reveal the name of his accomplice, the defendant invoked his right to remain silent, requiring that all interrogation cease.

State v. Forte, 360 N.C. 427 (2006). Officers were investigating the defendant's alleged involvement in three murders. They asked the defendant at work whether he would accompany them to the police station for an interview. He was told that he was not under arrest and that he could return to work later. The defendant was not given *Miranda* warnings. He went with the officers to the police station, where he admitted involvement with the three murders; he then went with the officers to the locations where the murders were committed. The officers and the defendant returned to the police station, where the defendant was given *Miranda* warnings and asked if he wanted to answer any more questions at that time. When the defendant answered "no," the officer asked what he meant. The defendant responded that he was tired and would answer more questions after he had had a chance to sleep. When the defendant awoke after several hours of sleep, he said that he felt like talking some more. The officers readvised the defendant of his *Miranda* rights, and the defendant affirmed his willingness to continue answering questions. The court ruled, citing *State v. Golphin*, 352 N.C. 364 (2000), that under these circumstances, the defendant's "no" response was ambiguous (that is, it was not a clear assertion of the right to remain silent), and the officer did not violate the defendant's constitutional rights by asking for amplification. The defendant had been cooperative from the beginning of his encounter with the police and had been forthcoming with his answers to the officers' questions. When the defendant unexpectedly answered "no" on being asked if he wished to answer any more questions, the officer did no more than ask him what he meant.

State v. Golphin, 352 N.C. 364 (2000). Two defendants were charged with several offenses, including the murders of two law enforcement officers. During the interrogation of the defendant about a shooting at a vehicle, the defendant said that he did not want to say anything about it and that he did not know who shot at the vehicle or he would have told the officer. The officer asked again, and the defendant stated that his codefendant shot at the vehicle.

The court noted that *Davis v. United States*, 512 U.S. 452 (1994), ruled that an officer is not required to stop interrogation when a defendant makes an ambiguous request for counsel and that the Fourth Circuit in *Burket v. Angelone*, 208 F.3d 172 (4th Cir. 2000), ruled that the same rule applies when a defendant makes an ambiguous request to remain silent. [Author's note: The later ruling in *Berghuis v. Thompkins*, 560 U.S. 370 (2010), applied *Davis* to the assertion of the right to remain silent.] The court ruled that the defendant in this case made an ambiguous request to remain silent, and the officer's continuing question did not violate the defendant's *Miranda* rights. The court stated that it was not unreasonable for the officer to believe that the defendant wanted to talk about what happened to the vehicle, because the defendant had indicated that had he known whom the incident involved, he would have made a statement about it.

State v. Murphy, 342 N.C. 813 (1996). The defendant, a murder suspect, was in custody on other charges. Officers gave him *Miranda* warnings, and he waived his rights. After the defendant talked about some other matters, the officers informed him that he was going to be charged with murder. The defendant twice denied any knowledge of the killing. When one officer indicated a willingness to stay and continue talking, the defendant stood up and said, "I got nothing to say." The officers stopped their interrogation, charged the defendant with murder,

and began the booking process. During the booking process, an officer (without readvising the defendant of his *Miranda* rights) encouraged the defendant to "tell the truth" about the murder so the "bad feeling in his stomach" would go away. The defendant responded, "Man, you know the position I'm in, I can't tell you about it." This statement was made about 15 minutes after the initial interrogation, which had ended when the defendant advised the officers that he had nothing to say.

(1) The court ruled that the defendant's conduct in abruptly standing up, combined with his unambiguous statement, "I got nothing to say," was an invocation of the right to remain silent, based on the facts in this case. (2) Relying on *Michigan v. Mosley*, 423 U.S. 96 (1975), the court ruled that a defendant's assertion of the right to remain silent permits reinterrogation (unlike the assertion of the right to counsel) if officers "scrupulously honor" the assertion—that is, the officers immediately stop questioning and do not attempt reinterrogation until a significant period of time has elapsed. (3) Distinguishing *Mosley*, the court ruled that the officer in this case did not scrupulously honor the defendant's assertion of the right to remain silent, because the officer initiated conversation with the defendant about the same subject matter 15 minutes after the assertion. (4) The court ruled that a readvisement of *Miranda* rights is not a prerequisite to reinterrogation under the Mosley ruling; it is but one factor in determining if the defendant's rights have been "scrupulously honored." The defendant's statement was ordered suppressed because of the ruling in (3) above.

State v. Walls, 342 N.C. 1 (1995). The defendant was arrested and orally informed of his *Miranda* rights, and he orally waived them. At the sheriff's department, a detective took the defendant to the fingerprinting room and asked him if he remembered his rights; the defendant said that he did. Nevertheless, the detective read him his *Miranda* rights again, provided him with a written copy, and obtained a written waiver. After being told of the crimes (two assaults) for which he was charged, the defendant denied any knowledge of them and signed a writing that he no longer wished to make a statement. The detective did not ask any questions and began to fingerprint the defendant. When the detective took his right hand, the defendant exclaimed, "Ouch, take it easy." The detective noticed that the defendant's hand was badly swollen and cut, so he asked him, "What happened to your hand?" The defendant answered, "I hit an oak tree." The detective asked, "[W]hat did you hit a tree for? A tree had never hurt anybody." The defendant replied, "I should have hit her a little harder so I could really hurt my hand." The court ruled that the defendant's remarks were volunteered statements, and the detective's questions did not convert the conversation into an interrogation under *Miranda*.

State v. Lambert, 341 N.C. 36 (1995). The defendant was in jail and requested that an officer come and speak to her. After the defendant spoke with her father, she approached the officer and told him that she had "blacked out" and could not remember anything. The court ruled that her statement was admissible under *Miranda* because (1) it was not made as a result of interrogation and (2) it was not an invocation of the right to silence— her specific request to speak to the officer and her statement indicated a desire not to remain silent.

State v. Robbins, 319 N.C. 465 (1987). The defendant's statement, "I told you everything I know," to an officer during custodial interrogation was not an invocation of his right to remain silent. Although the statement may have conveyed a message that the defendant had nothing else to tell, it could not reasonably be interpreted as indicating that he had said all he wished to say.

State v. Westmoreland, 314 N.C. 442 (1985). The mere failure of a defendant, who had consented to interrogation, to answer some questions was not sufficient, by itself, to indicate that the defendant had asserted the right to remain silent, when the defendant never explicitly asserted the right to remain silent.

State v. Fincher, 309 N.C. 1 (1983). The defendant did not invoke the right to remain silent when he stated to an officer that he would not give another written statement until his accomplice confronted him with the truth. Even if the defendant made an equivocal assertion of the right to remain silent, the officer properly clarified the defendant's intentions by inquiring whether he could ask another question.

NORTH CAROLINA COURT OF APPEALS

State v. Bordeaux, 207 N.C. App. 645 (2010). Citing *Berghuis v. Thompkins*, 560 U.S. 370 (2010), the court ruled that the defendant's silence or refusal to answer the officers' questions was not an invocation of the right to remain silent.

State v. Jacobs, 174 N.C. App. 1 (2005). [Author's note: There was a dissenting opinion in this case, but not on the issue discussed below.] The defendant was arrested for the armed robbery of James Morgan and committed to jail.

On August 6, 2002, after Officer A gave *Miranda* warnings to the defendant, the defendant asserted his right to remain silent and no interrogation was conducted about the robbery of Morgan. The defendant did not assert his right to counsel, however. On August 8, 2002, Officer B initiated interrogation about a different armed robbery case (the victims were Mr. and Mrs. Chavis), after giving *Miranda* warnings and obtaining a proper waiver. The defendant made statements that were introduced at the trial involving Mr. and Mrs. Chavis. The court ruled that the second interrogation was proper under *Michigan v. Mosley*, 423 U.S. 96 (1975), because the officers had "scrupulously honored" the defendant's assertion of his right to remain silent.

State v. Ash, 169 N.C. App. 715 (2005). The defendant was arrested for murder and other offenses. After being advised during an officer's giving of *Miranda* rights of his right to have an attorney present, the defendant asked, "Now?" The officer responded affirmatively. The defendant then asked, "Where's my lawyer at? [Inaudible] come down here?" The officer replied that the lawyer who was representing the defendant on a pending, but unrelated, breaking and entering charge had nothing to do "with what [he was] going to talk to [defendant] about." The defendant responded, "Oh, okay," and signed the waiver of rights form. The court ruled that the defendant did not clearly invoke his right to counsel under the ruling in *Davis v. United States*, 512 U.S. 452 (1994), and thus his *Miranda* rights were not violated. During the officer's interrogation, the defendant confessed that he and others had planned to commit a robbery but ended their plan when they drove by the murder victim's mobile home and observed all the interior lights illuminated there. After the officer asked the defendant whether he was "scared" when the gun "went off," the defendant stated, "I don't want to talk no more 'cause you're talking some crazy shit now." The officer continued to question the defendant, stating, "You didn't even know how many people was [sic] in the house, did you?" The defendant responded, "That's why the fuck I didn't stop," and the interrogation continued. The defendant continued to deny his involvement in the crime, but he admitted his participation after further questioning. The court ruled, relying on *State v. Golphin*, 352 N.C. 364 (2000), that the defendant did not clearly invoke his right to remain silent under *Miranda*. The court upheld the trial judge's finding that despite the defendant's statement about not talking any more, the defendant continued to talk without significant prompting by the officer.

State v. Johnson, 136 N.C. App. 683 (2000). An officer gave juvenile interrogation warnings to a 15-year-old juvenile while his mother was present. The juvenile responded affirmatively to the question of whether he understood his rights. He then responded "no" when asked if he wished to answer questions. His mother then turned to him and said, "No, we need to get this straightened out today. We'll talk with him anyway." The juvenile looked at his mother, lowered his head, and appeared to be considering what his mother had said. He then turned to the officer and nodded his head affirmatively. The officer asked the juvenile if he wished to answer questions without a lawyer present, and he answered "yes." Citing State v. Bragg, 67 N.C. App. 759 (1984), and State v. Crawford, 83 N.C. App. 135 (1986), the court ruled that by nodding affirmatively to the officer, the defendant communicated with him and thus initiated further communication. Thus, the officer properly was permitted to continue the interrogation process and the resulting confession was admissible. [Author's note: Although the result of the court's ruling is clearly correct, its citation to and reliance on the standard set out in the Bragg and Crawford rulings rests on an erroneous interpretation of federal constitutional standards. The requirement that a defendant initiate communication applies only after an assertion of the right to counsel, not an assertion of the right to remain silent.]

State v. Fortner, 93 N.C. App. 753 (1989). The defendant was arrested for murder and committed to jail. He made an incriminating statement after officers had properly given him Miranda warnings and obtained a waiver. He then told them that he did not want to answer any more questions, and the officers immediately stopped the interrogation. Several hours later, an SBI agent questioned the defendant after properly giving him Miranda warnings and obtaining a waiver. The court ruled that the SBI agent did not violate the defendant's Miranda rights, based on Michigan v. Mosley, 423 U.S. 96 (1975), and State v. Temple, 302 N.C. 1 (1981). [Author's note: The court did not discuss the prior court of appeals cases of State v. Crawford, 83 N.C. App. 135 (1987), and State v. Bragg, 67 N.C. App. 759 (1984), which had incorrectly ruled that the assertion of the right to remain silent barred further interrogation under Edwards v. Arizona, 451 U.S. 477 (1981).]

State v. Toms, 28 N.C. App. 394 (1976). The defendant's Miranda rights were violated when an officer continued interrogation for about 30 or more minutes immediately after the defendant asserted his right to remain silent. See also United States v. Barone, 968 F.2d 1378 (1st Cir. 1992) (officers violated the defendant's right to remain silent by repeatedly questioning him after he told them he did not want to talk with them until he got back to Boston).

Assertion of the Right to Counsel

(*This topic is discussed on page 579.*)

UNITED STATES SUPREME COURT

Maryland v. Shatzer, 559 U.S. 98 (2010). In 2003, a detective went to a Maryland prison to question the defendant about his alleged sexual abuse of his son, for which he then was not charged. The defendant was serving a prison sentence for a conviction of a different offense. The defendant asserted his right to counsel under Miranda, and the detective terminated the custodial interrogation. The defendant was released back to the general prison population to continue serving his sentence, and the child abuse investigation was closed. Another detective reopened the investigation in 2006 and went to another prison where the defendant was still serving his sentence. The detective gave Miranda warnings to the defendant; the defendant waived his Miranda rights and then gave a statement that was introduced at his child sexual abuse trial. The United States Supreme Court in Edwards v. Arizona, 451 U.S. 477 (1981), ruled that once a defendant has asserted his or her right to counsel at a custodial interrogation, an officer may not conduct custodial interrogation of the defendant until a lawyer is made available for the interrogation or the defendant initiates further communication with the officer. The Court in Shatzer ruled that when a break in custody lasting 14 days or more has occurred after a defendant previously asserted his right to counsel at a custodial interrogation, an officer may reinitiate custodial interrogation after giving Miranda warnings and obtaining a waiver of Miranda rights. The Court also ruled that although the defendant remained in prison after asserting his right to counsel, there was a break in custody under its ruling. The Court reasoned that when a prisoner is released after an officer's interrogation to return to the general prison population, the prisoner returns to his or her accustomed routine and regains the degree of control over his or her life that existed before the interrogation. Sentenced prisoners, in contrast to defendants being subjected to custodial interrogation under *Miranda*, are not isolated with their accusers (law enforcement officers). They live among other inmates, guards, and workers and often can receive visitors and communicate with people on the outside by mail or telephone. The "inherently compelling pressures" of custodial interrogation ended when this defendant returned to his normal life in prison. [Author's note: For a detailed analysis of the *Shatzer* ruling, see Robert L. Farb, *The United States Supreme Court's Ruling in Maryland v. Shatzer* (UNC School of Government, 2010), www.sog.unc.edu/sites/www.sog.unc.edu/files/marylandshatzer2010.pdf.]

Davis v. United States, 512 U.S. 452 (1994). Investigators gave the in-custody defendant *Miranda* warnings and received a proper waiver of his rights. About an hour and a half into the interrogation, the defendant said, "Maybe I should talk to a lawyer." The investigators told the defendant that they did not want to violate his rights, that if he wanted a lawyer then they would stop questioning him, and that they would not pursue the matter unless it was clarified whether he was asking for a lawyer or was just making a comment about a lawyer. The defendant said, "No, I'm not asking for a lawyer," and continued on, and said, "No, I don't want a lawyer." After a short break, the investigators reminded the defendant of his rights to remain silent and to counsel. The defendant then made incriminating statements that he later sought to suppress at trial, arguing that the investigators violated the ruling in *Edwards v. Arizona*, 384 U.S. 436 (1981) (officers must immediately stop interrogation if the suspect has clearly asserted the right to counsel).

The Court stated that the determination as to whether a defendant actually invoked the right to counsel is an objective one, requiring some statement that can reasonably be construed to be an expression of the desire for the assistance of counsel. The Court ruled that if a defendant makes a reference to an attorney that is ambiguous or equivocal so that a reasonable officer under the circumstances would have understood only that the defendant might be invoking the right to counsel, the officer is not required to stop the interrogation—rather, the defendant must unambiguously request counsel. The Court specifically rejected a requirement that an officer must stop interrogation immediately when a defendant makes an ambiguous or equivocal request for counsel. [Author's note: It is unclear whether the Court's ruling applies only when a defendant makes an ambiguous or equivocal

request for counsel during custodial interrogation after proper *Miranda* warnings have been given and a waiver of rights has been obtained. If a defendant makes an ambiguous or equivocal request for counsel when the officer is giving *Miranda* warnings or obtaining a waiver of rights, the officer should clarify whether or not the defendant wants a lawyer, because the State has the burden of proving that the defendant waived his or her rights, including the right to counsel.]

The Court noted that when a defendant makes an ambiguous or equivocal request for counsel, it often will be good law enforcement practice for officers to clarify whether or not the defendant wants a lawyer. Clarifying questions protect the rights of the defendant by ensuring that the defendant gets a lawyer if he or she wants one and will minimize the risk of a confession being suppressed by later judicial second-guessing of the meaning of the defendant's statement about counsel. But the Court reiterated that if the defendant's statement is not an unambiguous or unequivocal request for counsel, officers are not obligated to stop questioning the defendant.

The Court upheld the lower court ruling that the defendant's remark to the officers in this case, "Maybe I should talk to a lawyer," was not a request for counsel. Therefore, the officers were not required to stop questioning the defendant.

[Author's note: The Court's ruling now casts substantial doubt on the validity of a ruling in *State v. Torres*, 330 N.C. 517 (1992), that the defendant unequivocally invoked her right to counsel when she asked law enforcement officers whether she needed a lawyer.]

McNeil v. Wisconsin, 501 U.S. 171 (1991). The defendant was arrested for armed robbery and advised of his *Miranda* rights. He refused to answer questions, although he did not request an attorney. A public defender represented the defendant in court at a bail hearing, at which a preliminary examination was scheduled. Officers from another county investigating an unrelated murder visited the defendant in jail three times, properly gave him *Miranda* warnings, obtained a waiver each time, and obtained incriminating statements about the murder.

The Court noted that it was undisputed that when the defendant gave the incriminating statements about the murder, his Sixth Amendment right to counsel had attached and had been invoked for the robbery charge (apparently at a court hearing on that charge). However, the Court ruled that this invocation was offense-specific (that is, only for the robbery charge) and did not constitute an invocation of the right to counsel under the Fifth Amendment. Therefore, the officers did not violate the defendant's Fifth or Sixth Amendment rights to counsel by initiating interrogation about the murder, because (1) his Sixth Amendment right to counsel had not attached for the murder because he had not yet been charged with that crime, and (2) he had never asserted his right to counsel under the Fifth Amendment. The Court did not decide if the Fifth Amendment right to counsel can be properly asserted at a time other than during custodial interrogation, although it indicated in footnote 3 that it can be asserted only during custodial interrogation.

See United States v. Wright, 962 F.2d 953 (9th Cir. 1992) (defense attorney at plea hearing for in-custody defendant, who had not previously invoked counsel during custodial interrogation, told the government that she wanted to be present during interviews with the defendant; court ruled that this request was not an assertion of counsel under Fifth Amendment that barred officers from initiating custodial interrogation about unrelated crimes); United States v. Wyatt, 179 F.3d 532 (7th Cir. 1999) (defendant's assertion of right to counsel when he was not in custody was not assertion under *Miranda*, even if assertion was made in anticipation of future custodial interrogation).

Minnick v. Mississippi, 498 U.S. 146 (1990). The defendant was arrested for murder and asserted his right to counsel during interrogation by federal law enforcement officers. He then communicated with counsel two or three times. A state law enforcement officer then initiated interrogation with the defendant about the same offense, properly executed *Miranda* warnings and waiver, and obtained a statement from him. The Court ruled that under *Miranda*, when a defendant requests counsel, interrogation must stop, and officers may not reinitiate interrogation without counsel being present (assuming the defendant has remained in continuous custody)—regardless of whether the defendant has consulted with counsel. Thus, the state officer violated the defendant's *Miranda* rights by reinitiating interrogation.

Arizona v. Roberson, 486 U.S. 675 (1988). When a defendant who is in custody asserts the right to counsel under *Miranda*, the ruling of *Edwards v. Arizona*, 451 U.S. 477 (1981) (officers may not initiate interrogation until a lawyer has been provided or until defendant initiates further communication with officers), applies not only to the crime for which the defendant is being interrogated but also to interrogation about unrelated crimes. The Court also ruled that the *Edwards v. Arizona* rule applies to an interrogating officer from a different agency even if the officer does not know the defendant's assertion of the right to counsel. [Author's note: This ruling effectively reversed a contrary ruling in *State v. Dampier*, 314 N.C. 292 (1985).]

The Court stated, however, that officers are free to inform a defendant of the facts of the investigation of the unrelated crimes as long as such communication does not constitute interrogation. *See* United States v. Jackson, 189 F.3d 502 (7th Cir. 1989) (relying on this statement in *Arizona v. Roberson*, court ruled that officer did not interrogate a defendant under the standard of *Rhode Island v. Innis*, 446 U.S. 291 (1980), when he merely explained to a jailed defendant, who had asserted the right to counsel after his arrest for crime A, that he was the subject of an ongoing investigation for unrelated crime B, and the officer asked the defendant's assistance if he was willing to give it after he was released from jail; the officer also told him he had no interest in obtaining a statement from him; defendant shortly thereafter initiated communication with another officer and gave an incriminating statement about crime A).

Arizona v. Mauro, 481 U.S. 520 (1987). The defendant was arrested for the murder of his son and asserted his right to counsel after being given *Miranda* warnings. The defendant's wife insisted on seeing her husband, who was being held in a police captain's office. The officers allowed the meeting, but only on the condition that an officer could be present and the conversation could be tape recorded. The conversation between the defendant and his wife was later admitted at the defendant's trial. The Court ruled that the officer did not engage in "interrogation" as defined in *Rhode Island v. Innis*, 446 U.S. 291 (1980). The Court stated, "Officers do not interrogate a suspect simply by hoping that he will incriminate himself."

Connecticut v. Barrett, 479 U.S. 523 (1987). The defendant was properly given his *Miranda* warnings and waived his rights. He said that he would not give a written statement without the presence of counsel, but he was willing to talk about the alleged crime. He then orally confessed. The Court ruled that the defendant's invocation of his right to counsel was limited only to making written statements and did not prohibit further oral discussion with officers. *See also* Bruni v. Lewis, 847 F.2d 561 (9th Cir. 1988) (in response to officer's request to answer questions, defendant replied, "Not without my attorney," and then immediately waived that right by adding, "Well, ask your questions and I will answer those I see fit."); United States v. Ivy, 929 F.2d 147 (5th Cir. 1991) (defendant's response, "I'll tell you, let me talk to my lawyer before I answer that," to officer's question, "Who can you get dynamite from?" was not general assertion of right to counsel, and officer honored request and moved to a different subject).

Moran v. Burbine, 475 U.S. 412 (1986). The defendant validly waived his *Miranda* rights, even though officers did not inform him of his attorney's efforts to contact him (in this case, the defendant's Sixth Amendment right to counsel had not attached when his attorney was trying to contact him). The attorney's effort to contact him, unknown by the defendant, did not affect the defendant's capacity to waive his *Miranda* rights. The Court also ruled that the officers' conduct was not so outrageous as to constitute a due process violation. *See also* Blair v. Armontrout, 916 F.2d 1310 (8th Cir. 1990) (defendant charged with murder made two detailed oral confessions and then agreed to make a videotaped confession; he was informed that he could have an attorney present, but he repeatedly stated that he did not want an attorney; an assistant public defender, who represented the defendant on an unrelated charge but did not and could not represent him on the murder charge, saw the defendant in a hallway and demanded to speak to the defendant but was refused by officers; the court ruled that there was no *Miranda* violation).

Smith v. Illinois, 469 U.S. 91 (1984). When a defendant makes a clear request for counsel under *Edwards v. Arizona*, questioning must cease, and the defendant's responses to further interrogation conducted after he or she makes a clear request may not be used to cast doubt on the initial request for counsel. The Court ruled that in this case the defendant's statement, "Uh, yeah, I'd like to do that," after being told of his right to counsel was a clear request for counsel, particularly since he earlier had mentioned to the officers that a woman had told him to get his lawyer because the officers would railroad him.

Oregon v. Bradshaw, 462 U.S. 1039 (1983). After being arrested and given his *Miranda* rights, the defendant talked with an officer for a while but then stated, "I do want an attorney before it goes very much further." The officer immediately stopped his questioning. Sometime before or during the trip to the county jail, the defendant asked an officer, "Well, what is going to happen to me

now?" The officer reminded the defendant that he did not have to talk with the officer because he had requested an attorney and said that he did not want the defendant talking to him unless the defendant wanted to. In the discussion that followed, the officer suggested a polygraph examination, and the defendant agreed to take one. The next day, after being given *Miranda* warnings, the defendant took a polygraph examination and eventually gave an incriminating statement.

The Court ruled that a two-part test applies when determining the admissibility of statements made after a defendant asserts a right to counsel. [Author's note: Although it is a four-Justice plurality opinion, the ruling clearly states the prevailing law.] First, did the defendant initiate further conversation? In this case, the Court ruled that his statement showed a willingness to discuss the investigation; it was not simply a question about the custodial relationship, such as a request for water or to use a telephone. Second, did the defendant validly waive his right to counsel, which he had previously asserted? The Court ruled that the State in this case had satisfied its burden of showing that the defendant had done so.

Wyrick v. Fields, 459 U.S. 42 (1983). The Court ruled that, considering all the circumstances, the defendant's Fifth Amendment right to counsel under *Edwards v. Arizona* was properly waived before officers interrogated him after he had taken a polygraph examination. The Court did not decide whether the defendant's Sixth Amendment rights were violated. *But see* State v. Stephens, 300 N.C. 321 (1980) (defendant was tricked into waiving his right to counsel and privilege against self-incrimination when polygraph operator interrogated him after test phase was completed, without giving him opportunity—contrary to understanding between operator, defendant, and his lawyer—to consult with his lawyer, who was outside room; because defendant was not in custody, this case appears to be based on Sixth Amendment violation rather than *Miranda* right to counsel under Fifth Amendment).

Edwards v. Arizona, 451 U.S. 477 (1981). The defendant was arrested for murder, robbery, and burglary and was taken to a police station. He was properly given his *Miranda* warnings, properly waived his rights, and began to answer questions. However, he later told the officers, "I want an attorney before making a deal." Questioning then stopped, and the defendant was taken to the county jail. The next morning, two detectives, neither of whom had interrogated the defendant the night before, came to the jail to question him. When the jailer told the defendant that the detectives wanted to speak with him, he said that he did not want to talk with anyone. The jailer told him that he "had" to talk and then took him to meet with the detectives. After being given his *Miranda* rights, the defendant agreed to talk and confessed to the crimes.

The Court ruled that once a defendant has asserted his right to counsel, officers may not question the defendant until a lawyer is made available or the "[defendant] himself initiates further communication, exchanges, or conversations" with an officer. The State may not show a valid waiver of the right to counsel, after the defendant has asserted that right, by merely establishing that the defendant waived that right later after being given another set of *Miranda* warnings. The Court further ruled that in this case the defendant's rights were violated when the officers returned the following day to interrogate him. The Court noted that if the defendant had initiated the meeting, he could have properly waived his right to counsel, which he had asserted the day before. [Author's note: The *Edwards* ruling was modified in part in *Maryland v. Shatzer*, 559 U.S. 98 (2010).]

Fare v. Michael C., 442 U.S. 707 (1979). Under the facts of this case, the juvenile's request to speak with his probation officer was neither a request for counsel nor a request to remain silent under *Miranda v. Arizona*, and all the circumstances showed that he voluntarily and knowingly waived his rights and consented to interrogation.

NORTH CAROLINA SUPREME COURT

State v. Boggess, 358 N.C. 676 (2004). During custodial interrogation about a murder, one of the officers told the defendant that he was a "lying piece of shit." The defendant responded, "I'm not lying. I'm telling you the truth. If y'all going to treat me this way, then I probably would want a lawyer." The court ruled that the defendant's statement was not a clear request for counsel under *Davis v. United States*, 512 U.S. 452 (1994), to require the officers to stop interrogation. The court stated that the defendant's words reflected that he understood perfectly well his right to an attorney and was threatening to exercise it unless the officers improved their behavior.

State v. Hyatt, 355 N.C. 642 (2002). The court ruled, relying on *Fare v. Michael C.*, 442 U.S. 707 (1979), and *Davis v. United States*, 512 U.S. 452 (1994), that the defendant's statements during interrogation that his father wanted him to have an attorney present and the defendant's request to speak to his father did not constitute unambiguous requests for counsel.

State v. Warren, 348 N.C. 80 (1998). [Author's note: This case involved the trial and conviction of the defendant for a murder committed in High Point.] On May 29, 1990, the defendant requested counsel during custodial interrogation by an Asheville detective, who was questioning him about a murder committed in Asheville. When the interrogation concluded, the defendant was arrested on an outstanding warrant for a motor vehicle violation and for misdemeanor larceny of the Asheville murder victim's pocketbook. He was not, however, arrested or charged for the Asheville murder. He was represented by an attorney in Asheville district court for these charges and released on bond on June 7, 1990. The defendant was later arrested in High Point on July 20, 1990, for a South Carolina murder. He was properly given *Miranda* warnings and confessed to murders in South Carolina, New York, Asheville, and High Point.

The court rejected the defendant's argument that the interrogation about the High Point murder violated his Fifth Amendment right to counsel. The court ruled, relying on a statement in *McNeil v. Wisconsin*, 501 U.S. 171 (1991), that the rule prohibiting reinitiation of interrogation after a defendant's assertion of the right to counsel during custodial interrogation does not apply when there has been a break in custody (here, the defendant was released from custody on June 7, 1990, and was not arrested again until July 20, 1990).

The court rejected the defendant's argument that the interrogation violated his Sixth Amendment right to counsel on grounds that the Sixth Amendment right to counsel is offense-specific and adversary judicial proceedings had not begun for the High Point murder at the time of the interrogation. The court also rejected the defendant's argument that, despite the offense-specific requirement, his Sixth Amendment right to counsel had begun for the Asheville charges and they were inextricably intertwined with the High Point murder. [Author's note: The later ruling in *Texas v. Cobb*, 532 U.S. 167 (2001), discussed below, would also reject the defendant's argument.]

State v. Jackson, 348 N.C. 52 (1998). Two detectives went to the defendant's workplace and, after telling him he was not under arrest, requested that he accompany them to the sheriff's office to answer some questions. The defendant agreed. He was told at the sheriff's office that he was a suspect in the murder of Karen Styles. He denied involvement. He was given *Miranda* rights and was again told that he was not under arrest. The defendant consented to a search of his person and to the taking of fingerprints and blood and hair samples. He was again told that he was not under arrest. After the defendant had been questioned for about three hours, the sheriff entered the interrogation room and asked the defendant, "What did you do with the rifle that Karen Styles was shot with?" The defendant replied, "I think I need a lawyer present." (A detective's handwritten notes, taken during the interview, read, "2:04 p.m. on 12-20-94, wants a lawyer present.") In response to the defendant's statement, the sheriff told the defendant that he did not want the defendant to answer any more questions, but he wanted to tell him something. The sheriff then stated, "Son, I know you bought the rifle and the duct tape at K-Mart on the 28th of October. I know you were in Bent Creek on the day she was killed, and that's fine, but you need help." The defendant then began crying and stated, "But I didn't mean to kill nobody. I didn't." He continued crying and said, "I'm sorry; I didn't mean to kill her."

The court ruled that the defendant was in custody under *Miranda* when he inquired about an attorney. The court stated that a reasonable person in the defendant's position who had been interrogated for about three hours and thought the sheriff believed that he had committed murder would have believed that the sheriff intended to hold him to be prosecuted for murder. [Author's note: The North Carolina Supreme Court, in the later case of *State v. Buchanan*, 353 N.C. 332 (2001), expressly disavowed the "free to leave" test used in this case to determine custody under *Miranda*. Thus, it is unclear whether the court would now reach a different result on the custody issue.]

The court ruled, distinguishing *Davis v. United States*, 512 U.S. 452 (1994) (defendant's statement during custodial interrogation, "Maybe I should talk to a lawyer," was not an assertion of the right to counsel), that the defendant in this case asserted the right to counsel. The court stated that the "use of the word '[m]aybe' by the defendant in *Davis* connotes uncertainty. There was no uncertainty by the defendant. When he said, 'I think I need a lawyer present,' he told the officers what he thought. He thought he needed a lawyer. This was not an ambiguous statement. The interrogation should have stopped at that time." The court also stated that the detective's handwritten notes (see above), although not binding on the court, were an indication of how a reasonable officer conducting an interrogation would have interpreted the defendant's statement. The court ruled that the defendant's statements should have been suppressed because they resulted from interrogation that was conducted after he asserted the right to counsel. *Compare with* Burket v. Angelone, 208 F.3d 172 (4th Cir. 2000) (defendant's statement, "I think I need a lawyer," was not clear assertion of right to counsel); Mueller v. Angelone, 181 F.3d 557 (4th Cir. 1999) (about two hours into interrogation, defendant's question, "Do you think I need an attorney here?" was not unequivocal request for counsel).

State v. Coffey, 345 N.C. 389 (1997). The defendant was arrested for murder, and two attorneys were appointed to represent him. The attorneys requested that the district attorney have a polygraph examination conducted on the defendant but did not express any desire to accompany their client to the polygraph site. When the defendant was being removed from his cell for the polygraph examination, he told a deputy sheriff that he wanted to call his attorney. The deputy declined to allow the defendant to do so, because the policy of the sheriff's office did not permit a prisoner to make a telephone call while being transported from one facility to another. Later, when the polygraph operator was explaining the polygraph procedures to the defendant, the defendant stated that he did not tell the investigating officers the truth about the money taken from the murder victim. The operator asked him what he did not tell the truth about. The defendant said that he was handed the money by his accomplice and the accomplice "went off." The operator did not ask any further questions; instead, he conducted the polygraph examination. After the examination, the operator informed the defendant that he had not passed the polygraph about the murder and robbery. The defendant then made an incriminating statement. The operator asked the defendant if he would be willing to talk to one of the investigating officers. The defendant named a particular officer and later repeated the same incriminating statement to that officer.

The court ruled that the defendant was not being interrogated in violation of *Edwards v. Arizona*, 451 U.S. 477 (1981) (interrogation is not permitted after defendant has asserted right to counsel), when he made his statements to the polygraph operator and the investigating officer. These statements were volunteered by the defendant. Thus, neither his Fifth nor Sixth Amendment rights to counsel were violated. The court alternatively ruled, assuming that the defendant was being interrogated, that the defendant initiated the communication with the polygraph operator and investigating officer. *See, e.g.,* Oregon v. Bradshaw, 462 U.S. 1039 (1983).

State v. Munsey, 342 N.C. 882 (1996). After the defendant had been arrested and given *Miranda* rights, he told officers that he would like to have a lawyer. At the defendant's request, an officer called a particular lawyer but was unable to reach him. The defendant then asked the officer to call his brother and said "that would do instead of" the lawyer. In response to an officer's telephone call, the defendant's brother came to the law enforcement office where the defendant was located and conferred in private with him for about 15 to 20 minutes. After the defendant's brother left, the officers went into the office and asked the defendant if he was ready to talk to them now. The defendant answered affirmatively. The officers then questioned the defendant and obtained a statement. The court ruled that this evidence showed that the defendant did not initiate the conversation with officers after his brother left, and therefore the officers' questioning violated the ruling in *Edwards v. Arizona,* 451 U.S. 477 (1981).

State v. Gibson, 342 N.C. 142 (1995). Officers who were investigating a homicide properly gave a 15-year-old his juvenile custodial interrogation rights under G.S. 7A-595(a) (now, G.S. 7B-2101(a)) and obtained a waiver of those rights. The juvenile argued on appeal that his waiver of rights was involuntary as a matter of law because the officers did not inform the juvenile that his parents and attorney were at the police station at the time of the interrogation. The court, relying on *Moran v. Burbine*, 475 U.S. 412 (1986), and *State v. Reese*, 319 N.C. 110 (1987), rejected the defendant's argument. The court stated that law enforcement officers are not required to inform a juvenile that his parents or attorney are present before taking a voluntary confession, and the failure to do so does not make the juvenile's confession involuntary as a matter of law or otherwise inadmissible. [Author's note: This ruling would not apply to a juvenile under 14, because a juvenile's parent, guardian, custodian, or attorney must be present during custodial interrogation.]

State v. Daughtry, 340 N.C. 488 (1995). The defendant voluntarily went with two officers to the police station to be questioned about a murder. The officers advised the defendant that he was not under arrest and could leave at any time. One officer advised the defendant of his *Miranda* rights as a precaution. The defendant waived those rights. After some conversation between the officers and the defendant, the defendant said, "I think I need to speak to a lawyer." One officer handed the defendant the telephone directory opened to the yellow pages with attorney listings. As he did so, the officer told the defendant that he could talk to a lawyer and continue to talk to the officers if he wished. The defendant briefly looked at the yellow pages and then told the officers that he was willing to talk to them. One officer reminded the defendant of his right to remain silent and his right to an attorney; the defendant indicated that he understood his rights. The defendant had not been placed under arrest. He then confessed.

The court ruled that because the defendant was not in custody when he requested an attorney, his rights under *Miranda* and *Edwards v. Arizona*, 451 U.S. 477 (1981), were inapplicable. Therefore, the court did not need to decide whether the trial judge had erred in concluding that the defendant had voluntarily reinitiated interrogation after requesting an attorney. *See also* Burket v. Angelone, 208 F.3d 172 (4th Cir. 2000) (defendant's assertion in police station, "I'm gonna need a lawyer," when he was there voluntarily, was not an assertion of counsel under *Miranda* because he was not in custody when he made that statement).

State v. Harris, 338 N.C. 129 (1994). North Carolina law enforcement officers went to Georgia to return the defendant to North Carolina for a first-degree murder charge pending in North Carolina. After properly being advised of his *Miranda* rights, the defendant asserted his right to counsel. No interrogation was conducted. After his return to North Carolina 12 hours later, the defendant—through his brother (who was visiting the defendant in jail)—asked to talk to the sheriff.

The court ruled as follows: (1) The defendant initiated communication with the sheriff by telling his brother to inform the sheriff that he wanted to speak with him. (2) The sheriff was not required to give *Miranda* warnings again before interrogating the defendant, based on the facts in this case; *see generally* State v. McZorn, 288 N.C. 417 (1975). The court stated that there was no reason to believe that the defendant, having been properly advised of his *Miranda* rights 12 hours earlier, had forgotten them. For example, he should have known of his right to an attorney, because he had exercised that right 12 hours earlier.

State v. Barber, 335 N.C. 120 (1993). A fire occurred at a home in which the 15-year-old defendant and her grandparents lived. Both grandparents died as a result of the fire. The court, assuming without deciding that the defendant was in custody when she was given *Miranda* and juvenile warnings in the sheriff's office hours after the fire, ruled—distinguishing *State v. Torres*, 330 N.C. 517 (1992)—that the defendant did not assert her Fifth Amendment right to counsel when she asked an officer during his recitation of the warnings if she needed a lawyer. Her inquiry constituted an ambiguous or equivocal invocation of her right to counsel. The officer's response—that he could not advise her whether she needed a lawyer or not, but he was merely advising her about her right to a lawyer—was a proper narrow response to clarify her intent. Immediately thereafter, her specific affirmative waiver of her rights (including whether she wished to answer questions without a lawyer, parents, guardian, or custodian present) demonstrated that she had not invoked her right to counsel when she asked the officer if she needed a lawyer.

State v. Gibbs, 335 N.C. 1 (1993). On May 31, 1990, the defendant was in custody at a police department as a murder suspect. He had not yet been given *Miranda* warnings or interrogated. About 15 minutes before being taken to the magistrate's office for service of arrest warrants charging him with murder and other offenses, the defendant asked Officer Batchelor if he had to get an attorney (defendant's inquiry was not in response to questions by the officer). Batchelor told the defendant that the question of a lawyer had to be his decision and asked the defendant if he could afford to hire an attorney. The defendant said that he could not, and Batchelor then told him that the court would appoint an attorney to represent him if he asked for one. About an hour later, Batchelor and another officer gave the defendant *Miranda* warnings, properly obtained a waiver, and took a statement from the defendant. The officers obtained another statement from the defendant on June 3, 1990. The defendant had a first appearance in district court on June 4, 1990, which was within 96 hours of his arrest on May 31, 1990.

Distinguishing *State v. Torres*, 330 N.C. 517 (1992), the court ruled that the defendant did not assert his Fifth Amendment right to counsel when he asked Officer Batchelor if he had to get an attorney. Unlike in *Torres*, in this case interrogation was not impending and the defendant had not been told that he would be questioned. Batchelor's responses to the defendant's question about an attorney constituted narrow clarification, and the defendant did not ask for an attorney afterward. Moreover, Batchelor did not attempt to dissuade the defendant from exercising his right to an attorney. Based on the entire context in which the defendant's inquiry was made, the defendant did not assert his right to counsel.

State v. Medlin, 333 N.C. 280 (1993). Atlantic Beach officers arrested the defendant in a breezeway outside a motel room in Atlantic Beach for a murder and robbery committed in Wake County, based on a mistaken belief that an arrest warrant had been issued in Wake County for these offenses. The court determined, however, that the Atlantic Beach officers had sufficient information to establish probable cause to arrest, based on the facts in this case. Therefore, the warrantless arrest was proper. When the Atlantic Beach officers learned, after they had brought the defendant to the police station, that there were no arrest warrants for him, they told him that he was not under arrest and was free to leave. They also told him that investigators were coming from Wake County and wanted to talk to him, that he could stay and move around the police station at will, and that he should let them know if he needed anything. The defendant indicated that he wanted to stay and in fact remained there and later gave statements to the officers. Based on these and other facts, the court concluded that the defendant was no longer in custody, and therefore he was not entitled to *Miranda* rights, including the right to counsel under *Edwards v. Arizona,* 451 U.S. 477 (1981). Therefore, the court ruled that it was unnecessary to decide whether the defendant properly waived his right to counsel.

State v. Pope, 333 N.C. 106 (1992). The defendant invoked his right to counsel on two occasions: (1) on September 17, 1987, when he told a detective that he did not want to answer any questions then but that he might be willing to make a statement after he talked with a lawyer; and (2) on October 2, 1987, when he told a detective that he did not want to talk until he conferred with an attorney. The court ruled that, based on the facts in this case, the detectives later improperly initiated interrogation about unrelated crimes (the defendant had remained in continuous custody after his assertions for counsel) in violation of the ruling in *Arizona v. Roberson,* 486 U.S. 675 (1988).

State v. Morris, 332 N.C. 600 (1992). An officer advised an in-custody defendant of his *Miranda* rights and asked him if he would like to waive his right to counsel. The defendant responded, "I don't know." The officer then asked him if he would sign a waiver-of-counsel form. The defendant responded, "No, because I don't know how much I want to tell you." The court ruled that the defendant invoked his right to counsel when he refused to sign the waiver form.

State v. Tucker, 331 N.C. 12 (1992). The defendant was indicted for murder on April 18, 1988. On April 20, 1988, the defendant made his first appearance in district court, and a lawyer was appointed to represent him. Later that day the defendant met with his lawyer, who told him not to talk with anyone without counsel. On April 21, 1988, the investigating officer met with the defendant (not at the defendant's initiative) in the county jail and stated that he wanted the defendant to go with him to another county to look for the murder victim's body. The defendant told the officer what his lawyer had said. The defendant also tried twice unsuccessfully to call his lawyer. The officer told the defendant that they needed to hurry and commented that he was after the defendant's accomplice, not necessarily the defendant. The officer later obtained incriminating statements from the defendant, which were introduced at his murder trial. The court ruled that the officer violated the defendant's Fifth and Sixth Amendment rights to counsel.

State v. Torres, 330 N.C. 517 (1992). The defendant shot and killed her husband in their home in the early evening. Deputy sheriffs arrived to investigate the shooting. A deputy sheriff transported the defendant and her close friend to the sheriff's department. From 7:00 p.m. to 10:00 p.m., she was in the department's conference room with that deputy sheriff—and during that time she was informed that her husband had died. Sometime during that period, the sheriff entered the room. The defendant asked him whether she needed a lawyer and was told that she did not need a lawyer right now. About 10:00 p.m., the defendant was taken to the sheriff's office, where she was told that she would be interviewed by two other officers. Although she was never informed that she was under arrest, she also was never told that she was free to leave.

(1) The court ruled that a reasonable person in the defendant's position—knowing that she had just shot her spouse and having been brought to the sheriff's department by a deputy, kept under constant supervision there, and never informed that she was free to leave—would feel compelled to stay and was therefore in custody under *Miranda*.

(2) The court rejected the State's argument that the defendant could not have invoked her right to counsel because she was not being questioned when she asked about a lawyer. The court ruled that a defendant in custody may assert her right to have counsel present during her impending interrogation before *Miranda* warnings are given and interrogation begins. [Author's note: The

court distinguished contrary dicta in *McNeil v. Wisconsin*, 501 U.S. 171 (1991), by noting that the United States Supreme Court suggested that a defendant cannot anticipatorily invoke *Miranda* rights when not in custody. However, the court incorrectly described the dicta, because the dicta gave an example—arraignment in court—that clearly can occur when someone is in custody and attempting to invoke *Miranda* rights anticipatorily.]

(3) The court rejected the State's argument that a defendant's invocation of the right to counsel must be precise and unequivocal. The court stated that the crucial determination is whether the defendant has indicated in any manner a desire to have the assistance of a lawyer during custodial interrogation; thus, a court must examine not only the defendant's spoken words but also the context in which they are spoken. The court ruled, based on facts of this case, that the defendant indicated, at least once, a desire to have an attorney during interrogation. Even if the defendant's statements are construed to be an equivocal request for counsel (in which case officers must immediately stop interrogation, except for questions narrowly designed to clarify the defendant's actual intent), the result—suppression of the confession—remains the same, because the officers did not seek to clarify the defendant's intent. Instead, they dissuaded the defendant from exercising her right to have a lawyer present during custodial interrogation. The court concluded that the defendant invoked her right to counsel, and the later officer-initiated custodial interrogation violated her *Miranda* rights. Therefore, her statements were inadmissible as substantive evidence at trial.

[Author's note: The court's ruling and analysis discussed in (3), above, now appear to be inconsistent with the later ruling in *Davis v. United States*, 512 U.S. 452 (1994). See the discussion in *State v. Little*, 203 N.C. App. 684 (2010).] *See also* United States v. Kelsey, 951 F.2d 1196 (10th Cir. 1991) (after being arrested in his home for drug charges, defendant asked to see his lawyer three or four times; officers told him that they could not question him further if they allowed him to see his lawyer; they later give him *Miranda* warnings; court ruled that defendant's request for counsel came within *Edwards v. Arizona*); Tukes v. Dugger, 911 F.2d 508 (11th Cir. 1990) (court stated in dicta that if defendant was given *Miranda* warnings when not in custody and invoked his right to counsel, officers would not be free to ignore defendant's invocation). *But see* United States v. Lennick, 917 F.2d 974 (7th Cir. 1990) (officer's conversation in courthouse hallway occurred while the defendant was not in custody; officer therefore did not have to stop conversation when defendant said he had a lawyer who wanted to be present at any questioning).

State v. McQueen, 324 N.C. 118 (1989). (1) The defendant, after being arrested in a river gorge and given *Miranda* warnings, asserted his right to counsel. As they were leaving the gorge, a highway patrolman stated, "I guess you're tired and hungry." The court ruled that this statement and subsequent conversations between them in the river gorge were not interrogation, just "generalized questions," and therefore did not violate the defendant's *Miranda* rights. (2) Later, SBI agents at a law enforcement facility, without knowing that the defendant had asserted his right to counsel in the river gorge, gave the defendant *Miranda* warnings and began interrogation. Eventually the defendant, after asserting his right to counsel to the agents but then later initiating a conversation with them, made incriminating statements. The court ruled that the SBI agents' actions did not violate *Arizona v. Roberson* and *Edwards v. Arizona*, discussed above. [Author's note: It is unclear whether this ruling is consistent with those United States Supreme Court decisions, because the SBI agents at the law enforcement facility initiated questioning after the defendant had asserted his right to counsel in the river gorge. The ruling in *Oregon v. Bradshaw*, discussed above, might justify the agents' actions, but the court did not discuss that ruling and its applicability to the defendant's conversations with the highway patrolman in the river gorge.]

State v. Allen, 323 N.C. 208 (1988). When a defendant who was in custody asserted his right to counsel, officers stopped interrogating him. One officer told the defendant that all he wanted was the truth, that the defendant would be returned to his jail cell, and that there would be no further interviews with him. He informed the defendant that if he wished to have a further conversation, he should call an officer. Another officer told the defendant the name of the specific officer he should contact if he decided to call an officer. The defendant then said, "Okay," and added, "I want to talk to you now, man." The court ruled that the officers' statements after the defendant's assertion of the right to counsel did not violate *Edwards v. Arizona*, because they were not interrogation.

State v. Nations, 319 N.C. 318; 319 N.C. 329 (1987). The defendant was arrested for a sex offense with a child, placed in jail, and given *Miranda* warnings. He asserted his right to counsel and interrogation stopped. The defen-

dant was provided a first appearance in district court and counsel was appointed. About a week later, the defendant told a volunteer jailer that he wanted to speak with someone from mental health services. The protective services supervisor of the social services department was visiting in the jail and spoke with the defendant, who confessed to him. The defendant told the supervisor that he would be willing to talk with an officer. An officer arrived and gave him *Miranda* warnings and obtained a waiver. The defendant also confessed to the officer. The court ruled that the social services worker was not an agent of any law enforcement officer, the defendant initiated both contacts and volunteered his confession, and therefore no interrogation took place. Neither his Fifth nor Sixth Amendment rights were violated.

State v. Reese, 319 N.C. 110 (1987). The defendant was arrested for murder, he asserted his right to counsel during custodial interrogation, and interrogation stopped. He was appointed counsel at his first appearance in district court. The defendant's lawyer instructed officers not to question his client. However, in his lawyer's absence, the defendant sought out an officer to make a statement. The officer reminded the defendant that he had appointed counsel, truthfully told him that his lawyer was unavailable because he was out of town, and asked the defendant if he still wanted to talk with him. The defendant stated that he still wanted to make a statement. He then voluntarily, knowingly, and intelligently waived his Fifth and Sixth Amendment rights to counsel before he gave a statement; the officer specifically reminded him that he had appointed counsel.

The court ruled that the defendant's waiver was valid despite the fact that the officer did not inform the defendant of his lawyer's instruction to the officers; his lawyer's instruction was irrelevant in determining the validity of the defendant's waiver of counsel. The Fifth and Sixth Amendment right to counsel belongs to the defendant; a defendant's attorney cannot control the defendant's own exercise of constitutional rights. To the extent that *State v. Bauguss*, 310 N.C. 259 (1984), indicated that a lawyer can control access to his client under these circumstances, it is overruled. *See also* State v. Hyatt, 355 N.C. 642 (2002) (similar ruling).

State v. Jenkins, 311 N.C. 194 (1984). After receiving proper *Miranda* warnings and waiving his rights, the defendant asserted his right to counsel and questioning stopped. As he was entering the booking area, the defendant asked an officer—for whom he had been acting as an informant—to come see him the next morning in jail. When the officer arrived there the following day, he asked the jailer to check whether the defendant still wanted to see him; the defendant did. The officer gave the defendant his *Miranda* warnings and obtained a waiver. The defendant then confessed.

The court ruled that the officer's conduct was proper under the rulings of *Edwards v. Arizona* and *Oregon v. Bradshaw. See also* State v. Williams, 314 N.C. 337 (1985) (delivery of inventory form to defendant after he asserted right to counsel was not initiation of conversation); State v. Thomas, 310 N.C. 369 (1984) (officer's statement to defendant after he asserted his right to counsel, "Be sure to tell your attorney that you had the opportunity to help yourself and didn't," was not interrogation in violation of *Edwards v. Arizona*); State v. Lang, 309 N.C. 512 (1983) (court set out trial judge's duty to make findings resolving material conflicts about who initiated conversation after defendant asserted right to counsel and whether defendant waived his right to counsel and right to silence under all the circumstances).

State v. Bauguss, 310 N.C. 259 (1984). The defendant's lawyer could not control an officer's access to the defendant so that the officer could question him on charges unrelated to the charges for which the lawyer represented him. Thus, the lawyer could not assert the defendant's right to counsel under *Edwards v. Arizona*. In this case, the defendant himself validly waived his *Miranda* rights (his Sixth Amendment right to counsel had not attached yet) and agreed to talk with the officers.

State v. Franklin, 308 N.C. 682 (1983). The defendant invoked his right to counsel under *Edwards v. Arizona* for one murder but had not yet invoked his right to counsel for an unrelated murder. While the defendant was in jail for a third set of unrelated charges, an officer wanted to renew questioning for the murder for which the defendant had invoked his right to counsel—although the officer did not know that the defendant had done so. Before the officer questioned him about any case, the defendant began to discuss and then confessed to the murder for which he had not invoked his right to counsel. The court stated that it need not decide whether the officer could have initiated questioning about either murder, because the defendant gave an unsolicited confession about a murder that the officer had not intended to question him about, and therefore there was no *Edwards v. Arizona* violation.

NORTH CAROLINA COURT OF APPEALS

State v. Taylor, ___ N.C. App. ___, 784 S.E.2d 224 (2016). The court ruled that the defendant, a 19-year-old, never invoked his right to counsel in a custodial interrogation. It summarized the relevant facts as follows:

> [D]uring the police interview, after defendant asked to speak to his grandmother, Detective Morse called defendant's grandmother from his phone and then handed his phone to defendant. While on the phone, defendant told his grandmother that he called her to "let [her] know that [he] was alright." From defendant's responses on the phone, it appears that his grandmother asked him if the police had informed him of his right to speak to an attorney. Defendant responded, "An attorney? No, not yet. They didn't give me a chance yet." Defendant then responds, "Alright," as if he is listening to his grandmother's advice. Defendant then looked up at Detective Morse and asked, "Can I speak to an attorney?" Detective Morse responded: "You can call one, absolutely." Defendant then relayed Detective Morse's answer to his grandmother: "Yeah, they said I could call one." Defendant then told his grandmother that the police had not yet made any charges against him, listened to his grandmother for several more seconds, and then hung up the phone.

After the defendant refused to sign a *Miranda* waiver form, explaining that his grandmother told him not to sign anything, Morse asked, "Are you willing to talk to me today?" The defendant responded, "I will. But [my grandmother] said—um—that I need an attorney or a lawyer present." Morse responded, "Okay. Well you're nineteen. You're an adult. Um—that's really your decision whether or not you want to talk to me and kind-of clear your name or—" The defendant then interrupted, "But I didn't do anything, so I'm willing to talk to you." The defendant then orally waived his *Miranda* rights. The defendant's question, "Can I speak to an attorney?"—made during his phone conversation with his grandmother—"is ambiguous whether defendant was conveying his own desire to receive the assistance of counsel or whether he was merely relaying a question from his grandmother." The defendant's later statement—"But [my grandmother] said—um—that I need an attorney or a lawyer present"— "is also not an invocation since it does not unambiguously convey *defendant's* desire to receive the assistance of counsel." (quotation omitted). The court went on to note: "A few minutes later, after Detective Morse advised defendant of his *Miranda* rights, he properly clarified that the decision to invoke the right to counsel was defendant's decision, not his grandmother's."

State v. Quick, 226 N.C. App. 541 (2013). The court rejected the State's argument that the defendant initiated contact with the police following his initial request for counsel and thus waived his right to counsel. After the defendant asserted his right to counsel, the police returned him to the interrogation room and again asked if he wanted counsel; he said yes. Then, on the way from the interrogation room back to the jail, a detective told the defendant that an attorney would not be able to help him and that he would be served with warrants regardless of whether an attorney was there. The police knew or should have known that telling the defendant that an attorney could not help him with the warrants would be reasonably likely to elicit an incriminating response. It was only after this statement by police that the defendant agreed to talk. Therefore, the court concluded, the defendant did not initiate the communication. The court also concluded that even if the defendant had initiated communication with police, his waiver was not knowing and intelligent. The trial court had found that the prosecution failed to meet its burden of showing that the defendant made a knowing and intelligent waiver, relying on the facts that the defendant was 18 years old and had limited experience with the criminal justice system. There was a period of time between 12:39 and 12:54 p.m. on the day the defendant was questioned when there was no evidence as to what occurred and no audio or video recording of the interview. The court found that the defendant's age and inexperience, when combined with the circumstances of his interrogation, supported the trial court's conclusion that the State failed to prove the defendant's waiver was knowing and intelligent.

State v. Cureton, 223 N.C. App. 274, 286 (2012). The court ruled that the defendant did not unambiguously ask to speak to a lawyer. The court rejected the defendant's argument that he made a clear request for counsel, concluding as follows: "Defendant never expressed a clear desire to speak with an attorney. Rather, he appears to have been seeking clarification regarding whether he had a right to speak with an attorney before answering any of the detective's questions." The court added: "There is a distinct difference between inquiring whether one

has the right to counsel and actually requesting counsel. Once defendant was informed that it was his decision whether to invoke the right to counsel, he opted not to exercise that right."

State v. Moses, 205 N.C. App. 629 (2010). The court ruled that the trial court did not err by denying the defendant's motion to suppress when, although the defendant initially invoked his *Miranda* right to counsel during a custodial interrogation, he later reinitiated conversation with the officer. The defendant was not under the influence of impairing substances, no promises or threats were made to him, and the defendant was again fully advised of and waived his *Miranda* rights before he made the statement at issue.

State v. Little, 203 N.C. App. 684 (2010). The defendant was convicted of first-degree murder. He voluntarily drove to the police station about six hours after the shooting. There was no warrant for the defendant's arrest, and the police had not attempted to contact him or request his presence for an interview. A detective who knew the defendant met him in the public lobby and invited him into a secure area that required a passkey for entry, but anyone could leave the secure area without a key. The detective patted him down for weapons (the defendant did not object to the frisk) and told him that a detective wanted to speak with him. The other detective arrived and told the defendant that he was not under arrest and was free to leave. The defendant voluntarily accompanied the detective and another officer upstairs. The defendant was later told on two different occasions that he was not under arrest and was free to leave. Unknown to the defendant, the other officer entered an adjacent room and took notes on the interview. Also, a detective stayed in the hallway to keep the defendant from leaving, but the defendant was unaware of the detective's intentions. The detective began to question the defendant about his actions during the day and about the shooting. At one point, the defendant asked if he needed an attorney. The detective replied, "I don't know, I can't answer that for you, are you asking for one?" The defendant did not reply to this question and continued talking with the detective. At another point the defendant stood up and said, "I'm trying to leave, I didn't do it." The detective did not restrain the defendant, who then sat back down and continued talking. The defendant made inculpatory statements that he sought to suppress.

The court ruled that the defendant was not in custody to require *Miranda* warnings. The facts did not show the indicia of an arrest. The court relied on *State v. Gaines,*

345 N.C. 647 (1997), and other cases. Also, the presence of a note-taking officer and an officer's unarticulated determination not to let the defendant leave had no bearing on whether the defendant was in custody, because the defendant was unaware of these facts. The defendant argued on appeal, relying on *State v. Torres*, 330 N.C. 517 (1992) (when defendant makes ambiguous request for counsel, interrogation must stop except for narrow questions designed to clarify the defendant's intent), that he made a sufficiently unambiguous request for counsel to require that questioning be stopped. The court first noted that because the defendant was not in custody when the interview occurred, the defendant was not entitled to *Miranda* protections. [Author's note: That is, the defendant's purported assertion of the right to counsel did not require the officer to stop the noncustodial interrogation, because *Miranda* protections were inapplicable.] The court then stated that as a guide to trial courts, it would address the defendant's argument about the request for counsel. The court noted that *Torres* was decided before *Davis v. United States*, 512 U.S. 452 (1994) (Court rejected requirement that officer must stop interrogation when defendant makes ambiguous or equivocal request for counsel to ask questions clarifying whether defendant wants a lawyer.) The later ruling in *State v. Dix*, 194 N.C. App. 151 (2008), stated that the trial court's assumption that the officer was required to ask clarifying questions, and its later conclusion that it was required to resolve any ambiguity in the defendant's favor, was error. In *Little*, the defendant did not unambiguously ask for an attorney; rather, he asked for the detective's opinion about the matter. The detective went beyond federal and state case law when he asked a clarifying question: "Are you asking for one?"

State v. Allen, 200 N.C. App. 709 (2009). After being advised of his *Miranda* rights at the police station, the defendant asserted his right to counsel by naming an attorney he wanted to be present before answering questions. During a conversation with the defendant about the officer's unsuccessful efforts to locate the attorney, the officer told the defendant that he was being detained and charged with second-degree murder. The defendant told the officer that he wanted to talk with the officer "right now." The court ruled, relying on *State v. Leak*, 90 N.C. App. 351 (1988), that the officer did not violate the defendant's assertion of the right to counsel when he informed the defendant of the charge against him.

State v. Herrera, 195 N.C. App. 181 (2009). Officers obtained an arrest warrant charging the defendant with first-degree murder. They notified Virginia authorities of the warrant because it was believed he might be there. A Spanish interpreter called the defendant's grandmother in Honduras to determine if the defendant had returned there. The grandmother expressed concern about the defendant and asked the interpreter to notify her if law enforcement found him. The defendant was eventually arrested in Virginia and taken to Durham. During interrogation, in which the same interpreter was used, the defendant asserted the right to counsel, and questioning stopped. The officer then prepared to take the defendant to a magistrate. The interpreter advised the officer of his call to the grandmother in Honduras and her desire to be notified when the defendant was in custody. The officer then allowed the interpreter to place a call on speaker phone to the defendant's grandmother and offered to let the defendant speak with her, to which he assented. He and his grandmother conversed in Spanish over the speaker phone in the presence of the officer and interpreter, with the interpreter translating for the officer. During the call, the grandmother asked the defendant, "Son, did you do this?" and he replied affirmatively. The grandmother told him to tell the truth to the police, and he indicated that he would. Thereafter, the defendant reinitiated interrogation with the officer by informing the interpreter that he wanted to tell the truth.

The court ruled, relying on *Arizona v. Mauro*, 481 U.S. 520 (1987), that the officer did not conduct interrogation after the defendant had asserted the right to counsel. There was no evidence to show that the phone call to the defendant's grandmother was made to elicit incriminating statements from the defendant or that she was acting as an agent of the officer. In addition, a suspect in the defendant's position would not have felt coerced to incriminate himself by being permitted to speak with his grandmother via speaker phone in the presence of the officer and interpreter.

State v. Dix, 191 N.C. App. 151 (2008). Officers arrested the defendant at his residence for various felony sex offenses. Before being transported to the police station, the defendant indicated his willingness to talk to one of the arresting officers (hereafter, detective). The detective told the defendant to wait until they arrived at the jail. She said that at the police station she would first advise the defendant of his rights and then listen to his side of the story. While being transported, the defendant made a brief unsolicited oral confession to another officer, who related this information to the detective. At the police station, the detective gave *Miranda* warnings to the defendant. She asked the defendant if he understood his rights, and the defendant responded, "Yeah." The detective then said, "Okay. And will you answer some questions for me?" The defendant said, "I'm probably gonna have to have a lawyer." The officer explained that it was up to him whether he wanted to answer questions or not, and the defendant eventually agreed to talk and signed a *Miranda* waiver of rights form. The court ruled, relying on *Davis v. United States*, 512 U.S. 452 (1994) (suspect must unambiguously request counsel), and distinguishing *State v. Torres*, 330 N.C. 517 (1992), that the defendant's statement was not a clear request for counsel. The court noted that the defendant's statement must be considered in the context of what had occurred beforehand. The court stated that the defendant's statement was ambiguous because no reasonable officer under the circumstances would have understood the defendant's words as an unambiguous request for a lawyer at that moment, as opposed to a mere comment about the likelihood that the defendant would eventually require an attorney in this matter, which he surely anticipated would involve criminal proceedings.

State v. Shelly, 181 N.C. App. 196 (2007). The defendant was convicted of first-degree murder. During custodial interrogation the defendant asked general questions about when he would get a lawyer, and the officer truthfully told him that unless he had a personal lawyer, one would be appointed when he went to court. The court noted the informative nature of the conversation: the defendant asked questions and received answers from the officer in an effort to understand his rights and the interview process before choosing to invoke or forego his right to counsel. The court ruled, distinguishing *State v. Torres*, 330 N.C. 517 (1992), and *State v. Steptoe*, 296 N.C. 711 (1979), that the defendant did not make a clear request for counsel so as to require the officer to stop the interrogation.

State v. Ash, 169 N.C. App. 715 (2005). The defendant was arrested for murder and other offenses. After being advised during an officer's giving of *Miranda* rights of his right to have an attorney present, the defendant asked, "Now?" The officer responded affirmatively. The defendant then asked, "Where's my lawyer at? [Inaudible] come down here?" The officer replied that the lawyer who was representing the defendant on a pending, but unrelated,

breaking and entering charge had nothing to do "with what [he was] going to talk to [defendant] about." The defendant responded, "Oh, okay," and signed the waiver of rights form. The court ruled that the defendant did not clearly invoke his right to counsel under the ruling in *Davis v. United States*, 512 U.S. 452 (1994), and thus his *Miranda* rights were not violated. During the officer's interrogation, the defendant confessed that he and others had planned to commit a robbery but ended their plan when they drove by the murder victim's mobile home and observed all the interior lights illuminated there. After the officer asked the defendant whether he was "scared" when the gun "went off," the defendant stated, "I don't want to talk no more 'cause you're talking some crazy shit now." The officer continued to question the defendant, stating, "You didn't even know how many people was [*sic*] in the house, did you?" The defendant responded, "That's why the fuck I didn't stop," and the interrogation continued. The defendant continued to deny his involvement in the crime, but he admitted his participation after further questioning. The court ruled, relying on *State v. Golphin*, 352 N.C. 364 (2000), that the defendant did not clearly invoke his right to remain silent under *Miranda*. The court upheld the trial judge's finding that despite the defendant's statement about not talking any more, the defendant continued to talk without significant prompting by the officer.

State v. Strobel, 164 N.C. App. 310 (2004). Three people were involved in an armed robbery. The defendant was arrested for conspiracy to commit the armed robbery, appeared in district court, and requested and was appointed an attorney in December 2001. Based on additional information implicating her as a participant in the robbery, an officer arrested the defendant in January 2002 for armed robbery. The officer did not orally advise the defendant of her *Miranda* rights. Instead, he gave her a written form and asked her to read it. She signed each page of the statement that acknowledged that she had read it. During her interrogation, the defendant mentioned that she had a court-appointed attorney representing her on the conspiracy charge. The officer told the defendant that she could use the telephone and telephone book located in the room to call her attorney. He also told her that he would stop the interrogation until she had the opportunity to talk to her lawyer. The court ruled, relying on *Davis v. United States*, 512 U.S. 452 (1994), that the defendant did not unequivocally assert her right to counsel during custodial interrogation when she mentioned that she had an attorney for a related charge.

State v. Little, 133 N.C. App. 601 (1999). The defendant asserted his right to counsel after his arrest. A detective, who did not know of this assertion, approached the defendant and began to read *Miranda* rights to the defendant. [Author's note: A defendant's assertion of the right to counsel is imputed to all officers regardless of their knowledge of the defendant's assertion. *See* Arizona v. Roberson, 486 U.S. 675 (1988).] The defendant interrupted the detective and informed him that although he had told another officer that he wanted an attorney, he had changed his mind and now wanted to talk about the criminal charges. The detective properly gave *Miranda* warnings and obtained a waiver of rights, and then the defendant gave a statement to the detective.

The court ruled, relying on *State v. Underwood*, 84 N.C. App. 408 (1987), and other cases, that the defendant reinitiated conversation with the detective after asserting his right to counsel. Thus, the defendant's statement was admissible at trial. [Author's note: This ruling does not appear to be consistent with *Arizona v. Roberson*, cited above, and statements in *Minnick v. Mississippi*, 498 U.S. 146 (1990) ("we now hold that when counsel is requested, interrogation must cease, and officials may not reinitiate interrogation without counsel present, whether or not the accused has consulted with his attorney"). Although an officer's reading of *Miranda* rights may not constitute interrogation, it is a part of the process of reinitiating interrogation that is prohibited once a defendant has asserted the right to counsel.]

State v. Davis, 124 N.C. App. 93 (1996). The defendant was given his *Miranda* warnings and properly waived them. Before questioning began, the defendant requested permission to make a phone call and was allowed to do so. After the phone call, the defendant told a law enforcement officer that "somebody at [his] office told [him he] needed a lawyer." The officer responded, "Well, that's your decision." The defendant then asked, "Do I need a lawyer?" and the officer replied, "That is your decision; I can't make that decision for you." The defendant did not respond and followed the officer into an office to be questioned. He eventually confessed. The court ruled, relying on *State v. Barber*, 335 N.C. 120 (1993), discussed above, that the defendant did not invoke his right to counsel based on the facts in this case. *See also* Diaz v. Senkowski, 76 F.3d 61

(2d Cir. 1996) ("Do you think I need a lawyer?" was not clear assertion of right to counsel).

State v. Easterling, 119 N.C. App. 22 (1995). [Author's note: To better understand the summary of this appellate case, one should know that the defendant was tried and convicted of multiple counts of rape and sexual offense that he committed with his accomplice, Sherman White.] After a detective gave the defendant his *Miranda* warnings, the defendant asserted his right to counsel. The detective later informed the defendant that he would be taken to the magistrate's office to be served with arrest warrants. The detective then said, "Who was Sherman?" The defendant said, "White." Just a few moments later the defendant indicated that he wanted to talk about the case. The detective then gave him *Miranda* warnings and obtained a waiver, and the defendant gave an incriminating statement that was introduced in the State's case in chief at trial.

The court ruled that the detective's question constituted interrogation: it was designed to elicit an incriminating response and therefore was improper under *Edwards v. Arizona*, 384 U.S. 436 (1981), because it was made after the defendant's assertion of his right to counsel. In addition, the defendant's statement a few moments later that he was willing to talk about the case was a continuation of the improper interrogation (that is, it was not simply the defendant's initiation of communication with the detective). Thus, the defendant's confession was inadmissible. The court also ruled that, based on the State's overwhelming evidence against the defendant in this case, the defendant was not induced to testify in his behalf because of the introduction in the State's case in chief of this illegally obtained confession; *see generally* Harrison v. United States, 392 U.S. 219 (1968).

State v. Willis, 109 N.C. App. 184 (1993). The defendant did not validly assert a Fifth Amendment violation when he requested counsel during an interview with law enforcement officers, because he was not in custody when he requested counsel.

State v. Greime, 97 N.C. App. 409 (1990). An officer discussed *Miranda* warnings with the defendant, who said that he understood them and then answered "yes" to the officer's question, "Having these rights in mind, do you wish to answer questions?" The defendant then answered "no" to the officer's question, "You now wish to answer questions now without a lawyer present?" In response to the officer's question as to whether the defendant had an attorney, the defendant said that he did and that the attorney had advised him that he should not say anything. However, the defendant asked the officer if he could stop answering questions at any time. The officer said, "Right." The defendant then said that he would answer questions but would stop if he wanted to. The officer replied, "Okay, but you don't have to without your attorney being present." The defendant then said that he would talk with the officer. The court ruled that the defendant properly waived his right to counsel.

State v. Underwood, 84 N.C. App. 408 (1987). The defendant was arrested, invoked his right to counsel, and was committed to jail. The court ruled that an officer did not improperly initiate interrogation by reading and delivering arrest warrants to the defendant while he was in jail. Shortly after the officer left, the defendant notified the jailer that he wanted to speak with the officer. The officer then returned and gave *Miranda* warnings, received a waiver, and obtained a statement.

Evidentiary Use of a Defendant's Silence or Assertion of Right to Counsel or Right to Remain Silent

UNITED STATES SUPREME COURT

Salinas v. Texas, 133 S. Ct. 2174 (2013). The Court ruled that the use at trial of the defendant's silence during a noncustodial interview did not violate the Fifth Amendment. Without being placed in custody or receiving *Miranda* warnings, the defendant voluntarily answered an officer's questions about a murder. But when asked whether his shotgun would match shells recovered at the murder scene, the defendant declined to answer. Instead, he looked at the floor, shuffled his feet, bit his bottom lip, clenched his hands in his lap, and began "to tighten up." After a few moments, the officer asked additional questions, which the defendant answered. The defendant was charged with murder, and at trial prosecutors argued that his reaction to the officer's question suggested that he was guilty. A three-Justice plurality found it unnecessary to reach the primary issue, concluding instead that the defendant's argument that the prosecutor's jury argument based on the defendant's silence violated his Fifth Amendment privilege against self-incrimination failed because he did not expressly invoke the privilege in response to the officer's question and that no exception applied to excuse his failure to invoke the privilege.

A separate two-Justice plurality concurred in the judgment but for a different reason: the defendant's argument would fail even if he had invoked the privilege because the prosecutor's comments regarding his pre-custodial silence did not compel him to give self-incriminating testimony. [Author's note: Because the three-Justice plurality represents the narrower ground to reverse the judgment, it is the controlling opinion. *See* Marks v. United States, 430 U.S. 188 (1977) (when a fragmented Court decides a case and no single rationale explaining the result enjoys the assent of five Justices, the holding of the Court may be viewed as the position taken by the Justices who concurred in the judgment on the narrowest grounds).]

Greer v. Miller, 483 U.S. 756 (1987). When the prosecutor asked the defendant on cross-examination, "Why didn't you tell this story to anybody when you got arrested?" (defendant had been given *Miranda* warnings after his arrest), the defendant's lawyer objected, and the trial judge sustained his objection and gave a curative instruction to the jury. The Court ruled that no due process violation occurred, because the trial judge prevented the prosecutor from impermissibly using the defendant's post-arrest silence.

Wainwright v. Greenfield, 474 U.S. 284 (1986). A prosecutor's use of a defendant's assertion of his *Miranda* right to remain silent and right to counsel as evidence of his sanity—by showing his ability to comprehend and to assert his rights—violated due process. The Court indicated, however, that a prosecutor may offer evidence of the defendant's behavior after his arrest if it avoids mention of the defendant's exercise of his constitutional rights.

Fletcher v. Weir, 455 U.S. 603 (1982). The defendant stabbed the homicide victim with a knife during a fight. At trial, he testified that he acted in self-defense. His trial statement was the first occasion on which he offered an exculpatory statement. The prosecutor cross-examined him by asking why, when he was arrested, he had not offered his exculpatory explanation or disclosed the location of the knife used in the stabbing. There was no evidence that the defendant was given *Miranda* warnings when he was arrested.

The Court ruled that the cross-examination did not violate due process because the defendant had not been given *Miranda* warnings, which implicitly assure him that his silence will not be used against him. A state may specify under its rules of evidence the extent to which post-arrest silence, in the absence of *Miranda* warnings, may be used to impeach a defendant's testimony. [Author's note: For a discussion of North Carolina cases on the use of a defendant's silence as evidence, see 2 KENNETH S. BROUN, BRANDIS AND BROUN ON NORTH CAROLINA EVIDENCE § 211 (7th ed. 2011)—although some of these cases were decided before *Fletcher v. Weir* and may be affected by the ruling of that case. *See, e.g.,* State v. Lane, 301 N.C. 382 (1980) (although the court's Fifth Amendment analysis is now inconsistent with *Fletcher v. Weir*, its ruling that the defendant's silence after his arrest about his alibi was not an inconsistent statement when compared with his trial testimony is still valid); State v. Westbrooks, 345 N.C. 43 (1996) (using *State v. Lane* analysis, defendant's pre-arrest silence about who killed her husband was admissible as prior inconsistent statement, when compared to her trial testimony).]

Anderson v. Charles, 447 U.S. 404 (1980). After being given *Miranda* warnings, the defendant gave a statement to an officer. The court ruled that it is not a due process violation if the prosecutor cross-examines the defendant at trial about inconsistencies between his post-arrest statement and his trial testimony by asking in essence why, if his trial testimony is true, did he not tell the same version to the officer after his arrest. *See also* State v. Westbrooks, 345 N.C. 43 (1996); State v. Mitchell, 317 N.C. 661 (1986); State v. Fair, 354 N.C. 131 (2001) (State properly cross-examined defendant about his voluntary statements to news media after arrest that were inconsistent with trial testimony).

Jenkins v. Anderson, 447 U.S. 231 (1980). The defendant was arrested for murder about two weeks after the homicide had occurred. When he testified at trial, the prosecutor attempted to impeach him by referring to his pre-arrest silence—that is, his failure to surrender himself or tell his self-defense story to the police. The Court ruled that the use in this case of pre-arrest silence to impeach did not violate the defendant's Fifth Amendment or due process rights. A state may resolve under its rules of evidence the extent to which pre-arrest silence may be used to impeach a defendant's testimony. *But see* Coppola v. Powell, 878 F.2d 1562 (1st Cir. 1989) (defendant's pre-arrest statement that he would not confess was sufficient to invoke his Fifth Amendment privilege, and State's using that statement in its case in chief was constitutional error).

Doyle v. Ohio, 426 U.S. 610 (1976). The use of a defendant's post-arrest silence (that is, defendant's having remained silent after being given *Miranda* warnings) to impeach the defendant's exculpatory testimony at trial violated due process.

NORTH CAROLINA SUPREME COURT

State v. Moore, 366 N.C. 100 (2012). On direct examination an officer testified that after he read the defendant his *Miranda* rights, the defendant "refused to talk about the case." Because this testimony referred to the defendant's exercise of his right to silence, its admission was error. The court rejected the State's argument that no error occurred because the comments were neither made by the prosecutor nor the result of a question by the prosecutor designed to elicit a comment on the defendant's exercise of his right to silence. The court stated: "An improper adverse inference of guilt from a defendant's exercise of his right to remain silent cannot be made, regardless of who comments on it."

State v. Buckner, 342 N.C. 198 (1995). The court ruled that the prosecutor's jury argument recounting the defendant's failure to tell officers at his interrogation that another person had shot the murder victim did not violate the ruling in *Doyle v. Ohio*, 426 U.S. 610 (1976), because there was no evidence that the defendant had been given his *Miranda* warnings during the interrogation. The court relied on *Jenkins v. Anderson*, 447 U.S. 231 (1980).

State v. Quick, 337 N.C. 359 (1994). Five law enforcement officers were questioning the defendant about a murder. They informed him that he was not under arrest and was free to leave at any time. The officers gave him *Miranda* warnings and obtained a waiver. The defendant denied his involvement in the murder. During the interview, an officer received a telephone call from the SBI lab that the defendant's fingerprints had been found in an ashtray in the victim's home. Another officer told the defendant that he was under arrest for first-degree murder. The officer then made accusatory remarks to the defendant, including asking him how it felt to have killed a 78-year-old helpless man. The trial judge permitted the officer to testify how the defendant reacted to these accusatory remarks: "He had no reaction. He acted like I was talking about the weather."

Relying on *State v. Hoyle*, 325 N.C. 232 (1989), and *Doyle v. Ohio*, 426 U.S. 610 (1976), the court ruled that this evidence impermissibly referred to the defendant's exercise of his right to remain silent. The court also ruled that the State's cross-examination of the defendant (which again elicited the defendant's silence in response to the officer's accusation) was improper.

State v. Carter, 335 N.C. 422 (1994). A detective was permitted to testify that in the police department's interrogation room, he advised the defendant of his *Miranda* rights and the defendant indicated that he understood those rights. The court ruled that (1) the testimony did not violate *Doyle v. Ohio*, 426 U.S. 610 (1976), because no evidence was introduced showing that the defendant exercised his right to remain silent; and (2) the testimony was relevant in this case because defense counsel consistently throughout the trial had attacked the professionalism of the investigating officers, and the testimony tended to refute the characterization of the officers' conduct as unprofessional.

State v. Hoyle, 325 N.C. 232 (1989). Officers arrested the defendant and advised him of his *Miranda* rights. The defendant said that he would not sign a waiver of his rights without a lawyer being present but that he would answer questions. The defendant answered some questions, but when asked what happened when the male (the alleged homicide victim) followed him to his truck, he said that he would "rather not say" without having talked with his lawyer. The court ruled that in the trial of the defendant for murder, in which the defendant asserted the defense of self-defense, the prosecutor's cross-examination of the defendant and jury argument about the defendant's failure to tell officers of his defense of self-defense violated *Doyle v. Ohio* and *State v. Lane*, discussed above. *See also* State v. Shores, 155 N.C. App. 342 (2002) (similar ruling).

State v. Ladd, 308 N.C. 272 (1983). The content of the defendant's statement invoking his right to counsel as well as his right to remain silent after receiving *Miranda* warnings was inadmissible at trial.

NORTH CAROLINA COURT OF APPEALS

State v. Taylor, ___ N.C. App. ___, 780 S.E.2d 222 (2015). The court ruled: "[t]estimony that the investigating detective was unable to reach defendant to question him during her investigation was admissible to describe the course of her investigation, and was not improper testimony of defendant's pre-arrest silence." The testimony at issue involved the State's questioning of the detective about her repeated unsuccessful efforts to contact the defendant and his lack of participation in the investigation. Noting that pre-arrest silence may not be used as substantive evidence of guilt, the court noted that none of the relevant cases involve a situation when "there has been no direct contact between the defendant and a law enforcement officer." It continued: "Pre-arrest silence has

no significance if there is no indication that a defendant was questioned by a law enforcement officer and refused to answer." Here, the detective never made contact with the defendant, never confronted him in person, and never requested that he submit to questioning. Additionally, the court noted that there was no indication that the defendant knew the detective was trying to talk to him and that he refused to speak to her. Thus, the court concluded: "it cannot be inferred that defendant's lack of response to indirect attempts to speak to him about an ongoing investigation was evidence of pre-arrest silence."

State v. Barbour, 229 N.C. App. 635 (2013). The court ruled that the State did not impermissibly present evidence of the defendant's post-*Miranda* silence. After being advised of his *Miranda* rights, the defendant did not remain silent but, rather, made statements to the police. Thus, no error occurred when an officer indicated that after his arrest the defendant never asked to speak with the officer or anyone else in the officer's agency.

State v. Harrison, 218 N.C. App. 546 (2012). The court of appeals ruled that the trial court committed error by allowing the State to use the defendant's pre- and post-arrest silence as substantive evidence of guilt. When explaining the circumstances of the defendant's initial interview, an officer testifying for the State said, "He provided me—he denied any involvement, wished to give me no statement, written or verbal." Also, when the State asked the officer whether the defendant had made any statements after arrest, the officer responded, "After he was mirandized [*sic*], he waived his rights and provided no further verbal or written statements." The court noted that neither a defendant's pre-arrest silence nor post-arrest, pre–*Miranda* warnings silence may be used as substantive evidence of guilt, though either or both may be used to impeach the defendant by suggesting that his or her prior silence is inconsistent with statements made at trial. A defendant's post-arrest, post–*Miranda* warnings silence, however, may not be used for any purpose. Here, the defendant testified after the officer, so the State could not use the officer's statement for impeachment. Also, the officer's testimony was admitted as substantive evidence during the State's case in chief.

State v. Mendoza, 206 N.C. App. 391 (2010). The court ruled that the trial court erred by allowing the State to introduce evidence, during its case in chief, of the defendant's pre-arrest, post-arrest, and pre-*Miranda* warnings silence. The only permissible purpose for such evidence is impeachment; because the defendant had not yet testified when the State presented the evidence, the testimony could not have been used for that purpose. Also, the State's use of the defendant's post-arrest, post-*Miranda* warnings silence was forbidden for any purpose.

State v. Smith, 206 N.C. App. 404 (2010). The court ruled that the trial court did not improperly allow use of the defendant's post-arrest silence when it allowed the State to impeach him with his failure to provide information about an alleged meeting with a drug dealer. In this murder case, the defendant claimed that the child victim drowned in a bathtub while the defendant met with the dealer. The defendant's pretrial statements to the police never mentioned the meeting. The court ruled that because the defendant waived his rights and made pretrial statements to the police, the case did not involve the use of post-arrest silence for impeachment. Rather, it involved only the evidentiary issue of impeachment with a prior inconsistent statement.

State v. Adu, 195 N.C. App. 269 (2009). The court ruled, relying on *State v. Hoyle*, 325 N.C. 232 (1989), *State v. Ward*, 354 N.C. 231 (2001), and *State v. Shores*, 155 N.C. App. 342 (2002), that the State on cross-examination of the defendant and during jury argument violated the defendant's Fifth Amendment rights by using the defendant's silence as substantive evidence of guilt. (See the court's discussion of the facts in this case.)

State v. Boston, 191 N.C. App. 637 (2008). The State was allowed to introduce evidence that the defendant, who had not been arrested, refused a law enforcement officer's request to come to the police department to answer questions about an arson. This evidence was admitted as substantive evidence of the defendant's guilt. The defendant did not testify at trial. The court ruled, distinguishing *Jenkins v. Anderson*, 447 U.S. 231 (1980), and relying on several federal appellate cases, that it was constitutional error to admit this pre-arrest silence as substantive evidence; it could only be introduced as impeachment evidence.

State v. Ezzell, 182 N.C. App. 417 (2007). The defendant was arrested for murder at the crime scene and spoke to an officer after waiving his *Miranda* rights. He made several statements concerning the events surrounding the murder. After arriving at the sheriff's office and being given *Miranda* warnings, the defendant asserted his right to remain silent. The prosecutor cross-examined the defendant at trial about what he did and did not tell the officer at the crime scene. The court noted that it would have been natural and expected for the defendant

to have mentioned certain details to the officer then. The court ruled that the prosecutor's cross-examination did not impermissibly comment on the defendant's assertion of his right to remain silent at the sheriff's office.

State v. Shores, 155 N.C. App. 342 (2002). The defendant was arrested for murder and given *Miranda* warnings. He gave a brief statement asserting self-defense and exercised his right to remain silent from then until trial. The defendant testified on direct examination at trial and added details about the alleged victim's actions toward him. The prosecutor's cross-examination repeatedly questioned the defendant as to whether he had ever informed law enforcement about these details. The prosecutor also mentioned this matter in jury argument. The court ruled, relying on *Doyle v. Ohio*, 426 U.S. 610 (1976), *State v. Hoyle*, 325 N.C. 232 (1989), and *State v. Lane*, 301 N.C. 382 (1980), that the prosecutor's cross-examination of the defendant and jury argument impermissibly commented on the defendant's right to remain silent.

State v. Hanton, 140 N.C. App. 679 (2000). The defendant was arrested and given *Miranda* warnings, which he waived. He then gave an oral statement to an officer but refused to provide a written statement. The officer testified at trial that the defendant told him "that he was no dummy and that he was not going to put anything in writing [and] don't try to trick me into your little games." The court ruled, relying on *Connecticut v. Barrett*, 479 U.S. 523 (1987), that the defendant's refusal to put his oral statement into writing was not an assertion of the right to remain silent, and thus the officer's testimony was not improper.

State v. Salmon, 140 N.C. App. 567 (2000). An officer arrested the defendant (who was 15 but was tried as an adult) for murder and placed him in a patrol car. He was not given *Miranda* warnings. During the ride to the police station, the defendant voluntarily stated, "I didn't mean to do it." The defendant called the officer during the presentation of his defense to introduce this statement to support his primary defense, that he did not intend to kill the victim because he did not believe the gun was loaded. During the State's cross-examination of the officer, he testified that after this voluntary statement, the defendant was informed that a youth detective would be speaking with him on his arrival at the station. The defendant then responded, "Not without my lawyer." The trial judge permitted the State to use this statement to rebut the defendant's mistake-of-fact defense. The State argued to the jury that if the killing was truly a mistake, the defendant would not have needed to speak with a lawyer.

The court ruled that the admission of the defendant's statement about his lawyer did not unconstitutionally violate his exercise of the right to counsel. The court reasoned, relying on the analysis in *Fletcher v. Weir*, 455 U.S. 603 (1982), that the prohibition against using evidence of a defendant's invocation of the right to counsel after *Miranda* warnings have been given (*see* State v. Ladd, 308 N.C. 272 (1983)) does not apply to such an invocation before a defendant has been given those warnings.

State v. Alkano, 119 N.C. App. 256 (1995). The defendant, who had not been given *Miranda* warnings, volunteered several inculpatory statements after his arrest. At trial, the prosecutor asked officers about the defendant's failure to explain several matters surrounding the crime. The court ruled that the State did not impermissibly comment on the defendant's silence in violation of *Doyle v. Ohio*, 426 U.S. 610 (1976), because the defendant in this case was not silent about the facts of the crime when he was arrested.

Use of Evidence Obtained as the Result of a *Miranda* Violation

UNITED STATES SUPREME COURT

Bobby v. Dixon, 132 S. Ct. 26 (2011). The Court ruled that a federal appellate court erroneously concluded that a state supreme court ruling affirming the defendant's murder conviction was contrary to or involved an unreasonable application of clearly established federal law. The defendant and an accomplice murdered the victim, obtained an identification card in the victim's name, and sold the victim's car. An officer first spoke with the defendant during a chance encounter when the defendant was voluntarily at the police station for completely unrelated reasons. The officer gave the defendant *Miranda* warnings and asked to talk to him about the victim's disappearance. The defendant declined to answer questions without his lawyer and left. Five days later, after receiving information that the defendant had sold the victim's car and forged his name, officers arrested the defendant for forgery and interrogated him. They decided not to give the defendant *Miranda* warnings for fear that he would again refuse to speak with them. The defendant admitted to obtaining an identification card in the victim's name

but claimed ignorance about the victim's disappearance. An officer told the defendant that "now is the time to say" whether he had any involvement in the murder because "if [the accomplice] starts cutting a deal over there, this is kinda like, a bus leaving. The first one that gets on it is the only one that's gonna get on." When the defendant continued to deny knowledge of the victim's disappearance, the interrogation ended. That afternoon the accomplice led the police to the victim's body, saying that the defendant told him where it was. The defendant was brought back for questioning. Before questioning began, the defendant said that he heard they had found a body and asked whether the accomplice was in custody. When the police said that the accomplice was not in custody, the defendant replied, "I talked to my attorney, and I want to tell you what happened." Officers read him *Miranda* rights and obtained a signed waiver of those rights. At this point, the defendant admitted to murdering the victim. The defendant's confession to murder was admitted at trial, and the defendant was convicted of murder, among other things, and sentenced to death. After the state supreme court affirmed, the defendant filed for federal habeas relief. The district court denied relief, but a federal appellate court reversed.

The Supreme Court found that the federal appellate court erred in three respects. First, it erred by concluding that federal law clearly established that police could not speak to the defendant when five days earlier he had refused to speak to them without his lawyer. The defendant was not in custody during the chance encounter, and no law says that a person can invoke his or her *Miranda* rights anticipatorily in a context other than custodial interrogation. Second, the federal appellate court erroneously ruled that police violated the Fifth Amendment by urging the defendant to "cut a deal" before his accomplice did so. No precedent holds that this common police tactic is unconstitutional. Third, the federal appellate court erroneously concluded that the state supreme court unreasonably applied *Oregon v. Elstad*, 470 U.S. 298 (1985), when it ruled that the defendant's second confession was voluntary. As the state supreme court explained, the defendant's statements were voluntary. During the first interrogation, he received several breaks, was given water and offered food, and was not abused or threatened. He freely acknowledged that he forged the victim's name and had no difficulty denying involvement with the victim's disappearance. Prior to his second interrogation, the defendant made an unsolicited declaration that he had spoken with his attorney and wanted to tell the police what happened. Then, before giving his confession, the defendant received *Miranda* warnings and signed a waiver-of-rights form. The state court recognized that the defendant's first interrogation involved an intentional *Miranda* violation but concluded that the breach of *Miranda* procedures did not involve actual compulsion, and thus there was no reason to suppress the later, warned confession. The federal appellate court erred by concluding that *Missouri v. Seibert*, 542 U.S. 600 (2004), mandated a different result. The nature of the interrogation here was different from that in *Seibert*. Here, the Court explained, the defendant denied involvement in the murder and then after *Miranda* warnings were given changed his mind and confessed (in *Seibert* the defendant confessed both times). Additionally, the Court noted, in contrast to *Seibert*, the two interrogations at issue here did not occur in one continuum.

United States v. Patane, 542 U.S. 630 (2004). An officer arrested the defendant at his residence for violating a restraining order involving his ex-girlfriend. When another officer began to give *Miranda* warnings, the defendant interrupted the officer, asserting that he knew his rights, and neither officer attempted to complete the *Miranda* warnings. Because one of the officers had been previously informed that the defendant, a convicted felon, illegally possessed a Glock pistol, he asked the defendant about it. The defendant, after persistent questioning, told the officer that the pistol was in his bedroom. The officer received consent from the defendant to retrieve the pistol. The pistol was admitted at the defendant's trial, and he was convicted of possession of a firearm by a convicted felon. An opinion representing the views of three Justices and announcing the judgment of the Court ruled, distinguishing *Dickerson v. United States*, 530 U.S. 428 (2000) (*Miranda* announced a constitutional rule that Congress may not supersede legislatively), that the Fifth Amendment's self-incrimination privilege is not implicated by the admission into evidence of the physical fruit of a voluntary statement taken in violation of the *Miranda* ruling. An opinion representing the views of two other Justices and concurring in the judgment stated that it agreed with the opinion announcing the judgment of the Court that the nontestimonial physical fruit of the defendant's unwarned statement, the Glock pistol, was admissible—although it did not necessarily agree with all of the statements in the opinion. [Author's note: The ruling in *State v. May*, 334 N.C. 609 (1993) (physical evidence

discovered as a result of a voluntary statement taken in violation of *Miranda* is admissible), is consistent with this ruling.]

Missouri v. Seibert, 542 U.S. 600 (2004). An officer arrested the defendant for her involvement with an unlawful burning of a mobile home and the resulting death of a person inside. As part of an interrogation technique, the officer deliberately failed to give the defendant *Miranda* warnings, interrogated her for 30 to 40 minutes, and obtained a confession. The defendant was then given a 20-minute break. The same officer then gave *Miranda* warnings to the defendant, obtained a waiver, interrogated her again (referring in this second interrogation to statements she had made in the first interrogation), and obtained another confession. The trial judge suppressed the first confession but admitted the second confession. The issue before the United States Supreme Court was the admissibility of the second confession.

Distinguishing *Oregon v. Elstad*, 470 U.S. 298 (1985) (second voluntary incriminating statement obtained with *Miranda* warnings and waiver at police station was admissible even though it occurred after the defendant had made voluntary incriminating statement at his house that was inadmissible under *Miranda* because warnings had not been given), an opinion announcing the judgment of the Court and representing the views of four Justices (a plurality opinion) ruled that the second confession was inadmissible. The opinion stated that it would have been reasonable for the defendant to regard the two interrogation sessions as a continuum in which it would have been unnatural to refuse to repeat at the second interrogation what had been said before. These circumstances challenged the comprehensibility and efficacy of the *Miranda* warnings given before the second interrogation: a reasonable person in the defendant's shoes would not have understood the warnings to convey a message that she retained a choice about continuing to talk.

A fifth Justice (Justice Kennedy) concurred in the judgment that the second confession was inadmissible, although he disagreed with the reasoning of the plurality opinion. He stated that the admissibility of post-*Miranda* warning statements should continue to be governed by *Oregon v. Elstad* except when the second statement is obtained in the two-step interrogation technique deliberately used in this case to undermine the *Miranda* warning. In such a case, post-*Miranda* warning statements that are related to the substance of the pre-*Miranda* warning statements must be excluded unless curative measures are taken before the post-*Miranda* warning statement is made. The curative measures discussed in his opinion were not taken in this case, so he concluded that the second confession was inadmissible. [Author's note: When a fifth vote is necessary to support a judgment of the Court, the concurring opinion defines the scope of the ruling if it rests on the narrowest ground that supports the judgment, which it does in this case. *See, e.g.,* Chandler v. Florida, 449 U.S. 560 (1981); Grutter v. Bollinger, 539 U.S. 306 (2003); Marks v. United States, 430 U.S. 188 (1977); United States v. Capers, 627 F.3d 470, 476 (2d Cir. 2010) (Justice Kennedy's concurring opinion in *Seibert* is controlling).] For a post-*Seibert* North Carolina case, see *State v. Hartley,* 212 N.C. App. 1 (2011) (court distinguished *Seibert* by noting that both confessions in *Seibert* were obtained while the defendant was in custody, while the defendant in *Hartley* was not in custody when the first confession was obtained).

Oregon v. Elstad, 470 U.S. 298 (1985). The fact that an officer has obtained a voluntary statement from a defendant that is not admissible because it was obtained as a result of a *Miranda* violation does not prohibit the admission at trial of a defendant's later voluntary statements made after proper *Miranda* warnings and a proper waiver. A simple failure to give *Miranda* warnings is not a violation of a defendant's Fifth Amendment rights. Instead, the defendant's unwarned statement merely must be excluded in the State's case in chief. Therefore, a voluntary statement, tainted by the failure to give *Miranda* warnings, does not bar the admissibility of a later voluntary statement that was taken in compliance with the *Miranda* rule.

For similar rulings in North Carolina, see *State v. Edgerton,* 328 N.C. 319 (1991); *State v. Barlow,* 330 N.C. 133 (1991); *State v. Greene,* 332 N.C. 565 (1992); *State v. Morrell,* 108 N.C. App. 465 (1993); *State v. Bunnell,* 340 N.C. 74 (1995); *State v. Soles,* 119 N.C. App. 375 (1995). *Compare* United States v. Carter, 884 F.2d 368 (8th Cir. 1989) (court ruled inadmissible a written confession taken with proper *Miranda* warnings immediately after oral confession that had been taken unconstitutionally without *Miranda* warnings) *with* United States v. Gale, 952 F.2d 1412 (D.C. Cir. 1992) (distinguishing *Carter,* court ruled admissible a statement that was given one hour after inadmissible statements were obtained).

[Author's note: The United States Supreme Court strongly indicated in *Dickerson v. United States,* 530 U.S. 428 (2000) (*Miranda* ruling is constitutionally based and may not be modified by legislative act), that its ruling in *Dickerson* did not adversely affect its *Elstad* ruling; see discussion of this issue in *United States v. Sterling,* 283 F.3d 216 (4th Cir. 2002), and *United States v. DeSumma,* 272 F.3d 176 (3d Cir. 2001).]

Michigan v. Tucker, 417 U.S. 433 (1974). The defendant made a voluntary statement that was inadmissible because it was obtained as a result of a *Miranda* violation. The officers learned the name of a witness from the statement, and that witness later testified against the defendant at trial. The Court ruled that the *Miranda* violation did not require exclusion of the witness's testimony, because the defendant's voluntary statement was not taken in violation of his Fifth, Sixth, or Fourteenth Amendment rights.

Harris v. New York, 401 U.S. 222 (1971). A statement taken in violation of *Miranda* that is not involuntary may be used to impeach the defendant's credibility if the defendant testifies at trial. *See also* Oregon v. Hass, 420 U.S. 714 (1975); State v. Bryant, 280 N.C. 551 (1972).

Miranda v. Arizona, 384 U.S. 436 (1966). Any statement, whether inculpatory or exculpatory, obtained from a defendant as a result of a *Miranda* violation is inadmissible. But see *Harris v. New York* and *Oregon v. Elstad,* discussed above.

NORTH CAROLINA SUPREME COURT

State v. Stokes, 357 N.C. 220 (2003). The court ruled, relying on *State v. McQueen,* 324 N.C. 118 (1989), and assuming without deciding that the defendant's statements were taken in violation of *Miranda,* that the State was properly permitted to use those statements in cross-examination to impeach the defendant when he testified at trial. The court also ruled that the State was properly permitted to call the law enforcement officer who took the statements as a rebuttal witness after the defendant had testified, because the testimony was material to the central issue at the murder trial—how the child died.

State v. Wallace, 351 N.C. 481 (2000). The court ruled that a three-hour delay in giving the defendant his *Miranda* warnings did not taint his later confessions given after *Miranda* warnings. He did not make any incriminating statements during those three hours that would affect his later confessions.

State v. May, 334 N.C. 609 (1993). The court ruled that physical evidence found as a result of a *Miranda* violation (in this case, the defendant's statement led officers to a knife, a pair of gloves, and a rag in the defendant's backyard) is admissible when the defendant was not coerced into giving the statement (that is, the statement was voluntarily given). The court relied on *Michigan v. Tucker*, 417 U.S. 433 (1974), and *Oregon v. Elstad*, 470 U.S. 298 (1985), in ruling that although the officers violated the prophylactic rules of *Miranda* and *Edwards v. Arizona*, they did not violate the defendant's right against compelled self-incrimination. The rule's deterrent value is satisfied by excluding the defendant's statement but not the physical evidence.

State v. Hicks, 333 N.C. 467 (1993). The court ruled that the first confession that was taken without *Miranda* warnings should have been ruled inadmissible. The court also ruled that the second confession, taken after *Miranda* warnings had been properly given and waived, was admissible under the ruling in *Oregon v. Elstad*, 470 U.S. 298 (1985). The court adopted the *Elstad* ruling to determine alleged constitutional violations under Article I, Sections 19 and 23, of the North Carolina Constitution.

State v. McQueen, 324 N.C. 118 (1989). The defendant testified on direct examination at trial that he had two knives but no "weapons" and did not know where the two guns used in the murder were located. The State called as a rebuttal witness a law enforcement officer who testified that during interrogation, in response to the agent's question as to where the guns were located, the defendant said, "After I talk to my lawyer and if he tells me to, I'll tell you where they are at." The State also had cross-examined the defendant about this statement. Although an assertion of the right to counsel is generally inadmissible, the court ruled that the cross-examination and rebuttal evidence was proper for impeachment under *Harris v. New York*, discussed above, to question the defendant about a prior inconsistent statement.

NORTH CAROLINA COURT OF APPEALS

In re L.I., 205 N.C. App. 155 (2010). The juvenile was a passenger in a vehicle stopped by an officer. When the officer ordered the juvenile out of the vehicle, he asked, "[Where is] the marijuana I know you have[?]" The juvenile turned away and appeared to reach into her pants. When the officer tried to see what the juvenile was reaching for, she told him that he could not look in her pants. After handcuffing and placing the juvenile in the back of the patrol car, the officer—without giving *Miranda* and juvenile statutory warnings—told her that he was going to "take her downtown" and that "if [she] t[ook] drugs into the jail it[] [would be] an additional charge." The juvenile

shortly thereafter told the officer that she had marijuana and that it was in her coat pocket.

(1) The Court ruled, relying on *State v. Johnston*, 154 N.C. App. 500 (2002), that the juvenile was in custody when the officer spoke to her. She had been detained, handcuffed, and placed in the backseat of the officer's vehicle. (2) The court ruled, relying on *State v. Phelps*, 156 N.C. App. 119 (2003), that the officer's statements to the juvenile constituted interrogation under *Rhode Island v. Innis*, 446 U.S. 291 (1980), because the officer knew or should have known that they were reasonably likely to elicit an incriminating response from her. The officer's objective purpose was to obtain the juvenile's admission that she possessed the marijuana that he knew she had. The trial court erred in admitting the juvenile's statements made in response to the officer's custodial interrogation. (3) The court ruled, relying on *State v. May*, 334 N.C. 609 (1993), and other cases, that the physical evidence (marijuana) discovered as a result of statements inadmissible under *Miranda* was admissible when the juvenile's statements were not coerced.

State v. Houston, 169 N.C. App. 367 (2005). Officers arrested the defendant in a parking lot, did not give him *Miranda* warnings, and took him to an apartment where he consented to a search—including the search of a safe to which the defendant gave officers the combination. Cocaine, cash, and a handgun were found in the safe. The officers transported the defendant to the police station, where they advised him of his *Miranda* rights and took a statement. None of the defendant's pre–*Miranda* warning statements were admitted at his trial. However, the evidence in the safe was admitted into evidence, as were the defendant's statements at the police station. The court ruled, relying on *United States v. Patane*, 542 U.S. 630 (2004), *State v. May*, 334 N.C. 609 (1993), and *State v. Goodman*, 165 N.C. App. 865 (2004), that the fruit of the poisonous tree doctrine did not apply to bar admission of physical evidence discovered after the *Miranda* violation (questioning the defendant after his arrest and obtaining the combination to the safe without giving *Miranda* warnings). Thus, evidence seized from the safe was admissible at the defendant's trial based on the defendant's valid consent to search it. [Author's note: An officer's request for a consent search is not interrogation. State v. Cummings, 188 N.C. App. 598 (2008).]

State v. Goodman, 165 N.C. App. 865 (2004). The defendant, after waiving his *Miranda* rights, talked to officers but later asserted his right to counsel. Five days later, officers went to the jail and told the defendant that they were not going to question him about the murder, but that they had information that he had killed someone and might know where the body was. The defendant made some incriminating statements and took the officers to the body. The trial judge ordered the statements suppressed based on the officers' *Miranda* violation. However, the trial judge did not suppress the physical evidence (the body and items found near the body) that had been obtained as a result of the *Miranda* violation. The court ruled, relying on *State v. May*, 334 N.C. 609 (1993), and *United States v. Patane*, 542 U.S. 630 (2004), that the physical evidence found as a result of the non-coerced statement obtained from the defendant after the *Miranda* violation was admissible, and it upheld the trial judge's ruling on that ground.

North Carolina Statutory Warnings for Young Arrestees

(*This topic is discussed on page 572.*)

NORTH CAROLINA SUPREME COURT

State v. Oglesby, 361 N.C. 550 (2007). Officers did not stop questioning the 16-year-old defendant during custodial interrogation when he requested permission to telephone his aunt. Although the aunt testified that she was a "mother figure" to the defendant, the court ruled that this evidence did not constitute the legal authority inherent in a guardian or custodial relationship. Thus, the aunt was not a "guardian" under G.S. 7B-2101(a)(3) so as to require the officers to stop their questioning of the defendant.

State v. Miller, 344 N.C. 658 (1996). Officers arrested a 17-year-old for murder. They could not find a juvenile rights form, so they used an adult *Miranda* form and inserted an additional question: "Do you wish to answer questions without your parents/parent present?" The defendant waived all of his rights except that he stated that he wanted his mother present. No questioning was conducted until his mother was present. During the questioning the defendant appeared embarrassed and ill at ease. An officer asked the defendant if he was comfortable talking in front of his mom or if he wanted her to step out of the room. He replied, "She might as well leave." His mother left the interrogation room and sat on a bench

outside the open doorway where the defendant could see her if he leaned forward. She was told that she could come back into the room at any time. The defendant then confessed to the murder.

The court ruled that the additional language added to the adult *Miranda* form adequately conveyed the substance of the defendant's right to have his parent(s) present during questioning. It was clear that the defendant understood his rights because he asked that his mother be present, he did not give any statement until she arrived, and he answered questions in her presence. The court also ruled that the defendant's statements and conduct that resulted in his mother leaving the interrogation room were a knowing and intelligent waiver of his right to have her present during the custodial interrogation.

State v. Smith, 317 N.C. 100 (1986). The court applied the ruling of *Edwards v. Arizona*, 451 U.S. 477 (1981), to a juvenile's assertion of the statutory right to have a parent present during custodial interrogation and ruled that the resumption of questioning in the absence of counsel or a parent was improper in this case; therefore, the resulting confession was inadmissible.

State v. Fincher, 309 N.C. 1 (1983). The court ruled that custodial interrogation warnings listed in G.S. 7A-595 (now, G.S. 7B-2101) must be given to a person under 18 who is unemancipated, unmarried, and not in the armed forces.

NORTH CAROLINA COURT OF APPEALS

State v. Williams, 209 N.C. App. 255 (2011). The court ruled that the trial court did not err by denying the defendant's motion to suppress statements made during officers' interrogation, because no violation of G.S. 7B-2101 occurred. The defendant, a 17-year-old juvenile, was already in custody on unrelated charges when he was brought to an interview room for questioning. When the defendant invoked his statutory right to have his mother present during questioning, the detectives stopped all questioning. After the detectives had trouble determining how to contact the defendant's mother, they returned to the room and asked the defendant how to reach her. The defendant then asked them when he would be able to talk to them about the new charges (robbery and murder) and explained that the detectives had "misunderstood" him when he requested the presence of his mother for questioning. He explained that he only wanted his mother present for questioning related to the charges for which he was already in custody, not the new crimes of robbery and murder. Although the defendant initially invoked his right to have his mother present during his custodial interrogation, he thereafter initiated further communication with the detectives; that communication was not the result of any further interrogation by the detectives. The defendant voluntarily and knowingly waived his rights.

In re M.L.T.H., 200 N.C. App. 476 (2009). The court ruled that an officer improperly advised a juvenile of custodial interrogation rights when the form the officer used advised the juvenile that he had the right to have a parent, guardian, custodian, or any other person present during questioning. G.S. 7B-2101 does not allow the advisement to include "any other person." The officer's advisement gave the juvenile an improper choice.

State v. Oglesby, 174 N.C. App. 658 (2005). The court ruled that the request of the defendant (who was 16 years old) for his aunt to be present during custodial interrogation did not require officers to stop interrogation, because his aunt was not a guardian under the juvenile interrogation statute, G.S. 7B-2101. Distinguishing *State v. Jones*, 147 N.C. App. 527 (2001), the court noted that no governmental entity had conferred legal authority over the defendant to the aunt.

State v. Branham, 153 N.C. App. 91 (2002). The court ruled, relying on *State v. Smith*, 317 N.C. 100 (2001), that officers violated the juvenile's statutory interrogation rights by continuing to question him after he had requested that his mother be present during custodial interrogation. There was evidence that the mother, when informed of her son's request that she be present during custodial interrogation, refused to be with him. The court stated that even if she did not want to be present, she could not waive his right to have her present during the custodial interrogation. The court ordered that the juvenile's statement must be suppressed.

State v. Jones, 147 N.C. App. 527 (2001). The defendant, a 13-year-old juvenile who was subjected to custodial interrogation in his aunt's presence, was tried as an adult and convicted of several felonies. The court ruled that the custodial interrogation complied with G.S. 7A-595(b) (now, G.S. 7B-2101(b)), because his aunt was a guardian under the juvenile rights provisions. The court noted that the term "guardian" is not defined in the juvenile code, and it rejected the defendant's argument that a guardian means only someone who is court appointed. The court ruled that a guardian under G.S. 7A-595(b) means a person upon whom government has conferred any authority over the juvenile. Because both the department of social

services and the local school system had given authority over the defendant to the aunt, the court ruled that she was a guardian under G.S. 7A-595(b). [Author's note: This ruling would clearly also apply to G.S. 7B-2101(b).]

State v. McKeithan, 140 N.C. App. 422 (2000). An officer gave a juvenile an interrogation rights warning that included the statement: "If you cannot afford a lawyer, one will be appointed for you before questioning if you wish." The defendant argued that the warning was deficient because it was contrary to statutory law that a juvenile is always entitled to an attorney regardless of financial resources. The court rejected this argument, citing rulings in *State v. Flowers*, 128 N.C. App. 697 (1998), and *State v. Miller*, 344 N.C. 658 (1996). However, the court stated that it urged law enforcement officers to comply literally with the provisions of G.S. 7B-2101, which in pertinent part provides that an officer must advise a juvenile that "the juvenile has a right to consult with an attorney and that one will be appointed for the juvenile if the juvenile is not represented and wants representation."

State v. Flowers, 128 N.C. App. 697 (1998). When the mother of the defendant, who was 13 years old, learned that the police were looking for him, she brought him to the police department. Before asking any questions, an officer read the defendant his juvenile rights in the mother's presence. After each right was read, the officer asked the defendant and his mother if they understood, and they answered "yes" each time. The defendant did not make any affirmative statement as to whether he would agree to talk with officers or whether he wanted a lawyer to be present. The officer interrogated the defendant in his mother's presence for about two hours.

The defendant argued that he never expressly waived his right to remain silent and his right to counsel. The court, citing *North Carolina v. Butler*, 441 U.S. 369 (1979), noted that an express waiver of *Miranda* rights is not required and ruled that a juvenile need not make an express waiver of juvenile rights. The defendant argued that he lacked the capacity to understand his rights because of his youth and low mental ability (a psychologist testified that the defendant was mildly retarded with a full-scale IQ of 56 and a verbal IQ of 48). The court discussed the evidence presented at the suppression hearing and upheld the trial judge's findings that the defendant knowingly, intelligently, and voluntarily waived his rights. The court stated, citing *State v. Fincher*, 309 N.C. 1 (1995), that a defendant's youth or subnormal mental capacity does not necessarily make him incapable of waiving his rights knowingly and voluntarily.

State v. Taylor, 128 N.C. App. 394 (1998). The court rejected the defendant's argument that an officer is required to advise a juvenile, before conducting custodial interrogation, that the juvenile could be tried as an adult for the offense being investigated. The court declined to follow rulings from other state courts that require an officer to advise the juvenile in that manner.

Fifth Amendment Issues and Court-Ordered Mental Examinations

Kansas v. Cheever, 134 S. Ct. 596 (2013). The Court ruled that the Fifth Amendment does not prohibit the government from introducing evidence from a court-ordered mental evaluation of a criminal defendant to rebut that defendant's presentation of expert testimony in support of a defense of voluntary intoxication. It explained:

> [We hold] that where a defense expert who has examined the defendant testifies that the defendant lacked the requisite mental state to commit an offense, the prosecution may present psychiatric evidence in rebuttal. . . . Any other rule would undermine the adversarial process, allowing a defendant to provide the jury, through an expert operating as proxy, with a one-sided and potentially inaccurate view of his mental state at the time of the alleged crime.

The Court noted that "admission of this rebuttal testimony harmonizes with the principle that when a defendant chooses to testify in a criminal case, the Fifth Amendment does not allow him to refuse to answer related questions on cross-examination."

State v. Huff, 325 N.C. 1 (1989). After the defendant filed notice of his intent to rely on the insanity defense and to introduce expert testimony supporting it, the court—on the State's motion—ordered the defendant to undergo examination at a state hospital about his mental state at the time of the offenses. Seven months later, when the defense counsel questioned the defendant's capacity to stand trial, the court ordered the defendant to undergo examination on that issue. At trial, after the defendant offered expert testimony on the insanity issue (including

that of a doctor who had examined the defendant at the first court-ordered examination), the State offered, over the defendant's objection, expert testimony on the insanity issue from the second court-ordered examination.

The court ruled that when a defendant relies on the insanity defense and introduces expert testimony about the defendant's mental status, the State may introduce expert testimony based on prior court-ordered psychiatric examinations to rebut that testimony without violating the Fifth Amendment or Article I, Section 23, of the North Carolina Constitution, because these constitutional provisions are inapplicable to these court-ordered psychiatric examinations. The court distinguished this case from *Estelle v. Smith*, 451 U.S. 454 (1981), and modified the rationale of *State v. Jackson*, 77 N.C. App. 491 (1985).

The court also ruled that the defendant's Sixth Amendment right to counsel (as well as his state constitutional right to counsel) was not violated by the court-ordered psychiatric examinations. Distinguishing *Estelle v. Smith* and relying on *Buchanan v. Kentucky*, 483 U.S. 402 (1987), the court ruled that the defendant's right to effective assistance of counsel was not violated by the counsel's failure to anticipate that the examination results might be used to rebut his insanity defense. It was sufficient under the Sixth Amendment that the defendant had an opportunity to discuss with his lawyer whether or not to submit to the second court-ordered examination and to discuss its scope as well. It was irrelevant that the second court order, which was to determine the defendant's competency to stand trial, did not specify that the examination was also to determine his mental state at the time of the offenses. [Author's note: The court also ruled that, based on the facts of this case, the State was entitled to a second court-ordered mental examination of the defendant.]

The Defendant's Sixth Amendment Right to Counsel

(*This topic is discussed on page 586.*)

Generally

UNITED STATES SUPREME COURT

Montejo v. Louisiana, 556 U.S. 778 (2009). The defendant was arrested for murder, waived his *Miranda* rights, and gave statements in response to officers' interrogation.

He was brought before a judge for a preliminary hearing; the judge ordered that the defendant be held without bond and appointed the Office of Indigent Defender to represent him. Later that day, two officers visited the defendant in prison and requested that he accompany them to locate the murder weapon. He was read his *Miranda* rights again and agreed to go with the officers. During the trip, he wrote an inculpatory letter of apology to the murder victim's widow. Only on his return did the defendant finally meet his court-appointed attorney. The issue in this case was whether the letter of apology was erroneously admitted in the defendant's trial, based on a violation of his Sixth Amendment right to counsel. In *Michigan v. Jackson*, 475 U.S. 625 (1986), the Court ruled that when a defendant requests counsel at an arraignment or similar proceeding that takes place at or after the attachment (beginning) of the Sixth Amendment right to counsel, an officer is thereafter prohibited under the Sixth Amendment from initiating interrogation of the defendant. (To put it another way, any waiver of counsel for the interrogation is automatically invalid.) Instead of deciding whether *Jackson* barred the officers from initiating interrogation of Montejo after a lawyer had been appointed for him, the Court overruled *Jackson* and remanded the case to a Louisiana court to determine unresolved factual and legal issues.

[Author's note: The effect of *Montejo*'s overruling of *Jackson* is to allow an officer to initiate interrogation provided the defendant is advised of his or her rights and knowingly and voluntarily waives the Sixth Amendment right to counsel. A defendant may execute a waiver of counsel without the presence of his or her attorney. Generally, a *Miranda* Fifth Amendment waiver of counsel would suffice as well for a Sixth Amendment waiver, although a cautious officer may want to add the name of the defendant's counsel to the waiver. There are several other issues to consider before the initiation of interrogation: (1) possible bars to the initiation of interrogation under the Fifth Amendment *Miranda* right-to-counsel cases of *Arizona v. Roberson*, 486 U.S. 675 (1988), and *Maryland v. Shatzer*, 559 U.S. 98 (2010); (2) the fact that any waiver of the Sixth Amendment right to counsel must be obtained even when the defendant is not in custody, because the Sixth Amendment right applies to a defendant whether or not he or she is in custody; and (3) the fact that surreptitious questioning of a defendant by an officer or officer's agent violates the Sixth Amendment right to counsel, even after the overruling of *Jackson*.]

Rothgery v. Gillespie County, 554 U.S. 191 (2008). Local Texas officers arrested Rothgery and brought him before a Texas state magistrate who found probable cause, formally apprised him of the accusation, and set bail. Rothgery was soon released after posting bond. Based on an unwritten county policy of denying appointed counsel for indigent defendants out on bond until at least the entry of an information or indictment, Rothgery was not appointed counsel for six months. The only issue before the Court was whether the proceeding before the magistrate was the initiation of adversary judicial proceedings under the Sixth Amendment right to counsel so that the right to counsel attached (began) then. The Court, citing *Brewer v. Williams*, 430 U.S. 387 (1997), and other cases, ruled that the proceeding was the initiation of adversary judicial proceedings, with the consequent State obligation to appoint counsel within a reasonable time once a defendant's request for assistance was made. A prosecutor need not be aware of or be involved with the proceeding for it to be considered the initiation of adversary judicial proceedings.

[Author's note: (1) North Carolina's current statutory law on appointment of counsel for judicial proceedings does not appear to be inconsistent with *Rothgery*. A defendant, if not released for a felony charge, is entitled under G.S. 15A-601(c) to a first appearance before a district court judge (which is when appointment of counsel for indigents is made) within 96 hours of being taken into custody or at the next district court session, whichever occurs first—or, if the defendant is released, at the next district court session. Although it was not decided in this case, it is highly likely that the Court would rule that neither a proceeding before a magistrate nor a first appearance before a district court judge is a critical stage of a prosecution at which a defendant has a Sixth Amendment right to counsel to represent him or her at these proceedings. There is a distinction between when the Sixth Amendment right to counsel attaches (begins) and a critical stage of a prosecution, at which a defendant has a Sixth Amendment right to have counsel represent him or her (the Court in *Rothgery* noted that distinction). A probable cause hearing is a critical stage, Coleman v. Alabama, 399 U.S. 1 (1970), and in any event there is a statutory right to counsel for an indigent defendant under G.S. 7A-451(b)(4) and for a nonindigent defendant under G.S. 15A-606(e). (2) The Court's ruling does affect North Carolina case law on investigative activities, which had ruled that the Sixth Amendment right to counsel does not attach (begin) for a felony until the first appearance in district court or indictment, whichever occurs first. Thus, for a typical felony case that begins with an arrest either with or without a warrant and an appearance before a magistrate or other judicial official, the Sixth Amendment right to counsel attaches (begins) with the appearance before a magistrate. That means that a critical stage occurring thereafter (for example, an officer's deliberate elicitation of information from the defendant by interrogation or conversation or the defendant's appearance in a lineup) is subject to case law concerning the Sixth Amendment right to counsel. The attachment (beginning) of the Sixth Amendment right to counsel no longer awaits the defendant's first appearance in district court. Based on *Patterson v. Illinois*, 487 U.S. 285 (1988), it is highly likely that the Court would rule that an officer's interrogation of a defendant at or after the defendant's appearance before a magistrate can be accomplished with *Miranda* warnings and waiver even though the defendant also has a Sixth Amendment right to counsel. North Carolina Supreme Court rulings are in accord. Of course, if the defendant requests counsel at or after the appearance before a magistrate, that request prevents interrogation even if the defendant is no longer in custody because the Sixth Amendment right to counsel, unlike *Miranda*'s Fifth Amendment right to counsel, applies whether or not the defendant is in custody.]

Fellers v. United States, 540 U.S. 519 (2004). A grand jury indicted the defendant for conspiracy to distribute methamphetamine. Law enforcement officers went to the defendant's home to arrest him. They knocked on the door, the defendant answered, and they identified themselves and asked if they could come in. The defendant invited them in. The officers advised him that they wanted to discuss his involvement in methamphetamine distribution. They informed him that they had a federal warrant for his arrest and that a grand jury had indicted him for conspiracy to distribute methamphetamine. They then told him that the indictment referred to his involvement with certain people, four of whom they named. The defendant then told the officers that he knew the four people and had used methamphetamine during his association with them. After spending 15 minutes in the defendant's home, the officers took the defendant to a county jail. There they advised the defendant for the first time of his *Miranda* rights. He waived those rights and reiterated the incriminating statements that he had made in his home. The Court ruled, relying on *Massiah*

v. United States, 377 U.S. 201 (1964), and other cases, that the officers deliberately elicited the statements made by the defendant in his home in violation of his Sixth Amendment right to counsel. The discussion at home occurred after the defendant had been indicted, outside the presence of counsel, and in the absence of any waiver of the defendant's Sixth Amendment rights. Responding to the argument that the defendant's statements were not the product of interrogation by the officers, the Court noted that the legal standard for deliberately eliciting statements under the Sixth Amendment is different from the legal standard for custodial interrogation under the Fifth Amendment. [Author's note: If the officers had advised the defendant of his *Miranda* rights and had obtained a valid waiver of those rights at his home, then under *Patterson v. Illinois*, 487 U.S. 285 (1988), the statements likely would have been properly obtained.] The Court remanded the case to the federal court of appeals to determine whether the defendant's statements at the county jail were admissible—that is, whether the rationale of *Oregon v. Elstad*, 470 U.S. 298 (1985), applies to the Sixth Amendment violation in this case.

Texas v. Cobb, 532 U.S. 167 (2001). A home was burglarized, and a mother and daughter living there were missing. The defendant confessed to the burglary but denied any knowledge of the missing mother and daughter. He was indicted for the burglary, and a lawyer was appointed to represent him. Officers later received information that the defendant had murdered the mother and daughter; they obtained arrest warrants for the murders and arrested the defendant. They then gave him *Miranda* warnings and received a proper waiver, and the defendant confessed to the murders. The defendant argued, relying on *Michigan v. Jackson*, 475 U.S. 625 (1986), that his Sixth Amendment right to counsel had been violated because officers interrogated him about the murders, which were closely related factually to the burglary; thus, his Sixth Amendment right to counsel attached to the murders when he was indicted for the burglary even though he had not yet been charged with those murders. The Court rejected the defendant's argument, although it noted that some lower federal court and state courts had adopted it.

The Court noted its ruling in *McNeil v. Wisconsin*, 501 U.S. 171 (1991), that the Sixth Amendment right to counsel is offense-specific. The Court ruled, however, that the term "offense" in its double jeopardy jurisprudence (*see* Blockburger v. United States, 284 U.S. 299 (1932)) applies to the determination of whether the Sixth Amendment right to counsel applies to related offenses, so that a defendant has a Sixth Amendment right to counsel for an uncharged offense only if it is the same offense under the *Blockburger* test (an offense is not the same "offense" as another offense if each of two offenses has an element that is not in the other offense). The Court ruled that murder and burglary were not the same offense under the *Blockburger* test. Therefore, the defendant in this case did not have a Sixth Amendment right to counsel for the murder charges as a result of the burglary indictment, and thus the officers did not violate that right when they interrogated the defendant about the murders. *See also* United States v. Avants, 278 F.3d 510 (5th Cir. 2002) (court applied *Cobb* ruling to murder that was first prosecuted in state court and then prosecuted in federal court; murder prosecutions were different offenses under Sixth Amendment because they also were different offenses under Double Jeopardy Clause).

McNeil v. Wisconsin, 501 U.S. 171 (1991). The defendant was arrested for armed robbery and advised of his *Miranda* rights. He refused to answer questions, although he did not request an attorney. A public defender represented the defendant in court at a bail hearing, at which a preliminary examination was scheduled. Officers from another county investigating an unrelated murder there visited the defendant in jail three times, properly gave him *Miranda* warnings, obtained a waiver each time, and secured incriminating statements about the murder. The Court noted that it is undisputed that when the defendant gave the incriminating statements about the murder, his Sixth Amendment right to counsel had attached and had been invoked for the robbery charge (apparently at a court hearing on that charge). However, the Court ruled that that invocation was offense-specific (that is, only for the robbery charge) and did not constitute an invocation of the right to counsel under the Fifth Amendment. Therefore, the officers did not violate the defendant's Fifth or Sixth Amendment rights to counsel by initiating interrogation about the murder: (1) his Sixth Amendment right to counsel had not attached for the murder because he had not yet been charged with that crime, and (2) he had never asserted his right to counsel under the Fifth Amendment. The Court did not decide if the Fifth Amendment right to counsel can properly be asserted at a time other than during custodial interrogation, although it indicated in footnote 3 that it can be asserted only during custodial interrogation.

Patterson v. Illinois, 487 U.S. 285 (1988). The defendant was arrested and then indicted for murder. Before he requested counsel, was assigned counsel, or retained counsel (*see* Maine v. Moulton, 474 U.S. 159 (1985); Michigan v. Jackson, 475 U.S. 625 (1986)), he was questioned by an officer and later by a prosecutor—after properly having been given *Miranda* warnings and having waived them. The Court ruled that (1) no Sixth Amendment violation occurred in questioning the defendant in this case, because he had not asserted his right to counsel, and (2) in the context of this case, involving a Sixth Amendment right to counsel for post-indictment questioning, *Miranda* warnings and waiver were sufficient to waive the defendant's Sixth Amendment right to counsel. *See also* State v. Wynne, 329 N.C. 507 (1991) (assuming, without deciding, that defendant had a Sixth Amendment right to counsel (which he clearly did not), the court ruled that the officers' giving of *Miranda* warnings and obtaining a waiver constituted a proper waiver of his Sixth Amendment right to counsel); United States v. Charria, 919 F.2d 842 (2d Cir. 1990) (*Miranda* warnings were sufficient to waive Sixth Amendment right to counsel); United States v. Muca, 945 F.2d 88 (4th Cir. 1991) (similar ruling).

In dicta, the Court stated that it need not decide whether a valid waiver must include a statement to the defendant that he or she has been indicted. [Author's note: It appears that the Court would not require such a statement.]

The Court also noted that some post-indictment questioning that is permissible under the Fifth Amendment under *Miranda* would not be permissible under the Sixth Amendment: (1) an officer's not telling the defendant that his lawyer was trying to reach him during questioning (Moran v. Burbine, 475 U.S. 412 (1986)) or (2) surreptitious, noncustodial questioning (United States v. Henry, 447 U.S. 264 (1980)).

Satterwhite v. Texas, 486 U.S. 249 (1988). Following *Estelle v. Smith*, discussed below, the Court ruled that the defendant's Sixth Amendment right to counsel was violated when, after the defendant had been indicted, the trial court ordered him, without actual notice to the defendant's counsel, to undergo a psychiatric examination to determine his future dangerousness. Therefore, the psychiatrist's testimony was inadmissible at the defendant's capital sentencing hearing. The Court also ruled that a violation of *Estelle v. Smith* is subject to a harmless error analysis. However, the Court determined that the violation in this case was not harmless error. *See also*

Powell v. Texas, 492 U.S. 680 (1989) (defendant's Sixth Amendment right to counsel was violated when, without notice to his lawyer, he was ordered to undergo psychiatric examination to determine his future dangerousness).

Buchanan v. Kentucky, 483 U.S. 402 (1987). When the defendant at trial offered the defense of "extreme emotional disturbance" by introducing psychological evaluations of his mental condition, the prosecutor in rebuttal offered psychological evidence from involuntary hospitalization proceedings that had resulted from a petition for involuntary hospitalization (which had been conducted before trial by motion of the prosecutor and defense counsel). Because the defendant had joined in the petition that led to this psychological evidence, neither his Fifth nor Sixth Amendment rights were violated. *Estelle v. Smith*, discussed below, was distinguished. *See also* Pawlyk v. Wood, 237 F.3d 1054 (9th Cir. 2001), *opinion amended*, 248 F.3d 815 (9th Cir. 2001) (no due process violation when State introduced testimony of former defense psychiatrist funded by State, whom defendant had elected not to offer as a witness, in rebuttal to insanity evidence presented by second defense psychiatrist funded by State).

Moran v. Burbine, 475 U.S. 412 (1986). A defendant's Sixth Amendment right to counsel is not violated by an officer's interference with a relationship between a defendant and a lawyer that occurs before the initiation of adversary judicial proceedings, although a due process violation may be committed.

Estelle v. Smith, 451 U.S. 454 (1981). The defendant, indicted for murder, was in jail awaiting trial. A judge ordered a prosecutor to arrange a psychiatric examination of the defendant to determine his competency to stand trial. (The defendant did not request a psychiatric evaluation or attempt to introduce any psychiatric evidence at trial.) The psychiatrist later testified at a capital sentencing hearing about the defendant's future dangerousness, based on the defendant's statements at his examination.

The Court ruled that because the defendant's counsel was not notified in advance that the psychiatric examination would include the issue of future dangerousness, the defendant's Sixth Amendment right to counsel was violated—he was denied the assistance of his attorneys in deciding whether to submit to the examination and not told how the psychiatrist's findings would be used. The Court also ruled that the statements were admitted in violation of the defendant's Fifth Amendment rights,

because he had not been given *Miranda* warnings before the examination. The Court noted that this was not a case involving a routine competency examination or a court's ordering a defendant to undergo a State-requested psychiatric examination because the defendant asserts an insanity defense and will introduce supporting psychiatric testimony. For such a case, see *State v. Jackson*, 77 N.C. App. 491 (1985).

Brewer v. Williams, 430 U.S. 387 (1977). The defendant was arraigned before a judge in court under a warrant charging him with the murder of a young girl (whose body had not yet been found), and he was committed to jail. His lawyer specifically told the officers, who were about to transport the defendant to another jail, that they were not to question him about the girl's disappearance during the trip. While the defendant was being transported, the detective—who knew that the defendant was a former mental patient and deeply religious—spoke to him about the need to find the girl's body to give her a decent Christian burial and how the falling snow might prevent her body from ever being found. The defendant then led the detective to the body.

The Court ruled that the defendant's Sixth Amendment right to counsel was violated by the detective's deliberate attempt to elicit information from him in the absence of counsel during the trip. The Court noted that although the defendant could have waived his right to counsel without notice to his lawyer, the State failed to satisfy its heavy burden of showing that this had happened. *See also* State v. Smith, 294 N.C. 365 (1978) (defendant may waive his rights in the absence of counsel and agree to be questioned by officers); State v. Bauguss, 310 N.C. 259 (1984).

McLeod v. Ohio, 381 U.S. 356 (1965). The defendant was indicted for a murder committed during a robbery. Before he had retained or had been assigned counsel, he voluntarily made an oral confession while he, a deputy sheriff, and a prosecutor were riding in the deputy's car searching for the gun used in the robbery. He had not waived his right to counsel before he confessed. The Ohio Supreme Court in *Ohio v. McLeod*, 203 N.E.2d 349 (Ohio 1964), ruled that McLeod's Sixth Amendment right to counsel had not been violated and his confession was admissible. It stated that *Massiah v. United States*, 377 U.S. 201 (1964), was distinguishable, because although McLeod had confessed without counsel or waiver of counsel, he had done so willingly and in the presence of these two public officers. It also noted that McLeod had not requested counsel before he confessed. The United States Supreme Court, citing *Massiah*, summarily reversed (without an opinion) the judgment of the Ohio Supreme Court. Compare this case with *Patterson v. Illinois*, discussed above.

NORTH CAROLINA SUPREME COURT

State v. Phillips, 365 N.C. 103 (2011). (1) The court ruled that officers did not violate the capital defendant's Sixth Amendment right to counsel by continuing to question him after an attorney who had been appointed provisional counsel arrived at the sheriff's office and was denied access to the defendant. The interrogation had begun before the attorney arrived, the defendant had waived his *Miranda* rights, and the defendant never stated that he wanted the questioning to stop or that he wanted to speak with an attorney. The court cited *Moran v. Burbine*, 475 U.S. 412 (1986); *State v. Hyatt*, 355 N.C. 642 (2002); and *State v. Reese*, 319 N.C. 110 (1987). (2) The court ruled that Office of Indigent Defense Services statutes and rules concerning an indigent's entitlement to counsel did not make the defendant's statement inadmissible. Although the relevant statutes create an entitlement to counsel and authorize provisional counsel to seek access to a potential capital defendant, they do not override a defendant's waiver of the right to counsel, which the defendant had executed in this case.

State v. Davis, 349 N.C. 1 (1998). A defendant does not have a Sixth Amendment right to have counsel present during a competency evaluation.

State v. Warren, 348 N.C. 80 (1998). [Author's note: This case involved the trial and conviction of the defendant for a murder committed in High Point.] On May 29, 1990, the defendant requested counsel during custodial interrogation by an Asheville detective, who was questioning him about a murder committed in Asheville. When the interrogation concluded, the defendant was arrested on an outstanding warrant for a motor vehicle violation and for misdemeanor larceny of the Asheville murder victim's pocketbook. He was not, however, arrested or charged for the Asheville murder. He was represented by an attorney in Asheville district court for these charges and released on bond on June 7, 1990. The defendant was later arrested in High Point on July 20, 1990, for a South Carolina murder. He was properly given *Miranda* warnings and confessed to murders in South Carolina, New York, Asheville, and High Point.

(1) The defendant argued on appeal that the interrogation about the High Point murder violated his Fifth Amendment right to counsel. The court ruled, relying on a statement in *McNeil v. Wisconsin*, 501 U.S. 171 (1991), that the rule prohibiting reinitiation of interrogation after a defendant's assertion of the right to counsel during custodial interrogation does not apply when there has been a break in custody (in this case, the defendant was released from custody on June 7, 1990, and was not arrested again until July 20, 1990). (2) The defendant argued on appeal that the interrogation violated his Sixth Amendment right to counsel. The court rejected this argument because the Sixth Amendment right to counsel is offense-specific and adversary judicial proceedings had not begun for the High Point murder at the time of the interrogation. The defendant also argued on appeal that, despite the offense-specific requirement, his Sixth Amendment right to counsel had begun for the Asheville charges and they were inextricably intertwined with the High Point murder. While the court acknowledged that some cases had recognized the principle of inextricably intertwined cases triggering the Sixth Amendment right to counsel, the High Point murder and the Asheville charges were not such a case. In fact, the High Point murder had not even been committed when the Asheville charges were brought. [Author's note: The later ruling in *Texas v. Cobb*, 532 U.S. 167 (2001), would require the same ruling in this case because the Asheville charges and the High Point murder were not the same offenses under the Sixth Amendment as set out in *Cobb*.]

State v. Adams, 345 N.C. 745 (1997). The court ruled that the defendant did not have a Sixth Amendment right to counsel when the State brought a civil petition for child abuse. The Sixth Amendment right to counsel applies only to criminal charges.

State v. Palmer, 334 N.C. 104 (1993). The court ruled that an officer who gave *Miranda* warnings sufficiently established the defendant's valid waiver of his Sixth Amendment and state constitutional right to counsel. The officer was not required to explain specifically to the defendant that he was waiving his right to counsel under these constitutional provisions. *See also* United States v. Chadwick, 999 F.2d 1282 (8th Cir. 1993) (*Miranda* warnings sufficient to waive Sixth Amendment right to counsel; officer is not required to inform defendant that he or she has been indicted).

State v. Tucker, 331 N.C. 12 (1992). The defendant was indicted for murder on April 18, 1988. On April 20,

1988, the defendant made his first appearance in district court, and a lawyer was appointed to represent him. Later that day the defendant met with his appointed lawyer, who told him not to talk with anyone without counsel. On April 21, 1988, the investigating officer met with the defendant (not at the defendant's initiative) in the county jail and stated that he wanted the defendant to go with him to another county to look for the murder victim's body. The defendant told the officer what his lawyer had said. The defendant also tried twice unsuccessfully to call his lawyer. The officer told the defendant that they needed to hurry and commented that he was after the defendant's accomplice, not necessarily the defendant. The officer later obtained incriminating statements from the defendant, which were introduced at his murder trial. The court ruled that the officer violated the defendant's Sixth Amendment rights to counsel.

The court also ruled that the officer violated the defendant's Fifth Amendment right to counsel. Although under *McNeil v. Wisconsin*, 501 U.S. 171 (1991), the defendant's request for counsel at the first appearance was not considered an assertion of the Fifth Amendment right to counsel, the court ruled that the defendant invoked his Fifth Amendment right to counsel by informing the officer of his desire to call his lawyer and in attempting to do so. Thus, under *Edwards v. Arizona*, 451 U.S. 477 (1981), the officer could not interrogate the defendant unless the defendant initiated communication with the officer. The officer's continued interrogation of the defendant after he invoked his Fifth Amendment right to counsel violated *Edwards*, and the defendant's later waiver of the right to counsel was invalid. Therefore, the incriminating statements were inadmissible.

State v. Huff, 325 N.C. 1 (1989). After the defendant filed notice of his intent to rely on the insanity defense and to introduce expert testimony supporting it, the court—on the State's motion—ordered the defendant to undergo examination at a state hospital about his mental state at the time of the offenses. Seven months later, when the defense counsel questioned the defendant's capacity to stand trial, the court ordered the defendant to undergo examination on that issue. At trial, after the defendant offered expert testimony on the insanity issue (including that of a doctor who had examined the defendant at the first court-ordered examination), the State offered, over the defendant's objection, expert testimony on the insanity issue from the second court-ordered examination.

The court ruled that when a defendant relies on the insanity defense and introduces expert testimony about the defendant's mental status, the State may introduce expert testimony based on prior court-ordered psychiatric examinations to rebut that testimony without violating the Fifth Amendment or Article I, Section 23, of the North Carolina Constitution, because these constitutional provisions are inapplicable to these court-ordered psychiatric examinations. The court distinguished this case from *Estelle v. Smith*, discussed above, and modified the rationale of *State v. Jackson*, 77 N.C. App. 491 (1985). The court also ruled that the defendant's Sixth Amendment right to counsel (as well as his state constitutional right to counsel) was not violated by the court-ordered psychiatric examinations. Distinguishing *Estelle v. Smith* and relying on *Buchanan v. Kentucky*, discussed above, the court ruled that the defendant's right to effective assistance of counsel was not violated by the counsel's failure to anticipate that the examination results might be used to rebut his insanity defense. It was sufficient under the Sixth Amendment that the defendant had an opportunity to discuss with his lawyer whether or not to submit to the second court-ordered examination and to discuss its scope as well. It was irrelevant that the second court order, which was to determine the defendant's competency to stand trial, did not specify that the examination was also to determine his mental state at the time of the offenses. (The court also ruled that, based on the facts of this case, the State was entitled to a second court-ordered mental examination of the defendant.)

State v. Nations, 319 N.C. 318; 319 N.C. 329 (1987). The defendant was arrested for a sex offense with a child, placed in jail, and given *Miranda* warnings. He asserted his right to counsel and interrogation stopped. The defendant was provided a first appearance in district court, and counsel was appointed (his Sixth Amendment right to counsel attached at first appearance). About a week later, the defendant told a volunteer jailer that he wanted to speak with someone from mental health services. The protective services supervisor of the social services department was visiting in the jail and spoke with the defendant, who confessed to him. The defendant told the supervisor that he would be willing to talk with an officer. An officer arrived and gave him *Miranda* warnings and obtained a waiver. The defendant also confessed to the officer. The court ruled that the social services worker was not an agent of any law enforcement officer, the defendant initiated both contacts and volunteered his confession, and therefore no interrogation took place. Neither his Fifth nor Sixth Amendment rights were violated.

State v. Reese, 319 N.C. 110 (1987). The defendant was arrested for murder, he asserted his right to counsel during custodial interrogation, and interrogation stopped. He was appointed counsel at his first appearance in district court. The defendant's lawyer instructed officers not to question his client. However, in his lawyer's absence, the defendant sought out an officer to make a statement. The officer reminded the defendant that he had appointed counsel, truthfully told him that his lawyer was unavailable because he was out of town, and asked the defendant if he still wanted to talk with him. The defendant stated that he still wanted to make a statement. He then voluntarily, knowingly, and intelligently waived his Fifth and Sixth Amendment rights to counsel before he gave a statement; the officer specifically reminded him that he had appointed counsel.

The court ruled that the defendant's waiver was valid despite the fact that the officer did not inform the defendant of his lawyer's instruction to the officers. His lawyer's instruction was irrelevant in determining the validity of the defendant's waiver of counsel. The Fifth and Sixth Amendment right to counsel belongs to the defendant; an attorney cannot control the defendant's exercise of the defendant's constitutional rights. To the extent that *State v. Baguss,* 310 N.C. 259 (1984), indicated that a lawyer can control access to the client under these circumstances, it was overruled.

NORTH CAROLINA COURT OF APPEALS

State v. Williams, 209 N.C. App. 255 (2011). The court ruled, relying on *State v. Strobel,* 164 N.C. App. 310 (2004), that no violation of the defendant's Sixth Amendment right to counsel occurred when detectives interviewed him on new charges while he was in custody on other unrelated charges. The Sixth Amendment right to counsel is offense-specific and had not attached for the new crimes.

State v. Strobel, 164 N.C. App. 310 (2004). Three people were involved in an armed robbery. The defendant was arrested for conspiracy to commit the armed robbery, appeared in district court, and requested and was appointed an attorney in December 2001. Based on additional information implicating her as a participant in the robbery, in January 2002 an officer arrested the defendant for armed robbery. The officer did not orally advise the defendant of her *Miranda* rights. Instead,

he gave her a written form and asked her to read it. She signed each page of the statement that acknowledged that she had read it. During her interrogation, the defendant mentioned that she had a court-appointed attorney representing her on the conspiracy charge. The officer told the defendant that she could use the telephone and telephone book located in the room to call her attorney. He also told her that he would stop interrogation until she had the opportunity to talk to her lawyer. The court ruled, relying on *Texas v. Cobb,* 532 U.S. 162 (2001), and *State v. Warren,* 348 N.C. 80 (1998), that the officer did not violate the defendant's Sixth Amendment right to counsel when he arrested and interrogated her for the armed robbery charge after she already had been charged and had an attorney for the related charge of conspiracy to commit armed robbery. The two charges are separate under the standard set out in the *Cobb* ruling.

State v. Harris, 111 N.C. App. 58 (1993). The defendant was arrested for an armed robbery of a Fast Fare store, committed to jail, and given his first appearance in district court, where he declined appointed counsel (he stated he would hire his own attorney). He remained in jail for that charge. The next day he changed his mind and requested and was appointed counsel. Later that day, a detective who was investigating an unrelated armed robbery of a Circle K store interrogated the defendant after properly giving him *Miranda* warnings and obtaining a waiver of rights. Relying on *McNeil v. Wisconsin,* 501 U.S. 171 (1991), the court ruled that the defendant, when he invoked his Sixth Amendment right to counsel for the Fast Fare robbery, did not invoke his Fifth Amendment right to counsel concerning the interrogation about the Circle K robbery (he did not have a Sixth Amendment right to counsel because he had not yet been charged for that offense). The court also rejected the defendant's arguments under Article I, Section 23, of the North Carolina Constitution.

FEDERAL APPELLATE COURTS

United States v. Montgomery, 262 F.3d 233 (4th Cir. 2001). The defendant was charged with murder in state court and invoked his Sixth Amendment right to counsel. The State later dismissed the murder charge. Thereafter, federal authorities obtained a statement from the defendant about the murder and prosecuted him for that murder. The court ruled that the defendant's invocation of his right to counsel did not bar federal authorities from eliciting statements from him, absent evidence that the federal and state authorities attempted to circumvent the defendant's Sixth Amendment right to counsel.

United States v. Hayes, 231 F.3d 663 (9th Cir. 2000). The defendant, who was not charged with an offense, was informed that he was a target of federal investigation and hired counsel (counsel was later appointed for him when he no longer had retained counsel). However, he did not have a Sixth Amendment right to counsel to require the suppression of an incriminating tape recording of his conversation with a co-conspirator without his counsel being present. The Sixth Amendment right to counsel applies only when a formal charge has been brought. The fact that a defendant has counsel does not by itself create a Sixth Amendment right to counsel to bar interrogation by the government.

Chewning v. Rogerson, 29 F.3d 418 (8th Cir. 1994). The court ruled that the defendant's representation by an attorney at an extradition hearing was not an invocation of his Sixth Amendment right to counsel for the murder charge for which he was being extradited.

Polygraph Examination Issues

State v. Coffey, 345 N.C. 389 (1997). The defendant was arrested for murder, and two attorneys were appointed to represent him. The attorneys requested that the district attorney have a polygraph examination conducted on the defendant but did not express any desire to accompany their client to the polygraph site. When the defendant was being removed from his cell for the polygraph examination, he told a deputy sheriff that he wanted to call his attorney. The deputy declined to allow the defendant to do so, because the policy of the sheriff's office did not permit a prisoner to make a telephone call while being transported from one facility to another. Later, when the polygraph operator was explaining the polygraph procedures to the defendant, the defendant stated that he did not tell the investigating officers the truth about the money taken from the murder victim. The operator asked him what he did not tell the truth about. The defendant said that he was handed the money by his accomplice and the accomplice "went off." The operator did not ask any further questions; instead, he conducted the polygraph examination. After the examination, the operator informed the defendant that he had not passed the polygraph about the murder and robbery. The defendant then made an incriminating statement. The operator asked the defendant if he would be willing to talk to one of the investigating officers. The defendant named a par-

ticular officer and later repeated the same incriminating statement to that officer.

The court ruled that the defendant was not being interrogated in violation of *Edwards v. Arizona*, 451 U.S. 477 (1981) (interrogation is not permitted after defendant has asserted right to counsel), when he made his statements to the polygraph operator and the investigating officer. These statements were volunteered by the defendant. Thus, neither his Fifth nor Sixth Amendment rights to counsel were violated. The court alternatively ruled, assuming that the defendant was being interrogated, that the defendant initiated the communication with the polygraph operator and investigating officer. *See, e.g.,* Oregon v. Bradshaw, 462 U.S. 1039 (1983).

State v. Shepherd, 163 N.C. App. 646 (2004). The defendant was arrested and charged with several sex offenses. He requested, through his attorney, to take a polygraph test concerning the offenses. Before the polygraph test, the defendant and his attorney signed documents waiving the attorney's presence at the polygraph examination. During the polygraph examiner's post-test interview, the defendant made incriminating statements that were introduced at trial. The court noted the examiner's testimony that the examination consists of a pre-test examination, the instrumentation phase, and the post-test interview. The court ruled, relying on *State v. Soles*, 119 N.C. App. 375 (1995), that the defendant's waiver of counsel applied to all phases of the examination and thus permitted the introduction of the defendant's incriminating statements made without his counsel's presence.

State v. Soles, 119 N.C. App. 375 (1995). Officers took the defendant, with his consent, for questioning. The defendant was not handcuffed during a four-hour interview, was left alone, and was allowed to use the vending machines. The defendant conceded on appeal that he was free to leave and voluntarily gave a statement to the officers. The court ruled that the defendant was not in custody to require *Miranda* warnings. At a second interview six days later, a polygraph examiner confronted the defendant about patterns of deception and questioned him in addition to the polygraph testing. The operator had given *Miranda* warnings to the defendant and obtained a waiver before the testing. In any event, the court ruled that the defendant was not in custody to require *Miranda* warnings, because the defendant had voluntarily come to the police station for the polygraph and was free to leave at any time. The court also ruled, based on the facts in this case, that the defendant's second statement was voluntarily given.

Mental Examination Issues

Satterwhite v. Texas, 486 U.S. 249 (1988). Following *Estelle v. Smith*, discussed below, the Court ruled that the defendant's Sixth Amendment right to counsel was violated when, after the defendant had been indicted, the trial court ordered him, without actual notice to the defendant's counsel, to undergo a psychiatric examination to determine his future dangerousness. Therefore, the psychiatrist's testimony was inadmissible at his capital sentencing hearing. The Court also ruled that a violation of *Estelle v. Smith* is subject to a harmless error analysis. However, the Court determined that the violation in this case was not harmless error. *See also* Powell v. Texas, 492 U.S. 680 (1989) (defendant's Sixth Amendment right to counsel was violated when, without notice to his lawyer, he was ordered to undergo psychiatric examination to determine his future dangerousness).

Buchanan v. Kentucky, 483 U.S. 402 (1987). When the defendant at trial offered the defense of "extreme emotional disturbance" by introducing psychological evaluations of his mental condition, the prosecutor in rebuttal offered psychological evidence from involuntary hospitalization proceedings that had resulted from a petition for involuntary hospitalization (which had been conducted before trial by motion of the prosecutor and defense counsel). Because the defendant had joined in the petition that led to this psychological evidence, neither his Fifth nor Sixth Amendment rights were violated. *Estelle v. Smith*, discussed below, was distinguished. *See also* Pawlyk v. Wood, 237 F.3d 1054 (9th Cir. 2001), *opinion amended*, 248 F.3d 815 (9th Cir. 2001) (no due process violation when State introduced testimony of former defense psychiatrist funded by State, whom defendant had elected not to offer as a witness, in rebuttal to insanity evidence presented by second defense psychiatrist funded by State).

Estelle v. Smith, 451 U.S. 454 (1981). The defendant, indicted for murder, was in jail awaiting trial. A judge ordered a prosecutor to arrange a psychiatric examination of the defendant to determine his competency to stand trial. (The defendant did not request a psychiatric evaluation or attempt to introduce any psychiatric evidence at trial.) The psychiatrist later testified at a capital sentencing hearing about the defendant's future dangerousness, based on the defendant's statements at his examination.

The Court ruled that because the defendant's counsel was not notified in advance that the psychiatric examination would include the issue of future dangerousness, the defendant's Sixth Amendment right to counsel was violated—he was denied the assistance of his attorneys in deciding whether to submit to the examination and not told how the psychiatrist's findings would be used. The Court also ruled that the statements were admitted in violation of the defendant's Fifth Amendment rights, because he had not been given *Miranda* warnings before the examination. The Court noted that this was not a case involving a routine competency examination or a court's ordering a defendant to undergo a State-requested psychiatric examination because the defendant asserts an insanity defense and will introduce supporting psychiatric testimony. For such a case, see *State v. Jackson*, 77 N.C. App. 491 (1985).

State v. Huff, 325 N.C. 1 (1989). After the defendant filed notice of his intent to rely on the insanity defense and to introduce expert testimony supporting it, the court—on the State's motion—ordered the defendant to undergo examination at a state hospital about his mental state at the time of the offenses. Seven months later, when the defense counsel questioned the defendant's capacity to stand trial, the court ordered the defendant to undergo examination on that issue. At trial, after the defendant offered expert testimony on the insanity issue (including that of a doctor who had examined the defendant at the first court-ordered examination), the State offered, over the defendant's objection, expert testimony on the insanity issue from the second court-ordered examination.

The court ruled that when a defendant relies on the insanity defense and introduces expert testimony about the defendant's mental status, the State may introduce expert testimony based on prior court-ordered psychiatric examinations to rebut that testimony without violating the Fifth Amendment or Article I, Section 23, of the North Carolina Constitution, because these constitutional provisions are inapplicable to these court-ordered psychiatric examinations. The court distinguished this case from *Estelle v. Smith*, discussed above, and modified the rationale of *State v. Jackson*, 77 N.C. App. 491 (1985). The court also ruled that the defendant's Sixth Amendment right to counsel (as well as his state constitutional right to counsel) was not violated by the court-ordered psychiatric examinations. Distinguishing *Estelle v. Smith* and relying on *Buchanan v. Kentucky*, discussed above, the court ruled that the defendant's right to effective assistance of counsel was not violated by the counsel's failure to anticipate that the examination results might be used to rebut his insanity defense. It was sufficient under the Sixth Amendment that the defendant had an opportunity to discuss with his lawyer whether or not to submit to the second court-ordered examination and to discuss its scope as well. It was irrelevant that the second court order, which was to determine the defendant's competency to stand trial, did not specify that the examination was also to determine his mental state at the time of the offenses. (The court also ruled that, based on the facts of this case, the State was entitled to a second court-ordered mental examination of the defendant.)

Use of Informants to Obtain Statements

(*This topic is discussed on page 590.*)

UNITED STATES SUPREME COURT

Kuhlmann v. Wilson, 477 U.S. 436 (1986). The defendant was arrested for robbery and murder. He told officers that he witnessed the robbery but denied being involved. He was arraigned before a judge and committed to jail. A detective placed a police informant in the defendant's cell (the defendant did not know he was an informant). He instructed the informant not to ask the defendant any questions but simply to "keep [his] ear open" for the names of accomplices in the robbery and murder. At first the defendant told the informant the same story he had told the officers, although the informant told the defendant that his explanation "didn't sound too good." A few days later, the defendant's brother visited him and told him that his family was upset because they believed that the defendant was involved in the crimes. After the visit, the defendant essentially confessed to the informant. The informant told the detective about the confession and gave him notes about it that he had written surreptitiously in his cell.

Distinguishing *United States v. Henry* and *Maine v. Moulton*, discussed below, the Court ruled that the defendant's confession was not taken in violation of his Sixth Amendment right to counsel. The Court stated that a defendant's right to counsel is not violated by the fact, standing alone, that an informant, either voluntarily or by prior agreement, reports incriminating statements to a law enforcement officer. Instead, some evidence must exist that an officer and his informant deliberately

intended to elicit incriminating statements—not merely to listen for information. In this case, the detective only instructed the informant to listen to the defendant to determine the identities of other participants in the robbery and murder (solid evidence already linked the defendant to these crimes). The informant never asked the defendant about the pending charges; he only listened to the defendant's spontaneous and unsolicited statements. The mere fact that the informant commented unfavorably to the defendant about his initial version of noninvolvement in the crimes was not sufficient to find in this case that the informant deliberately elicited the defendant's later incriminating statements. *See also* United States v. York, 933 F.2d 1343 (7th Cir. 1991) (although inmate was government agent, he did not deliberately elicit information from defendant); United States v. Stubbs, 944 F.2d 828 (11th Cir. 1991) (similar ruling).

Maine v. Moulton, 474 U.S. 159 (1985). The defendant was indicted for theft charges along with his codefendant, Colson. The defendant retained a lawyer, pled not guilty, and was released on bail. Sometime later, the defendant met with Colson and suggested killing one of the State's witnesses, and they discussed how to commit the murder. Colson eventually confessed to officers about his involvement with the thefts and some other crimes, and he also told them about the plan to kill the witness. The officers offered Colson a deal: they would bring no further charges if he would testify against the defendant and cooperate with them. Colson also agreed to have his telephone conversations recorded in order to pick up conversations with the defendant and any anonymous threats (Colson had told the officers of having received threatening calls). The defendant, unaware that Colson was cooperating with the officers, asked Colson to meet him to discuss their defense at their upcoming theft trial. The officers wired Colson for this meeting and told him not to question the defendant but just to have a conversation. During this meeting, the defendant made incriminating statements, which were used at his theft trial.

The Court ruled that the officers "deliberately elicited" these incriminating statements in violation of the defendant's Sixth Amendment right to counsel. The officer's instructions to Colson were not sufficient to protect against Colson's discussing the pending theft charges with the defendant, especially because they knew that the defendant had set up the meeting for that purpose. Although the State argued that it had a legitimate reason to record the conversations—the proposed killing of a State's witness—the Court stated that the officers had a dual purpose: the continued investigation of the theft charges and the proposed murder. The Court clearly stated that the defendant's incriminating statements about the proposed murder would be admissible in a trial for that charge, because his Sixth Amendment right to counsel had not attached for that crime.

United States v. Henry, 447 U.S. 264 (1980). The defendant was indicted (thus, his Sixth Amendment right to counsel had attached) for armed robbery and was in jail awaiting trial. A federal officer, who was investigating the robbery, asked a paid government informant who was incarcerated in the same jail (he eventually shared a cell with the defendant) to be alert to any statements made by federal prisoners there. He instructed the informant that he should not initiate any conversations with the defendant or any other prisoner but should pay attention to any information the defendant might furnish. The defendant eventually revealed information to the informant about his participation in the robbery.

The Court stated that the issue is whether the informant, a government agent, "deliberately elicited" statements from the defendant, and it ruled that the informant did so in violation of the defendant's Sixth Amendment right to counsel. First, the defendant was unaware that the informant was acting as a government agent. Second, the informant had an incentive to produce useful information—he was paid only if he produced useful information. Third, the fact that the informant and defendant were confined together made the defendant particularly susceptible to the informant's ploys.

The Court noted that although the federal officers instructed the informant not to question the defendant, the informant was not a passive listener—rather, he talked with the defendant, and the statements resulted from these conversations. Even if the federal agent did not intend that the informant affirmatively take steps to secure information from the defendant, he must have known that the close proximity of the two would probably lead to that result. This was not a case of a passive listener or a passive listening device that overhears statements. (See *Kuhlmann v. Wilson*, discussed above.) The Court noted that it did not question its prior rulings concerning the permissive use of undercover agents in obtaining statements from people not in custody and before their Sixth Amendment right to counsel had attached, as in *Hoffa v. United States*, 385 U.S. 293 (1966) (defendant's incriminating statements made to a secret government

informant during the course of a labor-racketeering trial were admissible at later jury-tampering charge, because he made them before his Sixth Amendment right to counsel had attached for that charge), and *United States v. White*, 401 U.S. 745 (1971) (no Fourth Amendment violation occurred when a government agent was wired to transmit to officers his conversations about drug transactions with the defendant; conversations took place before his Sixth Amendment right to counsel had attached for the drug charges). *See also* State v. Thompson, 322 N.C. 204 (1992) (no Fourth or Sixth Amendment violations occurred when officers used accomplice to elicit incriminating statements from a defendant who had not been charged with any offense).

Massiah v. United States, 377 U.S. 201 (1964). The defendant was indicted for importing drugs into the United States, retained a lawyer, pled not guilty, and was released on bail. A federal agent wired an accomplice's car (with the accomplice's permission but without the defendant's knowledge) with a radio transmitter. While the accomplice and the defendant sat in the car and talked about the case, the agent listened to their conversations and heard the defendant make incriminating statements about the drug charges. The Court ruled that the defendant's right to counsel had been violated because the government deliberately elicited statements from the defendant after his right to counsel had attached.

NORTH CAROLINA SUPREME COURT

State v. Taylor, 332 N.C. 372 (1992). The defendant was in jail awaiting trial for murder. An inmate reported the defendant's incriminating statements to an SBI agent. The SBI agent told the inmate that he should not make any further contact with the defendant and that the inmate was not working for anyone on behalf of the State. The agent also refused to make any deals with the inmate for the information. The agent had five more meetings with the inmate, who revealed additional incriminating statements by the defendant. Relying on *Kuhlmann v. Wilson*, discussed above, the court ruled that the defendant's statements to the inmate were not taken in violation of the defendant's Sixth Amendment right to counsel.

NORTH CAROLINA COURT OF APPEALS

State v. Brown, 67 N.C. App. 223 (1984). The defendant's Sixth Amendment right to counsel was not violated when an officer recorded conversations between an undercover informant and the defendant concerning (1) a crime (solicitation to murder) for which his Sixth Amendment right to counsel had not attached and (2) crimes for which his Sixth Amendment right to counsel had attached (he had been indicted), because the defendant had waived his right to counsel in court. [Author's note: Although decided before *Maine v. Moulton*, discussed above, this case appears to be consistent with it, because the defendant had waived his right to counsel and had agreed to represent himself.]

FEDERAL APPELLATE COURTS

United States v. LaBare, 191 F.3d 60 (1st Cir. 1999). When a jail inmate simply agrees to report whatever he or she learns about crimes from other inmates in general (without a focus on a particular inmate), the inmate is not a government agent for the purpose of the ruling in *Massiah v. United States*, 377 U.S. 201 (1964), discussed above.

United States v. Ford, 176 F.3d 376 (6th Cir. 1999). The government did not violate the defendant's Sixth Amendment right to counsel by sending an informant into the defendant's jail cell to tape record conversations about uncharged offenses that the defendant may have committed. The court also ruled that the federal prosecutors did not violate Rule 4.2 of the Kentucky Rules of Professional Conduct (which is substantially identical to Rule 4.2 of the North Carolina Rules of Professional Conduct) by doing so. The court noted that Rule 4.2 ("a lawyer shall not communicate about the subject of the representation . . .") does not apply, because the prosecutors were investigating an offense other than the offense for which the defendant was indicted. [Author's note: See 97 Formal Ethics Opinion 10 of the North Carolina State Bar, which is not inconsistent with the ruling on the ethical issue in this case.]

United States v. Ingle, 157 F.3d 1147 (8th Cir. 1998). The defendant was appointed a lawyer to represent him during custodial interrogation and grand jury proceedings concerning a murder for which he was a suspect but was not charged. The court ruled that the government did not violate the defendant's Sixth Amendment right to counsel when it arranged for inmates to elicit incriminating statements from the defendant. The appointment of counsel did not trigger the right to counsel when the defendant had not been charged with the murder.

Brooks v. Kincheloe, 848 F.2d 940 (9th Cir. 1988). Although the jail inmate asked questions of the defendant (about the defendant's murder of a young boy) while they were in jail together, the inmate did so before the detectives had ever talked to the inmate. Therefore, the detectives did not violate the defendant's Sixth Amendment right to counsel. The inmate was not a government agent when the defendant made his incriminating statements to him. *See also* United States v. Watson, 894 F.2d 1345 (D.C. Cir. 1990) (government informant in jail spoke to defendant without any encouragement from officers; no violation of defendant's Sixth Amendment right to counsel; informant's mere hope of reward for giving government the contents of conversation did not make government responsible for informant's actions); United States v. Love, 134 F.3d 595 (4th Cir. 1998) (similar ruling); United States v. Birbal, 113 F.3d 342 (2d Cir. 1997) (similar ruling).

Use of Evidence Obtained as the Result of a Violation of the Sixth Amendment Right to Counsel

Kansas v. Ventris, 556 U.S. 586 (2009). The Court ruled that the defendant's incriminating statement to a jailhouse informant, assumed to have been obtained in violation of the defendant's Sixth Amendment right to counsel, was admissible on rebuttal to impeach the defendant's trial testimony that conflicted with the statement. [Author's note: The statement would not have been admissible during the State's presentation of evidence in its case in chief.]

Michigan v. Harvey, 494 U.S. 344 (1990). Officers obtained a statement from the defendant by violating the ruling in *Michigan v. Jackson*, 475 U.S. 625 (1986). [Author's note: *Jackson* was overruled by *Montejo v. Louisiana*, 556 U.S. 778 (2009).] The prosecutor used the statement to impeach the defendant when he testified at his trial. The Court ruled that using the statement for impeachment is permissible, at least when the defendant knowingly and voluntarily waived his right to counsel before he gave the statement.

Nix v. Williams, 467 U.S. 431 (1984). [Author's note: For the facts of this case, see *Brewer v. Williams*, 430 U.S. 387 (1997).] The Court ruled that although a defendant's statements are inadmissible at trial when they are obtained in violation of the Sixth Amendment right to counsel, other evidence obtained as a result of the statements is admissible if the State proves by a preponderance of evidence that the evidence would inevitably have been discovered by lawful means without using the defendant's illegally obtained statements. The Court ruled that the State satisfied its burden of proving that the victim's body would have been discovered by a searching party even if the defendant's illegally obtained statements had not been used to find it. The Court rejected the contention that, as part of the inevitable discovery rule, the State must prove that the officer committed the Sixth Amendment violation in a good faith belief that he was acting lawfully. [Author's note: The inevitable discovery rule also may apply—under appropriate circumstances—to Fourth Amendment and other constitutional violations.] *See* United States v. Satterfield, 743 F.2d 827 (11th Cir. 1984); United States v. Merriweather, 777 F.2d 503 (9th Cir. 1985); United States v. Andrade, 784 F.2d 1431 (9th Cir. 1986) (routine inventory would have inevitably discovered drugs in defendant's garment bag after arrest).

Admission of Defendant's Statements after an Alleged Unconstitutional Arrest
When an Unconstitutional Arrest Occurred

New York v. Harris, 495 U.S. 14 (1990). Officers with probable cause to arrest the defendant entered his apartment without an arrest warrant, consent, or exigent circumstances in violation of *Payton v. New York*, 445 U.S. 573 (1980), and arrested him. He was taken to the police station and properly given his *Miranda* rights; he then waived them and confessed. Thus, his confession was obtained outside the place—his apartment—where the Fourth Amendment violation occurred. Distinguishing *Brown v. Illinois*, 422 U.S. 590 (1975); *Dunaway v. New York*, 442 U.S. 200 (1979); and *Taylor v. Alabama*, discussed below, in which the officers lacked probable cause to arrest the defendants, the Court ruled that a defendant's statement is admissible when the officers have probable cause to arrest and the statement is obtained outside the place where the *Payton* violation occurred. The Court explained that once the defendant was outside his apartment, he was no longer in unlawful custody, because the arrest was supported by probable cause and therefore the statement was no longer the fruit of the unconstitutional arrest made in the apartment.

Taylor v. Alabama, 457 U.S. 687 (1982). When a defendant is arrested without probable cause, a statement made as a result of interrogation is inadmissible at trial unless the State proves that intervening events broke the causal connection between the unconstitutional arrest and the statement, so that the statement is an act of free will that purges the primary "taint" of the unconstitu-

tional arrest. The fact that the statement is voluntarily given under the Fifth Amendment (and in compliance with the *Miranda* rule) is not sufficient by itself to purge the taint. Factors to consider in determining the admissibility of a statement include (1) the time between the arrest and statement, (2) the presence of intervening circumstances, and (3) the purpose and flagrancy of the officer's misconduct. *See also* Dunaway v. New York, 442 U.S. 200 (1979); Brown v. Illinois, 422 U.S. 590 (1975); Lanier v. South Carolina, 474 U.S. 25 (1985); State v. Freeman, 307 N.C. 357 (1983); State v. Allen, 332 N.C. 123 (1992). *But see* Rawlings v. Kentucky, 448 U.S. 98 (1980) (statement made after illegal detention admissible under *Brown v. Illinois* analysis).

When an Unconstitutional Arrest or Seizure Did Not Occur

State v. Knight, 340 N.C. 531 (1995). The murder victim was stabbed 27 times, was castrated, and his penis was inserted in his mouth. Officers went to the defendant's home to execute arrest and search warrants for this murder. They knocked on the front door several times and announced, "Police! Search warrant!" at least two or three times. After waiting 30 to 60 seconds and hearing no response from inside the residence, the officers used a battering ram to open the door. They entered the residence, conducted a quick sweep for weapons, and arrested the defendant. The defendant was taken to the police station, where he confessed to his participation in the murder and also told the officers the location in the residence of one of the knives used in the murder.

The court ruled that the officers' forcible entry into the premises was reasonable under the Fourth Amendment (*see* Wilson v. Arkansas, 514 U.S. 927 (1995)) and that it complied with the provisions of G.S. Chapter 15A. They had probable cause to believe that further delay in entering the residence or the giving of more specific notice would endanger their own safety or the safety of the other occupants of the residence. They knew that the defendant was dangerous, armed with a hunting knife and possibly firearms; there was at least one other suspect who had not been arrested; they were concerned about the safety of a woman and her children inside the residence, who might become hostages; and if the entry was not forced, it would not be safe. The court ruled, citing *New York v. Harris*, 495 U.S. 14 (1990) (confession is not to be suppressed, even though officers made unconstitutional entry into home to arrest defendant, when officers had probable cause to arrest and the confession was taken outside home), that even assuming the forcible entry was unconstitutional, the defendant's confession at the police station was still admissible. The confession was not the fruit of the alleged illegal entry into the home when the confession was taken at another location and the officers had probable cause to arrest the defendant in any event.

State v. Simpson, 303 N.C. 439 (1981). The defendant was not arrested or otherwise seized under the Fourth Amendment when he voluntarily accompanied officers to a law enforcement building at their request, was taken to an unlocked interrogation room, and was interviewed throughout the day but was never arrested, handcuffed, restrained, or otherwise treated as if in custody until an arrest warrant was served in the evening. An officer's statement at a court hearing that the defendant was in his "custody" during the day was not dispositive when the evidence showed that the restraint on the defendant's freedom was not so great as to constitute a seizure under the Fourth Amendment. *See also* State v. Bromfield, 332 N.C. 24 (1992); State v. Johnson, 317 N.C. 343 (1986); State v. Jackson, 308 N.C. 549 (1983), *later appeal*, 317 N.C. 1 (1986); State v. Davis, 305 N.C. 400 (1982); State v. Morgan, 299 N.C. 191 (1980); State v. Reynolds, 298 N.C. 380 (1979); State v. Cass, 55 N.C. App. 291 (1982).

Defendant's Statements after a North Carolina Statutory Violation

State v. Wallace, 351 N.C. 481 (2000). The defendant was arrested pursuant to an outstanding arrest warrant for a larceny, but he also was a suspect in three murders. Before giving *Miranda* warnings, officers spoke with the defendant for about three hours, mostly about sports, his employment and military experience, and his biographical information. The defendant also voluntarily raised the issue of his drug use. The officers did not interrogate him about the murders for which he was a suspect and did not ask any questions designed to elicit incriminating responses. After properly being given *Miranda* warnings, the defendant confessed to nine murders. He was given opportunities to use the restroom and was fed. At some point during the interrogation, the defendant requested to see his girlfriend and daughter. An officer told the defendant that the police would attempt to contact them but that they had no control over whether either of them

would come to see him. The defendant was taken to a magistrate 19 hours after his arrest (he had slept four hours just before being taken to the magistrate).

(1) The court ruled that the officers did not violate G.S. 15A-501(2) by taking the defendant to a magistrate 19 hours after his arrest. Because of the number of crimes to which the defendant confessed and the amount of time needed to record the details of the crimes—along with the officers' accommodation of the defendant's request to sleep—the delay was not unnecessary under the statute. (2) The court also ruled that there was not a substantial violation of any of the provisions of G.S. 15A-501 that would require the defendant's confession to be suppressed.

State v. Chapman, 343 N.C. 495 (1996). On August 23, 1993, about 9:30 a.m., the defendant was arrested at a bank for attempting to cash a forged check. He waived his *Miranda* rights and admitted that he had attempted to cash a check that he had forged after taking it in a robbery. Officers took the defendant to a school to search for a purse that had been taken in the robbery. They then returned the defendant to the police station, where he confessed to forgery and uttering charges. A detective procured arrest warrants for these charges at 12:15 p.m. and served them on the defendant. The defendant then was questioned by another detective who was investigating the robbery in which the checks were taken, and the defendant confessed to the robbery at 1:27 p.m. Officers prepared an arrest warrant to charge the robbery, but it was not presented to the magistrate at that time.

The defendant then was interviewed by another detective about a robbery and murder (not related to the crimes discussed previously). The detective put nine photos of the murder victim on the walls of the interrogation room and one photo of the victim on the floor directly in front of the chair in which the defendant sat during the interrogation. Thus the defendant saw a photo of the victim in every direction he turned. During the interview, the detective falsely implied to the defendant that a note found next to the victim's body had been the subject of handwriting analysis that showed it was the defendant's handwriting and that the defendant's fingerprints were on the note. The defendant confessed to the murder at about 7:05 p.m. and was taken to the magistrate about 8:00 p.m.

(1) The court ruled that there was no unreasonable delay in a magistrate's determination of whether there was probable cause to issue an arrest warrant. Distinguishing *County of Riverside v. McLaughlin*, 500 U.S. 44

(1991), and *Gerstein v. Pugh*, 420 U.S. 1034 (1975), the court noted that the defendant was arrested at 9:30 a.m. without a warrant and that a magistrate issued an arrest warrant based on probable cause at 12:30 p.m. This procedure satisfied the rulings in these cases that a magistrate promptly determine probable cause. The court noted that the defendant was then in lawful custody and could be interrogated about other crimes. (2) The court ruled that the defendant's statutory right under G.S. 15A-501(2) to be taken to a magistrate without unnecessary delay was not violated. The court noted that much of the time between the defendant's arrest at 9:30 a.m. and his being taken before a magistrate at 8:00 p.m. was spent interrogating the defendant about several crimes. The court stated that the officers had the right to conduct these interrogations and that they did not cause an unnecessary delay by doing so. (3) The officers failed to advise the defendant of his right to communicate with friends in violation of G.S. 15A-501(5). The court ruled that, based on *State v. Curmon*, 295 N.C. 453 (1978), the defendant was not prejudiced by this violation, based on the facts in this case.

State v. Simpson, 320 N.C. 313 (1987). A magistrate's failure to set bail, assuming it was an error under G.S. 15A-511(e), did not render inadmissible a voluntary confession obtained later. The assumed violation of G.S. Chapter 15A was not a "substantial violation" under G.S. 15A-974(2) (now, G.S. 15A-974(a)(2)). [Author's note: Legislation enacted in 2011 (S.L. 2011-6) added a good faith exception to the application of G.S. 15A-974.] The court also ruled that an otherwise voluntary confession was not to be suppressed as the fruit of an unreasonable seizure under the Fourth Amendment when the defendant had been arrested under a proper warrant but was temporarily denied the opportunity to post reasonable bail by a magistrate's good faith misinterpretation of law.

State v. Richardson, 295 N.C. 309 (1978). The court assumed without deciding that (1) the four-and-one-half-hour delay between the defendant's arrest and his being taken before a magistrate was a violation of G.S. 15A-501(2), and (2) the officers' failure to comply with this statute was a "substantial violation." The court then ruled that the defendant's confession—obtained during the interval between his arrest and his appearance before a magistrate—was not obtained "as a result of" the alleged substantial violation, as is necessary to invoke G.S. 15A-974(2) (now, G.S. 15A-974(a)(2)). The statutory exclusionary rule requires, at a minimum, a causal con-

nection between the violation and the resulting evidence. After reviewing the evidence, the court concluded that the defendant's confession was not causally related to the delay in bringing him before a magistrate. [Author's note: Legislation enacted in 2011 (S.L. 2011-6) added a good faith exception to the application of G.S. 15A-974.] *See also* State v. Hunter, 305 N.C. 106 (1982) (similar ruling).

State v. Caudill, 227 N.C. App. 119 (2013). The trial court did not err by denying the defendant's motion to suppress statements to officers on grounds that they were obtained in violation of G.S. 15A-501(2) (arrested person must be taken before a judicial official without unnecessary delay). After a consensual search of his residence produced controlled substances, the defendant and three colleagues were arrested for drug possession. The defendant, who previously had waived his *Miranda* rights, was checked into the county jail at 11:12 a.m. After again being informed of his rights, the defendant was interviewed from 1:59 p.m. to 2:53 p.m. and made incriminating statements about a murder. After the interview the defendant was taken before a magistrate and charged with drug offenses and murder. The defendant argued that the delay between his arrival at the jail and his initial appearance required suppression of his statements regarding the murder. The court noted that under G.S. 15A-974(2), evidence obtained as a result of a substantial violation of Chapter 15A must be suppressed upon timely motion; the statutory term "result" indicates that a causal relationship between a violation of the statute and the acquisition of the evidence to be suppressed must exist. The court concluded that the delay in this case was not unnecessary and there was no causal relationship between the delay and the defendant's incriminating statements made during his interview. The court rejected the defendant's constitutional arguments asserted on similar grounds.

State v. Jones, 112 N.C. App. 337 (1993). The trial judge ruled that officers violated G.S. 15A-501(2) (taking the defendant to magistrate without unnecessary delay) and G.S. 15A-501(5) (advising the defendant without unnecessary delay of right to communicate with counsel and friends), but these violations had not proximately caused the defendant's incriminating statements. The court affirmed the trial judge's ruling, citing *State v. Richardson*, 295 N.C. 309 (1978), and noted that the defendant did not argue a causal connection before the trial judge.

Voluntariness of a Witness's Statement

State v. Montgomery, 291 N.C. 235 (1976). A defendant's due process rights are not violated if a witness's statement, allegedly obtained by an officer's coercive tactics, is introduced at trial—if the jury is informed of the facts surrounding the statement. *See also* State v. Williams, 304 N.C. 3947 (1981).

Defendant's Trial Testimony Allegedly Induced by Introduction of Illegally Obtained Statement

State v. Hunt, 339 N.C. 622 (1995). The introduction at the defendant's second trial of his testimony at his first trial did not violate the defendant's Fifth Amendment rights under *Harrison v. United States*, 392 U.S. 219 (1968). The defendant was not compelled to testify at his first trial by the admission of unconstitutionally obtained evidence. *See also* State v. McNeill, 140 N.C. App. 450 (2000) (defendant's testimony at accomplice's trial was freely and voluntarily given and defendant's Fifth Amendment privilege against self-incrimination did not apply to that testimony—thus, the trial judge did not err in admitting testimony at defendant's trial).

State v. Easterling, 119 N.C. App. 22 (1995). [Author's note: The defendant was tried and convicted of multiple counts of rape and sexual offense that he committed with his accomplice, Sherman White.] After a detective gave the defendant his *Miranda* warnings, the defendant asserted his right to counsel. The detective later informed the defendant that he would be taken to the magistrate's office to be served with arrest warrants. The detective then said, "Who was Sherman?" The defendant said, "White." Just a few moments later the defendant indicated that he wanted to talk about the case. The detective then gave him *Miranda* warnings and obtained a waiver, and the defendant gave an incriminating statement that was introduced in the State's case in chief at trial.

The court ruled that the detective's question constituted interrogation: it was designed to elicit an incriminating response and therefore was improper under *Edwards v. Arizona*, 384 U.S. 436 (1981), because it was made after the defendant's assertion of his right to counsel. In addition, the defendant's statement a few moments later that he was willing to talk about the case was a continuation of the improper interrogation (that is, it was not

simply the defendant's initiation of communication with the detective). Thus, the trial judge erred in admitting the defendant's confession. The court also ruled that, based on the State's overwhelming evidence against the defendant in this case, the defendant was not induced to testify in his behalf because of the introduction in the State's case in chief of this illegally obtained confession; *see generally* Harrison v. United States, 392 U.S. 219 (1968). The court also ruled that the introduction of the confession was harmless error beyond a reasonable doubt.

Scope of Fifth Amendment Privilege of a Defendant or Witness at Trial

UNITED STATES SUPREME COURT

Hiibel v. Sixth Judicial District Court of Nevada, 542 U.S. 177 (2004). A caller to a sheriff's department reported seeing a man assault a woman in a truck on a certain road. When the officer arrived there, he found the truck parked on the side of the road, the defendant standing by the truck, and a young woman sitting inside. The defendant was stopped by the law enforcement officer based on reasonable suspicion that the defendant had committed the assault. The officer asked the defendant for identification, explaining that he wanted to determine who he was and what he was doing there. The defendant refused to provide identification. The defendant was convicted of willfully obstructing and delaying the officer in attempting to discharge a legal duty, based on a Nevada statute that requires a person subject to an investigative stop to disclose his name.

(1) The Court ruled that the officer's request for the defendant's name was reasonably related in scope to the circumstances that justified the stop and did not violate the Fourth Amendment. (2) The Court ruled that the defendant's conviction did not violate his Fifth Amendment privilege against compelled self-incrimination because in this case the defendant's refusal to disclose his name was not based on any articulated real and appreciable fear that his name would be used to incriminate him or that it would furnish a link in the chain of evidence needed to prosecute him. The Court noted that a case may arise in which there is a substantial allegation that furnishing identity at the time of an investigative stop would have given an officer a link in the chain of evidence needed to convict the defendant of a separate offense. In

such a case, a court can then consider whether the Fifth Amendment privilege applies, and, if the privilege has been violated, what remedy must follow. But those questions need not be resolved in the case before the Court.

[Author's note: The ruling in this case that the Nevada law is constitutional does not resolve the issue of whether it is a violation of North Carolina law when a person refuses to give his or her name during an investigative stop. That is a matter for North Carolina state courts to decide. Unlike under Nevada law, there is no North Carolina statute that requires a person who is the subject of an investigative stop based on reasonable suspicion to disclose his or her name. (There is a limited provision in G.S. 20-29 that it is a Class 2 misdemeanor for a person operating a motor vehicle, when requested by a uniformed officer, to refuse to write his or her name for identification or give his or her name.) Without such a statute, it does not appear that a person's mere refusal to disclose his or her name is sufficient evidence by itself to arrest or convict the person of violating G.S. 14-223 (resisting, delaying, or obstructing a public officer in discharging or attempting to discharge a duty of office) absent a showing of how the mere refusal to disclose resisted, delayed, or obstructed the officer in that particular investigative stop. Although a mere refusal may be insufficient to arrest a person for violating G.S. 14-223, the refusal under certain circumstances may allow an officer additional time to detain the person to determine whether a crime was committed.]

Chavez v. Martinez, 538 U.S. 760 (2003). While the plaintiff was being treated for a gunshot wound received during an altercation with law enforcement officers, an officer—without giving *Miranda* warnings—conducted an allegedly coercive interrogation of the plaintiff. The plaintiff was never charged with a criminal offense, and thus his answers during the interrogation were never used against him in a criminal trial. The plaintiff sued the interrogating officer for violating his constitutional rights.

(1) The Court ruled (representing a majority of the Justices in several opinions) that the officer's alleged coercive questioning of the plaintiff did not violate the Self-Incrimination Clause of the Fifth Amendment when the compelled statements were not introduced against the plaintiff at a criminal trial. (2) The Court remanded to the federal court of appeals the issue of whether the plaintiff could pursue a claim of liability against the officer for a substantive due process violation based on the alleged coercive questioning.

McKune v. Lile, 536 U.S. 24 (2002). A four-Justice plurality ruled that a prison's sexual abuse treatment program and consequences for nonparticipation in the program did not violate the prisoner's Fifth Amendment privilege against compelled self-incrimination. Inmates participating in the program were required to admit responsibility for the crime(s) for which they were convicted and admit to any other sexual crimes they had committed, without receiving any immunity from prosecution. In addition, a refusal to participate in the program resulted in the loss of specified prison privileges. A fifth Justice agreed that the prisoner's Fifth Amendment privilege was not violated but did not agree with the plurality's reasoning.

Ohio v. Reiner, 532 U.S. 17 (2001). The Court ruled, based on the facts in this case, that a witness who denied culpability in a child's death validly asserted the privilege against self-incrimination when she feared that answers to questions might tend to incriminate her.

United States v. Hubbell, 530 U.S. 27 (2000). The government served the defendant with a grand jury subpoena requiring the defendant to produce financial and other documents containing potentially incriminating evidence. The defendant refused to produce the documents, asserting his Fifth Amendment privilege against compelled self-incrimination. The government then granted the defendant use immunity under federal law that protects the use or derivative use of the testimonial act of producing them. The government later indicted the defendant after he had produced the documents.

The Court, relying on principles set out in *United States v. Doe*, 465 U.S. 605 (1984), and distinguishing *Fisher v. United States*, 425 U.S. 391 (1976), ruled that the government's use of the subpoenaed documents at trial would violate the defendant's Fifth Amendment privilege, because the documents the government would offer against the defendant at trial derived either directly or indirectly from the testimonial aspects of the defendant's immunized act of producing the documents. In this case, the government had no prior knowledge of either the existence or the whereabouts of the documents produced by the defendant.

United States v. Balsys, 524 U.S. 666 (1998). The Fifth Amendment privilege against self-incrimination may not be used because of a fear of prosecution in a foreign country.

Ohio Adult Parole Authority v. Woodard, 523 U.S. 272 (1998). Giving an inmate the option of voluntarily participating in an interview as part of a clemency process does not violate the inmate's Fifth Amendment rights.

Doe v. United States, 487 U.S. 201 (1988). A federal district court order required the defendant to execute a consent directive authorizing foreign banks to disclose records of any accounts over which the defendant had a right of withdrawal, without identifying or acknowledging the existence of any account. The Court ruled that the consent directive did not violate the defendant's Fifth Amendment rights, because it was not testimonial. A defendant's oral or written communication or act is "testimonial" when it explicitly or implicitly relates a factual assertion or discloses information. The consent directive in this case did not involve the defendant's revealing that an account existed or that, if there was an account, records were there, and the execution of the defendant's consent directive would reveal only the bank's implicit declaration, by its act of producing records, that it believes that the account is the defendant's account.

Braswell v. United States, 487 U.S. 99 (1988). (1) The custodian of corporate records may not resist a subpoena for records on the ground that the act of production will incriminate the custodian. However, the government may not make evidentiary use of the "individual act" of production against the individual. (2) A corporation does not have a Fifth Amendment privilege against self-incrimination. *See also* United States v. Wujkowski, 929 F.2d 981 (4th Cir. 1991); *In re* Grand Jury Witnesses, 92 F.3d 710 (8th Cir. 1996).

Andresen v. Maryland, 427 U.S. 463 (1976). The execution of a search warrant of the defendant's office for business records did not violate his Fifth Amendment rights, because he was not required to aid in the discovery, production, or authentication of the evidence that was seized. *See also* State v. Downing, 31 N.C. App. 743 (1976). [Author's note: For a discussion of the Fifth Amendment issues involved when the State issues a subpoena for records, see *Doe v. United States,* discussed above, and *Fisher v. United States,* 425 U.S. 391 (1976). For a discussion of a related issue, involving whether a mother-custodian of a child may assert her Fifth Amendment privilege to resist a court order to produce the child, see *Baltimore City Department of Social Services v. Bouknight,* 493 U.S. 549 (1990).]

NORTH CAROLINA SUPREME COURT

Herndon v. Herndon, ___ N.C. ___, 785 S.E.2d 922 (2016). The court ruled that the trial court did not vio-late a civil defendant's Fifth Amendment rights in a hearing concerning a civil domestic violence protective order. During the defendant's case in chief, but before the defendant took the stand, the trial court asked defense counsel whether the defendant intended to invoke the Fifth Amendment, to which counsel twice responded in the negative.

While the defendant was on the stand, the trial court posed questions to her. The court noted that never during direct examination nor during the trial court's questioning did the defendant, a voluntary witness, give any indication that answering any question posed to her would tend to incriminate her. "Put simply," the court stated, the "defendant never attempted to invoke the privilege against self-incrimination." The court continued: "We are not aware of, and the parties do not cite to, any case holding that a trial court infringes upon a witness's Fifth Amendment rights when the witness does not invoke the privilege." The court further noted that in questioning the defendant, the trial court inquired into matters within the scope of issues that were put into dispute on direct examination by the defendant. Therefore, even if the defendant had attempted to invoke the Fifth Amendment, the privilege was unavailable during the trial court's inquiry.

State v. Pickens, 346 N.C. 628 (1997). The court ruled that because there was an asserted fear of future prosecution for other crimes, a witness's plea of guilty did not act as a complete waiver of his privilege against self-incrimination. The court also ruled that the trial court did not abuse its discretion by not requiring a proposed witness to assert his Fifth Amendment privilege in the presence of the jury; the court distinguished *State v. Thompson,* 332 N.C. 204 (1992) (trial court did not err in allowing prosecutor to call witness to stand knowing witness would assert Fifth Amendment privilege). *See also* State v. Harris, 139 N.C. App. 153 (2000) (defendant failed to properly support his claim that he should have been allowed to compel his codefendants to take witness stand and assert their Fifth Amendment privileges before jury).

State v. Hunt, 339 N.C. 622 (1995). The introduction at the defendant's second trial of his testimony at his first trial did not violate the defendant's Fifth Amendment rights under *Harrison v. United States,* 392 U.S. 219 (1968). The defendant was not compelled to testify at his first trial by the admission of unconstitutionally obtained evidence. *See also* State v. McNeill, 140 N.C. App. 450 (2000) (defendant's testimony at accomplice's trial was freely and voluntarily given and defendant's Fifth Amendment privilege against self-incrimination did not apply to that testimony—thus, the trial judge did not err in admitting testimony at defendant's trial).

State v. Ray, 336 N.C. 463 (1994). The defendant was convicted of first-degree murder that was drug related. During direct examination of a State's witness—an eyewitness to the murder—the State asked the witness about his and the murder victim's involvement with drug dealing. On cross-examination, the witness refused to answer some questions about drug dealing, asserting his Fifth Amendment privilege against compelled self-incrimination. The trial judge found that some of the answers to the cross-examination questions could be incriminating and that the witness had a right to refuse to answer those questions. After the witness had completed his testimony, the defendant requested that the trial judge either direct the witness to answer the questions to which he had invoked the privilege or strike the witness's entire testimony.

The court noted that the issue of whether the witness was properly allowed to assert the privilege was not raised on appeal. However, the court ruled that the defendant's right to confront witnesses through cross-examination was unreasonably limited by the witness's assertion of the testimonial privilege. The court discussed several cases, particularly *United States v. Cardillo*, 316 F.2d 606 (2d Cir. 1963), and noted that courts have distinguished between the assertion of the privilege preventing inquiry into matters about which the witness testified on direct examination (in which case the defendant's motion to strike the testimony should be granted) and the assertion of the privilege preventing inquiry into collateral matters, such as the credibility of the witness (in which case the defendant's motion to strike the testimony should be denied). The court examined the facts in this case and ruled that the trial judge erred in not striking the testimony of the witness, because the prohibited inquiry on cross-examination involved matters discussed on direct examination—drug dealing that was the basis of the relationship between the victim, the defendant, and the witness.

Debnam v. Department of Correction, 334 N.C. 380 (1993). The court ruled that the State did not violate a public employee's Fifth Amendment right against compelled self-incrimination by firing the employee for refusing to answer questions relating to his employment—in this case, questions about an incident involving a ring allegedly stolen from an inmate. The employee

was informed that his failure to answer might result in his dismissal, and the State did not seek the employee's waiver of his immunity from the State's use of any of his answers in a criminal action against him. The court rejected the employee's argument that the Fifth Amendment prohibited the State from firing him for refusing to answer questions during its internal investigation because he was not advised that his responses could not be used against him in any criminal prosecution and that the questions would relate specifically and narrowly to his performance of official duties.

In re Estate of Trogdon, 330 N.C. 143 (1991). The finder of fact in a civil case may use a witness's invocation of the Fifth Amendment privilege against self-incrimination to infer that the witness's truthful testimony would have been unfavorable to the witness.

State v. Eason, 328 N.C. 409 (1991). A witness properly was permitted to invoke her Fifth Amendment privilege to refuse to answer questions when the questions related to a criminal case pending in superior court.

State v. Perry, 291 N.C. 284 (1976). The defendant's Fifth Amendment rights were not violated when he was required to put on, before the jury, an orange stocking mask found at the scene of the armed robbery. *See also* State v. Suddreth, 105 N.C. App. 122 (1992) (similar ruling; mask worn during sexual assault); State v. Summers, 105 N.C. App. 420 (1992) (similar ruling; defendant displaying his teeth—victim had described assailant as a man with missing teeth).

NORTH CAROLINA COURT OF APPEALS

Lovendahl v. Wicker, 208 N.C. App. 193 (2010). The civil defendant was being sued for negligence in the operation of a vehicle that resulted in the death of a passenger. The defendant asserted affirmative defenses of contributory negligence and gross contributory negligence. The defendant was also awaiting trial for second-degree murder and other offenses arising from the operation of the vehicle. The defendant asserted his Fifth Amendment privilege and refused to answer questions about the accident in a deposition in the civil case. The court ruled that the trial court did not abuse its discretion in striking the defendant's affirmative defenses based on his refusal to testify at the deposition.

Roadway Express, Inc. v. Hayes, 178 N.C. App. 165 (2006). Plaintiffs sued the defendant for a vehicular accident in which a death resulted. Plaintiffs alleged that the defendant was impaired when the accident occurred. The court ruled, relying on *Schmerber v. California*, 384 U.S. 757 (1966), that the Fifth Amendment privilege against self-incrimination did not protect the production in discovery of the defendant's medical records that contained blood test results concerning impairing substances. The court ruled, however, that the privilege protected the defendant from having to answer interrogatories and requests for admissions about alcohol and medications that the defendant may have taken before the accident. (There was a pending criminal prosecution of the defendant.) The court noted that the defendant's assertion of the privilege may bar the defendant's assertion of his affirmative defense of sudden emergency.

In re Lineberry, 154 N.C. App. 246 (2002). The court ruled that the trial judge erred in finding that the juvenile's refusal during court-ordered therapeutic treatment to admit to the offenses for which he had been adjudicated delinquent was a factor justifying his continued custody pending his appeal to the court of appeals. The court ruled that the trial judge violated the juvenile's Fifth Amendment privilege against compelled self-incrimination in relying on this factor.

Davis v. Town of Stallings Board of Adjustment, 141 N.C. App. 489 (2000). The Town of Stallings Board of Adjustment held a hearing to determine whether petitioner Davis was operating an unauthorized adult establishment. At the hearing both Davis and his wife invoked their Fifth Amendment privilege against self-incrimination and refused to testify. The court ruled, relying on *Gray v. Hoover*, 94 N.C. App. 724 (1989), and other cases, that the Board of Adjustment properly could use their assertions of the privilege to infer that Davis was running an unauthorized adult establishment.

Sugg v. Field, 139 N.C. App. 160 (2000). Plaintiff brought a civil action against the defendants for various torts. During the defendants' deposition of the plaintiff, the plaintiff asserted the Fifth Amendment and refused to answer questions on matters that were relevant and material to his claims. The trial judge ruled that the plaintiff's refusal to provide the information was prejudicial to the rights of the defendants and their ability to defend themselves, and the judge dismissed the civil action. The court ruled, relying on *Qurneh v. Colie*, 122 N.C. App. 553 (1996), that the judge did not err in dismissing the civil action.

McKillop v. Onslow County, 139 N.C. App. 53 (2000). McKillop was ordered to comply with a county ordinance regulating adult sexually oriented businesses. A show cause hearing was later held to determine whether she should be held in civil contempt. After the county presented evidence, McKillop refused to present evidence on her behalf on the Fifth Amendment ground that she might incriminate herself in a pending criminal case. The court ruled, relying on *Cantwell v. Cantwell*, 109 N.C. App. 395 (1993), and *Gray v. Hoover*, 94 N.C. App. 724 (1989), that the defendant's assertion of the Fifth Amendment was an abandonment of her defense to the contempt charge.

State v. Linney, 138 N.C. App. 169 (2000). The defendant, an attorney, was convicted of two counts of embezzlement and two counts of perjury involving his role as a guardian of the person and estate of Georgiana Alexander. Before the State prosecuted the defendant, the North Carolina State Bar had investigated the defendant for possible disbarment. The State during the criminal trial used statements that the defendant had made to a state bar investigator.

The court ruled, distinguishing *Garrity v. New Jersey*, 385 U.S. 493 (1967), that the defendant's Fifth Amendment rights were not violated by the admission of these statements. The defendant was not compelled by threat of disbarment if he failed to give any statements. He could have asserted his Fifth Amendment privilege and not spoken to the investigator, but he voluntarily chose not to assert the privilege. The State during the criminal trial used bank records that the defendant had provided to a state bar investigator. The court ruled, citing *Shapiro v. United States*, 335 U.S. 1 (1948), and other cases, that even if the defendant had asserted his Fifth Amendment privilege during bar proceedings, the privilege would not have protected these records. The Fifth Amendment does not apply to the production of records that an attorney is required by law to maintain.

Staton v. Brame, 136 N.C. App. 170 (1999). Brame allegedly mishandled and misappropriated funds belonging to others. In 1996, he was civilly sued for recovery of these funds in state court. The Internal Revenue Service later informed him that he was the target of an ongoing criminal investigation concerning these funds. On March 27, 1997, Brame asserted his Fifth Amendment privilege not to testify at a deposition in the civil lawsuit. On August 1, 1997, Brame answered questions about these matters in a deposition conducted as part of a pending bankruptcy action (he and his former wife had filed petitions for bankruptcy, and the deposition was given in an equitable distribution action that had been removed to federal bankruptcy court). After learning of the August 1, 1997, deposition, the plaintiffs in the civil lawsuit moved to compel Brame's deposition testimony. The court ruled, relying on *State v. Pearsall*, 38 N.C. App. 600 (1978), and *State v. Hart*, 66 N.C. App. 702 (1984), that the defendant had not waived the right to assert his Fifth Amendment privilege by testifying in bankruptcy court. The bankruptcy proceeding and the civil lawsuit were separate proceedings.

State v. Teague, 134 N.C. App. 702 (1999). The court ruled, relying on *State v. McNeil*, 99 N.C. App. 235 (1990), that the trial judge did not err in admitting evidence at trial of the defendant's refusal to provide handwriting samples pursuant to a search warrant. The admission of this evidence was relevant to the trial and did not violate the defendant's Fifth Amendment rights.

Qurneh v. Colie, 122 N.C. App. 553 (1996). Plaintiff (natural father) filed a civil lawsuit against the defendant (natural mother) seeking custody of his child. The defendant and intervenors (the child's maternal grandparents) alleged that the plaintiff was unfit to have custody. When the plaintiff was cross-examined about his alleged illegal drug use, he asserted his Fifth Amendment privilege against compelled self-incrimination. The court ruled that when the plaintiff failed to make a prima facie showing that he was fit to have custody and the trial judge could not determine the plaintiff's fitness because he had asserted his Fifth Amendment privilege, the trial judge properly dismissed the plaintiff's claim for custody and awarded custody to the intervenors. The court noted a similar ruling in *Cantwell v. Cantwell*, 109 N.C. App. 395 (1993).

State v. Locklear, 117 N.C. App. 255 (1994). The trial judge during the trial ordered the defendant to speak the exact words of the robber so that a State's witness could attempt to make a voice identification. The court ruled, relying on *State v. Perry*, 291 N.C. 284 (1976), and other cases, that the defendant's Fifth Amendment privilege against compelled self-incrimination was not violated by the judge's order. *See also* State v. Thompson, 129 N.C. App. 13 (1998) (similar ruling).

In re Jones, 116 N.C. App. 695 (1994). Jones, who had a pending murder charge against him, was called as a defense witness in a related murder trial of another person. Jones refused, by asserting his Fifth Amendment privilege against compelled self-incrimination, to answer two questions asked by the prosecutor on cross-examina-tion. The trial judge held Jones in contempt of court for refusing to answer the questions.

The court reversed. One question—whether the defendant owed money for drugs to some specified people—was a matter that the State was seeking to prove at Jones's upcoming murder trial. Thus, the answer to this question could incriminate Jones. The other question—whether Jones had a reputation for robbing drug dealers—could be used to undermine Jones's credibility if charged with a crime in the future. Thus, the court stated that it was possible that the answer to this question could incriminate Jones.

Leonard v. Williams, 100 N.C. App. 512 (1990). A witness may not invoke the Fifth Amendment privilege against self-incrimination if a prosecution for the criminal offense is barred by the statute of limitations.

FEDERAL APPELLATE COURTS

Barrett v. Acevedo, 169 F.3d 1155 (8th Cir. 1999). The Fifth Amendment does not protect the contents of a personal diary, because a person has voluntarily created it. Thus, the diary was admissible at trial.

Johnson v. Baker, 108 F.3d 10 (2d Cir. 1997). A state prison did not violate a convicted sex offender's Fifth Amendment privilege against self-incrimination by requiring him to admit to his alleged sex offenses as a condition of entry into the prison's sex offender program, admission to which was itself required for entry into a family reunion program. The State did not seek a court order compelling answers to its questions about the alleged offenses, require waiver of immunity, or insist that answers be used in a criminal proceeding. The inmate's unwillingness to admit to the offenses rendered him unlikely to benefit from the rehabilitative process. *See also* Asherman v. Meachum, 957 F.2d 978 (2d Cir. 1992).

Harvey v. Shillinger, 76 F.3d 1528 (10th Cir. 1996). A defendant's statement that he voluntarily made at the sentencing hearing of his first trial was properly admitted at his second trial without violating his Fifth Amendment rights.

Admissibility of Written Confession

State v. Wagner, 343 N.C. 250 (1996). The State sought to introduce the detective's handwritten notes of the defendant's confession. The notes were not read to the defendant and were not signed by him or otherwise admitted to be correct. The court ruled that *State v. Walker*, 269 N.C. 135 (1967) (setting out the rules for the admission of a written confession), does not bar the admissibility of an unsigned statement taken in longhand of a defendant's actual responses to recorded questions. The court noted that the evidence showed that the notes were an exact word-for-word rendition of the interview of the defendant.

State v. Spencer, 192 N.C. App. 143 (2008). The court ruled, relying on *State v. Walker*, 269 N.C. 135 (1967), and *State v. Bartlett*, 121 N.C. App. 521 (1996), that the admission of the defendant's confession by reading it to the jury from an officer's handwritten notes was error because the officer did not have the defendant review and confirm the notes as an accurate representation of the defendant's answers, nor were the notes a verbatim account of the defendant's confession.

State v. Bartlett, 121 N.C. App. 521 (1996). While the defendant spoke to law enforcement officers, one of the officers attempted to write down the defendant's answers to the questions asked by another officer. The officer's questions were not written down. When the paper writing was given to the defendant, he refused to sign it. The court ruled that the trial judge erroneously permitted the State to introduce the paper writing into evidence. The court noted the general rule that a defendant's written statement may not be introduced into evidence unless (1) it was read to or by the defendant and the defendant signed or otherwise admitted to its being correct, or (2) it was a verbatim record of the questions asked and answers given by the defendant. In this case, the officer did not write down the questions asked and never testified that the answers given by the defendant were correctly reflected on the paper writing. In addition, there was no evidence that the defendant acquiesced in the correctness of the paper writing. [Author's note: This ruling applies only to the admissibility of the paper writing, not to the admissibility of oral testimony of the conversation between the officers and the defendant.]

Foreign National's Notification under Vienna Convention and Admissibility of Defendant's Statements

Sanchez-Llamas v. Oregon, 548 U.S. 331 (2006). The Court ruled, assuming without deciding that the Vienna Convention on Consular Relations (an international treaty requiring law enforcement to inform an arrested foreign national of the right to consular notification) creates judicially enforceable rights, that (1) suppression of a defendant's statements to law enforcement is not a remedy for a violation of the treaty, and (2) a state may subject claims of treaty violations to the same procedural default rules that apply generally to other federal law claims.

State v. Herrera, 195 N.C. App. 181 (2009). The court ruled, relying on *Sanchez-Llamas v. Oregon*, 548 U.S. 331 (2006), that a violation of the Vienna Convention on Consular Relations (requiring notification to arrested foreign national of right to have consul of national's country notified of arrest) does not provide the remedy of suppression of a confession.

Motions to Suppress and Suppression Hearings

(See also pertinent cases on page 534.)

State v. Williams, 308 N.C. 47 (1983). A defendant may not raise on appeal a ground attacking a confession that the defendant did not properly raise at the trial level. *See also* State v. Jenkins, 311 N.C. 194 (1984); State v. Hunter, 305 N.C. 106 (1982).

State v. Barnett, 307 N.C. 608 (1983). A trial judge decides whether a confession was voluntary. This issue is not submitted to the jury. However, a defendant is entitled to present evidence to the jury about how the confession was taken so that the defendant may challenge its reliability and credibility. *See* Crane v. Kentucky, 476 U.S. 683 (1986).

State v. Johnson, 304 N.C. 680 (1982). The State must prove voluntariness of a confession by a preponderance of the evidence.

State v. Bracey, 303 N.C. 112 (1981). The State may impeach a defendant with the defendant's testimony at a suppression hearing if the defendant testifies at trial.

State v. Weakley, 176 N.C. App. 642 (2006). The defendant argued on appeal that the State was improperly permitted to cross-examine a defense witness concerning her failure to give a statement to a law enforcement officer, because the cross-examination violated the witness's Fifth Amendment rights. The court ruled, relying on *State v. Lipford*, 81 N.C. App. 464 (1986), and other cases, that the defendant had no standing to assert the witness's constitutional right against self-incrimination.

State v. Graves, 135 N.C. App. 216 (1999). The court noted that statements obtained as a result of an illegal search must be suppressed. However, the officer in this case obtained statements from the defendant without mentioning the illegal drugs and drug paraphernalia that were discovered pursuant to an illegal search. Thus, only those statements from the defendant after the officer told the defendant about what he had discovered must be suppressed.

State v. Lipford, 81 N.C. App. 464 (1986). The defendant had no standing to contest the admission of a codefendant's statement on the ground that it had been obtained in violation of the codefendant's Fifth Amendment rights.

II. Lineups and Other Identification Procedures

The Sixth Amendment Right to Counsel at Identification Procedures

(*This topic is discussed on page 596.*)

Nature of the Identification Procedure
In-Person Lineup or Showup

Kirby v. Illinois, 406 U.S. 682 (1972). A defendant who appears in a lineup or showup has a Sixth Amendment right to counsel, but the right attaches only at or after the adversary judicial proceedings begin against the defendant. The defendant's right to counsel had not attached in this case when a showup identification occurred after the defendant's arrest but before indictment, the probable cause hearing, or the beginning of any other adversary judicial proceeding. *See also* United States v. Gouveia, 467 U.S. 180 (1984) (Court majority recognized *Kirby*, which was a plurality opinion, as prevailing law); Moore v. Illinois, 434 U.S. 220 (1977) (defendant's Sixth Amendment right to counsel had attached at an in-court showup at

a preliminary hearing) [Author's note: The preliminary hearing was equivalent to a North Carolina probable cause hearing.]; United States v. Wade, 388 U.S. 218 (1967) (defendant had Sixth Amendment right to counsel at post-indictment lineup); Gilbert v. California, 388 U.S. 263 (1967) (same). For a discussion of when the Sixth Amendment right to counsel attaches in North Carolina, see page 596 of this chapter.

United States v. Jones, 907 F.2d 456 (4th Cir. 1990). A lawyer for a defendant who was appearing in a lineup did not have a right to be present in the witness's viewing room to monitor the remarks of law enforcement officers who were conducting the lineup.

Photographic Lineup

United States v. Ash, 413 U.S. 300 (1973). A defendant has no Sixth Amendment right to counsel when an officer conducts a photographic identification procedure in which witnesses attempt to identify an offender, regardless of whether the photographic lineup occurs before or after an indictment. *See also* State v. Miller, 288 N.C. 582 (1975).

When the Right to Counsel Attaches

Kirby v. Illinois, 406 U.S. 682 (1972). A defendant who appears in a lineup or showup has a Sixth Amendment right to counsel, but the right attaches only at or after the adversary judicial proceedings begin against the defendant. The defendant's right to counsel had not attached in this case when a showup identification occurred after the defendant's arrest but before indictment, the probable cause hearing, or the beginning of any other adversary judicial proceeding. *See also* United States v. Gouveia, 467 U.S. 180 (1984) (Court majority recognized *Kirby*, which was a plurality opinion, as prevailing law); Moore v. Illinois, 434 U.S. 220 (1977) (defendant's Sixth Amendment right to counsel had attached at in-court showup at preliminary hearing) [Author's note: The preliminary hearing was equivalent to a North Carolina probable cause hearing.]; United States v. Wade, 388 U.S. 218 (1967) (defendant had Sixth Amendment right to counsel at post-indictment lineup); Gilbert v. California, 388 U.S. 263 (1967) (same). For a discussion of when the Sixth Amendment right to counsel attaches in North Carolina, see page 596 of this chapter.

State v. Leggett, 305 N.C. 213 (1982). The point at which a defendant's Sixth Amendment right to counsel attaches must be determined for each criminal charge.

The mere fact that the defendant was in custody for an unrelated charge did not constitute the initiation of adversary judicial proceedings sufficient to provide a Sixth Amendment right to counsel.

Thompson v. Mississippi, 914 F.2d 736 (5th Cir. 1990). A robbery victim's encounter with the defendant in a jail facility did not violate the defendant's Sixth Amendment right to counsel, because the victim's presence was not authorized, arranged, or requested by law enforcement officers (that is, there was no state action).

The Exclusionary Rule When the Right to Counsel Is Violated

United States v. Wade, 388 U.S. 218 (1967). When a defendant's Sixth Amendment right to counsel is violated at a lineup, evidence resulting from the lineup is automatically inadmissible in court, and a witness's in-court identification of the defendant is also inadmissible unless the State proves by clear and convincing evidence that the identification originated independent of the unconstitutional lineup. Various factors to consider in determining independent origin include prior opportunity to observe the offense, any discrepancy between any pre-lineup description and the defendant's actual description, any identification of another person or of the defendant by a picture before the lineup takes place, failure to identify the defendant on a prior occasion, the time elapsed between the offense and the lineup identification, and facts concerning the conduct of the illegal lineup. *See also* Gilbert v. California, 388 U.S. 263 (1967).

Due Process Review of Identification Procedures

(*This topic is discussed on page 595.*)

Generally

UNITED STATES SUPREME COURT

Perry v. New Hampshire, 132 S. Ct. 716 (2012). The Court ruled that the Due Process Clause does not require a preliminary judicial inquiry into the reliability of an eyewitness identification when the identification was not procured under unnecessarily suggestive circumstances arranged by law enforcement. New Hampshire police received a call reporting that an African American male was trying to break into cars parked in the lot of the call-

er's apartment building. When an officer responding to the call asked eyewitness Nubia Blandon to describe the man, Blandon, who was standing in her apartment building just outside the open door to her apartment, pointed to her kitchen window and said that the man she saw breaking into a car was standing in the parking lot, next to a police officer. The defendant, Perry, who was that person, was arrested. About a month later, when the police showed Blandon a photographic array that included a picture of Perry and asked her to point out the man who had broken into the car, she was unable to identify Perry. At trial Perry unsuccessfully moved to suppress Blandon's identification on the ground that admitting it would violate due process.

The Supreme Court began by noting that an identification infected by improper police influence is not automatically excluded. Instead, the Court explained, the trial judge at a pretrial proceeding must screen the evidence for reliability. If there is a very substantial likelihood of irreparable misidentification, the judge must exclude the evidence at trial. But, it continued, if the indicia of reliability are strong enough to outweigh the corrupting effect of the police-arranged suggestive circumstances, the identification evidence ordinarily will be admitted, and the jury will ultimately determine its worth. In this case, Perry asked the Court to extend pretrial screening for reliability to cases in which the suggestive circumstances were not arranged by law enforcement officers because of the grave risk that mistaken identification will yield a miscarriage of justice. The Court declined to do so, ruling: "When no improper law enforcement activity is involved . . . it suffices to test reliability through the rights and opportunities generally designed for that purpose, notably, the presence of counsel at postindictment lineups, vigorous cross-examination, protective rules of evidence, and jury instructions on both the fallibility of eyewitness identification and the requirement that guilt be proved beyond a reasonable doubt."

Neil v. Biggers, 409 U.S. 188 (1972). The due process test for determining whether an in-court identification is admissible at trial is whether the out-of-court identification procedure was so impermissibly suggestive as to give rise to a very substantial likelihood of irreparable misidentification. The due process test for determining whether evidence of the out-of-court identification procedure is admissible at trial is whether it was so impermissibly suggestive as to raise a very substantial likelihood of misidentification. [Author's note: The test is the same as for the in-court identification except for the deletion of the word "irreparable."]

The central issue in determining the admissibility of identification evidence is whether—considering the totality of circumstances—the identification was reliable even though the confrontation procedure was suggestive. The factors to consider in evaluating the likelihood of misidentification include (1) the witness's opportunity to view the suspect when the offense was committed, (2) the degree of attention, (3) the degree of certainty at the identification procedure, (4) the accuracy of a prior description of the suspect, and (5) the length of time between the crime and the identification procedure. Applying these factors, the Court analyzed the identification of the defendant by the victim at a police station showup conducted seven months after the crime and ruled that evidence of the showup and identification was admissible.

See also Manson v. Brathwaite, 432 U.S. 98 (1977) (Court reaffirmed tests set out in *Neil v. Biggers*, rejected a per se exclusionary rule for impermissibly suggestive identification procedures, analyzed a one-photo identification procedure in this case, and found it admissible as evidence). [Author's note: The Court appeared to use the word "irreparable" incorrectly when testing the admissibility of evidence of the out-of-court one-photo identification.] Other Supreme Court cases include *Stovall v. Denno*, 388 U.S. 293 (1967) (evidence of injured witness who identified defendant at hospital showup was admissible); *Simmons v. United States*, 390 U.S. 377 (1968) (in-court identification of defendants was admissible, although pretrial photo-identification procedure may have been suggestive); *Coleman v. Alabama*, 399 U.S. 1 (1970) (in-court identification did not result from allegedly improper lineup); *Foster v. California*, 394 U.S. 440 (1969) (use of suggestive three-man lineup, then one-man showup, and then five-man lineup in which defendant was the only one who had appeared in the first lineup violated due process).

NORTH CAROLINA SUPREME COURT

State v. Hunt, 339 N.C. 622 (1995). The witness's identification of the defendant was independent of an illegal lineup and thus admissible.

State v. Pigott, 320 N.C. 96 (1987). Assuming that photo lineups were unnecessarily suggestive (only two of the ten photos presented a real choice), the court ruled that evidence of the witnesses' identifications of the defendant during the photo lineups was properly admit-

ted at trial because their identifications were reliable, based on the facts in the case.

State v. Flowers, 318 N.C. 208 (1986). Assuming that a one-on-one showup conducted between the victim and the defendant one week after the crime was unnecessarily suggestive, the court ruled that evidence of the witness's identification of the defendant during the showup was properly admitted at trial because her identification was reliable.

State v. Wilson, 313 N.C. 516 (1985). Although both the pretrial photo lineup and the in-person lineup were made suggestive by an officer's statement to the witness that the offender was in each, evidence of both lineups was admissible because they were not impermissibly suggestive and did not create a substantial likelihood of misidentification.

See also State v. Simpson, 327 N.C. 178 (1990) (photo lineup was not impermissibly suggestive, although two photos were of light-complexioned black males, one of whom was the defendant, and four were of dark-complexioned black males); State v. Harris, 308 N.C. 159 (1983) (evidence of photo lineup was admissible, even though photo of the defendant had same kind of cap and scarf that the victim said offender wore during offense); State v. White, 307 N.C. 42 (1982) (similar ruling); State v. Leggett, 305 N.C. 213 (1982) (fact that defendant's photo was only one common to two groups of photographs shown to victim was not sufficient by itself to make photo-identification procedure impermissibly suggestive); State v. Jones, 98 N.C. App. 342 (1990) (although pretrial photo identification procedure was impermissibly suggestive because an officer showed an undercover drug officer one photo with suspect's name on it, in-court identification was admissible because the pretrial procedure did not result in "very substantial likelihood of irreparable misrepresentation," based on totality of circumstances in this case); State v. Vest, 104 N.C. App. 771 (1991) (in-court identification was admissible despite a one-photo lineup).

State v. Turner, 305 N.C. 356 (1982). Evidence of showup conducted by officers about 15 minutes after the crime occurred was admissible, because it was sufficiently reliable despite the procedure's suggestiveness.

See also State v. Richardson, 328 N.C. 505 (1991) (evidence of showup was admissible, despite being unnecessarily suggestive, because witnesses' identifications were sufficiently reliable, based on facts in this case); State v. Oliver, 302 N.C. 28 (1980) (evidence of showup was admissible, despite being unnecessarily suggestive, because witness's identification was sufficiently reliable; time between crime and showup was a few hours); Willis v. Garrison, 624 F.2d 491 (4th Cir. 1980) (evidence of showup after robbery was admissible); Stanley v. Cox, 486 F.2d 48 (4th Cir. 1973) (evidence of showup after robbery was admissible); United States v. Watson, 76 F.3d 4 (1st Cir. 1996) (evidence of showup after assault was admissible); Brodnicki v. City of Omaha, 75 F.3d 1261 (8th Cir. 1996) (showup after kidnapping was not impermissibly suggestive); United States v. Henderson, 719 F.2d 934 (8th Cir. 1983) (in-court identification was admissible, even though there was an unnecessarily suggestive one-photo identification procedure; government did not introduce evidence of out-of-court identification, so it was not an issue in the case); Graham v. Solem, 728 F.2d 1533 (8th Cir. 1984) (in-court identification was admissible, even though there was an unnecessarily suggestive showup; State did not introduce evidence of showup, so it was not an issue in the case). *But see* Velez v. Schmer, 724 F.2d 249 (1st Cir. 1984) (unnecessarily suggestive showup made in-court identification unreliable and therefore inadmissible); United States v. Eltayib, 88 F.3d 157 (2d Cir. 1996) (photo array was impermissibly suggestive because defendant's photo, matching descriptions given by witness, was significantly different from other photos in array).

State v. Bass, 280 N.C. 435 (1972). Testimony of witness that she identified the defendant at a preliminary hearing (now called a probable cause hearing) in district court was admissible when there was no evidence that the hearing was "rigged" by officers for the purpose of identifying the defendant. The witness testified that she was subpoenaed to testify at the hearing and recognized the defendant when he was brought into court: no one prompted her to identify him or pointed him out. *See also* State v. McGraw, 300 N.C. 610 (1980); State v. Dunlap, 298 N.C. 725 (1979); State v. Long, 293 N.C. 286 (1977); State v. Fowler, 353 N.C. 599 (2001).

NORTH CAROLINA COURT OF APPEALS

State v. Macon, 236 N.C. App. 182 (2014). The court ruled that the trial court did not err by admitting in-court identifications of the defendant by two officers. The defendant argued that the trial court erred in denying his motion to suppress the officers' in-court identifications because the procedure they used to identify him violated the Eyewitness Identification Reform Act (EIRA) and his constitutional due process rights. After the officers observed the defendant at the scene of a suspected drug transaction, they returned to the police station and put the suspect's name into their computer database. When a picture appeared, both officers identified the defendant as the perpetrator. The officers then pulled up another photograph of the defendant and confirmed that he was the perpetrator. This occurred within 10 to 15 minutes of the incident in question. The court concluded that the identification based on two photographs was not a "lineup" and therefore was not subject to the EIRA. The court also ruled that even assuming that the procedure was impermissibly suggestive, the officers' in-court identifications were admissible because each was based on an independent source—the officers' clear, close, and unobstructed view of the suspect at the scene.

State v. Jackson, 229 N.C. App. 644 (2013). The court ruled that an out-of-court showup identification was not impermissibly suggestive. Officers told a victim that they "believed they had found the suspect." The victim was then taken to the place where the defendant was standing in a front yard with officers. With a light shining on the defendant while he was standing in the yard, the victim (who was in a patrol car) identified the defendant as the perpetrator. For reasons discussed in the opinion, the court concluded that the showup possessed sufficient aspects of reliability to outweigh its suggestiveness.

State v. Stowes, 220 N.C. App. 330 (2012). In a robbery trial, the court of appeals found no plain error in the trial court's determination that a photo lineup was not impermissibly suggestive. The defendant argued that the photo lineup was impermissibly suggestive because one of the officers administering the procedure was involved in the investigation and because that officer may have made unintentional movements or displayed body language that could have influenced the eyewitness. The court noted that the eyewitness (an employee of the store that was robbed) was 75 percent certain of his identification; the investigating officer's presence was the only irregularity in the identification procedure. The eyewitness did not describe any suggestive actions on the part of the investigating officer, and there was no testimony from other officers to indicate such. Also, the lineup was conducted within days of the crime. Finally, the perpetrator was in the store for 45 to 50 minutes and spoke with the employee several times.

State v. Watkins, 218 N.C. App. 94 (2012). The court ruled that a pretrial showup was not impermissibly suggestive. The robbery victim had ample opportunity to view the defendant at the time of the crime, and there was no suggestion that the description of the perpetrator given by the victim to the police officer was inaccurate. During the showup, the victim stood in close proximity to the defendant, and the defendant was illuminated by spotlights and a flashlight. The victim stated both at the scene and in court that he was "sure" that the defendant was the perpetrator. Also, the time interval between the crime and the showup was relatively short.

State v. Jones, 216 N.C. App. 225 (2011). The court of appeals ruled that the trial court's admission of photo identification evidence did not violate the defendant's right to due process. The day after a break-in at her house, one of the victims, a high school student, became upset in school. Her mother was called to school and brought along the student's sister, who was also present when the crime occurred. After the student told the principal about the incident, the principal took the student, her sister, and her mother into his office and showed the sisters photographs from the North Carolina Sex Offender Registry website to identify the perpetrator. Both youths identified the perpetrator from one of the pictures. The mother then contacted the police, and the defendant was eventually arrested. At trial both youths identified the defendant as the perpetrator. The court rejected the defendant's argument that the principal acted as an agent of the State when he showed the youths the photos, finding that his actions "were more akin to that of a parent, friend, or other concerned citizen offering to help the victim of a crime." Because the principal was not a state actor when he presented the photographs, the defendant's due process rights were not implicated in the identification. Even if the principal was a state actor and the procedure used was unnecessarily suggestive, the procedure did not give rise to a substantial likelihood of irreparable misidentification given the circumstances of the identification, the court found. Finally, because the photo identification evidence was properly admitted, the trial court also properly admitted the in-court identifications of the defendant.

State v. Boozer, 210 N.C. App. 391 (2011). (1) The court ruled that the trial court properly denied the defendant's motion to suppress asserting that an eyewitness's pretrial identification was unduly suggestive. The eyewitness had the opportunity to view the defendant at close range for an extended period of time and was focused on and paying attention to the defendant for at least 15 minutes. Additionally, the eyewitness described the defendant by name as someone he knew and had interacted with previously and immediately identified a photograph of him, indicating high levels of accuracy and confidence in the eyewitness's description and identification. Although the eyewitness stated that he recognized but could not name all of the suspects on the night of the attack, he named the defendant and identified a photograph of him the next day.

State v. Rawls, 207 N.C. App. 415 (2010). Two men broke into a house, a third man stayed outside the door, and they all fled when confronted by a resident. Shortly thereafter, the three men were detained by officers. The resident was brought to them for a showup identification, and she identified all of the men as having been involved in the break-in. One of the three men was the defendant. Although the showup procedure was unduly suggestive, there was no substantial likelihood of irreparable misidentification, and thus the trial judge did not err by denying a motion to suppress the resident's showup identification. The showup was unduly suggestive when an officer told the resident beforehand that "they think they found the guy" and the defendant at the showup was detained with several officers present. However, there was no substantial likelihood of irreparable misidentification when, although only having viewed the suspects for a short time, the resident looked "dead at" the suspect and made eye contact with him from a table's length away during daylight hours with nothing obstructing her view, the showup occurred 15 minutes later, and the resident was "positive" about her identification of the three suspects, as "she could not forget their faces."

State v. Williams, 201 N.C. App. 103 (2009). The victim's friend called her to identify the defendant the night he was arrested. The friend did so on her own volition and was not acting on behalf of law enforcement. The court rejected the defendant's argument that the trial court erred by admitting the victim's identification testimony because it resulted from an improper showup. Absent government involvement, there was no violation of the defendant's constitutional rights.

State v. Pinchback, 140 N.C. App. 512 (2000). The State's evidence showed that the defendant and an accomplice robbed the victim in Yanceyville. A law enforcement officer took the victim to a restaurant parking lot in Virginia, where two suspects had been stopped. The victim viewed the suspects while they were standing next to a vehicle that was surrounded by law enforcement vehicles. The victim said that these two men robbed him, but he could only positively identify the accomplice. This identification procedure took place about an hour after the robbery.

The issue on appeal was the admissibility at trial of this pretrial identification procedure under the Due Process Clause. The court noted, citing *State v. Pigott*, 320 N.C. 96 (1987), that even when a pretrial identification procedure is suggestive, the pretrial identification is nevertheless admissible unless under the totality of circumstances "there is a substantial likelihood of irreparable misidentification." The court then examined the due process factors set out in *Pigott* and ruled that the trial judge erred in admitting evidence of the pretrial identification. Here, the victim did not have an opportunity to view the defendant when the robbery occurred, the victim's degree of attention to the defendant's identity was minimal because the victim was unable to view the defendant, and the victim's description of the defendant was unreliable.

State v. Capps, 114 N.C. App. 156 (1994). Although one-on-one showups were unnecessarily suggestive, they were not impermissibly suggestive to result in a substantial likelihood of irreparable misidentification. Therefore, the trial judge did not err in admitting evidence of the witnesses' out-of-court identifications of the defendant that occurred during the showups. Also, the in-court identifications by the witnesses were properly admitted.

State v. Bartow, 77 N.C. App. 103 (1985). The court ruled that the trial judge did not err in not suppressing an out-of-court photographic identification when the photographs had been altered by drawing eyeglasses on each picture to conform to the victim's description of the robber and the defendant was the only person pictured having cuts and bruises on his face and wearing dark clothing. The alteration of the photographs was not impermissibly suggestive because all the photographs had been similarly altered, and the dark clothing, cuts, and bruises were not unduly suggestive because the victim had not described the robber as having those features. *See also* State v. Smith, 130 N.C. App. 71 (1998) (procedures in conducting photographic and in-person lineup were not impermissibly suggestive).

Identification after an Unconstitutional Arrest

United States v. Crews, 445 U.S. 463 (1980). The defendant was arrested without probable cause for an assault, his photograph was taken, and he was compelled to appear in a lineup. The assault victim identified the defendant's photograph from a photo lineup and also identified him in an in-person lineup. The Court ruled that the victim's in-court identification (neither of her out-of-court identifications was introduced at trial) of the defendant was admissible despite his unconstitutional arrest, because her in-court identification rested on her independent recollection of the robbery, uninfluenced by the out-of-court identifications.

Johnson v. Louisiana, 406 U.S. 356 (1972). The defendant was arrested, brought before a magistrate, and advised of his rights. Bail was set, and he was committed to jail. A lineup then was held at which the defendant was represented by counsel. Responding to the defendant's argument that the lineup identification should have been suppressed because it resulted from an illegal arrest, the Court ruled that the identification evidence was not a fruit of the illegal arrest because the defendant was being detained under the magistrate's commitment when the lineup was held. Therefore, the lineup was not conducted through the exploitation of the illegal arrest but rather by means sufficiently distinguishable to be purged of the illegal arrest.

State v. Matthews, 295 N.C. 265 (1978). An out-of-court identification that follows an unconstitutional arrest is admissible if it otherwise satisfies due process standards. The court stated that the only fruit of the illegal arrest was the identification of defendants, and the federal constitution does not protect a person from being viewed. *See also* United States v. Young, 512 F.2d 321 (4th Cir. 1975).

State v. Accor, 277 N.C. 65 (1970), *later appeal*, 281 N.C. 287 (1972). Photographs and evidence of the photographic lineup in which they were used are inadmissible at trial when the photographs were taken while the defendants were in custody as a result of unconstitutional arrests.

Statutory Procedures Involving Lineups

(*This topic is discussed on page 598.*)

State v. Gamble, ___ N.C. App. ___, 777 S.E.2d 158 (2015). The court rejected the defendant's argument that the identification procedure used violated the Eyewitness Identification Reform Act (EIRA). Although a non-independent administrator was used, the administrator satisfied the requirements of G.S. 15A-284.52(c) for such administrators (he used the folder method specified in the statute). Additionally, the administrator met the other requirements of the EIRA. The court rejected the defendant's argument that plain error occurred because the administrator could not identify the specific five filler photographs that were used out of the seven total selected for the lineup. The court concluded that the administrator's failure to recall which of the five filler photographs were used affected the weight of his testimony, not its admissibility. The court ruled that the trial court did not err by admitting the filler photographs into evidence.

State v. Macon, 236 N.C. App. 182 (2014). The court ruled that the trial court did not err by admitting in-court identifications of the defendant by two officers. The defendant argued that the trial court erred in denying his motion to suppress the officers' in-court identifications because the procedure they used to identify him violated the Eyewitness Identification Reform Act (EIRA) and his constitutional due process rights. After the officers observed the defendant at the scene of a suspected drug transaction, they returned to the police station and put the suspect's name into their computer database. When a picture appeared, both officers identified the defendant as the perpetrator. The officers then pulled up another photograph of the defendant and confirmed that he was the perpetrator. This occurred within 10 to 15 minutes of the incident in question. The court concluded that the identification based on two photographs was not a "lineup" and therefore was not subject to the EIRA. The court also ruled that even assuming that the procedure was impermissibly suggestive, the officers' in-court identifications were admissible because each was based on an independent source—the officers' clear, close, and unobstructed view of the suspect at the scene.

State v. Stowes, 220 N.C. App. 330 (2012). While the court of appeals ruled that the trial court did not commit plain error by granting the defendant relief under the Eyewitness Identification Reform Act (EIRA), it did not exclude evidence of a pretrial identification. The trial court found that an EIRA violation occurred because one of the officers administering the identification procedure was involved in the investigation. The court of appeals concluded: "We are not persuaded that the trial court committed plain error by granting Defendant all other available remedies under EIRA, rather than excluding the evidence."

State v. Boozer, 210 N.C. App. 391 (2011). (1) The court ruled that the trial court properly denied the defendant's motion to suppress asserting that an eyewitness's pretrial identification was unduly suggestive. The eyewitness had the opportunity to view the defendant at close range for an extended period of time and was focused on and paying attention to the defendant for at least 15 minutes. Additionally, the eyewitness described the defendant by name as someone he knew and had interacted with previously and immediately identified a photograph of him, indicating high levels of accuracy and confidence in the eyewitness's description and identification. Although the eyewitness stated that he recognized but could not name all of the suspects on the night of the attack, he named the defendant and identified a photograph of him the next day. (2) The court ruled that there was no violation of G.S. 15A-284.52 (eyewitness identification procedures). The eyewitness told the detective that he had seen one of the perpetrators in a weekly newspaper called the *Slammer* but did not recall his name. The detective allowed the eyewitness to look through pages of photographs in the *Slammer*, and from this process the eyewitness identified one of the defendants. The detective did not know who the eyewitness was looking for and thus could not have pressured him to select one of the defendants, nor does any evidence suggest that this occurred. The court noted that G.S. 15A-284.52(c) permits the use of any photo identification procedure that achieves neutral administration, and any alternative method must be carefully structured to achieve neutral administration and to prevent the administrator from knowing which photo is being presented to the eyewitness during the identification procedure.

State v. Rawls, 207 N.C. App. 415 (2010). Two men broke into a house, a third man stayed outside the door, and they all fled when confronted by a resident. Shortly thereafter, the three men were detained by officers. The resident was brought to them for a showup identification, and she identified all of the men as having been involved in the break-in. One of the three men was the defendant. The court ruled that the Eyewitness Identification Reform Act (G.S. 15A-284.50 through 15A-284.53), which sets out procedures for conducting live and photo lineups, does not apply to showups.

Statutory Restrictions on the Use of Identification Procedures with Young People

(This topic is discussed on page 594.)

In re Stallings, 318 N.C. 565 (1986). A one-on-one showup between a victim and a juvenile suspect may be conducted without a juvenile nontestimonial identification order (G.S. 7A-596; now, G.S. 7B-2103) when the showup does not violate due process. In this case the showup was conducted within about an hour after the crime occurred and, based on the totality of circumstances, was constitutionally permissible. The court's ruling reversed the opinion of the North Carolina Court of Appeals, 77 N.C. App. 592 (1985). [Author's note: The *Stallings* ruling effectively reversed the ruling in *State v. Norris*, 77 N.C. App. 525 (1985) (one-on-one showup cannot be conducted with a juvenile without a nontestimonial identification order).]

Chapter 6

Rules of Evidence in Criminal Cases

Chapter 6

Rules of Evidence in Criminal Cases

This chapter discusses the rules of evidence in criminal cases to assist law enforcement officers in understanding why evidence may or may not be admitted at trial. The discussion of exclusionary rules and informants in Chapter 4 on page 407 and Chapter 5 on page 599 will not be repeated here.

Introduction

North Carolina has an evidence code[1] with rules of evidence that are substantially similar to the federal rules of evidence. Judges are guided by these rules of evidence and appellate cases interpreting the rules when they make their evidentiary rulings. In addition, they are guided by federal and state constitutional requirements, miscellaneous state statutes, and the common law.

Judges have considerable discretion in deciding whether evidence should be admitted in a trial. For example, a judge must decide whether evidence, although otherwise admissible, should be excluded from a trial because

- Its probative value is substantially outweighed by the danger of unfair prejudice to the State or the defendant

- The evidence may confuse the issues in the case or mislead the jury
- The evidence is unnecessarily repetitious (and other specified reasons)[2]

For example, a judge could limit the number of character witnesses who testify at trial. Or, in a robbery case, a judge could exclude the testimony of an expert witness on identification testimony if the expert's testimony would confuse the jurors and therefore would not assist them in understanding the robbery victim's identification testimony.[3] Thus, officers should realize that identical or similar evidence admitted in one trial may be excluded in another trial, and the discretionary rulings by the judges in both trials may be correct.

Officers also should realize that lawyers often may not object to improper questions or inadmissible evidence because (1) the evidence may not be harmful or even may be helpful to the lawyer's case, and therefore an objection is unnecessary; (2) lawyers may be concerned that the jurors may not like their objecting too often; (3) admission

---

1. N.C. Gen. Stat. (hereafter, G.S.) § 8C-1, Rules of Evidence (hereafter, Rule).

2. Rule 403. *See, e.g.,* State v. Mason, 315 N.C. 724 (1986); State v. Darden, 323 N.C. 356 (1988). A judge may not make a discretionary decision under Rule 403 in at least two circumstances: (1) see *State v. Scott,* 331 N.C. 39 (1992) (acquittal of offense automatically disqualifies, under Rule 403, use of that offense under Rule 404(b)—with one exception) and (2) convictions under 10 years old admissible under Rule 609(a) are not subject to review under Rule 403—see *State v. McConico,* 153 N.C. App. 723 (2002).

3. State v. Summers, 105 N.C. App. 420 (1992).

of evidence may permit the nonobjecting lawyer to intro-duce evidence later to refute the admitted evidence and actually help the lawyer's case; or (4) the lawyer was inat-tentive or misunderstood the rules. Although trial judges may object on their own to the introduction of evidence, they rarely do so. Thus, evidence may be admitted in a trial that should have been excluded. Officers should remem-ber that evidence may have been admitted only because a lawyer did not object—not because it was admissible. At another trial, similar evidence may be excluded because a lawyer properly objects. And, of course, judges sometimes make errors in admitting or excluding evidence.

Kinds of Evidence

It is useful to understand the different kinds of evidence that may be introduced at trial.

Direct and Circumstantial Evidence

Evidence is sometimes categorized as direct or circum-stantial evidence. *Direct* evidence directly proves a fact. For example, testimony that the witness saw the defen-dant shoot the victim is direct evidence. *Circumstantial* evidence does not directly prove a fact but provides an inference to assist in proving a fact. For example, a defen-dant's fingerprint found at a murder scene is circumstan-tial evidence, because it provides an inference that the defendant may have committed the murder but does not directly prove that the defendant did so.

Contrary to popular belief, a defendant may be con-victed solely by circumstantial evidence, which often may be more valuable than direct evidence. Physical facts may be more reliable in proving that a defendant com-mitted a crime than an eyewitness or accomplice, whose credibility or ability to observe or recall events may be questioned.

Testimonial, Real, Documentary, Illustrative, and Substantive Evidence

Evidence also may be categorized as testimonial, real, documentary, illustrative, or substantive. *Testimonial* evidence is what a witness says under oath. *Real* evidence is a physical object, such as a murder weapon, the vic-tim's clothing, illegal drugs, and the like. *Documentary* evidence is information in the form of business records, letters, and so on. *Illustrative* evidence (also known as *demonstrative* evidence) is used to help explain evidence.

It may consist of a photograph or chart to assist in explain-ing testimony. When a photograph is introduced solely to illustrate a witness's testimony, a jury may only consider the photograph for that purpose. However, a photograph also may be introduced as *substantive* evidence, which means that the jury may consider it to prove a fact in issue.[4] For example, a photograph of a person committing a bank robbery may be offered solely to illustrate the bank teller's testimony about the robbery. However, it could also be introduced as substantive evidence, which means that the jury may use the photograph to determine the robber's identity.

Judicial Notice

A judge may take judicial notice of facts capable of accu-rate and ready determination by referring to sources whose accuracy cannot reasonably be questioned.[5] A law-yer does not need to offer evidence of judicially noticed facts, which include the existence of federal and state laws and established medical and scientific facts (for example, oil floats on water); the dates of a calendar (for example, the fact that April 30, 2011, was a Saturday); and the times of sunrise, sunset, or tides from recognized sources.

Witnesses
Competence of Witnesses
Generally

A person is disqualified from testifying as a witness if a judge determines that the person is incapable of (1) understanding the duty to tell the truth or (2) express-ing himself or herself in a manner that can be under-stood.[6] Generally, this issue arises with young children or people with mental or other disabilities.

Spouses

In criminal cases one spouse may choose to testify against the other spouse, but the State cannot compel a spouse to testify—except in prosecutions for assault or communication of a threat to the testifying spouse, any criminal offense against a minor child of either of the spouses, child abuse, abandonment or nonsupport of the spouse or their children, trespass when living separate

---

4. G.S. 8-97.
5. Rule 201.
6. Rule 601(b).

and apart, and other specified offenses.[7] For example, a wife may testify against her husband charged with murdering a neighbor, but the State cannot compel her to testify under threat of contempt. She alone makes that decision.[8] On the other hand, the State may compel a wife to testify against her husband when he is charged with assaulting her.

A spouse's marital status at the time of testifying determines whether the rules of spousal competency apply. Thus, a divorced spouse may be compelled to testify in all cases, but see the privilege for confidential communications between spouses, discussed below.[9]

Direct Examination of Witnesses

Direct examination is the questioning of a witness by the attorney who has called the witness to testify. After direct examination, the opposing attorney then cross-examines the witness. Additional questioning is *redirect* and *re-cross* examination.

Leading Questions

A leading question suggests the desired answer; for example, "Isn't it true that you saw the defendant shoot Paula Smith?" Leading questions are often those that may be answered "yes" or "no." Although leading questions generally are not permitted on direct examination (to prevent the attorney from suggesting the answer to his or her own witness), exceptions may be made for preliminary matters, such as a witness's employment and educational background, and for the questioning of a hostile witness or a child or other witness who has difficulty understanding questions.

Support of a Witness's Testimony

There are various ways to support the credibility of a witness's testimony:

- Offering a witness's pretrial statement that is consistent with the witness's trial testimony—for example, a statement to an officer at the crime scene that is consistent with the witness's trial testimony
- Offering evidence that the witness accurately perceived and remembered the events about which he or she is testifying

- Showing that the witness is not biased or prejudiced against the other party
- Offering evidence that the witness has no prior convictions and has not committed acts of misconduct related to truthfulness
- Showing that the witness's testimony is corroborated by physical evidence and by other witnesses' testimony
- Offering evidence that the witness has a good character trait for truthfulness

Cross-Examining Witnesses

An attorney who cross-examines a witness usually seeks to discredit or to minimize any harmful testimony given on direct examination and to elicit evidence favorable to the attorney's case. Unlike on direct examination, leading questions are almost always permitted on cross-examination.

Impeaching a Witness's Testimony

The various ways to impeach (discredit) a witness on cross-examination are essentially the opposite of the six ways of supporting a witness's testimony (discussed above):

- Offering a prior inconsistent statement by the witness
- Showing that the witness inaccurately perceived and recollected the events about which the witness has testified
- Showing that the witness is biased or prejudiced against the other party
- Offering evidence that the witness has prior convictions (discussed below) and has committed acts of misconduct related to truthfulness
- Offering evidence that the witness has a bad character trait for truthfulness
- Showing that the State's witness has received favorable treatment from the prosecutor concerning his or her own pending criminal charges—for example, the prosecutor accepted a guilty plea to second-degree murder, reduced from first-degree murder, for the witness's testimony against the defendant

---

7. G.S. 8-57.

8. State v. Britt, 320 N.C. 705 (1987).

9. 1 Kenneth S. Broun, Brandis & Broun on North Carolina Evidence § 135 (7th ed. 2011).

Impeaching a Witness with a Prior Conviction

Any witness, including a defendant, may be impeached by being asked about a prior conviction of a felony or a Class A1, 1, or 2 misdemeanor[10] if the date of the conviction or the witness's release from imprisonment for the conviction, whichever is later, occurred within 10 years of the witness's testimony.[11] Convictions over 10 years old may be used only if a judge finds that their probative value substantially outweighs their prejudicial effect.[12] In addition to asking a witness about a prior conviction, an attorney may introduce evidence of the conviction—usually by a certified copy of the public record.

A prosecutor may not ask a defendant about prior juvenile adjudications. However, a witness other than the defendant may be asked about these adjudications if the judge finds that the evidence is necessary for a fair determination of guilt or innocence—for example, a defense lawyer usually may ask a juvenile accomplice of the defendant whether the juvenile was adjudicated delinquent of the robbery.[13]

Impeaching One's Own Witness

The rules of evidence permit a party to attack the credibility of any witness, even a witness the party has called to testify. However, there are limitations to impeaching one's own witness, particularly when a prosecutor impeaches a State's witness. For example, it is not uncommon for a State's witness to give a written or oral statement to a law enforcement officer that incriminates the defendant and then, before trial, retract the statement or deny having made the statement. In such a case, a prosecutor is not permitted to call the witness at trial solely to have the witness deny making the statement and then, in an effort to impeach the witness, call the officer to testify about the witness's prior inconsistent statement.[14]

Recollection
Refreshing Recollection

Witnesses—particularly investigating officers—are not expected to remember details of events that may have occurred months or years ago. They sometimes need to refer to their notes or to an investigative report.

Officers (or any other witnesses) may use their notes, an investigative report, or any other item to refresh their memory when they are testifying. For example, if an officer is asked to provide a vehicle's license plate number and cannot remember it, the officer may look at notes or an investigative report to refresh his or her memory. This is commonly known as *refreshing recollection*.[15] The defense lawyer has a right to inspect the notes or investigative report used to refresh recollection. However, a judge must determine what portion of the notes or report will be provided to the defense lawyer and must exclude privileged information[16] (for example, an informant's information) and information not directly related to the subject matter of the testimony. The defense lawyer may introduce into evidence those portions of the notes or report that relate to the witness's testimony.

If officers use their notes, an investigative report, or any other item to refresh their memory before testifying, a judge may allow the defense lawyer to inspect and to introduce into evidence the notes, report, or other item in the same manner as described in the preceding paragraph. Note, however, that the judge's decision to allow a defense lawyer's inspection under these circumstances is discretionary.

Officers should not hesitate to refresh their recollection simply because a defense lawyer may have the right to inspect their notes or investigative report. They should consult with the prosecuting attorney or their agency's legal advisor if they have any questions about doing so.

Recorded Past Recollection

Recorded past recollection is an exception to hearsay rules, discussed below. It permits the introduction of a written statement, memorandum, or recording concerning a matter about which a witness once knew but now has insufficient recollection to testify fully, made or adopted by the witness when the matter was fresh in his or her memory.[17] In effect, although the witness cannot

---

10. Rule 609(a). *See also* State v. Gregory, 154 N.C. App. 178 (2002) (DWI conviction may be subject to impeachment under Rule 609 because DWI is equivalent of Class 1 misdemeanor).

11. Rule 609(b) does not specify the event from which the 10-year period is calculated, but it is probably from the last event specified in the rule to the beginning of the trial. State v. Lynch, 337 N.C. 415 (1994).

12. Rule 609(b); State v. Ross, 329 N.C. 108 (1991).

13. Rule 609(d).

14. State v. Hunt, 324 N.C. 343 (1989); State v. Hyleman, 324 N.C. 506 (1989).

15. Rule 612.

16. State v. Hall, 330 N.C. 808 (1992).

17. Rule 803(5).

remember enough about the matter to testify fully, he or she admits that the prior written statement was accurate when taken. The written statement then may be read into evidence, but it may not be received as an exhibit unless offered by the other party.

The following is an example of recorded past recollection. An officer interviews a witness to a homicide and writes down what the witness says. The witness at trial testifies that he does not remember what happened. The prosecutor shows the witness the written statement that he signed when the officer interviewed him. The witness testifies that he remembers that he made the statement to the officer, saw the officer write it, told the truth to the officer, signed the statement, and saw the officer sign it. The statement then may be read into evidence because it qualifies as recorded past recollection.[18] However, officers should remember that when a witness at trial denies having made a prior statement or says that the statement is not true, the prior statement is not admissible as recorded past recollection.

Opinion Evidence, Including Expert Testimony
Lay Opinion

Generally, lay (nonexpert) witnesses may testify only about their personal knowledge of facts, not their opinions. Opinions are evaluations of or inferences made from facts. However, lay witnesses may offer opinions that are rationally based on their perceptions and helpful to the jury in understanding their testimony or determining a fact in issue.[19]

A lawyer seeking an opinion from a witness must lay a foundation for it by showing that the witness had a basis to form the opinion—for example, knowledge of the underlying facts, ability to see and hear, and so forth. Some permissible lay opinions include (1) whether a person was dead, sane or insane, or under the influence of alcohol or drugs; (2) the speed of a vehicle; (3) the fair market value of property; and (4) identification of a person's voice or handwriting.

Also admissible is a *shorthand statement of fact*, which is a conclusion about a variety of facts in one statement; for example, that the person "lost control of the vehicle"

or that the person's shoes were muddy and "didn't look like they had been unlaced in several days."[20]

Expert Opinion

A witness qualified as an expert by knowledge, skill, experience, training, or education may give an opinion, even about an ultimate issue—for example, whether the defendant was insane—when the expert's scientific, technical, or other specialized knowledge will help the jury understand the evidence or determine a fact in issue.[21] Typical experts in a criminal case are physicians, psychiatrists, and scientific laboratory personnel. They offer opinions about cause of death, nature of injuries, insanity, and whether the defendant had the specific intent to kill. Experts also offer opinions about tests and examinations of drugs, blood and bodily fluids, DNA, fingerprints, hair, handwriting, footprints, tire tracks, fibers, bullets, firearms, toolmarks, questioned documents, and so on.

Expert testimony is admissible on the issue of impairment (but not on a specific alcohol concentration level) concerning (1) the results of a Horizontal Gaze Nystagmus (HGN) Test, when the test was administered by a person who has successfully completed HGN training; and (2) whether a person was under the influence of one or more impairing substances and the category of the impairing substance or substances, when the witness has received training and holds a current certification, issued by the State Department of Health and Human Services, as a Drug Recognition Expert.[22]

An expert in accident reconstruction who has performed a reconstruction of a crash or has reviewed the report of an investigation may with a proper foundation give an opinion about the speed of a vehicle, even if the expert did not observe the vehicle in motion.[23]

Law enforcement officers sometimes may qualify as experts in drug cases. Although the case law may still be evolving, appellate courts have recognized that officers, when properly qualified by training and experience, may be experts in identifying a substance such as marijuana,[24]

---

18. *See* State v. Nickerson, 320 N.C. 603 (1987).
19. Rule 701.

20. *See* 2 Kenneth S. Broun, Brandis & Broun on North Carolina Evidence § 178 (7th ed. 2011).
21. Rules 702, 703.
22. Rule 702(a1).
23. Rule 701(i).
24. State v. Fletcher, 92 N.C. App. 50 (1988); State v. Morris, 102 N.C. App. 541 (1991). But see the discussion of officers' identification of drugs, including marijuana, in Shea Denning,

the manner in which marijuana is packaged,[25] how drug paraphernalia is used, and how heroin is cut.[26] On the other hand, officers are generally not permitted to identify substances as powder or crack cocaine.[27]

Character Evidence

Evidence of character traits of a witness, a homicide or assault victim, or a defendant is admissible under certain circumstances. To be admissible, the character trait must be pertinent to the case. For example, the defendant's character trait of peacefulness would be pertinent in a homicide case but not in a forgery case. Pertinent traits of character may be proved by either of two types of evidence, or by both:

1. Reputation evidence, which is what others believe about the witness's character traits
2. Opinion evidence, which is an individual's personal belief about the witness's character traits[28]

Character Traits of Testifying Witnesses

The character trait of truthfulness is pertinent for all witnesses who testify at trial, including a defendant who testifies. Thus, both the prosecutor and defense counsel may offer character witnesses to testify about a testifying witness's character trait for truthfulness or untruthfulness. As discussed above, character witnesses may offer opinion or reputation evidence, or both, about a character trait.

Character Traits of Criminal Defendants

Even if the defendant does not testify, evidence of a defendant's pertinent character traits may be introduced on his or her behalf. In any criminal case, the trait of obeying the law (being "law-abiding") is always pertinent.[29] In homicide or assault cases, peacefulness is a pertinent character trait.[30]

A prosecutor may cross-examine a defendant's character witnesses about their knowledge of the defendant's prior acts that reflect adversely on a pertinent character trait,[31] and the prosecutor may offer character witnesses to rebut the testimony of the defendant's character witnesses.[32]

If the defendant testifies at trial, the prosecutor may question the defendant about his or her prior misconduct that did not result in a conviction (prior convictions were discussed above), but only if the misconduct is relevant to the character trait of truthfulness.[33] For example, the defendant may be asked about lying on an application for employment, but he or she may not be asked about committing prior assaults or sexual abuse.[34]

Character Traits of Homicide or Assault Victims

In any criminal case, a defendant may offer character witnesses to testify about pertinent character traits of the victim.[35] For example, the victim's character trait of being a violent person would be pertinent in a homicide or assault case when there is evidence that the defendant acted in self-defense. If the defendant offers such evidence, the prosecutor may offer character witnesses to testify about the victim's character trait of peacefulness.[36]

Prior Sexual Behavior of Sexual Assault Victims

The prior sexual behavior of a victim of rape or other sexual offenses is not admissible unless it fits within one of the following four categories:

1. It was between the alleged victim and the defendant.

Where Are We with Drug ID? NC CRIM. L. BLOG (Mar. 3, 2011), http://sogweb.sog.unc.edu/blogs/ncclaw/?p=2001.

25. State v. Chisholm, 90 N.C. App. 526 (1988).

26. State v. Covington, 22 N.C. App. 250 (1974).

27. See the discussion of the case law, some of which is unsettled, in Shea Denning, *Where Are We with Drug ID?* NC CRIM. L. BLOG (Mar. 3, 2011), http://sogweb.sog.unc.edu/blogs/ncclaw/?p=2001.

28. Rule 405(a).

29. State v. Squire, 321 N.C. 541 (1988).

30. *Id.*

31. State v. Gappins, 320 N.C. 64 (1987).

32. Rule 404(a)(1).

33. Rule 608(b); State v. Morgan, 315 N.C. 626 (1986). Under Rule 608(b), a prosecutor may not offer extrinsic evidence of the misconduct by calling a witness to testify about it. However, such evidence would be permitted if it also qualified under Rule 404(b). State v. Bagley, 321 N.C. 201 (1987).

34. State v. Morgan, 315 N.C. 626 (1986); State v. Scott, 318 N.C. 237 (1986).

35. Rule 404(a)(2). *See generally* JOHN RUBIN, THE LAW OF SELF-DEFENSE IN NORTH CAROLINA (UNC Institute of Government, 1996).

36. Rule 404(a)(2). Even if the defendant in a homicide case does not offer character witnesses about the victim's character trait for violence, the prosecutor may offer character witnesses for the trait of peacefulness to rebut evidence that the victim was the initial aggressor. *But see* State v. Faison, 330 N.C. 347 (1991).

2. The evidence shows that the alleged sexual act was not committed by the defendant—for example, the defendant could not have been the source of semen found in the victim's vagina.

3. The prior sexual behavior is so distinctive and so closely resembling the act being tried that the behavior tends to prove that the victim consented.

4. The prior sexual behavior is the basis of expert opinion that the alleged victim invented the charged act.[37]

Even if evidence of prior sexual behavior is admissible under one of these four categories, it may not be proved by reputation or opinion evidence.[38]

Rule 404(b): Other Offenses or Bad Acts Committed by the Defendant

Under Rule 404(b), evidence of other crimes or misconduct is admissible to prove a defendant's identity, motive, intent, plan, and the like, unless the evidence is offered only to prove that the defendant has a bad character.[39] For example, evidence of the defendant's prior assaults on a homicide victim may be admissible to show that the defendant acted with malice in killing the victim.[40] In a child sexual offense trial, evidence of the defendant's sexual assaults against the victim and the victim's siblings may be admissible to show a common plan to sexually abuse children.[41] In a rape and burglary trial, evidence that the defendant committed a similar rape and burglary may be admissible to prove the defendant's identity in committing the charged offenses.[42] In determining whether prior offenses are admissible under this rule, courts consider not only the relevance of the prior offense to the offense being tried but also how similar the prior

offense is to the charged offense and how long before the charged offense it occurred.[43]

A defendant also may offer evidence under Rule 404(b); for example, evidence of similar offenses that tends to show that someone other than the defendant committed the charged crime.[44]

Privileges

Confidential Communications between Spouses

Confidential communications between spouses are privileged when the communications are induced by the confidence of their relationship. The privilege also includes acts intended as communications. For example: a husband takes a gun from a cabinet while only his wife is present and tells her that he is going to shoot and kill someone. The privilege would prevent the State—over the husband's objection—from eliciting testimony from the wife about the incident.[45]

This privilege continues after divorce.[46] However, the privilege does not apply at any time to communications about child abuse or neglect.[47]

Attorney–Client Privilege

The attorney–client privilege applies to confidential communications between an attorney and client made during the attorney–client relationship if the communications concern a matter for which the attorney is employed or being consulted.[48] The privilege may be waived only by the client—that is, the attorney may not testify about the communications if the client objects.

---

37. Rule 412. *See generally* Jeff Welty, *Special Evidentiary Issues in Sexual Assault Cases: The Rape Shield Law and Evidence of Prior Sexual Misconduct by the Defendant*, Admin. of Just. Bull. 2009/04 (Aug. 2009), http://sogpubs.unc.edu/electronicversions/pdfs/aojb0904.pdf.

38. Rule 412(c).

39. State v. Coffey, 326 N.C. 268 (1990). With a limited exception, such evidence is not admissible if the defendant was found not guilty of the conduct sought to be introduced under Rule 404(b). *See* State v. Scott, 331 N.C. 39 (1992).

40. State v. Simpson, 327 N.C. 178 (1990).

41. State v. Shamsid-Deen, 324 N.C. 437 (1989).

42. State v. Jeter, 326 N.C. 457 (1990).

43. State v. Hipps, 348 N.C. 377 (1998).

44. State v. Cotton, 318 N.C. 663 (1987). Although the court in *Cotton* indicated that Rule 404(b) may support the admission of this kind of evidence, it ultimately based its ruling on the relevance of the evidence under Rule 401.

45. State v. Holmes, 330 N.C. 826 (1992). However, the privilege does not apply when spouses are communicating about crimes in which they are jointly participating. *See* United States v. Parker, 834 F.2d 408 (4th Cir. 1987); United States v. Mendoza, 574 F.2d 1373 (5th Cir. 1978); United States v. Estes, 793 F.2d 465 (2d Cir. 1986).

46. 1 Kenneth S. Broun, Brandis & Broun on North Carolina Evidence § 127 (7th ed. 2011).

47. G.S. 8-57.1.

48. 1 Kenneth S. Broun, Brandis & Broun on North Carolina Evidence § 129 (7th ed. 2011). For cases construing the attorney–client privilege in criminal investigations or trials, see *In re Investigation of the Death of Miller*, 357 N.C. 316 (2003), *later appeal*, 358 N.C. 364 (2004); *State v. McLean*, 183 N.C. App. 429 (2007).

Physician–Patient Privilege

The physician–patient privilege applies to information that a physician (or someone working at the physician's direction) needs in treating a patient. The privilege may be waived only by the patient. However, a judge may set aside the privilege and order the disclosure of the information when the judge finds that it is "necessary to a proper administration of justice."[49] For example, a judge could order a physician to testify about finding illegal drugs on a patient during treatment.[50]

This privilege does not apply to information about child abuse.[51]

Other Privileges

Other privileges include communications between a member of the clergy and a communicant;[52] between a patient and a nurse;[53] and between a client and a psychologist,[54] school counselor,[55] certified marital and family therapist,[56] social worker,[57] optometrist,[58] domestic violence or rape crisis center employee,[59] law enforcement peer group counselor,[60] or registered professional counselor.[61] A journalist has a qualified privilege against disclosing information in a legal proceeding that was obtained or prepared while he or she was acting as a journalist.[62] The confidential relationship between a law enforcement officer and an informant is discussed in Chapters 4 and 5.

Hearsay

Hearsay is not admissible except as provided by the rules of evidence or statutory law.[63] Hearsay is not admissible because the party against whom it is offered does not have the opportunity to cross-examine the person who made the statement, the statement is usually not under oath, and the statement may be unreliable evidence.

A criminal defendant also has a Sixth Amendment right to confront the State's witnesses. United States Supreme Court cases interpreting the Sixth Amendment's Confrontation Clause have effectively narrowed the admissibility of hearsay offered by the State. For an analysis of the complex issues involved in these cases, see the resource cited in the accompanying footnote.[64]

Definition

Hearsay is defined as a statement of another person that is offered to prove the truth of the matter asserted in the statement.[65] A *statement* is (1) an oral or written assertion—for example, a written statement or letter—or (2) a person's nonverbal conduct that is intended as an assertion.[66] Such nonverbal conduct would include a witness at a lineup pointing at a person in response to an officer's request to identify the person who committed a robbery.

If a law enforcement officer testifies that a rape victim told the officer shortly after the rape that John Smith forced her to have sexual intercourse, and the rape victim's statement is offered to prove that John Smith raped her, that statement is hearsay and therefore inadmissible—unless it fits an exception to the hearsay rule, discussed below. On the other hand, if the statement is offered solely to corroborate the rape victim's trial testimony that she was forced to have sexual intercourse with John Smith, the statement is not hearsay.

If a law enforcement officer testifies that he or she went to 21 Elm Street in response to a radio communication

---

49. G.S. 8-53; State v. Drdak, 330 N.C. 587 (1992); *In re Albemarle Mental Health Ctr.*, 42 N.C. App. 292 (1979).

50. *Cf.* State v. Wooten, 18 N.C. App. 269 (1973).

51. G.S. 7B-310; G.S. 8-53.1; State v. Etheridge, 319 N.C. 34 (1987).

52. G.S. 8-53.2.

53. G.S. 8-53.13.

54. G.S. 8-53.3.

55. G.S. 8-53.4.

56. G.S. 8-53.5.

57. G.S. 8-53.7.

58. G.S. 8-53.9.

59. G.S. 8-53.12.

60. G.S. 8-53.10.

61. G.S. 8-53.8.

62. G.S. 8-53.11.

---

63. Rule 802. For a discussion of hearsay and its exceptions, see Jessica Smith, *Criminal Evidence: Hearsay*, in NORTH CAROLINA SUPERIOR COURT JUDGES' BENCHBOOK (UNC School of Government, Oct. 2013), http://benchbook.sog.unc.edu/evidence/hearsay-rules.

64. Jessica Smith, *A Guide to Crawford and the Confrontation Clause*, in NORTH CAROLINA SUPERIOR COURT JUDGES' BENCHBOOK (UNC School of Government, Aug. 2015), http://benchbook.sog.unc.edu/evidence/guide-crawford-confrontation-clause.

65. Rule 801(c).

66. Rule 801(a).

that a murder was committed there, the communication is not hearsay if it is offered solely to explain why the officer went to that address. However, it is hearsay if it is offered to prove that a murder occurred there.

A witness's affidavit is hearsay if the statements within the affidavit are offered to prove the truth of the matter asserted in them. A statement under oath is not excluded from the definition of hearsay.[67]

Exceptions to the Hearsay Rule

There are more than 20 exceptions to the hearsay rule. The exceptions are divided into two categories, depending on whether or not the party offering the statement must prove that the declarant is unavailable as a witness to testify. Remember, however, that under some circumstances the Sixth Amendment's Confrontation Clause may require the State to produce the witness for cross-examination even though the hearsay rule does not.[68]

When It Is Unnecessary to Prove That Hearsay Declarant Is Unavailable to Testify

The statements under the hearsay exceptions discussed below are admissible whether or not the declarant is available to testify as a witness. For example, if a person's statement was made for medical diagnosis and treatment, discussed below, the State may introduce the statement into evidence even though the person is available as a witness and is not called to testify. Remember, however, that under some circumstances the Sixth Amendment's Confrontation Clause may require the State to produce the witness for cross-examination even though the hearsay rule does not.[69]

Admissions, including statements by co-conspirators. Any statement of the defendant offered by the State is admissible as an admission.[70] A statement includes not only the defendant's verbal and written statements but also implied admissions—also known as admissions by silence.[71] An *implied admission* is a statement made by someone other than the defendant in the defendant's presence—including over the telephone—under circumstances in which a denial would be naturally expected if the statement were untrue. The defendant must have been able to hear and understand what was said and must have had an opportunity to speak.[72] For example, if an accomplice and the defendant committed a murder together, the accomplice later explained the details of the murder to a third person while the defendant was in the same room listening to the explanation, and the defendant said nothing, then the defendant's silence is an implied admission of the accomplice's statements.[73] However, when a defendant remains silent in response to questioning about a crime by law enforcement officers, it is not an implied admission.[74]

Statements made by the defendant's co-conspirators are admissible as admissions against the defendant if the statements are made during the course of and in furtherance of the conspiracy.[75] On the other hand, statements made before the conspiracy begins or after the conspiracy ends are not admissions.[76]

Statement made for medical diagnosis or treatment. Statements are admissible if they are made for medical diagnosis and treatment and describe a person's medical history, past or present symptoms, pain or sensations, or the cause or source of the medical problem.[77] The statement may be made to medical personnel or to lay people who, as a result of the statement, contact medical personnel to treat the declarant. However, there are significant restrictions on the admissibility of these statements in

---

67. 2 Kenneth S. Broun, Brandis & Broun on North Carolina Evidence § 193 (7th ed. 2011).

68. *See* the publication cited *supra* note 64.

69. *Id.*

70. Rule 801(d)(A). A defendant's statement offered by the defense is not an admission. If the defendant has not testified and the statement is offered for the truth of the matter asserted, it is hearsay (commonly known as a self-serving declaration) and inadmissible—unless the statement fits within one of the hearsay exceptions. 2 Kenneth S. Broun, Brandis & Broun on North Carolina Evidence § 194 (7th ed. 2011); State v. Maness, 321 N.C. 454 (1988); State v. Stanton, 319 N.C. 180 (1987); State v. Pearce, 296 N.C. 281 (1979); State v. Davis, 289 N.C. 500 (1976).

71. Rule 801(d)(B).

72. State v. Moore, 301 N.C. 262 (1980); State v. Hunt, 325 N.C. 187 (1989); State v. Thompson, 332 N.C. 204 (1992) (admission by silence during telephone conversation); 2 Kenneth S. Broun, Brandis & Broun on North Carolina Evidence § 211 (7th ed. 2011).

73. State v. Moore, 301 N.C. 262 (1980).

74. *See generally* 2 Kenneth S. Broun, Brandis & Broun on North Carolina Evidence § 211 (7th ed. 2011); State v. Hoyle, 325 N.C. 232 (1989).

75. Rule 801(d)(E). *See generally* 2 Kenneth S. Broun, Brandis & Broun on North Carolina Evidence § 205 (7th ed. 2011).

76. State v. Branch, 288 N.C. 514 (1975); State v. Gary, 78 N.C. App. 29 (1985).

77. Rule 803(4).

child abuse cases.[78] If the statement includes the identity of the perpetrator who caused the medical problem, it also is admissible if the perpetrator's identity aids proper medical treatment.[79]

Excited utterance. Statements that relate to a startling event or condition are admissible if the declarant was under the stress of excitement caused by the event or condition.[80] Examples of statements that qualify under this exception include the following:

- A bystander (the declarant) to a shooting telling the defendant immediately after the defendant had shot the victim and was bending over her with the gun still in his hand "not to shoot her no more because he had already killed her"[81]
- An extremely excited declarant—15 minutes after a fire had started in a house—running to an officer and telling him that he had been inside the house and had gone to sleep, and the defendant had poured some fuel oil and set it on fire and left[82]

A greater time period between the startling event and the statement is recognized for statements by young children—particularly when the event is child abuse—because the stress and spontaneity on which the exception is based is often present longer than with adults.[83]

Existing mental, emotional, or physical conditions. Statements of the declarant's then existing state of mind, emotion, sensation, or physical condition—such as intent, plan, motive, mental feeling, pain, and physical health—are admissible under this exception.[84] Statements within this exception include a murder victim's expression of fear of the alleged murderer or the victim's statements about prior threats made by the alleged murderer against the victim.[85]

Present sense impression. Statements describing or explaining an event or condition are admissible when they were made while the declarant was perceiving the event or condition, or immediately thereafter.[86] When a victim came over to her mother's house crying and told her that the defendant had kicked her out of his house, the statement was made "immediately thereafter" and was admissible under this exception.[87]

Business records. The business records exception includes records, memoranda, or reports or data compilations in any form—for example, computer data—made or transmitted in a timely manner by a knowledgeable person if the records were kept in the course of a regularly conducted business activity and it was the business's regular practice to make the records. These facts must be proved by testimony of the records custodian or other qualified witness.[88] The exception would permit, for example, the introduction of hospital or private laboratory test records,[89] computer-generated records,[90] telephone bills,[91] and firearm sales records.[92]

Public records or reports. The public records exception includes records, reports, statements, and data compilations, in any form, of public agencies setting forth (1) the agency's activities; (2) matters observed pursuant to a legal duty for which there was a duty to report—excluding in a criminal case, however, matters observed by law enforcement officers and personnel; or (3) against the State in criminal cases, factual findings from an investigation made under legal authority, unless the sources of information or other circumstances indicate a lack of

---

78. State v. Hinnant, 351 N.C. 277 (2000) (objective circumstances must show that child declarant intended to make statements to obtain medical diagnosis or treatment and that the statements were reasonably pertinent to diagnosis or treatment).

79. State v. Smith, 315 N.C. 76 (1985). But statements are generally not admissible when they are made in preparing the State's witness for trial, rather than for medical diagnosis or treatment. *See* State v. Stafford, 317 N.C. 568 (1986).

80. Rule 803(2).

81. State v. Wingard, 317 N.C. 590 (1986).

82. State v. Kerley, 87 N.C. App. 240 (1987).

83. State v. Smith, 315 N.C. 76 (1985).

84. Rule 803(3). Excluded are statements of memory or belief to prove the fact remembered or believed, unless they involve certain matters involving the declarant's will. *See* State v. Artis, 325 N.C. 278 (1989).

85. State v. Stager, 329 N.C. 278 (1991); State v. Lynch, 327 N.C. 210 (1990).

86. Rule 803(1).

87. State v. Cummings, 326 N.C. 298 (1990).

88. Rule 803(6). However, evidence is inadmissible if the source of information or the method or circumstances of preparation of a business record indicate a lack of trustworthiness.

89. State v. Deanes, 323 N.C. 508 (1989); State v. Miller, 80 N.C. 425 (1986).

90. State v. Springer, 283 N.C. 627 (1973) (however, foundation evidence was insufficient to support admissibility in this case); State v. Agudelo, 89 N.C. App. 640 (1988) (similar ruling).

91. State v. Price, 326 N.C. 56 (1990) (however, foundation evidence was insufficient to support admissibility in this case).

92. State v. Holden, 321 N.C. 125 (1987).

trustworthiness.[93] Under this exception, a defendant—but not the State—may introduce, for example, a State Crime Laboratory report on hair analysis.[94] (Note that drug laboratory reports may be introduced by the State under certain circumstances, discussed below.)

Residual hearsay exception. The residual hearsay exception permits the introduction of a statement that does not qualify under any specified exception, but only if the party seeking to introduce the statement satisfies rigorous criteria to show that the statement is sufficiently reliable to be admitted into evidence.[95]

When It Is Necessary to Prove That Hearsay Declarant Is Unavailable to Testify

Statements under the hearsay exceptions discussed below are admissible only if the declarant is unavailable to testify as a witness. Remember, however, that under some circumstances the Sixth Amendment's Confrontation Clause may require the State to produce the witness for cross-examination even though the hearsay rule does not.[96]

A declarant is unavailable as a witness if any one of the following occurs:

- A judge rules that the declarant has a privilege not to testify—for example, the declarant has asserted the Fifth Amendment privilege against self-incrimination
- The declarant refuses to testify about the subject matter of the hearsay statement, despite a judge's order to do so
- The declarant testifies that he or she does not remember the subject matter of the hearsay statement
- The declarant is unable to be present or to testify because of death or physical or mental illness or infirmity[97]
- The declarant is absent from the trial and the party seeking to offer the hearsay statement has been

unable to procure the declarant's attendance or testimony by legal process, such as a subpoena[98]

Former testimony. Former testimony is admissible if it was given by an unavailable declarant at a prior court proceeding and the party against whom it is offered had an opportunity and similar motive to develop the testimony by direct, cross, or redirect examination.[99] For example, the testimony of an unavailable witness from a prior trial against the same defendant or a probable cause hearing for the offense being tried may be admitted if it otherwise qualifies under the exception.[100]

Statement under belief of impending death (dying declaration). An unavailable declarant's statement about the cause or circumstances of what the declarant believes to be his or her impending death—for example, "Tom Smith shot me"—is admissible if the statement is made while the declarant believes that death is imminent.[101] The statement may be admissible even if the declarant does not die, as long as the declarant is unavailable at trial—for example, when the declarant is in a coma.

Statement against interest. An unavailable declarant's statement is admissible if, when it was made, it was so contrary to the declarant's pecuniary (money) or proprietary (property) interest, or so tended to subject the declarant to criminal liability, that a reasonable person in his or her position would not have made the statement unless the person believed it was true.[102] A statement exposing the declarant to criminal liability is not admissible unless corroborating circumstances clearly indicate the statement's trustworthiness.[103] Under this exception, an unavailable declarant's statement admitting involvement in criminal activity and implicating others, including the defendant, is admissible if corroborating circumstances clearly indicate the statement's trustworthiness.[104]

---

93. Rule 803(8).

94. State v. Acklin, 317 N.C. 677 (1986).

95. Rule 803(24); State v. Smith, 315 N.C. 76 (1985). *See generally* 2 KENNETH S. BROUN, BRANDIS & BROUN ON NORTH CAROLINA EVIDENCE § 241 (7th ed. 2011).

96. *See* the publication cited *supra* note 64.

97. State v. Chandler, 324 N.C. 172 (1989).

98. Rule 804(a).

99. Rule 804(b)(1).

100. *See* 2 KENNETH S. BROUN, BRANDIS & BROUN ON NORTH CAROLINA EVIDENCE § 236 (7th ed. 2011); State v. Giles, 83 N.C. App. 487 (1986).

101. Rule 804(b)(2). *See* 2 KENNETH S. BROUN, BRANDIS & BROUN ON NORTH CAROLINA EVIDENCE § 237 (7th ed. 2011); State v. Penley, 318 N.C. 30 (1986); State v. Hamlette, 302 N.C. 490 (1981).

102. Rule 804(b)(3).

103. *Id.*

104. State v. Wilson, 322 N.C. 117 (1988). A defendant also may seek to introduce evidence under this rule. *See* State v. Tucker, 331 N.C. 12 (1992) (defendant was improperly prohibited from introducing a statement against penal interest made

Residual hearsay exception. The residual hearsay exception permits the introduction of a statement that does not qualify under any specified exception, but only if the party seeking to introduce the unavailable declarant's statement satisfies rigorous criteria to show that the statement is sufficiently reliable to be admitted into evidence.[105]

Constitutional and Related Statutory Issues

Constitutional Duty to Provide Evidence Materially Favorable to a Defendant; Related Statutory Obligations

Prosecutors have a constitutional duty under the Due Process Clause of the Fourteenth Amendment to disclose to a defendant evidence that is materially favorable to the defendant at a trial or a sentencing hearing.[106] Prosecutors may violate a defendant's constitutional rights even when they are unaware of materially favorable evidence in law enforcement files, because knowledge of that evidence is imputed to them.[107] Therefore, law enforcement officers should always attempt to provide prosecutors with all relevant information about a pending case.

Prosecutors also have statutory duties to disclose information, whether or not it is favorable to the defense.[108] For example, they must make available to a defendant the complete files of all law enforcement agencies, other investigatory agencies, and prosecutors' offices involved in the investigation of the crimes committed or the prosecution of the defendant.[109] Law enforcement and other investigatory agencies must provide on a timely basis a complete copy of their complete files concerning the investigation and prosecution. Also, if they obtain discoverable information and material, they must ensure that it

is fully disclosed to the prosecutor on a timely basis for disclosure to the defendant.[110] Any person who willfully omits or misrepresents evidence or information required to be disclosed to a defendant or to a prosecutor's office commits a Class H felony or Class 1 misdemeanor (the punishment varies depending on the type of evidence or information). [111]

Lost or Destroyed Evidence; Related Statutory Obligations

Officers should take appropriate care of relevant evidence in a pending case so that it is not lost or inadvertently destroyed or disposed of. Officers should consult with a prosecutor or their agency's legal advisor before deliberately destroying or disposing of relevant evidence in a pending case or a case on appeal or review in state or federal courts, unless they are sure that they can do so.

Officers do not violate a defendant's constitutional rights unless they act in bad faith in failing to preserve potentially useful evidence for the defense at trial.[112]

North Carolina statutory law requires government entities, including law enforcement agencies, to preserve DNA and biological evidence for specified time periods.[113]

Confessions That Implicate Another at a Joint Trial

Two people, Pete Smith and Sandra Jones, commit an armed robbery and murder. Smith is arrested and confesses to committing the crimes with Jones. Jones is

---

by his codefendant); State v. Artis, 325 N.C. 278 (1989) (letter was inadmissible under Rule 804(b)(3)); State v. Agubata, 92 N.C. App. 651 (1989) (similar ruling).

105. State v. Triplett, 316 N.C. 1 (1986); State v. Nichols, 321 N.C. 616 (1988). *See generally* 2 Kenneth S. Broun, Brandis & Broun on North Carolina Evidence § 241 (7th ed. 2011).

106. Kyles v. Whitley, 514 U.S. 419 (1995); United States v. Bagley, 473 U.S. 667 (1985).

107. Kyles v. Whitley, 514 U.S. 419 (1995); State v. Smith, 337 N.C. 658 (1994); Smith v. Cain, 132 S. Ct. 627 (2012).

108. G.S. Ch. 15A, Art. 48 (G.S. 15A-901 through -910).

109. G.S. 15A-903(a)(1).

110. G.S. 15A-903(c).

111. G.S. 15A-903(d). It is a Class H felony if the evidence or information is required to be disclosed under G.S. 15A-903(a)(1) (requiring disclosure of complete files of law enforcement agencies, other investigatory agencies, and prosecutors' offices). It is a Class 1 misdemeanor if the evidence or information is required to be disclosed under other provision of G.S. 15A-903.

112. Illinois v. Fisher, 540 U.S. 544 (2004); Arizona v. Youngblood, 488 U.S. 51 (1988); California v. Trombetta, 467 U.S. 479 (1984) (no constitutional duty to preserve breath test ampoule); State v. Jones, 106 N.C. App. 214 (1992) (same ruling under state constitution); State v. Drdak, 330 N.C. 587 (1991); State v. Cummings, 326 N.C. 298 (1990); State v. Graham, 118 N.C. App. 231 (1995) (police department's inadvertent destruction of rape kit and victim's clothing did not violate the defendant's due process rights); State v. Anderson, 57 N.C. App. 602 (1982) (destruction of marijuana was done in good faith because of inadequate storage facilities, based on facts in this case); State v. Hudson, 56 N.C. App. 172 (1982) (inadvertent destruction of bloodstained paper towels did not violate defendant's constitutional rights).

113. G.S. 15A-266 through -270.1.

arrested and denies any involvement in the crimes. If the two defendants are tried together, the prosecution may not introduce Smith's confession—at least that part of the confession that implicates Jones—unless Smith testifies and thus provides Jones with her constitutional right to confront any witnesses against her. This rule of evidence is commonly known as the *Bruton* rule, named after a United States Supreme Court case.[114]

In deciding how to deal with Smith's confession, a prosecutor must proceed in one of three ways: (1) a joint trial where the confession is not admitted into evidence; (2) a joint trial where the confession is admitted into evidence only after references to Jones have been effectively deleted so that the confession will not prejudice Jones—editing the confession in this manner is commonly known as *redaction*; or (3) separate trials for Smith and Jones.[115]

Miscellaneous Evidentiary Issues
Introduction of Forensic and Chemical Analysis Reports and Affidavits through Notice and Demand Statutes

To comply with a United States Supreme Court ruling[116] involving a defendant's right to confront witnesses at trial, the North Carolina General Assembly enacted legislation amending existing notice and demand statutes and creating others.[117] Notice and demand statutes set up procedures by which the State may procure the defendant's waiver of his or her confrontation right concerning foren-

sic laboratory reports and chemical analyst affidavits.[118] If a defendant declines to waive that right, the State generally will be required to produce the appropriate analyst to testify in court.

Forensic Analyses

Section 8-58.20 of the North Carolina General Statutes (hereafter, G.S.) sets out a notice and demand procedure for a laboratory report of a written forensic analysis, including an analysis of the defendant's DNA. It provides that in any criminal proceeding, a laboratory report that states the results of the analysis and is signed and sworn to by the person performing the analysis is admissible in evidence without the testimony of the analyst who prepared the report. The State must give notice of its intent to use the report no later than five business days after receiving it or 30 business days before any proceeding in which the report may be used against the defendant, whichever occurs first. The defendant then has 15 business days to file a written objection to its use. If the defense fails to file an objection, the report is admissible without the testimony of the analyst, subject to the presiding judge ruling otherwise. If an objection is filed, the special admissibility provision in the statute does not apply.

Chemical Analyses of Blood or Urine

G.S. 20-139.1(c1) provides for the use of chemical analyses of blood or urine in any court without the testimony of the analyst. It applies to cases tried in both district and superior courts as well as to adjudicatory hearings in juvenile court. Under this provision, the State must notify the defendant at least 15 business days before the proceeding of its intent to introduce the report into evidence and provide a copy of the report to the defendant. The defendant has until five business days before the proceeding to file a written objection with the court. If the defendant fails to object, then the evidence may be admitted without the testimony of the analyst. If the defense objects, the special admissibility provision in the statute does not apply.

Chemical Analyst's Affidavit in District Court

G.S. 20-139.1(e1) provides for the use of a chemical analyst's affidavit in district court. Under this statute, a sworn affidavit is admissible in evidence, without further

---

114. Bruton v. United States, 391 U.S. 123 (1968). The example in the text assumes that an exception to the hearsay rule does not exist to make Smith's confession admissible against Jones. Because the conspiracy had clearly ended when Smith confessed, his confession is not admissible as a statement of a co-conspirator made during the course of and in furtherance of the conspiracy.

115. *See* G.S. 15A-927(c)(1); *see also* Gray v. Maryland, 523 U.S. 185 (1998).

116. Melendez-Diaz v. Massachusetts, 557 U.S. 305 (2009). *See also* Bullcoming v. New Mexico, 131 S. Ct. 2705 (2011); Williams v. Illinois, 132 S. Ct. 2221 (2012).

117. S.L. 2009-473. In *State v. Steele*, 201 N.C. App. 689, 696 (2010), the court upheld the constitutionality of G.S. 90-95(g), the notice and demand statute that applies in drug cases. That holding is likely to apply to North Carolina's other similarly worded notice and demand statutes.

---

118. The legislation also provides notice and demand procedures involving the chain of custody of evidence, mentioned later in this chapter.

authentication and without the testimony of the analyst, with regard to, among other things, alcohol concentration or the presence of an impairing substance. G.S. 20-139.1(e2) sets out a simple notice and demand procedure for this evidence. Specifically, the State must provide notice to the defendant at least 15 business days before the proceeding that it intends to use the affidavit and must provide the defendant with a copy of that document. The defendant must file a written objection to the use of the affidavit at least five business days before the proceeding at which it will be used. Failure to file an objection is considered a waiver of the right to object to the affidavit's admissibility. If an objection is timely filed, the special admissibility provision does not apply. However, the case must be continued until the analyst can be present and may not be dismissed due to the failure of the analyst to appear, unless the analyst willfully fails to appear after being ordered to do so by the court.

Chemical Analyses in Drug Cases

G.S. 90-95(g) contains a simple notice and demand procedure for the use of chemical analyses in drug cases that applies in all court proceedings. It requires the State to provide notice 15 business days before the proceeding at which the report will be used. The defendant has until five business days before the proceeding to object. If no objection is filed, the report is admissible without the testimony of the analyst. If an objection is filed, the special admissibility provision does not apply.[119]

Breath-Testing Instrument Records and Permits

A judge must take judicial notice of preventive maintenance records involving breath-testing instruments used for chemical analysis, chemical analyst permits, and related information.[120]

Division of Motor Vehicles Records

A certified copy of a driver's license record maintained by the Division of Motor Vehicles (DMV) and sent by the Police Information Network (PIN, also known as DCI or Division of Criminal Information) is sufficient evidence to prove the status of a person's license—for

example, whether the license was revoked.[121] A copy of a defendant's conviction records maintained by the DMV or other state agency and sent by PIN (DCI) is sufficient evidence of those convictions to prove aggravating factors in a sentencing hearing for a defendant convicted of impaired driving.[122] Evidence of the numbers and letters on a license plate attached to a motor vehicle or a motor vehicle identification number (VIN), together with certified DMV records showing the name of the owner of the vehicle to which the license plate or VIN is assigned—or a certified copy of the motor vehicle title on file with the DMV—is sufficient evidence of the ownership of the motor vehicle.[123]

Public Records

Copies of public records—for example, conviction records—are admissible when properly certified under seal by the records custodian.[124] Certified copies of criminal conviction records in a criminal index maintained by a clerk of superior court are also admissible if the original documents on which the records are based have been destroyed pursuant to law.[125]

Authentication of Physical Evidence or Documents: Chain of Custody

Before a physical object or document may be introduced in evidence, it must be properly identified as being what the party introducing the evidence asserts it is.[126] For example, if the State wants to introduce a white powdery substance to prove that the defendant possessed it at his or her home, it must show—before the substance is introduced—that it is the same substance that officers seized from that home.

A trial judge in each case exercises discretionary authority whether to allow evidence to be introduced.[127] There are no standard rules to determine whether the

---

119. The North Carolina Court of Appeals in *State v. Steele*, 201 N.C. App. 689 (2010), upheld the constitutionality of this statute under *Melendez-Diaz v. Massachusetts*, 557 U.S. 305 (2009).

120. G.S. 20-139.1(b2), -139.1(b6).

121. G.S. 20-26(b).

122. G.S. 20-179(o). *See also* G.S. 8-35.1 (certified copy of DMV records sufficient evidence of an impaired driving conviction).

123. G.S. 8-37.

124. G.S. 8-35. Various public records and documents may be admitted and authenticated under Rules 803, 901, 902, or 1005. *See generally* 2 KENNETH S. BROUN, BRANDIS & BROUN ON NORTH CAROLINA EVIDENCE §§ 229, 243 (7th ed. 2011).

125. G.S. 8-35.2.

126. Rule 901(a).

127. State v. Harbison, 293 N.C. 474 (1977).

State or the defendant has sufficiently identified an object so that it may be introduced at trial. One common way to identify a physical object sufficiently is to establish a chain of custody, which consists of accounting for the location and condition of the object from the time it is discovered until the time it is presented in court.[128] Mailing evidence in a sealed envelope is a common and proper way to maintain a chain of custody.[129] A chain of custody is not always required[130]—nor is an unbroken chain always required[131]—to introduce evidence at trial. Any

weak links in a chain of custody affect only the weight the jury gives the evidence, not its admissibility.[132] However, as a matter of caution, officers should attempt to establish a chain of custody with all evidence they collect

---

128. *See, e.g.*, State v. Stalls, 22 N.C. App. 265 (1974).

129. State v. Poplin, 56 N.C. App. 304 (1982); State v. Jordan, 14 N.C. App. 453 (1972) (unnecessary to show which postal employees may have handled sealed package); State v. Sealey, 41 N.C. App. 175 (1979) (unnecessary to show which laboratory personnel picked up sealed package from post office). *See also* G.S. 8-103 (sending evidence with state courier service or common or contract carrier considered the same as first-class mail in maintaining chain of custody).

130. Generally, if the evidence is unique, readily identifiable, and relatively resistant to change, testimony that identifies the evidence is sufficient without a chain of custody. A chain of custody must be established only when the evidence is not readily identifiable or is susceptible to alteration and there is reason to believe that it may have been altered. State v. Campbell, 311 N.C. 386 (1984); State v. Oliver, 302 N.C. 28 (1981) (witness's failure to testify directly that evidence did not materially change was not fatal to its admissibility when witness made positive identification and it was unlikely that evidence would have changed); State v. Silhan, 302 N.C. 223 (1981) (unnecessary to show chain of custody when officer positively identified boots taken from defendant after his arrest); State v. Dellinger, 308 N.C. 288 (1983) (chain of custody unnecessary for rifle bolt found near deceased's body when officer sufficiently identified it at trial ("does . . . look like the same one")); State v. Hunt, 305 N.C. 238 (1982) (unnecessary to show chain of custody when officer positively identified pocketknife and pistol); State v. Moore, 301 N.C. 262 (1980) (same; weapon); State v. Smith, 291 N.C. 505 (1977) (same; weapon); State v. Boyd, 287 N.C. 131 (1975) (positive identification of weapon by serial number and make; unnecessary to show chain of custody to introduce weapon and ballistics evidence about it).

131. The custodians in the chain of custody need not all testify at trial when there are no concrete facts showing that the evidence was tampered with or exchanged with other evidence. United States v. Harrington, 923 F.2d 1371 (9th Cir. 1991) (testimony of police department's evidence custodian unnecessary to establish chain of custody in this case); State v. Campbell, 311 N.C. 386 (1984) (sealed rape evidence kit positively identified by physician; there was only speculation about possibility of tampering); State v. Detter, 298 N.C. 604 (1979) (adequate chain shown; unnecessary to show which lab employee picked up evidence at post office); State v. Grier, 307 N.C. 628 (1983) (chain of custody for blood sample sufficiently

established, although person who drew blood from rape victim did not testify, when doctor testified that although she did not see the blood drawn from the victim, she signed a blood sample that was supposedly taken from the victim by a lab technician either immediately before or after the examination; no evidence that blood sample had been contaminated or confused with another person's sample); State v. Montgomery, 291 N.C. 91 (1976) (chain of custody sufficient although two doctors were not sure whether a third person handled Pap smear); State v. Abernathy, 295 N.C. 147 (1978) (chain of custody sufficient when three witnesses positively identified evidence, even though there may have been some missing custodians of evidence); State v. Carr, 122 N.C. App. 369 (1996) (evidence sufficient to establish chain of custody of drugs sent by officer to SBI laboratory chemist and returned to officer; testimony of laboratory evidence technician unnecessary); State v. Hairston, 123 N.C. App. 753 (1996) (person who draws blood sample is not always required to testify to establish proper foundation for chain of custody of blood sample); State v. Greenlee, 146 N.C. App. 729 (2001) (officer sealed crack cocaine in evidence envelope with date, initials, etc., completed SBI request for examination form, and placed it in the drop box in his agency's property control room; two other people were involved in transfer of envelope to SBI chemist; each person upon receipt and delivery signed their names in chain of custody section of request form; only the officer and SBI chemist testified at trial; chemist testified that envelope was still sealed when he received it; both officer and chemist testified that substance appeared to be in same condition as when they had last seen it; sufficient chain of custody); State v. Feimster, 21 N.C. App. 602 (1974) (chain of custody was sufficient although an officer in the chain had died before trial); State v. Coble, 20 N.C. App. 575 (1974) (when complete chain of custody was shown from the time the officer obtained evidence to the time the chemist analyzed it, evidence was admissible; court rejected defendant's argument that chain of custody from chemist to time of trial also must be shown).

132. State v. Frye, 341 N.C. 470 (1995) (State's failure to offer evidence concerning which of two people drew blood from the murder victim at the autopsy did not constitute insufficient evidence of chain of custody; any weakness in the chain of custody affected weight, not admissibility, of evidence concerning blood sample); State v. Campbell, 311 N.C. 386 (1984) (rape kit admissible; tampering with kit was mere speculation); State v. Sloan, 316 N.C. 714 (1986) (similar ruling); United States v. Cardenas, 864 F.2d 1528 (10th Cir. 1989) (chain of custody need not be perfect for evidence to be admissible; unavailable officer in chain of custody did not adversely affect admissibility of evidence). *See generally* 2 Kenneth S. Broun, Brandis & Broun on North Carolina Evidence §§ 248, 249 (7th ed. 2011).

during an investigation, because they obviously cannot know in advance how a trial judge may rule on whether the State has sufficiently identified an object to allow it to be introduced.

There are some steps officers may take to avoid problems in establishing a chain of custody. First, they should limit the number of people who handle the evidence. Second, those who take control of evidence may want to mark it with their initials or some other notation if it is appropriate to do so with the particular kind of evidence. Third, evidence may be placed in sealed containers or tagged, if appropriate, with labels that have spaces for recording the time, date, and name of each recipient of the material whenever it is transferred from one person to another. Fourth, evidence should be stored in a place where unauthorized access is minimized.[133]

Statutory Methods for Establishing Chain of Custody for Evidence Concerning Forensic and Chemical Analyses

North Carolina statutes set out procedures to allow, under certain circumstances, proof of a chain of custody of evidence without witness testimony concerning forensic and chemical analyses.[134] For a discussion of these statutes, see the publication cited in the accompanying footnote.[135]

Authentication of Audio and Video Recordings

To authenticate an audiotape recording, the rules of evidence require only a witness's testimony that he or she personally recognized the identity of the voice(s) on the recording.[136] The rules concerning the authentication of video recordings are set out in the cases and blog posts cited in the accompanying footnote.[137]

Authentication of Text Messages and Cell Phone Records

Text messages may be authenticated in several ways; for example, by taking a screen shot of a text message[138] or by circumstantial evidence.[139] Cell phone records typically may be authenticated by the testimony of a custodian of records of the cell phone company.[140]

---

133. The fact that others may have had access to the evidence does not by itself destroy a chain of custody. State v. Detter, 298 N.C. 604 (1979) (access of several laboratory employees to bench where evidence was placed; adequate chain shown); State v. Fulton, 299 N.C. 491 (1980) (officer left evidence unattended for an hour in his unlocked office; unknown employee took evidence to mail-pickup point; adequate chain shown); State v. Essick, 67 N.C. App. 697 (1984) (access to evidence locker by others does not destroy chain of custody); State v. Newcomb, 36 N.C. App. 137 (1978) (fact that unknown people may have had access to evidence does not destroy chain of custody).

134. G.S. 8-58.20(g) (forensic analysis); 20-139.1(c3) (tested blood or urine); 90-95(g1) (drug analysis).

135. Jessica Smith, *Understanding the New Confrontation Clause Analysis: Crawford, Davis, and Melendez-Diaz,* ADMIN. OF JUST. BULL. 2010/02, at 22–24 (Apr. 2010), http:// sogpubs.unc.edu/electronicversions/pdfs/aojb1002.pdf.

136. State v. Stager, 329 N.C. 278 (1991) (court ruled that the authentication requirements under Rule 901 have superseded the seven-pronged test of *State v. Lynch,* 279 N.C. 1 (1971)).

137. State v. Snead, ___ N.C. ___, 783 S.E.2d 733 (2016) (authentication of surveillance video upheld); State v. Fleming, ___ N.C. App. ___, 786 S.E.2d 760 (2016) (similar ruling); State v. Cannon, 92 N.C. App. 246, *rev'd on other grounds,* 326 N.C. 37 (1990) (similar ruling). *See* Jeff Welty, *State Supreme Court Reverses Court of Appeals Regarding Authentication of Surveillance Video,* NC CRIM. L. BLOG (April 18, 2016), http:// nccriminallaw.sog.unc.edu/state-supreme-court-reverses-court-appeals-regarding-authentication-surveillance-video/ *and* Jeff Welty, *One Case, Two Ways of Authenticating Video,* NC CRIM. L. BLOG (June 27, 2016), http://nccriminallaw. sog.unc.edu/one-case-two-ways-authenticating-video/. *See also* State v. Redd, 144 N.C. App. 248 (2001) (State properly authenticated videotape of drug deal that contained deliberate deletions of extraneous material); State v. Sibley, 140 N.C. App. 584 (2000) (videotapes were not properly authenticated); State v. Mason, 144 N.C. App. 20 (2001) (State failed to properly authenticate videotape of convenience store robbery).

138. State v. Gray, 234 N.C. App. 197 (2014) (detective took screen shots of text messages and testified that they were in substantially the same condition as when he obtained them; accomplice also testified as to their authenticity).

139. In *State v. Wilkerson,* 223 N.C. App. 195 (2012), the court ruled that circumstantial evidence supported the admission of an incriminating text message sent from the defendant's cell phone. A witness saw a suspicious car driving up and down the victim's street on the day of the breaking or entering and reported its description and license plate to law enforcement; she also testified that the driver appeared to be using a cell phone. Stolen property was found in a car parked at the defendant's home and a cell phone was found on the defendant's person. Around the time of the crime, multiple calls were made from and to the phone, and a text message referenced a stolen item. Cell tower information traced a path of transit of the phone from and back to the area of the defendant's and victim's homes.

140. State v. Crawley, 217 N.C. App. 509 (2011).

Polygraph (Lie Detector) Evidence

Polygraph testing evidence is not admissible in North Carolina courts for any purpose, although officers may use polygraph testing as an investigative tool.[141] If a defendant confesses during or after polygraph testing, the confession is admissible as long as the test results are not presented to the jury.[142]

Hypnotically Refreshed Testimony

Although officers may hypnotize a person for investigative purposes, testimony about the hypnotic session and any hypnotically refreshed testimony (that is, testimony given after a person has been hypnotized) is generally inadmissible in North Carolina courts.[143] When a party attempts to offer testimony by a person who previously has been hypnotized, that party has the burden of proving that the person is relating information that he or she knew before the hypnotic session.[144] Thus, officers need to record carefully a person's statements before he or she is hypnotized.

Officers should consider consulting a prosecutor or their agency's legal advisor before placing a person under hypnosis.

Admissibility of a Defendant's Written Confession

A law enforcement officer may orally testify about what the defendant told the officer during a confession, including a confession that was later reduced to writing. However, before the State may introduce into evidence a written document containing a defendant's confession,[145] the State must show that the written document (1) was read to or by the defendant and signed or otherwise acknowledged to be correct or (2) is a verbatim record of the questions asked by the officer and the answers given by the defendant.[146]

Best Evidence Rule

The best evidence rule applies only to writings, recordings, and photographs, which includes still photographs, x-ray films, videotapes, and motion pictures. It does not apply to physical evidence, for example. Thus, a witness may testify about a shotgun in a murder case without the shotgun being introduced into evidence.

The best evidence rule provides that to prove the contents of a writing, recording, or photograph, the original is required, except as provided by other rules or statutes.[147] An officer who listens to and records—by audiotape or videotape—a defendant's confession may testify about the confession without producing the recording, because the State is not attempting to prove the contents of the recording.[148] The State is only proving the contents of the confession. Similarly, the best evidence rule does not apply to a photograph that a witness is using solely to illustrate his or her testimony, because proof of its contents is not involved.

If a party is seeking to prove the contents of a writing, recording, or photograph, the rule allows many alternatives to the original. For example, (1) an original of a photograph is defined to include the negative or any print from the negative, and (2) an original of computer data includes any printout readable by sight that accurately reflects the data. Duplicates of the original are admissible to the same extent as an original, with limited exceptions.[149] Thus, photocopies of written confessions and search warrants and copies of audiotapes and videotapes are admissible to prove their contents just as if they were

---

141. State v. Grier, 307 N.C. 628 (1983).

142. State v. Harris, 315 N.C. 556 (1986); State v. Payne, 327 N.C. 194 (1990).

143. State v. Peoples, 311 N.C. 515 (1984). However, an automatic rule prohibiting testimony of a criminal defendant after undergoing hypnosis is unconstitutional. *See* Rock v. Arkansas, 483 U.S. 44 (1987).

144. State v. Peoples, 311 N.C. 515 (1984).

145. The rules govern a defendant's statement as well as a confession, but the text uses confession for ease of reading.

146. State v. Wagner, 343 N.C. 250 (1996) (written confession was admissible because it was an exact word-for-word rendition of the officer's interview of the defendant); State v. Bartlett, 121 N.C. App. 521 (1996) (written confession was

inadmissible because it did not comply with rules of admissibility); State v. Spencer, 192 N.C. App. 143 (2008) (admission of defendant's confession through reading of officer's handwritten notes was error because officer did not have defendant review and confirm notes as accurate representation of defendant's answer, nor were notes a verbatim account of defendant's confession).

147. Rule 1002. *See, e.g.*, State v. Clark, 324 N.C. 146 (1989) (insurance policy's contents were not in issue; testimony about contents was offered only to show defendant's knowledge that the policy existed). The best evidence rule also does not apply to collateral matters; see Rule 1004(4).

148. State v. Davis, 284 N.C. 701 (1974). *See also* State v. Branch, 288 N.C. 514 (1975) (witness's testimony about telephone conversation did not violate best evidence rule, even though prosecutor possessed recording of conversation). *See generally* 2 Kenneth S. Broun, Brandis & Broun on North Carolina Evidence § 254 (7th ed. 2011).

149. Rule 1003. Certified copies of public records are made admissible by Rule 1005.

the originals—unless, of course, there is a genuine question about their authenticity. Therefore, officers should consider making copies of important writings, recordings, and photographs.

Testimony about an original to prove its contents is admissible when all originals have been lost or destroyed, unless the party offering the testimony lost or destroyed them in bad faith.[150] For example, a witness may testify about the contents of letters that have not been lost in bad faith.[151]

Proof of Local Ordinances

In charging a violation of a city or county ordinance, the criminal pleading (arrest warrant, criminal summons, citation, or magistrate's order) must allege the section number and caption; for example, "Livingston City Code, Section 7. No Loitering for Purpose of Selling Drugs." If the ordinance has not been codified, it must be pleaded by its caption. At trial, the State must prove the validity of the ordinance, usually by offering the city or county code book containing the ordinance or by a certified copy of the ordinance.[152]

Return of Property to Owner

North Carolina law provides a procedure for property owners to apply to a court for return of their property (even before trial) if a district attorney refuses to release it.[153] The court must hold a hearing after notice to all parties, including the defendant. The court may order the property returned to the lawful owner under conditions that assure that it will be available for use at trial and will otherwise protect the rights of all parties.

---

150. Rule 1004.
151. State v. Eason, 328 N.C. 409 (1991).

152. G.S. 160A-79; 153A-50.
153. G.S. 15-11.1. Photographs of property may be admissible in evidence at trial. *See* State v. Alston, 91 N.C. App. 707 (1988); State v. Jones, 97 N.C. App. 189 (1990).

Index of the Cases in the Case Summaries

Note: United States Supreme Court Cases are in **bold**.

Subject Index

CPSIA information can be obtained
at www.ICGtesting.com
Printed in the USA
LVHW062059171221
706489LV00013B/590

9 781560 118596